# BEGINNING VISUAL C#® 2012 PROGRAMMING

*Continued*

BEGINNING

# Visual C#® 2012 Programming

BEGINNING

# Visual C#® 2012 Programming

Karli Watson
Jacob Vibe Hammer
John D. Reid
Morgan Skinner
Daniel Kemper
Christian Nagel

John Wiley & Sons, Inc.

# Beginning Visual C#® 2012 Programming

Published by
John Wiley & Sons, Inc.
10475 Crosspoint Boulevard
Indianapolis, IN 46256
www.wiley.com

Copyright © 2013 by John Wiley & Sons, Inc., Indianapolis, Indiana

Published simultaneously in Canada

ISBN: 978-1-118-31441-8
ISBN: 978-1-118-33194-1 (ebk)
ISBN: 978-1-118-33540-6 (ebk)
ISBN: 978-1-118-39637-7 (ebk)

Manufactured in the United States of America

10 9 8 7 6 5 4 3 2 1

For general information on our other products and services please contact our Customer Care Department within the United States at (877) 762-2974, outside the United States at (317) 572-3993 or fax (317) 572-4002.

Wiley publishes in a variety of print and electronic formats and by print-on-demand. Some material included with standard print versions of this book may not be included in e-books or in print-on-demand. If this book refers to media such as a CD or DVD that is not included in the version you purchased, you may download this material at http://booksupport.wiley.com. For more information about Wiley products, visit www.wiley.com.

Library of Congress Control Number: 2012946841

*for donna*

— KARLI WATSON

*Love is as strong as death;*
*Many waters cannot quench love,*
*neither can the floods drown it.*

*From the inside of my Mum's hymnbook, of which I*
*now have the privilege of being the custodian.*

— MORGAN SKINNER

# ABOUT THE AUTHORS

**KARLI WATSON** is an IT contractor and author currently working in London in the financial sector. For the most part, he immerses himself in .NET (in particular C#) and has written numerous books in the field for several publishers. He specializes in communicating complex ideas in a way that is accessible to anyone with a passion to learn, and spends much of his time playing with new technology to find new things to teach people about.

During those (seemingly few) times where he isn't doing the above, Karli will probably be wishing he was hurtling down a mountain on a snowboard. Or possibly trying to get his novel published. Either way, you'll know him by his brightly colored clothes. You can also find him tweeting online as @karlequin, and maybe one day he'll get round to making himself a website.

**JACOB VIBE HAMMER** is a software architect and developer at Kamstrup, where he is helping the company develop world class Smart Grid solutions for large public utilities. He started programming just about the time when he was able to spell the word "BASIC" — which, incidentally, is the first programming language he ever used. Since then, he has worked with numerous programming languages and solution architectures; however, since the turn of the century, he has worked primarily with the .NET platform. Today, his programming time is spent working primarily with C# and WPF, as well as toying with NoSQL databases.

A Danish citizen, Jacob lives in Aarhus, Denmark, with his wife and son.

**JON D. REID** is the Director of Software Technology for IFS Metrix Service Management (www.IFSWORLD .com/Metrix). He has coauthored a number of .NET books, including *Beginning Visual C# 2010, Fast Track C#, Pro Visual Studio .NET*, and many others.

**MORGAN SKINNER** started messing with computers in 1980 when he first started programming at school in assembly language. Since then he's used many languages commercially, including Pascal, Modula-2, VAX Macro assembly language, Smalltalk, PowerBuilder, C, C++ and C# (to name the more well-known ones). He joined Microsoft in 2001 after getting his hands on .NET for the first time, and he spent nearly 10 years there as an Application Development Consultant, working with some of the smallest — and largest — companies in the UK. Morgan left Microsoft in 2011 and is now an independent contractor working on bespoke systems; see www.morganskinner.com for more details.

**DANIEL KEMPER** is a software architect with a couple of Microsoft certifications. He specializes in rich Internet application, desktop client, and reporting technologies.

**CHRISTIAN NAGEL** is a Microsoft Regional Director and Microsoft MVP, an associate of thinktecture, and founder of CN innovation. A software architect and developer, he offers training and consulting on how to develop solutions using the Microsoft platform. He draws on more than 25 years of software development experience. Christian started his computing career with PDP 11 and VAX/VMS systems, covering a variety of languages and platforms. Since 2000, when .NET was just a technology preview, he has been working with various .NET technologies to build .NET solutions. Currently, he mainly coaches the development of Windows 8 apps accessing Windows Azure services. With his profound knowledge of Microsoft technologies, he has written numerous books and is certified as a Microsoft Certified Trainer and Professional Developer. Christian speaks at international conferences such as TechEd, Basta!, and TechDays, and he founded INETA Europe to support .NET user groups. You can contact Christian via his websites, www.cninnovation.com and www.thinktecture.com. You can also follow his tweets at @christiannagel.

# ABOUT THE TECHNICAL EDITORS

**DOUG HOLLAND** is an architect with Microsoft's Developer and Platform Evangelism team and works with Microsoft's strategic ISV partners to help bring new and exciting experiences to consumers on Windows 8 and Windows Phone 8.

**RICHARD HOPTON** has been developing business software systems for 10 years, currently focusing on designing and building highly scalable REST-based API solutions using C# for a digital media company in London, UK. Richard has been published in Microsoft's monthly developer newsletter, MSDN Flash, and has spoken at numerous developer community events throughout the UK.

**MARCEL MEIJER** has lived in the world of information and communications technologies for more than 15 years. Currently, he is mainly concerned with Windows Azure, the cloud, C#, software development, and architecture. He works as a senior architect at VX Company. In his spare time, he is a board member of the SDN (Software Development Network; www.sdn.nl). At SDN, he is responsible for arranging speakers for the SDN Events (SDE); selecting content for SDN Conferences; and arranging and editing content for SDN Magazine.

# CREDITS

**ACQUISITIONS EDITOR**
Mary James

**PROJECT EDITOR**
Patrick Meader

**TECHNICAL EDITORS**
Doug Holland
Richard Hopton
Marcel Meijer

**PRODUCTION EDITOR**
Christine Mugnolo

**COPY EDITOR**
Kezia Endsley

**EDITORIAL MANAGER**
Mary Beth Wakefield

**FREELANCER EDITORIAL MANAGER**
Rosemarie Graham

**ASSOCIATE DIRECTOR OF MARKETING**
David Mayhew

**MARKETING MANAGER**
Ashley Zurcher

**BUSINESS MANAGER**
Amy Knies

**PRODUCTION MANAGER**
Tim Tate

**VICE PRESIDENT AND EXECUTIVE GROUP PUBLISHER**
Richard Swadley

**VICE PRESIDENT AND EXECUTIVE PUBLISHER**
Neil Edde

**ASSOCIATE PUBLISHER**
Jim Minatel

**PROJECT COORDINATOR, COVER**
Katie Crocker

**PROOFREADERS**
Sarah Kaikini, Word One New York
Scott Klemp, Word One New York
James Saturnio, Word One New York

**INDEXER**
Robert Swanson

**COVER DESIGNER**
LeAndra Young

**COVER IMAGE**
© Lisa Loyd / iStockphoto

# ACKNOWLEDGMENTS

**THANKS ONCE AGAIN TO EVERYONE AT WILEY** for help, encouragement, and understanding. Striking the balance between getting the book done quickly and ensuring it's accurate in the face of numerous product and naming changes is never easy, but between us I think we've just about managed it. Special thanks to Patrick Meader for remaining (mostly) calm throughout the project — or at least calmer than me... As ever, no acknowledgements would be complete without thanks to my wife, donna, who very nearly succeeds in keeping me sane during writing periods. And, of course, thanks to you for (hopefully) buying this book, and the very best of luck in your coding adventures!

— KARLI WATSON

# CONTENTS

# INTRODUCTION

**C# IS A RELATIVELY NEW LANGUAGE** that was unveiled to the world when Microsoft announced the first version of its .NET Framework in July 2000. Since then its popularity has rocketed, and it has arguably become the language of choice for both desktop and web developers who use the .NET Framework. Part of the appeal of C# comes from its clear syntax, which derives from C/C++ but simplifies some things that have previously discouraged some programmers. Despite this simplification, C# has retained the power of C++, and there is now no reason not to move into C#. The language is not difficult and it's a great one to learn elementary programming techniques with. This ease of learning, combined with the capabilities of the .NET Framework, make C# an excellent way to start your programming career.

The latest release of C#, C# 5, which is included with version 4.5 of the .NET Framework, builds on the existing successes and adds even more attractive features. The latest release of Visual Studio (Visual Studio 2012) and the Visual Studio Express 2012 line of development tools also bring many tweaks and improvements to make your life easier and dramatically increase your productivity.

This book is intended to teach you about all aspects of C# programming, from the language itself, through desktop and web programming, to making use of data sources, and finally to some new and advanced techniques. You'll also learn about the capabilities of Visual Studio 2012, and all the ways that this product can aid your application development.

The book is written in a friendly, mentor-style fashion, with each chapter building on previous ones, and every effort is made to ease you into advanced techniques painlessly. At no point will technical terms appear from nowhere to discourage you from continuing; every concept is introduced and discussed as required. Technical jargon is kept to a minimum; but where it is necessary, it, too, is properly defined and laid out in context.

The authors of this book are all experts in their field, and are all enthusiastic in their passion for both the C# language and the .NET Framework. Nowhere will you find a group of people better qualified to take you under their collective wing and nurture your understanding of C# from first principles to advanced techniques. Along with the fundamental knowledge it provides, this book is packed full of helpful hints, tips, exercises, and full-fledged example code (available for download at p2p.wrox.com) that you will find yourself returning to repeatedly as your career progresses.

We pass this knowledge on without begrudging it, and hope that you will be able to use it to become the best programmer you can be. Good luck, and all the best!

## WHO THIS BOOK IS FOR

This book is for everyone who wants to learn how to program in C# using the .NET Framework. It is for absolute beginners who want to give programming a try by learning a clean, modern, elegant programming language. But it also for people familiar with other programming languages who want to explore the .NET platform, as well as for existing .NET developers who want to give Microsoft's .NET flagship language a try.

## WHAT THIS BOOK COVERS

The early chapters cover the language itself, assuming no prior programming experience. If you have programmed in other languages before, then much of the material in these chapters will be familiar. Many aspects of C# syntax are shared with other languages, and many structures are common to practically all programming languages (such as looping and branching structures). However, even if you are an experienced programmer you will benefit from looking through these chapters to learn the specifics of how these techniques apply to C#.

If you are new to programming, you should start from the beginning, where you will learn basic programming concepts and become acquainted with both C# and the .NET platform that underpins it. If you are new to the .NET Framework but know how to program, you should read Chapter 1 and then skim through the next few chapters before continuing with the application of the C# language. If you know how to program but haven't encountered an object-oriented programming language before, you should read the chapters from Chapter 8 onward.

Alternatively, if you already know the C# language, you might want to concentrate on the chapters dealing with the most recent .NET Framework and C# language developments, specifically the chapters on collections, generics, and C# language enhancements (Chapters 11 to 14), or skip the first section of the book completely and start with Chapter 15.

The chapters in this book have been written with a dual purpose in mind: they can be read sequentially to provide a complete tutorial in the C# language, and they can be dipped into as required reference material.

In addition to the core material, starting with Chapter 3 each chapter also includes a selection of exercises at the end, which you can work through to ensure that you have understood the material. The exercises range from simple multiple choice or true/false questions to more complex exercises that require you to modify or build applications. The answers to all the exercises are provided in Appendix A. You can also find these exercises as part of the wrox.com code downloads for this book at www.wrox.com/remtitle .cgi?isbn=9781118314418 on the Download Code tab.

This book also gives plenty of love and attention to coincide with the release of C# 5 and .NET 4.5. Every chapter received an overhaul, with less relevant material removed, and new material added. All of the code has been tested against the latest version of the development tools used, and all of the screenshots have been retaken in Windows 8 to provide the most current windows and dialog boxes.

Although we hate to admit our own fallibility, any errors from previous editions have been fixed, and many other reader comments have been addressed. Hopefully, we haven't introduced many new errors, but any that have slipped through our web of experts will be corrected online as soon as we find them.

New highlights of this edition include the following:

➤ Additional and improved code examples for you to try out

➤ A shift of focus in desktop applications from the old way of doing things (Windows Forms) to the new way (Windows Presentation Foundation), so you won't be left behind

➤ Coverage of everything that's new in C# 5 and .NET 4.5, including how to create Windows Store applications

➤ Streamlined coverage of advanced techniques to focus on those most appropriate to beginners without getting too obscure

## HOW THIS BOOK IS STRUCTURED

This book is divided into six sections:

➤ **Introduction**—Purpose and general outline of the book's contents

➤ **The C# Language**—Covers all aspects of the C# language, from the fundamentals to object-oriented techniques

➤ **Windows Programming**—How to write and deploy desktop and Windows Store applications

➤ **Web Programming**—Web application development and deployment

➤ **Data Access**—How to use data in your applications, including data stored in files on your hard disk, data stored in XML format, and data in databases

➤ **Additional Techniques**—An examination of some extra ways to use C# and the .NET Framework, including Windows Communication Foundation (WCF) and Windows Workflow Foundation (WF)—technologies introduced with .NET 3.0 and enhanced for .NET 4 and .NET 4.5.

The following sections describe the chapters in the five major parts of this book.

## The C# Language (Chapters 1–14)

Chapter 1 introduces you to C# and how it fits into the .NET landscape. You'll learn the fundamentals of programming in this environment, and how Visual Studio 2012 (VS) fit in.

Chapter 2 starts you off with writing C# applications. You'll look at the syntax of C# and put the language to use with sample command-line and Windows applications. These examples demonstrate just how quick and easy it can be to get up and running, and along the way you'll be introduced to the VS development environment and the basic windows and tools that you'll be using throughout the book.

Next you'll learn more about the basics of the C# language. You'll learn what variables are and how to manipulate them in Chapter 3. You'll enhance the structure of your applications with flow control (looping and branching) in Chapter 4, and see some more advanced variable types such as arrays in Chapter 5. In Chapter 6 you'll start to encapsulate your code in the form of functions, which make it much easier to perform repetitive operations and make your code much more readable.

By the beginning of Chapter 7 you'll have a handle on the fundamentals of the C# language, and will focus on debugging your applications. This involves looking at outputting trace information as your applications are executed, and at how VS can be used to trap errors and lead you to solutions for them with its powerful debugging environment.

From Chapter 8 onward you'll learn about object-oriented programming (OOP), starting with a look at what this term means, and an answer to the eternal question, "What is an object?" OOP can seem quite difficult at first. The whole of Chapter 8 is devoted to demystifying it and explaining what makes it so great, and you won't actually deal with much C# code until the very end of the chapter.

Everything changes in Chapter 9, when you put theory into practice and start using OOP in your C# applications. This is where the true power of C# lies. You'll start by looking at how to define classes and interfaces, and then move on to class members (including fields, properties, and methods) in Chapter 10. At the end of that chapter you'll start to assemble a card game application, which is developed over several chapters, and will help to illustrate OOP.

Once you've learned how OOP works in C#, Chapter 11 moves on to look at common OOP scenarios, including dealing with collections of objects, and comparing and converting objects. Chapter 12 takes a look at a very useful feature of C# that was introduced in .NET 2.0: generics, which enable you to create very flexible classes. Next, Chapter 13 continues the discussion of the C# language and OOP with some additional techniques, notably events, which become very important in, for example, Windows programming. Finally, Chapter 14 focuses on C# language features that were introduced with versions 3.0, 4, and 5 of the language.

## Windows Programming (Chapters 15–18)

Chapter 15 starts by introducing you to what is meant by Windows programming, and looks at how this is achieved in VS. It focuses on WPF as a tool that enables you to build desktop applications in a graphical way, and assemble advanced applications with the minimum of effort and time. You'll start with the basics of WPF programming, and build up your knowledge in both this chapter and Chapter 16, which demonstrates how you can use the wealth of controls supplied by the .NET Framework in your applications.

Chapter 17 shows you how you can create Windows Store applications, which are new to Windows 8. This is an exciting new way to provide users with beautiful, full-screen user experiences. You will also see how you can make your applications ready to be sold from the Windows Store.

Chapter 18 discusses how to deploy your applications, including how to make installation programs that enable your users to get up and running with your applications in double-quick time.

## Web Programming (Chapters 19–20)

This section is structured in a similar way to the desktop programming section. It starts with Chapter 19, which describes the controls that make up the simplest of web applications, and how you can fit them together and make them perform tasks using ASP.NET. The chapter then moves on to look at more advanced techniques, ASP.NET AJAX, versatile controls, and state management in the context of the web, as well as how to conform to web standards.

Next, Chapter 20 examines the deployment of web applications and services, in particular the features of VS that enable you to publish applications to the web with the click of a button.

## Data Access (Chapters 21–24)

Chapter 21 looks at how your applications can save and retrieve data to disk, both as simple text files and as more complex representations of data. You'll also learn how to compress data, how to work with legacy data such as comma-separated value (CSV) files, and how to monitor and act on file system changes.

In Chapter 22 you'll learn about the de facto standard for data exchange—namely, XML. By this point in the book, you'll have touched on XML several times in preceding chapters, but this chapter lays out the ground rules and shows you what all the excitement is about.

The remainder of this part looks at LINQ, which is a query language built in to the latest versions of the .NET Framework. You start in Chapter 23 with a general introduction to LINQ, and then you will use LINQ to access a database and other data in Chapter 24.

## Additional Techniques (Chapters 25–26)

Finally, in this part of the book you will look at some exciting new technologies that have emerged with the most recent .NET Framework releases. Chapter 25 is an introduction to Windows Communication Foundation (WCF), which provides you with the tools you need for enterprise-level programmatic access to information and capabilities across local networks and the Internet. You will see how you can use WCF to expose complex data and functionality to web and desktop applications in a platform-independent way.

The last chapter of the book, Chapter 26, looks at Windows Workflow Foundation (WF). WF enables you to implement workflow functionality in your applications, which means you can define operations that are performed in a specific order controlled by external interactions, which is very useful for many types of applications.

## WHAT YOU NEED TO USE THIS BOOK

The code and descriptions of C# and the .NET Framework in this book apply to C# 5 and .NET 4.5. You don't need anything other than the Framework to understand this aspect of the book, but many of the examples require a development tool. This book uses Visual Studio 2012 as its primary development tool; however, if you don't have this, you will be able to use the free Visual Studio Express 2012 line of products. For the first part of the book, Visual Studio Express 2012 for Windows Desktop will enable you to create desktop and console applications. For later chapters, you may also use Visual Studio Express 2012 for Windows 8 in order to create Windows Store applications, Visual Studio Express 2012 for Web to create web applications, and SQL Server Express 2012 for applications that access databases. Some functionality is available only in Visual Studio 2012, but this won't stop you from working through any of the examples in this book.

The source code for the samples is available for download from the Wrox website at:

```
www.wrox.com/remtitle.cgi?isbn=9781118314418
```

## CONVENTIONS

To help you get the most from the text and keep track of what's happening, we've used a number of conventions throughout the book.

**TRY IT OUT**

The *Try It Out* is an exercise you should work through, following the text in the book.

1. They usually consist of a set of steps.
2. Each step has a number.
3. Follow the steps through with your copy of the database.

*How It Works*

After each *Try It Out*, the code you've typed will be explained in detail.

> **WARNING** *Warnings hold important, not-to-be-forgotten information that is directly relevant to the surrounding text.*

> **NOTE** *Notes indicates notes, tips, hints, tricks, or and asides to the current discussion.*

As for styles in the text:

➤ We *highlight* new terms and important words when we introduce them.
➤ We show keyboard strokes like this: Ctrl+A.
➤ We show filenames, URLs, and code within the text like so: `persistence.properties`.
➤ We present code in two different ways:

```
We use a monofont type with no highlighting for most code examples.
```

```
We use bold to emphasize code that is particularly important in the present context or to show
changes from a previous code snippet.
```

## SOURCE CODE

As you work through the examples in this book, you may choose either to type in all the code manually or to use the source code files that accompany the book. All the source code used in this book is available for download at `http://www.wrox.com`. A file name is provided for each code snippet or listing presented in the book and this file name corresponds to the source code on the `www.wrox.com` site. When at the site, simply locate the book's title (either by using the Search box or by using one of the title lists) and click the Download Code link on the book's detail page to obtain all the source code for the book.

> **NOTE** *Because many books have similar titles, you may find it easiest to search by ISBN; this book's ISBN is 978-1-118-31441-8.*

After you download the code, just decompress it with your favorite compression tool. Alternatively, you can go to the main Wrox code download page at `http://www.wrox.com/dynamic/books/download.aspx` to see the code available for this book and all other Wrox books.

## ERRATA

We make every effort to ensure that there are no errors in the text or in the code. However, no one is perfect, and mistakes do occur. If you find an error in one of our books, like a spelling mistake or faulty piece of code, we would be grateful for your feedback. By sending in errata you may save another reader hours of frustration and at the same time you can help us provide even higher quality information.

To find the errata page for this book, go to `http://www.wrox.com` and locate the title using the Search box or one of the title lists. Then, on the book details page, click the Book Errata link. On this page you can view all errata that has been submitted for this book and posted by Wrox editors.

> **NOTE** *A complete book list including links to each book's errata is also available at* `www.wrox.com/misc-pages/booklist.shtml`.

If you don't spot "your" error on the Book Errata page, go to `www.wrox.com/contact/techsupport.shtml` and complete the form there to send us the error you have found. We'll check the information and, if appropriate, post a message to the book's errata page and fix the problem in subsequent editions of the book.

## P2P.WROX.COM

For author and peer discussion, join the P2P forums at `http://p2p.wrox.com`. The forums are a Web-based system for you to post messages relating to Wrox books and related technologies and interact with other readers and technology users. The forums offer a subscription feature to e-mail you topics of interest of your choosing when new posts are made to the forums. Wrox authors, editors, other industry experts, and your fellow readers are present on these forums.

At `http://p2p.wrox.com`, you will find a number of different forums that will help you, not only as you read this book, but also as you develop your own applications. To join the forums, just follow these steps:

1. Go to `http://p2p.wrox.com` and click the Register link.
2. Read the terms of use and click Agree.

3. Complete the required information to join, as well as any optional information you wish to provide, and click Submit.

4. You will receive an e-mail with information describing how to verify your account and complete the joining process.

> **NOTE** *You can read messages in the forums without joining P2P, but in order to post your own messages, you must join.*

Once you join, you can post new messages and respond to messages other users post. You can read messages at any time on the web. If you would like to have new messages from a particular forum e-mailed to you, click the Subscribe to this Forum icon by the forum name in the forum listing.

For more information about how to use the Wrox P2P, be sure to read the P2P FAQs for answers to questions about how the forum software works, as well as many common questions specific to P2P and Wrox books. To read the FAQs, click the FAQ link on any P2P page.

# PART I
# The C# Language

# Introducing C#

## WHAT YOU WILL LEARN IN THIS CHAPTER

➤    What the .NET Framework is and what it contains

➤    How .NET applications work

➤    What C# is and how it relates to the .NET Framework

➤    Which tools are available for creating .NET applications with C#

Welcome to the first chapter of the first section of this book. This section provides you with the basic knowledge you need to get up and running with the most recent version of C#. Specifically, this chapter provides an overview of C# and the .NET Framework, including what these technologies are, the motivation for using them, and how they relate to each other.

It begins with a general discussion of the .NET Framework. This technology contains many concepts that are tricky to come to grips with initially. This means that the discussion, by necessity, covers many new concepts in a short amount of space. However, a quick look at the basics is essential to understanding how to program in C#. Later in the book, you revisit many of the topics covered here, exploring them in more detail.

After that general introduction, the chapter provides a basic description of C# itself, including its origins and similarities to C++. Finally, you look at the primary tool used throughout this book: Visual Studio 2012 (VS). VS 2012 is the latest in a long line of development environments that Microsoft has produced, and it includes all sorts of new features (including full support for Windows Store applications) that you will learn about throughout this book.

## WHAT IS THE .NET FRAMEWORK?

The .NET Framework (now at version 4.5) is a revolutionary platform created by Microsoft for developing applications. The most interesting thing about this statement is how vague it is—but there are good reasons for this. For a start, note that it doesn't "develop applications on the Windows operating system." Although the Microsoft release of the .NET Framework runs on the Windows and Windows Phone operating systems, it is possible to find alternative versions that will work on other systems. One example of this is Mono, an open-source version of the .NET Framework (including a C# compiler) that runs on several operating systems, including various flavors of Linux and Mac OS. There are also variants of Mono that run on iPhone (MonoTouch) and Android (Mono for Android, a.k.a. MonoDroid) smartphones. One of the key motivations behind the .NET Framework is its intended use as a means of integrating disparate operating systems.

In addition, the preceding definition of the .NET Framework includes no restriction on the type of applications that are possible. That's because there is no restriction—the .NET Framework enables the creation of desktop applications, Windows Store applications, web applications, web services, and pretty much anything else you can think of. Also, with web applications it's worth noting that these are, by definition, multi-platform applications, since any system with a web browser can access them.

The .NET Framework has been designed so that it can be used from any language, including C# (the subject of this book) as well as C++, Visual Basic, JScript, and even older languages such as COBOL. For this to work, .NET-specific versions of these languages have also appeared, and more are being released all the time. Not only do all of these have access to the .NET Framework, but they can also communicate with each other. It is possible for C# developers to make use of code written by Visual Basic programmers, and vice versa.

All of this provides an extremely high level of versatility and is part of what makes using the .NET Framework such an attractive prospect.

## What's in the .NET Framework?

The .NET Framework consists primarily of a gigantic library of code that you use from your client languages (such as C#) using object-oriented programming (OOP) techniques. This library is categorized into different modules—you use portions of it depending on the results you want to achieve. For example, one module contains the building blocks for Windows applications, another for network programming, and another for web development. Some modules are divided into more specific submodules, such as a module for building web services within the module for web development.

The intention is for different operating systems to support some or all of these modules, depending on their characteristics. A smartphone, for example, includes support for all the core .NET functionality but is unlikely to require some of the more esoteric modules.

Part of the .NET Framework library defines some basic *types*. A type is a representation of data, and specifying some of the most fundamental of these (such as "a 32-bit signed integer") facilitates interoperability between languages using the .NET Framework. This is called the *Common Type System* (CTS).

As well as supplying this library, the .Net Framework also includes the .NET *Common Language Runtime* (CLR), which is responsible for the execution of all applications developed using the .NET library.

## Writing Applications Using the .NET Framework

Writing an application using the .NET Framework means writing code (using any of the languages that support the Framework) using the .NET code library. In this book you use VS for your development. VS is a powerful, integrated development environment that supports C# (as well as managed and unmanaged C++, Visual Basic, and some others). The advantage of this environment is the ease with which .NET features can be integrated into your code. The code that you create will be entirely C# but use the .NET Framework throughout, and you'll make use of the additional tools in VS where necessary.

In order for C# code to execute, it must be converted into a language that the target operating system understands, known as *native code*. This conversion is called *compiling* code, an act that is performed by a *compiler*. Under the .NET Framework, this is a two-stage process.

### CIL and JIT

When you compile code that uses the .NET Framework library, you don't immediately create operating system–specific native code. Instead, you compile your code into *Common Intermediate Language* (CIL) code. This code isn't specific to any operating system (OS) and isn't specific to C#. Other

.NET languages—Visual Basic .NET, for example—also compile to this language as a first stage. This compilation step is carried out by VS when you develop C# applications.

Obviously, more work is necessary to execute an application. That is the job of a *just-in-time* (JIT) compiler, which compiles CIL into native code that is specific to the OS and machine architecture being targeted. Only at this point can the OS execute the application. The *just-in-time* part of the name reflects the fact that CIL code is compiled only when it is needed. This compilation can happen on the fly while your application is running, although luckily this isn't something that you normally need to worry about as a developer. Unless you are writing extremely advanced code where performance is critical, it's enough to know that this compilation process will churn along merrily in the background, without interfering.

In the past, it was often necessary to compile your code into several applications, each of which targeted a specific operating system and CPU architecture. Typically, this was a form of optimization (to get code to run faster on an AMD chipset, for example), but at times it was critical (for applications to work in both Win9*x* and WinNT/2000 environments, for example). This is now unnecessary, because JIT compilers (as their name suggests) use CIL code, which is independent of the machine, operating system, and CPU. Several JIT compilers exist, each targeting a different architecture, and the CLR uses the appropriate one to create the native code required.

The beauty of all this is that it requires a lot less work on your part—in fact, you can forget about system-dependent details and concentrate on the more interesting functionality of your code.

> **NOTE** *You might come across references to Microsoft Intermediate Language (MSIL) or just IL. MSIL was the original name for CIL, and many developers still use this terminology.*

## Assemblies

When you compile an application, the CIL code is stored in an *assembly*. Assemblies include both executable application files that you can run directly from Windows without the need for any other programs (these have a `.exe` file extension) and libraries (which have a `.dll` extension) for use by other applications.

In addition to containing CIL, assemblies also include *meta* information (that is, information about the information contained in the assembly, also known as *metadata*) and optional *resources* (additional data used by the CIL, such as sound files and pictures). The meta information enables assemblies to be fully self-descriptive. You need no other information to use an assembly, meaning you avoid situations such as failing to add required data to the system registry and so on, which was often a problem when developing with other platforms.

This means that deploying applications is often as simple as copying the files into a directory on a remote computer. Because no additional information is required on the target systems, you can just run an executable file from this directory and (assuming the .NET CLR is installed) you're good to go.

Of course, you won't necessarily want to include everything required to run an application in one place. You might write some code that performs tasks required by multiple applications. In situations like that, it is often useful to place the reusable code in a place accessible to all applications. In the .NET Framework, this is the *global assembly cache* (GAC). Placing code in the GAC is simple—you just place the assembly containing the code in the directory containing this cache.

## Managed Code

The role of the CLR doesn't end after you have compiled your code to CIL and a JIT compiler has compiled that to native code. Code written using the .NET Framework is *managed* when it is executed (a stage usually referred to as *runtime*). This means that the CLR looks after your applications by managing memory, handling security, allowing cross-language debugging, and so on. By contrast, applications that do not run under the control of the CLR are said to be *unmanaged,* and certain languages such as C++ can be used to write such applications, which, for example, access low-level functions of the operating system. However, in C# you can write only code that runs in a managed environment. You will make use of the managed features of the CLR and allow .NET itself to handle any interaction with the operating system.

## Garbage Collection

One of the most important features of managed code is the concept of *garbage collection.* This is the .NET method of making sure that the memory used by an application is freed up completely when the application is no longer in use. Prior to .NET this was mostly the responsibility of programmers, and a few simple errors in code could result in large blocks of memory mysteriously disappearing as a result of being allocated to the wrong place in memory. That usually meant a progressive slowdown of your computer, followed by a system crash.

.NET garbage collection works by periodically inspecting the memory of your computer and removing anything from it that is no longer needed. There is no set time frame for this; it might happen thousands of times a second, once every few seconds, or whenever, but you can rest assured that it will happen.

There are some implications for programmers here. Because this work is done for you at an unpredictable time, applications have to be designed with this in mind. Code that requires a lot of memory to run should tidy itself up, rather than wait for garbage collection to happen, but that isn't as tricky as it sounds.

## Fitting It Together

Before moving on, let's summarize the steps required to create a .NET application as discussed previously:

1. Application code is written using a .NET-compatible language such as C# (see Figure 1-1).
2. That code is compiled into CIL, which is stored in an assembly (see Figure 1-2).

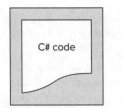

FIGURE 1-1

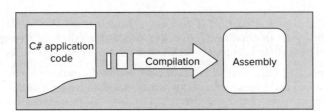

FIGURE 1-2

3. When this code is executed (either in its own right if it is an executable or when it is used from other code), it must first be compiled into native code using a JIT compiler (see Figure 1-3).

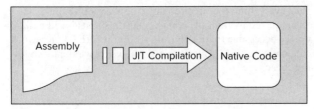

FIGURE 1-3

4. The native code is executed in the context of the managed CLR, along with any other running applications or processes, as shown in Figure 1-4.

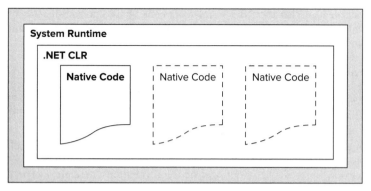

**FIGURE 1-4**

## Linking

Note one additional point concerning this process. The C# code that compiles into CIL in step 2 needn't be contained in a single file. It's possible to split application code across multiple source-code files, which are then compiled together into a single assembly. This extremely useful process is known as *linking*. It is required because it is far easier to work with several smaller files than one enormous one. You can separate logically related code into an individual file so that it can be worked on independently and then practically forgotten about when completed. This also makes it easy to locate specific pieces of code when you need them and enables teams of developers to divide the programming burden into manageable chunks, whereby individuals can "check out" pieces of code to work on without risking damage to otherwise satisfactory sections or sections other people are working on.

## WHAT IS C#?

C#, as mentioned earlier, is one of the languages you can use to create applications that will run in the .NET CLR. It is an evolution of the C and C++ languages and has been created by Microsoft specifically to work with the .NET platform. The C# language has been designed to incorporate many of the best features from other languages, while clearing up their problems.

Developing applications using C# is simpler than using C++, because the language syntax is simpler. Still, C# is a powerful language, and there is little you might want to do in C++ that you can't do in C#. Having said that, those features of C# that parallel the more advanced features of C++, such as directly accessing and manipulating system memory, can be carried out only by using code marked as *unsafe*. This advanced programmatic technique is potentially dangerous (hence its name) because it is possible to overwrite system-critical blocks of memory with potentially catastrophic results. For this reason, and others, this book does not cover that topic.

At times, C# code is slightly more verbose than C++. This is a consequence of C# being a *typesafe* language (unlike C++). In layperson's terms, this means that once some data has been assigned to a type, it cannot subsequently transform itself into another unrelated type. Consequently, strict rules must be adhered to when converting between types, which means you will often need to write more code to carry out the same task in C# than you might write in C++. However, there are benefits to this—The code is more robust, debugging is simpler, and .NET can always track the type of a piece of data at any time. In C#, you therefore might not be able to do things such as "take the region of memory 4 bytes into this data and 10 bytes long and interpret it as X," but that's not necessarily a bad thing.

C# is just one of the languages available for .NET development, but it is certainly the best. It has the advantage of being the only language designed from the ground up for the .NET Framework and is the principal language used in versions of .NET that are ported to other operating systems. To keep languages such as the .NET version of Visual Basic as similar as possible to their predecessors yet compliant with the CLR, certain features of the .NET code library are not fully supported, or at least require unusual syntax.

By contrast, C# can make use of every feature that the .NET Framework code library has to offer. Also, each new version of .NET has included additions to the C# language, partly in response to requests from developers, making it even more powerful.

## Applications You Can Write with C#

The .NET Framework has no restrictions on the types of applications that are possible, as discussed earlier. C# uses the framework and therefore has no restrictions on possible applications. However, here are a few of the more common application types:

➤ **Desktop applications**—Applications, such as Microsoft Office, that have a familiar Windows look and feel about them. This is made simple by using the Windows Presentation Foundation (WPF) module of the .NET Framework, which is a library of *controls* (such as buttons, toolbars, menus, and so on) that you can use to build a Windows user interface (UI).

➤ **Windows Store applications**—Windows 8 has introduced a new type of application, known as a Windows Store application. This type of application is designed primarily for touch devices, and it is usually run full-screen, with a minimum of clutter, and an emphasis on simplicity. You can create these applications in several ways, including using WPF.

➤ **Web applications**—Web pages such as those that might be viewed through any web browser. The .NET Framework includes a powerful system for generating web content dynamically, enabling personalization, security, and much more. This system is called ASP.NET (Active Server Pages .NET), and you can use C# to create ASP.NET applications using Web Forms. You can also write applications that run inside the browser with Silverlight.

➤ **WCF services**—A way to create versatile distributed applications. Using WCF you can exchange virtually any data over local networks or the Internet, using the same simple syntax regardless of the language used to create a service or the system on which it resides.

Any of these types might also require some form of database access, which can be achieved using the ADO.NET (Active Data Objects .NET) section of the .NET Framework, through the ADO.NET Entity Framework, or through the LINQ (Language Integrated Query) capabilities of C#. Many other resources can be drawn on, such as tools for creating networking components, outputting graphics, performing complex mathematical tasks, and so on.

## C# in this Book

The first part of this book deals with the syntax and usage of the C# language without too much emphasis on the .NET Framework. This is necessary because you can't use the .NET Framework at all without a firm grounding in C# programming. You'll start off even simpler, in fact, and leave the more involved topic of OOP until you've covered the basics. These are taught from first principles, assuming no programming knowledge at all.

After that, you'll be ready to move on to developing more complex (but more useful) applications. Part II of this book looks at desktop and Windows Store application programming, Part III tackles web application programming, Part IV examines data access (for database, filesystem, and XML data) and LINQ, and Part V covers some other .NET topics of interest.

## VISUAL STUDIO 2012

In this book, you use the Visual Studio 2012 development tool for all of your C# programming, from simple command-line applications to more complex project types. A development tool, or integrated development environment (IDE), such as VS isn't essential for developing C# applications, but it makes things much easier. You can (if you want to) manipulate C# source code files in a basic text editor, such as the ubiquitous Notepad application, and compile code into assemblies using the command-line compiler that is part of the .NET Framework. However, why do this when you have the power of an IDE to help you?

The following is a short list of some Visual Studio features that make it an appealing choice for .NET development:

➤ VS automates the steps required to compile source code but at the same time gives you complete control over any options used should you want to override them.

➤ The VS text editor is tailored to the languages VS supports (including C#) so that it can intelligently detect errors and suggest code where appropriate as you are typing. This feature is called *IntelliSense*.

➤ VS includes designers for XAML, ASP.NET, and other UI languages, enabling simple drag-and-drop design of UI elements.

➤ Many types of C# projects can be created with "boilerplate" code already in place. Instead of starting from scratch, you will often find that various code files are started for you, reducing the amount of time spent getting started on a project.

➤ VS includes several wizards that automate common tasks, many of which can add appropriate code to existing files without you having to worry about (or even, in some cases, remember) the correct syntax.

➤ VS contains many powerful tools for visualizing and navigating through elements of your projects, whether they are C# source code files or other resources such as bitmap images or sound files.

➤ As well as simply writing applications in VS, you can create deployment projects, making it easy to supply code to clients and for them to install it without much trouble.

➤ VS enables you to use advanced debugging techniques when developing projects, such as the capability to step through code one instruction at a time while keeping an eye on the state of your application.

There is much more than this, but you get the idea!

## Visual Studio Express 2012 Products

In addition to Visual Studio 2012, Microsoft also supplies several simpler development tools known as Visual Studio Express 2012 Products. These are freely available at `http://www.microsoft.com/express`.

The various express products enable you to create almost any C# application you might need. They function as slimmed-down versions of VS and retain the same look and feel. While they offer many of the same features as VS, some notable feature are absent, although not so many that they would prevent you from using these tools to work through the chapters of this book.

> **NOTE** *This book was written using the Professional version of Visual Studio 2012 because the Express products were not available. At the time of writing, there is an Express product scheduled for release called Visual Studio Express 2012 for Windows Desktop that should be sufficient for the following along with the first part of this book. The remainder of the book may also allow you to use Visual Studio Express 2012 for Windows 8 and Visual Studio Express 2012 for web, but at the time of writing we can't say for certain whether that will hold true.*

## Solutions

When you use VS to develop applications, you do so by creating *solutions*. A solution, in VS terms, is more than just an application. Solutions contain *projects*, which might be WPF projects, Web Application projects, and so on. Because solutions can contain multiple projects, you can group together related code in one place, even if it will eventually compile to multiple assemblies in various places on your hard disk.

This is very useful because it enables you to work on shared code (which might be placed in the GAC) at the same time as applications that use this code. Debugging code is a lot easier when only one development environment is used, because you can step through instructions in multiple code modules.

## SUMMARY

In this chapter, you looked at the .NET Framework in general terms and discovered how it makes it easy for you to create powerful and versatile applications. You saw what is necessary to turn code in languages such as C# into working applications, and what benefits you gain from using managed code running in the .NET CLR.

You also learned what C# actually is and how it relates to the .NET Framework, and you were introduced to the tool that you'll use for C# development—Visual Studio 2012.

In the next chapter, you get some C# code running, which will give you enough knowledge to sit back and concentrate on the C# language itself, rather than worry too much about how the IDE works.

## ▶ WHAT YOU LEARNED IN THIS CHAPTER

| TOPIC | KEY CONCEPTS |
| --- | --- |
| **.NET Framework fundamentals** | The .NET Framework is Microsoft's latest development platform, and is currently in version 4.5. It includes a common type system (CTS) and common language runtime (CLR). .NET Framework applications are written using object-oriented programming (OOP) methodology, and usually contain managed code. Memory management of managed code is handled by the .NET runtime; this includes garbage collection. |
| **.NET Framework applications** | Applications written using the .NET Framework are first compiled into CIL. When an application is executed, the CLR uses a JIT to compile this CIL into native code as required. Applications are compiled and different parts are linked together into assemblies that contain the CIL. |
| **C# basics** | C# is one of the languages included in the .NET Framework. It is an evolution of previous languages such as C++, and can be used to write any number of applications, including web and desktop applications. |
| **Integrated Development Environments (IDEs)** | You can use Visual Studio 2012 to write any type of .NET application using C#. You can also use the free, but less powerful, Express product range to create .NET applications in C#. Both of these IDEs work with solutions, which can consist of multiple projects. |

# Writing a C# Program

➤ A basic working knowledge of Visual Studio 2012

➤ How to write a simple console application

➤ How to write a simple desktop application

**WROX.COM CODE DOWNLOADS FOR THIS CHAPTER**

The wrox.com code downloads for this chapter are found at www.wrox.com/remtitle
.cgi?isbn=9781118314418 on the Download Code tab. The code is in the Chapter 2 download and
individually named according to the names throughout the chapter.

Now that you've spent some time learning what C# is and how it fits into the .NET Framework, it's
time to get your hands dirty and write some code. You use Visual Studio 2012 (VS) throughout this
book, so the first thing to do is have a look at some of the basics of this development environment.

VS is an enormous and complicated product, and it can be daunting to first-time users, but using it to
create basic applications can be surprisingly simple. As you start to use VS in this chapter, you will see
that you don't need to know a huge amount about it to begin playing with C# code. Later in the book
you'll see some of the more complicated operations that VS can perform, but for now a basic working
knowledge is all that is required.

After you've looked at the IDE, you put together two simple applications. You don't need to worry too
much about the code in these for now; you just want to prove that things work. By working through
the application-creation procedures in these early examples, they will become second nature before
too long.

You will learn how to create two basic types of applications in this chapter: a *console application* and
a *desktop application*.

The first application you create is a simple console application. Console applications don't use the
graphical windows environment, so you won't have to worry about buttons, menus, interaction with
the mouse pointer, and so on. Instead, you run the application in a command prompt window and
interact with it in a much simpler way.

The second application is a desktop application, which you create using Windows Presentation Foundation (WPF). The look and feel of a desktop application is very familiar to Windows users, and (surprisingly) the application doesn't require much more effort to create. However, the syntax of the code required is more complicated, even though in many cases you don't actually have to worry about details.

You use both types of application over the next two parts of the book, with more emphasis on console applications at the beginning. The additional flexibility of desktop applications isn't necessary when you are learning the C# language, while the simplicity of console applications enables you to concentrate on learning the syntax without worrying about the look and feel of the application.

## THE VISUAL STUDIO 2012 DEVELOPMENT ENVIRONMENT

When VS is first loaded, it immediately presents you with a host of windows, most of which are empty, along with an array of menu items and toolbar icons. You will be using most of these in the course of this book, and you can rest assured that they will look far more familiar before too long.

If this is the first time you've run VS, you will be presented with a list of preferences intended for users who have experience with previous releases of this development environment. The choices you make here affect a number of things, such as the layout of windows, the way that console windows run, and so on. Therefore, choose Visual C# Development Settings; otherwise, you might find that things don't quite work as described in this book. Note that the options available vary depending on the options you chose when installing VS, but as long as you chose to install C# this option will be available.

If this isn't the first time that you've run VS, but you chose a different option the first time, don't panic. To reset the settings to Visual C# Development settings, you simply have to import them. To do this, select Tools ⇨ Import and Export Settings, and choose the Reset All Settings option, shown in Figure 2-1.

Click Next, and indicate whether you want to save your existing settings before proceeding. If you have customized things, you might want to do this; otherwise, select No and click Next again. From the next dialog box, select Visual C# Development Settings, shown in Figure 2-2. Again, the available options may vary.

Finally, click Finish to apply the settings.

The VS environment layout is completely customizable, but the default is fine here. With C# Developer Settings selected, it is arranged as shown in Figure 2-3.

FIGURE 2-1

FIGURE 2-2

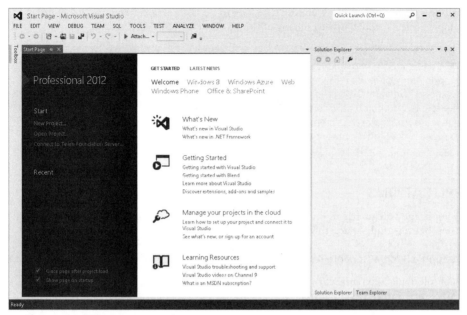

**FIGURE 2-3**

The main window, which contains a helpful Start Page by default when VS is started, is where all your code is displayed. This window can contain many documents, each indicated by a tab, so you can easily switch between several files by clicking their filenames. It also has other functions: It can display GUIs that you are designing for your projects, plain-text files, HTML, and various tools that are built into VS. You will come across all of these in the course of this book.

Above the main window are toolbars and the VS menu. Several different toolbars can be placed here, with functionality ranging from saving and loading files to building and running projects to debugging controls. Again, you are introduced to these as you need to use them.

Here are brief descriptions of each of the main features that you will use the most:

➤ The Toolbox window pops up when you click its tab. It provides access to, among other things, the user interface building blocks for desktop applications. Another tab, Server Explorer, can also appear here (selectable via the View ➪ Server Explorer menu option) and includes various additional capabilities, such as providing access to datasources, server settings, services, and more.

➤ The Solution Explorer window displays information about the currently loaded *solution*. A solution, as you learned in the previous chapter, is VS terminology for one or more projects along with their configurations. The Solution Explorer window displays various views of the projects in a solution, such as what files they contain and what is contained in those files.

➤ The Team Explorer window displays information about the current Team Foundation Server or Team Foundation Service connection. This allows you access to source control, bug tracking, build automation, and other functionality. However, this is an advanced subject and is not covered in this book.

➤ Just below the Solution Explorer window you can display a Properties window, not shown in Figure 2-3 because it appears only when you are working on a project (you can also toggle its display using View ➪ Properties Window). This window provides a more detailed view of the project's contents, enabling you to perform additional configuration of individual elements. For example, you can use this window to change the appearance of a button in a desktop application.

➤ Also not shown in the screenshot is another extremely important window: the Error List window, which you can display using View ➪ Error List. It shows errors, warnings, and other project-related information. The window updates continuously, although some information appears only when a project is compiled.

This might seem like a lot to take in, but it doesn't take long to get comfortable. You start by building the first of your example projects, which involves many of the VS elements just described.

> **NOTE** *VS is capable of displaying many other windows, both informational and functional. Many of these can share screen space with the windows mentioned here, and you can switch between them using tabs, dock them elsewhere, or even detach them and place them on other displays if you have multiple monitors. Several of these windows are used later in the book, and you'll probably discover more yourself when you explore the VS environment in more detail.*

## CONSOLE APPLICATIONS

You use console applications regularly in this book, particularly at the beginning, so the following Try It Out provides a step-by-step guide to creating a simple one.

**TRY IT OUT** Creating a Simple Console Application: ConsoleApplication1\Program.cs

**1.** Create a new console application project by selecting File ⇨ New ⇨ Project, as shown in Figure 2-4.

**2.** Ensure that the Visual C# node is selected in the left pane of the window that appears, and choose the Console Application project type in the middle pane (see Figure 2-5). Change the Location text box to C:\BegVCSharp\Chapter02 (this directory is created automatically if it doesn't already exist). Leave the default text in the Name text box (ConsoleApplication1) and the other settings as they are (refer to Figure 2-5).

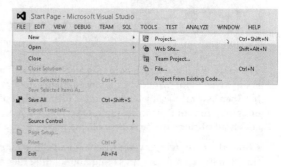

**FIGURE 2-4**

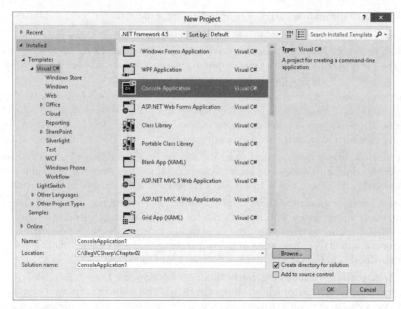

**FIGURE 2-5**

**3.** Click the OK button.

**4.** Once the project is initialized, add the following lines of code to the file displayed in the main window:

```
namespace ConsoleApplication1
{
    class Program
    {
        static void Main(string[] args)
        {
            // Output text to the screen.
            Console.WriteLine("The first app in Beginning Visual C# 2012!");
            Console.ReadKey();
        }
    }
}
```

**5.** Select the Debug ➪ Start Debugging menu item. After a few moments you should see the window shown in Figure 2-6.

**FIGURE 2-6**

**6.** Press any key to exit the application (you might need to click on the console window to focus on it first).

The display in Figure 2-6 appears only if the Visual C# Developer Settings are applied, as described earlier in this chapter. For example, with Visual Basic Developer Settings applied, an empty console window is displayed, and the application output appears in a window labeled `Immediate`. In this case, the `Console.ReadKey()` code also fails, and you see an error. If you experience this problem, the best solution for working through the examples in this book is to apply the Visual C# Developer Settings—that way, the results you see match the results shown here. If this problem persists, then open the Tools ➪ Options window and uncheck the Debugging ➪ Redirect All Output Window text to the Immediate Window option, as shown in Figure 2-7.

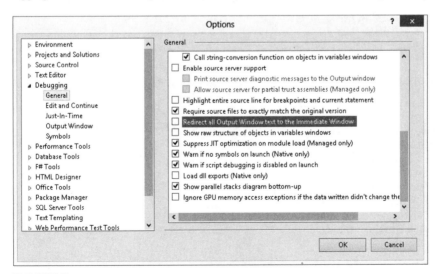

**FIGURE 2-7**

### How It Works

For now, I won't dissect the code used thus far because the focus here is on how to use the development tools to get code up and running. Clearly, VS does a lot of the work for you and makes the process of compiling and executing code simple. In fact, there are multiple ways to perform even these basic steps—for instance, you can create a new project by using the menu item mentioned earlier, by pressing Ctrl+Shift+N, or by clicking the corresponding icon in the toolbar.

Similarly, your code can be compiled and executed in several ways. The process you used in the example—selecting Debug ➪ Start Debugging—also has a keyboard shortcut (F5) and a toolbar icon. You can also run code without being in debugging mode using the Debug ➪ Start Without Debugging menu item (or by pressing Ctrl+F5), or compile your project without running it (with debugging on or off) using Build ➪ Build Solution or pressing F6. Note that you can execute a project without debugging or build a project using toolbar icons, although these icons don't appear on the toolbar by default. After you have compiled your code, you can also execute it simply by running the .exe file produced in Windows Explorer, or from the command prompt. To do this, open a command prompt window, change the directory to C:\BegVCSharp\Chapter02\ConsoleApplication1\ConsoleApplication1\bin\Debug\, type **ConsoleApplication1**, and press Enter.

> **NOTE**  *In future examples, when you see the instructions "create a new console project" or "execute the code," you can choose whichever method you want to perform these steps. Unless otherwise stated, all code should be run with debugging enabled. In addition, the terms "start," "execute," and "run" are used interchangeably in this book, and discussions following examples always assume that you have exited the application in the example.*
>
> *Console applications terminate as soon as they finish execution, which can mean that you don't get a chance to see the results if you run them directly through the IDE. To get around this in the preceding example, the code is told to wait for a key press before terminating, using the following line:*
>
> ```
> Console.ReadKey();
> ```
>
> *You will see this technique used many times in later examples. Now that you've created a project, you can take a more detailed look at some of the regions of the development environment.*

## The Solution Explorer

By default, the Solution Explorer window is docked in the top-right corner of the screen. As with other windows, you can move it wherever you like, or you can set it to auto-hide by clicking the pin icon. The Solution Explorer window shares space with another useful window called Class View, which you can display using View ➪ Class View. Figure 2-8 shows both of these windows with all nodes expanded (you can toggle between them by clicking on the tabs at the bottom of the window when the window is docked).

This Solution Explorer view shows the files that make up the ConsoleApplication1 project. The file to which you added code, Program.cs, is shown

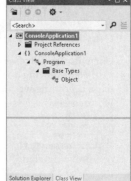

**FIGURE 2-8**

along with another code file, AssemblyInfo.cs, and several references.

You don't have to worry about the `AssemblyInfo.cs` file for the moment. It contains extra information about your project that doesn't concern you yet.

You can use this window to change what code is displayed in the main window by double-clicking `.cs` files; right-clicking them and selecting View Code; or by selecting them and clicking the toolbar button that appears at the top of the window. You can also perform other operations on files here, such as renaming them or deleting them from your project. Other file types can also appear here, such as project resources (resources are files used by the project that might not be C# files, such as bitmap images and sound files). Again, you can manipulate them through the same interface.

You can also expand code items such as `Program.cs` to see what is contained. This overview of your code structure can be a very useful tool; it also enables you to navigate directly to specific parts of your code file, instead of opening the code file and scrolling to the part you want.

The `References` entry contains a list of the .NET libraries you are using in your project. You'll look at this later; the standard references are fine for now. Class View presents an alternative view of your project by showing the structure of the code you created. You'll come back to this later in the book; for now the Solution Explorer display is appropriate. As you click on files or other icons in these windows, notice that the contents of the Properties window (shown in Figure 2-9) changes.

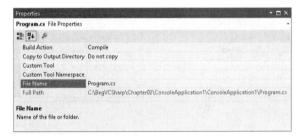

**FIGURE 2-9**

## The Properties Window

The Properties window (select View ⇨ Properties Window if it isn't already displayed) shows additional information about whatever you select in the window above it. For example, the view shown in Figure 2-9 is displayed when the `Program.cs` file from the project is selected. This window also displays information about other selected items, such as user interface components (as shown in the "Desktop Applications" section of this chapter).

Often, changes you make to entries in the Properties window affect your code directly, adding lines of code or changing what you have in your files. With some projects, you spend as much time manipulating things through this window as making manual code changes.

## The Error List Window

Currently, the Error List window (View ⇨ Error List) isn't showing anything interesting because there is nothing wrong with the application. However, this is a very useful window indeed. As a test, remove the semicolon from one of the lines of code you added in the previous section. After a moment, you should see a display like the one shown in Figure 2-10.

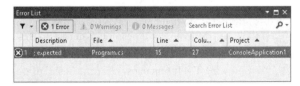

**FIGURE 2-10**

In addition, the project will no longer compile.

> **NOTE** *In Chapter 3, when you start looking at C# syntax, you will learn that semicolons are expected throughout your code — at the end of most lines, in fact.*

This window helps you eradicate bugs in your code because it keeps track of what you have to do to compile projects. If you double-click the error shown here, the cursor jumps to the position of the error in your source code (the source file containing the error will be opened if it isn't already open), so you can fix it quickly. Red wavy lines appear at the positions of errors in the code, so you can quickly scan the source code to see where problems lie.

The error location is specified as a line number. By default, line numbers aren't displayed in the VS text editor, but that is something well worth turning on. To do so, tick the Line numbers check box in the Options dialog box (selected via the Tools ➪ Options menu item). It appears in the Text Editor ➪ All Languages ➪ General category, as shown in Figure 2-11.

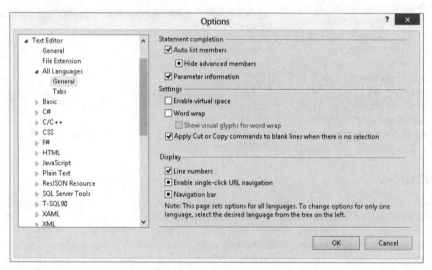

**FIGURE 2-11**

You can also change this setting on a per-language basis through the language-specific settings pages in the dialog box. Many other useful options can be found through this dialog box, and you will use several of them later in this book.

## DESKTOP APPLICATIONS

It is often easier to demonstrate code by running it as part of a desktop application than through a console window or via a command prompt. You can do this using user interface building blocks to piece together a user interface.

The following Try It Out shows just the basics of doing this, and you'll see how to get a desktop application up and running without a lot of details about what the application is actually doing. You'll use WPF here, which is Microsoft's recommended technology for creating desktop applications. Later, you take a detailed look at desktop applications and learn much more about what WPF is and what it's capable of.

Creating a Simple Windows Application: WpfApplication1\MainWindow.xaml and WpfApplication1\MainWindow.xaml.cs

**1.** Create a new project of type WPF Application in the same location as before (C:\BegVCSharp\Chapter02), with the default name WpfApplication1. If the first project is still open, make sure the Create New Solution option is selected to start a new solution. These settings are shown in Figure 2-12.

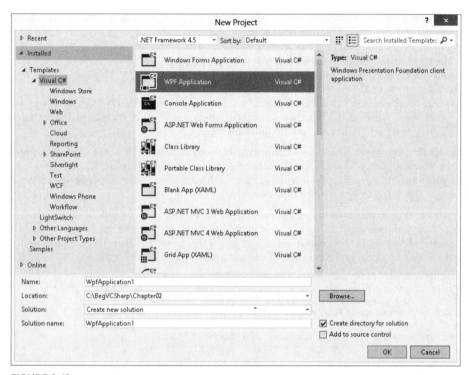

**FIGURE 2-12**

**2.** Click OK to create the project. You should see a new tab that's split into two panes. The top pane shows an empty window called MainWindow and the bottom pane shows some text. This text is actually the code that is used to generate the window, and you'll see it change as you modify the UI.

**3.** Click the Toolbox tab on the top left of the screen, then double-click the Button entry in the Common WPF Controls section to add a button to the window.

**4.** Double-click the button that has been added to the window.

**5.** The C# code in MainWindow.xaml.cs should now be displayed. Modify it as follows (only part of the code in the file is shown here for brevity):

```
private void Button_Click_1(object sender, EventArgs e)
{
    MessageBox.Show("The first desktop app in the book!");
}
```

**6.** Run the application.

**7.** Click the button presented to open a message dialog box, as shown in Figure 2-13.

**8.** Click OK, and then exit the application by clicking the X in the top-right corner, as is standard for desktop applications.

### How It Works

Again, it is plain that the IDE has done a lot of work for you and made it simple to create a functional desktop application with little effort. The application you created behaves just like other windows—you can move it around, resize it, minimize it, and so on. You don't have to write the code to do that—it just

**FIGURE 2-13**

works. The same is true for the button you added. Simply by double-clicking it, the IDE knew that you wanted to write code to execute when a user clicked the button in the running application. All you had to do was provide that code, getting full button-clicking functionality for free.

Of course, desktop applications aren't limited to plain windows with buttons. Look at the Toolbox window where you found the Button option and you'll see a whole host of user interface building blocks (known as *controls*), some of which might be familiar. You will use most of these at some point in the book, and you'll find that they are all easy to use and save you a lot of time and effort.

The code for your application, in `MainWindow.xaml.cs`, doesn't look much more complicated than the code in the previous section, and the same is true for the code in the other files in the Solution Explorer window. The code you saw in `MainWindow.xaml` (the split-pane view where you added the button) also looks pretty straightforward. Below the graphical representation of the window, you can see the following:

```
<Window x:Class="WpfApplication1.MainWindow"
    xmlns="http://schemas.microsoft.com/winfx/2006/xaml/presentation"
    xmlns:x="http://schemas.microsoft.com/winfx/2006/xaml"
    Title="MainWindow" Height="350" Width="525">
    <Grid>
        <Button Content="Button" HorizontalAlignment="Left"
            VerticalAlignment="Top" Width="75" Click="Button_Click_1" />
    </Grid>
</Window>
```

This code is written in XAML, which is the language used to define user interfaces in WPF applications.

Now take a closer look at the button you added to the window. In the top pane of `MainWindow.xaml`, click once on the button to select it. When you do so, the Properties window in the bottom-right corner of the screen shows the properties of the button control (controls have properties much like the files shown in the last example). Ensure that the application isn't currently running, scroll down to the `Content` property, which is currently set to `Button`, and change the value to `Click Me`, as shown in Figure 2-14.

The text written on the button in the designer should also reflect this change, as should the XAML code, as shown in Figure 2-15.

**FIGURE 2-14**

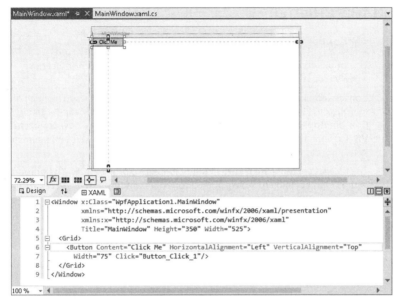

**FIGURE 2-15**

There are many properties for this button, ranging from simple formatting of the color and size to more obscure settings such as data binding, which enables you to establish links to data. As briefly mentioned in the previous example, changing properties often results in direct changes to code, and this is no exception, as you saw with the XAML code change. However, if you switch back to the code view of MainWindow.xaml.cs, you won't see any changes there. This is because WPF applications are capable of keeping design aspects of your applications (such as the text on a button) separate from the functionality aspects (such as what happens when you click a button).

> **NOTE** *Note that it is also possible to use Windows Forms to create desktop applications. WPF is a newer technology that is intended to replace Windows Forms and provides a far more flexible and powerful way to create desktop applications, which is why this book doesn't cover Windows Forms.*

## SUMMARY

This chapter introduced some of the tools that you will use throughout the rest of this book. You took a quick tour around the Visual Studio 2012 development environment and used it to build two types of applications. The simpler of these, the console application, is quite enough for most needs, and it enables you to focus on the basics of C# programming. Desktop applications are more complicated but are visually more impressive and intuitive to use for anyone accustomed to a Windows environment (and let's face it, that's most of us).

Now that you know how to create simple applications, you can get down to the real task of learning C#. After dealing with basic C# syntax and program structure, you move on to more advanced object-oriented methods. Once you've covered all those, you can begin to learn how to use C# to gain access to the power available in the .NET Framework.

## ▶ WHAT YOU LEARNED IN THIS CHAPTER

| TOPIC | KEY CONCEPTS |
| --- | --- |
| **Visual Studio 2012 settings** | This book requires the C# development settings option, which you choose when you first run Visual Studio or by resetting the settings. |
| **Console applications** | Console applications are simple command-line applications, used in much of this book to illustrate techniques. Create a new console application with the Console Application template that you see when you create a new project in VS. To run a project in debug mode, use the Debug ⇨ Start Debugging menu item, or press F5. |
| **IDE windows** | The project contents are shown in the Solution Explorer window. The properties of the selected item are shown in the Properties window. Errors are shown in the Error List window. |
| **Desktop applications** | Desktop applications are applications that have the look and feel of standard Windows applications, including the familiar icons to maximize, minimize, and close an application. They are created with the WPF Application template in the New Project dialog box. |

# Variables and Expressions

**WHAT YOU WILL LEARN IN THIS CHAPTER**

➤ Basic C# syntax

➤ Variables and how to use them

➤ Expressions and how to use them

**WROX.COM CODE DOWNLOADS FOR THIS CHAPTER**

You can find the wrox.com code downloads for this chapter at www.wrox.com/remtitle .cgi?isbn=9781118314418 on the Download Code tab. The code is in the Chapter 3 download and individually named according to the names throughout the chapter.

To use C# effectively, it's important to understand what you're actually doing when you create a computer program. Perhaps the most basic description of a computer program is that it is a series of operations that manipulate data. This is true even of the most complicated examples, including vast, multi-featured Windows applications (such as the Microsoft Office Suite). Although this is often completely hidden from users of applications, it is always going on behind the scenes.

To illustrate this further, consider the display unit of your computer. What you see onscreen is often so familiar that it is difficult to imagine it as anything other than a "moving picture." In fact, what you see is only a representation of some data, which in its raw form is merely a stream of 0s and 1s stashed away somewhere in the computer's memory. Any onscreen action—moving a mouse pointer, clicking on an icon, typing text into a word processor—results in the shunting around of data in memory.

Of course, simpler situations show this just as well. When using a calculator application, you are supplying data as numbers and performing operations on the numbers in much the same way as you would with paper and pencil—but a lot quicker!

If computer programs are fundamentally performing operations on data, this implies that you need a way to store that data, and some methods to manipulate it. These two functions are provided by *variables* and *expressions*, respectively, and this chapter explores what that means, both in general and specific terms.

First, though, you'll take a look at the basic syntax involved in C# programming, because you need a context in which you can learn about and use variables and expressions in the C# language.

## BASIC C# SYNTAX

The look and feel of C# code is similar to that of C++ and Java. This syntax can look quite confusing at first and it's a lot less like written English than some other languages. However, as you immerse yourself in the world of C# programming, you'll find that the style used is a sensible one, and it is possible to write very readable code without much effort.

Unlike the compilers of some other languages, C# compilers ignore additional spacing in code, whether it results from spaces, carriage returns, or tab characters (collectively known as *whitespace characters*). This means you have a lot of freedom in the way that you format your code, although conforming to certain rules can help make your code easier to read.

C# code is made up of a series of *statements*, each of which is terminated with a semicolon. Because whitespace is ignored, multiple statements can appear on one line, although for readability it is usual to add carriage returns after semicolons, to avoid multiple statements on one line. It is perfectly acceptable (and quite normal), however, to use statements that span several lines of code.

C# is a *block-structured language*, meaning statements are part of a block of code. These blocks, which are delimited with curly brackets ({ and }), may contain any number of statements, or none at all. Note that the curly bracket characters do not need accompanying semicolons.

For example, a simple block of C# code could take the following form:

```
{
   <code line 1, statement 1>;
   <code line 2, statement 2>
      <code line 3, statement 2>;
}
```

Here the `<code line x, statement y>` sections are not actual pieces of C# code; this text is used as a placeholder where C# statements would go. In this case, the second and third lines of code are part of the same statement, because there is no semicolon after the second line.

The following simple example uses *indentation* to clarify the C# itself. This is actually standard practice, and in fact VS automatically does this for you by default. In general, each block of code has its own level of indentation, meaning how far to the right it is. Blocks of code may be nested inside each other (that is, blocks may contain other blocks), in which case nested blocks will be indented further:

```
{
   <code line 1>;
   {
      <code line 2>;
      <code line 3>;
   }
   <code line 4>;
}
```

In addition, lines of code that are continuations of previous lines are usually indented further as well, as in the third line of code in the first code example.

> **NOTE** Look in the VS Options dialog box (select Tools ⇨ Options) to see the rules that VS uses for formatting your code. There are many of these, in subcategories of the Text Editor ⇨ C# ⇨ Formatting node. Most of the settings here reflect parts of C# that haven't been covered yet, but you might want to return to these settings later if you want to tweak them to suit your personal style better. For clarity, this book shows all code snippets as they would be formatted by the default settings.

Of course, this style is by no means mandatory. If you don't use it, however, you will quickly find that things can get very confusing as you move through this book!

*Comments* are something else you often see in C# code. A comment is not, strictly speaking, C# code at all, but it happily cohabits with it. Comments are self-explanatory: They enable you to add descriptive text to your code—in plain English (or French, German, Mongolian, and so on)—which is ignored by the compiler. When you start dealing with lengthy code sections, it's useful to add reminders about exactly what you are doing, such as "this line of code asks the user for a number" or "this code section was written by Bob."

C# provides two ways of doing this. You can either place markers at the beginning and end of a comment or you can use a marker that means "everything on the rest of this line is a comment." The latter method is an exception to the rule mentioned previously about C# compilers ignoring carriage returns, but it is a special case.

To indicate comments using the first method, you use /* characters at the start of the comment and */ characters at the end. These may occur on a single line, or on different lines, in which case all lines in between are part of the comment. The only thing you can't type in the body of a comment is */, because that is interpreted as the end marker. For example, the following are okay:

```
/* This is a comment */

/* And so…
```

```
                … is this! */
```

The following, however, causes problems:

```
/* Comments often end with "*/" characters */
```

Here, the end of the comment (the characters after "*/") will be interpreted as C# code, and errors will occur.

The other commenting approach involves starting a comment with //. After that, you can write whatever you like—as long as you keep to one line! The following is okay:

```
// This is a different sort of comment.
```

The following fails, however, because the second line is interpreted as C# code:

```
// So is this,
   but this bit isn't.
```

This sort of commenting is useful to document statements because both can be placed on a single line:

```
<A statement>;          // Explanation of statement
```

It was stated earlier that there are two ways of commenting C# code, but there is a third type of comment in C#—although strictly speaking this is an extension of the // syntax. You can use single-line comments that start with three / symbols instead of two, like this:

```
/// A special comment
```

Under normal circumstances, they are ignored by the compiler—just like other comments—but you can configure VS to extract the text after these comments and create a specially formatted text file when a project is compiled. You can then use it to create documentation. In order for this documentation to be created, the comments must follow the rules of XML documentation—a subject not covered in this book but one that is well worth learning about if you have some spare time.

A *very* important point about C# code is that it is *case sensitive*. Unlike some other languages, you must enter code using exactly the right case, because using an uppercase letter instead of a lowercase one will prevent a project from compiling. For example, consider the following line of code, taken from Chapter 2:

```
Console.WriteLine("The first app in Beginning C# Programming!");
```

This code is understood by the C# compiler, as the case of the `Console.WriteLine()` command is correct. However, none of the following lines of code work:

```
console.WriteLine("The first app in Beginning C# Programming!");
CONSOLE.WRITELINE("The first app in Beginning C# Programming!");
Console.Writeline("The first app in Beginning C# Programming!");
```

Here, the case used is wrong, so the C# compiler won't know what you want. Luckily, as you will soon discover, VS is very helpful when it comes to entering code, and most of the time it knows (as much as a program can know) what you are trying to do. As you type, it suggests commands that you might like to use, and it tries to correct case problems.

## BASIC C# CONSOLE APPLICATION STRUCTURE

Here, you'll take a closer look at the console application example from Chapter 2 (`ConsoleApplication1`) and break down the structure a bit. Here's the code:

```
using System;
using System.Collections.Generic;
using System.Linq;
using System.Text;
using System.Threading.Tasks;

namespace ConsoleApplication1
{
    class Program
    {
        static void Main(string[] args)
        {
            // Output text to the screen.
            Console.WriteLine("The first app in Beginning C# Programming!");
            Console.ReadKey();
        }
    }
}
```

You can immediately see that all the syntactic elements discussed in the previous section are present here—semicolons, curly braces, and comments, along with appropriate indentation.

The most important section of code at the moment is the following:

```
static void Main(string[] args)
{
    // Output text to the screen.
    Console.WriteLine("The first app in Beginning C# Programming!");
    Console.ReadKey();
}
```

This is the code that is executed when you run your console application. Well, to be more precise, the code block enclosed in curly braces is executed. The comment line doesn't do anything, as mentioned earlier; it's just there for clarity. The other two code lines output some text to the console window and wait for a response, respectively, although the exact mechanisms of this don't need to concern you for now.

Note how to achieve the code outlining functionality shown in the previous chapter, albeit for a Windows application, since it is such a useful feature. You can do this with the `#region` and `#endregion` keywords, which define the start and end of a region of code that can be expanded and collapsed. For example, you could modify the generated code for `ConsoleApplication1` as follows:

```
#region Using directives

using System;
using System.Collections.Generic;
```

```
using System.Linq;
using System.Text;
using System.Threading.Tasks;
```

**#endregion**

This enables you to collapse this code into a single line and expand it again later should you want to look at the details. The `using` statements contained here, and the `namespace` statement just underneath, are explained at the end of this chapter.

> **NOTE** *Any keyword that starts with a # is actually a preprocessor directive and not, strictly speaking, a C# keyword. Other than the two described here,* #region *and* #endregion, *these can be quite complicated, and they have very specialized uses. This is one subject you might like to investigate yourself after you've worked through this book.*

For now, don't worry about the other code in the example, because the purpose of these first few chapters is to explain basic C# syntax, so the exact method of how the application execution gets to the point where `Console.WriteLine()` is called is of no concern. Later, the significance of this additional code is made clear.

## VARIABLES

As mentioned earlier, variables are concerned with the storage of data. Essentially, you can think of variables in computer memory as boxes sitting on a shelf. You can put things in boxes and take them out again, or you can just look inside a box to see if anything is there. The same goes for variables; you place data in them and can take it out or look at it, as required.

Although all data in a computer is effectively the same thing (a series of 0s and 1s), variables come in different flavors, known as *types*. Using the box analogy again, boxes come in different shapes and sizes, so some items fit only in certain boxes. The reasoning behind this type system is that different types of data may require different methods of manipulation, and by restricting variables to individual types you can avoid mixing them up. For example, it wouldn't make much sense to treat the series of 0s and 1s that make up a digital picture as an audio file.

To use variables, you have to *declare* them. This means that you have to assign them a *name* and a *type*. After you have declared variables, you can use them as storage units for the type of data that you declared them to hold.

C# syntax for declaring variables merely specifies the type and variable name:

```
<type> <name>;
```

If you try to use a variable that hasn't been declared, your code won't compile, but in this case the compiler tells you exactly what the problem is, so this isn't really a disastrous error. Trying to use a variable without assigning it a value also causes an error, but, again, the compiler detects this.

There are an almost infinite number of types that you can use. This is because you can define your own types to hold whatever convoluted data you like. Having said this, though, there are certain types of data that just about everyone will need to use at some point or another, such as a variable that stores a number. Therefore, you should be aware of several simple, predefined types.

## Simple Types

Simple types include types such as numbers and Boolean (true or false) values that make up the fundamental building blocks for your applications. Unlike complex types, simple types cannot have children or attributes. Most of the simple types available are numeric, which at first glance seems a bit strange—surely, you only need one type to store a number?

The reason for the plethora of numeric types is because of the mechanics of storing numbers as a series of 0s and 1s in the memory of a computer. For integer values, you simply take a number of *bits* (individual digits that can be 0 or 1) and represent your number in binary format. A variable storing N bits enables you to represent any number between 0 and $(2^N - 1)$. Any numbers above this value are too big to fit into this variable.

For example, suppose you have a variable that can store two bits. The mapping between integers and the bits representing those integers is therefore as follows:

```
0 = 00
1 = 01
2 = 10
3 = 11
```

In order to store more numbers, you need more bits (three bits enable you to store the numbers from 0 to 7, for example).

The inevitable result of this system is that you would need an infinite number of bits to be able to store every imaginable number, which isn't going to fit in your trusty PC. Even if there were a quantity of bits you could use for every number, it surely wouldn't be efficient to use all these bits for a variable that, for example, was required to store only the numbers between 0 and 10 (because storage would be wasted). Four bits would do the job fine here, enabling you to store many more values in this range in the same space of memory.

Instead, a number of different integer types can be used to store various ranges of numbers, which take up differing amounts of memory (up to 64 bits). These types are shown in Table 3-1.

> **NOTE** *Each of these types uses one of the standard types defined in the .NET Framework. As discussed in Chapter 1, this use of standard types is what enables language interoperability. The names you use for these types in C# are aliases for the types defined in the framework. Table 3-1 lists the names of these types as they are referred to in the .NET Framework library.*

**TABLE 3-1:** Integer Types

| TYPE | ALIAS FOR | ALLOWED VALUES |
| --- | --- | --- |
| sbyte | System.SByte | Integer between −128 and 127 |
| byte | System.Byte | Integer between 0 and 255 |
| short | System.Int16 | Integer between −32768 and 32767 |
| ushort | System.UInt16 | Integer between 0 and 65535 |
| int | System.Int32 | Integer between −2147483648 and 2147483647 |
| uint | System.UInt32 | Integer between 0 and 4294967295 |
| long | System.Int64 | Integer between −9223372036854775808 and 9223372036854775807 |
| ulong | System.UInt64 | Integer between 0 and 18446744073709551615 |

The u characters before some variable names are shorthand for *unsigned*, meaning that you can't store negative numbers in variables of those types, as shown in the Allowed Values column of the preceding table.

Of course, you also need to store *floating-point* values, those that aren't whole numbers. You can use three floating-point variable types: float, double, and decimal. The first two store floating points in the form $\pm m \times 2^e$, where the allowed values for m and e differ for each type. decimal uses the alternative form $\pm m \times 10^e$. These three types are shown in the following table, along with their allowed values of m and e, and these limits in real numeric terms (see Table 3-2).

**TABLE 3-2:** Floating-point Types

| TYPE | ALIAS FOR | MIN M | MAX M | MIN E | MAX E | APPROX MIN VALUE | APPROX MAX VALUE |
|------|-----------|-------|-------|-------|-------|------------------|------------------|
| float | System.Single | 0 | $2^{24}$ | –149 | 104 | $1.5 \times 10^{-45}$ | $3.4 \times 10^{38}$ |
| double | System.Double | 0 | $2^{53}$ | –1075 | 970 | $5.0 \times 10^{-324}$ | $1.7 \times 10^{308}$ |
| decimal | System.Decimal | 0 | $2^{96}$ | –28 | 0 | $1.0 \times 10^{-28}$ | $7.9 \times 10^{28}$ |

In addition to numeric types, three other simple types are available (see Table 3-3).

**TABLE 3-3:** Text and Boolean Types

| TYPE | ALIAS FOR | ALLOWED VALUES |
|------|-----------|----------------|
| char | System.Char | Single Unicode character, stored as an integer between 0 and 65535 |
| bool | System.Boolean | Boolean value, true or false |
| string | System.String | A sequence of characters |

Note that there is no upper limit on the amount of characters making up a string, because it can use varying amounts of memory.

The Boolean type bool is one of the most commonly used variable types in C#, and indeed similar types are equally prolific in code in other languages. Having a variable that can be either true or false has important ramifications when it comes to the flow of logic in an application. As a simple example, consider how many questions can be answered with true or false (or yes and no). Performing comparisons between variable values or validating input are just two of the programmatic uses of Boolean variables that you will examine very soon.

Now that you've seen these types, consider a short example that declares and uses them. In the following Try It Out you use some simple code that declares two variables, assigns them values, and then outputs these values.

**TRY IT OUT** Using Simple Type Variables: Ch03Ex01\Program.cs

**1.** Create a new console application called Ch03Ex01 and save it in the directory C:\BegVCSharp\Chapter03.

**2.** Add the following code to Program.cs:

```
static void Main(string[] args)
{
    int myInteger;
    string myString;
    myInteger = 17;
    myString = "\"myInteger\" is";
    Console.WriteLine("{0} {1}.", myString, myInteger);
    Console.ReadKey();
}
```

**3.** Execute the code. The result is shown in Figure 3-1.

file:///C:/BegVCSharp/Chapter03/Ch03Ex01/Ch03Ex01/bin/Debug/Ch03Ex01.EXE

"myInteger" is 17.

**FIGURE 3-1**

*How It Works*

The added code performs three tasks:

➤   It declares two variables.

➤   It assigns values to those two variables.

➤   It outputs the values of the two variables to the console.

Variable declaration occurs in the following code:

```
int myInteger;
string myString;
```

The first line declares a variable of type `int` with a name of `myInteger`, and the second line declares a variable of type `string` called `myString`.

> **NOTE** *Variable naming is restricted; you can't use just any sequence of characters. You learn about this in the section entitled "Variable Naming."*

The next two lines of code assign values:

```
myInteger = 17;
myString = "\"myInteger\" is";
```

Here, you assign two fixed values (known as *literal* values in code) to your variables using the = *assignment operator* (the "Expressions" section of this chapter has more details about operators). You assign the integer value 17 to `myInteger`, and you assigned the following string (including the quotes) to `myString`:

**"myInteger" is**

When you assign string literal values in this way, double quotation marks are required to enclose the string. Therefore, certain characters might cause problems if they are included in the string itself, such as the double quotation characters, and you must escape some characters by substituting a sequence of other characters (an *escape sequence*) that represents the character(s) you want to use. In this example, you use the sequence \" to escape a double quotation mark:

```
myString = "\"myInteger\" is";
```

If you didn't use these escape sequences and tried coding this as follows, you would get a compiler error:

```
myString = ""myInteger" is";
```

Note that assigning string literals is another situation in which you must be careful with line breaks—the C# compiler rejects string literals that span more than one line. If you want to add a line break, then use the escape sequence for a newline character in your string, which is \n. For example, consider the following assignment:

```
myString = "This string has a\nline break.";
```

This string would be displayed on two lines in the console view as follows:

```
This string has a
line break.
```

All escape sequences consist of the backslash symbol followed by one of a small set of characters (you'll see the full set later). Because this symbol is used for this purpose, there is also an escape sequence for the backslash symbol itself, which is simply two consecutive backslashes (\\).

Getting back to the code, there is one more new line to look at:

```
Console.WriteLine("{0} {1}.", myString, myInteger);
```

This looks similar to the simple method of writing text to the console that you saw in the first example, but now you are specifying your variables. It's too soon to dive into the details of this line of code, but suffice it to say that it is the technique you will be using in the first part of this book to output text to the console window. Within the brackets you have two things:

➤ A string

➤ A list of variables whose values you want to insert into the output string, separated by commas

The string you are outputting, "{0} {1}.", doesn't seem to contain much useful text. As shown earlier, however, this is not what you actually see when you run the code. This is because the string is actually a template into which you insert the contents of your variables. Each set of curly brackets in the string is a placeholder that will contain the contents of one of the variables in the list. Each placeholder (or format string) is represented as an integer enclosed in curly brackets. The integers start at 0 and are incremented by 1, and the total number of placeholders should match the number of variables specified in the comma-separated list following the string. When the text is output to the console, each placeholder is replaced by the corresponding value for each variable. In the preceding example, the {0} is replaced with the actual value of the first variable, myString, and {1} is replaced with the contents of myInteger.

This method of outputting text to the console is what you use to display output from your code in the examples that follow. Finally, the code includes the line shown in the earlier example for waiting for user input before terminating:

```
Console.ReadKey();
```

Again, the code isn't dissected now, but you will see it frequently in later examples. For now, understand that it pauses code execution until you press a key.

## Variable Naming

As mentioned in the previous section, you can't just choose any sequence of characters as a variable name. This isn't as worrying as it might sound, however, because you're still left with a very flexible naming system.

The basic variable naming rules are as follows:

➤ The first character of a variable name must be either a letter, an underscore character(_), or the *at* symbol (@).

➤ Subsequent characters may be letters, underscore characters, or numbers.

There are also certain keywords that have a specialized meaning to the C# compiler, such as the using and namespace keywords shown earlier. If you use one of these by mistake, the compiler complains, however, so don't worry about it.

For example, the following variable names are fine:

```
myBigVar
VAR1
_test
```

These are not, however:

```
99BottlesOfBeer
namespace
It's-All-Over
```

Remember that C# is case sensitive, so be careful not to forget the exact case used when you declare your variables. References to them made later in the program with even so much as a single letter in the wrong case prevents compilation. A further consequence of this is that you can have multiple variables whose names differ only in case. For example, the following are all separate names:

```
myVariable
MyVariable
MYVARIABLE
```

## Naming Conventions

Variable names are something you will use *a lot*, so it's worth spending a bit of time learning the sort of names you should use. Before you get started, though, bear in mind that this is controversial ground. Over the years, different systems have come and gone, and many developers will fight tooth and nail to justify their personal system.

Until recently the most popular system was what is known as *Hungarian notation*. This system involves placing a lowercase prefix on all variable names that identify the type. For example, if a variable were of type int, then you might place an i (or n) in front of it, for example iAge. Using this system, it is easy to see a variable's type at a glance.

More modern languages, however, such as C#, make this system tricky to implement. For the types you've seen so far, you could probably come up with one- or two-letter prefixes signifying each type. However, because you can create your own types, and there are many hundreds of these more complex types in the basic .NET Framework, this quickly becomes unworkable. With several people working on a project, it would be easy for different people to come up with different and confusing prefixes, with potentially disastrous consequences.

Developers have realized that it is far better to name variables appropriately for their purpose. If any doubt arises, it is easy enough to determine what the type of a variable is. In VS, you just have to hover the mouse pointer over a variable name and a pop-up box indicates the type soon enough.

Currently, two naming conventions are used in the .NET Framework namespaces: *PascalCase* and *camelCase*. The case used in the names indicates their usage. They both apply to names that comprise multiple words and they both specify that each word in a name should be in lowercase except for its first letter, which should be uppercase. For camelCase terms, there is an additional rule: The first word should start with a lowercase letter.

The following are camelCase variable names:

```
age
firstName
timeOfDeath
```

These are PascalCase:

```
Age
LastName
WinterOfDiscontent
```

For your simple variables, stick to camelCase. Later in this book, you'll use PascalCase for certain, more advanced naming, following Microsoft's recommendations. Finally, note that many past naming systems involved frequent use of the underscore character, usually as a separator between words in variable names, such as yet_another_variable. This usage is now discouraged (which is just as well; it looks ugly!).

## Literal Values

The previous Try It Out showed two examples of literal values: an integer (17) and a string ("\"myInteger\" is"). The other variable types also have associated literal values, as shown in Table 3-4. Many of these involve *suffixes*, whereby you add a sequence of characters to the end of the literal value to specify the type desired. Some literals have multiple types, determined at compile time by the compiler based on their context (also shown in Table 3-4).

**TABLE 3-4:** Literal Values

| TYPE(S) | CATEGORY | SUFFIX | EXAMPLE/ALLOWED VALUES |
|---------|----------|--------|------------------------|
| bool | Boolean | None | True or false |
| int, uint, long, ulong | Integer | None | 100 |
| uint, ulong | Integer | u or U | 100U |
| long, ulong | Integer | l or L | 100L |
| ulong | Integer | ul, uL, Ul, UL, lu, lU, Lu, or LU | 100UL |
| float | Real | f or F | 1.5F |
| double | Real | None, d, or D | 1.5 |
| decimal | Real | m or M | 1.5M |
| char | Character | None | 'a', or escape sequence |
| string | String | None | "a…a", may include escape sequences |

## String Literals

Earlier in the chapter, you saw a few of the escape sequences you can use in `string` literals. Table 3-5 lists these for reference purposes.

**TABLE 3-5:** Escape Sequences for String Literals

| ESCAPE SEQUENCE | CHARACTER PRODUCED | UNICODE VALUE OF CHARACTER |
|-----------------|--------------------|-----------------------------|
| \' | Single quotation mark | 0x0027 |
| \" | Double quotation mark | 0x0022 |
| \\ | Backslash | 0x005C |
| \0 | Null | 0x0000 |
| \a | Alert (causes a beep) | 0x0007 |
| \b | Backspace | 0x0008 |
| \f | Form feed | 0x000C |
| \n | New line | 0x000A |
| \r | Carriage return | 0x000D |
| \t | Horizontal tab | 0x0009 |
| \v | Vertical tab | 0x000B |

The Unicode Value of Character column of the preceding table shows the hexadecimal values of the characters as they are found in the Unicode character set. As well as the preceding, you can specify any Unicode character using a Unicode escape sequence. These consist of the standard \ character followed by a u and a four-digit hexadecimal value (for example, the four digits after the x in Table 3-5).

This means that the following strings are equivalent:

```
"Karli\'s string."
"Karli\u0027s string."
```

Obviously, you have more versatility using Unicode escape sequences.

You can also specify strings *verbatim*. This means that all characters contained between two double quotation marks are included in the string, including end-of-line characters and characters that would otherwise need escaping. The only exception to this is the escape sequence for the double quotation mark character, which must be specified to avoid ending the string. To do this, place the @ character before the string:

```
@"Verbatim string literal."
```

This string could just as easily be specified in the normal way, but the following requires the @ character:

```
@"A short list:
item 1
item 2"
```

Verbatim strings are particularly useful in filenames, as these use plenty of backslash characters. Using normal strings, you'd have to use double backslashes all the way along the string:

```
"C:\\Temp\\MyDir\\MyFile.doc"
```

With verbatim string literals you can make this more readable. The following verbatim string is equivalent to the preceding one:

```
@"C:\Temp\MyDir\MyFile.doc"
```

> **NOTE** As shown later in the book, strings are reference types. This is in contrast to the other types you've seen in this chapter, which are value types. One consequence of this is that strings can also be assigned the value `null`, which means that the string variable doesn't reference a string (or anything else, for that matter).

## Variable Declaration and Assignment

To recap, recall that you declare variables simply using their type and name:

```
int age;
```

You then assign values to variables using the = assignment operator:

```
age = 25;
```

> **NOTE** Remember that variables must be initialized before you use them. The preceding assignment could be used as an initialization.

There are a couple of other things you can do here that you are likely to see in C# code. One, you can declare multiple variables of the same type at the same time by separating their names with commas after the type, as follows:

```
int xSize, ySize;
```

Here, xSize and ySize are both declared as integer types.

The second technique you are likely to see is assigning values to variables when you declare them, which basically means combining two lines of code:

```
int age = 25;
```

You can use both techniques together:

```
int xSize = 4, ySize = 5;
```

Here, both xSize and ySize are assigned different values. Note that

```
int xSize, ySize = 5;
```

results in only `ySize` being initialized—`xSize` is just declared, and it still needs to be initialized before it's used.

## EXPRESSIONS

Now that you've learned how to declare and initialize variables, it's time to look at manipulating them. C# contains a number of *operators* for this purpose. By combining operators with variables and literal values (together referred to as *operands* when used with operators), you can create *expressions*, which are the basic building blocks of computation.

The operators available range from the simple to the highly complex, some of which you might never encounter outside of mathematical applications. The simple ones include all the basic mathematical operations, such as the + operator to add two operands; the complex ones include manipulations of variable content via the binary representation of this content. There are also logical operators specifically for dealing with Boolean values, and assignment operators such as =.

This chapter focuses on the mathematical and assignment operators, leaving the logical ones for the next chapter, where you examine Boolean logic in the context of controlling program flow.

Operators can be roughly classified into three categories:

➤ **Unary**—Act on single operands

➤ **Binary**—Act on two operands

➤ **Ternary**—Act on three operands

Most operators fall into the binary category, with a few unary ones, and a single ternary one called the *conditional operator* (the conditional operator is a logical one and is discussed in Chapter 4, "Flow Control"). Let's start by looking at the mathematical operators, which span both the unary and binary categories.

## Mathematical Operators

There are five simple mathematical operators, two of which (+ and -) have both binary and unary forms. Table 3-6 lists each of these operators, along with a short example of its use and the result when it's used with simple numeric types (integer and floating point).

**TABLE 3-6:** Simple Mathematical Operators

| OPERATOR | CATEGORY | EXAMPLE EXPRESSION | RESULT |
|---|---|---|---|
| + | Binary | `var1 = var2 + var3;` | `var1` is assigned the value that is the sum of `var2` and `var3`. |
| - | Binary | `var1 = var2 - var3;` | `var1` is assigned the value that is the value of `var3` subtracted from the value of `var2`. |
| * | Binary | `var1 = var2 * var3;` | `var1` is assigned the value that is the product of `var2` and `var3`. |
| / | Binary | `var1 = var2 / var3;` | `var1` is assigned the value that is the result of dividing `var2` by `var3`. |
| % | Binary | `var1 = var2 % var3;` | `var1` is assigned the value that is the remainder when `var2` is divided by `var3`. |
| + | Unary | `var1 = +var2;` | `var1` is assigned the value of `var2`. |
| - | Unary | `var1 = -var2;` | `var1` is assigned the value of `var2` multiplied by `-1`. |

> **NOTE** The + (unary) operator is slightly odd, as it has no effect on the result. It doesn't force values to be positive, as you might assume—if var2 is -1, then +var2 is also -1. However, it is a universally recognized operator, and as such is included. The most useful fact about this operator is shown later in this book when you look at operator overloading.

The examples use simple numeric types because the result can be unclear when using the other simple types. What would you expect if you added two Boolean values, for example? In this case, nothing, because the compiler complains if you try to use + (or any of the other mathematical operators) with bool variables. Adding char variables is also slightly confusing. Remember that char variables are actually stored as numbers, so adding two char variables also results in a number (of type int, to be precise). This is an example of *implicit conversion*, which you'll learn a lot more about shortly (along with explicit conversion), because it also applies to cases where var1, var2, and var3 are of mixed types.

The binary + operator *does* make sense when used with string type variables. In this case, the table entry should read as shown in Table 3-7.

**TABLE 3-7.** The String Concatenation Operator

| OPERATOR | CATEGORY | EXAMPLE EXPRESSION | RESULT |
|---|---|---|---|
| + | Binary | var1 = var2 + var3; | var1 is assigned the value that is the concatenation of the two strings stored in var2 and var3. |

None of the other mathematical operators, however, work with strings.

The other two operators you should look at here are the increment and decrement operators, both of which are unary operators that can be used in two ways: either immediately before or immediately after the operand. The results obtained in simple expressions are shown in Table 3-8.

**TABLE 3-8:** Increment and Decrement Operators

| OPERATOR | CATEGORY | EXAMPLE EXPRESSION | RESULT |
|---|---|---|---|
| ++ | Unary | var1 = ++var2; | var1 is assigned the value of var2 + 1. var2 is incremented by 1. |
| -- | Unary | var1 = --var2; | var1 is assigned the value of var2 - 1. var2 is decremented by 1. |
| ++ | Unary | var1 = var2++; | var1 is assigned the value of var2. var2 is incremented by 1. |
| -- | Unary | var1 = var2--; | var1 is assigned the value of var2. var2 is decremented by 1. |

These operators always result in a change to the value stored in their operand:

➤ ++ always results in its operand being incremented by one.

➤ -- always results in its operand being decremented by one.

The differences between the results stored in var1 are a consequence of the fact that the placement of the operator determines when it takes effect. Placing one of these operators before its operand means that the operand is affected before any other computation takes place. Placing it after the operand means that the operand is affected after all other computation of the expression is completed.

This merits another example! Consider this code:

```
int var1, var2 = 5, var3 = 6;
var1 = var2++ * --var3;
```

What value will be assigned to var1? Before the expression is evaluated, the -- operator preceding var3 takes effect, changing its value from 6 to 5. You can ignore the ++ operator that follows var2, as it won't take effect until after the calculation is completed, so var1 will be the product of 5 and 5, or 25.

These simple unary operators come in very handy in a surprising number of situations. They are really just shorthand for expressions such as this:

```
var1 = var1 + 1;
```

This sort of expression has many uses, particularly where *looping* is concerned, as shown in the next chapter. The following Try It Out provides an example demonstrating how to use the mathematical operators, and it introduces a couple of other useful concepts as well. The code prompts you to type in a string and two numbers and then demonstrates the results of performing some calculations.

**TRY IT OUT** **Manipulating Variables with Mathematical Operators: Ch03Ex02\Program.cs**

**1.** Create a new console application called Ch03Ex02 and save it to the directory C:\BegVCSharp\Chapter03.

**2.** Add the following code to Program.cs:

```csharp
static void Main(string[] args)
{
    double firstNumber, secondNumber;
    string userName;
    Console.WriteLine("Enter your name:");
    userName = Console.ReadLine();
    Console.WriteLine("Welcome {0}!", userName);
    Console.WriteLine("Now give me a number:");
    firstNumber = Convert.ToDouble(Console.ReadLine());
    Console.WriteLine("Now give me another number:");
    secondNumber = Convert.ToDouble(Console.ReadLine());
    Console.WriteLine("The sum of {0} and {1} is {2}.", firstNumber,
            secondNumber, firstNumber + secondNumber);
    Console.WriteLine("The result of subtracting {0} from {1} is {2}.",
            secondNumber, firstNumber, firstNumber - secondNumber);
    Console.WriteLine("The product of {0} and {1} is {2}.", firstNumber,
            secondNumber, firstNumber * secondNumber);
    Console.WriteLine("The result of dividing {0} by {1} is {2}.",
            firstNumber, secondNumber, firstNumber / secondNumber);
    Console.WriteLine("The remainder after dividing {0} by {1} is {2}.",
            firstNumber, secondNumber, firstNumber % secondNumber);
    Console.ReadKey();
}
```

**3.** Execute the code. The display shown in Figure 3-2 appears.

**FIGURE 3-2**

**4.** Enter your name and press Enter. Figure 3-3 shows the display.

**FIGURE 3-3**

**5.** Enter a number, press Enter, enter another number, and then press Enter again. Figure 3-4 shows an example result.

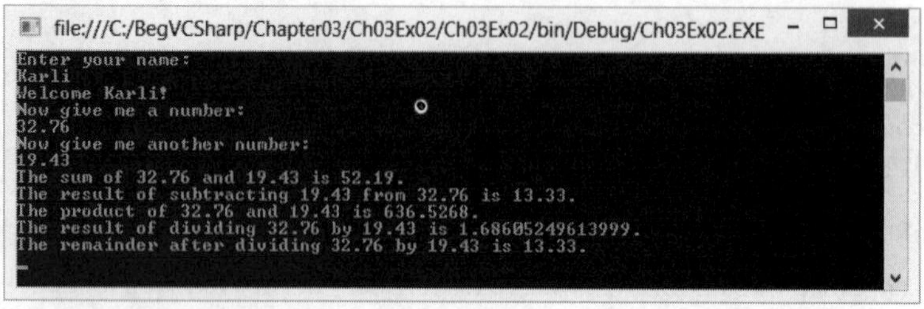

**FIGURE 3-4**

### How It Works

As well as demonstrating the mathematical operators, this code introduces two important concepts that you will often come across:

➤ User input

➤ Type conversion

User input uses a syntax similar to the `Console.WriteLine()` command you've already seen—you use `Console.ReadLine()`. This command prompts the user for input, which is stored in a `string` variable:

```
string userName;
Console.WriteLine("Enter your name:");
userName = Console.ReadLine();
Console.WriteLine("Welcome {0}!", userName);
```

This code writes the contents of the assigned variable, `userName`, straight to the screen.

You also read in two numbers in this example. This is slightly more involved, because the `Console .ReadLine()` command generates a string, but you want a number. This introduces the topic of *type conversion*, which is covered in more detail in Chapter 5, "More About Variables," but let's have a look at the code used in this example.

First, you declare the variables in which you want to store the number input:

```
double firstNumber, secondNumber;
```

Next, you supply a prompt and use the command `Convert.ToDouble()` on a string obtained by `Console .ReadLine()` to convert the string into a `double` type. You assign this number to the `firstNumber` variable you have declared:

```
Console.WriteLine("Now give me a number:");
firstNumber = Convert.ToDouble(Console.ReadLine());
```

This syntax is remarkably simple, and many other conversions can be performed in a similar way.

The remainder of the code obtains a second number in the same way:

```
Console.WriteLine("Now give me another number:");
secondNumber = Convert.ToDouble(Console.ReadLine());
```

Next, you output the results of adding, subtracting, multiplying, and dividing the two numbers, in addition to displaying the remainder after division, using the remainder (%) operator:

```
Console.WriteLine("The sum of {0} and {1} is {2}.", firstNumber,
         secondNumber, firstNumber + secondNumber);
Console.WriteLine("The result of subtracting {0} from {1} is {2}.",
         secondNumber, firstNumber, firstNumber - secondNumber);
Console.WriteLine("The product of {0} and {1} is {2}.", firstNumber,
         secondNumber, firstNumber * secondNumber);
Console.WriteLine("The result of dividing {0} by {1} is {2}.",
         firstNumber, secondNumber, firstNumber / secondNumber);
Console.WriteLine("The remainder after dividing {0} by {1} is {2}.",
         firstNumber, secondNumber, firstNumber % secondNumber);
```

Note that you are supplying the expressions, `firstNumber + secondNumber` and so on, as a parameter to the `Console.WriteLine()` statement, without using an intermediate variable:

```
Console.WriteLine("The sum of {0} and {1} is {2}.", firstNumber,
         secondNumber, firstNumber + secondNumber);
```

This kind of syntax can make your code very readable, and reduce the number of lines of code you need to write.

## Assignment Operators

So far, you've been using the simple = assignment operator, and it may come as a surprise that any other assignment operators exist at all. There are more, however, and they're quite useful! All of the assignment operators other than = work in a similar way. Like =, they all result in a value being assigned to the variable on their left side based on the operands and operators on their right side.

Table 3-9 describes the operators.

**TABLE 3-9:** Assignment Operators

| OPERATOR | CATEGORY | EXAMPLE EXPRESSION | RESULT |
|---|---|---|---|
| = | Binary | var1 = var2; | var1 is assigned the value of var2. |
| += | Binary | var1 += var2; | var1 is assigned the value that is the sum of var1 and var2. |
| -= | Binary | var1 -= var2; | var1 is assigned the value that is the value of var2 subtracted from the value of var1. |
| *= | Binary | var1 *= var2; | var1 is assigned the value that is the product of var1 and var2. |
| /= | Binary | var1 /= var2; | var1 is assigned the value that is the result of dividing var1 by var2. |
| %= | Binary | var1 %= var2; | var1 is assigned the value that is the remainder when var1 is divided by var2. |

As you can see, the additional operators result in var1 being included in the calculation, so code like

```
var1 += var2;
```

has exactly the same result as

```
var1 = var1 + var2;
```

> **NOTE** *The += operator can also be used with strings, just like +.*

Using these operators, especially when employing long variable names, can make code much easier to read.

## Operator Precedence

When an expression is evaluated, each operator is processed in sequence, but this doesn't necessarily mean evaluating these operators from left to right. As a trivial example, consider the following:

```
var1 = var2 + var3;
```

Here, the + operator acts before the = operator. There are other situations where operator precedence isn't so obvious, as shown here:

```
var1 = var2 + var3 * var4;
```

In the preceding example, the * operator acts first, followed by the + operator, and finally the = operator. This is standard mathematical order, and it provides the same result as you would expect from working out the equivalent algebraic calculation on paper.

Similarly, you can gain control over operator precedence by using parentheses, as shown in this example:

```
var1 = (var2 + var3) * var4;
```

Here, the content of the parentheses is evaluated first, meaning that the + operator acts before the * operator.

Table 3-10 shows the order of precedence for the operators you've encountered so far. Operators of equal precedence (such as * and /) are evaluated from left to right:

**TABLE 3-10:** Operator Precedence

| PRECEDENCE | OPERATORS |
| --- | --- |
| Highest | ++, -- (used as prefixes); +, - (unary) |
| | *, /, % |
| | +, - |
| | =, *=, /=, %=, +=, -= |
| Lowest | ++, -- (used as suffixes) |

> **NOTE** *You can use parentheses to override this precedence order, as described previously. In addition, note that ++ and --, when used as suffixes, only have lowest priority in conceptual terms, as described in the preceding table. They don't operate on the result of, say, an assignment expression, so you can consider them to have a higher priority than all other operators. However, because they change the value of their operand after expression evaluation, it's easier to think of their precedence as shown in Table 3-10.*

## Namespaces

Before moving on, it's worthwhile to consider one more important subject—*namespaces*. These are the .NET way of providing containers for application code, such that code and its contents may be uniquely identified. Namespaces are also used as a means of categorizing items in the .NET Framework. Most of these items are type definitions, such as the simple types in this chapter (System.Int32 and so on).

C# code, by default, is contained in the *global namespace*. This means that items contained in this code are accessible from other code in the global namespace simply by referring to them by name. You can use the `namespace` keyword, however, to explicitly define the namespace for a block of code enclosed in curly brackets. Names in such a namespace must be *qualified* if they are used from code outside of this namespace.

A qualified name is one that contains all of its hierarchical information, which basically means that if you have code in one namespace that needs to use a name defined in a different namespace, you must include a reference to this namespace. Qualified names use period characters (.) between namespace levels, as shown here:

```
namespace LevelOne
{
    // code in LevelOne namespace

    // name "NameOne" defined
}

// code in global namespace
```

This code defines one namespace, `LevelOne`, and a name in this namespace, `NameOne` (no actual code is shown here to keep the discussion general; instead, a comment appears where the definition would go). Code written inside the `LevelOne` namespace can simply refer to this name using `NameOne`—no classification is necessary. Code in the global namespace, however, must refer to this name using the classified name `LevelOne.NameOne`.

> **NOTE** *By convention, namespaces are usually written in PascalCase.*

Within a namespace, you can define nested namespaces, also using the `namespace` keyword. Nested namespaces are referred to via their hierarchy, again using periods to classify each level of the hierarchy. This is best illustrated with an example. Consider the following namespaces:

```
namespace LevelOne
{
    // code in LevelOne namespace

    namespace LevelTwo
    {
        // code in LevelOne.LevelTwo namespace

        // name "NameTwo" defined
    }
}

// code in global namespace
```

Here, `NameTwo` must be referred to as `LevelOne.LevelTwo.NameTwo` from the global namespace, `LevelTwo.NameTwo` from the `LevelOne` namespace, and `NameTwo` from the `LevelOne.LevelTwo` namespace.

The important point here is that names are uniquely defined by their namespace. You could define the name `NameThree` in the `LevelOne` and `LevelTwo` namespaces:

```
namespace LevelOne
{
    // name "NameThree" defined
```

```
    namespace LevelTwo
    {
        // name "NameThree" defined
    }
}
```

This defines two separate names, `LevelOne.NameThree` and `LevelOne.LevelTwo.NameThree`, which can be used independently of each other.

After namespaces are set up, you can use the `using` statement to simplify access to the names they contain. In effect, the `using` statement says, "Okay, I'll be needing names from this namespace, so don't bother asking me to classify them every time." For example, the following code says that code in the `LevelOne` namespace should have access to names in the `LevelOne.LevelTwo` namespace without classification:

```
namespace LevelOne
{
    using LevelTwo;

    namespace LevelTwo
    {
        // name "NameTwo" defined
    }
}
```

Code in the `LevelOne` namespace can now refer to `LevelTwo.NameTwo` by simply using `NameTwo`.

Sometimes, as with the `NameThree` example shown previously, this can lead to problems with clashes between identical names in different namespaces (if you use such a name, then your code won't compile—and the compiler will let you know that there is an ambiguity). In cases such as these, you can provide an *alias* for a namespace as part of the `using` statement:

```
namespace LevelOne
{
    using LT = LevelTwo;

    // name "NameThree" defined

    namespace LevelTwo
    {
        // name "NameThree" defined
    }
}
```

Here, code in the `LevelOne` namespace can refer to `LevelOne.NameThree` as `NameThree` and `LevelOne.LevelTwo.NameThree` as `LT.NameThree`.

`using` statements apply to the namespace they are contained in, and any nested namespaces that might also be contained in this namespace. In the preceding code, the global namespace can't use `LT.NameThree`. However, if this `using` statement were declared as

```
using LT = LevelOne.LevelTwo;

namespace LevelOne
{
    // name "NameThree" defined

    namespace LevelTwo
    {
        // name "NameThree" defined
    }
}
```

then code in the global namespace and the `LevelOne` namespace could use `LT.NameThree`.

Note one more important point here: The using statement doesn't in itself give you access to names in another namespace. Unless the code in a namespace is in some way linked to your project, by being defined in a source file in the project or being defined in some other code linked to the project, you won't have access to the names contained. In addition, if code containing a namespace is linked to your project, then you have access to the names contained in that code, regardless of whether you use using. using simply makes it easier for you to access these names, and it can shorten otherwise lengthy code to make it more readable.

Going back to the code in ConsoleApplication1 shown at the beginning of this chapter, the following lines that apply to namespaces appear:

```
using System;
using System.Collections.Generic;
using System.Linq;
using System.Text;
using System.Threading.Tasks;

namespace ConsoleApplication1
{
    ...
}
```

The five lines that start with the using keyword are used to declare that the System, System .Collections.Generic, System.Linq, System.Text, and System.Threading.Tasks namespaces will be used in this C# code and should be accessible from all namespaces in this file without classification. The System namespace is the root namespace for .NET Framework applications and contains all the basic functionality you need for console applications. The other four namespaces are very often used in console applications, so they are there just in case.

Finally, a namespace is declared for the application code itself, ConsoleApplication1.

## SUMMARY

This chapter covered a fair amount of ground on the way to creating usable (if basic) C# applications. You've looked at the basic C# syntax and analyzed the basic console application code that VS generates for you when you create a console application project.

The major part of this chapter concerned the use of variables. You have seen what variables are, how you create them, how you assign values to them, and how you manipulate them and the values that they contain. Along the way, you've also looked at some basic user interaction, which showed how you can output text to a console application and read user input back in. This involved some very basic type conversion, a complex subject that is covered in more depth in Chapter 5.

You also learned how you can assemble operators and operands into expressions, and looked at the way these are executed and the order in which this takes place.

Finally, you looked at namespaces, which will become increasingly important as the book progresses. By introducing this topic in a fairly abstract way here, the groundwork is completed for later discussions.

So far, all of your programming has taken the form of line-by-line execution. In the next chapter, you learn how to make your code more efficient by controlling the flow of execution using looping techniques and conditional branching.

## EXERCISES

**3.1**   In the following code, how would you refer to the name great from code in the namespace fabulous?

```
namespace fabulous
{
    // code in fabulous namespace
}
```

```
namespace super
{
    namespace smashing
    {
        // great name defined
    }
}
```

**3.2**   Which of the following is not a legal variable name?

➤   `myVariableIsGood`

➤   `99Flake`

➤   `_floor`

➤   `time2GetJiggyWidIt`

➤   `wrox.com`

**3.3**   Is the string `"supercalifragilisticexpialidocious"` too big to fit in a `string` variable? If so, why?

**3.4**   The *, %, and / operators have equal highest precedence here, followed by + and finally +=. The precedence in the exercise can be illustrated using parentheses as follows:

```
resultVar += (var1 * var2) + (var3 % (var4 / var5));
```

Or:

```
resultVar += (var1 * var2) + ((var3 % var4) / var5));
```

The result is the same in both cases.

**3.5**   Write a console application that obtains four `int` values from the user and displays the product. Hint: You may recall that the `Convert.ToDouble()` command was used to convert the input from the console to a `double`; the equivalent command to convert from a `string` to an `int` is `Convert.ToInt32()`.

Answers to the exercises can be found in Appendix A.

## ▶ WHAT YOU LEARNED IN THIS CHAPTER

| TOPIC | KEY CONCEPTS |
| --- | --- |
| **Basic C# syntax** | C# is a case-sensitive language, and each line of code is terminated with a semicolon. Lines can be indented for ease of reading if they get too long, or to identify nested blocks. You can include non-compiled comments with // or /* ... */ syntax. Blocks of code can be collapsed into regions, also to ease readability. |
| **Variables** | Variables are chunks of data that have a name and a type. The .NET Framework defines plenty of simple types, such as numeric and string (text) types for you to use. Variables must be declared and initialized for you to use them. You can assign literal values to variables to initialize them, and variables can be declared and initialized in a single step. |
| **Expressions** | Expressions are built from operators and operands, where operators perform operations on operands. There are three types of operators—unary, binary, and ternary—that operate on 1, 2, and 3 operands, respectively. Mathematical operators perform operations on numeric values, and assignment operators place the result of an expression into a variable. Operators have a fixed precedence that determines the order in which they are processed in an expression. |
| **Namespaces** | All names defined in a .NET application, including variable names, are contained in a namespace. Namespaces are hierarchical, and you often have to qualify names according to the namespace that contains them in order to access them. |

# Flow Control

## WHAT YOU WILL LEARN IN THIS CHAPTER

- ➤ Boolean logic and how to use it
- ➤ How to branch code
- ➤ How to loop code

### WROX.COM CODE DOWNLOADS FOR THIS CHAPTER

You can find the wrox.com code downloads for this chapter at www.wrox.com/remtitle
.cgi?isbn=9781118314418 on the Download Code tab. The code is in the Chapter 4 download and
individually named according to the names throughout the chapter.

All of the C# code you've seen so far has had one thing in common. In each case, program execution
has proceeded from one line to the next in top-to-bottom order, missing nothing. If all applications
worked like this, then you would be very limited in what you could do. This chapter describes two
methods for controlling program flow—that is, the order of execution of lines of C# code: *branching*
and *looping*. Branching executes code conditionally, depending on the outcome of an evaluation, such
as "Execute this code only if the variable myVal is less than 10." Looping repeatedly executes the
same statements, either a certain number of times or until a test condition has been reached.

Both of these techniques involve the use of *Boolean logic*. In the last chapter, you saw the bool
type, but didn't actually do much with it. In this chapter, you'll use it a lot, so the chapter begins
by discussing what is meant by Boolean logic, and then goes on to cover how you can use it in flow
control scenarios.

## BOOLEAN LOGIC

The bool type introduced in the previous chapter can hold one of only two values: true or false.
This type is often used to record the result of some operation, so that you can act on this result. In
particular, bool types are used to store the result of a *comparison*.

> **NOTE** *As a historical aside, it is the work of the mid-nineteenth-century English
> mathematician George Boole that forms the basis of Boolean logic.*

For instance, consider the situation (mentioned in the chapter introduction) in which you want to execute code based on whether a variable, `myVal`, is less than 10. To do this, you need some indication of whether the statement "`myVal` is less than 10" is `true` or `false`—that is, you need to know the Boolean result of a comparison.

Boolean comparisons require the use of Boolean *comparison operators* (also known as *relational operators*), which are shown in Table 4-1.

**TABLE 4-1:** Boolean Comparison Operators

| OPERATOR | CATEGORY | EXAMPLE EXPRESSION | RESULT |
|---|---|---|---|
| == | Binary | `var1 = var2 == var3;` | var1 is assigned the value `true` if var2 is equal to var3, or `false` otherwise. |
| != | Binary | `var1 = var2 != var3;` | var1 is assigned the value `true` if var2 is not equal to var3, or `false` otherwise. |
| < | Binary | `var1 = var2 < var3;` | var1 is assigned the value `true` if var2 is less than var3, or `false` otherwise. |
| > | Binary | `var1 = var2 > var3;` | var1 is assigned the value `true` if var2 is greater than var3, or `false` otherwise. |
| <= | Binary | `var1 = var2 <= var3;` | var1 is assigned the value `true` if var2 is less than or equal to var3, or `false` otherwise. |
| >= | Binary | `var1 = var2 >= var3;` | var1 is assigned the value `true` if var2 is greater than or equal to var3, or `false` otherwise. |

In all cases in Table 4-1, `var1` is a `bool` type variable, whereas the types of `var2` and `var3` may vary.

You might use operators such as these on numeric values in code:

```
bool isLessThan10;
isLessThan10 = myVal < 10;
```

The preceding code results in `isLessThan10` being assigned the value `true` if `myVal` stores a value less than 10, or `false` otherwise.

You can also use these comparison operators on other types, such as strings:

```
bool isKarli;
isKarli = myString == "Karli";
```

Here, `isKarli` is true only if `myString` stores the string `"Karli"`.

You can also compare variables with Boolean values:

```
bool isTrue;
isTrue = myBool == true;
```

Here, however, you are limited to the use of the `==` and `!=` operators.

> **NOTE** *A common code error occurs if you unintentionally assume that because* `val1 < val2` *is* `false`, `val1 > val2` *is* `true`. *If* `val1 == val2`, *both these statements are* `false`.

Some other Boolean operators are intended specifically for working with Boolean values, as shown in Table 4-2.

**TABLE 4-2:** Boolean Operators for Boolean Values

| OPERATOR | CATEGORY | EXAMPLE EXPRESSION | RESULT |
|---|---|---|---|
| ! | Unary | `var1 = !var2;` | var1 is assigned the value true if var2 is false, or false if var2 is true. (Logical NOT) |
| & | Binary | `var1 = var2 & var3;` | var1 is assigned the value true if var2 and var3 are both true, or false otherwise. (Logical AND) |
| \| | Binary | `var1 = var2 \| var3;` | var1 is assigned the value true if either var2 or var3 (or both) is true, or false otherwise. (Logical OR) |
| ^ | Binary | `var1 = var2 ^ var3;` | var1 is assigned the value true if either var2 or var3, but not both, is true, or false otherwise. (Logical XOR or exclusive OR) |

Therefore, the previous code snippet could also be expressed as follows:

```
bool isTrue;
isTrue = myBool & true;
```

The & and | operators also have two similar operators, known as *conditional Boolean* operators, shown in Table 4-3.

**TABLE 4-3:** Conditional Boolean Operators

| OPERATOR | CATEGORY | EXAMPLE EXPRESSION | RESULT |
|---|---|---|---|
| && | Binary | `var1 = var2 && var3;` | var1 is assigned the value true if var2 and var3 are both true, or false otherwise. (Logical AND) |
| \|\| | Binary | `var1 = var2 \|\| var3;` | var1 is assigned the value true if either var2 or var3 (or both) is true, or false otherwise. (Logical OR) |

The result of these operators is exactly the same as & and |, but there is an important difference in the way this result is obtained, which can result in better performance. Both of these look at the value of their first operands (var2 in the preceding table) and, based on the value of this operand, may not need to process the second operands (var3 in the preceding table) at all.

If the value of the first operand of the && operator is false, then there is no need to consider the value of the second operand, because the result will be false regardless. Similarly, the || operator returns true if its first operand is true, regardless of the value of the second operand. This isn't the case for the & and | operators shown earlier. With these, both operands are always evaluated.

Because of this conditional evaluation of operands, you get a small performance increase if you use && and || instead of & and |. This is particularly apparent in applications that use these operators a lot. As a rule of thumb, *always* use && and || where possible. These operators really come into their own in more complicated situations, where computation of the second operand is possible only with certain values of the first operand, as shown in this example:

```
var1 = (var2 != 0) && (var3 / var2 > 2);
```

Here, if `var2` is zero, dividing `var3` by `var2` results in either a "division by zero" error or `var1` being defined as infinite (the latter is possible, and detectable, with some types, such as `float`).

> **NOTE** At this point, you may be asking why the `&` and `|` operators exist at all. The reason is that these operators may be used to perform operations on numeric values. In fact, as you will see shortly in the section "Bitwise Operators," they operate on the series of bits stored in a variable, rather than the value of the variable.

## Boolean Assignment Operators

Boolean comparisons can be combined with assignments by using Boolean assignment operators. These work in the same way as the mathematical assignment operators that were introduced in the preceding chapter (`+=`, `*=`, and so on). The Boolean versions are shown in Table 4-4.

**TABLE 4-4:** Boolean Assignment Operators

| OPERATOR | CATEGORY | EXAMPLE EXPRESSION | RESULT |
|---|---|---|---|
| `&=` | Binary | `var1 &= var2;` | `var1` is assigned the value that is the result of `var1 & var2`. |
| `|=` | Binary | `var1 |= var2;` | `var1` is assigned the value that is the result of `var1 | var2`. |
| `^=` | Binary | `var1 ^= var2;` | `var1` is assigned the value that is the result of `var1 ^ var2`. |

These work with both Boolean and numeric values in the same way as `&`, `|`, and `^`.

> **NOTE** Note that the `&=` and `|=` assignment operators do not make use of the `&&` and `||` conditional Boolean operators; that is, all operands are processed regardless of the value to the left of the assignment operator.

In the Try It Out that follows, you type in an integer and then the code performs various Boolean evaluations using that integer.

**TRY IT OUT** Using Boolean Operators: Ch04Ex01\Program.cs

1. Create a new console application called Ch04Ex01 and save it in the directory `C:\BegVCSharp\Chapter04`.

2. Add the following code to `Program.cs`:

```
static void Main(string[] args)
{
    Console.WriteLine("Enter an integer:");
    int myInt = Convert.ToInt32(Console.ReadLine());
    bool isLessThan10 = myInt < 10;
    bool isBetween0And5 = (0 <= myInt) && (myInt <= 5);
    Console.WriteLine("Integer less than 10? {0}", isLessThan10);
    Console.WriteLine("Integer between 0 and 5? {0}", isBetween0And5);
    Console.WriteLine("Exactly one of the above is true? {0}",
        isLessThan10 ^ isBetween0And5);
    Console.ReadKey();
}
```

**3.** Execute the application and enter an integer when prompted. The result is shown in Figure 4-1.

**FIGURE 4-1**

*How It Works*

The first two lines of code prompt for and accept an integer value using techniques you've already seen:

```
Console.WriteLine("Enter an integer:");
int myInt = Convert.ToInt32(Console.ReadLine());
```

You use `Convert.ToInt32()` to obtain an integer from the string input, which is simply another conversion command in the same family as the `Convert.ToDouble()` command used previously.

Next, two Boolean variables, `isLessThan10` and `isBetween0And5`, are declared and assigned values with logic that matches the description in their names:

```
bool isLessThan10 = myInt < 10;
bool isBetween0And5 = (0 <= myInt) && (myInt <= 5);
```

These variables are used in the next three lines of code, the first two of which output their values, whereas the third performs an operation on them and outputs the result. You work through this code assuming that the user enters 7, as shown in the screenshot.

The first output is the result of the operation `myInt < 10`. If `myInt` is 6, which is less than 10, the result is `true`, which is what you see displayed. Values of `myInt` of 10 or higher result in `false`.

The second output is a more involved calculation: `(0 <= myInt) && (myInt <= 5)`. It uses two comparison operations to determine whether `myInt` is greater than or equal to 0 and less than or equal to 5, and a Boolean AND operation on the results obtained. With a value of 6, `(0 <= myInt)` returns `true`, and `(myInt <= 5)` returns `false`. The result is then `(true) && (false)`, which is `false`, as you can see from the display.

Finally, you perform a logical exclusive OR on the two Boolean variables `isLessThan10` and `isBetween0And5`. This will return `true` if one of the values is `true` and the other `false`; that is, it returns `true` only if `myInt` is 6, 7, 8, or 9. With a value of 6, as in the example, the result is `true`.

## Bitwise Operators

The `&` and `|` operators you saw earlier serve an additional purpose: They may be used to perform operations on numeric values. When used in this way, they operate on the series of bits stored in a variable, rather than the value of the variable, which is why they are referred to as *bitwise* operators.

In this section you will look at these and other bitwise operators that are defined by the C# language. Using this functionality is fairly uncommon in most development, apart from mathematical applications. For that reason there is no Try it Out for this section.

Start by considering `&` and `|` in turn. Each bit in the first operand is compared with the bit in the same position in the second operand, resulting in the bit in the same position in the resultant value being assigned a value, as shown in Table 4-5.

**TABLE 4-5:** Using the & Bitwise Operator

| OPERAND 1 BIT | OPERAND 2 BIT | & RESULT BIT |
|---|---|---|
| 1 | 1 | 1 |
| 1 | 0 | 0 |
| 0 | 1 | 0 |
| 0 | 0 | 0 |

| is similar, but the result bits are different, as shown in Table 4-6.

**TABLE 4-6:** Using the | Bitwise Operator

| OPERAND 1 BIT | OPERAND 2 BIT | | RESULT BIT |
|---|---|---|
| 1 | 1 | 1 |
| 1 | 0 | 1 |
| 0 | 1 | 1 |
| 0 | 0 | 0 |

For example, consider the operation shown here:

```
int result, op1, op2;
op1 = 4;
op2 = 5;
result = op1 & op2;
```

In this case, you must consider the binary representations of op1 and op2, which are 100 and 101, respectively. The result is obtained by comparing the binary digits in equivalent positions in these two representations as follows:

➤ The leftmost bit of result is 1 if the leftmost bits of op1 and op2 are both 1, or 0 otherwise.

➤ The next bit of result is 1 if the next bits of op1 and op2 are both 1, or 0 otherwise.

➤ Continue for all remaining bits.

In this example, the leftmost bits of op1 and op2 are both 1, so the leftmost bit of result will be 1, too. The next bits are both 0, and the third bits are 1 and 0, respectively, so the second and third bits of result will be 0. The final value of result in binary representation is therefore 100, so the result is assigned the value 4. This is shown graphically in the following equations:

```
  1 0 0    4
& 1 0 1  & 5
  1 0 0    4
```

The same process occurs if you use the | operator, except that in this case each result bit is 1 if either of the operand bits in the same position is 1, as shown in the following equations:

```
  1 0 0    4
| 1 0 1  | 5
  1 0 1    5
```

You can also use the ^ operator in the same way, where each result bit is 1 if one or other of the operand bits in the same position is 1, but not both, as shown in Table 4-7.

**TABLE 4-7:** Using the ^ Operator

| OPERAND 1 BIT | OPERAND 2 BIT | ^ RESULT BIT |
| --- | --- | --- |
| 1 | 1 | 0 |
| 1 | 0 | 1 |
| 0 | 1 | 1 |
| 0 | 0 | 0 |

C# also allows the use of a unary bitwise operator (~), which acts on its operand by inverting each of its bits, so that the result is a variable having values of 1 for each bit in the operand that is 0, and vice versa. This is shown in Table 4-8.

**TABLE 4-8:** Using the ~ Operator

| OPERAND BIT | ~ RESULT BIT |
| --- | --- |
| 1 | 0 |
| 0 | 1 |

The way integer numbers are stored in .NET, known as *two's complement*, means that using the ~ unary operator can lead to results that look a little odd. If you remember that an int type is a 32-bit number, for example, knowing that the ~ operator acts on all 32 of those bits can help you to see what is going on. For example, the number 5 in its full binary representation is as follows:

```
00000000000000000000000000000101
```

This is the number −5:

```
11111111111111111111111111111011
```

In fact, by the two's complement system, (−x) is defined as (~x + 1). That may seem odd, but this system is very useful when it comes to adding numbers. For example, adding 10 and −5 (that is, subtracting 5 from 10) looks like this in binary format:

```
  00000000000000000000000000001010
+ 11111111111111111111111111111011
= 100000000000000000000000000000101
```

> **NOTE** By ignoring the 1 on the far left, you are left with the binary representation for 5, so while results such as ~1 = −2 may look odd, the underlying structures force this result.

The bitwise operations you've seen in this section are quite useful in certain situations, because they enable an easy method of using individual variable bits to store information. Consider a simple representation of a color using three bits to specify red, green, and blue content. You can set these bits independently to change the three bits to one of the configurations shown in Table 4-9.

**TABLE 4-9:** Sample Scheme for Binary Color Representation

| BITS | DECIMAL REPRESENTATION | MEANING |
|------|------------------------|---------|
| 000 | 0 | black |
| 100 | 4 | red |
| 010 | 2 | green |
| 001 | 1 | blue |
| 101 | 5 | magenta |
| 110 | 6 | yellow |
| 011 | 3 | cyan |
| 111 | 7 | white |

Suppose you store these values in a variable of type int. Starting from a black color—that is, an int variable with the value of 0—you can perform operations like this:

```
int myColor = 0;
bool containsRed;
myColor = myColor | 2;         // Add green bit, myColor now stores 010
myColor = myColor | 4;         // Add red bit, myColor now stores 110
containsRed = (myColor & 4) == 4; // Check value of red bit
```

The final line of code assigns a value of true to containsRed, as the red bit of myColor is 1. This technique can be quite useful for making efficient use of information, particularly because the operations involved can be used to check the values of multiple bits simultaneously (32 in the case of int values). However, there are better ways to store extra information in single variables (making use of the advanced variable types discussed in the next chapter).

In addition to these four bitwise operators, this section considers two others, shown in Table 4-10.

**TABLE 4-10:** Bitwise Shift Operators

| OPERATOR | CATEGORY | EXAMPLE EXPRESSION | RESULT |
|----------|----------|--------------------|--------|
| >> | Binary | var1 = var2 >> var3; | var1 is assigned the value obtained when the binary content of var2 is shifted var3 bits to the right. |
| << | Binary | var1 = var2 << var3; | var1 is assigned the value obtained when the binary content of var2 is shifted var3 bits to the left. |

These operators, commonly called *bitwise shift operators,* are best illustrated with a quick example:

```
int var1, var2 = 10, var3 = 2;
var1 = var2 << var3;
```

Here, var1 is assigned the value 40. This can be explained by considering that the binary representation of 10 is 1010, which shifted to the left by two places is 101000—the binary representation of 40. In effect, you have carried out a multiplication operation. Each bit shifted to the left multiplies the value by 2, so two bit-shifts to the left result in multiplication by 4. Conversely, each bit shifted to the right has the effect of dividing the operand by 2, with any non-integer remainder being lost:

```
int var1, var2 = 10;
var1 = var2 >> 1;
```

In this example, `var1` contains the value 5, whereas the following code results in a value of 2:

```
int var1, var2 = 10;
var1 = var2 >> 2;
```

You are unlikely to use these operators in most code, but it is worth being aware of their existence. Their primary use is in highly optimized code, where the overhead of other mathematical operations just won't do. For this reason, they are often used in, for example, device drivers or system code.

The bitwise shift operators also have assignment operators, as shown in the Table 4-11.

**TABLE 4-11:** Bitwise Shift Assignment Operators

| OPERATOR | CATEGORY | EXAMPLE EXPRESSION | RESULT |
|---|---|---|---|
| >>= | Unary | `var1 >>= var2;` | var1 is assigned the value obtained when the binary content of `var1` is shifted `var2` bits to the right. |
| <<= | Unary | `var1 <<= var2;` | var1 is assigned the value obtained when the binary content of `var1` is shifted `var2` bits to the left. |

## Operator Precedence Updated

Now that you have a few more operators to consider, Table 3-10: "Operator Precedence" from the previous chapter should be updated to include them. The new order is shown in Table 4-12.

**TABLE 4-12:** Operator Precedence (Updated)

| PRECEDENCE | OPERATORS |
|---|---|
| Highest | ++, −− (used as prefixes); ( ), +, − (unary), !, ~ |
| | *, /, % |
| | +, − |
| | <<, >> |
| | <, >, <=, >= |
| | ==, != |
| | & |
| | ^ |
| | \| |
| | && |
| | \|\| |
| | =, *=, /=, %=, +=, −=, <<=, >>=, &=, ^=, \|= |
| Lowest | ++, −− (used as suffixes) |

This adds quite a few more levels but explicitly defines how expressions such as the following will be evaluated, where the `&&` operator is processed after the `<=` and `>=` operators (in this code `var2` is an `int` value):

```
var1 = var2 <= 4 && var2 >= 2;
```

It doesn't hurt to add parentheses to make expressions such as this one clearer. The compiler knows what order to process operators in, but we humans are prone to forget such things (and you might want to change the order). Writing the previous expression as

```
var1 = (var2 <= 4) && (var2 >= 2);
```

solves this problem by explicitly ordering the computation.

## THE GOTO STATEMENT

C# enables you to label lines of code and then jump straight to them using the goto statement. This has its benefits and problems. The main benefit is that it's a simple way to control what code is executed when. The main problem is that excessive use of this technique can result in spaghetti code that is difficult to understand.

The goto statement is used as follows:

```
goto <labelName>;
```

Labels are defined as follows:

```
<labelName>:
```

For example, consider the following:

```
int myInteger = 5;
goto myLabel;
myInteger += 10;
myLabel:
Console.WriteLine("myInteger = {0}", myInteger);
```

Execution proceeds as follows:

➤ myInteger is declared as an int type and assigned the value 5.

➤ The goto statement interrupts normal execution and transfers control to the line marked myLabel:.

➤ The value of myInteger is written to the console.

The highlighted line in the following code is never executed:

```
int myInteger = 5;
goto myLabel;
myInteger += 10;
myLabel:
Console.WriteLine("myInteger = {0}", myInteger);
```

In fact, if you try to compile this code in an application, the Error List window will show a warning labeled "Unreachable code detected," along with location details. You will also see a wavy green line under myInteger on the unreachable line of code.

goto statements have their uses, but they can make things very confusing indeed. In fact, if you can avoid it (and by using the techniques you'll learn in the remainder of this chapter you'll be able to), *never* use goto. The following example shows some spaghetti code arising from the use of this unfortunate keyword:

```
start:
int myInteger = 5;
goto addVal;
writeResult:
Console.WriteLine("myInteger = {0}", myInteger);
goto start;
addVal:
myInteger += 10;
goto writeResult;
```

This is perfectly valid code but very difficult to read! Try it out for yourself and see what happens. Before doing that, though, try to first determine what this code will do by looking at it, and then give yourself a pat on the back if you're right. You'll revisit this statement a little later, because it has implications for use with some of the other structures in this chapter.

## BRANCHING

Branching is the act of controlling which line of code should be executed next. The line to jump to is controlled by some kind of conditional statement. This conditional statement is based on a comparison between a test value and one or more possible values using Boolean logic.

This section describes three branching techniques available in C#:

➤ The ternary operator
➤ The if statement
➤ The switch statement

## The Ternary Operator

The simplest way to perform a comparison is to use the *ternary* (or *conditional*) operator mentioned in the last chapter. You've already seen unary operators that work on one operand, and binary operators that work on two operands, so it won't come as a surprise that this operator works on three operands. The syntax is as follows:

```
<test> ? <resultIfTrue>: <resultIfFalse>
```

Here, <test> is evaluated to obtain a Boolean value, and the result of the operator is either <resultIfTrue> or <resultIfFalse> based on this value.

You might use this as follows to test the value of an int variable called myInteger:

```
string resultString = (myInteger < 10) ? "Less than 10"
                                        : "Greater than or equal to 10";
```

The result of the ternary operator is one of two strings, both of which may be assigned to resultString. The choice of which string to assign is made by comparing the value of myInteger to 10. In this case, a value of less than 10 results in the first string being assigned, and a value of greater than or equal to 10 results in the second string being assigned. For example, if myInteger is 4, then resultString will be assigned the string Less than 10.

This operator is fine for simple assignments such as this, but it isn't really suitable for executing larger amounts of code based on a comparison. A much better way to do this is to use the if statement.

## The if Statement

The if statement is a far more versatile and useful way to make decisions. Unlike ?: statements, if statements don't have a result (so you can't use them in assignments); instead, you use the statement to conditionally execute other statements.

The simplest use of an if statement is as follows, where <test> is evaluated (it must evaluate to a Boolean value for the code to compile) and the line of code that follows the statement is executed if <test> evaluates to true:

```
if (<test>)
   <code executed if <test> is true>;
```

After this code is executed, or if it isn't executed due to <test> evaluating to false, program execution resumes at the next line of code.

You can also specify additional code using the `else` statement in combination with an `if` statement. This statement is executed if `<test>` evaluates to `false`:

```
if (<test>)
    <code executed if <test> is true>;
else
    <code executed if <test> is false>;
```

Both sections of code can span multiple lines using blocks in braces:

```
if (<test>)
{
    <code executed if <test> is true>;
}
else
{
    <code executed if <test> is false>;
}
```

As a quick example, you could rewrite the code from the last section that used the ternary operator:

```
string resultString = (myInteger < 10) ? "Less than 10"
                                        : "Greater than or equal to 10";
```

Because the result of the `if` statement cannot be assigned to a variable, you have to assign a value to the variable in a separate step:

```
string resultString;
if (myInteger < 10)
    resultString = "Less than 10";
else
    resultString = "Greater than or equal to 10";
```

Code such as this, although more verbose, is far easier to read and understand than the equivalent ternary form, and enables far more flexibility.

The following Try It Out illustrates the use of the `if` statement.

**TRY IT OUT** **Using the if Statement: Ch04Ex02\Program.cs**

1. Create a new console application called Ch04Ex02 and save it in the directory `C:\BegVCSharp\Chapter04`.

2. Add the following code to `Program.cs`:

```
static void Main(string[] args)
{
    string comparison;
    Console.WriteLine("Enter a number:");
    double var1 = Convert.ToDouble(Console.ReadLine());
    Console.WriteLine("Enter another number:");
    double var2 = Convert.ToDouble(Console.ReadLine());
    if (var1 < var2)
        comparison = "less than";
    else
    {
        if (var1 == var2)
            comparison = "equal to";
        else
            comparison = "greater than";
    }
    Console.WriteLine("The first number is {0} the second number.",
                        comparison);
    Console.ReadKey();
}
```

**3.** Execute the code and enter two numbers at the prompts (see Figure 4-2).

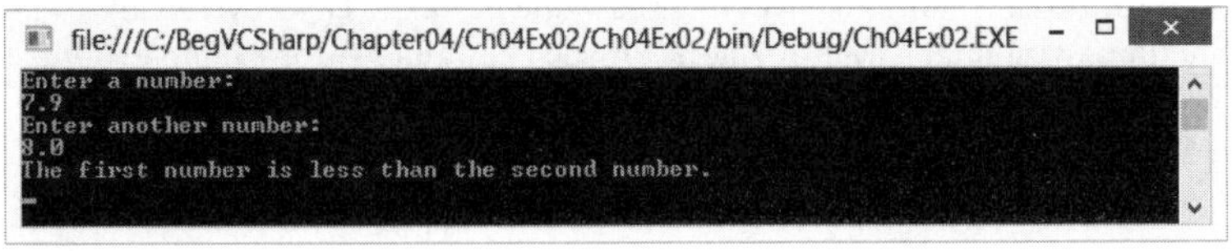

**FIGURE 4-2**

*How It Works*

The first section of code is very familiar. It simply obtains two `double` values from user input:

```
string comparison;
Console.WriteLine("Enter a number:");
double var1 = Convert.ToDouble(Console.ReadLine());
Console.WriteLine("Enter another number:");
double var2 = Convert.ToDouble(Console.ReadLine());
```

Next, you assign a string to the `string` variable `comparison` based on the values obtained for `var1` and `var2`. First, you check whether `var1` is less than `var2`:

```
if (var1 < var2)
    comparison = "less than";
```

If this isn't the case, then `var1` is either greater than or equal to `var2`. In the `else` section of the first comparison, you need to nest a second comparison:

```
else
{
    if (var1 == var2)
        comparison = "equal to";
```

The `else` section of this second comparison is reached only if `var1` is greater than `var2`:

```
    else
        comparison = "greater than";
}
```

Finally, you write the value of `comparison` to the console:

```
Console.WriteLine("The first number is {0} the second number.",
                  comparison);
```

The nesting used here is just one method of performing these comparisons. You could equally have written this:

```
if (var1 < var2)
    comparison = "less than";
if (var1 == var2)
    comparison = "equal to";
if (var1 > var2)
    comparison = "greater than";
```

The disadvantage to this method is that you are performing three comparisons regardless of the values of `var1` and `var2`. With the first method, you perform only one comparison if `var1 < var2` is true, and two comparisons otherwise (you also perform the `var1 == var2` comparison), resulting in fewer lines of code being executed. The difference in performance here is slight, but it would be significant in applications where speed of execution is crucial.

## Checking More Conditions Using if Statements

In the preceding example, you checked for three conditions involving the value of var1. This covered all possible values for this variable. Sometimes, you might want to check for specific values—for example, if var1 is equal to 1, 2, 3, or 4, and so on. Using code such as the preceding can result in annoyingly nested code:

```
if (var1 == 1)
{
   // Do something.
}
else
{
   if (var1 == 2)
   {
      // Do something else.
   }
   else
   {
      if (var1 == 3 || var1 == 4)
      {
         // Do something else.
      }
      else
      {
         // Do something else.
      }
   }
}
```

> **WARNING** *It's a common mistake to write conditions such as* if (var1 == 3 || var1 == 4) *as* if (var1 == 3 || 4). *Here, owing to operator precedence, the* == *operator is processed first, leaving the* || *operator to operate on a Boolean and a numeric operand, which causes an error.*

In these situations, consider using a slightly different indentation scheme and contracting the section of code for the else blocks (that is, using a single line of code after the else blocks, rather than a block of code). That way, you end up with a structure involving else if statements:

```
if (var1 == 1)
{
   // Do something.
}
else if (var1 == 2)
{
   // Do something else.
}
else if (var1 == 3 || var1 == 4)
{
   // Do something else.
}
else
{
   // Do something else.
}
```

These else if statements are really two separate statements, and the code is functionally identical to the previous code, but much easier to read. When making multiple comparisons such as this, consider using the switch statement as an alternative branching structure.

## The switch Statement

The switch statement is similar to the if statement in that it executes code conditionally based on the value of a test. However, switch enables you to test for multiple values of a test variable in one go, rather than just a single condition. This test is limited to discrete values, rather than clauses such as "greater than X," so its use is slightly different; however, it can be a powerful technique.

The basic structure of a switch statement is as follows:

```
switch (<testVar>)
{
   case <comparisonVal1>:
      <code to execute if <testVar> == <comparisonVal1> >
      break;
   case <comparisonVal2>:
      <code to execute if <testVar> == <comparisonVal2> >
      break;
   ...
   case <comparisonValN>:
      <code to execute if <testVar> == <comparisonValN> >
      break;
   default:
      <code to execute if <testVar> != comparisonVals>
      break;
}
```

The value in *<testVar>* is compared to each of the *<comparisonValX>* values (specified with case statements). If there is a match, then the code supplied for this match is executed. If there is no match, then the code in the default section is executed if this block exists.

On completion of the code in each section, you have an additional command, break. It is illegal for the flow of execution to reach a second case statement after processing one case block.

> **NOTE** *The behavior where the flow of execution is forbidden from flowing from one* case *block to the next is one area in which C# differs from C++. In C++ the processing of* case *statements is allowed to run from one to another.*

The break statement here simply terminates the switch statement, and processing continues on the statement following the structure.

There are alternative methods for preventing flow from one case statement to the next in C# code. You can use the return statement, which results in termination of the current function, rather than just the switch structure (see Chapter 6 for more details about this), or a goto statement. goto statements (as detailed earlier) work here because case statements actually define labels in C# code. Here is an example:

```
switch (<testVar>)
{
   case <comparisonVal1>:
      <code to execute if <testVar> == <comparisonVal1> >
      goto case <comparisonVal2>;
   case <comparisonVal2>:
      <code to execute if <testVar> == <comparisonVal2> >
      break;
   ...
```

Here's one exception to the rule that the processing of one case statement can't run freely into the next: If you place multiple case statements together (*stack* them) before a single block of code, then you are in effect checking for multiple conditions at once. If any of these conditions is met, then the code is executed. Here's an example:

```
switch (<testVar>)
{
   case <comparisonVal1>:
   case <comparisonVal2>:
      <code to execute if <testVar> == <comparisonVal1> or
                              <testVar> == <comparisonVal2> >
      break;
   ...
```

These conditions also apply to the `default` statement. There is no rule stipulating that this statement must be the last in the list of comparisons, and you can stack it with `case` statements if you want. Adding a breakpoint with `break`, `goto`, or `return` ensures that a valid execution path exists through the structure in all cases.

Each of the `<comparisonValX>` comparisons must be a constant value. One way of doing this is to provide literal values, like this:

```
switch (myInteger)
{
   case 1:
      <code to execute if myInteger == 1>
      break;
   case -1:
      <code to execute if myInteger == -1>
      break;
   default:
      <code to execute if myInteger != comparisons>
      break;
}
```

Another way is to use *constant variables*. Constant variables (also known as just "constants," avoiding the oxymoron) are just like any other variable except for one key factor: The value they contain never changes. Once you assign a value to a constant variable, then that is the value it has for the duration of code execution. Constant variables can come in handy here, because it is often easier to read code where the actual values being compared are hidden from you at the time of comparison.

You declare constant variables using the `const` keyword in addition to the variable type, and you *must* assign them values at this time, as shown here:

```
const int intTwo = 2;
```

The preceding code is perfectly valid, but if you try

```
const int intTwo;
intTwo = 2;
```

you will get an error and won't be able to compile your code. This also happens if you try to change the value of a constant variable through any other means after initial assignment.

The following Try It Out uses a `switch` statement to write different strings to the console, depending on the value you enter for a test string.

**TRY IT OUT**    **Using the switch Statement: Ch04Ex03\Program.cs**

1.  Create a new console application called Ch04Ex03 and save it to the directory `C:\BegVCSharp\Chapter04`.

2.  Add the following code to Program.cs:

```
static void Main(string[] args)
{
   const string myName = "karli";
```

```
            const string sexyName = "angelina";
            const string sillyName = "ploppy";
            string name;
            Console.WriteLine("What is your name?");
            name = Console.ReadLine();
            switch (name.ToLower())
            {
               case myName:
                  Console.WriteLine("You have the same name as me!");
                  break;
               case sexyName:
                  Console.WriteLine("My, what a sexy name you have!");
                  break;
               case sillyName:
                  Console.WriteLine("That's a very silly name.");
                  break;
            }
            Console.WriteLine("Hello {0}!", name);
            Console.ReadKey();
         }
```

**3.** Execute the code and enter a name. The result is shown in Figure 4-3.

**FIGURE 4-3**

### How It Works

The code sets up three constant strings, accepts a string from the user, and then writes out text to the console based on the string entered. Here, the strings are names.

When you compare the name entered (in the variable name) to your constant values, you first force it into lowercase with name.ToLower(). This is a standard command that works with all string variables, and it comes in handy when you're not sure what the user entered. Using this technique, the strings Karli, kArLi, karli, and so on all match the test string karli.

The switch statement itself attempts to match the string entered with the constant values you have defined, and, if successful, writes out a personalized message to greet the user. If no match is made, you offer a generic greeting.

switch statements place no limit on the amount of case sections they contain, so you could extend this code to cover every name you can think of should you want... but it might take a while!

## LOOPING

*Looping* refers to the repeated execution of statements. This technique comes in very handy because it means that you can repeat operations as many times as you want (thousands, even millions, of times) without having to write the same code each time.

As a simple example, consider the following code for calculating the amount of money in a bank account after 10 years, assuming that interest is paid each year and no other money flows into or out of the account:

```
double balance = 1000;
double interestRate = 1.05; // 5% interest/year
balance *= interestRate;
```

```
balance *= interestRate;
balance *= interestRate;
balance *= interestRate;
balance *= interestRate;
balance *= interestRate;
balance *= interestRate;
balance *= interestRate;
balance *= interestRate;
balance *= interestRate;
```

Writing the same code 10 times seems a bit wasteful, and what if you wanted to change the duration from 10 years to some other value? You'd have to manually copy the line of code the required amount of times, which would be a bit of a pain! Luckily, you don't have to do this. Instead, you can have a loop that executes the instruction you want the required number of times.

Another important type of loop is one in which you loop until a certain condition is fulfilled. These loops are slightly simpler than the situation detailed previously (although no less useful), so they're a good starting point.

## do Loops

do loops operate as follows. The code you have marked out for looping is executed, a Boolean test is performed, and the code executes again if this test evaluates to `true`, and so on. When the test evaluates to `false`, the loop exits.

The structure of a do loop is as follows, where `<Test>` evaluates to a Boolean value:

```
do
{
    <code to be looped>
} while (<Test>);
```

> **NOTE** The semicolon after the `while` statement is required.

For example, you could use the following to write the numbers from 1 to 10 in a column:

```
int i = 1;
do
{
    Console.WriteLine("{0}", i++);
} while (i <= 10);
```

Here, you use the suffix version of the `++` operator to increment the value of `i` after it is written to the screen, so you need to check for `i <= 10` to include 10 in the numbers written to the console.

The following Try It Out uses this for a slightly modified version of the code shown earlier, where you calculated the balance in an account after 10 years. Here, you use a loop to calculate how many years it will take to get a specified amount of money in the account, based on a starting amount and a fixed interest rate.

**TRY IT OUT** Using do Loops: Ch04Ex04\Program.cs

1. Create a new console application called Ch04Ex04 and save it to the directory `C:\BegVCSharp\Chapter04`.

2. Add the following code to `Program.cs`:

```
static void Main(string[] args)
{
    double balance, interestRate, targetBalance;
    Console.WriteLine("What is your current balance?");
    balance = Convert.ToDouble(Console.ReadLine());
    Console.WriteLine("What is your current annual interest rate (in %)?");
    interestRate = 1 + Convert.ToDouble(Console.ReadLine()) / 100.0;
    Console.WriteLine("What balance would you like to have?");
```

```
            targetBalance = Convert.ToDouble(Console.ReadLine());
            int totalYears = 0;
            do
            {
               balance *= interestRate;
               ++totalYears;
            }
            while (balance < targetBalance);
            Console.WriteLine("In {0} year{1} you'll have a balance of {2}.",
                              totalYears, totalYears == 1 ? "" : "s", balance);
            Console.ReadKey();
        }
```

**3.** Execute the code and enter some values. A sample result is shown in Figure 4-4.

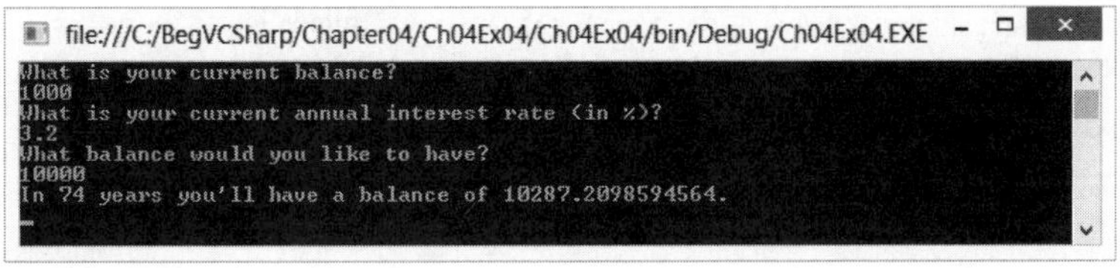

**FIGURE 4-4**

*How It Works*

This code simply repeats the simple annual calculation of the balance with a fixed interest rate as many times as is necessary for the balance to satisfy the terminating condition. You keep a count of how many years have been accounted for by incrementing a counter variable with each loop cycle:

```
            int totalYears = 0;
            do
            {
               balance *= interestRate;
               ++totalYears;
            }
            while (balance < targetBalance);
```

You can then use this counter variable as part of the result output:

```
            Console.WriteLine("In {0} year{1} you'll have a balance of {2}.",
                              totalYears, totalYears == 1 ? "" : "s", balance);
```

> **NOTE** *Perhaps the most common usage of the* ?: *(ternary) operator is to conditionally format text with the minimum of code. Here, you output an "s" after "year" if* totalYears *isn't equal to 1.*

Unfortunately, this code isn't perfect. Consider what happens when the target balance is less than the current balance. The output will be similar to what is shown in Figure 4-5.

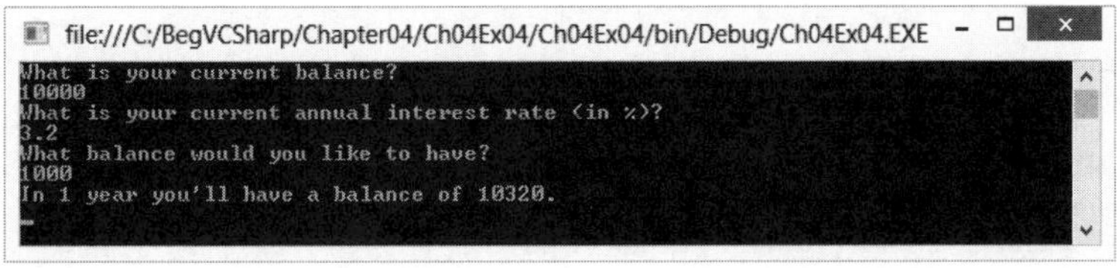

**FIGURE 4-5**

do loops always execute at least once. Sometimes, as in this situation, this isn't ideal. Of course, you could add an `if` statement:

```
int totalYears = 0;
if (balance < targetBalance)
{
    do
    {
        balance *= interestRate;
        ++totalYears;
    }
    while (balance < targetBalance);
}
Console.WriteLine(
    "In {0} year{1} you'll have a balance of {2}.",
                    totalYears, totalYears == 1 ? "": "s",
                    balance);
```

Clearly, this adds unnecessary complexity. A far better solution is to use a `while` loop.

## while Loops

`while` loops are very similar to `do` loops, but they have one important difference: The Boolean test in a `while` loop takes place at the start of the loop cycle, not at the end. If the test evaluates to `false`, then the loop cycle is never executed. Instead, program execution jumps straight to the code following the loop.

Here's how `while` loops are specified:

```
while (<Test>)
{
    <code to be looped>
}
```

They can be used in almost the same way as `do` loops:

```
int i = 1;
while (i <= 10)
{
    Console.WriteLine("{0}", i++);
}
```

This code has the same result as the `do` loop shown earlier; it outputs the numbers 1 to 10 in a column. The following Try It Out demonstrates how you can modify the last example to use a `while` loop.

**TRY IT OUT** Using while Loops: Ch04Ex05\Program.cs

1. Create a new console application called Ch04Ex05 and save it to the directory C:\BegVCSharp\ Chapter04.

2. Modify the code as follows (use the code from Ch04Ex04 as a starting point, and remember to delete the `while` statement at the end of the original do loop):

```
static void Main(string[] args)
{
    double balance, interestRate, targetBalance;
    Console.WriteLine("What is your current balance?");
    balance = Convert.ToDouble(Console.ReadLine());
    Console.WriteLine("What is your current annual interest rate (in %)?");
    interestRate = 1 + Convert.ToDouble(Console.ReadLine()) / 100.0;
    Console.WriteLine("What balance would you like to have?");
    targetBalance = Convert.ToDouble(Console.ReadLine());
    int totalYears = 0;
```

```
    while (balance < targetBalance)
    {
        balance *= interestRate;
        ++totalYears;
    }
    Console.WriteLine("In {0} year{1} you'll have a balance of {2}.",
                    totalYears, totalYears == 1 ? "": "s", balance);
        if (totalYears == 0)
            Console.WriteLine(
                "To be honest, you really didn't need to use this calculator.");
    Console.ReadKey();
}
```

**3.** Execute the code again, but this time use a target balance that is less than the starting balance, as shown in Figure 4-6.

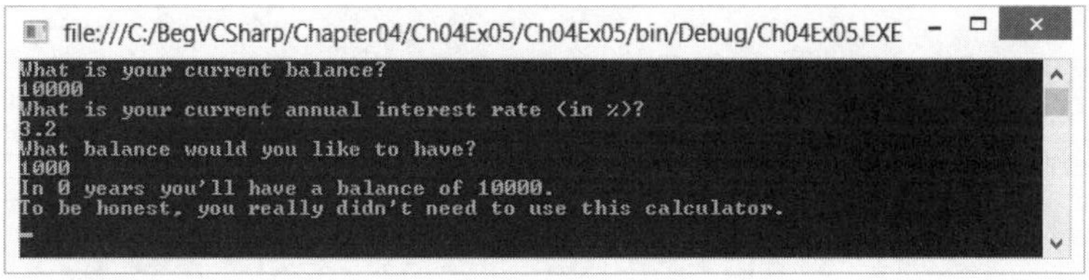

FIGURE 4-6

*How It Works*

This simple change from a do loop to a while loop has solved the problem in the last example. By moving the Boolean test to the beginning, you provide for the circumstance where no looping is required, and you can jump straight to the result.

Of course, other alternatives are possible in this situation. For example, you could check the user input to ensure that the target balance is greater than the starting balance. In that case, you can place the user input section in a loop as follows:

```
    Console.WriteLine("What balance would you like to have?");
    do
    {
        targetBalance = Convert.ToDouble(Console.ReadLine());
        if (targetBalance <= balance)
            Console.WriteLine("You must enter an amount greater than " +
                    "your current balance!\nPlease enter another value.");
    }
    while (targetBalance <= balance);
```

This rejects values that don't make sense, so the output looks like Figure 4-7.

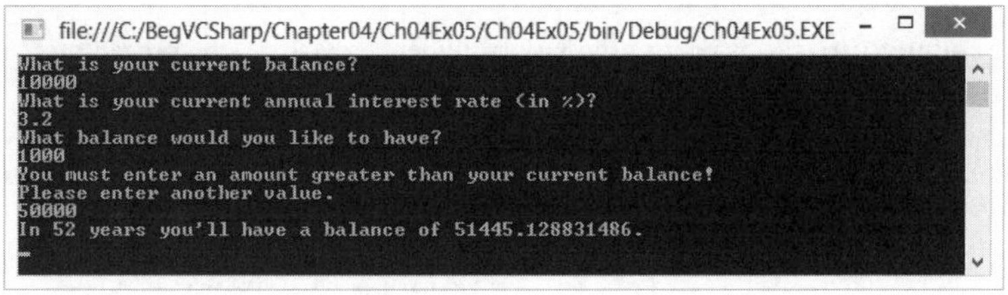

FIGURE 4-7

This *validation* of user input is an important topic when it comes to application design, and many examples of it appear throughout this book.

# for Loops

The last type of loop to look at in this chapter is the for loop. This type of loop executes a set number of times and maintains its own counter. To define a for loop you need the following information:

➤ A starting value to initialize the counter variable

➤ A condition for continuing the loop, involving the counter variable

➤ An operation to perform on the counter variable at the end of each loop cycle

For example, if you want a loop with a counter that increments from 1 to 10 in steps of one, then the starting value is 1; the condition is that the counter is less than or equal to 10; and the operation to perform at the end of each cycle is to add 1 to the counter.

This information must be placed into the structure of a for loop as follows:

```
for (<initialization>; <condition>; <operation>)
{
    <code to loop>
}
```

This works exactly the same way as the following while loop:

```
<initialization>
while (<condition>)
{
    <code to loop>
    <operation>
}
```

The format of the for loop makes the code easier to read, however, because the syntax involves the complete specification of the loop in one place, rather than dividing it over several statements in different areas of the code.

Earlier, you used do and while loops to write out the numbers from 1 to 10. The code that follows shows what is required to do this using a for loop:

```
int i;
for (i = 1; i <= 10; ++i)
{
    Console.WriteLine("{0}", i);
}
```

The counter variable, an integer called i, starts with a value of 1 and is incremented by 1 at the end of each cycle. During each cycle, the value of i is written to the console.

When the code resumes after the loop, i has a value of 11. That's because at the end of the cycle where i is equal to 10, i is incremented to 11. This happens before the condition i <= 10 is processed, at which point the loop ends. As with while loops, for loops execute only if the condition evaluates to true before the first cycle, so the code in the loop doesn't necessarily run at all.

As a final note, you can declare the counter variable as part of the for statement, rewriting the preceding code as follows:

```
for (int i = 1; i <= 10; ++i)
{
    Console.WriteLine("{0}", i);
}
```

If you do this, though, the variable i won't be accessible from code outside this loop (see the "Variable Scope" section in Chapter 6).

The next Try It Out uses for loops. And because you have already used several loops now, this example is a bit more interesting. It displays a *Mandelbrot set*, which is one of many types of *fractal* images. A fractal is a mathematical concept that describes data that is "self-similar"—that is, it describes data that looks more-or-less the same, however closely you look. A great example of a fractal is the coastline of any country you care to mention. On a map showing the whole country, a coastline looks pretty crinkly. A close up of a mile or two of coastline would look equally crinkly, and so on right down to the pebbles on a beach or the atoms that make up those pebbles. Try entering the term "Mandelbrot set" into your favorite search engine, and you'll see a great many beautiful images that look like they might be sections of coastline on an alien word. Rather than being photos, though, these images are generated using (surprisingly simple) mathematics. You'll do the same thing here; but to keep things simple you'll use plain-text characters, so it won't look quite so spectacular.

**TRY IT OUT**   Using for Loops: Ch04Ex06\Program.cs

1. Create a new console application called Ch04Ex06 and save it to the directory C:\BegVCSharp\ Chapter04.

2. Add the following code to Program.cs:

```
static void Main(string[] args)
{
    double realCoord, imagCoord;
    double realTemp, imagTemp, realTemp2, arg;
    int iterations;
    for (imagCoord = 1.2; imagCoord >= -1.2; imagCoord -= 0.05)
    {
        for (realCoord = -0.6; realCoord <= 1.77; realCoord += 0.03)
        {
            iterations = 0;
            realTemp = realCoord;
            imagTemp = imagCoord;
            arg = (realCoord * realCoord) + (imagCoord * imagCoord);
            while ((arg < 4) && (iterations < 40))
            {
                realTemp2 = (realTemp * realTemp)-(imagTemp * imagTemp)
                    -realCoord;
                imagTemp = (2 * realTemp * imagTemp) -imagCoord;
                realTemp = realTemp2;
                arg = (realTemp * realTemp) + (imagTemp * imagTemp);
                iterations += 1;
            }
            switch (iterations % 4)
            {
                case 0:
                    Console.Write(".");
                    break;
                case 1:
                    Console.Write("o");
                    break;
                case 2:
                    Console.Write("O");
                    break;
                case 3:
                    Console.Write("@");
                    break;
            }
        }
        Console.Write("\n");
    }
    Console.ReadKey();
}
```

3. Execute the code. The result is shown in Figure 4-8.

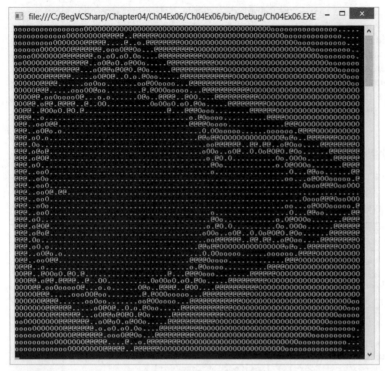

**FIGURE 4-8**

*How It Works*

Details about calculating Mandelbrot sets are beyond the scope of this chapter, but you should understand why you need the loops used in this code. Feel free to skim through the following two paragraphs if the mathematics doesn't interest you; it's an understanding of the code that is important here.

Each position in a Mandelbrot image corresponds to an imaginary number of the form N = x + y*i, where the real part is x, the imaginary part is y, and i is the square root of -1. The x and y coordinates of the position in the image correspond to the x and y parts of the imaginary number.

For each position on the image, you look at the argument of N, which is the square root of x*x + y*y. If this value is greater than or equal to 2, you say that the position corresponding to this number has a value of 0. If the argument of N is less than 2, you change N to a value of N*N-N (giving you N = (x*x-y*y-x) + (2*x*y-y)*i) and check the argument of this new value of N again. If this value is greater than or equal to 2, you say that the position corresponding to this number has a value of 1. This process continues until you either assign a value to the position on the image or perform more than a certain number of iterations.

Based on the values assigned to each point in the image, you would, in a graphical environment, place a pixel of a certain color on the screen. However, because you are using a text display, you simply place characters onscreen instead.

Now, turn your attention back to the code and the loops contained in it. You begin by declaring the variables you need for your calculation:

```
double realCoord, imagCoord;
double realTemp, imagTemp, realTemp2, arg;
int iterations;
```

Here, `realCoord` and `imagCoord` are the real and imaginary parts of `N`, and the other `double` variables are for temporary information during computation. `iterations` records how many iterations it takes before the argument of `N` (`arg`) is 2 or greater.

Next, you start two `for` loops to cycle through coordinates covering the whole of the image (using a slightly more complex syntax for modifying your counters than ++ or --, a common and powerful technique):

```
for (imagCoord = 1.2; imagCoord >= -1.2; imagCoord -= 0.05)
{
    for (realCoord = -0.6; realCoord <= 1.77; realCoord += 0.03)
    {
```

Here, appropriate limits have been used to show the main section of the Mandelbrot set. Feel free to play around with these if you want to try "zooming in" on the image.

Within these two loops you have code that pertains to a single point in the Mandelbrot set, giving you a value for `N` to play with. This is where you perform your calculation of iterations required, giving you a value to plot for the current point.

First, initialize some variables:

```
iterations = 0;
realTemp = realCoord;
imagTemp = imagCoord;
arg = (realCoord * realCoord) + (imagCoord * imagCoord);
```

Next, you have a `while` loop to perform your iterating. Use a `while` loop rather than a `do` loop, in case the initial value of `N` has an argument greater than 2 already, in which case `iterations == 0` is the answer you are looking for and no further calculations are necessary.

Note that you're not quite calculating the argument fully here. You're just getting the value of x*x + y*y and checking whether that value is less than 4. This simplifies the calculation, because you know that 2 is the square root of 4 and don't have to calculate any square roots yourself:

```
while ((arg < 4) && (iterations < 40))
{
    realTemp2 = (realTemp * realTemp)-(imagTemp * imagTemp)
        -realCoord;
    imagTemp = (2 * realTemp * imagTemp)-imagCoord;
    realTemp = realTemp2;
    arg = (realTemp * realTemp) + (imagTemp * imagTemp);
    iterations += 1;
}
```

The maximum number of iterations of this loop, which calculates values as detailed above, is 40.

Once you have a value for the current point stored in `iterations`, you use a `switch` statement to choose a character to output. You just use four different characters here, instead of the 40 possible values, and use the modulus operator (`%`) so that values of 0, 4, 8, and so on provide one character; values of 1, 5, 9, and so on provide another character, and so forth:

```
switch (iterations % 4)
{
    case 0:
        Console.Write(".");
        break;
    case 1:
        Console.Write("o");
        break;
    case 2:
        Console.Write("O");
        break;
    case 3:
        Console.Write("@");
        break;
}
```

You use `Console.Write()` here, rather than `Console.WriteLine()`, because you don't want to start a new line every time you output a character. At the end of one of the innermost `for` loops, you do want to end a line, so you simply output an end-of-line character using the escape sequence shown earlier:

```
        }
        Console.Write("\n");
    }
```

This results in each row being separated from the next and lining up appropriately. The final result of this application, although not spectacular, is fairly impressive, and certainly shows how useful looping and branching can be.

## Interrupting Loops

Sometimes you want finer-grained control over the processing of looping code. C# provides four commands to help you here, three of which were shown in other situations:

➤ `break`—Causes the loop to end immediately

➤ `continue`—Causes the current loop cycle to end immediately (execution continues with the next loop cycle)

➤ `goto`—Allows jumping out of a loop to a labeled position (not recommended if you want your code to be easy to read and understand)

➤ `return`—Jumps out of the loop and its containing function (see Chapter 6)

The `break` command simply exits the loop, and execution continues at the first line of code after the loop, as shown in the following example:

```
int i = 1;
while (i <= 10)
{
    if (i == 6)
        break;
    Console.WriteLine("{0}", i++);
}
```

This code writes out the numbers from 1 to 5 because the `break` command causes the loop to exit when `i` reaches 6.

`continue` only stops the current cycle, not the whole loop, as shown here:

```
int i;
for (i = 1; i <= 10; i++)
{
    if ((i % 2) == 0)
        continue;
    Console.WriteLine(i);
}
```

In the preceding example, whenever the remainder of `i` divided by 2 is zero, the `continue` statement stops the execution of the current cycle, so only the numbers 1, 3, 5, 7, and 9 are displayed.

The third method of interrupting a loop is to use `goto`, as shown earlier:

```
int i = 1;
while (i <= 10)
{
    if (i == 6)
        goto exitPoint;
    Console.WriteLine("{0}", i++);
}
```

```
Console.WriteLine("This code will never be reached.");
exitPoint:
Console.WriteLine("This code is run when the loop is exited using goto.");
```

Note that exiting a loop with `goto` is legal (if slightly messy), but it is illegal to use `goto` to jump into a loop from outside.

## Infinite Loops

It is possible, through both coding errors and design, to define loops that never end, so-called *infinite loops*. As a very simple example, consider the following:

```
while (true)
{
    // code in loop
}
```

This can be useful, and you can always exit such loops using code such as `break` statements or manually by using the Windows Task Manager. However, when this occurs by accident, it can be annoying. Consider the following loop, which is similar to the `for` loop in the previous section:

```
int i = 1;
while (i <= 10)
{
    if ((i % 2) == 0)
        continue;
    Console.WriteLine("{0}", i++);
}
```

Here, `i` isn't incremented until the last line of code in the loop, which occurs after the `continue` statement. If this `continue` statement is reached (which it will be when `i` is 2), the next loop cycle will be using the same value of `i`, continuing the loop, testing the same value of `i`, continuing the loop, and so on. This will cause the application to freeze. Note that it's still possible to quit the frozen application in the normal way, so you won't have to reboot if this happens.

## SUMMARY

In this chapter, you increased your programming knowledge by considering various structures that you can use in your code. The proper use of these structures is essential when you start making more complex applications, and you will see them used throughout this book.

You first spent some time looking at Boolean logic, with a bit of bitwise logic thrown in for good measure. Looking back on this after working through the rest of the chapter should confirm the suggestion that this topic is very important when it comes to implementing branching and looping code in your programs. It is essential to become very familiar with the operators and techniques detailed in this section.

Branching enables you to conditionally execute code, which, when combined with looping, enables you to create convoluted structures in your C# code. When you have loops inside loops inside `if` structures inside loops, you start to see why code indentation is so useful! If you shift all your code to the left of the screen, it instantly becomes difficult to parse by eye, and even more difficult to debug. Make sure you've got the hang of indentation at this stage—you'll appreciate it later! VS does a lot of this for you, but it's a good idea to indent code as you type it anyway.

The next chapter covers variables in more depth.

## EXERCISES

**4.1** If you have two integers stored in variables `var1` and `var2`, what Boolean test can you perform to determine whether one or the other (but not both) is greater than 10?

**4.2** Write an application that includes the logic from Exercise 1, obtains two numbers from the user, and displays them, but rejects any input where both numbers are greater than 10 and asks for two new numbers.

**4.3** What is wrong with the following code?

```
int i;
for (i = 1; i <= 10; i++)
{
    if ((i % 2) = 0)
        continue;
    Console.WriteLine(i);
}
```

**4.4** Modify the Mandelbrot set application to request image limits from the user and display the chosen section of the image. The current code outputs as many characters as will fit on a single line of a console application; consider making every image chosen fit in the same amount of space to maximize the viewable area.

Answers to the exercises can be found in Appendix A.

## ▶ WHAT YOU LEARNED IN THIS CHAPTER

| TOPIC | KEY CONCEPTS |
| --- | --- |
| **Boolean logic** | Boolean logic involves using Boolean (`true` or `false`) values to evaluate conditions. Boolean operators are used to perform comparisons between values and return Boolean results. Some Boolean operators are also used to perform bitwise operations on the underlying bit structure of values, and there are some specialized bitwise operators too. |
| **Branching** | You can use Boolean logic to control program flow. The result of an expression that evaluates to a Boolean value can be used to determine whether a block of code is executed. You do this with `if` statements or the `?:` (ternary) operator for simple branching, or the `switch` statement to check multiple conditions simultaneously. |
| **Looping** | Looping allows you to execute blocks of code a number of times according to conditions you specify. You can use `do` and `while` loops to execute code while a Boolean expression evaluates to `true`, and `for` loops to include a counter in your looping code. Loops can be interrupted by cycle (with `continue`) or completely (with `break`). Some loops end only if you interrupt them; these are called infinite loops. |

# More About Variables

## WHAT YOU WILL LEARN IN THIS CHAPTER

➤ How to perform implicit and explicit conversions between types

➤ How to create and use enum types

➤ How to create and use struct types

➤ How to create and use arrays

➤ How to manipulate string values

## WROX.COM CODE DOWNLOADS FOR THIS CHAPTER

You can find the wrox.com code downloads for this chapter at www.wrox.com/remtitle
.cgi?isbn=9781118314418 on the Download Code tab. The code is in the Chapter 5 download and
individually named according to the names throughout the chapter.

Now that you've seen a bit more of the C# language, you can go back and tackle some of the more
involved topics concerning variables.

The first subject you look at in this chapter is *type conversion*, whereby you convert values from
one type into another. You've already seen a bit of this, but you look at it formally here. A grasp of
this topic gives you a greater understanding of what happens when you mix types in expressions
(intentionally or unintentionally), as well as tighter control over the way that data is manipulated.
This helps you to streamline your code and avoid nasty surprises.

Then you'll look at a few more types of variables that you can use:

➤ **Enumerations**—Variable types that have a user-defined discrete set of possible values that can
be used in a human-readable way.

➤ **Structs**—Composite variable types made up of a user-defined set of other variable types.

➤ **Arrays**—Types that hold multiple variables of one type, allowing index access to the individual
value.

These are slightly more complex than the simple types you've been using up to now, but they can
make your life much easier. Finally, you'll explore another useful subject concerning strings: basic
string manipulation.

## TYPE CONVERSION

Earlier in this book, you saw that all data, regardless of type, is simply a sequence of bits—that is, a sequence of zeros and ones. The meaning of the variable is determined by the way in which this data is interpreted. The simplest example of this is the `char` type. This type represents a character in the Unicode character set using a number. In fact, the number is stored in exactly the same way as a `ushort`—both of them store a number between 0 and 65535.

However, in general, the different types of variables use varying schemes to represent data. This implies that even if it were possible to place the sequence of bits from one variable into a variable of a different type (perhaps they use the same amount of storage, or perhaps the target type has enough storage space to include all the source bits), the results might not be what you expect.

Instead of this one-to-one mapping of bits from one variable into another, you need to use *type conversion* on the data. Type conversion takes two forms:

➤ **Implicit conversion**—Conversion from type A to type B is possible in all circumstances, and the rules for performing the conversion are simple enough for you to trust in the compiler.

➤ **Explicit conversion**—Conversion from type A to type B is possible only in certain circumstances or where the rules for conversion are complicated enough to merit additional processing of some kind.

### Implicit Conversions

Implicit conversion requires no work on your part and no additional code. Consider the code shown here:

```
var1 = var2;
```

This assignment may involve an implicit conversion if the type of `var2` can be implicitly converted into the type of `var1`; however, it could just as easily involve two variables with the same type, in which case no implicit conversion is necessary. For example, the values of `ushort` and `char` are effectively interchangeable, because both store a number between 0 and 65535. You can convert values between these types implicitly, as demonstrated by the following code:

```
ushort destinationVar;
char sourceVar = 'a';
destinationVar = sourceVar;
Console.WriteLine("sourceVar val: {0}", sourceVar);
Console.WriteLine("destinationVar val: {0}", destinationVar);
```

Here, the value stored in `sourceVar` is placed in `destinationVar`. When you output the variables with the two `Console.WriteLine()` commands, you get the following output:

```
sourceVar val: a
destinationVar val: 97
```

Even though the two variables store the same information, they are interpreted in different ways using their type.

There are many implicit conversions of simple types; `bool` and `string` have no implicit conversions, but the numeric types have a few. For reference, Table 5-1 shows the numeric conversions that the compiler can perform implicitly (remember that `char`s are stored as numbers, so `char` counts as a numeric type).

**TABLE 5-1:** Implicit Numeric Conversions

| TYPE | CAN SAFELY BE CONVERTED TO |
| --- | --- |
| byte | short, ushort, int, uint, long, ulong, float, double, decimal |
| sbyte | short, int, long, float, double, decimal |
| short | int, long, float, double, decimal |

| | |
|---|---|
| ushort | int, uint, long, ulong, float, double, decimal |
| int | long, float, double, decimal |
| uint | long, ulong, float, double, decimal |
| long | float, double, decimal |
| ulong | float, double, decimal |
| float | double |
| char | ushort, int, uint, long, ulong, float, double, decimal |

Don't worry—you don't need to learn this table by heart, because it's actually quite easy to work out which conversions the compiler can do implicitly. Back in Chapter 3, Table 3-6 showed the range of possible values for every simple numeric type. The implicit conversion rule for these types is this: Any type A whose range of possible values completely fits inside the range of possible values of type B can be implicitly converted into that type.

The reasoning for this is simple. If you try to fit a value into a variable, but that value is outside the range of values the variable can take, then there will be a problem. For example, a short type variable is capable of storing values up to 32767, and the maximum value allowed into a byte is 255, so there could be problems if you try to convert a short value into a byte value. If the short holds a value between 256 and 32767, then it simply won't fit into a byte.

If you know that the value in your short type variable is less than 255, then you should be able to convert the value, right? The simple answer is that, of course, you can. The slightly more complex answer is that, of course, you can, but you must use an *explicit* conversion. Performing an explicit conversion is a bit like saying "Okay, I know you've warned me about doing this, but I'll take responsibility for what happens."

## Explicit Conversions

As the name suggests, an explicit conversion occurs when you explicitly ask the compiler to convert a value from one data type to another. These conversions require extra code, and the format of this code may vary, depending on the exact conversion method. Before you look at any of this explicit conversion code, look at what happens if you *don't* add any.

For example, the following modification to the code from the last section attempts to convert a short value into a byte:

```
byte destinationVar;
short sourceVar = 7;
destinationVar = sourceVar;
Console.WriteLine("sourceVar val: {0}", sourceVar);
Console.WriteLine("destinationVar val: {0}", destinationVar);
```

If you attempt to compile the preceding code, you will receive the following error:

```
Cannot implicitly convert type 'short' to 'byte'. An explicit conversion exists
(are you missing a cast?)
```

Luckily for you, the C# compiler can detect missing explicit conversions!

To get this code to compile, you need to add the code to perform an explicit conversion. The easiest way to do that in this context is to *cast* the short variable into a byte (as suggested by the preceding error string). Casting basically means forcing data from one type into another, and it uses the following simple syntax:

```
(<destinationType>)<sourceVar>
```

This will convert the value in *<sourceVar>* into *<destinationType>*.

> **NOTE** Casting is only possible in some situations. Types that bear little or no relation to each other are likely not to have casting conversions defined.

You can, therefore, modify your example using this syntax to force the conversion from a short to a byte:

```
byte destinationVar;
short sourceVar = 7;
destinationVar = (byte)sourceVar;
Console.WriteLine("sourceVar val: {0}", sourceVar);
Console.WriteLine("destinationVar val: {0}", destinationVar);
```

This results in the following output:

```
sourceVar val: 7
destinationVar val: 7
```

What happens when you try to force a value into an incompatible variable type. For example, you can't fit a large integer into a numeric type that's too small. Modifying your code as follows illustrates this:

```
byte destinationVar;
short sourceVar = 281;
destinationVar = (byte)sourceVar;
Console.WriteLine("sourceVar val: {0}", sourceVar);
Console.WriteLine("destinationVar val: {0}", destinationVar);
```

This results in the following:

```
sourceVar val: 281
destinationVar val: 25
```

What happened? Well, look at the binary representations of these two numbers, along with the maximum value that can be stored in a byte, which is 255:

```
281 = 100011001
 25 = 000011001
255 = 011111111
```

You can see that the leftmost bit of the source data has been lost. This immediately raises a question: How can you tell when this happens? Obviously, there will be times when you will need to explicitly cast one type into another, and it would be nice to know if any data has been lost along the way. Not detecting this could cause serious errors—for example, in an accounting application or an application determining the trajectory of a rocket to the moon.

One way to do this is simply to check the value of the source variable and compare it with the known limits of the destination variable. Another technique is to force the system to pay special attention to the conversion at runtime. Attempting to fit a value into a variable when that value is too big for the type of that variable results in an *overflow*, and this is the situation you want to check for.

Two keywords exist for setting what is called the *overflow checking context* for an expression: checked and unchecked. You use these in the following way:

```
checked(<expression>)
unchecked(<expression>)
```

You can force overflow checking in the last example:

```
byte destinationVar;
short sourceVar = 281;
destinationVar = checked((byte)sourceVar);
Console.WriteLine("sourceVar val: {0}", sourceVar);
Console.WriteLine("destinationVar val: {0}", destinationVar);
```

When this code is executed, it will crash with the error message shown in Figure 5-1 (this was compiled in a project called OverflowCheck).

```
static void Main(string[] args)
{
    byte destinationVar;
    short sourceVar = 281;
    destinationVar = checked((byte)sourceVar);
    Console.WriteLine("sourceVar val: {0}", sourceVar);
    Console.WriteLine("destinationVar val: {0}", destinationVar);
}
```

**OverflowException was unhandled**        ✕

Arithmetic operation resulted in an overflow.

**Troubleshooting tips:**

Make sure you are not dividing by zero.

Get general help for this exception.

Search for more Help Online...

**Exception settings:**
☐ Break when this exception type is thrown

**Actions:**
View Detail...

Copy exception detail to the clipboard

Open exception settings

**FIGURE 5-1**

However, if you replace checked with unchecked in this code, you get the result shown earlier, and no error occurs. That is identical to the default behavior, also shown earlier.

You also can configure your application to behave as if every expression of this type includes the checked keyword, unless that expression explicitly uses the unchecked keyword (in other words, you can change the default setting for overflow checking). To do this, you modify the properties for your project by right-clicking on it in the Solution Explorer window and selecting the Properties option. Click Build on the left side of the window to bring up the Build settings, as shown in Figure 5-2.

OverflowCheck ✱ ✕ Program.cs

| Application | | | | |
| Build | Configuration: | Active (Debug) | Platform: | Active (Any CPU) |
| Build Events | | | | |
| Debug | General | | | |
| Resources | Conditional compilation symbols: | | | |
| Services | ☑ Define DEBUG constant | | | |
| Settings | ☑ Define TRACE constant | | | |
| Reference Paths | Platform target: | Any CPU | | |
| Signing | ☑ Prefer 32-bit | | | |
| Security | ☐ Allow unsafe code | | | |
| Publish | ☐ Optimize code | | | |
| Code Analysis | | | | |

Errors and warnings

Warning level: 4

Suppress warnings:

Treat warnings as errors

◉ None

○ All

○ Specific warnings:

Output

Output path: bin\Debug\   Browse...

☐ XML documentation file:

☐ Register for COM interop

Generate serialization assembly: Auto

Advanced...

**FIGURE 5-2**

The property you want to change is one of the Advanced settings, so click the Advanced button. In the dialog box that appears, enable the Check for Arithmetic Overflow/Underflow box, as shown in Figure 5-3. By default, this setting is disabled; enabling it provides the `checked` behavior detailed previously.

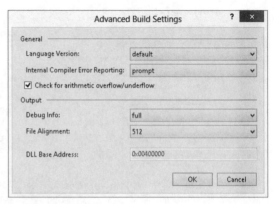

**FIGURE 5-3**

## Explicit Conversions Using the Convert Commands

The type of explicit conversion you have been using in many of the Try It Out examples in this book is a bit different from those you have seen so far in this chapter. You have been converting string values into numbers using commands such as `Convert.ToDouble()`, which is obviously something that won't work for every possible string.

If, for example, you try to convert a string like `Number` into a double value using `Convert.ToDouble()`, you will see the dialog box shown in Figure 5-4 when you execute the code.

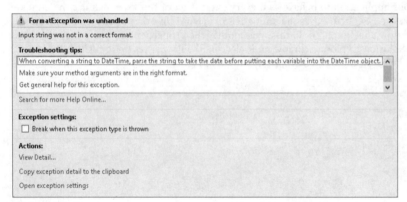

**FIGURE 5-4**

As you can see, the operation fails. For this type of conversion to work, the string supplied *must* be a valid representation of a number, and that number must be one that won't cause an overflow. A valid representation of a number is one that contains an optional sign (that is, plus or minus), zero or more digits, an optional period followed by one or more digits, and an optional "e" or "E" followed by an optional sign, one or more digits, and nothing else except spaces (before or after this sequence). Using all of these optional extras, you can recognize strings as complex as `-1.2451e-24` as being a number.

You can specify many such explicit conversions in this way, as Table 5-2 shows.

**TABLE 5-2:** Convert Commands

| COMMAND | RESULT |
| --- | --- |
| `Convert.ToBoolean(val)` | val converted to `bool` |
| `Convert.ToByte(val)` | val converted to `byte` |
| `Convert.ToChar(val)` | val converted to `char` |
| `Convert.ToDecimal(val)` | val converted to `decimal` |

| | |
|---|---|
| `Convert.ToDouble(val)` | `val` converted to `double` |
| `Convert.ToInt16(val)` | `val` converted to `short` |
| `Convert.ToInt32(val)` | `val` converted to `int` |
| `Convert.ToInt64(val)` | `val` converted to `long` |
| `Convert.ToSByte(val)` | `val` converted to `sbyte` |
| `Convert.ToSingle(val)` | `val` converted to `float` |
| `Convert.ToString(val)` | `val` converted to `string` |
| `Convert.ToUInt16(val)` | `val` converted to `ushort` |
| `Convert.ToUInt32(val)` | `val` converted to `uint` |
| `Convert.ToUInt64(val)` | `val` converted to `ulong` |

Here, `val` can be most types of variable (if it's a type that can't be handled by these commands, the compiler will tell you).

Unfortunately, as Table 5-2 shows, the names of these conversions are slightly different from the C# type names; for example, to convert to an `int` you use `Convert.ToInt32()`. That's because these commands come from the .NET Framework `System` namespace, rather than being native C#. This enables them to be used from other .NET-compatible languages besides C#.

The important thing to note about these conversions is that they are *always* overflow-checked, and the `checked` and `unchecked` keywords and project property settings have no effect.

The next Try It Out is an example that covers many of the conversion types from this section. It declares and initializes a number of variables of different types and then converts between them implicitly and explicitly.

**TRY IT OUT**   Type Conversions in Practice: Ch05Ex01\Program.cs

1. Create a new console application called Ch05Ex01 and save it in the directory `C:\BegVCSharp\Chapter05`.

2. Add the following code to `Program.cs`:

```
static void Main(string[] args)
{
    short  shortResult, shortVal = 4;
    int    integerVal = 67;
    long   longResult;
    float  floatVal = 10.5F;
    double doubleResult, doubleVal = 99.999;
    string stringResult, stringVal = "17";
    bool   boolVal = true;

    Console.WriteLine("Variable Conversion Examples\n");

    doubleResult = floatVal * shortVal;
    Console.WriteLine("Implicit, -> double: {0} * {1} -> {2}", floatVal,
        shortVal, doubleResult);

    shortResult = (short)floatVal;
    Console.WriteLine("Explicit, -> short: {0} -> {1}", floatVal,
        shortResult);

    stringResult = Convert.ToString(boolVal) +
        Convert.ToString(doubleVal);
    Console.WriteLine("Explicit, -> string: \"{0}\" + \"{1}\" -> {2}",
        boolVal, doubleVal, stringResult);

    longResult = integerVal + Convert.ToInt64(stringVal);
    Console.WriteLine("Mixed,    -> long:   {0} + {1} -> {2}",
```

```
        integerVal, stringVal, longResult);
    Console.ReadKey();
}
```

**3.** Execute the code. The result is shown in Figure 5-5.

```
file:///C:/BegVCSharp/Chapter05/Ch05Ex01/Ch05Ex01/bin/Debug/Ch05Ex01.EXE

Variable Conversion Examples

Implicit, -> double: 10.5 * 4 -> 42
Explicit, -> short:  10.5 -> 10
Explicit, -> string: "True" + "99.999" -> True99.999
Mixed,    -> long:   67 + 17 -> 84
```

**FIGURE 5-5**

*How It Works*

This example contains all of the conversion types you've seen so far—both in simple assignments, as in the short code examples in the preceding discussion, and in expressions. You need to consider both cases because the processing of *every* non-unary operator may result in type conversions, not just assignment operators. For example, the following multiplies a `short` value by a `float` value:

```
shortVal * floatVal
```

In situations such as this, where no explicit conversion is specified, implicit conversion will be used if possible. In this example, the only implicit conversion that makes sense is to convert the `short` into a `float` (as converting a `float` into a `short` requires explicit conversion), so this is the one that will be used.

However, you can override this behavior should you want, as shown here:

```
shortVal * (short)floatVal
```

> **NOTE** *Interestingly, multiplying two* `short` *values together doesn't return a* `short` *value. Because the result of this operation is quite likely to exceed 32767 (the maximum value a* `short` *can hold), it actually returns an* `int`.

Explicit conversions performed using this casting syntax take the same operator precedence as other unary operators (such as ++ used as a prefix)—that is, the highest level of precedence.

When you have statements involving mixed types, conversions occur as each operator is processed, according to operator precedence. This means that "intermediate" conversions may occur:

```
doubleResult = floatVal + (shortVal * floatVal);
```

The first operator to be processed here is *, which, as discussed previously, will result in `shortVal` being converted to a `float`. Next, you process the + operator, which won't require any conversion because it acts on two `float` values (`floatVal` and the `float` type result of `shortVal * floatVal`). Finally, the `float` result of this calculation is converted into a `double` when the = operator is processed.

The conversion process can seem complex at first glance, but as long as you break expressions down into parts by taking the operator precedence order into account, you should be able to work things out.

## COMPLEX VARIABLE TYPES

In addition to all the simple variable types, C# also offers three slightly more complex (but very useful) sorts of variables: enumerations (often referred to as enums), structs (occasionally referred to as structures), and arrays.

# Enumerations

Each of the types you've seen so far (with the exception of `string`) has a clearly defined set of allowed values. Admittedly, this set is so large in types such as `double` that it can practically be considered a continuum, but it is a fixed set nevertheless. The simplest example of this is the `bool` type, which can take only one of two values: `true` or `false`.

There are many other circumstances in which you might want to have a variable that can take one of a fixed set of results. For example, you might want to have an `orientation` type that can store one of the values `north`, `south`, `east`, or `west`.

In situations like this, *enumerations* can be very useful. Enumerations do exactly what you want in this `orientation` type: They allow the definition of a type that can take one of a finite set of values that you supply. What you need to do, then, is create your own enumeration type called `orientation` that can take one of the four possible values.

Note that there is an additional step involved here—you don't just declare a variable of a given type; you declare and detail a user-defined type and then declare a variable of this new type.

## Defining Enumerations

You can use the `enum` keyword to define enumerations as follows:

```
enum <typeName>
{
   <value1>,
   <value2>,
   <value3>,
   ...
   <valueN>
}
```

Next, you can declare variables of this new type as follows:

```
<typeName> <varName>;
```

You can assign values using the following:

```
<varName> = <typeName>.<value>;
```

Enumerations have an *underlying type* used for storage. Each of the values that an enumeration type can take is stored as a value of this underlying type, which by default is `int`. You can specify a different underlying type by adding the type to the enumeration declaration:

```
enum <typeName> : <underlyingType>
{
   <value1>,
   <value2>,
   <value3>,
   ...
   <valueN>
}
```

Enumerations can have underlying types of `byte`, `sbyte`, `short`, `ushort`, `int`, `uint`, `long`, and `ulong`.

By default, each value is assigned a corresponding underlying type value automatically according to the order in which it is defined, starting from zero. This means that `<value1>` gets the value 0, `<value2>` gets 1, `<value3>` gets 2, and so on. You can override this assignment by using the = operator and specifying actual values for each enumeration value:

```
enum <typeName> : <underlyingType>
{
   <value1> = <actualVal1>,
   <value2> = <actualVal2>,
   <value3> = <actualVal3>,
```

```
    ...
    <valueN> = <actualValN>
}
```

In addition, you can specify identical values for multiple enumeration values by using one value as the underlying value of another:

```
enum <typeName> : <underlyingType>
{
    <value1> = <actualVal1>,
    <value2> = <value1>,
    <value3>,
    ...
    <valueN> = <actualValN>
}
```

Any values left unassigned are given an underlying value automatically, whereby the values used are in a sequence starting from 1 greater than the last explicitly declared one. In the preceding code, for example, `<value3>` will get the value `<value1>` + 1.

Note that this can cause problems, with values specified after a definition such as `<value2>` = `<value1>` being identical to other values. For example, in the following code `<value4>` will have the same value as `<value2>`:

```
enum <typeName> : <underlyingType>
{
    <value1> = <actualVal1>,
    <value2>,
    <value3> = <value1>,
    <value4>,
    ...
    <valueN> = <actualValN>
}
```

Of course, if this is the behavior you want, then this code is fine. Note also that assigning values in a circular fashion will cause an error:

```
enum <typeName> : <underlyingType>
{
    <value1> = <value2>,
    <value2> = <value1>
}
```

The following Try It Out shows an example of all of this. The code defines and then uses an enumeration called `orientation`.

**TRY IT OUT**   Using an Enumeration: Ch05Ex02\Program.cs

**1.** Create a new console application called Ch05Ex02 and save it in the directory C:\BegVCSharp\Chapter05.

**2.** Add the following code to Program.cs:

```
namespace Ch05Ex02
{
    enum orientation : byte
    {
        north = 1,
        south = 2,
        east  = 3,
        west  = 4
    }

    class Program
    {
        static void Main(string[] args)
        {
```

```
            orientation myDirection = orientation.north;
            Console.WriteLine("myDirection = {0}", myDirection);
            Console.ReadKey();
        }
    }
}
```

**3.** Execute the application. You should see the output shown in Figure 5-6.

**FIGURE 5-6**

**4.** Quit the application and modify the code as follows:

```
byte directionByte;
string directionString;
orientation myDirection = orientation.north;
Console.WriteLine("myDirection = {0}", myDirection);
directionByte = (byte)myDirection;
directionString = Convert.ToString(myDirection);
Console.WriteLine("byte equivalent = {0}", directionByte);
Console.WriteLine("string equivalent = {0}", directionString);
Console.ReadKey();
```

**5.** Execute the application again. The output is shown in Figure 5-7.

**FIGURE 5-7**

### How It Works

This code defines and uses an enumeration type called `orientation`. The first thing to notice is that the type definition code is placed in your namespace, `Ch05Ex02`, but not in the same place as the rest of your code. That is because definitions are not executed; that is, at runtime you don't step through the code in a definition as you do the lines of code in your application. Application execution starts in the place you're used to and has access to your new type because it belongs to the same namespace.

The first iteration of the example demonstrates the basic method of creating a variable of your new type, assigning it a value, and outputting it to the screen. Next, you modify the code to show the conversion of enumeration values into other types. Note that you must use explicit conversions here. Even though the underlying type of `orientation` is byte, you still have to use the `(byte)` cast to convert the value of `myDirection` into a byte type:

```
directionByte = (byte)myDirection;
```

The same explicit casting is necessary in the other direction, too, if you want to convert a byte into an `orientation`. For example, you could use the following code to convert a byte variable called `myByte` into an `orientation` and assign this value to `myDirection`:

```
myDirection = (orientation)myByte;
```

Of course, you must be careful here because not all permissible values of byte type variables map to defined `orientation` values. The `orientation` type can store other byte values, so you won't get an error straight away, but this may break logic later in the application.

To get the string value of an enumeration value you can use `Convert.ToString()`:

```
directionString = Convert.ToString(myDirection);
```

Using a `(string)` cast won't work because the processing required is more complicated than just placing the data stored in the enumeration variable into a `string` variable. Alternatively, you can use the `ToString()` command of the variable itself. The following code gives you the same result as using `Convert.ToString()`:

```
directionString = myDirection.ToString();
```

Converting a `string` to an enumeration value is also possible, except that here the syntax required is slightly more complex. A special command exists for this sort of conversion, `Enum.Parse()`, which is used in the following way:

```
(enumerationType)Enum.Parse(typeof(enumerationType), enumerationValueString);
```

This uses another operator, `typeof`, which obtains the type of its operand. You could use this for your `orientation` type as follows:

```
string myString = "north";
orientation myDirection = (orientation)Enum.Parse(typeof(orientation),
                                                  myString);
```

Of course, not all string values will map to an `orientation` value! If you pass in a value that doesn't map to one of your enumeration values, you will get an error. Like everything else in C#, these values are case sensitive, so you still get an error if your string agrees with a value in everything but case (for example, if `myString` is set to `North` rather than `north`).

## Structs

The *struct* (short for structure) is just that. That is, structs are data structures are composed of several pieces of data, possibly of different types. They enable you to define your own types of variables based on this structure. For example, suppose that you want to store the route to a location from a starting point, where the route consists of a direction and a distance in miles. For simplicity, you can assume that the direction is one of the compass points (such that it can be represented using the `orientation` enumeration from the last section), and that distance in miles can be represented as a `double` type.

You could use two separate variables for this using code you've seen already:

```
orientation myDirection;
double      myDistance;
```

There is nothing wrong with using two variables like this, but it is far simpler (especially where multiple routes are required) to store this information in one place.

### Defining Structs

Structs are defined using the `struct` keyword as follows:

```
struct <typeName>
{
   <memberDeclarations>
}
```

The `<memberDeclarations>` section contains declarations of variables (called the *data members* of the struct) in almost the same format as usual. Each member declaration takes the following form:

```
<accessibility> <type> <name>;
```

To allow the code that calls the struct to access the struct's data members, you use the keyword `public` for `<accessibility>`. For example:

```
struct route
{
    public orientation direction;
    public double      distance;
}
```

Once you have a struct type defined, you use it by defining variables of the new type:

```
route myRoute;
```

In addition, you have access to the data members of this composite variable via the period character:

```
myRoute.direction = orientation.north;
myRoute.distance  = 2.5;
```

This is demonstrated in the following Try It Out, where the `orientation` enumeration from the last Try It Out is used with the `route` struct shown earlier. This struct is then manipulated in code to give you a feel for how structs work.

**TRY IT OUT** Using a Struct: Ch05Ex03\Program.cs

**1.** Create a new console application called Ch05Ex03 and save it in the directory `C:\BegVCSharp\Chapter05`.

**2.** Add the following code to `Program.cs`:

```
namespace Ch05Ex03
{
    enum orientation: byte
    {
        north = 1,
        south = 2,
        east  = 3,
        west  = 4
    }

    struct route
    {
        public orientation direction;
        public double      distance;
    }

    class Program
    {
        static void Main(string[] args)
        {
            route myRoute;
            int myDirection = -1;
            double myDistance;
            Console.WriteLine("1) North\n2) South\n3) East\n4) West");
            do
            {
                Console.WriteLine("Select a direction:");
                myDirection = Convert.ToInt32(Console.ReadLine());
            }
            while ((myDirection < 1) || (myDirection > 4));
            Console.WriteLine("Input a distance:");
            myDistance = Convert.ToDouble(Console.ReadLine());
            myRoute.direction = (orientation)myDirection;
            myRoute.distance = myDistance;
            Console.WriteLine("myRoute specifies a direction of {0} and a " +
                "distance of {1}", myRoute.direction, myRoute.distance);
            Console.ReadKey();
        }
    }
}
```

**3.** Execute the code, select a direction by entering a number between 1 and 4, and then enter a distance. The result is shown in Figure 5-8.

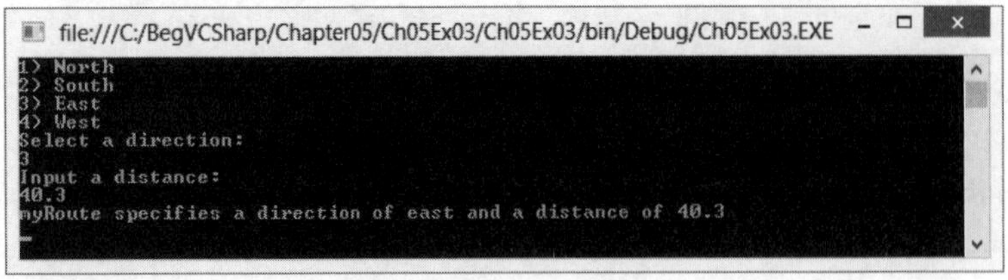

**FIGURE 5-8**

*How It Works*

Structs, like enumerations, are declared outside of the main body of the code. You declare your `route` struct just inside the namespace declaration, along with the `orientation` enumeration that it uses:

```
enum orientation: byte
{
    north = 1,
    south = 2,
    east  = 3,
    west  = 4
}

struct route
{
    public orientation direction;
    public double      distance;
}
```

The main body of the code follows a structure similar to some of the example code you've already seen, requesting input from the user and displaying it. You perform some simple validation of user input by placing the direction selection in a `do` loop, rejecting any input that isn't an integer between 1 and 4 (with values chosen such that they map onto the enumeration members for easy assignment).

> **NOTE** *Input that cannot be interpreted as an integer will result in an error. You'll see why this happens, and what to do about it, later in the book.*

The interesting point to note is that when you refer to members of `route` they are treated exactly the same way that variables of the same type as the member are. The assignment is as follows:

```
myRoute.direction = (orientation)myDirection;
myRoute.distance = myDistance;
```

You could simply take the input value directly into `myRoute.distance` with no ill effects as follows:

```
myRoute.distance = Convert.ToDouble(Console.ReadLine());
```

The extra step allows for more validation, although none is performed in this code. Any access to members of a structure is treated in the same way. Expressions of the form `<structVar>.<memberVar>` can be said to evaluate to a variable of the type of `<memberVar>`.

## Arrays

All the types you've seen so far have one thing in common: Each of them stores a single value (or a single set of values in the case of structs). Sometimes, in situations where you want to store a lot of data, this isn't very convenient. You may want to store several values of the same type at the same time, without having to use a different variable for each value.

For example, suppose you want to perform some processing that involves the names of all your friends. You could use simple string variables as follows:

```
string friendName1 = "Robert Barwell";
string friendName2 = "Mike Parry";
string friendName3 = "Jeremy Beacock";
```

But this looks like it will require a lot of effort, especially because you need to write different code to process each variable. You couldn't, for example, iterate through this list of strings in a loop.

The alternative is to use an *array*. Arrays are indexed lists of variables stored in a single array type variable. For example, you might have an array called `friendNames` that stores the three names shown in the preceding string variables. You can access individual members of the array by specifying their index in square brackets, as shown here:

```
friendNames[<index>]
```

The index is simply an integer, starting with 0 for the first entry, using 1 for the second, and so on. This means that you can go through the entries using a loop:

```
int i;
for (i = 0; i < 3; i++)
{
    Console.WriteLine("Name with index of {0}: {1}", i, friendNames[i]);
}
```

Arrays have a single *base type*—that is, individual entries in an array are all of the same type. This `friendNames` array has a base type of `string` because it is intended for storing `string` variables. Array entries are often referred to as *elements*.

## Declaring Arrays

Arrays are declared in the following way:

```
<baseType>[] <name>;
```

Here, `<baseType>` may be any variable type, including the enumeration and struct types you've seen in this chapter. Arrays must be initialized before you have access to them. You can't just access or assign values to the array elements like this:

```
int[] myIntArray;
myIntArray[10] = 5;
```

Arrays can be initialized in two ways. You can either specify the complete contents of the array in a literal form or specify the size of the array and use the `new` keyword to initialize all array elements.

Specifying an array using literal values simply involves providing a comma-separated list of element values enclosed in curly braces:

```
int[] myIntArray = { 5, 9, 10, 2, 99 };
```

Here, `myIntArray` has five elements, each with an assigned integer value.

The other method requires the following syntax:

```
int[] myIntArray = new int[5];
```

Here, you use the `new` keyword to explicitly initialize the array, and a constant value to define the size. This method results in all the array members being assigned a default value, which is 0 for numeric types. You can also use nonconstant variables for this initialization:

```
int[] myIntArray = new int[arraySize];
```

In addition, you can combine these two methods of initialization if you want:

```
int[] myIntArray = new int[5] { 5, 9, 10, 2, 99 };
```

With this method the sizes *must* match. You can't, for example, write the following:

```
int[] myIntArray = new int[10] { 5, 9, 10, 2, 99 };
```

Here, the array is defined as having 10 members, but only five are defined, so compilation will fail. A side effect of this is that if you define the size using a variable, then that variable must be a constant:

```
const int arraySize = 5;
int[] myIntArray = new int[arraySize] { 5, 9, 10, 2, 99 };
```

If you omit the `const` keyword, this code will fail.

As with other variable types, there is no need to initialize an array on the same line that you declare it. The following is perfectly legal:

```
int[] myIntArray;
myIntArray = new int[5];
```

In the following Try It Out you create and use an array of strings, using the example from the introduction to this section.

**TRY IT OUT**   Using an Array: Ch05Ex04\Program.cs

**1.** Create a new console application called Ch05Ex04 and save it in the directory `C:\BegVCSharp\Chapter05`.

**2.** Add the following code to `Program.cs`:

```
static void Main(string[] args)
{
    string[] friendNames = { "Robert Barwell", "Mike Parry",
                             "Jeremy Beacock" };
    int i;
    Console.WriteLine("Here are {0} of my friends:",
                     friendNames.Length);
    for (i = 0; i < friendNames.Length; i++)
    {
        Console.WriteLine(friendNames[i]);
    }
    Console.ReadKey();
}
```

**3.** Execute the code. The result is shown in Figure 5-9.

**FIGURE 5-9**

*How It Works*

This code sets up a `string` array with three values and lists them in the console in a `for` loop. Note that you have access to the number of elements in the array using `friendNames.Length`:

```
Console.WriteLine("Here are {0} of my friends:", friendNames.Length);
```

This is a handy way to get the size of an array. Outputting values in a `for` loop is easy to get wrong. For example, try changing < to <= as follows:

```
for (i = 0; i <= friendNames.Length; i++)
{
    Console.WriteLine(friendNames[i]);
}
```

Compiling and executing the preceding code results in the dialog box shown in Figure 5-10.

Here, the code attempted to access `friendNames[3]`. Remember that array indices start from 0, so the last element is `friendNames[2]`. If you attempt to access elements outside of the array size, the code will fail. It just so happens that there is a more resilient method of accessing all the members of an array: using `foreach` loops.

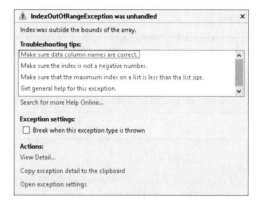

**FIGURE 5-10**

## foreach Loops

A `foreach` loop enables you to address each element in an array using this simple syntax:

```
foreach (<baseType> <name> in <array>)
{
    // can use <name> for each element
}
```

This loop will cycle through each element, placing it in the variable `<name>` in turn, without danger of accessing illegal elements. You don't have to worry about how many elements are in the array, and you can be sure that you'll get to use each one in the loop. Using this approach, you can modify the code in the last example as follows:

```
static void Main(string[] args)
{
    string[] friendNames = { "Robert Barwell", "Mike Parry",
                             "Jeremy Beacock" };
    Console.WriteLine("Here are {0} of my friends:",
                      friendNames.Length);
    foreach (string friendName in friendNames)
    {
        Console.WriteLine(friendName);
    }
    Console.ReadKey();
}
```

The output of this code will be exactly the same as that of the previous Try It Out. The main difference between using this method and a standard `for` loop is that `foreach` gives you *read-only* access to the array contents, so you can't change the values of any of the elements. You couldn't, for example, do the following:

```
foreach (string friendName in friendNames)
{
    friendName = "Rupert the bear";
}
```

If you try this, compilation will fail. If you use a simple `for` loop, however, you can assign values to array elements.

## Multidimensional Arrays

A multidimensional array is simply one that uses multiple indices to access its elements. For example, suppose you want to plot the height of a hill against the position measured. You might specify a position using two coordinates, x and y. You want to use these two coordinates as indices, such that an array called `hillHeight` would store the height at each pair of coordinates. This involves using multidimensional arrays.

A two-dimensional array such as this is declared as follows:

```
<baseType>[,] <name>;
```

Arrays of more dimensions simply require more commas:

```
<baseType>[,,,] <name>;
```

This would declare a four-dimensional array. Assigning values also uses a similar syntax, with commas separating sizes. Declaring and initializing the two-dimensional array `hillHeight`, with a base type of `double`, an x size of 3, and a y size of 4 requires the following:

```
double[,] hillHeight = new double[3,4];
```

Alternatively, you can use literal values for initial assignment. Here, you use nested blocks of curly braces, separated by commas:

```
double[,] hillHeight = { { 1, 2, 3, 4 }, { 2, 3, 4, 5 }, { 3, 4, 5, 6 } };
```

This array has the same dimensions as the previous one—that is, three rows and four columns. By providing literal values, these dimensions are defined implicitly.

To access individual elements of a multidimensional array, you simply specify the indices separated by commas:

```
hillHeight[2,1]
```

You can then manipulate this element just as you can other elements. This expression will access the second element of the third nested array as defined previously (the value will be 4). Remember that you start counting from 0 and that the first number is the nested array. In other words, the first number specifies the pair of curly braces, and the second number specifies the element within that pair of braces. You can represent this array visually, as shown in Figure 5-11.

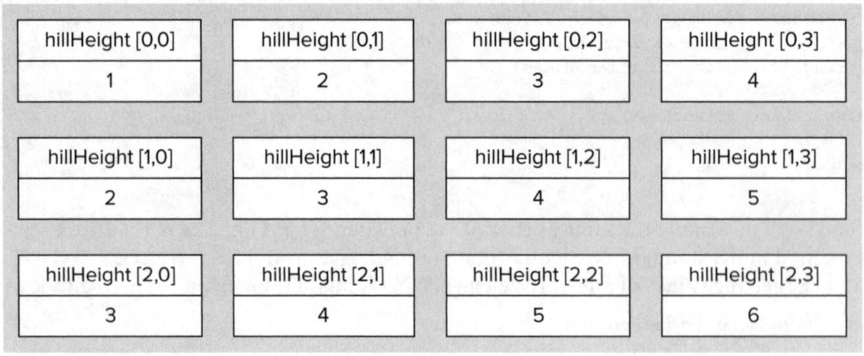

| hillHeight [0,0] | hillHeight [0,1] | hillHeight [0,2] | hillHeight [0,3] |
| :---: | :---: | :---: | :---: |
| 1 | 2 | 3 | 4 |

| hillHeight [1,0] | hillHeight [1,1] | hillHeight [1,2] | hillHeight [1,3] |
| :---: | :---: | :---: | :---: |
| 2 | 3 | 4 | 5 |

| hillHeight [2,0] | hillHeight [2,1] | hillHeight [2,2] | hillHeight [2,3] |
| :---: | :---: | :---: | :---: |
| 3 | 4 | 5 | 6 |

**FIGURE 5-11**

The `foreach` loop gives you access to all elements in a multidimensional way, just as with single-dimensional arrays:

```
double[,] hillHeight = { { 1, 2, 3, 4 }, { 2, 3, 4, 5 }, { 3, 4, 5, 6 } };
foreach (double height in hillHeight)
{
    Console.WriteLine("{0}", height);
}
```

The order in which the elements are output is the same as the order used to assign literal values. This sequence is as follows (the element identifiers are shown here rather than the actual values):

```
hillHeight[0,0]
hillHeight[0,1]
hillHeight[0,2]
hillHeight[0,3]
hillHeight[1,0]
hillHeight[1,1]
hillHeight[1,2]
...
```

## Arrays of Arrays

Multidimensional arrays, as discussed in the last section, are said to be *rectangular* because each "row" is the same size. Using the last example, you can have a y coordinate of 0 to 3 for any of the possible x coordinates.

It is also possible to have *jagged* arrays, whereby "rows" may be different sizes. For this, you need an array in which each element is another array. You could also have arrays of arrays of arrays, or even more complex situations. However, all this is possible only if the arrays have the same base type.

The syntax for declaring arrays of arrays involves specifying multiple sets of square brackets in the declaration of the array, as shown here:

```
int[][] jaggedIntArray;
```

Unfortunately, initializing arrays such as this isn't as simple as initializing multidimensional arrays. You can't, for example, follow the preceding declaration with this:

```
jaggedIntArray = new int[3][4];
```

Even if you could do this, it wouldn't be that useful because you can achieve the same effect with simple multidimensional arrays with less effort. Nor can you use code such as this:

```
jaggedIntArray = { { 1, 2, 3 }, { 1 }, { 1, 2 } };
```

You have two options. You can initialize the array that contains other arrays (let's call these sub-arrays for clarity) and then initialize the sub-arrays in turn:

```
jaggedIntArray = new int[2][];
jaggedIntArray[0] = new int[3];
jaggedIntArray[1] = new int[4];
```

Alternatively, you can use a modified form of the preceding literal assignment:

```
jaggedIntArray = new int[3][] { new int[] { 1, 2, 3 }, new int[] { 1 },
                                new int[] { 1, 2 } };
```

This can be simplified if the array is initialized on the same line as it is declared, as follows:

```
int[][] jaggedIntArray = { new int[] { 1, 2, 3 }, new int[] { 1 },
                           new int[] { 1, 2 } };
```

You can use foreach loops with jagged arrays, but you often need to nest these to get to the actual data. For example, suppose you have the following jagged array that contains 10 arrays, each of which contains an array of integers that are divisors of an integer between 1 and 10:

```
int[][] divisors1To10 = { new int[] { 1 },
                          new int[] { 1, 2 },
                          new int[] { 1, 3 },
                          new int[] { 1, 2, 4 },
                          new int[] { 1, 5 },
                          new int[] { 1, 2, 3, 6 },
                          new int[] { 1, 7 },
                          new int[] { 1, 2, 4, 8 },
                          new int[] { 1, 3, 9 },
                          new int[] { 1, 2, 5, 10 } };
```

The following code will fail:

```
foreach (int divisor in divisors1To10)
{
    Console.WriteLine(divisor);
}
```

The failure occurs because the array `divisors1To10` contains `int []` elements, not `int` elements. Instead, you have to loop through every sub-array, as well as through the array itself:

```
foreach (int[] divisorsOfInt in divisors1To10)
{
    foreach(int divisor in divisorsOfInt)
    {
        Console.WriteLine(divisor);
    }
}
```

As you can see, the syntax for using jagged arrays can quickly become complex! In most cases, it is easier to use rectangular arrays or a simpler storage method. Nonetheless, there may well be situations in which you are forced to use this method, and a working knowledge can't hurt.

## STRING MANIPULATION

Your use of strings so far has consisted of writing strings to the console, reading strings from the console, and concatenating strings using the + operator. In the course of programming more interesting applications, you will discover that manipulating strings is something that you end up doing *a lot*. Therefore, it is worth spending a few pages looking at some of the more common string-manipulation techniques available in C#.

To start with, a `string` type variable can be treated as a read-only array of `char` variables. This means that you can access individual characters using syntax like the following:

```
string myString = "A string";
char myChar = myString[1];
```

However, you can't assign individual characters this way. To get a `char` array that you can write to, you can use the following code. This uses the `ToCharArray()` command of the array variable:

```
string myString = "A string";
char[] myChars = myString.ToCharArray();
```

Then you can manipulate the `char` array the standard way. You can also use strings in `foreach` loops, as shown here:

```
foreach (char character in myString)
{
    Console.WriteLine("{0}", character);
}
```

As with arrays, you can also get the number of elements using `myString.Length`. This gives you the number of characters in the string:

```
string myString = Console.ReadLine();
Console.WriteLine("You typed {0} characters.", myString.Length);
```

Other basic string manipulation techniques use commands with a format similar to this `<string>.ToCharArray()` command. Two simple, but useful, ones are `<string>.ToLower()` and `<string>.ToUpper()`. These enable strings to be converted into lowercase and uppercase, respectively. To see why this is useful, consider the situation in which you want to check for a specific response from a user—for example, the string `yes`. If you convert the string entered by the user into lowercase, then you can also check for the strings `YES`, `Yes`, `yeS`, and so on—you saw an example of this in the previous chapter:

```
string userResponse = Console.ReadLine();
if (userResponse.ToLower() == "yes")
{
    // Act on response.
}
```

This command, like the others in this section, doesn't actually change the string to which it is applied. Instead, combining this command with a string results in the creation of a new string, which you can compare to another string (as shown here) or assign to another variable. The other variable may be the same one that is being operated on:

```
userResponse = userResponse.ToLower();
```

This is an important point to remember, because just writing

```
userResponse.ToLower();
```

 doesn't actually achieve very much!

There are other things you can do to ease the interpretation of user input. What if the user accidentally put an extra space at the beginning or end of the input? In this case, the preceding code won't work. You need to trim the string entered, which you can do using the `<string>`.Trim() command:

```
string userResponse = Console.ReadLine();
userResponse = userResponse.Trim();
if (userResponse.ToLower() == "yes")
{
    // Act on response.
}
```

The preceding code is also able detect strings like this:

```
" YES"
"Yes "
```

You can also use these commands to remove any other characters, by specifying them in a char array, for example:

```
char[] trimChars = {' ', 'e', 's'};
string userResponse = Console.ReadLine();
userResponse = userResponse.ToLower();
userResponse = userResponse.Trim(trimChars);
if (userResponse == "y")
{
    // Act on response.
}
```

This eliminates any occurrences of spaces, as well as the letters "e" and "s" from the beginning or end of your string. Providing there aren't any other characters in the string, this will result in the detection of strings such as

```
"Yeeeees"
" y"
```

and so on.

You can also use the `<string>`.TrimStart() and `<string>`.TrimEnd() commands, which will trim spaces from the beginning and end of a string, respectively. These can also have char arrays specified.

You can use two other string commands to manipulate the spacing of strings: `<string>`.PadLeft() and `<string>`.PadRight(). They enable you to add spaces to the left or right of a string to force it to the desired length. You use them as follows:

```
<string>.PadX(<desiredLength>);
```

Here is an example:

```
myString = "Aligned";
myString = myString.PadLeft(10);
```

This would result in three spaces being added to the left of the word `Aligned` in `myString`. These methods can be helpful when aligning strings in columns, which is particularly useful for positioning strings containing numbers.

As with the trimming commands, you can also use these commands in a second way, by supplying the character to pad the string with. This involves a single `char`, not an array of `chars` as with trimming:

```
myString = "Aligned";
myString = myString.PadLeft(10, '-');
```

This would add three dashes to the start of `myString`.

There are many more of these string-manipulation commands, many of which are only useful in very specific situations. These are discussed as you use them in the forthcoming chapters. Before moving on, though, it is worth looking at one of the features contained in Visual Studio 2012 that you may have noticed over the course of the last few chapters, and especially this one. In the following Try It Out, you examine auto-completion, whereby the IDE tries to help you out by suggesting what code you might like to insert.

**TRY IT OUT** Statement Auto-Completion in VS: Ch05Ex05\Program.cs

1. Create a new console application called Ch05Ex05 and save it in the directory `C:\BegVCSharp\Chapter05`.

2. Type the following code into `Program.cs`, exactly as written, noting windows that pop up as you do so:

```
static void Main(string[] args)
{
    string myString = "This is a test.";
    char[] separator = {' '};
    string[] myWords;
    myWords = myString.
}
```

3. As you type the final period, the window shown in Figure 5-12 appears.

4. Without moving the cursor, type `sp`. The pop-up window changes, and the Tooltip shown in Figure 5-13 appears.

**FIGURE 5-12**

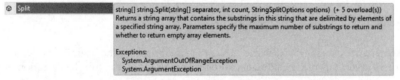

**FIGURE 5-13**

5. Type the following characters: (`se`. Another pop-up window and Tooltip appears, as shown in Figure 5-14.

6. Then, type these two characters: `);`. The code should look as follows, and the pop-up windows should disappear:

```
static void Main(string[] args)
{
    string myString = "This is a test.";
    char[] separator = {' '};
    string[] myWords;
    myWords = myString.Split(separator);
}
```

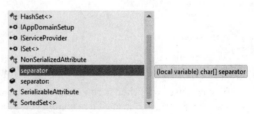

**FIGURE 5-14**

**7.** Add the following code, noting the windows as they pop up:

```
static void Main(string[] args)
{
    string myString = "This is a test.";
    char[] separator = {' '};
    string[] myWords;
    myWords = myString.Split(separator);
    foreach (string word in myWords)
    {
        Console.WriteLine("{0}", word);
    }
    Console.ReadKey();
}
```

**8.** Execute the code. The result is shown in Figure 5-15.

**FIGURE 5-15**

*How It Works*

Two main aspects of this code are the new string command used and the use of the auto-completion functionality. The command, *<string>*.Split(), converts a string into a string array by splitting it at the points specified. These points take the form of a char array, which in this case is simply populated by a single element, the space character:

```
char[] separator = {' '};
```

The following code obtains the substrings you get when the string is split at each space—that is, you get an array of individual words:

```
string[] myWords;
myWords = myString.Split(separator);
```

Next, you loop through the words in this array using foreach and write each one to the console:

```
foreach (string word in myWords)
{
    Console.WriteLine("{0}", word);
}
```

> **NOTE** *Each word obtained has no spaces, either embedded in the word or at either end. The separators are removed when you use* Split().

Next, it's time to move on to auto-completion. VS is a very intelligent package that works out a lot of information about your code as you type it. Even as you type the first character on a new line, the IDE tries to help you by suggesting a keyword, a variable name, a type name, and so on. Only three letters into the preceding code (str), the IDE correctly guessed that you want to type string. Even more useful is when you type variable names. In long pieces of code, you often forget the names of variables you want to use. Because the IDE pops up a list of these as you type, you can find them easily, without having to refer to earlier code.

By the time you type the period after myString, it knows that myString is a string, detects that you want to specify a string command, and presents the available options. At this point, you can stop typing if desired, and select the command you want using the up and down arrow keys. As you move through the available options, the IDE describes the currently selected command and indicates what syntax it uses.

As you start typing more characters, the IDE moves the selected command to the top of the commands you might mean automatically. Once it shows the command you want, you can simply carry on typing as if you'd typed the whole name, so typing (takes you straight to the point where you specify the additional information that some commands require—and the IDE even tells you the format this extra information must be in, presenting options for those commands that accept varying amounts of information.

This feature of the IDE, known as IntelliSense, comes in very handy, enabling you to find information about strange types with ease. You might find it interesting to look at all the commands that the `string` type exposes and experiment—nothing you do is going to break the computer, so play away!

> **NOTE** *Sometimes the displayed information can obscure some of the code you have already typed, which can be annoying. This is because the hidden code may be something that you need to refer to when typing. However, you can press the Ctrl key to make the command list transparent, enabling you to see what was hidden.*

## SUMMARY

In this chapter, you've spent some time expanding your knowledge of variables. Perhaps the most important topic covered in this chapter is type conversion, which will appear again throughout this book. Getting a sound grasp of the concepts involved now will make things a lot easier later.

You've also seen a few more variable types that you can use to help you store data in a more developer-friendly way. You've learned how enumerations can make your code much more readable with easily discernible values; how structs can be used to combine multiple, related data elements in one place; and how you can group similar data together in arrays. You see all of these types used many times throughout the rest of this book.

Finally, you looked at string manipulation, including some of the basic techniques and principles involved. Many individual string commands are available, and although you only examined a few, you now know how to view the available commands in your IDE. Using this technique, you can have some fun trying things out. At least one of the following exercises can be solved using one or more string commands you haven't seen yet, but you'll have to figure out which!

This chapter extended your knowledge of variables to cover the following:

➤ Type conversions

➤ Enumerations

➤ Structs

➤ Arrays

➤ String manipulation

In the next chapter, you'll learn a bit more about what the "string commands" you've used in this chapter actually are. You will also see other ways to organize your code and manipulate data as you investigate *functions*.

### EXERCISES

**5.1** Which of the following conversions can't be performed implicitly?

**a.** `int to short`

**b.** `short to int`

**c.** `bool to string`

**d.** `byte to float`

**5.2** Show the code for a `color` enumeration based on the `short` type containing the colors of the rainbow plus black and white. Can this enumeration be based on the `byte` type?

**5.3** Modify the Mandelbrot set generator example from the last chapter to use the following struct for complex numbers:

```
struct imagNum
{
    public double real, imag;
}
```

**5.4** Will the following code compile? Why or why not?

```
string[] blab = new string[5]
blab[5] = 5th string.
```

**5.5** Write a console application that accepts a string from the user and outputs a string with the characters in reverse order.

**5.6** Write a console application that accepts a string and replaces all occurrences of the string `no` with `yes`.

**5.7** Write a console application that places double quotes around each word in a string.

Answers to the exercises can be found in Appendix A.

▶ **WHAT YOU LEARNED IN THIS CHAPTER**

| TOPIC | KEY CONCEPT |
| --- | --- |
| **Type conversion** | You can convert values from one type into another, but there are rules that apply when you do so. Implicit conversion happens automatically, but only when all possible values of the source value type are available in the target value type. Explicit conversion is also possible, but you run the risk of values not being assigned as expected, or even causing errors. |
| **Enumerations** | Enums, or enumerations, are types that have a discrete set of values, each of which has a name. Enums are defined with the `enum` keyword. This makes them easy to understand in code because they are very readable. Enums have an underlying numeric type (`int` by default), and you can use this property of enum values to convert between enum values and numeric values, or to identify enum values. |
| **Structs** | Structs, or structures, are types that contain several different values at the same time. Structs are defined with the `struct` keyword. The values contained in a struct each have a name and a type; there is no requirement that every value stored in a struct is the same type. |
| **Arrays** | An array is a collection of values of the same type. Arrays have a fixed size, or length, which determines how many values they can contain. You can define multidimensional or jagged arrays to hold different amounts and shapes of data. You can also iterate through the values in an array with a `foreach` loop. |

# Functions

**WROX.COM CODE DOWNLOADS FOR THIS CHAPTER**

You can find the wrox.com code downloads for this chapter at www.wrox.com/remtitle .cgi?isbn=9781118314418 on the Download Code tab. The code is in the Chapter 6 download and individually named according to the names throughout the chapter.

All the code you have seen so far has taken the form of a single block, perhaps with some looping to repeat lines of code, and branching to execute statements conditionally. Performing an operation on your data has meant placing the code required right where you want it to work.

This kind of code structure is limited. Often, some tasks—such as finding the highest value in an array, for example—might need to be performed at several points in a program. You can place identical (or nearly identical) sections of code in your application whenever necessary, but this has its own problems. Changing even one minor detail concerning a common task (to correct a code error, for example) can require changes to multiple sections of code, which can be spread throughout the application. Missing one of these can have dramatic consequences and cause the whole application to fail. In addition, the application can get very lengthy.

The solution to this problem is to use *functions*. Functions in C# are a means of providing blocks of code that can be executed at any point in an application.

> **NOTE** *Functions of the specific type examined in this chapter are known as methods, but this term has a very specific meaning in .NET programming that will only become clear later in this book. Therefore, for now, the term method will not be used.*

For example, you could have a function that calculates the maximum value in an array. You can use the function from any point in your code, and use the same lines of code in each case. Because you need to supply this code only once, any changes you make to it will affect this calculation wherever it is used. The function can be thought of as containing *reusable* code.

Functions also have the advantage of making your code more readable, as you can use them to group related code together. This way, your application body can be very short, as the inner workings of the code are separated out. This is similar to the way in which you can collapse regions of code together in the IDE using the outline view, and it gives your application a more logical structure.

Functions can also be used to create multipurpose code, enabling them to perform the same operations on varying data. You can supply a function with information to work with in the form of arguments, and you can obtain results from functions in the form of return values. In the preceding example, you could supply an array to search as a argument and obtain the maximum value in the array as a return value. This means that you can use the same function to work with a different array each time. A function definition consists of a name, a return type, and a list of parameters that specify the number and type of arguments that the function requires. The name and parameters of a function (but not its return type) collectively define the *signature* of a function.

## DEFINING AND USING FUNCTIONS

This section describes how you can add functions to your applications and then use (call) them from your code. Starting with the basics, you look at simple functions that don't exchange any data with code that calls them, and then look at more advanced function usage. The following Try It Out gets things moving.

**TRY IT OUT** Defining and Using a Basic Function: Ch06Ex01\Program.cs

**1.** Create a new console application called Ch06Ex01 and save it in the directory C:\BegVCSharp\Chapter06.

**2.** Add the following code to Program.cs:

```
class Program
{
    static void Write()
    {
        Console.WriteLine("Text output from function.");
    }

    static void Main(string[] args)
    {
        Write();
        Console.ReadKey();
    }
}
```

**3.** Execute the code. The result is shown in Figure 6-1.

file:///C:/BegVCSharp/Chapter06/Ch06Ex01/Ch06Ex01/bin/Debug/Ch06Ex01.EXE
Text output from function.

**FIGURE 6-1**

*How It Works*

The following four lines of your code define a function called `Write()`:

```
static void Write()
{
    Console.WriteLine("Text output from function.");
}
```

The code contained here simply outputs some text to the console window, but this behavior isn't that important at the moment, because the focus here is on the mechanisms behind function definition and use.

The function definition consists of the following:

➤ Two keywords: `static` and `void`

➤ A function name followed by parentheses: `Write()`

➤ A block of code to execute, enclosed in curly braces

> **NOTE** *Function names are usually written in PascalCase.*

The code that defines the `Write()` function looks very similar to some of the other code in your application:

```
static void Main(string[] args)
{
    ...
}
```

That's because all the code you have written so far (apart from type definitions) has been part of a function. This function, `Main()`, is the entry point function for a console application. When a C# application is executed, the entry point function it contains is called; and when that function is completed, the application terminates. All C# executable code must have an entry point.

The only difference between the `Main()` function and your `Write()` function (apart from the lines of code they contain) is that there is some code inside the parentheses after the function name `Main`. This is how you specify parameters, which you see in more detail shortly.

As mentioned earlier, both `Main()` and `Write()` are defined using the `static` and `void` keywords. The `static` keyword relates to object-oriented concepts, which you come back to later in the book. For now, you only need to remember that all the functions you use in your applications in this section of the book must use this keyword.

In contrast, `void` is much simpler to explain. It's used to indicate that the function does not return a value. Later in this chapter, you'll see the code that you need to use when a function has a return value.

Moving on, the code that calls your function is as follows:

```
Write();
```

You simply type the name of the function followed by empty parentheses. When program execution reaches this point, the code in the `Write()` function runs.

> **NOTE** *The parentheses used both in the function definition and where the function is called are mandatory. Try removing them if you like—the code won't compile.*

## Return Values

The simplest way to exchange data with a function is to use a return value. Functions that have return values *evaluate* to that value exactly the same way that variables evaluate to the values they contain when you use them in expressions. Just like variables, return values have a type.

For example, you might have a function called GetString() whose return value is a string. You could use this in code, such as the following:

```
string myString;
myString = GetString();
```

Alternatively, you might have a function called GetVal() that returns a double value, which you could use in a mathematical expression:

```
double myVal;
double multiplier = 5.3;
myVal = GetVal() * multiplier;
```

When a function returns a value, you have to modify your function in two ways:

➤ Specify the type of the return value in the function declaration instead of using the void keyword.

➤ Use the return keyword to end the function execution and transfer the return value to the calling code.

In code terms, this looks like the following in a console application function of the type you've been looking at:

```
static <returnType> <FunctionName>()
{
    ...
    return <returnValue>;
}
```

The only limitation here is that <returnValue> must be a value that either is of type <returnType> or can be implicitly converted to that type. However, <returnType> can be any type you want, including the more complicated types you've seen. This might be as simple as the following:

```
static double GetVal()
{
    return 3.2;
}
```

However, return values are usually the result of some processing carried out by the function; the preceding could be achieved just as easily using a const variable.

When the return statement is reached, program execution returns to the calling code immediately. No lines of code after this statement are executed, although this doesn't mean that return statements can only be placed on the last line of a function body. You can use return earlier in the code, perhaps after performing some branching logic. Placing return in a for loop, an if block, or any other structure causes the structure to terminate immediately and the function to terminate:

```
static double GetVal()
{
    double checkVal;
    // checkVal assigned a value through some logic (not shown here).
    if (checkVal < 5)
        return 4.7;
    return 3.2;
}
```

Here, one of two values is returned, depending on the value of `checkVal`. The only restriction in this case is that a `return` statement must be processed before reaching the closing } of the function. The following is illegal:

```
static double GetVal()
{
   double checkVal;
   // checkVal assigned a value through some logic.
   if (checkVal < 5)
      return 4.7;
}
```

If `checkVal` is >= 5, then no `return` statement is met, which isn't allowed. All processing paths must reach a `return` statement. In most cases, the compiler detects this and gives you the error "not all code paths return a value."

As a final note, `return` can be used in functions that are declared using the `void` keyword (those that don't have a return value). In that case, the function simply terminates. When you use `return` this way, it is an error to provide a return value between the `return` keyword and the semicolon that follows.

## Parameters

When a function needs to accept parameters, you must specify the following:

➤  A list of the parameters accepted by the function in its definition, along with the types of those parameters

➤  A matching list of arguments in each function call

> **NOTE** *Note that careful reading of the C# specification shows a subtle distinction between* parameters *and* arguments. *Parameters are defined as part of a function definition, whereas arguments are passed to a function by calling code. However, these terms are often used interchangeably, and nobody seems to get too upset about that.*

This involves the following code, where you can have any number of parameters, each with a type and a name:

```
static <returnType> <FunctionName>(<paramType> <paramName>, ...)
{
   ...
   return <returnValue>;
}
```

The parameters are separated using commas, and each of these parameters is accessible from code within the function as a variable. For example, a simple function might take two `double` parameters and return their product:

```
static double Product(double param1, double param2)
{
   return param1 * param2;
}
```

The following Try It Out provides a more complex example.

1. Create a new console application called Ch06Ex02 and save it in the directory `C:\BegVCSharp\Chapter06`.

2. Add the following code to `Program.cs`:

```
class Program
{
    static int MaxValue(int[] intArray)
    {
        int maxVal = intArray[0];
        for (int i = 1; i < intArray.Length; i++)
        {
            if (intArray[i] > maxVal)
                maxVal = intArray[i];
        }
        return maxVal;
    }

    static void Main(string[] args)
    {
        int[] myArray = { 1, 8, 3, 6, 2, 5, 9, 3, 0, 2 };
        int maxVal = MaxValue(myArray);
        Console.WriteLine("The maximum value in myArray is {0}", maxVal);
        Console.ReadKey();
    }
}
```

3. Execute the code. The result is shown in Figure 6-2.

**FIGURE 6-2**

*How It Works*

This code contains a function that does what the example function at the beginning of this chapter hoped to do. It accepts an array of integers as a parameter and returns the highest number in the array. The function definition is as follows:

```
static int MaxValue(int[] intArray)
{
    int maxVal = intArray[0];
    for (int i = 1; i < intArray.Length; i++)
    {
        if (intArray[i] > maxVal)
            maxVal = intArray[i];
    }
    return maxVal;
}
```

The function, `MaxValue()`, has a single parameter defined, an `int` array called `intArray`. It also has a return type of `int`. The calculation of the maximum value is simple. A local integer variable called `maxVal` is initialized to the first value in the array, and then this value is compared with each of the subsequent elements in the array. If an element contains a higher value than `maxVal`, then this value replaces the current value of `maxVal`. When the loop finishes, `maxVal` contains the highest value in the array, and is returned using the `return` statement.

The code in `Main()` declares and initializes a simple integer array to use with the `MaxValue()` function:

```
int[] myArray = { 1, 8, 3, 6, 2, 5, 9, 3, 0, 2 };
```

The call to `MaxValue()` is used to assign a value to the `int` variable `maxVal`:

```
int maxVal = MaxValue(myArray);
```

Next, you write that value to the screen using `Console.WriteLine()`:

```
Console.WriteLine("The maximum value in myArray is {0}", maxVal);
```

## Parameter Matching

When you call a function, you must supply arguments that match the parameters as specified in the function definition exactly. This means matching the parameter types, the number of parameters, and the order of the parameters. For example, the function

```
static void MyFunction(string myString, double myDouble)
{
    ...
}
```

can't be called using the following:

```
MyFunction(2.6, "Hello");
```

Here, you are attempting to pass a `double` value as the first argument, and a `string` value as the second argument, which is not the order in which the parameters are defined in the function definition.

You also can't use

```
MyFunction("Hello");
```

because you are only passing a single `string` argument, where two arguments are required. Attempting to use either of the two preceding function calls will result in a compiler error, because the compiler forces you to match the signatures of the functions you use.

> **NOTE** Recall from the introduction that the signature of a function is defined by the name and parameters of the function.

Going back to the example, `MaxValue()` can be used only to obtain the maximum `int` in an array of `int` values. If you replace the code in `Main()` with

```
static void Main(string[] args)
{
    double[] myArray = { 1.3, 8.9, 3.3, 6.5, 2.7, 5.3 };
    double maxVal = MaxValue(myArray);
    Console.WriteLine("The maximum value in myArray is {0}", maxVal);
    Console.ReadKey();
}
```

the code won't compile because the parameter type is wrong. In the "Overloading Functions" section later in this chapter, you'll learn a useful technique for getting around this problem.

## Parameter Arrays

C# enables you to specify one (and only one) special parameter for a function. This parameter, which must be the last parameter in the function definition, is known as a *parameter array*. Parameter arrays enable you to call functions using a variable amount of parameters, and they are defined using the `params` keyword.

Parameter arrays can be a useful way to simplify your code because you don't have to pass arrays from your calling code. Instead, you pass several arguments of the same type, which are placed in an array you can use from within your function.

The following code is required to define a function that uses a parameter array:

```
static <returnType> <FunctionName>(<p1Type> <p1Name>, ...,
                                    params <type>[] <name>)
{
   ...
   return <returnValue>;
}
```

You can call this function using code like the following:

```
<FunctionName>(<p1>, ..., <val1>, <val2>, ...)
```

`<val1>`, `<val2>`, and so on are values of type `<type>`, which are used to initialize the `<name>` array. The number of arguments that you can specify here is almost limitless; the only restriction is that they must all be of type `<type>`. You can even specify no arguments at all.

This final point makes parameter arrays particularly useful for specifying additional information for functions to use in their processing. For example, suppose you have a function called `GetWord()` that takes a `string` value as its first parameter and returns the first word in the string:

```
string firstWord = GetWord("This is a sentence.");
```

Here, `firstWord` will be assigned the string `This`.

You might add a `params` parameter to `GetWord()`, enabling you to optionally select an alternative word to return by its index:

```
string firstWord = GetWord("This is a sentence.", 2);
```

Assuming that you start counting at 1 for the first word, this would result in `firstWord` being assigned the string `is`.

You might also add the capability to limit the number of characters returned in a third parameter, also accessible through the `params` parameter:

```
string firstWord = GetWord("This is a sentence.", 4, 3);
```

Here, `firstWord` would be assigned the string `sen`.

The following Try It Out defines and uses a function with a `params` type parameter.

**TRY IT OUT**   Exchanging Data with a Function (Part 2): Ch06Ex03\Program.cs

**1.** Create a new console application called Ch06Ex03 and save it in the directory `C:\BegVCSharp\Chapter06`.

**2.** Add the following code to `Program.cs`:

```
class Program
{
    static int SumVals(params int[] vals)
    {
        int sum = 0;
        foreach (int val in vals)
        {
            sum += val;
        }
        return sum;
    }

    static void Main(string[] args)
```

```
        {
            int sum = SumVals(1, 5, 2, 9, 8);
            Console.WriteLine("Summed Values = {0}", sum);
            Console.ReadKey();
        }
    }
```

**3.** Execute the code. The result is shown in Figure 6-3.

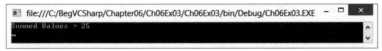

**FIGURE 6-3**

*How It Works*

The function SumVals() is defined using the params keyword to accept any number of int arguments (and no others):

```
static int SumVals(params int[] vals)
{
    . . .
}
```

The code in this function simply iterates through the values in the vals array and adds the values together, returning the result.

In Main(), you call SumVals() with five integer arguments:

```
int sum = SumVals(1, 5, 2, 9, 8);
```

You could just as easily call this function with none, one, two, or 100 integer arguments—there is no limit to the number you can specify.

> **NOTE** *C# version 4 introduced alternative ways to specify function parameters, including a far more readable way to include optional parameters. You will learn about these methods in Chapter 14, which looks at how the C# language has evolved since it was created.*

## Reference and Value Parameters

All the functions defined so far in this chapter have had value parameters. That is, when you have used parameters, you have passed a value into a variable used by the function. Any changes made to this variable in the function have no effect on the argument specified in the function call. For example, consider a function that doubles and displays the value of a passed parameter:

```
static void ShowDouble(int val)
{
    val *= 2;
    Console.WriteLine("val doubled = {0}", val);
}
```

Here, the parameter, val, is doubled in this function. If you call it like this,

```
int myNumber = 5;
Console.WriteLine("myNumber = {0}", myNumber);
ShowDouble(myNumber);
Console.WriteLine("myNumber = {0}", myNumber);
```

then the text output to the console is as follows:

```
myNumber = 5
val doubled = 10
myNumber = 5
```

Calling `ShowDouble()` with `myNumber` as an argument doesn't affect the value of `myNumber` in `Main()`, even though the parameter it is assigned to, `val`, is doubled.

That's all very well, but if you *want* the value of `myNumber` to change, you have a problem. You could use a function that returns a new value for `myNumber`, like this:

```
static int DoubleNum(int val)
{
    val *= 2;
    return val;
}
```

You could call this function using the following:

```
int myNumber = 5;
Console.WriteLine("myNumber = {0}", myNumber
myNumber = DoubleNum(myNumber);
Console.WriteLine("myNumber = {0}", myNumber);
```

However, this code is hardly intuitive and won't cope with changing the values of multiple variables used as arguments (as functions have only one return value).

Instead, you want to pass the parameter by *reference*, which means that the function will work with exactly the same variable as the one used in the function call, not just a variable that has the same value. Any changes made to this variable will, therefore, be reflected in the value of the variable used as an argument. To do this, you simply use the `ref` keyword to specify the parameter:

```
static void ShowDouble(ref int val)
{
    val *= 2;
    Console.WriteLine("val doubled = {0}", val);
}
```

Then, specify it again in the function call (this is mandatory):

```
int myNumber = 5;
Console.WriteLine("myNumber = {0}", myNumber);
ShowDouble(ref myNumber);
Console.WriteLine("myNumber = {0}", myNumber);
```

The text output to the console is now as follows:

```
myNumber = 5
val doubled = 10
myNumber = 10
```

This time `myNumber` has been modified by `ShowDouble()`.

Note two limitations on the variable used as a `ref` parameter. First, the function might result in a change to the value of a reference parameter, so you must use a *nonconstant* variable in the function call. The following is therefore illegal:

```
const int myNumber = 5;
Console.WriteLine("myNumber = {0}", myNumber);
ShowDouble(ref myNumber);
Console.WriteLine("myNumber = {0}", myNumber);
```

Second, you must use an initialized variable. C# doesn't allow you to assume that a `ref` parameter will be initialized in the function that uses it. The following code is also illegal:

```
int myNumber;
ShowDouble(ref myNumber);
Console.WriteLine("myNumber = {0}", myNumber);
```

## Out Parameters

In addition to passing values by reference, you can specify that a given parameter is an *out parameter* by using the out keyword, which is used in the same way as the ref keyword (as a modifier to the parameter in the function definition and in the function call). In effect, this gives you almost exactly the same behavior as a reference parameter, in that the value of the parameter at the end of the function execution is returned to the variable used in the function call. However, there are important differences:

➤ Whereas it is illegal to use an unassigned variable as a ref parameter, you can use an unassigned variable as an out parameter.

➤ An out parameter must be treated as an unassigned value by the function that uses it.

This means that while it is permissible in calling code to use an assigned variable as an out parameter, the value stored in this variable is lost when the function executes.

As an example, consider an extension to the MaxValue() function shown earlier, which returns the maximum value of an array. Modify the function slightly so that you obtain the index of the element with the maximum value within the array. To keep things simple, obtain just the index of the first occurrence of this value when there are multiple elements with the maximum value. To do this, you add an out parameter by modifying the function as follows:

```
static int MaxValue(int[] intArray, out int maxIndex)
{
    int maxVal = intArray[0];
    maxIndex = 0;
    for (int i = 1; i < intArray.Length; i++)
    {
        if (intArray[i] > maxVal)
        {
            maxVal = intArray[i];
            maxIndex = i;
        }
    }
    return maxVal;
}
```

You might use the function like this:

```
int[] myArray = { 1, 8, 3, 6, 2, 5, 9, 3, 0, 2 };
int maxIndex;
Console.WriteLine("The maximum value in myArray is {0}",
                MaxValue(myArray, out maxIndex));
Console.WriteLine("The first occurrence of this value is at element {0}",
                maxIndex + 1);
```

That results in the following:

```
The maximum value in myArray is 9
The first occurrence of this value is at element 7
```

You must use the out keyword in the function call, just as with the ref keyword.

> **NOTE** One has been added to the value of maxIndex returned here when it is displayed onscreen. This is to translate the index to a more readable form so that the first element in the array is referred to as element 1, rather than element 0.

## VARIABLE SCOPE

Throughout the last section, you might have been wondering why exchanging data with functions is necessary. The reason is that variables in C# are accessible only from localized regions of code. A given variable is said to have a *scope* from which it is accessible.

Variable scope is an important subject and one best introduced with an example. The following Try It Out illustrates a situation in which a variable is defined in one scope, and an attempt to use it is made in a different scope.

**TRY IT OUT** Variable Scope: Ch06Ex01\Program.cs

**1.** Make the following changes to Ch06Ex01 in `Program.cs`:

```
class Program
{
    static void Write()
    {
        Console.WriteLine("myString = {0}", myString);
    }

    static void Main(string[] args)
    {
        string myString = "String defined in Main()";
        Write();
        Console.ReadKey();
    }
}
```

**2.** Compile the code and note the error and warning that appear in the error list:

```
The name 'myString' does not exist in the current context
The variable 'myString' is assigned but its value is never used
```

### How It Works

What went wrong? Well, the variable `myString` defined in the main body of your application (the `Main()` function) isn't accessible from the `Write()` function.

The reason for this inaccessibility is that variables have a scope within which they are valid. This scope encompasses the code block that they are defined in and any directly nested code blocks. The blocks of code in functions are separate from the blocks of code from which they are called. Inside `Write()`, the name `myString` is undefined, and the `myString` variable defined in `Main()` is *out of scope*—it can be used only from within `Main()`.

In fact, you can have a completely separate variable in `Write()` called `myString`. Try modifying the code as follows:

```
class Program
{
    static void Write()
    {
        string myString = "String defined in Write()";
        Console.WriteLine("Now in Write()");
        Console.WriteLine("myString = {0}", myString);
    }

    static void Main(string[] args)
    {
        string myString = "String defined in Main()";
        Write();
        Console.WriteLine("\nNow in Main()");
```

```
        Console.WriteLine("myString = {0}", myString);
        Console.ReadKey();
    }
}
```

This code does compile, resulting in the output shown in Figure 6-4.

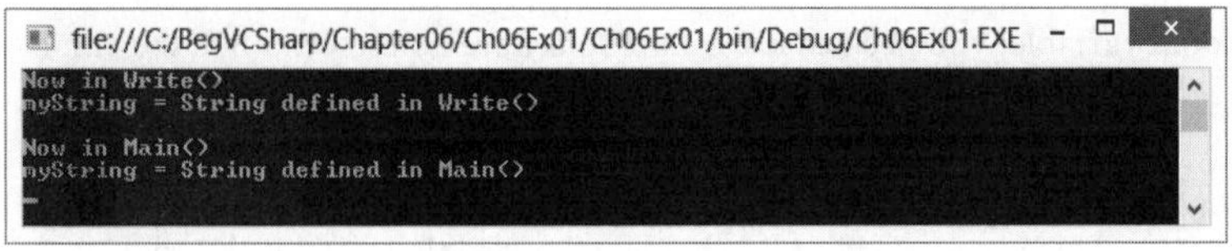

**FIGURE 6-4**

The operations performed by this code are as follows:

➤   `Main()` defines and initializes a string variable called `myString`.

➤   `Main()` transfers control to `Write()`.

➤   `Write()` defines and initializes a string variable called `myString`, which is a different variable from the `myString` defined in `Main()`.

➤   `Write()` outputs a string to the console containing the value of `myString` as defined in `Write()`.

➤   `Write()` transfers control back to `Main()`.

➤   `Main()` outputs a string to the console containing the value of `myString` as defined in `Main()`.

Variables whose scopes cover a single function in this way are known as *local variables*. It is also possible to have *global variables*, whose scopes cover multiple functions. Modify the code as follows:

```
    class Program
    {
        static string myString;

        static void Write()
        {
            string myString = "String defined in Write()";
            Console.WriteLine("Now in Write()");
            Console.WriteLine("Local myString = {0}", myString);
            Console.WriteLine("Global myString = {0}", Program.myString);
        }

        static void Main(string[] args)
        {
            string myString = "String defined in Main()";
            Program.myString = "Global string";
            Write();
            Console.WriteLine("\nNow in Main()");
            Console.WriteLine("Local myString = {0}", myString);
            Console.WriteLine("Global myString = {0}", Program.myString);
            Console.ReadKey();
        }
    }
```

The result is now as shown in Figure 6-5.

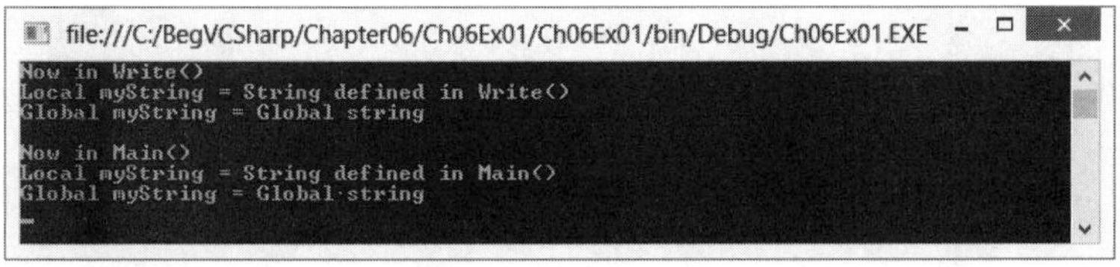

**FIGURE 6-5**

Here, you have added another variable called myString, this time further up the hierarchy of names in the code. The variable is defined as follows:

```
static string myString;
```

Again, the static keyword is required. Without going into too much detail, understand that in this type of console application, you must use either the static or the const keyword for global variables of this form. If you want to modify the value of the global variable, you need to use static because const prohibits the value of the variable from changing.

To differentiate between this variable and the local variables in Main() and Write() with the same names, you have to classify the variable name using a fully qualified name, as described in Chapter 3. Here, you refer to the global version as Program.myString. This is necessary only when you have global and local variables with the same name; if there were no local myString variable, you could simply use myString to refer to the global variable, rather than Program.myString. When you have a local variable with the same name as a global variable, the global variable is said to be *hidden*.

The value of the global variable is set in Main() with

```
Program.myString = "Global string";
```

and accessed in Write() with

```
Console.WriteLine("Global myString = {0}", Program.myString);
```

You might be wondering why you shouldn't just use this technique to exchange data with functions, rather than the parameter passing shown earlier. There are indeed situations where this is the preferable way to exchange data, but there are just as many scenarios (if not more) where it isn't. The choice of whether to use global variables depends on the intended use of the function in question. The problem with using global variables is that they are generally unsuitable for "general-purpose" functions, which are capable of working with whatever data you supply, not just data in a specific global variable. You look at this in more depth a little later.

## Variable Scope in Other Structures

One of the points made in the last section has consequences above and beyond variable scope between functions: that the scopes of variables encompass the code blocks in which they are defined and any directly nested code blocks. You can find the code discussed next in the chapter download in VariableScopeInLoops\Program.cs. This also applies to other code blocks, such as those in branching and looping structures. Consider the following code:

```
int i;
for (i = 0; i < 10; i++)
{
    string text = "Line " + Convert.ToString(i);
    Console.WriteLine("{0}", text);
}
Console.WriteLine("Last text output in loop: {0}", text);
```

Here, the string variable text is local to the for loop. This code won't compile because the call to Console.WriteLine() that occurs outside of this loop attempts to use the variable text, which is out of scope outside of the loop. Try modifying the code as follows:

```
int i;
string text;
for (i = 0; i < 10; i++)
{
    text = "Line " + Convert.ToString(i);
    Console.WriteLine("{0}", text);
}
Console.WriteLine("Last text output in loop: {0}", text);
```

This code will also fail because variables must be declared and initialized before use, and text is only initialized in the for loop. The value assigned to text is lost when the loop block is exited as it isn't initialized outside the block. However, you can make the following change:

```
int i;
string text = "";
for (i = 0; i < 10; i++)
{
    text = "Line " + Convert.ToString(i);
    Console.WriteLine("{0}", text);
}
Console.WriteLine("Last text output in loop: {0}", text);
```

This time text is initialized outside of the loop, and you have access to its value. The result of this simple code is shown in Figure 6-6.

**FIGURE 6-6**

The last value assigned to text in the loop is accessible from outside the loop. As you can see, this topic requires a bit of effort to come to grips with. It is not immediately obvious why, in light of the earlier example, text doesn't retain the empty string it is assigned before the loop in the code after the loop.

The explanation for this behavior is related to memory allocation for the text variable, and indeed any variable. Merely declaring a simple variable type doesn't result in very much happening. It is only when values are assigned to the variables that values are allocated a place in memory to be stored. When this allocation takes place inside a loop, the value is essentially defined as a local value and goes out of scope outside of the loop.

Even though the variable itself isn't localized to the loop, the value it contains is. However, assigning a value outside of the loop ensures that the value is local to the main code, and is still in scope inside the loop. This means that the variable doesn't go out of scope before the main code block is exited, so you have access to its value outside of the loop.

Luckily for you, the C# compiler detects variable scope problems, and responding to the error messages it generates certainly helps you to understand the topic of variable scope.

Finally, be aware of best practices. In general, it is worth declaring and initializing all variables before any code blocks that use them. An exception to this is when you declare looping variables as part of a loop block:

```
for (int i = 0; i < 10; i++)
{
    ...
}
```

Here, i is localized to the looping code block, but that's fine because you will rarely require access to this counter from external code.

## Parameters and Return Values versus Global Data

Let's take a closer look at exchanging data with functions via global data and via parameters and return values. To recap, consider the following code:

```
class Program
{
    static void ShowDouble(ref int val)
    {
        val *= 2;
        Console.WriteLine("val doubled = {0}", val);
    }

    static void Main(string[] args)
    {
        int val = 5;
        Console.WriteLine("val = {0}", val);
        ShowDouble(ref val);
        Console.WriteLine("val = {0}", val);
    }
}
```

> **NOTE** This code is slightly different from the code shown earlier in this chapter, when you used the variable name myNumber in Main(). This illustrates the fact that local variables can have identical names and yet not interfere with each other. It also means that the two code samples shown here are more similar, enabling you to focus on the specific differences without worrying about variable names.

Now compare it with this code:

```
class Program
{
    static int val;

    static void ShowDouble()
    {
        val *= 2;
        Console.WriteLine("val doubled = {0}", val);
    }

    static void Main(string[] args)
    {
        val = 5;
        Console.WriteLine("val = {0}", val);
        ShowDouble();
        Console.WriteLine("val = {0}", val);
    }
}
```

The results of these ShowDouble() functions are identical.

There are no hard-and-fast rules for using one technique rather than another, and both techniques are perfectly valid, but you might want to consider the following guidelines.

To start with, as mentioned when this topic was first introduced, the ShowDouble() version that uses the global value only uses the global variable val. To use this version, you must use this global variable. This limits the versatility of the function slightly and means that you must continuously copy the global variable value into other variables if you intend to store the results. In addition, global data might be modified by code elsewhere in your application, which could causeunpredictable results (values might change without you realizing it until it's too late).

However, this loss of versatility can often be a bonus. Sometimes you only want to use a function for one purpose, and using a global datastore reduces the possibility that you will make an error in a function call, perhaps passing it the wrong variable.

Of course, it could also be argued that this simplicity actually makes your code more difficult to understand. Explicitly specifying parameters enables you to see at a glance what is changing. If you see a call that reads FunctionName(val1, out val2), you instantly know that val1 and val2 are the important variables to consider and that val2 will be assigned a new value when the function is completed. Conversely, if this function took no parameters, then you would be unable to make any assumptions about what data it manipulated.

Finally, remember that using global data isn't always possible. Later in this book, you will see code written in different files and/or belonging to different namespaces communicating with each other via functions. In these cases, the code is often separated to such a degree that there is no obvious choice for a global storage location.

Feel free to use either technique to exchange data. In general, use parameters rather than global data; however, there are certainly cases where global data might be more suitable, and it certainly isn't an error to use that technique.

## THE MAIN( ) FUNCTION

Now that you've covered most of the simple techniques used in the creation and use of functions, it's time to take a closer look at the Main() function.

Earlier, you saw that Main() is the entry point for a C# application and that execution of this function encompasses the execution of the application. That is, when execution is initiated, the Main() function executes, and when the Main() function finishes, execution ends.

The Main() function can return either void or int, and can optionally include a string[] args parameter, so you can use any of the following versions:

```
static void Main()
static void Main(string[] args)
static int Main()
static int Main(string[] args)
```

The third and fourth versions return an int value, which can be used to signify how the application terminates, and often is used as an indication of an error (although this is by no means mandatory). In general, returning a value of 0 reflects normal termination (that is, the application has completed and can terminate safely).

The optional args parameter of Main() provides you with a way to obtain information from outside the application, specified at runtime. This information takes the form of *command-line parameters*.

You might well have come across command-line parameters already. When you execute an application from the command line, you can often specify information directly, such as a file to load on application execution. For example, consider the Notepad application in Windows. You can run Notepad simply by typing **notepad** in a command prompt window or in the window that appears when you select the Run option from the Windows Start menu. You can also type something like **notepad "myfile.txt"** in these locations. The result is that Notepad will either load the file myfile.txt when it runs or offer to create this file if it doesn't already exist. Here, "myfile.txt" is a command-line argument. You can write console applications that work similarly by making use of the args parameter.

When a console application is executed, any specified command-line parameters are placed in this args array. You can then use these parameters in your application. The following Try It Out shows this in action. You can specify any number of command-line arguments, each of which will be output to the console.

**TRY IT OUT** Command-Line Arguments: Ch06Ex04\Program.cs

1. Create a new console application called Ch06Ex04 and save it in the directory C:\BegVCSharp\Chapter06.

2. Add the following code to Program.cs:

```
class Program
{
    static void Main(string[] args)
    {
        Console.WriteLine("{0} command line arguments were specified:",
                          args.Length);
        foreach (string arg in args)
            Console.WriteLine(arg);
        Console.ReadKey();
    }
}
```

3. Open the property pages for the project (right-click on the Ch06Ex04 project name in the Solution Explorer window and select Properties).

4. Select the Debug page and add any command-line arguments you want to the Command Line Arguments setting. Figure 6-7 shows an example.

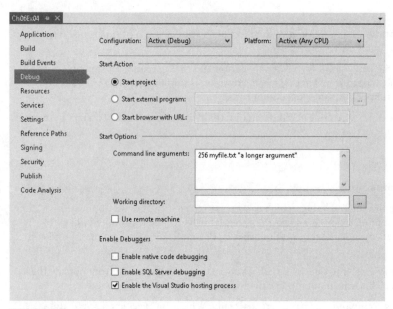

**FIGURE 6-7**

5. Run the application. Figure 6-8 shows the output.

```
file:///C:/BegVCSharp/Chapter06/Ch06Ex04/Ch06Ex04/bin/Debug/Ch06Ex04.EXE
3 command line arguments were specified:
256
myfile.txt
a longer argument
```

**FIGURE 6-8**

*How It Works*

The code used here is very simple:

```
Console.WriteLine("{0} command line arguments were specified:",
                  args.Length);
foreach (string arg in args)
    Console.WriteLine(arg);
```

You're just using the `args` parameter as you would any other string array. You're not doing anything fancy with the arguments; you're just writing whatever is specified to the screen. You supplied the arguments via the project properties in the IDE. This is a handy way to use the same command-line arguments whenever you run the application from the IDE, rather than type them at a command-line prompt every time. The same result can be obtained by opening a command prompt window in the same directory as the project output (`C:\BegCSharp\Chapter06\Ch06Ex04\Ch06Ex04\bin\Debug`) and typing this:

```
Ch06Ex04 256 myFile.txt "a longer argument"
```

Each argument is separated from the next by spaces. To supply an argument that includes spaces, you can enclose it in double quotation marks, which prevents it from being interpreted as multiple arguments.

## STRUCT FUNCTIONS

The last chapter covered struct types for storing multiple data elements in one place. Structs are actually capable of a lot more than this. For example, they can contain functions as well as data. That might seem a little strange at first, but it is, in fact, very useful. As a simple example, consider the following struct:

```
struct CustomerName
{
    public string firstName, lastName;
}
```

If you have variables of type `CustomerName` and you want to output a full name to the console, you are forced to build the name from its component parts. You might use the following syntax for a `CustomerName` variable called `myCustomer`, for example:

```
CustomerName myCustomer;
myCustomer.firstName = "John";
myCustomer.lastName = "Franklin";
Console.WriteLine("{0} {1}", myCustomer.firstName, myCustomer.lastName);
```

By adding functions to structs, you can simplify this by centralizing the processing of common tasks. For example, you can add a suitable function to the struct type as follows:

```
struct CustomerName
{
    public string firstName, lastName;

    public string Name()
    {
        return firstName + " " + lastName;
    }
}
```

This looks much like any other function you've seen in this chapter, except that you haven't used the `static` modifier. The reasons for this will become clear later in the book; for now, it is enough to know that this keyword isn't required for struct functions. You can use this function as follows:

```
CustomerName myCustomer;
myCustomer.firstName = "John";
myCustomer.lastName = "Franklin";
Console.WriteLine(myCustomer.Name());
```

This syntax is much simpler, and much easier to understand, than the previous syntax. The `Name()` function has direct access to the `firstName` and `lastName` struct members. Within the `customerName` struct, they can be thought of as global.

## OVERLOADING FUNCTIONS

Earlier in this chapter, you saw how you must match the signature of a function when you call it. This implies that you need to have separate functions to operate on different types of variables. Function overloading provides you with the capability to create multiple functions with the same name, but each working with different parameter types. For example, earlier you used the following code, which contains a function called `MaxValue()`:

```
class Program
{
    static int MaxValue(int[] intArray)
    {
        int maxVal = intArray[0];
        for (int i = 1; i < intArray.Length; i++)
        {
            if (intArray[i] > maxVal)
                maxVal = intArray[i];
        }
        return maxVal;
    }

    static void Main(string[] args)
    {
        int[] myArray = { 1, 8, 3, 6, 2, 5, 9, 3, 0, 2 };
        int maxVal = MaxValue(myArray);
        Console.WriteLine("The maximum value in myArray is {0}", maxVal);
        Console.ReadKey();
    }
}
```

This function can be used only with arrays of `int` values. You could provide different named functions for different parameter types, perhaps renaming the preceding function as `IntArrayMaxValue()` and adding functions such as `DoubleArrayMaxValue()` to work with other types. Alternatively, you could just add the following function to your code:

```
static double MaxValue(double[] doubleArray)
{
    double maxVal = doubleArray[0];
    for (int i = 1; i < doubleArray.Length; i++)
    {
        if (doubleArray[i] > maxVal)
            maxVal = doubleArray[i];
    }
    return maxVal;
}
```

The difference here is that you are using `double` values. The function name, `MaxValue()`, is the same, but (crucially) its *signature* is different. That's because the signature of a function, as shown earlier, includes both the name of the function and its parameters. It would be an error to define two functions with the same signature, but because these two functions have different signatures, this is fine.

> **NOTE** *The return type of a function isn't part of its signature, so you can't define two functions that differ only in return type; they would have identical signatures.*

After adding the preceding code, you have two versions of `MaxValue()`, which accept `int` and `double` arrays, returning an `int` or `double` maximum, respectively.

The beauty of this type of code is that you don't have to explicitly specify which of these two functions you want to use. You simply provide an array parameter, and the correct function is executed depending on the type of parameter used.

Note another aspect of the IntelliSense feature in VS: When you have the two functions shown previously in an application and then proceed to type the name of the function, for example, `Main()`, the IDE shows you the available overloads for that function. For example, if you type

```
double result = MaxValue(
```

the IDE gives you information about both versions of `MaxValue()`, which you can scroll between using the Up and Down arrow keys, as shown in Figure 6-9.

**FIGURE 6-9**

All aspects of the function signature are included when overloading functions. You might, for example, have two different functions that take parameters by value and by reference, respectively:

```
static void ShowDouble(ref int val)
{
    ...
}
static void ShowDouble(int val)
{
    ...
}
```

Deciding which version to use is based purely on whether the function call contains the `ref` keyword. The following would call the reference version:

```
ShowDouble(ref val);
```

This would call the value version:

```
ShowDouble(val);
```

Alternatively, you could have functions that differ in the number of parameters they require, and so on.

## USING DELEGATES

A *delegate* is a type that enables you to store references to functions. Although this sounds quite involved, the mechanism is surprisingly simple. The most important purpose of delegates will become clear later in the book when you look at events and event handling, but it's useful to briefly consider them here. Delegates are declared much like functions, but with no function body and using the `delegate` keyword. The delegate declaration specifies a return type and parameter list.

After defining a delegate, you can declare a variable with the type of that delegate. You can then initialize the variable as a reference to any function that has the same return type and parameter list as that delegate. Once you have done this, you can call that function by using the delegate variable as if it were a function.

When you have a variable that refers to a function, you can also perform other operations that would be otherwise impossible. For example, you can pass a delegate variable to a function as a parameter, and then that function can use the delegate to call whatever function it refers to, without knowing which function will be called until runtime. The following Try It Out demonstrates using a delegate to access one of two functions.

**TRY IT OUT**   Using a Delegate to Call a Function: Ch06Ex05\Program.cs

**1.**   Create a new console application called Ch06Ex05 and save it in the directory `C:\BegVCSharp\Chapter06`.

**2.**   Add the following code to `Program.cs`:

```
class Program
{
    delegate double ProcessDelegate(double param1, double param2);

    static double Multiply(double param1, double param2)
    {
        return param1 * param2;
    }

    static double Divide(double param1, double param2)
    {
        return param1 / param2;
    }

    static void Main(string[] args)
    {
        ProcessDelegate process;
        Console.WriteLine("Enter 2 numbers separated with a comma:");
        string input = Console.ReadLine();
        int commaPos = input.IndexOf(',');
        double param1 = Convert.ToDouble(input.Substring(0, commaPos));
        double param2 = Convert.ToDouble(input.Substring(commaPos + 1,
                                    input.Length - commaPos - 1));
        Console.WriteLine("Enter M to multiply or D to divide:");
        input = Console.ReadLine();
        if (input == "M")
            process = new ProcessDelegate(Multiply);
        else
            process = new ProcessDelegate(Divide);
        Console.WriteLine("Result: {0}", process(param1, param2));
        Console.ReadKey();
    }
}
```

**3.**   Execute the code and enter the values when prompted. Figure 6-10 shows the result.

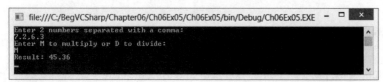

```
file:///C:/BegVCSharp/Chapter06/Ch06Ex05/Ch06Ex05/bin/Debug/Ch06Ex05.EXE
Enter 2 numbers separated with a comma:
7.2,6.3
Enter M to multiply or D to divide:
M
Result: 45.36
```

**FIGURE 6-10**

*How It Works*

This code defines a delegate (`ProcessDelegate`) whose return type and parameters match those of the two functions (`Multiply()` and `Divide()`). The delegate definition is as follows:

```
delegate double ProcessDelegate(double param1, double param2);
```

The `delegate` keyword specifies that the definition is for a delegate, rather than a function (the definition appears in the same place that a function definition might). Next, the definition specifies a `double` return value and two `double` parameters. The actual names used are arbitrary; you can call the delegate type and parameter names whatever you like. This example uses a delegate called `ProcessDelegate` and double parameters called `param1` and `param2`.

The code in `Main()` starts by declaring a variable using the new delegate type:

```
static void Main(string[] args)
{
    ProcessDelegate process;
```

Next, you have some fairly standard C# code that requests two numbers separated by a comma, and then places these numbers in two `double` variables:

```
Console.WriteLine("Enter 2 numbers separated with a comma:");
string input = Console.ReadLine();
int commaPos = input.IndexOf(',');
double param1 = Convert.ToDouble(input.Substring(0, commaPos));
double param2 = Convert.ToDouble(input.Substring(commaPos + 1,
                                 input.Length - commaPos - 1));
```

> **NOTE** For demonstration purposes, no user input validation is included here. If this were "real" code, you'd spend much more time ensuring that you had valid values in the local `param1` and `param2` variables.

Next, you ask the user to multiply or divide these numbers:

```
Console.WriteLine("Enter M to multiply or D to divide:");
input = Console.ReadLine();
```

Based on the user's choice, you initialize the `process` delegate variable:

```
if (input == "M")
    process = new ProcessDelegate(Multiply);
else
    process = new ProcessDelegate(Divide);
```

To assign a function reference to a delegate variable, you use slightly odd-looking syntax. Much like assigning array values, you can use the `new` keyword to create a new delegate. After this keyword, you specify the delegate type and supply an argument referring to the function you want to use—namely, the `Multiply()` or `Divide()` function. This argument doesn't match the parameters of the delegate type or the target function; it is a syntax unique to delegate assignment. The argument is simply the name of the function to use, without any parentheses.

In fact, you can use slightly simpler syntax here, if you want:

```
if (input == "M")
    process = Multiply;
else
    process = Divide;
```

The compiler recognizes that the delegate type of the process variable matches the signature of the two functions, and automatically initializes a delegate for you. Which syntax you use is up to you, although some people prefer to use the longhand version, as it is easier to see at a glance what is happening.

Finally, call the chosen function using the delegate. The same syntax works, regardless of which function the delegate refers to:

```
Console.WriteLine("Result: {0}", process(param1, param2));
Console.ReadKey();
}
```

Here, you treat the delegate variable as if it were a function name. Unlike a function, though, you can also perform additional operations on this variable, such as passing it to a function via a parameter, as shown in this simple example:

```
static void ExecuteFunction(ProcessDelegate process)
{
    process(2.2, 3.3);
}
```

This means that you can control the behavior of functions by passing them function delegates, much like choosing a "snap-in" to use. For example, you might have a function that sorts a string array alphabetically. You can use several techniques to sort lists, with varying performance depending on the characteristics of the list being sorted. By using delegates, you can specify the function to use by passing a sorting algorithm function delegate to a sorting function.

There are many such uses for delegates, but, as mentioned earlier, their most prolific use is in event handling, covered in Chapter 13.

## SUMMARY

This chapter provided a fairly complete overview of the use of functions in C# code. Many of the additional features that functions offer (delegates in particular) are more abstract, and you need to understand them in regard to object-oriented programming, the subject of Chapter 8.

Knowing how to use functions is central to all of the programming you are likely to do. Later chapters, particularly when you get to OOP (from Chapter 8 onward), explain a more formal structure for functions and how they apply to classes. You will likely find that the capability to abstract code into reusable blocks is the most useful aspect of C# programming.

### EXERCISES

**6.1**  The following two functions have errors. What are they?

```
static bool Write()
{
    Console.WriteLine("Text output from function.");
}

static void MyFunction(string label, params int[] args, bool showLabel)
{
    if (showLabel)
        Console.WriteLine(label);
    foreach (int i in args)
        Console.WriteLine("{0}", i);
}
```

**6.2**  Write an application that uses two command-line arguments to place values into a string and an integer variable, respectively. Then display those values.

**6.3**  Create a delegate and use it to impersonate the `Console.ReadLine()` function when asking for user input.

**6.4**  Modify the following struct to include a function that returns the total price of an order:

```
struct order
{
    public string itemName;
    public int    unitCount;
    public double unitCost;
}
```

**6.5**  Add another function to the order struct that returns a formatted string as follows (as a single line of text, where italic entries enclosed in angle brackets are replaced by appropriate values):

```
Order Information: <unit count> <item name> items at $<unit cost> each,
total cost $<total cost>
```

Answers to the exercises can be found in Appendix A.

► **WHAT YOU LEARNED IN THIS CHAPTER**

| TOPIC | KEY CONCEPTS |
|---|---|
| **Defining functions** | Functions are defined with a name, zero or more parameters, and a return type. The name and parameters of a function collectively define the signature of the function. It is possible to define multiple functions whose signatures are different even though their names are the same—this is called *function overloading*. Functions can also be defined within struct types. |
| **Return values and parameters** | The return type of a function can be any type, or `void` if the function does not return a value. Parameters can also be of any type, and consist of a comma-separated list of type and name pairs. A variable number of parameters of a specified type can be specified through a parameter array. Parameters can be specified as `ref` or `out` parameters in order to return values to the caller. When calling a function, any arguments specified must match the parameters in the definition both in type and in order and must include matching `ref` and `out` keywords if these are used in the parameter definition. |
| **Variable scope** | Variables are scoped according to the block of code where they are defined. Blocks of code include methods as well as other structures, such as the body of a loop. It is possible to define multiple, separate variables with the same name at different scope levels. |
| **Command-line parameters** | The `Main()` function in a console application can receive command-line parameters that are passed to the application when it is executed. When executing the application, these parameters are specified by arguments separated by spaces, and longer arguments can be passed in quotes. |
| **Delegates** | As well as calling functions directly, it is possible to call them through delegates. Delegates are variables that are defined with a return type and parameter list. A given delegate type can match any method whose return type and parameters match the delegate definition. |

# Debugging and Error Handling

**WHAT YOU WILL LEARN IN THIS CHAPTER**

➤   Debugging methods available in the IDE
➤   Error-handling techniques available in C#

**WROX.COM CODE DOWNLOADS FOR THIS CHAPTER**

You can find the wrox.com code downloads for this chapter at www.wrox.com/remtitle
.cgi?isbn=9781118314418 on the Download Code tab. The code is in the Chapter 7 download and
individually named according to the names throughout the chapter.

So far this book has covered all the basics of simple programming in C#. Before you move on to
object-oriented programming in the next part, you need to look at debugging and error handling in
C# code.

Errors in code are something that will always be with you. No matter how good a programmer is,
problems will always slip through, and part of being a good programmer is realizing this and being
prepared to deal with it. Of course, some problems are minor and don't affect the execution of an
application, such as a spelling mistake on a button, but glaring errors are also possible, including
those that cause applications to fail completely (usually known as *fatal errors*). Fatal errors include
simple errors in code that prevent compilation (syntax errors), or more serious problems that occur
only at runtime. Some errors are subtle. Perhaps your application fails to add a record to a database
because a requested field is missing, or adds a record with the wrong data in other restricted
circumstances. Errors such as these, where application logic is in some way flawed, are known as
*semantic errors* or *logic errors*.

Often, you won't know about these subtle errors until a user complains that something isn't working
properly. This leaves you with the task of tracing through your code to find out what's happening and
fixing it so that it does what it was intended to do. In these situations, the debugging capabilities of VS
are a fantastic help. The first part of this chapter looks at some of the techniques available and applies
them to some common problems.

Then, you'll learn the error-handling techniques available in C#. These enable you to take precautions
in cases where errors are likely, and to write code that is resilient enough to cope with errors that
might otherwise be fatal. The techniques are part of the C# language, rather than a debugging
feature, but the IDE provides some tools to help you here too.

## DEBUGGING IN VISUAL STUDIO

Earlier, you learned that you can execute applications in two ways: with debugging enabled or without debugging enabled. By default, when you execute an application from Visual Studio (VS), it executes with debugging enabled. This happens, for example, when you press F5 or click the green Play arrow in the toolbar. To execute an application without debugging enabled, choose Debug ➪ Start Without Debugging, or press Ctrl+F5.

VS allows you to build applications in two configurations: Debug (the default) and Release. (In fact, you can define additional configurations, but that's an advanced technique not covered here.) You can switch between these configurations using the Solution Configurations drop-down menu in the Standard toolbar.

When you build an application in debug configuration and execute it in debug mode, more is going on than the execution of your code. Debug builds maintain *symbolic information* about your application, so that the IDE knows exactly what is happening as each line of code is executed. Symbolic information means keeping track of, for example, the names of variables used in uncompiled code, so they can be matched to the values in the compiled machine code application, which won't contain such human-readable information. This information is contained in .pdb files, which you may have seen in your computer's Debug directories. This enables you to perform many useful operations:

➤ Outputting debugging information to the IDE

➤ Examining the values of variables in scope during application execution

➤ Pausing and restarting program execution

➤ Automatically halting execution at certain points in the code

➤ Stepping through program execution one line at a time

➤ Monitoring changes in variable content during application execution

➤ Modifying variable content at runtime

➤ Performing test calls of functions

In the release configuration, application code is optimized, and you cannot perform these operations. However, release builds also run faster; when you have finished developing an application, you will typically supply users with release builds because they won't require the symbolic information that debug builds include.

This section describes debugging techniques you can use to identify and fix areas of code that don't work as expected, a process known as *debugging*. The techniques are grouped into two sections according to how they are used. In general, debugging is performed either by interrupting program execution or by making notes for later analysis. In VS terms, an application is either running or in break mode—that is, normal execution is halted. You'll look at the nonbreak mode (runtime or normal) techniques first.

## Debugging in Nonbreak (Normal) Mode

One of the commands you've been using throughout this book is the `Console.WriteLine()` function, which outputs text to the console. As you are developing applications, this function comes in handy for getting extra feedback about operations:

```
Console.WriteLine("MyFunc() Function about to be called.");
MyFunc("Do something.");
Console.WriteLine("MyFunc() Function execution completed.");
```

This code snippet shows how you can get extra information concerning a function called `MyFunc()`. This is all very well, but it can make your console output a bit cluttered; and when you develop other types of applications, such as desktop applications, you won't have a console to output information to. As an alternative, you can output text to a separate location—the Output window in the IDE.

Chapter 2, which describes the Error List window, mentions that other windows can also be displayed in the same place. One of these, the Output window, can be very useful for debugging. To display this window, select View ➪ Output. This window provides information related to compilation and execution of code, including errors encountered during compilation. You can also use this window, shown in Figure 7-1, to display custom diagnostic information by writing to it directly.

> **NOTE** *The Output window contains a drop-down menu from which different modes can be selected, including Build and Debug. These modes display compilation and runtime information, respectively. When you read "writing to the Output window" in this section, it actually means "writing to the debug mode view of the Output window."*

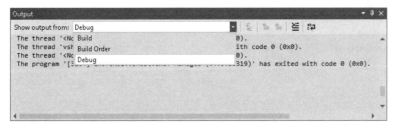

**FIGURE 7-1**

Alternatively, you might want to create a logging file, which has information appended to it when your application is executed. The techniques for doing this are much the same as those for writing text to the Output window, although the process requires an understanding of how to access the filesystem from C# applications. For now, leave that functionality on the back burner because there is plenty you can do without getting bogged down by file-access techniques.

## Outputting Debugging Information

Writing text to the Output window at runtime is easy. You simply replace calls to `Console.WriteLine()` with the required call to write text where you want it. There are two commands you can use to do this:

➤ `Debug.WriteLine()`

➤ `Trace.WriteLine()`

These commands function in almost exactly the same way, with one key difference—the first command works in debug builds only; the latter works for release builds as well. In fact, the `Debug.WriteLine()` command won't even be compiled into a release build; it just disappears, which certainly has its advantages (the compiled code will be smaller, for one thing). You can, in effect, create two versions of your application from a single source file. The debug version displays all kinds of extra diagnostic information, whereas the release version won't have this overhead, and won't display messages to users that might otherwise be annoying!

These functions don't work exactly like `Console.WriteLine()`. They work with only a single string parameter for the message to output, rather than letting you insert variable values using {X} syntax. This means you must use an alternative technique to embed variable values in strings—for example, the + concatenation operator. You can also (optionally) supply a second string parameter, which displays a category for the output text. This enables you to see at a glance which output messages are displayed in the Output window, which is useful when similar messages are output from different places in the application.

The general output of these functions is as follows:

```
<category>: <message>
```

For example, the following statement, which has `"MyFunc"` as the optional category parameter,

```
Debug.WriteLine("Added 1 to i", "MyFunc");
```

would result in the following:

```
MyFunc: Added 1 to i
```

The next Try It Out demonstrates outputting debugging information in this way.

---

**TRY IT OUT** Writing Text to the Output Window: Ch07Ex01\Program.cs

**1.** Create a new console application called Ch07Ex01 and save it in the directory `C:\BegVCSharp\Chapter07`.

**2.** Modify the code as follows:

```csharp
using System;
using System.Collections.Generic;
using System.Diagnostics;
using System.Linq;
using System.Text;
using System.Threading.Tasks;

namespace Ch07Ex01
{
    class Program
    {
        static void Main(string[] args)
        {
            int[] testArray = {4, 7, 4, 2, 7, 3, 7, 8, 3, 9, 1, 9};
            int[] maxValIndices;
            int maxVal = Maxima(testArray, out maxValIndices);
            Console.WriteLine("Maximum value {0} found at element indices:",
                              maxVal);
            foreach (int index in maxValIndices)
            {
                Console.WriteLine(index);
            }
            Console.ReadKey();
        }

        static int Maxima(int[] integers, out int[] indices)
        {
            Debug.WriteLine("Maximum value search started.");
            indices = new int[1];
            int maxVal = integers[0];
            indices[0] = 0;
            int count = 1;
            Debug.WriteLine(string.Format(
                "Maximum value initialized to {0}, at element index 0.", maxVal));
            for (int i = 1; i < integers.Length; i++)
            {
                Debug.WriteLine(string.Format(
                    "Now looking at element at index {0}.", i));
                if (integers[i] > maxVal)
                {
                    maxVal = integers[i];
                    count = 1;
                    indices = new int[1];
                    indices[0] = i;
                    Debug.WriteLine(string.Format(
                        "New maximum found. New value is {0}, at element index {1}.",
                        maxVal, i));
                }
```

```
        else
        {
            if (integers[i] == maxVal)
            {
                count++;
                int[] oldIndices = indices;
                indices = new int[count];
                oldIndices.CopyTo(indices, 0);
                indices[count - 1] = i;
                Debug.WriteLine(string.Format(
                    "Duplicate maximum found at element index {0}.", i));
            }
        }
    }

    Trace.WriteLine(string.Format(
        "Maximum value {0} found, with {1} occurrences.", maxVal, count));
    Debug.WriteLine("Maximum value search completed.");
    return maxVal;
        }
    }
}
```

**3.** Execute the code in debug mode. The result is shown in Figure 7-2.

**FIGURE 7-2**

**4.** Terminate the application and check the contents of the Output window (in debug mode). A truncated version of the output is shown here:

```
...

Maximum value search started.
Maximum value initialized to 4, at element index 0.
Now looking at element at index 1.
New maximum found. New value is 7, at element index 1.
Now looking at element at index 2.
Now looking at element at index 3.
Now looking at element at index 4.
Duplicate maximum found at element index 4.
Now looking at element at index 5.
Now looking at element at index 6.
Duplicate maximum found at element index 6.
Now looking at element at index 7.
New maximum found. New value is 8, at element index 7.
Now looking at element at index 8.
Now looking at element at index 9.
New maximum found. New value is 9, at element index 9.
Now looking at element at index 10.
Now looking at element at index 11.
Duplicate maximum found at element index 11.
Maximum value 9 found, with 2 occurrences.
Maximum value search completed.
The thread '<No Name>' (0xdcc) has exited with code 0 (0x0).
The thread 'vshost.RunParkingWindow' (0x5bc) has exited with code 0 (0x0).
The thread '<No Name>' (0x528) has exited with code 0 (0x0).
The program '[2436] Ch07Ex01.vshost.exe: Managed (v4.0.30319)' has exited with
code 0 (0x0).
```

**5.** Change to release mode using the drop-down menu on the Standard toolbar, as shown in Figure 7-3.

**6.** Run the program again, this time in release mode, and recheck the Output window when execution terminates. The output (again truncated) is as follows:

**FIGURE 7-3**

```
...
Maximum value 9 found, with 2 occurrences.
The thread 'vshost.RunParkingWindow' (0xde4) has exited with code 0 (0x0).
The thread '<No Name>' (0xfec) has exited with code 0 (0x0).
The program '[1700] Ch07Ex01.vshost.exe: Managed (v4.0.30319)' has exited with
code 0 (0x0).
```

### How It Works

This application is an expanded version of one shown in Chapter 6, using a function to calculate the maximum value in an integer array. This version also returns an array of the indices where maximum values are found in an array, so that the calling code can manipulate these elements.

First, an additional `using` directive appears at the beginning of the code:

```
using System.Diagnostics;
```

This simplifies access to the functions discussed earlier because they are contained in the `System.Diagnostics` namespace. Without this `using` directive, code such as,

```
Debug.WriteLine("Bananas");
```

would need further qualification, and would have to be rewritten as:

```
System.Diagnostics.Debug.WriteLine("Bananas");
```

The `using` directive keeps your code simple and reduces verbosity.

The code in `Main()` simply initializes a test array of integers called `testArray`; it also declares another integer array called `maxValIndices` to store the index output of `Maxima()` (the function that performs the calculation), and then calls this function. Once the function returns, the code simply outputs the results.

`Maxima()` is slightly more complicated, but it doesn't use much code that you haven't already seen. The search through the array is performed in a similar way to the `MaxVal()` function in *Chapter 6*, but a record is kept of the indices of maximum values.

Note the function used to keep track of the indices (other than the lines that output debugging information). Rather than return an array that would be large enough to store every index in the source array (needing the same dimensions as the source array), `Maxima()` returns an array just large enough to hold the indices found. It does this by continually recreating arrays of different sizes as the search progresses. This is necessary because arrays can't be resized once they are created.

The search is initialized by assuming that the first element in the source array (called `integers` locally) is the maximum value and that there is only one maximum value in the array. Values can therefore be set for `maxVal` (the return value of the function and the maximum value found) and `indices`, the `out` parameter array that stores the indices of the maximum values found. `maxVal` is assigned the value of the first element in `integers`, and `indices` is assigned a single value, simply 0, which is the index of the array's first element. You also store the number of maximum values found in a variable called `count`, which enables you to keep track of the `indices` array.

The main body of the function is a loop that cycles through the values in the `integers` array, omitting the first one because it has already been processed. Each value is compared to the current value of `maxVal` and ignored if `maxVal` is greater. If the currently inspected array value is greater than `maxVal`, then `maxVal` and `indices` are changed to reflect this. If the value is equal to `maxVal`, then `count` is incremented and a new array is substituted for `indices`. This new array is one element bigger than the old `indices` array, containing the new index.

The code for this last piece of functionality is as follows:

```
if (integers[i] == maxVal)
{
    count++;
    int[] oldIndices = indices;
    indices = new int[count];
    oldIndices.CopyTo(indices, 0);
    indices[count - 1] = i;
    Debug.WriteLine(string.Format(
        "Duplicate maximum found at element index {0}.", i));
}
```

This works by backing up the old `indices` array into `oldIndices`, an integer array local to this `if` code block. Note that the values in `oldIndices` are copied into the new `indices` array using the `<array>.CopyTo()` function. This function simply takes a target array and an index to use for the first element to copy to and pastes all values into the target array.

Throughout the code, various pieces of text are output using the `Debug.WriteLine()` and `Trace.WriteLine()` functions. These functions use the `string.Format()` function to embed variable values in strings in the same way as `Console.WriteLine()`. This is slightly more efficient than using the + concatenation operator.

When you run the application in debug mode, you see a complete record of the steps taken in the loop that give you the result. In release mode, you see just the result of the calculation, because no calls to `Debug.WriteLine()` are made in release builds.

In addition to these `WriteLine()` functions, there are a few more functions you should be aware of. To start with, there are equivalents to `Console.Write()`:

➤ `Debug.Write()`
➤ `Trace.Write()`

Both functions use the same syntax as the `WriteLine()` functions (one or two parameters, with a message and an optional category), but differ in that they don't add end-of-line characters.

There are also the following functions:

➤ `Debug.WriteLineIf()`
➤ `Trace.WriteLineIf()`
➤ `Debug.WriteIf()`
➤ `Trace.WriteIf()`

Each of these has the same parameters as the non-`If` counterparts, with the addition of an extra, mandatory parameter that precedes them in the parameter list. This parameter takes a Boolean value (or an expression that evaluates to a Boolean value) and results in the function writing text only if this value evaluates to `true`. You can use these functions to conditionally output text to the Output window.

For example, you might require debugging information to be output only in certain situations, so you can have a great many `Debug.WriteLineIf()` statements in your code that all depend on a certain condition being met. If this condition doesn't occur, then they aren't displayed, which prevents the Output window from being cluttered with superfluous information.

### Tracepoints

An alternative to writing information to the Output window is to use *tracepoints*. These are a feature of VS, rather than C#, but they serve the same function as using `Debug.WriteLine()`. Essentially, they enable you to output debugging information without modifying your code.

To demonstrate tracepoints, you can use them to replace the debugging commands in the previous example. (See the Ch07Ex01TracePoints file in the downloadable code for this chapter.) The process for adding a tracepoint is as follows:

1. Position the cursor at the line where you want the tracepoint to be inserted. The tracepoint will be processed *before* this line of code is executed.

2. Right-click the line of code and select Breakpoint ➪ Insert Tracepoint.

3. Type the string to be output in the Print a Message text box in the When Breakpoint Is Hit dialog box that appears. If you want to output variable values, enclose the variable name in curly braces.

4. Click OK. A red diamond appears to the left of the line of code containing a tracepoint, and the line of code itself is shown in red.

As implied by the title of the dialog box for adding tracepoints and the menu selections required for them, tracepoints are a form of breakpoint (and can cause application execution to pause, just like a breakpoint, if desired). You look at breakpoints, which typically serve a more advanced debugging purpose, a little later in the chapter.

Figure 7-4 shows the tracepoint required for line 31 of Ch07Ex01TracePoints, where line numbering applies to the code after the existing Debug.WriteLine() statements have been removed.

> **NOTE** *As shown in the text in Figure 7-4, tracepoints enable you to insert other useful information concerning the location and context of the tracepoint. Experiment with these values, particularly $FUNCTION and $CALLER, to see what additional information you can glean. You can also see that it is possible for the tracepoint to execute a macro, an advanced feature that isn't covered here.*

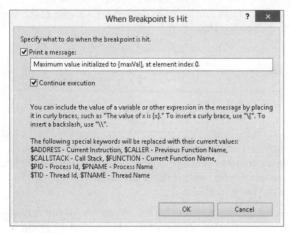

**FIGURE 7-4**

There is another window that you can use to quickly see the tracepoints in an application. To display this window, select Debug ➪ Windows ➪ Breakpoints from the VS menu. This is a general window for displaying breakpoints (tracepoints, as noted earlier, are a form of breakpoint). You can customize the display to show more tracepoint-specific information by adding the When Hit column from the Columns drop-down in this window. Figure 7-5 shows the display with this column configured and all the tracepoints added to Ch07Ex01TracePoints.

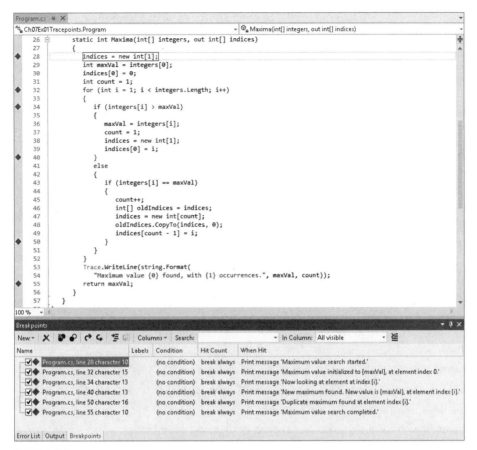

**FIGURE 7-5**

Executing this application in debug mode has the same result as before. You can remove or temporarily disable tracepoints by right-clicking on them in the code window or via the Breakpoints window. In the Breakpoints window, the check box to the left of the tracepoint indicates whether the tracepoint is enabled; disabled tracepoints are unchecked and displayed in the code window as diamond outlines, rather than solid diamonds.

## Diagnostics Output Versus Tracepoints

Now that you have seen two methods of outputting essentially the same information, consider the pros and cons of each. First, tracepoints have no equivalent to the `Trace` commands; that is, there is no way to output information in a release build using tracepoints. This is because tracepoints are not included in your application. Tracepoints are handled by Visual Studio and, as such, do not exist in the compiled version of your application. You will see tracepoints doing something only when your application is running in the VS debugger.

The chief disadvantage of tracepoints is also their major advantage, which is that they are stored in VS. This makes them quick and easy to add to your applications as you need them, but also makes them all too easy to delete. Deleting a tracepoint is as simple as clicking on the red diamond indicating its position, which can be annoying if you are outputting a complicated string of information.

One bonus of tracepoints, though, is the additional information that can be easily added, such as `$FUNCTION`, as noted in the previous section. Although this information is available to code written using

`Debug` and `Trace` commands, it is trickier to obtain. In summary, use these two methods of outputting debug information as follows:

➤ **Diagnostics output**—Use when debug output is something you always want to output from an application, particularly when the string you want to output is complex, involving several variables or a lot of information. In addition, `Trace` commands are often the only option should you want output during execution of an application built in release mode.

➤ **Tracepoints**—Use these when debugging an application to quickly output important information that may help you resolve semantic errors.

## Debugging in Break Mode

The rest of the debugging techniques described in this chapter work in break mode. This mode can be entered in several ways, all of which result in the program pausing in some way.

### Entering Break Mode

The simplest way to enter break mode is to click the Pause button in the IDE while an application is running. This Pause button is found on the Debug toolbar, which you should add to the toolbars that appear by default in VS. To do this, right-click in the toolbar area and select Debug. Figure 7-6 shows the Debug toolbar that appears.

**FIGURE 7-6**

The first three buttons on the toolbar allow manual control of breaking. In Figure 7-6, these are grayed out because they don't work with a program that isn't currently executing. The following sections describe the rest of the buttons as needed.

When an application is running, the toolbar changes to look like Figure 7-7.

The three buttons that were grayed out now enable you to do the following:

**FIGURE 7-7**

➤ Pause the application and enter break mode.

➤ Stop the application completely (this doesn't enter break mode; it just quits).

➤ Restart the application.

Pausing the application is perhaps the simplest way to enter break mode, but it doesn't give you fine-grained control over exactly where to stop. You are likely to stop in a natural pause in the application, perhaps where you request user input. You might also be able to enter break mode during a lengthy operation, or a long loop, but the exact stop point is likely to be fairly random. In general, it is far better to use breakpoints.

### Breakpoints

A *breakpoint* is a marker in your source code that triggers automatic entry into break mode. Breakpoints can be configured to do the following:

➤ Enter break mode immediately when the breakpoint is reached.

➤ Enter break mode when the breakpoint is reached if a Boolean expression evaluates to `true`.

➤ Enter break mode once the breakpoint is reached a set number of times.

➤ Enter break mode once the breakpoint is reached and a variable value has changed since the last time the breakpoint was reached.

➤ Output text to the Output window or execute a macro (see the section called "Tracepoints" earlier in the chapter).

These features are available only in debug builds. If you compile a release build, all breakpoints are ignored.

There are several ways to add breakpoints. To add simple breakpoints that break when a line is reached, just left-click on the far left of the line of code. Alternatively, you can right-click on the line and select Breakpoint ⇨ Insert Breakpoint, select Debug ⇨ Toggle Breakpoint from the menu, or press F9.

A breakpoint appears as a red circle next to the line of code, which is highlighted, as shown in Figure 7-8.

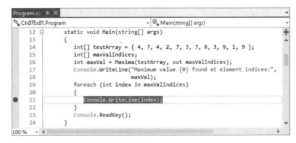

**FIGURE 7-8**

You can also see information about a file's breakpoints using the Breakpoints window (you saw how to enable this window earlier). You can use the Breakpoints window to disable breakpoints (by removing the tick to the left of a description; a disabled breakpoint shows up as an unfilled red circle), to delete breakpoints, and to edit the properties of breakpoints. You can also add labels to breakpoints, which is a handy way to group selected breakpoints. You can see labels in the Labels column and filter the items shown in this window by label.

The other columns shown in this window, Condition and Hit Count, are only two of the available ones, but they are the most useful. You can edit these by right-clicking a breakpoint (in code or in this window) and selecting Condition or Hit Count.

Selecting Condition opens a dialog box in which you can type any Boolean expression, which may involve any variables in scope at the breakpoint. For example, you could configure a breakpoint that triggers when it is reached and the value of maxVal is greater than 4 by entering the expression "maxVal > 4" and selecting the Is true option. You can also check whether the value of this expression has changed and only trigger the breakpoint then (you might trigger it if maxVal changed from 2 to 6 between breakpoint encounters, for example).

Selecting Hit Count opens a dialog box in which you can specify how many times a breakpoint needs to be hit before it is triggered. A drop-down list offers the following options:

➤ Break always
➤ Break when the hit count is equal to
➤ Break when the hit count is a multiple of
➤ Break when the hit count is greater than or equal to

The option you choose, combined with the value entered in the text box next to the options, determines the behavior of the breakpoint. The hit count is useful in long loops, when you might want to break after, say, the first 5,000 cycles. It would be a pain to break and restart 5,000 times if you couldn't do this!

> **NOTE** *A breakpoint with additional properties set (such as a condition or hit count) is displayed slightly differently. Instead of a simple red circle, a configured breakpoint consists of a red circle containing a white + (plus) symbol. This can be useful because it enables you to see at a glance which breakpoints will always cause break mode to be entered and which will do so only in certain circumstances.*

### Other Ways to Enter Break Mode

There are two more ways to get into break mode. One is to enter it when an unhandled exception is thrown. This subject is covered later in this chapter, when you look at error handling. The other way is to break when an assertion is generated.

*Assertions* are instructions that can interrupt application execution with a user-defined message. They are often used during application development to test whether things are going smoothly. For example, at some point in your application you might require a given variable to have a value less than 10. You can use an assertion to confirm that this is true, interrupting the program if it isn't. When the assertion occurs, you have the option to Abort, which terminates the application; Retry, which causes break mode to be entered; or Ignore, which causes the application to continue as normal.

As with the debug output functions shown earlier, there are two versions of the assertion function:

➤   `Debug.Assert()`

➤   `Trace.Assert()`

Again, the debug version is only compiled into debug builds.

These functions take three parameters. The first is a Boolean value, whereby a value of `false` causes the assertion to trigger. The second and third are string parameters to write information both to a pop-up dialog box and the Output window. The preceding example would need a function call such as the following:

```
Debug.Assert(myVar < 10, "myVar is 10 or greater.",
             "Assertion occurred in Main().");
```

Assertions are often useful in the early stages of user adoption of an application. You can distribute release builds of your application containing `Trace.Assert()` functions to keep tabs on things. Should an assertion be triggered, the user will be informed, and this information can be passed on to you. You can then determine what has gone wrong even if you don't know how it went wrong.

You might, for example, provide a brief description of the error in the first string, with instructions as to what to do next as the second string:

```
Trace.Assert(myVar < 10, "Variable out of bounds.",
             "Please contact vendor with the error code KCW001.");
```

Should this assertion occur, the user will see the dialog box shown in Figure 7-9.

Admittedly, this isn't the most user-friendly dialog box in the world, as it contains a lot of information that could confuse users, but if they send you a screenshot of the error, you could quickly track down the problem.

Now it's time to look at what you can actually do after application execution is halted and you are in break mode. In general, you enter break mode to find an error in your code (or to reassure yourself that things are working properly). Once you are in break mode, you can use various techniques, all of which enable you to analyze your code and the exact state of the application at the point in its execution where it is paused.

**FIGURE 7-9**

## Monitoring Variable Content

Monitoring variable content is just one example of how VS helps you a great deal by simplifying things. The easiest way to check the value of a variable is to hover the mouse over its name in the source code while in break mode. A tooltip showing information about the variable appears, including the variable's current value.

You can also highlight entire expressions to get information about their results in the same way. For more complex values, such as arrays, you can even expand values in the tooltip to see individual element entries.

It is possible to pin these tooltip windows to the code view, which can be useful if there is a variable you are particularly interested in. Pinned tooltips persist, so they are available even if you stop and restart debugging. You can also add comments to pinned tooltips, move them around, and see the value of the last variable value, even when the application isn't running.

You may have noticed that when you run an application, the layout of the various windows in the IDE changes. By default, the following changes are likely to occur at runtime (this behavior may vary slightly depending on your installation):

➤ The Properties window disappears, along with some other windows, probably including the Solution Explorer window.

➤ The Error List window is replaced with two new windows across the bottom of the IDE window.

➤ Several new tabs appear in the new windows.

The new screen layout is shown in Figure 7-10. This may not match your display exactly, and some of the tabs and windows may not look exactly the same, but the functionality of these windows as described later will be the same, and this display is customizable via the View and Debug ⇨ Windows menus (during break mode), as well as by dragging windows around the screen to reposition them.

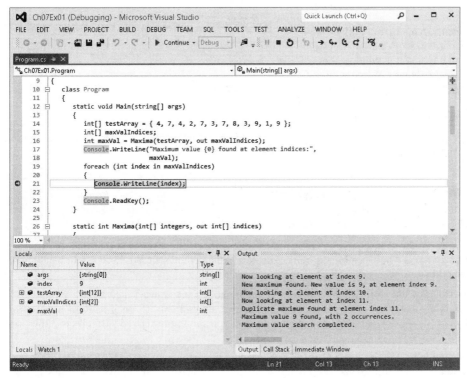

**FIGURE 7-10**

The new window that appears in the bottom-left corner is particularly useful for debugging. It enables you to keep tabs on the values of variables in your application when in break mode:

➤ **Autos**—Variables in use in the current and previous statements (Ctrl+D, A)

➤ **Locals**—All variables in scope (Ctrl+D, L)

➤ **Watch N**—Customizable variable and expression display (where N is 1 to 4, found on Debug ⇨ Windows ⇨ Watch)

All these tabs work in more or less the same way, with various additional features depending on their specific function. In general, each tab contains a list of variables, with information on each variable's name, value, and type. More complex variables, such as arrays, may be further examined using the + and – tree expansion/contraction symbols to the left of their names, enabling a tree view of their content. For example, Figure 7-11 shows the Locals tab obtained by placing a breakpoint in the example code. It shows the expanded view for one of the array variables, maxValIndices.

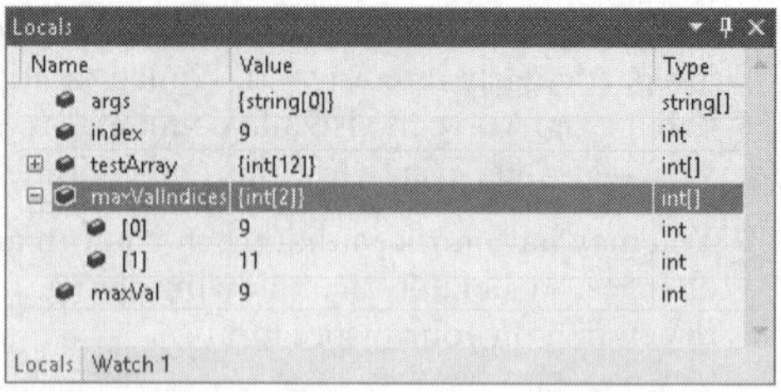

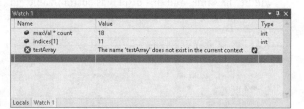

**FIGURE 7-11**

You can also edit the content of variables from this view. This effectively bypasses any other variable assignment that might have happened in earlier code. To do this, simply type a new value into the Value column for the variable you want to edit. You might do this to try out some scenarios that would otherwise require code changes, for example.

The Watch windows enable you to monitor specific variables, or expressions involving specific variables. To use this window, type the name of a variable or expression into the Name column and view the results. Note that not all variables in an application are in scope all the time, and are labeled as such in a Watch window. For example, Figure 7-12 shows a Watch window with a few sample variables and expressions in it, obtained when a breakpoint just before the end of the Maxima() function is reached.

**FIGURE 7-12**

The testArray array is local to Main(), so you don't see a value here. Instead, you get a message informing you that the variable isn't in scope.

> **NOTE** *You can also add variables to a Watch window by dragging them from the source code into the window.*

One nice feature about the various displays of variables accessible in this window is that they show you variables that have changed between breakpoints. Any new value is shown in red, rather than black, making it easy to see whether a value has changed.

As mentioned earlier, to add more Watch windows, in break mode you can use the Debug ➪ Windows ➪ Watch ➪ Watch N menu options to toggle the four possible windows on or off. Each window may contain an individual set of watches on variables and expressions, so you can group related variables together for easy access.

As well as these windows, VS also has a QuickWatch window that provides detailed information about a variable in the source code. To use this, simply right-click the variable you want to examine and select the QuickWatch menu option. In most cases, though, it is just as easy to use the standard Watch windows or to pin the variable view tooltip, as described earlier.

Watches are maintained between application executions. If you terminate an application and then rerun it, you don't have to add watches again—the IDE remembers what you were looking at the last time.

## Stepping Through Code

So far, you've learned how to discover what is going on in your applications at the point where break mode is entered. Now it's time to see how you can use the IDE to step through code while remaining in break mode, which enables you to see the exact results of the code being executed. This is an extremely valuable technique for those of us who can't think as fast as computers can.

When VS enters break mode, a yellow arrow cursor appears to the left of the code view (which may initially appear inside the red circle of a breakpoint if a breakpoint was used to enter break mode) next to the line of code that is about to be executed, as shown in Figure 7-13.

```
Program.cs
Ch07Ex01.Program                              Main(string[] args)
   12        static void Main(string[] args)
   13        {
   14            int[] testArray = { 4, 7, 4, 2, 7, 3, 7, 8, 3, 9, 1, 9 };
   15            int[] maxValIndices;
   16            int maxVal = Maxima(testArray, out maxValIndices);
   17            Console.WriteLine("Maximum value {0} found at element indices:",
   18                              maxVal);
   19            foreach (int index in maxValIndices)
   20            {
   21                Console.WriteLine(index);
   22            }
   23            Console.ReadKey();
   24        }
100 %
```

**FIGURE 7-13**

This shows you what point execution has reached when break mode is entered. At this point, you can execute the program on a line-by-line basis. To do so, you use some of the Debug toolbar buttons shown in Figure 7-14.

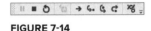

**FIGURE 7-14**

The sixth, seventh, and eighth icons control program flow in break mode. In order, they are as follows:

➤ **Step Into**—Execute and move to the next statement to execute.

➤ **Step Over**—Similar to Step Into, but won't enter nested blocks of code, including functions.

➤ **Step Out**—Run to the end of the code block and resume break mode at the statement that follows.

To look at every single operation carried out by the application, you can use Step Into to follow the instructions sequentially. This includes moving inside functions, such as Maxima() in the preceding example. Clicking this icon when the cursor reaches line 15, which is the call to Maxima(), results in the cursor moving to the first line inside the Maxima() function. Alternatively, clicking Step Over when you reach line 15 moves the cursor straight to line 16, without going through the code in Maxima() (although this code is still executed). If you do step into a function that you aren't interested in, you can click Step Out to return to the code that called the function. As you step through code, the values of variables are likely to change. If you keep an eye on the monitoring windows just discussed, you can clearly see this happening.

You can also change which line of code will be executed next by right-clicking on a line of code and selecting Set Next Statement, or by dragging the yellow arrow to a different line of code. This doesn't always work, such as when skipping variable initialization. However, it can be very useful for skipping problematic lines of code to see what will happen, or for repeating the execution of code by moving the arrow backward.

In code that has semantic errors, these techniques may be the most useful ones at your disposal. You can step through code right up to the point where you expect problems to occur, and the errors will be generated as if you were running the program normally. Or you can cause statements to be executed more than once by changing the executing code. Along the way, you can watch the data to see just what is going wrong. Later in this chapter, you'll step through some code to find out what is happening in an example application.

## Immediate and Command Windows

The Command and Immediate windows (found on the Debug Windows menu) enable you to execute commands while an application is running. The Command window enables you to perform VS operations manually (such as menu and toolbar operations), and the Immediate window enables you to execute additional code besides the source code lines being executed, and to evaluate expressions.

These windows are intrinsically linked (in fact, earlier versions of VS treated them as the same thing). You can even switch between them by entering commands—immed to move from the Command window to the Immediate window and cmd to move back.

This section concentrates on the Immediate window because the Command window is only really useful for complex operations. The simplest use of this window is to evaluate expressions, a bit like a one-shot use of the Watch windows. To do this, type an expression and press Return. The information requested will then be displayed. An example is shown in Figure 7-15.

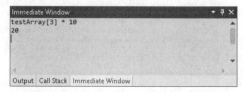

**FIGURE 7-15**

You can also change variable content here, as demonstrated in Figure 7-16.

In most cases, you can get the effects you want more easily using the variable monitoring windows shown earlier, but this technique is still handy for tweaking values, and it's good for testing expressions.

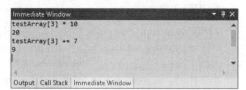

**FIGURE 7-16**

## The Call Stack Window

The final window to look at is the Call Stack window, which shows you the way in which the program reached the current location. In simple terms, this means showing the current function along with the function that called it, the function that called that, and so on (that is, a list of nested function calls). The exact points where calls are made are also recorded.

In the earlier example, entering break mode when in Maxima(), or moving into this function using code stepping, reveals the information shown in Figure 7-17.

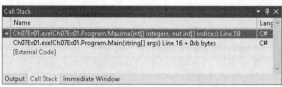

**FIGURE 7-17**

If you double-click an entry, you are taken to the appropriate location, enabling you to track the way code execution has reached the current point. This window is particularly useful when errors are first detected, because you can see what happened immediately before the error. Where errors occur in commonly used functions, this helps you determine the source of the error.

> **NOTE** Sometimes the Call Stack window shows some very confusing information. For example, errors may occur outside of your applications due to using external functions in the wrong way. In such cases, this window could contain a long list of entries, but only one or two might look familiar. You can see external references (should you ever need to) by right-clicking in the window and selecting Show External Code.

# ERROR HANDLING

The first part of this chapter explained how to find and correct errors during application development so that they don't occur in release-level code. Sometimes, however, you know that errors are likely to occur and there is no way to be 100 percent sure that they won't. In those situations, it may be preferable to anticipate problems and write code that is robust enough to deal with these errors gracefully, without interrupting execution.

*Error handling* is the term for all techniques of this nature, and this section looks at exceptions and how you can deal with them. An exception is an error generated either in your code or in a function called by your code that occurs at runtime. The definition of error here is more vague than it has been up until now, because exceptions may be generated manually, in functions and so on. For example, you might generate an exception in a function if one of its string parameters doesn't start with the letter "a." Strictly speaking, this isn't an error outside of the context of the function, although the code that calls the function treats it as an error.

You've seen exceptions a few times already in this book. Perhaps the simplest example is attempting to address an array element that is out of range:

```
int[] myArray = { 1, 2, 3, 4 };
int myElem = myArray[4];
```

This outputs the following exception message and then terminates the application:

```
Index was outside the bounds of the array.
```

> **NOTE** *You've already seen some examples of the exception helper window that is displayed in previous chapters. It has a line connecting it to the offending code and includes links to reference topics in the .NET help files, as well as a View Detail link to more information about the exception.*

Exceptions are defined in namespaces, and most have names that make their purpose clear. In this example, the exception generated is called `System.IndexOutOfRangeException`, which makes sense because you have supplied an index that is not in the range of indices permissible in `myArray`. This message appears, and the application terminates, only when the exception is unhandled. In the next section, you'll see exactly what you have to do to handle an exception.

## try...catch...finally

The C# language includes syntax for *structured exception handling* (SEH). Three keywords mark code as being able to handle exceptions, along with instructions specifying what to do when an exception occurs: `try`, `catch`, and `finally`. Each of these has an associated code block and must be used in consecutive lines of code. The basic structure is as follows:

```
try
{
   ...
}
catch (<exceptionType> e)
{
   ...
}
finally
{
   ...
}
```

It is also possible, however, to have a try block and a finally block with no catch block, or a try block with multiple catch blocks. If one or more catch blocks exist, then the finally block is optional; otherwise, it is mandatory. The usage of the blocks is as follows:

➤ try—Contains code that might throw exceptions ("throw" is the C# way of saying "generate" or "cause" when talking about exceptions).

➤ catch—Contains code to execute when exceptions are thrown. catch blocks can respond only to specific exception types (such as System.IndexOutOfRangeException) using *<exceptionType>*, hence the ability to provide multiple catch blocks. It is also possible to omit this parameter entirely, to get a general catch block that responds to all exceptions.

➤ finally—Contains code that is always executed, either after the try block if no exception occurs, after a catch block if an exception is handled, or just before an unhandled exception moves "up the call stack." This phrase means that SEH allows you to nest try...catch...finally blocks inside one another, either directly or because of a call to a function within a try block. For example, if an exception isn't handled by any catch blocks in the called function, it might be handled by a catch block in the calling code. Eventually, if no catch blocks are matched, then the application will terminate. The fact that the finally block is processed before this happens is the reason for its existence; otherwise, you might just as well place code outside of the try...catch...finally structure. This nested functionality is discussed further in the "Notes on Exception Handling" section a little later, so don't worry if it sounds a little confusing.

Here's the sequence of events that occurs after an exception occurs in code in a try block:

➤ The try block terminates at the point where the exception occurred.

➤ If a catch block exists, then a check is made to determine whether the block matches the type of exception that was thrown. If no catch block exists, then the finally block (which must be present if there are no catch blocks) executes.

➤ If a catch block exists but there is no match, then a check is made for other catch blocks.

➤ If a catch block matches the exception type, then the code it contains executes, and then the finally block executes if it is present.

➤ If no catch blocks match the exception type, then the finally block of code executes if it is present.

The following Try It Out demonstrates handling exceptions. It shows throwing and handling them in several ways so you can see how things work.

**TRY IT OUT** Exception Handling: Ch07Ex02\Program.cs

**1.** Create a new console application called Ch07Ex02 and save it in the directory C:\BegVCSharp\Chapter07.

**2.** Modify the code as follows (the line number comments shown here will help you match up your code to the discussion afterward, and they are duplicated in the downloadable code for this chapter for your convenience):

```
class Program
{
    static string[] eTypes = { "none", "simple", "index", "nested index" };

    static void Main(string[] args)
    {
        foreach (string eType in eTypes)
        {
            try
            {
                Console.WriteLine("Main() try block reached.");          // Line 19
                Console.WriteLine("ThrowException(\"{0}\") called.", eType);
```

```
                ThrowException(eType);
                Console.WriteLine("Main() try block continues.");     // Line 22
            }
            catch (System.IndexOutOfRangeException e)                 // Line 24
            {
                Console.WriteLine("Main() System.IndexOutOfRangeException catch"
                            + " block reached. Message:\n\"{0}\"",
                            e.Message);
            }
            catch                                                     // Line 30
            {
                Console.WriteLine("Main() general catch block reached.");
            }
            finally
            {
                Console.WriteLine("Main() finally block reached.");
            }
            Console.WriteLine();
        }
        Console.ReadKey();
    }

    static void ThrowException(string exceptionType)
    {
        Console.WriteLine("ThrowException(\"{0}\") reached.", exceptionType);
        switch (exceptionType)
        {
            case "none":
              Console.WriteLine("Not throwing an exception.");
              break;                                                 // Line 50
            case "simple":
              Console.WriteLine("Throwing System.Exception.");
              throw new System.Exception();                          // Line 53
            case "index":
              Console.WriteLine("Throwing System.IndexOutOfRangeException.");
              eTypes[4] = "error";                                   // Line 56
              break;
            case "nested index":
              try                                                    // Line 59
              {
                 Console.WriteLine("ThrowException(\"nested index\") " +
                             "try block reached.");
                 Console.WriteLine("ThrowException(\"index\") called.");
                 ThrowException("index");                            // Line 64
              }
              catch                                                  // Line 66
              {
                 Console.WriteLine("ThrowException(\"nested index\") general"
                             + " catch block reached.");
              }
              finally
              {
                 Console.WriteLine("ThrowException(\"nested index\") finally"
                             + " block reached.");
              }
              break;
        }
    }
}
```

**3.** Run the application. The result is shown in Figure 7-18.

**FIGURE 7-18**

*How It Works*

This application has a `try` block in `Main()` that calls a function called `ThrowException()`. This function may throw exceptions, depending on the parameter it is called with:

➤   `ThrowException("none")`—Doesn't throw an exception

➤   `ThrowException("simple")`—Generates a general exception

➤   `ThrowException("index")`—Generates a `System.IndexOutOfRangeException` exception

➤   `ThrowException("nested index")`—Contains its own `try` block, which contains code that calls `ThrowException("index")` to generate a `System.IndexOutOfRangeException` exception

Each of these `string` parameters is held in the global `eTypes` array, which is iterated through in the `Main()` function to call `ThrowException()` once with each possible parameter. During this iteration, various messages are written to the console to indicate what is happening. This code gives you an excellent opportunity to use the code-stepping techniques shown earlier in the chapter. By working your way through the code one line at a time, you can see exactly how code execution progresses.

Add a new breakpoint (with the default properties) to line 19 of the code, which reads as follows:

```
Console.WriteLine("Main() try block reached.");
```

> **NOTE** *Code is referred to by line numbers as they appear in the downloadable version of this code. If you have line numbers turned off, remember that you can turn them back on (select Tools ⇨ Options and then change the Line numbers setting in the Text Editor ⇨ C# ⇨ General options section). Comments are included in the preceding code so that you can follow the text without having the file open in front of you.*

Run the application in debug mode. Almost immediately, the program will enter break mode, with the cursor on line 19. If you select the Locals tab in the variable monitoring window, you should see that `eType` is currently "none". Use the Step Into button to process lines 19 and 20, and confirm that the first line of text has been written to the console. Next, use the Step Into button to step into the `ThrowException()` function on line 21.

Once in the `ThrowException()` function, the Locals window changes. `eType` and `args` are no longer in scope (they are local to `Main()`); instead, you see the local `exceptionType` argument, which is, of course, `"none"`. Keep pressing Step Into and you'll reach the `switch` statement that checks the value of `exceptionType` and executes the code that writes out the string `Not throwing an exception` to the screen. When you execute the `break` statement (on line 50), you exit the function and resume processing in `Main()` at line 22. Because no exception was thrown, the `try` block continues.

Next, processing continues with the `finally` block. Click Step Into a few more times to complete the `finally` block and the first cycle of the `foreach` loop. The next time you reach line 21, `ThrowException()` is called using a different parameter, `"simple"`.

Continue using Step Into through `ThrowException()`, and you'll eventually reach line 53:

```
throw new System.Exception();
```

You use the C# `throw` keyword to generate an exception. This keyword simply needs to be provided with a new-initialized exception as a parameter, and it will throw that exception. Here, you are using another exception from the `System` namespace, `System.Exception`.

> **NOTE** When you use `throw` in a case *block, no* `break;` *statement is necessary.* `throw` *is enough to end execution of the block.*

When you process this statement with Step Into, you find yourself at the general `catch` block starting on line 30. There was no match with the earlier `catch` block starting on line 24, so this one is processed instead. Stepping through this code takes you through this block, through the `finally` block, and back into another loop cycle that calls `ThrowException()` with a new parameter on line 21. This time the parameter is "index".

Now `ThrowException()` generates an exception on line 56:

```
eTypes[4] = "error";
```

The `eTypes` array is global, so you have access to it here. However, here you are attempting to access the fifth element in the array (remember that counting starts at 0), which generates a `System.IndexOutOfRangeException` exception.

This time there is a matched `catch` block in `Main()`, and stepping into the code takes you to this block, starting at line 24. The `Console.WriteLine()` call in this block writes out the message stored in the exception using `e.Message` (you have access to the exception through the parameter of the `catch` block). Again, stepping through takes you through the `finally` block (but not the second `catch` block, as the exception is already handled) and back into the loop cycle, again calling `ThrowException()` on line 21.

When you reach the `switch` structure in `ThrowException()`, this time you enter a new `try` block, starting on line 59. When you reach line 64, you perform a nested call to `ThrowException()`, this time with the parameter "index". You can use the Step Over button to skip the lines of code that are executed here because you've been through them already. As before, this call generates a `System.IndexOutOfRangeException` exception, but this time it's handled in the nested `try...catch...finally` structure, the one in `ThrowException()`. This structure has no explicit match for this type of exception, so the general `catch` block (starting on line 66) deals with it.

As with the earlier exception handling, you now step through this `catch` block and the associated `finally` block, and reach the end of the function call, but with one crucial difference. Although an exception was thrown, it was also handled—by the code in `ThrowException()`. This means there is no exception left to handle in `Main()`, so you go straight to the `finally` block, at which point the application terminates.

## Listing and Configuring Exceptions

The .NET Framework contains a host of exception types, and you are free to throw and handle any of these in your own code. The IDE supplies a dialog box for examining and editing the available exceptions, which can be called up with the Debug ⇨ Exceptions menu item (or by pressing Ctrl+D, E). Figure 7-19 shows the Exceptions dialog box.

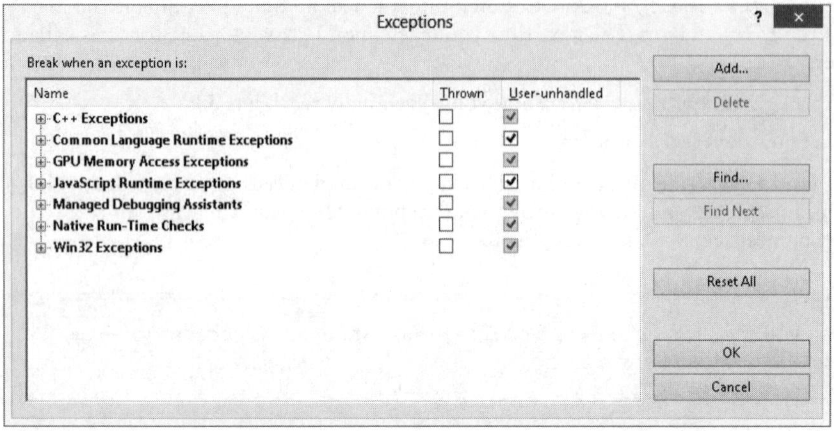

**FIGURE 7-19**

Exceptions are listed by category and .NET library namespace. You can see the exceptions in the System namespace by expanding the Common Language Runtime Exceptions tab, and then the System tab. The list includes the System.IndexOutOfRangeException exception you used earlier.

Each exception may be configured using the check boxes shown. You can use the first option, (break when) Thrown, to cause a break into the debugger even for exceptions that are handled. The second option enables you to ignore unhandled exceptions and suffer the consequences. In most cases, this results in break mode being entered, so you will likely need to do this only in exceptional circumstances.

Typically, the default settings here are fine.

## Notes on Exception Handling

You must always supply catch blocks for more specific exceptions before more general catching. If you get this wrong, the application will fail to compile. Note also that you can throw exceptions from within catch blocks, either in the ways used in the previous example or simply by using the following expression:

```
throw;
```

This expression results in the exception handled by the catch block being rethrown. If you throw an exception in this way, it will not be handled by the current try...catch...finally block, but by parent code (although the finally block in the nested structure will still execute).

For example, if you changed the try...catch...finally block in ThrowException() as follows:

```
try
{
    Console.WriteLine("ThrowException(\"nested index\") " +
                      "try block reached.");
    Console.WriteLine("ThrowException(\"index\") called.");
    ThrowException("index");
}
catch
```

```
        {
            Console.WriteLine("ThrowException(\"nested index\") general"
                + " catch block reached.");
            throw;
        }
        finally
        {
            Console.WriteLine("ThrowException(\"nested index\") finally"
                + " block reached.");
        }
```

Execution would proceed first to the `finally` block shown here, then with the matching `catch` block in `Main()`. The resulting console output changes, as shown in Figure 7-20.

**FIGURE 7-20**

This screenshot shows extra lines of output from the `Main()` function, as the `System.IndexOutOfRangeException` is caught in this function.

## SUMMARY

This chapter concentrates on techniques that you can use to debug your applications. A variety of techniques are possible, most of which are available for whatever type of project you are creating, not just for console applications.

You have now covered everything that you need to produce simple console applications, along with the methods for debugging them. From the next chapter onward, you'll look at the powerful technique of object-oriented programming.

**EXERCISES**

**7.1**  "Using `Trace.WriteLine()` is preferable to using `Debug.WriteLine()`, as the `Debug` version works only in debug builds." Do you agree with this statement? If so, why?

**7.2**  Provide code for a simple application containing a loop that generates an error after 5,000 cycles. Use a breakpoint to enter break mode just before the error is caused on the 5,000th cycle. (Note: A simple way to generate an error is to attempt to access a nonexistent array element, such as `myArray[1000]` in an array with 100 elements.)

**7.3**  "`finally` code blocks execute only if a `catch` block isn't executed." True or false?

**7.4** Given the enumeration data type `orientation` defined in the following code, write an application that uses structured exception handling (SEH) to cast a `byte`-type variable into an `orientation`-type variable in a safe way. (Note: You can force exceptions to be thrown using the `checked` keyword, an example of which is shown here. This code should be used in your application.)

```
enum Orientation : byte
{
    North = 1,
    South = 2,
    East  = 3,
    West  = 4
}
myDirection = checked((Orientation)myByte);
```

Answers to these exercises are in Appendix A.

## ▶ WHAT YOU LEARNED IN THIS CHAPTER

| TOPIC | KEY CONCEPTS |
|---|---|
| **Error types** | Fatal errors cause your application to fail completely, either at compile time (syntax errors) or at runtime. Semantic, or logic, errors are more insidious, and may cause your application to function incorrectly or unpredictably. |
| **Outputting debugging information** | You can write code that outputs helpful information to the Output window to aid debugging in the IDE. You do this with the `Debug` and `Trace` family of functions, where `Debug` functions are ignored in release builds. For production applications, you may want to write debugging output to a log file instead. You can also use tracepoints to output debugging information. |
| **Break mode** | You can enter break mode (essentially a state where the application is paused) manually, through breakpoints, through assertions, or when unhandled exceptions occur. You can add breakpoints anywhere in your code and you can configure breakpoints to break execution only under specific conditions. When in break mode, you can inspect the content of variables (with the help of various debug information windows) and step through code a line at a time to assist you in determining where the errors are. |
| **Exceptions** | Exceptions are errors that occur at runtime and that you can trap and process programmatically to prevent your application from terminating. There are many types of exceptions that can occur when you call functions or manipulate variables. You can also generate exceptions with the `throw` keyword. |
| **Exception handling** | Exceptions that are not handled in your code will cause the application to terminate. You handle exceptions with `try`, `catch`, and `finally` code blocks. `try` blocks mark out a section of code for which exception handling is enabled. `catch` blocks consist of code that is executed only if an exception occurs, and can match specific types of exceptions. You can include multiple `catch` blocks. `finally` blocks specify code that is executed after exception handling has occurred, or after the `try` block finishes if no exception occurs. You can include only a single `finally` block, and if you include any `catch` blocks, then the `finally` block is optional. |

# Introduction to Object-Oriented Programming

At this point in the book, you've covered all the basics of C# syntax and programming, and have learned how to debug your applications. Already, you can assemble usable console applications. However, to access the real power of the C# language and the .NET Framework, you need to make use of *object-oriented programming* (OOP) techniques. In fact, as you will soon see, you've been using these techniques already, although to keep things simple we haven't focused on this.

This chapter steers away from code temporarily and focuses instead on the principles behind OOP. This leads you back into the C# language because it has a symbiotic relationship with OOP. All of the concepts introduced in this chapter are revisited in later chapters, with illustrative code—so don't panic if you don't grasp everything in the first read-through of this material.

To start with, you'll look at the basics of OOP, which include answering that most fundamental of questions, "What is an *object*?" You will quickly find that a lot of terminology related to OOP can be confusing at first, but plenty of explanations are provided. You will also see that using OOP requires you to look at programming in a different way.

As well as discussing the general principles of OOP, this chapter looks at an area requiring a thorough understanding of OOP: desktop applications. This type of application relies on the Windows environment, with features such as menus, buttons, and so on. As such, it provides plenty of scope for description, and you will be able to observe OOP points effectively in the Windows environment.

> **NOTE** OOP as presented in this chapter is really .NET OOP, and some of the techniques presented here don't apply to other OOP environments. When programming in C#, you use .NET-specific OOP, so it makes sense to concentrate on these aspects.

## WHAT IS OBJECT-ORIENTED PROGRAMMING?

Object-oriented programming is a relatively new approach to creating computer applications that seeks to address many of the problems with traditional programming techniques. The type of programming you have seen so far is known as *functional programming* (also known as *procedural programming*), often resulting in so-called monolithic applications, meaning all functionality is contained in a few modules of code (often just one). With OOP techniques, you often use many more modules of code, with each offering specific functionality. Also, each module can be isolated or even completely independent of the others. This modular method of programming gives you much more versatility and provides more opportunity for code reuse.

To illustrate this further, imagine that a high-performance application on your computer is a top-of-the-range race car. Written with traditional programming techniques, this sports car is basically a single unit. If you want to improve this car, then you have to replace the whole unit by sending it back to the manufacturer and getting their expert mechanics to upgrade it, or by buying a new one. If OOP techniques are used, however, you can simply buy a new engine from the manufacturer and follow their instructions to replace it yourself, rather than taking a hacksaw to the bodywork.

In a more traditional application, the flow of execution is often simple and linear. Applications are loaded into memory, begin executing at point A, end at point B, and are then unloaded from memory. Along the way various other entities might be used, such as files on storage media, or the capabilities of a video card, but the main body of the processing occurs in one place. The code along the way is generally concerned with manipulating data through various mathematical and logical means. The methods of manipulation are usually quite simple, using basic types such as integers and Boolean values to build more complex representations of data.

With OOP, things are rarely so linear. Although the same results are achieved, the way of getting there is often very different. OOP techniques are firmly rooted in the structure and meaning of data, and the interaction between that data and other data. This usually means putting more effort into the design stages of a project, but it has the benefit of extensibility. After an agreement is made as to the representation of a specific type of data, that agreement can be worked into later versions of an application, and even entirely new applications. The fact that such an agreement exists can reduce development time dramatically. This explains how the race car example works. The agreement here is how the code for the "engine" is structured, such that new code (for a new engine) can be substituted with ease, rather than requiring a trip back to the manufacturer. It also means that the engine, once created, can be used for other purposes. You could put it in a different car, or use it to power a submarine, for example.

OOP programming often simplifies things by providing an agreement about the approach to data representation, as well as about the structure and usage of more abstract entities. For example, an agreement can be made not just on the format of data that should be used to send output to a device such as a printer, but also on the methods of data exchange with that device, including what instructions it understands, and so on. In the race car analogy, the agreement would include how the engine connects to the fuel tank, how it passes drive power to the wheels, and so on.

As the name of the technology suggests, this is achieved using objects.

## What Is an Object?

An *object* is a building block of an OOP application. This building block encapsulates part of the application, which can be a process, a chunk of data, or a more abstract entity.

In the simplest sense, an object can be very similar to a struct type such as those shown earlier in the book, containing members of variable and function types. The variables contained make up the data stored in the object, and the functions contained allow access to the object's functionality. Slightly more complex objects might not maintain any data; instead, they can represent a process by containing only functions. For example, an object representing a printer might be used, which would have functions enabling control over a printer (so you can print a document, a test page, and so on).

Objects in C# are created from types, just like the variables you've seen already. The type of an object is known by a special name in OOP, its *class*. You can use class definitions to *instantiate* objects, which means creating a real, named *instance* of a class. The phrases *instance of a class* and *object* mean the same thing here; but *class* and *object* mean fundamentally different things.

> **NOTE** *The terms* class *and* object *are often confused, and it is important to understand the distinction. It might help to visualize these terms using the earlier race car analogy. Think of a class as the template for the car, or perhaps the plans used to build the car. The car itself is an instance of those plans, so it could be referred to as an object.*

In this chapter, you work with classes and objects using *Unified Modeling Language* (UML) syntax. UML is designed for modeling applications, from the objects that build them to the operations they perform to the use cases that are expected. Here, you use only the basics of this language, which are explained as you go along. UML is a specialized subject to which entire books are devoted, so its more complex aspects are not covered here.

> **NOTE** *VS has a class viewer that is a powerful tool in its own right that can be used to display classes in a similar way. For simplicity, though, the figures in this chapter were hand drawn.*

Figure 8-1 shows a UML representation of your printer class, called `Printer`. The class name is shown in the top section of this box (you learn about the bottom two sections a little later).

Figure 8-2 shows a UML representation of an instance of this `Printer` class called `myPrinter`.

Here, the instance name is shown first in the top section, followed by the name of its class. The two names are separated by a colon.

**FIGURE 8-1**

## Properties and Fields

Properties and fields provide access to the data contained in an object. This object data differentiates separate objects because it is possible for different objects of the same class to have different values stored in properties and fields.

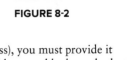

**FIGURE 8-2**

The various pieces of data contained in an object together make up the *state* of that object. Imagine an object class that represents a cup of coffee, called `CupOfCoffee`. When you instantiate this class (that is, create an object of this class), you must provide it with a state for it to be meaningful. In this case, you might use properties and fields to enable the code that uses this object to set the type of coffee used, whether the coffee contains milk and/or sugar, whether the coffee is instant, and so on. A given coffee cup object would then have a given state, such as "Columbian filter coffee with milk and two sugars."

Both fields and properties are typed, so you can store information in them as `string` values, as `int` values, and so on. However, properties differ from fields in that they don't provide direct access to data. Objects can shield users from the nitty-gritty details of their data, which needn't be represented on a one-to-one basis in the properties that exist. If you used a field for the number of sugars in a CupOfCoffee instance, then users could place whatever values they liked in the field, limited only by the limits of the type used to store this information. If, for example, you used an int to store this data, then users could use any value between –2147483648 and 2147483647, as shown in Chapter 3. Obviously, not all values make sense, particularly the negative ones, and some of the large positive amounts might require an inordinately large cup. If you use a property for this information, you could limit this value to, say, a number between 0 and 2.

In general, it is better to provide properties rather than fields for state access because you have more control over various behaviors. This choice doesn't affect code that uses object instances because the syntax for using properties and fields is the same.

Read/write access to properties can also be clearly defined by an object. Certain properties can be read-only, allowing you to see what they are but not change them (at least not directly). This is often a useful technique for reading several pieces of state simultaneously. You might have a read-only property of the CupOfCoffee class called Description, returning a string representing the state of an instance of this class (such as the string given earlier) when requested. You might be able to assemble the same data by interrogating several properties, but a property such as this one might save you time and effort. You might also have write-only properties that operate in a similar way.

As well as this read/write access for properties, you can also specify a different sort of access permission for both fields and properties, known as *accessibility*. Accessibility determines which code can access these members—that is, whether they are available to all code (public), only to code within the class (private), or should use a more complex scheme (covered in more detail later in the chapter, when it becomes pertinent). One common practice is to make fields private and provide access to them via public properties. This means that code within the class has direct access to data stored in the field, while the public property shields external users from this data and prevents them from placing invalid content there. Public members are said to be *exposed* by the class.

One way to visualize this is to equate it with variable scope. Private fields and properties, for example, can be thought of as local to the object that possesses them, whereas the scope of public fields and properties also encompasses code external to the object.

In the UML representation of a class, you use the second section to display properties and fields, as shown in Figure 8-3.

This is a representation of the CupOfCoffee class, with five members (properties or fields, because no distinction is made in UML) defined as discussed earlier. Each of the entries contains the following information:

| **CupOfCoffee** |
| --- |
| +BeanType : string |
| +Instant : bool |
| +Milk : bool |
| +Sugar : byte |
| +Description : string |
| |

**FIGURE 8-3**

➤ Accessibility—A + symbol is used for a public member, a – symbol is used for a private member. In general, though, private members are not shown in the diagrams in this chapter because this information is internal to the class. No information is provided as to read/write access.

➤ The member name.

➤ The type of the member.

A colon is used to separate the member names and types.

## Methods

*Method* is the term used to refer to functions exposed by objects. These can be called in the same way as any other function and can use return values and parameters in the same way—you looked at functions in detail in Chapter 6.

Methods are used to provide access to the object's functionality. Like fields and properties, they can be public or private, restricting access to external code as necessary. They often make use of an object's state to affect their operations, and have access to private members, such as private fields, if required. For example, the CupOfCoffee class might define a method called AddSugar(), which would provide a more readable syntax for incrementing the amount of sugar than setting the corresponding Sugar property.

In UML, class boxes show methods in the third section, as shown in Figure 8-4.

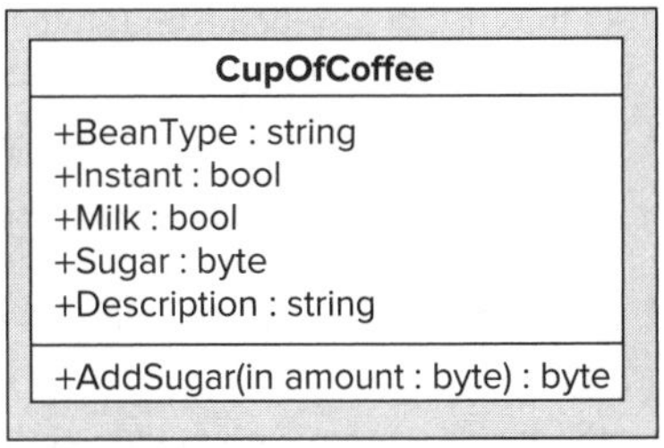

The syntax here is similar to that for fields and properties, except that the type shown at the end is the return type, and method parameters are shown. Each parameter is displayed in UML with one of the following identifiers: in, out, or inout. These are used to signify the direction of data flow, where out and inout roughly correspond to the use of the C# keywords out and ref described in Chapter 6. in roughly corresponds to the default C# behavior, where neither the out nor ref keyword is used.

| **CupOfCoffee** |
| --- |
| +BeanType : string |
| +Instant : bool |
| +Milk : bool |
| +Sugar : byte |
| +Description : string |
| +AddSugar(in amount : byte) : byte |

**FIGURE 8-4**

## Everything's an Object

At this point, it's time to come clean: You have been using objects, properties, and methods throughout this book. In fact, everything in C# and the .NET Framework is an object! The Main() function in a console application is a method of a class. Every variable type you've looked at is a class. Every command you have used has been a property or a method, such as *<String>*.Length, *<String>*.ToUpper(), and so on. (The period character here separates the object instance's name from the property or method name, and methods are shown with () at the end to differentiate them from properties.)

Objects really are everywhere, and the syntax to use them is often very simple. It has certainly been simple enough for you to concentrate on some of the more fundamental aspects of C# up until now. From this point on, you'll begin to look at objects in detail. Bear in mind that the concepts introduced here have far-reaching consequences—applying even to that simple little int variable you've been happily playing around with.

## The Life Cycle of an Object

Every object has a clearly defined life cycle. Apart from the normal state of "being in use," this life cycle includes two important stages:

➤ **Construction**—When an object is first instantiated it needs to be initialized. This initialization is known as *construction* and is carried out by a constructor function, often referred to simply as a *constructor* for convenience.

➤ **Destruction**—When an object is destroyed, there are often some clean-up tasks to perform, such as freeing memory. This is the job of a destructor function, also known as a *destructor*.

### Constructors

Basic initialization of an object is automatic. For example, you don't have to worry about finding the memory to fit a new object into. However, at times you will want to perform additional tasks during an object's initialization stage, such as initializing the data stored by an object. A constructor is what you use to do this.

All class definitions contain at least one constructor. These constructors can include a *default constructor*, which is a parameter-less method with the same name as the class itself. A class definition might also include several constructor methods with parameters, known as *nondefault constructors*. These enable code that instantiates an object to do so in many ways, perhaps providing initial values for data stored in the object.

In C#, constructors are called using the new keyword. For example, you could instantiate a CupOfCoffee object using its default constructor in the following way:

```
CupOfCoffee myCup = new CupOfCoffee();
```

Objects can also be instantiated using nondefault constructors. For example, the `CupOfCoffee` class might have a nondefault constructor that uses a parameter to set the bean type at instantiation:

```
CupOfCoffee myCup = new CupOfCoffee("Blue Mountain");
```

Constructors, like fields, properties, and methods, can be public or private. Code external to a class can't instantiate an object using a private constructor; it must use a public constructor. In this way, you can, for example, force users of your classes to use a nondefault constructor (by making the default constructor private).

Some classes have no public constructors, meaning it is impossible for external code to instantiate them (they are said to be *noncreatable*). However, that doesn't make them completely useless, as you will see shortly.

### Destructors

Destructors are used by the .NET Framework to clean up after objects. In general, you don't have to provide code for a destructor method; instead, the default operation does the work for you. However, you can provide specific instructions if anything important needs to be done before the object instance is deleted.

For example, when a variable goes out of scope, it may not be accessible from your code; however, it might still exist somewhere in your computer's memory. Only when the .NET runtime performs its garbage collection clean-up is the instance completely destroyed.

> **NOTE** *Don't rely on the destructor to free up resources used by an object instance, as this might occur long after the object is of no further use to you. If the resources in use are critical, then this can cause problems. However, there is a solution to this — described in "Disposable Objects" later in this chapter.*

## Static and Instance Class Members

As well as having members such as properties, methods, and fields that are specific to object instances, it is also possible to have *static* (also known as *shared*, particularly to our Visual Basic brethren) members, which can be methods, properties, or fields. Static members are shared between instances of a class, so they can be thought of as global for objects of a given class. Static properties and fields enable you to access data that is independent of any object instances, and static methods enable you to execute commands related to the class type but not specific to object instances. When using static members, in fact, you don't even need to instantiate an object.

For example, the `Console.WriteLine()` and `Convert.ToString()` methods you have been using are static. At no point do you need to instantiate the `Console` or `Convert` classes (indeed, if you try, you'll find that you can't, as the constructors of these classes aren't publicly accessible, as discussed earlier).

There are many situations such as these where static properties and methods can be used to good effect. For example, you might use a static property to keep track of how many instances of a class have been created. In UML syntax, static members of classes appear with underlining, as shown in Figure 8-5.

### Static Constructors

When using static members in a class, you might want to initialize these members beforehand. You can supply a static member with an initial value as part of its declaration, but sometimes you might want to perform a more complex initialization, or perhaps perform some operations before assigning values or allowing static methods to execute.

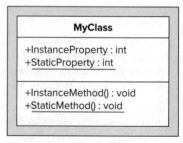

FIGURE 8-5

You can use a static constructor to perform initialization tasks of this type. A class can have a single static constructor, which must have no access modifiers and cannot have any parameters. A static constructor can never be called directly; instead, it is executed when one of the following occurs:

➤ An instance of the class containing the static constructor is created.

➤ A static member of the class containing the static constructor is accessed.

In both cases, the static constructor is called first, before the class is instantiated or static members accessed. No matter how many instances of a class are created, its static constructor will be called only once. To differentiate between static constructors and the constructors described earlier in this chapter, all nonstatic constructors are also known as *instance constructors*.

### Static Classes

Often, you will want to use classes that contain only static members and cannot be used to instantiate objects (such as `Console`). A shorthand way to do this, rather than make the constructors of the class private, is to use a *static class*. A static class can contain only static members and can't have instance constructors, since by implication it can never be instantiated. Static classes can, however, have a static constructor, as described in the preceding section.

> **NOTE** *If you are completely new to OOP, you might like to take a break before embarking on the remainder of this chapter. It is important to fully grasp the fundamentals before learning about the more complicated aspects of this methodology.*

## OOP TECHNIQUES

Now that you know the basics, and what objects are and how they work, you can spend some time looking at some of the other features of objects. This section covers all of the following:

➤ Interfaces

➤ Inheritance

➤ Polymorphism

➤ Relationships between objects

➤ Operator overloading

➤ Events

➤ Reference versus value types

## Interfaces

An *interface* is a collection of public instance (that is, nonstatic) methods and properties that are grouped together to encapsulate specific functionality. After an interface has been defined, you can implement it in a class. This means that the class will then support all of the properties and members specified by the interface.

Interfaces cannot exist on their own. You can't "instantiate an interface" as you can a class. In addition, interfaces cannot contain any code that implements its members; it just defines the members. The implementation must come from classes that implement the interface.

In the earlier coffee example, you might group together many of the more general-purpose properties and methods into an interface, such as `AddSugar()`, `Milk`, `Sugar`, and `Instant`. You could call this interface something like `IHotDrink` (interface names are normally prefixed with a capital I). You could use this interface on other objects, perhaps those of a `CupOfTea` class. You could therefore treat these objects in a similar way, and they can still have their own individual properties (`BeanType` for `CupOfCoffee` and `LeafType` for `CupOfTea`, for example).

Interfaces implemented on objects in UML are shown using *lollipop* syntax. In Figure 8-6, members of `IHotDrink` are split into a separate box using class-like syntax.

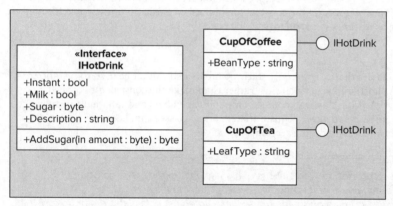

**FIGURE 8-6**

A class can support multiple interfaces, and multiple classes can support the same interface. The concept of an interface, therefore, makes life easier for users and other developers. For example, you might have some code that uses an object with a certain interface. Provided that you don't use other properties and methods of this object, it is possible to replace one object with another (code using the `IHotDrink` interface shown earlier could work with both `CupOfCoffee` and `CupOfTea` instances, for example). In addition, the developer of the object itself could supply you with an updated version of an object, and as long as it supports an interface already in use, it would be easy to use this new version in your code.

Once an interface is published—that is, it has been made available to other developers or end users—it is good practice not to change it. One way of thinking about this is to imagine the interface as a contract between class creators and class consumers. You are effectively saying, "Every class that supports interface X will support these methods and properties." If the interface changes later, perhaps due to an upgrade of the underlying code, this could cause consumers of that interface to run it incorrectly, or even fail. Instead, you should create a new interface that extends the old one, perhaps including a version number, such as X2. This has become the standard way of doing things, and you are likely to come across numbered interfaces frequently.

## Disposable Objects

One interface of particular interest is `IDisposable`. An object that supports the `IDisposable` interface must implement the `Dispose()` method—that is, it must provide code for this method. This method can be called when an object is no longer needed (just before it goes out of scope, for example) and should be used to free up any critical resources that might otherwise linger until the destructor method is called on garbage collection. This gives you more control over the resources used by your objects.

C# enables you to use a structure that makes excellent use of this method. The `using` keyword enables you to initialize an object that uses critical resources in a code block, where `Dispose()` is automatically called at the end of the code block:

OOP Techniques | 165

```
<ClassName> <VariableName> = new <ClassName>();

...


using (<VariableName>)
{
    ...
}
```

Alternatively, you can instantiate the object *<VariableName>* as part of the `using` statement:

```
using (<ClassName> <VariableName> = new <ClassName>())
{
    ...
}
```

In both cases, the variable *<VariableName>* will be usable within the `using` code block and will be disposed of automatically at the end (that is, `Dispose()` is called when the code block finishes executing).

## Inheritance

*Inheritance* is one of the most important features of OOP. Any class may *inherit* from another, which means that it will have all the members of the class from which it inherits. In OOP terminology, the class being inherited from (*derived* from) is the *parent* class (also known as the *base* class). Classes in C# can derive only from a single base class directly, although of course that base class can have a base class of its own, and so on.

Inheritance enables you to extend or create more specific classes from a single, more generic base class. For example, consider a class that represents a farm animal (as used by ace octogenarian developer Old MacDonald in his livestock application). This class might be called `Animal` and possess methods such as `EatFood()` or `Breed()`. You could create a derived class called `Cow`, which would support all of these methods but might also supply its own, such as `Moo()` and `SupplyMilk()`. You could also create another derived class, `Chicken`, with `Cluck()` and `LayEgg()` methods.

In UML, you indicate inheritance using arrows, as shown in Figure 8-7.

> **NOTE** *In Figure 8-7, the member return types are omitted for clarity.*

When using inheritance from a base class, the question of member accessibility becomes an important one. Private members of the base class are not accessible from a derived class, but public members are. However, public members are accessible to both the derived class and external code. Therefore, if you could use only these two levels of accessibility, you couldn't have a member that was accessible both by the base class and the derived class but not external code.

To get around this, there is a third type of accessibility, *protected*, in which only derived classes have access to a member. As far as external code is aware, this is identical to a private member—it doesn't have access in either case.

As well as defining the protection level of a member, you can also define an inheritance behavior for it. Members of a base class can be *virtual*, which means that the member

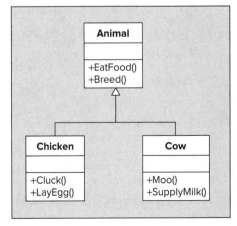

**FIGURE 8-7**

can be overridden by the class that inherits it. Therefore, the derived class can provide an alternative implementation for the member. This alternative implementation doesn't delete the original code, which is still accessible from within the class, but it does shield it from external code. If no alternative is supplied, then any external code that uses the member through the derived class automatically uses the base class implementation of the member.

> **NOTE** *Virtual members cannot be private because that would cause a paradox—it is impossible to say that a member can be overridden by a derived class at the same time you say that it is inaccessible from the derived class.*

In the animals example, you could make EatFood() virtual and provide a new implementation for it on any derived class—for example, just on the Cow class, as shown in Figure 8-8. This displays the EatFood() method on the Animal and Cow classes to signify that they have their own implementations.

Base classes may also be defined as *abstract* classes. An abstract class can't be instantiated directly; to use it you need to inherit from it. Abstract classes can have abstract members, which have no implementation in the base class, so an implementation must be supplied in the derived class. If Animal were an abstract class, then the UML would look as shown in Figure 8-9.

> **NOTE** *Abstract class names are shown in italics (or with a dashed line for their boxes).*

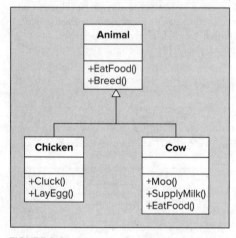

FIGURE 8-8

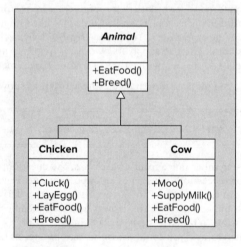

FIGURE 8-9

In Figure 8-9, both EatFood() and Breed() are shown in the derived classes Chicken and Cow, implying that these methods are either abstract (and, therefore, must be overridden in derived classes) or virtual (and, in this case, have been overridden in Chicken and Cow). Of course, abstract base classes can provide implementation of members, which is very common. The fact that you can't instantiate an abstract class doesn't mean you can't encapsulate functionality in it.

Finally, a class may be *sealed*. A sealed class cannot be used as a base class, so no derived classes are possible.

C# provides a common base class for all objects called `object` (which is an alias for the `System.Object` class in the .NET Framework). You take a closer look at this class in Chapter 9.

> **NOTE** *Interfaces, described earlier in this chapter, can also inherit from other interfaces. Unlike classes, interfaces can inherit from multiple base interfaces (in the same way that classes can support multiple interfaces).*

## Polymorphism

One consequence of inheritance is that classes deriving from a base class have an overlap in the methods and properties that they expose. Because of this, it is often possible to treat objects instantiated from classes with a base type in common using identical syntax. For example, if a base class called `Animal` has a method called `EatFood()`, then the syntax for calling this method from the derived classes `Cow` and `Chicken` will be similar:

```
Cow myCow = new Cow();
Chicken myChicken = new Chicken();
myCow.EatFood();
myChicken.EatFood();
```

Polymorphism takes this a step further. You can assign a variable that is of a derived type to a variable of one the base types, as shown here:

```
Animal myAnimal = myCow;
```

No casting is required for this. You can then call methods of the base class through this variable:

```
myAnimal.EatFood();
```

This results in the implementation of `EatFood()` in the derived class being called. Note that you can't call methods defined on the derived class in the same way. The following code won't work:

```
myAnimal.Moo();
```

However, you can cast a base type variable into a derived class variable and call the method of the derived class that way:

```
Cow myNewCow = (Cow)myAnimal;
myNewCow.Moo();
```

This casting causes an exception to be raised if the type of the original variable was anything other than `Cow` or a class derived from `Cow`. There are ways to determine the type of an object, which you'll learn in the next chapter.

Polymorphism is an extremely useful technique for performing tasks with a minimum of code on different objects descending from a single class. It isn't just classes sharing the same parent class that can make use of polymorphism. It is also possible to treat, say, a child and a grandchild class in the same way, as long as there is a common class in their inheritance hierarchy.

As a further note here, remember that in C# all classes derive from the base class `object` at the root of their inheritance hierarchies. It is therefore possible to treat all objects as instances of the class `object`. This is how `Console.WriteLine()` can process an almost infinite number of parameter combinations when building strings. Every parameter after the first is treated as an `object` instance, allowing output from any object to be written to the screen. To do this, the method `ToString()` (a member of `object`) is called. You can override this method to provide an implementation suitable for your class, or simply use the default, which returns the class name (qualified according to any namespaces it is in).

### Interface Polymorphism

Although you can't instantiate interfaces in the same way as objects, you can have a variable of an interface type. You can then use the variable to access methods and properties exposed by this interface on objects that support it.

For example, suppose that instead of an `Animal` base class being used to supply the `EatFood()` method, you place this `EatFood()` method on an interface called `IConsume`. The `Cow` and `Chicken` classes could both support this interface, the only difference being that they are forced to provide an implementation for `EatFood()` because interfaces contain no implementation. You can then access this method using code such as the following:

```
Cow myCow = new Cow();
Chicken myChicken = new Chicken();
IConsume consumeInterface;
consumeInterface = myCow;
consumeInterface.EatFood();
consumeInterface = myChicken;
consumeInterface.EatFood();
```

This provides a simple way for multiple objects to be called in the same manner, and it doesn't rely on a common base class. For example, this interface could be implemented by a class called `VenusFlyTrap` that derives from `Vegetable` instead of `Animal`:

```
VenusFlyTrap myVenusFlyTrap = new VenusFlyTrap();
IConsume consumeInterface;
consumeInterface = myVenusFlyTrap;
consumeInterface.EatFood();
```

In the preceding code snippets, calling `consumeInterface.EatFood()` results in the `EatFood()` method of the `Cow`, `Chicken`, or `VenusFlyTrap` class being called, depending on which instance has been assigned to the interface type variable.

Note here that derived classes inherit the interfaces supported by their base classes. In the first of the preceding examples, it might be that either `Animal` supports `IConsume` or that both `Cow` and `Chicken` support `IConsume`. Remember that classes with a base class in common do not necessarily have interfaces in common, and vice versa.

## Relationships Between Objects

Inheritance is a simple relationship between objects that results in a base class being completely exposed by a derived class, where the derived class can also have some access to the inner workings of its base class (through protected members). There are other situations in which relationships between objects become important.

This section takes a brief look at the following

➤ Containment—One class contains another. This is similar to inheritance but allows the containing class to control access to members of the contained class and even perform additional processing before using members of a contained class.

➤ Collections—One class acts as a container for multiple instances of another class. This is similar to having arrays of objects, but collections have additional functionality, including indexing, sorting, resizing, and more.

### Containment

Containment is simple to achieve by using a member field to hold an object instance. This member field might be public, in which case users of the container object have access to its exposed methods and properties, much like with inheritance. However, you won't have access to the internals of the class via the derived class, as you would with inheritance.

Alternatively, you can make the contained member object a private member. If you do this, then none of its members will be accessible directly by users, even if they are public. Instead, you can provide access to these members using members of the containing class. This means that you have complete control over which members of the contained class to expose, if any, and you can perform additional processing in the containing class members before accessing the contained class members.

For example, a `Cow` class might contain an `Udder` class with the public method `Milk()`. The `Cow` object could call this method as required, perhaps as part of its `SupplyMilk()` method, but these details will not be apparent (or important) to users of the `Cow` object.

Contained classes can be visualized in UML using an association line. For simple containment, you label the ends of the lines with 1s, showing a one-to-one relationship (one `Cow` instance will contain one `Udder` instance). You can also show the contained `Udder` class instance as a private field of the `Cow` class for clarity (see Figure 8-10).

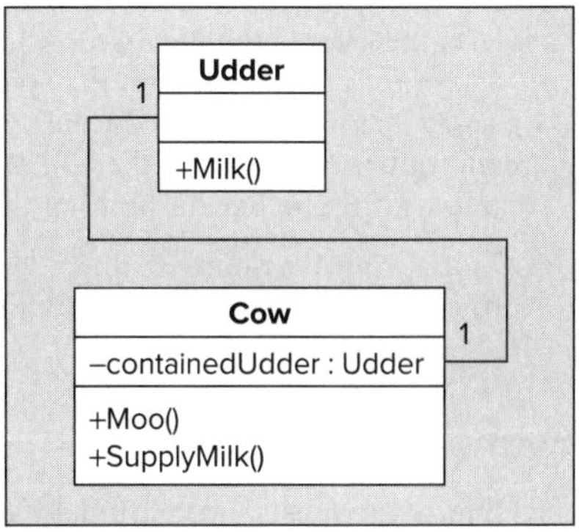

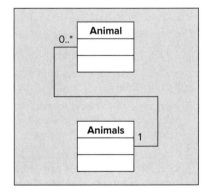

FIGURE 8-10

### Collections

Chapter 5 described how you can use arrays to store multiple variables of the same type. This also works for objects (remember, the variable types you have been using are really objects, so this is no real surprise). Here's an example:

```
Animal[] animals = new Animal[5];
```

A *collection* is basically an array with bells and whistles. Collections are implemented as classes in much the same way as other objects. They are often named in the plural form of the objects they store—for example, a class called `Animals` might contain a collection of `Animal` objects.

The main difference from arrays is that collections usually implement additional functionality, such as `Add()` and `Remove()` methods to add and remove items to and from the collection. There is also usually an `Item` property that returns an object based on its index. More often than not this property is implemented in such a way as to allow more sophisticated access. For example, it would be possible to design `Animals` so that a given `Animal` object could be accessed by its name.

In UML you can visualize this as shown in Figure 8-11.

Members are not included in Figure 8-11 because it's the relationship that is being illustrated. The numbers on the ends of the connecting lines show that one `Animals` object will contain zero or more `Animal` objects. You take a more detailed look at collections in Chapter 11.

## Operator Overloading

Earlier in the book, you saw how operators can be used to manipulate simple variable types. There are times when it is logical to use operators with objects instantiated from your own classes. This is possible because classes can contain instructions regarding how operators should be treated.

FIGURE 8-11

For example, you might add a new property to the `Animal` class called `Weight`. You could then compare animal weights using the following:

```
if (cowA.Weight > cowB.Weight)
{
    ...
}
```

Using operator overloading, you can provide logic that uses the `Weight` property implicitly in your code, so that you can write code such as the following:

```
if (cowA > cowB)
{
    ...
}
```

Here, the greater-than operator (`>`) has been *overloaded*. An overloaded operator is one for which you have written the code to perform the operation involved—this code is added to the class definition of one of the classes that it operates on. In the preceding example, you are using two `Cow` objects, so the operator overload definition is contained in the `Cow` class. You can also overload operators to work with different classes in the same way, where one (or both) of the class definitions contains the code to achieve this.

You can only overload existing C# operators in this way; you can't create new ones. However, you can provide implementations for both unary and binary usages of operators such as `+`. You see how to do this in C# in Chapter 13.

## Events

Objects can raise (and consume) *events* as part of their processing. Events are important occurrences that you can act on in other parts of code, similar to (but more powerful than) exceptions. You might, for example, want some specific code to execute when an `Animal` object is added to an `Animals` collection, where that code isn't part of either the `Animals` class or the code that calls the `Add()` method. To do this, you need to add an *event handler* to your code, which is a special kind of function that is called when the event occurs. You also need to configure this handler to listen for the event you are interested in.

You can create *event-driven applications*, which are far more prolific than you might think. For example, bear in mind that Windows-based applications are entirely dependent on events. Every button click or scroll bar drag you perform is achieved through event handling, as the events are triggered by the mouse or keyboard.

Later in this chapter you will see how this works in Windows applications, and there is a more in-depth discussion of events in Chapter 13.

## Reference Types Versus Value Types

Data in C# is stored in a variable in one of two ways, depending on the type of the variable. This type will fall into one of two categories: reference or value. The difference is as follows:

➤   Value types store themselves and their content in one place in memory.

➤   Reference types hold a reference to somewhere else in memory (called the *heap*) where content is stored.

In fact, you don't have to worry about this too much when using C#. So far, you've used `string` variables (which are reference types) and other simple variables (most of which are value types, such as `int`) in pretty much the same way.

One key difference between value types and reference types is that value types always contain a value, whereas reference types can be `null`, reflecting the fact that they contain no value. It is, however, possible to create a value type that behaves like a reference type in this respect (that is, it can be `null`) by using *nullable types*. These are described in Chapter 12, when you look at the advanced technique of *generic types* (which include nullable types).

The only simple types that are reference types are `string` and `object`, although arrays are implicitly *reference types as well. Every class you create will be a reference type, which is why* this is stressed here.

> **NOTE** The key difference between struct types and classes is that struct types are value types. The fact that struct types and classes are similar might have occurred to you, particularly when you saw, in Chapter 6, how you can use functions in struct types. You learn more about this in Chapter 9.

## OOP IN DESKTOP APPLICATIONS

In Chapter 2, you created a simple desktop application in C# using Windows Presentation Foundation (WPF). WPF desktop applications are heavily dependent on OOP techniques, and this section takes a look at this to illustrate some of the points made in this chapter. The following Try It Out enables you to work through a simple example.

**TRY IT OUT** Objects in Action: Ch08Ex01

1. Create a new WPF application called Ch08Ex01 and save it in the directory `C:\BegVCSharp\Chapter08`.

2. Add a new `Button` control using the Toolbox, and position it in the center of `MainWindow`, as shown in Figure 8-12.

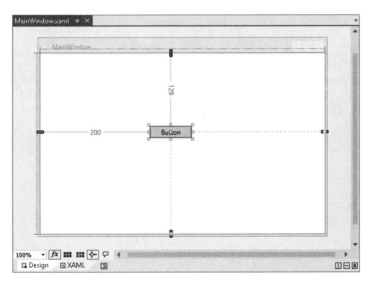

**FIGURE 8-12**

3. Double-click on the button to add code for a mouse click. Modify the code that appears as follows:

```
private void Button_Click_1(object sender, RoutedEventArgs e)
{
    ((Button)sender).Content = "Clicked!";
    Button newButton = new Button();
    newButton.Content = "New Button!";
    newButton.Margin = new Thickness(10, 10, 200, 200);
    newButton.Click += newButton_Click;
```

```
            ((Grid)((Button)sender).Parent).Children.Add(newButton);
    }

    private void newButton_Click(object sender, RoutedEventArgs e)
    {
        ((Button)sender).Content = "Clicked!!";
    }
```

**4.** Run the application. The window is shown in Figure 8-13.

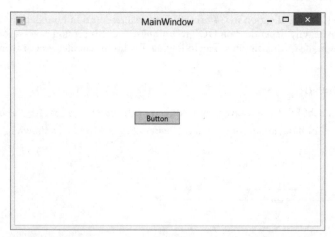

**FIGURE 8-13**

**5.** Click the button marked Button. The display changes (see Figure 8-14).

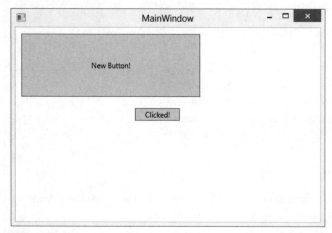

**FIGURE 8-14**

**6.** Click the button marked New Button! The display changes (see Figure 8-15).

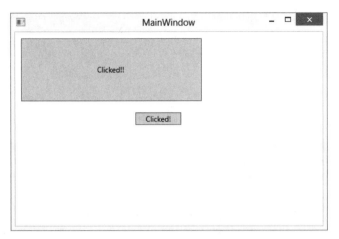

**FIGURE 8-15**

### How It Works

By adding just a few lines of code you've created a desktop application that does something, while at the same time illustrating some OOP techniques in C#. The phrase "everything's an object" is even more true when it comes to desktop applications. From the form that runs to the controls on the form, you need to use OOP techniques all the time. This example highlights some of the concepts you looked at earlier in this chapter to show how everything fits together.

The first thing you do in this application is add a new button to the MainWindow window. The button is an object; it's an instance of a class called Button, and the window is an instance of a class called MainWindow, which is derived from a class called Window. Next, by double-clicking the button, you add an event handler to listen for the Click event that the Button class exposes. The event handler is added to the code for the MainWindow object that encapsulates your application, as a private method:

```
private void Button_Click_1(object sender, RoutedEventArgs e)
{
}
```

The code uses the C# keyword private as a qualifier. Don't worry too much about that for now; the next chapter explains the C# code required for the OOP techniques covered in this chapter.

The first line of code you add changes the text on the button that is clicked. This makes use of polymorphism, described earlier in the chapter. The Button object representing the button that you click is sent to the event handler as an object parameter, which you cast into a Button type (this is possible because the Button object inherits from System.Object, which is the .NET class that object is an alias for). You then change the Content property of the object to change the text displayed:

```
((Button)sender).Content = "Clicked!";
```

Next, you create a new Button object with the new keyword (note that namespaces are set up in this project to enable this simple syntax; otherwise, you need to use the fully qualified name of this object, System.Windows .Forms.Button):

```
Button newButton = new Button();
```

You also set the Content and Margin properties of the newly created Button object to suitable values for displaying the button. Note that the Margin property is of type Thickness, so you create a Thickness object using a non-default constructor before assigning it to the property:

```
newButton.Content = "New Button!";
newButton.Margin = new Thickness(10, 10, 200, 200);
```

Elsewhere in the code a new event handler is added, which you use to respond to the `Click` event generated by the new button:

```
private void newButton_Click(object sender, RoutedEventArgs e)
{
    ((Button)sender).Content = "Clicked!!";
}
```

You register the event handler as a listener for the `Click` event, using overloaded operator syntax:

```
newButton.Click += newButton_Click;
```

Finally, you add the new button to the window. To do this, you find the parent of the existing button (using its `Parent` property), cast it to the correct type (which is `Grid`), and use the `Add()` method of the `Grid.Children` property to add the button, passing the button as a method parameter:

```
((Grid)((Button)sender).Parent).Children.Add(newButton);
```

This code looks more complicated than it actually is. Once you get the hang of the way that WPF represents the content of a window through a hierarchy of controls (including buttons and containers), this sort of thing will become second nature.

This short example used almost all of the techniques introduced in this chapter. As you can see, OOP programming needn't be complicated—it just requires a different point of view to get right.

## SUMMARY

This chapter has presented a full description of object-oriented techniques. You have worked through this in the context of C# programming, but this has mainly been illustrative. The vast majority of this chapter is relevant to OOP in any language.

You first covered the basics, such as what is meant by the term *object* and how an object is an instance of a class. Next, you learned how objects can have various members, such as fields, properties, and methods. These members can have restricted accessibility, and you learned what is meant by public and private members. Later, you saw that members can also be protected, as well as being virtual and abstract (where abstract methods are only permissible for abstract classes). You also learned the difference between static (shared) and instance members, and why you might want to use static classes.

Next, you took a quick look at the life cycle of an object, including how constructors are used in object creation, and how destructors are used in object deletion. Later, after examining groups of members in interfaces, you looked at more advanced object destruction with disposable objects supporting the `IDisposable` interface.

Most of the remainder of the chapter covered the features of OOP, many of which you'll explore in more depth in the chapters that follow. You looked at inheritance, whereby classes inherit from base classes; two versions of polymorphism, through base classes and shared interfaces; and how objects can be used to contain one or more other objects (through containment and collections). Finally, you saw how operator overloading can be used to simplify the syntax of object usage and how objects often raise events.

The last part of this chapter demonstrated much of the theory in this chapter, using a WPF desktop application example. The next chapter looks at defining classes using C#.

**EXERCISES**

**8.1** Which of the following are real levels of accessibility in OOP?

    **a.** Friend

    **b.** Public

    **c.** Secure

    **d.** Private

    **e.** Protected

    **f.** Loose

    **g.** Wildcard

**8.2** "You must call the destructor of an object manually or it will waste memory." True or false?

**8.3** Do you need to create an object to call a static method of its class?

**8.4** Draw a UML diagram similar to the ones shown in this chapter for the following classes and interface:

An abstract class called `HotDrink` that has the methods `Drink`, `AddMilk`, and `AddSugar`, and the properties `Milk` and `Sugar`

An interface called `ICup` that has the methods `Refill` and `Wash`, and the properties `Color` and `Volume`

A class called `CupOfCoffee` that derives from `HotDrink`, supports the `ICup` interface, and has the additional property `BeanType`

A class called `CupOfTea` that derives from `HotDrink`, supports the `ICup` interface, and has the additional property `LeafType`

**8.5** Write some code for a function that will accept either of the two cup objects in the preceding example as a parameter. The function should call the `AddMilk`, `Drink`, and `Wash` methods for any cup object it is passed.

Answers to the exercises can be found in Appendix A.

## ▶ WHAT YOU LEARNED IN THIS CHAPTER

| TOPIC | KEY CONCEPTS |
|---|---|
| **Objects and classes** | Objects are the building blocks of OOP applications. Classes are type definitions that are used to instantiate objects. Objects can contain data and/or expose operations that other code can use. Data can be made available to external code through properties, and operations can be made available to external code through methods. Both properties and methods are referred to as class members. Properties can allow read access, write access, or both. Class members can be public (available to all code), or private (available only to code inside the class definition). In .NET, everything is an object. |
| **Object life cycle** | An object is instantiated by calling one of its constructors. When an object is no longer needed, it is destroyed by executing its destructor. To clean up after an object, it is often necessary to manually dispose of it. |
| **Static and instance members** | Instance members are available only on object instances of a class. Static members are available only through the class definition directly, and are not associated with an instance. |
| **Interfaces** | Interfaces are a collection of public properties and methods that can be implemented on a class. An instance-typed variable can be assigned a value of any object whose class definition implements that interface. Only the interface-defined members are then available through the variable. |
| **Inheritance** | Inheritance is the mechanism through which one class definition can derive from another. A class inherits members from its parent, of which it can have only one. Child classes cannot access private members in its parent, but it is possible to define protected members that are available only within a class or classes that derive from that class. Child classes can override members that are defined as virtual in a parent class. All classes have an inheritance chain that ends in `System.Object`, which has the alias `object` in C#. |
| **Polymorphism** | All objects instantiated from a derived class can be treated as if they were instances of a parent class. |
| **Object relationships and features** | Objects can contain other objects, and can also represent collections of other objects. To manipulate objects in expressions, you often need to define how operators work with objects, through operator overloading. Objects can expose events that are triggered due to some internal process, and client code can respond to events by providing event handlers. |

# Defining Classes

**WHAT YOU WILL LEARN IN THIS CHAPTER**

- ➤ How to define classes and interfaces in C#
- ➤ How to use the keywords that control accessibility and inheritance
- ➤ What the `System.Object` class is and its role in class definitions
- ➤ How to use some helpful tools provided by Visual Studio (VS)
- ➤ How to define class libraries
- ➤ The differences and similarities between interfaces and abstract classes
- ➤ More about struct types
- ➤ Some important information about copying objects

**WROX.COM CODE DOWNLOADS FOR THIS CHAPTER**

You can find the wrox.com code downloads for this chapter at `www.wrox.com/remtitle` `.cgi?isbn=9781118314418` on the Download Code tab. The code is in the Chapter 9 download and individually named according to the names throughout the chapter.

In Chapter 8, you looked at the features of object-oriented programming (OOP). In this chapter, you put theory into practice and define classes in C#. You won't go so far as to define class members in this chapter, but you will concentrate on the class definitions themselves. That might sound a little limiting, but don't worry—there's plenty here to sink your teeth into!

To begin, you explore the basic class definition syntax, the keywords you can use to determine class accessibility and more, and the way in which you can specify inheritance. You also look at interface definitions because they are similar to class definitions in many ways.

The rest of the chapter covers various related topics that apply when defining classes in C#.

## CLASS DEFINITIONS IN C#

C# uses the `class` keyword to define classes:

```
class MyClass
{
    // Class members.
}
```

This code defines a class called `MyClass`. Once you have defined a class, you are free to instantiate it anywhere else in your project that has access to the definition. By default, classes are declared as *internal*, meaning that only code in the current project will have access to them. You can specify this explicitly using the `internal` access modifier keyword as follows (although you don't have to):

```
internal class MyClass
{
    // Class members.
}
```

Alternatively, you can specify that the class is public and should also be accessible to code in other projects. To do so, you use the `public` keyword:

```
public class MyClass
{
    // Class members.
}
```

> **NOTE** Classes declared in their own right like this cannot be private or protected, but you can use these modifiers to declare classes as class members, as shown in the next chapter.

In addition to these two access modifier keywords, you can also specify that the class is either *abstract* (cannot be instantiated, only inherited, and can have abstract members) or *sealed* (cannot be inherited). To do this, you use one of the two mutually exclusive keywords, `abstract` or `sealed`. An abstract class is declared as follows:

```
public abstract class MyClass
{
    // Class members, may be abstract.
}
```

Here, `MyClass` is a public abstract class, while internal abstract classes are also possible.

Sealed classes are declared as follows:

```
public sealed class MyClass
{
    // Class members.
}
```

As with abstract classes, sealed classes can be public or internal.

Inheritance can also be specified in the class definition. You simply put a colon after the class name, followed by the base class name:

```
public class MyClass : MyBase
{
    // Class members.
}
```

Only one base class is permitted in C# class definitions; and if you inherit from an abstract class, you must implement all the abstract members inherited (unless the derived class is also abstract).

The compiler does not allow a derived class to be more accessible than its base class. This means that an internal class can inherit from a public base, but a public class can't inherit from an internal base. This code is legal:

```
public class MyBase
{
    // Class members.
}

internal class MyClass : MyBase
{
    // Class members.
}
```

The following code won't compile:

```
internal class MyBase
{
    // Class members.
}

public class MyClass : MyBase
{
    // Class members.
}
```

If no base class is used, the class inherits only from the base class System.Object (which has the alias object in C#). Ultimately, all classes have System.Object at the root of their inheritance hierarchy. You will take a closer look at this fundamental class a little later.

In addition to specifying base classes in this way, you can also specify interfaces supported after the colon character. If a base class is specified, it must be the first thing after the colon, with interfaces specified afterward. If no base class is specified, you specify the interfaces immediately after the colon. Commas must be used to separate the base class name (if there is one) and the interface names from one another.

For example, you could add an interface to MyClass as follows:

```
public class MyClass : IMyInterface
{
    // Class members.
}
```

All interface members must be implemented in any class that supports the interface, although you can provide an "empty" implementation (with no functional code) if you don't want to do anything with a given interface member, and you can implement interface members as abstract in abstract classes.

The following declaration is invalid because the base class MyBase isn't the first entry in the inheritance list:

```
public class MyClass : IMyInterface, MyBase
{
    // Class members.
}
```

The correct way to specify a base class and an interface is as follows:

```
public class MyClass : MyBase, IMyInterface
{
    // Class members.
}
```

Remember that multiple interfaces are possible, so the following is also valid:

```
public class MyClass : MyBase, IMyInterface, IMySecondInterface
{
    // Class members.
}
```

Table 9-1 shows the allowed access modifier combinations for class definitions.

**TABLE 9-1:** Access Modifiers for Class Definitions

| MODIFIER | DESCRIPTION |
|---|---|
| none or internal | Class is accessible only from within the current project |
| public | Class is accessible from anywhere |
| abstract or internal abstract | Class is accessible only from within the current project, and cannot be instantiated, only derived from |
| public abstract | Class is accessible from anywhere, and cannot be instantiated, only derived from |
| sealed or internal sealed | Class is accessible only from within the current project, and cannot be derived from, only instantiated |
| public sealed | Class is accessible from anywhere, and cannot be derived from, only instantiated |

## Interface Definitions

Interfaces are declared in a similar way to classes, but using the `interface` keyword, rather than `class`:

```
interface IMyInterface
{
    // Interface members.
}
```

The access modifier keywords `public` and `internal` are used in the same way; and as with classes, interfaces are defined as internal by default. To make an interface publicly accessible, you must use the `public` keyword:

```
public interface IMyInterface
{
    // Interface members.
}
```

The keywords `abstract` and `sealed` are not allowed because neither modifier makes sense in the context of interfaces (they contain no implementation, so they can't be instantiated directly, and they must be inheritable to be useful).

Interface inheritance is also specified in a similar way to class inheritance. The main difference here is that multiple base interfaces can be used, as shown here:

```
public interface IMyInterface : IMyBaseInterface, IMyBaseInterface2
{
    // Interface members.
}
```

Interfaces are not classes, and thus do not inherit from `System.Object`. However, the members of `System.Object` are available via an interface type variable, purely for convenience. In addition, as already discussed, it is impossible to instantiate an interface in the same way as a class. The following Try It Out provides an example of some class definitions, along with some code that uses them.

**TRY IT OUT**    Defining Classes: Ch09Ex01\Program.cs

1.  Create a new console application called Ch09Ex01 and save it in the directory C:\BegVCSharp\ Chapter09.

2.  Modify the code in Program.cs as follows:

```
namespace Ch09Ex01
{
    public abstract class MyBase
    {
    }

    internal class MyClass : MyBase
    {
    }

    public interface IMyBaseInterface
    {
    }

    internal interface IMyBaseInterface2
    {
    }

    internal interface IMyInterface : IMyBaseInterface, IMyBaseInterface2
    {
    }

    internal sealed class MyComplexClass : MyClass, IMyInterface
    {
    }

    class Program
    {
        static void Main(string[] args)
        {
            MyComplexClass myObj = new MyComplexClass();
            Console.WriteLine(myObj.ToString());
            Console.ReadKey();
        }
    }
}
```

3.  Execute the project. Figure 9-1 shows the output.

**FIGURE 9-1**

*How It Works*

This project defines classes and interfaces in the inheritance hierarchy shown in Figure 9-2.

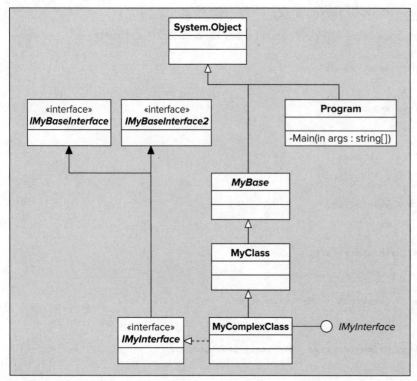

**FIGURE 9-2**

Program is included because it is a class defined in the same way as the other classes, even though it isn't part of the main class hierarchy. The Main() method possessed by this class is the entry point for your application.

MyBase and IMyBaseInterface are public definitions, so they are available from other projects. The other classes and interfaces are internal, and only available in this project.

The code in Main() calls the ToString() method of myObj, an instance of MyComplexClass:

```
MyComplexClass myObj = new MyComplexClass();
Console.WriteLine(myObj.ToString());
```

ToString() is one of the methods inherited from System.Object (not shown in the diagram because members of this class are omitted for clarity) and simply returns the class name of the object as a string, qualified by any relevant namespaces.

This example doesn't do a lot, but you will return to it later in this chapter, where it is used to demonstrate several key concepts and techniques.

## SYSTEM.OBJECT

Because all classes inherit from System.Object, all classes have access to the protected and public members of this class. Therefore, it is worthwhile to take a look at what is available there. System.Object contains the methods described in Table 9-2.

**TABLE 9-2:** Methods of System.Object

| METHOD | RETURN TYPE | VIRTUAL | STATIC | DESCRIPTION |
|---|---|---|---|---|
| Object() | N/A | No | No | Constructor for the System.Object type. Automatically called by constructors of derived types. |
| ~Object() (also known as Finalize()—see the next section) | N/A | No | No | Destructor for the System.Object type. Automatically called by destructors of derived types; cannot be called manually. |
| Equals(object) | bool | Yes | No | Compares the object for which this method is called with another object and returns true if they are equal. The default implementation checks whether the object parameter refers to the same object (because objects are reference types). This method can be overridden if you want to compare objects in a different way, for example, to compare the state of two objects. |
| Equals(object, object) | bool | No | Yes | Compares the two objects passed to it and checks whether they are equal. This check is performed using the Equals(object) method. If both objects are null references, then this method returns true. |
| ReferenceEquals (object, object) | bool | No | Yes | Compares the two objects passed to it and checks whether they are references to the same instance. |
| ToString() | string | Yes | No | Returns a string corresponding to the object instance. By default, this is the qualified name of the class type, but this can be overridden to provide an implementation appropriate to the class type. |
| Memberwise Clone() | object | No | No | Copies the object by creating a new object instance and copying members. This member copying does not result in new instances of these members. Any reference type members of the new object refer to the same objects as the original class. This method is protected, so it can be used only from within the class or from derived classes. |
| GetType() | System .Type | No | No | Returns the type of the object in the form of a System.Type object. |
| GetHashCode() | int | Yes | No | Used as a hash function for objects where this is required. A hash function returns a value identifying the object state in some compressed form. |

These are the basic methods that must be supported by object types in the .NET Framework, although you might never use some of them (or you might use them only in special circumstances, such as GetHashCode()).

GetType() is helpful when you are using polymorphism because it enables you to perform different operations with objects depending on their type, rather than the same operation for all objects, as is often the case. For example, if you have a function that accepts an object type parameter (meaning you can pass it just about anything), you might perform additional tasks if certain objects are encountered. Using a combination of GetType() and typeof (a C# operator that converts a class name into a System.Type object), you can perform comparisons such as the following:

```
if (myObj.GetType() == typeof(MyComplexClass))
{
    // myObj is an instance of the class MyComplexClass.
}
```

The System.Type object returned is capable of a lot more than that, but only this is covered here. It can also be very useful to override the ToString() method, particularly in situations where the contents of an object can be easily represented with a single human-readable string. You see these System.Object methods repeatedly in subsequent chapters, so you'll learn more details as necessary.

## CONSTRUCTORS AND DESTRUCTORS

When you define a class in C#, it's often unnecessary to define associated constructors and destructors because the compiler adds them for you when you build your code if you don't supply them. However, you can provide your own, if required, which enables you to initialize and clean up after your objects, respectively.

You can add a simple constructor to a class using the following syntax:

```
class MyClass
{
    public MyClass()
    {
        // Constructor code.
    }
}
```

This constructor has the same name as the class that contains it, has no parameters (making it the default constructor for the class), and is public so that objects of the class can be instantiated using this constructor (refer to Chapter 8 for more information about this).

You can also use a private default constructor, meaning that object instances of this class cannot be created using this constructor (it is *non-creatable*—again, see the discussion in Chapter 8):

```
class MyClass
{
    private MyClass()
    {
        // Constructor code.
    }
}
```

Finally, you can add nondefault constructors to your class in a similar way, simply by providing parameters:

```
class MyClass
{
    public MyClass()
    {
        // Default constructor code.
    }
```

```
    public MyClass(int myInt)
    {
        // Nondefault constructor code (uses myInt).
    }
}
```

You can supply an unlimited number of constructors (until you run out of memory or out of distinct sets of parameters, so maybe "almost unlimited" is more appropriate).

Destructors are declared using a slightly different syntax. The destructor used in .NET (and supplied by the `System.Object` class) is called `Finalize()`, but this isn't the name you use to declare a destructor. Instead of overriding `Finalize()`, you use the following:

```
class MyClass
{
    MyClass()
    {
        // Destructor body.
    }
}
```

Thus, the destructor of a class is declared by the class name (just as the constructor is), with the tilde (~) prefix. The code in the destructor is executed when garbage collection occurs, enabling you to free resources. After the destructor is called, implicit calls to the destructors of base classes also occur, including a call to `Finalize()` in the `System.Object` root class. This technique enables the .NET Framework to ensure that this occurs, because overriding `Finalize()` would mean that base class calls would need to be explicitly performed, which is potentially dangerous (you learn how to call base class methods in the next chapter).

## Constructor Execution Sequence

If you perform multiple tasks in the constructors of a class, it can be handy to have this code in one place, which has the same benefits as splitting code into functions, as shown in Chapter 6. You could do this using a method (see Chapter 10), but C# provides a nice alternative. You can configure any constructor to call any other constructor before it executes its own code.

First, though, you need to take a closer look at what happens by default when you instantiate a class instance. Apart from facilitating the centralization of initialization code, as noted previously, this is worth knowing about in its own right. During development, objects often don't behave quite as you expect them to due to errors during constructor calling—usually a base class somewhere in the inheritance hierarchy of your class that you are not instantiating correctly, or information that is not being properly supplied to base class constructors. Understanding what happens during this phase of an object's lifecycle can make it much easier to solve this sort of problem.

For a derived class to be instantiated, its base class must be instantiated. For this base class to be instantiated, its own base class must be instantiated, and so on all the way back to `System.Object` (the root of all classes). As a result, whatever constructor you use to instantiate a class, `System.Object.Object()` is always called first.

Regardless of which constructor you use in a derived class (the default constructor or a nondefault constructor), unless you specify otherwise, the default constructor for the base class is used. (You'll see how to change this behavior shortly.) Here's a short example illustrating the sequence of execution. Consider the following object hierarchy:

```
public class MyBaseClass
{
    public MyBaseClass()
    {
    }
```

```
    public MyBaseClass(int i)
    {
    }
}

public class MyDerivedClass : MyBaseClass
{
    public MyDerivedClass()
    {
    }

    public MyDerivedClass(int i)
    {
    }

    public MyDerivedClass(int i, int j)
    {
    }
}
```

You could instantiate `MyDerivedClass` as follows:

```
MyDerivedClass myObj = new MyDerivedClass();
```

In this case, the following sequence of events will occur:

➤   The `System.Object.Object()` constructor will execute.

➤   The `MyBaseClass.MyBaseClass()` constructor will execute.

➤   The `MyDerivedClass.MyDerivedClass()` constructor will execute.

Alternatively, you could use the following:

```
MyDerivedClass myObj = new MyDerivedClass(4);
```

The sequence is as follows:

➤   The `System.Object.Object()` constructor will execute.

➤   The `MyBaseClass.MyBaseClass()` constructor will execute.

➤   The `MyDerivedClass.MyDerivedClass(int i)` constructor will execute.

Finally, you could use this:

```
MyDerivedClass myObj = new MyDerivedClass(4, 8);
```

The result is the following sequence:

➤   The `System.Object.Object()` constructor will execute.

➤   The `MyBaseClass.MyBaseClass()` constructor will execute.

➤   The `MyDerivedClass.MyDerivedClass(int i, int j)` constructor will execute.

This system works fine most of the time, but sometimes you will want a little more control over the events that occur. For example, in the last instantiation example, you might want to have the following sequence:

➤   The `System.Object.Object()` constructor will execute.

➤   The `MyBaseClass.MyBaseClass(int i)` constructor will execute.

➤   The `MyDerivedClass.MyDerivedClass(int i, int j)` constructor will execute.

Using this sequence you could place the code that uses the `int i` parameter in `MyBaseClass(int i)`, which means that the `MyDerivedClass(int i, int j)` constructor would have less work to do—it would only need to process the int j parameter. (This assumes that the int i parameter has an identical meaning in both scenarios, which might not always be the case; but in practice, with this kind of arrangement, it usually is.) C# allows you to specify this kind of behavior if you want.

To do this, you can use a *constructor initializer*, which consists of code placed after a colon in the method definition. For example, you could specify the base class constructor to use in the definition of the constructor in your derived class, as follows:

```
public class MyDerivedClass : MyBaseClass
{
    ...

    public MyDerivedClass(int i, int j) : base(i)
    {
    }
}
```

The base keyword directs the .NET instantiation process to use the base class constructor, which has the specified parameters. Here, you are using a single int parameter (the value of which is the value passed to the MyDerivedClass constructor as the parameter i), so MyBaseClass(int i) will be used. Doing this means that MyBaseClass will not be called, giving you the sequence of events listed prior to this example—exactly what you want here.

You can also use this keyword to specify literal values for base class constructors, perhaps using the default constructor of MyDerivedClass to call a nondefault constructor of MyBaseClass:

```
public class MyDerivedClass : MyBaseClass
{
    public MyDerivedClass() : base(5)
    {
    }

    ...
}
```

This gives you the following sequence:

➤    The System.Object.Object() constructor will execute.

➤    The MyBaseClass.MyBaseClass(int i) constructor will execute.

➤    The MyDerivedClass.MyDerivedClass() constructor will execute.

As well as this base keyword, you can use one more keyword as a constructor initializer: this. This keyword instructs the .NET instantiation process to use a nondefault constructor on the current class before the specified constructor is called:

```
public class MyDerivedClass : MyBaseClass
{
    public MyDerivedClass() : this(5, 6)
    {
    }

    ...

    public MyDerivedClass(int i, int j) : base(i)
    {
    }
}
```

Here, using the MyDerivedClass.MyDerivedClass() constructor gives you the following sequence:

➤    The System.Object.Object() constructor will execute.

➤    The MyBaseClass.MyBaseClass(int i) constructor will execute.

➤ The `MyDerivedClass.MyDerivedClass(int i, int j)` constructor will execute.

➤ The `MyDerivedClass.MyDerivedClass()` constructor will execute.

The only limitation here is that you can specify only a single constructor using a constructor initializer. However, as demonstrated in the last example, this isn't much of a limitation, because you can still construct fairly sophisticated execution sequences.

> **NOTE** *If you don't specify a constructor initializer for a constructor, the compiler adds one for you:* `base()`. *This results in the default behavior described earlier in this section.*

Be careful not to accidentally create an infinite loop when defining constructors. For example, consider this code:

```
public class MyBaseClass
{
    public MyBaseClass() : this(5)
    {
    }

    public MyBaseClass(int i) : this()
    {
    }
}
```

Using either one of these constructors requires the other to execute first, which in turn requires the other to execute first, and so on. This code will compile, but if you try to instantiate `MyBaseClass` you will receive a `SystemOverflowException`.

## OOP TOOLS IN VISUAL STUDIO

Because OOP is such a fundamental aspect of the .NET Framework, several tools are provided by VS to aid development of OOP applications. This section describes some of these.

## The Class View Window

In Chapter 2, you saw that the Solution Explorer window shares space with a window called Class View. This window shows you the class hierarchy of your application and enables you to see at a glance the characteristics of the classes you use. Figure 9-3 shows a view of the example project in the previous Try It Out.

The window is divided into two main sections; the bottom section shows members of types. Note that Figure 9-3 shows the display when all items in the Class View Settings drop-down, at the top of the Class View window, are checked.

Many symbols can be used here, including the ones shown in Table 9-3.

**FIGURE 9-3**

**TABLE 9-3:** Class View Icons

| ICON | MEANING | ICON | MEANING | ICON | MEANING |
|---|---|---|---|---|---|
| C# | Project | 🔧 | Property | ⚡ | Event |
| { } | Namespace | ● | Field | 🗄 | Delegate |
| ⚙ | Class | ▬▬ | Struct | ∎·∎ | Assembly |
| •■O | Interface | ⬚ | Enumeration | | |
| ⬡ | Method | ⬚ | Enumeration item | | |

Some of these are used for type definitions other than classes, such as enumerations and struct types.

Some of the entries can have other symbols placed below them, signifying their access level (no symbol appears for public entries). These are listed in Table 9-4.

**TABLE 9-4:** Additional Class View Icons

| ICON | MEANING | ICON | MEANING | ICON | MEANING |
|---|---|---|---|---|---|
| 🔒 | Private | ★ | Protected | ♥ | Internal |

No symbols are used to denote abstract, sealed, or virtual entries.

As well as being able to look at this information here, you can also access the relevant code for many of these items. Double-clicking on an item, or right-clicking and selecting Go To Definition, takes you straight to the code in your project that defines the item, if it is available. If the code isn't available, such as code in an inaccessible base type (for example, System.Object), you instead have the option to select Browse Definition, which will take you to the Object Browser view (described in the next section).

One other entry that appears in Figure 9-3 is Project References. This enables you to see which assemblies are referenced by your projects, which in this case includes (among others) the core .NET types in mscorlib and System, data access types in System.Data, and XML manipulation types in System.Xml. The references here can be expanded, showing you the namespaces and types contained within these assemblies.

You can find occurrences of types and members in your code by right-clicking on an item and selecting Find All References; a list of search results displays in the Find Symbol Results window, which appears at the bottom of the screen as a tabbed window in the Error List display area. You can also rename items using the Class View window. If you do this, you're given the option to rename references to the item wherever it occurs in your code. This means you have no excuse for spelling mistakes in class names because you can change them as often as you like!

In addition, you can navigate through your code with a view called *Call Hierarchy*, which is accessible from the Class View window through the View Call Hierarchy right-click menu option. This functionality is extremely useful for looking at how class members interact with each other, and you'll look at it in the next chapter.

## The Object Browser

The Object Browser is an expanded version of the Class View window, enabling you to view other classes available to your project, and even external classes. It is entered either automatically (for example, in the situation noted in the last section) or manually via View ⇨ Object Browser. The view appears in the main window, and you can browse it in the same way as the Class View window.

This window provides the same information as Class View but also shows you more of the .NET types. When an item is selected, you also get information about it in a third window, as shown in Figure 9-4.

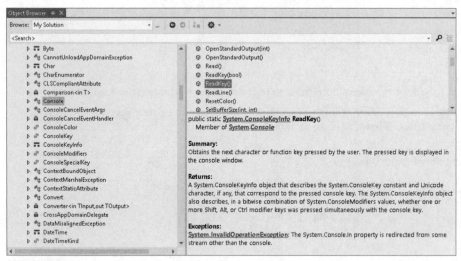

**FIGURE 9-4**

Here, the `ReadKey()` method of the `Console` class has been selected. (`Console` is found in the `System` namespace in the `mscorlib` assembly.) The information window in the bottom-right corner shows you the method signature, the class to which the method belongs, and a summary of the method function. This information can be useful when you are exploring the .NET types, or if you are just refreshing your memory about what a particular class can do.

Additionally, you can make use of this information window in types that you create. Make the following change to the code created previously in Ch09Ex01:

```
/// <summary>
/// This class contains my program!
/// </summary>
class Program
{
    static void Main(string[] args)
    {
        MyComplexClass myObj = new MyComplexClass();
        Console.WriteLine(myObj.ToString());
        Console.ReadKey();
    }
}
```

Return to the Object Browser. The change is reflected in the information window. This is an example of XML documentation, a subject not covered in this book but well worth learning about when you have a spare moment.

**NOTE** *If you made this code change manually, then you noticed that simply typing the three slashes (///) causes the IDE to add most of the rest of the code for you. It automatically analyzes the code to which you are applying XML documentation and builds the basic XML documentation—more evidence, should you need any, that VS is a great tool to work with!*

## Adding Classes

VS contains tools that can speed up some common tasks, and some of these are applicable to OOP. One of these tools, the Add New Item Wizard, enables you to add new classes to your project with a minimum amount of typing.

This tool is accessible through the Project ➪ Add New Item menu item or by right-clicking on your project in the Solution Explorer window and selecting the appropriate item. Either way, a dialog box appears, enabling you to choose the item to add. To add a class, select the Class item in the templates window, as shown in Figure 9-5, provide a filename for the file that will contain the class, and click Add. The class created is named according to the filename you provided.

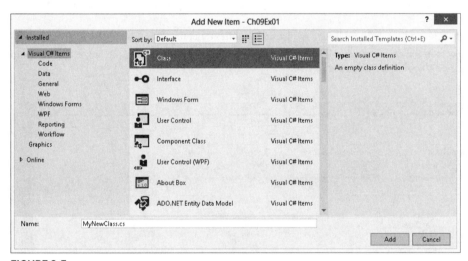

**FIGURE 9-5**

In the Try It Out earlier in this chapter, you added class definitions manually to your `Program.cs` file. Often, keeping classes in separate files makes it easier to keep track of your classes. Entering the information in the Add New Item dialog box when the Ch09Ex01 project is open results in the following code being generated in `MyNewClass.cs`:

```csharp
using System;
using System.Collections.Generic;
using System.Linq;
using System.Text;
using System.Threading.Tasks;

namespace Ch09Ex01
{
    class MyNewClass
    {
    }
}
```

This class, `MyNewClass`, is defined in the same namespace as your entry point class, `Program`, so you can use it from code just as if it were defined in the same file. As shown in the code, the class generated for you contains no constructor. Recall that if a class definition doesn't include a constructor, then the compiler adds a default constructor when you compile your code.

## Class Diagrams

One powerful feature of VS that you haven't looked at yet is the capability to generate class diagrams from code and use them to modify projects. The class diagram editor in VS enables you to generate UML-like diagrams of your code with ease. You'll see this in action in the following Try It Out when you generate a class diagram for the Ch09Ex01 project you created earlier.

**TRY IT OUT** Generating a Class Diagram

1. Open the Ch09Ex01 project created earlier in this chapter.
2. In the Solution Explorer window, right-click the Ch09Ex01 project and then select the View Class Diagram menu item.
3. A class diagram appears, called `ClassDiagram1.cd`.
4. Click the `IMyInterface` lollipop and, using the Properties window, change its `Position` property to `Right`.
5. Right-click `MyBase` and select Show Base Type from the context menu.
6. Move the objects in the drawing around by dragging them to achieve a more pleasing layout. At this point, the diagram should look a little like Figure 9-6.

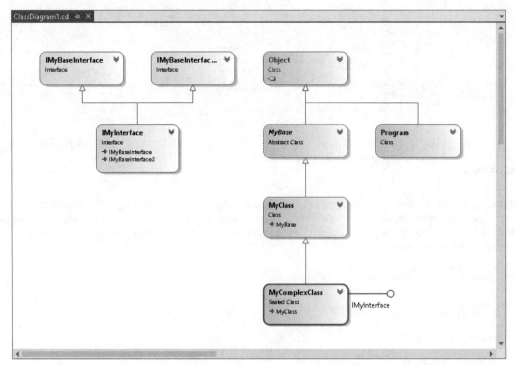

**FIGURE 9-6**

### How It Works

With very little effort, you have created a class diagram not unlike the UML diagram presented in Figure 9-2 (without the color, of course). The following features are evident:

➤ Classes are shown as blue boxes, including their name and type.

➤ Interfaces are shown as green boxes, including their name and type.

➤ Inheritance is shown with arrows with white heads (and in some cases, text inside class boxes).

➤ Classes implementing interfaces have lollipops.

➤ Abstract classes are shown with a dotted outline and italicized name.

➤ Sealed classes are shown with a thick black outline.

Clicking on an object shows you additional information in a Class Details window at the bottom of the screen (right-click an object and select Class Details if this window doesn''t appear). Here, you can see (and modify) class members. You can also modify class details in the Properties window.

> **NOTE** *Chapter 10 takes a detailed look at adding members to classes using the class diagram.*

From the Toolbox, you can add new items such as classes, interfaces, and enums to the diagram, and define relationships between objects in the diagram. When you do this, the code for the new items is automatically generated for you.

Using this editor, you can design whole families of types graphically, without ever having to use the code editor. Obviously, when it comes to actually adding the functionality you have to do things by hand, but this is a great way to get started. You'll return to this view in subsequent chapters and learn more about what it can do for you. For now, though, you can explore things on your own.

## CLASS LIBRARY PROJECTS

As well as placing classes in separate files within your project, you can also place them in completely separate projects. A project that contains nothing but classes (along with other relevant type definitions, but no entry point) is called a *class library*.

Class library projects compile into .dll assemblies, and you can access their contents by adding references to them from other projects (which might be part of the same solution, but don't have to be). This extends the encapsulation that objects provide because class libraries can be revised and updated without touching the projects that use them. That means you can easily upgrade services provided by classes (which might affect multiple consumer applications).

The following Try It Out provides an example of a class library project and a separate project that makes use of the classes that it contains.

**TRY IT OUT** | **Using a Class Library: Ch09ClassLib and Ch09Ex02\Program.cs**

1. Create a new project of type Class Library called Ch09ClassLib and save it in the directory `C:\BegVCSharp\Chapter09`, as shown in Figure 9-7.

2. Rename the file `Class1.cs` to `MyExternalClass.cs` (by right-clicking on the file in the Solution Explorer window and selecting Rename). Click Yes on the dialog box that appears.

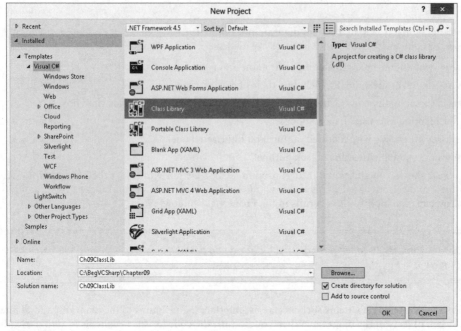

**FIGURE 9-7**

**3.** The code in `MyExternalClass.cs` automatically changes to reflect the class name change:

```
public class MyExternalClass
{
}
```

**4.** Add a new class to the project, using the filename `MyInternalClass.cs`.

**5.** Modify the code to make the class `MyInternalClass` explicitly internal:

```
internal class MyInternalClass
{
}
```

**6.** Compile the project (this project has no entry point, so you can't run it as normal—instead, you can build it by selecting Build ⇨ Build Solution).

**7.** Create a new console application project called Ch09Ex02 and save it in the directory `C:\BegVCSharp\Chapter09`.

**8.** Select Project ⇨ Add Reference, or select the same option after right-clicking References in the Solution Explorer window.

**9.** Click the Browse tab, navigate to `C:\BegVCSharp\Chapter09\Chapter09\Ch09ClassLib\bin\Debug\`, and double-click on `Ch09ClassLib.dll`.

**10.** When the operation completes, confirm that a reference was added in the Solution Explorer window, as shown in Figure 9-8.

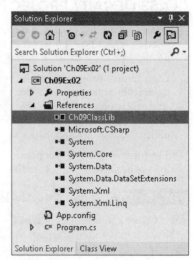

**FIGURE 9-8**

**11.** Open the Object Browser window and examine the new reference to see what objects it contains (see Figure 9-9).

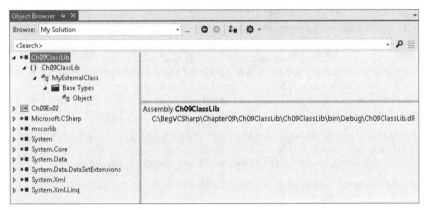

**FIGURE 9-9**

**12.** Modify the code in `Program.cs` as follows:

```
using System;
using System.Collections.Generic;
using System.Linq;
using System.Text;
using System.Threading.Tasks;
using Ch09ClassLib;

namespace Ch09Ex02
{
    class Program
    {
        static void Main(string[] args)
        {
            MyExternalClass myObj = new MyExternalClass();
            Console.WriteLine(myObj.ToString());
            Console.ReadKey();
        }
    }
}
```

**13.** Run the application. The result is shown in Figure 9-10.

**FIGURE 9-10**

### How It Works

This example created two projects: a class library project and a console application project. The class library project, Ch09ClassLib, contains two classes: `MyExternalClass`, which is publicly accessible, and `MyInternalClass`, which is internally accessible. Note that this class was implicitly internal by default when you created it, as it had no access modifier. It is good practice to be explicit about accessibility, though, because it makes your code more readable, which is why you add the `internal` keyword. The console application project, Ch09Ex02, contains simple code that makes use of the class library project.

> **NOTE** *When an application uses classes defined in an external library, you can call that application a client application of the library. Code that uses a class that you define is often similarly referred to as client code.*

To use the classes in Ch09ClassLib, you added a reference to `Ch09ClassLib.dll` to the console application. For the purposes of this example, you simply point at the output file for the class library, although it would be just as easy to copy this file to a location local to Ch09Ex02, enabling you to continue development of the class library without affecting the console application. To replace the old assembly version with the new one, simply copy the newly generated DLL file over the old one.

After adding the reference, you took a look at the available classes using the Object Browser. Because the `MyInternalClass` is internal, you can't see it in this display—it isn't accessible to external projects. However, `MyExternalClass` is accessible, and it's the one you use in the console application.

You could replace the code in the console application with code attempting to use the internal class as follows:

```
static void Main(string[] args)
{
    MyInternalClass myObj = new MyInternalClass();
    Console.WriteLine(myObj.ToString());
    Console.ReadKey();
}
```

If you attempt to compile this code, you receive the following compilation error:

```
'Ch09ClassLib.MyInternalClass' is inaccessible due to its protection level
```

This technique of making use of classes in external assemblies is key to programming with C# and the .NET Framework. It is, in fact, exactly what you are doing when you use any of the classes in the .NET Framework because they are treated in the same way.

## INTERFACES VERSUS ABSTRACT CLASSES

This chapter has demonstrated how you can create both interfaces and abstract classes (without members for now—you get to them in Chapter 10). The two types are similar in a number of ways, so it would be useful to know how to determine when you should use one technique or the other.

First the similarities: both abstract classes and interfaces can contain members that can be inherited by a derived class. Neither interfaces nor abstract classes can be directly instantiated, but it is possible to declare variables of these types. If you do, you can use polymorphism to assign objects that inherit from these types to variables of these types. In both cases, you can then use the members of these types through these variables, although you don't have direct access to the other members of the derived object.

Now the differences: derived classes can only inherit from a single base class, which means that only a single abstract class can be inherited directly (although it is possible for a chain of inheritance to include multiple abstract classes). Conversely, classes can use as many interfaces as they want, but this doesn't make a massive difference—similar results can be achieved either way. It's just that the interface way of doing things is slightly different.

Abstract classes can possess both *abstract members* (these have no code body and must be implemented in the derived class unless the derived class is itself abstract) and *non-abstract members* (these possess a code body, and can be virtual so that they can be overridden in the derived class). *Interface members*, conversely, must be implemented on the class that uses the interface—they do not possess code bodies. Moreover, interface members are by definition public (because they are intended for external use), but members of abstract classes can also be private (as long as they aren't abstract), protected, internal, or protected internal (where protected internal members are accessible only from code within the application or from a derived class). In addition, interfaces can't contain fields, constructors, destructors, static members, or constants.

> **NOTE** *Abstract classes are intended for use as the base class for families of objects that share certain central characteristics, such as a common purpose and structure. Interfaces are intended for use by classes that might differ on a far more fundamental level, but can still do some of the same things.*

For example, consider a family of objects representing trains. The base class, `Train`, contains the core definition of a train, such as wheel gauge and engine type (which could be steam, diesel, and so on). However, this class is abstract because there is no such thing as a "generic" train. To create an "actual" train, you add characteristics specific to that train. For example, you derive classes such as `PassengerTrain`, `FreightTrain`, and `424DoubleBogey`, as shown in Figure 9-11.

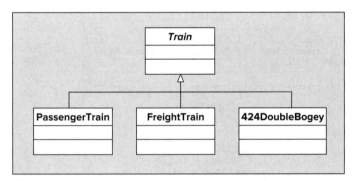

**FIGURE 9-11**

A family of car objects might be defined in the same way, with an abstract base class of `Car` and derived classes such as `Compact`, `SUV`, and `PickUp`. `Car` and `Train` might even derive from a common base class, such as `Vehicle`. This is shown in Figure 9-12.

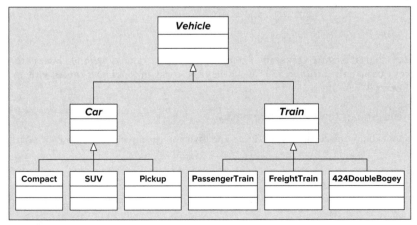

**FIGURE 9-12**

Some of the classes lower in the hierarchy can share characteristics because of their purpose, not just because of what they are derived from. For example, PassengerTrain, Compact, SUV, and Pickup are all capable of carrying passengers, so they might possess an IPassengerCarrier interface. FreightTrain and Pickup can carry heavy loads, so they might both have an IHeavyLoadCarrier interface as well. This is illustrated in Figure 9-13.

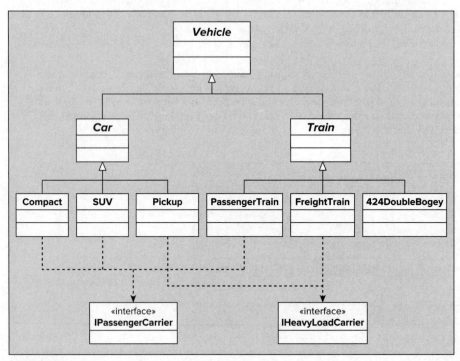

**FIGURE 9-13**

By breaking down an object system in this way before going about assigning specifics, you can clearly see which situations should use abstract classes rather than interfaces, and vice versa. The result of this example couldn't be achieved using only interfaces or only abstract inheritance.

## STRUCT TYPES

Chapter 8 noted that structs and classes are very similar but that structs are value types and classes are reference types. What does this actually mean to you? Well, the easiest way of looking at this is with an example, such as the following Try It Out.

**TRY IT OUT** Classes versus Structs: Ch09Ex03\Program.cs

1. Create a new console application project called Ch09Ex03 and save it in the directory C:\BegVCSharp\ Chapter09.

2. Modify the code as follows:

```
namespace Ch09Ex03
{
    class MyClass
    {
```

```
        public int val;
    }

    struct myStruct
    {
        public int val;
    }

    class Program
    {
        static void Main(string[] args)
        {
            MyClass objectA = new MyClass();
            MyClass objectB = objectA;
            objectA.val = 10;
            objectB.val = 20;
            myStruct structA = new myStruct();
            myStruct structB = structA;
            structA.val = 30;
            structB.val = 40;
            Console.WriteLine("objectA.val = {0}", objectA.val);
            Console.WriteLine("objectB.val = {0}", objectB.val);
            Console.WriteLine("structA.val = {0}", structA.val);
            Console.WriteLine("structB.val = {0}", structB.val);
            Console.ReadKey();
        }
    }
}
```

**3.** Run the application. Figure 9-14 shows the output.

**FIGURE 9-14**

*How It Works*

This application contains two type definitions: one for a struct called `myStruct`, which has a single public `int` field called `val`, and one for a class called `MyClass` that contains an identical field (you look at class members such as fields in Chapter 10; for now just understand that the syntax is the same here). Next, you perform the same operations on instances of both of these types:

**1.** Declare a variable of the type.

**2.** Create a new instance of the type in this variable.

**3.** Declare a second variable of the type.

**4.** Assign the first variable to the second variable.

**5.** Assign a value to the `val` field in the instance in the first variable.

**6.** Assign a value to the `val` field in the instance in the second variable.

**7.** Display the values of the `val` fields for both variables.

Although you are performing the same operations on variables of both types, the outcome is different. When you display the values of the `val` field, both object types have the same value, whereas the struct types have different values. What has happened?

Objects are *reference* types. When you assign an object to a variable you are actually assigning that variable with a *pointer* to the object to which it refers. A pointer, in real code terms, is an address in memory. In this case, the address is the point in memory where the object is found. When you assign the first object reference to the second variable of type `MyClass` with the following line, you are actually copying this address:

```
MyClass objectB = objectA;
```

This means that both variables contain pointers to the same object.

Structs are *value* types. Instead of the variable holding a pointer to the struct, the variable contains the struct itself. When you assign the first struct to the second variable of type `myStruct` with the following line, you are actually copying all the information from one struct to the other:

```
myStruct structB = structA;
```

You saw behavior like this earlier in this book for simple variable types such as `int`. The upshot is that the two struct type variables contain different structs. The entire technique of using pointers is hidden from you in managed C# code, making your code much simpler. It is possible to access lower-level operations such as pointer manipulation in C# using unsafe code, but that is an advanced topic not covered here.

## SHALLOW COPYING VERSUS DEEP COPYING

Copying objects from one variable to another by value instead of by reference (that is, copying them in the same way as structs) can be quite complex. Because a single object can contain references to many other objects, such as field members and so on, a lot of processing can be involved. Simply copying each member from one object to another might not work because some of these members might be reference types in their own right.

The .NET Framework takes this into account. You can create a simple copy of an object where each member is copied to the new object by using the method `MemberwiseClone()`, inherited from `System.Object`. This is a protected method, but it would be easy to define a public method on an object that called this method. This copying method is known as a *shallow copy*, in that it doesn't take reference type members into account. This means that reference members in the new object refer to the same objects as equivalent members in the source object, which isn't ideal in many cases. If you want to create new instances of the members in question by copying the values across (rather than the references), you need to perform a *deep copy*.

There is an interface you can implement that enables you to deep copy in a standard way: `ICloneable`. If you use this interface, then you must implement the single method it contains, `Clone()`. This method returns a value of type `System.Object`. You can use whatever processing you want to obtain this object, by implementing the method body however you choose. That means you can implement a deep copy if you want to, although the exact behavior isn't mandatory, so you could perform a shallow copy if desired. There are no rules or restrictions on what you actually return from this method, so many people recommend avoiding it. Instead, they recommend implementing your own deep-copy method. You take a closer look at this interface in Chapter 11.

## SUMMARY

This chapter showed how you can define classes and interfaces in C#, putting the theory from the last chapter into a more concrete form. You've learned the C# syntax required for basic declarations, as well as the accessibility keywords you can use, the way in which you can inherit from interfaces and other classes, how to define abstract and sealed classes to control this inheritance, and how to define constructors and destructors.

You then looked at `System.Object`, the root base class of any class that you define. It supplies several methods, some of which are virtual, so you can override their implementation. This class also enables you to treat any object instance as an instance of this type, enabling polymorphism with any object.

You also examined some of the tools supplied by VS for OOP development, including the Class View window, the Object Browser window, and a quick way to add new classes to a project. As an extension of this multifile concept, you learned how to create assemblies that can't be executed but that contain class definitions that you can use in other projects.

After that, you took a more detailed look at abstract classes and interfaces, including their similarities and differences, and situations in which you use one or the other.

Finally, you revisited the subject of reference and value types, looking at structs (the value type equivalent of objects) in slightly more detail. This led to a discussion about shallow and deep copying of objects, a subject covered in more detail later in the book.

The next chapter looks at defining class members, such as properties and methods, which enables you to take OOP in C# to the level required to create real applications.

## EXERCISES

**9.1** What is wrong with the following code?

```
public sealed class MyClass
{
    // Class members.
}

public class myDerivedClass : MyClass
{
    // Class members.
}
```

**9.2** How would you define a non-creatable class?

**9.3** Why are non-creatable classes still useful? How do you make use of their capabilities?

**9.4** Write code in a class library project called Vehicles that implements the Vehicle family of objects discussed earlier in this chapter. There are nine objects and two interfaces that require implementation.

**9.5** Create a console application project, Traffic, that references Vehicles.dll (created in Question 4). Include a function called AddPassenger that accepts any object with the IPassengerCarrier interface. To prove that the code works, call this function using instances of each object that supports this interface, calling the ToString method inherited from System.Object on each one and writing the result to the screen.

Answers to the exercises can be found in Appendix A.

▶ **WHAT YOU LEARNED IN THIS CHAPTER**

| TOPIC | KEY CONCEPTS |
| --- | --- |
| **Class and interface definitions** | Classes are defined with the `class` keyword, and interfaces with the `interface` keyword. You can use the `public` and `internal` keywords to define class and interface accessibility, and classes can be defined as `abstract` or `sealed` to control inheritance. Parent classes and interfaces are specified in a comma-separated list after a colon following the class or interface name. Only a single parent class can be specified in a class definition, and it must be the first item in the list. |
| **Constructors and destructors** | Classes come ready-equipped with a default constructor and destructor implementation, and you rarely have to provide your own destructor. You can define constructors with an accessibility, the name of the class, and any required parameters. Constructors of base classes are executed before those of derived classes, and you can control the execution sequence within a class with the `this` and `base` constructor initializer keywords. |
| **Class libraries** | You can create class library projects that only contain class definitions. These projects cannot be executed directly; they must be accessed through client code in an executable application. VS provides various tools for creating, modifying, and examining classes. |
| **Class families** | Classes can be grouped into families that exhibit common behavior or that share common characteristics. You can do this by inheriting from a shared base class (which can be abstract), or by implementing interfaces. |
| **Struct definitions** | A struct is defined in a very similar way to a class, but remember that structs are value types whereas classes are reference types. |
| **Copying objects** | When you make a copy of an object, you must be careful to copy any objects that it might contain, rather than simply copying the references to those objects. Copying references is referred to as shallow copying, whereas a full copy is referred to as a deep copy. You can use the `ICloneable` interface as a framework for providing deep-copy capabilities in a class definition. |

# 10

# Defining Class Members

**WHAT YOU WILL LEARN IN THIS CHAPTER**

- ➤ How to define class members
- ➤ How to use the class diagram to add members
- ➤ How to control class member inheritance
- ➤ How to define nested classes
- ➤ How to implement interfaces
- ➤ How to use partial class definitions
- ➤ How to use the Call Hierarchy window

**WROX.COM CODE DOWNLOADS FOR THIS CHAPTER**

You can find the wrox.com code downloads for this chapter at www.wrox.com/remtitle .cgi?isbn=9781118314418 on the Download Code tab. The code is in the Chapter 10 download and individually named according to the names throughout the chapter.

This chapter continues exploring class definitions in C# by looking at how you define field, property, and method class members. You start by examining the code required for each of these types, and learn how to generate the structure of this code using wizards. You also learn how to modify members quickly by editing their properties.

After covering the basics of member definition, you'll learn some advanced techniques involving members: hiding base class members, calling overridden base class members, nested type definitions, and partial class definitions.

Finally, you put theory into practice by creating a class library that you can build on and use in later chapters.

## MEMBER DEFINITIONS

Within a class definition, you provide definitions for all members of the class, including fields, methods, and properties. All members have their own accessibility levels, defined in all cases by one of the following keywords:

➤ `public`—Members are accessible from any code.

➤ `private`—Members are accessible only from code that is part of the class (the default if no keyword is used).

➤ `internal`—Members are accessible only from code within the assembly (project) where they are defined.

➤ `protected`—Members are accessible only from code that is part of either the class or a derived class.

The last two of these can be combined, so `protected internal` members are also possible. These are only accessible from code-derived classes within the project (more accurately, the assembly).

Fields, methods, and properties can also be declared using the keyword `static`, which means that they are static members owned by the class, rather than by object instances, as discussed in Chapter 8.

## Defining Fields

Fields are defined using standard variable declaration format (with optional initialization), along with the modifiers discussed previously:

```
class MyClass
{
    public int MyInt;
}
```

> **NOTE** Public fields in the .NET Framework are named using PascalCasing, rather than camelCasing, and that's the casing methodology used here. That's why the field in this example is called `MyInt` instead of `myInt`. This is only a suggested casing scheme, but it makes a lot of sense. There is no recommendation for private fields, which are usually named using camelCasing.

Fields can also use the keyword `readonly`, meaning the field can be assigned a value only during constructor execution or by initial assignment:

```
class MyClass
{
    public readonly int MyInt = 17;
}
```

As noted in the chapter introduction, fields can be declared as static using the `static` keyword:

```
class MyClass
{
    public static int MyInt;
}
```

Static fields are accessed via the class that defines them (`MyClass.MyInt` in the preceding example), not through object instances of that class. You can use the keyword `const` to create a constant value. `const` members are static by definition, so you don't need to use the `static` modifier (in fact, it is an error to do so).

## Defining Methods

Methods use standard function format, along with accessibility and optional `static` modifiers, as shown in this example:

```
class MyClass
{
    public string GetString()
    {
        return "Here is a string.";
    }
}
```

> **NOTE** Like public fields, public methods in the .NET Framework are named using PascalCasing.

Remember that if you use the `static` keyword, then this method is accessible only through the class, not the object instance. You can also use the following keywords with method definitions:

➤ `virtual`—The method can be overridden.

➤ `abstract`—The method must be overridden in non-abstract derived classes (only permitted in abstract classes).

➤ `override`—The method overrides a base class method (it must be used if a method is being overridden).

➤ `extern`—The method definition is found elsewhere.

Here's an example of a method override:

```
public class MyBaseClass
{
   public virtual void DoSomething()
   {
      // Base implementation.
   }
}

public class MyDerivedClass : MyBaseClass
{
   public override void DoSomething()
   {
      // Derived class implementation, overrides base implementation.
   }
}
```

If `override` is used, then `sealed` can also be used to specify that no further modifications can be made to this method in derived classes—that is, the method can't be overridden by derived classes. Here is an example:

```
public class MyDerivedClass : MyBaseClass
{
   public override sealed void DoSomething()
   {
      // Derived class implementation, overrides base implementation.
   }
}
```

Using `extern` enables you to provide the implementation of a method externally to the project, but this is an advanced topic not covered here.

## Defining Properties

Properties are defined in a similar way to fields, but there's more to them. Properties, as already discussed, are more involved than fields in that they can perform additional processing before modifying state—and, indeed, might not modify state at all. They achieve this by possessing two function-like blocks: one for getting the value of the property and one for setting the value of the property.

These blocks, also known as *accessors*, are defined using `get` and `set` keywords respectively, and can be used to control the access level of the property. You can omit one or the other of these blocks to create read-only or write-only properties (where omitting the `get` block gives you write-only access, and omitting the `set` block gives you read-only access). Of course, that only applies to external code because code elsewhere within the class will have access to the same data that these code blocks have. You can also include accessibility modifiers on accessors—making a `get` block public while the `set` block is protected, for example. You must include at least one of these blocks to obtain a valid property (and, let's face it, a property you can't read or change wouldn't be very useful).

The basic structure of a property consists of the standard access modifying keyword (`public`, `private`, and so on), followed by a type name, the property name, and one or both of the `get` and `set` blocks that contain the property processing:

```
public int MyIntProp
{
   get
   {
      // Property get code.
   }
   set
   {
      // Property set code.
   }
}
```

> **NOTE** Public properties in .NET are also named using PascalCasing, rather than camelCasing; as with fields and methods, PascalCasing is used here.

The first line of the definition is the bit that is very similar to a field definition. The difference is that there is no semicolon at the end of the line; instead, you have a code block containing nested `get` and `set` blocks.

`get` blocks must have a return value of the type of the property. Simple properties are often associated with a single private field controlling access to that field, in which case the `get` block can return the field's value directly:

```
// Field used by property.
private int myInt;

// Property.
public int MyIntProp
{
   get
   {
      return myInt;
   }
   set
   {
      // Property set code.
   }
}
```

Code external to the class cannot access this `myInt` field directly due to its accessibility level (it is private). Instead, external code must use the property to access the field. The `set` function assigns a value to the field similarly. Here, you can use the keyword `value` to refer to the value received from the user of the property:

```
// Field used by property.
private int myInt;

// Property.
public int MyIntProp
{
   get
   {
      return myInt;
```

```
        }
        set
        {
            myInt = value;
        }
    }
```

`value` equates to a value of the same type as the property, so if the property uses the same type as the field, then you never have to worry about casting in situations like this.

This simple property does little more than shield direct access to the `myInt` field. The real power of properties is apparent when you exert a little more control over the proceedings. For example, you might implement your `set` block as follows:

```
    set
    {
        if (value >= 0 && value <= 10)
            myInt = value;
    }
```

Here, you modify `myInt` only if the value assigned to the property is between 0 and 10. In situations like this, you have an important design choice to make. What should you do if an invalid value is used? You have four options:

➤ Do nothing (as in the preceding code).

➤ Assign a default value to the field.

➤ Continue as if nothing went wrong but log the event for future analysis.

➤ Throw an exception.

In general, the last two options are preferable. Deciding between them depends on how the class will be used and how much control should be assigned to the users of the class. Exception throwing gives users a fair amount of control and lets them know what is going on so that they can respond appropriately. You can use one of the standard exceptions in the `System` namespace for this:

```
    set
    {
        if (value >= 0 && value <= 10)
            myInt = value;
        else
            throw (new ArgumentOutOfRangeException("MyIntProp", value,
                    "MyIntProp must be assigned a value between 0 and 10."));
    }
```

This can be handled using `try...catch...finally` logic in the code that uses the property, as you saw in Chapter 7.

Logging data, perhaps to a text file, can be useful, such as in production code where problems really shouldn't occur. It enables developers to check on performance and perhaps debug existing code if necessary.

Properties can use the `virtual`, `override`, and `abstract` keywords just like methods, something that isn't possible with fields. Finally, as mentioned earlier, accessors can have their own accessibilities, as shown here:

```
    // Field used by property.
    private int myInt;

    // Property.
    public int MyIntProp
    {
        get
        {
            return myInt;
        }
```

```
        protected set
        {
            myInt = value;
        }
    }
```

Here, only code within the class or derived classes can use the set accessor.

The accessibilities that are permitted for accessors depend on the accessibility of the property, and it is forbidden to make an accessor more accessible than the property to which it belongs. This means that a private property cannot contain any accessibility modifiers for its accessors, whereas public properties can use all modifiers on their accessors. The following Try It Out enables you to experiment with defining and using fields, methods, and properties.

**TRY IT OUT**   Using Fields, Methods, and Properties: Ch10Ex01

1. Create a new console application called Ch10Ex01 and save it in the directory C:\BegVCSharp\Chapter10.

2. Add a new class called MyClass, using the Add Class shortcut, which will cause the new class to be defined in a new file called MyClass.cs.

3. Modify the code in MyClass.cs as follows:

```
public class MyClass
{
    public readonly string Name;
    private int intVal;

    public int Val
    {
        get
        {
            return intVal;
        }
        set
        {
            if (value >= 0 && value <= 10)
                intVal = value;
            else
                throw (new ArgumentOutOfRangeException("Val", value,
                    "Val must be assigned a value between 0 and 10."));
        }
    }

    public override string ToString()
    {
        return "Name: " + Name + "\nVal: " + Val;
    }

    private MyClass() : this("Default Name")
    {
    }

    public MyClass(string newName)
    {
        Name = newName;
        intVal = 0;
    }
}
```

4. Modify the code in Program.cs as follows:

```
static void Main(string[] args)
{
    Console.WriteLine("Creating object myObj...");
    MyClass myObj = new MyClass("My Object");
```

```
        Console.WriteLine("myObj created.");
        for (int i = -1; i <= 0; i++)
        {
           try
           {
              Console.WriteLine("\nAttempting to assign {0} to myObj.Val...",
                                i);
              myObj.Val = i;
              Console.WriteLine("Value {0} assigned to myObj.Val.", myObj.Val);
           }
           catch (Exception e)
           {
              Console.WriteLine("Exception {0} thrown.", e.GetType().FullName);
              Console.WriteLine("Message:\n\"{0}\"", e.Message);
           }
        }
        Console.WriteLine("\nOutputting myObj.ToString()...");
        Console.WriteLine(myObj.ToString());
        Console.WriteLine("myObj.ToString() Output.");
        Console.ReadKey();
     }
```

**5.** Run the application. The result is shown in Figure 10-1.

**FIGURE 10-1**

### How It Works

The code in `Main()` creates and uses an instance of the `MyClass` class defined in `MyClass.cs`. The code must instantiate this class by using a nondefault constructor because the default constructor of `MyClass` is private:

```
        private MyClass() : this("Default Name")
        {
        }
```

Using `this("Default Name")` ensures that `Name` gets a value if this constructor is ever called, which is possible if this class is used to derive a new class. This is necessary because not assigning a value to the `Name` field could be a source of errors later.

The nondefault constructor used assigns values to the `readonly` field `Name` (you can only do this by assignment in the field declaration or in a constructor) and the private field `intVal`.

Next, `Main()` attempts two assignments to the `Val` property of `myObj` (the instance of `MyClass`). A `for` loop is used to assign the values -1 and 0 in two cycles, and a `try...catch` structure is used to check for any exception thrown. When -1 is assigned to the property, an exception of type `System.ArgumentOutOfRangeException` is thrown, and code in the `catch` block outputs information about the exception to the console window. In the next loop cycle, the value 0 is successfully assigned to the `Val` property, and through that property to the private `intVal` field.

Finally, you use the overridden `ToString()` method to output a formatted string representing the contents of the object:

```
public override string ToString()
{
    return "Name: " + Name + "\nVal: " + Val;
}
```

This method must be declared using the `override` keyword, because it is overriding the virtual `ToString()` method of the base `System.Object` class. The code here uses the property `Val` directly, rather than the private field `intVal`. There is no reason why you shouldn"t use properties from within classes in this way, although there may be a small performance hit (so small that you are unlikely to notice it). Of course, using the property also gives you the validation inherent in property use, which may be beneficial for code within the class as well.

## Adding Members from a Class Diagram

The last chapter described how you can use the class diagram to explore the classes in a project. You also learned that you can use the class diagram to add members, and this is what you will examine in this section.

All the tools for adding and editing members are shown in the Class Details window in the Class Diagram view. To see this in action, create a class diagram for the `MyClass` class created in Ch10Ex01. You can see the existing members by expanding the view of the class in the class designer (by clicking the icon that looks like two downward-pointing chevrons). The resulting view is shown in Figure 10-2.

Figure 10-3 shows the information you'll see in the Class Details window when a class is selected.

**FIGURE 10-2**

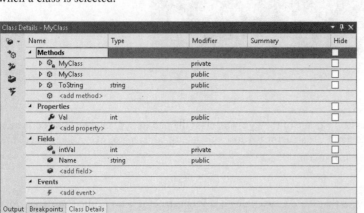

**FIGURE 10-3**

The window shows all the currently defined members for the class and includes spaces so you can add new members simply by typing their names.

### Adding Methods

To add a method to your class, simply type it in the box labeled `<add method>`. After you have named a method, you can use the Tab key to navigate to subsequent settings, starting with the return type of the method, and moving on to the accessibility of the method, summary information (which translates to XML documentation), and whether to hide the method in the class diagram.

Once you have added a method, you can expand the entry and add parameters in the same way. For parameters, you also have the option to use the modifiers out, ref, and params. Figure 10-4 shows an example of a new method.

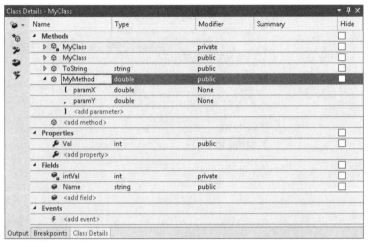

**FIGURE 10-4**

With the new method shown in Figure 10-4, the following code is added to your class:

```
public double MyMethod(double paramX, double paramY)
{
    throw new System.NotImplementedException();
}
```

You can configure other method settings in the Properties window, shown in Figure 10-5.

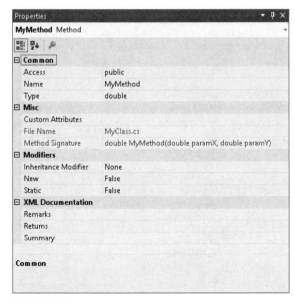

**FIGURE 10-5**

Among other things, you can make the method static here. Obviously, this technique can't provide the method implementation for you, but it does provide the basic structure, and certainly reduces typing errors!

## Adding Properties

Adding properties is achieved in much the same way. Figure 10-6 shows a new property added using the Class Details window.

This adds the property shown here:

```
public int MyInt
{
    get
    {
        throw new System.NotImplementedException();
    }
    Set
    {
    }
}
```

| Class Details | | | | | |
|---|---|---|---|---|---|
| Name | Type | Modifier | Summary | Hide | |
| **Methods** | | | | ☐ | |
| ▷ MyClass | | private | | ☐ | |
| ▷ MyClass | | public | | ☐ | |
| ▷ ToString | string | public | | ☐ | |
| ▷ MyMethod | double | public | | ☐ | |
| \<add method> | | | | | |
| **Properties** | | | | ☐ | |
| Val | int | public | | ☐ | |
| MyInt | int | public | | ■ | |
| \<add property> | | | | | |
| **Fields** | | | | ☐ | |
| intVal | int | private | | ☐ | |
| Name | string | public | | ☐ | |
| \<add field> | | | | | |
| **Events** | | | | | |
| \<add event> | | | | | |

Output | Breakpoints | Class Details

**FIGURE 10-6**

You are left to provide the complete implementation yourself, which includes matching the property with a field for simple properties, removing an accessor if you want the property to be read- or write-only, or applying accessibility modifiers to accessors. However, the basic structure is provided for you.

## Adding Fields

Adding fields is just as simple. Just type the name of the field, choose a type and access modifier, and away you go.

# Refactoring Members

One technique that comes in handy when adding properties is the capability to generate a property from a field. This is an example of *refactoring*, which simply means modifying your code using a tool, rather than by hand. This can be accomplished by right-clicking a member in a class diagram or in code view.

For example, if the MyClass class contained the field,

```
public string myString;
```

you could right-click on the field and select Refactor ⇨ Encapsulate Field. That would bring up the dialog box shown in Figure 10-7.

Accepting the default options modifies the code for MyClass as follows:

```
private string myString;
public string MyString
{
    get
    {
        return myString;
    }
    set
    {
        myString = value;
    }
}
```

**Encapsulate Field**

Field name:

myString

Property name:

MyString

Update references:
- ⦿ External
- ○ All

☑ Preview reference changes
☐ Search in comments
☐ Search in strings

OK    Cancel

**FIGURE 10-7**

Here, the accessibility of the `myString` field has been changed to `private`, and a public property called `MyString` has been created and automatically linked to `myString`. Clearly, reducing the time required to monotonously create properties for fields is a big plus!

## Automatic Properties

Properties are the preferred way to access the state of an object because they shield external code from the implementation of data storage within the object. They also give you greater control over how internal data is accessed, as you have seen several times in this chapter's code. However, you'll typically define properties in a very standard way—that is, you will have a private member that is accessed directly through a public property. The code for this is almost invariably similar to the code in the previous section, which was autogenerated by the VS refactoring tool.

Refactoring certainly speeds things up when it comes to typing, but C# has another trick up its sleeve: automatic properties. With an *automatic property*, you declare a property with a simplified syntax and the C# compiler fills in the blanks for you. Specifically, the compiler declares a private field that is used for storage, and uses that field in the `get` and `set` blocks of your property—without you having to worry about the details.

Use the following code structure to define an automatic property:

```
public int MyIntProp
{
   get;
   set;
}
```

You can even define an automatic property on a single line of code to save space, without making the property much less readable:

```
public int MyIntProp { get; set; }
```

You define the accessibility, type, and name of the property in the usual way, but you don't provide any implementation for the `get` or `set` block. Instead, the compiler provides the implementations of these blocks (and the underlying field).

When you use an automatic property, you only have access to its data through the property, not through its underlying private field. This is because you can't access the private field without knowing its name, which is defined during compilation. However, that's not really a limitation because using the property name directly is fine. The only limitation of automatic properties is that they must include both a `get` and a `set` accessor—you cannot define read- or write-only properties in this way. However, you can change the accessibility of these accessors. For example, this means you can create an externally read-only property as follows:

```
public int MyIntProp { get; private set; }
```

Here you can access the value of `MyIntProp` only from code in the class definition.

## ADDITIONAL CLASS MEMBER TOPICS

Now you're ready to look at some more advanced member topics. This section tackles the following:

➤ Hiding base class methods
➤ Calling overridden or hidden base class methods
➤ Using nested type definitions

## Hiding Base Class Methods

When you inherit a (non-abstract) member from a base class, you also inherit an implementation. If the inherited member is virtual, then you can override this implementation with the `override` keyword.

Regardless of whether the inherited member is virtual, you can, if you want, *hide* the implementation. This is useful when, for example, a public inherited member doesn't work quite as you want it to.

You can do this simply by using code such as the following:

```
public class MyBaseClass
{
    public void DoSomething()
    {
        // Base implementation.
    }
}

public class MyDerivedClass : MyBaseClass
{
    public void DoSomething()
    {
        // Derived class implementation, hides base implementation.
    }
}
```

Although this code works fine, it generates a warning that you are hiding a base class member. That warning gives you the chance to correct it if you have accidentally hidden a member that you want to use. If you really do want to hide the member, you can use the new keyword to explicitly indicate that this is what you want to do:

```
public class MyDerivedClass : MyBaseClass
{
    new public void DoSomething()
    {
        // Derived class implementation, hides base implementation.
    }
}
```

This works in exactly the same way but won't show a warning. At this point, it's worthwhile to note the difference between hiding and overriding base class members. Consider the following code:

```
public class MyBaseClass
{
    public virtual void DoSomething()
    {
        Console.WriteLine("Base imp");
    }
}

public class MyDerivedClass : MyBaseClass
{
    public override void DoSomething()
    {
        Console.WriteLine("Derived imp");
    }
}
```

Here, the overriding method replaces the implementation in the base class, such that the following code uses the new version even though it does so through the base class type (using polymorphism):

```
MyDerivedClass myObj = new MyDerivedClass();
MyBaseClass myBaseObj;
myBaseObj = myObj;
myBaseObj.DoSomething();
```

This results in the following output:

```
Derived imp
```

Alternatively, you could hide the base class method:

```
public class MyBaseClass
{
   public virtual void DoSomething()
   {
      Console.WriteLine("Base imp");
   }
}

public class MyDerivedClass : MyBaseClass
{
   new public void DoSomething()
   {
      Console.WriteLine("Derived imp");
   }
}
```

The base class method needn't be virtual for this to work, but the effect is exactly the same and the preceding code only requires changes to one line. The result for a virtual or nonvirtual base class method is as follows:

```
Base imp
```

Although the base implementation is hidden, you still have access to it through the base class.

## Calling Overridden or Hidden Base Class Methods

Whether you override or hide a member, you still have access to the base class member from the derived class. There are many situations in which this can be useful, such as the following:

➤ When you want to hide an inherited public member from users of a derived class but still want access to its functionality from within the class

➤ When you want to add to the implementation of an inherited virtual member rather than simply replace it with a new overridden implementation

To achieve this, you use the base keyword, which refers to the implementation of the base class contained within a derived class (in a similar way to its use in controlling constructors, as shown in the last chapter):

```
public class MyBaseClass
{
   public virtual void DoSomething()
   {
      // Base implementation.
   }
}

public class MyDerivedClass : MyBaseClass
{
   public override void DoSomething()
   {
      // Derived class implementation, extends base class implementation.
      base.DoSomething();
      // More derived class implementation.
   }
}
```

This code executes the version of DoSomething() contained in MyBaseClass, the base class of MyDerivedClass, from within the version of DoSomething() contained in MyDerivedClass. As base works using object instances, it is an error to use it from within a static member.

### The this Keyword

As well as using `base` in the last chapter, you also used the `this` keyword. As with `base`, `this` can be used from within class members, and, like `base`, `this` refers to an object instance, although it is the current object instance (which means you can't use this keyword in static members because static members are not part of an object instance).

The most useful function of the `this` keyword is the capability to pass a reference to the current object instance to a method, as shown in this example:

```
public void doSomething()
{
    MyTargetClass myObj = new MyTargetClass();
    myObj.DoSomethingWith(this);
}
```

Here, the `MyTargetClass` instance that is instantiated (`myObj`) has a method called `DoSomethingWith()`, which takes a single parameter of a type compatible with the class containing the preceding method. This parameter type might be of this class type, a class type from which this class derives, an interface implemented by the class, or (of course) `System.Object`.

Another common use of the `this` keyword is to use it to qualify local type members, for example:

```
public class MyClass
{
    private int someData;

    public int SomeData
    {
        get
        {
            return this.someData;
        }
    }
}
```

Many developers like this syntax, which can be used with any member type, as it is clear at a glance that you are referring to a member rather than a local variable.

## Using Nested Type Definitions

You can define types such as classes in namespaces, and you can also define them inside other classes. Then you can use the full range of accessibility modifiers for the definition, rather than just `public` and `internal`, and you can use the `new` keyword to hide a type definition inherited from a base class. For example, the following code defining `MyClass` also defines a nested class called `MyNestedClass`:

```
public class MyClass
{
    public class MyNestedClass
    {
        public int NestedClassField;
    }
}
```

To instantiate `MyNestedClass` from outside `MyClass`, you must qualify the name, as shown here:

```
MyClass.MyNestedClass myObj = new MyClass.MyNestedClass();
```

However, you might not be able to do this, for example if the nested class is declared as `private`. One reason for the existence of this feature is to define classes that are private to the containing class so that no other code in the namespace has access to them. Another reason is that nested classes have access to private and protected members of their containing class. The next Try it Out examines this feature.

**TRY IT OUT**  Using Nested Classes: Ch10Ex02

1. Create a new console application called Ch10Ex02 and save it in the directory `C:\BegVCSharp\Chapter10`.

2. Modify the code in `Program.cs` as follows:

```
namespace Ch10Ex02
{
    public class ClassA
    {
        private int state = -1;

        public int State
        {
            get
            {
                return state;
            }
        }

        public class ClassB
        {
            public void SetPrivateState(ClassA target, int newState)
            {
                target.state = newState;
            }
        }
    }

    class Program
    {
        static void Main(string[] args)
        {
            ClassA myObject = new ClassA();
            Console.WriteLine("myObject.State = {0}", myObject.State);
            ClassA.ClassB myOtherObject = new ClassA.ClassB();
            myOtherObject.SetPrivateState(myObject, 999);
            Console.WriteLine("myObject.State = {0}", myObject.State);
            Console.ReadKey();
        }
    }
}
```

3. Run the application. The result is shown in Figure 10-8.

file:///C:/BegVCSharp/Chapter10/Ch10Ex02/Ch10Ex02/bin/Debug/Ch10Ex02.EXE

```
myObject.State = -1
myObject.State = 999
```

**FIGURE 10-8**

*How It Works*

The code in `Main()` creates and uses an instance of `ClassA`, which has a read-only property called `State`. Next, the code creates an instance of the nested class `ClassA.ClassB`. This class has access to the backing field for `ClassA.State`, which is the `ClassA.state` field, even though the field is private. Because of this, the nested class method `SetPrivateState()` can change the value of the read-only `State` property of `ClassA`.

It is important to reiterate that this is possible only because `ClassB` is defined as a nested class of `ClassA`. If you were to move the definition of `ClassB` outside of `ClassA`, then the code wouldn't compile due to this error:

```
'Ch10Ex02.ClassA.state' is inaccessible due to its protection level.
```

Being able to expose the internal state of your classes to nested classes can be extremely useful in some circumstances. However, most of the time it's enough simply to manipulate the internal state through methods that your class exposes.

## INTERFACE IMPLEMENTATION

Before moving on, this section takes a closer look at how you go about defining and implementing interfaces. In the last chapter, you learned that interfaces are defined in a similar way as classes, using code such as the following:

```
interface IMyInterface
{
    // Interface members.
}
```

Interface members are defined like class members except for a few important differences:

➤ No access modifiers (`public`, `private`, `protected`, or `internal`) are allowed—all interface members are implicitly public.

➤ Interface members can't contain code bodies.

➤ Interfaces can't define field members.

➤ Interface members can't be defined using the keywords `static`, `virtual`, `abstract`, or `sealed`.

➤ Type definition members are forbidden.

You can, however, define members using the `new` keyword if you want to hide members inherited from base interfaces:

```
interface IMyBaseInterface
{
    void DoSomething();
}

interface IMyDerivedInterface : IMyBaseInterface
{
    new void DoSomething();
}
```

This works exactly the same way as hiding inherited class members.

Properties defined in interfaces define either or both of the access blocks—`get` and `set`—which are permitted for the property, as shown here:

```
interface IMyInterface
{
    int MyInt { get; set; }
}
```

Here the `int` property `MyInt` has both `get` and `set` accessors. Either of these can be omitted for a property with more restricted access.

> **NOTE** *This syntax is similar to automatic properties, but remember that automatic properties are defined for classes, not interfaces, and that automatic properties must have both* get *and* set *accessors.*

Interfaces do not specify how the property data should be stored. Interfaces cannot specify fields, for example, that might be used to store property data. Finally, interfaces, like classes, can be defined as members of classes (but not as members of other interfaces because interfaces cannot contain type definitions).

## Implementing Interfaces in Classes

A class that implements an interface must contain implementations for all members of that interface, which must match the signatures specified (including matching the specified `get` and `set` blocks), and must be public, as shown here:

```
public interface IMyInterface
{
    void DoSomething();
    void DoSomethingElse();
}

public class MyClass : IMyInterface
{
    public void DoSomething()
    {
    }

    public void DoSomethingElse()
    {
    }
}
```

It is possible to implement interface members using the keyword `virtual` or `abstract`, but not `static` or `const`. Interface members can also be implemented on base classes:

```
public interface IMyInterface
{
    void DoSomething();
    void DoSomethingElse();
}

public class MyBaseClass
{
    public void DoSomething()
    {
    }
}

public class MyDerivedClass : MyBaseClass, IMyInterface
{
    public void DoSomethingElse()
    {
    }
}
```

Inheriting from a base class that implements a given interface means that the interface is implicitly supported by the derived class. Here's an example:

```
public interface IMyInterface
{
    void DoSomething();
    void DoSomethingElse();
}

public class MyBaseClass : IMyInterface
{
    public virtual void DoSomething()
    {
    }

    public virtual void DoSomethingElse()
    {
```

```
        }
    }

    public class MyDerivedClass : MyBaseClass
    {
        public override void DoSomething()
        {
        }
    }
```

Clearly, it is useful to define implementations in base classes as virtual so that derived classes can replace the implementation, rather than hide it. If you were to hide a base class member using the new keyword, rather than override it in this way, the method IMyInterface.DoSomething() would always refer to the base class version even if the derived class were being accessed via the interface.

## Explicit Interface Member Implementation

Interface members can also be implemented *explicitly* by a class. If you do that, the member can only be accessed through the interface, not the class. *Implicit* members, which you used in the code in the last section, can be accessed either way.

For example, if the class MyClass implemented the DoSomething() method of IMyInterface implicitly, as in the preceding example, then the following code would be valid:

```
MyClass myObj = new MyClass();
myObj.DoSomething();
```

This would also be valid:

```
MyClass myObj = new MyClass();
IMyInterface myInt = myObj;
myInt.DoSomething();
```

Alternatively, if MyDerivedClass implements DoSomething() explicitly, then only the latter technique is permitted. The code for doing that is as follows:

```
public class MyClass : IMyInterface
{
    void IMyInterface.DoSomething()
    {
    }

    public void DoSomethingElse()
    {
    }
}
```

Here, DoSomething() is implemented explicitly, and DoSomethingElse() implicitly. Only the latter is accessible directly through an object instance of MyClass.

## Additional Property Accessors

Earlier you learned that if you implement an interface with a property, you must implement matching get/set accessors. That isn't strictly true—it is possible to add a get block to a property in a class in which the interface defining that property only contains a set block, and vice versa. However, this is possible only if you implement the interface implicitly. Also, in most cases you will want to add the accessor with an accessibility modifier that is more restrictive than the accessibility modifier on the accessor defined in the interface. Because the accessor defined by the interface is, by definition, public, this means that you would add nonpublic accessors. Here's an example:

```
public interface IMyInterface
{
   int MyIntProperty
   {
      get;
   }
}

public class MyBaseClass : IMyInterface
{
   public int MyIntProperty { get; protected set; }
}
```

If you define the additional accessor as public, then code with access to the class implementing the interface can access it. However, code that has access only to the interface won't be able to access it.

## PARTIAL CLASS DEFINITIONS

When you create classes with a lot of members of one type or another, the code can get quite confusing, and code files can get very long. One technique that can help, which you've looked at in earlier chapters, is to use code outlining. By defining regions in code, you can collapse and expand sections to make the code easier to read. For example, you might have a class defined as follows:

```
public class MyClass
{
   #region Fields
   private int myInt;
   #endregion

   #region Constructor
   public MyClass()
   {
      myInt = 99;
   }
   #endregion

   #region Properties
   public int MyInt
   {
      get
      {
         return myInt;
      }
      set
      {
         myInt = value;
      }
   }
   #endregion

   #region Methods
   public void DoSomething()
   {
      // Do something..
   }
   #endregion
}
```

Here, you can expand and contract fields, properties, the constructor, and methods for the class, enabling you to focus only on what you are interested in. It is even possible to nest regions this way, so some regions are visible only when the region that contains them is expanded.

However, even using this technique, things can still get out of hand (and many developers find regions very annoying). One alternative is to use *partial class definitions*. Put simply, you use partial class definitions to split the definition of a class across multiple files. You can, for example, put the fields, properties, and constructor in one file, and the methods in another. To do that, you just use the `partial` keyword with the class in each file that contains part of the definition, as follows:

```
public partial class MyClass
{
    ...
}
```

If you use partial class definitions, the `partial` keyword must appear in this position in every file containing part of the definition.

For example, a WPF window in a class called `MainWindow` has code stored in both `MainWindow.xaml.cs` and `MainWindow.g.i.cs` (visible if Show All Files is selected in the Solution Explorer window if you drill down into `obj\Debug` folder). This enables you to concentrate on the functionality of your forms, without worrying about your code being cluttered with information that doesn't really interest you.

One final note about partial classes: Interfaces applied to one partial class part apply to the whole class, meaning that the definition,

```
public partial class MyClass : IMyInterface1
{
    ...
}

public partial class MyClass : IMyInterface2
{
    ...
}
```

is equivalent to:

```
public class MyClass : IMyInterface1, IMyInterface2
{
    ...
}
```

Partial class definitions can include a base class in a single partial class definition, or more than one partial class definition. If a base class is specified in more than one definition, though, it must be the *same* base class; recall that classes in C# can inherit only from a single base class.

## PARTIAL METHOD DEFINITIONS

Partial classes can also define partial methods. Partial methods are defined in one partial class definition without a method body, and implemented in another partial class definition. In both places, the `partial` keyword is used:

```
public partial class MyClass
{
    partial void MyPartialMethod();
}

public partial class MyClass
{
    partial void MyPartialMethod()
```

```
        {
            // Method implementation
        }
    }
```

Partial methods can also be static, but they are always private and can't have a return value. Any parameters they use can't be out parameters, although they can be `ref` parameters. They also can't use the `virtual`, `abstract`, `override`, `new`, `sealed`, or `extern` modifiers.

Given these limitations, it is not immediately obvious what purpose partial methods fulfill. In fact, they are important when it comes to code compilation, rather than usage. Consider the following code:

```
public partial class MyClass
{
    partial void DoSomethingElse();

    public void DoSomething()
    {
        Console.WriteLine("DoSomething() execution started.");
        DoSomethingElse();
        Console.WriteLine("DoSomething() execution finished.");
    }
}

public partial class MyClass
{
    partial void DoSomethingElse()
    {
        Console.WriteLine("DoSomethingElse() called.");
    }
}
```

Here, the partial method `DoSomethingElse()` is defined and called in the first partial class definition, and implemented in the second. The output, when `DoSomething()` is called from a console application, is what you might expect:

```
DoSomething() execution started.
DoSomethingElse() called.
DoSomething() execution finished.
```

If you were to remove the second partial class definition or partial method implementation entirely (or comment out the code), the output would be as follows:

```
DoSomething() execution started.
DoSomething() execution finished.
```

You might assume that what is happening here is that when the call to `DoSomethingElse()` is made, the runtime discovers that the method has no implementation and therefore continues executing the next line of code. What actually happens is a little subtler. When you compile code that contains a partial method definition without an implementation, the compiler actually removes the method entirely. It also removes any calls to the method. When you execute the code, no check is made for an implementation because there is no call to check. This results in a slight—but nevertheless significant—improvement in performance.

As with partial classes, partial methods are useful when it comes to customizing autogenerated or designer-created code. The designer may declare partial methods that you can choose to implement or not depending on the situation. If you don't implement them, you incur no performance hit because effectively the method does not exist in the compiled code.

Consider at this point why partial methods can't have a return type. If you can answer that to your own satisfaction, you can be sure that you fully understand this topic—so that is left as an exercise for you.

## EXAMPLE APPLICATION

To illustrate some of the techniques you've been using so far, in this section you'll develop a class module that you can build on and make use of in subsequent chapters. The class module contains two classes:

➤ Card—Representing a standard playing card, with a suit of club, diamond, heart, or spade, and a rank that lies between ace and king

➤ Deck—Representing a full deck of 52 cards, with access to cards by position in the deck and the capability to shuffle the deck

You'll also develop a simple client to ensure that things are working, but you won't use the deck in a full card game application—yet.

## Planning the Application

The class library for this application, Ch10CardLib, will contain your classes. Before you get down to any code, though, you should plan the required structure and functionality of your classes.

### The Card Class

The Card class is basically a container for two read-only fields: suit and rank. The reason for making the fields read-only is that it doesn't make sense to have a "blank" card, and cards shouldn't be able to change once they have been created. To facilitate this, you'll make the default constructor private, and provide an alternative constructor that builds a card from a supplied suit and rank.

Other than that, the Card class will override the ToString() method of System.Object, so that you can easily obtain a human-readable string representing the card. To make things a little simpler, you'll provide enumerations for the two fields suit and rank.

The Card class is shown in Figure 10-9.

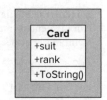

**FIGURE 10-9**

### The Deck Class

The Deck class will maintain 52 Card objects. You can use a simple array type for this. The array won't be directly accessible because access to the Card object is achieved through a GetCard() method, which returns the Card object with the given index. This class should also expose a Shuffle() method to rearrange the cards in the array. The Deck class is shown in Figure 10-10.

## Writing the Class Library

For the purposes of this example, it is assumed that you are familiar enough with the IDE to bypass the standard Try It Out format, so the steps aren't listed explicitly, as they are the same steps you've used many times. The important thing here is a detailed look at the code. Nonetheless, several pointers are included to ensure that you don't run into any problems along the way.

Both your classes and your enumerations will be contained in a class library project called Ch10CardLib. This project will contain four .cs files: Card.cs, which contains the Card class definition, Deck.cs, which contains the Deck class definition, and the Suit.cs and Rank.cs files containing enumerations.

You can put together a lot of this code using the VS class diagram tool.

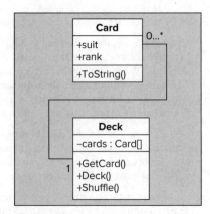

**FIGURE 10-10**

> **NOTE** *If you'd prefer not to use the class diagram tool, don't worry. Each of the following sections also includes the code generated by the class diagram, so you'll be able to follow along just fine.*

To get started, you need to do the following:

**1.** Create a new class library project called Ch10CardLib and save it in the directory C:\BegVCSharp\Chapter10.

**2.** Remove Class1.cs from the project.

**3.** Open the class diagram for the project using the Solution Explorer window (right-click the project and then click View Class Diagram). The class diagram should be blank to start with because the project contains no classes.

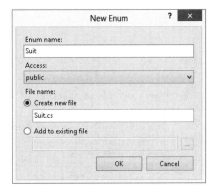

### Adding the Suit and Rank Enumerations

You can add an enumeration to the class diagram by dragging an Enum from the Toolbox into the diagram, and then filling in the New Enum dialog box that appears. For example, for the Suit enumeration, fill out the dialog box as shown in Figure 10-11.

Next, add the members of the enumeration using the Class Details window. Figure 10-12 shows the values that are required.

**FIGURE 10-11**

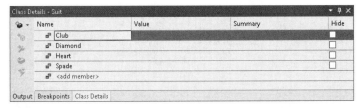

**FIGURE 10-12**

Add the Rank enumeration from the Toolbox in the same way. The values required are shown in Figure 10-13.

> **NOTE** *The value entry for the first member, Ace, is set to 1 so that the underlying storage of the Enum matches the rank of the card, such that Six is stored as 6, for example.*

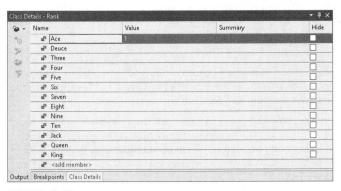

**FIGURE 10-13**

You can find the code generated for these two enumerations in the code files, `Suit.cs` and `Rank.cs`. First, you can find the full code for this example in `Ch10CardLib folder/Suit.cs`:

```
using System;
using System.Collections.Generic;
using System.Linq;
using System.Text;

namespace Ch10CardLib
{
    public enum Suit
    {
        Club,
        Diamond,
        Heart,
        Spade,
    }
}
```

And you can find the full code for this example in `Ch10CardLib folder/Rank.cs`:

```
using System;
using System.Collections.Generic;
using System.Linq;
using System.Text;

namespace Ch10CardLib
{
    public enum Rank
    {
        Ace = 1,
        Deuce,
        Three,
        Four,
        Five,
        Six,
        Seven,
        Eight,
        Nine,
        Ten,
        Jack,
        Queen,
        King,
    }
}
```

Alternatively, you can add this code manually by adding `Suit.cs` and `Rank.cs` code files and then entering the code. Note that the extra commas added by the code generator after the last enumeration member do not prevent compilation and do not result in an additional "empty" member being created—although they are a little messy.

## Adding the Card Class

To add the `Card` class, you'll use a mix of the class designer and code editor. Adding a class in the class designer is much like adding an enumeration—you drag the appropriate entry from the Toolbox into the diagram. In this case, you drag a `Class` into the diagram and name the new class `Card`.

Use the Class Details window to add the fields `rank` and `suit`, and then use the Properties window to set the Constant Kind of the field to `readonly`. You also need to add two constructors—a private default constructor, and a public constructor that takes two parameters, `newSuit` and `newRank`, of types `Suit` and `Rank`, respectively. Finally, you override `ToString()`, which requires you to change the Inheritance Modifier in the Properties window to `override`.

Figure 10-14 shows the Class Details window and the `Card` class with all the information entered. (You can find this code in `Ch10CardLib\Card.cs`.)

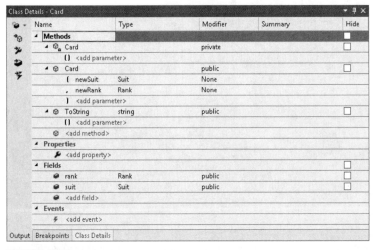

**FIGURE 10-14**

Next, modify the code for the class in `Card.cs` as follows (or add the code shown to a new class called `Card` in the `Ch10CardLib` namespace):

```
public class Card
{
    public readonly Suit suit;
    public readonly Rank rank;

    public Card(Suit newSuit, Rank newRank)
    {
        suit = newSuit;
        rank = newRank;
    }

    private Card()
    {

    }

    public override string ToString()
    {
        return "The " + rank + " of " + suit + "s";
    }
}
```

The overridden `ToString()` method writes the string representation of the enumeration value stored to the returned string, and the nondefault constructor initializes the values of the `suit` and `rank` fields.

## Adding the Deck Class

The `Deck` class needs the following members defined using the class diagram:

➤ A private field called `cards`, of type `Card[]`

➤ A public default constructor

➤ A public method called `GetCard()`, which takes one `int` parameter called `cardNum` and returns an object of type `Card`

➤ A public method called `Shuffle()`, which takes no parameters and returns `void`

When these are added, the Class Details window for the `Deck` class will appear as shown in Figure 10-15.

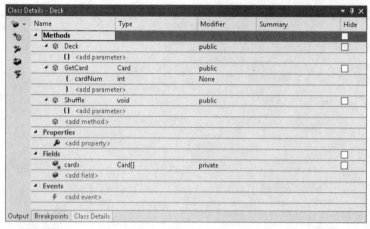

**FIGURE 10-15**

To make things clearer in the diagram, you can show the relationships among the members and types you have added. In the class diagram, right-click on each of the following in turn and select Show as Association from the menu:

➤ `cards` in `Deck`

➤ `suit` in `Card`

➤ `rank` in `Card`

When you have finished, the diagram should look like Figure 10-16.

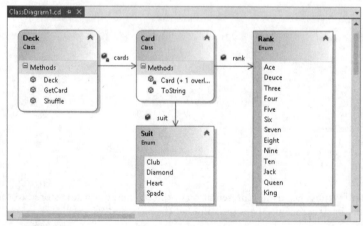

**FIGURE 10-16**

Next, modify the code in `Deck.cs` (if you aren't using the class designer, you must add this class first with the code shown here). You can find this code in `Ch10CardLib\Deck.cs`. First you implement the constructor, which simply creates and assigns 52 cards in the `cards` field. You iterate through all combinations of the two enumerations, using each to create a card. This results in `cards` initially containing an ordered list of cards:

```
using System;
using System.Collections.Generic;
using System.Linq;
using System.Text;
using System.Threading.Tasks;

namespace Ch10CardLib
{
    public class Deck
    {
        private Card[] cards;

        public Deck()
        {
            cards = new Card[52];
            for (int suitVal = 0; suitVal < 4; suitVal++)
            {
                for (int rankVal = 1; rankVal < 14; rankVal++)
                {
                    cards[suitVal * 13 + rankVal -1] = new Card((Suit)suitVal,
                                                         (Rank)rankVal);
                }
            }
        }
```

Next, implement the GetCard() method, which either returns the Card object with the requested index or throws an exception as shown earlier:

```
public Card GetCard(int cardNum)
{
    if (cardNum >= 0 && cardNum <= 51)
        return cards[cardNum];
    else
        throw (new System.ArgumentOutOfRangeException("cardNum", cardNum,
                "Value must be between 0 and 51."));
}
```

Finally, you implement the Shuffle() method. This method works by creating a temporary card array and copying cards from the existing cards array into this array at random. The main body of this function is a loop that counts from 0 to 51. On each cycle, you generate a random number between 0 and 51, using an instance of the System.Random class from the .NET Framework. Once instantiated, an object of this class generates a random number between 0 and X, using the method Next(X). When you have a random number, you simply use that as the index of the Card object in your temporary array in which to copy a card from the cards array.

To keep a record of assigned cards, you also have an array of bool variables, and assign these to true as each card is copied. As you are generating random numbers, you check against this array to see whether you have already copied a card to the location in the temporary array specified by the random number. If so, you simply generate another.

This isn't the most efficient way of doing things because many random numbers will be generated before finding a vacant slot into which a card can be copied. However, it works, it's very simple, and C# code executes so quickly you will hardly notice a delay. The code is as follows:

```
public void Shuffle()
{
    Card[] newDeck = new Card[52];
    bool[] assigned = new bool[52];
    Random sourceGen = new Random();
    for (int i = 0; i < 52; i++)
    {
        int destCard = 0;
        bool foundCard = false;
```

```
            while (foundCard == false)
            {
                destCard = sourceGen.Next(52);
                if (assigned[destCard] == false)
                    foundCard = true;
            }
            assigned[destCard] = true;
            newDeck[destCard] = cards[i];
        }
        newDeck.CopyTo(cards, 0);
    }
  }
}
```

The last line of this method uses the `CopyTo()` method of the `System.Array` class (used whenever you create an array) to copy each of the cards in `newDeck` back into `cards`. This means you are using the same set of `Card` objects in the same `cards` object, rather than creating any new instances. If you had instead used `cards = newDeck`, then you would be replacing the object instance referred to by `cards` with another. This could cause problems if code elsewhere were retaining a reference to the original `cards` instance—which wouldn't be shuffled!

That completes the class library code.

## A Client Application for the Class Library

To keep things simple, you can add a client console application to the solution containing the class library. To do so, simply right-click on the solution in Solution Explorer and select Add ⇨ New Project. The new project is called Ch10CardClient.

To use the class library you have created from this new console application project, add a reference to your Ch10CardLib class library project. You can do that through the Projects tab of the Add Reference dialog box, as shown in Figure 10-17.

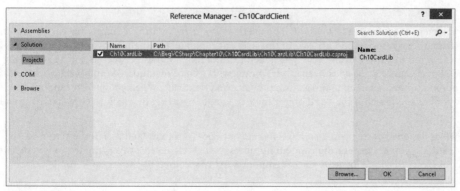

**FIGURE 10-17**

Select the project and click OK to add the reference.

Because this new project is the second one you've created, you also need to specify that it is the startup project for the solution, meaning the one that is executed when you click Run. To do so, simply right-click on the project name in the Solution Explorer window and select the Set as StartUp Project menu option.

Next, add the code that uses your new classes. That doesn't require anything particularly special, so the following code will do (you can find this code in `Ch10CardClient\Program.cs`):

```
using System;
using System.Collections.Generic;
using System.Linq;
using System.Text;
using System.Threading.Tasks;
using Ch10CardLib;

namespace Ch10CardClient
{
    class Program
    {
        static void Main(string[] args)
        {
            Deck myDeck = new Deck();
            myDeck.Shuffle();
            for (int i = 0; i < 52; i++)
            {
                Card tempCard = myDeck.GetCard(i);
                Console.Write(tempCard.ToString());
                if (i != 51)
                    Console.Write(", ");
                else
                    Console.WriteLine();
            }
            Console.ReadKey();
        }
    }
}
```

Figure 10-18 shows the result you'll get if you run this application.

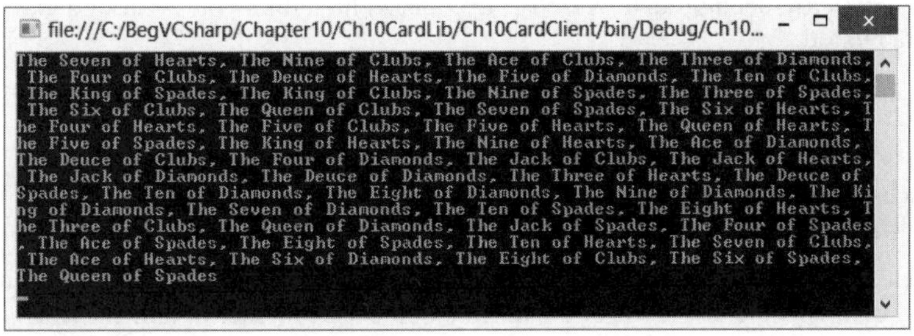

**FIGURE 10-18**

This is a random arrangement of the 52 playing cards in the deck. You'll continue to develop and use this class library in later chapters.

## THE CALL HIERARCHY WINDOW

Now is a good time to take a quick look at another feature of VS (introduced in VS 2010): the Call Hierarchy window. This window enables you to interrogate code to find out where your methods are called from and how they relate to other methods. The best way to illustrate this is with an example.

Open the example application from the previous section, and open the Deck.cs code file. Find the Shuffle() method, right-click on it, and select the View Call Hierarchy menu item. The window that appears is shown in Figure 10-19 (which has some regions expanded).

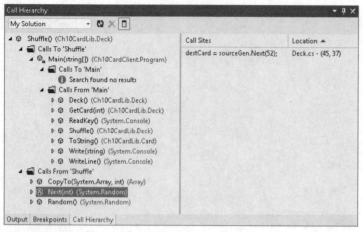

**FIGURE 10-19**

Starting from the Shuffle() method, you can drill into the tree view in the window to find all the code that calls the method, and all the calls that the method makes. For example, the highlighted method, Next(int), is called from Shuffle(), so it appears in the Calls From 'Shuffle' section. When you click on a call you can see the line of code that makes the call on the right, along with its location. You can double-click on the location to navigate instantly to the line of code that is referred to.

You can also drill into methods further down the hierarchy—in Figure 10-19 this has been done for Main(), and the display shows calls from and to the Main() method.

This window is very useful when you are debugging or refactoring code, as it enables you to see at a glance how different pieces of code are related.

## SUMMARY

This chapter completes the discussion of how to define basic classes. There's still plenty to cover, but the techniques covered so far enable you to create quite complicated applications.

You looked at how to define fields, methods, and properties, including the various access levels and modifier keywords. You also looked at the tools you can use to get the outline of a class together in half the time.

You explored inheritance behavior in detail, learning how to hide unwanted inherited members with the new keyword, and extending base class members rather than replacing their implementation, using the base keyword. You also looked at nested class definitions, looked in detail at interface definition and implementation, including the concepts of explicit and implicit implementation, and learned how to split definitions between code files using partial class and method definitions.

Finally, you developed and used a simple class library representing a deck of playing cards, making use of the handy class diagram tool to make things easier. You'll make further use of this library in later chapters.

In the next chapter, you look at collections, a type of class you will frequently use in your development.

**10.1**  Write code that defines a base class, `MyClass`, with the virtual method `GetString()`. This method should return the string stored in the protected field `myString`, accessible through the write-only public property `ContainedString`.

**10.2**  Derive a class, `MyDerivedClass`, from `MyClass`. Override the `GetString()` method to return the string from the base class, using the base implementation of the method, but add the text " `(output from derived class)` " to the returned string.

**10.3**  Partial method definitions must use the `void` return type. Provide a reason why this is so.

**10.4**  Write a class called `MyCopyableClass` that is capable of returning a copy of itself using the method `GetCopy()`. This method should use the `MemberwiseClone()` method inherited from `System.Object`. Add a simple property to the class, and write client code that uses the class to confirm that everything is working.

**10.5**  Write a console client for the Ch10CardLib library that draws five cards at one time from a shuffled `Deck` object. If all five cards are the same suit, then the client should display the card names onscreen along with the text `Flush!`; otherwise, it should quit after 50 cards with the text `No flush`.

Answers to the exercises can be found in Appendix A.

▶ **WHAT YOU LEARNED IN THIS CHAPTER**

| TOPIC | KEY CONCEPTS |
| --- | --- |
| **Member definitions** | You can define field, method, and property members in a class. Fields are defined with an accessibility, name, and type. Methods are defined with an accessibility, return type, name, and parameters. Properties are defined with an accessibility, name, and a `get` and/or `set` accessor. Individual property accessors can have their own accessibility, which must be less accessible than the property as a whole. |
| **Member hiding and overrides** | Properties and methods can be defined as `abstract` or `virtual` in base classes to define inheritance. Derived classes must implement abstract members, and can override virtual members, with the `override` keyword. They can also provide new implementations with the `new` keyword, and prevent further overrides of `virtual` members with the `sealed` keyword. Base implementations can be called with the `base` keyword. |
| **Interface implementation** | A class that implements an interface must implement all of the members defined by that interface as public. You can implement interfaces implicitly or explicitly, where explicit implementations are only available through an interface reference. |
| **Partial definitions** | You can split class definitions across multiple code files with the `partial` keyword. You can also create partial methods with the `partial` keyword. Partial methods have certain restrictions, including no return value or `out` parameters, and are not compiled if no implementation is provided. |

# 11

# Collections, Comparisons, and Conversions

## WHAT YOU WILL LEARN IN THIS CHAPTER

- ➤ How to define and use collections
- ➤ The different types of collections that are available
- ➤ How to compare types and use the `is` operator
- ➤ How to compare values and overload operators
- ➤ How to define and use conversions
- ➤ How to use the `as` operator

## WROX.COM CODE DOWNLOADS FOR THIS CHAPTER

You can find the wrox.com code downloads for this chapter at `www.wrox.com/remtitle .cgi?isbn=9781118314418` on the Download Code tab. The code is in the Chapter 11 download and individually named according to the names throughout the chapter.

You've covered all the basic OOP techniques in C# now, but there are some more advanced techniques that are worth becoming familiar with. These techniques relate to certain problems that you must solve regularly when you are writing code. Learning about them will make it much easier to progress and allow you to concentrate on other, potentially more important aspects of your applications. In this chapter, you look at the following:

- ➤ **Collections**—Collections enable you to maintain groups of objects. Unlike arrays, which you've used in earlier chapters, collections can include more advanced functionality, such as controlling access to the objects they contain, searching and sorting, and more. You'll learn how to use and create collection classes and learn about some powerful techniques for getting the most out of them.

- ➤ **Comparisons**—When dealing with objects, you often want to make comparisons between them. This is especially important in collections, because it is how sorting is achieved. You'll look at how to compare objects in a number of ways, including operator overloading, and how to use the `IComparable` and `IComparer` interface to sort collections.

- ➤ **Conversions**—Earlier chapters showed you how to cast objects from one type into another. In this chapter, you'll learn how to customize type conversions to suit your needs.

## COLLECTIONS

In Chapter 5, you learned how to use arrays to create variable types that contain a number of objects or values. Arrays, however, have their limitations. The biggest limitation is that once arrays have been created, they have a fixed size, so you can't add new items to the end of an existing array without creating a new one. This often means that the syntax used to manipulate arrays can become overly complicated. OOP techniques enable you to create classes that perform much of this manipulation internally, simplifying the code that uses lists of items or arrays.

Arrays in C# are implemented as instances of the System.Array class and are just one type of what are known as *collection classes*. Collection classes in general are used for maintaining lists of objects, and they may expose more functionality than simple arrays. Much of this functionality comes through implementing interfaces from the System.Collections namespace, thus standardizing collection syntax. This namespace also contains some other interesting things, such as classes that implement these interfaces in ways other than System.Array.

Because the collection's functionality (including basic functions such as accessing collection items by using [index] syntax) is available through interfaces, you aren't limited to using basic collection classes such as System.Array. Instead, you can create your own customized collection classes. These can be made more specific to the objects you want to enumerate (that is, the objects you want to maintain collections of). One advantage of doing this, as you will see, is that custom collection classes can be *strongly typed*. That is, when you extract items from the collection, you don't need to cast them into the correct type. Another advantage is the capability to expose specialized methods. For example, you can provide a quick way to obtain subsets of items. In the deck of cards example, you could add a method to obtain all Card items of a particular suit.

Several interfaces in the System.Collections namespace provide basic collection functionality:

➤ IEnumerable—Provides the capability to loop through items in a collection

➤ ICollection—Provides the capability to obtain the number of items in a collection and copy items into a simple array type (inherits from IEnumerable)

➤ IList—Provides a list of items for a collection along with the capabilities for accessing these items, and some other basic capabilities related to lists of items (inherits from IEnumerable and ICollection)

➤ IDictionary—Similar to IList, but provides a list of items accessible via a key value, rather than an index (inherits from IEnumerable and ICollection)

The System.Array class implements IList, ICollection, and IEnumerable. However, it doesn't support some of the more advanced features of IList, and it represents a list of items by using a fixed size.

## Using Collections

One of the classes in the Systems.Collections namespace, System.Collections.ArrayList, also implements IList, ICollection, and IEnumerable, but does so in a more sophisticated way than System.Array. Whereas arrays are fixed in size (you can't add or remove elements), this class can be used to represent a variable-length list of items. To give you more of a feel for what is possible with such a highly advanced collection, the following Try It Out uses this class, as well as a simple array.

**TRY IT OUT** **Arrays versus More Advanced Collections: Ch11Ex01**

1. Create a new console application called Ch11Ex01 and save it in the directory C:\BegVCSharp\Chapter11.

2. Add three new classes, Animal, Cow, and Chicken, to the project by right-clicking on the project in the Solution Explorer window and selecting Add ⇨ Class for each.

3. Modify the code in Animal.cs as follows:

```
namespace Ch11Ex01
{
    public abstract class Animal
    {
        protected string name;

        public string Name
        {
            get
            {
                return name;
            }
            set
            {
                name = value;
            }
        }

        public Animal()
        {
            name = "The animal with no name";
        }

        public Animal(string newName)
        {
            name = newName;
        }

        public void Feed()
        {
            Console.WriteLine("{0} has been fed.", name);
        }
    }
}
```

4. Modify the code in Cow.cs as follows:

```
namespace Ch11Ex01
{
    public class Cow : Animal
    {
        public void Milk()
        {
            Console.WriteLine("{0} has been milked.", name);
        }

        public Cow(string newName) : base(newName)
        {
        }
    }
}
```

5. Modify the code in Chicken.cs as follows:

```
namespace Ch11Ex01
{
    public class Chicken : Animal
    {
        public void LayEgg()
        {
            Console.WriteLine("{0} has laid an egg.", name);
        }

        public Chicken(string newName) : base(newName)
```

```
                {
                }
            }
        }
    }
```

**6.** Modify the code in `Program.cs` as follows:

```
using System;
using System.Collections;
using System.Collections.Generic;
using System.Linq;
using System.Text;
using System.Threading.Tasks;

namespace Ch11Ex01

{
    class Program
    {
        static void Main(string[] args)
        {
            Console.WriteLine("Create an Array type collection of Animal " +
                            "objects and use it:");

            Animal[] animalArray = new Animal[2];
            Cow myCow1 = new Cow("Deirdre");
            animalArray[0] = myCow1;
            animalArray[1] = new Chicken("Ken");

            foreach (Animal myAnimal in animalArray)
            {
                Console.WriteLine("New {0} object added to Array collection, " +
                            "Name = {1}", myAnimal.ToString(), myAnimal.Name);
            }

            Console.WriteLine("Array collection contains {0} objects.",
                            animalArray.Length);
            animalArray[0].Feed();
            ((Chicken)animalArray[1]).LayEgg();
            Console.WriteLine();

            Console.WriteLine("Create an ArrayList type collection of Animal " +
                            "objects and use it:");
            ArrayList animalArrayList = new ArrayList();
            Cow myCow2 = new Cow("Hayley");
            animalArrayList.Add(myCow2);
            animalArrayList.Add(new Chicken("Roy"));

            foreach (Animal myAnimal in animalArrayList)
            {
                Console.WriteLine("New {0} object added to ArrayList collection," +
                            " Name = {1}", myAnimal.ToString(), myAnimal.Name);
            }
            Console.WriteLine("ArrayList collection contains {0} objects.",
                    animalArrayList.Count);
            ((Animal)animalArrayList[0]).Feed();
            ((Chicken)animalArrayList[1]).LayEgg();
            Console.WriteLine();

            Console.WriteLine("Additional manipulation of ArrayList:");
            animalArrayList.RemoveAt(0);
            ((Animal)animalArrayList[0]).Feed();
            animalArrayList.AddRange(animalArray);
            ((Chicken)animalArrayList[2]).LayEgg();
            Console.WriteLine("The animal called {0} is at index {1}.",
```

```
                                        myCow1.Name, animalArrayList.IndexOf(myCow1));
                myCow1.Name = "Janice";
                Console.WriteLine("The animal is now called {0}.",
                                  ((Animal)animalArrayList[1]).Name);
                Console.ReadKey();
            }
        }
    }
```

7. Run the application. The result is shown in Figure 11-1.

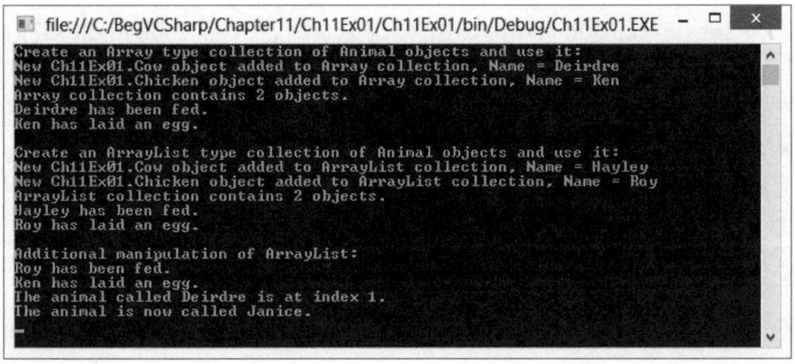

**FIGURE 11-1**

### How It Works

This example creates two collections of objects: the first uses the System.Array class (that is, a simple array), and the second uses the System.Collections.ArrayList class. Both collections are of Animal objects, which are defined in Animal.cs. The Animal class is abstract, so it can't be instantiated, although you can have items in your collection that are instances of the Cow and Chicken classes, which are derived from Animal. You achieve this by using polymorphism, discussed in Chapter 8.

Once created in the Main() method in Class1.cs, these arrays are manipulated to show their characteristics and capabilities. Several of the operations performed apply to both Array and ArrayList collections, although their syntax differs slightly. Some, however, are possible only by using the more advanced ArrayList type.

You'll learn the similar operations first, comparing the code and results for both types of collection. First, collection creation. With simple arrays you must initialize the array with a fixed size in order to use it. You do this to an array called animalArray by using the standard syntax shown in Chapter 5:

```
Animal[] animalArray = new Animal[2];
```

ArrayList collections, conversely, don't need a size to be initialized, so you can create your list (called animalArrayList) as follows:

```
ArrayList animalArrayList = new ArrayList();
```

You can use two other constructors with this class. The first copies the contents of an existing collection to the new instance by specifying the existing collection as a parameter; the other sets the capacity of the collection, also via a parameter. This capacity, specified as an int value, sets the initial number of items that can be contained in the collection. This is not an absolute capacity, however, because it is doubled automatically if the number of items in the collection ever exceeds this value.

With arrays of reference types (such as the Animal and Animal-derived objects), simply initializing the array with a size doesn't initialize the items it contains. To use a given entry, that entry needs to be initialized, which means that you need to assign initialized objects to the items:

```
Cow myCow1 = new Cow("Deirdre");
animalArray[0] = myCow1;
animalArray[1] = new Chicken("Ken");
```

The preceding code does this in two ways: once by assignment using an existing `Cow` object, and once by assignment through the creation of a new `Chicken` object. The main difference here is that the former method creates a reference to the object in the array—a fact that you make use of later in the code.

With the `ArrayList` collection, there are no existing items, not even `null`-referenced ones. This means you can't assign new instances to indices in the same way. Instead, you use the `Add()` method of the `ArrayList` object to add new items:

```
Cow myCow2 = new Cow("Hayley");
animalArrayList.Add(myCow2);
animalArrayList.Add(new Chicken("Roy"));
```

Apart from the slightly different syntax, you can add new or existing objects to the collection in the same way. Once you have added items in this way, you can overwrite them by using syntax identical to that for arrays:

```
animalArrayList[0] = new Cow("Alma");
```

You won't do that in this example, though.

Chapter 5 showed how the `foreach` structure can be used to iterate through an array. This is possible because the `System.Array` class implements the `IEnumerable` interface, and the only method on this interface, `GetEnumerator()`, allows you to loop through items in the collection. You'll look at this in more depth a little later in the chapter. In your code, you write out information about each `Animal` object in the array:

```
foreach (Animal myAnimal in animalArray)
{
    Console.WriteLine("New {0} object added to Array collection, " +
                "Name = {1}", myAnimal.ToString(), myAnimal.Name);
}
```

The `ArrayList` object you use also supports the `IEnumerable` interface and can be used with `foreach`. In this case, the syntax is identical:

```
foreach (Animal myAnimal in animalArrayList)
{
    Console.WriteLine("New {0} object added to ArrayList collection, " +
                "Name = {1}", myAnimal.ToString(), myAnimal.Name);
}
```

Next, you use the array's `Length` property to output to the screen the number of items in the array:

```
Console.WriteLine("Array collection contains {0} objects.",
                animalArray.Length);
```

You can achieve the same thing with the `ArrayList` collection, except that you use the `Count` property that is part of the `ICollection` interface:

```
Console.WriteLine("ArrayList collection contains {0} objects.",
                animalArrayList.Count);
```

Collections—whether simple arrays or more complex collections—aren't very useful unless they provide access to the items that belong to them. Simple arrays are strongly typed—that is, they allow direct access to the type of the items they contain. This means you can call the methods of the item directly:

```
animalArray[0].Feed();
```

The type of the array is the abstract type `Animal`; therefore, you can't call methods supplied by derived classes directly. Instead you must use casting:

```
((Chicken)animalArray[1]).LayEgg();
```

The `ArrayList` collection is a collection of `System.Object` objects (you have assigned `Animal` objects via polymorphism). This means that you must use casting for all items:

```
((Animal)animalArrayList[0]).Feed();
((Chicken)animalArrayList[1]).LayEgg();
```

The remainder of the code looks at some of the `ArrayList` collection's capabilities that go beyond those of the `Array` collection. First, you can remove items by using the `Remove()` and `RemoveAt()` methods, part of the `IList` interface implementation in the `ArrayList` class. These methods remove items from an array based on an item reference or index, respectively. This example uses the latter method to remove the list's first item, the `Cow` object with a `Name` property of `Hayley`:

```
animalArrayList.RemoveAt(0);
```

Alternatively, you could use

```
animalArrayList.Remove(myCow2);
```

because you already have a local reference to this object—you added an existing reference to the array via `Add()`, rather than create a new object. Either way, the only item left in the collection is the `Chicken` object, which you access as follows:

```
((Animal)animalArrayList[0]).Feed();
```

Any modifications to items in the `ArrayList` object resulting in N items being left in the array will be executed in such a way as to maintain indices from 0 to N-1. For example, removing the item with the index 0 results in all other items being shifted one place in the array, so you access the `Chicken` object with the index 0, not 1. You no longer have an item with an index of 1 (because you only had two items in the first place), so an exception would be thrown if you tried the following:

```
((Animal)animalArrayList[1]).Feed();
```

`ArrayList` collections enable you to add several items at once with the `AddRange()` method. This method accepts any object with the `ICollection` interface, which includes the `animalArray` array created earlier in the code:

```
animalArrayList.AddRange(animalArray);
```

To check that this works, you can attempt to access the third item in the collection, which is the second item in `animalArray`:

```
((Chicken)animalArrayList[2]).LayEgg();
```

The `AddRange()` method isn't part of any of the interfaces exposed by `ArrayList`. This method is specific to the `ArrayList` class and demonstrates the fact that you can exhibit customized behavior in your collection classes, beyond what is required by the interfaces you have looked at. This class exposes other interesting methods too, such as `InsertRange()`, for inserting an array of objects at any point in the list, and methods for tasks such as sorting and reordering the array.

Finally, you make use of the fact that you can have multiple references to the same object. Using the `IndexOf()` method (part of the `IList` interface), you can see that `myCow1` (an object originally added to `animalArray`) is now not only part of the `animalArrayList` collection, but also its index:

```
Console.WriteLine("The animal called {0} is at index {1}.",
                  myCow1.Name, animalArrayList.IndexOf(myCow1));
```

As an extension of this, the next two lines of code rename the object via the object reference and display the new name via the collection reference:

```
myCow1.Name = "Janice";
Console.WriteLine("The animal is now called {0}.",
                  ((Animal)animalArrayList[1]).Name);
```

## Defining Collections

Now that you know what is possible using more advanced collection classes, it's time to learn how to create your own strongly typed collection. One way of doing this is to implement the required methods manually, but this can be a time-consuming and complex process. Alternatively, you can derive your collection from a class, such as `System.Collections.CollectionBase`, an abstract class that supplies much of the implementation of a collection for you. This option is strongly recommended.

The `CollectionBase` class exposes the interfaces `IEnumerable`, `ICollection`, and `IList` but provides only some of the required implementation—notably, the `Clear()` and `RemoveAt()` methods of `IList` and the `Count` property of `ICollection`. You need to implement everything else yourself if you want the functionality provided.

To facilitate this, `CollectionBase` provides two protected properties that enable access to the stored objects themselves. You can use `List`, which gives you access to the items through an `IList` interface, and `InnerList`, which is the `ArrayList` object used to store items.

For example, the basics of a collection class to store `Animal` objects could be defined as follows (you'll see a fuller implementation shortly):

```
public class Animals : CollectionBase
{
    public void Add(Animal newAnimal)
    {
        List.Add(newAnimal);
    }

    public void Remove(Animal oldAnimal)
    {
        List.Remove(oldAnimal);
    }

    public Animals()
    {
    }
}
```

Here, `Add()` and `Remove()` have been implemented as strongly typed methods that use the standard `Add()` method of the `IList` interface used to access the items. The methods exposed will now only work with `Animal` classes or classes derived from `Animal`, unlike the `ArrayList` implementations shown earlier, which work with any object.

The `CollectionBase` class enables you to use the `foreach` syntax with your derived collections. For example, you can use code such as this:

```
Console.WriteLine("Using custom collection class Animals:");
Animals animalCollection = new Animals();
animalCollection.Add(new Cow("Sarah"));
foreach (Animal myAnimal in animalCollection)
{
    Console.WriteLine("New {0} object added to custom collection, " +
                "Name = {1}", myAnimal.ToString(), myAnimal.Name);
}
```

You can't, however, do the following:

```
animalCollection[0].Feed();
```

To access items via their indices in this way, you need to use an indexer.

## Indexers

An *indexer* is a special kind of property that you can add to a class to provide array-like access. In fact, you can provide more complex access via an indexer, because you can define and use complex parameter types with the square bracket syntax as you want. Implementing a simple numeric index for items, however, is the most common usage.

You can add an indexer to the `Animals` collection of `Animal` objects as follows:

```
public class Animals : CollectionBase
{
    ...

    public Animal this[int animalIndex]
    {
        get
        {
            return (Animal)List[animalIndex];
        }
        set
        {
            List[animalIndex] = value;
        }
    }
}
```

The `this` keyword is used along with parameters in square brackets, but otherwise the indexer looks much like any other property. This syntax is logical, because you access the indexer by using the name of the object followed by the index parameter(s) in square brackets (for example, `MyAnimals[0]`).

The indexer code uses an indexer on the `List` property (that is, on the `IList` interface that provides access to the `ArrayList` in `CollectionBase` that stores your items):

```
return (Animal)List[animalIndex];
```

Explicit casting is necessary here, as the `IList.List` property returns a `System.Object` object. The important point to note here is that you define a type for this indexer. This is the type that will be obtained when you access an item by using this indexer. This strong typing means that you can write code such as

```
animalCollection[0].Feed();
```

rather than:

```
((Animal)animalCollection[0]).Feed();
```

This is another handy feature of strongly typed custom collections. In the following Try It Out, you expand the previous Try It Out to put this into action.

**TRY IT OUT**  Implementing an Animals Collection: Ch11Ex02

1. Create a new console application called Ch11Ex02 and save it in the directory `C:\BegVCSharp\Chapter11`.
2. Right-click on the project name in the Solution Explorer window and select Add ➪ Existing Item.
3. Select the `Animal.cs`, `Cow.cs`, and `Chicken.cs` files from the `C:\BegVCSharp\Chapter11\Ch11Ex01\Ch11Ex01` directory, and click Add.
4. Modify the namespace declaration in the three files you added as follows:
```
namespace Ch11Ex02
```
5. Add a new class called `Animals`.
6. Modify the code in `Animals.cs` as follows:
```
using System;
using System.Collections;
using System.Collections.Generic;
using System.Linq;
using System.Text;
using System.Threading.Tasks;

namespace Ch11Ex02
{
    public class Animals : CollectionBase
    {
        public void Add(Animal newAnimal)
        {
```

```
                    List.Add(newAnimal);
                }

                public void Remove(Animal newAnimal)
                {
                    List.Remove(newAnimal);
                }

                public Animal this[int animalIndex]
                {
                    get
                    {
                        return (Animal)List[animalIndex];
                    }
                    set
                    {
                        List[animalIndex] = value;
                    }
                }
            }
        }
```

**7.** Modify `Program.cs` as follows:

```
        static void Main(string[] args)
        {
            Animals animalCollection = new Animals();
            animalCollection.Add(new Cow("Jack"));
            animalCollection.Add(new Chicken("Vera"));
            foreach (Animal myAnimal in animalCollection)
            {
                myAnimal.Feed();
            }
            Console.ReadKey();
        }
```

**8.** Execute the application. The result is shown in Figure 11-2.

**FIGURE 11-2**

*How It Works*

This example uses code detailed in the last section to implement a strongly typed collection of `Animal` objects in a class called `Animals`. The code in `Main()` simply instantiates an `Animals` object called `animalCollection`, adds two items (an instance of `Cow` and `Chicken`), and uses a `foreach` loop to call the `Feed()` method that both objects inherit from their base class, `Animal`.

## Adding a Cards Collection to CardLib

In the last chapter, you created a class library project called Ch10CardLib that contained a `Card` class representing a playing card, and a `Deck` class representing a deck of cards—that is, a collection of `Card` classes. This collection was implemented as a simple array.

In this chapter, you'll add a new class to this library, renamed Ch11CardLib. This new class, `Cards`, will be a custom collection of `Card` objects, giving you all the benefits described earlier in this chapter. Create a new class library called Ch11CardLib in the `C:\BegVCSharp\Chapter11` directory. Next, delete the autogenerated `Class1.cs` file; select Project ⇨ Add Existing Item; select the `Card.cs`, `Deck.cs`, `Suit.cs`, and `Rank.cs` files from the `C:\BegVCSharp\Chapter10\Ch10CardLib\Ch10CardLib` directory; and add the files to your project. As with the previous version of this project, introduced in Chapter 10, these changes are presented without using the standard Try It Out format. Should you want to jump straight to the code, feel free to open the version of this project included in the downloadable code for this chapter.

> **NOTE** *Don't forget that when copying the source files from* `Ch10CardLib` *to* `Ch11CardLib`, *you must change the namespace declarations to refer to* `Ch11CardLib`. *This also applies to the* `Ch10CardClient` *console application that you will use for testing.*
>
> *The downloadable code for this chapter includes a* `Ch11CardLib` *folder that contains all the code you need for the various expansions to the* `Ch11CardLib` *project. Because of this, you may notice some extra code that isn't included in this example, but this won't affect how it works at this stage. Often you will find that code is commented out; however, when you reach the relevant example, you can uncomment the section you want to experiment with.*

If you decide to create this project yourself, add a new class called `Cards` and modify the code in `Cards.cs` as follows:

```
using System;
using System.Collections;
using System.Collections.Generic;
using System.Linq;
using System.Text;
using System.Threading.Tasks;

namespace Ch11CardLib
{
    public class Cards : CollectionBase
    {
        public void Add(Card newCard)
        {
            List.Add(newCard);
        }

        public void Remove(Card oldCard)
        {
            List.Remove(oldCard);
        }

        public Card this[int cardIndex]
        {
            get
            {
                return (Card)List[cardIndex];
            }
            set
            {
                List[cardIndex] = value;
            }
        }

        /// <summary>
        /// Utility method for copying card instances into another Cards
        /// instance—used in Deck.Shuffle(). This implementation assumes that
        /// source and target collections are the same size.
```

```
        /// </summary>
        public void CopyTo(Cards targetCards)
        {
            for (int index = 0; index < this.Count; index++)
            {
                targetCards[index] = this[index];
            }
        }

        /// <summary>
        /// Check to see if the Cards collection contains a particular card.
        /// This calls the Contains() method of the ArrayList for the collection,
        /// which you access through the InnerList property.
        /// </summary>
        public bool Contains(Card card)
        {
            return InnerList.Contains(card);
        }
    }
}
```

Next, modify Deck.cs to use this new collection, rather than an array:

```
using System;
using System.Collections.Generic;
using System.Linq;
using System.Text;

namespace Ch11CardLib
{
    public class Deck
    {
        private Cards cards = new Cards();

        public Deck()
        {
            // Line of code removed here
            for (int suitVal = 0; suitVal < 4; suitVal++)
            {
                for (int rankVal = 1; rankVal < 14; rankVal++)
                {
                    cards.Add(new Card((Suit)suitVal, (Rank)rankVal));
                }
            }
        }

        public Card GetCard(int cardNum)
        {
            if (cardNum >= 0 && cardNum <= 51)
                return cards[cardNum];
            else
                throw (new System.ArgumentOutOfRangeException("cardNum", cardNum,
                        "Value must be between 0 and 51."));
        }

        public void Shuffle()
        {
            Cards newDeck = new Cards();
            bool[] assigned = new bool[52];
            Random sourceGen = new Random();
            for (int i = 0; i < 52; i++)
            {
                int sourceCard = 0;
```

```
                bool foundCard = false;
                while (foundCard == false)
                {
                    sourceCard = sourceGen.Next(52);
                    if (assigned[sourceCard] == false)
                        foundCard = true;
                }
                assigned[sourceCard] = true;
                newDeck.Add(cards[sourceCard]);
            }
            newDeck.CopyTo(cards);
        }
    }
}
```

Not many changes are necessary here. Most of them involve changing the shuffling logic to allow for the fact that cards are added to the beginning of the new `Cards` collection `newDeck` from a random index in `cards`, rather than to a random index in `newDeck` from a sequential position in `cards`.

The client console application for the `Ch10CardLib` solution, `Ch10CardClient`, can be used with this new library with the same result as before, as the method signatures of `Deck` are unchanged. Clients of this class library can now make use of the `Cards` collection class, however, rather than rely on arrays of `Card` objects—for example, to define hands of cards in a card game application.

## Keyed Collections and IDictionary

Instead of implementing the `IList` interface, it is also possible for collections to implement the similar `IDictionary` interface, which allows items to be indexed via a key value (such as a string name), rather than an index. This is also achieved using an indexer, although here the indexer parameter used is a key associated with a stored item, rather than an `int` index, which can make the collection a lot more user-friendly.

As with indexed collections, there is a base class you can use to simplify implementation of the `IDictionary` interface: `DictionaryBase`. This class also implements `IEnumerable` and `ICollection`, providing the basic collection-manipulation capabilities that are the same for any collection.

`DictionaryBase`, like `CollectionBase`, implements some (but not all) of the members obtained through its supported interfaces. Like `CollectionBase`, the `Clear` and `Count` members are implemented, although `RemoveAt()` isn't because it's a method on the `IList` interface and doesn't appear on the `IDictionary` interface. `IDictionary` does, however, have a `Remove()` method, which is one of the methods you should implement in a custom collection class based on `DictionaryBase`.

The following code shows an alternative version of the `Animals` class, this time derived from `DictionaryBase`. Implementations are included for `Add()`, `Remove()`, and a key-accessed indexer:

```
public class Animals : DictionaryBase
{
    public void Add(string newID, Animal newAnimal)
    {
        Dictionary.Add(newID, newAnimal);
    }

    public void Remove(string animalID)
    {
        Dictionary.Remove(animalID);
    }

    public Animals()
    {
    }

    public Animal this[string animalID]
```

```
    {
        get
        {
            return (Animal)Dictionary[animalID];
        }
        set
        {
            Dictionary[animalID] = value;
        }
    }
}
```

The differences in these members are as follows:

➤ Add() —Takes two parameters, a key and a value, to store together. The dictionary collection has a member called Dictionary inherited from DictionaryBase, which is an IDictionary interface. This interface has its own Add() method, which takes two object parameters. Your implementation takes a string value as a key and an Animal object as the data to store alongside this key.

➤ Remove() —Takes a key parameter, rather than an object reference. The item with the key value specified is removed.

➤ Indexer—Uses a string key value, rather than an index, which is used to access the stored item via the Dictionary inherited member. Again, casting is necessary here.

One other difference between collections based on DictionaryBase and collections based on CollectionBase is that foreach works slightly differently. The collection from the last section allowed you to extract Animal objects directly from the collection. Using foreach with the DictionaryBase derived class gives you DictionaryEntry structs, another type defined in the System.Collections namespace. To get to the Animal objects themselves, you must use the Value member of this struct, or you can use the Key member of the struct to get the associated key. To get code equivalent to the earlier

```
foreach (Animal myAnimal in animalCollection)
{
    Console.WriteLine("New {0} object added to custom collection, " +
                "Name = {1}", myAnimal.ToString(), myAnimal.Name);
}
```

you need the following:

```
foreach (DictionaryEntry myEntry in animalCollection)
{
    Console.WriteLine("New {0} object added to custom collection, " +
                "Name = {1}", myEntry.Value.ToString(),
                ((Animal)myEntry.Value).Name);
}
```

It is possible to override this behavior so that you can access Animal objects directly through foreach. There are several ways to do this, the simplest being to implement an iterator.

## Iterators

Earlier in this chapter, you saw that the IEnumerable interface enables you to use foreach loops. It's often beneficial to use your classes in foreach loops, not just collection classes such as those shown in previous sections.

However, overriding this behavior, or providing your own custom implementation of it, is not always simple. To illustrate this, it's necessary to take a detailed look at foreach loops. The following steps show you what actually happens in a foreach loop iterating through a collection called collectionObject:

1. collectionObject.GetEnumerator() is called, which returns an IEnumerator reference. This method is available through implementation of the IEnumerable interface, although this is optional.

2. The MoveNext() method of the returned IEnumerator interface is called.

**3.** If MoveNext() returns true, then the Current property of the IEnumerator interface is used to get a reference to an object, which is used in the foreach loop.

**4.** The preceding two steps repeat until MoveNext() returns false, at which point the loop terminates.

To enable this behavior in your classes, you must override several methods, keep track of indices, maintain the Current property, and so on. This can be a lot of work to achieve very little.

A simpler alternative is to use an iterator. Effectively, using iterators generates a lot of the code for you behind the scenes and hooks it all up correctly. Moreover, the syntax for using iterators is much easier to get a grip on.

A good definition of an iterator is a block of code that supplies all the values to be used in a foreach block in sequence. Typically, this block of code is a method, although you can also use property accessors and other blocks of code as iterators. To keep things simple, you'll just look at methods here.

Whatever the block of code is, its return type is restricted. Perhaps contrary to expectations, this return type isn't the same as the type of object being enumerated. For example, in a class that represents a collection of Animal objects, the return type of the iterator block can't be Animal. Two possible return types are the interface types mentioned earlier, IEnumerable or IEnumerator. You use these types as follows:

➤   To iterate over a class, use a method called GetEnumerator() with a return type of IEnumerator.

➤   To iterate over a class member, such as a method, use IEnumerable.

Within an iterator block, you select the values to be used in the foreach loop by using the yield keyword. The syntax for doing this is as follows:

```
yield return <value>;
```

That information is all you need to build a very simple example, as follows (you can find this code in SimpleIterators\Program.cs):

```
public static IEnumerable SimpleList()
{
   yield return "string 1";
   yield return "string 2";
   yield return "string 3";
}

static void Main(string[] args)
{
   foreach (string item in SimpleList())
      Console.WriteLine(item);

   Console.ReadKey();
}
```

> **NOTE** To test this code yourself, remember to add a using statement for the System .Collections namespace or fully qualify the System.Collections.IEnumerable interface. Alternately, you can find all the code for this project in the SimpleIterators folder in the downloadable code for this chapter.

Here, the static method SimpleList() is the iterator block. Because it is a method, you use a return type of IEnumerable. SimpleList() uses the yield keyword to supply three values to the foreach block that uses it, each of which is written to the screen. The result is shown in Figure 11-3.

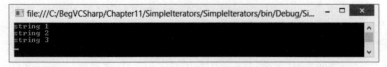

**FIGURE 11-3**

Obviously, this iterator isn't a particularly useful one, but it does show how this works in action and how simple the implementation can be. Looking at the code, you might wonder how the code knows to return `string` type items. In fact, it doesn't; it returns `object` type values. As you know, `object` is the base class for all types, so you can return anything from the `yield` statements.

However, the compiler is intelligent enough that you can interpret the returned values as whatever type you want in the context of the `foreach` loop. Here, the code asks for `string` type values, so those are the values you get to work. Should you change one of the `yield` lines so that it returns, say, an integer, you would get a bad cast exception in the `foreach` loop.

One more thing about iterators. It is possible to interrupt the return of information to the `foreach` loop by using the following statement:

```
yield break;
```

When this statement is encountered in an iterator, the iterator processing terminates immediately, as does the `foreach` loop using it.

Now it's time for a more complicated—and useful!—example. In this Try It Out, you'll implement an iterator that obtains prime numbers.

**TRY IT OUT** Implementing an Iterator: Ch11Ex03

1. Create a new console application called Ch11Ex03 and save it in the directory `C:\BegVCSharp\Chapter11`.

2. Add a new class called `Primes` and modify the code in `Primes.cs` as follows:

```csharp
using System;
using System.Collections;
using System.Collections.Generic;
using System.Linq;
using System.Text;
using System.Threading.Tasks;

namespace Ch11Ex03
{
    public class Primes
    {
        private long min;
        private long max;

        public Primes() : this(2, 100)
        {
        }

        public Primes(long minimum, long maximum)
        {
            if (minimum < 2)
                min = 2;
            else
                min = minimum;

            max = maximum;
        }

        public IEnumerator GetEnumerator()
```

```
        {
            for (long possiblePrime = min; possiblePrime <= max; possiblePrime++)
            {
                bool isPrime = true;
                for (long possibleFactor = 2; possibleFactor <=
                    (long)Math.Floor(Math.Sqrt(possiblePrime)); possibleFactor++)
                {
                    long remainderAfterDivision = possiblePrime % possibleFactor;
                    if (remainderAfterDivision == 0)
                    {
                        isPrime = false;
                        break;
                    }
                }
                if (isPrime)
                {
                    yield return possiblePrime;
                }
            }
        }
    }
}
```

**3.** Modify the code in `Program.cs` as follows:

```
static void Main(string[] args)
{
    Primes primesFrom2To1000 = new Primes(2, 1000);
    foreach (long i in primesFrom2To1000)
        Console.Write("{0} ", i);

    Console.ReadKey();
}
```

**4.** Execute the application. The result is shown in Figure 11-4.

**FIGURE 11-4**

### How It Works

This example consists of a class that enables you to enumerate over a collection of prime numbers between an upper and lower limit. The class that encapsulates the prime numbers uses an iterator to provide this functionality.

The code for `Primes` starts off with the basics: two fields to hold the maximum and minimum values to search between, and constructors to set these values. Note that the minimum value is restricted—it can't be less than 2. This makes sense, because 2 is the lowest prime number. The interesting code is all in the `GetEnumerator()` method. The method signature fulfils the rules for an iterator block in that it returns an `IEnumerator` type:

```
public IEnumerator GetEnumerator()
{
```

To extract prime numbers between limits, you need to test each number in turn, so you start with a `for` loop:

```
for (long possiblePrime = min; possiblePrime <= max; possiblePrime++)
{
```

Because you don't know whether a number is prime, you first assume that it is and then check to see if it isn't. That means checking whether any number between 2 and the square root of the number to be tested is a factor. If this is `true`, then the number isn't prime, so you move on to the next one. If the number is indeed prime, then you pass it to the `foreach` loop using `yield`:

```
bool isPrime = true;
for (long possibleFactor = 2; possibleFactor <=
    (long)Math.Floor(Math.Sqrt(possiblePrime)); possibleFactor++)
{
    long remainderAfterDivision = possiblePrime % possibleFactor;
    if (remainderAfterDivision == 0)
    {
        isPrime = false;
        break;
    }
}
if (isPrime)
{
    yield return possiblePrime;
}
}
}
```

An interesting fact reveals itself through this code if you set the minimum and maximum limits to very big numbers. When you execute the application, the results appear one at a time, with pauses in between, rather than all at once. This is evidence that the iterator code returns results one at a time, despite the fact that there is no obvious place where the code terminates between `yield` calls. Behind the scenes, calling `yield` does interrupt the code, which resumes when another value is requested—that is, when the `foreach` loop using the iterator begins a new cycle.

## Iterators and Collections

Earlier you were promised an explanation of how iterators can be used to iterate over the objects stored in a dictionary-type collection without having to deal with `DictionaryItem` objects. In the downloadable code for this chapter, you will find the code for the next project in the `DictionaryAnimals` folder. Recall the collection class `Animals`:

```
public class Animals : DictionaryBase
{
    public void Add(string newID, Animal newAnimal)
    {
        Dictionary.Add(newID, newAnimal);
    }

    public void Remove(string animalID)
    {
        Dictionary.Remove(animalID);
    }

    public Animal this[string animalID]
    {
        get
        {
            return (Animal)Dictionary[animalID];
        }
        set
        {
            Dictionary[animalID] = value;
        }
    }
}
```

You can add this simple iterator to the code to get the desired behavior:

```
public new IEnumerator GetEnumerator()
{
    foreach (object animal in Dictionary.Values)
        yield return (Animal)animal;
}
```

Now you can use the following code to iterate through the Animal objects in the collection:

```
foreach (Animal myAnimal in animalCollection)
{
    Console.WriteLine("New {0} object added to custom collection, " +
                      "Name = {1}", myAnimal.ToString(), myAnimal.Name);
}
```

## Deep Copying

Chapter 9 described how you can perform shallow copying with the System.Object.MemberwiseClone() protected method, by using a method like the GetCopy() one shown here:

```
public class Cloner
{
    public int Val;

    public Cloner(int newVal)
    {
        Val = newVal;
    }

    public object GetCopy()
    {
        return MemberwiseClone();
    }
}
```

Suppose you have fields that are reference types, rather than value types (for example, objects):

```
public class Content
{
    public int Val;
}

public class Cloner
{
    public Content MyContent = new Content();

    public Cloner(int newVal)
    {
        MyContent.Val = newVal;
    }

    public object GetCopy()
    {
        return MemberwiseClone();
    }
}
```

In this case, the shallow copy obtained though GetCopy() has a field that refers to the same object as the original object. The following code, which uses this Cloner class, illustrates the consequences of shallow copying reference types:

```
Cloner mySource = new Cloner(5);
Cloner myTarget = (Cloner)mySource.GetCopy();
Console.WriteLine("myTarget.MyContent.Val = {0}", myTarget.MyContent.Val);
mySource.MyContent.Val = 2;
Console.WriteLine("myTarget.MyContent.Val = {0}", myTarget.MyContent.Val);
```

The fourth line, which assigns a value to `mySource.MyContent.Val`, the `Val` public field of the `MyContent` public field of the original object, also changes the value of `myTarget.MyContent.Val`. That's because `mySource.MyContent` refers to the same object instance as `myTarget.MyContent`. The output of the preceding code is as follows:

```
myTarget.MyContent.Val = 5
myTarget.MyContent.Val = 2
```

To get around this, you need to perform a deep copy. You could just modify the `GetCopy()` method used previously to do this, but it is preferable to use the standard .NET Framework way of doing things: implement the `ICloneable` interface, which has the single method `Clone()`. This method takes no parameters and returns an `object` type result, giving it a signature identical to the `GetCopy()` method used earlier.

To modify the preceding classes, try using the following deep copy code:

```
public class Content
{
    public int Val;
}

public class Cloner : ICloneable
{
    public Content MyContent = new Content();

    public Cloner(int newVal)
    {
        MyContent.Val = newVal;
    }

    public object Clone()
    {
        Cloner clonedCloner = new Cloner(MyContent.Val);
        return clonedCloner;
    }
}
```

This created a new `Cloner` object by using the `Val` field of the `Content` object contained in the original `Cloner` object (`MyContent`). This field is a value type, so no deeper copying is necessary.

Using code similar to that just shown to test the shallow copy—but using `Clone()` instead of `GetCopy()`—gives you the following result:

```
myTarget.MyContent.Val = 5
myTarget.MyContent.Val = 5
```

This time, the contained objects are independent. Note that sometimes calls to `Clone()` are made recursively, in more complex object systems. For example, if the `MyContent` field of the `Cloner` class also required deep copying, then you might need the following:

```
public class Cloner : ICloneable
{
    public Content MyContent = new Content();

    ...

    public object Clone()
    {
        Cloner clonedCloner = new Cloner();
        clonedCloner.MyContent = MyContent.Clone();
        return clonedCloner;
    }
}
```

You're calling the default constructor here to simplify the syntax of creating a new `Cloner` object. For this code to work, you would also need to implement `ICloneable` on the `Content` class.

## Adding Deep Copying to CardLib

You can put this into practice by implementing the capability to copy `Card`, `Cards`, and `Deck` objects by using the `ICloneable` interface. This might be useful in some card games, where you might not necessarily want two decks with references to the same set of `Card` objects, although you might conceivably want to set up one deck to have the same card order as another.

Implementing cloning functionality for the `Card` class in `Ch11CardLib` is simple because shallow copying is sufficient (`Card` contains only value-type data, in the form of fields). Begin by making the following changes to the `class` definition:

```
public class Card : ICloneable
{
    public object Clone()
    {
        return MemberwiseClone();
    }
}
```

This implementation of `ICloneable` is just a shallow copy. There is no rule determining what should happen in the `Clone()` method, and this is sufficient for your purposes.

Next, implement `ICloneable` on the `Cards` collection class. This is slightly more complicated because it involves cloning every `Card` object in the original collection—so you need to make a deep copy:

```
public class Cards : CollectionBase, ICloneable
{
    public object Clone()
    {
        Cards newCards = new Cards();
        foreach (Card sourceCard in List)
        {
            newCards.Add((Card)sourceCard.Clone());
        }
        return newCards;
    }
}
```

Finally, implement `ICloneable` on the `Deck` class. Note a slight problem here: The `Deck` class in `Ch11CardLib` has no way to modify the cards it contains, short of shuffling them. There is no way, for example, to modify a `Deck` instance to have a given card order. To get around this, define a new private constructor for the `Deck` class that allows a specific `Cards` collection to be passed in when the `Deck` object is instantiated. Here's the code to implement cloning in this class:

```
public class Deck : ICloneable
{
    public object Clone()
    {
        Deck newDeck = new Deck(cards.Clone() as Cards);
        return newDeck;
    }

    private Deck(Cards newCards)
    {
        cards = newCards;
    }
}
```

Again, you can test this with some simple client code. As before, place this code within the `Main()` method of a client project for testing (you can find this code in `Ch11CardClient\Program.cs` in the chapter's online download):

```
Deck deck1 = new Deck();
Deck deck2 = (Deck)deck1.Clone();
Console.WriteLine("The first card in the original deck is: {0}",
```

```
                           deck1.GetCard(0));
            Console.WriteLine("The first card in the cloned deck is: {0}",
                           deck2.GetCard(0));
            deck1.Shuffle();
            Console.WriteLine("Original deck shuffled.");
            Console.WriteLine("The first card in the original deck is: {0}",
                           deck1.GetCard(0));
            Console.WriteLine("The first card in the cloned deck is: {0}",
                           deck2.GetCard(0));
            Console.ReadKey();
```

The output will be similar to what is shown in Figure 11-5.

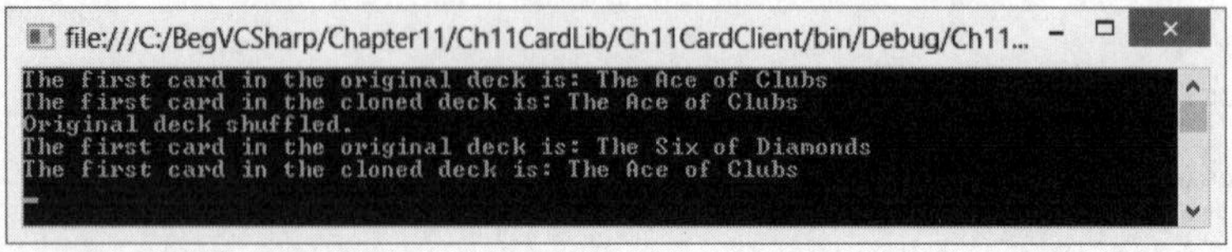

**FIGURE 11-5**

## COMPARISONS

This section covers two types of comparisons between objects:

➤ Type comparisons

➤ Value comparisons

Type comparisons—that is, determining what an object is, or what it inherits from—are important in all areas of C# programming. Often when you pass an object—to a method, for example—what happens next depends on the type of the object. You've seen this in passing in this and earlier chapters, but here you will see some more useful techniques.

Value comparisons are also something you've seen a lot of, at least with simple types. When it comes to comparing values of objects, things get a little more complicated. You have to define what is meant by a comparison for a start, and what operators such as > mean in the context of your classes. This is especially important in collections, for which you might want to sort objects according to some condition, perhaps alphabetically or according to a more complicated algorithm.

### Type Comparisons

When comparing objects, you often need to know their type, which enables you to determine whether a value comparison is possible. In Chapter 9 you saw the GetType() method, which all classes inherit from System.Object, and how this method can be used in combination with the typeof() operator to determine (and take action depending on) object types:

```
if (myObj.GetType() == typeof(MyComplexClass))
{
    // myObj is an instance of the class MyComplexClass.
}
```

You've also seen how the default implementation of ToString(), also inherited from System.Object, will get you a string representation of an object's type. You can compare these strings too, although that's a rather messy way to accomplish this.

This section demonstrates a handy shorthand way of doing things: the is operator. This operator allows for much more readable code and, as you will see, has the advantage of examining base classes. Before looking at the is operator, though, you need to be aware of what often happens behind the scenes when dealing with value types (as opposed to reference types): *boxing* and *unboxing*.

## Boxing and Unboxing

In Chapter 8, you learned the difference between reference types and value types, which was illustrated in Chapter 9 by comparing structs (which are value types) with classes (which are reference types). Boxing is the act of converting a value type into the System.Object type or to an interface type that is implemented by the value type. Unboxing is the opposite conversion.

For example, suppose you have the following struct type:

```
struct MyStruct
{
    public int Val;
}
```

You can box a struct of this type by placing it into an object-type variable:

```
MyStruct valType1 = new MyStruct();
valType1.Val = 5;
object refType = valType1;
```

Here, you create a new variable (valType1) of type MyStruct, assign a value to the Val member of this struct, and then box it into an object-type variable (refType).

The object created by boxing a variable in this way contains a reference to a copy of the value-type variable, not a reference to the original value-type variable. You can verify this by modifying the original struct's contents and then unboxing the struct contained in the object into a new variable and examining its contents:

```
valType1.Val = 6;
MyStruct valType2 = (MyStruct)refType;
Console.WriteLine("valType2.Val = {0}", valType2.Val);
```

This code gives you the following output:

```
valType2.Val = 5
```

When you assign a reference type to an object, however, you get a different behavior. You can see this by changing MyStruct into a class (ignoring the fact that the name of this class isn't appropriate now):

```
class MyStruct
{
    public int Val;
}
```

With no changes to the client code shown previously (again ignoring the misnamed variables), you get the following output:

```
valType2.Val = 6
```

You can also box value types into interface types, so long as they implement that interface. For example, suppose the MyStruct type implements the IMyInterface interface as follows:

```
interface IMyInterface
{
}

struct MyStruct : IMyInterface
{
    public int Val;
}
```

You can then box the struct into an IMyInterface type as follows:

```
MyStruct valType1 = new MyStruct();
IMyInterface refType = valType1;
```

You can unbox it by using the normal casting syntax:

```
MyStruct ValType2 = (MyStruct)refType;
```

As shown in these examples, boxing is performed without your intervention—that is, you don't have to write any code to make it possible. Unboxing a value requires an explicit conversion, however, and requires you to make a cast (boxing is implicit and doesn't have this requirement).

You might be wondering why you would actually want to do this. There are two very good reasons why boxing is extremely useful. First, it enables you to use value types in collections (such as `ArrayList`) where the items are of type `object`. Second, it's the internal mechanism that enables you to call `object` methods on value types, such as `int`s and structs.

It is worth noting that unboxing is necessary before access to the value type contents is possible.

## The is Operator

Despite its name, the `is` operator isn't a way to determine whether an object is a certain type. Instead, the `is` operator enables you to check whether an object either is or *can be converted into* a given type. If this is the case, then the operator evaluates to `true`.

Earlier examples showed a `Cow` and a `Chicken` class, both of which inherit from `Animal`. Using the `is` operator to compare objects with the `Animal` type will return `true` for objects of all three of these types, not just `Animal`. This is something you'd have a hard time achieving with the `GetType()` method and `typeof()` operator shown previously.

The `is` operator has the following syntax:

```
<operand> is <type>
```

The possible results of this expression are as follows:

➤ If `<type>` is a class type, then the result is `true` if `<operand>` is of that type, if it inherits from that type, or if it can be boxed into that type.

➤ If `<type>` is an interface type, then the result is `true` if `<operand>` is of that type or it is a type that implements the interface.

➤ If `<type>` is a value type, then the result is `true` if `<operand>` is of that type or it is a type that can be unboxed into that type.

The following Try It Out shows how this works in practice.

**TRY IT OUT** | Using the is Operator: Ch11Ex04\Program.cs

**1.** Create a new console application called Ch11Ex04 in the directory `C:\BegVCSharp\Chapter11`.

**2.** Modify the code in `Program.cs` as follows:

```
namespace Ch11Ex04
{
    class Checker
    {
        public void Check(object param1)
        {
            if (param1 is ClassA)
                Console.WriteLine("Variable can be converted to ClassA.");
            else
                Console.WriteLine("Variable can't be converted to ClassA.");

            if (param1 is IMyInterface)
                Console.WriteLine("Variable can be converted to IMyInterface.");
            else
                Console.WriteLine("Variable can't be converted to IMyInterface.");

            if (param1 is MyStruct)
```

```
                 Console.WriteLine("Variable can be converted to MyStruct.");
            else
                 Console.WriteLine("Variable can't be converted to MyStruct.");
        }
    }

    interface IMyInterface
    {
    }

    class ClassA : IMyInterface
    {
    }

    class ClassB : IMyInterface
    {
    }

    class ClassC
    {
    }

    class ClassD : ClassA
    {
    }

    struct MyStruct : IMyInterface
    {
    }

    class Program
    {
        static void Main(string[] args)
        {
            Checker check = new Checker();
            ClassA try1 = new ClassA();
            ClassB try2 = new ClassB();
            ClassC try3 = new ClassC();
            ClassD try4 = new ClassD();
            MyStruct try5 = new MyStruct();
            object try6 = try5;
            Console.WriteLine("Analyzing ClassA type variable:");
            check.Check(try1);
            Console.WriteLine("\nAnalyzing ClassB type variable:");
            check.Check(try2);
            Console.WriteLine("\nAnalyzing ClassC type variable:");
            check.Check(try3);
            Console.WriteLine("\nAnalyzing ClassD type variable:");
            check.Check(try4);
            Console.WriteLine("\nAnalyzing MyStruct type variable:");
            check.Check(try5);
            Console.WriteLine("\nAnalyzing boxed MyStruct type variable:");
            check.Check(try6);
            Console.ReadKey();
        }
    }
}
```

**3.** Execute the code. The result is shown in Figure 11-6.

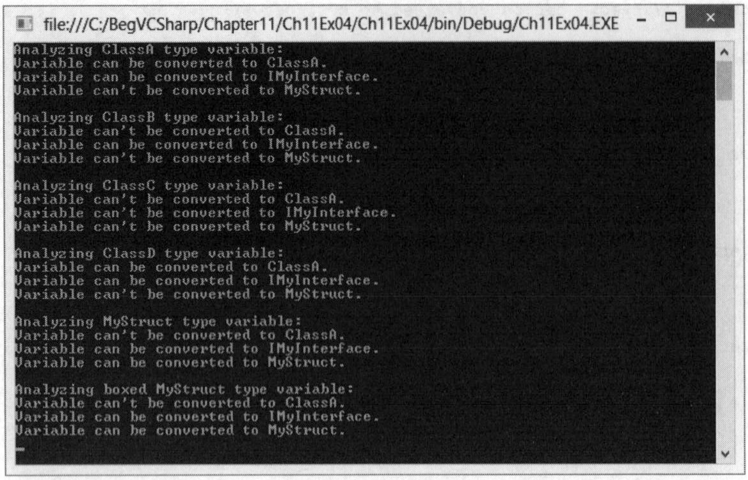

**FIGURE 11-6**

*How It Works*

This example illustrates the various results possible when using the `is` operator. Three classes, an interface, and a structure are defined and used as parameters to a method of a class that uses the `is` operator to determine whether they can be converted into the `ClassA` type, the interface type, and the struct type.

Only the `ClassA` and `ClassD` (which inherits from `ClassA`) types are compatible with `ClassA`. Types that don't inherit from a class are not compatible with that class.

The `ClassA`, `ClassB`, and `MyStruct` types all implement `IMyInterface`, so these are all compatible with the `IMyInterface` type. `ClassD` inherits from `ClassA`, so it too is compatible. Therefore, only `ClassC` is incompatible.

Finally, only variables of type `MyStruct` itself and boxed variables of that type are compatible with `MyStruct`, because you can't convert reference types to value types (although, of course, you can unbox previously boxed variables).

## Value Comparisons

Consider two `Person` objects representing people, each with an integer `Age` property. You might want to compare them to see which person is older. You can simply use the following code:

```
if (person1.Age > person2.Age)
{
    ...
}
```

This works fine, but there are alternatives. You might prefer to use syntax such as the following:

```
if (person1 > person2)
{
    ...
}
```

This is possible using *operator overloading*, which you'll look at in this section. This is a powerful technique, but it should be used judiciously. In the preceding code, it is not immediately obvious that ages are being compared—it could be height, weight, IQ, or just general "greatness."

Another option is to use the `IComparable` and `IComparer` interfaces, which enable you to define how objects will be compared to each other in a standard way. This technique is supported by the various collection classes in the .NET Framework, making it an excellent way to sort objects in a collection.

## Operator Overloading

*Operator overloading* enables you to use standard operators, such as +, >, and so on, with classes that you design. This is called "overloading" because you are supplying your own implementations for these operators when used with specific parameter types, in much the same way that you overload methods by supplying different parameters for methods with the same name.

Operator overloading is useful because you can perform whatever processing you want in the implementation of the operator overload, which might not be as simple as, for example, +, meaning "add these two operands together." Later, you'll see a good example of this in a further upgrade of the `CardLib` library, whereby you'll provide implementations for comparison operators that compare two cards to see which would beat the other in a trick (one round of card game play).

Because a trick in many card games depends on the suits of the cards involved, this isn't as straightforward as comparing the numbers on the cards. If the second card laid down is a different suit from the first, then the first card wins regardless of its rank. You can implement this by considering the order of the two operands. You can also take a trump suit into account, whereby trumps beat other suits even if that isn't the first suit laid down. This means that calculating that `card1 > card2` is `true` (that is, `card1` will beat `card2` if `card1` is laid down first), doesn't necessarily imply that `card2 > card1` is `false`. If neither `card1` nor `card2` are trumps and they belong to different suits, then both of these comparisons will be `true`.

To start with, though, here's a look at the basic syntax for operator overloading. Operators can be overloaded by adding operator type members (which must be static) to a class. Some operators have multiple uses (such as -, which has unary and binary capabilities); therefore, you also specify how many operands you are dealing with and the types of these operands. In general, you will have operands that are the same type as the class in which the operator is defined, although it's possible to define operators that work on mixed types, as you'll see shortly.

As an example, consider the simple type `AddClass1`, defined as follows:

```
public class AddClass1
{
    public int val;
}
```

This is just a wrapper around an `int` value but it illustrates the principles. With this class, code such as the following will fail to compile:

```
AddClass1 op1 = new AddClass1();
op1.val = 5;
AddClass1 op2 = new AddClass1();
op2.val = 5;
AddClass1 op3 = op1 + op2;
```

The error you get informs you that the + operator cannot be applied to operands of the `AddClass1` type. This is because you haven't defined an operation to perform yet. Code such as the following works, but it won't give you the result you might want:

```
AddClass1 op1 = new AddClass1();
op1.val = 5;
AddClass1 op2 = new AddClass1();
op2.val = 5;
bool op3 = op1 == op2;
```

Here, `op1` and `op2` are compared by using the == binary operator to determine whether they refer to the same object, not to verify whether their values are equal. `op3` will be `false` in the preceding code, even though `op1.val` and `op2.val` are identical.

To overload the + operator, use the following code:

```
public class AddClass1
{
    public int val;

    public static AddClass1 operator +(AddClass1 op1, AddClass1 op2)
    {
        AddClass1 returnVal = new AddClass1();
        returnVal.val = op1.val + op2.val;
        return returnVal;
    }
}
```

As you can see, operator overloads look much like standard `static` method declarations, except that they use the keyword `operator` and the operator itself, rather than a method name. You can now successfully use the + operator with this class, as in the previous example:

```
AddClass1 op3 = op1 + op2;
```

Overloading all binary operators fits the same pattern. Unary operators look similar but have only one parameter:

```
public class AddClass1
{
    public int val;

    public static AddClass1 operator +(AddClass1 op1, AddClass1 op2)
    {
        AddClass1 returnVal = new AddClass1();
        returnVal.val = op1.val + op2.val;
        return returnVal;
    }

    public static AddClass1 operator -(AddClass1 op1)
    {
        AddClass1 returnVal = new AddClass1();
        returnVal.val = -op1.val;
        return returnVal;
    }
}
```

Both these operators work on operands of the same type as the class and have return values that are also of that type. Consider, however, the following class definitions:

```
public class AddClass1
{
    public int val;

    public static AddClass3 operator +(AddClass1 op1, AddClass2 op2)
    {
        AddClass3 returnVal = new AddClass3();
        returnVal.val = op1.val + op2.val;
        return returnVal;
    }
}

public class AddClass2
{
    public int val;
}

public class AddClass3
{
    public int val;
}
```

This will allow the following code:

```
AddClass1 op1 = new AddClass1();
op1.val = 5;
AddClass2 op2 = new AddClass2();
op2.val = 5;
AddClass3 op3 = op1 + op2;
```

When appropriate, you can mix types in this way. Note, however, that if you added the same operator to `AddClass2`, then the preceding code would fail because it would be ambiguous as to which operator to use. You should, therefore, take care not to add operators with the same signature to more than one class.

In addition, if you mix types, then the operands must be supplied in the same order as the parameters to the operator overload. If you attempt to use your overloaded operator with the operands in the wrong order, the operation will fail. For example, you can't use the operator like,

```
AddClass3 op3 = op2 + op1;
```

unless, of course, you supply another overload with the parameters reversed:

```
public static AddClass3 operator +(AddClass2 op1, AddClass1 op2)
{
    AddClass3 returnVal = new AddClass3();
    returnVal.val = op1.val + op2.val;
    return returnVal;
}
```

The following operators can be overloaded:

➤ Unary operators—`+, -, !, ~, ++, --, true, false`

➤ Binary operators—`+, -, *, /, %, &, |, ^, <<, >>`

➤ Comparison operators—`==, !=, <, >, <=, >=`

> **NOTE** *If you overload the* `true` *and* `false` *operators, then you can use classes in Boolean expressions, such as* `if(op1){}`*.*

You can't overload assignment operators, such as `+=`, but these operators use their simple counterparts, such as `+`, so you don't have to worry about that. Overloading `+` means that `+=` will function as expected. The `=` operator can't be overloaded because it has such a fundamental usage, but this operator is related to the user-defined conversion operators, which you'll look at in the next section.

You also can't overload `&&` and `||`, but these operators use the `&` and `|` operators to perform their calculations, so overloading these is enough.

Some operators, such as `<` and `>`, must be overloaded in pairs. That is, you can't overload `<` unless you also overload `>`. In many cases, you can simply call other operators from these to reduce the code required (and the errors that might occur), as shown in this example:

```
public class AddClass1
{
    public int val;

    public static bool operator >=(AddClass1 op1, AddClass1 op2)
    {
        return (op1.val >= op2.val);
    }

    public static bool operator <(AddClass1 op1, AddClass1 op2)
    {
```

```
            return !(op1 >= op2);
        }

        // Also need implementations for <= and > operators.
    }
```

In more complex operator definitions, this can reduce the lines of code. It also means that you have less code to change if you later decide to modify the implementation of these operators.

The same applies to == and !=, but with these operators it is often worth overriding `Object.Equals()` and `Object.GetHashCode()`, because both of these functions can also be used to compare objects. By overriding these methods, you ensure that whatever technique users of the class use, they get the same result. This isn't essential, but it's worth adding for completeness. It requires the following nonstatic override methods:

```
public class AddClass1
{
    public int val;

    public static bool operator ==(AddClass1 op1, AddClass1 op2)
    {
        return (op1.val == op2.val);
    }

    public static bool operator !=(AddClass1 op1, AddClass1 op2)
    {
        return !(op1 == op2);
    }

    public override bool Equals(object op1)
    {
        return val == ((AddClass1)op1).val;
    }

    public override int GetHashCode()
    {
        return val;
    }
}
```

`GetHashCode()` is used to obtain a unique `int` value for an object instance based on its state. Here, using `val` is fine, because it is also an `int` value.

Note that `Equals()` uses an `object` type parameter. You need to use this signature or you will be overloading this method, rather than overriding it, and the default implementation will still be accessible to users of the class. Instead, you must use casting to get the required result. It is often worth checking the object type using the `is` operator discussed earlier, in code such as this:

```
public override bool Equals(object op1)
{
    if (op1 is AddClass1)
    {
        return val == ((AddClass1)op1).val;
    }
    else
    {
        throw new ArgumentException(
            "Cannot compare AddClass1 objects with objects of type "
            + op1.GetType().ToString());
    }
}
```

In this code, an exception is thrown if the operand passed to `Equals` is of the wrong type or cannot be converted into the correct type. Of course, this behavior might not be what you want. You might want to be able to compare objects of one type with objects of another type, in which case more branching would be necessary. Alternatively, you might want to restrict comparisons to those in which both objects are of exactly the same type, which would require the following change to the first `if` statement:

```
if (op1.GetType() == typeof(AddClass1))
```

## Adding Operator Overloads to CardLib

Now you'll upgrade your `Ch11CardLib` project again, adding operator overloading to the `Card` class. Again, you can find the code for the classes that follow in the `Ch11CardLib` folder of this chapter's code download. First, though, you'll add the extra fields to the `Card` class that allow for trump suits and an option to place aces high. You make these static, because when they are set, they apply to all `Card` objects:

```
public class Card
{
    /// <summary>
    /// Flag for trump usage. If true, trumps are valued higher
    /// than cards of other suits.
    /// </summary>
    public static bool useTrumps = false;

    /// <summary>
    /// Trump suit to use if useTrumps is true.
    /// </summary>
    public static Suit trump = Suit.Club;

    /// <summary>
    /// Flag that determines whether aces are higher than kings or lower
    /// than deuces.
    /// </summary>
    public static bool isAceHigh = true;
```

These rules apply to all `Card` objects in every `Deck` in an application. It's not possible to have two decks of cards with cards contained in each that obey different rules. That's fine for this class library, however, as you can safely assume that if a single application wants to use separate rules, then it could maintain these itself, perhaps setting the static members of `Card` whenever decks are switched.

Because you have done this, it is worth adding a few more constructors to the `Deck` class to initialize decks with different characteristics:

```
    /// <summary>
    /// Nondefault constructor. Allows aces to be set high.
    /// </summary>
    public Deck(bool isAceHigh) : this()
    {
        Card.isAceHigh = isAceHigh;
    }

    /// <summary>
    /// Nondefault constructor. Allows a trump suit to be used.
    /// </summary>
    public Deck(bool useTrumps, Suit trump) : this()
    {
        Card.useTrumps = useTrumps;
        Card.trump = trump;
    }

    /// <summary>
    /// Nondefault constructor. Allows aces to be set high and a trump suit
    /// to be used.
```

```
/// </summary>
public Deck(bool isAceHigh, bool useTrumps, Suit trump) : this()
{
    Card.isAceHigh = isAceHigh;
    Card.useTrumps = useTrumps;
    Card.trump = trump;
}
```

Each of these constructors is defined by using the `: this()` syntax shown in Chapter 9, so in all cases the default constructor is called before the nondefault one, initializing the deck.

Now add your operator overloads (and suggested overrides) to the `Card` class:

```
public static bool operator ==(Card card1, Card card2)
{
    return (card1.suit == card2.suit) && (card1.rank == card2.rank);
}

public static bool operator !=(Card card1, Card card2)
{
    return !(card1 == card2);
}

public override bool Equals(object card)
{
    return this == (Card)card;
}

public override int GetHashCode()
{
    return 13 * (int)suit + (int)rank;
}

public static bool operator >(Card card1, Card card2)
{
    if (card1.suit == card2.suit)
    {
        if (isAceHigh)
        {
            if (card1.rank == Rank.Ace)
            {
                if (card2.rank == Rank.Ace)
                    return false;
                else
                    return true;
            }
            else
            {
                if (card2.rank == Rank.Ace)
                    return false;
                else
                    return (card1.rank > card2.rank);
            }
        }
        else
        {
            return (card1.rank > card2.rank);
        }
    }
    else
    {
```

```
            if (useTrumps && (card2.suit == Card.trump))
                return false;
            else
                return true;
        }
    }

    public static bool operator <(Card card1, Card card2)
    {
        return !(card1 >= card2);
    }

    public static bool operator >=(Card card1, Card card2)
    {
        if (card1.suit == card2.suit)
        {
            if (isAceHigh)
            {
                if (card1.rank == Rank.Ace)
                {
                    return true;
                }
                else
                {
                    if (card2.rank == Rank.Ace)
                        return false;
                    else
                        return (card1.rank >= card2.rank);
                }
            }
            else
            {
                return (card1.rank >= card2.rank);
            }
        }
        else
        {
            if (useTrumps && (card2.suit == Card.trump))
                return false;
            else
                return true;
        }
    }

    public static bool operator <=(Card card1, Card card2)
    {
        return !(card1 > card2);
    }
```

There's not much to note here, except perhaps the slightly lengthy code for the > and >= overloaded operators. If you step through the code for >, you can see how it works and why these steps are necessary.

You are comparing two cards, card1 and card2, where card1 is assumed to be the first one laid down on the table. As discussed earlier, this becomes important when you are using trump cards, because a trump will beat a non-trump even if the non-trump has a higher rank. Of course, if the suits of the two cards are identical, then whether the suit is the trump suit or not is irrelevant, so this is the first comparison you make:

```
public static bool operator >(Card card1, Card card2)
{
    if (card1.suit == card2.suit)
    {
```

If the static `isAceHigh` flag is `true`, then you can't compare the cards' ranks directly via their value in the `Rank` enumeration, because the rank of ace has a value of `1` in this enumeration, which is less than that of all other ranks. Instead, use the following steps:

➤ If the first card is an ace, then check whether the second card is also an ace. If it is, then the first card won't beat the second. If the second card isn't an ace, then the first card wins:

```
if (isAceHigh)
{
    if (card1.rank == Rank.Ace)
    {
        if (card2.rank == Rank.Ace)
            return false;
        else
            return true;
    }
```

➤ If the first card isn't an ace, then you also need to check whether the second one is. If it is, then the second card wins; otherwise, you can compare the rank values because you know that aces aren't an issue:

```
    else
    {
        if (card2.rank == Rank.Ace)
            return false;
        else
            return (card1.rank > card2.rank);
    }
}
```

➤ If aces aren't high, then you just compare the rank values:

```
else
{
    return (card1.rank > card2.rank);
}
```

The remainder of the code concerns the case where the suits of `card1` and `card2` are different. Here, the static `useTrumps` flag is important. If this flag is `true` and `card2` is of the trump suit, then you can say definitively that `card1` isn't a trump (because the two cards have different suits); and trumps always win, so `card2` is the higher card:

```
else
{
    if (useTrumps && (card2.suit == Card.trump))
        return false;
```

If `card2` isn't a trump (or `useTrumps` is `false`), then `card1` wins, because it was the first card laid down:

```
    else
        return true;
    }
}
```

Only one other operator (`>=`) uses code similar to this, and the other operators are very simple, so there's no need to go into more detail about them.

The following simple client code tests these operators. Simply place it in the `Main()` method of a client project to test it, like the client code shown earlier in the `CardLib` examples (you can find this code in `Ch11CardClient\Program.cs`):

```
Card.isAceHigh = true;
Console.WriteLine("Aces are high.");
Card.useTrumps = true;
Card.trump = Suit.Club;
```

```
    Console.WriteLine("Clubs are trumps.");

    Card card1, card2, card3, card4, card5;
    card1 = new Card(Suit.Club, Rank.Five);
    card2 = new Card(Suit.Club, Rank.Five);
    card3 = new Card(Suit.Club, Rank.Ace);
    card4 = new Card(Suit.Heart, Rank.Ten);
    card5 = new Card(Suit.Diamond, Rank.Ace);
    Console.WriteLine("{0} == {1} ? {2}",
        card1.ToString(), card2.ToString(), card1 == card2);
    Console.WriteLine("{0} != {1} ? {2}",
        card1.ToString(), card3.ToString(), card1 != card3);
    Console.WriteLine("{0}.Equals({1}) ? {2}",
        card1.ToString(), card4.ToString(), card1.Equals(card4));
    Console.WriteLine("Card.Equals({0}, {1}) ? {2}",
        card3.ToString(), card4.ToString(), Card.Equals(card3, card4));
    Console.WriteLine("{0} > {1} ? {2}",
        card1.ToString(), card2.ToString(), card1 > card2);
    Console.WriteLine("{0} <= {1} ? {2}",
        card1.ToString(), card3.ToString(), card1 <= card3);
    Console.WriteLine("{0} > {1} ? {2}",
        card1.ToString(), card4.ToString(), card1 > card4);
    Console.WriteLine("{0} > {1} ? {2}",
        card4.ToString(), card1.ToString(), card4 > card1);
    Console.WriteLine("{0} > {1} ? {2}",
        card5.ToString(), card4.ToString(), card5 > card4);
    Console.WriteLine("{0} > {1} ? {2}",
        card4.ToString(), card5.ToString(), card4 > card5);
    Console.ReadKey();
```

The results are as shown in Figure 11-7.

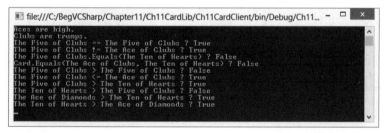

**FIGURE 11-7**

In each case, the operators are applied taking the specified rules into account. This is particularly apparent in the last four lines of output, demonstrating how trump cards always beat non-trumps.

### The IComparable and IComparer Interfaces

The IComparable and IComparer interfaces are the standard way to compare objects in the .NET Framework. The difference between the interfaces is as follows:

➤  IComparable is implemented in the class of the object to be compared and allows comparisons between that object and another object.

➤  IComparer is implemented in a separate class, which allows comparisons between any two objects.

Typically, you give a class default comparison code by using IComparable, and nondefault comparisons using other classes.

`IComparable` exposes the single method `CompareTo()`, which accepts an object. You could, for example, implement it in a way that enables you to pass a `Person` object to it and determine whether that person is older or younger than the current person. In fact, this method returns an `int`, so you could also determine how much older or younger the second person is:

```
if (person1.CompareTo(person2) == 0)
{
    Console.WriteLine("Same age");
}
else if (person1.CompareTo(person2) > 0)
{
    Console.WriteLine("person 1 is Older");
}
else
{
    Console.WriteLine("person1 is Younger");
}
```

`IComparer` exposes the single method `Compare()`, which accepts two objects and returns an integer result just like `CompareTo()`. With an object supporting `IComparer`, you could use code like the following:

```
if (personComparer.Compare(person1, person2) == 0)
{
    Console.WriteLine("Same age");
}
else if (personComparer.Compare(person1, person2) > 0)
{
    Console.WriteLine("person 1 is Older");
}
else
{
    Console.WriteLine("person1 is Younger");
}
```

In both cases, the parameters supplied to the methods are of the type `System.Object`. This means that you can compare one object to another object of any other type, so you usually have to perform some type comparison before returning a result, and maybe even throw exceptions if the wrong types are used.

The .NET Framework includes a default implementation of the `IComparer` interface on a class called `Comparer`, found in the `System.Collections` namespace. This class is capable of performing culture-specific comparisons between simple types, as well as any type that supports the `IComparable` interface. You can use it, for example, with the following code:

```
string firstString = "First String";
string secondString = "Second String";
Console.WriteLine("Comparing '{0}' and '{1}', result: {2}",
    firstString, secondString,
    Comparer.Default.Compare(firstString, secondString));

int firstNumber = 35;
int secondNumber = 23;
Console.WriteLine("Comparing '{0}' and '{1}', result: {2}",
    firstNumber, secondNumber,
    Comparer.Default.Compare(firstNumber, secondNumber));
```

This uses the `Comparer.Default` static member to obtain an instance of the `Comparer` class, and then uses the `Compare()` method to compare first two strings, and then two integers.

The result is as follows:

```
Comparing 'First String' and 'Second String', result: -1
Comparing '35' and '23', result: 1
```

Because F comes before S in the alphabet, it is deemed "less than" S, so the result of the first comparison is –1. Similarly, 35 is greater than 23, hence the result of 1. Note that the results do not indicate the magnitude of the difference.

When using `Comparer`, you must use types that can be compared. Attempting to compare `firstString` with `firstNumber`, for instance, will generate an exception.

Here are a few more points about the behavior of this class:

➤ Objects passed to `Comparer.Compare()` are checked to determine whether they support `IComparable`. If they do, then that implementation is used.

➤ Null values are allowed, and are interpreted as being "less than" any other object.

➤ Strings are processed according to the current culture. To process strings according to a different culture (or language), the `Comparer` class must be instantiated using its constructor, which enables you to pass a `System.Globalization.CultureInfo` object specifying the culture to use.

➤ Strings are processed in a case-sensitive way. To process them in a non-case-sensitive way, you need to use the `CaseInsensitiveComparer` class, which otherwise works exactly the same.

## Sorting Collections

Many collection classes allow sorting, either by default comparisons between objects or by custom methods. `ArrayList` is one example. It contains the method `Sort()`, which can be used without parameters, in which case default comparisons are used, or it can be passed an `IComparer` interface to use to compare pairs of objects.

When you have an `ArrayList` filled with simple types, such as integers or strings, the default comparer is fine. For your own classes, you must either implement `IComparable` in your class definition or create a separate class supporting `IComparer` to use for comparisons.

Note that some classes in the `System.Collections` namespace, including `CollectionBase`, don't expose a method for sorting. If you want to sort a collection you have derived from this class, then you have to do a bit more work and sort the internal `List` collection yourself.

The following Try It Out shows how to use a default and nondefault comparer to sort a list.

**TRY IT OUT** Sorting a List: Ch11Ex05

1. Create a new console application called Ch11Ex05 in the directory `C:\BegVCSharp\Chapter11`.

2. Add a new class called `Person` and modify the code in `Person.cs` as follows:

```
namespace Ch11Ex05
{
    public class Person : IComparable
    {
        public string Name;
        public int Age;

        public Person(string name, int age)
        {
            Name = name;
            Age = age;
        }

        public int CompareTo(object obj)
        {
            if (obj is Person)
            {
                Person otherPerson = obj as Person;
                return this.Age - otherPerson.Age;
            }
            else
```

```
                {
                    throw new ArgumentException(
                        "Object to compare to is not a Person object.");
                }
            }
        }
    }
}
```

3. Add another new class called `PersonComparerName` and modify the code as follows:

```
using System;
using System.Collections;
using System.Collections.Generic;
using System.Linq;
using System.Text;
using System.Threading.Tasks;

namespace Ch11Ex05
{
    public class PersonComparerName : IComparer
    {
        public static IComparer Default = new PersonComparerName();

        public int Compare(object x, object y)
        {
            if (x is Person && y is Person)
            {
                return Comparer.Default.Compare(
                    ((Person)x).Name, ((Person)y).Name);
            }
            else
            {
                throw new ArgumentException(
                    "One or both objects to compare are not Person objects.");
            }
        }
    }
}
```

4. Modify the code in `Program.cs` as follows:

```
using System;
using System.Collections;
using System.Collections.Generic;
using System.Linq;
using System.Text;
using System.Threading.Tasks;

namespace Ch11Ex05
{
    class Program
    {
        static void Main(string[] args)
        {
            ArrayList list = new ArrayList();
            list.Add(new Person("Jim", 30));
            list.Add(new Person("Bob", 25));
            list.Add(new Person("Bert", 27));
            list.Add(new Person("Ernie", 22));

            Console.WriteLine("Unsorted people:");
            for (int i = 0; i < list.Count; i++)
            {
                Console.WriteLine("{0} ({1})",
                    (list[i] as Person).Name, (list[i] as Person).Age);
```

```
            }
            Console.WriteLine();

            Console.WriteLine(
                "People sorted with default comparer (by age):");
            list.Sort();
            for (int i = 0; i < list.Count; i++)
            {
                Console.WriteLine("{0} ({1})",
                    (list[i] as Person).Name, (list[i] as Person).Age);
            }
            Console.WriteLine();

            Console.WriteLine(
                "People sorted with nondefault comparer (by name):");
            list.Sort(PersonComparerName.Default);
            for (int i = 0; i < list.Count; i++)
            {
                Console.WriteLine("{0} ({1})",
                    (list[i] as Person).Name, (list[i] as Person).Age);
            }

            Console.ReadKey();
        }
    }
}
```

5.  Execute the code. The result is shown in Figure 11-8.

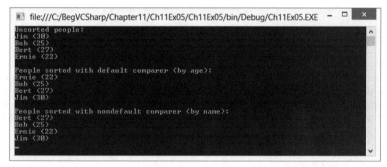

**FIGURE 11-8**

### How It Works

An `ArrayList` containing `Person` objects is sorted in two different ways here. By calling the
`ArrayList.Sort()` method with no parameters, the default comparison is used, which is the `CompareTo()`
method in the `Person` class (because this class implements `IComparable`):

```
public int CompareTo(object obj)
{
    if (obj is Person)
    {
        Person otherPerson = obj as Person;
        return this.Age - otherPerson.Age;
    }
    else
    {
        throw new ArgumentException(
            "Object to compare to is not a Person object.");
    }
}
```

This method first checks whether its argument can be compared to a `Person` object—that is, whether the object can be converted into a `Person` object. If there is a problem, then an exception is thrown. Otherwise, the `Age` properties of the two `Person` objects are compared.

Next, a nondefault comparison sort is performed using the `PersonComparerName` class, which implements `IComparer`. This class has a `public static` field for ease of use:

```
public static IComparer Default = new PersonComparerName();
```

This enables you to get an instance using `PersonComparerName.Default`, just like the `Comparer` class shown earlier. The `CompareTo()` method of this class is as follows:

```
public int Compare(object x, object y)
{
    if (x is Person && y is Person)
    {
        return Comparer.Default.Compare(
            ((Person)x).Name, ((Person)y).Name);
    }
    else
    {
        throw new ArgumentException(
            "One or both objects to compare are not Person objects.");
    }
}
```

Again, arguments are first checked to determine whether they are `Person` objects. If they aren't, then an exception is thrown. If they are, then the default `Comparer` object is used to compare the two string `Name` fields of the `Person` objects.

## CONVERSIONS

Thus far, you have used casting whenever you have needed to convert one type into another, but this isn't the only way to do things. Just as an `int` can be converted into a `long` or a `double` implicitly as part of a calculation, you can define how classes you have created can be converted into other classes (either implicitly or explicitly). To do this, you overload conversion operators, much like other operators were overloaded earlier in this chapter. You'll see how in the first part of this section. You'll also see another useful operator, the `as` operator, which in general is preferable to casting when using reference types.

### Overloading Conversion Operators

As well as overloading mathematical operators, as shown earlier, you can define both implicit and explicit conversions between types. This is necessary if you want to convert between types that aren't related—if there is no inheritance relationship between them and no shared interfaces, for example.

Suppose you define an implicit conversion between `ConvClass1` and `ConvClass2`. This means that you can write code such as the following:

```
ConvClass1 op1 = new ConvClass1();
ConvClass2 op2 = op1;
```

Alternatively, you can define an explicit conversion:

```
ConvClass1 op1 = new ConvClass1();
ConvClass2 op2 = (ConvClass2)op1;
```

As an example, consider the following code:

```
public class ConvClass1
{
    public int val;

    public static implicit operator ConvClass2(ConvClass1 op1)
```

```
    {
        ConvClass2 returnVal = new ConvClass2();
        returnVal.val = op1.val;
        return returnVal;
    }
}

public class ConvClass2
{
    public double val;

    public static explicit operator ConvClass1(ConvClass2 op1)
    {
        ConvClass1 returnVal = new ConvClass1();
        checked {returnVal.val = (int)op1.val;};
        return returnVal;
    }
}
```

Here, ConvClass1 contains an int value and ConvClass2 contains a double value. Because int values can be converted into double values implicitly, you can define an implicit conversion between ConvClass1 and ConvClass2. The reverse is not true, however, and you should define the conversion operator between ConvClass2 and ConvClass1 as explicit.

You specify this using the implicit and explicit keywords as shown. With these classes, the following code is fine:

```
ConvClass1 op1 = new ConvClass1();
op1.val = 3;
ConvClass2 op2 = op1;
```

A conversion in the other direction, however, requires the following explicit casting conversion:

```
ConvClass2 op1 = new ConvClass2();
op1.val = 3e15;
ConvClass1 op2 = (ConvClass1)op1;
```

Because you have used the checked keyword in your explicit conversion, you will get an exception in the preceding code, as the val property of op1 is too large to fit into the val property of op2.

## The as Operator

The as operator converts a type into a specified reference type, using the following syntax:

```
<operand> as <type>
```

This is possible only in certain circumstances:

➤   If <operand> is of type <type>
➤   If <operand> can be implicitly converted to type <type>
➤   If <operand> can be boxed into type <type>

If no conversion from <operand> to <type> is possible, then the result of the expression will be null.

Conversion from a base class to a derived class is possible by using an explicit conversion, but it won't always work. Consider the two classes ClassA and ClassD from an earlier example, where ClassD inherits from ClassA:

```
class ClassA : IMyInterface
{
}

class ClassD : ClassA
{
}
```

The following code uses the as operator to convert from a ClassA instance stored in obj1 into the ClassD type:

```
ClassA obj1 = new ClassA();
ClassD obj2 = obj1 as ClassD;
```

This will result in obj2 being null.

However, it is possible to store ClassD instances in ClassA-type variables by using polymorphism. The following code illustrates this, using the as operator to convert from a ClassA-type variable containing a ClassD-type instance into the ClassD type:

```
ClassD obj1 = new ClassD();
ClassA obj2 = obj1;
ClassD obj3 = obj2 as ClassD;
```

This time the result is that obj3 ends up containing a reference to the same object as obj1, not null.

This functionality makes the as operator very useful, because the following code (which uses simple casting) results in an exception being thrown:

```
ClassA obj1 = new ClassA();
ClassD obj2 = (ClassD)obj1;
```

The as equivalent of this code results in a null value being assigned to obj2 — no exception is thrown. This means that code such as the following (using two of the classes developed earlier in this chapter, Animal and a class derived from Animal called Cow) is very common in C# applications:

```
public void MilkCow(Animal myAnimal)
{
    Cow myCow = myAnimal as Cow;
    if (myCow != null)
    {
        myCow.Milk();
    }
    else
    {
        Console.WriteLine("{0} isn't a cow, and so can't be milked.",
            myAnimal.Name);
    }
}
```

This is much simpler than checking for exceptions!

## SUMMARY

This chapter covered many of the techniques that you can use to make your OOP applications far more powerful—and more interesting. Although these techniques take a little effort to accomplish, they can make your classes much easier to work with and therefore simplify the task of writing the rest of the code.

Each of the topics covered has many uses. You're likely to come across collections in one form or another in almost any application, and creating strongly typed collections can make your life much easier if you need to work with a group of objects of the same type. You also learned how you can add indexers and iterators to get easy access to objects within the collection.

Comparisons and conversions are another topic that crops up repeatedly. You learned how to perform various comparisons, and saw some of the underlying functionality of boxing and unboxing. You also learned how to overload operators for both comparisons and conversions, and how to link things together with list sorting.

The next chapter covers something entirely new—generics. These enable you to create classes that automatically customize themselves to work with dynamically chosen types. This is especially useful with collections, and you'll see how a lot of the code in this chapter can be simplified dramatically using generic collections.

**11.1** Create a collection class called `People` that is a collection of the following `Person` class. The items in the collection should be accessible via a string indexer that is the name of the person, identical to the `Person.Name` property.

```
public class Person
{
    private string name;
    private int age;

    public string Name
    {
        get
        {
            return name;
        }
        set
        {
            name = value;
        }
    }

    public int Age
    {
        get
        {
            return age;
        }
        set
        {
            age = value;
        }
    }
}
```

**11.2** Extend the `Person` class from the preceding exercise so that the `>`, `<`, `>=`, and `<=` operators are overloaded, and compare the `Age` properties of `Person` instances.

**11.3** Add a `GetOldest()` method to the `People` class that returns an array of `Person` objects with the greatest `Age` property (one or more objects, as multiple items can have the same value for this property), using the overloaded operators defined in Exercise 11.2.

**11.4** Implement the `ICloneable` interface on the `People` class to provide deep copying capability.

**11.5** Add an iterator to the `People` class that enables you to get the ages of all members in a `foreach` loop as follows:

```
foreach (int age in myPeople.Ages)
{
    // Display ages.
}
```

Answers to the exercises can be found in Appendix A.

▶ **WHAT YOU LEARNED IN THIS CHAPTER**

| KEY CONCEPT | DESCRIPTION |
|---|---|
| **Defining collections** | Collections are classes that can contain instances of other classes. You can define a collection by deriving from `CollectionBase`, or implement collection interfaces such as `IEnumerable`, `ICollection`, and `IList` yourself. Typically, you will define an indexer for your collection in order to use `collection[index]` syntax to access members. |
| **Dictionaries** | You can also define keyed collections, or dictionaries, whereby each item has an associated key. In this case, the key can be used to identify an item, rather than using the item's index. You can define a dictionary by implementing `IDictionary` or by deriving a class from `DictionaryBase`. |
| **Iterators** | You can implement an iterator to control how looping code obtains values in its loop cycles. To iterate over a class, implement a method called `GetEnumerator()` with a return type of `IEnumerator`. To iterate over a class member, such as a method, use a return type of `IEnumerable`. In iterator code blocks, return values with the `yield` keyword. |
| **Type comparisons** | You can use the `GetType()` method to obtain the type of an object, or the `typeof()` operator to get the type of a class. You can then compare these type values. You can also use the `is` operator to determine whether an object is compatible with a certain class type. |
| **Value comparisons** | If you want to make classes whose instances can be compared using standard C# operators, you must overload those operators in the class definition. For other types of value comparison, you can use classes that implement the `IComparable` or `IComparer` interfaces. These interfaces are particularly useful for sorting collections. |
| **The as operator** | You can use the `as` operator to convert a value to a reference type. If no conversion is possible, the `as` operator returns a `null` value. |

# 12

# Generics

## WHAT YOU WILL LEARN IN THIS CHAPTER

- ➤ What generics are
- ➤ How to use some of the generic classes provided by the .NET Framework
- ➤ How to define your own generics
- ➤ How variance works with generics

## WROX.COM CODE DOWNLOADS FOR THIS CHAPTER

You can find the wrox.com code downloads for this chapter at www.wrox.com/remtitle .cgi?isbn=9781118314418 on the Download Code tab. The code is in the Chapter 12 download and individually named according to the names throughout the chapter.

One of the (admittedly few) criticisms leveled against the first version of C# was its lack of support for *generics*. Generics in C++ (known as *templates* in that language) had long been regarded as an excellent way of doing things, as they enabled a single type definition to spawn a multitude of specialized types at compile time and thus save a lot of time and effort. For whatever reason, generics didn't quite make it into the first release of C#, and the language suffered because of it. Perhaps it was because generics are often seen as being quite difficult to get a handle on, or maybe it was decided that they weren't necessary. Fortunately, generics joined the party in version 2.0 of C#. Even better, they aren't very difficult to use, although they do require a slightly different way of looking at things.

This chapter begins by looking at what generics are. You learn about generics in fairly abstract terms at first, because learning the concepts behind generics is crucial to being able to use them effectively.

Next, you see some of the generic types in the .NET Framework in action. This will help you understand their functionality and power, as well as the new syntax required in your code. You'll then move on to define your own generic types, including generic classes, interfaces, methods, and delegates. You also learn additional techniques for further customizing generic types: the `default` keyword and type constraints.

Finally, you'll look at covariance and contravariance, two forms of variance that were introduced in C# 4 and that allow greater flexibility when using generic classes.

# WHAT ARE GENERICS?

To best illustrate what generics are, and why they are so useful, recall the collection classes from the previous chapter. You saw how basic collections can be contained in classes such as `ArrayList`, but that such collections suffer from being untyped. This requires that you cast `object` items into whatever type of objects you actually stored in the collection. Because anything that inherits from `System.Object` (that is, practically anything) can be stored in an `ArrayList`, you need to be careful. Assuming that certain types are all that is contained in a collection can lead to exceptions being thrown, and code logic breaking down. You learned some techniques to deal with this, including the code required to check the type of an object.

However, you discovered that a much better solution is to use a strongly typed collection class initially. By deriving from `CollectionBase` and providing your own methods for adding, removing, and otherwise accessing members of the collection, you learned how you could restrict collection members to those derived from a certain base type or supporting a certain interface. This is where you encounter a problem. Every time you create a new class that needs to be held in a collection, you must do one of the following:

➤ Use a collection class you've already made that can contain items of the new type.

➤ Create a new collection class that can hold items of the new type, implementing all the required methods.

Typically, with a new type you need extra functionality, so more often than not, you need a new collection class anyway. Therefore, making collection classes can take up a fair amount of your time!

*Generic classes*, conversely, make coding a lot simpler. A generic class is built around whatever type, or types, you supply during instantiation, enabling you to strongly type an object with hardly any effort at all. In the context of collections, creating a "collection of type `T` objects" is as simple as saying it aloud—and achievable in a single line of code. Instead of code such as,

```
CollectionClass items = new CollectionClass();
items.Add(new ItemClass());
```

you can use this:

```
CollectionClass<ItemClass> items = new CollectionClass<ItemClass>();
items.Add(new ItemClass());
```

The angle bracket syntax is the way you pass type parameters to generic types. In the preceding code, read `CollectionClass<ItemClass>` as CollectionClass of ItemClass. You will, of course, examine this syntax in more detail later in the chapter.

There's more to the subject of generics than just collections, but they are particularly suited to this area, as you will see later in the chapter when you look at the `System.Collections.Generic` namespace. By creating a generic class, you can generate methods that have a signature that can be strongly typed to any type you want, even catering to the fact that a type can be a value or reference type, and deal with individual cases as they occur. You can even allow only a subset of types to be used, by restricting the types used to instantiate a generic class to those that support a given interface or are derived from a certain type. Moreover, you're not restricted to generic classes—you can create generic interfaces, generic methods (which can be defined on nongeneric classes), and even generic delegates. All this adds a great deal of flexibility to your code, and judicious use of generics can eliminate hours of development time.

You're probably wondering how all this is possible. Usually, when you create a class, it is compiled into a type that you can then use in your code. You might think that when you create a generic class, it would have to be compiled into a plethora of types, so that you could instantiate it. Fortunately, that's not the case—and given the infinite amount of classes possible in .NET, that's just as well. Behind the scenes, the .NET runtime allows generic classes to be dynamically generated as and when you need them. A given generic class `A` of `B` won't exist until you ask for it by instantiating it.

> **NOTE** For those who are familiar with C++, or are interested, this is one difference between C++ templates and C# generic classes. In C++ the compiler detects where you used a specific type of template—for example, A of B—and compiles the code necessary to create this type. In C# everything happens at runtime.

To summarize, generics enable you to create flexible types that process objects of one or more specific types. These types are determined when you instantiate or otherwise use the generic. Now it's time to see them in action.

## USING GENERICS

Before you look at how to create your own generic types, it's worth looking at the ones supplied by the .NET Framework. These include the types in the `System.Collections.Generic` namespace, a namespace that you've seen several times in your code because it is included by default in console applications. You haven't yet used any of the types in this namespace, but that's about to change. This section looks at the types in this namespace and how you can use them to create strongly typed collections and improve the functionality of your existing collections.

First, though, you'll look at another simpler generic type that gets around a minor issue with value types: *nullable types.*

## Nullable Types

In earlier chapters, you saw that one of the ways in which value types (which include most of the basic types such as `int` and `double` as well as all structs) differ from reference types (`string` and any class) is that they must contain a value. They can exist in an unassigned state, just after they are declared and before a value is assigned, but you can't make use of the value type in that state in any way. Conversely, reference types can be `null`.

There are times, and they crop up more often than you might think (particularly when you work with databases), when it is useful to have a value type that can be `null`. Generics give you a way to do this using the `System.Nullable<T>` type, as shown in this example:

```
System.Nullable<int> nullableInt;
```

This code declares a variable called `nullableInt`, which can have any value that an `int` variable can, plus the value `null`. This enables you to write code such as the following:

```
nullableInt = null;
```

If `nullableInt` were an `int` type variable, then the preceding code wouldn't compile.

The preceding assignment is equivalent to the following:

```
nullableInt = new System.Nullable<int>();
```

As with any other variable, you can't just use it before some kind of initialization, whether to `null` (through either syntax shown previously) or by assigning a value.

You can test nullable types to determine whether they are `null`, just like you test reference types:

```
if (nullableInt == null)
{
    ...
}
```

Alternatively, you can use the `HasValue` property:

```
if (nullableInt.HasValue)
{
    ...
}
```

This wouldn't work for reference types, even one with a `HasValue` property of its own, because having a `null`-valued reference type variable means that no object exists through which to access this property, and an exception would be thrown.

You can also look at the value of a nullable type by using the `Value` property. If `HasValue` is `true`, then you are guaranteed a non-`null` value for `Value`; but if `HasValue` is `false`—that is, `null` has been assigned to the variable—then accessing `Value` will result in an exception of type `System.InvalidOperationException`.

Note that nullable types are so useful that they have resulted in a modification of C# syntax. Rather than use the syntax shown previously to declare a nullable type variable, you can instead use the following:

```
int? nullableInt;
```

`int?` is simply a shorthand for `System.Nullable<int>` but is much more readable. In subsequent sections, you'll use this syntax.

## Operators and Nullable Types

With simple types, such as `int`, you can use operators such as +, -, and so on to work with values. With nullable type equivalents, there is no difference: The values contained in nullable types are implicitly converted to the required type and the appropriate operators are used. This also applies to structs with operators that you have supplied:

```
int? op1 = 5;
int? result = op1 * 2;
```

Note that here the `result` variable is also of type `int?`. The following code will not compile:

```
int? op1 = 5;
int result = op1 * 2;
```

To get this to work you must perform an explicit conversion or access the value through the `Value` property, which requires code such as,

```
int? op1 = 5;
int result = (int)op1 * 2;
```

or:

```
int? op1 = 5;
int result = op1.Value * 2;
```

This works fine as long as `op1` has a value—if it is `null`, then you will get an exception of type `System.InvalidOperationException`.

This raises the obvious question: What happens when one or both values in an operator evaluation that involves two nullable values are `null`, such as `op1` in the following code?

```
int? op1 = null;
int? op2 = 5;
int? result = op1 * op2;
```

The answer is that for all simple nullable types other than `bool?`, the result of the operation is `null`, which you can interpret as "unable to compute." For structs you can define your own operators to deal with this situation (as shown later in this chapter), and for `bool?` there are operators defined for & and | that might result in non-`null` return values. These are shown in Table 12-1.

**TABLE 12-1:** Resolving Bool? Comparisons with null Value

| OP1 | OP2 | OP1 & OP2 | OP1 \| OP2 |
|------|-------|-----------|-----------|
| true | true | true | true |
| true | false | false | true |
| true | null | null | true |
| false | true | false | true |
| false | false | false | false |
| false | null | false | null |
| null | true | null | true |
| null | false | false | null |
| null | null | null | null |

The results in the table make perfect sense logically—if there is enough information to work out the answer of the computation without needing to know the value of one of the operands, then it doesn't matter if that operand is null.

## The ?? Operator

To further reduce the amount of code you need in order to deal with nullable types, and to make it easier to deal with variables that can be null, you can use the ?? operator. Known as the *null coalescing operator,* it is a binary operator that enables you to supply an alternative value to use for expressions that might evaluate to null. The operator evaluates to its first operand if the first operand is not null, or to its second operator if the first operand is null. Functionally, the following two expressions are equivalent:

```
op1 ?? op2
op1 == null ? op2 : op1
```

In this code, op1 can be any nullable expression, including a reference type and, importantly, a nullable type. This means that you can use the ?? operator to provide default values to use if a nullable type is null, as shown here:

```
int? op1 = null;
int result = op1 * 2 ?? 5;
```

Because in this example op1 is null, op1 * 2 will also be null. However, the ?? operator detects this and assigns the value 5 to result. Importantly, note here that no explicit conversion is required to put the result in the int type variable result. The ?? operator handles this conversion for you. Alternatively, you can pass the result of a ?? evaluation into an int? with no problems:

```
int? result = op1 * 2 ?? 5;
```

This behavior makes the ?? operator a versatile one to use when dealing with nullable variables, and a handy way to supply defaults without using either a block of code in an if structure or the often confusing ternary operator.

Use the following Try It Out to experiment with a nullable Vector type.

**TRY IT OUT** Nullable Types: Ch12Ex01

1. Create a new console application project called Ch12Ex01 and save it in the directory C:\BegVCSharp\ Chapter12.
2. Add a new class called Vector in the file Vector.cs.

**3.** Modify the code in `Vector.cs` as follows:

```
public class Vector
{
    public double? R = null;
    public double? Theta = null;

    public double? ThetaRadians
    {
        get
        {
            // Convert degrees to radians.
            return (Theta * Math.PI / 180.0);
        }
    }
    public Vector(double? r, double? theta)
    {
        // Normalize.
        if (r < 0)
        {
            r = -r;
            theta += 180;
        }
        theta = theta % 360;

        // Assign fields.
        R = r;
        Theta = theta;
    }

    public static Vector operator +(Vector op1, Vector op2)
    {
        try
        {
            // Get (x, y) coordinates for new vector.
            double newX = op1.R.Value * Math.Sin(op1.ThetaRadians.Value)
                + op2.R.Value * Math.Sin(op2.ThetaRadians.Value);
            double newY = op1.R.Value * Math.Cos(op1.ThetaRadians.Value)
                + op2.R.Value * Math.Cos(op2.ThetaRadians.Value);

            // Convert to (r, theta).
            double newR = Math.Sqrt(newX * newX + newY * newY);
            double newTheta = Math.Atan2(newX, newY) * 180.0 / Math.PI;

            // Return result.
            return new Vector(newR, newTheta);
        }
        catch
        {
            // Return "null" vector.
            return new Vector(null, null);
        }
    }

    public static Vector operator -(Vector op1)
    {
        return new Vector(-op1.R, op1.Theta);
    }

    public static Vector operator -(Vector op1, Vector op2)
    {
        return op1 + (-op2);
    }
```

```
      public override string ToString()
      {
         // Get string representation of coordinates.
         string rString = R.HasValue ? R.ToString(): "null";
         string thetaString = Theta.HasValue ? Theta.ToString(): "null";

         // Return (r, theta) string.
         return string.Format("({0}, {1})", rString, thetaString);
      }
   }
```

**4.** Modify the code in `Program.cs` as follows:

```
class Program
{
   static void Main(string[] args)
   {
      Vector v1 = GetVector("vector1");
      Vector v2 = GetVector("vector1");
      Console.WriteLine("{0} + {1} = {2}", v1, v2, v1 + v2);
      Console.WriteLine("{0} - {1} = {2}", v1, v2, v1 - v2);
      Console.ReadKey();
   }

   static Vector GetVector(string name)
   {
      Console.WriteLine("Input {0} magnitude:", name);
      double? r = GetNullableDouble();
      Console.WriteLine("Input {0} angle (in degrees):", name);
      double? theta = GetNullableDouble();
      return new Vector(r, theta);
   }

   static double? GetNullableDouble()
   {
      double? result;
      string userInput = Console.ReadLine();
      try
      {
         result = double.Parse(userInput);
      }
      catch
      {
         result = null;
      }
      return result;
   }
}
```

**5.** Execute the application and enter values for two vectors. The sample output is shown in Figure 12-1.

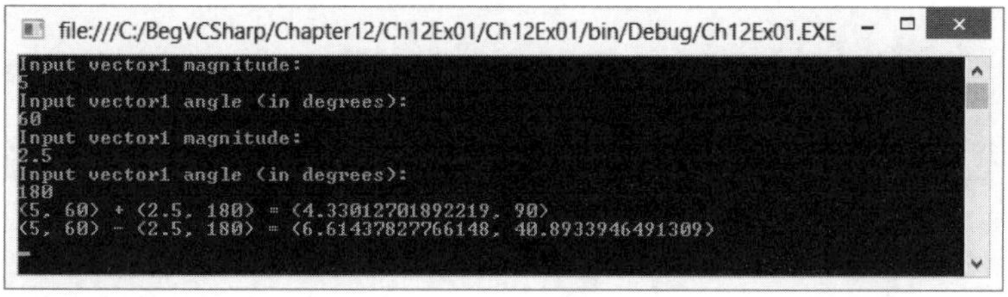

**FIGURE 12-1**

6. Execute the application again, but this time skip at least one of the four values. The sample output is shown in Figure 12-2.

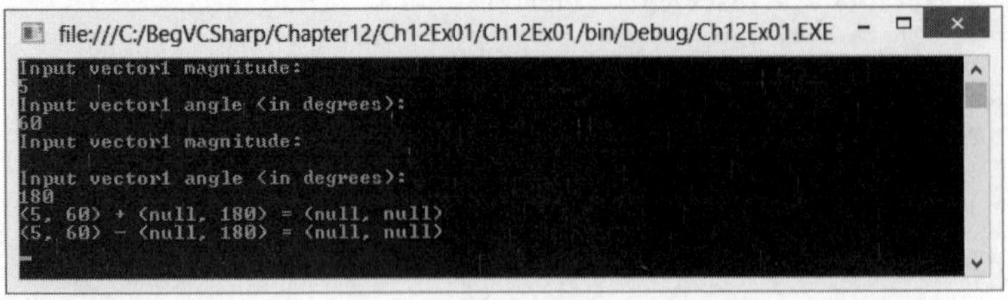

```
file:///C:/BegVCSharp/Chapter12/Ch12Ex01/Ch12Ex01/bin/Debug/Ch12Ex01.EXE    -  □  ×
Input vector1 magnitude:
5
Input vector1 angle (in degrees):
60
Input vector1 magnitude:

Input vector1 angle (in degrees):
180
(5, 60) + (null, 180) = (null, null)
(5, 60) - (null, 180) = (null, null)
```

**FIGURE 12-2**

### How It Works

This example created a class called `Vector` that represents a vector with polar coordinates (that is, with a magnitude and an angle), as shown in Figure 12-3.

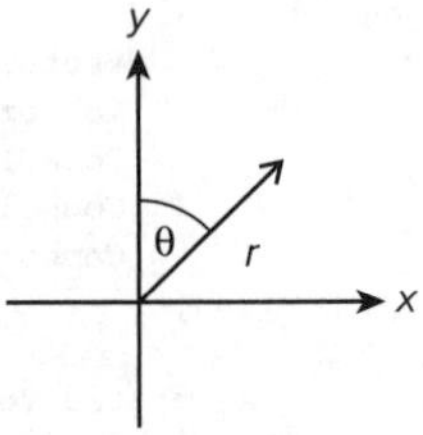

The coordinates $r$ and $\theta$ are represented in code by the public fields R and Theta, where Theta is expressed in degrees. ThetaRadians is supplied to obtain the value of Theta in radians—this is necessary because the Math class uses radians in its static methods. Both R and Theta are of type `double?`, so they can be `null`:

**FIGURE 12-3**

```csharp
public class Vector
{
    public double? R = null;
    public double? Theta = null;

    public double? ThetaRadians
    {
        get
        {
            // Convert degrees to radians.
            return (Theta * Math.PI / 180.0);
        }
    }
}
```

The constructor for `Vector` normalizes the initial values of R and Theta and then assigns the public fields:

```csharp
public Vector(double? r, double? theta)
{
    // Normalize.
    if (r < 0)
    {
        r = -r;
        theta += 180;
    }
    theta = theta % 360;
    // Assign fields.
    R = r;
    Theta = theta;
}
```

The main functionality of the `Vector` class is to add and subtract vectors using operator overloading, which requires some fairly basic trigonometry not covered here. The important point about the code is that if an exception is thrown when obtaining the `Value` property of R or ThetaRadians—that is, if either is `null`—then a "null" vector is returned:

```csharp
public static Vector operator +(Vector op1, Vector op2)
{
    try
    {
        {
```

```
            // Get (x, y) coordinates for new vector.
            . . .
    }
    catch
    {
        // Return "null" vector.
        return new Vector(null, null);
    }
}
```

If either of the coordinates making up a vector is `null`, then the vector is invalid, which is signified here by a `Vector` class with `null` values for both `R` and `Theta`. The rest of the code in the `Vector` class overrides the other operators required to extend the addition functionality to include subtraction, and overrides `ToString()` to obtain a string representation of a `Vector` object.

The code in `Program.cs` tests the `Vector` class by enabling the user to initialize two vectors, and then adds and subtracts them to and from one another. Should the user omit a value, it will be interpreted as `null`, and the rules mentioned previously apply.

## The System.Collections.Generic Namespace

In practically every application used so far in this book, you have seen the following namespaces:

```
using System;
using System.Collections.Generic;
using System.Linq;
using System.Text;
using System.Threading.Tasks;
```

The `System` namespace contains most of the basic types used in .NET applications. The `System.Text` namespace includes types relating to string processing and encoding. You'll look at the `System.Linq` namespace later in this book, from Chapter 23 onward. The `System.Threading.Tasks` namespace contains types that help you to write asynchronous code, which isn't covered in this book. But what about `System.Collections.Generic`, and why is it included by default in console applications?

The answer is that this namespace contains generic types for dealing with collections, and it is likely to be used so often that it is configured with a `using` statement, ready for you to use without qualification.

As promised earlier in the chapter, you'll now look at these types, which are guaranteed to make your life easier. They make it possible for you to create strongly typed collection classes with hardly any effort. Table 12-2 lists two types from the `System.Collections.Generic` namespace that are covered in this section. More of the types in this namespace are covered later in this chapter.

**TABLE 12-2:** Generic Collection Type

| TYPE | DESCRIPTION |
| --- | --- |
| List<T> | Collection of type T objects |
| Dictionary<K, V> | Collection of items of type V, associated with keys of type K |

This section also describes various interfaces and delegates used with these classes.

### List<T>

Rather than derive a class from `CollectionBase` and implement the required methods as you did in the last chapter, it can be quicker and easier simply to use the `List<T>` generic collection type. An added bonus here is that many of the methods you normally have to implement, such as `Add()`, are implemented for you.

Creating a collection of type T objects requires the following code:

```
List<T> myCollection = new List<T>();
```

That's it. You don't have to define any classes, implement any methods, or do anything else. You can also set a starting list of items in the collection by passing a List<T> object to the constructor. An object instantiated using this syntax supports the methods and properties shown in Table 12-3 (where the type supplied to the List<T> generic is T).

**TABLE 12-3:** Supported Methods and Properties for List<T>

| MEMBER | DESCRIPTION |
|--------|-------------|
| int Count | Property providing the number of items in the collection. |
| void Add(T item) | Adds an item to the collection. |
| void AddRange(IEnumerable<T>) | Adds multiple items to the collection. |
| IList<T> AsReadOnly() | Returns a read-only interface to the collection. |
| int Capacity | Gets or sets the number of items that the collection can contain. |
| void Clear() | Removes all items from the collection. |
| bool Contains(T item) | Determines whether the item is contained in the collection. |
| void CopyTo(T[] array, int index) | Copies the items in the collection into the array array, starting from index index in the array. |
| IEnumerator<T> GetEnumerator() | Obtains an IEnumerator<T> instance for iteration through the collection. Note that the interface returned is strongly typed to T, so no casting is required in foreach loops. |
| int IndexOf(T item) | Obtains the index of the item, or –1 if the item is not contained in the collection. |
| void Insert(int index, T item) | Inserts the item into the collection at the specified index. |
| bool Remove(T item) | Removes the first occurrence of the item from the collection and returns true. If the item is not contained in the collection, it returns false. |
| void RemoveAt(int index) | Removes the item at index index from the collection. |

List<T> also has an Item property, enabling array-like access:

```
T itemAtIndex2 = myCollectionOfT[2];
```

This class supports several other methods, but that's plenty to get you started. The following Try It Out demonstrates how to use List<T> in practice.

**TRY IT OUT** Using List<T>: Ch12Ex02

1. Create a new console application called Ch12Ex02 and save it in the directory C:\BegVCSharp\ Chapter12.

2. Right-click on the project name in the Solution Explorer window and select the Add ⇨ Existing Item option.

3. Select the Animal.cs, Cow.cs, and Chicken.cs files from the C:\BegVCSharp\Chapter11\Ch11Ex01\ Ch11Ex01 directory and click Add.

4. Modify the namespace declaration in the three files you added as follows:

```
namespace Ch12Ex02
```

**5.** Modify `Program.cs` as follows:

```
static void Main(string[] args)
{
    List<Animal> animalCollection = new List<Animal>();
    animalCollection.Add(new Cow("Jack"));
    animalCollection.Add(new Chicken("Vera"));
    foreach (Animal myAnimal in animalCollection)
    {
        myAnimal.Feed();
    }
    Console.ReadKey();
}
```

**6.** Execute the application. The result is exactly the same as the result for `Ch11Ex02` in the last chapter.

*How It Works*

There are only two differences between this example and `Ch11Ex02`. The first is that the line of code

```
Animals animalCollection = new Animals();
```

has been replaced with:

```
List<Animal> animalCollection = new List<Animal>();
```

The second, and more crucial, difference is that there is no longer an `Animals` collection class in the project. All that hard work you did earlier to create this class was achieved in a single line of code by using a generic collection class.

An alternative way to get the same result is to leave the code in `Program.cs` as it was in the last chapter, and use the following definition of `Animals`:

```
public class Animals : List<Animal>
{
}
```

Doing this has the advantage that the code in `Program.cs` is slightly easier to read, plus you can add members to the `Animals` class as you see fit.

You might, of course, be wondering why you'd ever want to derive classes from `CollectionBase`, which is a good question. In fact, there aren't many situations where you would do this. It's certainly good to know how the code works internally because `List<T>` works in much the same way, but `CollectionBase` is basically there for backward compatibility. The only situation in which you might want to use `CollectionBase` is when you want much more control over the members exposed to users of the class. For example, if you wanted a collection class with an internal access modifier on its `Add()` method, then using `CollectionBase` might be the best option.

> **NOTE** *You can also pass an initial capacity to use to the constructor of* `List<T>` *(as an int), or an initial list of items using an* `IEnumerable<T>` *interface. Classes supporting this interface include* `List<T>`.

## Sorting and Searching Generic Lists

Sorting a generic list is much the same as sorting any other list. The last chapter described how you can use the `IComparer` and `IComparable` interfaces to compare two objects and thereby sort a list of that type of object. The only difference here is that you can use the generic interfaces `IComparer<T>` and `IComparable<T>`, which expose slightly different, type-specific methods. Table 12-4 explains these differences.

**TABLE 12-4:** Sorting with Generic Types

| GENERIC METHOD | NONGENERIC METHOD | DIFFERENCE |
|---|---|---|
| `int IComparable<T>`<br>`.CompareTo(T otherObj)` | `int IComparable`<br>`.CompareTo(object otherObj)` | Strongly typed in generic versions. |
| `bool IComparable<T>`<br>`.Equals(T otherObj)` | N/A | Doesn't exist on a nongeneric interface; can use inherited `object.Equals()` instead. |
| `int IComparer<T>.Compare`<br>`(T objectA, T objectB)` | `int IComparer`<br>`.Compare(object objectA,`<br>`object objectB)` | Strongly typed in generic versions. |
| `bool IComparer<T>.Equals`<br>`(T objectA, T objectB)` | N/A | Doesn't exist on a nongeneric interface; can use inherited `object.Equals()` instead. |
| `int IComparer<T>`<br>`.GetHashCode(T objectA)` | N/A | Doesn't exist on a nongeneric interface; can use inherited `object.GetHashCode()` instead. |

To sort a `List<T>`, you can supply an `IComparable<T>` interface on the type to be sorted, or supply an `IComparer<T>` interface. Alternatively, you can supply a *generic delegate* as a sorting method. From the perspective of seeing how the code works, this is far more interesting because implementing the interfaces described here takes no more effort than implementing their nongeneric cousins.

In general terms, all you need to sort a list is a method that compares two objects of type `T`; and to search, all you need is a method that checks an object of type `T` to determine whether it meets certain criteria. It is a simple matter to define such methods, and to aid you there are two generic delegate types that you can use:

➤ `Comparison<T>`—A delegate type for a method used for sorting, with the following return type and parameters:

```
int method(T objectA, T objectB)
```

➤ `Predicate<T>`—A delegate type for a method used for searching, with the following return type and parameters:

```
bool method(T targetObject)
```

You can define any number of such methods, and use them to "snap-in" to the searching and sorting methods of `List<T>`. The next Try It Out illustrates this technique.

**TRY IT OUT**   Sorting and Searching List<T>: Ch12Ex03

1. Create a new console application called Ch12Ex03 and save it in the directory `C:\BegVCSharp\Chapter12`.

2. Right-click on the project name in the Solution Explorer window and select the Add Existing Item option.

3. Select the `Vector.cs` file from the `C:\BegVCSharp\Chapter12\Ch12Ex01\Ch12Ex01` directory and click Add.

4. Modify the namespace declaration in the file you added as follows:

```
namespace Ch12Ex03
```

5. Add a new class called `Vectors`.

**6.** Modify `Vectors.cs` as follows:

```csharp
public class Vectors : List<Vector>
{
    public Vectors()
    {
    }

    public Vectors(IEnumerable<Vector> initialItems)
    {
        foreach (Vector vector in initialItems)
        {
            Add(vector);
        }
    }

    public string Sum()
    {
        StringBuilder sb = new StringBuilder();
        Vector currentPoint = new Vector(0.0, 0.0);
        sb.Append("origin");
        foreach (Vector vector in this)
        {
            sb.AppendFormat(" + {0}", vector);
            currentPoint += vector;
        }
        sb.AppendFormat(" = {0}", currentPoint);
        return sb.ToString();
    }
}
```

**7.** Add a new class called `VectorDelegates`.

**8.** Modify `VectorDelegates.cs` as follows:

```csharp
public static class VectorDelegates
{
    public static int Compare(Vector x, Vector y)
    {
        if (x.R > y.R)
        {
            return 1;
        }
        else if (x.R < y.R)
        {
            return -1;
        }
        return 0;
    }

    public static bool TopRightQuadrant(Vector target)
    {
        if (target.Theta >= 0.0 && target.Theta <= 90.0)
        {
            return true;
        }
        else
        {
            return false;
        }
    }
}
```

**9.** Modify `Program.cs` as follows:

```
static void Main(string[] args)
{
    Vectors route = new Vectors();
    route.Add(new Vector(2.0, 90.0));
    route.Add(new Vector(1.0, 180.0));
    route.Add(new Vector(0.5, 45.0));
    route.Add(new Vector(2.5, 315.0));

    Console.WriteLine(route.Sum());

    Comparison<Vector> sorter = new Comparison<Vector>(
        VectorDelegates.Compare);
    route.Sort(sorter);
    Console.WriteLine(route.Sum());

    Predicate<Vector> searcher =
        new Predicate<Vector>(VectorDelegates.TopRightQuadrant);
    Vectors topRightQuadrantRoute = new Vectors(route.FindAll(searcher));
    Console.WriteLine(topRightQuadrantRoute.Sum());

    Console.ReadKey();
}
```

**10.** Execute the application. The result is shown in Figure 12-4.

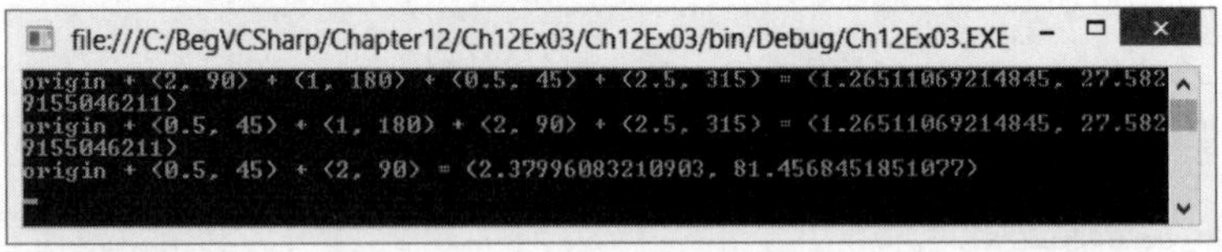

**FIGURE 12-4**

### How It Works

In this example, you created a collection class, `Vectors`, for the `Vector` class created in `Ch12Ex01`. You could just use a variable of type `List<Vector>`, but because you want additional functionality you use a new class, `Vectors`, and derive from `List<Vector>`, which enables you to add whatever additional members you want.

One member, `Sum()`, returns a string listing each vector in turn, along with the result of summing them all together (using the overloaded + operator from the original `Vector` class). Because each vector can be thought of as a direction and a distance, this effectively constitutes a route with an endpoint:

```
public string Sum()
{
    StringBuilder sb = new StringBuilder();
    Vector currentPoint = new Vector(0.0, 0.0);
    sb.Append("origin");
    foreach (Vector vector in this)
    {
        sb.AppendFormat(" + {0}", vector);
        currentPoint += vector;
    }
    sb.AppendFormat(" = {0}", currentPoint);
    return sb.ToString();
}
```

This method uses the handy `StringBuilder` class, found in the `System.Text` namespace, to build the response string. This class has members such as `Append()` and `AppendFormat()` (used here), which make it easy to assemble a string—the performance is better than concatenating individual strings. You use the `ToString()` method of this class to obtain the resultant string.

You also create two methods to be used as delegates, as static members of `VectorDelegates.Compare()` is used for comparison (sorting), and `TopRightQuadrant()` for searching. You'll look at these as you review the code in `Program.cs`.

The code in `Main()` starts with the initialization of a `Vectors` collection, to which are added several `Vector` objects (you can find this code in `Ch12Ex03\Program.cs`):

```
Vectors route = new Vectors();
route.Add(new Vector(2.0, 90.0));
route.Add(new Vector(1.0, 180.0));
route.Add(new Vector(0.5, 45.0));
route.Add(new Vector(2.5, 315.0));
```

The `Vectors.Sum()` method is used to write out the items in the collection as noted earlier, this time in their initial order:

```
Console.WriteLine(route.Sum());
```

Next, you create the first of your delegates, `sorter`. This delegate is of type `Comparison<Vector>` and, therefore, can be assigned a method with the following return type and parameters:

```
int method(Vector objectA, Vector objectB)
```

This matches `VectorDelegates.Compare()`, which is the method you assign to the delegate:

```
Comparison<Vector> sorter = new Comparison<Vector>(
    VectorDelegates.Compare);
```

`Compare()` compares the magnitudes of two vectors as follows:

```
public static int Compare(Vector x, Vector y)
{
    if (x.R > y.R)
    {
        return 1;
    }
    else if (x.R < y.R)
    {
        return -1;
    }
    return 0;
}
```

This enables you to order the vectors by magnitude:

```
route.Sort(sorter);
Console.WriteLine(route.Sum());
```

The output of the application gives the result you'd expect—the result of the summation is the same because the endpoint of following the "vector route" is the same regardless of the order in which you carry out the individual steps.

Next, you obtain a subset of the vectors in the collection by searching. This uses `VectorDelegates.TopRightQuadrant()`:

```
public static bool TopRightQuadrant(Vector target)
{
    if (target.Theta >= 0.0 && target.Theta <= 90.0)
    {
        return true;
    }
    else
    {
        return false;
    }
}
```

This method returns `true` if its `Vector` argument has a value of `Theta` between 0 and 90 degrees—that is, if it points up and/or right in a diagram of the sort shown earlier.

In the `Main()` method, you use this method via a delegate of type `Predicate<Vector>` as follows:

```
Predicate<Vector> searcher =
    new Predicate<Vector>(VectorDelegates.TopRightQuadrant);
Vectors topRightQuadrantRoute = new Vectors(route.FindAll(searcher));
Console.WriteLine(topRightQuadrantRoute.Sum());
```

This requires the constructor defined in `Vectors`:

```
public Vectors(IEnumerable<Vector> initialItems)
{
    foreach (Vector vector in initialItems)
    {
        Add(vector);
    }
}
```

Here, you initialize a new `Vectors` collection using an interface of `IEnumerable<Vector>`, which is necessary because `List<Vector>.FindAll()` returns a `List<Vector>` instance, not a `Vectors` instance.

The result of the searching is that only a subset of `Vector` objects is returned, so (again, as you'd expect) the result of the summation is different. The use of these generic delegate types to sort and search generic collections can take a little while to get used to, but the result is code that is streamlined and efficient, and which has a highly logical structure. It is well worth investing the time to learn the techniques presented in this section.

As an aside to this example, note that the code,

```
Comparison<Vector> sorter = new Comparison<Vector>(
    VectorDelegates.Compare);
route.Sort(sorter);
```

can be simplified to the following:

```
route.Sort(VectorDelegates.Compare);
```

This removes the necessity to implicitly reference the `Comparison<Vector>` type. In fact, an instance of this type is still created, but it is created implicitly. The `Sort()` method obviously needs an instance of this type to work, but the compiler realizes this and creates one for you from the method that you supply. In this situation, the reference to `VectorDelegates.Compare()` (without the parentheses) is referred to as a *method group*. There are many situations in which you can use method groups to implicitly create delegates in this way, which can make your code more readable.

## Dictionary<K, V>

The `Dictionary<K, V>` type enables you to define a collection of key-value pairs. Unlike the other generic collection types you've looked at in this chapter, this class requires instantiating two types: the types for both the key and the value that represent each item in the collection.

Once a `Dictionary<K, V>` object is instantiated, you can perform much the same operations on it as you can on a class that inherits from `DictionaryBase`, but with type-safe methods and properties already in place. You can, for example, add key-value pairs using a strongly typed `Add()` method:

```
Dictionary<string, int> things = new Dictionary<string, int>();
things.Add("Green Things", 29);
things.Add("Blue Things", 94);
things.Add("Yellow Things", 34);
things.Add("Red Things", 52);
things.Add("Brown Things", 27);
```

You can iterate through keys and values in the collection by using the `Keys` and `Values` properties:

```
foreach (string key in things.Keys)
{
    Console.WriteLine(key);
}

foreach (int value in things.Values)
{
    Console.WriteLine(value);
}
```

In addition, you can iterate through items in the collection by obtaining each as a `KeyValuePair<K, V>` instance, much like you can with the `DictionaryEntry` objects shown in the last chapter:

```
foreach (KeyValuePair<string, int> thing in things)
{
    Console.WriteLine("{0} = {1}", thing.Key, thing.Value);
}
```

One point to note about `Dictionary<K, V>` is that the key for each item must be unique. Attempting to add an item with an identical key will cause an `ArgumentException` exception to be thrown. Because of this, `Dictionary<K, V>` allows you to pass an `IComparer<K>` interface to its constructor. This might be necessary if you use your own classes as keys and they don't support an `IComparable` or `IComparable<K>` interface, or if you want to compare objects using a nondefault process. For instance, in the preceding example, you could use a case-insensitive method to compare string keys:

```
Dictionary<string, int> things =
    new Dictionary<string, int>(StringComparer.CurrentCultureIgnoreCase);
```

Now you'll get an exception if you use keys such as this:

```
things.Add("Green Things", 29);
things.Add("Green things", 94);
```

You can also pass an initial capacity (with an `int`) or a set of items (with an `IDictionary<K, V>` interface) to the constructor.

## Modifying CardLib to Use a Generic Collection Class

One simple modification you can make to the `CardLib` project you've been building over recent chapters is to change the `Cards` collection class to use a generic collection class, thus saving many lines of code. The required modification to the class definition for `Cards` is as follows (you can find this code in `Ch12CardLib\ Cards.cs`):

```
public class Cards : List<Card>, ICloneable
{
    ...
}
```

You can also remove all the methods of `Cards` except `Clone()`, which is required for `ICloneable`, and `CopyTo()`, because the version of `CopyTo()` supplied by `List<Card>` works with an array of `Card` objects, not a `Cards` collection. `Clone()` requires a minor modification because the `List<T>` class does not define a `List` property to use:

```
public object Clone()
{
    Cards newCards = new Cards();
    foreach (Card sourceCard in this)
    {
        newCards.Add((Card)sourceCard.Clone());
    }
    return newCards;
}
```

Rather than show the code here for what is a very simple modification, the updated version of `CardLib`, called `Ch12CardLib`, is included in the downloadable code for this chapter, along with the client code from the last chapter.

## DEFINING GENERIC TYPES

You've now learned enough about generics to create your own. You've seen plenty of code involving generic types and have had plenty of practice using generic syntax. This section looks at defining the following:

➤   Generic classes

➤   Generic interfaces

➤   Generic methods

➤   Generic delegates

You'll also look at the following more advanced techniques for dealing with the issues that come up when defining generic types:

➤   The `default` keyword

➤   Constraining types

➤   Inheriting from generic classes

➤   Generic operators

## Defining Generic Classes

To create a generic class, merely include the angle bracket syntax in the class definition:

```
class MyGenericClass<T>
{
   ...
}
```

Here, `T` can be any identifier you like, following the usual C# naming rules, such as not starting with a number and so on. Typically, though, you can just use `T`. A generic class can have any number of type parameters in its definition, separated by commas:

```
class MyGenericClass<T1, T2, T3>
{
   ...
}
```

Once these types are defined, you can use them in the class definition just like any other type. You can use them as types for member variables, return types for members such as properties or methods, and parameter types for method arguments:

```
class MyGenericClass<T1, T2, T3>
{
   private T1 innerT1Object;

   public MyGenericClass(T1 item)
   {
      innerT1Object = item;
   }

   public T1 InnerT1Object
   {
      get
      {
```

```
            return innerT1Object;
        }
    }
}
```

Here, an object of type `T1` can be passed to the constructor, and read-only access is permitted to this object via the property `InnerT1Object`. Note that you can make practically no assumptions as to what the types supplied to the class are. The following code, for example, will not compile:

```
class MyGenericClass<T1, T2, T3>
{
    private T1 innerT1Object;

    public MyGenericClass()
    {
        innerT1Object = new T1();
    }

    public T1 InnerT1Object
    {
        get
        {
            return innerT1Object;
        }
    }
}
```

Because you don't know what `T1` is, you can't use any of its constructors—it might not even have any, or it might have no publicly accessible default constructor. Without more complicated code involving the techniques shown later in this section, you can make only the following assumption about `T1`: you can treat it as a type that either inherits from or can be boxed into `System.Object`.

Obviously, this means that you can't really do anything very interesting with instances of this type, or any of the other types supplied to the generic class `MyGenericClass`. Without using *reflection,* which is an advanced technique used to examine types at runtime (and not covered in this chapter), you're limited to code that's no more complicated than the following:

```
public string GetAllTypesAsString()
{
    return "T1 = " + typeof(T1).ToString()
        + ", T2 = " + typeof(T2).ToString()
        + ", T3 = " + typeof(T3).ToString();
}
```

There is a bit more that you can do, particularly in terms of collections, because dealing with groups of objects is a pretty simple process and doesn't need any assumptions about the object types—which is one good reason why the generic collection classes you've seen in this chapter exist.

Another limitation that you need to be aware of is that using the operator `==` or `!=` is permitted only when comparing a value of a type supplied to a generic type to `null`. That is, the following code works fine:

```
public bool Compare(T1 op1, T1 op2)
{
    if (op1 != null && op2 != null)
    {
        return true;
    }
    else
    {
        return false;
    }
}
```

Here, if T1 is a value type, then it is always assumed to be non-null, so in the preceding code Compare will always return true. However, attempting to compare the two arguments op1 and op2 fails to compile:

```
public bool Compare(T1 op1, T1 op2)
{
    if (op1 == op2)
    {
        return true;
    }
    else
    {
        return false;
    }
}
```

That's because this code assumes that T1 supports the == operator. In short, to do anything interesting with generics, you need to know a bit more about the types used in the class.

## The default Keyword

One of the most basic things you might want to know about types used to create generic class instances is whether they are reference types or value types. Without knowing this, you can't even assign null values with code such as this:

```
public MyGenericClass()
{
    innerT1Object = null;
}
```

If T1 is a value type, then innerT1Object can't have the value null, so this code won't compile. Luckily, this problem has been addressed, resulting in a new use for the default keyword (which you've seen being used in switch structures earlier in the book). This is used as follows:

```
public MyGenericClass()
{
    innerT1Object = default(T1);
}
```

The result of this is that innerT1Object is assigned a value of null if it is a reference type, or a default value if it is a value type. This default value is 0 for numeric types, while structs have each of their members initialized to 0 or null in the same way. The default keyword gets you a bit further in terms of doing a little more with the types you are forced to use, but to truly get ahead, you need to constrain the types that are supplied.

## Constraining Types

The types you have used with generic classes until now are known as *unbounded* types because no restrictions are placed on what they can be. By *constraining* types, it is possible to restrict the types that can be used to instantiate a generic class. There are a number of ways to do this. For example, it's possible to restrict a type to one that inherits from a certain type. Referring back to the Animal, Cow, and Chicken classes used earlier, you could restrict a type to one that was or inherited from Animal, so this code would be fine:

```
MyGenericClass<Cow> = new MyGenericClass<Cow>();
```

The following, however, would fail to compile:

```
MyGenericClass<string> = new MyGenericClass<string>();
```

In your class definitions this is achieved using the where keyword:

```
class MyGenericClass<T> where T : constraint
{
    ...
}
```

Here, *constraint* defines what the constraint is. You can supply a number of constraints in this way by separating them with commas:

```
class MyGenericClass<T> where T : constraint1, constraint2
{
   ...
}
```

You can define constraints on any or all of the types required by the generic class by using multiple `where` statements:

```
class MyGenericClass<T1, T2> where T1 : constraint1 where T2 : constraint2
{
   ...
}
```

Any constraints that you use must appear after the inheritance specifiers:

```
class MyGenericClass<T1, T2> : MyBaseClass, IMyInterface
   where T1 : constraint1 where T2 : constraint2
{
   ...
}
```

The available constraints are shown in Table 12-5.

**TABLE 12-5:** Generic Type Constraints

| CONSTRAINT | DEFINITION | EXAMPLE USAGE |
| --- | --- | --- |
| struct | Type must be a value type. | In a class that requires value types to function—for example, where a member variable of type T being 0 means something |
| class | Type must be a reference type. | In a class that requires reference types to function—for example, where a member variable of type T being null means something |
| base-class | Type must be, or inherit from, *base-class*. You can supply any class name as this constraint. | In a class that requires certain baseline functionality inherited from *base-class* in order to function |
| interface | Type must be, or implement, *interface*. | In a class that requires certain baseline functionality exposed by *interface* in order to function |
| new() | Type must have a public, parameterless constructor. | In a class where you need to be able to instantiate variables of type T, perhaps in a constructor |

> **NOTE** If `new()` is used as a constraint, it must be the last constraint specified for a type.

It is possible to use one type parameter as a constraint on another through the base-class constraint as follows:

```
class MyGenericClass<T1, T2> where T2 : T1
{
   ...
}
```

Here, T2 must be the same type as T1 or inherit from T1. This is known as a *naked type constraint*, meaning that one generic type parameter is used as a constraint on another.

Circular type constraints, as shown here, are forbidden:

```
class MyGenericClass<T1, T2> where T2 : T1 where T1 : T2
{
    ...
}
```

This code will not compile. In the following Try It Out, you'll define and use a generic class that uses the `Animal` family of classes shown in earlier chapters.

**TRY IT OUT** Defining a Generic Class: Ch12Ex04

**1.** Create a new console application called Ch12Ex04 and save it in the directory C:\BegVCSharp\Chapter12.

**2.** Right-click on the project name in the Solution Explorer window and select the Add Existing Item option.

**3.** Select the `Animal.cs`, `Cow.cs`, and `Chicken.cs` files from the C:\BegVCSharp\Chapter12\Ch12Ex02\ Ch12Ex02 directory and click Add.

**4.** Modify the namespace declaration in the file you have added as follows:

```
namespace Ch12Ex04
```

**5.** Modify `Animal.cs` as follows:

```
public abstract class Animal
{
    ...

    public abstract void MakeANoise();
}
```

**6.** Modify `Chicken.cs` as follows:

```
public class Chicken : Animal
{
    ...

    public override void MakeANoise()
    {
        Console.WriteLine("{0} says 'cluck!';", name);
    }
}
```

**7.** Modify `Cow.cs` as follows:

```
public class Cow : Animal
{
    ...

    public override void MakeANoise()
    {
        Console.WriteLine("{0} says 'moo!'", name);
    }
}
```

**8.** Add a new class called `SuperCow` and modify the code in `SuperCow.cs` as follows:

```
public class SuperCow : Cow
{
    public void Fly()
    {
        Console.WriteLine("{0} is flying!", name);
    }

    public SuperCow(string newName): base(newName)
    {
```

```
    }

    public override void MakeANoise()
    {
        Console.WriteLine(
            "{0} says 'here I come to save the day!'", name);
    }
}
```

**9.** Add a new class called `Farm` and modify the code in `Farm.cs` as follows:

```
using System;
using System.Collections;
using System.Collections.Generic;
using System.Linq;
using System.Text;
using System.Threading.Tasks;

namespace Ch12Ex04
{
    public class Farm<T> : IEnumerable<T>
        where T : Animal
    {
        private List<T> animals = new List<T>();

        public List<T> Animals
        {
            get
            {
                return animals;
            }
        }

        public IEnumerator<T> GetEnumerator()
        {
            return animals.GetEnumerator();
        }

        IEnumerator IEnumerable.GetEnumerator()
        {
            return animals.GetEnumerator();
        }

        public void MakeNoises()
        {
            foreach (T animal in animals)
            {
                animal.MakeANoise();
            }
        }

        public void FeedTheAnimals()
        {
            foreach (T animal in animals)
            {
                animal.Feed();
            }
        }

        public Farm<Cow> GetCows()
        {
            Farm<Cow> cowFarm = new Farm<Cow>();
            foreach (T animal in animals)
            {
```

```
            if (animal is Cow)
            {
                cowFarm.Animals.Add(animal as Cow);
            }
        }
        return cowFarm;
    }
  }
}
```

**10.** Modify `Program.cs` as follows:

```
static void Main(string[] args)
{
    Farm<Animal> farm = new Farm<Animal>();
    farm.Animals.Add(new Cow("Jack"));
    farm.Animals.Add(new Chicken("Vera"));
    farm.Animals.Add(new Chicken("Sally"));
    farm.Animals.Add(new SuperCow("Kevin"));
    farm.MakeNoises();

    Farm<Cow> dairyFarm = farm.GetCows();
    dairyFarm.FeedTheAnimals();

    foreach (Cow cow in dairyFarm)
    {
        if (cow is SuperCow)
        {
            (cow as SuperCow).Fly();
        }
    }
    Console.ReadKey();
}
```

**11.** Execute the application. The result is shown in Figure 12-5.

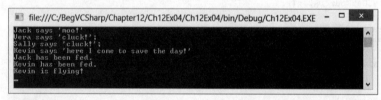

**FIGURE 12-5**

### How It Works

In this example, you created a generic class called `Farm<T>`, which, rather than inheriting from a generic list class, exposes a generic list class as a public property. The type of this list is determined by the type parameter `T` that is passed to `Farm<T>` and is constrained to be, or inherit from, `Animal`:

```
public class Farm<T> : IEnumerable<T>
    where T : Animal
{
    private List<T> animals = new List<T>();

    public List<T> Animals
    {
        get
        {
            return animals;
        }
    }
```

Farm<T> also implements IEnumerable<T>, where T is passed into this generic interface and is therefore also constrained in the same way. You implement this interface to make it possible to iterate through the items contained in Farm<T> without needing to explicitly iterate over Farm<T>.Animals. This is simple to achieve: you simply return the enumerator exposed by Animals, which is a List<T> class that also implements IEnumerable<T>:

```
public IEnumerator<T> GetEnumerator()
{
    return animals.GetEnumerator();
}
```

Because IEnumerable<T> inherits from IEnumerable, you also need to implement IEnumerable .GetEnumerator():

```
IEnumerator IEnumerable.GetEnumerator()
{
    return animals.GetEnumerator();
}
```

Next, Farm<T> includes two methods that make use of methods of the abstract Animal class:

```
public void MakeNoises()
{
    foreach (T animal in animals)
    {
        animal.MakeANoise();
    }
}

public void FeedTheAnimals()
{
    foreach (T animal in animals)
    {
        animal.Feed();
    }
}
```

Because T is constrained to Animal, this code compiles fine—you are guaranteed to have access to the MakeANoise() and Feed() methods, whatever type T actually is.

The next method, GetCows(), is more interesting. This method simply extracts all the items in the collection that are of type Cow (or that inherit from Cow, such as the new SuperCow class):

```
public Farm<Cow> GetCows()
{
    Farm<Cow> cowFarm = new Farm<Cow>();
    foreach (T animal in animals)
    {
        if (animal is Cow)
        {
            cowFarm.Animals.Add(animal as Cow);
        }
    }
    return cowFarm;
}
```

What is interesting here is that this method seems a bit wasteful. If you wanted other methods of the same sort, such as GetChickens() and so on, you'd need to implement them explicitly too. In a system with many more types, you'd need many more methods. A far better solution is to use a *generic method*, which you'll implement a little later in the chapter.

The client code in Program.cs simply tests the various methods of Farm and doesn't contain much you haven't already seen, so there's no need to examine this code in any greater detail—despite the flying cow.

## Inheriting from Generic Classes

The `Farm<T>` class in the preceding example, as well as several other classes you've seen in this chapter, inherit from a generic type. In the case of `Farm<T>`, this type was an interface: `IEnumerable<T>`. Here, the constraint on `T` supplied by `Farm<T>` resulted in an additional constraint on `T` used in `IEnumerable<T>`. This can be a useful technique for constraining otherwise unbounded types. However, you do need to follow some rules.

First, you can't "unconstrain" types that are constrained in a type from which you are inheriting. In other words, a type `T` that is used in a type you are inheriting from must be constrained at least as much as it is in that type. For example, the following code is fine:

```
class SuperFarm<T> : Farm<T>
      where T : SuperCow
{
}
```

This works because `T` is constrained to `Animal` in `Farm<T>`, and constraining it to `SuperCow` is constraining `T` to a subset of these values. However, the following won't compile:

```
class SuperFarm<T> : Farm<T>
      where T : struct
{
}
```

Here, you can say definitively that the type `T` supplied to `SuperFarm<T>` cannot be converted into a `T` usable by `Farm<T>`, so the code won't compile.

Even situations in which the constraint is a superset have the same problem:

```
class SuperFarm<T> : Farm<T>
      where T : class
{
}
```

Even though types such as `Animal` would be allowed by `SuperFarm<T>`, other types that satisfy the class constraint won't be allowed in `Farm<T>`. Again, compilation will fail. This rule applies to all the constraint types shown earlier in this chapter.

Also note that if you inherit from a generic type, then you must supply all the required type information, either in the form of other generic type parameters, as shown, or explicitly. This also applies to nongeneric classes that inherit from generic types, as you've seen elsewhere. Here's an example:

```
public class Cards : List<Card>, ICloneable
{
}
```

This is fine, but attempting the following will fail:

```
public class Cards : List<T>, ICloneable
{
}
```

Here, no information is supplied for `T`, so no compilation is possible.

> **NOTE** If you supply a parameter to a generic type, as in `List<Card>`, then you can refer to the type as closed. Similarly, inheriting from `List<T>` is inheriting from an open generic type.

## Generic Operators

Operator overrides are implemented in C# just like other methods and can be implemented in generic classes. For example, you could define the following implicit conversion operator in `Farm<T>`:

```
public static implicit operator List<Animal>(Farm<T> farm)
{
   List<Animal> result = new List<Animal>();
   foreach (T animal in farm)
   {
      result.Add(animal);
   }
   return result;
}
```

This allows the `Animal` objects in a `Farm<T>` to be accessed directly as a `List<Animal>` should you require it. This comes in handy if you want to add two `Farm<T>` instances together, such as with the following operators:

```
public static Farm<T> operator +(Farm<T> farm1, List<T> farm2)
{
   Farm<T> result = new Farm<T>();

   foreach (T animal in farm1)
   {
      result.Animals.Add(animal);
   }

   foreach (T animal in farm2)
   {
      if (!result.Animals.Contains(animal))
      {
         result.Animals.Add(animal);
      }
   }
   return result;
}

public static Farm<T> operator +(List<T> farm1, Farm<T> farm2)
{
   return farm2 + farm1;
}
```

You could then add instances of `Farm<Animal>` and `Farm<Cow>` as follows:

```
Farm<Animal> newFarm = farm + dairyFarm;
```

In this code, `dairyFarm` (an instance of `Farm<Cow>`) is implicitly converted into `List<Animal>`, which is usable by the overloaded + operator in `Farm<T>`.

You might think that this could be achieved simply by using the following:

```
public static Farm<T> operator +(Farm<T> farm1, Farm<T> farm2)
{
   ...
}
```

However, because `Farm<Cow>` cannot be converted into `Farm<Animal>`, the summation will fail. To take this a step further, you could solve this using the following conversion operator:

```
public static implicit operator Farm<Animal>(Farm<T> farm)
{
   Farm <Animal> result = new Farm <Animal>();
   foreach (T animal in farm)
```

```
    {
        result.Animals.Add(animal);
    }
    return result;
}
```

With this operator, instances of `Farm<T>`, such as `Farm<Cow>`, can be converted into instances of `Farm<Animal>`, solving the problem. You can use either of the methods shown, although the latter is preferable for its simplicity.

### Generic Structs

You learned in earlier chapters that structs are essentially the same as classes, barring some minor differences and the fact that a struct is a value type, not a reference type. Because this is the case, *generic structs* can be created in the same way as generic classes, as shown here:

```
public struct MyStruct<T1, T2>
{
    public T1 item1;
    public T2 item2;
}
```

## Defining Generic Interfaces

You've now seen several generic interfaces in use—namely, those in the `Systems.Collections.Generic` namespace such as `IEnumerable<T>` used in the last example. Defining a generic interface involves the same techniques as defining a generic class:

```
interface MyFarmingInterface<T>
    where T : Animal
{
    bool AttemptToBreed(T animal1, T animal2);

    T OldestInHerd { get; }
}
```

Here, the generic parameter `T` is used as the type of the two arguments of `AttemptToBreed()` and the type of the `OldestInHerd` property.

The same inheritance rules apply as for classes. If you inherit from a base generic interface, you must obey the rules, such as keeping the constraints of the base interface generic type parameters.

## Defining Generic Methods

The previous Try It Out used a method called `GetCows()`, and in the discussion of the example it was stated that you could make a more general form of this method using a *generic method*. In this section you'll see how this is possible. A generic method is one in which the return and/or parameter types are determined by a generic type parameter or parameters:

```
public T GetDefault<T>()
{
    return default(T);
}
```

This trivial example uses the default keyword you looked at earlier in the chapter to return a default value for a type `T`. This method is called as follows:

```
int myDefaultInt = GetDefault<int>();
```

The type parameter `T` is provided at the time the method is called.

This T is quite separate from the types used to supply generic type parameters to classes. In fact, generic methods can be implemented by nongeneric classes:

```
public class Defaulter
{
   public T GetDefault<T>()
   {
      return default(T);
   }
}
```

If the class is generic, though, then you must use different identifiers for generic method types. The following code won't compile:

```
public class Defaulter<T>
{
   public T GetDefault<T>()
   {
      return default(T);
   }
}
```

The type T used by either the method or the class must be renamed.

Constraints can be used by generic method parameters in the same way that they are for classes, and in this case you can make use of any class type parameters:

```
public class Defaulter<T1>
{
   public T2 GetDefault<T2>()
      where T2 : T1
   {
      return default(T2);
   }
}
```

Here, the type T2 supplied to the method must be the same as, or inherit from, T1 supplied to the class. This is a common way to constrain generic methods.

In the Farm<T> class shown earlier, you could include the following method (included, but commented out, in the downloadable code for Ch12Ex04):

```
public Farm<U> GetSpecies<U>() where U : T
{
   Farm<U> speciesFarm = new Farm<U>();
   foreach (T animal in animals)
   {
      if (animal is U)
      {
         speciesFarm.Animals.Add(animal as U);
      }
   }
   return speciesFarm;
}
```

This can replace GetCows() and any other methods of the same type. The generic type parameter used here, U, is constrained by T, which is in turn constrained by the Farm<T> class to Animal. This enables you to treat instances of T as instances of Animal, should you want to do so.

In the client code for Ch12Ex04, in Program.cs, using this new method requires one modification:

```
Farm<Cow> dairyFarm = farm.GetSpecies<Cow>();
```

In a similar vein, you could write:

```
Farm<Chicken> poultryFarm = farm.GetSpecies<Chicken>();
```

You can take this same approach with any class that inherits from `Animal`.

Note here that having generic type parameters on a method changes the signature of the method. This means you can have several overloads of a method differing only in generic type parameters, as shown in this example:

```
public void ProcessT<T>(T op1)
{
   ...
}

public void ProcessT<T, U>(T op1)
{
   ...
}
```

Which method should be used is determined by the amount of generic type parameters specified when the method is called.

## Defining Generic Delegates

The last generic type to consider is the *generic delegate*. You saw these delegates in action earlier in the chapter when you learned how to sort and search generic lists. You used the `Comparison<T>` and `Predicate<T>` delegates, respectively, for this.

Chapter 6 described how to define delegates using the parameters and return type of a method, the `delegate` keyword, and a name for the delegate:

```
public delegate int MyDelegate(int op1, int op2);
```

To define a generic delegate, you simply declare and use one or more generic type parameters:

```
public delegate T1 MyDelegate<T1, T2>(T2 op1, T2 op2) where T1: T2;
```

As you can see, constraints can be applied here too. You'll learn a lot more about delegates in the next chapter, including how you can use them in a common C# programming technique—events.

## VARIANCE

Variance is the collective term for *covariance* and *contravariance*, two concepts that were introduced in .NET 4. In fact, they have been around longer than that (they were available in .NET 2.0), but until .NET 4 it was very difficult to implement them, as this required custom compilation procedures.

The easiest way to grasp what these terms mean is to compare them with polymorphism. Polymorphism, as you will recall, is what enables you to put objects of a derived type into variables of a base type, for example:

```
Cow myCow = new Cow("Geronimo");
Animal myAnimal = myCow;
```

Here, an object of type `Cow` has been placed into a variable of type `Animal`—which is possible because `Cow` derives from `Animal`.

However, the same cannot be said for interfaces. That is to say, the following code will not work:

```
IMethaneProducer<Cow> cowMethaneProducer = myCow;
IMethaneProducer<Animal> animalMethaneProducer = cowMethaneProducer;
```

The first line of code is fine, assuming that `Cow` supports the interface `IMethaneProducer<Cow>`. However, the second line of code presupposes a relationship between the two interface types that doesn't exist, so there is no way of converting one into the other. Or is there? There certainly isn't a way using the techniques you've seen so far in this chapter, as all the type parameters for generic types have been *invariant*. However, it is possible to define variant type parameters on generic interfaces and generic delegates that cater to exactly the situation illustrated in the previous code.

To make the previous code work, the type parameter T for the IMethaneProducer<T> interface must be *covariant*. Having a covariant type parameter effectively sets up an inheritance relationship between IMethaneProducer<Cow> and IMethaneProducer<Animal>, so that variables of one type can hold values of the other, just like with polymorphism (although a little more complicated).

To round off this introduction to variance, you need to look at the other kind, *contravariance*. This is similar but works in the other direction. Rather than being able to place a generic interface value into a variable that includes a base type as in covariance, contravariance enables you to place that interface into a variable that uses a derived type, for example:

```
IGrassMuncher<Cow> cowGrassMuncher = myCow;
IGrassMuncher<SuperCow> superCowGrassMuncher = cowGrassMuncher;
```

At first glance this seems a little odd, as you couldn't do the same with polymorphism. However, this is a useful technique in certain circumstances, as you will see in the section called, "Contravariance."

In the next two sections, you look at how to implement variance in generic types and how the .NET Framework uses variance to make your life easier.

> **NOTE** *All of the code in this section is included in a demo project called* VarianceDemo *if you want to work through it as you go along.*

## Covariance

To define a generic type parameter as covariant, you use the out keyword in the type definition, as shown in the following example:

```
public interface IMethaneProducer<out T>
{
    ...
}
```

For interface definitions, covariant type parameters can be used only as return values of methods or property get accessors.

A good example of how this is useful is found in the .NET Framework, in the IEnumerable<T> interface that you've used previously. The item type T in this interface is defined as being covariant. This means that you can put an object that supports, say, IEnumerable<Cow> into a variable of type IEnumerable<Animal>.

This enables the following code:

```
static void Main(string[] args)
{
    List<Cow> cows = new List<Cow>();
    cows.Add(new Cow("Geronimo"));
    cows.Add(new SuperCow("Tonto"));
    ListAnimals(cows);
    Console.ReadKey();
}

static void ListAnimals(IEnumerable<Animal> animals)
{
    foreach (Animal animal in animals)
    {
        Console.WriteLine(animal.ToString());
    }
}
```

Here the cows variable is of type List<Cow>, which supports the IEnumerable<Cow> interface. This variable can, through covariance, be passed to a method that expects a parameter of type IEnumerable<Animal>. Recalling what you know about how foreach loops work, you know that the GetEnumerator() method is used to get an enumerator of IEnumerator<T>, and the Current property of that enumerator is used to access items. IEnumerator<T> also defines its type parameter as covariant, which means that it's okay to use it as the get accessor of a parameter, and everything works perfectly.

## Contravariance

To define a generic type parameter as contravariant, you use the in keyword in the type definition:

```
public interface IGrassMuncher<in T>
{
    ...
}
```

For interface definitions, contravariant type parameters can be used only as method parameters, not as return types.

Again, the best way to understand this is to look at an example of how contravariance is used in the .NET Framework. One interface that has a contravariant type parameter, again one that you've already used, is IComparer<T>. You might implement this interface for animals as follows:

```
public class AnimalNameLengthComparer : IComparer<Animal>
{
    public int Compare(Animal x, Animal y)
    {
        return x.Name.Length.CompareTo(y.Name.Length);
    }
}
```

This comparer compares animals by name length, so you could use it to sort, for example, an instance of List<Animal>. However, through contravariance, you can also use it to sort an instance of List<Cow>, even though the List<Cow>.Sort() method expects an instance of IComparer<Cow>:

```
List<Cow> cows = new List<Cow>();
cows.Add(new Cow("Geronimo"));
cows.Add(new SuperCow("Tonto"));
cows.Add(new Cow("Gerald"));
cows.Add(new Cow("Phil"));
cows.Sort(new AnimalNameLengthComparer());
```

In most circumstances, contravariance is something that simply happens—and it's been worked into the .NET Framework to help with just this sort of operation. The good thing about both types of variance in .NET 4 and above, though, is that you can now implement them with the techniques shown in this section whenever you need them.

## SUMMARY

This chapter examined how to use generic types in C# and create your own generic types, including classes, interfaces, methods, and delegates. You also looked at how to use structs, including how to create nullable types, and how to use the classes in the System.Collections.Generic namespace.

Generics, as you saw, are an extremely powerful technique in C#. You can use them to create classes that satisfy several purposes at the same time, and they can be used in a variety of situations. Even if you don't have any reason to create your own generic types, you're almost certain to use the generic collection classes repeatedly.

In the next chapter, you''ll continue your examination of the basic C# language by tying up a few loose ends and looking at events.

## EXERCISES

**12.1** Which of the following can be generic?

a. Classes

b. Methods

c. Properties

d. Operator overloads

e. Structs

f. Enumerations

**12.2** Extend the `Vector` class in `Ch12Ex01` such that the * operator returns the dot product of two vectors.

> **NOTE** *The dot product of two vectors is defined as the product of their magnitudes multiplied by the cosine of the angle between them.*

**12.3** What is wrong with the following code? Fix it.

```
public class Instantiator<T>
{
    public T instance;

    public Instantiator()
    {
        instance = new T();
    }
}
```

**12.4** What is wrong with the following code? Fix it.

```
public class StringGetter<T>
{
    public string GetString<T>(T item)
    {
        return item.ToString();
    }
}
```

**12.5** Create a generic class called `ShortList<T>` that implements `IList<T>` and consists of a collection of items with a maximum size. This maximum size should be an integer that can be supplied to the constructor of `ShortList<T>` or defaults to 10. The constructor should also be able to take an initial list of items via an `IEnumerable<T>` parameter. The class should function exactly like `List<T>` but throw an exception of type `IndexOutOfRangeException` if an attempt is made to add too many items to the collection, or if the `IEnumerable<T>` passed to the constructor contains too many items.

**12.6** Will the following code compile? If not, why not?

```
public interface IMethaneProducer<out T>
{
    void BelchAt(T target);
}
```

Answers to the exercises can be found in Appendix A.

▶ **WHAT YOU HAVE LEARNED IN THIS CHAPTER**

| TOPIC | KEY CONCEPTS |
|---|---|
| **Using generic types** | Generic types require one or more type parameters to work. You can use a generic type as the type of a variable by passing the type parameters you require when you declare a variable. You do this by enclosing a comma-separated list of type names in angle brackets. |
| **Nullable types** | Nullable types are types that can take any value of a specified value type or the value null. You can use the syntax Nullable<T> or T? to declare a nullable type variable. |
| **The ?? operator** | The null coalescing operator returns either the value of its first operand, or, if the first operand is null, its second operand. |
| **Generic collections** | Generic collections are extremely useful as they come with strong typing built-in. You can use List<T>, Collection<T>, and Dictionary<K, V> among other collection types. These also expose generic interfaces. To sort and search generic collections, you use the IComparer<T> and IComparable<T> interfaces. |
| **Defining generic classes** | You define a generic type much like any other type, with the addition of generic type parameters where you specify the type name. As with using generic types, you specify these as a comma-separated list enclosed in angle brackets. You can use the generic type parameters in your code anywhere you'd use a type name, for example, in method return values and parameters. |
| **Generic type parameter constraints** | In order to use generic type parameters more effectively in your generic type code, you can constrain the types that can be supplied when the type is used. You can constrain type parameters by base class, supported interface, whether they must be value or reference types, and whether they support parameterless constructors. Without such constraints, you must use the default keyword to instantiate a variable of a generic type. |
| **Other generic types** | As well as classes, you can define generic interfaces, delegates, and methods. |
| **Variance** | Variance is a concept similar to polymorphism, but applied to type parameters. It allows you to use one generic type in place of another, where those generic types vary only in the generic type parameters used. Covariance allows conversion between two types where the target type has a type parameter that is a base class of the type parameter of the source type. Contravariance allows conversion where this relationship is inverted. Covariant type parameters are defined with the out parameter, and can only be used as return types and property get accessor types. Contravariant type parameters are defined with the in parameter and can only be used as method parameters. |

# 13

# Additional OOP Techniques

**WHAT YOU WILL LEARN IN THIS CHAPTER**

- ➤ What the :: operator is
- ➤ What the global namespace qualifier is
- ➤ How to create custom exceptions
- ➤ How to use events
- ➤ How to use anonymous methods
- ➤ How to use C# attributes

**WROX.COM CODE DOWNLOADS FOR THIS CHAPTER**

You can find the wrox.com code downloads for this chapter at www.wrox.com/remtitle .cgi?isbn=9781118314418 on the Download Code tab. The code is in the Chapter 13 download and individually named according to the names throughout the chapter.

In this chapter, you continue exploring the C# language by looking at a few bits and pieces that haven't quite fit in elsewhere. This isn't to say that these techniques aren't useful—it's just that they don't fall under any of the headings you've worked through so far.

You also make some final modifications to the CardLib code that you've been building in the last few chapters, and even use CardLib to create a card game.

## THE :: OPERATOR AND THE GLOBAL NAMESPACE QUALIFIER

The :: operator provides an alternative way to access types in namespaces. This might be necessary if you want to use a namespace alias and there is ambiguity between the alias and the actual namespace hierarchy. If that's the case, then the namespace hierarchy is given priority over the namespace alias. To see what this means, consider the following code:

```
using MyNamespaceAlias = MyRootNamespace.MyNestedNamespace;

namespace MyRootNamespace
{
   namespace MyNamespaceAlias
   {
```

```
        public class MyClass
        {
        }
    }

    namespace MyNestedNamespace
    {
        public class MyClass
        {
        }
    }
}
```

Code in `MyRootNamespace` might use the following to refer to a class:

```
MyNamespaceAlias.MyClass
```

The class referred to by this code is the `MyRootNamespace.MyNamespaceAlias.MyClass`
class, not the `MyRootNamespace.MyNestedNamespace.MyClass` class. That is, the namespace
`MyRootNamespace.MyNamespaceAlias` has hidden the alias defined by the `using` statement, which
refers to `MyRootNamespace.MyNestedNamespace`. You can still access the `MyRootNamespace.`
`MyNestedNamespace` namespace and the class contained within, but it requires different syntax:

```
MyNestedNamespace.MyClass
```

Alternatively, you can use the :: operator:

```
MyNamespaceAlias::MyClass
```

Using this operator forces the compiler to use the alias defined by the `using` statement, and therefore the
code refers to `MyRootNamespace.MyNestedNamespace.MyClass`.

You can also use the keyword `global` with the :: operator, which is essentially an alias to the top-level, root
namespace. This can be useful to make it clearer which namespace you are referring to, as
shown here:

```
global::System.Collections.Generic.List<int>
```

This is the class you'd expect it to be, the generic `List<T>` collection class. It definitely isn't the class defined
with the following code:

```
namespace MyRootNamespace
{
    namespace System
    {
        namespace Collections
        {
            namespace Generic
            {
                class List<T>
                {
                }
            }
        }
    }
}
```

Of course, you should avoid giving your namespaces names that already exist as .NET namespaces,
although similar problems can arise in large projects, particularly if you are working as part of a
large team. Using the :: operator and the `global` keyword might be the only way you can access the
types you want.

## CUSTOM EXCEPTIONS

Chapter 7 covered exceptions and explained how you can use `try...catch...finally` blocks to act on them. You also saw several standard .NET exceptions, including the base class for exceptions, `System.Exception`. Sometimes it's useful to derive your own exception classes from this base class for use in your applications, instead of using the standard exceptions. This enables you to be more specific with the information you send to whatever code catches the exception, and it enables catching code to be more specific about which exceptions it handles. For example, you might add a new property to your exception class that permits access to some underlying information, making it possible for the exception's receiver to make the required changes, or just provide more information about the exception's cause.

Once you have defined an exception class, you can add it to the list of exceptions recognized by VS using the Debug ⇨ Exceptions dialog box's Add button, and then defining exception-specific behavior, as shown in Chapter 7.

> **NOTE** Two fundamental exception classes exist in the `System` namespace and derive from `Exception`: `ApplicationException` and `SystemException`. `SystemException` is used as the base class for exceptions that are predefined by the .NET Framework. `ApplicationException` was provided for developers to derive their own exception classes, but more recent best practice dictates that you should not derive your exceptions from this class; you should use `Exception` instead. The `ApplicationException` class will likely be deprecated at some point in the future.

## Adding Custom Exceptions to CardLib

How to use custom exceptions is, once again, best illustrated by upgrading the CardLib project. The `Deck.GetCard()` method currently throws a standard .NET exception if an attempt is made to access a card with an index less than 0 or greater than 51, but you'll modify that to use a custom exception.

First, you need to create a new class library project called Ch13CardLib, save it in the `BegVCSharp\Chapter13` directory, and copy the classes from Ch12CardLib as before, changing the namespace to `Ch13CardLib` as applicable. Next, define the exception. You do this with a new class defined in a new class file called `CardOutOfRangeException.cs`, which you can add to the Ch13CardLib project with Project ⇨ Add Class (you can find this code in `Ch13CardLib\CardOutOfRangeException.cs`):

```
public class CardOutOfRangeException : Exception
{
    private Cards deckContents;

    public Cards DeckContents
    {
        get
        {
            return deckContents;
        }
    }

    public CardOutOfRangeException(Cards sourceDeckContents)
        : base("There are only 52 cards in the deck.")
    {
        deckContents = sourceDeckContents;
    }
}
```

An instance of the `Cards` class is required for the constructor of this class. It allows access to this `Cards` object through a `DeckContents` property and supplies a suitable error message to the base `Exception` constructor so that it is available through the `Message` property of the class.

Next, add code to throw this exception to `Deck.cs`, replacing the old standard exception (you can find this code in `Ch13CardLib\Deck.cs`):

```
public Card GetCard(int cardNum)
{
    if (cardNum >= 0 && cardNum <= 51)
        return cards[cardNum];
    else
        throw new CardOutOfRangeException(cards.Clone() as Cards);
}
```

The `DeckContents` property is initialized with a deep copy of the current contents of the `Deck` object, in the form of a `Cards` object. This means that you see the contents at the point where the exception was thrown, so subsequent modification to the deck contents won't "lose" this information.

To test this, use the following client code (you can find this code in in `Ch13CardClient\Program.cs`):

```
Deck deck1 = new Deck();
try
{
    Card myCard = deck1.GetCard(60);
}
catch (CardOutOfRangeException e)
{
    Console.WriteLine(e.Message);
    Console.WriteLine(e.DeckContents[0]);
}
Console.ReadKey();
```

This code results in the output shown in Figure 13-1.

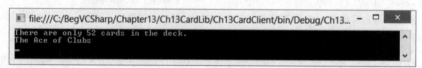

file:///C:/BegVCSharp/Chapter13/Ch13CardLib/Ch13CardClient/bin/Debug/Ch13...

```
There are only 52 cards in the deck.
The Ace of Clubs
```

**FIGURE 13-1**

Here, the catching code has written the exception `Message` property to the screen. You also displayed the first card in the `Cards` object obtained through `DeckContents`, just to prove that you can access the `Cards` collection through your custom exception object.

## EVENTS

This section covers one of the most frequently used OOP techniques in .NET: *events*. You start, as usual, with the basics—looking at what events actually are. After that, you'll see some simple events in action and learn what you can do with them. Then, you learn how you can create and use events of your own.

At the end of this chapter, you'll complete your `CardLib` class library by adding an event. Finally, because this is the last port of call before arriving at some advanced topics, you'll have a bit of fun creating a card game application that uses this class library.

### What Is an Event?

Events are similar to exceptions in that they are *raised* (thrown) by objects, and you can supply code that acts on them. However, there are several important differences, the most important of which is that there is no equivalent to the `try...catch` structure for handling events. Instead, you must *subscribe* to them. Subscribing to an event means supplying code that will be executed when an event is raised, in the form of an *event handler*.

Many handlers can be subscribed to a single event, all of which are called when the event is raised. This can include event handlers that are part of the class of the object that raises the event, but event handlers are just as likely to be found in other classes.

Event handlers themselves are simply methods. The only restriction on an event handler method is that it must match the return type and parameters required by the event. This restriction is part of the definition of an event and is specified by a *delegate*.

> **NOTE** *The fact that delegates are used in events is one of the reasons why delegates are so useful. This is why some space was devoted to them in Chapter 6. You might want to review that material to refresh your memory about delegates and how you use them.*

The basic sequence of processing is as follows: First, an application creates an object that can raise an event. For example, suppose an instant messaging application creates an object that represents a connection to a remote user. That connection object might raise an event when a message arrives through the connection from the remote user (see Figure 13-2).

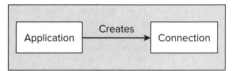

**FIGURE 13-2**

Next, the application subscribes to the event. Your instant messaging application would do this by defining a method that could be used with the delegate type specified by the event, passing a reference to this method to the event. The event handler method might be a method on another object, such as an object representing a display device to show instant messages when they arrive (see Figure 13-3).

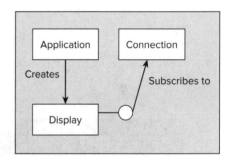

**FIGURE 13-3**

When the event is raised, the subscriber is notified. When an instant message arrives through the connection object, the event handler method on the display device object is called. Because you are using a standard method, the object that raises the event can pass any relevant information via parameters, making events very versatile. In the example case, one parameter might be the text of the instant message, which the event handler could display on the display device object. This is shown in Figure 13-4.

## Handling Events

As previously discussed, to handle an event you need to subscribe to it by providing an event handler method whose return type and parameters match that of the delegate specified for use with the event. The following example uses a simple timer object to raise events, which results in a handler method being called.

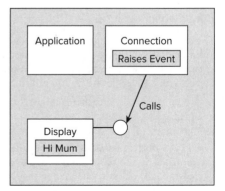

**FIGURE 13-4**

**TRY IT OUT** Handling Events: Ch13Ex01\Program.cs

**1.** Create a new console application called Ch13Ex01 and save it in the directory C:\BegVCSharp\Chapter13.

**2.** Modify the code in Program.cs as follows:

```
using System;
using System.Collections.Generic;
using System.Linq;
using System.Text;
using System.Threading.Tasks;
using System.Timers;

namespace Ch13Ex01
{
    class Program
    {
        static int counter = 0;

        static string displayString =
                        "This string will appear one letter at a time. ";
        static void Main(string[] args)
        {
            Timer myTimer = new Timer(100);
            myTimer.Elapsed += new ElapsedEventHandler(WriteChar);
            myTimer.Start();
            System.Threading.Thread.Sleep(200);
            Console.ReadKey();
        }
        static void WriteChar(object source, ElapsedEventArgs e)
        {
            Console.Write(displayString[counter++ % displayString.Length]);
        }
    }
}
```

**3.** Run the application (once it is running, pressing a key will terminate the application). The result, after a short period, is shown in Figure 13-5.

**FIGURE 13-5**

*How It Works*

The object you are using to raise events is an instance of the System.Timers.Timer class. This object is initialized with a time period (in milliseconds). When the Timer object is started using its Start() method, a stream of events is raised, spaced out in time according to the specified time period. Main() initializes a Timer object with a timer period of 100 milliseconds, so it will raise events 10 times a second when started:

```
static void Main(string[] args)
{
    Timer myTimer = new Timer(100);
```

The Timer object possesses an event called Elapsed, and the event handler required by this event must match the return type and parameters of the System.Timers.ElapsedEventHandler delegate type, which is one of the standard delegates defined in the .NET Framework. This delegate specifies the following return type and parameters:

```
void <MethodName>(object source, ElapsedEventArgs e);
```

The `Timer` object sends a reference to itself in the first parameter and an instance of an `ElapsedEventArgs` object in its second parameter. It is safe to ignore these parameters for now; you'll take a look at them a little later.

In your code you have a suitable method:

```
static void WriteChar(object source, ElapsedEventArgs e)
{
    Console.Write(displayString[counter++ % displayString.Length]);
}
```

This method uses the two static fields of `Program`, `counter` and `displayString`, to display a single character. Every time the method is called, a different character is displayed.

The next task is to hook this handler up to the event—to subscribe to it. To do this, you use the `+=` operator to add a handler to the event in the form of a new delegate instance initialized with your event handler method:

```
static void Main(string[] args)
{
    Timer myTimer = new Timer(100);
    myTimer.Elapsed += new ElapsedEventHandler(WriteChar);
```

This command (which uses slightly strange-looking syntax, specific to delegates) adds a handler to the list that will be called when the `Elapsed` event is raised. You can add as many handlers as you like to this list as long as they all meet the criteria required. Each handler is called in turn when the event is raised.

All that remains for `Main()` to do is start the timer running:

```
    myTimer.Start();
```

You don't want the application terminating before you have handled any events, so you put the `Main()` method on hold. The simplest way to do this is to request user input, as this command won't finish processing until the user has pressed a key:

```
    Console.ReadKey();
```

Although processing in `Main()` effectively ceases here, processing in the `Timer` object continues. When it raises events it calls the `WriteChar()` method, which runs concurrently with the `Console.ReadLine()` statement. The `System.Threading.Thread.Sleep(200)` statement is included to give the timer the opportunity to start sending messages to the console application.

Note that the syntax for adding an event handler can be simplified slightly using the method group concept introduced in the previous chapter, as follows:

```
    myTimer.Elapsed += WriteChar;
```

The end result is exactly the same, but you do not have to explicitly specify the delegate type; it is inferred by the compiler from the context in which you use it. However, many programmers dislike this syntax because it reduces readability—it is no longer possible to tell at a glance what delegate type you are using. Feel free to use this syntax if you prefer, but in this chapter all the delegates you use will be referenced explicitly to make things clearer.

## Defining Events

Now it's time to define and use your own events. The following Try It Out implements an example version of the instant messaging scenario introduced earlier in this chapter, creating a `Connection` object that raises events that are handled by a `Display` object.

**TRY IT OUT**   Defining Events: Ch13Ex02

1. Create a new console application called Ch13Ex02 and save it in the directory C:\BegVCSharp\
   Chapter13.

2. Add a new class called Connection and modify Connection.cs as follows:

```
using System;
using System.Collections.Generic;
using System.Linq;
using System.Text;
using System.Threading.Tasks;
using System.Timers;

namespace Ch13Ex02
{
    public delegate void MessageHandler(string messageText);

    public class Connection
    {
        public event MessageHandler MessageArrived;
        private Timer pollTimer;

        public Connection()
        {
            pollTimer = new Timer(100);
            pollTimer.Elapsed += new ElapsedEventHandler(CheckForMessage);
        }

        public void Connect()
        {
            pollTimer.Start();
        }

        public void Disconnect()
        {
            pollTimer.Stop();
        }

        private static Random random = new Random();

        private void CheckForMessage(object source, ElapsedEventArgs e)
        {
            Console.WriteLine("Checking for new messages.");
            if ((random.Next(9) == 0) && (MessageArrived != null))
            {
                MessageArrived("Hello Mum!");
            }
        }
    }
}
```

3. Add a new class called Display and modify Display.cs as follows:

```
namespace Ch13Ex02
{
    public class Display
    {
        public void DisplayMessage(string message)
        {
            Console.WriteLine("Message arrived: {0}", message);
        }
    }
}
```

4. Modify the code in `Program.cs` as follows:

```
static void Main(string[] args)
{
    Connection myConnection = new Connection();
    Display myDisplay = new Display();
    myConnection.MessageArrived +=
            new MessageHandler (myDisplay.DisplayMessage);
    myConnection.Connect();
    Console.ReadKey();
}
```

5. Run the application. The result is shown in Figure 13-6.

**FIGURE 13-6**

### How It Works

The `Connection` class does most of the work in this application. Instances of this class make use of a `Timer` object much like the one shown in the first example of this chapter, initializing it in the class constructor and providing access to its state (enabled or disabled) via `Connect()` and `Disconnect()`:

```
public class Connection
{
    private Timer pollTimer;

    public Connection()
    {
        pollTimer = new Timer(100);
        pollTimer.Elapsed += new ElapsedEventHandler(CheckForMessage);
    }

    public void Connect()
    {
        pollTimer.Start();
    }

    public void Disconnect()
    {
        pollTimer.Stop();
    }

    ...
}
```

Also in the constructor, you register an event handler for the `Elapsed` event, just as you did in the first example. The handler method, `CheckForMessage()`, raises an event on average once every 10 times it is called. You will look at the code for this, but first it would be useful to look at the event definition itself.

Before you define an event, you must define a delegate type to use with the event—that is, a delegate type that specifies the return type and parameters to which an event handling method must conform. You do this using standard delegate syntax, defining it as public inside the `Ch13Ex02` namespace to make the type available to external code:

```
namespace Ch13Ex02
{
    public delegate void MessageHandler(string messageText);
```

This delegate type, called `MessageHandler` here, is a `void` method that has a single `string` parameter. You can use this parameter to pass an instant message received by the `Connection` object to the `Display` object. Once a delegate has been defined (or a suitable existing delegate has been located), you can define the event itself, as a member of the `Connection` class:

```
public class Connection
{
    public event MessageHandler MessageArrived;
```

You simply name the event (here it is `MessageArrived`) and declare it by using the `event` keyword and specifying the delegate type to use (the `MessageHandler` delegate type defined earlier). After you have declared an event in this way, you can raise it simply by calling it by name as if it were a method with the return type and parameters specified by the delegate. For example, you could raise this event using the following:

```
MessageArrived("This is a message.");
```

If the delegate had been defined without any parameters, then you could simply use the following:

```
MessageArrived();
```

Alternatively, you could define more parameters, which would require more code to raise the event. The `CheckForMessage()` method looks like this:

```
private static Random random = new Random();

private void CheckForMessage(object source, ElapsedEventArgs e)
{
    Console.WriteLine("Checking for new messages.");
    if ((random.Next(9) == 0) && (MessageArrived != null))
    {
        MessageArrived("Hello Mum!");
    }
}
```

You use an instance of the `Random` class shown in earlier chapters to generate a random number between 0 and 9, and raise an event if the number generated is 0, which should happen 10 percent of the time. This simulates polling the connection to determine whether a message has arrived, which won't be the case every time you check. To separate the timer from the instance of `Connection`, you use a private static instance of the `Random` class.

Note that you supply additional logic. You raise an event only if the expression `MessageArrived != null` evaluates to `true`. This expression, which again uses the delegate syntax in a slightly unusual way, means "Does the event have any subscribers?" If there are no subscribers, then `MessageArrived` evaluates to `null`, and there is no point in raising the event.

The class that will subscribe to the event is called `Display` and contains the single method, `DisplayMessage()`, defined as follows:

```
public class Display
{
    public void DisplayMessage(string message)
```

```
        {
            Console.WriteLine("Message arrived: {0}", message);
        }
    }
```

This method matches the delegate type (and is public, which is a requirement of event handlers in classes other than the class that generates the event), so you can use it to respond to the `MessageArrived` event.

All that is left now is for the code in `Main()` to initialize instances of the `Connection` and `Display` classes, hook them up, and start things going. The code required here is similar to the first example:

```
static void Main(string[] args)
{
    Connection myConnection = new Connection();
    Display myDisplay = new Display();
    myConnection.MessageArrived +=
            new MessageHandler(myDisplay.DisplayMessage);
    myConnection.Connect();
    System.Threading.Thread.Sleep(200);
    Console.ReadKey();
}
```

Again, you call `Console.ReadKey()` to pause the processing of `Main()` once you have started things moving with the `Connect()` method of the `Connection` object and inserted a short delay.

## Multipurpose Event Handlers

The delegate you saw earlier, for the `Timer.Elapsed` event, contained two parameters that are of a type often seen in event handlers:

➤ `object source`—A reference to the object that raised the event

➤ `ElapsedEventArgs e`—Parameters sent by the event

The reason the `object` type parameter is used in this event, and indeed in many other events, is that you often need to use a single event handler for several identical events generated by different objects and still tell which object generated the event.

To explain and illustrate this concept, the next Try It Out extends the last example a little.

**TRY IT OUT**   Using a Multipurpose Event Handler: Ch13Ex03

**1.** Create a new console application called Ch13Ex03 and save it in the directory `C:\BegVCSharp\Chapter13`.

**2.** Copy the code across for `Program.cs`, `Connection.cs`, and `Display.cs` from Ch13Ex02, making sure that you change the namespaces in each file from `Ch13Ex02` to `Ch13Ex03`.

**3.** Add a new class called `MessageArrivedEventArgs` and modify `MessageArrivedEventArgs.cs` as follows:

```
namespace Ch13Ex03
{
    public class MessageArrivedEventArgs : EventArgs
    {
        private string message;

        public string Message
        {
            get
            {
                return message;
            }
        }
    }
```

```
        public MessageArrivedEventArgs()
        {
            message = "No message sent.";
        }

        public MessageArrivedEventArgs(string newMessage)
        {
            message = newMessage;
        }
    }
}
```

**4.** Modify `Connection.cs` as follows:

```
namespace Ch13Ex03
{
    // delegate definition removed

    public class Connection
    {
        public event EventHandler<MessageArrivedEventArgs> MessageArrived;

        public string Name { get; set; }

        ...

        private void CheckForMessage(object source, EventArgs e)
        {
            Console.WriteLine("Checking for new messages.");
            if ((random.Next(9) == 0) && (MessageArrived != null))
            {
                MessageArrived(this, new MessageArrivedEventArgs("Hello Mum!"));
            }
        }

        ...

    }
}
```

**5.** Modify `Display.cs` as follows:

```
        public void DisplayMessage(object source, MessageArrivedEventArgs e)
        {
            Console.WriteLine("Message arrived from: {0}",
                              ((Connection)source).Name);
            Console.WriteLine("Message Text: {0}", e.Message);
        }
```

**6.** Modify `Program.cs` as follows:

```
        static void Main(string[] args)
        {
            Connection myConnection1 = new Connection();
            myConnection1.Name = "First connection.";
            Connection myConnection2 = new Connection();
            myConnection2.Name = "Second connection.";
            Display myDisplay = new Display();
            myConnection1.MessageArrived += myDisplay.DisplayMessage;
            myConnection2.MessageArrived += myDisplay.DisplayMessage;
            myConnection1.Connect();
            myConnection2.Connect();
            System.Threading.Thread.Sleep(200);
            Console.ReadKey();
        }
```

**7.** Run the application. The result is shown in Figure 13-7.

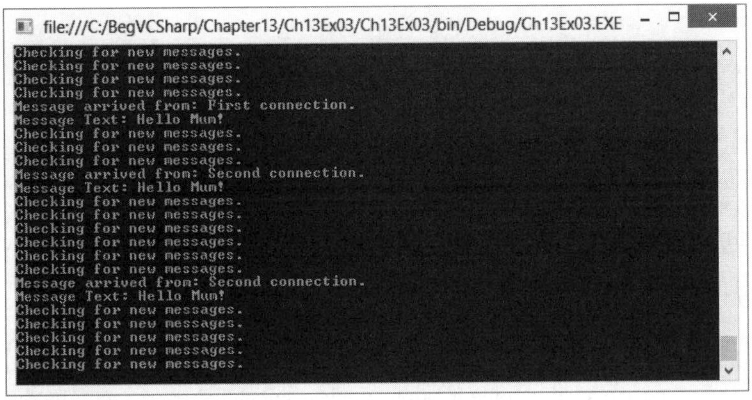

**FIGURE 13-7**

*How It Works*

By sending a reference to the object that raises an event as one of the event handler parameters, you can customize the response of the handler to individual objects. The reference gives you access to the source object, including its properties.

By sending parameters that are contained in a class that inherits from System.EventArgs (as ElapsedEventArgs does), you can supply whatever additional information is necessary as parameters (such as the Message parameter on the MessageArrivedEventArgs class).

In addition, these parameters benefit from polymorphism. You could define a handler for the MessageArrived event such as this:

```
public void DisplayMessage(object source, EventArgs e)
{
    Console.WriteLine("Message arrived from: {0}",
                       ((Connection)source).Name);
    Console.WriteLine("Message Text: {0}",
                       ((MessageArrivedEventArgs)e).Message);
}
```

The application will execute exactly as it did before, but the DisplayMessage() method is now more versatile (in theory at least—more implementation is needed to make this production quality). This same handler could work with other events, such as the Timer.Elapsed, although you'd have to modify the internals of the handler a bit more such that the parameters sent when this event is raised are handled properly. (Casting them to Connection and MessageArrivedEventArgs objects in this way will cause an exception; you should use the as operator instead and check for null values.)

## The EventHandler and Generic EventHandler<T> Types

In most cases, you will follow the pattern outlined in the previous section and use event handlers with a void return type and two parameters. The first parameter will be of type object, and will be the event source. The second parameter will be of a type that derives from System.EventArgs, and will contain any event arguments. As this is so common, .NET provides two delegate types to make it easier to define events: EventHandler and EventHandler<T>. Both of these are delegates that use the standard event handler pattern. The generic version enables you to specify the type of event argument you want to use.

In the previous Try It Out, you saw this in action as you used the generic `EventHandler<T>` delegate type as follows:

```
public class Connection
{
    public event EventHandler<MessageArrivedEventArgs> MessageArrived;

    ...
}
```

This is obviously a good thing to do because it simplifies your code. In general, it is best practice to use these delegate types whenever you define an event. Note that if you have an event that doesn't need event argument data, you can still use the `EventHandler` delegate type. You can simply pass `EventArgs.Empty` as the argument value.

### Return Values and Event Handlers

All the event handlers you've seen so far have had a return type of `void`. It is possible to provide a return type for an event, but this can lead to problems because a given event can result in several event handlers being called. If all of these handlers return a value, then it can be unclear which value was actually returned.

The system deals with this by allowing you access to only the last value returned by an event handler. That will be the value returned by the last event handler to subscribe to an event. Although this functionality might be of use in some situations, it is recommended that you use `void` type event handlers, and avoid `out` type parameters (which would lead to the same ambiguity regarding the source of the value returned by the parameter).

### Anonymous Methods

Instead of defining event handler methods, you can choose to use *anonymous methods*. An anonymous method doesn't actually exist as a method in the traditional sense—that is, it isn't a method on any particular class. Instead, an anonymous method is created purely for use as a target for a delegate.

To create an anonymous method, you need the following code:

```
delegate (parameters)
{
    // Anonymous method code.
};
```

`parameters` is a list of parameters matching those of the delegate type you are instantiating, as used by the anonymous method code:

```
delegate(Connection source, MessageArrivedEventArgs e)
{
    // Anonymous method code matching MessageHandler event in Ch13Ex03.
};
```

For example, you could use this code to completely bypass the `Display.DisplayMessage()` method in Ch13Ex03:

```
myConnection1.MessageArrived +=
    delegate(Connection source, MessageArrivedEventArgs e)
    {
        Console.WriteLine("Message arrived from: {0}", source.Name);
        Console.WriteLine("Message Text: {0}", e.Message);
    };
```

An interesting point about anonymous methods is that they are effectively local to the code block that contains them, and they have access to local variables in this scope. If you use such a variable, then it becomes an *outer* variable. Outer variables are not disposed of when they go out of scope as other local variables are; instead, they live on until the anonymous methods that use them are destroyed. This might be some time later than you expect, so it's definitely something to be careful about. If an outer variable takes up a large amount of memory, or if it uses resources that are expensive in other ways (for example, resources that are limited in number), then this could cause memory or performance problems.

## EXPANDING AND USING CARDLIB

Now that you've had a look at defining and using events, you can use them in Ch13CardLib. The event you'll add to your library will be generated when the last Card object in a Deck object is obtained by using GetCard, and it will be called LastCardDrawn. The event enables subscribers to reshuffle the deck automatically, cutting down on the processing necessary by a client. The event will use the EventHandler delegate type and will pass as its source a reference to the Deck object, such that the Shuffle() method will be accessible from wherever the handler is. Add the following code to Deck.cs (you can find this code in Ch13CardLib\Deck.cs) to define and raise the event:

```
namespace Ch13CardLib
{
    public event EventHandler LastCardDrawn;

    ...

    public Card GetCard(int cardNum)
    {
        if (cardNum >= 0 && cardNum <= 51)
        {
            if ((cardNum == 51) && (LastCardDrawn != null))
                LastCardDrawn(this, EventArgs.Empty);
            return cards[cardNum];
        }
        else
            throw new CardOutOfRangeException((Cards)cards.Clone());
    }
```

This is all the code required to add the event to the Deck class definition.

## A Card Game Client for CardLib

After spending all this time developing the CardLib library, it would be a shame not to use it. Before finishing this section on OOP in C# and the .NET Framework, it's time to have a little fun and write the basics of a card game application that uses the familiar playing card classes.

As in previous chapters, you'll add a client console application to the Ch13CardLib solution, add a reference to the Ch13CardLib project, and make it the startup project. This application will be called Ch13CardClient.

To begin, you'll create a new class called Player in a new file in Ch13CardClient, Player.cs. You can find this code in Ch13CardClient\Player.cs in this chapter's online download. This class will contain two automatic properties: Name (a string) and PlayHand (of type Cards). Both of these properties have private set accessors, but despite this the PlayHand provides write-access to its contents, enabling you to modify the cards in the player's hand.

You'll also hide the default constructor by making it private, and supply a public nondefault constructor that accepts an initial value for the Name property of Player instances.

Finally, you'll provide a bool type method called HasWon(), which returns true if all the cards in the player's hand are the same suit (a simple winning condition, but that doesn't matter too much).

Here's the code for Player.cs:

```
using System;
using System.Collections.Generic;
using System.Linq;
using System.Text;
using System.Threading.Tasks;
using Ch13CardLib;
```

```csharp
namespace Ch13CardClient
{
    public class Player
    {
        public string Name { get; private set; }

        public Cards PlayHand { get; private set; }

        private Player()
        {
        }

        public Player(string name)
        {
            Name = name;
            PlayHand = new Cards();
        }

        public bool HasWon()
        {
            bool won = true;
            Suit match = PlayHand[0].suit;
            for (int i = 1; i < PlayHand.Count; i++)
            {
                won &= PlayHand[i].suit == match;
            }
            return won;
        }
    }
}
```

Next, define a class that will handle the card game itself, called `Game`. This class is found in the file `Game.cs` of the Ch13CardClient project. The class has four private member fields:

➤ `playDeck`—A `Deck` type variable containing the deck of cards to use

➤ `currentCard`—An `int` value used as a pointer to the next card in the deck to draw

➤ `players`—An array of `Player` objects representing the players of the game

➤ `discardedCards`—A `Cards` collection for the cards that have been discarded by players but not shuffled back into the deck

The default constructor for the class initializes and shuffles the `Deck` stored in `playDeck`, sets the `currentCard` pointer variable to 0 (the first card in `playDeck`), and wires up an event handler called `Reshuffle()` to the `playDeck.LastCardDrawn` event. The handler simply shuffles the deck, initializes the `discardedCards` collection, and resets `currentCard` to 0, ready to read cards from the new deck.

The `Game` class also contains two utility methods: `SetPlayers()` for setting the players for the game (as an array of `Player` objects) and `DealHands()` for dealing hands to the players (seven cards each). The allowed number of players is restricted to between two and seven to ensure that there are enough cards to go around.

Finally, there is a `PlayGame()` method that contains the game logic itself. You'll come back to this method shortly, after you've looked at the code in `Program.cs`. The rest of the code in `Game.cs` is as follows (you can find this code in `Ch13CardClient\Game.cs`):

```csharp
using System;
using System.Collections.Generic;
using System.Linq;
using System.Text;
using System.Threading.Tasks;
using Ch13CardLib;

namespace Ch13CardClient
{
```

```csharp
public class Game
{
    private int currentCard;
    private Deck playDeck;
    private Player[] players;
    private Cards discardedCards;

    public Game()
    {
        currentCard = 0;
        playDeck = new Deck(true);
        playDeck.LastCardDrawn += Reshuffle;
        playDeck.Shuffle();
        discardedCards = new Cards();
    }

    private void Reshuffle(object source, EventArgs args)
    {
        Console.WriteLine("Discarded cards reshuffled into deck.");
        ((Deck)source).Shuffle();
        discardedCards.Clear();
        currentCard = 0;
    }

    public void SetPlayers(Player[] newPlayers)
    {
        if (newPlayers.Length > 7)
            throw new ArgumentException(
                "A maximum of 7 players may play this game.");

        if (newPlayers.Length < 2)
            throw new ArgumentException(
                "A minimum of 2 players may play this game.");

        players = newPlayers;
    }

    private void DealHands()
    {
        for (int p = 0; p < players.Length; p++)
        {
            for (int c = 0; c < 7; c++)
            {
                players[p].PlayHand.Add(playDeck.GetCard(currentCard++));
            }
        }
    }

    public int PlayGame()
    {
        // Code to follow.
    }
}
```

Program.cs contains the Main() method, which initializes and runs the game. This method performs the following steps:

1. An introduction is displayed.
2. The user is prompted for a number of players between 2 and 7.
3. An array of Player objects is set up accordingly.
4. Each player is prompted for a name, used to initialize one Player object in the array.

5. A `Game` object is created and players are assigned using the `SetPlayers()` method.

6. The game is started by using the `PlayGame()` method.

7. The `int` return value of `PlayGame()` is used to display a winning message (the value returned is the index of the winning player in the array of `Player` objects).

The code for this follows, with comments added for clarity (you can find this code in `Ch13CardClient\ Program.cs`):

```
static void Main(string[] args)
{
    // Display introduction.
    Console.WriteLine("KarliCards: a new and exciting card game.");
    Console.WriteLine("To win you must have 7 cards of the same suit in" +
                      " your hand.");
    Console.WriteLine();

    // Prompt for number of players.
    bool inputOK = false;
    int choice = -1;
    do
    {
        Console.WriteLine("How many players (2-7)?");
        string input = Console.ReadLine();
        try
        {
            // Attempt to convert input into a valid number of players.
            choice = Convert.ToInt32(input);
            if ((choice >= 2) && (choice <= 7))
                inputOK = true;
        }
        catch
        {
            // Ignore failed conversions, just continue prompting.
        }
    } while (inputOK == false);

    // Initialize array of Player objects.
    Player[] players = new Player[choice];

    // Get player names.
    for (int p = 0; p < players.Length; p++)
    {
        Console.WriteLine("Player {0}, enter your name:", p + 1);
        string playerName = Console.ReadLine();
        players[p] = new Player(playerName);
    }

    // Start game.
    Game newGame = new Game();
    newGame.SetPlayers(players);
    int whoWon = newGame.PlayGame();

    // Display winning player.
    Console.WriteLine("{0} has won the game!", players[whoWon].Name);
    Console.ReadKey();
}
```

Now you come to `PlayGame()`, the main body of the application. Space limitations preclude us from providing a lot of detail about this method, but the code is commented to make it more comprehensible. None of the code is complicated; there's just quite a bit of it.

Play proceeds with each player viewing his or her cards and an upturned card on the table. They can either pick up this card or draw a new one from the deck. After drawing a card, each player must discard one, replacing the card on the table with another one if it has been picked up, or placing the discarded card on top of the one on the table (also adding the discarded card to the discardedCards collection).

As you consider this code, bear in mind how the Card objects are manipulated. The reason why these objects are defined as reference types, rather than value types (using a struct), should now be clear. A given Card object can appear to exist in several places at once because references can be held by the Deck object, the hand fields of the Player objects, the discardedCards collection, and the playCard object (the card currently on the table). This makes it easy to keep track of the cards and is used in particular in the code that draws a new card from the deck. The card is accepted only if it isn't in any player's hand or in the discardedCards collection.

The code is as follows:

```
public int PlayGame()
{
    // Only play if players exist.
    if (players == null)
        return -1;

    // Deal initial hands.
    DealHands();

    // Initialize game vars, including an initial card to place on the
    // table: playCard.
    bool GameWon = false;
    int currentPlayer;
    Card playCard = playDeck.GetCard(currentCard++);
    discardedCards.Add(playCard);

    // Main game loop, continues until GameWon == true.
    do
    {
        // Loop through players in each game round.
        for (currentPlayer = 0; currentPlayer < players.Length;
                currentPlayer++)
        {
            // Write out current player, player hand, and the card on the
            // table.
            Console.WriteLine("{0}'s turn.", players[currentPlayer].Name);
            Console.WriteLine("Current hand:");
            foreach (Card card in players[currentPlayer].PlayHand)
            {
                Console.WriteLine(card);
            }
            Console.WriteLine("Card in play: {0}", playCard);

            // Prompt player to pick up card on table or draw a new one.
            bool inputOK = false;
            do
            {
                Console.WriteLine("Press T to take card in play or D to " +
                            "draw:");
                string input = Console.ReadLine();
                if (input.ToLower() == "t")
                {
                    // Add card from table to player hand.
                    Console.WriteLine("Drawn: {0}", playCard);

                    // Remove from discarded cards if possible (if deck
                    // is reshuffled it won't be there any more)
                    if (discardedCards.Contains(playCard))
                    {
                        discardedCards.Remove(playCard);
                    }
```

```
                          players[currentPlayer].PlayHand.Add(playCard);
                          inputOK = true;
                      }
                  if (input.ToLower() == "d")
                  {
                      // Add new card from deck to player hand.
                      Card newCard;
                      // Only add card if it isn't already in a player hand
                      // or in the discard pile
                      bool cardIsAvailable;
                      do
                      {
                          newCard = playDeck.GetCard(currentCard++);
                          // Check if card is in discard pile
                          cardIsAvailable = !discardedCards.Contains(newCard);
                          if (cardIsAvailable)
                          {
                              // Loop through all player hands to see if newCard
                              // is already in a hand.
                              foreach (Player testPlayer in players)
                              {
                                  if (testPlayer.PlayHand.Contains(newCard))
                                  {
                                      cardIsAvailable = false;
                                      break;
                                  }
                              }
                          }
                      } while (!cardIsAvailable);
                      // Add the card found to player hand.
                      Console.WriteLine("Drawn: {0}", newCard);
                      players[currentPlayer].PlayHand.Add(newCard);
                      inputOK = true;
                  }
              } while (inputOK == false);

              // Display new hand with cards numbered.
              Console.WriteLine("New hand:");
              for (int i = 0; i < players[currentPlayer].PlayHand.Count; i++)
              {
                  Console.WriteLine("{0}: {1}", i + 1,
                                  players[currentPlayer].PlayHand[i]);
              }

              // Prompt player for a card to discard.
              inputOK = false;
              int choice = -1;
              do
              {
                  Console.WriteLine("Choose card to discard:");
                  string input = Console.ReadLine();
                  try
                  {
                      // Attempt to convert input into a valid card number.
                      choice = Convert.ToInt32(input);
                      if ((choice > 0) && (choice <= 8))
                          inputOK = true;
                  }
                  catch
                  {
                      // Ignore failed conversions, just continue prompting.
                  }
              } while (inputOK == false);
```

```
                        // Place reference to removed card in playCard (place the card
                        // on the table), then remove card from player hand and add
                        // to discarded card pile.
                        playCard = players[currentPlayer].PlayHand[choice - 1];
                        players[currentPlayer].PlayHand.RemoveAt(choice - 1);
                        discardedCards.Add(playCard);
                        Console.WriteLine("Discarding: {0}", playCard);

                        // Space out text for players
                        Console.WriteLine();

                        // Check to see if player has won the game, and exit the player
                        // loop if so.
                        GameWon = players[currentPlayer].HasWon();
                        if (GameWon == true)
                            break;
                    }
                } while (GameWon == false);

                // End game, noting the winning player.
                return currentPlayer;
            }
```

Figure 13-8 shows a game in progress.

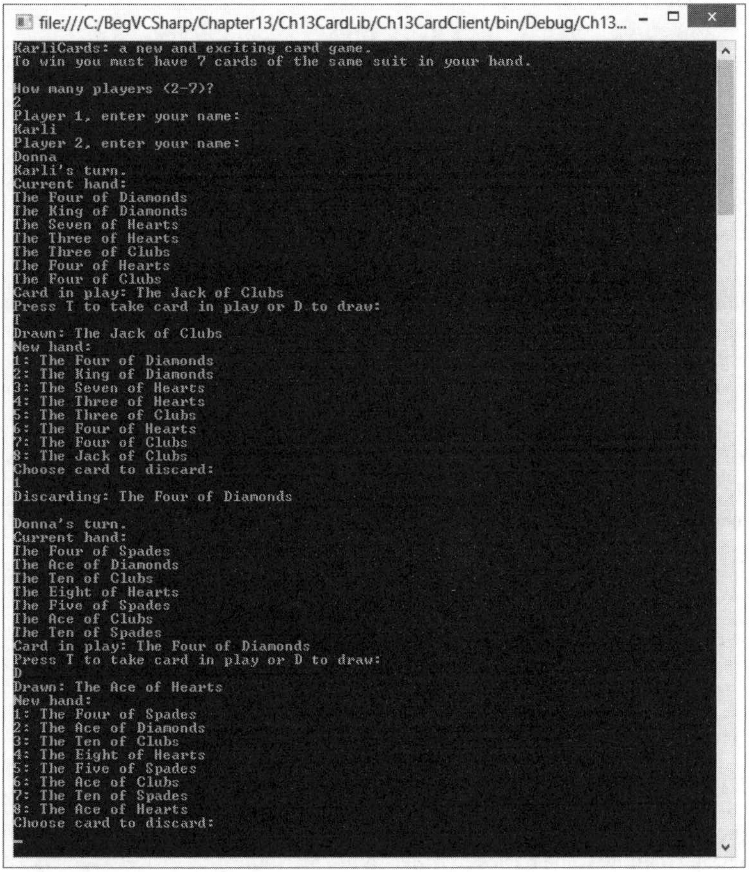

**FIGURE 13-8**

Have fun playing the game—and make sure that you spend some time going through it in detail. Try putting a breakpoint in the `Reshuffle()` method and playing the game with seven players. If you keep drawing cards and discarding the cards drawn, it won't take long for reshuffles to occur, because with seven players there are only three cards to spare. This way, you can prove to yourself that things are working properly by noting the three cards when they reappear.

As a final exercise, have a close look at the code in `Player.HasWon()`. Can you think of a way that you could make this code more efficient, perhaps without having to examine every card in the player's hand every time this method is called?

## ATTRIBUTES

This section takes a brief look at a useful way to provide additional information to code that consumes types that you create: *attributes*. Attributes give you a way to mark sections of code with information that can be read externally and used in any number of ways to affect how your types are used. This is often referred to as *decorating* the code. You can find the code for this section in `CustomAttributes\Program.cs` in this chapter's online download.

For example, let's say you create a class with a really simple method. In fact, it's so simple that you really aren't that interested in stepping through it. Unfortunately—and to your considerable annoyance—you keep doing precisely that as you debug the code in your application. In this situation, it's possible to add an attribute to the method that tells VS not to step into the code when you debug it; instead, VS should step through it and onto the next statement. The code for this is as follows:

```
[DebuggerStepThrough]
public void DullMethod()
{
   ...
}
```

The attribute in this code is `[DebuggerStepThrough]`. All attributes are added in this way, by enclosing the name of the attribute in square brackets just before the target to which they apply. You can add multiple attributes to a single target either by separating them with commas or by enclosing each one in square brackets.

The attribute used in the preceding code is actually implemented in a class called `DebuggerStepThroughAttribute`, and is found in the `System.Diagnostics` namespace, so you need a `using` statement for that namespace if you want to use this attribute. You can refer to this attribute either by its full name or, as in the code you saw, with an abbreviated name that doesn't include the suffix `Attribute`.

When you add an attribute in this way, the compiler creates an instance of the attribute class and associates it with the class method. Some attributes are customizable through constructor parameters or properties, and these can be specified when you add the attribute, for example:

```
[DoesInterestingThings(1000, WhatDoesItDo = "voodoo")]
public class DecoratedClass
{
}
```

This attribute is passing a value of 1000 to the constructor of `DoesInterestingThingsAttribute` and setting the value of a property called `WhatDoesItDo` to the string `"voodoo"`.

### Reading Attributes

In order to read attribute values, you have to use a technique called *reflection*. This is a fairly advanced technique that allows you to dynamically inspect type information at runtime, even to the point where you can create objects and call methods without knowing what those objects are. This book doesn't cover this technique in detail, but you do need to know some basics in order to use attributes.

Essentially, reflection involves using information stored in `Type` objects (which you've seen in several places in this book) along with types in the `System.Reflection` namespace to work with type information. You've already seen a quick way to get type information from a class with the `typeof` operator, and from an object instance using the `GetType()` method. Using reflection you can proceed to interrogate member information from the `Type` object. You can then obtain attribute information from the class or its various members.

The simplest way to do this—and the only way you'll see in this book—is to use the `Type.GetCustomAttributes()` method. This method takes up to two parameters and returns an array of `object` instances, each of which is an attribute instance. First, you can optionally pass the type or types of attributes you are interested in (any other attributes will be ignored). If you omit this parameter, then all attributes will be returned. Second, you must pass a Boolean value indicating whether to look just at the class or at the class and all classes that the class derives from.

For example, the following code would list the attributes of a class called `DecoratedClass`:

```
Type classType = typeof(DecoratedClass);
object[] customAttributes = classType.GetCustomAttributes(true);
foreach (object customAttribute in customAttributes)
{
    Console.WriteLine("Attribute of type {0} found.", customAttribute);
}
```

Once you have found attributes in this way, you can take whatever action is appropriate for the attribute. This is exactly what VS does when it encounters the `DebuggerStepThroughAttribute` attribute discussed earlier.

## Creating Attributes

You can create your own attributes simply by deriving from the `System.Attribute` class. Sometimes, you don't need to do anything else, as no additional information is required if your code is interested only in the presence or absence of your attribute. However, you can supply nondefault constructors and/or writeable properties if you want the attribute to be customizable.

You also need to decide two things about your attribute: what type of target it can be applied to (class, property, and so on) and whether it can be applied more than once to the same target. You specify this information through an attribute that you apply to your attribute (this has a certain Zen feeling of correctness to it!) called `AttributeUsageAttribute`. This attribute has a constructor parameter of type `AttributeTargets`, which is an enum that allows you to combine its values with the | operator. It also has a Boolean property called `AllowMultiple` that specifies whether the attribute can be applied more than once.

For example, the following code specifies an attribute that can be applied (once) to a class or property:

```
[AttributeUsage(AttributeTargets.Class | AttributeTargets.Method,
                AllowMultiple = false)]
class DoesInterestingThingsAttribute : Attribute
{
    public DoesInterestingThingsAttribute(int howManyTimes)
    {
        HowManyTimes = howManyTimes;
    }

    public string WhatDoesItDo { get; set; }

    public int HowManyTimes { get; private set; }
}
```

This attribute, `DoesInterestingThingsAttribute`, can be used as in the earlier code snippet:

```
[DoesInterestingThings(1000, WhatDoesItDo = "voodoo")]
public class DecoratedClass
{
}
```

And by modifying the code in the previous section, you can gain access to the properties of the attribute:

```
Type classType = typeof(DecoratedClass);
object[] customAttributes = classType.GetCustomAttributes(true);
foreach (object customAttribute in customAttributes)
{
    Console.WriteLine("Attribute of type {0} found.", customAttribute);
    DoesInterestingThingsAttribute interestingAttribute =
        customAttribute as DoesInterestingThingsAttribute;
    if (interestingAttribute != null)
    {
        Console.WriteLine("This class does {0} x {1}!",
            interestingAttribute.WhatDoesItDo,
            interestingAttribute.HowManyTimes);
    }
}
```

Putting everything in this section together and using this code would give you the result shown in Figure 13-9.

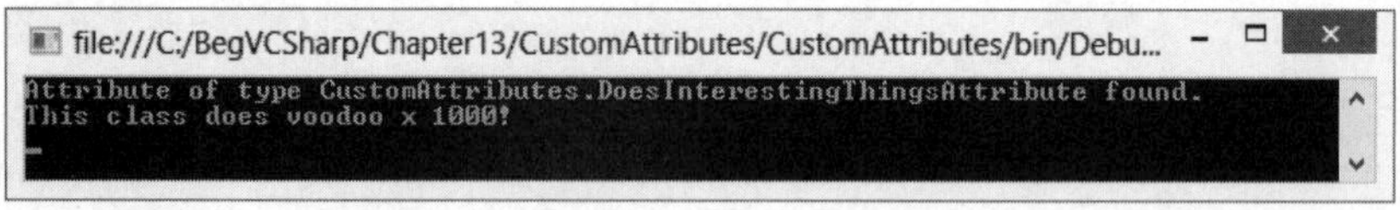

**FIGURE 13-9**

Attributes can be extremely useful and crop up all over .NET applications—and WPF and Windows Store applications in particular. You will encounter them repeatedly throughout the remainder of this book.

## SUMMARY

This chapter explained some advanced techniques that extend your knowledge of the C# language. You first looked at namespace qualification, the `::` operator, and the `global` keyword, which ensure that references to types are references to the types you want. Next, you saw how to implement your own exception objects and pass more detailed information to the exception handler. You then used a custom exception in the code for CardLib—the card game library you've been developing in the last few chapters.

Next, you looked at the important topic of events and event handling. Although quite subtle, and initially difficult to get your head around, the code involved is quite simple—and you'll certainly be using event handlers a lot in the rest of the book. You saw some simple illustrative examples of events and how to handle them, and modified the CardLib library and used it to create a simple card game application. This application demonstrates nearly all the techniques you've looked at so far in this book.

Finally, you looked at attributes and how you can use them to add information to the types that you create. Often you will do this because the framework demands it (this happens a lot in WPF programming, for example). Sometimes, you will create your own attributes if you want to provide additional information to types.

With this chapter, you have completed not only a full description of OOP as applied to C# programming, but also a full description of the fundamentals of the C# language. The next chapter describes the new features of C# that have been added with versions 3, 4, and 5 of the language.

**13.1.** Write the code for an event handler that uses the general-purpose `(object sender, EventArgs e)` syntax that will accept either the `Timer.Elapsed` event or the `Connection.MessageArrived` event from the code shown earlier in this chapter. The handler should output a string specifying which type of event has been received, along with the `Message` property of the `MessageArrivedEventArgs` parameter or the `SignalTime` property of the `ElapsedEventArgs` parameter, depending on which event occurs.

**13.2.** Modify the card game example to check for the more interesting winning condition of the popular card game, rummy. This means that a player wins the game if his or her hand contains two "sets" of cards, one of which consists of three cards and one of which consists of four cards. A set is defined as either a sequence of cards of the same suit (such as 3H, 4H, 5H, 6H) or several cards of the same rank (such as 2H, 2D, 2S).

Answers to the exercises can be found in Appendix A.

▶ **WHAT YOU LEARNED IN THIS CHAPTER**

| TOPIC | KEY CONCEPTS |
|---|---|
| **Namespace qualification** | To avoid ambiguity in namespace qualification, you can use the :: operator to force the compiler to use aliases that you have created. You can also use the `global` namespace as an alias for the top-level namespace. |
| **Custom exceptions** | You can create your own exception classes by deriving from the root `Exception` class. This is helpful because it gives you greater control over catching specific exceptions, and allows you to customize the data that is contained in an exception in order to deal with it effectively. |
| **Event handling** | Many classes expose events that are raised when certain triggers occur in their code. You can write handlers for these events to execute code at the point where they are raised. This two-way communication is a great mechanism for responsive code, and prevents you from having to write what would otherwise be complex, convoluted code that might poll an object for changes. |
| **Event definitions** | You can define your own event types, which involves creating a named event and a delegate type for any handlers for the event. You can use the standard delegate type with no return type and custom event arguments that derive from `System.EventArgs` to allow for multipurpose event handlers. You can also use the `EventHandler` and `EventHandler<T>` delegate types to define events with simpler code. |
| **Anonymous methods** | Often, to make your code more readable, you can use an anonymous method instead of a full event handler method. This means defining the code to execute when an event is raised in-line at the point where you add the event handler. You achieve this with the `delegate` keyword. |
| **Attributes** | Occasionally, either because the framework you are using demands it or because you choose to, you will make use of attributes in your code. You can add attributes to classes, methods and other members using `[AttributeName]` syntax, and you can create your own attributes by deriving from `System.Attribute`. You can read attribute values through reflection. |

# 14

# C# Language Enhancements

## WHAT YOU WILL LEARN IN THIS CHAPTER

- ➤ How to use initializers
- ➤ What the `var` type is and how to use type inference
- ➤ How to use anonymous types
- ➤ What the `dynamic` type is and how to use it
- ➤ How to use named and optional method parameters
- ➤ How to use extension methods
- ➤ What lambda expressions are and how to use them
- ➤ How to use caller information attributes

## WROX.COM CODE DOWNLOADS FOR THIS CHAPTER

You can find the wrox.com code downloads for this chapter at www.wrox.com/remtitle .cgi?isbn=9781118314418 on the Download Code tab. The code is in the Chapter 14 download and individually named according to the names throughout the chapter.

The C# language is not static. Anders Hejlsberg (the inventor of C#) and others at Microsoft continue to update and refine the language. At the time of this writing, the most recent changes are part of version 5 of the C# language, which is released as part of the Visual Studio 2012 product line, along with .NET 4.5. At this point in the book, you might be wondering what else could be needed; indeed, previous versions of C# lack little in terms of functionality. However, this doesn't mean that it isn't possible to make some aspects of C# programming easier, or that the relationships between C# and other technologies can't be streamlined.

Perhaps the best way to understand this is to consider an addition that was made between versions 1.0 and 2.0 of the language—*generics*. You could argue that while generics are extremely useful, they don't provide any functionality that you couldn't achieve before. True, they simplify things a great deal, and you would have to write a lot more code without them. None of us would want to go back to the days before generic collection classes. Nonetheless, generics aren't an essential part of C#. They are, though, a definite improvement to the language.

The subsequent language enhancements are much the same. They provide new ways of achieving things that would have been difficult to accomplish before without lengthy and/or advanced programming techniques. In this chapter, you'll look at several of these enhancements. Some, such as *variance*, have already been covered in the appropriate sections earlier in the book.

## INITIALIZERS

In earlier chapters you learned to instantiate and initialize objects in various ways. Invariably, that has required you either to add code to class definitions to enable initialization or to instantiate and initialize objects with separate statements. You have also learned how to create collection classes of various types, including generic collection classes. Again, you might have noticed that there was no easy way to combine the creation of a collection with adding items to the collection.

Object initializers provide a way to simplify your code by enabling you to combine instantiation and initialization of objects. Collection initializers give you a simple, elegant syntax to create and populate collections in a single step. This section explains how to use both of these features.

## Object Initializers

Consider the following simple class definition:

```
public class Curry
{
    public string MainIngredient { get; set; }
    public string Style { get; set; }
    public int Spiciness { get; set; }
}
```

This class has three properties that are defined using the automatic property syntax shown in Chapter 10. If you want to instantiate and initialize an object instance of this class, you must execute several statements:

```
Curry tastyCurry = new Curry();
tastyCurry.MainIngredient = "panir tikka";
tastyCurry.Style = "jalfrezi";
tastyCurry.Spiciness = 8;
```

This code uses the default, parameter-less constructor that is supplied by the C# compiler if you don't include a constructor in your class definition. To simplify this initialization, you can supply an appropriate nondefault constructor:

```
public class Curry
{
    public Curry(string mainIngredient, string style,
                 int spiciness)
    {
        MainIngredient = mainIngredient;
        Style = style;
        Spiciness = spiciness;
    }

    ...
}
```

That enables you to write code that combines instantiation with initialization:

```
Curry tastyCurry = new Curry("panir tikka", "jalfrezi", 8);
```

This works fine, although it forces code that uses this class to use this constructor, which would prevent the previous code, which used a parameter-less constructor, from working. Often, particularly when classes must be serializable, it is necessary to provide a parameter-less constructor:

```
public class Curry
{
   public Curry()
   {
   }

   ...
}
```

Now you have a situation where you can instantiate and initialize the Curry class any way you like. However, you have added several lines of code to the initial class definition that don't do anything much other than provide the basic plumbing required for this flexibility.

Enter *object initializers*, which are a way to instantiate and initialize objects without having to add code (such as the constructors detailed here) to a class. When you instantiate an object, you supply values for publicly accessible properties or fields using a name/value pair for each property you want to initialize. The syntax for this is as follows:

```
<ClassName> <variableName> = new <ClassName>
{
   <propertyOrField1> = <value1>,
   <propertyOrField2> = <value2>,
   ...
   <propertyOrFieldN> = <valueN>
};
```

For example, you could rewrite the code shown earlier, which instantiates and initializes an object of type Curry, as follows:

```
Curry tastyCurry = new Curry
{
   MainIngredient = "panir tikka",
   Style = "jalfrezi",
   Spiciness = 8
};
```

Often you can put code like that on a single line without seriously degrading readability.

When you use an object initializer, you don't have to explicitly call a constructor of the class. If you omit the constructor parentheses (as in the previous code), the default parameter-less constructor is called automatically. This happens before any parameter values are set by the initializer, which enables you to provide default values for parameters in the default constructor if desired. Alternatively, you can call a specific constructor. Again, this constructor is called first, so any initialization of public properties that takes place in the constructor might be overridden by values that you provide in the initializer. You must have access to the constructor that you use (or the default one if you aren't explicit) in order for object initializers to work.

If one of the properties you want to initialize with an object initializer is more complex than the simple types used in this example, then you might find yourself using a *nested object initializer*. That simply means using the exact same syntax you've already seen:

```
Curry tastyCurry = new Curry
{
   MainIngredient = "panir tikka",
   Style = "jalfrezi",
   Spiciness = 8,
   Origin = new Restaurant
   {
      Name = "King's Balti",
      Location = "York Road",
      Rating = 5
   }
};
```

Here, a property called `Origin` of type `Restaurant` (not shown here) is initialized. The code initializes three properties of the `Origin` property—`Name`, `Location`, and `Rating`—with values of type `string`, `string`, and `int`, respectively. This initialization uses a nested object initializer.

Note that object initializers are not a replacement for nondefault constructors. The fact that you can use object initializers to set property and field values when you instantiate an object does not mean that you will always know what state needs initializing. With constructors you can specify exactly which values are required for an object to function, and then execute code in response to those values immediately.

Also, in the previous example there is another (admittedly quite subtle) difference between using a nested object initializer and using constructors. This difference is the order in which objects get created. With a nested initializer, the top level object (`Curry`) gets created first. Next, the nested object (`Restaurant`) is created and assigned to the property `Origin`. If you used a constructor, you would reverse this construction order and pass the `Restaurant` instance to the constructor of `Curry`. In this simple example, there is no practical difference, but in some circumstances this might be significant.

## Collection Initializers

Chapter 5 described how arrays can be initialized with values using the following syntax:

```
int[] myIntArray = new int[5] { 5, 9, 10, 2, 99 };
```

This is a quick and easy way to combine the instantiation and initialization of an array. Collection initializers simply extend this syntax to collections:

```
List<int> myIntCollection = new List<int> { 5, 9, 10, 2, 99 };
```

By combining object and collection initializers, it is possible to configure collections with simple and elegant code. Rather than code like this:

```
List<Curry> curries = new List<Curry>();
curries.Add(new Curry("Chicken", "Pathia", 6));
curries.Add(new Curry("Vegetable", "Korma", 3));
curries.Add(new Curry("Prawn", "Vindaloo", 9));
```

You can use the following:

```
List<Curry> moreCurries = new List<Curry>
{
    new Curry
    {
        MainIngredient = "Chicken",
        Style = "Pathia",
        Spiciness = 6
    },
    new Curry
    {
        MainIngredient = "Vegetable",
        Style = "Korma",
        Spiciness = 3
    },
    new Curry
    {
        MainIngredient = "Prawn",
        Style = "Vindaloo",
        Spiciness = 9
    }
};
```

This works very well for types that are primarily used for data representation, and as such, collection initializers are a great accompaniment to the LINQ technology described later in the book.

The following Try It Out illustrates how you can use object and collection initializers.

**TRY IT OUT** Using Initializers: Ch14Ex01

**1.** Create a new console application called Ch14Ex01 and save it in the directory C:\BegVCSharp\Chapter14.

**2.** Right-click on the project name in the Solution Explorer window and select the Add Existing Item option.

**3.** Select the Animal.cs, Cow.cs, Chicken.cs, SuperCow.cs, and Farm.cs files from the C:\BegVCSharp\Chapter12\Ch12Ex04\Ch12Ex04 directory, and click Add.

**4.** Modify the namespace declaration in the file you have added as follows:

```
namespace Ch14Ex01
```

**5.** Remove the constructors from the Cow, Chicken, and SuperCow classes.

**6.** Modify the code in Program.cs as follows:

```
static void Main(string[] args)
{
    Farm<Animal> farm = new Farm<Animal>
    {
        new Cow { Name="Norris" },
        new Chicken { Name="Rita" },
        new Chicken(),
        new SuperCow { Name="Chesney" }
    };
    farm.MakeNoises();
    Console.ReadKey();
}
```

**7.** Build the application. You should receive the build errors shown in Figure 14-1.

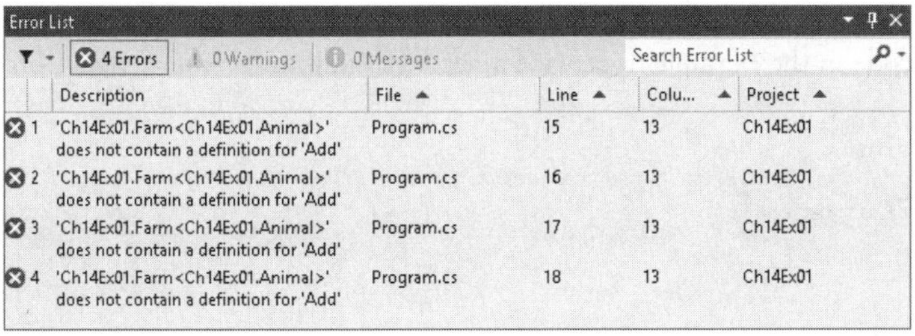

| | Description | File ▲ | Line ▲ | Colu... ▲ | Project ▲ |
|---|---|---|---|---|---|
| ❌ 1 | 'Ch14Ex01.Farm<Ch14Ex01.Animal>' does not contain a definition for 'Add' | Program.cs | 15 | 13 | Ch14Ex01 |
| ❌ 2 | 'Ch14Ex01.Farm<Ch14Ex01.Animal>' does not contain a definition for 'Add' | Program.cs | 16 | 13 | Ch14Ex01 |
| ❌ 3 | 'Ch14Ex01.Farm<Ch14Ex01.Animal>' does not contain a definition for 'Add' | Program.cs | 17 | 13 | Ch14Ex01 |
| ❌ 4 | 'Ch14Ex01.Farm<Ch14Ex01.Animal>' does not contain a definition for 'Add' | Program.cs | 18 | 13 | Ch14Ex01 |

*Error List — 4 Errors, 0 Warnings, 0 Messages — Search Error List*

**FIGURE 14-1**

**8.** Add the following code to Farm.cs:

```
public class Farm<T> : IEnumerable<T>
    where T : Animal
{
    public void Add(T animal)
    {
        animals.Add(animal);
    }

    ...
```

**9.** Run the application. The result is shown in Figure 14-2.

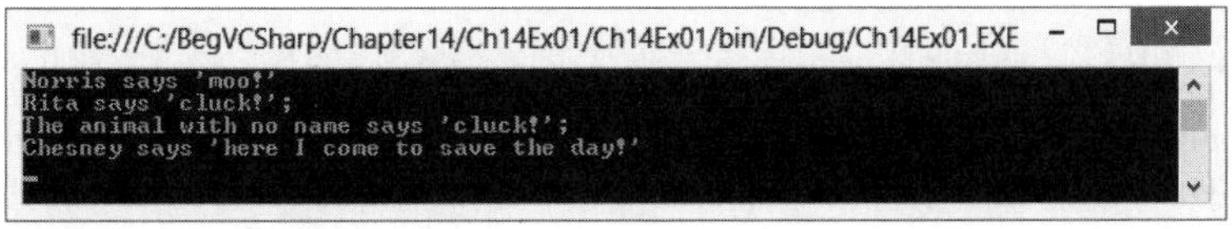

```
file:///C:/BegVCSharp/Chapter14/Ch14Ex01/Ch14Ex01/bin/Debug/Ch14Ex01.EXE
Norris says 'moo!';
Rita says 'cluck!';
The animal with no name says 'cluck!';
Chesney says 'here I come to save the day!'
```

**FIGURE 14-2**

*How It Works*

This example combines object and collection initializers to create and populate a collection of objects in a single step. It uses the farmyard collection of objects that you have seen in previous chapters, although two modifications are necessary for initializers to be used with these classes.

First, you remove the constructors from the classes derived from the base `Animal` class. You can remove these constructors because they set the animal's `Name` property, which you will do with object initializers instead. Alternatively, you could have added default constructors. In either case, when using default constructors, the `Name` property is initialized according to the default constructor in the base class, which has code as follows:

```
public Animal()
{
    name = "The animal with no name";
}
```

However, when an object initializer is used with a class that derives from `Animal`, recall that any properties set by the initializer are set after the object is instantiated, and therefore after this base class constructor is executed. If a value for the `Name` property is supplied as part of an object initializer, it will override this default value. In the example code, the `Name` property is set for all but one of the items added to the collection.

Second, you add an `Add()` method to the `Farm` class. This is in response to a series of compiler errors of the following form:

```
'Ch14Ex01.Farm<Ch14Ex01.Animal>' does not contain a definition for 'Add'
```

This error exposes part of the underlying functionality of collection initializers. Behind the scenes, the compiler calls the `Add()` method of a collection for each item that you supply in a collection initializer. The `Farm` class exposes a collection of `Animal` objects through a property called `Animals`. The compiler cannot guess that this is the property you want to populate (through `Animals.Add()`), so the code fails. To correct this problem, you add an `Add()` method to the class, which is initialized through the object initializer.

Alternatively, you could modify the code in the example to provide a nested initializer for the `Animals` property as follows:

```
static void Main(string[] args)
{
    Farm<Animal> farm = new Farm<Animal>
    {
        Animals =
        {
            new Cow { Name="Norris" },
            new Chicken { Name="Rita" },
            new Chicken(),
            new SuperCow { Name="Chesney" }
        }
    };
    farm.MakeNoises();
    Console.ReadKey();
}
```

With this code there is no need to provide an `Add()` method for the `Farm` class. This alternative technique is appropriate when you have a class that contains multiple collections. In this case, there is no obvious candidate for a collection to add to with an `Add()` method of the containing class.

## TYPE INFERENCE

Earlier in this book you saw how C# is a *strongly typed* language, which means that every variable has a fixed type and can be used only in code that takes that type into account. In every code example you've seen so far, you have declared variables in one of two ways:

```
<type> <varName>;
<type> <varName> = <value>;
```

The following code shows at a glance what type of variable `<varName>` is:

```
int myInt = 5;
Console.WriteLine(myInt);
```

You can also see that the IDE is aware of the variable type simply by hovering the mouse pointer over the variable identifier, as shown in Figure 14-3.

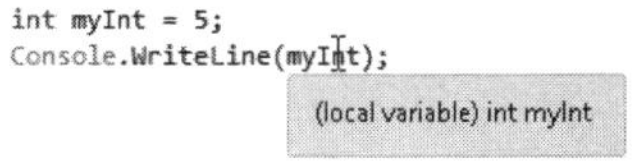

```
int myInt = 5;
Console.WriteLine(myInt);
        (local variable) int myInt
```

**FIGURE 14-3**

C# 3 introduced the new keyword `var`, which you can use as an alternative for `type` in the preceding code:

```
var <varName> = <value>;
```

In this code, the variable `<varName>` is *implicitly typed* to the type of `<value>`. Note that there is no type called `var`. In the code:

```
var myVar = 5;
```

myVar is a variable of type `int`, not of type `var`. Again, as shown in Figure 14-4, the IDE is aware of this.

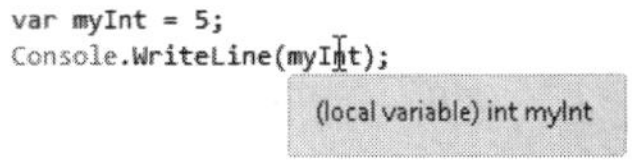

```
var myInt = 5;
Console.WriteLine(myInt);
        (local variable) int myInt
```

**FIGURE 14-4**

This is an extremely important point. When you use `var` you are not declaring a variable with no type, or even a type that can change. If that were the case, C# would no longer be a strongly typed language. All you are doing is relying on the compiler to determine the type of the variable.

> **NOTE** *The introduction of dynamic types in .NET 4 stretched the definition of C# being a strongly typed language, as you will see in the section "Dynamic Lookup" later in this chapter.*

If the compiler is unable to determine the type of variable declared using `var`, then your code will not compile. Therefore, you can't declare a variable using `var` without initializing the variable at the same time. If you do this, there is no value that the compiler can use to determine the type of the variable. The following code, therefore, will not compile:

```
var myVar;
```

The `var` keyword can also be used to infer the type of an array through the array initializer:

```
var myArray = new[] { 4, 5, 2 };
```

In this code, the type `myArray` is implicitly `int []`. When you implicitly type an array in this way, the array elements used in the initializer must be one of the following:

➤  All the same type

➤  All the same reference type or `null`

➤  All elements that can be implicitly converted to a single type

If the last of these rules is applied, then the type that elements can be converted to is referred to as the *best* type for the array elements. If there is any ambiguity as to what this best type might be—that is, if there are two or more types that all the elements can be implicitly converted to—your code will not compile. Instead, you receive the error indicating that no best type is available, as in the following code:

```
var myArray = new[] { 4, "not an int", 2 };
```

Note also that numeric values are never interpreted as nullable types, so the following code will not compile:

```
var myArray = new[] { 4, null, 2 };
```

You can, however, use a standard array initializer to make this work:

```
var myArray = new int?[] { 4, null, 2 };
```

A final point: The identifier var is not a forbidden identifier to use for a class name. This means, for example, that if your code has a class called var in scope (in the same namespace or in a referenced namespace), then you cannot use implicit typing with the var keyword.

In itself, type inference is not particularly useful because in the code you've seen in this section it only serves to complicate things. Using var makes it more difficult to see at a glance the type of a given variable. However, as you will see later in this chapter, the concept of inferred types is important because it underlies other techniques. The next subject, anonymous types, is one for which inferred types are essential.

## ANONYMOUS TYPES

After programming for a while you might find, especially in database applications, that you spend a lot of time creating simple, dull classes for data representation. It is not unusual to have families of classes that do absolutely nothing other than expose properties. The Curry class shown earlier in this chapter is a perfect example:

```
public class Curry
{
    public string MainIngredient { get; set; }
    public string Style { get; set; }
    public int Spiciness { get; set; }
}
```

This class doesn't do anything—it merely stores structured data. In database or spreadsheet terms, you could think of this class as representing a row in a table. A collection class that was capable of holding instances of this class would be a representation of multiple rows in a table or spreadsheet.

This is a perfectly acceptable use of classes, but writing the code for these classes can become monotonous, and any modifications to the underlying data schema requires you to add, remove, or modify the code that defines the classes.

*Anonymous types* are a way to simplify this programming model. The idea behind anonymous types is that rather than define these simple data storage types, you can instead use the C# compiler to automatically create types based on the data that you want to store in them.

The preceding Curry type can be instantiated as follows:

```
Curry curry = new Curry
{
    MainIngredient = "Lamb",
    Style = "Dhansak",
    Spiciness = 5
};
```

Alternatively, you could use an anonymous type, as in the following code:

```
var curry = new
{
    MainIngredient = "Lamb",
    Style = "Dhansak",
    Spiciness = 5
};
```

There are two differences here. First, the var keyword is used. That's because anonymous types do not have an identifier that you can use. Internally they do have an identifier, as you will see in a moment, but it is not available to you in your code. Second, no type name is specified after the new keyword. That's how the compiler knows you want to use an anonymous type.

The IDE detects the anonymous type definition and updates IntelliSense accordingly. With the preceding declaration, you can see the anonymous type, as shown in Figure 14-5.

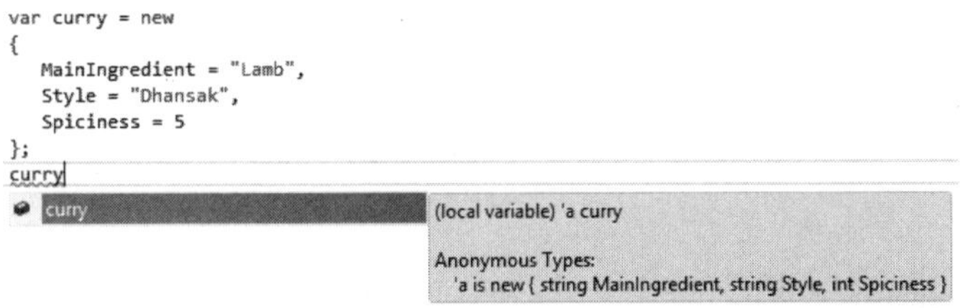

```
var curry = new
{
    MainIngredient = "Lamb",
    Style = "Dhansak",
    Spiciness = 5
};
curry
```

| 🔵 curry | (local variable) 'a curry |
|---|---|
| | Anonymous Types: |
| | 'a is new { string MainIngredient, string Style, int Spiciness } |

**FIGURE 14-5**

Here, internally, the type of the variable `curry` is `'a`. Obviously, you can't use this type in your code—it's not even a legal identifier name. The `'` is simply the symbol used to denote an anonymous type in IntelliSense. IntelliSense also enables you to inspect the members of the anonymous type, as shown in Figure 14-6.

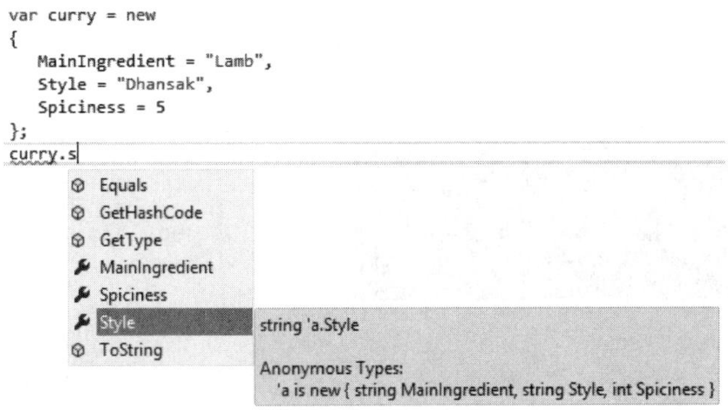

```
var curry = new
{
    MainIngredient = "Lamb",
    Style = "Dhansak",
    Spiciness = 5
};
curry.s
```

| ⊘ Equals | |
|---|---|
| ⊘ GetHashCode | |
| ⊘ GetType | |
| 🔧 MainIngredient | |
| 🔧 Spiciness | |
| 🔧 Style | string 'a.Style |
| ⊘ ToString | Anonymous Types: |
| | 'a is new { string MainIngredient, string Style, int Spiciness } |

**FIGURE 14-6**

Note that the properties shown here are defined as *read-only* properties. This means that if you want to be able to change the values of properties in your data storage objects, you cannot use anonymous types.

The other members of anonymous types are implemented, as shown in the following Try It Out.

**TRY IT OUT** **Using Anonymous Types: Ch14Ex02\Program.cs**

**1.** Create a new console application called Ch14Ex02 and save it in the directory `C:\BegVCSharp\Chapter14`.

**2.** Modify the code in `Program.cs` as follows:

```
static void Main(string[] args)
{
    var curries = new[]
    {
        new
        {
            MainIngredient = "Lamb",
            Style = "Dhansak",
            Spiciness = 5
        },
    }
}
```

```
        new
        {
            MainIngredient = "Lamb",
            Style = "Dhansak",
            Spiciness = 5
        },
        new
        {
            MainIngredient = "Chicken",
            Style = "Dhansak",
            Spiciness = 5
        }
    };
    Console.WriteLine(curries[0].ToString());
    Console.WriteLine(curries[0].GetHashCode());
    Console.WriteLine(curries[1].GetHashCode());
    Console.WriteLine(curries[2].GetHashCode());
    Console.WriteLine(curries[0].Equals(curries[1]));
    Console.WriteLine(curries[0].Equals(curries[2]));
    Console.WriteLine(curries[0] == curries[1]);
    Console.WriteLine(curries[0] == curries[2]);

    Console.ReadKey();
}
```

**3.** Run the application. The result is shown in Figure 14-7.

**FIGURE 14-7**

### How It Works

In this example you create an array of anonymous type objects that you then proceed to use to perform tests of the members supplied by anonymous types. The code to create the array of anonymously typed objects is as follows:

```
var curries = new[]
{
    new
    {
        MainIngredient = "Lamb",
        Style = "Dhansak",
        Spiciness = 5
    },
    ...
};
```

This uses an array that is implicitly typed to an anonymous type, using a combination of syntax from this section and the "Type Inference" section earlier in this chapter. The result is that the `curries` variable contains three instances of an anonymous type.

The first thing the code does after creating this array is output the result of calling `ToString()` on the anonymous type:

```
Console.WriteLine(curries[0].ToString());
```

This results in the following output:

```
{ MainIngredient = Lamb, Style = Dhansak, Spiciness = 5 }
```

The implementation of `ToString()` in an anonymous type outputs the values of each property defined for the type.

The code next calls `GetHashCode()` on each of the array's three objects:

```
Console.WriteLine(curries[0].GetHashCode());
Console.WriteLine(curries[1].GetHashCode());
Console.WriteLine(curries[2].GetHashCode());
```

When implemented, `GetHashCode()` should return a unique integer for an object based on the object's state. The first two objects in the array have the same property values, and therefore the same state. The result of these calls is the same integer for each of these objects, but a different integer for the third object. The output is as follows:

```
294897435
294897435
621671265
```

Next, the `Equals()` method is called to compare the first object with the second object, and then to compare the first object with the third object:

```
Console.WriteLine(curries[0].Equals(curries[1]));
Console.WriteLine(curries[0].Equals(curries[2]));
```

The result is as follows:

```
True
False
```

The implementation of `Equals()` in anonymous types compares the state of objects. The result is `true` where every property of one object contains the same value as the comparable property on another object.

That is not what happens when you use the `==` operator, however. The `==` operator, as shown in previous chapters, compares object references. The last section of code performs the same comparisons as the previous section of code but uses `==` instead of `Equals()`:

```
Console.WriteLine(curries[0] == curries[1]);
Console.WriteLine(curries[0] == curries[2]);
```

Each entry in the `curries` array refers to a different instance of the anonymous type, so the result is `false` in both cases. The output is as expected:

```
False
False
```

Interestingly, when you create instances of the anonymous types in this example, the compiler notices that the parameters are the same and creates three instances of the *same* anonymous type—not three separate anonymous types. However, this doesn't mean that when you instantiate an object from an anonymous type the compiler looks for a type to match it with. Even if you have defined a class elsewhere that has matching properties, if you use anonymous type syntax, then an anonymous type will be created (or reused as in this example).

## DYNAMIC LOOKUP

The var keyword, as described earlier, is not in itself a type, and so doesn't break the "strongly typed" methodology of C#. From C# 4 onward, though, things have become a little less fixed. C# 4 introduced the concept of *dynamic variables*, which, as their name suggests, are variables that do not have a fixed type.

The main motivation for this is that there are many situations where you will want to use C# to manipulate objects created by another language. This includes interoperability with older technologies such as the Component Object Model (COM), as well as dealing with dynamic languages such as JavaScript, Python, and Ruby. Without going into too much implementation detail, using C# to access methods and properties of objects created by these languages has, in the past, involved awkward syntax. For example, say you had code that obtained an object from JavaScript with a method called Add() that added two numbers. Without dynamic lookup, your code to call this method might look something like the following:

```
ScriptObject jsObj = SomeMethodThatGetsTheObject();
int sum = Convert.ToInt32(jsObj.Invoke("Add", 2, 3));
```

The ScriptObject type (not covered in depth here) provides a way to access a JavaScript object, but even this is unable to give you the capability to do the following:

```
int sum = jsObj.Add(2, 3);
```

Dynamic lookup changes everything—enabling you to write code just like the preceding. However, as you will see in the following sections, this power comes at a price.

Another situation in which dynamic lookup can assist you is when you are dealing with a C# object whose type you do not know. This might sound like an odd situation, but it happens more often than you might think. It is also an important capability when writing generic code that can deal with whatever input it receives. The "old" way to deal with this situation is called *reflection*, which involves using type information to access types and members. You saw some simple reflection in the previous chapter, where you used it to access attributes associated with types. The syntax for using reflection to access type members such as methods is quite similar to the syntax used to access the JavaScript object, as shown in the preceding code. In other words, it's messy.

Under the hood, dynamic lookup is supported by the Dynamic Language Runtime (DLR). This is part of .NET 4.5, just as the CLR is. An exact description of the DLR and how it makes interoperability easier is beyond the scope of this book; here you're more interested in how to use it in C#.

## The dynamic Type

C# 4 introduced the dynamic keyword, which you can use to define variables, as in this example:

```
dynamic myDynamicVar;
```

Unlike the var keyword introduced earlier, there really is a dynamic type, so there is no need to initialize the value of myDynamicVar when it is declared.

> **NOTE** *Unusually, the* dynamic *type exists only at compile time; at runtime the* System.Object *type is used instead. This is a minor implementation detail but one that is worth remembering, as it might clarify some of the discussion that follows.*

Once you have a dynamic variable, you can proceed to access its members (the code to obtain a value for the variable is not shown here):

```
myDynamicVar.DoSomething("With this!");
```

Regardless of the value that myDynamicVar contains, this code will compile. However, if the requested member does not exist, you will get an exception when this code is executed, of type RuntimeBinderException.

In effect, what you are doing with code like this is providing a "recipe" that should be applied at runtime. The value of myDynamicVar will be examined, and a method called DoSomething() with a single string parameter will be located and called at the point where it is required.

This is best illustrated with an example.

> **WARNING** *The following example is for illustrative purposes only! In general, you should use dynamic types only when they are your only option—for example, when you are dealing with non-.NET objects.*

**TRY IT OUT** Using Dynamic Types: Ch14Ex03\Program.cs

**1.** Create a new console application called Ch14Ex03 and save it in the directory C:\BegVCSharp\Chapter14.

**2.** Modify the code in Program.cs as follows:

```
using System;
using System.Collections.Generic;
using System.Linq;
using System.Text;
using System.Threading.Tasks;
using Microsoft.CSharp.RuntimeBinder;

namespace Ch14Ex03
{
    class MyClass1
    {
        public int Add(int var1, int var2)
        {
            return var1 + var2;
        }
    }

    class MyClass2
    {
    }

    class Program
    {
        static int callCount = 0;

        static dynamic GetValue()
        {
            if (callCount++ == 0)
            {
                return new MyClass1();
            }
            return new MyClass2();
        }

        static void Main(string[] args)
        {
            try
            {
                dynamic firstResult = GetValue();
                dynamic secondResult = GetValue();
                Console.WriteLine("firstResult is: {0}",
                    firstResult.ToString());
                Console.WriteLine("secondResult is: {0}",
```

```
            secondResult.ToString());
        Console.WriteLine("firstResult call: {0}",
            firstResult.Add(2, 3));
        Console.WriteLine("secondResult call: {0}",
            secondResult.Add(2, 3));
    }
    catch (RuntimeBinderException ex)
    {
        Console.WriteLine(ex.Message);
    }
    Console.ReadKey();
    }
  }
}
```

**3.** Run the application. The result is shown in Figure 14-8.

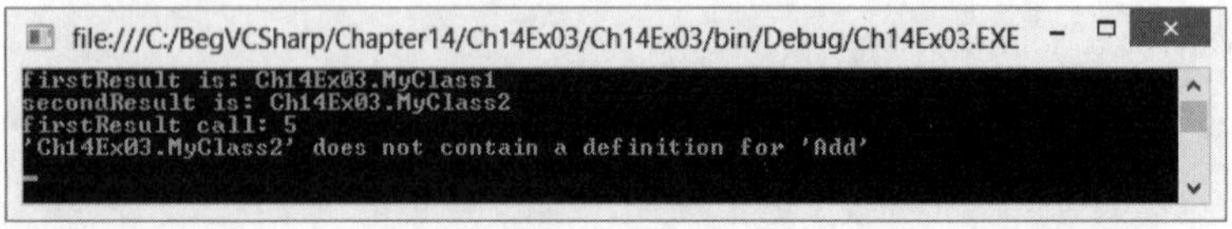

**FIGURE 14-8**

### How It Works

In this example you use a method that returns one of two types of objects to obtain a dynamic value, and then attempts to use the object obtained. The code compiles without any trouble, but an exception is thrown (and handled) when an attempt is made to access a non-existent method.

To begin, you add a using statement for the namespace that contains the `RuntimeBinderException` exception:

```
using Microsoft.CSharp.RuntimeBinder;
```

Next, you define two classes, `MyClass1` and `MyClass2`, where `MyClass1` has an `Add()` method and `MyClass2` has no members:

```
class MyClass1
{
    public int Add(int var1, int var2)
    {
        return var1 + var2;
    }
}

class MyClass2
{
}
```

You also add a field (`callCount`) and a method (`GetValue()`) to the `Program` class to provide a way to obtain an instance of one of these classes:

```
static int callCount = 0;

static dynamic GetValue()
{
    if (callCount++ == 0)
    {
        return new MyClass1();
    }

    return new MyClass2();
}
```

A simple call counter is used so that this method returns an instance of MyClass1 the first time it is called, and instances of MyClass2 thereafter. Note that the dynamic keyword can be used as a return type for a method.

Next, the code in Main() calls the GetValue() method twice and then attempts to call GetString() and Add() on both values returned in turn. This code is placed in a try...catch block to trap any exceptions of type RuntimeBinderException that occur:

```
static void Main(string[] args)
{
    try
    {
        dynamic firstResult = GetValue();
        dynamic secondResult = GetValue();
        Console.WriteLine("firstResult is: {0}",
            firstResult.ToString());
        Console.WriteLine("secondResult is: {0}",
            secondResult.ToString());
        Console.WriteLine("firstResult call: {0}",
            firstResult.Add(2, 3));
        Console.WriteLine("secondResult call: {0}",
            secondResult.Add(2, 3));
    }
    catch (RuntimeBinderException ex)
    {
        Console.WriteLine(ex.Message);
    }

    Console.ReadKey();
}
```

Sure enough, an exception is thrown when secondResult.Add() is called, as no such method exists on MyClass2. The exception message tells you exactly that.

The dynamic keyword can also be used in other places where a type name is required, such as for method parameters. You could rewrite the Add() method as follows:

```
public int Add(dynamic var1, dynamic var2)
{
    return var1 + var2;
}
```

This would have no effect on the result. In this case, at runtime the values passed to var1 and var2 are inspected to determine whether a compatible operator definition for + exists. In the case of two int values being passed, such an operator does exist. If incompatible values are used, a RuntimeBinderException exception is thrown. For example, if you try,

```
Console.WriteLine("firstResult call: {0}", firstResult.Add("2", 3));
```

the exception message will be as follows:

```
Cannot implicitly convert type 'string' to 'int'
```

The lesson to be learned here is that dynamic types are very powerful, but there's a warning to learn too. These sorts of exceptions are entirely avoidable if you use strong typing instead of dynamic typing. For most C# code that you write, avoid the dynamic keyword. However, if a situation arises where you need to use it, use it and love it—and spare a thought for those poor programmers of the past who didn't have this powerful tool at their disposal.

# IDynamicMetaObjectProvider

Before moving on, it's worthwhile to note how dynamic types are used, or, to be more precise, what happens when a "recipe" for member access is applied at runtime. In fact, there are three ways that this might happen:

➤ If the dynamic value is a COM object, then COM techniques are used to access members (through an interface called `IUnknown`, although you don't need to know that here).

➤ If the dynamic value supports the `IDynamicMetaObjectProvider` interface, then that interface is used to access type members.

➤ If neither of the above applies, then reflection is used.

The interesting case is the second one, which involves the `IDynamicMetaObjectProvider` interface. Without delving into the details, note that you can implement this interface to control exactly what happens when members are accessed at runtime. However, this is a subject for a more advanced level book, and therefore not covered here.

# ADVANCED METHOD PARAMETERS

C# 4 extended what is possible when defining and using method parameters. This is primarily in response to a specific problem that arises when using interfaces defined externally, such as the Microsoft Office programming model. Here, certain methods expose a vast number of parameters, many of which are not required for every call. In the past, this has meant that a way to specify missing parameters has been necessary, or that a lot of nulls appear in code:

```
RemoteCall(var1, var2, null, null, null, null, null);
```

In this code it is not at all obvious what the `null` values refer to, or why they have been omitted.

Perhaps, in an ideal world, there would be multiple overloads of this `RemoteCall()` method, including one that only required two parameters as follows:

```
RemoteCall(var1, var2);
```

However, this would require many more methods with alternative combinations of parameters, which in itself would cause more problems (more code to maintain, increased code complexity, and so on).

Languages such as Visual Basic have dealt with this situation in a different way, by allowing named and optional parameters. From version 4, this became possible in C#, demonstrating one way in which the evolution of all .NET languages is converging.

In the following sections you will see how to use these parameter types.

## Optional Parameters

Often when you call a method, you pass in the same value for a particular parameter. This can be a Boolean value, for example, which might control a nonessential part of the method's operation. To be more specific, consider the following method definition:

```
public List<string> GetWords(
    string sentence,
    bool capitalizeWords)
{
    ...
}
```

Regardless of the value passed into the `capitalizeWords` parameter, this method will return a list of `string` values, each of which is a word from the input sentence. Depending on how this method was used, you might occasionally want to capitalize the list of words returned (perhaps you are formatting a heading such as the one for this section, "Optional Parameters"). In most cases, though, you might not want to do this, so most calls would be as follows:

```
List<string> words = GetWords(sentence, false);
```

To make this the "default" behavior, you might declare a second method as follows:

```
public List<string> GetWords(string sentence)
{
    return GetWords(sentence, false);
}
```

This method calls into the second method, passing a value of `false` for `capitalizeWords`.

There is nothing wrong with doing this, but you can probably imagine how complicated this would become in a situation where many more parameters were used.

An alternative is to make the `capitalizeWords` parameter an *optional parameter*. This involves defining the parameter as optional in the method definition by providing a default value that will be used if none is supplied, as follows:

```
public List<string> GetWords(
    string sentence,
    bool capitalizeWords = false)
{
    ...
}
```

If you were to define a method in this way, then you could supply either one or two parameters, where the second parameter is required only if you want `capitalizeWords` to be `true`.

## Optional Parameter Values

As described in the previous section, a method definition defines an optional parameter with syntax as follows:

```
<parameterType> <parameterName> = <defaultValue>
```

There are restrictions on what you can use for the `<defaultValue>` default value. Default values must be literal values, constant values, or default value type values. The following, therefore, will not compile:

```
public bool CapitalizationDefault;

public List<string> GetWords(
    string sentence,
    bool capitalizeWords = CapitalizationDefault)
{
    ...
}
```

In order to make this work, the `CapitalizationDefault` value must be defined as a constant:

```
public const bool CapitalizationDefault = false;
```

Whether it makes sense to do this depends on the situation; in most cases you will probably be better off providing a literal value as in the previous section.

### The OptionalAttribute Attribute

As an alternative to the syntax described in the previous sections, you can define optional parameters using the `OptionalAttribute` attribute as follows:

```
[Optional] <parameterType> <parameterName>
```

This attribute is found in the `System.Runtime.InteropServices` namespace. Note that if you use this syntax there is no way to provide a default value for the parameter.

### Optional Parameter Order

When you use optional values, they must appear at the end of the list of parameters for a method. No parameters without default values can appear after any parameters with default values.

The following code, therefore, is illegal:

```
public List<string> GetWords(
    bool capitalizeWords = false,
    string sentence)
{
    . . .
}
```

Here, `sentence` is a required parameter, and must therefore appear before the optional `capitalizedWords` parameter.

## Named Parameters

When you use optional parameters, you might find yourself in a situation where a particular method has several optional parameters. It's not beyond the realm of the imagination, then, to conceive of a situation where you want to pass a value to, say, only the third optional parameter. With just the syntax from the previous section there is no way to do this without supplying values for the first and second optional parameters.

C# 4 also introduced *named parameters* that enable you to specify whichever parameters you want. This doesn't require you to do anything in particular in your method definition; it is a technique that you use when you are calling a method. The syntax is as follows:

```
MyMethod(
    <param1Name>: <param1Value>,
    . . .
    <paramNName>: <paramNValue>);
```

The names of parameters are the names of the variables used in the method definition.

You can specify any number of parameters you like in this way, as long as the named parameters exist, and you can do so in any order. Named parameters can be optional as well.

You can, if you want, use named parameters for only some of the parameters in a method call. This is particularly useful when you have several optional parameters in a method signature, but some required parameters. You might specify the required parameters first, then finish off with named optional parameters. For example:

```
MyMethod(
    requiredParameter1Value,
    optionalParameter5: optionalParameter5Value);
```

If you mix named and positional parameters, though, note that you must include all positional parameters first, before the named parameters. However, you can use a different order if you prefer as long as you use named parameters throughout, as in this example:

```
MyMethod(
    optionalParameter5: optionalParameter5Value,
    requiredParameter1: requiredParameter1Value);
```

If you do this you must include values for all required parameters.

In the following Try It Out, you will see how you can use named and optional parameters.

**TRY IT OUT** Using Named and Optional Parameters: Ch14Ex04

**1.** Create a new console application called Ch14Ex04 and save it in the directory `C:\BegVCSharp\Chapter14`.

**2.** Add a class called `WordProcessor` to the project and modify its code as follows:

```csharp
public static class WordProcessor
{
    public static List<string> GetWords(
        string sentence,
        bool capitalizeWords = false,
        bool reverseOrder = false,
        bool reverseWords = false)
    {
        List<string> words = new List<string>(sentence.Split(' '));
        if (capitalizeWords)
            words = CapitalizeWords(words);
        if (reverseOrder)
            words = ReverseOrder(words);
        if (reverseWords)
            words = ReverseWords(words);
        return words;
    }

    private static List<string> CapitalizeWords(
        List<string> words)
    {
        List<string> capitalizedWords = new List<string>();
        foreach (string word in words)
        {
            if (word.Length == 0)
                continue;
            if (word.Length == 1)
                capitalizedWords.Add(
                    word[0].ToString().ToUpper());
            else
                capitalizedWords.Add(
                    word[0].ToString().ToUpper()
                    + word.Substring(1));
        }

        return capitalizedWords;
    }

    private static List<string> ReverseOrder(List<string> words)
    {
        List<string> reversedWords = new List<string>();
        for (int wordIndex = words.Count - 1;
            wordIndex >= 0; wordIndex--)
            reversedWords.Add(words[wordIndex]);

        return reversedWords;
    }
    private static List<string> ReverseWords(List<string> words)
    {
        List<string> reversedWords = new List<string>();
        foreach (string word in words)
```

```
            reversedWords.Add(ReverseWord(word));

        return reversedWords;
    }

    private static string ReverseWord(string word)
    {
        StringBuilder sb = new StringBuilder();
        for (int characterIndex = word.Length - 1;
            characterIndex >= 0; characterIndex--)
            sb.Append(word[characterIndex]);

        return sb.ToString();
    }
}
```

**3.** Modify the code in `Program.cs` as follows:

```
static void Main(string[] args)
{
    string sentence = "'twas brillig, and the slithy toves did gyre "
        + "and gimble in the wabe:";
    List<string> words;

    words = WordProcessor.GetWords(sentence);
    Console.WriteLine("Original sentence:");
    foreach (string word in words)
    {
        Console.Write(word);
        Console.Write(' ');
    }

    Console.WriteLine('\n');

    words = WordProcessor.GetWords(
        sentence,
        reverseWords: true,
        capitalizeWords: true);
    Console.WriteLine("Capitalized sentence with reversed words:");
    foreach (string word in words)
    {
        Console.Write(word);
        Console.Write(' ');
    }

    Console.ReadKey();
}
```

**4.** Run the application. The result is shown in Figure 14-9.

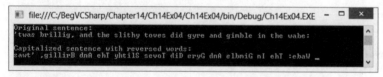

**FIGURE 14-9**

### How It Works

In this example you have created a utility class that performs some simple string manipulation, and used that class to modify a string. The single public method exposed by the class contains one required parameter and three optional ones:

```
public static List<string> GetWords(
    string sentence,
    bool capitalizeWords = false,
    bool reverseOrder = false,
    bool reverseWords = false)
{
    ...
}
```

This method returns a collection of `string` values, each of which is a word from the original input. Depending on which (if any) of the three optional parameters are specified, additional transformations can be made—on the string collection as a whole or on individual word values.

> **NOTE** You won't look at the functionality of the WordProcessor class in any more depth here; you are free to browse the code at your leisure. Along the way you might like to think about how this code might be improved. For example, should the word `'twas` be capitalized as `'Twas`? How would you go about making that change?

When this method is called, only two of the available optional parameters are used; the third parameter (`reverseOrder`) will have its default value of `false`:

```
words = WordProcessor.GetWords(
    sentence,
    reverseWords: true,
    capitalizeWords: true);
```

Also, note that the two parameters specified are placed in a different order from how they are defined.

As a final point to note, IntelliSense can be quite handy when dealing with methods that have optional parameters. When entering the code for this Try It Out, you might have noticed the tooltip for the `GetWords()` method, shown in Figure 14-10 (you can also see this tooltip by hovering the mouse pointer over the method call as shown).

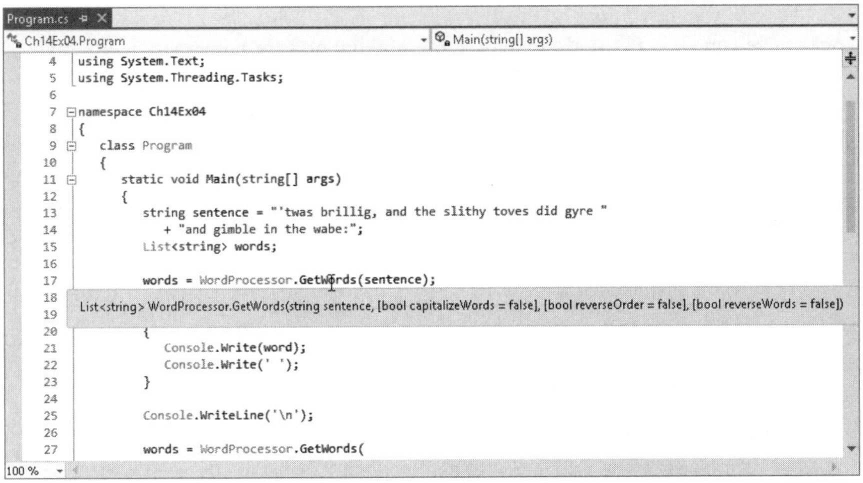

**FIGURE 14-10**

This is a very useful tooltip, as it shows not only the names of available parameters, but also the default values for optional parameters, so you can tell at a glance if you need to override a particular default.

## Named and Optional Parameter Guidelines

Since named and optional parameters were announced, they have received a mixed reaction. Some developers—and those who work with Microsoft Office in particular—have been very enthusiastic about them. However, many others see them as unnecessary changes to the C# language, arguing that a well-defined user interface should not need such a means of access—at least not at the level of a change to the language.

Personally, I think that there are some good points about named and optional parameters, but I worry that their overuse could be detrimental to code. Some situations, such as the aforementioned Microsoft Office scenario, will certainly benefit. Also, code similar to that shown in the preceding Try It Out, where many options are defined to control the operation of a method, becomes much simpler—both to write and to use. In most cases, though, I don't think it's a good idea to use named and optional parameters without a good reason. Perhaps a good test would be to look at a method call and see if you can determine what the result might be without knowing beforehand what the method should do. If the parameters and how they are used is obvious (which, in well-written code, they should be), then there is no need to use named and/or optional parameters to refactor your code.

## EXTENSION METHODS

*Extension methods* are a way to extend the functionality of types without modifying the types themselves. You can even use extension methods to extend types that you cannot modify—including types defined in the .NET Framework. Using an extension method, for example, you could even add functionality to something as fundamental as the System.string type.

In this context, to *extend the functionality* of a type means to provide a method that can be called through an instance of that type. The method you create to do this, known as the *extension method*, can take any number of parameters and return any return type (including void). To create and use an extension method, you must do the following:

1. Create a nongeneric static class.

2. Add the extension method to the class you have created as a static method, using extension method syntax (described shortly).

3. Ensure that the code where you want to use the extension method imports the namespace containing the extension method class with a using statement.

4. Call the extension method through an instance of the extended type as if you were calling any other method of the extended type.

The C# compiler works its magic between Step 3 and Step 4. The IDE is instantly aware that you have created an extension method, and even displays it in IntelliSense, as shown in Figure 14-11.

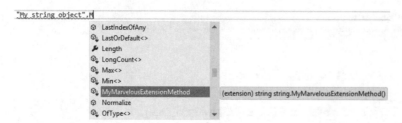

**FIGURE 14-11**

In Figure 14-11, an extension method called MyMarvelousExtensionMethod() is available through a string object (here just a literal string). This method, which is denoted with a slightly different method icon that includes a downward-pointing arrow, takes no additional parameters, and returns a string.

To define an extension method, you define a method in the same way as any other method, but it must meet the requirements of extension method syntax:

➤ The method must be static.

➤ The method must include a parameter to represent the instance of the type that the extension method will be called on. (This parameter will be referred to here as the *instance parameter*.)

➤ The instance parameter must be the first parameter defined for the method (as with other methods, you can define as many additional parameters as you want).

➤ The instance parameter must have no other modifier other than the `this` keyword.

The syntax for an extension method is as follows:

```
public static class ExtensionClass
{
    public static <ReturnType> <ExtensionMethodName>(
        this <TypeToExtend> instance, <OtherParameters>)
    {
        ...
    }
}
```

Once you have imported the namespace containing the static class that includes this method (which is known as making the extension method available), you can write code as follows:

```
<TypeToExtend> myVar;
// myVar is initialized by code not shown here.
myVar.<ExtensionMethodName>();
```

You can also include any additional parameters you want in the extension method, and make use of its return type.

Effectively, this call is identical to the following, but with simpler syntax:

```
<TypeToExtend> myVar;
// myVar is initialized by code not shown here.
ExtensionClass.<ExtensionMethodName>(myVar);
```

The other advantage is that once it is imported, you can find the functionality you need much more easily by looking at extension methods through IntelliSense. Extension methods can be spread across multiple extension classes, or even libraries, but they will all show up in the member list of the extended type.

When you define an extension method that can be used with a particular type, you can use it with any types that derive from this type. Referring back to an example used earlier in this chapter, if you defined an extension method for the `Animal` class, you could call it on, for example, a `Cow` object.

You can also define extension methods that operate on a particular interface, which you can then use for any type that implements that interface.

Extension methods provide a fantastic way to provide libraries of utility code that you can reuse across your applications. They are also used extensively in LINQ, which you will learn about later in this book. To better understand them, work through a full Try It Out example.

**TRY IT OUT** Defining and Using Extension Methods: Ch14Ex05

**1.** Create a new console application called Ch14Ex05 and save it in the directory `C:\BegVCSharp\Chapter14`.

**2.** Add a new Class Library project to the solution called ExtensionLib.

**3.** Remove the existing `Class1.cs` class file from ExtensionLib and add the `WordProcessor.cs` class file from Ch14Ex04 to the project.

**4.** Modify the code in `WordProcessor.cs` as follows (you can find this code in `ExtensionLib\WordProcessor.cs`):

```
namespace ExtensionLib
{
    public static class WordProcessor
    {
        public static List<string> GetWords(
            this string sentence,
            bool capitalizeWords = false,
            bool reverseOrder = false,
            bool reverseWords = false)
        {
            ...
        }
        ...
        public static string ToStringReversed(this object inputObject)
        {
            return ReverseWord(inputObject.ToString());
        }

        public static string AsSentence(this List<string> words)
        {
            StringBuilder sb = new StringBuilder();
            for (int wordIndex = 0; wordIndex < words.Count; wordIndex++)
            {
                sb.Append(words[wordIndex]);
                if (wordIndex != words.Count - 1)
                {
                    sb.Append(' ');
                }
            }
            return sb.ToString();
        }
    }
}
```

**5.** Add a project reference to the ExtensionLib project to the Ch14Ex05 project.

**6.** Modify the code in `Program.cs` as follows:

```
using ExtensionLib;

namespace Ch14Ex05
{
    class Program
    {
        static void Main(string[] args)
        {
            Console.WriteLine("Enter a string to convert:");
            string sourceString = Console.ReadLine();
            Console.WriteLine("String with title casing: {0}",
                sourceString.GetWords(capitalizeWords: true)
                    .AsSentence());
            Console.WriteLine("String backwards: {0}",
                sourceString.GetWords(reverseOrder: true,
                    reverseWords: true).AsSentence());
            Console.WriteLine("String length backwards: {0}",
                sourceString.Length.ToStringReversed());
            Console.ReadKey();
        }
    }
}
```

**7.** Run the application. When prompted, type in a string (at least 10 characters long and more than one word for the best effect). An example result is shown in Figure 14-12.

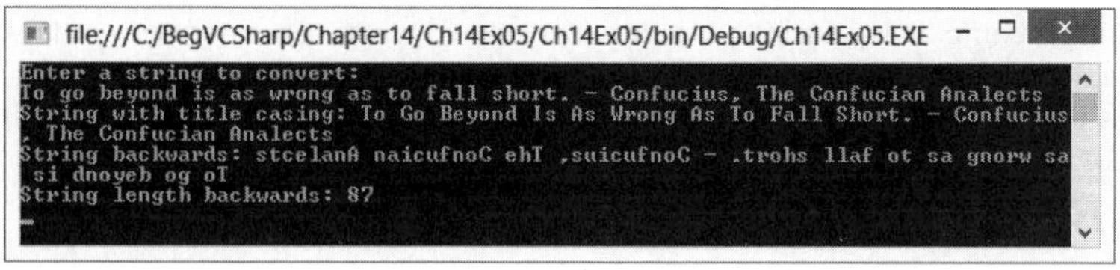

**FIGURE 14-12**

*How It Works*

This example created a class library containing utility extension methods, which you used in a simple client application. The class library includes an extended version of the static class WordProcessor from the preceding Try It Out that contains the extension methods, and you imported the ExtensionLib namespace that contains this class into the client application, thus making the extension methods available.

You created the three extension methods shown in Table 14-1.

**TABLE 14-1:** Extension Methods

| METHOD | DESCRIPTION |
| --- | --- |
| GetWords() | Flexible method for manipulating a string, as described in the previous Try It Out. In this example, the method has been changed to be an extension method. Returns a List<string>. |
| ToStringReversed() | Uses ReverseWord() to reverse the order of letters in the string returned by calling ToString() on an object. Returns a string. |
| AsSentence() | "Flattens" a List<string> object to return a string consisting of the words it contains. |

The client code used each of these methods to modify the string you input in various ways. As the GetWords() method defined previously returns a List<string>, its output is flattened to a string with AsSentence() for ease of use.

The ToStringReversed() extension method is an example of a more general extension method. Rather than require a string type instance parameter, this method instead has an instance parameter of type object. This means that this extension method can be called on *any* object and will show up in IntelliSense on every object you use. There isn't a lot you can do in this extension method, as you cannot assume very much about the object that might be used. You could use the is operator or try conversion to find out what the instance parameter type is and act accordingly, or you could do what is done in this example and use basic functionality that is supported by all objects—the ToString() method:

```
public static string ToStringReversed(this object inputObject)
{
    return ReverseWord(inputObject.ToString());
}
```

This method simply calls the ToString() method on its instance parameter and reverses it using the ReverseWord() method described earlier. In the example client application, the ToStringReversed() method is called on an int variable, which results in a string representation of the integer with its digits reversed.

Extension methods that can be used with multiple types can be very useful. Remember as well that you can define generic extension methods, which can apply constraints to the types that can be used, as shown in Chapter 12.

# LAMBDA EXPRESSIONS

*Lambda expressions* are a construct introduced in C# 3 that you can use to simplify certain aspects of C# programming, in particular when combined with LINQ. They can be difficult to grasp at first, mainly because they are so flexible in their usage. Lambda expressions are extremely useful when combined with other C# language features, such as anonymous methods. Without looking at LINQ, a subject left until later in the book, anonymous methods are the best entry point for examining this subject. Start with a quick refresher.

## Anonymous Methods Recap

In Chapter 13 you learned about anonymous methods—methods that you supply inline, where a delegate type variable would otherwise be required. When you add an event handler to an event, the sequence of events is as follows:

**1.** Define an event handler method whose return type and parameters match those of the delegate required for the event to which you want to subscribe.

**2.** Declare a variable of the delegate type used for the event.

**3.** Initialize the delegate variable to an instance of the delegate type that refers to the event handler method.

**4.** Add the delegate variable to the list of subscribers for the event.

In practice, things are a bit simpler than this because you typically won't bother with a variable to store the delegate—you will just use an instance of the delegate when you subscribe to the event.

This was the case when you used the following code in Chapter 13:

```
Timer myTimer = new Timer(100);
myTimer.Elapsed += new ElapsedEventHandler(WriteChar);
```

This code subscribes to the `Elapsed` event of a `Timer` object. This event uses the `ElapsedEventHandler` delegate type, which is instantiated using a method identifier, `WriteChar`. The result here is that when the `Timer` raises the `Elapsed` event, the `WriteChar()` method is called. The parameters passed to `WriteChar()` depend on the parameter types defined by the `ElapsedEventHandler` delegate and the values passed by the code in `Timer` that raises the event.

In fact, as noted in Chapter 13, the C# compiler can achieve the same result with even less code through method group syntax:

```
myTimer.Elapsed += WriteChar;
```

The C# compiler knows the delegate type required by the `Elapsed` event, so it can fill in the blanks. However, you should use this syntax with care because it can make it harder to read your code and know exactly what is happening. When you use an anonymous method, the sequence of events shown earlier is reduced to a single step:

**1.** Use an inline, anonymous method that matches the return type and the parameters of the delegate required by an event to subscribe to that event.

The inline, anonymous method is defined by using the `delegate` keyword:

```
myTimer.Elapsed +=
    delegate(object source, ElapsedEventArgs e)
    {
        Console.WriteLine(
            "Event handler called after {0} milliseconds.",
            (source as Timer).Interval);
    };
```

This code works just as well as using the event handler separately. The main difference is that the anonymous method used here is effectively hidden from the rest of your code. You cannot, for example, reuse this event handler elsewhere in your application. In addition, the syntax used here is, for want of a better description, a little clunky. The `delegate` keyword is immediately confusing because it is effectively being overloaded—you use it both for anonymous methods and for defining delegate types.

## Lambda Expressions for Anonymous Methods

This brings you to lambda expressions. Lambda expressions are a way to simplify the syntax of anonymous methods. In fact, they are more than that, but this section will keep things simple for now. Using a lambda expression, you can rewrite the code at the end of the previous section as follows:

```
myTimer.Elapsed += (source, e) => Console.WriteLine(
    "Event handler called after {0} milliseconds.",
    (source as Timer).Interval);
```

At first glance this looks... well, a little baffling (unless you are familiar with so-called functional programming languages such as Lisp or Haskell, that is). However, if you look closer you can see, or at least infer, how this works and how it relates to the anonymous method that it replaces. The lambda expression is made up of three parts:

➤ A list of (untyped) parameters in parentheses

➤ The `=>` operator

➤ A C# statement

The types of the parameters are inferred from the context, using the same logic shown in the section, "Anonymous Types" earlier in this chapter. The `=>` operator simply separates the parameter list from the expression body. The expression body is executed when the lambda expression is called.

The compiler takes this lambda expression and creates an anonymous method that works exactly the same way as the anonymous method in the previous section. In fact, it will be compiled into the same or similar Common Intermediate Language (CIL) code.

The following Try It Out clarifies what occurs in lambda expressions.

**TRY IT OUT** Using Simple Lambda Expressions: Ch14Ex06\Program.cs

**1.** Create a new console application called Ch14Ex06 and save it in the directory C:\BegVCSharp\Chapter14.

**2.** Modify the code in `Program.cs` as follows:

```
namespace Ch14Ex06
{
    delegate int TwoIntegerOperationDelegate(int paramA, int paramB);

    class Program
    {
        static void PerformOperations(TwoIntegerOperationDelegate del)
        {
            for (int paramAVal = 1; paramAVal <= 5; paramAVal++)
            {
                for (int paramBVal = 1; paramBVal <= 5; paramBVal++)
                {
                    int delegateCallResult = del(paramAVal, paramBVal);
                    Console.Write("f({0},{1})={2}",
                        paramAVal, paramBVal, delegateCallResult);
                    if (paramBVal != 5)
                    {
                        Console.Write(", ");
                    }
                }
                Console.WriteLine();
            }
        }

        static void Main(string[] args)
```

```
        {
            Console.WriteLine("f(a, b) = a + b:");
            PerformOperations((paramA, paramB) => paramA + paramB);
            Console.WriteLine();
            Console.WriteLine("f(a, b) = a * b:");
            PerformOperations((paramA, paramB) => paramA * paramB);
            Console.WriteLine();
            Console.WriteLine("f(a, b) = (a - b) % b:");
            PerformOperations((paramA, paramB) => (paramA - paramB)
                % paramB);
            Console.ReadKey();
        }
    }
}
```

**3.** Run the application. The result is shown in Figure 14-13.

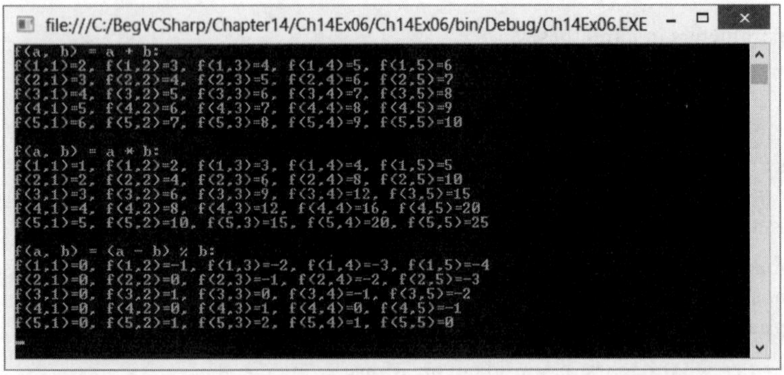

**FIGURE 14-13**

### How It Works

This example uses lambda expressions to generate functions that can be used to return the result of performing specific processing on two input parameters. Those functions then operate on 25 pairs of values and output the results to the console.

You start by defining a delegate type called TwoIntegerOperationDelegate to represent a method that takes two int parameters and returns an int result:

```
delegate int TwoIntegerOperationDelegate(int paramA, int paramB);
```

This delegate type is used later when you define your lambda expressions. These lambda expressions compile into methods whose return type and parameter types match this delegate type, as you will see shortly.

Next, you add a method called PerformOperations(), which takes a single parameter of type TwoIntegerOperationDelegate:

```
static void PerformOperations(TwoIntegerOperationDelegate del)
{
```

The idea behind this method is that you can pass it a delegate instance (or an anonymous method or lambda expression, because these constructs compile to delegate instances) and the method will call the method represented by the delegate instance with an assortment of values:

```
for (int paramAVal = 1; paramAVal <= 5; paramAVal++)
{
    for (int paramBVal = 1; paramBVal <= 5; paramBVal++)
    {
        int delegateCallResult = del(paramAVal, paramBVal);
```

The parameters and results are then output to the console:

```
            Console.Write("f({0},{1})={2}",
                paramAVal, paramBVal, delegateCallResult);
            if (paramBVal != 5)
            {
                Console.Write(", ");
            }
        }
        Console.WriteLine();
    }
}
```

In the `Main()` method you create three lambda expressions and use them to call `PerformOperations()` in turn. The first of these calls is as follows:

```
        Console.WriteLine("f(a, b) = a + b:");
        PerformOperations((paramA, paramB) => paramA + paramB);
```

The lambda expression used here is as follows:

```
    (paramA, paramB) => paramA + paramB
```

Again, this breaks down into three parts:

**1.** A parameter definition section. Here there are two parameters, `paramA` and `paramB`. These parameters are untyped, meaning the compiler can infer the types of these parameters according to the context. In this case the compiler can determine that the `PerformOperations()` method call requires a delegate of type `TwoIntegerOperationDelegate`. This delegate type has two `int` parameters, so by inference both `paramA` and `paramB` are typed as `int` variables.

**2.** The `=>` operator. This separates the lambda expression parameters from the lambda expression body.

**3.** The expression body. This specifies a simple operation, which is the summation of `paramA` and `paramB`. Notice that there is no need to specify that this is a return value. The compiler knows that in order to create a method that can be used with `TwoIntegerOperationDelegate`, the method must have a return type of `int`. Because the operation specified, `paramA + paramB`, evaluates to an `int`, and no additional information is supplied, the compiler infers that the result of this expression should be the return type of the method.

In longhand then, you can expand the code that uses this lambda expression to the following code that uses an anonymous method:

```
        Console.WriteLine("f(a, b) = a + b:");
        PerformOperations(delegate(int paramA, int paramB)
        {
            return paramA + paramB;
        });
```

The remaining code performs operations using two different lambda expressions in the same way:

```
        Console.WriteLine();
        Console.WriteLine("f(a, b) = a * b:");
        PerformOperations((paramA, paramB) => paramA * paramB);
        Console.WriteLine();
        Console.WriteLine("f(a, b) = (a - b) % b:");
        PerformOperations((paramA, paramB) => (paramA - paramB)
            % paramB);
        Console.ReadKey();
```

The last lambda expression involves more calculations but is no more complicated than the others. The syntax for lambda expressions enables you to perform far more complicated operations, as you will see shortly.

## Lambda Expression Parameters

In the code you have seen so far, the lambda expressions have used type inference to determine the types of the parameters passed. In fact, this is not mandatory; you can define types if you want. For example, you could use the following lambda expression:

```
(int paramA, int paramB) => paramA + paramB
```

This has the advantage of making your code more readable, although you lose out in both brevity and flexibility. You could use the implicitly typed lambda expressions from the previous Try It Out for delegate types that used other numeric types, such as `long` variables.

Note that you cannot use implicit and explicit parameter types in the same lambda expression. The following lambda expressions will not compile because `paramA` is explicitly typed and `paramB` is implicitly typed:

```
(int paramA, paramB) => paramA + paramB
```

Parameter lists in lambda expressions always consist of a comma-separated list of either all implicitly typed parameters or all explicitly typed parameters. If you have only one implicitly typed parameter, then you can omit the parentheses; otherwise, they are required as part of the parameter list, as shown earlier. For example, you could have the following as a single-parameter, implicitly typed lambda expression:

```
param1 => param1 * param1
```

You can also define lambda expressions that have no parameters. This is denoted by using empty parentheses, `()`:

```
() => Math.PI
```

This could be used where a delegate requiring no parameters but returning a `double` value is required.

## Lambda Expression Statement Bodies

In all the code that you have seen so far, a single expression has been used in the statement body of lambda expressions. You have also seen how this single expression has been interpreted as the return value of the lambda expression, which is, for example, how you can use the expression `paramA + paramB` as the statement body for a lambda expression for a delegate with a return type of `int` (assuming both `paramA` and `paramB` are implicitly or explicitly typed to `int` values, as they were in the example code).

An earlier example showed how a delegate with a `void` return type was less fussy about the code used in the statement body:

```
myTimer.Elapsed += (source, e) => Console.WriteLine(
   "Event handler called after {0} milliseconds.",
   (source as Timer).Interval);
```

Here, the statement doesn't evaluate to anything, so it is simply executed without any return value being used anywhere.

Given that lambda expressions can be visualized as an extension of the anonymous method syntax, you might not be surprised to learn that you can also include multiple statements as a lambda expression statement body. To do so, you simply provide a block of code enclosed in curly braces, much like any other situation in C# where you must supply multiple lines of code:

```
(param1, param2) =>
{
   // Multiple statements ahoy!
}
```

If you use a lambda expression in combination with a delegate type that has a non-`void` return type, then you must return a value with the `return` keyword, just like any other method:

```
(param1, param2) =>
{
    // Multiple statements ahoy!
    return returnValue;
}
```

For example, earlier you saw how you could rewrite the following code from the Try It Out,

```
PerformOperations((paramA, paramB) => paramA + paramB);
```

as:

```
PerformOperations(delegate(int paramA, int paramB)
    {
        return paramA + paramB;
    });
```

Alternatively, you could rewrite the code as follows:

```
PerformOperations((paramA, paramB) =>
    {
        return paramA + paramB;
    });
```

This is more in keeping with the original code because it maintains implicit typing of the paramA and paramB parameters.

For the most part, lambda expressions are at their most useful—and certainly their most elegant—when used with single expressions. To be honest, if you require multiple statements, your code might read much better if you define a separate, nonanonymous method to use instead of a lambda expression; that also makes your code more reusable.

## Lambda Expressions as Delegates and Expression Trees

You have already seen some of the differences between lambda expressions and anonymous methods where lambda methods have more flexibility—for example, implicitly typed parameters. At this point it is worth noting another key difference, although the implications of this will not become apparent until later in the book when you learn about LINQ.

You can interpret a lambda expression in two ways. The first way, which you have seen throughout this chapter, is as a delegate. That is, you can assign a lambda expression to a delegate type variable, as you did in the previous Try It Out.

In general terms, you can represent a lambda expression with up to eight parameters as one of the following generic types, all defined in the System namespace:

➤   Action for lambda expressions with no parameters and a return type of void.

➤   Action<> for lambda expressions with up to eight parameters and a return type of void.

➤   Func<> for lambda expressions with up to eight parameters and a return type that is not void.

Action<> has up to eight generic type parameters, one for each parameter, and Func<> has up to nine generic type parameters, used for up to eight parameters and the return type. In Func<>, the return type is always the last in the list.

For example, the following lambda expression, which you saw earlier:

```
(int paramA, int paramB) => paramA + paramB
```

This expression can be represented as a delegate of type Func<int, int, int> because it has two parameters and a return type all of type int. Note that you can use these generic delegate types instead of defining your own in many circumstances. For example, you can use them instead of the TwoIntegerOperationDelegate delegate you defined in the previous Try It Out.

The second way to interpret a lambda expression is as an *expression tree*. An expression tree is an abstract representation of a lambda expression; and as such, it cannot be executed directly. Instead, you can use the expression tree to analyze the lambda expression programmatically and perform actions in response to the lambda expression.

This is, obviously, a complicated subject. However, expression trees are critical to the LINQ functionality you will learn about later in this book. To give a more concrete example, the LINQ framework includes a generic class called Expression<>, which you can use to encapsulate a lambda expression. One of the ways in which this class is used is to take a lambda expression that you have written in C# and convert it into an equivalent SQL script representation for executing directly in a database.

You don't need to know any more about that at this point. When you encounter this functionality later in the book, you will be better equipped to understand what is going on, as you now have a thorough grounding in the key concepts that the C# language provides.

## Lambda Expressions and Collections

Now that you have learned about the Func<> generic delegate, you can understand some of the extension methods that the System.Linq namespace provides for array types (which you might have seen popping up in IntelliSense at various points during your coding). For example, there is an extension method called Aggregate(), which is defined with three overloads as follows:

```
public static TSource Aggregate<TSource>(
    this IEnumerable<TSource> source,
    Func<TSource, TSource, TSource> func);

public static TAccumulate Aggregate<TSource, TAccumulate>(
    this IEnumerable<TSource> source,
    TAccumulate seed,
    Func<TAccumulate, TSource, TAccumulate> func);

public static TResult Aggregate<TSource, TAccumulate,
                                Aggregate<TSource, TAccumulate, TResult>( TResult>(
    this IEnumerable<TSource> source,
    TAccumulate seed,
    Func<TAccumulate, TSource, TAccumulate> func,
    Func<TAccumulate, TResult> resultSelector);
```

As with the extension method shown earlier, this looks at first glance to be impenetrable, but if you break it down you can work it out easily enough. The IntelliSense for this function tells you that it does the following:

```
Applies an accumulator function over a sequence.
```

This means that an accumulator function (which you can supply in the form of a lambda expression) will be applied to each element in a collection from beginning to end. This accumulator function must have two parameters and one return value. One input is the current element; the other input is either a seed value, the first value in the collection, or the result of the previous evaluation.

In the simplest of the three overloads, there is only one generic type specification, which can be inferred from the type of the instance parameter. For example, in the following code the generic type specification will be int (the accumulator function is left blank for now):

```
int[] myIntArray = { 2, 6, 3 };
int result = myIntArray.Aggregate(...);
```

This is equivalent to the following:

```
int[] myIntArray = { 2, 6, 3 };
int result = myIntArray.Aggregate<int>(...);
```

The lambda expression that is required here can be deduced from the extension method specification. Because the type TSource is int in this code, you must supply a lambda expression for the delegate Func<int, int, int>. For example, you could use one you've seen before:

```
int[] myIntArray = { 2, 6, 3 };
int result = myIntArray.Aggregate((paramA, paramB) => paramA + paramB);
```

This call results in the lambda expression being called twice, first with paramA = 2 and paramB = 6, and once with paramA = 8 (the result of the first calculation) and paramB = 3. The final result assigned to the variable result will be the int value 11—the summation of all the elements in the array.

The other two overloads of the Aggregate() extension method are similar, but enable you to perform slightly more complicated processing. This is illustrated in the following short Try It Out.

**TRY IT OUT**  **Using Lambda Expressions with Collections: Ch14Ex07\Program.cs**

**1.** Create a new console application called Ch14Ex07 and save it in the directory C:\BegVCSharp\Chapter14.

**2.** Modify the code in Program.cs as follows:

```
static void Main(string[] args)
{
    string[] curries = { "pathia", "jalfrezi", "korma" };
    Console.WriteLine(curries.Aggregate(
        (a, b) => a + " " + b));
    Console.WriteLine(curries.Aggregate<string, int>(
        0,
        (a, b) => a + b.Length));
    Console.WriteLine(curries.Aggregate<string, string, string>(
        "Some curries:",
        (a, b) => a + " " + b,
        a => a));
    Console.WriteLine(curries.Aggregate<string, string, int>(
        "Some curries:",
        (a, b) => a + " " + b,
        a => a.Length));
    Console.ReadKey();
}
```

**3.** Run the application. The result is shown in Figure 14-14.

**FIGURE 14-14**

## How It Works

In this example you experimented with each of the overloads of the Aggregate() extension method, using a string array with three elements as source data.

First, a simple concatenation is performed:

```
Console.WriteLine(curries.Aggregate(
    (a, b) => a + " " + b));
```

The first pair of elements is concatenated into a string using simple syntax. This is far from the best way to concatenate strings—ideally you would use string.Concat() or string.Format() to optimize performance—but here it provides a very simple way to see what is going on. After this first concatenation, the result is passed back into the lambda expression along with the third element in the array, in much the same way as you saw `int` values being summed earlier. The result is a concatenation of the entire array, with spaces separating entries. You can achieve this effect in a simpler way using the `string.Join()` method, but the remainer of the overloads illustrated in this example provide additional functionality that `string.Join()` doesn't.

The second overload of the `Aggregate()` function, which has the two generic type parameters `TSource` and `TAccumulate`, is used. In this case the lambda expression must be of the form `Func<TAccumulate, TSource, TAccumulate>`. In addition, a seed value of type `TAccumulate` must be specified. This seed value is used in the first call to the lambda expression, along with the first array element. Subsequent calls take the accumulator result of previous calls to the expression. The code used is as follows:

```
Console.WriteLine(curries.Aggregate<string, int>(
    0,
    (a, b) => a + b.Length));
```

The accumulator (and, by implication, the return value) is of type `int`. The accumulator value is initially set to the seed value of `0`, and with each call to the lambda expression it is summed with the length of an element in the array. The final result is the sum of the lengths of each element in the array.

Next you come to the last overload of `Aggregate()`. This takes three generic type parameters and differs from the previous version only in that the return value can be a different type from both the type of the elements in the array and the accumulator value. First, this overload is used to concatenate the string elements with a seed string:

```
Console.WriteLine(curries.Aggregate<string, string, string>(
    "Some curries:",
    (a, b) => a + " " + b,
    a => a));
```

The final parameter of this method, `resultSelector`, must be specified even if (as in this example) the accumulator value is simply copied to the result. This parameter is a lambda expression of type `Func<TAccumulate, TResult>`.

In the final section of code, the same version of `Aggregate()` is used again, but this time with an `int` return value. Here, `resultSelector` is supplied with a lambda expression that returns the length of the accumulator string:

```
Console.WriteLine(curries.Aggregate<string, string, int>(
    "Some curries:",
    (a, b) => a + " " + b,
    a => a.Length));
```

This example hasn't done anything spectacular, but it demonstrates how you can use more complicated extension methods that involve generic type parameters, collections, and seemingly complex syntax. You'll see more of this later in the book.

## CALLER INFORMATION ATTRIBUTES

Most of the changes in the latest version of C# and the .NET Framework (versions 5 and 4.5, respectively) are unfortunately not covered in this book. This is because they relate to asynchronous programming, which is an advanced subject. However, one quite minor, but very useful, improvement is the ability to access caller information using attributes that you apply to method parameters. What this means is that it's possible for a method to find out information about the code that calls it.

There are three attributes that you can use:

➤ `CallerFilePathAttribute`—This allows you to get the path to the file that contains the calling code.

➤ `CallerLineNumberAttribute`—This allows you to get the line number of the file that contains the calling code.

➤ `CallerMemberNameAttribute`—This allows you to get the name of the member that contains the calling code. In most cases, for example methods and properties, you get the name of the member. For some members you get a fixed string, such as ".`ctor`" for a constructor.

You use these attributes by applying them to a parameter of a method, which must be optional and must be a `string` for the file path and member name or an `int` for the line number.

The information you obtain can be useful in a number of ways, not the least being logging information about calls. However, it is most useful when used in WPF applications to notify calling code of property changes, as you will see later in this book.

The following Try It Out shows how to use these attributes, as well as clarifying a few points about how they work in practice.

**TRY IT OUT** Using Caller Information Attributes: Ch14Ex08\Program.cs

**1.** Create a new console application called Ch14Ex08 and save it in the directory `C:\BegVCSharp\Chapter14`.

**2.** Modify the code in `Program.cs` as follows:

```
using System.Runtime.CompilerServices;

namespace Ch14Ex08
{
    class Program
    {
        static void Main(string[] args)
        {
            DisplayCallerInformation();
            Action callerDelegate = new Action(() => DisplayCallerInformation());
            callerDelegate();
            CallerHelper(callerDelegate);
            Caller();
            DisplayCallerInformation(3, "Bob", @"C:\Temp\NotRealCode.cs");
            Console.ReadKey();
        }

        static void CallerHelper(Action callToMake)
        {
            callToMake();
        }

        static void Caller()
        {
            DisplayCallerInformation();
        }

        static void DisplayCallerInformation(
            [CallerLineNumber] int callerLineNumber = 0,
            [CallerMemberName] string callerMemberName = "",
            [CallerFilePath] string callerFilePath = "")
        {
            Console.WriteLine(
                string.Format(
                    "Method called from line {0} of member {1} in file {2}.",
                    callerLineNumber,
```

```
                callerMemberName,
                callerFilePath));
        }
    }
}
```

**3.** Run the application. The result is shown in Figure 14-15.

**FIGURE 14-15**

### How It Works

In this example you call a method that displayed caller information in a number of ways. The method you call, `DisplayCallerInformation()`, is defined as follows:

```
static void DisplayCallerInformation(
    [CallerLineNumber] int callerLineNumber = 0,
    [CallerMemberName] string callerMemberName = "",
    [CallerFilePath] string callerFilePath = "")
{
    ...
}
```

This method uses each of the caller information attributes you saw earlier to populate the parameters `callerLineNumber`, `callerMemberName`, and `callerFilePath`. These parameters used output a string to the console that reports their values.

The first call you make to this method is a simple call from `Main()`:

```
static void Main(string[] args)
{
    DisplayCallerInformation();
```

The string output to the console includes the name of the method, `Main`, along with the line number and the path to the file, exactly as expected.

Next, you call the method using a delegate, either directly or via a helper method:

```
Action callerDelegate = new Action(() => DisplayCallerInformation());
callerDelegate();
CallerHelper(callerDelegate);
```

In both cases the output shows the same information, which is the line in `Main()` where the delegate is defined. In fact, the report is showing the location of the lambda function you use to create the delegate.

Next you call the reporting method from a secondary method called `Caller()`:

```
Caller();
```

This time the report identifies the calling method as `Caller`, as you'd expect.

Finally, you call the reporting method with custom parameters:

```
DisplayCallerInformation(3, "Bob", @"C:\Temp\NotRealCode.cs");
```

These parameters are included in the reporting output. This behavior isn't exactly ideal, as it shows that you can override the caller information attributes. This illustrates that you must use them with caution.

Under the hood, these attributes are used by the compiler at compile time, which substitutes appropriate information according to what it knows as the default parameter values. It's worth remembering this because, for example, compiling code in one location will affect the value added by `CallerMemberNameAttribute` wherever the compiled application is executed.

## SUMMARY

This chapter examined the new or recently added features that are included in version 5 of the C# language, which is the version that you use in Visual Studio 2012. You learned how these features simplify some of the coding required to achieve commonly used and/or advanced functionality.

Highlights of this chapter included the following:

➤ How to use object and collection initializers to instantiate and initialize objects and collections in one step

➤ How the IDE and C# compiler are capable of inferring types from context, and how to use the var keyword to permit type inference to be used with any variable type

➤ How to create and use anonymous types, which combine the initializer and type inference topics already covered

➤ How to use dynamic lookup on variables that will be interrogated for members only at runtime

➤ How to use named and optional parameters to call methods in a flexible way

➤ How to create extension methods that can be called on instances of other types without adding code to the definition of these types, and how this technique can be used to supply libraries of utility methods

➤ How to use lambda methods to provide anonymous methods to delegate instances, and how the extended syntax of lambda methods makes additional functionality possible

➤ How to use called information attributes to find out information about the code that calls your methods

Most of the C# features that you learned about in this chapter have been added specifically to cater to the new LINQ capabilities of the .NET Framework. Much of the elegance, and many of the subtleties, of the code that you have seen will become apparent later. Having said that, you have learned some extremely powerful techniques that you can put to work straight away to improve your C# programming skills.

You have now covered pretty much the entire C# language as it stands with version 5. However, this is not the same thing as knowing everything about programming with the .NET Framework. The C# language gives you all the tools you need to write .NET applications, but it is the classes available to you in the .NET Framework that give you the raw materials to build with. From this point on in the book, you will become increasingly immersed in these classes, and you will learn how to perform a multitude of tasks with them. The next chapter moves away from the console applications you have thus far spent most of your time working with, and starts to use the rich functionality offered by WPF to create graphical user interfaces for desktop applications. As you do this, remember that the underlying principles are the same regardless of the type of application you create. The skills you learned in the first part of this book will serve you well as you progress through the following chapters.

**14.1** Why can't you use an object initializer with the following class? After modifying this class to enable the use of an object initializer, give an example of the code you would use to instantiate and initialize this class in one step:

```
public class Giraffe
{
    public Giraffe(double neckLength, string name)
    {
        NeckLength = neckLength;
        Name = name;
    }
    public double NeckLength {get; set;}
    public string Name {get; set;}
}
```

**14.2** True or false: If you declare a variable of type `var`, you will then be able to use it to hold any object type.

**14.3** When you use anonymous types, how can you compare two instances to determine whether they contain the same data?

**14.4** Try to correct the following code for an extension method, which contains an error:

```
public string ToAcronym(this string inputString)
{
    inputString = inputString.Trim();
    if (inputString == "")
    {
        return "";
    }
    string[] inputStringAsArray = inputString.Split(' ');
    StringBuilder sb = new StringBuilder();
    for (int i = 0; i < inputStringAsArray.Length; i++)
    {
        if (inputStringAsArray[i].Length > 0)
        {
            sb.AppendFormat("{0}",
                inputStringAsArray[i].Substring(
                    0, 1).ToUpper());
        }
    }
    return sb.ToString();
}
```

**14.5** How would you ensure that the extension method in Question 4 was available to your client code?

**14.6** Rewrite the `ToAcronym()` method shown here as a single statement. The code should ensure that strings including multiple spaces between words do not cause errors. Hint: You will require the `?:` tertiary operator, the `string.Aggregate<string, string>()` extension method, and a lambda expression to achieve this.

Answers to the exercises can be found in Appendix A.

## ▶ WHAT YOU LEARNED IN THIS CHAPTER

| TOPIC | KEY CONCEPTS |
|---|---|
| **Initializers** | You can use initializers to initialize an object or collection at the same time as creating it. Both types of initializers consist of a block of code surrounded by curly brackets. Object initializers allow you to set property values by providing a comma-separated list of property name/value pairs. Collection initializers simply require a comma-separated list of values. When you use an object initializer, you can also use a nondefault constructor. |
| **Type inference** | The `var` keyword allows you to omit the type of a variable when you declare it. However, this is possible only if the type can be determined at compile time. Using `var` does not break the strong typing methodology of C# as a variable declared with `var` has one and only one possible type. |
| **Anonymous types** | For many simple types used to structure data storage, defining a type is not necessary. Instead, you can use an anonymous type, whose members are inferred from usage. You define an anonymous type with object initializer syntax, and every property you set is defined as a read-only property. |
| **Dynamic lookup** | Use the `dynamic` keyword to define a dynamic type variable that can hold any value. You can then access members of the contained value with normal property or method syntax, and these are only checked at runtime. If, at runtime, you attempt to access a nonexistent member, an exception is thrown. This dynamic typing greatly simplifies the syntax required to access non-.NET types, or .NET types whose type information is not available at compile time. However, dynamic types must be used with caution as you lose compile time code checking. You can control the behavior of dynamic lookup by implementing the `IDynamicMetaObjectProvider` interface. |
| **Optional method parameters** | Often, you can define a method with lots of parameters, many of which are only rarely used. Instead of forcing client code to specify values for rarely used parameters, you might provide multiple method overloads. Alternatively, you can define these parameters as optional (and provide default values for parameters that are not specified). Client code that calls your method can then specify only as many parameters as are required. |
| **Named method parameters** | Client code can specify method parameter values by position or by name (or a mix of the two where positional parameters are specified first). Named parameters can be specified in any order. This is particularly useful when combined with optional parameters. |
| **Extension methods** | You can define extension methods for any existing type without modifying the type definition. This includes, for example, extending system-defined types such as `string`. Extension methods are defined as static methods of a nongeneric static class. The first parameter of an extension method is defined with the `this` keyword, and is the instance value for which the method is called. Once defined, an extension method can be called from any code that references the namespace that contains the class that defines the method. Extension methods can be called from instances of the type used in the method definition or any derived type, so you can define general purpose extension methods for families of types. Another way to create general-purpose extension methods is to create extension methods that can be used with a particular interface. |

| | |
|---|---|
| **Lambda expressions** | Lambda expressions are essentially a shorthand way of defining anonymous methods, although they have additional capabilities such as implicit typing. You define a lambda expression with a comma-separated list of parameters (or empty parentheses for no parameters), the => operator, and an expression. The expression can be a block of code enclosed in curly brackets. Lambda expressions with up to eight parameters and an optional return type can be represented with the `Action`, `Action<>`, and `Func<>` delegate types. Many LINQ extension methods that can be used with collections use lambda expression parameters. |
| **Caller information attributes** | If you apply the attributes `CallerFilePathAttribute`, `CallerLineNumberAttribute`, or `CallerMemberNameAttribute` to optional method parameters, then the compiler will insert appropriate default values for those parameters. Your method can use this to find out about calling code, although it is possible that these values will be overridden by that code, so you must use these attributes with caution. |

# PART II
# Windows Programming

# 15

# Basic Desktop Programming

## WHAT YOU WILL LEARN IN THIS CHAPTER

➤ How to use the WPF designer

➤ How to use controls for displaying information to the user, such as the `Label` and `TextBlock` controls

➤ How to use controls for triggering events, such as the `Button` control

➤ How to use the controls that enable users of your application to enter text, such as the `TextBox` control

➤ How to use controls that enable you to inform users of the current state of the application and allow the user to change that state, such as the `RadioButton` and `CheckButton` controls

➤ How to use controls that enable you to display lists of information, such as the `ListBox` and `ComboBox` controls

➤ How to use panels to lay out your user interfaces

## WROX.COM CODE DOWNLOADS FOR THIS CHAPTER

You can find the wrox.com code downloads for this chapter at www.wrox.com/remtitle .cgi?isbn=9781118314418 on the Download Code tab. The code is in the Chapter 15 download and individually named according to the names throughout the chapter.

The first part of this book has concerned itself with the ins and outs of C#, but now it is time to move away from the details of the programming language and into the world of the graphical user interface (GUI).

Over the past 10 years, Visual Studio has provided the Windows developers with a couple of choices for creating user interfaces: Windows Forms, which is a basic tool for creating applications that target classic Windows, and Windows Presentation Foundations (WPF), which provide a wider range of application types and attempts to solve a number of problems with Windows Forms. WPF is technically platform-independent, and some of its flexibility can be seen in the fact that a subset of WPF called Silverlight is used to create interactive web applications. In this and the next chapter you are going to learn how to use WPF to create Windows applications and then how to use XAML to create applications that target the new style of applications in Windows: Windows Store apps.

At the heart of the development of most graphical Windows applications is the Window Designer. You create a user interface by dragging and dropping controls from a Toolbox to your window, placing them where you want them to appear when you run the application. With WPF this is only partly true, as the user interface is in fact written entirely in another language called Extensible Application Markup Language (XAML, pronounced *zammel*). Visual Studio allows you to do both and as you get more comfortable with WPF, you are likely going to combine dragging and dropping controls with writing raw XAML.

In this chapter, you work with the Visual Studio WPF designer to create a number of windows for the card game that you wrote in previous chapters. You learn to use some of the many controls that ship with Visual Studio that cover a wide range of functionality. Through the design capabilities of Visual Studio, developing user interfaces and handling user interaction is very straightforward—and fun! Presenting all of Visual Studio's controls is impossible within the scope of this book, so this chapter looks at some of the most commonly used controls, ranging from labels and text boxes to menu bars and layout panels.

## XAML

XAML is a language that uses XML syntax and enables controls to be added to a user interface in a declarative, hierarchical way. That is to say, you can add controls in the form of XML elements, and specify control properties with XML attributes. You can also have controls that contain other controls, which is essential for both layout and functionality.

> **NOTE** *XML is covered in detail in Chapter 22. If you want a quick introduction to the basics of XML at this point, it might be a good idea to skip forward and read the first nine pages of that chapter.*

XAML is designed with today's powerful graphics cards in mind, and as such it enables you to use all the advanced capabilities that these graphics cards offer through DirectX. The following lists some of these capabilities:

➤  Floating-point coordinates and vector graphics to provide layout that can be scaled, rotated, and otherwise transformed with no loss of quality

➤  2D and 3D capabilities for advanced rendering

➤  Advanced font processing and rendering

➤  Solid, gradient, and texture fills with optional transparency for UI objects

➤  Animation storyboarding that can be used in all manner of situations, including user-triggered events such as mouse clicks on buttons

➤  Reusable resources that you can use to dynamically style controls

You will see some of this in action in Chapters 16 and 17 but the more advanced features are out of the scope of this book.

## Separation of Concerns

One problem that exists with maintaining Windows applications that has been written over the years is that they very often mix the code that generates the user interface and the code that executes based on users actions. This makes it difficult for multiple developers and designers to work on the same project. WPF solves this in two ways. First, by using XAML to describe the GUI rather than C#, the GUI becomes platform independent, and you can in fact render XAML without any code whatsoever. Second, this means that it feels natural to place the C# code in a different file than you place the GUI code. Visual Studio utilizes something called *code-behind* files, which are C# files that are dynamically linked to the XAML files.

Because the GUI is separated from the code, it is possible to create tailor-made applications for designing the GUI, and this is exactly what Microsoft has done. The design tool Expression Blend is the favored tool used by designers when creating GUIs for WPF. This tool can load the same projects as Visual Studio, but where Visual Studio targets the developer more than the designer, the opposite is true in Expression Blend. This means that on large projects with designers and developers, everyone can work together on the same project, using their preferred tool without fear of inadvertently influencing the others.

## XAML in Action

As stated, XAML is XML, which means that as long as the files are fairly small, it is possible to see immediately what it is describing. Take a look at this small example and see if you can tell what it does:

```
<Window x:Class="Ch15Ex01.MainWindow"
        xmlns="http://schemas.microsoft.com/winfx/2006/xaml/presentation"
        xmlns:x="http://schemas.microsoft.com/winfx/2006/xaml"
        Title="MainWindow" Height="350" Width="525">
  <Grid>
    <Button Content="Hello World"
            HorizontalAlignment="Left"
            Margin="220,151,0,0"
            VerticalAlignment="Top"
            Width="75"/>
  </Grid>
</Window>
```

The XAML in this example creates a window with a single button on it. Both the window and the button display the text "Hello World". XML allows you to place tags inside other tags as long as you close them properly. When an element in placed inside another in XAML, this element becomes the content of the enclosing element, meaning that the Button could also have been written like this:

```
<Button Content="Hello World"
        HorizontalAlignment="Left"
        Margin="220,151,0,0"
        VerticalAlignment="Top" Width="75"/>
```

Here, the Content property of the Button has been removed and the text is now a child node of the Button control. Content can be just about anything in XAML, which is also demonstrated in this example: the Button element is the content of the Grid element, which is itself the content of the Window element.

Most, if not all, controls can have content, and there are very few limits to what you can do to change the appearance of the built-in controls. Chapter 16 explores this more detail.

## Namespaces

The Window element of the previous example is the root element of the XAML file. This element usually includes a number of namespace declarations. By default, the Visual Studio designer includes two namespaces that you should be aware of: http://schemas.microsoft.com/winfx/2006/xaml/presentation and http://schemas.microsoft.com/winfx/2006/xaml. The first one is the default namespace of WPF and declares a lot of controls that you are going to use to create user interfaces. The second one declares the XAML language itself. Namespaces don't have to be declared on the root tag, but doing so ensures that their content can be easily accessed throughout the XAML file, so there is rarely any need to move the declarations.

When you create a new window in Visual Studio, the presentation namespace is always declared as the default and the language namespace as xmlns:x. As seen with the Window, Button, and Grid tags, this ensures that you don't have to prefix the controls you add to the window, but the language elements you specify must be prefixed with an x.

The last namespace that you will see quite often is the system namespace: `xmlns:sys="clr-namespace:S ystem;assembly=mscorlib"`. This namespace allows you to use the built-in types of the .NET Framework in your XAML. By doing this, the markup you write can explicitly declare the types of elements you are creating. For example, it is possible to declare an array in markup and state that the members of the array are strings:

```
<Window.Resources>
  <ResourceDictionary>
    <x:Array Type="sys:String" x:Key="localArray">
      <sys:String>"Karli Watson"</sys:String>
      <sys:String>"Jacob Vibe Hammer"</sys:String>
      <sys:String>"Christian Nagel"</sys:String>
      <sys:String>"Job D. Reid"</sys:String>
      <sys:String>"Morgan Skinner"</sys:String>
    </x:Array>
  </ResourceDictionary>
</Window.Resources>
```

### Code-Behind Files

Although XAML is a powerful way to declare user interfaces, it is not a programming language. Whenever you want to do more than presentation, you need C#. It is possible to embed C# code directly into XAML, but mixing code and markup is never recommended and you will not see it done in this book. What you will see quite a lot is the use of code-behind files. These files are normal C# files that have the same name as the XAML file, plus a `.cs` extension. Although you can call them whatever you like, it's best to stick to the naming convention. Visual Studio creates code-behind files automatically when you create a new window in your application, because it expects you to add code to the window. It also adds the `x:Class` property to the `Window` tag in the XAML:

```
<Window x:Class="Ch15Ex01.MainWindow"
```

This tells the compiler that it can find the code for this window in, not a file, but the class `GameClient .MainWindow`. Because you can specify only the fully qualified class name, and not the assembly in which the class is found, it is not possible to put the code-behind file somewhere outside of the project in which the XAML is defined. Visual Studio puts the code-behind files in the same directory as the XAML files so you never have to worry about this while working in Visual Studio. Over the course of the next few chapters it's going to become second nature for you to navigate between the code-behind files and the XAML files.

## THE PLAYGROUND

Now you know enough about how WPF is constructed to start getting your hands dirty, so it's time to look at the editor. You're going to be spending quite a lot of time with this editor in the next few chapters.

Start by creating a new WPF project by selecting File ➪ New ➪ Project. From the New Project dialog box, select the project template WPF Application and click OK. You are going to use this project only to explore the editor, so the name is not too important.

Visual Studio now displays an empty window and a number of panels around it. The greater part of the screen is divided in two sections. The upper section, known as the Design View, displays a WYSIWYG (What You See Is What You Get) representation of the window you are designing and the lower section, known as the XAML View, displays a textual representation of the same window.

To the right of the Design View, you see the Solution Explorer that you have seen in previous projects and a Properties panel that displays information about the current selection in the Design and XAML Views. It is worth noting that the selection in the Properties panel, XAML View, and Design View are always in sync, so if you move the cursor in the XAML View you will see the selection change in the other two.

Collapsed to the left of the Design View are three panels: The Toolbox, a document outline, and a Data Sources panel. This chapter shows you how to use many of the controls from the Toolbox panel to create dialog boxes for the card game, so expand it and pin it open by clicking the pin in the top-right corner. While you are at it, expand the Common WPF Controls node in the panel as well. You will be using most of the controls shown here in this chapter.

# WPF Controls

Controls combine prepackaged code and a GUI that can be reused to create more complex applications. They can define how they draw themselves by default and a set of standard behaviors. Some controls, such as the Label, Button, and TextBox controls are easily recognizable and have been used in Windows applications for about 20 years. Others, such as Canvas and StackPanel, don't display anything and simply help you create the GUI.

Out-of-the-box controls look exactly as you would expect a control to look in a standard Windows application and use the current Windows Theme to draw themselves. All of this is highly customizable and with only a few clicks you can completely change how a control is displayed. This customization is done using properties that are defined on the controls. WPF uses normal properties that you have seen before and adds a new type of property called a *dependency property*. These are examined in detail in Chapter 16, but for now it is enough to know that many of the properties of WPF do more than just get and set a value; for one, they are able to notify observers of changes.

Besides defining how something looks on the screen, controls also define standard behavior, such as the ability to click on a button and select something in a list. You can change what happens when a user performs an action on a control by "handling" the events that the control defines. When and how you implement the event handler will vary from application to application and from control to control, but generally speaking you will always handle the Click event for a button; for a ListBox control, you often have to react when the user changes the selection and so the SelectionChanged event should be handled. On other controls, such as the Label or TextBlock controls, you will rarely implement any event.

> **WARNING** *Although users are often happy when you take the time to provide a more interesting user interface than the standard Windows display, you must be careful when changing the standard behavior of controls. Imagine that you change a* Button *control to work only when users right-click it. Your users will think that your application is broken when nothing happens when they left-click on the button. In fact, even if there are fantastic reasons for changing the button like this, it is likely that you should be using another type of control instead of changing the behavior of the* Button *control.*

You can add controls to a window in a number of ways, but the most common way is to drag and drop them from the Toolbox onto the Design View or the XAML View.

**TRY IT OUT** Adding Controls to a Window

As you work your way through this chapter, you will add controls to the Design View by dragging them from the Toolbox panel or by typing the XAML manually.

1. Start by dragging a Button control from the Toolbox onto the Design View. Notice how the text in the XAML View is updated to reflect the change you made.

2. Now drag another Button, but this time drop it in the XAML View below the first Button, but above the </Grid> tag.

## How It Works

The result you see in the Design View might be somewhat surprising—the second button expands to fill the entire window. When you drop a control onto the Design View, Visual Studio will try to set properties and insert child elements to allow the controls to display themselves in a standard way. This does not happen when you drag controls into the XAML View, where only the tag that is used to define the control is inserted.

There are times when you want to position a control at a specific position on your window and it is difficult to drop it at exactly the right position. When this happens, you might want to drop the control directly in the XAML View or type it manually.

> **NOTE** *If you want the behavior of the Design View when you drop a control, but can't hit the right spot, just drop it anywhere and then cut and paste the XAML that was generated for you into the correct position.*

## Properties

As mentioned, all controls have a number of properties that are used to manipulate the behavior of the control. Some of these are easy to understand such as `height` and `width`, whereas others are less obvious such as `RenderTransform`. All of them can be set using the Properties panel, directly in XAML, or by manipulating the control on the Design View.

**TRY IT OUT**    Manipulating Properties: Ch15Ex01\MainWindow.xaml

Return to the previous example and follow these steps. As you change the properties, notice how your changes affect the XAML and Design Views. You are going to change the window to look like Figure 15-1.

1. Start by selecting the second `Button` control in Design View; this is the button that is currently filling the entire window.

2. You can change the name of the control in the Properties panel at the very top. Change it to `rotatedButton`.

3. Under the Common node, change the `Content` to `2nd Button`.

4. Under Layout, change width to 75 and height to 22.

5. Expand the Text node and change the text to bold by clicking the B icon.

6. Select the first button and drag it to a position above the second button. Visual Studio will assist with the positioning by snapping the control.

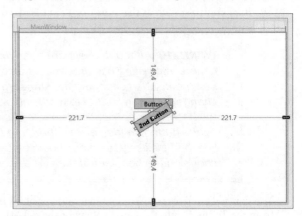

**FIGURE 15-1**

7. Select the second button again, and hover the mouse pointer over the top-left corner of it. The pointer changes to a quarter-circle with arrows on both ends. Drag down until the button is tilted down.

8. The XAML code for the window should now look like this:

```
<Window x:Class="Ch15Ex01.MainWindow"
        xmlns="http://schemas.microsoft.com/winfx/2006/xaml/presentation"
        xmlns:x="http://schemas.microsoft.com/winfx/2006/xaml"
        Title="MainWindow" Height="350" Width="525">
    <Grid>
        <Button Content="Button" HorizontalAlignment="Left" Margin="222,125,0,0"
VerticalAlignment="Top" Width="75"/>
        <Button x:Name="rotatedButton" Content="2nd Button" Width="75" Height="22"
```

```
      FontWeight="Bold" RenderTransformOrigin="0.5,0.5" >
          <Button.RenderTransform>
            <TransformGroup>
              <ScaleTransform/>
              <SkewTransform/>
              <RotateTransform Angle="-31.336"/>
              <TranslateTransform/>
            </TransformGroup>
          </Button.RenderTransform>
        </Button>
      </Grid>
    </Window>
```

**9.** Run the application by pressing F5. Try to resize the window. Notice that the second button moves with the window, whereas the first button stays fixed.

### How It Works

Any change that you apply in any of the three views is reflected in the other views, but some things are easier to do in certain views. Changing something trivial like the text displayed on a button can be done quickly in XAML View, but adding the information needed to perform a render transformation is much quicker from Design View.

In this exercise, you began by changing the name of the button, which added the x:Name property to the button. The name of a control must be unique within the scope of the namespace, so you can use the name for only one control.

Next you changed the Content property, set the Height and Width of the control, and then changed the font to bold. By doing so changed the way the control displayed itself within the window. It used to fill all the space of its container, but now you have limited it to a specific size.

Then you dragged the first button to a specific position on the Design View. As you see later in this chapter, this action will not always yield the same results but is dependent on the container in which the control is placed. In this case, with the Grid container, the control can be dragged to a specific position. The action sets the Margin property on the control. Two other properties should be mentioned here: HorizontalAlignment="Left" and VerticalAlignment="Top". With these two properties set, the margin becomes relative to the top-left corner of the window and thus the control is pushed to the position you placed it in the grid. If you compare the first and second buttons at this point, you will notice that the second control has none of these properties set. By omitting the alignment properties as well as the margin properties, the control is placed at the center of the container, even at runtime. This means that the first button with the margin and alignments set is fixed when the window resizes, but the second button always stays centered.

Finally, you performed a little bit of a party trick. By dragging the control when the Rotate mouse pointer is displayed, you can rotate the control. This is a standard feature of XAML and WPF and can be applied to all controls, although there are a few controls that fail to change their content when the control itself is rotated. This includes controls that rely on Windows Forms or old Windows controls to display content.

The transformations that you can do in WPF are covered in Chapter 16, but from the XML that was generated when you dragged the cursor, you can see that you can perform some advanced animation simply by manipulating these properties.

## Dependency Properties

For the most part, normal .NET properties are simple getters and setters, which is fine for most cases. However, when you are working with a dynamic user interface that can and should change when properties change, you have to write a lot of code in these get and set methods that will be repeated many times. A *dependency property* is a property that is registered with the WPF property system in such a way as to allow extended functionality. This extended functionality includes, but is not limited to, automatic property change notifications. Specifically, dependency properties have the following features:

➤ You can use styles to change the values of dependency properties.

➤ You can set the value of a dependency property by using resources or by data binding.

➤ You can change dependency property values in an animation.

➤ You can set dependency properties hierarchically in XAML—that is, a value for a dependency property that you set on a parent element can be used to set the default value for the same dependency property of its child elements.

➤ You can configure notifications for property value changes using a well-defined coding pattern.

➤ You can configure sets of related properties so that they all update in response to a change to one of them. This is known as *coercion*. The changed property is said to *coerce* the values of the other properties.

➤ You can apply metadata to a dependency property to specify other behavior characteristics. For example, you might specify that if a given property changes, then it might be necessary to rearrange the user interface.

In practice, because of the way in which dependency properties are implemented, you might not notice much of a difference compared to ordinary properties. However, when you create your own controls, you will quickly find that a lot of functionality suddenly disappears when you use ordinary .NET properties.

Chapter 16 shows how you can implement new dependency properties.

### Attached Properties

An *attached property* is a property that is made available to each child object of an instance of the class that defines the property. For example, as you will see later in this chapter, the Grid control that you used in the previous examples allows you to define columns and rows for ordering the child controls of the Grid. Each child control can then use the attached properties Column and Row to specify where it belongs in the grid:

```
<Grid HorizontalAlignment="Left" Height="167" VerticalAlignment="Top" Width="290">

   <Button Content="Button" HorizontalAlignment="Left" Margin="10,10,0,0"
VerticalAlignment="Top" Width="75" Grid.Column="0" Grid.Row="0"
Height="22" />
   ...
   </Grid>
```

Here, the attached property is referred to using the name of the parent element, a period, and the name of the attached property.

In WPF, attached properties serve a variety of uses. You will see a lot of attached properties shortly, when you look at how to position controls in the "Control Layout" section. You will learn how container controls define attached properties that enable child controls to define, for example, which edges of the container to dock to.

## Events

In Chapter 13, you learned what events are and how to use them. This section covers particular kinds of events—specifically, the events generated by WPF controls—and introduces *routed events,* which are usually associated with user actions. For example, when the user clicks a button, that button generates an event indicating what just happened to it. Handling the event is the means by which the programmer can provide some functionality for that button.

Many of the events you handle are common to most of the controls that you work with in this book. This includes events such as LostFocus and MouseEnter. This is because the events themselves are inherited from base classes such as Control or ContentControl. Other events such as the CalendarOpened event of the DatePicker are more specific and only found on specialized controls. Some of the most used events are listed in Table 15-1.

**TABLE 15-1:** Common Control Events

| EVENT | DESCRIPTION |
| --- | --- |
| Click | Occurs when a control is clicked. In some cases, this event also occurs when a user presses the Enter key. |
| Drop | Occurs when a drag-and-drop operation is completed—in other words, when an object has been dragged over the control, and the user releases the mouse button. |
| DragEnter | Occurs when an object being dragged enters the bounds of the control. |
| DragLeave | Occurs when an object being dragged leaves the bounds of the control. |
| DragOver | Occurs when an object has been dragged over the control. |
| KeyDown | Occurs when a key is pressed while the control has focus. This event always occurs before KeyPress and KeyUp. |
| KeyUp | Occurs when a key is released while a control has focus. This event always occurs after KeyDown event. |
| GotFocus | Occurs when a control receives focus. Do not use this event to perform validation of controls. Use Validating and Validated instead. |
| LostFocus | Occurs when a control loses focus. Do not use this event to perform validation of controls. Use Validating and Validated instead. |
| MouseDoubleClick | Occurs when a control is double-clicked. |
| MouseDown | Occurs when the mouse pointer is over a control and a mouse button is pressed. This is not the same as a Click event because MouseDown occurs as soon as the button is pressed and *before* it is released. |
| MouseMove | Occurs continually as the mouse travels over the control. |
| MouseUp | Occurs when the mouse pointer is over a control and a mouse button is released. |

You will see many of these events in the examples in this chapter.

## Handling Events

There are two basic ways to add a handler for an event. One way is to use the Events list in the Properties window, shown in Figure 15-2, which is displayed when you click the lightning bolt button.

To add a handler for a particular event, either type the name of the event and press Return, or double-click to the right of the event name in the Events list. This causes the event to be added to the XAML tag. The method signature to handle the event is added to the C# code-behind file.

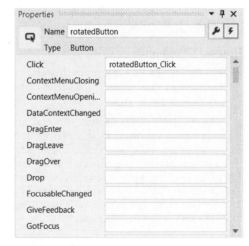

**FIGURE 15-2**

```
        <Button x:Name="rotatedButton" Content="2nd Button" Width="75" Height="22"
FontWeight="Bold" RenderTransformOrigin="0.5,0.5"
Click="rotatedButton_Click" >
        <Button.RenderTransform>
          <TransformGroup>
            <ScaleTransform/>
            <SkewTransform/>
            <RotateTransform Angle="-31.336"/>
            <TranslateTransform/>
          </TransformGroup>
        </Button.RenderTransform>
      </Button>
private void rotatedButton_Click(object sender, RoutedEventArgs e)
    {

    }
```

You can also type the name of the event directly in XAML and add the name of the handler there. If you do this, you can right-click on the event and chose Navigate to Event Handler. This will add the event handler to the code-behind file.

## Routed Events

WPF uses events that are called *routed events*. A standard .NET event is handled by the code that has explicitly subscribed to it and it is sent only to those subscribers. Routed events are different in that they can send the event to all controls in the hierarchy in which the control participates.

A routed event can travel up and down the hierarchy of the control on which the event occurred. So, if you right-click a button, the MouseRightButtonDown event will first be sent to the button itself, then to the parent of the control—in the case of the earlier example, the Grid control. If this doesn't handle it, then the event is finally sent to the window. If, on the other hand you don't want the event to travel further up the hierarchy, then you simply set the RoutedEventArgs property Handled to true, and no additional calls will be made at that point. When an event travels up the control hierarchy like this, it is called a *bobbling event*.

Routed events can also travel in the other direction, that is, from the root element to the control on which the action was performed. This is called a *tunneling event* and by convention all events like this are prefixed with the word Preview and always occur before their bobbling counterparts. An example of this is the PreviewMouseRightButtonDown event.

Finally, a routed event can behave exactly like a normal .NET event and only be sent to the control on which the action was made.

## Routed Commands

Routed commands serve much the same purpose as events in that they cause some code to execute. Where Events are bound directly to a single element in the XAML and a handler in the code, Routed Commands are more sophisticated.

The key difference between events and commands is in their use. An event should be used whenever you have a piece of code that has to respond to a user action that happens in only one place in your application. An example of such an event could be when the user clicks OK in a window to save and close it. A command can be used when you have code that will be executed to respond to actions that happen in many locations. An example of this is when the content of an application is saved. There is often a menu with a Save command that can be selected, as well as a toolbar button for the same purpose. It is possible to use event handlers to do this, but it would mean implementing the same code in many locations—a command allows you to write the code just once.

When you create a command, you must also implement code that can respond to the question, "Should this code be available to the user at the moment?" This means that when a command is associated with a button, that button can ask the command if it can execute and set its state accordingly.

A command is much more complicated to implement than an event, so you are not going to see them in use until Chapter 16, where they will be used with menu items.

**TRY IT OUT** Routed Events: Ch15Ex01\MainWindow.xaml

This example builds on the example from earlier in the chapter. If you added the rows and columns earlier, you should remove them to match the XAML in this example.

1. Select the button `rotatedButton` and add the event `KeyDown`. You can do this through the Properties panel or by typing the XAML directly. Name it `rotatedButton_KeyDown`.

2. Select the `Grid` by clicking on the tag it in the XAML View, and add the same event to it. Name it `Grid_KeyDown`.

3. Select the `Window` tag in the XAML View and add the event again. Name it `Window_KeyDown`.

4. Repeat Steps 1 through 3, but replace the event with `PreviewKeyDown` and change the name of the event to reflect that it is the `Preview` handler. The XAML should look like this:

```xml
<Window x:Class="Ch15Ex01.MainWindow"
        xmlns="http://schemas.microsoft.com/winfx/2006/xaml/presentation"
        xmlns:x="http://schemas.microsoft.com/winfx/2006/xaml"
        Title="MainWindow" Height="350" Width="525" KeyDown="Window_KeyDown"
  PreviewKeyDown="Window_ Window_PreviewKeyDown">
    <Grid KeyDown="Grid_KeyDown" PreviewKeyDown="Grid_PreviewKeyDown">
        <Button Content="Button" HorizontalAlignment="Left" Margin="222,125,0,0"
VerticalAlignment="Top" Width="75"/>
        <Button x:Name="rotatedButton" Content="2nd Button" Width="75" Height="22"
FontWeight="Bold" RenderTransformOrigin="0.5,0.5" Click"
KeyDown="rotatedButton_KeyDown"
PreviewKeyDown="rotatedButton_PreviewKeyDown" >
            <Button.RenderTransform>
              <TransformGroup>
                <ScaleTransform/>
                <SkewTransform/>
                <RotateTransform Angle="-31.336"/>
                <TranslateTransform/>
              </TransformGroup>
            </Button.RenderTransform>
        </Button>
    </Grid>
</Window>
```

5. If you typed the XAML directly, right-click each of the events and add the event handler to the code-behind by selecting the Navigate to Event Handler menu item.

6. Add this code to the event handlers:

```csharp
private void Grid_KeyDown(object sender, KeyEventArgs e)
{
  MessageBox.Show("Grid handler, bubbling up");
}

private void Grid_PreviewKeyDown(object sender, KeyEventArgs e)
{
  MessageBox.Show("Grid handler, tunneling down");
}

private void rotatedButton_KeyDown(object sender, KeyEventArgs e)
{
  MessageBox.Show("rotatedButton handler, bubbling up");
}

private void rotatedButton_PreviewKeyDown(object sender, KeyEventArgs e)
```

```
    {
      MessageBox.Show("rotatedButton handler, tunneling down");
    }

    private void Window_KeyDown(object sender, KeyEventArgs e)
    {
      MessageBox.Show("Window handler, bubbling up");
    }

    private void Window_PreviewKeyDown(object sender, KeyEventArgs e)
    {
      MessageBox.Show("Window handler, tunneling down");
    }
```

7.  Run the application by pressing F5.

8.  Select the rotated button by clicking it and pressing any key except Return, Tab, Escape, the spacebar, or the arrow keys. Observe the events being executed in turn.

9.  Stop the application.

10. Go to the `Grid_PreviewKeyDown` event handler and add this line below the `MessageBox` line:

    ```
    e.Handled = true;
    ```

11. Repeat Steps 7 and 8.

### How It Works

The `KeyDown` and `PreviewKeyDown` events demonstrate bubbling and tunneling events. When you press a key with `rotatedButton` selected, you see each of the event handlers executing, one after another.

First the `Preview` events execute, starting with the handler on `Window`, then the `Grid`, and finally the `rotatedButton`. Then the `KeyDown` events execute, but in the opposite order, starting with the event handler on the `rotatedButton` and finishing with the handler on `Window`.

If you use any of the keys explicitly stated not to use in Step 8, you will notice that the `Preview` event is fired only on `Window`. This is because these are not considered input keys and are ignored by the grid and buttons.

Then you added this line:

```
    e.Handled = true;
```

This changed the behavior dramatically. By setting the `Handled` property of the `RoutedEventArgs` you not only caused the execution of the tunneling events, but also of the bubbling events. This is generally true for all events like this. If you stop the execution of either the `Preview` or the "normal" version of the event handlers, you stop them both.

## Control Types

As stated, WPF has a lot of controls to choose from. Two types of interest are the Content and Items controls. Content controls, such as the `Button` control, have a `Content` property that can be set to any other control. This means that you can determine how the control is displayed, but you can specify only a single control directly in the content. That being said, you can specify an Items control, which is a control that allows you to insert multiple controls as content. An example of an Items control is the `Grid` control. When you are creating user interfaces, you are continually combining these two control types.

In addition to Content and Items controls, there are a number of other types of controls that don't allow you to use other controls as their content. One example of this is the `Image` control, which is used to display an image. Changing that behavior defeats the purpose of the control.

## CONTROL LAYOUT

So far in this chapter you have used the `Grid` element to lay out a few controls, primarily because that is the control supplied by default when you create a new WPF application. However, you haven't yet examined the full capabilities of this class, nor have you learned about the other layout containers that you can use to achieve alternative layouts. This section looks at control layout in more detail, as it is a fundamental concept of WPF.

All content layout controls derive from the abstract `Panel` class. This class simply defines a container that can contain a collection of objects that derive from `UIElement`. All WPF controls derive from `UIElement`. You cannot use the `Panel` class directly for control layout, but you can derive from it if you want to. Alternatively, you can use one of the following layout controls that derive from `Panel`:

➤ `Canvas`—This control enables you to position child controls any way you see fit. It doesn't place any restrictions on child control positioning, but nor does it provide any assistance in positioning.

➤ `DockPanel`—This control enables you to dock child controls against one of its four edges. The last child control fills the remaining space.

➤ `Grid`—This control enables flexible positioning of child controls. You can divide the layout of this control into rows and columns, which enables you to align controls in a grid layout.

➤ `StackPanel`—This control positions its child controls in a sequential horizontal or vertical layout.

➤ `WrapPanel`—This control positions its child controls in a sequential horizontal or vertical layout as `StackPanel`, but rather than a single row or column of controls, this control wraps its children into multiple rows or columns according to the space available.

You'll look at how to use these controls in more detail shortly. First, however, there are a few basic concepts to understand:

➤ How controls appear in stack order

➤ How to use alignment, margins, and padding to position controls and their content

➤ How to use the `Border` control

## Stack Order

When a container control contains multiple child controls, they are drawn in a specific stack order. You might be familiar with this concept from drawing packages. The best way to think of stack order is to imagine that each control is contained in a plate of glass, and the container contains a stack of these plates of glass. The appearance of the container, therefore, is what you would see if you looked down from the top through these layers of glass. The controls contained by the container overlap, so what you see is determined by the order of the glass plates. If a control is higher up the stack, then it will be the control that you see in the overlap area. Controls lower down may be partially or completely hidden by controls above them.

This also affects hit testing when you click on a window with the mouse. The target control will always be the one that is uppermost in the stack when considering overlapping controls. The stack order of controls is determined by the order in which they appear in the list of children for a container. The first child in a container is placed on the lowest layer in the stack, and the last child on the topmost layer. The children between the first and last child are placed on increasingly higher layers. The stack order of controls has additional implications for some of the layout controls that you can use in WPF, as you will see shortly.

## Alignment, Margins, Padding, and Dimensions

Earlier examples used the `Margin`, `HorizontalAlignment`, and `VerticalAlignment` properties to position controls in a `Grid` container, but without going into much detail about their use. You have also seen how you can use `Height` and `Width` to specify dimensions. These properties, along with `Padding`, which you haven't looked at yet, are useful for all of the layout controls (or most of them, as you will see), but in different ways. Different layout controls can also set default values for these properties. You'll see a lot of this by example in subsequent sections, but before doing that, it is worth covering the basics.

The two alignment properties, `HorizontalAlignment` and `VerticalAlignment`, determine how the control is aligned. `HorizontalAlignment` can be set to `Left`, `Right`, `Center`, or `Stretch`. `Left` and `Right` tend to position controls to the left or right edges of the container, `Center` positions controls in the middle, and `Stretch` changes the width of the control so that its edges reach to the sides of the container. `VerticalAlignment` is similar, and has the values `Top`, `Bottom`, `Center`, or `Stretch`.

`Margin` and `Padding` specify the space to leave blank around the edges of controls and inside the edges of controls, respectively. Earlier examples used `Margin` to position controls relative to the edges of a window. This worked because with `HorizontalAlignment` set to `Left` and `VerticalAlignment` set to `Top`, the control is positioned tight against the top-left corner, and `Margin` inserted a gap around the edge of the control. `Padding` is used similarly, but spaces out the content of a control from its edges. This is particularly useful for `Border`, as you will see in the next section. Both `Padding` and `Margin` can be specified in four parts (in the form `leftAmount, topAmount, rightAmount, bottomAmount`) or as a single value (a `Thickness` value).

Later, you will see how `Height` and `Width` are often controlled by other properties. For example, with `HorizontalAlignment` set to `Stretch`, the `Width` property of a control changes as the width of its container changes.

## Border

The `Border` control is a very simple, and very useful, container control. It holds a single child, not multiple children like the more complicated controls you'll look at in a moment. This child will be sized to completely fill the `Border` control. This might not seem particularly useful, but remember that you can use the `Margin` and `Padding` properties to position the `Border` within its container, and the content of the `Border` within the edges of the `Border`. You can also set, for example, the `Background` property of a `Border` so that it is visible. You will see this control in action shortly.

## Canvas

The `Canvas` control, as previously noted, provides complete freedom over control positioning. Another thing about `Canvas` is that the `HorizontalAligment` and `VerticalAlignment` properties used with a child element will have no effect whatsoever over the positioning of those elements.

You can use `Margin` to position elements in a `Canvas` as it was done in earlier examples, but a better way is to use the `Canvas.Left`, `Canvas.Top`, `Canvas.Right`, and `Canvas.Bottom` attached properties that the `Canvas` class exposes:

```
<Canvas...>
  <Button Canvas.Top="10" Canvas.Left="10"...>Button1</Button>
</Canvas>
```

The preceding code positions a `Button` so that its top edge is 10 pixels from the top edge of the `Canvas`, and its left edge is 10 pixels from the left edge of the `Canvas`. Note that the `Top` and `Left` properties take precedence over `Bottom` and `Right`. For example, if you specify both `Top` and `Bottom`, then the `Bottom` property is ignored.

Figure 15-3 shows two `Rectangle` controls positioned in a `Canvas` control, with the window resized to two sizes.

> **NOTE** All of the example layouts in this section can be found in the LayoutExamples project in the downloadable code for this chapter. See the "Wrox.com Code Downloads for this Chapter" section at the beginning of this chapter for information on how to download this chapter's code.

One `Rectangle` is positioned relative to the
top-left corner, and one is positioned relative to
the bottom-right corner. As you resize the window,
these relative positions are maintained. You can
also see the importance of the stacking order of the
`Rectangle` controls. The bottom-right `Rectangle`
is higher up in the stacking order, so when they
overlap this is the control that you see.

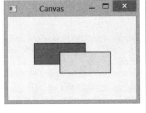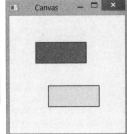

The code for this example is as follows (you can
find it in the downloaded code at `LayoutExamples\`
`Canvas.xaml`):

**FIGURE 15-3**

```xml
<Window x:Class="LayoutExamples.Canvas"
        xmlns="http://schemas.microsoft.com/winfx/2006/xaml/presentation"
        xmlns:x="http://schemas.microsoft.com/winfx/2006/xaml"
        Title="Canvas" Height="189.258" Width="264.751">
  <Canvas Background="AliceBlue">
    <Rectangle Canvas.Left="50" Canvas.Top="50" Height="40" Width="100"
    Stroke="Black" Fill="Chocolate" />
    <Rectangle Canvas.Right="50" Canvas.Bottom="50" Height="40" Width="100"
    Stroke="Black" Fill="Bisque" />
  </Canvas>
</Window>
```

## DockPanel

The `DockPanel` control, as its name suggests, enables you to dock controls to one of its edges. This sort of
layout should be familiar to you, even if you've never stopped to notice it before. It is how, for example, the
`Ribbon` control in Word remains at the top of the Word window, or how the various windows in VS are
positioned. In VS you can also change the docking of windows by dragging them around.

`DockPanel` has a single attached property that child controls can use to specify the edge to which controls
dock: `DockPanel.Dock`. You can set this property to `Left`, `Top`, `Right`, or `Bottom`.

The stack order of controls in a `DockPanel` is extremely important, as every time you dock a control to an
edge you also reduce the available space of subsequent child controls. For example, you might dock a toolbar
to the top of a `DockPanel` and then a second toolbar to the left of the `DockPanel`. The first control would
stretch across the entire top of the `DockPanel` display area, but the second control would only stretch from
the bottom of the first toolbar to the bottom of the `DockPanel` along the left edge.

The last child control you specify will (usually) fill the area that remains after all the previous children have
been positioned. (You can control this behavior, which is why this statement is qualified.)

When you position a control in a `DockPanel`, the area occupied by the control might be smaller than the area
of the `DockPanel` that is reserved for the control.
For example, if you dock a `Button` with a `Width` of
100, a `Height` of 50, and a `HorizontalAlingment`
of `Left` to the top of a `DockPanel`, then there will
be space to the right of the `Button` that isn't used
by other docked children. In addition, if the `Button`
control has a `Margin` of 20, then a total of 90
pixels at the top of the `DockPanel` will be reserved
(the height of the control plus the top and bottom
margins). You need to take this behavior into account
when you use `DockPanel` for layout; otherwise, you
can end up with unexpected results.

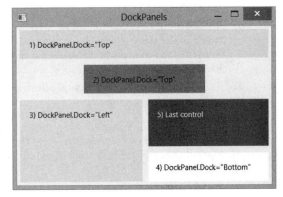

Figure 15-4 shows a sample `DockPanel` layout.

**FIGURE 15-4**

The code for this layout is as follows (you can find it in the downloadable code at `LayoutExamples\DockPanel.xaml`):

```xml
<Window x:Class="LayoutExamples.DockPanels"
        xmlns="http://schemas.microsoft.com/winfx/2006/xaml/presentation"
        xmlns:x="http://schemas.microsoft.com/winfx/2006/xaml"
        Title="DockPanels" Height="300" Width="300">
  <DockPanel Background="AliceBlue">
    <Border DockPanel.Dock="Top" Padding="10" Margin="5"
    Background="Aquamarine" Height="45">
      <Label>1) DockPanel.Dock="Top"</Label>
    </Border>
    <Border DockPanel.Dock="Top" Padding="10" Margin="5"
    Background="PaleVioletRed" Height="45" Width="200">
      <Label>2) DockPanel.Dock="Top"</Label>
    </Border>
    <Border DockPanel.Dock="Left" Padding="10" Margin="5"
    Background="Bisque" Width="200">
      <Label>3) DockPanel.Dock="Left"</Label>
    </Border>

    <Border DockPanel.Dock="Bottom" Padding="10" Margin="5"
    Background="Ivory" Width="200" HorizontalAlignment="Right">
      <Label>4) DockPanel.Dock="Bottom"</Label>
    </Border>
    <Border Padding="10" Margin="5" Background="BlueViolet">
      <Label Foreground="White">5) Last control</Label>
    </Border>
  </DockPanel>
</Window>
```

This code uses the `Border` control introduced earlier to clearly mark out the docked control regions in the example layout, along with `Label` controls to output simple informative text. To understand the layout, you must read it from top to bottom, looking at each control in turn:

1. The first `Border` control is docked to the top of the `DockPanel`. The total area taken up in the `DockPanel` is the top 55 pixels (Height + 2 × Margin). Note that the `Padding` property does not affect this layout, as it is inside the edge of the `Border`, but this property does control the positioning of the embedded `Label` control. The `Border` control fills any available space along the edge it is docked to if not constrained by `Height` or `Width` properties, which is why it stretches across the `DockPanel`.

2. The second `Border` control is also docked to the top of the `DockPanel`, and takes up another 55 pixels from the top of the display area. This `Border` control also includes a `Width` property, which causes the border to take up only a portion of the width of the `DockPanel`. It is positioned centrally, as the default value for `HorizonalAlignment` in a `DockPanel` is `Center`.

3. The third `Border` control is docked to the left of the `DockPanel` and takes up 210 pixels of the left of the display.

4. The fourth `Border` control is docked to the bottom of the `DockPanel` and takes up 30 pixels plus the height of the `Label` control it contains (whatever that is). This height is determined by the `Margin`, `Padding`, and contents of the `Border` control, as it is not specified explicitly. The `Border` control is locked to the bottom-right corner of the `DockPanel`, as it has a `HorizontalAlignment` of `Right`.

5. The fifth and final `Border` control fills the remaining space.

Run this example and experiment with resizing content. Note that the further up the stacking order a control is, the more priority is given to its space. By shrinking the window, the fifth `Border` control can be completely obscured by controls further up the stacking order. Be careful when using `DockPanel` control layout to avoid this, perhaps by setting minimum dimensions for the window.

## StackPanel

You can think of StackPanel as being a slimmed down version of DockPanel, where the edge to which child controls are docked is fixed for those controls. The other difference between these controls is that the last child control of a StackPanel doesn't fill the remaining space. However, controls will, by default, stretch to the edges of the StackPanel control.

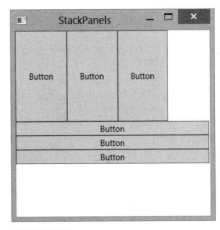

The direction in which controls are stacked is determined by three properties. Orientation can be set to Horizontal or Vertical, and HorizontalAlignment and VerticalAlignment can be used to determine whether control stacks are positioned next to the top, bottom, left, or right edge of the StackPanel. You can even make the stacked controls stack at the center of the StackPanel using the Center value for the alignment property you use.

**FIGURE 15-5**

Figure 15-5 shows two StackPanel controls, each of which contains three buttons. The top StackPanel has its Orientation property set to Horizontal and the bottom one has Orientation set to Vertical.

The code used here is as follows (you can find it in the downloaded code at LayoutExamples\StackPanels.xaml):

```xml
<Window x:Class="LayoutExamples.StackPanels"
        xmlns="http://schemas.microsoft.com/winfx/2006/xaml/presentation"
        xmlns:x="http://schemas.microsoft.com/winfx/2006/xaml"
        Title="StackPanels" Height="300" Width="300">
  <Grid>
    <StackPanel HorizontalAlignment="Left" Height="128" VerticalAlignment="Top"
Width="284" Orientation="Horizontal">
      <Button Content="Button" Height="128" VerticalAlignment="Top" Width="75"/>
      <Button Content="Button" Height="128" VerticalAlignment="Top" Width="75"/>
      <Button Content="Button" Height="128" VerticalAlignment="Top" Width="75"/>
    </StackPanel>
    <StackPanel HorizontalAlignment="Left" Height="128" VerticalAlignment="Top"
Width="284" Margin="0,128,0,0" Orientation="Vertical">
      <Button Content="Button" HorizontalAlignment="Left" Width="284"/>
      <Button Content="Button" HorizontalAlignment="Left" Width="284"/>
      <Button Content="Button" HorizontalAlignment="Left" Width="284"/>
    </StackPanel>
  </Grid>
</Window>
```

When you use the StackPanel layout, you often need to add scrollbars so that it is possible to view all the controls contained in the StackPanel. This is another area where WPF does a lot of the heavy lifting for you. You can use the ScrollViewer control to achieve this—simply enclose the StackPanel in this control:

```xml
<Grid Background="AliceBlue">
  <Grid.RowDefinitions>
    <RowDefinition />
    <RowDefinition />
  </Grid.RowDefinitions>
  <ScrollViewer>
    <StackPanel Grid.Row="0">
      <Button>Button1</Button>
      <Button>Button2</Button>
      <Button>Button3</Button>
    </StackPanel>
  </ScrollViewer>
```

```
  <StackPanel Grid.Row="1" Orientation="Horizontal">
    <Button>Button1</Button>
    <Button>Button2</Button>
    <Button>Button3</Button>
  </StackPanel>
</Grid>
```

You can use more complicated techniques to scroll in different ways, or to scroll programmatically, but often this is all you need to do.

### WrapPanel

WrapPanel is essentially an extended version of StackPanel; controls that "don't fit" are moved to additional rows (or columns). Figure 15-6 shows a WrapPanel control containing multiple shapes, with the window resized to two sizes.

The code to achieve this effect is shown here (you can find it in the downloaded code at LayoutExamples\WrapPanel.xaml):

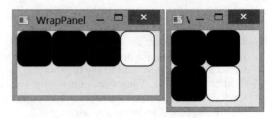

**FIGURE 15-6**

```
<Window x:Class="LayoutExamples.WrapPanel"
        xmlns="http://schemas.microsoft.com/winfx/2006/xaml/presentation"
        xmlns:x="http://schemas.microsoft.com/winfx/2006/xaml"
        Title="WrapPanel" Height="300" Width="300">
  <WrapPanel Background="AliceBlue">
    <Rectangle Fill="#FF000000" Height="50" Width="50" Stroke="Black"
    RadiusX="10" RadiusY="10", />
    <Rectangle Fill="#FF111111" Height="50" Width="50" Stroke="Black"
    RadiusX="10" RadiusY="10" />
    <Rectangle Fill="#FF222222" Height="50" Width="50" Stroke="Black"
    RadiusX="10" RadiusY="10" />
    <Rectangle Fill="#FFFFFFFF" Height="50" Width="50" Stroke="Black"
    RadiusX="10" RadiusY="10" />
  </WrapPanel>
</Window>
```

WrapPanel controls are a great way to create a dynamic layout that enables users to control exactly how content should be viewed.

## Grid

Grid controls can have multiple rows and columns that you can use to lay out child controls. You have used Grid controls several times already in this chapter, but in all cases you used a Grid with a single row and a single column. To add more rows and columns, you must use the RowDefinitions and ColumnDefinitions properties, which are collections of RowDefinition and ColumnDefinition objects, respectively, and are specified using property element syntax:

```
<Grid>
  <Grid.RowDefinitions>
    <RowDefinition />
    <RowDefinition />
  </Grid.RowDefinitions>
  <Grid.ColumnDefinitions>
    <ColumnDefinition />
    <ColumnDefinition />
  </Grid.ColumnDefinitions>

  ...
</Grid>
```

This code defines a `Grid` control with two rows and two columns. Note that no extra information is required here; with this code, each row and column is dynamically resized automatically as the `Grid` control resizes. Each row will be a third of the height of the `Grid`, and each column will be half the width. You can display lines between cells in a `Grid` by setting the `Grid.ShowGridlines` property to `true`.

> **NOTE** *You can also define rows and columns in the grid by clicking the edges of the grid in the Design View. If you move the mouse pointer to the edge of the grid, a yellow line is drawn across the Design View; if you click the edge, the necessary XAML is inserted. When you do this, the* Width *and* Height *properties of the rows and columns are always set by the designer, but you can delete them or drag the lines to suit your needs.*

You can control the resizing with the `Width`, `Height`, `MinWidth`, `MaxWidth`, `MinHeight`, and `MaxHeight` properties. For example, setting the `Width` property of a column ensures that the column stays at that width. You can also set the `Width` property of a column to `*`, which means "fill the remaining space after calculating the width of all other columns." This is actually the default. When you have multiple columns with a `Width` of `*`, then the remaining space is divided between them equally. The `*` value can also be used with the `Height` property of rows. The other possible value for `Height` and `Width` is `Auto`, which sizes the row or column according to its content. You can also use `GridSplitter` controls to enable users to customize the dimensions of rows and columns by clicking and dragging.

Child controls of a `Grid` control can use the attached `Grid.Column` and `Grid.Row` properties to specify which cell they are contained in. Both these properties default to `0`, so if you omit them, then the child control is placed in the top-left cell. Child controls can also use `Grid.ColumnSpan` and `Grid.RowSpan` to be positioned over multiple cells in a table, where the upper-left cell is specified by `Grid.Column` and `Grid.Row`.

**TRY IT OUT** Using Rows and Columns: Ch15Ex01\MainWindow.xaml

Return to the example from the beginning of the chapter with the two buttons and follow these steps.

1. Select the `Grid` control by clicking in the XAML View.
2. Move the mouse pointer to the top edge of the grid in Design View; you'll see an orange line appear across the surface of the grid. Allow room for a button and click to create two columns.
3. Repeat Step 2 on the left edge of the window, creating two rows.
4. Select the first of the two buttons. Note that the action of adding the rows and columns automatically added the `Grid.Row` and `Grid.Column` properties to the button. Change the `Grid.Row` and `Grid.Column` attached properties to `0`.
5. Adjust the `Margin` property to make the button fully visible in the cell.
6. The second button has also been adjusted. For example, a Margin has been added. Now delete the `Margin` property from the second button.
7. Add a `GridSplitter` control to the XAML View just before the closing tag of the `Grid` control and set its properties like this:

```
<GridSplitter Grid.RowSpan="2" Width="3" BorderThickness="2" BorderBrush="Black" />
```

8. Run the application. The complete XAML should look like this:

```
<Window x:Class="Ch15Ex01.MainWindow"
        xmlns="http://schemas.microsoft.com/winfx/2006/xaml/presentation"
        xmlns:x="http://schemas.microsoft.com/winfx/2006/xaml"
        Title="MainWindow" Height="219.025" Width="440.802" KeyDown="Window_KeyDown"
PreviewKeyDown="Window_PreviewKeyDown">
```

```
<Grid KeyDown="Grid_KeyDown" PreviewKeyDown="Grid_PreviewKeyDown">
  <Grid.RowDefinitions>
    <RowDefinition Height="52"/>
    <RowDefinition Height="92*"/>
  </Grid.RowDefinitions>
  <Grid.ColumnDefinitions>
    <ColumnDefinition Width="105"/>
    <ColumnDefinition Width="405*"/>
  </Grid.ColumnDefinitions>
  <Button Content="Button" HorizontalAlignment="Left" Margin="15,15,0,0"
VerticalAlignment="Top" Width="75" Grid.Column="0" Grid.Row="0"/>
  <Button x:Name="rotatedButton" Content="2nd Button" Width="75" Height="22"
FontWeight="Bold" RenderTransformOrigin="0.5,0.5" KeyDown="rotatedButton_KeyDown"
PreviewKeyDown="rotatedButton_PreviewKeyDown" Grid.Column="1" Grid.Row="1" >
    <Button.RenderTransform>
      <TransformGroup>
        <ScaleTransform/>
        <SkewTransform/>
        <RotateTransform Angle="-31.336"/>
        <TranslateTransform/>
      </TransformGroup>
    </Button.RenderTransform>
  </Button>
  <GridSplitter Grid.RowSpan="2" Width="3" BorderThickness="2" BorderBrush="Black" />
</Grid>
</Window>
```

Figure 15-7 shows the application running with the splitter pushed to two positions.

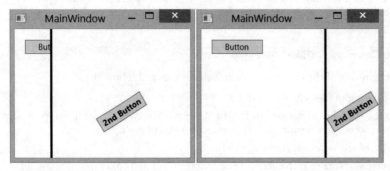

**FIGURE 15-7**

### How It Works

By dividing the grid into two columns and two rows, you have changed how the controls can be positioned in the grid. When you set the Grid.Row and Grid.Column to 0 for the first button, you move it from its previous position on the form to the top-left section.

The second button more or less stays put, but when you drag the GridSplitter slider, you see that the margin of the button is now relative to the left edge of the column in which it is placed, meaning that it slides across the window as you move the slider.

# THE GAME CLIENT

Now that you know the basics of what it means to work with WPF and Visual Studio, it is time to start working with the controls to create something useful. The remaining sections of this chapter and Chapter 16 are dedicated to writing a game client for the card game you have been developing over the previous chapters. You are going to use a lot of controls to write the game client, and you are even going to write one yourself.

In this chapter you are going to write the supporting dialog boxes of the game—this includes the About, Options, and New Game windows.

## The About Window

An About window, or About box as it's sometimes called, is used to display information about the developer of the application and the application itself. Some About windows are quite complex, like the one found in Microsoft Office applications and Visual Studio, and display version and licensing information. By convention, the About window can be accessed from the Help menu where it is usually the last item on the list.

Figure 15-8 shows a screenshot of the finished dialog box that you are about to create.

### Designing the User Interface

An About window is not something that the user is going to see very often. In fact, the reason that it is usually located on the Help menu is that it is very often only used when the user needs to find information about the version of the application or who to contact when something is wrong. But this also means that it is something the user has a specific purpose for visiting and if you include such a window in your application, you should treat it as important.

**FIGURE 15-8**

Whenever you are designing an application, you should strive to keep the look and feel as consistent as possible. This means that you should stick to a few select colors and use the same styling of controls everywhere in the application. In the case of Karli Cards, you are going to work with three main colors—red, black, and white.

If you look at Figure 15-8 you will see that the top-left corner of the window is occupied by a Wrox Press logo. You have not used images before, but adding a few select images to your applications can make the user interface look more professional.

### The Image Control

Image is a very simple control that can be used to great effect. It allows you to display a single image and to resize this image as you see fit. The control exposes two properties, as shown in Table 15-2:

**TABLE 15-2:** Image Control

| PROPERTY | DESCRIPTION |
|---|---|
| Source | Use this property to specify the location of the image. This can be a location on disk or somewhere on the web. As you will see in Chapter 16, it is also possible to create a static resource and use it as the source. |
| Stretch | It's actually pretty rare to have an image that is exactly the right size for your purpose, and sometimes the size of the image must change as the application window is resized. You can use this property to control how the image behaves. There are four possibilities:<br><br>None — The image doesn't resize.<br><br>Fill — The image resizes to fill the entire space. This may contort the image.<br><br>Uniform — The image keeps its aspect ratio and doesn't fill the available space if this would change the aspect ratio.<br><br>UniformToFill — The image keeps its aspect ratio and fills the available space. If the keeping the ratio means that some of the image is too large for the space available, the image is clipped to fit. |

## The Label Control

You have already seen this most simple of controls used in some of the previous examples. It displays simple text information to the user and in some cases relays information about shortcut keys. The control uses the Content property to display its text. The Label control displays text on a single line. If you prefix a letter with an underscore "_" character, the letter will become underlined and it will then be possible to access the control directly by using the prefixed letter and Alt. For example, _Name assigns the shortcut Alt+N to any control directly following the label.

## The TextBlock Control

Like Label, this control displays simple text without any complicated formatting. Unlike the Label, the TextBlock control is capable of displaying multiple lines of text. It is not possible to format individual parts of the text.

The TextBlock displays the text even if it will not fit in the space granted to the control. The control itself does not provide any scrollbars in this case, but it can be wrapped in a handy view control when needed: the ScrollViewer.

## The Button Control

Like the Label control, you have already seen quite a bit of the Button control. This control is used everywhere and is easily recognized on a user interface. Your users will expect that they can left-click it to perform an action—no more and no less. Altering this behavior will most likely lead to bad interface design and frustrated users.

By default, the button displays itself with a single short line of text or an image that describes what happens when you click on it.

The button does not contain any properties to display images or text, but you can use the Content property to display simple text or embed an Image control in the content to display an image. You can find this code in the downloaded code at Ch15Ex01\ImageButton.xaml:

```
<Button HorizontalAlignment="Left" VerticalAlignment="Top" Width="75" Margin="10" >
    <StackPanel Orientation="Horizontal">
        <Image Source=".\Images\Delete_black_32x32.png" Stretch="UniformToFill"
```

```
Width="16" Height="16" />
        <TextBlock>Delete</TextBlock>
    </StackPanel>
  </Button>
```

> **NOTE** The image for the button is included in the code download in `Ch15Ex01\`
> `Images`.

Figure 15-9 shows the Delete button with text and an image.

✗ Delete

**FIGURE 15-9**

> **NOTE** To complete the following example, you need an image for a banner. This
> image is included in the download for this chapter in `KarliCards Gui\Images\`
> `Banner.png`.

**TRY IT OUT** Creating the About Window: KarliCards Gui\About.xaml

Before you can start the About window, you need a project to work on. This is just one of many windows you
are going to make in the next couple of chapters, so go ahead and create a new WPF application project and
name it `KarliCards GUI`. Name the solution `KarliCards`.

1. In the Solution Explorer, right-click the KarliCards Gui project and select Add ➪ Window. Name the
   window `About.xaml`.

2. Resize the window by clicking and dragging it or by setting these properties:
   ```
   Height="300" Width="434" MinWidth="434" MinHeight="300"
   ResizeMode="CanResizeWithGrip"
   ```

3. Select the `Grid` and create four rows by clicking at the edges of the grid. Don't worry too much about the
   exact positioning of the rows, instead change the values like this:
   ```
   <Grid.RowDefinitions>
       <RowDefinition Height="58"/>
       <RowDefinition Height="20"/>
       <RowDefinition />
       <RowDefinition Height="42"/>
   </Grid.RowDefinitions>
   ```

4. Drag a `Canvas` control from the Toolbox into the top-most row. Remove any properties inserted by Visual
   Studio and add this:
   ```
   Grid.Row="0" Background="#C40D42"
   ```

5. Select the new canvas and drag an image control onto it. Change its properties like so:
   ```
   Height="56" Canvas.Left="0" Canvas.Top="0" Stretch="UniformToFill"
   Source=".\Images\Banner.png"
   ```

6. Right-click the project and Select Add ➪ New Folder. Create a directory called `Images`.

7. Right-click the new directory in the Solution Explorer and select Add ➪ Existing Item. Browse to the
   images of this chapter. Select them all and click Add. The banner is now displayed in Design View as
   shown in Figure 15-10.

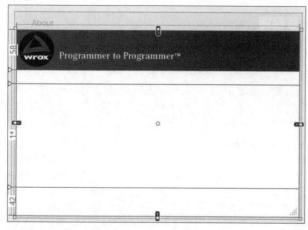

**FIGURE 15-10**

8.  Select Canvas and drag a Label control onto the it. Change its properties like this:

    ```
    Canvas.Right="10" Canvas.Top="25" Content="Karli Cards" Foreground="#FFF7EFEF"
    FontFamily="Times New Roman"
    ```

9.  Select Grid and drag a new canvas control onto it. Change its properties to:

    ```
    Grid.Row="1" Background="Black"
    ```

10. Select the new Canvas control and drag a Label onto it. Change its properties like this:

    ```
    Canvas.Left="5" Canvas.Top="0" FontWeight="Bold" FontFamily="Arial"
    Foreground="White"
    Content="Karli Cards (c) Copyright 2012 by Wrox Press and all readers"
    ```

11. Select Grid again, and drag the last Canvas into the bottom-most row. Change its properties like this:

    ```
    Grid.Row="3"
    ```

12. Select the new Canvas control and drag a Button onto it. Change its properties to this:

    ```
    Content="_OK" Canvas.Right="12" Canvas.Bottom="10" Width="75"
    ```

13. Select Grid again, and drag a StackPanel into the last center row. Change its properties to:

    ```
    Grid.Row="2"
    ```

14. Select StackPanel and drag two Label controls and one TextBlock into it, in that order.

15. Change the top-most Label like this:

    ```
    Content="CardLib and Idea developed by Karli Watson" HorizontalAlignment="Left"
    VerticalAlignment="Top" Padding="20,20,0,0" FontWeight="Bold"
    Foreground="#FF8B6F6F"
    ```

16. Change the next Label like this:

    ```
    Content="Graphical User Interface developed by Jacob Hammer" HorizontalAlignment="Left"
    Padding="20, 0,0,0" VerticalAlignment="Top" FontWeight="Bold" Foreground="#FF8B6F6F"
    ```

17. Change TextBlock like this:

    ```
    Text="Karli Cards developed with Visual C# 2012 for Wrox Press.
    You can visit Wrox Press at http://www.wrox.com."
    Margin="0, 10,0,0" Padding="20,0,0,0" TextWrapping="Wrap"
    HorizontalAlignment="Left" VerticalAlignment="Top" Height="39"
    ```

**18.** Double-click the button and, in the event handler, add this code:

```
private void Button_Click_1(object sender, RoutedEventArgs e)
{
    this.Close();
}
```

**19.** In the Solution Explorer, double-click the `App.xaml` file and change the name `NewWindow.xaml` to `About.xaml`.

**20.** Run the application.

### How It Works

You begin by setting some properties on the window. By setting `MinWidth` and `MinHeight`, you prevent the user from resizing the window to a point where it obscures the content. The `ResizeMode` is set to `CanResizeWithGrip`, which displays a small grip section in the bottom-right corner of the window that indicates to the user that the window can be resized.

Next you add four rows to the grid. By doing this, you define the basic structure of the window. By setting rows 1, 2, and 4 to fixed heights, you ensure that only the third row can change height; this is the row that holds the content.

Then you add the first `Canvas` control. This provides you with a handy place to set the background color of the first row. By ensuring that the canvas has no specific size, you force the canvas to fill the top row in the grid.

The `Image` control that is added to the canvas is fixed to the left and top edges of the canvas. This ensures that as the window resizes, the image stays put. You also gave the image a fixed height, but left the width open. With the `Stretch` property set to `UniformToFill`, this allows the `Image` control to use the height as a guide for the aspect ratio. The control simply changes its width to match the scale specified by the height and aspect ratio.

For the final part of the first row you add a single `Label` control and bind it to the top-right edge of the canvas, ensuring that when the window resizes, the `Label` moves with the right edge.

Then you start on the second row, which is filled by another `Canvas` control that has a `Label` added to it.

The bottom `Canvas` is more of the same, but this time you add a button to it and bind that button to the bottom-right side of the canvas. This ensures that when the window is resized, the button sticks to the bottom-right side of the window. The underscore "_" before the text OK creates a Alt+O shortcut for the button.

Finally, you add a `StackPanel` to the third row and add `Labels` and a `TextBlock` control to it. By setting the `Padding` of the first label to 20, 20, 0, 0, you push the content of the control down from the row above by 20 pixels and out from the left edge, also by 20 pixels.

The padding of the next label is set to 20,0,0,0, which pushes the content out from the edge because the space between the two labels is fine and doesn't need any extra space.

The `TextBlock` was then introduced. The property `TextWrapping` is set to `Wrap`, which causes the text to wrap if it can't fit on a single line. As the window resizes and the line becomes longer, the text is automatically fitted into as few lines as needed. Both the `Margin` and `Padding` properties are used here. The `Margin` property is set so it pushes the entire control down 10 pixels from the labels above, and the `Padding` is set so it pushes the content of the control in by 20 pixels from the left edge.

The code in the event handler closes the window. In this case, this is the same as closing the entire application, because in Step 19 you changed the startup window to be the About window, so closing it is the same as closing the application.

## The Options Window

The next window you are going to create is the Options window. This window will allow the players to set a number of parameters that will alter the game play. It will also allow you to use some controls that you haven't used yet: the `CheckBox`, `RadioButton`, `ComboBox`, `TextBox`, and `TabControl` controls.

Figure 15-11 shows the window with the first tab selected. At first glance the window looks much like the About window, but there is a lot more to do on this window.

### The TextBox Control

Previously in this chapter you used the `Label` and `TextBlock` controls. These controls are designed exclusively for displaying text to the user. The `TextBox` control allows the user to type text into the application. Although it can just display text as well, you should not use it for this purpose unless the user is allowed to edit the displayed text. If you decide that you want to display text using a textbox, be sure to set its `IsEnabled` property to `false` to prevent users from being able to edit it.

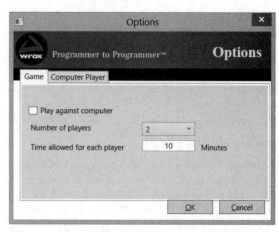

**FIGURE 15-11**

You control how the text is displayed and can be entered into the `TextBox` using a number of properties shown in Table 15-3.

**TABLE 15-3:** TextBox Properties

| PROPERTY | DESCRIPTION |
| --- | --- |
| `Text` | The text currently displayed in the `TextBox` control. |
| `IsEnabled` | When this is set to `true`, the user can edit the text in the `TextBox`. When it is `false`, the text is grayed out and the user cannot give focus to the control. |
| `TextWrapping` | Sometimes you want the `TextBox` to display only a single line of text. In this case, you can set this property to `NoWrap`. This is the default. If you want your text to be displayed on multiple lines, you can set it to either `Wrap` or `WrapWithOverflow`. `Wrap` will cause the text that extends beyond the edge of the box to be moved to the line below. `WrapWithOverflow` will in some cases allow very long words to extend beyond the edge if no suitable breakpoint can be determined. |
| `VerticalScrollBarVisibility` | If your `TextBox` allows the user to enter multiple lines of text, then the user can potentially type text that will disappear below the lower edge of the box. In that case, it's a good idea to display a scrollbar. Set this to `Auto` if you want the scrollbar to appear only if the text is too long to be displayed. Set it to `Visible` to always display it, and `Hidden` or `Disabled` to never display a scrollbar. |
| `AcceptsReturn` | This property controls how text can be entered into the control. If you set this to `false`, which is the default, then the user can't break the line with a Return. |

### The CheckBox Control

`CheckBoxes` present the users with options that they can select or clear. You should use a `CheckBox` if you have want to present an option to the users that can be turned on or off, or want the users to answer yes or no to a question. For example, in the Options dialog box, you want the user to answer to decide whether they should play against the computer. To this end a `CheckBox` with the text "Play Against Computer" is used.

A CheckBox is designed to be used as a single entity that is unaffected by other CheckBoxes on the view. You will sometimes see CheckBoxes used in a way that links them together so that selecting one causes another to become cleared, but this is not the intended use for this control. If you want this functionality, you should use a RadioButton, described in the next section.

CheckBoxes can also display a third state, which is known as "indeterminate" and is supposed to indicate that the yes/no answer could not be answered. This state is commonly used when a CheckBox is used to show information about something else. For example, CheckBoxes are sometimes used to indicate whether all child nodes in a Tree View are selected. In this case, the CheckBox will be selected if all nodes are selected, cleared if none are, and indeterminate if some, but not all, are selected.

Table 15-4 lists the properties commonly used to control the CheckBox control.

**TABLE 15-4:** CheckBox Properties

| PROPERTY | DESCRIPTION |
| --- | --- |
| Content | The CheckBox is a Content control and its display can therefore be heavily customized. Adding a text to the Content property yields the default view. |
| IsThreeState | Used to indicate if the control can have two or three states. The default is false, meaning that only two possible values exist. |
| IsChecked | This is either true or false. By default, setting it to true displays a checkmark. If IsThreeState is true, null is possible and indicates that the state is indeterminate. |

## The RadioButton Control

RadioButtons are used with other RadioButtons to allow users to choose between multiple options where only one can be selected at any time. You should use RadioButtons when you want the users to answer a question that has a very limited number of possible values. If there are more than four or five possible values, you should consider using a ListBox or a ComboBox instead. In the Options window you will create shortly, the user can choose the skill level of the computer player. There are three options: Dumb, Good, and Cheats. Only one should ever be selected at any given time.

When more than one RadioButton is displayed in the same view they will by default know about each other and as soon as any one of them is selected, all the others are cleared. If you have multiple unrelated RadioButtons on the same view, they can be grouped together to avoid controls clearing the values of unrelated controls.

You can control RadioButtons with the properties listed in Table 15-5.

**TABLE 15-5:** RadioButton Properties

| PROPERTY | DESCRIPTION |
| --- | --- |
| Content | RadioButtons are Content controls and can therefore have their display modified. By default, you enter a text in the Content. |
| IsChecked | This is either true or false. If IsThreeState is true, null is possible and indicates that the state is indeterminate. |
| GroupName | The name of the group the control belongs to. By default this is empty and any RadioButtons without a GroupName is considered in the same group. |

## The ComboBox Control

Like the RadioButton and CheckBox controls, ComboBoxes allow users to select exactly one option. However, ComboBoxes are fundamentally different from the other two in two ways:

➤ ComboBoxes display the possible choices in a drop-down list.

➤ It is possible to allow the users to type new values.

ComboBoxes are commonly used to display long lists of values, such as country or state names, but they can be used for many purposes. In the Options dialog box, a ComboBox is used to display a list from which the user can choose the number of players. Although this could just as well have been done using RadioButtons, the use of a ComboBox saves space in the view.

A ComboBox can be changed to display itself with a TextBox at the top that allows the users to type any values that they feel are missing. One of the exercises of this chapter asks you to add a ComboBox to the Options dialog box from which the users can either type their name or select it from a list.

The two properties—IsReadOnly and IsEditable—are very important for the behavior of the control and work together to provide four possible ways for the user to select the value of the ComboBox using the keyboard (see Table 15-6):

**TABLE 15-6:** IsReadOnly and IsEditable Combinations

|  | ISREADONLY IS TRUE | ISREADONLY IS FALSE |
| --- | --- | --- |
| IsEditable is true | The TextBox is displayed but the control does not react to key presses. If a selection is made in the list, the text can be selected in the TextBox. | The TextBox is displayed and the user can type anything she wishes. If something is typed that is in the list, it is selected. The control will display the best possible match as the user is typing. |
| IsEditable is false | When IsEditable is false, IsReadOnly no longer has any effect because the TextBox is not displayed. When the control is selected, the user can select a value from the list by typing but it is not possible to type a value that isn't in the list. | |

A ComboBox is an Items control, which means that you can add multiple items to it. Table 15-7 shows additional properties for the ComboBox control.

**TABLE 15-7:** Other ComboBox Properties

| COMBOBOX PROPERTY | DESCRIPTION |
| --- | --- |
| Text | The Text property represents the text displayed at the head of the ComboBox. It is either an element of the list or a new text typed by the user. |
| SelectedIndex | Represents the index of the selected item in the list. If this is -1 then no selection is made. This is also the case if the user has typed something that was not in the list. |
| SelectedItem | Represents the actual item of the list, not just the index or the text. If nothing is selected or the user has typed something new, this returns null. |

## The TabControl

The `TabControl` is radically different than the other controls presented this section. It is a layout control that is used to group controls on pages that can be selected by clicking on them.

Tab controls are used when you want to display a lot of information in a single window but don't want to clutter the view too much. In this case, you should divide the information into groups of related items and create a single page for each group. Generally speaking, you should never allow controls on one page to affect controls on another page. If you do so anyway, the user will not realize that something has changed on another page and will be confused when settings change behind her back.

By default each page is constructed of `TabItems` that, by default, are populated by a single `Grid` control, but you can change the `Grid` to any other control as you see fit. On each tab, you can lay out your UI and, by selecting the `TabItems`, you can change between the tabs. Each `TabItem` has a `Header` that can be used to display tab itself. This can be used as a `Content` control, meaning that you can customize how the header is displayed so that it can be more than just a text.

**TRY IT OUT**   Designing the Options Window: KarliCards Gui \Options.xaml

The first thing that you probably notice when you see the Options window is that it looks remarkably like the About window, and that is true. Because of that, it is possible to reuse at least some of the code from the previous example.

1. Right-click the project in the Solution Explorer and chose Add ⇨ Window. Name the window `Options.xaml`.

2. Delete the `Grid` control that is inserted by default.

3. Open the `About.xaml` window described earlier, copy the `Grid` control and all its content, and paste it into the new `Options.xaml` file.

4. Change the window properties like this:

   ```
   Title="Options" Height="345" Width="434" ResizeMode="NoResize"
   ```

5. Delete the `StackPanel` and all of its content.

6. Delete the `Canvas` control with the `Grid.Row` property set to 3 and all of its content.

7. Delete the `Label` control from the `Canvas` control with the `Grid.Row` property set to 1.

8. Change the `Label` control in the `Canvas` with the `Grid.Row` property set to 0 like this:

   ```
   <Label Canvas.Right="10" Canvas.Top="13" Content="Options" Foreground="#FFF7EFEF"
   FontFamily="Times New Roman" FontSize="24" FontWeight="Bold" />
   ```

9. Drag a `StackPanel` into the bottom row and set its properties to this:

   ```
   Grid.Row="3" Orientation="Horizontal" FlowDirection="RightToLeft"
   ```

10. Add two buttons to the `StackPanel` like this:

    ```
    <Button Content="_Cancel" Height="22" Width="75" Margin="10,0,0,0"
            Name="cancelButton" />
    <Button Content="_OK" Height="22" Width="75" Margin="10,0,0,0"
            Name="okButton" />
    ```

11. Drag a `TabControl` into the second row and set its properties like this:

    ```
    Grid.RowSpan="2" Canvas.Left="10" Canvas.Top="2" Width="408" Height="208"
    ```

12. Change the `Header` property of each of the two `TabItem` controls to Game and Computer Player, respectively.

    Your window now looks like Figure 15-12 and it is time to insert some content into the tab items.

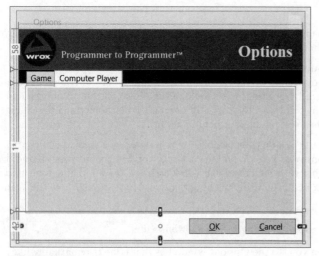

**FIGURE 15-12**

**13.** Select the Game `TabItem` and drag a `CheckBox` control onto it. Set its properties like this:

```
Content="Play against computer" HorizontalAlignment="Left" Margin="11,33,0,0"
VerticalAlignment="Top" Name="playAgainstComputerCheck"
```

**14.** Drag a `Label` control and then a `ComboBox` control into the `TabItem` and set their properties like this:

```
            <Label Content="Number of players" HorizontalAlignment="Left"
    Margin="10,54,0,0" VerticalAlignment="Top" />
            <ComboBox HorizontalAlignment="Left" Margin="196,58,0,0"
    VerticalAlignment="Top" Width="86" Name="numberOfPlayersComboBox" SelectedIndex="0"  >
                <ComboBoxItem>2</ComboBoxItem>
                <ComboBoxItem>3</ComboBoxItem>
                <ComboBoxItem>4</ComboBoxItem>
            </ComboBox>
```

**15.** Drag two more labels and a `TextBox` and drop them below the `ComboBox`. Set their properties like this:

```
            <Label Content="Time allowed for each player" HorizontalAlignment="Left"
    Margin="10,85,0,0" VerticalAlignment="Top"/>
            <TextBox HorizontalAlignment="Left" Margin="196,87,0,0"
    TextWrapping="WrapWithOverflow" Text="10" VerticalAlignment="Top" Width="86"
    TextAlignment="Center" Name="timeAllowedTextBox" />
            <Label Content="Minutes" HorizontalAlignment="Left" Margin="287,85,0,0"
    VerticalAlignment="Top"/>
```

**16.** Select the second `TabItem` with the header `Computer Player`. Drag a `Label` and three `RadioButtons` onto the `Grid` and set their properties like this:

```
            <Label Content="Skill Level" HorizontalAlignment="Left"
    Margin="10,10,0,0" VerticalAlignment="Top"/>
            <RadioButton Content="Dumb" HorizontalAlignment="Left"
    Margin="37,41,0,0" VerticalAlignment="Top" IsChecked="True"
    Name="dumbAIRadioButton"/>
            <RadioButton Content="Good" HorizontalAlignment="Left"
    Margin="37,62,0,0" VerticalAlignment="Top" Name="goodAIRadioButton"/>
            <RadioButton Content="Cheats" HorizontalAlignment="Left"
    Margin="37,83,0,0" VerticalAlignment="Top"
    Name="cheatingAIRadioButton"/>
```

**17.** The layout of the window is now complete. Open the `App.xaml` file and change `StartupUri` to `Options.xaml`.

**18.** Run the application.

*How It Works*

The window's `ResizeMode` is set to `NoResize`. You can therefore position the controls without regard to what happens if the window changes size, because the user can no longer resize the window.

The `StackPanel` in Step 9 has a new property, `FlowDirection`, which is set to `RightToLeft`. This causes the two buttons that are added to it to cling to the right edge of the dialog box rather than the left edge that is the default. Interestingly, this also changes the meaning of the `Margin` property of the two buttons, causing `Left` and `Right` to be swapped.

The `RadioButtons` on the second tab are set up without specifying a `GroupName`, which causes them to be grouped together. You set the `IsChecked` property to `true` on the first one, which makes this the default selection.

## Handling Events in the Options Window

The window looks fine at this point, and there are even a few things users can do with it, although nothing happens when a setting is changed. Users expect that the options they choose are stored and used by the application. You could do this by storing the values of the controls in the window, but this is not very flexible and mixes the data of the application with the GUI, which is not a good idea. Instead, you should create a class to hold the selections made by the users.

**TRY IT OUT** Handling Events: KarliCards Gui\Options.xaml

In this example, you will add a new class to the project that will contain the selections made by the user. Then you will handle events that happen as the user changes selections of the `RadioButtons` and finally you are going to change the default behavior of the `TextBox`.

**1.** Add a new class to the project and name it `GameOptions.cs`.

**2.** Enter this code:

```
using System;

namespace KarliCards_Gui
{
  [Serializable]
  public class GameOptions
  {
    public bool PlayAgainstComputer { get; set; }
    public int NumberOfPlayers { get; set; }
    public int MinutesBeforeLoss { get; set; }
    public ComputerSkillLevel ComputerSkill { get; set; }
  }

  [Serializable]
  public enum ComputerSkillLevel
  {
    Dumb,
    Good,
    Cheats
  }
}
```

**3.** Return to the `Options.xaml.cs` code-behind file and add a `private` field to hold the `GameOptions` instance:

```
private GameOptions _gameOptions;
```

**4.** Add this code to the constructor:

```
using System.IO;
using System.Windows;
using System.Windows.Controls;
using System.Windows.Input;
using System.Xml.Serialization;

namespace KarliCards_Gui
{
  public partial class Options : Window
  {
    private GameOptions _gameOptions;

    public Options()
    {
      if (_gameOptions == null)
      {
        if (File.Exists("GameOptions.xml"))
        {
          using (var stream = File.OpenRead("GameOptions.xml"))
          {
            var serializer = new XmlSerializer(typeof(GameOptions));
            _gameOptions = serializer.Deserialize(stream) as GameOptions;
          }
        }
        else
          _gameOptions = new GameOptions();
      }

      InitializeComponent();
    }
  }
}
```

**5.** Go to Design View and double-click each of the three RadioButtons to add the Checked event handler to the code-behind file. Change the handlers like this:

```
private void dumbAIRadioButton_Checked(object sender, RoutedEventArgs e)
{
  _gameOptions.ComputerSkill = ComputerSkillLevel.Dumb;
}

private void goodAIRadioButton_Checked(object sender, RoutedEventArgs e)
{
  _gameOptions.ComputerSkill = ComputerSkillLevel.Good;
}

private void cheatingAIRadioButton_Checked(object sender, RoutedEventArgs e)
{
  _gameOptions.ComputerSkill = ComputerSkillLevel.Cheats;
}
```

**6.** Return to Design View and select the TextBox on the Game tab. Click the lightning icon on the Properties panel and double-click the GotFocus event to add the handler to the code-behind file.

**7.** Enter this code:

```
private void timeAllowedTextBox_GotFocus(object sender, RoutedEventArgs e)
{
  timeAllowedTextBox.SelectAll();
}
```

**8.** Select the TextBox again in Design View and add the PreviewMouseLeftButtonDown event handler to the code-behind file.

**9.** Enter this code:

```
private void timeAllowedTextBox_PreviewMouseLeftButtonDown(object sender,
                    MouseButtonEventArgs e)
{
  var control = sender as TextBox;
  if (control == null)
    return;

    Keyboard.Focus(control);
  e.Handled = true;
}
```

**10.** Run the application.

### How It Works

The new class is currently just a number of properties that store the values from the Options window. It is marked as `Serializable` to make it possible to save it to a file.

The `Checked` event of a `RadioButton` is raised whenever the user selects it. You handle this event in order to set the value of the `ComputerSkillLevel` property of the `GameOptions` instance.

Next, you changed the `TextBox`. Did you notice what was changed? Normally, when a user selects the `TextBox`, the cursor is placed at the position where the control was clicked if the selection was done with the mouse or at the end of the text. But it is common in Windows to select all the text in the `TextBox` when it gets focus, because this allows the user to start typing without having to move the cursor and select the existing text. By handling the two events `GotFocus` and `PreviewLeftMouseButtonDown`, you can simulate this behavior.

The reason you have to use both of these events is because of the standard event handling of the `TextBox`. As long as the user uses the keyboard to select the `TextBox`, `GotFocus` is enough. This event is called whenever the control gets focus.

If the user selects the control using the mouse, handling `GotFocus` is not enough. `GotFocus` actually gets called and the text is selected, but immediately thereafter the selection is removed again. This is because the `TextBox` places the cursor at the position where the click happened. In order to prevent this from happening, you implement the `PreviewLeftMouseButtonDown` event and, after giving focus to the control, set the `Handled` property of the event arguments to `true`. This causes the processing of the event to stop and therefore prevents the cursor to be positioned within the `TextBox`.

## Data Binding

Data binding is a way of declaratively connecting controls with data. In the Options window, you handled the `Checked` event of the `RadioButtons` in order to set the value of the `ComputerSkillLevel` property in the `GameOptions` class. This works well, and you can use code and event handling to set all the values you have in a window, but very often it is better to bind the properties of your controls directly to the data.

A binding consists of four components:

➤ The binding target, which specifies the object on which the binding is used
➤ The target property, which specifies the property to set
➤ The binding source, which specifies the object used by the binding
➤ The source property, which specifies which property holds the data

You don't always set all of these elements explicitly; particularly the binding target is very often implicitly specified by the fact that you are setting a binding to a property on a control.

The binding source is always set in order to make a binding work, but it can be set in several ways. In the following sections and in Chapter 16, you are going to see several ways of binding data from sources.

### The DataContext

A `DataContext` control defines a data source that can be used for data binding on all child elements of an element. You will often have a single instance of a class that holds most of the data that is used in a view. If this is the case you can set the `DataContext` of the window to the instance of that object, which makes you able to bind properties from that class in your view. This is demonstrated in the "Dynamic Binding to External Objects" section.

### Binding to Local Objects

You can bind to any .NET object that has the data you need as long as the compiler can locate the object. If the object is found in the same context, that is the same XAML block, as the control using the object, you can specify the binding source by setting the `ElementName` property of the binding. Take a look at this changed `ComboBox` from the Options window:

```
<ComboBox HorizontalAlignment="Left" Margin="196,58,0,0" VerticalAlignment="Top"
Width="86" Name="numberOfPlayersComboBox" SelectedIndex="0"
IsEnabled="{Binding ElementName=playAgainstComputerCheck, Path=IsChecked}" >
```

Notice the `IsEnabled` property. Instead of specifying `true` or `false`, there is now lengthy text within a couple of curly brackets. This way of specifying property values is called *markup extension syntax*, and is a shorthand for specifying properties. The same could have been written like this:

```
        <ComboBox HorizontalAlignment="Left" Margin="196,58,0,0"
VerticalAlignment="Top" Width="86" Name="numberOfPlayersComboBox"
SelectedIndex="0" >
            <ComboBox.IsEnabled>
                <Binding ElementName="playAgainstComputerCheck"
Path="IsChecked" />
            </ComboBox.IsEnabled>
```

Both examples set the binding source to the `playAgainstComputerCheck` CheckBox. The source property is specified in the `Path` to be the `IsChecked` property.

The binding target is set to the `IsEnabled` property. Both examples do this by the specifying the binding as the content of the property—they just do it using different syntax. Finally, the binding target is implicitly specified by the fact that the binding is done on the `ComboBox`.

The binding in this example causes the `IsEnabled` property of the `ComboBox` to be set or cleared depending on the value of the `IsChecked` property of the `CheckBox`. The result is that without any code, the `ComboBox` is enabled and disabled when the user changes the value of the `CheckBox`.

### Static Binding to External Objects

It is possible to create object instances on the fly by specifying that a class is used as a resource in the XAML. This is done by adding a namespace to the XAML to allow the class to be located, and then declaring the class as a resource on an element in the XAML.

You can create resource references on parent elements of the object that you want to data bind.

**TRY IT OUT**    Creating a Static Data Binding: KarliCards Gui\NumberOfPlayers.cs

In this example you create a new class to hold the data for the `ComboBox` in the Options window and bind it to the control.

1. Add a new class to the project and name it `NumberOfPlayers.cs`.
2. Add this code:

```
using System.Collections.ObjectModel;

namespace KarliCards_Gui
{
  public class NumberOfPlayers : ObservableCollection<int>
```

```
      {
        public NumberOfPlayers()
          : base()
        {
          Add(2);
          Add(3);
          Add(4);
        }
      }
    }
```

3. Return to the `Options.xaml` file's Design View and select the `Window` root element.

4. Add a namespace declaration, as shown here. Note that if your classes are in another namespace, you should change it to match the namespace you are using.

   ```
   xmlns:src="clr-namespace:KarliCards_Gui"
   ```

5. Select the `Canvas` element that contains the `ComboBox` and add this code below it, and above the `TabControl` declaration.

   ```
   <Canvas.Resources>
     <src:NumberOfPlayers x:Key="numberOfPlayersData" />
   </Canvas.Resources>
   ```

6. Select the `ComboBox` and remove the three `ComboBoxItems` from it.

7. Add this property to it:

   ```
   ItemsSource="{Binding Source={StaticResource numberOfPlayersData}}"
   ```

### How It Works

There is a lot happening in this example. The class `NumberOfPlayers` derives from a special collection named `ObservableCollection`. This base class is a collection that has been extended to make it work better with WPF. In the constructor of the class, you add the values to the collection.

You then add a namespace to the `Window` control. This allows you to reference the classes defined in that namespace in the XAML.

Next you create a new resource on the `Canvas`. You could have created this resource on any parent element of the `ComboBox`. When a resource is specified on an element, all child elements can use it.

Finally you set the `ItemsSource` to a binding. The `ItemsSource` property is specifically designed to allow you to specify a binding for the collection of items on an Items control. In the binding you just need to specify the binding source. The binding target, target property, and source property settings are handled by the `ItemsSource` property.

## Dynamic Binding to External Objects

Now you can bind to objects that are created on the fly as they are needed in order to provide some data. What if you already have an instantiated object that you want to use for data binding? In that case, you need to do a little plumbing in the code.

In the case of the Options window, you don't want the options to be cleared every time the window is opened, and you want the selections the user made to persist and be used in the rest of the application.

You can do this in code by setting the value of the `DataContext` property to the instance.

**TRY IT OUT**   Creating Dynamic Bindings: KarliCards Gui\GameOptions.cs

In this example you bind the remaining controls to the `GameOptions` instance in the Options window.

1. Go to the `Options.xaml.cs` code-behind file.

**2.** At the bottom of the constructor, but above `InitializeComponent()`, add this line:

```
DataContext = _gameOptions;
```

**3.** Go to the `GameOptions` class and change it like this:

```csharp
using System;
using System.ComponentModel;

namespace KarliCards_Gui
{
  [Serializable]
  public class GameOptions : INotifyPropertyChanged
  {
    private bool _playAgainstComputer = true;
    private int _numberOfPlayers = 2;
    private int _minutedBeforeLoss = 10;
    private ComputerSkillLevel _computerSkill = ComputerSkillLevel.Dumb;

    public int NumberOfPlayers
    {
      get { return _numberOfPlayers; }
      set
      {
        _numberOfPlayers = value;
        OnPropertyChanged("NumberOfPlayers");
      }
    }

    public bool PlayAgainstComputer
    {
      get { return _playAgainstComputer; }
      set
      {
        _playAgainstComputer = value;
        OnPropertyChanged("PlayAgainstComputer");
      }
    }

    public int MinutesBeforeLoss
    {
      get { return _minutedBeforeLoss; }
      set
      {
        _minutedBeforeLoss = value;
        OnPropertyChanged("MinutesBeforeLoss");
      }
    }

    public ComputerSkillLevel ComputerSkill
    {
      get { return _computerSkill; }
      set
      {
        _computerSkill = value;
        OnPropertyChanged("ComputerSkill");
      }
    }

    public event PropertyChangedEventHandler PropertyChanged;
    private void OnPropertyChanged(string propertyName)
    {
      if (PropertyChanged != null)
        PropertyChanged(this, new PropertyChangedEventArgs(propertyName));
    }
```

```
        }

        [Serializable]
        public enum ComputerSkillLevel
        {
            Dumb,
            Good,
            Cheats
        }
    }
```

4. Return `Options.xaml` and select the `CheckBox`. Add the `IsChecked` property like this:

   ```
   IsChecked="{Binding Path=PlayAgainstComputer}"
   ```

5. Select the `ComboBox` and change it like this, removing the `SelectedIndex` property and changing the `ItemsSource` and `SelectedValue` properties:

   ```
   <ComboBox HorizontalAlignment="Left" Margin="196,58,0,0" VerticalAlignment="Top"
   Width="86" Name="numberOfPlayersComboBox"
   ItemsSource {Binding Source={StaticResource numberOfPlayersData}}"
   SelectedValue="{Binding Path=NumberOfPlayers}" />
   ```

6. Select the `TextBox` and change its `Text` property to this:

   ```
   Text="{Binding Path=MinutesBeforeLoss}"
   ```

7. Select and double-click the OK button to add the `Click` event handler to the code-behind file. Do the same with the Cancel button and add this code to the handlers:

   ```
   private void okButton_Click(object sender, RoutedEventArgs e)
   {
       using (var stream = File.Open("GameOptions.xml", FileMode.Create))
       {
           var serializer = new XmlSerializer(typeof(GameOptions));
           serializer.Serialize(stream, _gameOptions);
       }
       this.Close();
   }

   private void cancelButton_Click(object sender, RoutedEventArgs e)
   {
       _gameOptions = null;
       this.Close();
   }
   ```

8. Run the application.

### How It Works

Setting the `DataContext` of the window to an instance of `GameOptions` allows you to bind to this instance simply by specifying the property to use in the binding. This is done in Steps 4, 5, and 6. Note that the `ComboBox` is filled with items from a static resource, but the selected value is set in the `GameOptions` instance.

The `GameOptions` class is changed quite a bit. It now implements the `INotifyPropertyChanged` interface, which means that the class is now able to inform WPF that a property has changed. In order for this notification to work, you have to call the subscribers to the `PropertyChanged` event defined by the interface. For this to happen, the property setters have to actively call them, which is done using the helper method `OnPropertyChanged`.

The OK button event handler saves the settings to disk using an `XmlSerializer`. The Cancel event handler sets the game options field to null, ensuring that the selections made by the user are cleared. Both event handlers close the window.

## Starting a Game

You are now only one window short of having created all the supporting windows in the game. The last window before creating the game board is a window where the player can add new players and select the players who will be participating in a new game. This window will use a `ListBox` to display the names of the players.

### The ListBox Control

`ListBoxes` and `ComboBoxes` can often be used for the same purpose, but where a `ComboBox` normally allows you to select only a single entry, `ListBoxes` often allows the user to select multiple items. Another key difference is that a `ListBox` will display its content in a list that is always expanded. This means that it takes up more real estate on the window, but it allows to the user to see the options available right away.

Table 15-8 lists a few particularly interesting properties for the ListBox control.

**TABLE 15-8:** Interesting ListBox Properties

| PROPERTY | DESCRIPTION |
|---|---|
| SelectionMode | This property controls how the user can select items from the list. There are three possible values: `Single`, which allows the user to select only one item, `Multiple`, which allows the user to select multiple items without holding down the Ctrl key, and `Extended`, which allows the user to select multiple consecutive items by holding down the Shift key, and non-consecutive items by holding down the Ctrl key. |
| SelectedItem | Gets or sets the first selected item or null if nothing is selected. Even if multiple items are selected, only the first item is returned. |
| SelectedItems | Gets a list containing the items that are currently selected. |
| SelectedIndex | Works like `SelectedItem`, but returns the index instead of the item itself and -1 instead of null if nothing is selected. |

**TRY IT OUT** Creating the Start Game Window: KarliCards Gui\StartGame.xaml

This window is displayed to the players when a new game starts. It will allow the players to enter their names and select them from a list of known players.

1. Create a new window and name it `StartGame.xaml`.
2. Delete the `Grid` element from the window and copy the main `Grid` and its content from the `Options.xaml` window instead.
3. Remove all the content from the `Canvas` control that has its `Grid.Row` property set to 1.
4. Change the window title to "Start New Game" and set these properties:

   ```
   Height="345" Width="445" ResizeMode="NoResize"
   ```

5. Change the content of the label in grid row 0 to "New Game".
6. Open the `GameOptions.cs file` and add these fields at the top of the class:

   ```
   private ObservableCollection<string> _playerNames =
   new ObservableCollection<string>();
   public List<string> SelectedPlayers { get; set; }
   ```

7. The previous code used `System.Collections.Generic` and the `System.Collections.ObjectModel` namespaces, so include these:

   ```
   using System.Collections.Generic;
   using System.Collections.ObjectModel;
   ```

**8.** Add a constructor to initialize the `SelectedPlayers` collection:

```
public GameOptions()
{
    SelectedPlayers = new List<string>();
}
```

**9.** Add a property and two methods to the class like this:

```
public ObservableCollection<string> PlayerNames
{
  get
  {
    return _playerNames;
  }
  set
  {
    _playerNames = value;
    OnPropertyChanged("PlayerNames");
  }
}

public void AddPlayer(string playerName)
{
  if (_playerNames.Contains(playerName))
    return;
  _playerNames.Add(playerName);
  OnPropertyChanged("PlayerNames");
}
```

**10.** Return to the `StartGame.xaml` window.

**11.** Add a `ListBox`, two Labels, a `TextBox`, and a `Button` to the grid below the `Canvas` in grid row 1 and change the controls to look like those shown in Figure 15-13.

**FIGURE 15-13**

**12.** Set the `Name` property of the controls as shown in Table 15-9.

**TABLE 15-9:** The Name Property

| CONTROL | NAME |
| --- | --- |
| TextBox | newPlayerTextBox |
| Button | addNewPlayerButton |
| ListBox | playerNamesListBox |

**13.** Set the ItemsSource of the ListBox like this:

```
ItemsSource="{Binding Path=PlayerNames}"
```

**14.** Add the ListBox's SelectionChanged event handler to the code-behind file and add this code:

```
private void playerNamesListBox_SelectionChanged(object sender,
SelectionChangedEventArgs e)
    {
      if (_gameOptions.PlayAgainstComputer)
        okButton.IsEnabled = (playerNamesListBox.SelectedItems.Count == 1);
      else
        okButton.IsEnabled = (playerNamesListBox.SelectedItems.Count ==
_gameOptions.NumberOfPlayers);
    }
```

**15.** Set the IsEnabled property of the OK button to false.

**16.** Open the code-behind file and add this field to the top of the class:

```
private GameOptions _gameOptions;
```

**17.** Copy the constructor from the Options.xaml.cs code-behind (though not the name) and add these lines to the end after InitializeComponent (Note: You will need to add using declarations for System.IO and System.Xml.Serialization):

```
if (_gameOptions.PlayAgainstComputer)
  playerNamesListBox.SelectionMode = SelectionMode.Single;
else
  playerNamesListBox.SelectionMode = SelectionMode.Extended;
```

**18.** Select the Add button and add the Click event handler. Add this code:

```
private void addNewPlayerButton_Click(object sender, RoutedEventArgs e)
  {
    if (!string.IsNullOrWhiteSpace(newPlayerTextBox.Text))
      _gameOptions.AddPlayer(newPlayerTextBox.Text);
    newPlayerTextBox.Text = string.Empty;
  }
```

**19.** Copy the event handler for the OK and Cancel buttons from the Options.xaml.cs code-behind files to this code-behind.

**20.** Add these lines to the top of the OK button handler:

```
foreach (string item in playerNamesListBox.SelectedItems)
  {
    _gameOptions.SelectedPlayers.Add(item);
  }
```

**21.** Go to the App.xaml file and change the StartupUri to StartGame.xaml.

**22.** Run the application.

### How It Works

You started by adding code to the GameOptions class that holds information about all the known players and the current selection made in the StartGame window.

The ListBox's ItemsSource property is the same as you saw on the ComboBox earlier. But where you were able to bind the selected value of the ComboBox directly to a value, it is more complicated with a ListBox. If you try to bind the SelectedValues property you will find that it is read-only and therefore can't be used for data binding. The work-around used here is to use the OK button to store the values through code. Note that the cast to IList<string> works here because the content of the ListBox is strings at the moment, but if you decided to change the default behavior and display something else, then this selection of items must be changed as well.

The ListBox's SelectionChanged event is raised whenever something happens that changes the selection. In this case you want to handle this event to check if the number of items selected is correct. If the game is to be played against a computer, then there can only be one human player; otherwise the correct number of human players must be selected.

> **NOTE** Chapter 16 discusses the Styles, Control, and Item templates and shows why you can't always know what type the content of a control is.

## SUMMARY

This chapter covered the basics of creating Graphical User Interfaces using Windows Presentation Foundation. You used XAML and Design View in Visual Studio to create windows that leverage the standard controls that ship with WPF. You used the controls in their default style, which creates user interfaces that are highly recognizable in Windows. Chapter 16 goes beyond that and shows you how to customize the default behavior and styles.

In order to react to actions performed by the users of the application, you learned how to handle events to react to these actions using code defined in C# code-behind files.

You learned how to work with XAML to create windows that work and have behavior, simply by binding the state of some controls to properties of others. You learned how to use namespaces to add your code base into the scope of the XAML you are working on in order to bind directly to code instances. In addition to that, you used the DataContext of a window to set the data source of the entire window to an existing instance of an object, which allowed you to bind properties of your controls to an instance of a class defined outside of the window.

In Chapter 16, you will continue to work on the Karli Cards game. Specifically, you will use your knowledge of XAML to create user controls to represent the cards and hands of the game, and then bind everything together using data binding and C#.

### EXERCISES

**15.1** A TextBlock control can be used to display large amounts of text, but the control does not provide any way to scroll the text itself if the text extends beyond the viewport. By combining the TextBlock with another control, create a window that contains a TextBlock with a lot of text that can be scrolled and where the scrollbar appears only if the text extends beyond the viewport.

**15.2** The Slider and Progress controls have a few things in common, such as a minimum, maximum, and current value. Using only data binding on the ProgressBar, create a window with a slider and a progress bar, where the Slider control controls the minimum, maximum, and current value of the progress bar.

**15.3** Change the `ProgressBar` in the previous question to display itself diagonally from the bottom-left corner to the top-right corner of the window.

**15.4** Create a new class with the name `PersistentSlider` and three properties: `MinValue`, `MaxValue`, and `CurrentValue`. The class must be able to participate in data binding and all the properties must be able to notify bound controls of changes.

a. In the code-behind of the window you created in the two previous exercises, create a new field of type `PersistentSlider` and initialize it with some default values.

b. In the constructor, bind the instance to the windows data source.

c. Bind the slider's `Minimum`, `Maximum`, and `Value` properties to the data source.

## ▶ WHAT YOU LEARNED IN THIS CHAPTER

| KEY CONCEPT | DESCRIPTION |
|---|---|
| **XAML** | XAML is a language that uses XML syntax and enables controls to be added to a user interface in a declarative, hierarchical way. |
| **Data binding** | You can use data binding to connect properties of controls to the value of other controls. You can also define resources and use code defined in classes outside your views as a data source for both values of properties and as content for controls. `DataContexts` can be used to specify the binding source of existing object instances and thereby allow you to bind to instances that are created in other parts of your application. |
| **Routed events** | Routed events are special events used in WPF. They come in two flavors: bobbling and tunneling. Bobbling events are first called on the control on which they are activated and then bobble up through the view tree to the root element. Tunneling events move the other way, from the root element to the control that was activated by the user. Both bobbling and tunneling can be stopped by setting the `Handled` property of the event arguments to `true`. |
| **INotifyPropertyChanged** | The `INotifyPropertyChanged` interface is implemented by a class that will be used from a WPF view. When property setters of the class are called, they raise the event `PropertyChanged` with the name of the property that changed its value. Any control property that is bound to the property that raised the event will be notified of the change and can update itself accordingly. |
| **ObservableCollections** | An `ObservableCollection` is a collection that, among others, implement the `INotifyPropertyChanged` interface. You use this specialized collection when you want to provide properties or values that are lists to a WPF view for data binding. |
| **Content controls** | Content controls can contain a single control in their content. An example of such a control is `Button`. This control can be `Grid` or `StackPanel`; they allow you to create complex customizations. |
| **Items controls** | Items controls can contain a list of controls in their content. An example of such a control is the `ListBox`. Each control in the list can be customized. |
| **Layout controls** | You learned to use a number of controls that are used to help you create the view:<br>1. `Canvas` allows for explicit positioning of controls but little else.<br>2. `StackPanel` stacks controls horizontally or vertically.<br>3. `WrapPanel` stacks controls and wraps them to the next line or column depending on the orientation of the panel.<br>4. `DockPanel` allows you to dock controls to the edges of the control or fill the entire content.<br>5. `Grid` allows you to define rows and columns and use these to position the controls. |

**UI controls**

UI controls display themselves on the view, often using the layout controls to guide their positions. These controls were used:

1. `Label` controls display short text.

2. `TextBlock` controls display text that can need multiple lines to display.

3. `TextBox` controls allow the users to provide text input.

4. `Button` controls allow the users to perform a single action.

5. `Image` controls are used to display an image.

6. `CheckBoxes` let the users answer yes/no questions such as "Play Against Computer?"

7. `RadioButtons` let the users select exactly one from multiple options.

8. `ComboBoxes` display a drop-down list of items from which the user can select a single item. The control can also display a `TextBox`, letting the user enter new options.

9. `ListBox` controls display a list of items. Unlike the `ComboBox` the list is always expanded. The control allows for multiple items being selected.

10. `TabControls` allows you to group controls on pages.

# 16

# Advanced Desktop Programming

## WHAT YOU WILL LEARN IN THIS CHAPTER

- ➤ How to use routed commands instead of events
- ➤ How to create menus using the Menu control and routed commands
- ➤ How to use styling controls and applications using XAML styles
- ➤ How to create value converters
- ➤ How to use timelines to create animations
- ➤ How to define and reference static and dynamic resources
- ➤ How to create user controls when the common controls are not enough

## WROX.COM CODE DOWNLOADS FOR THIS CHAPTER

You can find the wrox.com code downloads for this chapter at www.wrox.com/remtitle.cgi?isbn=9781118314418 on the Download Code tab. The code is in the Chapter 16 download and individually named according to the names throughout the chapter.

Until this point you have used Windows Presentation Foundation in much the same way that you use the other major technology for creating windows applications in Visual Studio: Windows Forms. But that is about to change. WPF can style any control and use templates to change existing controls to look nothing like they do out-of-the-box. In addition to that, you are going to start working more and more by typing XAML. Although this might seem like a burden at first, the ability to move and fine-tune the display by setting properties will quickly become second nature, and you will find that there is quite a bit in XAML that cannot be done in the designer, such as creating animations.

Now it is time to continue where you left off in Chapter 15 and continue with the game client.

## THE MAIN WINDOW

The main window of the application is where the game is played, and it therefore doesn't have many controls on it. You'll construct the game in this chapter, but before you start, there are three things that you must do. You need to add the main window to the project, add menus to the window, and bind the windows you already constructed to the menu items.

## The Menu Control

Most applications include menus and toolbars of some kind. Both are a means to the same end: to provide easy navigation of the application's content. Toolbars generally contain a subset of the same entries that the menus provide and can be thought of as shortcuts to the menu items.

Visual Studio ships with both a `Menu` and a `Toolbar` control. The example here shows the use of the `Menu` control but using the Toolbar is very similar.

By default, the menu item appears as a horizontal bar from which you can drop down lists of items. The control is an `Items` control, so it is possible to change the default items contained in the content; however, you would normally use `MenuItems` in some form, as shown in the following example. Each `MenuItem` can contain other menu items, and you can build complex menus by nesting `MenuItems` within each other, but you should try to keep the menu structure as simple as possible.

You can control how the `MenuItem` displays using a number of properties (see Table 16-1).

**TABLE 16-1:** Displaying MenuItem Properties

| PROPERTY | DESCRIPTION |
| --- | --- |
| `Icon` | Displays an icon by the left edge of the control. |
| `IsCheckable` | Displays a `CheckBox` by the left edge of the control. |
| `IsChecked` | Gets or sets the value of a `CheckBox` on a `MenuItem`. |

## Routed Commands with Menus

*Routed commands* were briefly discussed in Chapter 15, but now you are going to see them in action for the first time. Recall that these commands are akin to events in that they execute code when a user performs an action, and they can return a state indicating whether they can be executed at any given time.

There are at least three reasons why you would want to use routed commands instead of events:

1. The action that will case an event to occur can be triggered from multiple locations in your application.
2. The UI element should be accessible only under certain conditions, such as a Save button being disabled if there's nothing to save.
3. You want to disconnect the code that handles the event from the code-behind file.

If any of these scenarios matches yours, consider using routed commands. In the case of the game, some of the items in the menu should also potentially be available from a toolbar. In addition, the Save action should be available only when a game is in progress and it should potentially be available from both a menu and the toolbar.

**TRY IT OUT** Creating the Main Window: KarliCards Gui\MainWindow.xaml

In this example you create the main window for the game. Because this window is the main window of the application, it will use the windows you have already created.

1. Add a new window to the project and name it `GameClient.xaml`.
2. Change the title to "Karli Cards Game Client" and remove the `Height` and `Width` properties.
3. Set the `WindowState` property to `Maximized`.
4. Add this namespace:

    ```
    xmlns:src="clr-namespace:KarliCards_Gui"
    ```

5. Remove the grid from the window and copy the grid and all its content from the `StartGame` window.

**6.** Delete everything that is not positioned in `Grid.Row = 0`.

**7.** Drag a `DockPanel` control into grid row 1. Set its properties like this:

```
Grid.Row="1" Margin="0"
```

**8.** Select `DockPanel` and drag a `Menu` control onto it. Note that the control expands to fill the entire `DockPanel`—this is what you want.

**9.** Change the menu's properties to give it a black background, bold text weight, and white foreground color:

```
Background="Black" FontWeight="Bold" Foreground="White"
```

**10.** Right-click the menu in the design view and choose Add MenuItem.

**11.** Change the `Header` property to _File. Note the leading underscore. Also set the foreground to white.

**12.** Add another `MenuItem` inside the _File item by right-clicking the _File item and selecting Add MenuItem. Set the `Height`, `Width`, `Header`, and `Foreground` properties like this:

```xml
<MenuItem Header="_File" Foreground="White">
  <MenuItem Header="_New Game..." Height="22"
      Width="200" Foreground="Black" />
</MenuItem>
```

**13.** Add the following `MenuItems` to the File menu:

```xml
<MenuItem Header="_Open" Width="200" Foreground="Black"/>
<MenuItem Header="_Save" Width="200" Foreground="Black" Command="Save">
  <MenuItem.Icon>
    <Image Source="Images\base_floppydisk_32.png" Width="20" />
  </MenuItem.Icon>
</MenuItem>
<Separator Width="145" Foreground="Black"/>
<MenuItem Header="_Close" Width="200" Foreground="Black" Command="Close"/>
```

**14.** Add these `MenuItems` to the menu on the same level as the `File MenuItem`.

```xml
<MenuItem Header="_Game" Background="Black" Foreground="White">
  <MenuItem Header="_Undo" HorizontalAlignment="Left"
      Width="145" Foreground="Black"/>
</MenuItem>
<MenuItem Header="_Tools" Background="Black" Foreground="White">
  <MenuItem Header="_Options" HorizontalAlignment="Left"
      Width="145" Foreground="Black"/>
</MenuItem>
<MenuItem Header="Help" Background="Black" Foreground="White">
  <MenuItem Header="_About" HorizontalAlignment="Left"
      Width="145" Foreground="Black"/>
</MenuItem>
```

**15.** Change the background color of the main grid control to green.

**16.** Before the first grid control, add this command binding to the window:

```xml
<Window.CommandBindings>
  <CommandBinding Command="ApplicationCommands.Close"
      CanExecute="CommandCanExecute" Executed="CommandExecuted" />
  <CommandBinding Command="ApplicationCommands.Save"
      CanExecute="CommandCanExecute" Executed="CommandExecuted" />
</Window.CommandBindings>
```

**17.** Change the content of the label in `Grid` row 0 from "New Game" to "Karli Cards".

**18.** Add a new grid to the grid in row 2 and name it `contentGrid`:

```xml
<Grid Grid.Row="2" x:Name="contentGrid" />
```

Your window should now look like Figure 16-1.

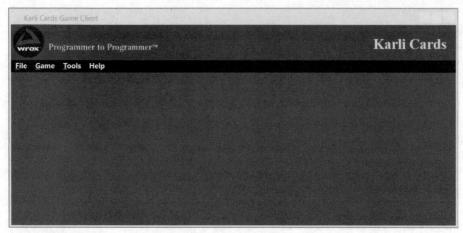

**FIGURE 16-1**

**19.** Go to the `GameClient.xaml.cs` code-behind file and add these two methods:

```
private void CommandCanExecute(object sender, CanExecuteRoutedEventArgs e)
{
    if (e.Command == ApplicationCommands.Close)
        e.CanExecute = true;
    if (e.Command == ApplicationCommands.Save)
        e.CanExecute = false;
    e.Handled = true;
}

private void CommandExecuted(object sender, ExecutedRoutedEventArgs e)
{
    if (e.Command == ApplicationCommands.Close)
        this.Close();
    e.Handled = true;
}
```

**20.** Change the `StartupUri` in the `App.xaml` file to `GameClient.xaml` and run the application.

### How It Works

When you run the application you will notice that the Game Client window is initially displayed as maximized, but you can resize the window as you like. When you hold down the Alt key, the File menu gets focus and the F in File is underlined, indicating that you can expand the menu by pressing F.

When you expand the menu you can see that the Save menu is disabled, but it displays a disk icon as well as the text "Ctrl-S" to the right of the element title. This means that you can access it by pressing Ctrl-S (when it is enabled). You might wonder why this is displayed, as you haven't set any shortcut keys anywhere. However, you did set a command for the menu item:

```
<MenuItem Header="_Save" Width="200" Foreground="Black" Command="Save">
```

The Save command is defined by WPF. Save and Close, which are used in the File menu, are defined in the `ApplicationCommands` class, which also defines Cut, Copy, Paste, and Print. When you specify the Save command for a `MenuItem`, the shortcut key Ctrl-S is assigned to the menu item because it's the standard key combination used to access that function in most Windows applications.

In the code-behind file, you added two methods used to determine the state and action taken by the commands. In the XAML, you created two command bindings that used the methods like this:

```
<Window.CommandBindings>
  <CommandBinding Command="ApplicationCommands.Close"
      CanExecute="CommandCanExecute" Executed="CommandExecuted" />
  <CommandBinding Command="ApplicationCommands.Save"
      CanExecute="CommandCanExecute" Executed="CommandExecuted" />
</Window.CommandBindings>
```

```
private void CommandCanExecute(object sender, CanExecuteRoutedEventArgs e)
{
    if (e.Command == ApplicationCommands.Close)
        e.CanExecute = true;
    if (e.Command == ApplicationCommands.Save)
        e.CanExecute = false;
    e.Handled = true;
}

private void CommandExecuted(object sender, ExecutedRoutedEventArgs e)
{
    if (e.Command == ApplicationCommands.Close)
        this.Close();
    e.Handled = true;
}
```

The CanExecute part of the command binding specifies a method that is called to determine whether the command should be available to the user at the moment. The Executed part specifies a method that should be called when the user activates the command. Note that it doesn't matter from where the command is activated. If a menu item and a button both include the Save command, the binding works for both.

The current implementation of CommandCanExecute is too simple for real life, where you would do some calculation to determine whether the application is ready to save anything. Since you don't have a game to save yet, just returning false for the Save command is appropriate. You do this by setting the e.CanExecute property on the CanExecuteRoutedEventArgs class. The Close command, on the other hand, can be executed just fine, so you return true for that one.

CommandExecuted performs the same test as CommandCanExecute. If it determines that the command to execute is the Close command, then it closes the current window.

## CREATING AND STYLING CONTROLS

It's time to step away from the client implementation of the game and start looking more at the game itself. One key feature of a graphical card game is…the cards. Obviously, you are not going to find a "Playing Card" control in the standard controls that ship with WPF, so you have to create it yourself.

One of the best features of WPF is the complete control it provides designers over the look and feel of user interfaces. Central to this is the capability to style controls however you want, in two or three dimensions. Until now, you have been using the basic styling for controls that is supplied with .NET, but the actual possibilities are endless.

This section describes two basic techniques:

➤ **Styles**—Sets of properties that are applied to a control as a batch

➤ **Templates**—The controls that are used to build the display for a control

There is some overlap here, as styles can contain templates.

## Styles

WPF controls have a property called Style (inherited from FrameworkElement) that can be set to an instance of the Style class. The Style class is quite complex and is capable of advanced styling functionality, but at its heart it is essentially a set of Setter objects. Each Setter object is responsible for setting the value of a property according to its Property property (the name of the property to set) and its Value property (the value to set the property to). You can either fully qualify the name you use in Property to the control type (for example, Button.Foreground), or you can set the TargetType property of the Style object (for example, Button), so that it is capable of resolving property names.

The following code shows how to use a Style object to set the Foreground property of a Button control:

```
<Button>
  Click me!
  <Button.Style>
    <Style TargetType="Button">
      <Setter Property="Foreground">
        <Setter.Value>
          <SolidColorBrush Color="Purple" />
        </Setter.Value>
      </Setter>
    </Style>
  </Button.Style>
</Button>
```

Obviously, in this case it would be far easier simply to set the Foreground property of the button in the usual way. Styles become much more useful when you turn them into resources, because resources can be reused. You will learn how to do this later in the chapter.

## Templates

Controls are constructed using templates, which you can customize. A template consists of a hierarchy of controls used to build the display of a control, which may include a content presenter for controls such as buttons that display content.

The template of a control is stored in its Template property, which is an instance of the ControlTemplate class. The ControlTemplate class includes a TargetType property that you can set to the type of control for which you are defining a template, and it can contain a single control. This control can be a container such as Grid, so this doesn't exactly limit what you can do.

Typically, you set the template for a class by using a style. This simply involves providing controls to use for the Template property in the following way:

```
<Button>
  Click me!
  <Button.Style>
    <Style TargetType="Button">
      <Setter Property="Template">
        <Setter.Value>
          <ControlTemplate TargetType="Button">
            ...
          </ControlTemplate>
        </Setter.Value>
      </Setter>
    </Style>
  </Button.Style>
</Button>
```

Some controls may require more than one template. For example, CheckBox controls use one template for a check box (CheckBox.Template) and one template to output text next to the check box (CheckBox.Content Template).

Templates that require content presenters can include a `ContentPresenter` control at the location where you want to output content. Some controls—especially those that output collections of items—use alternative techniques, which aren't covered in this chapter.

Again, replacing templates is most useful when combined with resources. However, as control styling is a very common technique, it is worth looking at how to do it in a Try It Out.

**TRY IT OUT** | Using Styles and Templates: Ch16Ex02\MainWindow.xaml

**1.** Create a new WPF application called Ch16Ex02.

**2.** Modify the code in `MainWindow.xaml` as follows:

```xml
<Grid Background="Black">
  <Button Margin="20" Click="Button_Click">
    Would anyone use a button like this?
    <Button.Style>
      <Style TargetType="Button">
        <Setter Property="FontSize" Value="18" />
        <Setter Property="FontFamily" Value="arial" />
        <Setter Property="FontWeight" Value="bold" />
        <Setter Property="Foreground">
          <Setter.Value>
            <LinearGradientBrush StartPoint="0.5,0" EndPoint="0.5,1">
              <LinearGradientBrush.GradientStops>
                <GradientStop Offset="0.0" Color="Purple" />
                <GradientStop Offset="0.5" Color="Azure" />
                <GradientStop Offset="1.0" Color="Purple" />
              </LinearGradientBrush.GradientStops>
            </LinearGradientBrush>
          </Setter.Value>
        </Setter>
        <Setter Property="Template">
          <Setter.Value>
            <ControlTemplate TargetType="Button">
              <Grid>

                <Grid.ColumnDefinitions>
                  <ColumnDefinition Width="50" />
                  <ColumnDefinition />
                  <ColumnDefinition Width="50" />
                </Grid.ColumnDefinitions>
                <Grid.RowDefinitions>
                  <RowDefinition MinHeight="50" />
                </Grid.RowDefinitions>
                <Ellipse Grid.Column="0" Height="50">
                  <Ellipse.Fill>
                    <RadialGradientBrush>
                      <RadialGradientBrush.GradientStops>
                        <GradientStop Offset="0.0" Color="Yellow" />
                        <GradientStop Offset="1.0" Color="Red" />
                      </RadialGradientBrush.GradientStops>
                    </RadialGradientBrush>
                  </Ellipse.Fill>
                </Ellipse>
                <Grid Grid.Column="1">
                  <Rectangle RadiusX="10" RadiusY="10">
                    <Rectangle.Fill>
                      <RadialGradientBrush>
                        <RadialGradientBrush.GradientStops>
                          <GradientStop Offset="0.0" Color="Yellow" />
                          <GradientStop Offset="1.0" Color="Red" />
                        </RadialGradientBrush.GradientStops>
```

```
                              </RadialGradientBrush>
                            </Rectangle.Fill>
                        </Rectangle>
                        <ContentPresenter Margin="20,0,20,0"
                          HorizontalAlignment="Center"
                          VerticalAlignment="Center" />
                      </Grid>
                      <Ellipse Grid.Column="2" Height="50">
                        <Ellipse.Fill>
                          <RadialGradientBrush>
                            <RadialGradientBrush.GradientStops>
                              <GradientStop Offset="0.0" Color="Yellow" />
                              <GradientStop Offset="1.0" Color="Red" />
                            </RadialGradientBrush.GradientStops>
                          </RadialGradientBrush>
                        </Ellipse.Fill>
                      </Ellipse>
                    </Grid>
                  </ControlTemplate>
                </Setter.Value>
              </Setter>
            </Style>
          </Button.Style>
        </Button>
      </Grid>
```

3. Modify the code in MainWindow.xaml.cs as follows:

```
public partial class MainWindow : Window
{
    ...

    private void Button_Click(object sender, RoutedEventArgs e)
    {
        MessageBox.Show("Button clicked.");
    }
}
```

4. Run the application and click the button once. Figure 16-2 shows the result.

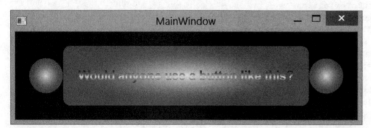

**FIGURE 16-2**

### How It Works

First, let me apologize for the truly nasty-looking button shown in this example. However, aesthetic considerations aside, this example does show that you can completely change how a button looks in WPF without a lot of effort. Note that changing the button template does not change the functionality of the button. That is, you can still click on the button and respond to that click in an event handler.

You probably noticed that certain things you associate with Windows buttons aren't implemented in the template used here. In particular, there is no visual feedback when you roll over the button or when you click it. This button also looks exactly the same whether it has focus or not. To achieve these missing effects, you need to learn about *triggers*, which are the subject of the next section.

Before doing that, though, consider the example code in a little more detail, focusing on styles and templates and looking at how the template was created.

The example starts with ordinary code that you would use to display a `Button` control:

```
<Button Margin="20" Click="Button_Click">
   Would anyone use a button like this?
```

This provides basic properties and content for the button. The `Style` property is set to a `Style` object, which begins by setting three simple font properties of the `Button` control:

```
<Button.Style>
  <Style TargetType="Button">
    <Setter Property="FontSize" Value="18" />
    <Setter Property="FontFamily" Value="arial" />
    <Setter Property="FontWeight" Value="bold" />
```

Next, the `Button.Foreground` property is set using property element syntax because a brush is used:

```
<Setter Property="Foreground">
  <Setter.Value>
    <LinearGradientBrush StartPoint="0.5,0" EndPoint="0.5,1">
      <LinearGradientBrush.GradientStops>
        <GradientStop Offset="0.0" Color="Purple" />
        <GradientStop Offset="0.5" Color="Azure" />
        <GradientStop Offset="1.0" Color="Purple" />
      </LinearGradientBrush.GradientStops>
    </LinearGradientBrush>
  </Setter.Value>
</Setter>
```

The remainder of the code for the `Style` object sets the `Button.Template` property to a `ControlTemplate` object:

```
<Setter Property="Template">
  <Setter.Value>
    <ControlTemplate TargetType="Button">
       ...
    </ControlTemplate>
  </Setter.Value>
</Setter>
      </Style>
  </Button.Style>
</Button>
```

The template code can be summarized as a `Grid` control that contains three cells in a single row. In turn, these cells contain an `Ellipse`, a `Rectangle`, the `ContentPresenter` for the template, and another `Ellipse`:

```
<Grid>
  <Ellipse Grid.Column="0" Height="50">
     ...
  </Ellipse>
  <Grid Grid.Column="1">
    <Rectangle RadiusX="10" RadiusY="10">
       ...
    </Rectangle>
    <ContentPresenter Margin="20,0,20,0"
      HorizontalAlignment="Center"
      VerticalAlignment="Center" />
  </Grid>
  <Ellipse Grid.Column="2" Height="50">
     ...
  </Ellipse>
</Grid>
```

# Value Converters

You may have wondered at some of the assignments that you have used in the examples so far: How, for example, can you assign the string value "true" to a Boolean property? You have learned that C# is type-safe and the compiler should not allow that kind of thing to happen! Happily, the reality is that it doesn't. XAML and WPF make extensive use of something called *value converters*, which can convert from one type to another behind the scenes.

WPF ships with converters for just about all the standard scenarios you can think of, so you can always convert from int to string or bool and integer. But what happens when you want to convert something that is not included? Then you have to implement the converter yourself.

Let's look at one example that is very common: The inversed bool converter. Imagine that you have a check box on a dialog box. Depending on whether it's checked, another part of the dialog box will be disabled or enabled. Quite often, the answer must be reversed for this to make sense. Take a look at the Options dialog box, for example. It has a check box with the question, "Play against computer?" Selecting this option should disable the ComboBox and TextBoxes on the dialog box. The value of IsChecked would be true, so binding that to IsEnabled of the other two controls will not work. Enter the InversedBoolConverter. This converter will simply inverse the bool value.

## The IValueConverter Interface

In order to create a ValueConverter, you must implement the IValueConverter interface. This interface has two methods: Convert and ConvertBack. These might seem self-explanatory, but they are actually a bit complicated.

```
object Convert(object value, Type targetType,
    object parameter, CultureInfo culture);
object ConvertBack(object value, Type targetType,
    object parameter, CultureInfo culture);
```

You use the Convert method when converting to a target type and use the ConvertBack method for the reverse operation. The value for these methods is the targetType that the type that is being converted to. The parameter can be used to set a helper. Exercise 16.1 at the end of this chapter requires you to use this parameter to create a specific value converter.

## ValueConversionAttribute

In addition to implementing the interface, you can set an attribute on the class that implements the converter. This is not needed, but it is a great help both for tools and users of your converter. TheValueConversionAttribute takes two parameters, both of which are Type objects. This means that you explicitly set the types that the converter will convert to and from.

**TRY IT OUT** Create a Value Converter: KarliCards Gui

This example builds on the KarliCards Gui project you created earlier.

1. Create a new class and name it ReversedBoolConverter.
2. Modify the class like this. You must also include the System.Windows.Data namespace:

```
[ValueConversion(typeof(bool), typeof(bool))]
public class InverseBoolConverter : IValueConverter
{
    public object Convert(object value, Type targetType, object parameter,
        System.Globalization.CultureInfo culture)
    {
        return !(bool)value;
    }
```

```
        public object ConvertBack(object value, Type targetType, object parameter,
            System.Globalization.CultureInfo culture)
        {
            return !(bool)value;
        }
    }
```

**3.** Go to the `Options.xaml` file and create a new static resource for the window:

```
<Window.Resources>
    <src:InverseBoolConverter x:Key="inverseBool" />
</Window.Resources>
```

**4.** Set the `IsEnabled` property of the combo box to this binding:

```
IsEnabled="{Binding ElementName=playAgainstComputerCheck,
    Path=IsChecked, Converter={StaticResource inverseBool}}
```

### How It Works

The conversion is obviously very simple in this case — it simply returns `false` if the value is true and vice-versa. You are going to see more complicated converters later in the chapter.

In the XAML, you create a resource for the converter to be able to reference it from the binding that needs it. In the binding, you set the `Converter` property to use the converter.

## Triggers

Events in WPF can include all manner of things, including button clicks, application startup and shutdown events, and so on. There are, in fact, several types of triggers in WPF, all of which inherit from a base `TriggerBase` class. One such trigger is the `EventTrigger` class, which contains a collection of actions, each of which is an object that derives from the base `TriggerAction` class. These actions are executed when the trigger is activated.

Not a lot of classes inherit from `TriggerAction` in WPF, but you can, of course, define your own. You can use `EventTrigger` to trigger animations using the `BeginStoryboard` action, manipulate storyboards using `ControllableStoryboardAction`, and trigger sound effects with `SoundPlayerAction`. As this latter trigger is mostly used in animations, you'll look at it in the next section.

Every control has a `Triggers` property that you can use to define triggers directly on that control. You can also define triggers further up the hierarchy — for example, on a `Window` object as shown earlier. The type of trigger you will use most often when you are styling controls is `Trigger` (although you will still use `EventTrigger` to trigger control animations). The `Trigger` class is used to set properties in response to changes to other properties, and is particularly useful when used in `Style` objects.

Trigger objects are configured as follows:

- ➤ To define what property a `Trigger` object monitors, you use the `Trigger.Property` property.
- ➤ To define when the `Trigger` object activates, you set the `Trigger.Value` property.
- ➤ To define the actions taken by a `Trigger`, you set the `Trigger.Setters` property to a collection of `Setter` objects.

The `Setter` objects referred to here are exactly the same objects that you saw in the "Styles" section earlier.

For example, the following trigger examines the value of a property called `MyBooleanValue`, and when that property is `true` it sets the value of the `Opacity` property to `0.5`:

```
<Trigger Property="MyBooleanValue" Value="true">
    <Setter Property="Opacity" Value="0.5" />
</Trigger>
```

On its own, this code doesn't tell you very much, as it is not associated with any control or style. The following code is much more explanatory; it shows a `Trigger` as you would use it in a `Style` object:

```
<Style TargetType="Button">
  <Style.Triggers>
    <Trigger Property="IsMouseOver" Value="true">
      <Setter Property="Foreground" Value="Yellow" />
    </Trigger>
  </Style.Triggers>
</Style>
```

This code changes the `Foreground` property of a `Button` control to `Yellow` when the `Button.IsMouseOver` property is `true`. `IsMouseOver` is one of several extremely useful properties that you can use as a shortcut to find out information about controls and control state. As its name suggests, it is `true` if the mouse is over the control. This enables you to code for mouse rollovers. Other properties like this include `IsFocused`, to determine whether a control has focus; `IsHitTestVisible`, which indicates whether it is possible to click on a control (that is, it is not obscured by controls further up the stacking order); and `IsPressed`, which indicates whether a button is pressed. The last of these only applies to buttons that inherit from `ButtonBase`, whereas the others are available on all controls.

You can also achieve a great deal by using the `ControlTemplate.Triggers` property, which enables you to create templates for controls that include triggers. This is how the default `Button` template is able to respond to mouse rollovers, clicks, and focus changes with its template. This is also what you must modify to implement this functionality for yourself.

## Animations

Animations are created by using storyboards. The absolute best way to define animations is, without a doubt, to use a designer such as Expression Blend. However, you can also define them by editing XAML code directly, and by implication from code-behind (as XAML is simply a way to build a WPF object model).

A storyboard is defined using a `Storyboard` object, which contains one or more timelines. You can define timelines by using key frames or by using one of several simpler objects that encapsulate entire animations. Complex storyboards may even contain nested storyboards.

A `Storyboard` is contained in a resource dictionary, so you must identify it with an `x:Key` property.

Within the timeline of a storyboard, you can animate properties of any element in your application that is of type `double`, `Point`, or `Color`. This covers most of the things that you may want to change, so it's quite flexible. There are some things that you can't do, such as replace one brush with another, but there are ways to achieve pretty much any effect you can imagine given these three types.

Each of these three types has two associated timeline controls that you can use as children of `Storyboard`. These six controls are `DoubleAnimation`, `DoubleAnimationUsingKeyFrames`, `PointAnimation`, `PointAnimationUsingKeyFrames`, `ColorAnimation`, and `ColorAnimationUsingKeyFrames`. Every timeline control can be associated with a specific property of a specific control by using the attached properties `Storyboard.TargetName` and `Storyboard.TargetProperty`. For example, you would set these properties to `MyRectangle` and `Width` if you wanted to animate the `Width` property of a `Rectangle` control with a `Name` property of `MyRectangle`. You would use either `DoubleAnimation` or `DoubleAnimationUsingKeyFrames` to animate this property. You will see examples of using storyboards as this chapter progresses and in Chapter 17.

Next, you'll look at the simple, animation timelines without key frames, and then move on to look at the timelines that use key frames.

### Timelines without Key Frames

The timelines without key frames are `DoubleAnimation`, `PointAnimation`, and `ColorAnimation`. These timelines have identical property names, although the types of these properties vary according to the type of the timeline (note that all duration properties are specified in the form `[days.]hours:minutes:seconds` in XAML code). Table 16-2 describes these properties.

**TABLE 16-2:** The Timeline Properties

| PROPERTY | DESCRIPTION |
|---|---|
| Name | The name of the timeline, so that you can refer to it from other places. |
| BeginTime | How long after the storyboard is triggered before the timeline starts. |
| Duration | How long the timeline lasts. |
| AutoReverse | Whether the timeline reverses when it completes and returns properties to their original values. This property is a Boolean value. |
| RepeatBehavior | Set this to a specified duration to make the timeline repeat as indicated—an integer followed by x (for example, 5x) to repeat the timeline a set number of times; or use Forever to make the timeline repeat until the storyboard is paused or stopped. |
| FillBehavior | How the timeline behaves if it completes while the storyboard is still continuing. You can use HoldEnd to leave properties at the values they are at when the timeline completes (the default), or Stop to return them to their original values. |
| SpeedRatio | Controls the speed of the animation relative to the values specified in other properties. The default value is 1, but you can change it from other code to speed up or slow down animations. |
| From | The initial value to set the property to at the start of the animation. You can omit this value to use the current value of the property. |
| To | The final value for the property at the end of the animation. You can omit this value to use the current value of the property. |
| By | Use this value to animate from the current value of a property to the sum of the current value and the value you specify. You can use this property on its own or in combination with From. |

For example, the following timeline will animate the Width property of a Rectangle control with a Name property of MyRectangle between 100 and 200 over five seconds:

```
<Storyboard x:Key="RectangleExpander">
<DoubleAnimation Storyboard.TargetName="MyRectangle"
  Storyboard.TargetProperty="Width" Duration="00:00:05"
  From="100" To="200" />
</Storyboard>
```

## Timelines with Key Frames

The timelines with key frames are DoubleAnimationUsingKeyFrames, PointAnimationUsingKeyFrames, and ColorAnimationUsingKeyFrames. These timeline classes use the same properties as the timeline classes in the previous section, except that they don't have From, To, or By properties. Instead, they have a KeyFrames property that is a collection of key frame objects.

These timelines can contain any number of key frames, each of which can cause the value being animated to behave in a different way. There are three types of key frames for each type of timeline:

➤ **Discrete**—A discrete key frame causes the value being animated to jump to a specified value with no transition.

➤ **Linear**—A linear key frame causes the value being animated to animate to a specified value in a linear transition.

➤ **Spline**—A spline key frame causes the value being animated to animate to a specified value in a non-linear transition defined by a cubic Bezier curve function.

There are therefore nine types of key frame objects: `DiscreteDoubleKeyFrame`, `LinearDoubleKeyFrame`, `SplineDoubleKeyFrame`, `DiscreteColorKeyFrame`, `LinearColorKeyFrame`, `SplineColorKeyFrame`, `DiscretePointKeyFrame`, `LinearPointKeyFrame`, and `SplinePointKeyFrame`.

The key frame classes have the same three properties as the timeline classes examined in the previous section. The four spline key frame classes add one additional property: `KeySpline` (see Table 16-3).

**TABLE 16-3:** Properties of the Spline Key Frame Classes

| PROPERTY | USAGE |
| --- | --- |
| Name | The name of the key frame, so that you can refer to it from other places. |
| KeyTime | The location of the key frame expressed as an amount of time after the timeline starts. |
| Value | The value that the property will reach or be set to when the key frame is reached. |
| KeySpline | Two sets of two numbers in the form `cp1x`, `cp1y`, `cp2x`, `cp2y` that define the cubic Bezier function to use to animate the property. (*Spline key frames only.*) |

For example, you could animate the position of an `Ellipse` in a square by animating its `Center` property, which is of type `Point`, as follows:

```
<Storyboard x:Key="EllipseMover">
  <PointAnimationUsingKeyFrames Storyboard.TargetName="MyEllipse"
    Storyboard.TargetProperty="Center" RepeatBehavior="Forever">
    <LinearPointKeyFrame KeyTime="00:00:00" Value="50,50" />
    <LinearPointKeyFrame KeyTime="00:00:01" Value="100,50" />
    <LinearPointKeyFrame KeyTime="00:00:02" Value="100,100" />
    <LinearPointKeyFrame KeyTime="00:00:03" Value="50,100" />
    <LinearPointKeyFrame KeyTime="00:00:04" Value="50,50" />
  </PointAnimationUsingKeyFrames>
</Storyboard>
```

Point values are specified in `x,y` form in XAML code.

## WPF USER CONTROLS

WPF provides a set of controls that are useful in many situations. However, as with all the .NET development frameworks, it also enables you to extend this functionality. Specifically, you can create your own controls by deriving your classes from classes in the WPF class hierarchy.

One of the most useful controls you can derive from is `UserControl`. This class gives you all the basic functionality that you are likely to require from a WPF control, and it enables your control to snap in beside the existing WPF control suite seamlessly. Everything you might hope to achieve with a WPF control—such as animation, styling, and templating—can be achieved with user controls.

You can add user controls to your project by using the Project ➪ Add User Control menu item. This gives you a blank canvas (well, actually a blank `Grid`) to work from. User controls are defined using the top-level `UserControl` element in XAML, and the class in the code-behind derives from the `System.Windows.Controls.UserControl` class.

Once you have added a user control to your project, you can add controls to lay out the control and code-behind to configure the control. When you have finished doing that, you can use it throughout your application, and even reuse it in other applications.

One of the crucial things you need to know when creating user controls is how to implement dependency properties. Chapter 15 briefly discussed dependency properties, and now that you are getting closer to writing your own controls, it is time to take a closer look at them.

## Implementing Dependency Properties

You can add dependency properties to any class that inherits from `System.Windows.DependencyObject`. This class is in the inheritance hierarchy for many classes in WPF, including all the controls and `UserControl`.

To implement a dependency property to a class, you add a public, static member to your class definition of type `System.Windows.DependencyProperty`. The name of this member is up to you, but best practice is to follow the naming convention `<PropertyName>Property`:

```
public static DependencyProperty MyStringProperty;
```

It might seem odd that this property is defined as static, as you end up with a property that can be uniquely defined for each instance of your class. The WPF property framework keeps track of things for you, so you don't have to worry about this for the moment.

The member you add must be configured by using the static `DependencyProperty.Register()` method:

```
public static DependencyProperty MyStringProperty =
    DependencyProperty.Register(…);
```

This method takes between three and five parameters, as shown in the Table 16-4 (these are shown in order, with the first three parameters being the mandatory ones).

**TABLE 16-4:** The Register ( ) Method's Parameters

| PARAMETER | USAGE |
|---|---|
| `string name` | The name of the property. |
| `Type propertyType` | The type of the property. |
| `Type ownerType` | The type of the class containing the property. |
| `PropertyMetadata typeMetadata` | Additional property settings: the default value of the property and callback methods to use for property change notifications and coercion. |
| `ValidateValueCallback validateValueCallback` | The callback method to use to validate property values. |

There are other methods that you can use to register dependency properties, such as `RegisterAttached()`, which you can use to implement an attached property. You won't look at these other methods in this chapter, but it's worth reading up on them.

For example, you could register the `MyStringProperty` dependency property using three parameters as follows:

```
public class MyClass : DependencyObject
{
    public static DependencyProperty MyStringProperty = DependencyProperty.Register(
        "MyString",
        typeof(string),
        typeof(MyClass));
}
```

You can also include a .NET property that can be used to access dependency properties directly (although this isn't mandatory, as you will see shortly). However, because dependency properties are defined as static members, you cannot use the same syntax you would use with ordinary properties. To access the value of a dependency property, you have to use methods that are inherited from `DependencyObject`, as follows:

```
public string MyString
{
```

```
            get { return (string)GetValue(MyStringProperty); }
            set { SetValue(MyStringProperty, value); }
    }
```

Here, the `GetValue()` and `SetValue()` methods get and set, respectively, the value of the `MyStringProperty`, dependency property for the current instance. These two methods are public, so client code can use them directly to manipulate dependency property values. This is why adding a .NET property to access a dependency property is not mandatory.

If you want to set metadata for a property, then you must use an object that derives from `PropertyMetadata`, such as `FrameworkPropertyMetadata`, and pass this instance as the fourth parameter to `Register()`. There are 11 overloads of the `FrameworkPropertyMetadata` constructor, and they take one or more of the parameters shown in Table 16-5.

**TABLE 16-5:** Overloads for the FrameworkPropertyMetadata Constructor

| PARAMETER TYPE | USAGE |
| --- | --- |
| `object defaultValue` | The default value for the property. |
| `FrameworkPropertyMetadata Options flags` | A combination of the flags (from the `FrameworkPropertyMetadataOptions` enum) that you can use to specify additional metadata for a property. For example, you might use `AffectsArrange` to declare that changes to the property might affect control layout. This would cause the layout engine for a window to recalculate control layout if the property changed. See the MSDN documentation for a full list of the options available here. |
| `PropertyChangedCallback propertyChangedCallback` | The callback method to use when the property value changes. |
| `CoerceValueCallback coerceValueCallback` | The callback method to use if the property value is coerced. |
| `bool isAnimationProhibited` | Specifies whether this property can be changed by an animation. |
| `UpdateSourceTrigger defaultUpdateSourceTrigger` | When property values are data-bound, this property determines when the data source is updated, according to values in the `UpdateSourceTrigger` enum. The default value is `PropertyChanged`, which means that the binding source is updated as soon as the property changes. This is not always appropriate—for example, the `TextBox` `.Text` property uses a value of `LostFocus` for this property. This ensures that the binding source is not updated prematurely. You can also use the value `Explicit` to specify that the binding source should be updated only when requested (by calling the `UpdateSource()` method of a class derived from `DependencyObject`). |

A simple example of using `FrameworkPropertyMetadata` is to use it to set the default value of a property:

```
public static DependencyProperty MyStringProperty =
        DependencyProperty.Register(
        "MyString",
        typeof(string),
        typeof(MyClass),
        new FrameworkPropertyMetadata("Default value"));
```

You have so far learned about three callback methods that you can specify, for property change notification, property coercion, and property value validation. These callbacks, like the dependency property itself, must all be implemented as public, static methods. Each callback has a specific return type and parameter list that you must use on your callback method.

Now it is time to get back on track and continue with the game client for Karli Cards. In the following Try It Out, you create a user control that can represent a playing card in the application.

User Controls: KarliCards Gui.CardControl.xaml

Return to the KarliCards Gui project from the previous Try It Out.

**1.** This example uses the CardLib project that you created in Chapter 13, so you have to add this to the solution.Begin by right-clicking the solution name in the Solution Explorer and choosing Add ⇨ Existing Project. Browse to and select the CardLib.csproj file from the Chapter 13 code examples.

**2.** Add a reference to the CardLib project by right-clicking References and choosing Add Reference in the KarliCards Gui project. Click Solution ⇨ Project from the tree on the left and select CardLib. Click OK.

**3.** Add a new user control called Card to the KarliCards Gui project, and modify the code in CardControl .xaml as follows:

```
<UserControl x:Class="KarliCards_Gui.CardControl"
             xmlns="http://schemas.microsoft.com/winfx/2006/xaml/presentation"
             xmlns:x="http://schemas.microsoft.com/winfx/2006/xaml"
             xmlns:mc="http://schemas.openxmlformats.org/markup-compatibility/2006"
             xmlns:d="http://schemas.microsoft.com/expression/blend/2008"
             xmlns:src="clr-namespace:KarliCards_Gui"
             mc:Ignorable="d"
             Height="154" Width="100" x:Name="UserControl">
  <UserControl.Resources>
    <src:RankNameConverter x:Key="rankConverter"/>
    <DataTemplate x:Key="SuitTemplate">
      <TextBlock Text="{Binding}"/>
    </DataTemplate>
    <Style TargetType="Image" x:Key="SuitImage">
      <Style.Triggers>
        <DataTrigger Binding="{Binding ElementName=UserControl, Path=Suit}"
Value="Club">
          <Setter Property="Source" Value="Images\Clubs.png" />
        </DataTrigger>
        <DataTrigger Binding="{Binding ElementName=UserControl, Path=Suit}"
Value="Heart">
          <Setter Property="Source" Value="Images\Hearts.png" />
        </DataTrigger>
        <DataTrigger Binding="{Binding ElementName=UserControl, Path=Suit}"
Value="Diamond">
          <Setter Property="Source" Value="Images\Diamonds.png" />
        </DataTrigger>
        <DataTrigger Binding="{Binding ElementName=UserControl, Path=Suit}"
Value="Spade">
          <Setter Property="Source" Value="Images\Spades.png" />
        </DataTrigger>
      </Style.Triggers>
    </Style>
  </UserControl.Resources>
  <Grid>
    <Rectangle Stroke="{x:Null}" RadiusX="12.5" RadiusY="12.5">
      <Rectangle.Fill>
        <LinearGradientBrush EndPoint="0.47,-0.167" StartPoint="0.86,0.92">
          <GradientStop Color="#FFD1C78F" Offset="0"/>
          <GradientStop Color="#FFFFFFFF" Offset="1"/>
        </LinearGradientBrush>
      </Rectangle.Fill>
      <Rectangle.Effect>
        <DropShadowEffect Direction="145" BlurRadius="10" ShadowDepth="0"  />
      </Rectangle.Effect>
    </Rectangle>
```

```
        <Label x:Name="SuitLabel"
          Content="{Binding Path=Suit, ElementName=UserControl, Mode=Default}"
          ContentTemplate="{DynamicResource SuitTemplate}"
          HorizontalAlignment="Center" VerticalAlignment="Center"
          Margin="8,51,8,60" />
        <Label x:Name="RankLabel"  Grid.ZIndex="1"
          Content="{Binding Path=Rank, ElementName=UserControl, Mode=Default,
   Converter={StaticResource ResourceKey=rankConverter}}"
          ContentTemplate="{DynamicResource SuitTemplate}"
          HorizontalAlignment="Left" VerticalAlignment="Top"
          Margin="8,8,0,0" />

        <Label x:Name="RankLabelInverted"
          Content="{Binding Path=Rank, ElementName=UserControl, Mode=Default,
   Converter={StaticResource ResourceKey=rankConverter}}"
          ContentTemplate="{DynamicResource SuitTemplate}"
          HorizontalAlignment="Right" VerticalAlignment="Bottom"
          Margin="0,0,8,8" RenderTransformOrigin="0.5,0.5">
          <Label.RenderTransform>
            <RotateTransform Angle="180"/>
          </Label.RenderTransform>
        </Label>
        <Image Name="TopRightImage" Style="{StaticResource ResourceKey=SuitImage}"
   Margin="12,12,8,0" HorizontalAlignment="Right" VerticalAlignment="Top"
   Width="18.5" Height="18.5" Stretch="UniformToFill" />
        <Image Name="BottomLeftImage" Style="{StaticResource ResourceKey=SuitImage}"
   Margin="12,0,8,12" HorizontalAlignment="Left" VerticalAlignment="Bottom"
   Width="18.5" Height="18.5" Stretch="UniformToFill"
   RenderTransformOrigin="0.5,0.5">
            <Image.RenderTransform>
              <RotateTransform Angle="180" />
            </Image.RenderTransform>
        </Image>
        <Path Fill="#FFFFFFFF" Stretch="Fill" Stroke="{x:Null}"
          Margin="0,0,35.218,-0.077" Data="F1 M110.5,51 L145.16457,51 C116.5986,
            76.731148 115.63518,132.69684 121.63533,149.34013 133.45299,
            182.12018 152.15821,195.69803 161.79765,200.07669 L110.5,200 C103.59644,
            200 98,194.40356 98,187.5 L98,63.5 C98,56.596439 103.59644,51 110.5,51 z">
          <Path.OpacityMask>
            <LinearGradientBrush EndPoint="0.957,1.127" StartPoint="0,-0.06">
              <GradientStop Color="#FF000000" Offset="0"/>
              <GradientStop Color="#00FFFFFF" Offset="1"/>
            </LinearGradientBrush>
          </Path.OpacityMask>
        </Path>
      </Grid>
    </UserControl>
```

4. Add three dependency properties to the class:

```
      public static DependencyProperty SuitProperty = DependencyProperty.Register(
        "Suit",
        typeof(CardLib.Suit),
        typeof(CardControl),
        new PropertyMetadata(CardLib.Suit.Club,
   new PropertyChangedCallback(OnSuitChanged)));

      public static DependencyProperty RankProperty = DependencyProperty.Register(
        "Rank",
        typeof(CardLib.Rank),
        typeof(CardControl),
        new PropertyMetadata(CardLib.Rank.Ace));
```

```
    public static DependencyProperty IsFaceUpProperty = DependencyProperty.Register(
    "IsFaceUp",
    typeof(bool),
    typeof(CardControl),
    new PropertyMetadata(true, new PropertyChangedCallback(OnIsFaceUpChanged)));

    public bool IsFaceUp
    {
      get { return (bool)GetValue(IsFaceUpProperty); }
      set { SetValue(IsFaceUpProperty, value); }
    }

    public CardLib.Suit Suit
    {
      get { return (CardLib.Suit)GetValue(SuitProperty); }
      set { SetValue(SuitProperty, value); }
    }

    public CardLib.Rank Rank
    {
      get { return (CardLib.Rank)GetValue(RankProperty); }
      set { SetValue(RankProperty, value); }
    }
```

**5.** Add the change event handlers to the class:

```
    public static void OnSuitChanged(DependencyObject source,
      DependencyPropertyChangedEventArgs args)
    {
      var control = source as CardControl;
      control.SetTextColor();
    }

    private static void OnIsFaceUpChanged(DependencyObject source,
            DependencyPropertyChangedEventArgs args)
    {
      var control = source as CardControl;
      control.RankLabel.Visibility = control.SuitLabel.Visibility =
              control.RankLabelInverted.Visibility =
    control.TopRightImage.Visibility =
    control.BottomLeftImage.Visibility = control.IsFaceUp ?
    Visibility.Visible : Visibility.Hidden;
      }
```

**6.** Add a property to the class:

```
    private CardLib.Card _card;
    public CardLib.Card Card
    {
      get { return _card; }
      private set { _card = value; Suit = _card.suit; Rank = _card.rank; }
    }
```

**7.** Add a helper method to set the text colors and overload the constructor to take a Card:

```
    public CardControl(Card card)
    {
      InitializeComponent();

      Card = card;
    }

    private void SetTextColor()
    {
      var color = (Suit == CardLib.Suit.Club || Suit == CardLib.Suit.Spade) ?
```

```
          new SolidColorBrush(Color.FromRgb(0, 0, 0)) :
          new SolidColorBrush(Color.FromRgb(255, 0, 0));
      RankLabel.Foreground = SuitLabel.Foreground = RankLabelInverted.Foreground =
                              color;
}
```

8. Add a new value converter by adding a new class to the project. Name it `RankNameConverter.cs` and add this code:

```
[ValueConversion(typeof(CardLib.Rank), typeof(string))]
public class RankNameConverter : IValueConverter
{
  public object Convert(object value, Type targetType,
object parameter, System.Globalization.CultureInfo culture)
  {
    int source = (int)value;
    if (source == 1 || source > 10)
    {
      switch (source)
      {
        case 1:
          return "Ace";
        case 11:
          return "Jack";
        case 12:
          return "Queen";
        case 13:
          return "King";
        default:
          return DependencyProperty.UnsetValue;
      }
    }
    else
      return source.ToString();
  }
  public object ConvertBack(object value, Type targetType,
object parameter, System.Globalization.CultureInfo culture)
  {
    return DependencyProperty.UnsetValue;
  }
}
```

6. Go to the `GameClient.xaml.cs` code-behind file and change the constructor like this:

```
public GameClient()
{
  InitializeComponent();

  var position = new Point(15, 15);
  for (var i = 0; i < 4; i++)
  {
    var suit = (CardLib.Suit)i;
    position.Y = 15;
    for (int rank = 1; rank < 14; rank++)
    {
      position.Y += 30;
      var card = new CardControl(new CardLib.Card((Suit)suit, (Rank)rank));
      card.VerticalAlignment = VerticalAlignment.Top;
      card.HorizontalAlignment = HorizontalAlignment.Left;
      card.Margin = new Thickness(position.X, position.Y, 0, 0);
      contentGrid.Children.Add(card);
```

```
        }
        position.X += 112;
    }
}
```

**7.** Run the application. The result is shown in Figure 16-3.

### How It Works

This example creates a user control with two dependent properties, and includes client code to use the control. This example covers plenty of ground, and the place to start looking at the code is with the Card control.

The Card control consists mostly of code that will be familiar to you from code you've seen earlier in this chapter. The layout code uses nothing new, although you might agree that the result is a bit prettier than the lurid button in the previous two examples.

The code in Card exposes three dependency properties, Suit, Rank, and IsFaceUp, to client code, and binds these properties to visual elements in the control layout. As a result, when you set Suit to Club, the word Club is displayed in the center of the card and the Club image is displayed in the top-right and bottom-left corners of the card. Similarly, the value of Rank is displayed in the other two corners of the card.

You'll look at the implementation of these properties in a moment. For now it is enough to know that they are enumerations originating from the CardLib project that you started in Chapter 10.

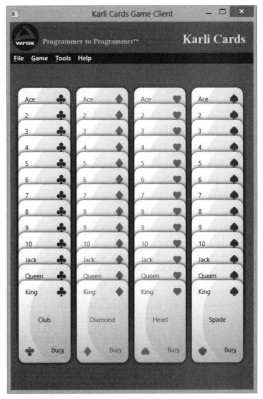

**FIGURE 16-3**

The three labels display the rank and suit of the card. Even though they are bound to different properties, they have a few things in common. They must display some text in red or black depending on the values of the bound properties. In this example, the color is set using the events raised when the Rank changes, but you can use triggers for this:

```
<Label x:Name="SuitLabel"
    Content="{Binding Path=Suit, ElementName=UserControl, Mode=Default}"
    ContentTemplate="{DynamicResource SuitTemplate}" HorizontalAlignment="Center"
    VerticalAlignment="Center" Margin="8,51,8,60" />
```

When you bind property values, you can also specify how to render the bound content, by using a data template. In this example, the *data template* is SuitTemplate, referenced as a dynamic resource (although in this case a static resource binding would also work fine). This template is defined in the user control resources section as follows:

```
<UserControl.Resources>
    <DataTemplate x:Key="SuitTemplate">
        <TextBlock Text="{Binding}"/>
    </DataTemplate>
</UserControl.Resources>
```

The string value of Suit is therefore used as the Text property of a TextBlock control. This same DataTemplate definition is reused for the two rank labels. Suit is an enumeration, and the name of the value in the enumeration is automatically converted to a string to be displayed in the Text property.

The two `Rank` labels include a value converter in the binding.

```
<Label x:Name="RankLabel" Grid.ZIndex="1"
       Content="{Binding Path=Rank, ElementName=UserControl, Mode=Default,
  Converter={StaticResource ResourceKey=rankConverter}}"
       ContentTemplate="{DynamicResource SuitTemplate}"
       HorizontalAlignment="Left" VerticalAlignment="Top"
       Margin="8,8,0,0" />
```

The converter is included in the `UserControl` resources through this declaration:

```
<src:RankNameConverter x:Key="rankConverter"/>
```

You will not break the control if you remove the value converter. Instead, you will see Ace, 2, 3, 4, and so on. You will also see the names of the enumeration values converted to string—Ace, Deuce, Three, Four, and so on. Although this is technically correct, it doesn't look quite right, so you convert the values to a combination of numbers and strings.

The final point to notice is the `Grid.ZIndex="1"` property assignment on the `RankLabel`. The `ZIndex` of a control on a `Grid` or `Canvas` determines the visual layer that holds the control. If two or more controls occupy the same space, then you can use the `ZIndex` to force one of them to go to the front. Normally all controls have a `ZIndex` of zero, so setting a single control to 1 means that it is moved to the front. This is necessary because the blur of the path would otherwise obscure the text.

For this data binding to work, you must define three dependency properties using techniques you learned in the previous section. These are defined in the code-behind for the user control as follows (they have simple .NET property wrappers, which there is no need to show here because of the simplicity of the code):

```
    public static DependencyProperty SuitProperty = DependencyProperty.Register(
        "Suit",
        typeof(CardLib.Suit),
        typeof(CardControl),
        new PropertyMetadata(CardLib.Suit.Club,
    new PropertyChangedCallback(OnSuitChanged)));

    public static DependencyProperty RankProperty = DependencyProperty.Register(
        "Rank",
        typeof(CardLib.Rank),
        typeof(CardControl),
        new PropertyMetadata(CardLib.Rank.Ace));

    public static DependencyProperty IsFaceUpProperty = DependencyProperty.Register(
        "IsFaceUp",typeof(bool),
        typeof(CardControl),
        new PropertyMetadata(true, new PropertyChangedCallback(OnIsFaceUpChanged)));
```

The dependency properties use a callback method to validate its values, and the `Suit` and `IsFaceUp` properties also have a callback method for when their values change.

When the value of `Suit` changes, the `OnSuitChanged()` callback method is called. This method is responsible for setting the text color to red (for hearts and diamonds) or black (for clubs and spades). It does this by calling a utility method on the source of the method call. This is necessary because the callback method is implemented as a static method, but it is passed the instance of the user control that raised the event as a parameter so that it can interact with it. The method called is `SetTextColor()`:

```
    public static void OnSuitChanged(DependencyObject source,
        DependencyPropertyChangedEventArgs args)
    {
      var control = source as CardControl;
      control.SetTextColor();
    }
```

The `SetTextColor()` method is private but is obviously still accessible from `OnSuitChanged()`, as they are both members of the same class, despite being instance and static methods, respectively. `SetTextColor()` simply sets the `Foreground` property of the various labels of the control to a solid color brush that is either black or red, depending on the `Suit` value.

When `IsFaceUp` changes, the control displays or hides the images and labels that are used to display the current value of the control.

This is all you need to look at in the `Card` control. The code in the `GameClient.xaml.cs` code-behind file is included to display the cards and is only temporary. It generates one card for each of the 13 possible values and displays each suit in a column.

## PUTTING IT ALL TOGETHER

At this point in the development of the game, you have two independent dialog boxes, a card library, and a main window that provides a blank space for the game to be displayed on. That still leaves quite a lot of work, but with the foundation build, it's time to start building the game. The classes in the CardLib describe the game "domain model," that is, the objects that a game can be broken down into, which need to be refactored a bit to make it work better with a Windows application. Next you are going to write the game's "View Model," which is a class that is able to control the display of the game. Then you will create two additional user controls that use the `Card` user control to display the game visually. Finally, you will bind it all together in the game client.

> **NOTE** The term "View Model" comes from a much used design pattern in WPF: Model - View - ViewModel (MVVM). This design pattern describes how to separate code from the view and link it together. Although this book doesn't attempt to confirm to this pattern, this example uses a lot of the elements from the pattern, such as separating the ViewModel from the views. In this context, the domain model described next is the "model" part of the MVVM name, and the Windows you have been creating are the views.

## Refactoring the Domain Model

As stated, the domain model is the code that describes the objects of the game. At the moment, you have these classes in the CardLib project that describe objects of the game:

➤ Card

➤ Deck

➤ Rank

➤ Suit

In addition to these classes, the game needs a `Player` and a `ComputerPlayer` class, so you are going to add those. You also need to modify the `Card` and `Deck` classes a bit to make them work better in a Windows application.

There is a lot of work to do, so let's get started.

> **NOTE** This example does not use the `CardClient` class from the earlier chapters because the differences between console and Windows applications are so great that very little code can be reused.

**TRY IT OUT** Finishing the Domain Model: KarliCards Gui

This example continues where the previous example left off.

1.  Each player in the game can be in a number of "states" during the game. You can model this in a `PlayerState` enumeration. Go to the CardLib project and create a new `PlayerState` enumeration for the project. You can simply create a new class and replace code like this:

    ```
    [Serializable]
    public enum PlayerState
    {
      Inactive,
      Active,
      MustDiscard,
      Winner,
      Loser
    }
    ```

2.  Next, you raise a few events when something happens on a player. For that, you need some custom event arguments, so add another class named `PlayerEventArgs`:

    ```
    public class PlayerEventArgs : EventArgs
    {
      public Player Player { get; set; }
      public PlayerState State { get; set; }
    }
    ```

3.  You also need to raise events when something happens to a card, so go ahead and create another class called `CardEventArgs`:

    ```
    public class CardEventArgs : EventArgs
    {
      public Card Card { get; set; }
    }
    ```

4.  The enumeration `ComputerSkillLevel` currently exists in the `GameOptions.cs` class (in the Karli Cards Gui project). Go ahead and cut it from there and move it to its own file in the CardLib project. This changes its namespace to `CardLib`, so you have to add the `CardLib` namespace to the `GameOptions .xaml.cs` and `Options.Xaml.cs` files:

    `using CardLib;`

5.  The `Deck` class should be changed. You will refactor the class a bit to make it more suitable for this application and add new code as well. First, start by selecting the code in the constructor. With this code selected, right-click and select Refactor ⇨ Extract Method (you can also press Ctrl-R+M). Visual Studio will create a new method containing the selected code. Name the method `InsertAllCards`.

6.  Whenever the deck is emptied, the discarded cards should be put back in play. In order to do this, add an overload of the `InsertAllCards` method that takes a list of the cards that are in play:

    ```
    private void InsertAllCards(List<Card> except)
    {
      for (int suitVal = 0; suitVal < 4; suitVal++)
      {
        for (int rankVal = 1; rankVal < 14; rankVal++)
        {
          var card = new Card((Suit)suitVal, (Rank)rankVal);
          if (except.Contains(card))
            continue;
          cards.Add(card);
        }
      }
    }
    ```

**7.** Add a new property called `CardsInDeck` that returns the number of cards in the deck:

```
public int CardsInDeck
{
  get { return cards.Count; }
}
```

**8.** Change the `Shuffle` method to reflect that there can be fewer than 52 cards in the deck. Do this by replacing the constant 52 with `cards.Count` in the three places it is used.

**9.** Insert the final three methods: `ReshuffleDiscarded`, `Draw`, and `SelectCardOfSpecificSuit`:

```
public void ReshuffleDiscarded(List<Card> cardsInPlay)
{
  InsertAllCards(cardsInPlay);
  Shuffle();
}
public Card Draw()
{
  if (cards.Count == 0)
    return null;
  else
  {
    var card = cards[0];
    cards.RemoveAt(0);
    return card;
  }
}

public Card SelectCardOfSpecificSuit(Suit suit)
{
  Card selectedCard = null;

  foreach (Card card in cards)
  {
    if (card.suit == suit)
    {
      selectedCard = card;
      break;
    }
  }
  if (selectedCard == null)
    return Draw(); // Can't cheat, no cards of the correct Suit
  else
  {
    cards.Remove(selectedCard);
  }
  return selectedCard;
}
```

**10.** Go to the `Card` class. During the game, card instances are going to be checked for null, which means you have to ensure that no properties are checked in the `==` operator on the cards. Change it like this:

```
public static bool operator ==(Card card1, Card card2)
{
  if (((object)card1) == null && ((object)card2) == null)
    return true;
  if (((object)card1) == null || ((object)card2) == null)
    return false;

  return (card1.suit == card2.suit) && (card1.rank == card2.rank);
}
```

**11.** Change the `Equals` method to test for the `Card` type:

```
public override bool Equals(object card)
{
  if (card == null)
    return false;

  if (card is Card)
    return this == (Card)card;
  return false;
}
```

**12.** Add a new method to the `Cards` class called `Discard`:

```
public void Discard(Card card)
{
  Remove(card);
}
```

**13.** There will be two types of players in the game: A Player, which is controlled by a real person; and a ComputerPlayer, which is controlled by the game. These two classes are omitted from the code listings here, but you can find them in the code download for the chapter as `Player.cs` and `ComputerPlayer.cs`. Go ahead and add them to the CardLib project.

### How It Works

That was a lot of code and a lot of changes! However, when you run the application, nothing seems to have changed. What you have done is called *refactoring*—the art of changing the code to work better or in another way, without actually changing the result. In Chapter 10 you saw an example of refactoring members, but here you have used it much more extensively. Strictly speaking, refactoring doesn't include adding behavior to the code, but you did that as well. Even though it can seem daft to change code that works, refactoring is actually an incredibly important task in programming because it allows you to utilize what you learn as you work on a project. Code that seemed to work perfect when it is written early in a project can become less perfect as new code needs to interact with it later. If you can identify a way to make the old code work better with the new, you should go ahead and refactor it. In the long run, you are going to end up with better code that is easier to maintain.

The dependency graph in Figure 16-4 shows the domain model of the Karli Cards game in its entirety.

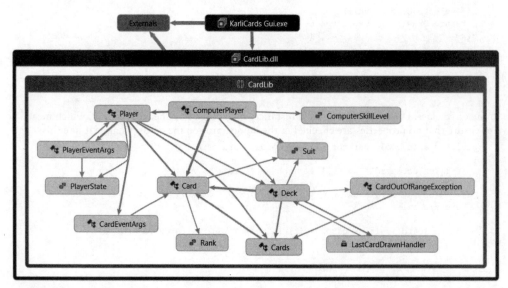

**FIGURE 16-4**

Most of the code in the `Player` and `ComputerPlayer` classes that you added to the project from the downloaded code is pretty easy to understand. The `Player` class can draw and discard cards. This is shared with the `ComputerPlayer`, but the computer is also equipped with the ability to decide which cards to draw and discard without user interaction. The `ComputerPlayer` class can also cheat:

```
public void PerformDraw(Deck deck, Card availableCard)
{
  switch (Skill)
  {
    case ComputerSkillLevel.Dumb:
      DrawCard(deck);
      break;
    default:
      DrawBestCard(deck, availableCard, (Skill == ComputerSkillLevel.Cheats));
      break;
  }
}

public void PerformDiscard(Deck deck)
{
  switch (Skill)
  {
    case ComputerSkillLevel.Dumb:
      int discardIndex = _random.Next(Hand.Count);
      DiscardCard(Hand[discardIndex]);
      break;
    default:
      DiscardWorstCard();
      break;
  }
}
private void DrawBestCard(Deck deck, Card availableCard, bool cheat = false)
{
  var bestSuit = CalculateBestSuit();
  if (availableCard.suit == bestSuit)
    AddCard(availableCard);
  else if (cheat == false)
    DrawCard(deck);
  else
    AddCard(deck.SelectCardOfSpecificSuit(bestSuit));
}
```

Cheating is assisted by a deck that allows the computer to select a card of a specific suit. If you allow the computer to cheat, you are going to have a hard time winning any games!

You will also notice that the `Player` class implements the `INotifyPropertyChanged` interface and the properties `PlayerName` and `State` use this to notify any observers of changes. Particularly, the `State` property is important later as changes to this property will drive the game forward.

## The View Models

The purpose of a view model is to hold the state of the view that displays it. In the case of the Karli Cards, this means that you already have a view model class: The `GameOptions` class. This class holds the state of the `Options` and `StartGame` windows. At the moment, you can't get the selected players from the options, so you have to add that ability. The view model of the Game Client window is missing, so that is the next task to do.

The view model for the execution of the game must reflect all the parts of the game as it is running. The parts of the game are:

➤  The deck from which the current player draw a card

➤  A card that can be taken by the current player instead of drawing a card

➤ A current player

➤ A number of participating players

The view model should also be able to notify observers of changes, and that means implementing
`INotifyPropertyChanged` again.

In addition to these abilities, the view model should also provide a way of starting a new game. You will
do this by creating a new routed command for the menu. The command is created in the view model, but is
called from the view.

---

**TRY IT OUT**   The View Model: KarliCards Gui

This example continues with the KarliCards Gui project.

**1.** Go to the KarliCards Gui project and create a new folder named `ViewModel` by right-clicking the project
and selecting Add ➪ New Folder.

**2.** Drag the `GameOptions.cs` class into this folder.

**3.** Change the namespace of the `GameOptions` class to `KarliCards_Gui.ViewModel`. You need to add the
using `KarliCards_Gui.ViewModel` directive in the `Options.xaml.cs` and `StartGame.xaml.cs` code-
behind files after this.

**4.** Add a new command to the `GameOptions` class:

```
public static RoutedCommand OptionsCommand = new RoutedCommand("Show Options",
typeof(GameOptions), new InputGestureCollection(new List<InputGesture>
{ new KeyGesture(Key.O, ModifierKeys.Control) }));
```

**5.** Add two new methods to the class:

```
public void Save()
{
  using (var stream = File.Open("GameOptions.xml", FileMode.Create))
  {
    var serializer = new XmlSerializer(typeof(GameOptions));
    serializer.Serialize(stream, this);
  }
}

public static GameOptions Create()
{
  if (File.Exists("GameOptions.xml"))
  {
    using (var stream = File.OpenRead("GameOptions.xml"))
    {
      var serializer = new XmlSerializer(typeof(GameOptions));
      return serializer.Deserialize(stream) as GameOptions;
    }
  }
  else
    return new GameOptions();
}
```

**6.** Change the OK click event handler of the `Options.xaml.cs` code-behind file like this:

```
private void okButton_Click(object sender, RoutedEventArgs e)
{
  this.DialogResult = true;
  _gameOptions.Save();
  this.Close();
}
```

**7.** Delete everything except the `InitializeComponent` call from the constructor and hook the `DataContextChanged` event like this:

```
public Options()
{
  _gameOptions = GameOptions.Create();
  DataContext = _gameOptions;

  InitializeComponent();
```

**8.** Open the `StartGame.xaml.cs` code-behind file and select the last four lines of the code in the constructor. Extract a new method called `ChangeListBoxOptions` by right-clicking the selected code and selecting Refactor ⇨ ExtractMethod:

```
private void ChangeListBoxOptions()
{
  if (_gameOptions.PlayAgainstComputer)
    playersListBox.SelectionMode = SelectionMode.Single;
  else
    playersListBox.SelectionMode = SelectionMode.Extended;
}
```

**9.** Delete everything except the `InitializeComponent` call from the constructor and hook the `Data ContextChanged` event like this:

```
public StartGame()
{
  InitializeComponent();

  DataContextChanged += StartGame_DataContextChanged;
}

void StartGame_DataContextChanged(object sender,
DependencyPropertyChangedEventArgs e)
{
  _gameOptions = DataContext as GameOptions;
  ChangeListBoxOptions();
}
```

**10.** Change the OK click event handler like this:

```
private void okButton_Click(object sender, RoutedEventArgs e)
{
  var gameOptions = DataContext as GameOptions;
  gameOptions.SelectedPlayers = new List<string>();
  foreach (string item in playerNamesListBox.SelectedItems)
  {
    gameOptions.SelectedPlayers.Add(item);
  }

  this.DialogResult = true;
  this.Close();
}
```

**11.** Create a new class in the new folder and name it `GameViewModel`. Start by implementing the `INotifyPropertyChanged` interface:

```
public event PropertyChangedEventHandler PropertyChanged;
private void OnPropertyChanged(string propertyName)
{
  if (PropertyChanged != null)
    PropertyChanged(this, new PropertyChangedEventArgs(propertyName));
}
```

**12.** Add a property to hold the current player. This property should use the `OnPropertyChanged` event:

```
private Player _currentPlayer;
public Player CurrentPlayer
{
  get { return _currentPlayer; }
  set
  {
    _currentPlayer = value;
    OnPropertyChanged("CurrentPlayer");
  }
}
```

**13.** Add four more properties and their related fields to the class, just as you did with the `CurrentPlayer` property. The property names and field names are shown in Table 16-6.

**TABLE 16-6:** Property and Field Names

| TYPE | PROPERTY NAME | FIELD NAME |
|---|---|---|
| List<Player> | Players | _players |
| Card | CurrentAvailableCard | _availableCard |
| Deck | GameDeck | _deck |
| bool | GameStarted | _gameStarted |

**14.** Add this private field to hold the game options:

```
private GameOptions _gameOptions;
```

**15.** Add two Routed commands:

```
public static RoutedCommand StartGameCommand =
new RoutedCommand("Start New Game", typeof(GameViewModel),
new InputGestureCollection(new List<InputGesture>
{ new KeyGesture(Key.N, ModifierKeys.Control) }));
    public static RoutedCommand ShowAboutCommand =
new RoutedCommand("Show About Dialog", typeof(GameViewModel));
```

**16.** Add a new default constructor:

```
public GameViewModel()
{
 _players = new List<Player>();
  this._gameOptions = GameOptions.Create();
}
```

**17.** When a game is started, the players and deck must be initialized. Add this code to the class:

```
public void StartNewGame()
{
    if (_gameOptions.SelectedPlayers.Count < 1 ||
(_gameOptions.SelectedPlayers.Count == 1
&& !_gameOptions.PlayAgainstComputer))
        return;

    CreateGameDeck();
    CreatePlayers();
    InitializeGame();
    GameStarted = true;
}

private void InitializeGame()
```

```
        {
          AssignCurrentPlayer(0);
          CurrentAvailableCard = GameDeck.Draw();
        }

        private void AssignCurrentPlayer(int index)
        {
          CurrentPlayer = Players[index];
          if (!Players.Any(x => x.State == PlayerState.Winner))
            Players.ForEach(x => x.State = (x == Players[index] ? PlayerState.Active :
    PlayerState.Inactive));
        }

        private void InitializePlayer(Player player)
        {
          player.DrawNewHand(GameDeck);
          player.OnCardDiscarded += player_OnCardDiscarded;
          player.OnPlayerHasWon += player_OnPlayerHasWon;
          Players.Add(player);
        }

        private void CreateGameDeck()
        {
          GameDeck = new CardLib.Deck();
          GameDeck.Shuffle();
        }

        private void CreatePlayers()
        {
          Players.Clear();
          for (var i = 0; i < _gameOptions.NumberOfPlayers; i++)
          {
            if (i < _gameOptions.SelectedPlayers.Count)
              InitializePlayer(new Player { Index = i, PlayerName =
    _gameOptions.SelectedPlayers[i] });
            else
              InitializePlayer(new ComputerPlayer { Index = i, Skill =
    _gameOptions.ComputerSkill });
          }
        }
```

**18.** Finally, add the two event handlers for the events generated by the players:

```
        void player_OnPlayerHasWon(object sender, PlayerEventArgs e)
        {
          Players.ForEach(x => x.State = (x == e.Player ? PlayerState.Winner :
                                          PlayerState.Loser));
        }

        void player_OnCardDiscarded(object sender, CardEventArgs e)
        {
          CurrentAvailableCard = e.Card;

          var nextIndex = CurrentPlayer.Index + 1 >= _gameOptions.NumberOfPlayers ? 0 :
                                          CurrentPlayer.Index + 1;

          if (GameDeck.CardsInDeck == 0)
          {
            var cardsInPlay = new List<Card>();
            foreach (var player in Players)
              cardsInPlay.AddRange(player.GetCards());
            cardsInPlay.Add(CurrentAvailableCard);
            GameDeck.ReshuffleDiscarded(cardsInPlay);
```

```
        }
      AssignCurrentPlayer(nextIndex);
    }
```

**19.** Go to the `GameClient.xaml` file and add a new namespace to the `Window` declaration:

```
xmlns:vm="clr-namespace:KarliCards_Gui.ViewModel"
```

**20.** Below the `Window` declaration, add a `DataContext` declaration:

```
<Window.DataContext >
  <vm:GameViewModel />
</Window.DataContext>
```

**21.** Add three command bindings to the `CommandBindings` declarations:

```
    <CommandBinding Command="vm:GameViewModel.StartGameCommand"
CanExecute="CommandCanExecute" Executed="CommandExecuted" />
<CommandBinding Command="vm:GameViewModel.ShowAboutCommand"
CanExecute="CommandCanExecute" Executed="CommandExecuted" />
    <CommandBinding Command="vm:GameOptions.OptionsCommand"
CanExecute="CommandCanExecute" Executed="CommandExecuted" />
```

**22.** Add a command to the New Game menu item like this:

```
<MenuItem Header="_New Game..." Foreground="Black" Width="200"
        Command="vm:GameViewModel.StartGameCommand" />
```

**23.** Add a command to the Options menu item and set the `width` to `200` like this:

```
<MenuItem Header="_Options" HorizontalAlignment="Left" Width="200"
Foreground="Black" Command="vm:GameOptions.OptionsCommand"/>
```

**24.** Add a command to the About menu item like this:

```
<MenuItem Header="_About" HorizontalAlignment="Left" Width="145"
Foreground="Black" Command="vm:GameViewModel.ShowAboutCommand"/>
```

**25.** Go to the code-behind file and change the `CommandCanExecute` and `CommandExecuted` methods like this:

```
private void CommandCanExecute(object sender, CanExecuteRoutedEventArgs e)
{
  if (e.Command == ApplicationCommands.Close)
    e.CanExecute = true;
  if (e.Command == ApplicationCommands.Save)
    e.CanExecute = false;
  if (e.Command == GameViewModel.StartGameCommand)
    e.CanExecute = true;
  if (e.Command == GameOptions.OptionsCommand)
    e.CanExecute = true;
  if (e.Command == GameViewModel.ShowAboutCommand)
    e.CanExecute = true;
  e.Handled = true;
}

private void CommandExecuted(object sender, ExecutedRoutedEventArgs e)
{
  if (e.Command == ApplicationCommands.Close)
    this.Close();
  if (e.Command == GameViewModel.StartGameCommand)
  {
    var model = new GameViewModel();
    StartGame startGameDialog = new StartGame();

    var options = GameOptions.Create();
    startGameDialog.DataContext = options;
    var result = startGameDialog.ShowDialog();
```

```
                if (result.HasValue && result.Value == true)
                {
                  options.Save();
                  model.StartNewGame();
                  DataContext = model;
                }
              }
              if (e.Command == GameOptions.OptionsCommand)
              {
                var dialog = new Options();
                dialog.DataContext = model;
                var result = dialog.ShowDialog();
                if (result.HasValue && result.Value == true)
                {

                  DataContext = new GameViewModel(); // Clear current game
                }
              }
              if (e.Command == GameViewModel.ShowAboutCommand)
              {
                var dialog = new About();
                dialog.ShowDialog();
              }
              e.Handled = true;
            }
```

**26.** Delete everything from the constructor except the `InitializeComponent()` call.

### *How It Works*

Once again you have done a lot of work with very little to show for it when you run the application, but the menus have changed. The Options and New Game menu items have been given shortcut keys and can now be accessed using Ctrl-O and Ctrl-N. This is displayed when you drop down the menus. This has happened because you created two new commands for the menu. You did this in `GameOptions.cs` and `GameViewModel.cs`, respectively:

```
        public static RoutedCommand OptionsCommand = new RoutedCommand("Show Options",
    typeof(GameOptions), new InputGestureCollection(new List<InputGesture>
    { new KeyGesture(Key.O, ModifierKeys.Control) }));

        public static RoutedCommand StartGameCommand =
    new RoutedCommand("Start New Game", typeof(GameViewModel),
    new InputGestureCollection(new List<InputGesture>
    { new KeyGesture(Key.N, ModifierKeys.Control) }));
```

When you assign a list of `InputGestures` to the command, the shortcuts are automatically associated with the menus.

In the code-behind for the game client, you also added code to display the two windows as dialog boxes.

```
              if (e.Command == GameViewModel.StartGameCommand)
              {
                var model = new GameViewModel();
                StartGame startGameDialog = new StartGame();
                startGameDialog.DataContext = model.GameOptions;
                var result = startGameDialog.ShowDialog();
                if (result.HasValue && result.Value == true)
                {
                  model.GameOptions.Save();
                  model.StartNewGame();
                  DataContext = model;
                }
              }
```

By showing the windows as dialog boxes, you can return a value that indicates whether the result of the dialog box should be used. You can't return a value directly from the window; instead, you set the window's `DialogResult` property to either true or false to indicate success or failure:

```
private void okButton_Click(object sender, RoutedEventArgs e)
{
  this.DialogResult = true;
  this.Close();
}
```

In Chapter 15 you were told that if you want to set the `DataContext` to an existing object instance, you had to do so from code. This happens in the previous code, but the XAML in `GameClient.xaml` also instantiates a new instance when the applications starts:

```
<Window.DataContext >
  <vm:GameViewModel />
</Window.DataContext>
```

This instance ensures that there is a `DataContext` for the view, but it isn't used for much before it is exchanged for a new instance in the `StartGame` command.

The `GameViewModel` contains a lot of code but much of it is just properties and instantiation of the players and the Deck instances.

Once the game has started, the state of the players and `GameViewModel` drive the game forward as the computer or the players make choices. The `PlayerHasWon` event is handled in `GameViewModel` and ensures that the state of the other players changes to `Loser`.

```
void player_OnPlayerHasWon(object sender, PlayerEventArgs e)
{
  Players.ForEach(x => x.State = (x == e.Player ? PlayerState.Winner :
PlayerState.Loser));
}
```

The other event you created for the player is also handled here: `CardDiscarded` is used to indicate that a player has completed her turn. This causes the `CurrentPlayer` to be set to the next available player:

```
void player_OnCardDiscarded(object sender, CardEventArgs e)
{
  CurrentAvailableCard = e.Card;
  var nextIndex = CurrentPlayer.Index + 1 >= _gameOptions.NumberOfPlayers ? 0 :
                    CurrentPlayer.Index + 1;
  if (GameDeck.CardsInDeck == 0)
  {
    var cardsInPlay = new List<Card>();
    foreach (var player in Players)
      cardsInPlay.AddRange(player.GetCards());
    cardsInPlay.Add(CurrentAvailableCard);
    GameDeck.ReshuffleDiscarded(cardsInPlay);
  }
  AssignCurrentPlayer(nextIndex);
}
```

This event handler also checks whether there are any more cards in the deck. If there are no more cards, the event handler collects a list of cards that are currently used in the game and makes the deck generate a new, shuffled deck containing only cards that have been discarded.

The `StartGame` method is called from the `CommandExecuted` method in the `GameClient.xaml.cs` code-behind file. This method uses three methods to create a new deck, to create and deal cards to the players, and finally to set the `CurrentPlayer` to start the game.

## Completing the Game

You now have a complete game that you can't play because nothing is being displayed in the game client. For the game to run, you need two additional user controls that will be positioned on the game client using a dock panel.

The two user controls are called `CardsInHand`, which displays a player's hand, and `GameDecks`, which displays the main deck and the available card.

> **NOTE** *You can add dependency properties by typing* `propdp` *and pressing Tab twice in the editor.*

**TRY IT OUT**  Completing the Game: KarliCards Gui

Once again, this example continues with the KarliCards Gui project you have been working on.

1. Create a new user control in the GameClient project by right-clicking the project and selecting Add ⇨ User Control. Name it `CardsInHandControl`.

2. Add a `Label` and a `Canvas` control to the `Grid` like this:

```
<Grid>
  <Label Name="PlayerNameLabel" Foreground="White" FontWeight="Bold"
FontSize="14" >
    <Label.Effect>
      <DropShadowEffect ShadowDepth="5" Opacity="0.5" Direction="145" />
    </Label.Effect>
  </Label>
  <Canvas Name="CardSurface">
  </Canvas>
</Grid>
```

3. Go to the code-behind file and use these using directives:

```
using CardLib;
using KarliCards_Gui.ViewModel;
using System;
using System.Threading;
using System.Windows;
using System.Windows.Controls;
using System.Windows.Input;
using System.Windows.Media;
using System.Windows.Threading;
```

4. There are four dependency properties. Type **propdp** and press the Tab key twice to insert the property template. Insert the `Type`, `Name`, `OwnerClass`, and default value. Use tab to switch from one value to the next. Set the values as shown in the table below. Press the Return key after you finish editing the values to complete the template (see Table 16-7).

**TABLE 16-7:** Cards in Hand Dependency Properties

| TYPE | NAME | OWNERCLASS | DEFAULT VALUE |
|---|---|---|---|
| Player | Owner | CardsInHandControl | null |
| GameViewModel | Game | CardsInHandControl | null |
| PlayerState | PlayerState | CardsInHandControl | PlayerState.Inactive |
| Orientation | PlayerOrientation | CardsInHandControl | Orientation.Horizontal |

**5.** The `Owner` property requires a callback that should be called whenever the property changes. You can specify this as the second parameter of the constructor of the `PropertyMetadata` class that is used as the fourth parameter of the `register()` method. Change the registration like this:

```
public static readonly DependencyProperty OwnerProperty =
DependencyProperty.Register(
"Owner",
typeof(Player),
typeof(CardsInHandControl),
new PropertyMetadata(null, new PropertyChangedCallback(OnOwnerChanged)));
```

**6.** Like the `Owner` property, the `PlayerState` and `PlayerOrientation` properties should also register a callback. Repeat Step 4 for these two properties using the names `OnPlayerStateChanged` and `OnPlayerOrientationChanged` for the callback methods.

**7.** Add the callback methods:

```
private static void OnOwnerChanged(DependencyObject source,
DependencyPropertyChangedEventArgs e)
    {
      var control = source as CardsInHandControl;
      control.RedrawCards();
    }

private static void OnPlayerStateChanged(DependencyObject source,
DependencyPropertyChangedEventArgs e)
    {
      var control = source as CardsInHandControl;
      var computerPlayer = control.Owner as ComputerPlayer;

      if (computerPlayer != null)
      {
        if (computerPlayer.State == PlayerState.MustDiscard)
        {
          Thread delayedWorker = new Thread(control.DelayDiscard);
          delayedWorker.Start(new Payload { Deck = control.Game.GameDeck,
AvailableCard = control.Game.CurrentAvailableCard, Player = computerPlayer });
        }
        else if (computerPlayer.State == PlayerState.Active)
        {
          Thread delayedWorker = new Thread(control.DelayDraw);
          delayedWorker.Start(new Payload { Deck = control.Game.GameDeck,
AvailableCard = control.Game.CurrentAvailableCard, Player = computerPlayer });
        }
      }
      control.RedrawCards();
    }

private static void OnPlayerOrientationChanged(DependencyObject source,
DependencyPropertyChangedEventArgs args)
    {
      var control = source as CardsInHandControl;
      control.RedrawCards();
    }
```

**8.** The callbacks require a number of helper methods. Start by adding the private class and two methods that are used by the `delayedWorker` threads in the `OnPlayerStateChanged` method:

```
private class Payload
{
  public Deck Deck { get; set; }
  public Card AvailableCard { get; set; }
  public ComputerPlayer Player { get; set; }
}

private void DelayDraw(object payload)
```

```
      {
        Thread.Sleep(1250);
        var data = payload as Payload;
        Dispatcher.Invoke(DispatcherPriority.Normal,
  new Action<Deck, Card>(data.Player.PerformDraw), data.Deck, data.AvailableCard);
      }

      private void DelayDiscard(object payload)
      {
        Thread.Sleep(1250);
        var data = payload as Payload;
        Dispatcher.Invoke(DispatcherPriority.Normal,
  new Action<Deck>(data.Player.PerformDiscard), data.Deck);
      }
```

**9.** Add the methods used to draw the control:

```
      private void RedrawCards()
      {
        CardSurface.Children.Clear();
        if (Owner == null)
        {
          PlayerNameLabel.Content = string.Empty;
          return;
        }
        DrawPlayerName();
        DrawCards();
      }

      private void DrawCards()
      {
        bool isFaceup = (Owner.State != PlayerState.Inactive);
        if (Owner is ComputerPlayer)
          isFaceup = (Owner.State == CardLib.PlayerState.Loser ||
  Owner.State == CardLib.PlayerState.Winner);

        var cards = Owner.GetCards();
        if (cards == null || cards.Count == 0)
          return;

        for (var i = 0; i < cards.Count; i++)
        {
          var cardControl = new CardControl(cards[i]);
          if (PlayerOrientation == Orientation.Horizontal)
            cardControl.Margin = new Thickness(i * 35, 35, 0, 0);
          else
            cardControl.Margin = new Thickness(5, 35 + i * 30, 0, 0);
          cardControl.MouseDoubleClick += cardControl_MouseDoubleClick;
          cardControl.IsFaceUp = isFaceup;
          CardSurface.Children.Add(cardControl);
        }
      }

      private void DrawPlayerName()
      {
        if (Owner.State == PlayerState.Winner || Owner.State == PlayerState.Loser)
          PlayerNameLabel.Content = Owner.PlayerName +
  (Owner.State == PlayerState.Winner ?
  " is the WINNER" : " has LOST");
        else
          PlayerNameLabel.Content = Owner.PlayerName;
        var isActivePlayer = (Owner.State == CardLib.PlayerState.Active ||
```

```
  Owner.State == CardLib.PlayerState.MustDiscard);
        PlayerNameLabel.FontSize = isActivePlayer ? 18 : 14;
        PlayerNameLabel.Foreground = isActivePlayer ?
new SolidColorBrush(Colors.Gold) :
new SolidColorBrush(Colors.White);
      }
```

10. Finally, add the double-click handler that is called when the player double-clicks a card:

```
    private void cardControl_MouseDoubleClick(object sender, MouseButtonEventArgs e)
    {
      var selectedCard = sender as CardControl;
      if (Owner == null)
        return;
      if (Owner.State == PlayerState.MustDiscard)
        Owner.DiscardCard(selectedCard.Card);
      RedrawCards();
    }
```

11. Create another user control like you did in Step 1 and name it GameDecksControl.

12. Remove the Grid and insert a Canvas control instead:

```
    <Canvas Name="controlCanvas" Width="250" />
```

13. Go to the code-behind file use these namespaces:

```
using CardLib;
using System.Collections.Generic;
using System.Linq;
using System.Windows;
using System.Windows.Controls;
using System.Windows.Documents;
using System.Windows.Input;
```

14. As you did in Step 4, add four dependency properties with these values (see Table 16-8).

**TABLE 16-8:** Game Decks Dependency Properties

| TYPE | NAME | OWNERCLASS | DEFAULT VALUE |
|------|------|------------|---------------|
| bool | GameStarted | GameDecksControl | false |
| Player | CurrentPlayer | GameDecksControl | null |
| Deck | Deck | GameDecksControl | null |
| Card | AvailableCard | GameDecksControl | null |

15. All four properties require a callback method for when the property changes. Add these as you did in Step 4 with the names OnGameStarted, OnPlayerChanged, OnDeckChanged, and OnAvailable CardChanged.

16. Add the callback methods:

```
    private static void OnGameStarted(DependencyObject source,
  DependencyPropertyChangedEventArgs e)
    {
      var control = source as GameDecksControl;
      control.DrawDecks();
    }

    private static void OnPlayerChanged(DependencyObject source,
        DependencyPropertyChangedEventArgs e)
    {
      var control = source as GameDecksControl;
      if (control.CurrentPlayer == null)
```

```
                return;

           control.CurrentPlayer.OnCardDiscarded +=
                         control.CurrentPlayer_OnCardDiscarded;
           control.DrawDecks();
         }

         private void CurrentPlayer_OnCardDiscarded(object sender, CardEventArgs e)
         {
           AvailableCard = e.Card;
           DrawDecks();
         }

         private static void OnDeckChanged(DependencyObject source,
     DependencyPropertyChangedEventArgs e)
         {
           var control = source as GameDecksControl;
           control.DrawDecks();
         }

         private static void OnAvailableCardChanged(DependencyObject source,
     DependencyPropertyChangedEventArgs e)
         {
           var control = source as GameDecksControl;
           control.DrawDecks();
         }
```

**17.** Add the `DrawDecks` method:

```
         private void DrawDecks()
         {
           controlCanvas.Children.Clear();
           if (CurrentPlayer == null || Deck == null || !GameStarted)
             return;

           List<CardControl> stackedCards = new List<CardControl>();
           for (int i = 0; i < Deck.CardsInDeck; i++)
             stackedCards.Add(new CardControl(Deck.GetCard(i)) { Margin =
     new Thickness(150 + (i * 1.25), 25 - (i * 1.25), 0, 0), IsFaceUp = false });

           if (stackedCards.Count > 0)
             stackedCards.Last().MouseDoubleClick += Deck_MouseDoubleClick;
           if (AvailableCard != null)
           {
             var availableCard = new CardControl(AvailableCard) { Margin =
     new Thickness(0, 25, 0, 0) };
             availableCard.MouseDoubleClick += AvailalbleCard_MouseDoubleClick;
             controlCanvas.Children.Add(availableCard);
           }
           stackedCards.ForEach(x => controlCanvas.Children.Add(x));
         }
```

**18.** Finally, add the event handlers for the cards:

```
         void AvailalbleCard_MouseDoubleClick(object sender, MouseButtonEventArgs e)
         {
           if (CurrentPlayer.State != PlayerState.Active)
             return;

           var control = sender as CardControl;
           CurrentPlayer.AddCard(control.Card);
           AvailableCard = null;
           DrawDecks();
         }
```

```
void Deck_MouseDoubleClick(object sender, MouseButtonEventArgs e)
{
  if (CurrentPlayer.State != PlayerState.Active)
    return;

  CurrentPlayer.DrawCard(Deck);
  DrawDecks();
}
```

**19.** Return to the `GameClient.xaml` file and remove the `Grid` that is currently in Row 2. Instead, insert a new dock panel like this:

```
<DockPanel Grid.Row="2">
    <src:CardsInHandControl x:Name="Player2Hand" DockPanel.Dock="Right"
 Height="380" Game="{Binding}"
        VerticalAlignment="Center" Width="180" PlayerOrientation="Vertical"
        Owner="{Binding Players[1]}" PlayerState="{Binding Players[1].State}" />
    <src:CardsInHandControl x:Name="Player4Hand" DockPanel.Dock="Left"
        HorizontalAlignment="Left" Height="380" VerticalAlignment="Center"
        PlayerOrientation="Vertical" Owner="{Binding Players[3]}" Width="180"
        PlayerState="{Binding Players[3].State}" Game="{Binding}"/>
    <src:CardsInHandControl x:Name="Player1Hand" DockPanel.Dock="Top"
        HorizontalAlignment="Center" Height="154" VerticalAlignment="Top"
        PlayerOrientation="Horizontal" Owner="{Binding Players[0]}" Width="380"
        PlayerState="{Binding Players[0].State}" Game="{Binding}"/>
    <src:CardsInHandControl x:Name="Player3Hand" DockPanel.Dock="Bottom"
        HorizontalAlignment="Center" Height="154" VerticalAlignment="Top"
        PlayerOrientation="Horizontal" Owner="{Binding Players[2]}" Width="380"
        PlayerState="{Binding Players[2].State}" Game="{Binding}"/>
    <src:GameDecksControl Height="180" x:Name="GameDecks" Deck="{Binding GameDeck}"
        AvailableCard="{Binding CurrentAvailableCard}"
        CurrentPlayer="{Binding CurrentPlayer}"
        GameStarted="{Binding GameStarted}"/>
</DockPanel>
```

**20.** Run the application. By default the `ComputerPlayer` class is enabled and the number of players is set to two. This means you select a single name in the Start Game dialog box. After that, you should be able to see something like Figure 16-5.

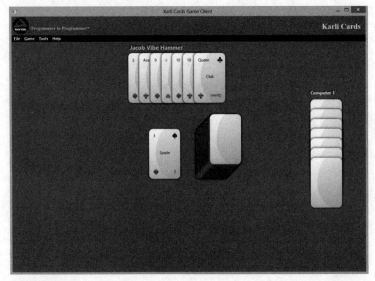

**FIGURE 16-5**

Double-click on the deck or available card to draw and then click a card from your hand to discard it.

### How It Works

Even though there is quite a bit of code in this example, most of it is the dependency properties, and the XAML is all about data binding these properties. The CardsInHandControl creates three properties that it uses to display itself and react to changes: Game, Owner, and PlayerState. Game and Owner are mostly used to draw , but the PlayerState is also used to control the ComputerPlayer actions.

```
private static void OnPlayerStateChanged(DependencyObject source,
                         DependencyPropertyChangedEventArgs e)
{
  var control = source as CardsInHandControl;
  var computerPlayer = control.Owner as ComputerPlayer;

  if (computerPlayer != null)
  {
    if (computerPlayer.State == PlayerState.MustDiscard)
    {
      Thread delayedWorker = new Thread(control.DelayDiscard);
      delayedWorker.Start(new Payload
      {
        Deck = control.Game.GameDeck,
        AvailableCard = control.Game.CurrentAvailableCard,
        Player = computerPlayer
      });
    }
    else if (computerPlayer.State == PlayerState.Active)
    {
      Thread delayedWorker = new Thread(control.DelayDraw);
      delayedWorker.Start(new Payload
      {
        Deck = control.Game.GameDeck,
        AvailableCard = control.Game.CurrentAvailableCard,
        Player = computerPlayer
      });
    }
  }
  control.RedrawCards();
}
```

The OnPlayerStateChanged method, which is used to react to changes in the state of the player, determines if the current player is a ComputerPlayer. If it is, it checks to make sure that the computer player draws or discards a card. If this is the case, it creates a worker thread for this to happen and executes the methods on this thread. This allows the application to continue working while the computer is waiting:

```
private void DelayDraw(object payload)
{
  Thread.Sleep(1250);

  var data = payload as Payload;
  Dispatcher.Invoke(DispatcherPriority.Normal,
    new Action<Deck, Card>(data.Player.PerformDraw), data.Deck, data.AvailableCard);
}
```

The Dispatcher is used to invoke the call. This ensures that the calls are made on the GUI thread.

Drawing the cards is pretty straightforward. The program simply stacks them vertically or horizontally depending on the settings in PlayerOrientation.

The GameDecksControl is even simpler. It uses the CurrentPlayer class to be notified that the CurrentPlayer has changed. When this happens, it hooks the CardDiscarded event on the player, and uses this event to be notified that the card was discarded.

Finally, you add a dock panel to the game client with a `CardsInHandControl` on each side and with a `GameDecksControl` in the middle:

```
<src:CardsInHandControl x:Name="Player1Hand" DockPanel.Dock="Top"
    HorizontalAlignment="Center" Height="154" VerticalAlignment="Top"
    PlayerOrientation="Horizontal" Owner="{Binding Players[0]}" Width="380"
    PlayerState="{Binding Players[0].State}" Game="{Binding}" />
```

The binding for `Game` simply binds the `DataContext` of the game client directly to the `Game` property of the `CardsInHandControl`. The `PlayerState` is bound to the `State` property of a player. In this case, the the player at index 0 is used to access the state.

## SUMMARY

This chapter covered a lot of ground while finishing the game client for the Karli Cards game. You used the `Menu` control to create a simple menu with menu items that included images and shortcut keys. The shortcut keys were assigned to the menu items through commands. You used built-in application commands that ship with WPF and created custom commands for starting the game and displaying dialog boxes.

You learned how to use styles to set properties on all or many controls of the same type and how to use control templates to define how controls should be displayed. By combining these techniques, you created a `Card` control that displayed itself entirely using XAML data binding.

Finally, you created two controls that used C# to add controls to child elements so the controls could display themselves.

### EXERCISES

**16.1** The current game client has a problem. From the Options dialog box, you can set the skill level of the computer. The problem is that the radio buttons are not updated to reflect the choice the next time you open the Options dialog box. This is partly because there is nothing that tries to update them and partly because there is no value converter from `ComputerSkillLevel`. Fix this problem by creating a new value converter and setting the `IsChecked` binding instead of using the `Checked` event that is currently being used.

Hint: You must use the `ConverterParameter` part of the `Converter` binding.

**16.2** The computer cheats, so you might want to allow the players to cheat as well. On the Options dialog box, create an option for the computer to play with open cards.

**16.3** Create a status bar at the bottom of the game client that displays the current state of the game.

## ▶ WHAT YOU HAVE LEARNED IN THIS CHAPTER

| TOPIC | KEY CONCEPTS |
|---|---|
| Styles | You can use styles to create styles for XAML elements that can be reused on many elements. Styles allow you to set the properties of an element. When you set the `Style` property of an element to point to a style you have defined, the properties of the element will use the values you specified in the `Style` property. |
| Templates | Templates are used to define the content of a control. Using templates you can change how standard controls are displayed. You can also build complex custom controls with them. |
| Value converters | Value converters are used to convert to and from two types. To create a value converter, you must implement the interface `IValueConverter` on a class. |
| User controls | User controls are used to create code and XAML that can be reused easily in your own project. This code and XAML can also be exported for use in other projects. |

# 17

# Windows Store Apps

**WHAT YOU WILL LEARN IN THIS CHAPTER**

- ➤ What a Windows 8 developer license is and how to get one
- ➤ The options you have for creating Windows Store apps
- ➤ How to develop Windows Store apps using XAML and C#
- ➤ What possible page and application types are available to you in Visual Studio and how to use them
- ➤ How to acquire and use a Windows Store account

**WROX.COM CODE DOWNLOADS FOR THIS CHAPTER**

You can find the wrox.com code downloads for this chapter at www.wrox.com/remtitle .cgi?isbn=9781118314418 on the Download Code tab. The code is in the Chapter 17 download and individually named according to the names throughout the chapter.

Windows Store apps is the new hot topic for Windows Developers all over the world. With the release of Windows 8, Microsoft is taking a huge leap from targeting the desktop and laptop computers almost exclusively toward becoming a real player on the market for tablet PCs and smartphones. Windows 8 ships with a new API for developing apps, a Windows Store that allows users to download apps in a secure and predictable way. At the same time, this new type of app makes it much easier for developers to reach their potential customers.

At the heart of the Windows Store is the Windows Store application. This chapter explores what that is and how you can develop applications using Visual C# and XAML.

## GETTING STARTED

Writing Windows Store apps requires a few initial steps before you can get going. Because it is useful to be able to see some of the features described in the following sections in Visual Studio, you should start by getting a Windows 8 developer license, as described next. You can then follow the descriptions and examples in the next sections.

## Windows 8 Developer License

Until now, you have been able to develop your applications and run them with a minimum of fuss. For traditional Windows development, you don't need any kind of license to create programs, even if your applications require administrative privileges on the local computer. For Windows Store apps, this is not the case. In order to develop these applications, you need to get a Windows 8 developer license. If you want to deploy your application to the app store, you need a Windows Store account.

### How to Get the License

The developer license is required to create Windows Store applications in Windows 8, and you are prompted by Visual Studio to get one the first time you create a Windows Store app. You cannot use the examples in this chapter unless you have a developer license, so the following Try It Out shows you how to get one.

**TRY IT OUT**    Getting a Developer License

1.  Start Visual Studio and create a new project by selecting File ➪ New ➪ Project.

2.  Under Installed ➪ Templates ➪ Visual C#, select Windows Store. In the list of templates, select Blank App (XAML). The name of the application is not important.

3.  At this point, Visual Studio will prompt you to get a developer license, as shown in Figure 17-1.

**FIGURE 17-1**

4.  If you agree to the terms and conditions, click I Agree.

5.  If you are prompted to allow Visual Studio to install changes, accept this.

6.  Now you need a Microsoft account. If you have a hotmail account you want to use, you can do that. Otherwise, you can click Sign Up to create the account. Once you have it, type the ID and password into the login screen, as shown in Figure 17-2.

**FIGURE 17-2**

**7.** At this point a developer license will be created for you and you will be presented with a window stating, among other things, that your license will soon expire. Click Close to return to Visual Studio.

### How It Works

The developer license is for deploying apps only for testing. You cannot get an app into the app store using this license, but it is enough to get started developing apps and testing them locally on your own computer.

A developer license expires a month after it is acquired. If you have a Store account, the developer license expiration is slower; however, renewing the license is easy. All you have to do is go to the Project ⇨ Store ⇨ Acquire developer license in Visual Studio.

## WINDOWS STORE APPS VERSUS DESKTOP APPLICATIONS

Windows Store apps are designed to run well on touch devices such as tablets and smartphones. They can run on normal laptops, but the visual design of your apps should be built for touch, and that requires a radical departure from the design you are likely familiar with in Windows 7. The design style suggested by Microsoft dictates a number of aspects about the look and feel of the apps, some of which you can ignore should you want to (although it's not a good idea to do so) and others you must comply with. The styles apply to all parts of an app, from resizing to how it presents itself on the Start screen. During this chapter you are going to see many of these styles in use.

In addition to the visual representation of the applications, Windows Store apps are Windows programs that run in a sandboxed environment in Windows, which limits what they can be used for.

Unlike desktop applications, Windows Store apps run on a new API called WinRT (not to be confused with the Windows edition, *Windows RT*). This API is developed on top of the old Win32 API and is designed to run fast and sandboxed. The API implements the UI for Windows Store apps. When you start developing apps for Windows 8, you will quickly realize that the .NET Framework for Windows Store apps is quite limited when compared to the full edition that you use when creating desktop applications. For example, the `File` class no longer exists. Obviously this doesn't mean that you can't store data locally, but you have to use secure methods to do so, and the direct access to the file system provided by the `File` class is not allowed.

WinRT has been designed with performance in mind, so Microsoft has made asynchronous any operation estimated to take more than 40 milliseconds to complete. This is also something that you should consider when you are writing apps. When you look at some of the new methods for opening a stream to a file, you will notice that these methods are marked as `awaitable`, which means you can use them with the async/await pattern you saw earlier in this book.

So far in this book, you've mainly seen desktop applications. They are usually displayed with a caption bar at the top of the window, an (x) button in the top-right corner of the screen, and an icon in the top-left corner that causes a drop-down menu to unfold when clicked. These applications use the Win32 API to access features in Windows, something that even the .NET Framework does behind the scenes. Because of this, they have access to the core components of Windows.

When you are planning to write an application that must run either on the desktop or as a Windows Store application, it is important that you consider the requirements of your application. There are two major factors to take into account: Do you want your application to run on touch devices such as phones, tablets, and touch-sensitive laptops? If you do, then the Windows Store app is the obvious choice unless you are explicitly hindered by the second factor: the Sandbox. If your applications require low-level access to the file system (for example, if you are developing a virus scanner or backup utility), then there is no way that you can do this as a Windows Store application and you must create a desktop application.

The last factor that you should consider when you decide between a desktop or Windows Store app is the distribution of your application. As a rule, Windows Store apps must be distributed using the Windows Store. This means that such apps must adhere to a number of rules set in stone by Microsoft. Desktop apps, on the other hand, can be packaged and distributed without the consent of Microsoft and the Windows Store. Although this grants you some freedom, the Windows Store makes it a lot easier to distribute the app to a potentially large audience.

## DEVELOPING WINDOWS STORE APPS

As already described, Windows Store apps use a long list of design styles to display themselves. They also have a number of common traits that you should be aware of when you develop the apps, so let's take a look at some of the many things that are new and compare how Windows Store apps match up against the desktop applications that you know.

### View Modes

All Windows Store apps are, by default, rendered in Full-Screen mode, but they should be able to display properly in two additional modes: Snapped and Fill. The reason for this is that users can have two apps running at the same time, side-by-side on the same screen. This is done by dragging one of the apps into a sidebar, causing the other app to fill the remaining space.

## Full-Screen Mode

When an application is in Full-Screen mode, it must fill the entire screen on which it is displayed, as illustrated in Figure 17-3.

This is the default way to display an app, and it is the most important one to get right; however, you must be aware of what happens to your app when it is resized.

**FIGURE 17-3**

## Snapped Mode

When a user drags your app into a sidebar, it enters Snapped mode (see Figure 17-4).

When this happens, your app should remain useable. This means that you can't just allow the app to display whatever part of the GUI happens to be visible in the snapped state. You must make a conscious decision as to what is displayed in this case.

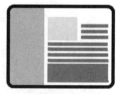

**FIGURE 17-4**

## Fill Mode

When another app moves into a sidebar, your app switches into the third view mode: Fill (see Figure 17-5).

This mode is closely related to Full-Screen mode since many apps will be able to retain the layout of the GUI in Fill mode, something that is rarely possible in Snapped mode.

**FIGURE 17-5**

## Screen Orientation

Although the view modes of Full-Screen, Fill, and Snapped can be said to be new, all Windows 7 applications should be able to resize themselves gracefully, so the change is not that great. But one aspect that is completely new to most Windows programmers is the fact that handheld devices can move in three dimensions. Your users will expect your app to move with the orientation of the screen. So, if the user flips her tablet around, your app should follow the movement, as shown in Figure 17-6.

**FIGURE 17-6**

## The Missing Caption Bar

In addition to the different view modes, one of the most immediately recognizable features of Windows Store apps is their lack of a caption bar at the top of the window. This is a radical break from desktop applications. The lack of a caption bar means that more space is available on the screen for the application, However, this can also cause experienced Windows users to wonder how to close an application. This question is answered in the "App Lifetime" section later in this chapter.

## Menus and Toolbars

Desktop apps use menus and toolbars for navigation in the application. Windows Store apps do so as well, but they are very different from the traditional menus and toolbars of desktop applications. For one thing, desktop apps usually display the visual components of the menu and toolbar all the time, but Windows Store apps do not. Once again, this saves space on the screen and allows users to focus on the content of the app rather than the menus and toolbars, which are rarely helpful while working with the content of the app.

Rather than forcing your users to look at the complexity of your app through the menu, the app style presents the application to the users, and they can activate the menu when needed. When the menu is displayed, it should be simple, containing only the main options. It is up to you to decide where to display the menu.

Figure 17-7 shows a screenshot of the Weather app in Windows 8 with the menus unfolded. (It also shows the sad truth about the weather in Denmark in the summer, which is that it's excellent for making plants grow, but not so great for working on your tan.)

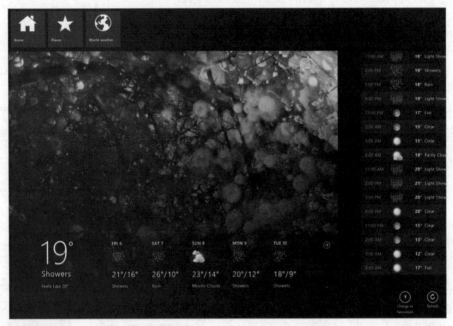

**FIGURE 17-7**

Notice the areas at the top and bottom of the screen. At the top, the app's developers provide its users with the basic navigation options. At the bottom, developers can present a few additional options. Both bars are instances of a control called the *App Bar*. This bar is the default menu provider in Windows Store apps.

## The App Bar

The App Bar is used in most Windows Store apps. It is hidden when the app is running normally, but users can activate it by right-clicking or swiping from the bottom of the screen. Figure 17-8 shows the App Bar of the Weather app when the temperature is displayed in Celsius.

**FIGURE 17-8**

This bar should contain the commands that cannot be performed directly from the surface of your app. You learn how to create App Bars later in this chapter.

## Charms

Windows Store apps use a set of contracts and extensions to allow apps to interact with each other and with Windows without knowing anything about each other. These contracts are represented in the Charms menu (see Figure 17-9), which is accessed by moving the mouse to the bottom-right side of the window or by swiping from the right.

Any app that wants to provide the user with the search functionality, to name one possibility, can implement something called a *Search contract*. Doing so enables the users to search through the common search interface in Windows. This also allows other apps to use the search functions provided by your application. One example of this is the Mail app that is installed by default with Windows. There is no Search button anywhere in the app; however, if you activate the *Search charm* with the Mail app open, you can search the mail items in the app using the standard Windows interface for searching.

### Contracts

Contracts allow apps to interact with other apps, and the possibilities include, but are not limited to, the ones listed in Table 17-1.

**TABLE 17-1:** Contracts

**FIGURE 17-9**

| NAME | DESCRIPTION |
|------|-------------|
| Search | This contract makes it possible for your app to use search content from other apps. You also agree to make the content of your own app searchable. |
| Settings | Using this contract ensures that your app is consistent with the settings model of Windows. |
| Share | By using this contract you can help users share content from your app and other apps. |
| App to App Picking | This contract lets your users pick files directly from your app and allows your users to pick files from other apps. |

### Extensions

Extensions allow apps to interact with Windows. This lets your app customize and use standard Windows features. There are many possibilities here, but Table 17-2 shows some of the more common ones.

**TABLE 17-2:** Extensions

| NAME | DESCRIPTION |
|------|-------------|
| Account Picture Provider | Allows you to get and change the picture associated with the current Microsoft Account. |
| Print Task Settings | Allows you to customize the print-related user interface and allows your app to communicate directly with the device. |
| AutoPlay | When a device is connected to the computer, Windows displays a menu with AutoPlay options. This extension allows your app to be listed as one of the possibilities. |

## Tiles and Badges

Windows uses something called *live tiles* to display the apps on the Start page. The "live" part of the name springs from the fact that the tiles can change based on the current content or state of the app. For example, you will see photo apps rotating through your pictures on the Start page, mail clients displaying the number of unread mails, games displaying screenshots from the last save, and so on. The possibilities are virtually endless.

Providing a good tile for your application is more important than providing a good icon for a desktop application, and that's pretty important as well. Tiles can be 310 × 150 or 150 × 150 pixels, and you should provide both for your application. Providing both sizes allows users to set the size of the tile to their preference. In addition to these two sizes, the app should provide a small image (30 × 30). This is not displayed as a tile, but can be used by Windows to display the app in searches. Tiles are embedded in the manifest for the application, and, as you will see later in the chapter, they are easy to include using Visual Studio.

A *badge* is a small (24 × 24) version of the tile that Windows can use on the Lock Screen and in other situations. You don't have to provide a badge for your app unless it will show notifications on the Lock Screen.

## App Lifetime

Remember the question from earlier this chapter—"How do you close an app?" The answer is that you can close these apps if you want to by pressing Alt+F4 from a keyboard or clicking at the top of the app and dragging it to the bottom of the screen, which is the same way you close an app using touch. But generally speaking, you don't need to close an app. Whenever a Windows Store app loses focus, it is suspended and will stop using processor resources entirely. This allows many apps to appear to be running at the same time, when in fact they are just suspended. The suspension happens automatically in Windows as soon as an app loses focus. It's not really something that you notice, except in the fact that Windows can keep a large number of apps apparently running without any loss of performance.

### Lock Screen Apps

Some apps should keep running when they lose focus. Examples of this kind of app include GPS navigation and audio-streaming apps. Users expect these types of apps to continue running even if they start driving or begin using other apps. If your app needs to keep running in the background, you must declare it as a Lock Screen app and provide information to display notifications on the Lock Screen.

## APP DEVELOPMENT

When you start developing Windows Store apps, you have a number of options regarding programming and UI language. This book uses C# and XAML, but other possibilities include using JavaScript and HTML5, C++ and DirectX, or Visual Basic and XAML.

You will notice that I am taking care to write XAML and not WPF. This is because WPF is a .NET technology that is not supported in WinRT. That is a little bit distressing for .NET developers. But as you saw in Chapters 15 and 16, WPF uses XAML extensively to create the user interfaces. Thus, even though the controls used in XAML for Windows Store apps are not the same as those used by WPF, many of the skills and much of the knowledge that you now have about WPF can be transferred to Windows Store apps.

## WPF and Windows Store App XAML Differences

At this point, you're ready to create your first Windows Store app. To do so, you'll use the blank template and take a look at the controls you have in the Toolbox. You will notice that many of the controls look a lot like something you have been working with in Chapters 15 and 16. The CheckBox, Button, ComboBox,

`StackPanel`, and many other controls are on display in the Toolbox. All of these controls work essentially like the ones you've worked with in WPF, albeit with some minor changes. However, they usually have a completely different visual appearance.

You will also notice a number of controls you have never seen before: a toggle switch, the App Bar, and more. These controls are designed specifically for working well with apps, and they provide a better experience for touch applications than the controls they replace. The `ToggleSwitch` control is a good example of this. Although it is possible to use check boxes in the XAML used in Windows Store apps, the `ToggleSwitch` control provides similar functionality, while also allowing users to swipe instead of pressing a small box with a finger (see Figure 17-10).

**FIGURE 17-10**

Finally, if you look closely, you will notice that a few controls are missing, such as the Label, Menu, and Toolbar controls. As you work with Windows Store apps, you will run into a number of things that are just slightly different, but your knowledge of WPF is nonetheless going to be quite helpful when creating these apps. The next sections go over some of the most important differences.

### Namespace Changes

Most of the namespaces that you will use in your Windows Store apps XAML are identical to those you have used in WPF so far. One change is that you no longer refer to namespaces in your applications using `clr-namespace`. Instead, you create the same reference with the `using` keyword.

WPF:

```
xmlns:src="clr-namespace:KarliCards_GUI"
```

Windows Store app XAML:

```
xmlns:src="using:KarliCards_GUI"
```

### Effects

If you recall the card game developed in Chapters 15 and 16, you will remember that the text and the cards themselves were both lifted off the background by the use of a drop shadow effect. This is not possible in the XAML you use with Windows Store apps because the `Effects` class is missing entirely. If you want effects like this in your apps, you have to fake it in some way, perhaps by using transparent images or by displaying text offset by a few pixels. In any case, it is much harder to achieve the desired effect in this way than it is in WPF.

### Opacity Mask

In WPF, opacity masks are used to set the transparency for images or shapes; and in the Card control you created earlier, such masks were used to control the transparency of the path drawn on the card. This caused the left side of the card to gradually transform from a white background to a color.

Opacity masks have been removed, which means that you once again have to resort to other tricks, such as using images or playing with the transparency of the colors you are using.

### Style Triggers

Triggers have been removed from the `Style` class, which means that you must find other ways to react to changes in properties and events. There are two possibilities: using `ValueConverters` to set values based on another type or using visual states. You have not seen visual states before, but you can use a Visual State manager to create visual states for your styles and then change the current state of the control to cause it to change into the specified state. You are going to see visual states in action in the examples later in this chapter.

## Commands

Although commands exists in Windows Store app XAML, they are much more limited in scope than the commands you use in WPF. They do not allow you to set input gestures on them and can generally be set only on button-type controls. This means that you don't get the application-wide use that you got from commands in WPF, where you were able to define code that was accessed from multiple sources in a single spot. You therefore have to rely a lot more on events in Windows Store app XAML than you did in WPF.

# Templates and Pages

You created windows in the WPF examples in Chapters 15 and 16; however, you might have noticed that you also had the option to create page objects as well. In Windows Store apps, you no longer have the option to create windows, and everything is going to be some kind of page. When you create a new Windows Store app in Visual Studio, you will notice that you have three templates available—Blank, Grid, and Split. The Grid and Split templates create an app with sample pages that you can use as a base for your own app or to discover how pages are bound together. Both of these templates include sample data that allows you to run the projects as soon as you have created them, so you can see how they work.

Each page type can be added to your app regardless of the template you chose when you first created it, but some of the pages are designed to work together.

## Blank Page

This is the simplest page type that you can add to your app and it gives you little except a blank surface to work on. This is the type of page that is created for you when you create a new project using the Blank template.

This page type is useful for testing XAML and creating custom views from the ground up, but it lacks something that you are given with almost all other page types that ship with Visual Studio—navigation. If you are simply creating a page that isn't related to anything else, that's not a problem; but if want your users to be able to jump between pages, consider using another template. You will see how to use navigation later in this chapter.

## Basic Page

The basic page is the simplest of the pages that support navigation. The page displays itself with a caption at the top of the screen and if the users have navigated to it, then it also displays a Back button to the left of the caption. Other than that, the page is blank.

The page might be blank, but you will notice that it includes a `VisualStateManager` element that defines four states that have already been mentioned in this chapter: `FullScreenLandscape`, `Filled`, `FullScreenPortrait`, and `Snapped`. These states are used to control how the page should display depending on the current position of the app. Recall that an app can be in Full-Screen, Fill, or Snapped mode, and in addition to those it can rotate to be displayed in landscape or portrait. You can use the states defined in the Visual State manager to display your page depending on the current display mode.

This page type and all of the pages presented in this chapter use a special page that is added to your project when you add an instance of the page type to your project: `LayoutAwarePage`. This class is itself derived from the Page Class and implements a number of helper methods that you can use to control navigation and the visual states of the app. This book does not dig into the class, but it's there in the project for you to go through if you are interested in knowing how it is implemented.

## Grouped Items and Group Details Pages

There are two page types that are designed to work together to present groups of data. The first is the Grouped Items Page, which displays a caption for each group that can be clicked to take the users to a details page for that group. Beneath each group, the page displays a list of previews for each item in the group. This is the main page that is displayed when you create a new project using the Grid template, where the Grid name refers to the way the items are displayed.

The second page type that can be used to display groups is called the Group Details page. This page type can be used to display information about a single group from the Grouped Items view. By default, it displays the information about the group on the left and a list of item previews on the right.

### Item Details Page

The Item Details page is the last type of page that is used in the Grid template. This page displays the details of a single item and allows users to navigate between items using arrows at the left and right sides of the screen.

### Items and Split Pages

The Items page displays a list of items. In the Split template project, this page type displays the items that are available. It presents the groups just as the Grouped Items page does. The difference here is that each group is displayed as a preview without the list of items. When the users click an item, they are taken to another page that uses the Split page.

The Split page presents a split view, with a list of items on the left and a detailed representation of the selected item on the right. This allows users to see the content of their selections immediately. The view shown on the right side is in effect the same as the Item Details page.

## Sandboxed Apps

Windows Store apps have limited access to the OS on which they run. This means that there are types of applications that you simply cannot write. If you require direct access to the file system, for instance, you must write a traditional Windows desktop application.

When you are writing apps in C#, you will find that the limiting factor is in the .NET Framework that is referenced from your application, where common namespaces and classes are missing entirely or have fewer methods available than before. If you open Visual Studio, create a new Blank app, and then expand the References node; then you will see that there are only two references—.NET for Windows Store apps and Windows. The first of these two is a changed version of .NET and the second is the WinRT API. At this point you might think that you could simply change the references to use the normal .NET Framework, and indeed this will work. That is, it will work right up to when you try to publish your app to the Windows Store, at which point it will be rejected for non-compliance with the specifications.

The sandboxed nature of the Windows Store apps and the process they must go through before they are admitted into the Windows Store means that the users should rarely have to fear downloading malicious apps through the store. Obviously, there are people who will try to circumvent this, and users should never let down their guard; however, it is considerably harder to place malicious programs on Windows computers through Windows Store apps.

### Disk Access

Desktop applications can access the disk pretty much as they like, with a few exceptions. One such exception is that they are normally prohibited from writing to the Program Files folder and other system folders. Windows Store apps can access only a few very specific locations on-disk directly. These locations include the folder in which the app is installed, the AppData folder associated with the app, and a few special folders such as the Documents folder. Access to the files and folders have also been moved in the .NET Framework for Windows Store apps to make sure that the developer can't accidentally write to a forbidden location.

In order to allow the user control over where files should be stored and read from in your app, Windows provides you with three File Picker contracts: `FolderOpenPicker`, `FileOpenPicker`, and `FileSavePicker`.

These picker classes can be used from your app to gain secure access to the local disk. In addition to the local disk, apps can implement the app to app picker contract. By doing so, an app allows other apps to pick files that they control. A good example of this contract in action is the SkyDrive app that is installed with Windows if you are logging on using a Microsoft account. Other apps that implement the app to app picker can access the files in the SkyDrive as if they were local files simply because the app provides a standard interface for doing so.

## Serialization, Streams, and Async Programming

In Chapter 16, you used the [Serializatiable] attribute to allow classes to be serialized. .NET for Windows Store apps do not include this attribute, but you can use a similar attribute called [DataContract] instead. The DataContract attribute works with the DataContractSerializer class to serialize the content of a class. In order to get the serialized content to or from disk, you need to use some file access types, and you will find that the namespace File.IO that you can use in desktop applications is nowhere to be found in .NET for Windows Store apps. Instead, you can use file pickers to create the stream objects, which you can use with the DataContractSerializer to save and load your files.

Disk access in Windows Store apps is asynchronous, which presents its own set of challenges and improvements compared with desktop applications. Traditionally when you load a file in code, everything is synchronous, which means that execution is blocked until the disk operation finishes. You can't know when the operations will finish in Windows Store apps, and that can be a little frustrating.

Imagine that a user clicks a button to load the content of a file into memory. The asynchronous nature of the file access means that even though you write the event handler in a way that appears to be synchronous, there are going to be "holes" in the execution wherever the await keyword appears. If the file access is slow for any reason, users might click on other parts of the app while the file actions are still ongoing. The lesson to learn here is that you should be careful when working with asynchronous methods.

> **NOTE** *The projects you can download for this chapter from* www.wrox.com/remtitle .cgi?isbn=9781118314418 *include a certificate file that you may not be able to use, but can generate yourself. Follow these steps to do so:*
>
> **1.** *With the project open, double-click the file Package.appxmanifest.*
> **2.** *Select the Packaging tab.*
> **3.** *Click Choose Certificate.*
> **4.** *Select Create test certificate from the Configure Certificate.*
> **5.** *Click OK.*

The next Try It Out demonstrates using DataContractSerializator with streams created by FileOpenPicker and FileSavePicker to load and save XML representations of a data model.

**TRY IT OUT** **Disk Access: Ch17Ex01**

**1.** Create a new project in Visual Studio by selecting Blank App (XAML).

**2.** Create a new class in the project named AppData.

**3.** Mark the class with the [DataContract] attribute and add the System.Runtime.Serialization namespace to the using section:

```
using System.Runtime.Serialization;

namespace Ch17Ex01
{
    [DataContract]
    public class AppData
```

```
      {
      }
   }
```

**4.** Add a property of type `int` to the class and mark it with the `[DataMember]` attribute:

```
[DataMember]
public int TheAnswer { get; set; }
```

**5.** Add a new enemy to the project called `AppStates`. Mark it with the `[DataContract]` attribute:

```
using System.Runtime.Serialization;

namespace Ch17Ex01
{
  [DataContract]
  public enum AppStates
  {
  }
}
```

**6.** Add three values to `AppStates`, taking care to mark each one with the `[EnumMember]` attribute:

```
[EnumMember]
Started,
[EnumMember]
Suspended,
[EnumMember]
Closing
```

**7.** Add two new properties to the `AppData` class:

```
[DataMember]
public AppStates State { get; set; }

[DataMember]
public object StateData { get; set; }
```

**8.** Add a new class with the name `AppStateData` and mark it with the `[DataContract]` attribute:

```
using System.Runtime.Serialization;

namespace Ch17Ex01
{
  [DataContract]
  public class AppStateData
  {
    [DataMember]
    public string Data { get; set; }
  }
}
```

**9.** Add a `[KnownType]` attribute to the `AppData` class like this:

```
[DataContract]
[KnownType(typeof(AppStateData))]
public class AppData
{
```

**10.** Double-click the `MainPage.xaml` file in the Solution Explorer and drag two buttons onto the page. Set their content and name properties to `Save` and `Load`.

**11.** Create a `click` event handler for the Save button and navigate to it in the code-behind file. Add this code (note the `async` keyword in the method declaration):

```
private async void Save_Click(object sender, RoutedEventArgs e)
{
  var data = new AppData
  {
```

```
                State = AppStates.Started,
                TheAnswer = 42,
                StateData = new AppStateData { Data = "The data is being saved" }
            };
            var fileSavePicker = new FileSavePicker
            {
                SuggestedStartLocation = PickerLocationId.DocumentsLibrary,
                DefaultFileExtension = ".xml",
            };
            fileSavePicker.FileTypeChoices.Add("XML file", new[] { ".xml" });
            var file = await fileSavePicker.PickSaveFileAsync();
            if (file != null)
            {
                var stream = await file.OpenStreamForWriteAsync();
                var serializer = new DataContractSerializer(typeof(AppData));
                serializer.WriteObject(stream, data);
            }
        }
```

**12.** Create the click event handler for the Load button and add this code (note the async keyword again):

```
        private async void Load_Click(object sender, RoutedEventArgs e)
        {
            var fileOpenPicker = new FileOpenPicker
            {
                SuggestedStartLocation = PickerLocationId.DocumentsLibrary,
                ViewMode = PickerViewMode.Thumbnail
            };
            fileOpenPicker.FileTypeFilter.Add(".xml");
            var file = await fileOpenPicker.PickSingleFileAsync();
            if (file != null)
            {
                var stream = await file.OpenStreamForReadAsync();
                var serializer = new DataContractSerializer(typeof(AppData));
                var data = serializer.ReadObject(stream);
            }
        }
```

**13.** You will need to add these two namespaces to the code-behind file:

```
    using System.Runtime.Serialization;
    using Windows.Storage.Pickers;
```

**14.** Run the app and click Load. This displays the FileOpenPicker as shown in Figure 17-11.

### How It Works

In Steps 1 through 9, you create the data model of the app. All classes and enumerations are marked with the [DataContract] attribute, but notice the difference in how members are marked. Properties and fields in classes can be marked with the [DataMember] attribute, but members of an enumeration must be marked with [EnumMember]:

```
        [DataContract]
    public class AppStateData
    {
        [DataMember]
        public string Data { get; set; }
    }
    [DataContract]
    public enum AppStates
```

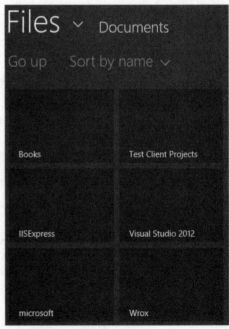

**FIGURE 17-11**

```
{
  [EnumMember]
  Started,
  [EnumMember]
  Suspended,
  [EnumMember]
  Closing
}
```

There is another attribute that is not shown here that can be of interest: `CollectionDataContract`. It can be set on custom collections.

You also add a property with a `type` object. In order for the serializer to be able to serialize this property, you must tell it what types it could be. You do this by setting the `[KnownTypes]` attribute on the class that contains the property. In this example, the property could also return the correct type; however, as you will see later, this is not always the case. In the `GameViewModel` of the KarliCards game, for example, the `CurrentPlayer` property returns a type `Player`, but the actual instance may be of the type `ComputerPlayer`. Unfortunately, the compiler can't know this from looking only at the declarations, so you have to declare it explicitly.

The `Save` and `Load` methods demonstrate some of the new file pickers. After displaying the pickers, you get a `StorageFile` instance back:

```
var file = await fileOpenPicker.PickSingleFileAsync();
if (file != null)
{
  var stream = await file.OpenStreamForReadAsync();
  var serializer = new DataContractSerializer(typeof(AppData));
  var data = serializer.ReadObject(stream);
}
```

This object can be used to open a stream for read or write operations. It is not shown directly here, but you can also use it directly with the `FileIO` class, which provides some simple methods for writing and reading data.

## Navigation Between Pages

Navigating between pages within an app is similar to doing it in web applications. You can call the method `Navigate` to go from one page to another; you can go back by calling the `Back` method. Both of these methods are defined and implemented in the custom class `LayoutAwarePage`, which is added to your project when you add a page type that allows navigation. In addition to these two methods, the `LayoutAwarePage` class provides methods to go forward and home.

The following Try It Out demonstrates how to move between pages in an app using three Basic pages.

**TRY IT OUT**    Navigation: Ch17Ex02

1.  Create a new Windows Store app project by selecting File ⇨ New ⇨ Project and expanding the Installed ⇨ Templates ⇨ Visual C# ⇨ Windows Store node. Select the Blank App (XAML) project and name it `BasicNavigation`.

2.  Select and delete the `MainPage.xaml` file.

3.  Right-click the project and select Add ⇨ New item. Add a new page using the Basic Page template and the default name.

4.  Visual Studio displays a dialog box telling you that the page depends on other files that are not currently in your project. You want these files to be added, so go ahead and select Yes.

5.  Repeat Step 3 twice so you have a total of three pages in the project.

6.  Open the `App.xaml.cs` code-behind file and locate the `OnLaunched` method. This method uses the `MainPage` that you just deleted, so change the reference to `BasicPage1` instead.

7. Open `BasicPage1` and change the `My Application` text in the resources to `Page 1`. Repeat this step with `BasicPage2` and `BasicPage3`, setting their text to `Page 2` and `Page 3`, respectively.

8. On the `BasicPage1`, insert a stack panel and two buttons just above the `VisualStateManager`:

```
<StackPanel Orientation="Horizontal" Grid.Row="1" HorizontalAlignment="Center">
  <Button Content="Page 2" Click="buttonGoto2_Click" />
  <Button Content="Page 3" Click="buttonGoto3_Click" />
</StackPanel>
```

9. Add the event handlers for the click events like this:

```
private void buttonGoto2_Click(object sender, RoutedEventArgs e)
{
  this.Frame.Navigate(typeof(BasicPage2));
}

private void buttonGoto3_Click(object sender, RoutedEventArgs e)
{
  this.Frame.Navigate(typeof(BasicPage3));
}
```

10. Open the second page (`BasicPage2`) and add a similar stack panel to it:

```
<StackPanel Orientation="Horizontal" Grid.Row="1" HorizontalAlignment="Center">
  <Button Content="Page 1" Click="buttonGoto1_Click" />
  <Button Content="Page 3" Click="buttonGoto3_Click" />
</StackPanel>
```

11. Add the navigation to the event handlers:

```
private void buttonGoto1_Click(object sender, RoutedEventArgs e)
{
  this.Frame.Navigate(typeof(BasicPage1));
}

private void buttonGoto3_Click(object sender, RoutedEventArgs e)
{
  this.Frame.Navigate(typeof(BasicPage3));
}
```

12. Open the third page and add another stack panel that includes a Home button:

```
<StackPanel Orientation="Horizontal" Grid.Row="1" HorizontalAlignment="Center">
  <Button Content="Page 1" Click="buttonGoto1_Click" />
  <Button Content="Page 2" Click="buttonGoto2_Click" />
  <Button Content="Home" Click="buttonGoHome_Click" />
</StackPanel>
```

13. Add the event handlers:

```
private void buttonGoto1_Click(object sender, RoutedEventArgs e)
{
  this.Frame.Navigate(typeof(BasicPage1));
}

private void buttonGoto2_Click(object sender, RoutedEventArgs e)
{
  this.Frame.Navigate(typeof(BasicPage2));
}

private void buttonGoHome_Click(object sender, RoutedEventArgs e)
{
  this.GoHome(this, e);
}
```

**14.** Run the app. The app displays the front page with two buttons and no Back button (see Figure 17-12).

### How It Works

When you run the application, it displays a splash screen when loading and then displays the first page. The first time you click one of the buttons, the Navigate method is called using the type of the page you want to navigate to.

**FIGURE 17-12**

```
this.Frame.Navigate(typeof(BasicPage2));
```

It is not shown in this example, but the Navigate method includes an overload that allows you to send parameters to the page that is being navigated to. When you navigate between the pages, you will notice that if you go back to Page 1 using one of the buttons, the Back button remains active.

On page three, you use the GoHome event implementation to go home.

```
this.GoHome(this, e);
```

This effectively causes the application to move back through all pages that have been displayed, ending on the first page. When you use this button method to return to Page 1, the Back button disappears.

Each time you navigate to a page like this, a new instance is created. You can change this behavior by enabling the property NavigationCacheMode in the constructor of your pages; for example, like this:

```
public BasicPage1()
{
    this.InitializeComponent();

    NavigationCacheMode = Windows.UI.Xaml.Navigation.NavigationCacheMode.Enabled;
}
```

This will cause the page to become cached.

After you close the app, you can right-click the tile that was added to your Start page and chose Uninstall to remove it again.

## Managing State

In most applications there are three kinds of state—User, Session, and Navigation. User state persists between invocations of the app. This kind of information should be managed using the Settings charm in Windows.

Session state is relevant only to the current instance of the app. In the KarliCards game, for example, this is the state of the game in progress. Session state should not be saved just because it changes—you don't want to waste the users' and operating system's time saving every time a user draw or discards a card. Instead, you want to save when the user abandons the app for some reason, which is when the app is suspended.

In addition to the data that is displayed on the pages, you must also store the app's navigation state so the app can remember which page it was on when it stopped.

The KarliCards Windows Store app that you develop in the next section manages all three kinds of state.

## CONVERTING KARLICARDS, PART 1

You now know enough about Windows Store apps to start creating one of your own, and in this section you are going to start converting the existing KarliCards WPF application to an app. This is quite an undertaking that requires you to make a lot of changes; but in the end, you will find that you have a game that can run and be deployed in the Windows Store.

The game will be built from three pages:

> ➤ A simple start page where the user can start a new game.
> ➤ A page where the user can add and select players.
> ➤ A game page where the game is played.

These three pages use navigation as described in the previous section to allow users to move back and forth in the game.

In addition to the three pages, it will be possible for the users to open the Settings charm in Windows from an App Bar at the bottom of the screen that is displayed when they right-click on the page. When the Settings panel is displayed, users can open the game's options or show the permissions required by the app. These options should persist between runs of the game, so the game will store both the user and session states.

The controls you created in Chapter 16 need to be converted into Windows Store app XAML. The Card control in particular needs some work because it uses both effects and opacity masks to display itself, and it can't do that anymore.

The classes in the CardLib project use the [Serialization] attribute, which has been removed. Instead, Windows Store apps can use the [DataContract] and [DataMember] attributes to achieve the same functionality. Because the game can save its current state, all the classes that participate in the game must be changed to allow them to be serialized.

Finally, the game will provide a splash screen and tiles.

## Creating the CardLib Project

The first part of the app that you will create is the CardLib project. The changes to that project are entirely related to serialization of the classes, which have to be changed in accordance with what you learned so far about Windows Store apps.

The following Try It Outs convert the existing CardLib project from Chapter 16 into something called CardLib.Store.

**TRY IT OUT** Creating CardLib.Store: KarliCards.Store\CardLib.Store

1. Create a new project by selecting File ➪ New ➪ Project. Select Installed ➪ Templates ➪ Visual C# ➪ Windows Store and pick the Class Library (Windows Store Apps). Name the project CardLib.Store and the solution KarliCards.Store.
2. Delete the file called Class1.cs.
3. Right-click the project file and select Add ➪ Existing Item.
4. Browse to the CardLib used in Chapter 16 and select all files with the .cs extension. Include them in the project.
5. Compile the project.

*How It Works*

At this point, you will get a number of compile errors, all of which have to do with serialization. You will have to correct these by using the [DataContract], [DataMember], and [EnumMember] attributes.

---

**TRY IT OUT** Converting CardLib: KarliCards.Store\CardLib.Store

1. Open the Player.cs class. Change the Serializable attribute to DataContract and add the using System.Runtime.Serialization directive to the class:

```
using System.Runtime.Serialization;

namespace CardLib
```

```
    {
      [DataContract]
      public class Player : INotifyPropertyChanged
```

2. Decorate the `Index`, `Hand`, `State`, and `PlayerName` properties with the `DataMember` attribute:

```
        [DataMember]
        public int Index { get; set; }
        [DataMember]
        protected Cards Hand { get; set; }
        [DataMember]
        public PlayerState State
        {
          get   {  return _state;   }
          set
          {
            _state = value;
            OnPropertyChanged("State");
          }
        }

        [DataMember]
        public virtual string PlayerName
        {
          get
          {
            return _name;
          }
          set
          {
            _name = value;
            OnPropertyChanged("PlayerName");
          }
        }
```

3. Repeat Step 1 for the classes and enums called `Card`, `ComputerPlayer`, `ComputerSkillLevel`, `Deck`, `PlayerState`, `Rank`, and `Suit`. Note that some of these was not serialized before. Just add the `[DataContract]` attribute in these cases.

4. Mark every member in the three enums called `ComputerSkillLevel`, `PlayerState`, `Rank`, and `Suit` with the `[EnumMember]` attribute like this:

```
    using System.Runtime.Serialization;

    namespace CardLib
    {
      [DataContract]
      public enum Suit
      {
        [EnumMember]
        Club,
        [EnumMember]
        Diamond,
        [EnumMember]
        Heart,
        [EnumMember]
        Spade,
      }
    }
```

5. Mark all the public properties in the `ComputerPlayer` class with the `[DataMember]` attribute.

6. Mark the field's suit and rank with the `[DataMember]` attribute in the `Card` class.

7. Mark the field `Cards` in the `Deck` class with the `[DataMember]` attribute.

8. Remove the `IClonable` interface from the classes `Card`, `Cards`, and `Deck`.

**9.** Add a new class called `PlayerNames` that will be used when managing state in the application (note the namespace is `CardLib`, not `CardLib.Store` as Visual Studio suggests when creating the class):

```
using System.Collections.Generic;
using System.Collections.ObjectModel;
using System.Text;

namespace CardLib
{
  public class PlayerNames : ObservableCollection<string>
  {
    public PlayerNames()
      : base()
    {
    }

    public PlayerNames(List<string> names)
    {
      foreach (var name in names)
        Add(name);
    }

    public override string ToString()
    {
      var sb = new StringBuilder();
      foreach (var player in Items)
      {
        if (sb.Length == 0)
          sb.Append(player);
        else
          sb.AppendFormat("¤{0}", player);
      }
      return sb.ToString();
    }

    public static PlayerNames FromString(string players)
    {
      var collection = new PlayerNames();
      var playerSplit = players.Split("¤".ToCharArray());
      foreach (var player in playerSplit)
        collection.Add(player);
      return collection;
    }
  }
}
```

### How It Works

The `DataContract` and `DataMember` attributes work with the `DataContractSerializer` that you saw earlier in the chapter to serialize data in much the same way that the `Serializable` and `XmlSerializer` attributes do for desktop applications.

Removing the `IClonable` interface from the classes will break any application that's using this interface to access the interface members, but there is no substitution for this interface in the new network.

The new class `PlayerNames` is a collection that's used as a handy way of storing names and converting the lists of strings to and from a single string. This is useful when passing parameters between pages.

## Converting the View Models

At this point the CardLib.Store is complete. Generally speaking, you are not going to encounter many problems when you convert the data models from a desktop application to a Windows Store app. That picture will change a little bit when you move on to the view models of the app. Even though this code is also isolated from the user interface, it has a closer relation with it and is therefore affected by the changes that will occur there. In the case of the KarliCards app, one thing in particular is going to affect the way the view models work—state management. Assume the user is in the middle of a game and switches to another app, causing the game to be suspended or even terminated. At this point, she should be returned to the correct page, and the game should resume from the place she ended the next time she starts the app.

You have already taken the first step toward allowing the game to save its entire state: You have marked most of the data model in CardLib.Store as `DataContracts`. Now it's time to take the next step and move to the view models. In the following Try It Out, you will start by creating the project for the game. Then you will convert the `GameOptions` and `GameViewModel` classes. The `GameOptions` class holds the data that should persist between invocations of the app and `GameViewModel` stores information about a single ongoing game.

---

**TRY IT OUT**   Converting KarliCards: KarliCards.Store\KarliCards.Gui

1. Add a new project to the solution from the previous example. Select a new Windows Store app using the Blank App (XAML) template and name the project `KarliCards.Gui`.

2. You will want to set this project as the startup project. Right-click on the project and select Set and Start Up Project.

3. Add a reference to the CardLib project by right-clicking on References and choosing Add Reference under the `KarliCards.Gui` project. Expand the Projects node and select the CardLib.Store project. Click OK.

4. Create a new folder in the KarliCards.Gui project named `ViewModels`.

5. Right-Click the `ViewModels` folder and select Add ➪ Existing Item. Browse to the KarliCards solution you created in Chapter 16. For now, just select the `GameOptions.cs` file.

6. Open the `GameOptions.cs` file and remove the `[Serializable]` attribute.

7. Delete the `OptionsCommand` from the class.

8. Change the constructor like this:

   ```
   public GameOptions()
       {
         LoadSettings();
       }
   ```

9. Change the `_playerNames` field to be of type `PlayerNames` instead of `ObservableCollection<string>`:

   ```
   private PlayerNames _playerNames = new PlayerNames();
   ```

10. Do the same for the `PlayerNames` property:

    ```
    public PlayerNames PlayerNames
    {
      get { return _playerNames; }
      set
      {
        _playerNames = value;
        OnPropertyChanged("PlayerNames");
      }
    }
    ```

11. Delete the `SelectedPlayers` property.

12. If you didn't complete the exercises in Chapter 16, add this field and property:

    ```
    private bool _computerPlaysWithOpenHand;
    public bool ComputerPlaysWithOpenHand
    {
    ```

```
            get { return _computerPlaysWithOpenHand; }
            set
            {
              _computerPlaysWithOpenHand = value;
              OnPropertyChanged("ComputerPlaysWithOpenHand");
            }
        }
```

**13.** Replace the `Save` and `Create` methods with these:

```
        public void Save()
        {
          ApplicationData.Current.LocalSettings.Values["PlayAgainstComputer"] =
                    _playAgainstComputer;
          ApplicationData.Current.LocalSettings.Values["ComputerSkillLevel"] =
                    (int)_computerSkill;
          ApplicationData.Current.LocalSettings.Values["NumberOfPlayers"] = _numberOfPlayers;
          ApplicationData.Current.LocalSettings.Values["ComputerPlaysWithOpenHand"] =
                    _computerPlaysWithOpenHand;
          ApplicationData.Current.LocalSettings.Values["PlayerNames"] =
                    _playerNames.ToString();
        }

        private void LoadSettings()
        {
          if (Windows.Storage.ApplicationData.Current.LocalSettings.Values
                        .ContainsKey("PlayAgainstComputer"))
          {
            _playAgainstComputer = (bool)ApplicationData.Current.LocalSettings.
        Values["PlayAgainstComputer"];
            _computerSkill = (ComputerSkillLevel)ApplicationData.Current.LocalSettings.
        Values["ComputerSkillLevel"];
            _numberOfPlayers = (int)ApplicationData.Current.LocalSettings.Values["NumberOfPlayers"];
            _computerPlaysWithOpenHand = (bool)ApplicationData.Current.LocalSettings.Values
        ["ComputerPlaysWithOpenHand"];
            _playerNames = CardLib.PlayerNames.FromString(ApplicationData.Current.LocalSettings
                        .Values["PlayerNames"] as string);
          }
        }
```

**14.** The class use these namespaces:

```
        using CardLib;
        using System.ComponentModel;
        using Windows.Storage;
```

**15.** The app should now compile again.

*How It Works*

You have now converted the first of the view models of the game to a Windows Store app. As you can see, there are minor changes but nothing too cumbersome. The one major change to the functionality is with the `Create` and `Save` methods.

Windows Store apps can use a special storage for their settings. This storage is accessed through the `ApplicationDataContainer` class in the `Windows.Storage` namespace. This container includes a `LocalSetitings` class, whereby you can use the `Values` `Dictionary` to store simple settings. This is by far the simplest way of storing state for an application, but be warned that you can only store simple types like `string`, `int`, `bool`, and so on. This is why this example creates the `PlayerNames` class. This class includes methods for converting the collection into a string and back again:

```
    _playerNames = CardLib.PlayerNames.FromString(
        ApplicationData.Current.LocalSettings.Values["PlayerNames"] as string);
```

That was the first of the two view models converted, so let's continue with the other one: GameViewModel. This class needs to be changed a bit more than the GameOptions did because it now has to participate in the state management of the app.

**TRY IT OUT** Converting GameViewModel: KarliCards.Store\KarliCards.Gui

**1.** Start by adding the GameViewModel.cs file to the ViewModels folder like you did with GameOptions.cs.

**2.** Delete the two RoutedCommands.

**3.** Add the [DataContract] and [KnownType] declarations to the class and add the namespace to the top of the file:

```
using System.Runtime.Serialization;
...
[DataContract]
[KnownType(typeof(ComputerPlayer))]
[KnownType(typeof(ComputerSkillLevel))]
[KnownType(typeof(ComputerPlayer))]
[KnownType(typeof(PlayerState))]
public class GameViewModel : INotifyPropertyChanged
```

**4.** Mark the _currentPlayer, _players, _availableCard, _deck and _gameStarted fields with the [DataMember] attribute.

**5.** Add these fields and properties to the class:

```
[DataMember]
private int _currentPlayerIndex;
[DataMember]
public bool ComputerPlaysWithOpenHand { get; set; }
[DataMember]
public int NumberOfPlayers { get; set; }
[DataMember]
public ComputerSkillLevel ComputerSkill { get; set; }
```

**6.** Locate the AssignCurrentPlayer method and change it like this:

```
private void AssignCurrentPlayer(int index)
{
  CurrentPlayer = Players[index];
  _currentPlayerIndex = index;
  if (!Players.Any(x => x.State == PlayerState.Winner))
    foreach (var player in Players)
      player.State = (player == CurrentPlayer ? PlayerState.Active :
                      PlayerState.Inactive);
}
```

**7.** Change the StartNewGame method like this:

```
if (playernNames == null || playernNames.Count == 0)
  return;

_gameOptions = new GameOptions();
NumberOfPlayers = _gameOptions.NumberOfPlayers;
ComputerPlaysWithOpenHand = _gameOptions.ComputerPlaysWithOpenHand;
ComputerSkill = _gameOptions.ComputerSkill;

CreateGameDeck();
CreatePlayers(playernNames);
InitializeGame();
GameStarted = true;
```

**8.** Change the `CreatePlayers` method like this:

```
private void CreatePlayers(PlayerNames players)
{
  Players.Clear();
  for (var i = 0; i < _gameOptions.NumberOfPlayers; i++)
  {
    if (i < players.Count)
      InitializePlayer(new Player { Index = i, PlayerName = players[i] });
    else
      InitializePlayer(new ComputerPlayer { Index = i, Skill = _gameOptions.ComputerSkill });
  }
}
```

**9.** Locate the `player_OnPlayerHasWon` event handler and change it like this:

```
void player_OnPlayerHasWon(object sender, PlayerEventArgs e)
{
  foreach (var player in Players)
    player.State = (player == e.Player ? PlayerState.Winner : PlayerState.Loser);
}
```

**10.** Add this method:

```
public void ContinueGame()
{
  foreach (var player in Players)
  {
    player.OnCardDiscarded += player_OnCardDiscarded;
    player.OnPlayerHasWon += player_OnPlayerHasWon;
  }
  CurrentPlayer = Players[_currentPlayerIndex];
}
```

**11.** Delete the constructor.

### How It Works

Many of the changes to the `GameViewModel` class spring from the fact that the `GameOptions` property is removed from the class. This is done to separate the session state from the user state, but it means that, although it is possible to use the same `GameOptions` instance everywhere in the WPF application, the information in the `GameOptions` that is unique to each game must be copied to the `GameViewModel`. Consider these fields:

```
[DataMember]
public bool ComputerPlaysWithOpenHand { get; set; }
[DataMember]
public int NumberOfPlayers { get; set; }
[DataMember]
public ComputerSkillLevel ComputerSkill { get; set; }
```

They are new to the class, and cause changes in the `StartNewGame` and `CreatePlayer` methods.

In addition to that, a new method called `ContinueGame` is introduced.

```
public void ContinueGame()
{
  foreach (var player in Players)
  {
    player.OnCardDiscarded += player_OnCardDiscarded;
    player.OnPlayerHasWon += player_OnPlayerHasWon;
  }
  CurrentPlayer = Players[_currentPlayerIndex];
}
```

This method is used by state management when the game has to be restored rather than restarted. The `GameViewModel` object is restored by the state manager, but you need to set up some event handlers on the players, which is done in this method.

## Visual Changes

Now that you have converted the view models and domain objects, it is time to turn to the visual parts of the game. As stated earlier in the chapter, there are a number of features of WPF XAML that are used in the existing game that cannot be used in the Windows Store app version. The next sections go through them so you can learn how to change them for the Windows Store app game.

### Drop Shadow and Opacity Masks

The `CardControl` uses both drop shadows and opacity masks to draw itself. Because these effects are unavailable in the Windows Store app game, you must decide what you want to do instead.

If the drop shadows are removed and the `CardControls` are stacked on top of each other, it becomes difficult to see where one card stops and the next starts. Therefore, you need something that will create a border around each card. You are going to do this by drawing an extra rectangle around the card:

```
<Rectangle Stroke="LightGray" RadiusX="12.5" RadiusY="12.5">
  <Rectangle.Fill>
    <SolidColorBrush Color="Transparent" />
  </Rectangle.Fill>
</Rectangle>
```

You simply remove the opacity mask that is used on the `Path` element of the card for now. The left side of the card becomes plain white because of this, but as there is text in the top corner and an image in the bottom corner, this doesn't affect the look of the card too much. You are also going to make the card smaller. Desktop applications often assume that the display is using a high resolution, but you can't make that assumption when you are targeting tablets.

### Style Triggers

The `CardControl` in WPF also uses triggers in the `Style SuitImage`, and this is no longer supported. When converting to the app, you are going to use a Visual State manager that will select the correct image for you.

## Converting User Controls

User controls are created in exactly the same way in a Windows Store app XAML as they are in WPF XAML; however, as the previous section detailed, there is work to do before the controls look more or less as they did in WPF.

In addition to the XAML changes, there are also changes to the Value converters that were used in WPF. Both of the methods in the interface have changed on the last parameter, which has changed to a string. Also, the `[ValueConversion]` attribute doesn't exist in the .NET Framework for Windows Store, so that will have to be removed as well. Finally, Dependency Properties no longer allow you to set a validation callback in the register method, so this must also be fixed.

In the next example, you convert the `CardControl` to a use Windows Store app XAML.

**TRY IT OUT**   Converting the Card: KarliCards.Store\KarliCards.Gui

**1.** The `CardControl` uses the `RankNameConverter.cs` class, so let's fix that one before you include the `CardControl` in the project. Add the file `KarliCards.Store` project by right-clicking the project and selecting Add ⇨ Existing Item from the Solution Explorer. Browse to the file in the project from Chapter 16. Include the `RankNameConverter.cs` file.

**2.** Open the `RankNameConverter.cs` file.

**3.** Delete the `[ValueConversion]` attribute.

**4.** Delete the `using System.Windows.Data;` statement and add these statements instead:

```
using Windows.UI.Xaml;
using Windows.UI.Xaml.Data;
```

**5.** Change the fourth parameter of both methods to a string instead of the current `System.Globalization.CultureInfo`.

**6.** The cards are using the four images for the suits. Right-click the `Assets` folder that was created by default to hold images. Next, click Add ⇨ Existing Item. Browse to the images that are located in the `Images` folder and include them.

**7.** Add the `CardControl.xaml` file to the project from the desktop application. When you select just this one file in the Add Existing Item window, Visual Studio will notice that the `CardControl.xaml.cs` file is needed as well and will include it. If, for some reason, it does not, just add the `CardControl.xaml.cs` file as well.

**8.** Change `xmlns:src="clr-namespace:KarliCards_GUI"` in the `UseControl` declaration to:

```
xmlns:src="using:KarliCards_Gui"
```

**9.** Delete the `DataTemplate` and `Style` elements from the `UserControl.Resources` element, and add a reference to the new `SuitToImageConverter`:

```
<UserControl.Resources>
  <src:RankNameConverter x:Key="rankConverter"/>
</UserControl.Resources>
```

**10.** Delete the `<Rectangle.Effect>` element.

**11.** There are no labels in Windows Store app XAML, so change the `<Label ...>` elements to `TextBlock` elements without changing any of their properties. There are three labels to change. You must also change any closing tags and the `Label.RenderTransform` elements should change to `TextBlock.RenderTransform`.

**12.** The text blocks you just created use the `Text` property instead of the `Content` property to display their values, so change the `Content` properties to `Text` properties in three places.

**13.** Delete the `ContentTemplate` property from the three text blocks.

**14.** Delete the `Grid.ZIndex="1"` setting from the `RankLabel` text block. `ZIndex` is no longer available on grids.

**15.** The final change to the text blocks is that the binding in the `Text` property includes a `Mode=Default` statement. Delete this statement.

**16.** Delete the `Path.OpacityMask` element from the `Path` element.

**17.** Move the `Path` element up to a position just below the `Rectangle` at the top of the file.

**18.** At this point, the `Card` should draw itself in Design View, but the images are still marked as problematic. This is because you removed the style they were using, so go ahead and change them like this:

```
<Image Name="TopRightImage"

    Margin="12,12,8,0"
    HorizontalAlignment="Right"
    VerticalAlignment="Top"
    Width="18.4"
    Height="18.4"
    Stretch="UniformToFill" />
<Image Name="BottomLeftImage"

        Margin="12,0,8,12"
        HorizontalAlignment="Left"
```

```
                VerticalAlignment="Bottom"
                Width="18.4"
                Height="18.4"
                Stretch="UniformToFill"
                RenderTransformOrigin="0.5,0.5">
        <Image.RenderTransform>
          <RotateTransform Angle="180" />
        </Image.RenderTransform>
      </Image>
```

**19.** Below the `Path` element, insert this rectangle:

```
      <Rectangle Stroke="LightGray" RadiusX="12.5" RadiusY="12.5">
        <Rectangle.Fill>
          <SolidColorBrush Color="Transparent" />
        </Rectangle.Fill>
      </Rectangle>
```

**20.** Just after the first `Grid` element, create this visual state:

```
      <VisualStateManager.VisualStateGroups>
          <VisualStateGroup x:Name="CommonStates">
            <VisualState x:Name="Heart">
              <Storyboard>
                <ObjectAnimationUsingKeyFrames Storyboard.TargetName="TopRightImage"
                    Storyboard.TargetProperty="Source" Duration="0">
                  <DiscreteObjectKeyFrame KeyTime="0" Value="Assets/Hearts.png" />
                </ObjectAnimationUsingKeyFrames>
                <ObjectAnimationUsingKeyFrames Storyboard.TargetName="BottomLeftImage"
                    Storyboard.TargetProperty="Source" Duration="0">
                  <DiscreteObjectKeyFrame KeyTime="0" Value="Assets/Hearts.png" />
                </ObjectAnimationUsingKeyFrames>
                <ObjectAnimationUsingKeyFrames Storyboard.TargetName="SuitLabel"
                    Storyboard.TargetProperty="Foreground" Duration="0">
                  <DiscreteObjectKeyFrame KeyTime="0" Value="Red" />
                </ObjectAnimationUsingKeyFrames>
                <ObjectAnimationUsingKeyFrames Storyboard.TargetName="RankLabel"
                    Storyboard.TargetProperty="Foreground" Duration="0">
                  <DiscreteObjectKeyFrame KeyTime="0" Value="Red" />
                </ObjectAnimationUsingKeyFrames>
                <ObjectAnimationUsingKeyFrames Storyboard.TargetName="RankLabelInverted"
                    Storyboard.TargetProperty="Foreground" Duration="0">
                  <DiscreteObjectKeyFrame KeyTime="0" Value="Red" />
                </ObjectAnimationUsingKeyFrames>
              </Storyboard>
            </VisualState>
          </VisualStateGroup>
        </VisualStateManager.VisualStateGroups>
```

**21.** Copy the `VisualState` tag with the name `x:name="Heart"` from the code in Step 20 and all its content and past it within the `VisualStateGroup`.

**22.** Change the name of the new state to `Diamond` and change the two `Hearts.png` image references to `Diamonds.png`.

**23.** Repeat Steps 21 and 22 to create two additional states called `Spade` and `Club` with the images changed to `Spades.png` and `Clubs.png`, respectively. For these two, you must also change the three color references from `Red` to `Black`.

**24.** Go to the `CardControl.xaml.cs` code-behind file and replace all `using` declarations with these:

```
using CardLib;
using Windows.UI;
using Windows.UI.Xaml;
using Windows.UI.Xaml.Controls;
using Windows.UI.Xaml.Media;
```

**25.** Change the constructor that takes a `Card` instance to set the visual state of the card:

```
public CardControl(Card card)
{
    InitializeComponent();

    Card = card;
    VisualStateManager.GoToState(this, Suit.ToString(), false);
}
```

**26.** Delete the method `SetTextColor`, which is obsolete now that you are setting it using the visual states.

**27.** To set the current visual state, change the `OnSuitChanged` method like this:

```
public static void OnSuitChanged(DependencyObject source, DependencyPropertyChangedEventArgs
args)
{
    var control = source as CardControl;
    VisualStateManager.GoToState(control, control.Suit.ToString(), false);
}
```

**28.** Finally, change the `Visibility.Hidden` possibility in the `OnIsFaceUpChanged` method to `Visibility.Collapsed`:

```
private static void OnIsFaceUpChanged(DependencyObject source,
            DependencyPropertyChangedEventArgs args)
{
    var control = source as CardControl;
    control.RankLabel.Visibility = control.SuitLabel.Visibility =
            control.RankLabelInverted.Visibility =
    control.TopRightImage.Visibility = control.BottomLeftImage.Visibility =
    control.IsFaceUp ? Visibility.Visible : Visibility.Collapsed;
}
```

### How It Works

You now have converted the first and most troublesome of the user controls used in the game. The card now uses a Visual State manager to set the values that are dependent on the suit of the current card. Let's examine one of the visual states:

```
<VisualState x:Name="Heart">
  <Storyboard>
    <ObjectAnimationUsingKeyFrames Storyboard.TargetName="TopRightImage"
        Storyboard.TargetProperty="Source" Duration="0">
      <DiscreteObjectKeyFrame KeyTime="0" Value="Assets/Hearts.png" />
    </ObjectAnimationUsingKeyFrames>
    <ObjectAnimationUsingKeyFrames Storyboard.TargetName="BottomLeftImage"
        Storyboard.TargetProperty="Source" Duration="0">
      <DiscreteObjectKeyFrame KeyTime="0" Value="Assets/Hearts.png" />
    </ObjectAnimationUsingKeyFrames>
    <ObjectAnimationUsingKeyFrames Storyboard.TargetName="SuitLabel"
        Storyboard.TargetProperty="Foreground" Duration="0">
      <DiscreteObjectKeyFrame KeyTime="0" Value="Red" />
    </ObjectAnimationUsingKeyFrames>
    <ObjectAnimationUsingKeyFrames Storyboard.TargetName="RankLabel"
        Storyboard.TargetProperty="Foreground" Duration="0">
      <DiscreteObjectKeyFrame KeyTime="0" Value="Red" />
    </ObjectAnimationUsingKeyFrames>
    <ObjectAnimationUsingKeyFrames Storyboard.TargetName="RankLabelInverted"
        Storyboard.TargetProperty="Foreground" Duration="0">
      <DiscreteObjectKeyFrame KeyTime="0" Value="Red" />
    </ObjectAnimationUsingKeyFrames>
  </Storyboard>
</VisualState>
```

You create four states because there are four suits: `Heart`, `Diamond`, `Club`, and `Spades`. For each of these states, you must set the `Source` property for the two images and the color of the text that displays the suit name and the rank.

The first state you define is for Heart. This includes a storyboard that holds all the animations that will happen when this state is activated. The ObjectAnimationUsingKeyFrames attribute allows you to set the value of the property you need, so this is used for all the controls.

In the code, you want to move to a specific state whenever the suit of the card changes. You do this by using the VisualStateManager.GotoState method:

```
VisualStateManager.GoToState(this, Suit.ToString(), false);
```

Label controls are not used in Windows Store XAML, so you change them to text blocks, which are more complex but in this case do the same thing. You also have to remove the ZIndex from one of them because Grids don't support this property. Happily, you don't need it anymore. The reason it is needed in the desktop version is due to the OpacityMask element on the Path, which causes the label to be partly transparent if it is below the path. With the opacity mask removed, this is no longer a problem.

Finally, the possibilities for visibility are limited to Visible and Collapsed.

---

The first user control is complete and the last two require only a quick to change, so this next Try It Out converts them both at once.

**TRY IT OUT**    Converting User Controls: KarliCards.Store\KarliCards.Gui

1. Add the file CardsInHandControl.xaml to the project from the existing desktop application in Chapter 16.

2. In the XAML, change the Label control to a TextBlock control and remove the Label.Effect element. This causes the control to draw itself.

3. Go to the code-behind file and replace the using declarations with these:

```
using System.Threading.Tasks;
using CardLib;
using KarliCards_Gui.ViewModel;
using Windows.UI;
using Windows.UI.Xaml;
using Windows.UI.Xaml.Controls;
using Windows.UI.Xaml.Input;
using Windows.UI.Xaml.Media;
```

4. Delete the methods DelayDraw and DelayDiscard.

5. Delete the class Payload, which is declared in the file.

6. Change the OnPlayerChanged method like this:

```
    private static async void OnPlayerStateChanged(DependencyObject source,
DependencyPropertyChangedEventArgs e)
    {
      var control = source as CardsInHandControl;
      var computerPlayer = control.Owner as ComputerPlayer;

      if (computerPlayer != null && computerPlayer.State == PlayerState.MustDiscard)
      {
        await Task.Delay(1250);
        computerPlayer.PerformDiscard(control.Game.GameDeck);
      }
      else if (computerPlayer != null && computerPlayer.State == PlayerState.Active)
      {
        await Task.Delay(1250);
        computerPlayer.PerformDraw(control.Game.GameDeck, control.Game.CurrentAvailableCard);
      }
      control.RedrawCards();
    }
```

**7.** In the `DrawCards` method, find this statement:

```
cardControl.MouseDoubleClick += cardControl_MouseDoubleClick;
```

Replace it with this:

```
cardControl.Tapped += cardControl_Tapped;
```

**8.** Add the event handler for the `Tapped` event:

```
void cardControl_Tapped(object sender, TappedRoutedEventArgs e)
{
    var selectedCard = sender as CardControl;
    if (Owner == null)
      return;
    if (Owner.State == PlayerState.MustDiscard)
    {
      Owner.DiscardCard(selectedCard.Card);
    }
    RedrawCards();
}
```

**9.** Delete the `cardControl_MouseDoubleClick` event handler.

**10.** Change the three places where `PlayerNameLabel.Content` is used to the following:

```
PlayerNameLabel.Text
```

**11.** Add a new `DependencyProperty` to the code:

```
public ComputerPlayer ComputerPlayer
{
    get { return (ComputerPlayer)GetValue(ComputerPlayerProperty); }
    set { SetValue(ComputerPlayerProperty, value); }
}

public static readonly DependencyProperty ComputerPlayerProperty =
    DependencyProperty.Register("ComputerPlayer", typeof(ComputerPlayer),
    typeof(CardsInHandControl),
    new PropertyMetadata(null, new PropertyChangedCallback(OnOwnerChanged)));
```

**12.** The `CardsInHandControl` is now complete, so let's move on to the `GameDecksControl`. Add the `GameDecksControl.xaml` file in the project.

**13.** There is nothing to change in the XAML, so go to the code-behind file and change the usings, as you did in Step 3.

**14.** Add two additional namespaces:

```
using System.Collections.Generic;
using System.Linq;
```

**15.** Change the `DrawDecks` method like this:

```
private void DrawDecks()
{
    controlCanvas.Children.Clear();

    if (CurrentPlayer == null || Deck == null | !GameStarted)
      return;

    List<CardControl> stackedCards = new List<CardControl>();
    for (int i = 0; i < Deck.CardsInDeck; i++)
      stackedCards.Add(new CardControl(Deck.GetCard(i))
{ Margin = new Thickness(150 + (i * 1.25), 25-(i * 1.25), 0, 0), IsFaceUp = false });

    if (stackedCards.Count > 0)
      stackedCardsLast().Tapped += GameDecksControl_Tapped;
    if (AvailableCard != null)
    {
```

```
            var availableCard = new CardControl(AvailableCard)
                                  { Margin = new Thickness(0, 25, 0, 0) };
            availableCard.Tapped += availableCard_Tapped;
            controlCanvas.Children.Add(availableCard);
        }
        foreach (var card in stackedCards)
          controlCanvas.Children.Add(card);}
```

**16.** Add the two event handlers like this:

```
        void availableCard_Tapped(object sender, TappedRoutedEventArgs e)
        {
          if (CurrentPlayer.State != PlayerState.Active)
            return;

          var control = sender as CardControl;
          CurrentPlayer.AddCard(control.Card);
          AvailableCard = null;
          DrawDecks();
        }

        void GameDecksControl_Tapped(object sender, TappedRoutedEventArgs e)
        {
          if (CurrentPlayer.State != PlayerState.Active)
            return;

          CurrentPlayer.DrawCard(Deck);
          DrawDecks();
        }
```

**17.** Delete the two event handlers for the double-clicks.

### How It Works

You are now done converting all the user controls. In both controls (in the `DrawDecks` method in `GameDeckControl`), you remove the event handlers for `DoubleClick` and replace them with a handler for `Tapped`. Doing this means that users with mice need only to single-click on the item for the event to fire; but more importantly, it means that users tapping on a touch-sensitive device can use the control better.

> **NOTE** *In Step 11 you added a new dependency property called* `ComputerPlayer`. *This is needed because of a bug in the current version of Windows 8 that causes the* `PropertyChangedCallback` *to fail to activate when the property is changed to an instance derived from the type declared in the property.*

At this point there is little left in the WPF application that is going to be useful in the Windows Store app. You will change the Options window to a Settings panel, and you'll change the Start window to a page of its own. You will create both of these elements from the ground up because they are going to participate in the state and navigation of the app.

For now, you are going to let KarliCards rest. You'll return to complete it after a brief discussion of some of the most common elements of Windows Store apps.

## COMMON ELEMENTS OF WINDOWS STORE APPS

There are two elements that are common to almost all Windows Store apps: App Bars and the Settings panel. Although you don't have to implement either if you have no settings that the users can manipulate or no options they can set, you should provide access to both otherwise.

All Windows Store apps should provide their own Tiles and Badges. Tiles give your app presence on the Start page in Windows and allow you to display information about the app. Badges allow Windows to display a small image that represents your app on the Lock Screen.

## The AppBar Control

An App Bar provides the users with much the same functionality that a menu bar provides in desktop applications, but you should keep them much more simple, limiting the available options to fewer than eight items in a bar.

You can display more than one App Bar at a time, but keep in mind that this clutters up the user interface, and you should not display more than one bar just to show more options. On the other hand, if you want to provide more than one kind of navigation, it is sometimes beneficial to show a top and bottom bar, in the same way that the Windows Store app version of Internet Explorer displays a bar at the bottom with options and a bar at the top with available windows.

Visual Studio ships with the `AppBar` control, which makes it very easy to create this kind of menu. Together with the common styles inserted into your project when you add one of the pages that provide navigation, you can very quickly create App Bars that provide access to common tasks.

The following Try It Out creates an App Bar with a number of standard items on it.

**TRY IT OUT**   Creating App Bars: Ch17Ex03\AppBars\MainPage.xaml

1. Create a new Windows Store app using the Blank App (XAML) template.
2. Delete the `MainPage.xaml` file.
3. Add a new page using the Basic Page template and name it `MainPage.xaml`.
4. Allow Visual Studio to add content to the project.
5. Compile the project to allow the changes to the project to be recognized.
6. Below the `<Page.Resources>` element, add this code:
   ```
   <Page.BottomAppBar>
     <AppBar x:Name="BottomAppBar1" Padding="10,0,10,0" Grid.ColumnSpan="10">
       <Grid>
         <Grid.ColumnDefinitions>
           <ColumnDefinition Width="50*"/>
           <ColumnDefinition Width="50*"/>
         </Grid.ColumnDefinitions>
         <StackPanel x:Name="RightPanel" Orientation="Horizontal" Grid.Column="1"
                     HorizontalAlignment="Right">
           <Button x:Name="StartGame" Style="{StaticResource PlayAppBarButtonStyle}"
                   Tag="StartGame" Click="StartGame_Click" />
           <Button x:Name="Settings" Style="{StaticResource SettingsAppBarButtonStyle}"
                   Tag="Settings" Click="GotoSettings" />
           <Button x:Name="Help" Style="{StaticResource HelpAppBarButtonStyle}" Tag="Help"/>
         </StackPanel>
       </Grid>
     </AppBar>
   </Page.BottomAppBar>
   ```
7. Add the event handlers for the Start Game and Settings buttons, but don't add any code to them yet.
8. Expand the `Common` folder that was added when you created the new page, and open the file `StandardStyles.xaml`.
9. Search for the style `PlayAppBarButtonStyle` and uncomment the entire section in which it is found.
10. Repeat Step 9, but search for `HelpAppBarButtonStyle`.
11. Run the app. When the app starts, you are greeted with an empty screen except for the caption. Right-click anywhere on the surface to display the App Bar shown in Figure 17-13.

**FIGURE 17-13**

### How It Works

The `AppBar` control by default defines two columns in a grid and a stack panel. Most apps display their App Bar buttons on the right side of the screen, but really this is a personal preference. A stack panel in column 0 should be aligned with the left edge and the stack panel in column 1 should be aligned with the right edge.

Wrapping the App Bar in the `Page.BottomAppBar` element ensures that the bar is positioned at the bottom of the screen.

The `StandardStyles.xaml` file is very important for apps that want to use the standard design provided by Microsoft. As you saw in this example, much is commented out, but if you want a style added to the project, all you have to do is uncomment the code. If you want to add common functionality to your app, go through this file first to see if there is a standard style before creating one yourself.

## The Settings Panel

If you are relatively new to Windows 8, you might not realize how integrated many apps are into the shared framework in Windows. Recall that charms, contracts, and extensions were discussed earlier in the chapter. Apps that implement and use these common contracts and extensions plug themselves into Windows and allow Windows to interact with them. One of the most common contracts for applications to implement is the Settings contract.

To see this in effect, run the Weather app. Once it has started, move the mouse pointer to the bottom-right corner of the screen to display the Charms panel. Select Settings. Notice how the information and options that are displayed are related to the app that is currently open. This happens because the Weather app has registered itself with the Settings panel and has added its own links.

Unlike the previous example with the App Bar, Visual Studio isn't much help when creating Settings panels, but it's pretty easy. There are, however, a few things that you should do when creating this panel.

First of all, the panel should "fly out" in the same way that the standard panels do in Windows. Second, the width of the panel should be exactly 346 pixels—or alternatively, exactly 646 pixels. If possible, stick with 346 and divide your options into more categories instead of creating a huge complex panel. Third, the panel should fold back in when it loses focus.

The next Try It Out builds on the previous example to add a Settings panel.

**TRY IT OUT** Creating Settings Panels: Ch17Ex03\AppBars\SettingsPanel.xaml

1. Return to the `AppBars` project from earlier in the chapter and add a new user control to the project. Name it `SettingsPanel.xaml`.

2. Change the `Width` property of the `Grid` to 346.

3. Set the `background` property of the `Grid` to `Gray`.

4. Add a toggle switch and a text block to the control like this:

```
<Grid Background="Gray">
    <ToggleSwitch Header="Settings panel is" HorizontalAlignment="Left" Margin="10,82,0,0"
            VerticalAlignment="Top" Foreground="Black" IsOn="True" />
    <TextBlock Style="{StaticResource PageSubheaderTextStyle}" HorizontalAlignment="Left"
Margin="10,21,0,0" TextWrapping="Wrap" Text="Settings" VerticalAlignment="Top"
Foreground="Black"/>
</Grid>
```

5. Open the `MainPage.xaml` file and add this just above the `VisualStateManager` element:

```
<local:SettingsPanel x:Name="SettingsPanel"
    HorizontalAlignment="Right" Margin="0, 0, -346, 0" Height="{Binding Height}"
    Grid.RowSpan="5">
    <local:SettingsPanel.Transitions>
```

```
         <TransitionCollection>
           <RepositionThemeTransition />
         </TransitionCollection>
       </local:SettingsPanel.Transitions>
     </local:SettingsPanel>
```

6. In the code behind, add this namespace to the using declarations:

   ```
   using Windows.UI.ApplicationSettings;
   ```

7. In the LoadState, add this line:

   ```
   SettingsPane.GetForCurrentView().CommandsRequested += MainPage_CommandsRequested;
   ```

8. Add this line to the SaveState method:

   ```
   SettingsPane.GetForCurrentView().CommandsRequested -= MainPage_CommandsRequested;
   ```

9. Add the event handler MainPage_CommandsRequested:

   ```
   private void MainPage_CommandsRequested(SettingsPane sender,
   SettingsPaneCommandsRequestedEventArgs args)
   {
   SettingsCommand cmd = new SettingsCommand("KarliCardsSettings", "Game Options",
       (x) =>
         {
           SettingsPanel.Height = Window.Current.Bounds.Height;
           SettingsPanel.Margin = new Thickness(0, 0, 0, 0);
         });
       args.Request.ApplicationCommands.Add(cmd);
   }
   ```

10. Override the OnPointerPressed method like this:

    ```
    protected override void OnPointerPressed(PointerRoutedEventArgs e)
    {
      var position = e.GetCurrentPoint(SettingsPanel).Position.X < 0;
      if (SettingsPanel.Margin.Right == 0 && position)
        SettingsPanel.Margin = new Thickness(0, 0, -346, 0);
      base.OnPointerPressed(e);
    }
    ```

11. Change the click event handler for the Settings button that you added in the previous example, like this:

    ```
    private void GotoSettings(object sender, RoutedEventArgs e)
    {
      Windows.UI.ApplicationSettings.SettingsPane.Show();
    }
    ```

12. Run the app.

### How It Works

The user control you created has no special features except that it sets its own width to the required 346 pixels. The magic of the panel happens in two places. First, in the XAML on the MainPage, the control is declared with a transition:

```
<local:SettingsPanel x:Name="SettingsPanel" HorizontalAlignment="Right"
        Margin="0, 0, -346, 0" Height="{Binding Height}" Grid.RowSpan="5">
  <local:SettingsPanel.Transitions>
    <TransitionCollection>
      <RepositionThemeTransition />
    </TransitionCollection>
  </local:SettingsPanel.Transitions>
</local:SettingsPanel>
```

RepositionThemeTransition causes the panel to appear to "fly out" when its position changes. For this animation to look right, it starts with the right side pushed out to 346 pixels beyond the right edge of the app, which causes the control to be visible, but out of view.

The second bit of magic happens when the command that is defined in the `MainPage_CommandsRequested` event handler is called:

```
private void MainPage_CommandsRequested(SettingsPane sender,
                      SettingsPaneCommandsRequestedEventArgs args)
{
  SettingsCommand cmd =
    new SettingsCommand("KarliCardsSettings", "Game Options", (x) =>
      {
        SettingsPanel.Height = Window.Current.Bounds.Height;
        SettingsPanel.Margin = new Thickness(0, 0, 0, 0);
      });
  args.Request.ApplicationCommands.Add(cmd);
}
```

When the panel should be displayed, you change the control to be aligned with the right edge instead of pushed out beyond it. `RepositionThemeTransition` then kicks in and performs an animation that makes the panel "fly out."

Later, when the user clicks anywhere in the display, the method `OnPointerPressed` is called.

```
protected override void OnPointerPressed(PointerRoutedEventArgs e)
{
  var position = e.GetCurrentPoint(SettingsPanel).Position.X < 0;
  if (SettingsPanel.Margin.Right == 0 && position)
    SettingsPanel.Margin = new Thickness(0, 0, -346, 0);
  base.OnPointerPressed(e);
}
```

This method checks two things. First, it determines whether the pointer was clicked on the surface of the panel, because you don't want to fold up the panel if the user clicked on it. If the position of the click was to the left of the panel and the panel is unfolded, you set the margin of the panel back to 346 pixels beyond the right edge, which causes the panel to fold back up.

In order to receive events from the Settings panel, you inserted this line in the `LoadState` method:

**`SettingsPane.GetForCurrentView().CommandsRequested += MainPage_CommandsRequested;`**

This adds the event handler to the `SettingsPane` for the current view. The reason that you remove it again in the `SaveState` method is that if you had more than one window, you must remove the event handler when you navigate to another page. If you don't, you will probably end up with the same entry multiple times on the Settings menu.

Finally, in the click event handler on the App Bar, you show the `Windows SettingsPane` using this command:

```
Windows.UI.ApplicationSettings.SettingsPane.Show();
```

## Tiles, Badges, and Splash Screens

Tiles are important because, if they look nice, users will more likely keep them on the Start page. Also, a tile should be easily identifiable; if you make your users search for a tile that disappears in the other tiles, then it's less likely that they will be happy by the time that they finally locate it.

The download for this book includes three tile images—`Tile30x30`, `Tile150x150`, and `Tile310x150`. Not coincidentally, there are three possible tile sizes in Windows Store apps. All apps should include a tile that is $150 \times 150$ pixels, but supplying the large tile ($310 \times 150$ pixels) is also recommended. The small tile ($30 \times 30$ pixels) is not used to display on the Start page and is less important, but if it is included, Windows will use it where appropriate (such as when the user chooses Uninstall).

Badges are smaller than the tiles ($24 \times 24$ pixels) and are used when Windows displays the app on the Lock Screen. If you set a badge image for your app, you must also enable Lock Screen notifications.

Splash screens are displayed while the app loads; and since that should take only a moment or two, they should not be too complex or provide any kind of information to the users, except for clearly identifying which app is currently starting. Splash screens are exactly 620 × 300 pixels, but you can make them smaller by making parts of the image transparent.

Tiles and badges are embedded in the apps package manifest, which can be edited easily in the Visual Studio Manifest Package editor. If you have downloaded the code for this book, you can use the tiles and badge supplied with the code (in the `Assets` folder), but otherwise you can quickly create the images in Paint or in a similar application.

**TRY IT OUT**   Adding Tiles and Badges: Ch17Ex04\Tiles

1. Use an image editor like Paint to create four PNG images with these sizes:
   - 620 × 300
   - 310 × 150
   - 150 × 150
   - 30 × 30

2. Name the images so you can recognize them without opening them. Name them `SplashScreen.png`, `Tile310x150.png`, `Tile150x150.png`, and so on.

3. Open the project from the previous example and add the images to the `Assets` folder.

4. Double-click the file `Package.appxmanifest` in the Solution Explorer to open the package editor.

5. Below the Tile heading, there are three entries that you can change that correspond to one of the tile sizes you created earlier. Add the three tiles here by clicking the buttons and browsing to them. If you add an image with an incorrect size, a red marker will be displayed.

6. Add the image for the splash screen below the Splash Screen heading farther down the page.

7. Run the app and close it again.

*How It Works*

When the app runs, the splash screen briefly appears. On the Start page in Windows, your app is now displayed with the large tile you provided. If you right-click the tile, you can change its size. This will cause the smaller (150 × 150) tile to be displayed. Finally, when you select Uninstall, the smallest tile of 30 × 30 is used.

## CONVERTING KARLICARDS, PART 2

It is time to finish KarliCards. You left the app having completed the controls, but no pages were yet displaying the game. In the following Try It Out, you are going to create three pages for the game and provide navigation between the pages. You will set up state management for the app in these examples. You have already seen how to add a settings panel and App Bars to an app, so performing these tasks are left as exercises at the end of the chapter.

**TRY IT OUT**   Converting KarliCards: KarliCards.Store\KarliCards.Gui

1. Return to the KarliCards.Store solution.
2. Delete the `MainPage.xaml` file.
3. Add a new page to the app using the Basic Page template. Name this page `MainPage.xaml`.
4. Allow Visual Studio to add the files it needs and compile the project.
5. Change the `AppName` in the Resources to `KarliCards`.
6. Above the `VisualStateManager` element, add a button like this:

```
<Button x:Name="startGameButton" Content="Create new game"
        Style="{StaticResource TextButtonStyle}" HorizontalAlignment="Center"
        VerticalAlignment="Center" Grid.ColumnSpan="2" Grid.RowSpan="2"
        Click="StartGame_Click" />
```

7. Navigate to the event handler to add it to the code. Leave it empty.

8. Add a second page to the project, again using the Basic Page template. Name this page StartGame.xaml.

9. Again, set the AppName to KarliCards.

10. Add this XAML to the page just above the VisualStateManager:

```
<ListBox x:Name="playersListBox" HorizontalAlignment="Left"
        Margin="10,110,0,0" Grid.Row="1" VerticalAlignment="Top" Width="273"
        ItemsSource="{Binding PlayerNames}" SelectionMode="Multiple"
        SelectionChanged="SelectedPlayersChanged"/>
<TextBlock Style="{StaticResource ItemTextStyle}" HorizontalAlignment="Left"
        Margin="11,79,0,0" Grid.Row="1" TextWrapping="Wrap" Text="Players"
        VerticalAlignment="Top"/>

<TextBlock Style="{StaticResource ItemTextStyle}" HorizontalAlignment="Left"
        Margin="10,10,0,0" Grid.Row="1" TextWrapping="Wrap" Text="New player"
        VerticalAlignment="Top"/>
<TextBox x:Name="playerNameTextBox"  HorizontalAlignment="Left" Margin="10,39,0,0"
        Grid.Row="1" TextWrapping="Wrap" Text="" VerticalAlignment="Top"
        Width="200"/>
<Button Content="Add"  HorizontalAlignment="Left" Margin="224,33,0,0" Grid.Row="1"
        VerticalAlignment="Top" Click="AddPlayer_Clicked"/>
<Button x:Name="startGameButton" Content="Start Game"  Style="{StaticResource
        TextButtonStyle}" HorizontalAlignment="Center" VerticalAlignment="Center"
        Grid.ColumnSpan="2" Grid.RowSpan="2" Visibility="Collapsed"
        Click="StartGame_Click" />
```

11. Add the three event handlers to the code-behind file.

12. Add the CardLib and KarliCards_Gui.ViewModel namespaces to the using declarations, and then add this field to the class:

```
using CardLib;
using KarliCards_Gui.ViewModel;
...
private GameOptions _options = new GameOptions();
```

13. Change the constructor like this:

```
public StartGame()
{
  this.InitializeComponent();
  DataContext = _options;
}
```

14. Add this code to the SelectedPlayersChanged and AddPlayer_Clicked event handlers:

```
private void SelectedPlayersChanged(object sender, SelectionChangedEventArgs e)
{
  if (playersListBox.SelectedItems.Count == 1 && _options.PlayAgainstComputer)
    startGameButton.Visibility = Windows.UI.Xaml.Visibility.Visible;
  else if (playersListBox.SelectedItems.Count == _options.NumberOfPlayers)
    startGameButton.Visibility = Windows.UI.Xaml.Visibility.Visible;
  else
    startGameButton.Visibility = Windows.UI.Xaml.Visibility.Collapsed;
}

private void AddPlayer_Clicked(object sender, RoutedEventArgs e)
{
  if (playerNameTextBox.Text.Length > 0)
  {
    _options.AddPlayer(playerNameTextBox.Text);
```

```
        playerNameTextBox.Text = string.Empty;
    }
}
```

**15.** Add yet another Basic Page to the project. Name this `GamePage.xaml`.

**16.** Change the `AppName` to `KarliCards`.

**17.** Add this namespace declaration to the `Page` element:

```
xmlns:src="using:KarliCards_Gui"
```

**18.** Add this XAML above the `VisualStateManager` element:

```xml
<src:CardsInHandControl
    x:Name="Player2Hand"
    Grid.Row="2"
    Height="400"
    Width="200"
    VerticalAlignment="Center"
    HorizontalAlignment="Right"
    PlayerOrientation="Vertical"
    Owner="{Binding Players[1], Mode=OneWay}"
    Game="{Binding}"
    PlayerState="{Binding Players[1].State, Mode=OneWay}"
    />
<src:CardsInHandControl
    Grid.Row="2"
    Height="400"
    Width="200"
    x:Name="Player4Hand"
    VerticalAlignment="Center"
    HorizontalAlignment="Left"
    PlayerOrientation="Vertical"
    Owner="{Binding Players[3], Mode=OneWay}"
    Game="{Binding}"
    PlayerState="{Binding Players[3].State, Mode=OneWay}"
    />
<src:CardsInHandControl
    Grid.Row="1"
    x:Name="Player1Hand"
    VerticalAlignment="Top"
    HorizontalAlignment="Center"
    Height="154"
    Width="400"
    PlayerOrientation="Horizontal"
    Owner="{Binding Players[0], Mode=OneWay}"
    Game="{Binding}"
    PlayerState="{Binding Players[0].State, Mode=OneWay}"
    />
<src:CardsInHandControl
    Grid.Row="2"
    x:Name="Player3Hand"
    VerticalAlignment="Bottom"
    HorizontalAlignment="Center"
    Height="200"
    Width="400"
    PlayerOrientation="Horizontal"
    Owner="{Binding Players[2], Mode=OneWay}"
    Game="{Binding}"
    PlayerState="{Binding Players[2].State, Mode=OneWay}"
    />
<src:GameDecksControl
    Grid.Row="1"
    VerticalAlignment="Center"
    HorizontalAlignment="Center"
```

```
        Height="175"
            x:Name="GameDecks"
            Deck="{Binding GameDeck, Mode=OneWay}"
            AvailableCard="{Binding CurrentAvailableCard, Mode=OneWay}"
            CurrentPlayer="{Binding CurrentPlayer, Mode=OneWay}"
            GameStarted="{Binding GameStarted, Mode=OneWay}"/>
```

**19.** Go to the code-behind file and add `CardLib` and `KarliCards_Gui` to the `using` declarations, and then change the `LoadState` method like this:

```csharp
using CardLib;
using KarliCards_Gui.ViewModel;

...

    protected override void LoadState(Object navigationParameter,
            Dictionary<String, Object> pageState)
    {
        if (pageState != null && pageState["CurrentGame"] != null)
        {
            var context = pageState["CurrentGame"] as GameViewModel;
            if (context != null)
            {
                this.DataContext = context;
                context.ContinueGame();
            }
        }
        else if (navigationParameter != null)
        {
            var players = navigationParameter as string;
            var newGame = new GameViewModel();
            newGame.StartNewGame(PlayerNames.FromString(players));
            DataContext = newGame;
        }
    }
```

**20.** Return to the `StartGame.xaml.cs` code-behind file and change the event handler for the Start game button like this:

```csharp
    private void StartGame_Click(object sender, RoutedEventArgs e)
    {
        var players = new PlayerNames();
        foreach (var player in playersListBox.SelectedItems)
            players.Add(player as string);
        _options.Save();
        Frame.Navigate(typeof(GamePage), players.ToString());
    }
```

**21.** Go back to the `MainPage.xaml.cs` code-behind file and change the same event for the Start game button like this:

```csharp
    private void StartGame_Click(object sender, RoutedEventArgs e)
    {
        Frame.Navigate(typeof(StartGame));
    }
```

**22.** Go to the `App.xaml.cs` file and change the `OnLaunched` and `OnSuspending` methods like this:

```csharp
        protected async override void OnLaunched(LaunchActivatedEventArgs args)
        {
            if (args.PreviousExecutionState == ApplicationExecutionState.Running)
            {
                Window.Current.Activate();
                return;
            }

            var rootFrame = new Frame();
```

```
            KarliCards.Gui.Common.SuspensionManager.RegisterFrame(
                    rootFrame, "karliCardsFrame");

            if (args.PreviousExecutionState == ApplicationExecutionState.Terminated)
            {
              KarliCards.Gui.Common.SuspensionManager.KnownTypes.Add(typeof(GameViewModel));
              await KarliCards.Gui.Common.SuspensionManager.RestoreAsync();
            }

            if (rootFrame.Content == null)
            {
              if (!rootFrame.Navigate(typeof(MainPage)))
              {
                throw new Exception("Failed to create initial page");
              }
            }

            Window.Current.Content = rootFrame;
            Window.Current.Activate();
        }
        private async void OnSuspending(object sender, SuspendingEventArgs e)
        {
            var deferral = e.SuspendingOperation.GetDeferral();
            KarliCards.Gui.Common.SuspensionManager.KnownTypes.Add(typeof(GameViewModel));
            await KarliCards.Gui.Common.SuspensionManager.SaveAsync();
            deferral.Complete();
        }
```

**23.** Return to the GamePage.xaml.cs code-behind file and change the SaveState method like this:

```
        protected override void SaveState(Dictionary<String, Object> pageState)
        {
            pageState["CurrentGame"] = DataContext as GameViewModel;
        }
```

**24.** Run the app. Note that if you suspend and close the app while it is on the GamePage, the game is saved and restored the next time you start the game. Figure 17-14 shows the game running with the _numberOfPlayers variable in the GameOptions class set to 4.

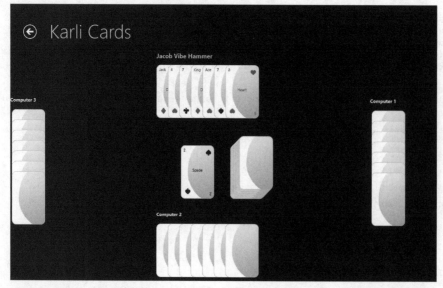

**FIGURE 17-14**

### How It Works

All of the code and XAML in this example is very simple and close to something that you have seen before; but in Step 19 and onward, you set up the management of the session state in the game. If the pageState dictionary includes the CurrentGame entry, then this is loaded and used as the DataContext instead of creating a new game. This is where the ContinueGame that was added to the GameViewModel previously is used.

In Step 20, you call the Navigate method with a string argument containing the selected players. This is used in the LoadState method of Step 19, where the navigationParameter is checked for null. If it isn't null, then the method knows that it can start a new game using the values extracted from the navigationParameter.

> **NOTE** *The reason that* navigationParameter *is converted into a string and back is that you are not allowed to pass complex types in the* Navigate *parameter. This is not readily apparent from the code because the parameter is of type object; however, your app will crash when it is suspended by Windows if you use the* PlayerNames *instance directly.*

## THE WINDOWS STORE

After you create your app, you will probably want to distribute it to the public—and the only way to do this is to use the Windows Store. Microsoft has gone to great lengths to create a store that is secure and lets Windows users download apps from it without too much fear of downloading malicious code. Unfortunately, this means you must endure a lengthy process to get your app in the store.

## Checking the Store Requirements

Your app must meet a set of requirements for it to be published to the store. When you installed Visual Studio, you also installed a toolkit for publishing apps to the app store. One of those tools is called the Windows App Cert Kit, which you can run from anywhere in Windows. You can use this kit to check if your app meets the requirements of the store.

> **NOTE** *Before you run the kit, be sure to compile your app in Release mode rather than in Debug mode.*

**TRY IT OUT** Checking Store Requirements

1. Compile your app in Release mode by selecting Release from the ComboBox control on the toolbar. This will normally display the selection Debug if you haven't changed it.

2. Run the app to install it.

3. On the Windows Start page, type **Windows App Cert Kit** to search for the tool, and press Return to start it.

4. When the tool starts, you have the option to validate three types of apps. Select the first one: Validate Windows Store App.

5. From the next window, select your app and click Next. The test now runs.

6. Save the report on disk.

7. Finally, you are told whether your app passes the test. If you have created the app using the templates in Visual Studio, there should be no problems. Click on the link to see the detailed results.

At this point you are ready to create your app store account. You will have to log into your Microsoft Account at the Microsoft website devoted to creating apps. At the time of writing this can be found here:

```
https://appdev.microsoft.com/StorePortals/en-us/Account/Signup/SelectAccountType
```

Please note that creating a Store Account is not free. At the time of writing, creating an individual account cost $49, but this is subject to change. If you want to create an account and pay the cost, follow the instructions on the website.

Once you have a Store Account, you can use the options on the Store menu in Visual Studio to continue. From there, you can reserve the name of your app on the store and launch a simulator to take screenshots that can be displayed to potential buyers. You can also create and upload the app package, which is required for the app to be available in the store.

## SUMMARY

Windows Store apps are a diverse lot, and the possibilities you have for creating apps is limited only by your imagination—well, your imagination and the limits set by the Windows Store. But you get the idea. And in this chapter, you have seen how to develop apps that meet these requirements. When you develop apps using C# and XAML, you are using a powerful toolset that can be easily used when developing applications for server or desktop applications for Windows. That makes the skill set you have required over these first two sections of the book very valuable.

### EXERCISES

**17.1** Add an App Bar to the KarliCards game. On the Main page the App Bar should include the following buttons: Play, Settings, and Help. On the Game page, the App Bar should include these buttons: Settings and Help. The Start button should use navigation to go to the Start Game page.

**17.2** Create a Settings panel and attach it to the Main and Game pages of the KarliCards application. On the Settings panel, the user should be able to set the options available in the GameOptions class: Number of Players, Computer Skill Level, Play Against Computer, and Computer Plays with Open Hand.

## ▶ WHAT YOU LEARNED IN THIS CHAPTER

| KEY CONCEPT | DESCRIPTION |
| --- | --- |
| **Windows Store XAML** | Windows Store XAML is used with C# to create the GUI for Windows Store apps. It includes many of the same controls that you know from WPF, but some have changed, others are missing, and new controls have been introduced. |
| **Visual State manager** | You saw how to use a Visual State manager to change the look of your controls and pages simply by changing the visual state of the control. This leads to a lot less code in exchange for slightly more complex XAML. |
| **Windows Developer License** | The Windows 8 developer license is required in order to be able to develop apps for the Windows Store. |
| **App store account** | This account is used for deploying apps to the Windows Store. |
| **Navigation** | Navigation in Windows Store apps is done in much the same way that is in web applications, using method calls to move back and forth in the page structure. |

# 18

# Deploying Desktop Applications

**WHAT YOU WILL LEARN IN THIS CHAPTER**

➤ An overview of deployment options

➤ How to deploy a Windows application with ClickOnce

➤ How to create a Windows Installer deployment package

➤ How to install an application with Windows Installer

There are several ways to install Windows applications. Simple applications can be installed with a basic xcopy deployment, but for installation to hundreds of clients, an xcopy deployment is not really useful. For that situation, you have two options: ClickOnce deployment or the Microsoft Windows Installer.

With ClickOnce deployment, the application is installed by clicking a link to a website. In situations where the user should select a directory in which to install the application, or when some registry entries are required, the Windows Installer is the deployment option to use.

This chapter covers both options for installing Windows applications.

> **NOTE** *The InstallShield Limited Edition tool that is used in the second section of this chapter is not part of Visual Studio out of the box. To get it, open Visual Studio and select File ➪ New ➪ Project, and then select Other Project Types ➪ Setup and Deployment. Double-click Enable InstallShield Limited Edition and follow the instructions in the browser window that opens. You will have to register with the creators of InstallShield in order to download the product. Once you install this tool, double-clicking the Enable InstallShield Limited Edition link gives you the option to activate the product. Once you do, you are ready to continue.*

> **NOTE** *This chapter covers how to install traditional desktop applications. To learn how to install Windows Store applications, the new type of application that can be made available to and acquired from Microsoft's Windows Store, please see Chapter 17, "Windows Store Apps."*

# DEPLOYMENT OVERVIEW

Deployment is the process of installing applications to the target systems. Traditionally, such an installation has been done by invoking a setup program. If one hundred or even one thousand clients must be installed, the installation can be very time-consuming. To alleviate this time commitment, the system administrator can create batch scripts to automate this activity. However, it still requires a lot of work to set up and support different client PCs and different versions of the operating system.

Because of these challenges, many companies have converted their intranet applications to web applications, even though Windows applications offer a much richer user interface. Web applications just need to be deployed to the server, and the client automatically gets the up-to-date user interface.

Using ClickOnce installation, you can avoid many of these challenges of deploying Windows applications. Applications can be installed just by clicking a link inside a web page. The user on the client system doesn't need administrative privileges, as the application is installed in a user-specific directory. With ClickOnce, you can install applications with a rich user interface. The application is installed to the client, so there's no need to remain connected with the client system after the installation is completed. In other words, the application can be used offline. This way, an application icon is available from the Start menu, the security issues are easier to resolve, and the application can easily be uninstalled.

A nice feature of ClickOnce is that updates can happen automatically when the client application starts or as a background task while the client application is running.

However, there are some restrictions accompanying ClickOnce deployment: ClickOnce cannot be used if you need to install shared components in the global assembly cache; if the application needs COM components that require registry settings; or if you want users to decide in what directory the application should be installed. In such cases, you must use the Windows Installer, which is the traditional way to install desktop applications on Windows. Before working with the Windows Installer packages, however, take a look at the next section, which covers ClickOnce deployment.

# CLICKONCE DEPLOYMENT

With ClickOnce deployment, there is no need to start a setup program on the client system. The client's user simply has to click a link on a web page, and the application is automatically installed. After the application is installed, the client can be offline—it doesn't need to access the server from the application that was installed.

ClickOnce installation can be done from a website, a UNC share, or a file location (such as, a CD). With ClickOnce, the application is installed on the client system, it is available with Start menu shortcuts, and it can be uninstalled from the Add/Remove Programs window.

ClickOnce deployment is described by the manifest files. The application manifest describes the application and permissions required by the application. The deployment manifest describes deployment configuration information, such as update policies. In the Try It Out exercises of this section, you configure ClickOnce deployment for the Karli Card game you created in Chapter 16, and you will need those code files again.

> **NOTE**  *When you are publishing with ClickOnce, you are always going to need administrative rights, and a real web server is also usually required. For testing and examining the files, you can publish to a local folder. When you start Visual Studio to do the examples in this chapter, please right-click the tile and select "Run as Administrator".*

## Implementing ClickOnce Deployment

In the following Try It Out exercise, you change the application name and define useful assembly settings.

Preparing the Application: Ch18Ex01

This example builds on the KarliCards Gui solution and CardLib projects you created in Chapter 16.

1. Open the game client solution you created for KarliCards in Chapter 16.
2. Double-click Properties of the KarliCards Gui project, and change the Assembly name to `KarliCards`.
3. Click the Assembly Information button.
4. Change the Title, Description, Company, Product, and Copyright information as shown in Figure 18-1.
5. Build the project by selecting Build ➪ Build Solution.

**FIGURE 18-1**

### How It Works

The assembly name defines the name of the assembly that is created from the build process. This assembly needs to be deployed when installing the application. The properties that are changed with the Assembly Information dialog box change assembly attributes in the file `AssemblyInfo.cs`. This metadata information is used by deployment tools. You can also read the metadata information from Windows Explorer by selecting the executable and clicking on Properties in the menu. With the Details tab, you can see the information you've added.

---

Successfully deploying the assembly across the network requires a manifest that is signed with a certificate. The certificate is used to show information to the user about the organization that created the application. This way the user can decide if he trusts the deployment. In the following Try It Out, you create a certificate that is associated with the ClickOnce manifests.

> **NOTE** *In the code download for this book, the password used for the included certificates is 1234.*

Signing the Projects: Ch18Ex01

This example continues where the previous example left, setting the properties of the project.

1. Select the Signing tab, as shown in Figure 18-2.
2. Check the Sign the ClickOnce manifests check box.
3. Click the Select from File... button and select the `KarliCards Gui_TemporaryKey.pfx` file. Next, click OK.
4. Check the Sign the Assembly check box.
5. From the dropdown, select `KarliCards Gui_TemporaryKey.pfx`.
6. In the Solution Explorer, double-click the properties node of the CardLib project.
7. Select the Signing tab and check the Sign the Assembly check box.

8. In the dropdown, select Browse...

9. Browse to the `KarliCards Gui_TemporaryKey.pfx` file in the KarliCards.Gui project.

**FIGURE 18-2**

### How It Works

A certificate is used so that the user installing the application can identify the creator of the installation package. By reading the certificate, users can decide whether they can trust the installation to approve the security requirements.

With the test certificate you just created, the user doesn't get real trust information and receives a warning that this certificate cannot be trusted, as you will see later. Such a certificate is for testing only. Before you make the application ready for deployment, you have to get a real certificate from a certification authority such as VeriSign. If the application is deployed only within an intranet, then you can also get a certificate from a local certificate server if one is installed with your local network. The Microsoft Certificate Server can be installed with Windows Server. If you have such a certificate, you can configure it by clicking Select from File within the Signing tab.

---

In the next Try It Out, you configure the security requirements of the assembly. When the assembly is installed on the client, the required trust must be defined.

**TRY IT OUT** Defining the Security Requirements: Ch18Ex01

This example continues where the previous example left off.

1. Double-click the properties node of the KarliCards.Gui project, select the Security tab (see Figure 18-3), and then select Enable ClickOnce Security Settings. Leave the default configuration for the full trust application.

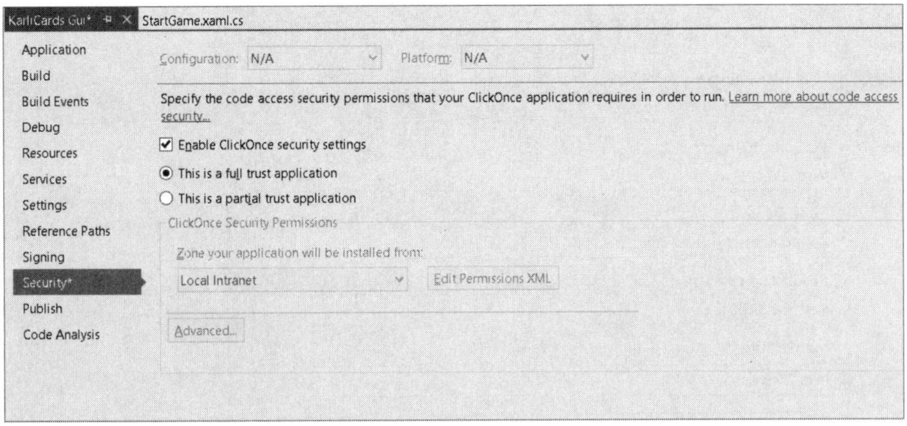

**FIGURE 18-3**

### How It Works

With ClickOnce settings, you can configure the application to require full trust or run with partial trust within a sandbox. With full trust, the application has full access to the system and can do anything the user running the application is allowed to do. With the installation of the application, the user is warned about these requirements. With a partial trust application, the application is not allowed to access any aspect of the file system other than the isolated storage or the registry. The application runs in a sandbox mode. Because the MDI editor application requires access to the file system, full trust is required.

With the defined security requirements, you can start to publish the application by creating a deployment manifest. This can easily be done with the Publish Wizard, as shown in the following Try It Out.

**TRY IT OUT** More Publish Configuration Options: Ch18Ex01

The previous examples have configured the project for ClickOnce deployment. Now it's time to specify in detail how and what to deploy.

1. Select the Publish tab with the project properties. Click the Options button to open the Publish Options dialog box (see Figure 18-4). Select Description from the list on the left. Enter the publisher name, the suite name, the product name, and a support URL.

2. Select the Deployment option in the list to the left and type a name for the deployment page. Then check the two boxes below it, as shown in Figure 18-5. This causes an HTML file to be generated that can be used to install the application. Click OK.

3. Configure the Update options by selecting the Updates button. Then select The Application Should Check for Updates check box, as shown in Figure 18-6. Click OK.

4. Click the ellipsis (...) next to the Publishing Folder Location textbox to select a location. In the window that is displayed, you can select how to publish. If you have IIS or IIS Express running, you can select Local IIS. For this example, create a new folder in the solution folder, name it DeploymentFiles, and then click OK.

5. You are publishing to a folder, so you need to provide a share from which the files can be reached. This folder must be on UNC form. In Windows Explorer, browse to the DeploymentFiles folder, right-click it, and select Share With ➪ Specific People.

6. Select Everyone from the dropdown menu and click Add.

7. As shown in Figure 18-7, type the path to the folder in the Installation Folder textbox. The path will look something like this:

```
\\your computer's name\DeploymentFiles
```

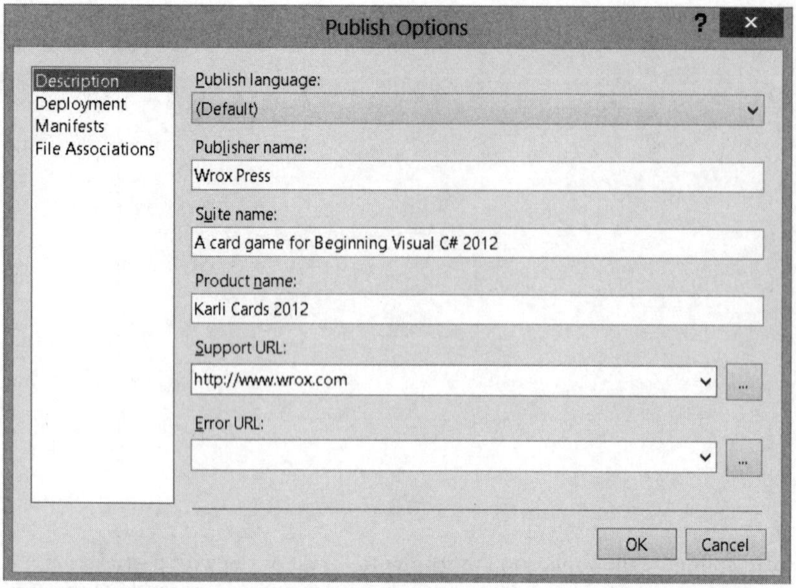

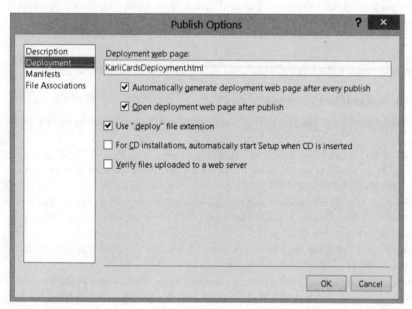

**FIGURE 18-4**

**FIGURE 18-5**

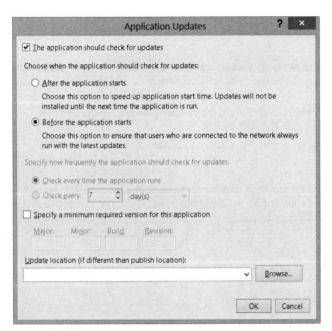

**FIGURE 18-6**

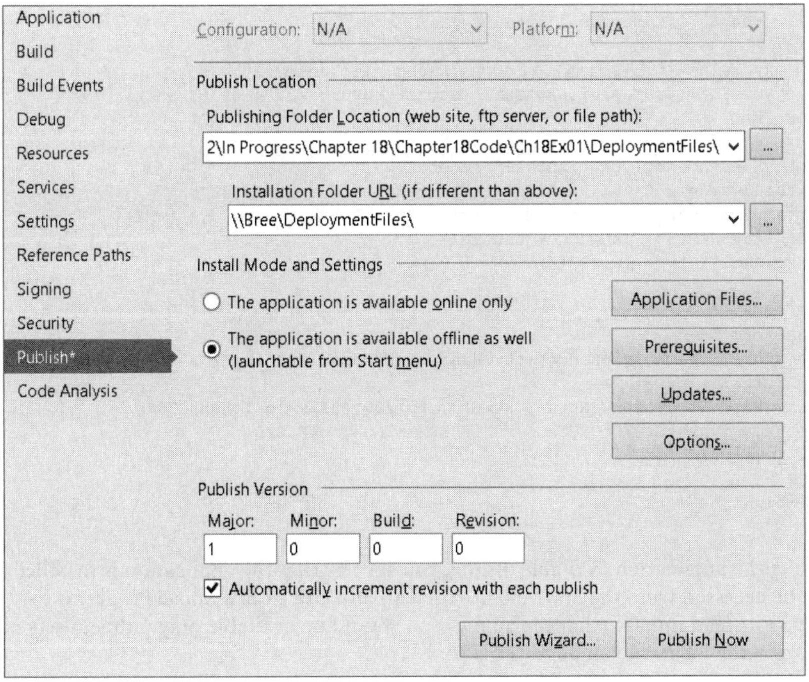

**FIGURE 18-7**

**Using the Publish Wizard: Ch18Ex01**

Finally, you are ready to deploy your application.

1. Start the Publish Wizard by clicking Publish Wizard. This feature is also available by selecting Build ⇨ Publish Wizard from the Visual Studio menu. The path you selected earlier should already be specified, so click the Next button.

2. The wizard shows three steps that display the information that you have provided in the previous examples. Click the Next button until you reach the summary.

3. The last window gives summary information, as you are ready to publish! Click the Finish button.

### How It Works

The Publish Wizard creates a number of files and folders, and then writes them to the location you specified. In this folder, you will find the HTML page that is generated by the deployment wizard (`KarliCardsDeployment .html`), alongside a deployment manifest file (`KarliCards.application`). The deployment manifest describes installation information. With Visual Studio, you can open the deployment manifest by opening the file `KarliCards.application` in the Solution Explorer.

With this manifest, you can see a dependency to the application manifest with the XML element `<dependentAssembly>`:

```
<deployment install="true" mapFileExtensions="true">
  <subscription>
    <update>
      <beforeApplicationStartup />
    </update>
  </subscription>
  <deploymentProvider codebase=
"http://lorien/KarliCards/KarliCards.application" />
</deployment>
<compatibleFrameworks xmlns="urn:schemas-microsoft-com:clickonce.v2">
  <framework targetVersion="4.5" profile="Full" supportedRuntime="4.0.30319" />
</compatibleFrameworks>
<dependency>
  <dependentAssembly dependencyType="install" codebase=
"Application Files\KarliCards_1_0_0_1\KarliCards.exe.manifest" size="8936">
    <assemblyIdentity name="KarliCards.exe" version="1.0.0.1"
publicKeyToken="ae25b3497596b45c" language="neutral"
processorArchitecture="msil" type="win32" />
    <hash>
      <dsig:Transforms>
        <dsig:Transform
        Algorithm="urn:schemas-microsoft-com:HashTransforms.Identity" />
      </dsig:Transforms>
      <dsig:DigestMethod Algorithm="http://www.w3.org/2000/09/xmldsig#sha256" />
      <dsig:DigestValue>vhrszCfNX0bQOUCst43KdXiFVExVmSlmtRQbo4ZJSfE=
</dsig:DigestValue>
    </hash>
  </dependentAssembly>
</dependency>
```

By selecting the option to make the application available offline, you specify that the application is installed on the client system and can be accessed from the Start menu. You can also use Add/Remove Programs to uninstall the application. If you instead indicate that the application should be available only online, users must always start the application from the location you deployed it to.

The files that belong to the application are defined by the project output. To see the application files with the properties of the application in the Publish settings, click the Application Files button. The Application Files dialog box opens (see Figure 18-8). By default, the assembly and the application manifest file are deployed.

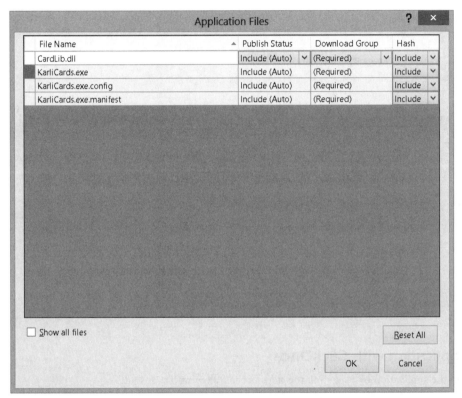

| File Name | Publish Status | Download Group | Hash |
|---|---|---|---|
| CardLib.dll | Include (Auto) | (Required) | Include |
| KarliCards.exe | Include (Auto) | (Required) | Include |
| KarliCards.exe.config | Include (Auto) | (Required) | Include |
| KarliCards.exe.manifest | Include (Auto) | (Required) | Include |

☐ Show all files

**FIGURE 18-8**

The prerequisites of the application are defined with the Prerequisites dialog box (see Figure 18-9), accessed by clicking the Prerequisites button. With .NET 4.5 applications, the prerequisite .NET Framework 4.5 is automatically detected, as the figure shows. You can also select other prerequisites using this dialog box.

> **NOTE** When installing ClickOnce applications, administrative privileges are not required. However, if prerequisites are not installed on the client system, administrative privileges are required to install the prerequisites.

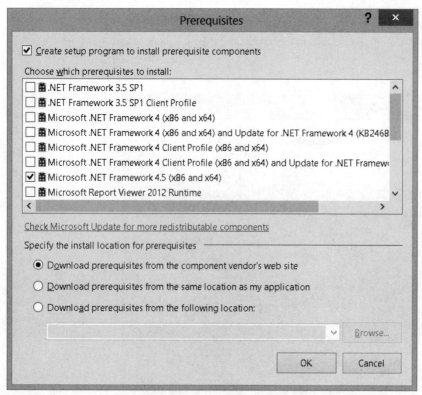

**FIGURE 18-9**

## Installing the Application with ClickOnce

Now you can install the application by executing the steps in the following Try It Out.

**TRY IT OUT** | **Installing Karli Cards: Ch18Ex01**

This exercise resumes with KarliCards deployment project.

1. Open the web page `KarliCardsDeployment.html`, shown in Figure 18-10.
2. Click the Install button to install the application. At this point Internet Explorer will ask you if you are sure you want to run an executable from the location you deployed it to. Click Run. You might also get warnings that the intranet setting is disabled, in which case you can choose to turn it on to remove some of the warnings. Then you will get yet another security warning (see Figure 18-11), this time because you are using a test certificate and the publisher cannot be verified.
3. Click the Install button if you trust the application you created.

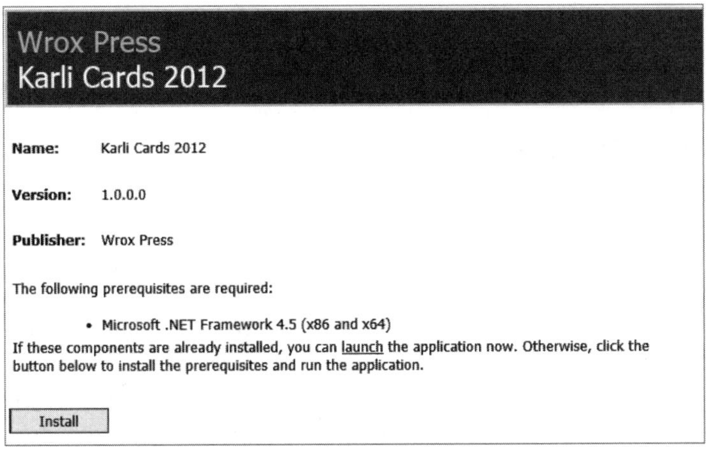

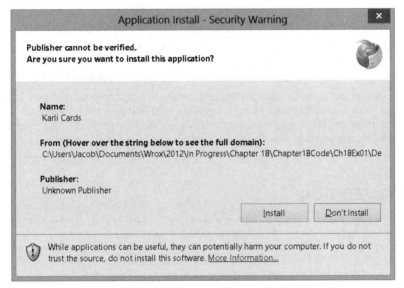

**FIGURE 18-10**

**FIGURE 18-11**

*How It Works*

When the file `KarliCardsDeployment.html` is opened, the target application is checked for version 4.5 of the .NET runtime. This check is done by a JavaScript function inside the HTML page. If the runtime is not there, it is installed before the client application. With the default publish settings, the runtime is copied from a Microsoft site.

By clicking the link to install the application, the deployment manifest is opened to install the application. Next, the user is informed about any possible security issues of the application. If the user clicks OK, the application is installed.

## Creating and Using Updates of the Application

With the update options you configured earlier, the client application automatically checks the web server for a new version. In the following Try It Out, you try such a scenario with the MDI Editor application.

**TRY IT OUT** Updating the installed Application: Ch18Ex01

If you make changes to an application after it has been installed by the user, ClickOnce will automatically detect this and install the update. Follow the steps in this Try It Out to test this behavior.

1. Make a change to the application that shows up immediately, such as setting the background color GameClient.xaml to blue.

2. Open the project properties and select the Publish tab. Verify that the publish version number changes to a new value in the project properties.

3. Build the application and click the Publish Now button in the Publish section of the project properties.

4. Do not click the KarliCardsDeployment.html link on the web page; instead, start the client application from the Start menu. When the application starts, the Update Available dialog box appears, asking whether a new version should be downloaded. Click OK to download the new version. When the new version launches, you can see the application with the colored rich text box.

*How It Works*

The update policy is defined by a setting in the deployment manifest with the XML <update> element. You can change the update policy by clicking the Updates button in the Publish settings. Remember to access the Publish settings within the properties of the project. The Application Updates dialog box is shown back in Figure 18-6.

Use this dialog box to specify whether the client should look for updates at all. If updates should be checked, then you can define whether the check should happen before the application starts or in the background while the application is running. If the update should occur in the background, you can set the time interval between them: with every start of the application or with a specific number of hours, days, or weeks.

## INSTALLSHIELD LIMITED EDITION

In previous editions, Visual Studio included a tool to create MSI installation packages, but this has now been removed. The tool worked, but it had a lot of problems and was never a fully integrated feature of Visual Studio, so having it replaced with a free edition from one of the major three party creators of installer tools is not a bad deal. That being said, the InstallShield Limited Edition is severely limited compared to other editions, but the commercial editions are quite expensive, so none of the features from those versions will be discussed here.

## The Project Assistant

In a little while you are going to work through an example that creates a new installer for the KarliCards game, and throughout that example you are going to work with the Project Assistant. This is a wizard that was installed into Visual Studio when you installed InstallShield (see Figure 18-12).

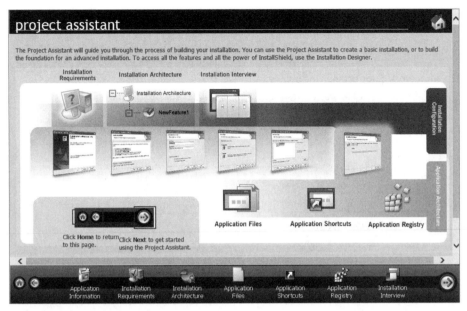

**FIGURE 18-12**

Across the bottom of the screen, you see seven steps that the assistant will take you through to create a new installation package, so let's go through them one by one.

### Step 1: Application Information

There are a few crucial bits of information about any application that you must provide no matter what application you are creating: The application name and version and this step allows you to set these two properties. It also allows you to specify the name and website of your company if any. Finally you can assign an icon to the application. This is the image that is displayed when the user sees the application installer or executable in Windows Explorer.

### Step 2: Installation Requirements

Applications written in C# have a specific set of requirements, just like most programs. In this step the assistant allows you to specify these requirements, but unfortunately it doesn't help you very much, so you have to know what the requirements actually are.

The top part of the page asks the question, "Does your application require any specific operating system?" Although the real answer to that question is a resounding "yes," it's a little bit more complicated than that, so let's start with the easy part. Microsoft .NET 4.5 is only supported on Windows 7, Windows 2008 Server, and newer. That means that any application that uses this framework—for example anything in this book—should change this setting to Yes and uncheck Windows Vista, Windows 2003 Server, Windows XP, and Windows 2000.

But then it becomes more complicated (see Table 18-1). If you want your application to install and run on older Windows versions, it is sometimes possible to do this. In any C# project you can open the Options dialog box and, on the Application page, change the target framework. The smaller the version number, the older the supported version of Windows. Doing this, however, can have drastic consequences for your application as this target is very important, and you should expect to do some work to make it work with an older framework.

**TABLE 18-1:** NET Framework Support in Windows

| .NET VERSION | OLDEST SUPPORTED WINDOWS VERSION |
| --- | --- |
| 4.5 | Windows 7 |
| | Windows 2008 |
| 4.0 | Windows XP SP3 |
| | Windows 2003 Server |
| 3.5 | Windows XP SP3 |
| | Windows 2003 Server |
| 2.0 | Windows 2000 SP3 |

Now, just because you can create something that runs on Windows 2000 doesn't mean that you should. Unless you have a very good reason for creating applications for this particular operating system, you should not bother.

The second question in this step pertains to the software that should be preinstalled on the OS. You always need the .NET Framework that your application targets.

### Step 3: Installation Architecture

This is not supported in the Limited Edition of InstallShield.

### Step 4: Application Files

An application consists of at least one file, and usually many more. For small projects a good guideline is that the files in the `bin` folder under the executable are all that are needed. For larger projects with more than one executable or with many support files that must be installed in specific locations, this can quickly become complicated.

The Application Files step (see Figure 18-13) allows you to specify both physical and virtual paths in which your files and folders can be placed. The tree on the left side of the page allows you to specify where your files go. The three folders displayed by default are the `AppDataFolder` folder in which, unsurprisingly, applications can store data, the `CommonFilesFolder`, in which shared files can be stored, and the `ProgramFilesFolder`, where the main application files are stored.

If you right-click on the root of the tree, you can select Show Predefined Folder and select another folder to use. One very important folder is `GlobalAssemblyCache`. Any DLLs that you place in this folder will be installed into the global assembly cache (GAC) on the target machine. There are a number of requirements for placing files into the GAC. For one thing the assemblies must be signed, but once the files are in the GAC, they can be accessed by all applications on the local computer.

At the bottom of the page there are three buttons. Using these three buttons, you can easily add your application files and folders to the list of files. If you add an existing project to the installer solution (you can do this without closing the assistant), you can use the Add Project outputs to have the files generated when you compile the projects to the list of files to install.

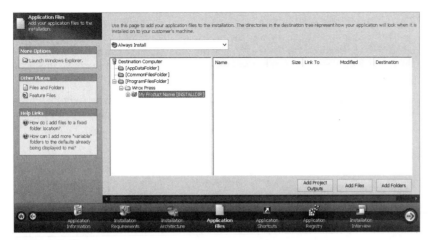

**FIGURE 18-13**

## Step 5: Application Shortcuts

Normally when a Windows application is installed a shortcut to the executable is placed inside the Start menu of Windows. This is of course true only if the application has an executable, but if you expect your users to be able to launch the application manually you have to provide at least this one shortcut. Otherwise it is highly unlikely that they will be able to find your application to run it after the installation finishes. You can use this step to create shortcuts to the files of your application. Help files and URLs can also be referenced this way, but the requirement is that the application files be included in Step 4 (see Figure 18-14).

On the right of this image, you can see the check boxes that define which types of shortcuts are required. Please note that your users are not going to thank you for creating numerous shortcuts on their desktop, so never place more than one link there.

Finally, you can associate a file extension with the target of the shortcut. This can be used, for example, to associate the extension .mp3 with your application and will cause all MP3s to open in your application by default. Again, your users are not going to thank you if you associate, for example, .docx with your application, because that would cause all Word documents to open in your application instead of in Word—unless of course that is the explicit purpose of your application. The bottom line—be very careful when associating file extensions!

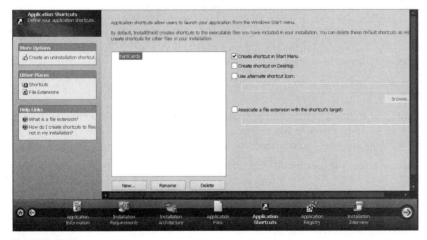

**FIGURE 18-14**

## Step 6: Application Registry

In what seems an ancient past, the Windows Registry was the preferred place for all Windows applications to store their configuration. .NET applications rarely need to do this. But there are times where it can be beneficial or even necessary to configure settings in the Windows Registry. If you need to do so, this is the page to do it.

Figure 18-15 shows this step. You add keys to the Hives displayed in the tree to the left by right-clicking them and selecting New ⇨ Key. Similarly you add values by right-clicking the key in which the value should be stored and selecting New ⇨ *<Type of the value>*.

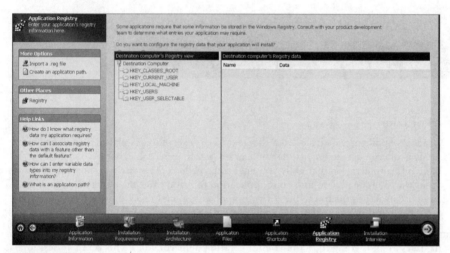

**FIGURE 18-15**

## Step 7: Installation Interview

This final page enables you to select the steps that the user will be presented with when the installation runs. There are four possible steps. First you can show a dialog box that displays a license agreement to the user. If users don't agree to the agreement, the installation is cancelled.

The user can then be prompted for a username and company name. If you require this information, you can have the installation collect it here.

The next available option is to display a page in which the user can specify an alternative destination for the application. You should never require your application to be installed in a specific location. Windows has been translated to more than a hundred languages and many of these use their own names for common folders, so make no assumptions about the names!

Finally, you can give the users the option to launch your application after installation completes. You will have to select the file to execute.

This completes the assistant. If you simply build your application after completing these steps, the installation package will be generated for you. If you right-click the installer project in the Solution Explorer, you can select Install or Uninstall directly from Visual Studio.

You can find the files generated under the solution in the folder at this location:\Express\CD_ROM\ DiskImages\Disk1.

Now it's time for you to try it for yourself.

**TRY IT OUT**   InstallShield Installer: Ch18Ex02

Before you create the installer for the KarliCards game, you need to make a small modification to the game. By default, applications are not allowed to write to the Program Files folders in Windows, and the game does so when it saves its state to disk, so you need to change this.

1. Open the Game Client from Chapter 16 and open the file `GameOptions.cs`.

2. Change the Save and Create methods like this:

```
public void Save()
{
    string filename = Path.Combine(System.Environment.GetFolderPath(
Environment.SpecialFolder.ApplicationData), "GameOptions.xml");
    using (var stream = File.Open(filename, FileMode.Create))
    {
      var serializer = new XmlSerializer(typeof(GameOptions));
      serializer.Serialize(stream, this);
    }
}

public static GameOptions Create()
{
    string filename = Path.Combine(System.Environment.GetFolderPath(
Environment.SpecialFolder.ApplicationData), "GameOptions.xml");
    if (File.Exists(filename))
    {
      using (var stream = File.OpenRead(filename))
      {
        var serializer = new XmlSerializer(typeof(GameOptions));
        return serializer.Deserialize(stream) as GameOptions;
      }
    }
    else
      return new GameOptions();
}
```

3. Open the Application tab on the properties window for the KarliCards Gui, and add an icon. One is provided with the download for this book.

4. Add a new project to the solution by selecting File ⇨ Add ⇨ New Project. In the dialog box that appears, select Installed ⇨ Templates ⇨ Other Project Types ⇨ Setup and Deployment.

5. Name the project `KarliCards Installer`.

6. Click the Application Information button at the bottom left of the assistant to start entering information.

7. When you are done, click Installation Requirements.

8. Select Yes to install specific versions of Windows, and uncheck Windows Vista, Windows Server 2003, Windows XP, and Windows 2000.

9. KarliCards requires the .NET Framework version 4.5, so select that.

10. Click Application Files.

11. Click Add Project Outputs and select Primary Output from both CardLib and KarliCards Gui.

12. Click Application Shortcuts.

13. Click New and under the `ProgramFilesFolder` node, browse to the project output and select the KarliCards Gui node.

14. Check the Create Shortcut on Desktop check box.

15. Skip the Application Registry step and click Installation Interview.

16. Select No when asked if you want to display a license agreement.

17. Select Yes to prompt the users for a name and company.

**18.** Select Yes to allow the users to change the installation location.

**19.** Select Yes to give the users the option to launch the application when installation completes.

**20.** Build the solution.

**21.** Right-click the KarliCards Installer in the Solution Explorer and select Install. Step through the wizard.

### How It Works

The Project Assistant is a very nice tool that creates installations that are good enough for most small projects. The main drawback is that you can't create an installation that allows users to select the features they want to install. Although this is not typically a problem with small projects, it can be something of a showstopper for large-scale projects. For such large-scale projects, you have no choice but to buy a license from either InstallShield or one of its competitors.

## SUMMARY

This chapter covered how to use ClickOnce deployment and the functionality of the Windows Installer, including how to create installer packages using Visual Studio 2012. The Windows Installer makes it easy to perform standardized installations, uninstalls, and repairs.

ClickOnce is a new technology that makes it easy to install Windows applications without the hassle of needing to be logged on as a system administrator. ClickOnce offers easy deployment as well as updates of client applications.

If you need more functionality than ClickOnce provides, try the Windows Installer, which does a good job. The Visual Studio 2010 Installer doesn't possess all the functionality of the Windows Installer, but for many applications its features are more than enough.

### EXERCISES

**18.1** Name the advantages of ClickOnce deployment.

**18.2** What is defined with a ClickOnce manifest?

**18.3** When is it necessary to use the Windows Installer?

Answers to the exercises can be found in Appendix A.

## ▶ WHAT YOU LEARNED IN THIS CHAPTER

| TOPIC | KEY CONCEPTS |
|---|---|
| **ClickOnce** | ClickOnce can be used to deploy applications without administrative rights. Just by clicking a link on a web page, a Windows Forms or WPF application is installed. This is the big advantage of ClickOnce, as it doesn't give the IT admins nightmares. ClickOnce deployment can be created from the Publish section of the project properties. |
| **Windows Installer package** | The Windows Installer allows shared applications to be installed on a system. With this technology you can install application components that require administrative privileges. An installer package can easily be created with the Visual Studio Installer template Setup Project. |
| **Customize installation windows** | The InstallShield Limited Edition provides some predefined windows for the installation that can be customized by setting properties such as the copyright text and the logos that are shown during installation. |

# PART III
## Web Programming

# 19

# ASP.NET Web Programming

## WHAT YOU WILL LEARN IN THIS CHAPTER

- ➤ An overview of ASP.NET development
- ➤ How to use ASP.NET server controls
- ➤ How to send an ASP.NET postback to different pages
- ➤ How to create ASP.NET Ajax postbacks
- ➤ How to validate user input
- ➤ How to manage state
- ➤ How to add styles to a web page
- ➤ How to use master pages
- ➤ How to implement page navigation
- ➤ How to authenticate and authorize users
- ➤ How to read from and write to SQL Server databases

## WROX.COM CODE DOWNLOADS FOR THIS CHAPTER

The `wrox.com` code downloads for this chapter are found at `www.wrox.com/remtitle .cgi?isbn=0123456789` on the Download Code tab. The code is in the Chapter 19 download and individually named according to the names throughout the chapter.

Windows Presentation Foundation is the technology for writing Windows applications; with ASP.NET you can build web applications that are displayed in any browser. ASP.NET enables you to write web applications in a similar way to Windows applications. This is made possible by server-side controls that abstract the HTML code and mimic the behavior of the Windows controls. Of course, there are still many differences between Windows and web applications because of the underlying technologies—HTTP and HTML—on which web applications are based.

This chapter provides an overview of programming web applications with ASP.NET, how to use web controls, how to deal with state management (which is very different from how it's handled in Windows applications), how to perform authentication, and how to read and write data to and from a database.

## OVERVIEW OF WEB APPLICATIONS

A web application causes a web server to send HTML code to a client. That code is displayed in a web browser such as Internet Explorer. When a user enters a URL string in the browser, an HTTP request is sent to the web server. The HTTP request contains the filename that is requested along with additional information such as a string identifying the client application, the languages that the client supports, and additional data belonging to the request. The web server returns an HTTP response that contains HTML code, which is interpreted by the web browser to display text boxes, buttons, and lists to the user. When you write your first ASP.NET application, you will encounter the ASP.NET `Page` object and its properties. In fact, two of the `Page` properties are `Request` and `Response`.

ASP.NET is a technology for dynamically creating web pages with server-side code. These web pages can be developed with many similarities to client-side Windows programs. Instead of dealing directly with the HTTP request and response and manually creating HTML code to send to the client, you can use controls such as `TextBox`, `Label`, `ComboBox`, and `Calendar`, which create HTML code.

## ASP.NET RUNTIME

Using ASP.NET for web applications on the client system requires only a simple web browser. You can use Internet Explorer, Opera, Chrome, Firefox, Safari, or any other web browser that supports HTML. The client system doesn't require .NET to be installed.

On the server system, the ASP.NET runtime is needed. If you have Internet Information Services (IIS) on the system, the ASP.NET runtime is configured with the server when the .NET Framework is installed. During development, there's no need to work with Internet Information Services because Visual Studio delivers its own ASP.NET Web Development server that you can use for testing and debugging the application.

To understand how the ASP.NET runtime goes into action, consider a typical web request from a browser (see Figure 19-1). The client requests a file, such as `default.aspx`, from the server. All ASP.NET web pages usually have the file extension `.aspx`. Because this file extension is registered with IIS, or known by the ASP.NET Web Development Server, the ASP.NET runtime and the ASP.NET worker process enter the picture. The ASP.NET worker process is named `w3wp.exe` and is host to your application on the web server. With the first request to the file `default.aspx`, the ASP.NET parser starts, and the compiler compiles the file together with a C# file, which is associated with the `.aspx` file and creates an assembly. Then the assembly is compiled to native code by the JIT compiler of the .NET runtime. The assembly contains a `Page` class that is invoked to return HTML code to the client. Then the `Page` object is destroyed. The assembly is kept for subsequent requests, though, so it is not necessary to compile the assembly again.

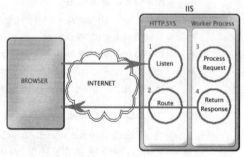

**FIGURE 19-1**

## CREATING A SIMPLE PAGE

In the following Try It Out, you create a simple web page using Visual Studio 2012. In the sample application used in this and the next chapter, a simple event registration website will be created where attendees can register for events.

**TRY IT OUT** Creating a Simple Web Page: Ex01

You will use Visual Studio 2012, ASP.NET and C# to create the layout of a page within what will become an event registration website. To create your event registration website with ASP.NET, follow these steps:

1. Create a new web project by selecting File ⇨ New ⇨ Project within Visual Studio. In the New Project dialog box (see Figure 19-2), select the category Visual C# and the subcategory Web, and then select the ASP.NET Empty web Application template. Name the project EventRegistration.

2. After creating the web project, create a new web page using the menu PROJECT ⇨ Add New Item. Select the Web Form template (see Figure 19-3), and name it `Registration.aspx`.

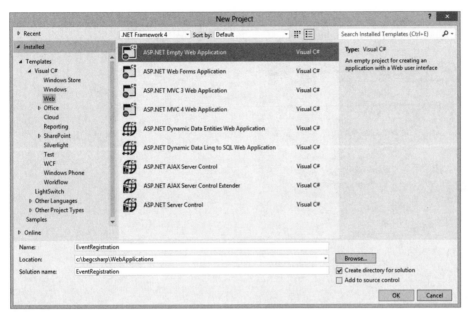

**FIGURE 19-2**

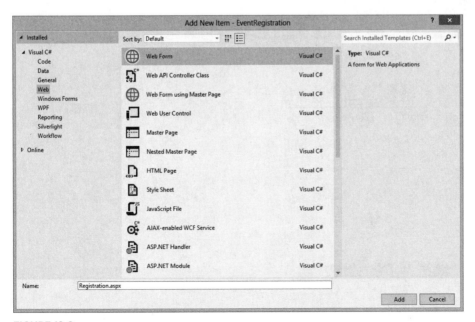

**FIGURE 19-3**

**3.** A table is useful for arranging the controls. Click into the Design View (option left just above the status bar) and add a table by selecting TABLE ⇨ Insert Table. In the Insert Table dialog box, set five rows and two columns, as shown in Figure 19-4.

**4.** Make the first column 100px by dragging the middle of the table to the left.

**5.** When in Design View, you can drag a control from the Toolbox. Add to the table four Label controls on each row in the first column, a DropDownList control, three TextBox controls and a Button in the second column, as shown in Figure 19-5.

**6.** Set the control properties as shown in Table 19-1. To set the properties, click on a control and edit the values in the properties part on the right.

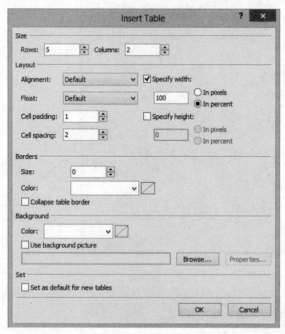

**FIGURE 19-4**

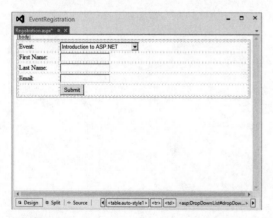

**FIGURE 19-5**

> **NOTE** *If the properties windows on the right is not shown, select the Properties window from the VIEW menu item.*

**TABLE 19-1:** Set Label Controls

| CONTROL TYPE | (ID) | TEXT |
|---|---|---|
| Label | labelEvent | Event: |
| Label | labelFirstName | First Name: |
| Label | labelLastName | Last Name: |
| Label | labelEmail | Email: |
| DropDownList | dropDownListEvents | |
| TextBox | textFirstName | |
| TextBox | textLastName | |
| TextBox | textEmail | |
| Button | buttonSubmit | Submit |

**7.** In the `DropDownList`, select the `Items` property in the Properties window, and enter the strings `Introduction to ASP.NET`, `Introduction to Windows Azure`, and `Beginning Visual C# 2012` in the ListItem Collection Editor, as shown in Figure 19-6.

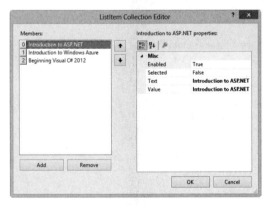

**FIGURE 19-6**

**8.** Switch the editor to source view and verify that the generated code looks similar to the following:

```
<%@ Page Language="C#" AutoEventWireup="true"
CodeBehind="Registration.aspx.cs"
Inherits="EventRegistration.Registration" %>

<!DOCTYPE html>

<html xmlns="http://www.w3.org/1999/xhtml">
<head runat="server">
    <title></title>
    <style type="text/css">
```

```
            .auto-style1 {
                width: 100%;
            }
            .auto-style2 {
                width: 100px;
            }
        </style>
</head>
<body>
    <form id="form1" runat="server">
    <div>

        <table class="auto-style1">
            <tr>
                <td class="auto-style2">
                    <asp:Label ID="labelEvent" runat="server"
                            Text="Event:"></asp:Label>
                </td>
                <td>
                    <asp:DropDownList ID="dropDownListEvents"
                                    runat="server">
                        <asp:ListItem>Introduction to ASP.NET
                        </asp:ListItem>
                        <asp:ListItem>Introduction to Windows Azure
                        </asp:ListItem>
                        <asp:ListItem>Beginning Visual C# 2012
                        </asp:ListItem>
                    </asp:DropDownList>
                </td>
            </tr>
            <tr>
                <td class="auto-style2">
                    <asp:Label ID="labelFirstName" runat="server"
                            Text="First Name:"></asp:Label>
                </td>
                <td>
                    <asp:TextBox ID="textFirstName" runat="server">
                    </asp:TextBox>
                </td>
            </tr>
            <tr>
                <td class="auto-style2">
                    <asp:Label ID="labelLastName" runat="server"
                            Text="Last Name:"></asp:Label>
                </td>
                <td>
                    <asp:TextBox ID="textLastName"
                                runat="server"></asp:TextBox>
                </td>
            </tr>
            <tr>
                <td class="auto-style2">
                    <asp:Label ID="labelEmail" runat="server"
                            Text="Email:"></asp:Label>
                </td>
                <td>
                    <asp:TextBox ID="textEmail"
                                runat="server"></asp:TextBox>
                </td>
            </tr>
            <tr>
                <td class="auto-style2"> </td>
```

```
        <td>
            <asp:Button ID="buttonSubmit"
                        runat="server"
                        Text="Submit" />
        </td>
    </tr>
</table>

    </div>
    </form>
</body>
</html>
```

**9.** Before starting the application, right click the project, select properties, and open the web settings, as shown in Figure 19-7. Verify that the start action is set to the Current Page; and within the Servers group, verify that the Visual Studio Development Server is selected.

**10.** Open the file `Registration.aspx` again in the editor. Start the web application by selecting DEBUG ⇨ Start Debugging. When you start the application, the ASP.NET Development Server is automatically started. You will find an icon for the ASP.NET Development Server in the Windows Explorer taskbar. Double-click that icon to see a dialog box similar to the one shown in Figure 19-8. This dialog box shows the physical and virtual paths of the web server, and the port the web server is listening to. This dialog box can also be used to stop the web server.

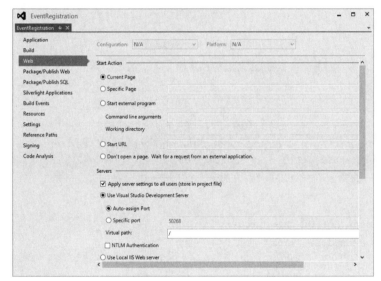

**FIGURE 19-7**

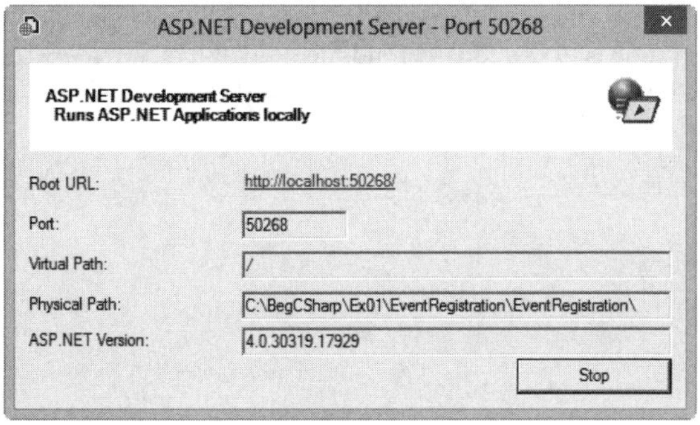

**FIGURE 19-8**

11. Starting the application causes Internet Explorer to show the web page, as shown in Figure 19-9. You can view the HTML code by selecting VIEW ➪ Source (or VIEW ➪ Markup). You'll see that the server-side controls are converted to pure HTML code.

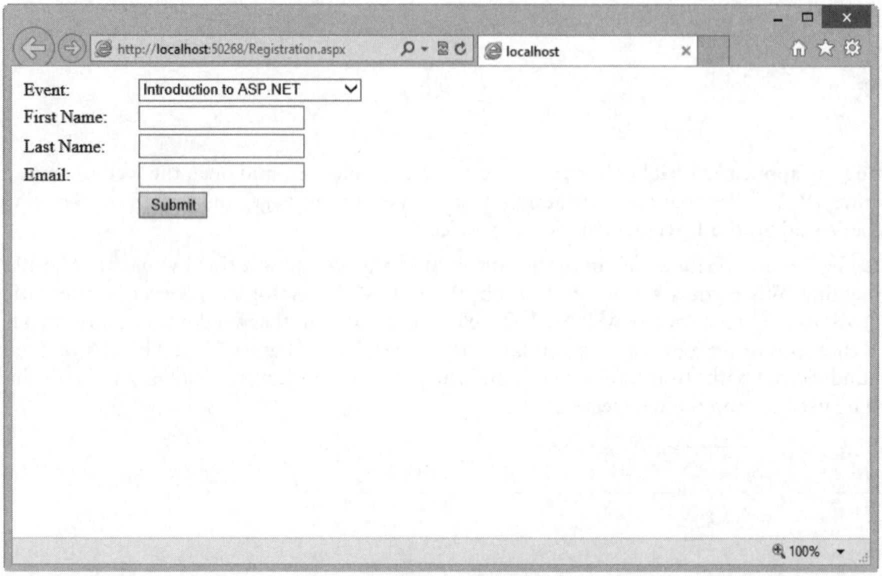

**FIGURE 19-9**

> **NOTE** *The port number (the part after the colon at the end of the URL) can and will differ from the one in the picture. This is no problem.*

### How It Works

The first line of the `Registration.aspx` file is the page directive:

```
<%@ Page Language="C#" AutoEventWireup="true"
CodeBehind="Registration.aspx.cs"
Inherits="EventRegistration. Registration" %>
```

This directive defines the programming language and the classes that are used. The property `AutoEventWireup="true"` automatically links the event handlers to specific method names, as shown later. `Inherits="EventRegistration.Default"` means that the class that is dynamically generated from the ASPX file derives from the base class `Registration`. This base code is in the code-behind file `Registration.aspx.cs`, as defined with the `CodeBehind` property. Later in the chapter, you add handler code to the `.cs` file. The generated code-behind file `Registration.aspx.cs` is shown here:

```
using System;
using System.Collections.Generic;
using System.Linq;
using System.Web;
using System.Web.UI;
using System.Web.UI.WebControls;
```

```
namespace EventRegistration
{
    public partial class Registration : System.Web.UI.Page
    {
        protected void Page_Load(object sender, EventArgs e)
        {

        }
    }
}
```

> **NOTE** The `partial` keyword used in the preceding code is discussed in Chapter 10.

Here is the code for the ASPX page. The client receives simple HTML code as it is; only the `runat="server"` attribute is removed from the `<head>` tag when the page is sent to the client:

```
<!DOCTYPE html>

<html xmlns="http://www.w3.org/1999/xhtml">
<head><title>

</title>
    <style type="text/css">
        .auto-style1 {
            width: 100%;
        }
        .auto-style2 {
            width: 100px;
        }
    </style>
</head>
```

`<!DOCTYPE html>` is a required tag that introduces the document to browsers that will parse and render it according to the HTML 5 specification. You will also find other HTML elements with the attribute `runat="server"`, such as the `<form>` element. When the `.aspx` page is created, a single `<form>` element is added to the page. All of the controls on the page are nested within this form element. With the `runat=server` attribute, an ASP.NET server control is associated with the HTML tag. The control can be used to write server-side code. Behind the `<form>` element is an object of type `System.Web.UI.HtmlControls.HtmlForm`. The object has the variable name `form1` as defined with the `id` attribute. `form1` can be used to invoke methods and properties of the `HtmlForm` class.

The `HtmlForm` object creates a `<form>` tag that is sent to the client:

```
<form id="form1" runat="server">
```

Of course, the `runat` attribute is not sent to the client.

The standard controls that you've dropped from the Toolbox onto the Forms Designer have elements that begin with `<asp:<asp:Label>` and `<asp:DropDownList>`. These are server-side ASP.NET web controls that are associated with .NET classes in the namespace `System.Web.UI.WebControls.<asp:Label>` is represented by the class `Label`, and `<asp:DropDownList>` is represented by the class `DropDownList`:

```
<td class="auto-style2">
    <asp:Label ID="labelEvent" runat="server"
            Text="Event:"></asp:Label>
</td>
<td>
    <asp:DropDownList ID="dropDownListEvents"
                    runat="server">
```

```
        <asp:ListItem>Introduction to ASP.NET</asp:ListItem>
        <asp:ListItem>Introduction to Windows Azure</asp:ListItem>
        <asp:ListItem>Beginning Visual C# 2012</asp:ListItem>
    </asp:DropDownList>
</td>
```

`<asp:Label>` doesn't send an `<asp:Label>` element to the client because this is not a valid HTML element. Instead, `<asp:Label>` returns a `<span>` tag. Similarly, `<asp:DropDownList>` returns a `<select>` element, and `<asp:TextBox>` returns the element `<input type="text">`.

ASP.NET has UI control classes in the namespaces `System.Web.UI.HtmlControls` and `System.Web.UI.WebControls`. Both of these namespaces have some similar controls, also known as HTML server controls and web server controls. Examples are the HTML server control `HtmlInputText` and the web server control `TextBox`. The HTML server controls offer methods and properties that are similar to the HTML controls. With the web server controls you will find much more complex controls such as `Calendar`, `DataGrid`, and `Wizard`. If you don't need to program a control from server-side code and just want to program it from JavaScript you can stick with the HTML controls and not add the `runat="server"` attribute.

## SERVER CONTROLS

In this section, you will learn about the server controls provided by the ASP.NET page framework. These controls are designed to provide a structured, event-driven, object-oriented model for programming web applications. Table 19-2 lists some of the principal web server controls available with ASP.NET, and the HTML code returned by these controls.

**TABLE 19-2:** Important ASP.NET Server Controls

| CONTROL | HTML | DESCRIPTION |
|---------|------|-------------|
| Label | `<span>` | Returns a span element containing text. |
| Literal | static text | Returns simple static text. With this control, it is possible to transform the content depending on the client application. |
| TextBox | `<input type="text">` | Returns HTML `<input type="text">` whereby the user can enter some values. You can write a server-side event handler when the text changes. |
| Button | `<input type="submit">` | Sends form values to the server. |
| LinkButton | `<a href="javascript:_____ dopostback()">` | Creates an anchor tag that includes JavaScript for doing a postback to the server. |
| ImageButton | `<input type="image">` | Generates an input tag of type image to show a referenced image. |
| HyperLink | `<a>` | Creates a simple anchor tag referencing a web page. |

| DropDownList | `<select>` | Creates a `select` tag whereby the user sees one item and can select one of multiple items by clicking on the drop-down list. |
|---|---|---|
| ListBox | `<select size="">` | Creates a `select` tag with a `size` attribute that shows multiple items at once. |
| CheckBox | `<input type="checkbox">` | Returns an `input` element of type check box to show a button that can be selected or deselected. Instead of using the `CheckBox`, you can use a `CheckBoxList`, which creates a table consisting of multiple check box elements. |
| RadioButton | `<input type="radio">` | Returns an `input` element of type radio. With a radio button, just one button of a group can be selected. Similar to the `CheckBoxList`, `RadioButtonList` provides a list of buttons. |
| Image | `<img src="">` | Returns an `img` tag to display a GIF or JPG file on the client. |
| Calendar | `<table>` | Displays a complete calendar from which a date can be selected, the month can be changed, and so on. For output, an HTML table with JavaScript code is generated. |
| TreeView | `<div><table>` | Returns a `div` tag that includes multiple `table` tags, depending on its content. JavaScript is used to open and close the tree on the client. |

If you have experience with ASP.NET you might have noticed that a number of controls are missing from this table. There are many other controls listed and explained throughout this chapter. What all these controls have in common is their ability to fire off events invoked by the user, automatically, or as part of the page event lifecycle. These events execute server-side event handlers. You will find ASP.NET applications are largely structured based on this event-driven model.

## ASP.NET POSTBACK

Web server controls can include event handlers that are invoked on the server. The `Button` control can include a `Click` event; the `DropDownList` offers the event `SelectedIndexChanged`, and the `TextBox` offers the event `TextChanged`.

The events occur on the server only when a postback occurs. When a value in a text box changes, the `TextChanged` event doesn't occur immediately; it occurs only when the form is submitted and sent to the server, which happens when the Submit button is clicked. The ASP.NET runtime verifies that the state of the control has changed before invoking the corresponding event handler. If the selection of the `DropDownList` has been changed, then the `SelectedIndexChanged` event is invoked; the `TextChanged` event is invoked accordingly when the value of a text box changes.

> **NOTE** *When you want a change event immediately posted to the server (for example, when the selection of a* `DropDownList` *changes), you can set the* `AutoPostBack` *property to* `true`. *That way, client-side JavaScript is used to submit the form data immediately to the server. Of course, network traffic is increased this way, so use this feature with care.*

To compare the old values of the control with the new values after the page is returned to the server, the view state is used. View state is a hidden field that is sent with the page content to the browser. When sending the page to the client, the view state contains the same values as the controls within a form. With a postback to the server, the view state is sent to the server together with the new values of the controls. That way, it can be verified whether the values change, and the event handler can be invoked.

Until now, the sample application has sent only a simple page to the client. Now you need to deal with the user-selected data.

**TRY IT OUT** Displaying User Input: Ex02

In this example, you echo user-selected data back to the page in the form of sentence that identifies the values chosen by the user:

**1.** Open the previously created web application EventRegistration using Visual Studio.

**2.** To display user input for the event registration, switch to the Source View of `Registration.aspx` and add another row to the table below the Submit button. In the second column, add a label with the name `labelResult` to the web page `Registration.aspx`. Clear the `Text` property of this label.

**3.** In the Design View of REGISTRATION.ASPX, double-click the Submit button to add a `Click` event handler to this button and add the following code to the handler in the file `Registration.aspx.cs`:

```
protected void buttonSubmit_Click(object sender, EventArgs e)
{
    string selectedEvent = dropDownListEvents.SelectedValue;
    string firstName = textFirstName.Text;
    string lastName = textLastName.Text;
    string email = textEmail.Text;

    labelResult.Text = String.Format(
                        "{0} {1} selected the event {2}.",
                        firstName, lastName, selectedEvent);
}
```

**4.** Start the web page using Visual Studio again. After you enter the data and click the Submit button, the same page displays the user input in the new label.

*How It Works*

Double-clicking the Submit button adds the `OnClick` attribute to the `<asp:Button>` element in the file `Registration.aspx`:

```
<asp:Button ID="buttonSubmit" runat="server" Text="Submit"
        onclick="buttonSubmit_Click" />
```

With the web server control, `OnClick` defines the server-side `Click` event that will be invoked when the button is clicked.

Within the implementation of the `buttonSubmit_Click()` method, the values of the controls can be read by using properties. `dropDownListEvents` is the variable that references the `DropDownList` control. In the ASPX file, the ID is set to `dropDownListEvents`, so a variable is automatically created. The property `SelectedValue` returns the current selection. With the `TextBox` controls, the `Text` property returns the strings that have been entered by the user:

```
string selectedEvent = dropDownListEvents.SelectedValue;
string firstName = textFirstName.Text;
string lastName = textLastName.Text;
string email = textEmail.Text;
```

The label `labelResult` again has a `Text` property where the result is set:

```
labelResult.Text = String.Format("{0} {1} selected the event {2}",
                                  firstName, lastName, selectedEvent);
```

Instead of displaying the results on the same page, ASP.NET makes it easy to display the results in a different page, as shown in the following Try It Out.

**TRY IT OUT** Displaying the Results in a Second Page: Ex03

In the previous examples, only one page was used. Follow these steps to take advantage of simple navigation by displaying the same user input on a separate page.

**1.** Create a new Web Form with the name `ResultsPage.aspx`.

**2.** Add a label to the `ResultsPage` with the name `labelResult`.

**3.** Add code to the `Page_Load` method to the class `ResultsPage` as shown here:

```
using System;
using System.Web.UI.WebControls;

namespace EventRegistration
{
    public partial class ResultsPage : System.Web.UI.Page
    {
        protected void Page_Load(object sender, EventArgs e)
        {
            try
            {
                DropDownList dropDownListEvents =
                    (DropDownList)PreviousPage.FindControl("dropDownListEvents");
                string selectedEvent = dropDownListEvents.SelectedValue;
                string firstName = ((TextBox)PreviousPage.FindControl(
                                    "textFirstName")).Text;
                string lastName = ((TextBox)PreviousPage.FindControl(
                                    "textLastName")).Text;
                string email = ((TextBox)PreviousPage.FindControl(
                                    "textEmail")).Text;
                labelResult.Text = String.Format("{0} {1} selected the event {2}",
                    firstName, lastName, selectedEvent);
            }
            catch
            {
                labelResult.Text = "The originating page must contain " +
                    "textFirstName, textLastName, textEmail controls";
            }
        }
    }
}
```

**4.** Set the `Registration.aspx` page's Submit button's `PostBackUrl` property to `ResultsPage.aspx`.

**5.** Remove the `Click` event handler of the Submit button because it is not required anymore.

**6.** Start the `Registration.aspx` page, fill in some data, and click the Submit button. You are redirected to the page `ResultsPage.aspx`, where the entered data is displayed.

> **NOTE** When assigning a path and filename to a control attribute, like
> `PostBackUrl`, you can use the tilde ~ character to represent the web applica-
> tion root folder. So, `PostBackUrl="~/ResultsPage.aspx"` will resolve to `http://`
> `your_web_server/ResultsPage.aspx` or a similar address. For instance,
> `PostBackUrl="~/ResultPages/ResultsPage.aspx"` would be valid if you were to
> group results pages in a folder named `ResultPages`.

*How It Works*

With ASP.NET, the `Button` control implements the property `PostBackUrl` to define the page that should be
requested from the web server. This property creates client-side JavaScript code to request the defined page with
the client-side `onclick` handler of the Submit button:

```
<input type="submit" name="buttonSubmit" value="Submit"
onclick="javascript:WebForm_DoPostBackWithOptions(
new&#32;WebForm_PostBackOptions(
&quot;buttonSubmit&quot;,,&#32;&quot;&quot;,,&#32;false,&#32;
&quot;&quot;,,&#32;&quot;
ResultsPage.aspx&quot;,,&#32;false,&#32;false))"
id="buttonSubmit" />
```

The browser sends all the data from the form inside the first page to the new page. However, inside the newly
requested page it is necessary to get the data from controls that have been defined with the previous page. To
access the controls from a previous page, the `Page` class defines the property `PreviousPage`. `PreviousPage` returns
a `Page` object, where the controls of this page can be accessed using the `FindControl()` method. `FindControl()`
is defined to return a `Control` object, so you must cast the return value to the control type that is searched:

```
DropDownList dropDownListEvents =
    (DropDownList)PreviousPage.FindControl(
                        "dropDownListEvents");
```

Instead of using the `FindControl()` method to access the values of the previous page, access to the previous
page can be strongly typed, which is less error prone during development. To make this possible, the next Try It
Out defines a custom struct that is returned with a property from the `default_aspx` class.

---

**TRY IT OUT** Creating a Strongly Typed PreviousPage: Ex04

In this example, you build on the simple two-page web application you have created thus far, and in the second
page, create a strongly typed reference to the first.

1. Add a new class item named `RegistrationInfo` to the project by selecting Project ➪ Add New Item.
   Make sure you choose the Code category from the tree on the right (as you saw in Figure 19-3).

2. Implement the class `RegistrationInfo` as shown:

```
public class RegistrationInfo
{
    public string FirstName { get; set; }
    public string LastName { get; set; }
    public string Email { get; set; }
    public string SelectedEvent { get; set; }
}
```

**3.** Add the public property `RegistrationInfo` to the class `Registration` in the file `Registration.aspx.cs`:

```
public RegistrationInfo RegistrationInfo
{
    get
    {
        return new RegistrationInfo
        {
            FirstName = textFirstName.Text,
            LastName = textLastName.Text,
            Email = textEmail.Text,
            SelectedEvent = dropDownListEvents.SelectedValue
        };
    }
}
```

**4.** Add the `PreviousPageType` directive to the file `ResultsPage.aspx` following the `Page` directive:

```
<%@ Page Language="C#" AutoEventWireup="true" CodeBehind="ResultsPage.aspx.cs"
    Inherits="EventRegistration.ResultsPage" %>
<%@ PreviousPageType VirtualPath="/Registration.aspx" %>
```

**5.** Within the `Page_Load()` method of the class `ResultsPage`, now the code can be simplified:

```
protected void Page_Load(object sender, EventArgs e)
{
    try
    {
        RegistrationInfo ri = PreviousPage.RegistrationInfo;

        labelResult.Text = String.Format("{0} {1} selected the event {2}",
            ri.FirstName, ri.LastName, ri.SelectedEvent);
    }
    catch
    {
        labelResult.Text = "The originating page must contain " +
            "textFirstName, textLastName, textEmail controls";
    }
}
```

### How It Works

The `PreviousPageType` directive creates a property of type `PreviousPage` that returns the type associated with the directive. Within its implementation, the `PreviousPage` property of the base class is invoked, as shown in the following code snippet:

```
public new EventRegistration.Default PreviousPage {
    get {
        return ((EventRegistrationWeb.Default)(base.PreviousPage));
    }
}
```

Instead of using the `VirtualPath` attribute of the `PreviousPageType` directive to define the type of the previous page, the attribute `TypeName` can be used. This is useful when multiple previous pages are possible. In that case you need to define a base class for all the previous pages and assign the base class to the `TypeName` attribute.

## ASP.NET AJAX POSTBACK

With a normal ASP.NET postback, a complete page is requested. With a postback to the same page the user already has loaded, the postback returns the complete page again. To reduce the traffic on the network, you can do an ASP.NET Ajax postback. With the Ajax postback, only a part of the page is returned and refreshed using JavaScript. You can do this easily with the `UpdatePanel`.

For easy comparison between a ASP.NET postback and an ASP.NET Ajax postback, you will write the current time to a label both with and without an `UpdatePanel` in the following Try It Out.

**TRY IT OUT** Using the Update Panel: Ex05

This exercise demonstrates how ASP.NET can refresh parts of a page without posting the page contents, in their entirety, back to the web server.

1. Open the previously created project EventRegistration using Visual Studio.
2. Add a new Web Form named `UpdatePanelDemo.aspx` to the existing website.
3. From the AJAX Extensions category in the Toolbox, add `ScriptManager` and `UpdatePanel` controls to the page.
4. Add a `Label` and a `Button` within the `UpdatePanel`, and another `Label` and `Button` outside of the `UpdatePanel`. Set the `Text` property of the `Button` within the `UpdatePanel` to AJAX PostBack and the `Text` property of the `Button` outside of the `UpdatePanel` to ASP.NET PostBack:

```
<form id="form1" runat="server">
    <div>
        <asp:ScriptManager ID="ScriptManager1" runat="server"></asp:ScriptManager>
    </div>
    <asp:UpdatePanel ID="UpdatePanel1" runat="server">
        <ContentTemplate>
            <asp:Label ID="Label1" runat="server" Text="Label"></asp:Label>
            <asp:Button ID="Button1" runat="server" Text="AJAX PostBack"
                        OnClick="OnButtonClick" />
        </ContentTemplate>
    </asp:UpdatePanel>
    <asp:Label ID="Label2" runat="server" Text="Label"></asp:Label>
    <asp:Button ID="Button2" runat="server" Text="ASP.NET PostBack"
                OnClick="OnButtonClick" />
</form>
```

5. Assign a `Click` event handler named `OnButtonClick()` to both buttons and implement it as shown:

```
protected void OnButtonClick(object sender, EventArgs e)
{
    DateTime now = DateTime.Now;
    Label1.Text = now.ToLongTimeString();
    Label2.Text = now.ToLongTimeString();
}
```

6. Start the application and navigate to the `UpdatePanelDemo.aspx` page. Click both buttons. Clicking the AJAX Postback button refreshes only the first label. With the ASP.NET Postback button, the entire page is refreshed (see Figure 19-10).

*How It Works*

For using AJAX functionality, a `ScriptManager` object is required. The `ScriptManager` class loads JavaScript functions for several features. You can also use this class to load your own custom scripts. `ScriptManager` properties are explained in Table 19-3.

**FIGURE 19-10**

**TABLE 19-3:** ScriptManager's Properties

| PROPERTY | DESCRIPTION |
|---|---|
| EnablePageMethods | Defines whether public static methods defined in the ASPX page should be callable from client script as web service methods. |
| EnablePartialRendering | To enable partial rendering with the UpdatePanel, this property must be set to true, which is the default. |
| LoadScriptsBeforeUI | Defines the position where the scripts are included in the returned HTML page. By placing them inside the <head> element, the scripts are loaded before the UI is loaded. |
| ScriptMode | Specifies whether the debug or the release version of scripts should be used. |
| ScriptPath | Specifies the root path of the directory where the custom scripts are located. |
| Scripts | Contains a collection of custom script files that should be rendered on the client. |
| Services | Contains a collection of web service references that can be called from within client script. |

The ASP.NET Button controls on the page result in the client creating HTML Submit buttons. Button2 makes a normal HTTP POST request to the server. Because Button1 is within an UpdatePanel, client script attaches to the Click event of the button to do an Ajax POST request. The Ajax POST request makes use of the XmlHttpRequest object to send a request to the server. The server returns only the data required to update the UI. The data is interpreted, and JavaScript code modifies HTML controls within the UpdatePanel for the new UI.

You can have multiple update panels in a page. Just by adding multiple panels to a page, every UpdatePanel is updated on an Ajax POST request. Updates can be controlled with triggers. You'll try that in the next Try it Out.

**TRY IT OUT** Update Panel with Triggers: Ex06

1. Open the previously created project EventRegistration using Visual Studio.
2. Add a new Web Form named UpdatePanelWithTrigger.aspx to the existing website.
3. Add one ScriptManager and two UpdatePanel controls.
4. Add a Label and a Button control in each of the UpdatePanel controls.
5. Assign the Click event handler of both Button controls to the OnButtonClick() method and implement the method as shown here:

```
protected void OnButtonClick(object sender, EventArgs e)
{
    DateTime now = DateTime.Now;
    Label1.Text = now.ToLongTimeString();
    Label2.Text = now.ToLongTimeString();
}
```

6. Run the application and navigate to the UpdatePanelWithTrigger.aspx page. Both labels change regardless of which Button control is clicked (see Figure 19-11).

7. Change the property `UpdateMode` for both `UpdatePanel` controls from `Always` to `Conditional`.

8. Run the application again. Now only the `Label` inside the `UpdatePanel` where the `Button` is clicked changes.

9. Select the first `UpdatePanel` and click the ellipsis with the `Triggers` property, which opens the dialog box shown in Figure 19-12. Add an `AsyncPostBack` trigger, set the `ControlID` property to the button of the second `UpdatePanel`, `Button2`, and set the `EventName` to `Click`.

10. Run the application. Clicking `Button2` updates the content of both `UpdatePanel` controls; clicking `Button1` updates only the content of the first `UpdatePanel`.

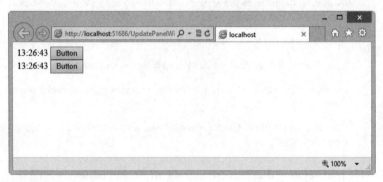

**FIGURE 19-11**

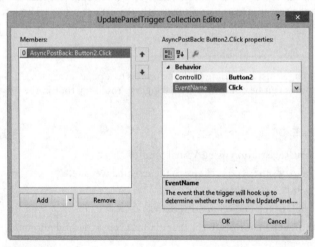

**FIGURE 19-12**

### How It Works

The update behavior of the `UpdatePanel` can be influenced. By default, it is updated every time an Ajax postback occurs. You can change the update so that controls are updated either when an update occurs from within the panel, or the update is triggered from controls outside of the panel.

Here is the ASPX code to define an `AsyncPostBackTrigger` for `UpdatePanel1`:

```
<asp:UpdatePanel ID="UpdatePanel1" runat="server" UpdateMode="Conditional">
    <ContentTemplate>
        <asp:Label ID="Label1" runat="server" Text="Label"></asp:Label>
```

```
        <asp:Button ID="Button1" runat="server" Text="Button"
            OnClick="OnButtonClick" />
    </ContentTemplate>
    <Triggers>
        <asp:AsyncPostBackTrigger ControlID="Button2" EventName="Click" />
    </Triggers>
</asp:UpdatePanel>
```

Table 19-4 describes the properties of the UpdatePanel control.

**TABLE 19-4:** The UpdatePanel Control's Properties

| PROPERTY | DESCRIPTION |
| --- | --- |
| ChildrenAsTriggers | When set to true, the content of UpdatePanel is updated when child controls of the UpdatePanel make a postback. |
| RenderMode | Defines how the panel should render. Possible values are UpdatePanelRenderMode.Block and UpdatePanelRenderMode.Inline. The Block enumeration value specifies that a <div> tag should be rendered; with Inline, a <span> tag is rendered. |
| UpdateMode | Set to one of the UpdatePanelUpdateMode enumeration values. Always updates the panel with every Ajax postback, Conditional only depending on the triggers. |
| Triggers | Specifies a collection of AsyncPostBackTrigger and PostBackTrigger elements to define when the content of the panel should update. |

## INPUT VALIDATION

When users enter data, it should be checked for validity. The check can happen on the client and on the server. You can check the data on the client using JavaScript. However, if the data is checked on the client using JavaScript, it should also be checked on the server, because you can never fully trust the client. It is possible to disable JavaScript in the browser, and hackers can use different JavaScript functions that accept incorrect input. It is absolutely necessary to check the data on the server. Checking the data on the client leads to better performance, as no round-trips occur to the server until the data is validated on the client.

With ASP.NET it is not necessary to write the validation functions yourself. Many validation controls exist that create both client- and server-side validation.

The following example shows the RequiredFieldValidator validation control that is associated with the text box textFirstname. All validator controls have the properties ErrorMessage and ControlToValidate in common. If the input is not correct, then ErrorMessage defines the message that is displayed. By default, the error message is displayed where the validator control is positioned. The property ControlToValidate defines the control where the input is checked.

```
<asp:TextBox ID="textFirstname" runat="server"></asp:TextBox>
<asp:RequiredFieldValidator ID="RequiredFieldValidator1" runat="server"
    ErrorMessage="Enter your first name" ControlToValidate="textFirstName">
</asp:RequiredFieldValidator>
```

Table 19-5 lists and describes all the validation controls.

**TABLE 19-5:** ASP.NET's Validation Controls

| CONTROL | DESCRIPTION |
|---|---|
| RequiredFieldValidator | Specifies that input is required with the control that is validated. If the control to validate has an initial value set, which the user has to change, you can set this initial value with the `InitialValue` property of the validator control. |
| RangeValidator | Defines a minimum and maximum value that the user is allowed to enter. The specific properties of the control are `MinimumValue` and `MaximumValue`. |
| RegularExpressionValidator | With the `ValidationExpression` property, a regular expression using Perl 5 syntax can be set to check the user input. |
| CompareValidator | Compares multiple values (such as passwords). Not only does this validator support comparing two values for equality, additional options can be set with the `Operator` property. The `Operator` property is of type `ValidationCompareOperator`, which defines enumeration values such as `Equal`, `NotEqual`, `GreaterThan`, and `DataTypeCheck`. Using `DataTypeCheck`, the input value can be checked to determine whether it is of a specific data type, for example, correct date input. |
| CustomValidator | If the other validator controls don't fulfill the requirements of the validation, the `CustomValidator` can be used. With the `CustomValidator`, both a client- and server-side validation function can be defined. |
| ValidationSummary | Writes a summary for a page instead of writing error messages directly to the input controls. |

With the sample application that you've created so far, users can input first name, last name, and e-mail address. In the following Try It Out, you extend the application by using validation controls.

**TRY IT OUT** Checking for Required Input and E-Mail Address: Ex07

1. Open the previously created project EventRegistration using Visual Studio.
2. Open the file `Registration.aspx`.
3. Add a new column to the table by selecting the right column in the Design View of the editor and choosing Table ⇨ Insert ⇨ Column to the Right.
4. First name, last name, and e-mail address are required inputs. A check is done to determine whether the e-mail address has the correct syntax. Add three `RequiredFieldValidator` controls and one `RegularExpressionValidator` control, as shown in Figure 19-13.
5. Configure the validation controls as defined in Table 19-6.

**TABLE 19-6:** Configuring Validation Controls

| VALIDATION CONTROL | PROPERTY | VALUE |
|---|---|---|
| RequiredFieldValidator | ErrorMessage | First name is required. |
|  | ControlToValidate | textFirstName |
| RequiredFieldValidator | ErrorMessage | Last name is required. |

| | ControlToValidate | textLastName |
|---|---|---|
| RequiredFieldValidator | ErrorMessage | Email is required. |
| | ControlToValidate | textEmail |
| | Display | Dynamic |
| RegularExpressionValidator1 | ErrorMessage | Enter a valid email. |
| | ControlToValidate | textEmail |
| | ValidationExpression | \w+([-+.']\w+)*@\w+([-.]\w+)*\.\w+([-.]\w+)* |
| | Display | Dynamic |

**6.** It is not necessary to enter the regular expression manually. Instead, you can click the ellipsis button of the `ValidationExpression` property in the Properties window to start the Regular Expression Editor, shown in Figure 19-14. This editor provides some predefined regular expressions, including the regular expression to check for an Internet e-mail address.

**7.** If a postback is done to a page other than the one that includes the validator controls (using the `PostBackUrl` property that was set earlier), in the new page you must verify that the result of the previous page was valid, using the `IsValid` property. Add the following code to the `Page_Load()` method of the `ResultsPage` class:

```
protected void Page_Load(object sender, EventArgs e)
{
    try
    {
        if (!PreviousPage.IsValid)
        {
            labelResult.Text = "Error in previous page";
            return;
        }
        //...
```

**8.** When you start the application, you might notice a page of error output as shown in Figure 19-15. This is due to new feature in ASP.NET 4.5 called *unobtrusive validation*. This feature allows the built-in validator controls to use unobtrusive JavaScript libraries for client-side validation logic. You can safely disable this feature for now by commenting out this line in the `Web.config` file of your project.

```
<add key="ValidationSettings:UnobtrusiveValidationMode" value="WebForms" />
```

Alternatively, you can add the following script definition, which represents one of a collection of mappings that indicate where a script resource is located. You must add this to the `Application_Start` method of the `Global.asax.cs` file.

```
System.Web.UI.ScriptManager.ScriptResourceMapping.AddDefinition("jquery",
        new System.Web.UI.ScriptResourceDefinition
    {
        Path = "~/scripts/jquery-1.7.1.min.js",
        DebugPath = "~/scripts/jquery-1.7.1.js",
        CdnPath = "http://ajax.microsoft.com/ajax/jQuery/jquery-1.7.1.min.js",
        CdnDebugPath = "http://ajax.microsoft.com/ajax/jQuery/jquery-1.7.1.js"
    }
);
```

**9.** Now you can start the application. As long as the `PostBackUrl` property on the Submit button is removed, when data is not entered or is not entered correctly, the validator controls show error messages, as shown in Figure 19-16.

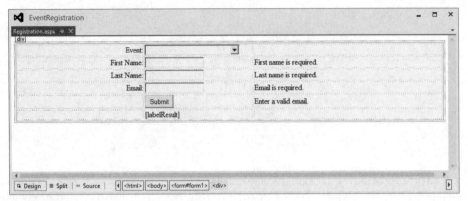

**FIGURE 19-13**

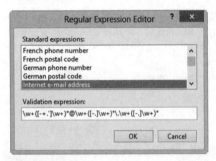

**FIGURE 19-14**

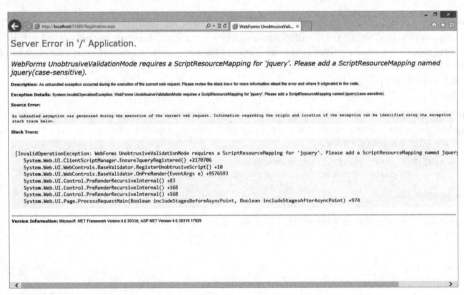

**FIGURE 19-15**

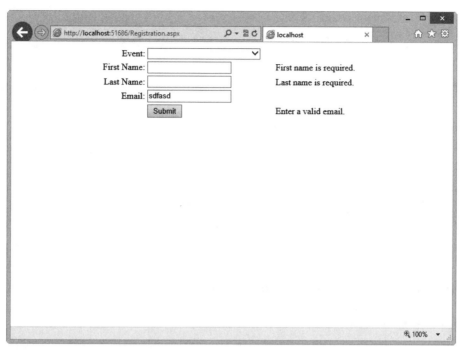

**FIGURE 19-16**

### How It Works

The validator controls create both client-side JavaScript code to verify input on the client, and server-side code to validate input on the server. It is also possible to turn JavaScript off by setting the validator property `EnableClientScript` to `false`. Instead of changing the property with every validator control, you can also turn off JavaScript by setting the property `ClientTarget` of the `Page` class.

Depending on the client type, the ASP.NET controls might return JavaScript to the client. This behavior depends on the `ClientTarget` property. By default, the `ClientTarget` is set to the string `"automatic"`, where, depending on the web browser's functionality, scripting code is returned or not. If the `ClientTarget` is set to `"downlevel"`, then scripting code is not returned for any clients, whereas setting the `ClientTarget` property to `"uplevel"` always returns scripting code.

You can set the `ClientTarget` property inside the `Page_Load()` method of the `Page` class:

```
protected void Page_Load(object sender, EventArgs e)
{
    ClientTarget = "downlevel";
}
```

## STATE MANAGEMENT

The HTTP protocol is stateless. The connection that is initiated from the client to the server can be closed after every request. However, normally it is necessary to remember some client information from one page to the other. There are several ways to accomplish this.

The main difference among the various ways to keep state is whether the state is stored on the client or on the server. Table 19-7 shows an overview of state management techniques and how long the state can be valid.

**TABLE 19-7:** State Management Techniques

| STATE TYPE | CLIENT OR SERVER RESOURCE | TIME VALID |
|---|---|---|
| View State | Client | Within a single page only. |
| Cookie | Client | Temporary cookies are deleted when the browser is closed; permanent cookies are stored on the disk of the client system. |
| Session | Server | Session state is associated with a browser session. The session is invalidated with a timeout (by default, 20 minutes). |
| Application | Server | Application state is shared among all clients. This state is valid until the server restarts. |
| Cache | Server | Similar to application state, cache is shared. However, when the cache should be invalidated, there's much better control. |

The following sections take a more detailed look at these techniques.

## Client-Side State Management

In this section, you are going to step into client-side state management by looking at two techniques: view state and cookies.

### View State

One technique to store state on the client was already discussed: view state. View state is used automatically by the web server controls to make events work. The view state contains the same state as the control when sent to the client. When the browser sends the form back to the server, the view state contains the original values, but the values of the controls that are sent contain the new values. If there's a difference, the corresponding event handlers are invoked.

The disadvantage of using view state is that data is always transferred from the server to the client, and vice versa, which increases network traffic. To reduce network traffic, view state can be turned off. To do so for all controls within the page, set the EnableViewState property to false with the Page directive:

```
<%@ Page Language="C#" AutoEventWireUp="true" CodeFile="Default.aspx.cs"
    Inherits="Default" EnableViewState="false" %>
```

The view state can also be configured on a control by setting the EnableViewState property of a control. Regardless of what the page configuration says, when the EnableViewState property is defined for the control, the control value is used. The value of the page configuration is used only for these controls when the view state is not configured.

It is also possible to store custom data inside the view state. Because the ViewState property of the Page class is a Dictionary, more specifically a System.Web.UI.StateBag, this can be done by using an indexer with the ViewState property of the Page class. You can define a name that is used to access the view state value with the index argument:

```
ViewState["mydata"] = "my data";
```

You can read the previously stored view state as shown here:

```
string mydata = (string)ViewState["mydata"];
```

In the HTML code that is sent to the client, you can see the view state of the complete page within a hidden field:

```
<input type="hidden" name="_____VIEWSTATE"
value="/wEPDwUKLTU4NzY5NTcwNw8WAh4HbXlzdGF0ZQUFbXl2YWwWAgIDD2QWAg
IFDw8WAh4EVGV4dAUFbXl2YWxkZGTCdCywUOcAW97aKpcjt1tzJ7ByUA==" />
```

Using hidden fields has the advantage that every browser can use this feature, and the users cannot turn it off.

The view state is remembered only within a page. If the state should be valid across different pages, then using cookies is an option for state on the client.

The data in the view state is not encrypted; it is just encoded using base64 encoding.

## Cookie

A cookie is defined in the HTTP header. Use the `HttpResponse` class to send a cookie to the client. `Response` is a property of the `Page` class, which returns an object of type `HttpResponse`. The `HttpResponse` class defines the `Cookies` property, which returns an `HttpCookieCollection`. Multiple cookies can be returned to the client with the `HttpCookieCollection`.

The following sample code shows how a cookie can be sent to the client. First, an `HttpCookie` object is instantiated. In the constructor of this class, the name of the cookie is set—here it is `mycookie`. The `HttpCookie` class has a `Values` property to add multiple cookie values. If you just have one cookie value to return, you can use the `Value` property instead. However, if you plan to send multiple cookie values, it is better to add the values to a single cookie instead of using multiple cookies.

```
string myval = "myval";
var cookie = new HttpCookie("mycookie");
cookie.Values.Add("mystate", myval);
Response.Cookies.Add(cookie);
```

Cookies can be temporary and valid within a browser session, or they can be stored on the client disk. To make the cookie permanent, the `Expires` property must be set with the `HttpCookie` object. With the `Expires` property, a date defines when the cookie is not valid anymore; in the following example, it is set to a date three months from the current date.

```
var cookie = new HttpCookie("mycookie");
cookie.Values.Add("mystate", "myval");
cookie.Expires = DateTime.Now.AddMonths(3);
Response.Cookies.Add(cookie);
```

Although a specific date can be set, there is no guarantee that the cookie is stored until the date is reached. The user can delete the cookie, and the browser application deletes the cookie if too many cookies are stored locally. Internet Explorer has a limit of 20 cookies for a single server, and 300 cookies for all servers. When the limit is reached, the cookies that haven't been used for some time are deleted.

When the client requests a page from the server, and a cookie for this server is available on the client, the cookie is sent to the server as part of the HTTP request. Reading the cookie in the ASP.NET page can be achieved by accessing the `cookies` collection in the `HttpRequest` object.

Similarly to the HTTP response, the `Page` class has a `Request` property that returns an object of type `HttpRequest`. The property `Cookies` returns an `HttpCookieCollection` that can be used to read the cookies sent by the client. A cookie can be accessed by its name with the indexer, and then the `Values` property of the `HttpCookie` is used to get the value from the cookie:

```
HttpCookie cookie = Request.Cookies["mycookie"];
string myval = cookie.Values["mystate"];
```

ASP.NET makes it easy to use cookies, but you must be aware of the cookie's restrictions. Recall that Internet Explorer accepts just 20 cookies from a single server and 300 cookies for all servers. In addition, a cookie cannot store more than 4KB of data. These restrictions ensure that the client disk won't be filled with cookies.

# Server-Side State Management

Instead of remembering state with the client, it is also possible to remember state with the server. Recall that using client-side state has the disadvantage that the data sent across the network increases. Using server-side state has the disadvantage that the server must allocate resources for its clients. The following sections look at the server-side state management techniques.

## Session

Session state is associated with a browser session. A session starts when the client first opens an ASP.NET page on the server, and ends when the client doesn't access the server for 20 minutes.

You can define your own code that should run when a session starts or ends within a global application class. To create such a class, select PROJECT ➪ Add New Item ➪ Global Application Class. By creating this class, the file `global.asax` is created. Inside this file, some handler routines are defined in the class Global that derives from the base class HttpApplication.

```
using System;
using System.Collections.Generic;
using System.Linq;
using System.Web;
using System.Web.Security;
using System.Web.SessionState;

namespace EventRegistration
{
    public class Global : System.Web.HttpApplication
    {

        protected void Application_Start(object sender, EventArgs e)
        {
            // Code that runs on application startup
        }

        protected void Session_Start(object sender, EventArgs e)
        {
            // Code that runs when a new session is started
        }

        protected void Application_BeginRequest(object sender, EventArgs e)
        {

        }

        protected void Application_AuthenticateRequest(object sender,
                                                       EventArgs e)
        {

        }

        protected void Application_Error(object sender, EventArgs e)
        {
            // Code that runs when an unhandled error occurs
        }

        protected void Session_End(object sender, EventArgs e)
        {
            // Code that runs when a session ends.
            // Note: The Session_End event is raised only when the session
            // state mode is set to InProc in the Web.config file. If session
            // mode is set to StateServer or SQLServer, the event
            // is not raised.
```

```
                }

                protected void Application_End(object sender, EventArgs e)
                {
                    // Code that runs on application shutdown
                }
            }
        }
```

Session state can be stored within an `HttpSessionState` object. The session state object associated with the current HTTP context can be accessed with the `Session` property of the `Page` class. In the `Session_Start()` event handler, session variables can be initialized; in the following example, the session state named `mydata` is initialized to 0:

```
        void Session_Start(Object sender, EventArgs e) {
            // Code that runs on application startup
            Session["mydata"] = 0;
        }
```

The following example shows how session state is read with the `Session` property using the session state name:

```
        void Button1_Click(object sender, EventArgs e)
        {
            int val = (int)Session["mydata"];
            Label1.Text = val.ToString();
            val += 4;
            Session["mydata"] = val;
        }
```

To associate the client with its session variables, by default ASP.NET uses a temporary cookie with a session identifier. ASP.NET also supports sessions without cookies, where URL identifiers are used to map the HTTP requests to the same session.

## Application

If data should be shared between different clients, then application state can be used. Application state can be used in a manner that's very similar to the way session state is used. With application state, the class `HttpApplicationState` is used, and it can be accessed with the `Application` property of the `Page` class.

In the following example, the application variable with the name `userCount` is initialized when the web application is started. `Application_Start()` is the event handler method in the file `global.asax` that is invoked when the first ASP.NET page of the website is started. This variable is used to count every user accessing the website:

```
        void Application_Start(Object sender, EventArgs e) {
            // Code that runs on application startup
            Application["userCount"] = 0;
        }
```

In the `Session_Start()` event handler, the value of the application variable `userCount` is incremented. Before changing an application variable, the application object must be locked with the `Lock()` method; otherwise, threading problems can occur because multiple clients can access an application variable concurrently. After the value of the application variable is changed, the `Unlock()` method must be called. Be aware that the time between locking and unlocking is very short — you shouldn't read files or data from the database during that time. Otherwise, other clients must wait until the data access is completed.

```
        void Session_Start(Object sender, EventArgs e) {
            // Code that runs when a new session is started
            Application.Lock();
            Application["userCount"] = (int)Application["userCount"] + 1;
            Application.UnLock();
        }
```

Reading the data from the application state is as easy as it was with the session state:

```
Label1.Text = this.Application["userCount"].ToString();
```

Don't store too much data in the application state because the application state requires server resources until the server is stopped or restarted.

## Cache

Cache is server-side state that is similar to application state insofar as it is shared with all clients. Cache is different from application state in that cache is much more flexible: there are many options to define when the state should be invalidated. Instead of reading a file with every request, or reading the database, the data can be stored inside the cache.

For the cache, the namespace System.Web.Caching and the class Cache are needed. Adding an object to the cache is shown in the following example:

```
Cache.Add("mycache", myobj, null, DateTime.MaxValue,
    TimeSpan.FromMinutes(10), CacheItemPriority.Normal, null);
```

The Page class has a Cache property that returns a Cache object. Using the Add() method of the Cache class, any object can be assigned to the cache. The first parameter of the Add() method defines the name of the cache item. The second parameter is the object that should be cached. With the third parameter, dependencies can be defined, for example, the cache item can be dependent on a file. When the file changes, the cache object is invalidated. In the preceding example there's no dependency because null is set with this parameter.

With parameters four and five, a time can be set specifying how long the cache item is valid. Parameter four defines an absolute time when the cache item should be invalidated, whereas parameter five requires a sliding time that invalidates the cache item after it hasn't been accessed for the time defined with the sliding expiration. In the preceding example, a sliding time span is used, invalidating the cache after the cache item hasn't been used for 10 minutes.

Parameter six defines a cache priority. CacheItemPriority is an enumeration for setting the cache priority. If the ASP.NET worker process has high memory usage, the ASP.NET runtime removes cache items according to their priority. Items with a lower priority are removed first. With the last parameter, it is possible to define a method that should be invoked when the cache item is removed. An example of how this can be used is when the cache is dependent on a file. When the file changes, the cache item is removed and the event handler is invoked. With the event handler, the cache can be reloaded by reading the file once more.

Cache items can be read by using the indexer, as you've already seen with the session and application state. Before using the object returned from the Cache property, always check whether the result is null, which happens when the cache is invalidated. When the returned value from the Cache indexer is not null, the returned object can be cast to the type that was used to store the cache item:

```
object o = Cache["mycache"];
if (o == null)
{
    // Reload the cache.
}
else
{
    // Use the cache.
    MyClass myObj = (MyClass)o;
    //...
}
```

# STYLES

Visual Studio supports styling web pages with Cascading Style Sheets (CSS). With CSS you can define the look and formatting of HTML pages. Instead of customizing each HTML element, with CSS you can define styles for specific elements (which you'll do in the following Try it Out), and then reference them by name for easy reuse. The colors used in the styles defined in the following sections are of high contrast and won't look very appealing. This approach is taken for demonstration purposes only. If you are interested in a balanced and attractive layout with an appropriate color palette, the ASP.NET Web Application template is a great starter solution and uses production-quality styles.

**TRY IT OUT**    Defining Styles for Elements: Ex08

**1.** Open the web application project named EventRegistration created previously.

**2.** Add a new folder named Styles by selecting Project ⇨ New Folder.

**3.** Select this folder in the Solution Explorer and create a new style sheet by selecting Project ⇨ Add New Item, and select Style Sheet. Give the style sheet the name Site.css.

**4.** By default, this style sheet contains an empty body element.

**5.** Click within the curly brackets of the body, open the context menu, and choose Build Style. The Modify Style dialog box shown in Figure 19-17 will open.

**6.** Select the Font category and change the font-family setting to Arial, Helvetica, sans-serif; change the font-size setting to .80 em, and change the color to #FFFF00.

**7.** Select the Background category in the same dialog box and change the background color to #0066CC.

**8.** Select the Box category and change the padding and margin to 0.

**9.** The style sheet should now look like the following code snippet:

```
body {
    font-family: Arial, Helvetica, sans-serif;
    font-size: .80em;
    color: #FFFF00;
    background-color: #0066CC;
    padding: 0px;
    margin: 0px;
}
```

**10.** Create a new style rule after the rule you have created for the body tag. This style rule will apply when the user hovers the mouse of a link. It should look like this:

```
a:hover
{
}
```

**11.** Open the Modify Style dialog box again. Select the Font category and change the color to #FF0000 and check the text-decoration underline and overline. The resulting CSS code should look like this:

```
a:hover
{
    color: #FF0000;
    text-decoration: underline overline;
}
```

**12.** Add style rules for a:active, a:link, a:visited, and h1 according to the following code:

```
a:link, a:visited
{
    color: #00FFFF;
}

a:active
{
    color: #00FFFF;
}

a:hover
```

```
    {
        color: #FF0000;
        text-decoration: underline overline;
    }
    h1
    {
        text-align: center;
    }
```

13. Create a new web page named `StylesDemo.aspx`. Drag and drop the file `Site.css` from the Solution Explorer to the Design View of the editor. The background color of the page changes immediately.

14. Change to the source view to verify the new `link` entry referencing the style sheet:

```
    <head runat="server">
        <title></title>
        <link href="Styles/Site.css" rel="stylesheet" type="text/css" />
    </head>
```

15. Add an `h1` tag and an anchor tag to the page within the body element as shown:

```
    <body>
        <form id="form1" runat="server">
        <h1>
            Styles Demo</h1>
        <div>
            <a href="http://www.wiley.com">Wiley Publishing</a>
        </div>
        </form>
    </body>
```

16. Run the application and navigate to the `StylesDemo.aspx` page The page should look like Figure 19-18. Verify the page styles are applied to the heading, the header, and the link; and hover over the link to see the change in color and text decorations.

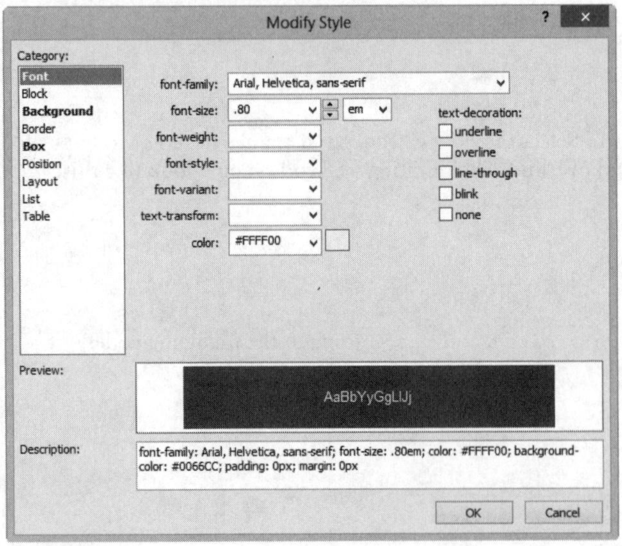

**FIGURE 19-17**

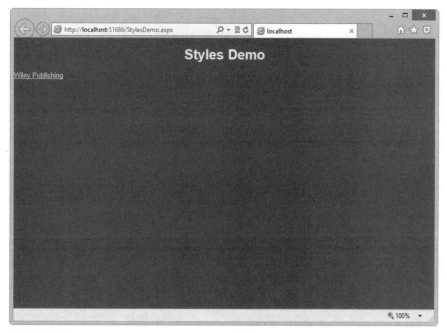

**FIGURE 19-18**

### How it Works

Because the CSS file is referenced with a link element, the browser requests this page alongside the HTML code. The browser then uses the styled elements from the CSS file to change the look of the HTML elements.

---

With CSS, you can change the style of specific HTML tags, as well as define classes that are referenced from HTML tags. You do the latter in the following Try It Out.

**TRY IT OUT**  Defining Style Classes: Ex09

In the last exercise, you created style rules for HTML elements like `body`, `h1`, and `a`. In this exercise you create CSS classes that you can apply to one or more elements within the markup of any `.aspx` page.

1. Open the style sheet `Site.css`.
2. Add a new class named `bottom`. Prefix the class name with a period (`.`), as shown:

   ```
   .bottom {

   }.
   ```

3. Open the Modify Style editor (by selecting Build Style from the context menu).
4. Select the Font category and choose a font-size of x-small.
5. Select the Block category and define vertical-align to text-bottom, and text-align to center.
6. Select the Box category and define a margin of 5 for all top, right, bottom, and left.
7. Select the Position category and define a height of 40px.
8. Verify the result in the `Site.css` file:

   ```
   .bottom
   {
       margin: 5px;
       height: 40px;
   ```

```
        text-align: center;
        vertical-align: text-bottom;
        font-size: x-small;
    }
```

**9.** Open the file `StylesDemo.aspx` and add a `div` element containing the following text:

```
<div class="bottom">
    Copyright (c) 2012 Wiley Publishing
</div>
```

**10.** Start the application and navigate to the `StylesDemo.aspx` page. Verify that the style for the `div` element is applied.

### How It Works

Instead of defining styles with every element in every page of the website, you can define styles in a common place. The Modify Style editor can give you a good glimpse of all the things that can be changed. When the page is opened, the browser is responsible for applying the styles and arranging the elements accordingly.

> **WARNING** *Some styles are applied differently in different browsers. Be sure to verify the look of your page with all browsers that should be supported.*

> **NOTE** *Using styles, you can apply font sizes and colors, as well as define the layout of a web page. Alternatively, instead of doing the layout with styles, it can be done with HTML tables. CSS not only offers more flexibility in the layout than HTML tables, it also provides advantages regarding accessibility by separating content from visual information. That's why nowadays a table-less web design is usually preferred.*
>
> *Because this book is on C# programming and doesn't focus on the design of HTML pages, it covers only a very brief introduction to CSS. For more information on CSS, you should read the book* Beginning HTML, XHTML, CSS, and JavaScript *by Jon Ducket (Wrox, 2009).*

## MASTER PAGES

Most websites reuse part of their content on every page—elements such as company logos and menus are often available on each page. It's not necessary to repeat the common user interface elements with every page; instead, the common elements can be added to a *master page*. Master pages look like normal ASP.NET pages but define placeholders that are replaced by *content pages*.

A master page has the file extension `.master` and uses the `Master` directive in the first line of the file, as shown here:

```
<%@ Master Language="C#" AutoEventWireup="true"
    CodeBehind="MasterPage.master.cs"
    Inherits="MasterPage" %>
```

Only the master pages in the website make use of `<html>`, `<head>`, `<body>`, and `<form>` HTML elements. The web pages contain only content that is embedded within the `<form>` element. The web pages can embed their own content within the `ContentPlaceHolder` control. The master page can define default content for the `ContentPlaceHolder` if the web page doesn't:

```
<html xmlns="http://www.w3.org/1999/xhtml">
<head runat="server">
    <title></title>
    <asp:ContentPlaceHolder ID="head" runat="server">
    </asp:ContentPlaceHolder>
</head>
<body>
    <form id="form1" runat="server">
    <div>
        <asp:ContentPlaceHolder ID="ContentPlaceHolder1"
                                runat="server">

        </asp:ContentPlaceHolder>
    </div>
    </form>
</body>
</html>
```

To use the master page, you must apply the `MasterPageFile` attribute to the `Page` directive. To replace the content of a master page, use the `Content` control. The `Content` control associates the `ContentPlaceHolder` with the `ContentPlaceHolderID`:

```
<%Page Language="C#" MasterPageFile="~/MasterPage.master"
    AutoEventWireUp="true" CodeFile="Default.aspx.cs"
    Inherits="default"
    Title="Untitled Page" %>
<asp:Content ID="Content1" ContentPlaceHolderID="head"
    Runat="Server"></asp:Content>
<asp:Content ID="Content2"
    ContentPlaceHolderID="ContentPlaceHolder1"
    Runat="Server"></asp:Content>
```

Instead of defining the master page with the `Page` directive, you can assign a default master page to all web pages with the `<pages>` element in the web configuration file, `Web.config`:

```
<configuration>
  <system.web>
    <pages masterPageFile="~/MasterPage.master">
      <!--...-->
    </pages>
  </system.web>
</configuration>
```

With the master page file configured within `Web.config`, the ASP.NET pages need a `Content` element as shown earlier; otherwise, the `masterPageFile` attribute would have no use. If you use both the `Page` directive's `MasterPageFile` attribute and the entry in `Web.config`, the setting of the `Page` directive overrides the setting from `Web.config`. This way, it's possible to define a default master page file (with `Web.config`), but override the default setting for specific web pages.

It is also possible to change the master page programmatically. By doing so, different master pages can be used for different devices or different browser types. The last place the master page can be changed is in the `Page_PreInit` handler method. In the following sample code, the `MasterPageFile` property of the `Page` class is set to `IE.master` if the browser sends the MSIE string with the browser name (which is done by Microsoft Internet Explorer), or to `Default.master` for all other browsers:

```
public partial class ChangeMaster: System.Web.UI.Page
{
    void Page_Load(object sender, EventArgs e)
    {
    }

    void Page_PreInit(object sender, EventArgs e)
    {
        if (Request.UserAgent.Contains("MSIE"))
```

```
        {
            this.MasterPageFile = "~/IE.master";
        }
        else
        {
            this.MasterPageFile = "~/Default.master";
        }
    }
}
```

Now try creating your own master page in the following Try It Out. The sample master page here have a heading and a body, and the main part of the master page will be replaced by individual pages.

**TRY IT OUT** Creating a Master Page: Ex10

In this exercise you create a master page and work with the ContentPlaceHolder elements within it.

1.  Open the web application project named EventRegistration.

2.  Add a new Master Page item and name it Events.Master.

3.  Change to the Design View of the editor and apply the style sheet Site.css. Drag and drop the file Site.css from the Solution Explorer to the editor.

4.  Rename the ID of the second ContentPlaceHolder to ContentPlaceHolderMain and assign the CSS class content to the div element as shown:

    ```
    <div class="content">
        <asp:ContentPlaceHolder ID="ContentPlaceHolderMain" runat="server">
        </asp:ContentPlaceHolder>
    </div>
    ```

5.  Add the following div and h1 elements before the previously changed div element:

    ```
    <div class="header">
        <h1>
            Event Registration
        </h1>
    </div>
    <div class="navigation">
        Menu will go here
    </div>
    ```

6.  Add the following div element after the div element surrounding the ContentPlaceHolder:

    ```
    <div class="bottom">
        Copyright (c) 2012  Wiley Publishing
    </div>
    ```

7.  The complete page should look similar to the following:

    ```
    <%@ Master Language="C#" AutoEventWireup="true" CodeBehind="Events.master.cs"
            Inherits="EventRegistration.Events" %>

    <!DOCTYPE html>
    <html xmlns="http://www.w3.org/1999/xhtml">
    <head runat="server">
        <title></title>
        <asp:ContentPlaceHolder ID="head" runat="server">
        </asp:ContentPlaceHolder>
        <link href="Styles/Site.css" rel="stylesheet" type="text/css" />
    </head>
    <body>
        <form id="form1" runat="server">
        <div class=""header"">
            <h1>Event Registration </h1>
        </div>
        <div class=""navigation"">
            Menu will go here
    ```

```
        </div>
        <div class="content">
            <asp:ContentPlaceHolder ID="ContentPlaceHolderMain" runat="server">
            </asp:ContentPlaceHolder>
        </div>
            <div class="bottom">
            Copyright (c) 2012 Wiley Publishing
        </div>
        </form>
    </body>
    </html>
```

### How It Works

As previously discussed, the master page contains the HTML, including the FORM tags that contain the content placeholders where the content will be replaced by the pages that use the master page. The HTML together with the linked CSS defines the layout of the page. Only the content placeholders are replaced from content pages. You can use multiple content placeholders if different parts of the page should be replaced.

After you have created the master page, you can use it from a web page, as shown in the following Try It Out.

**TRY IT OUT**  Using a Master Page: Ex11

1. Open the web application project named EventRegistration, and add a new item of type Web Form using the master page to the web application and name it Default.aspx.

2. The dialog box called Select a Master Page, shown in Figure 19-19, pops up. Select the master page Events.Master. Click OK.

3. The source view of the file Default.aspx shows just two Content controls after the Page directive that references the ContentPlaceHolder controls from the master page. Change the ID properties of the Content controls to ContentHead and ContentMain:

```
<%@ Page Title="" Language="C#" MasterPageFile="~/Events.Master"
        AutoEventWireup="true" CodeBehind="Default.aspx.cs"
        Inherits="EventRegistration.Default" %>
<asp:Content ID="ContentHead" ContentPlaceHolderID="head" runat="server">
</asp:Content>
<asp:Content ID="ContentMain" ContentPlaceHolderID="ContentPlaceHolderMain"
        runat="server">
</asp:Content>
```

4. Change to the Design View in Visual Studio. This view shows you the content of the master page that cannot be changed from the page, which includes the header and copyright information. Enter some text to the Content control and align it to center.

5. Change to the source view, which shows the code as follows. The center alignment is changed to a CSS style.

```
<%@ Page Title="" Language="C#" MasterPageFile="~/Events.Master"
        AutoEventWireup="true" CodeBehind="Default.aspx.cs"
        Inherits="EventRegistration.Default" %>
<asp:Content ID="ContentHead" ContentPlaceHolderID="head" runat="server">
    <style type="text/css">
        .auto-style1
        {
            text-align: center;
        }
    </style>
</asp:Content>
<asp:Content ID="ContentMain" ContentPlaceHolderID="ContentPlaceHolderMain"
        runat="server">
```

```
        <p class="auto-style1">
            Welcome to the</p>
        <p class="auto-style1">
            Event Registration</p>
        <p class="auto-style1">
            Sample application for Beginning Visual C# 2012!</p>
    </asp:Content>
```

**6.** Start the application and navigate to the `default.aspx` page. The result should look like what is shown in Figure 19-20.

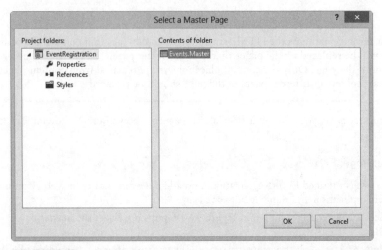

**FIGURE 19-19**

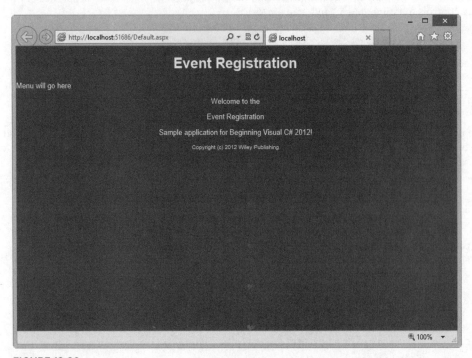

**FIGURE 19-20**

# SITE NAVIGATION

For navigation between multiple pages on a website, you can define an XML file that contains the structure of the site, and use some UI controls to display the navigation options. The important navigation controls are listed in Table 19-8.

**TABLE 19-8:** Navigation Controls

| CONTROL | DESCRIPTION |
| --- | --- |
| SiteMapDataSource | The SiteMapDataSource control is a data source control that references any site map data provider. In the Visual Studio Toolbox, you can find this control in the Data section. |
| Menu | The Menu control displays links to pages as defined with a site map data source. The Menu can be displayed horizontally or vertically, and it has many options to configure its style. |
| SiteMapPath | The SiteMapPath control uses minimal space to display the current position of a page within the hierarchy of the website. You can display text or image hyperlinks. |
| TreeView | The TreeView control displays a hierarchical view of the website. |

In the next Try It Out you add a site map and a menu control to navigate between pages of the website.

**TRY IT OUT**   Adding Navigation: Ex12

You add a Menu control that uses a SiteMapDataSource to the master page of the Event Registration website in this example. You also add and configure a SiteMapPath control, which will provide an intuitive and dynamic representation of the user's current location relative to the home page.

1. Open the web application project EventRegistration.
2. Add a new Site Map item to the website by right-clicking on the project in the Solution Explorer and selecting Add New Item. Keep the name Web.sitemap.
3. Change the content of the file as shown here:
   ```xml
   <?xml version="1.0" encoding="utf-8" ?>
   <siteMap xmlns="http://schemas.microsoft.com/AspNet/SiteMap-File-1.0" >
       <siteMapNode url="Default.aspx" title="Home">
         <siteMapNode url="EventRegister.aspx" title="Register"
                   description="Register to an Event" />
         <siteMapNode url="EventList.aspx" title="Event List"
                   description="Lists Events Worldwide" />
         <siteMapNode url="Admin/EventManagement.aspx" title="Event Management"
                   description="Management of Events" roles="Editors" />
       </siteMapNode>
   </siteMap>
   ```
4. Open the file Events.Master.
5. Locate the SiteMapDataSource control under the Data tab in your Toolbox and add it to the page.
6. Add a Menu control from the Navigation tab of your Toolbox, inside of the div tag that has been assigned the navigation class. Set the DataSourceID property to SiteMapDataSource1.
7. Configure the Menu control with the properties Orientation set to Horizontal, StaticDisplayLevels set to 2, and CssClass set to menu as shown in the following snippet:
   ```
   <div class="navigation">
        
       <asp:Menu ID="Menu1" runat="server" DataSourceID="SiteMapDataSource1"
   ```

```
                Orientation="Horizontal" StaticDisplayLevels="2" CssClass="menu">
            </asp:Menu>
            <asp:SiteMapDataSource ID="SiteMapDataSource1" runat="server" />
        </div>
```

8. Add the following style rules to the file `Site.css` to style the menu:

```css
.menu ul li a
{
    background-color: #008085;
    border: 1px #4e667d solid;
    color: #dde4ec;
    display: block;
    line-height: 1.35em;
    padding: 4px 20px;
    text-decoration: none;
    white-space: nowrap;
}

.menu ul li a:hover
{
    background-color: #bfcbd6;
    color: #465c71;
    text-decoration: none;
}
```

9. Add a `SiteMapPath` control below the `Menu` control.

10. Open the file `Default.aspx` in the browser. Notice the menu and the path that displays the position of the current file in the website.

11. Create new pages named `EventRegister.aspx` and `EventList.aspx` with the template Web Form using Master Page and select the master page `Events.Master`.

12. Create a new folder by selecting Project ➪ New Folder, and name it `Admin`. Create a new page called `EventManagement.aspx` within this folder. Again, use the template Web Form using Master Page to create this page.

13. You can add other pages that are referenced in the file `Web.sitemap` as needed by referencing the same master page to show the defined menus.

14. Add the `siteMap` element as shown to the `Web.config` file within the `system.web` element:

```xml
<siteMap defaultProvider="XmlSiteMapProvider" enabled="true">
  <providers>
    <clear />
    <add name="XmlSiteMapProvider"
        description="Default SiteMap Provider"
        type="System.Web.XmlSiteMapProvider"
        siteMapFile="Web.sitemap"
        securityTrimmingEnabled="true" />
  </providers>
</siteMap>
```

### How It Works

The structure of the website is defined by the web pages listed in the file `Web.sitemap`. This XML file contains XML `<siteMapNode>` elements inside a `<siteMap>` root element. The `<siteMapNode>` element defines a web page. The filename of the page is set with the `url` attribute, and the `title` attribute specifies the name as it should appear on menus. The hierarchy of the pages is defined by writing `<siteMapNode>` elements as child elements of the page on which the link to the children should occur.

The `SiteMapDataSource` control is a data source control with similarities to the data source controls shown in the previous chapter. This control can use different providers. By default, the `XmlSiteMapProvider` class is used to get to the data; and by default, the `XmlSiteMapProvider` class uses the file `Web.sitemap`.

Because the `roles` attribute is applied to the `siteMapNode EventManagement.aspx`, only users who are in the specified role `Editors` can see this menu entry. Because this authorization feature of the `XmlSiteMapProvider` is by default not enabled, the `Web.config` file is changed to set the `securityTrimmingEnabled` property of the `XmlSiteMapProvider`. Without requiring roles for menus, this configuration in `Web.config` wouldn't be needed.

With the `Menu` control you can edit menu items that appear in the ASPX source; or you can add menu items programmatically. The easiest way to add menu items is to use a site map data source by configuring the data source.

## AUTHENTICATION AND AUTHORIZATION

To secure the website, *authentication* is used to verify that the user has a valid logon; and authorization confirms that the user who was authenticated is allowed to use the resource.

ASP.NET offers both Windows and Forms authentication. The most frequently used authentication technique for web applications is Forms authentication, which is covered here. ASP.NET also has some great new features for Forms authentication. Windows authentication makes use of Windows accounts and IIS to authenticate users.

ASP.NET has many classes for user authentication. Figure 19-21 shows the structure of the new architecture. With ASP.NET, many new security controls, such as `Login` and `PasswordRecovery`, are available. These controls make use of the Membership API. With the Membership API, it is possible to create and delete users, validate logon information, or get information about currently logged-in users. The Membership API makes use of a *membership provider*. With ASP.NET 4.5, different providers exist to access users in an Access database, the SQL Server database, or the Active Directory. It is also possible to create a custom provider that accesses an XML file or any custom store.

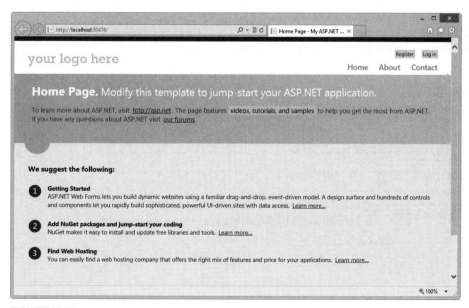

**FIGURE 19-21**

## Authentication Configuration

This chapter demonstrates Forms authentication with a Membership provider. In the following Try It Out, you configure security for the web application and assign different access lists to different folders.

**TRY IT OUT** Configuring Security: Ex13

1. Open the previously created web application EventRegistration using Visual Studio.

2. Within the solution, if a folder named Intro already exists, right-click the folder and choose Delete from the context menu.

3. Create a new folder named Intro by selecting Project ➪ New Folder. This folder will be configured for access by all users, while the main folder will be accessible only to authenticated users. The previously created folder Admin will be accessible only to users in the Editors role.

4. Start the ASP.NET Web Application Administration by selecting Project ➪ ASP.NET Configuration.

5. Select the Security tab, as shown in Figure 19-22.

6. Click the link to the Security Setup wizard. In the Welcome Screen, click the Next button. From step 2 of the wizard, select the access method From the Internet, as shown in Figure 19-23.

7. Click Next. In step 3, you can see the configured provider. The default provider is a SQL Server database provider. This configuration cannot be changed in the Wizard mode, but you can change it afterward.

8. Click the Next button. Within the Define Roles screen, click the checkbox Enable Roles for this Website.

9. Click the Next button. Create a new role named Editors.

10. Click the Next button, which takes you to step 5, where you add new users (see Figure 19-24). Create two new accounts. One of the accounts should be a member of the role Editors.

11. After the users are successfully created, click the Next button for step 6 of the wizard (see Figure 19-25). Here, you can configure which users are allowed or denied access to the website or specific directories. Add a rule to deny anonymous users. Next, select the Intro directory and add a rule to allow anonymous users. Select the Admin folder to deny access to authenticated users, and to allow access to users in the role Editors. Then click the Next button and finally the Finish button.

12. If you tried to start the website after the preceding steps, you should have received an error because a login.aspx page is missing. We will fix this in the next Try It Out.

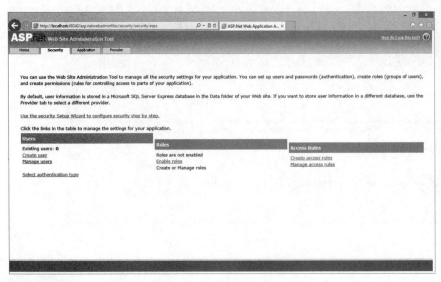

**FIGURE 19-22**

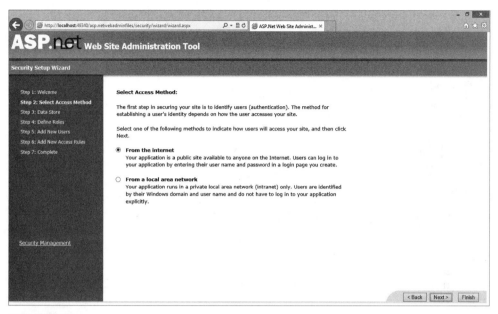

**FIGURE 19-23**

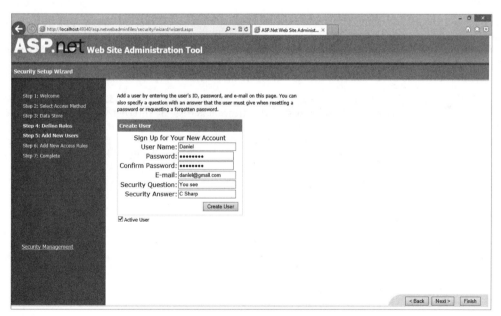

**FIGURE 19-24**

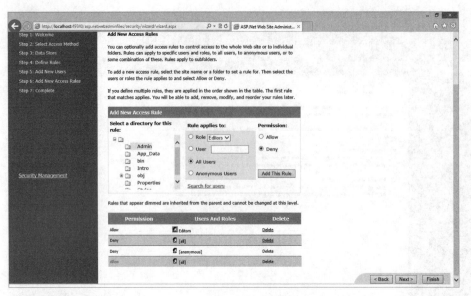

**FIGURE 19-25**

### How It Works

After you complete the security configuration, a new SQL Server database is created. An `App_Data` folder should now be included in the project tree of Solution Explorer within Visual Studio. If it does not show up, choose `Show All Files` from the Solution Explorer toolbar. Having refreshed the files in the Solution Explorer, you can see a new SQL Server Express database `ASPNETDB.mdf` in the directory `App_Data`. This database contains tables that are used by the SQL Membership provider.

Now, along with the web application you will also see the configuration file `Web.config`. This file contains the configuration for Forms authentication because authentication across the Internet was selected, and the `<authorization>` section denies access to anonymous users. If the Membership provider were changed, the new provider would be listed in the configuration file. Because the SQL provider is the default provider already defined with the machine configuration file, there is no need for it to be listed here:

```
<authorization>
  <deny users="?" />
</authorization>
<roleManager enabled="true" />
<authentication mode="Forms" />
```

Within the `Intro` subfolder, you can see another configuration file, `Web.config`. The authentication section is missing from this configuration file because the authentication configuration is taken from the parent directory. However, the authorization section is different. Here, anonymous users are allowed with `<allow users="?" />`:

```
<?xml version="1.0" encoding="utf-8"?>
<configuration>
    <system.web>
        <authorization>
            <allow users="?" />
        </authorization>
    </system.web>
</configuration>
```

Within the `Admin` subfolder, you can see another configuration file, `Web.config`. The authorization section allows the Editors role and denies authenticated users:

```
<?xml version="1.0" encoding="utf-8"?>
<configuration>
    <system.web>
        <authorization>
            <allow roles="Editors" />
            <deny users="*" />
        </authorization>
    </system.web>
</configuration>
```

# Using Security Controls

ASP.NET includes many security controls. Instead of writing a custom form to ask the user for a username and password, a ready-to-use `Login` control is available. The security controls and their functionality are described in Table 19-9.

**TABLE 19-9:** ASP.NET's Security Controls

| SECURITY CONTROL | DESCRIPTION |
|---|---|
| Login | A composite control that includes controls to ask for username and password. |
| LoginStatus | Includes hyperlinks to log in or log out, depending on whether the user is logged in. |
| LoginName | Displays the name of the user. |
| LoginView | Different content can be displayed depending on whether the user is logged in. |
| PasswordRecovery | A composite control to reset forgotten passwords. Depending on the security configurations, the user is asked for the answer to a previously set secret question or the password is sent by e-mail. |
| ChangePassword | A composite control that allows logged-in users to change their passwords. |
| CreateUserWizard | A wizard to create a new user and write the user information to the Membership provider. |

The following Try It Out adds a login page to the web application.

**TRY IT OUT** Creating a Login Page: Ex14

If you tried to start the website after it was configured to deny anonymous users, you should have received an error because a `login.aspx` page is missing. If a specific login page is not configured with Forms authentication, `login.aspx` is used by default. You now create a `login.aspx` page:

1. Add a new Web Form using Master Page and name it `login.aspx`.
2. From the `Login` group of the Visual Studio Toolbox, drag a `Login` control to the form.
3. That's all that's necessary to create a login page. Now when you start the site `default.aspx`, you are redirected to `login.aspx`, where you can enter the user credentials for the user you created earlier.
4. Add to the `Web.config` at the end before the `</configuration>`:

```
<location path="scripts">
  <system.web>
    <authorization>
      <allow users="*" />
    </authorization>
  </system.web>
</location>
```

> **NOTE** *The* `login.aspx` *page might not be styled according to the styles used in the site master page. This might be due to authorization restrictions on the* `Styles` *directory within the Visual Studio project. You can fix this problem by creating another access rule for the* `Styles` *directory that allows anonymous users access to the content within the* `Styles` *directory.*

### How It Works

After adding the `Login` control, you can see this code in the source view:

```
<%@ Page Title="" Language="C#" MasterPageFile="~/Events.Master"
        AutoEventWireup="true" CodeBehind="login.aspx.cs"
          Inherits="EventRegistration.login" %>
<asp:Content ID="Content1" ContentPlaceHolderID="head"
            runat="server">
</asp:Content>
<asp:Content ID="Content2"
            ContentPlaceHolderID="ContentPlaceHolderMain"
            runat="server">
    <asp:Login ID="Login1" runat="server"></asp:Login>
</asp:Content>
```

The properties for this control enable you to configure the text for the header, username, and password labels, and for the login button, too. You can make the Remember Me Next Time check box visible by setting the `DisplayRememberMe` property.

If you want more control over the look and feel of the `Login` control, you can convert the control to a template. You can do this in the Design View by clicking the smart tag and selecting Convert to Template. Next, when you click Edit Templates, you get a view where you can add and modify any controls.

JQuery scripts are being used to render the Login form and access to all is denied, which means we have to make an exception for the Script folder. Therefore you do so at the location part in the `Web.config`.

> **NOTE** *Notice that the solution in the code download does not contain a script folder. Nevertheless, the* `Web.config` *entry is still necessary; otherwise, you get a nasty critical error.*
>
> *For verifying the user credentials, when the Login button is clicked, the method* `Membership.ValidateUser()` *is invoked by the control, and you don't have to do this yourself.*

When users don't have an account to log in with the `EventRegistration` website, they should be able to create their own login. This can be done easily with the `CreateUserWizard` control, as shown in the next Try It Out.

**TRY IT OUT**    **Using the CreateUser Wizard: Ex15**

1. Add a new web page named `RegisterUser.aspx` in the `Intro` folder you previously created. This folder is configured to be accessed from anonymous users.

2. Add a `CreateUserWizard` control to this web page.

**3.** Set the property `ContinueDestinationPageUrl` to `~/Default.aspx`.

**4.** Add a `LinkButton` control to the `Login.aspx` page. Set the content of this control to `Register User`, and the `PostBackUrl` property of this control to the web page `Intro/RegisterUser.aspx`.

**5.** Now you can start the application. Clicking the link `Register User` on the `Login.aspx` page redirects to the page `RegisterUser.aspx`, where a new account will be created with the entered data.

### How It Works

The `CreateUserWizard` control is a wizard-like control that consists of multiple wizard steps, which are defined with the element `<WizardSteps>`:

```
<%@ Page Title="" Language="C#" MasterPageFile="~/Events.Master"
        AutoEventWireup="true" CodeBehind="RegisterUser.aspx.cs"
        Inherits="EventRegistration.Intro.RegisterUser" %>
<asp:Content ID="Content1" ContentPlaceHolderID="head" runat="server">
</asp:Content>
<asp:Content ID="Content2" ContentPlaceHolderID="ContentPlaceHolderMain"
runat="server">
    <asp:CreateUserWizard ID="CreateUserWizard1" runat="server"
                ContinueDestinationPageUrl="~/Default.aspx">
        <WizardSteps>
            <asp:CreateUserWizardStep ID="CreateUserWizardStep1" runat="server">
            </asp:CreateUserWizardStep>
            <asp:CompleteWizardStep ID="CompleteWizardStep1" runat="server">
            </asp:CompleteWizardStep>
        </WizardSteps>
    </asp:CreateUserWizard>
</asp:Content>
```

These wizard steps can be configured in the designer. The smart tag of the control enables you to configure each of these steps separately. Figure 19-26 shows configuration of the step Sign Up for Your New Account. You can also add custom steps with custom controls to add special requirements, such as having users accept a contract before signing up for an account.

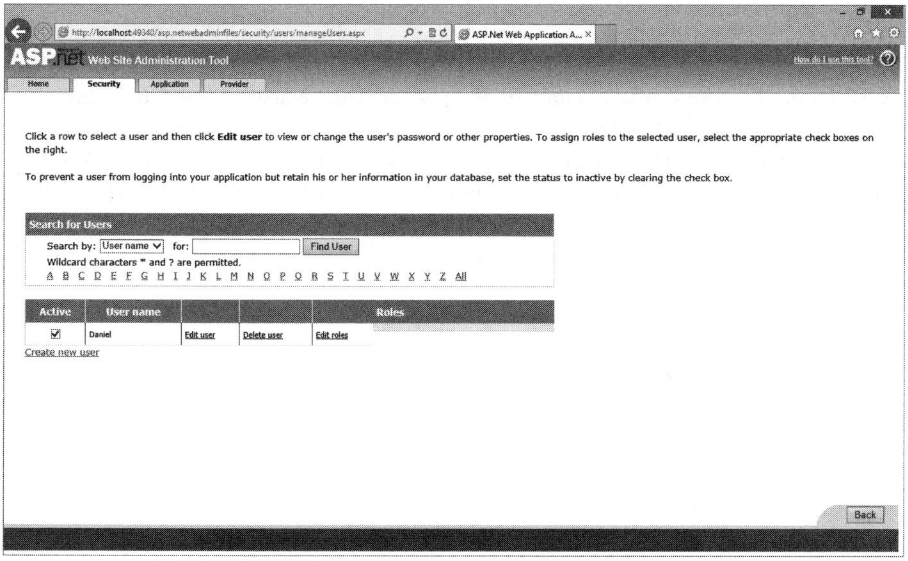

**FIGURE 19-26**

# READING FROM AND WRITING TO A SQL SERVER DATABASE

Most web applications need access to a database to read data from it and write data to it. In this section, you create a new database to store event information, and learn how to use this database from ASP.NET. First you create a new SQL Server database in the next Try It Out. This can be done directly from within Visual Studio 2012.

**TRY IT OUT** Creating a New Database: Ex16

1. Open the previously created web application `EventRegistration`.

2. Open the Database Explorer. If you cannot already see it in Visual Studio, you can open the window by selecting View ⇨ Server Explorer.

3. In the Server Explorer, select `Data Connections`, and expand the `ASPNETDB.mdf` database node. Notice the structure of your existing membership and roles database, as shown in Figure 19-28. This is the single database available within your existing project. Choose to add another by selecting the top-level PROJECT menu and choosing Add New Item. Choose the Data node under Visual C# and select SQL Server Database.

4. Enter the name `Events.mdf` for the database name, as shown in Figure 19-29. When prompted to place your new database in the `App_Data` file, choose `Yes`.

5. In the Database Explorer, expand the `Events.mdf` database node and right-click Tables. Choose Add New Table.

6. Enter the column names and data types shown in Table 19-10.

**TABLE 19-10:** Enter Column Names and Data Types

| COLUMN NAME | DATA TYPE |
|---|---|
| ID | Int |
| Title | nvarchar(50) |
| Date | Datetime |
| Location | nvarchar(50) |

7. Configure the ID column as a primary key column with an identity increment of 1 and an identity seed of 1. Configure all columns to not allow nulls.

8. Save the table with the name Events by changing `[dbo].[Table]` to `[dbo].[Events]` in the T-SQL tab, and then clicking the Update button shown in the top-left corner of the table designer shown in Figure 19-30.

9. Add a few events to the table with some sample titles, dates, and locations.

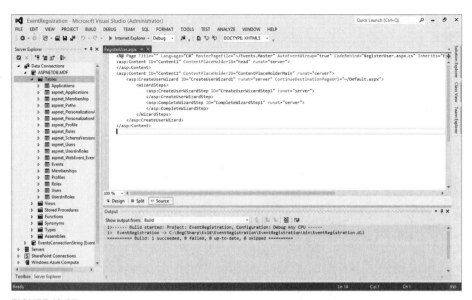

**FIGURE 19-27**

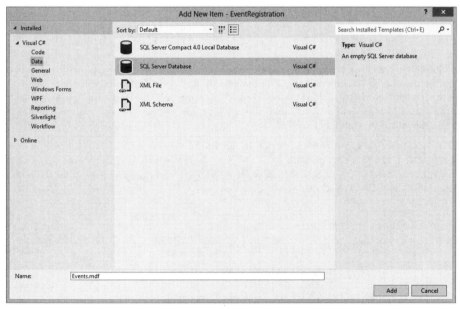

**FIGURE 19-28**

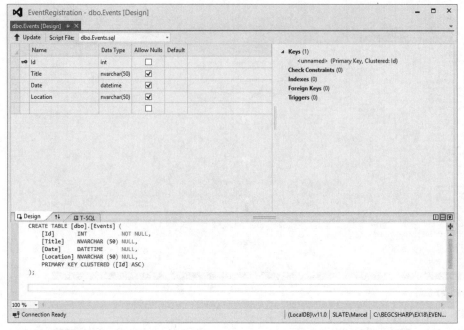

**FIGURE 19-29**

*How It Works*

Table creation is handled mostly by the Visual Studio design tools. By opening the single existing database connection within the project, the connection to your membership and roles database, you are presented with basic database management functions, such as table and query creation, via the Database Explorer. The SQL statement in the tab named T-SQL defines your table. To create a table named `Events`, and not just `Table`, change the table name in the SQL statement.

To display and edit data, there's a separate Data section in the Toolbox, representing data controls. The data controls can be categorized into two groups: data view and data source. A data source control is associated with a data source such as an XML file, a SQL database, or a .NET class; data views are connected with a data source to represent data. Table 19-11 describes all the data controls.

**TABLE 19-11:** The Data Controls

| DATA CONTROL | DESCRIPTION |
| --- | --- |
| GridView | Displays data with rows and columns |
| DataList | Displays a single column to display all items |
| DetailsView | Can be used together with a `GridView` if you have a master/detail relationship with your data |
| FormView | Displays a single row of the data source |
| Repeater | Template-based. You can define which HTML elements should be generated around the data from the data source |
| ListView | This is template-based, similar to the `Repeater` control |

The data source controls and their functionality are listed in Table 19-12.

**TABLE 19-12:** The Data Source Controls

| DATA SOURCE CONTROL | DESCRIPTION |
|---|---|
| SqlDataSource | Accesses the SQL Server or any other ADO.NET provider (for example, Oracle, ODBC, and OLEDB). Internally, it uses a `DataSet` or a `DataReader` class. |
| AccessDataSource | Enables you to use an Access database. |
| EntityDataSource | New as of .NET 4.0. Enables using the ADO.NET Entity Framework as a data source. |
| ObjectDataSource | Enables you to use .NET classes as the data source. |
| XmlDataSource | Enables you to access XML files. Using this data source, hierarchical structures can be displayed. |
| SiteMapDataSource | Uses XML files to define a site structure for creating links and references with a website. This feature is discussed in Chapter 20. |

In the next Try It Out, you use a `GridView` control to display and edit data from the previously created database.

**TRY IT OUT** Using a GridView Control to Display Data: Ex17

1. Open the previously created web page `EventsManagement.aspx` in the `Admin` folder.
2. Add a `GridView` control to the web page.
3. In the Choose Data Source combo box of the control's smart tag, select `<New data source.>` (see Figure 19-30). The dialog box shown in Figure 19-31 opens.
4. Select Database and enter the name **EventsDataSource** for this new data source.
5. Click OK to configure the data source. The Configure Data Source dialog box opens. Click the New Connection button to create a new connection.
6. In the next dialog box, select the previously created Events database. The next dialog box (see Figure 19-32) opens; it is here you store the connection string.
7. Click the check box to save the connection and enter the connection string name `EventsConnectionString`. Click Next.
8. In the next dialog box, select the Events table to read the data from this table, as shown in Figure 19-33. Select the ID, Title, Date, and Location columns to define the SQL command shown in the figure. Then click the Next button.
9. With the last window of the Configure Data Source dialog box, you can test the query. Finally, click the Finish button.
10. In the designer, you can now see the `GridView` control with dummy data, and the `SqlDataSource` with the name `EventsDataSource`.
11. For a more attractive layout of the `GridView` control, select AutoFormat from the smart tag and select the scheme Mocha, as shown in Figure 19-34.
12. Start the page with Visual Studio, where you will see the events in a nice table like the one shown in Figure 19-35.

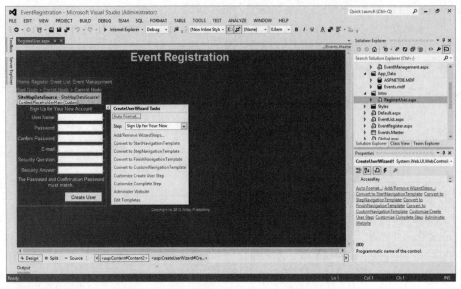

**FIGURE 19-30**

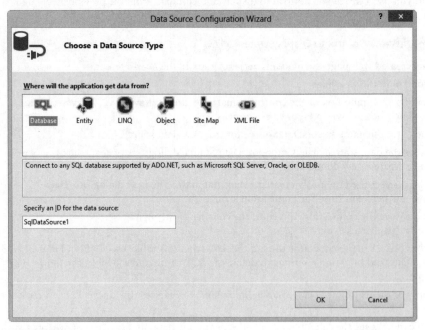

**FIGURE 19-31**

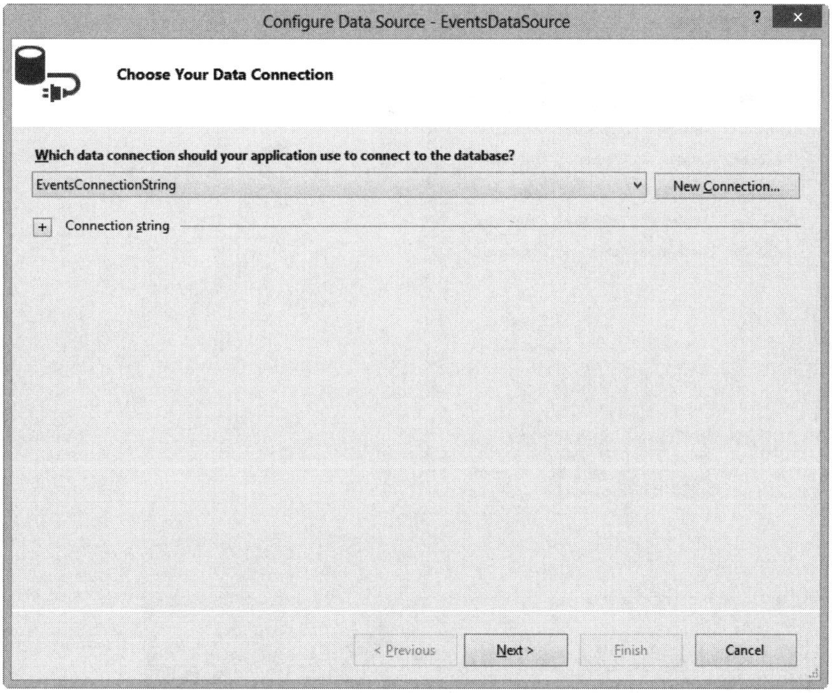

FIGURE 19-32

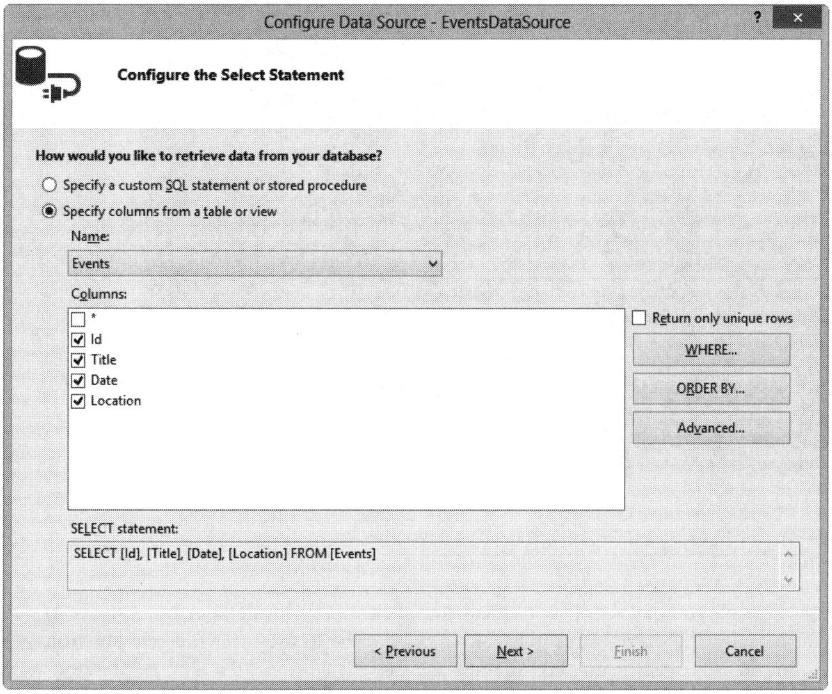

FIGURE 19-33

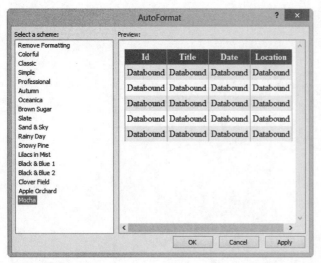

**FIGURE 19-34**

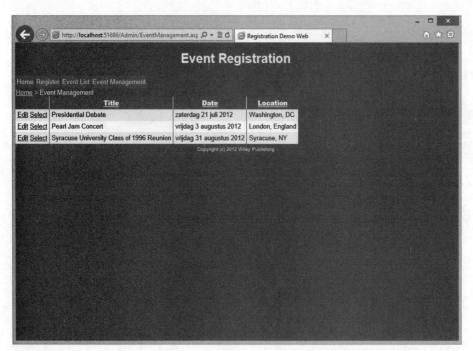

**FIGURE 19-35**

## How It Works

After you add the `GridView` control, you can see its configuration in the source code. The `DataSourceID` attribute defines the association with the data source control, which can be found after the grid control. Within the `<Columns>` element, all bound columns for displaying data are shown. `HeaderText` defines the text of the header and `DataField` defines the field name within the data source.

The data source is defined with the `<asp:SqlDataSource>` element, where the `SelectCommand` defines how the data is read from the database, and the `ConnectionString` defines how to connect with the database. Because you chose to save the connection string in the configuration file, `<%$` is used to make an association with a dynamically generated class from the configuration file:

```
<%@ Page Language="C#" MasterPageFile="~/Events.Master" AutoEventWireup="true"
        CodeBehind="EventManagement.aspx.cs"
        Inherits="EventRegistration.Admin.EventManagement" %>
<asp:Content ID="ContentHead" ContentPlaceHolderID="head" runat="server">
</asp:Content>
<asp:Content ID="ContentMain" ContentPlaceHolderID="ContentPlaceHolderMain"
            runat="server">
    <asp:GridView ID="GridView1" runat="server" AutoGenerateColumns="False"
                DataKeyNames="Id"
        DataSourceID="EventsDataSource" BackColor="White" BorderColor="#DEDFDE"
        BorderStyle="None" BorderWidth="1px" CellPadding="4" ForeColor="Black"
        GridLines="Vertical">
        <AlternatingRowStyle BackColor="White" />
        <Columns>
            <asp:BoundField DataField="Id" HeaderText="Id" ReadOnly="True"
                        SortExpression="Id">
            </asp:BoundField>
            <asp:BoundField DataField="Title" HeaderText="Title"
                        SortExpression="Title"></asp:BoundField>
            <asp:BoundField DataField="Date" HeaderText="Date"
                        SortExpression="Date"></asp:BoundField>
            <asp:BoundField DataField="Location" HeaderText="Location"
                        SortExpression="Location">
            </asp:BoundField>
        </Columns>
        <FooterStyle BackColor="#CCCC99" />
        <HeaderStyle BackColor="#6B696B" Font-Bold="True" ForeColor="White" />
        <PagerStyle BackColor="#F7F7DE" ForeColor="Black" HorizontalAlign="Right" />
        <RowStyle BackColor="#F7F7DE" />
        <SelectedRowStyle BackColor="#CE5D5A" Font-Bold="True" ForeColor="White" />
        <SortedAscendingCellStyle BackColor="#FBFBF2" />
        <SortedAscendingHeaderStyle BackColor="#848384" />
        <SortedDescendingCellStyle BackColor="#EAEAD3" />
        <SortedDescendingHeaderStyle BackColor="#575357" />
    </asp:GridView>
    <asp:SqlDataSource runat="server" ID="EventsDataSource"
        ConnectionString='<%$ ConnectionStrings:EventsConnectionString %>'
        SelectCommand="SELECT [Id], [Title], [Date], [Location] FROM [Events]">
    </asp:SqlDataSource>
</asp:Content>
```

In the `Web.config` configuration file, you can find the connection string to the database:

```
<connectionStrings>
    <add name="EventsConnectionString"
        connectionString="Data Source=
(LocalDB)\v11.0;AttachDbFilename=|DataDirectory|\Events.mdf;
Integrated Security=True"
        providerName="System.Data.SqlClient" />
</connectionStrings>
```

Now the `GridView` control should be configured differently. In the next Try It Out, the ID is no longer displayed to the user, and the date-time display shows only the date.

**TRY IT OUT** Configuring the GridView Control: Ex18

1. Select the smart tag of the GridView control and select the Edit Columns menu. The Fields dialog box, shown in Figure 19-36, appears. Select the Id field, and change the Visible property to False. You can arrange the columns with this dialog box, and you can change the colors and define the header text. Set the DataFormatString of the Date column to {0:D} to only show the date and not the time.

2. For editing the GridView, an update command must be defined with the data source. Select the SqlDataSource control with the name EventsDataSource, and select Configure Data Source from the smart tag. In the Configure Data Source dialog box, click the Next button until you can see the previously configured SELECT command. Click the Advanced button, and select the check box Generate INSERT, UPDATE, and DELETE Statements (see Figure 19-37). Click OK. Then click the Next and Finish buttons.

3. Select the smart tag of the GridView again. Now there's an Enable Editing item in the smart tag menu. After you've selected the check box to enable editing, a new column is added to the GridView control. You can also edit the columns with the smart tag menu to arrange the new Edit button. In addition, select the Enable Paging, Enable Sorting, and Enable Selection options.

4. Start the application and edit the existing event records. Click on a header to see it sorted.

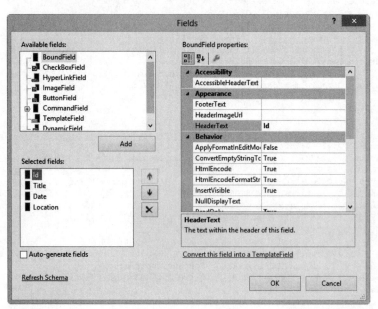

**FIGURE 19-36**

### How It Works

No line of code had to be written manually in this example; everything was handled using ASP.NET web controls. Behind the scenes, these controls make use of many features.

For example, the SqlDataSource control fills a DataSet with the help of a SqlDataAdapter with data from the database. The data used to fill the DataSet is defined with the connection string and the SELECT command. Just by changing a property of the SqlDataSource, the SqlDataReader can be

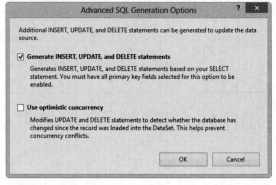

**FIGURE 19-37**

used instead of the DataSet. Also, by setting the property EnableCaching to true, the Cache object (discussed earlier in the chapter) is used automatically.

## SUMMARY

This chapter described the architecture of ASP.NET, how to work with server-side controls, and some base features of ASP.NET. ASP.NET offers several controls for which not much code is necessary, as shown with the login and data controls.

After learning about the base functionality of ASP.NET with server controls and the event handling mechanism, you learned about input validation, several methods for state management, authentication and authorization, and displaying data from the database.

The exercises that follow help you extend the web application developed in this chapter.

### EXERCISES

**19.1** Add the username to the master page you created in this chapter. You can use the LoginName control for this task. Use the LoginView to display this information only if the user is authenticated.

**19.2** Change the data source for the Registration.aspx page so that it uses the Events database for displaying the events.

**19.3** Create a new project of type ASP.NET web Application. Check all the files and folders that are created from this project template. All this should now look very familiar.

## ▶ WHAT YOU LEARNED IN THIS CHAPTER

| TOPIC | KEY CONCEPTS |
|---|---|
| **Using web server controls** | Web Server Controls are server-side controls that generate HTML code. The use of these controls is similar to using Windows controls. |
| **Using ASP.NET postbacks** | The ASP.NET postback model is a very important concept in writing ASP.NET web applications. The server-side code only comes into play on postbacks to the server. Now, with ASP.NET Ajax you can also define ASP.NET Ajax postbacks where only parts of the pages are updated. |
| **Verifying user input with validation controls** | ASP.NET offers several validation controls that can easily be used to validate user input on both the client and server sides. Validation on the client is done for performance reasons, but because the web client can never be trusted, validation must happen on the server as well. |
| **State management** | With web applications it is necessary to think about where to store state. State can be used on the client with cookies or view state; on the server with session, cache, and application objects. |
| **Master pages** | Master pages are used to separate the common parts of multiple pages into a master. |
| **Navigation** | Menu controls can be used to navigate between different pages on a website. Instead of needing to add the links to the pages directly to the menu control, a site map can be bound to the menu. |
| **Reading from and writing to a SQL server database** | Accessing a database is abstracted with the help of ASP.NET controls. The `GridView` can be easily customized from the designer. The data source of this grid can be a data source where all that needs to be done is set the properties to read and write data from a database (instead of writing C# code). |

# 20

# Deploying Web Applications

## WHAT YOU WILL LEARN IN THIS CHAPTER

➤   How to configure IIS for ASP.NET web applications

➤   How to copy Visual Studio websites

➤   How to publish web applications

In the previous chapter, you learned to develop web applications. For all these application types, different deployment options exist. You can copy the web pages, publish the website, or create an installation program. This chapter covers the advantages and disadvantages of these different options, as well as how to accomplish these tasks.

## INTERNET INFORMATION SERVICES

Internet Information Services (IIS) needn't be installed for developing web applications with Visual Studio 2012 because Visual Studio 2012 use a standalone web server: IIS Express. This is a full web server with respect to its features, but it is not suitable for real-world deployment of web applications. On a production system, a full version of IIS is needed to run the web application.

IIS is available only with Windows 8 Pro Edition or higher. On these editions, you can install IIS in the same way that you install other Windows components. From the desktop, open the Settings charm and select Control Panel, and then click Programs. Here you can find a category Programs and Features with a link called Turn Windows Features On or Off. Click this link. One of the features of Windows is Internet Information Services, which needs to be selected in order to install it. Unfold the node and browse down until you can select ASP.NET 4.5, as shown in Figure 20-1. Install these features.

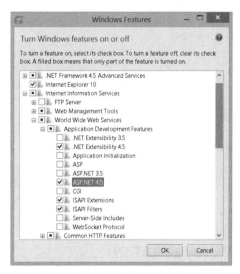

**FIGURE 20-1**

In addition to this selection, you must also install the IIS Management Console, which can be found under Web Management Tools. You can also ask your system administrator to install IIS on your system.

After installing IIS on your local computer, you can find the administration tool, called Internet Information Services (IIS) Manager, on the Start page or by searching for this name. When you first start the tool you get a dialog box asking you if you want to get the Microsoft Web Platform. If you do, click yes. This platform is beyond the scope of this book. It is used to deploy components such as IIS, SQL Server Express, and so on.

The ASP.NET runtime needs to be configured with IIS to allow it to run ASP.NET web applications. You can easily verify whether the ASP.NET runtime is configured by checking handler mappings (see Figure 20-2) with the IIS Manager tool.

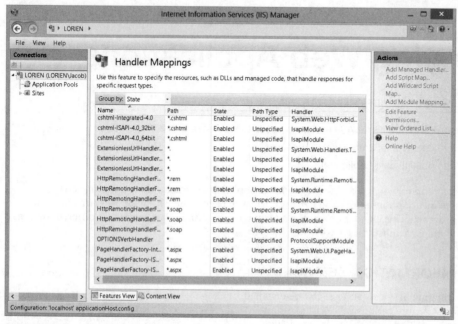

**FIGURE 20-2**

Within the Internet Information Services (IIS) Manager, double-click on Handler Mappings. Scrolling through the information, you can see that the *.aspx and *.cshtml paths are configured multiple times. You can find multiple versions of the .NET Framework and also native as well as managed configurations. The IsapiModule configuration for the .aspx extension defines the native configuration, System.Web .UI.PageHandlerFactory, which is the .NET class that handles the request.

If you see only a few handlers, you should install the ASP.NET 4.5 feature described earlier in the chapter.

The main process of IIS is inetinfo.exe. With the IsapiModule configured, a request to an ASPX file is forwarded to a worker process (w3wp.exe). Different worker processes can be configured to run different versions of the .NET runtime. You can also configure the user identity under which this process is running, and specify recycling options.

## IIS CONFIGURATION

IIS must be configured before you run a web application with it. In the following Try It Out, you create a website with the Internet Information Services (IIS) Manager. To begin, your website needs a virtual directory, which is the directory used by the client accessing the web application. For example, in `http://server/mydirectory`, `mydirectory` is a virtual directory. The virtual directory is independent of the physical directory where the files are stored on the disk. For example, the physical directory for `mydirectory` can be `D:\someotherdirectory`.

**TRY IT OUT** Creating a New Application Pool

**1.** Start the IIS Manager tool. You can find it by searching for Internet Information Services.

**2.** In the tree view, select Application Pools and right-click it. Choose Add Application Pool from the context menu.

**3.** The Add Application Pool window opens (see Figure 20-3). In the Name textbox, enter **Beginning Visual C# App Pool**, and then select the .NET Framework version v4. You will notice that the only .NET Framework options available to you are 4.x and 2.x. When you are developing on Visual Studio 2012, it is a safe bet that you will want to stick with 4.0. .NET 4.5 is directed to Metro Style apps and doesn't really affect the IIS, so you should continue to use .NET 4.0. The final option, No Managed Code, is for applications that don't require the .NET Framework. You will never want to choose this option when you have written your application in C#.

**4.** After the application pool is created, you can configure advanced settings (see Figure 20-4). The possibilities range from setting the user account that should be used to start the process, to indicating which CPU the process should prefer to run on. You rarely need to change these options, but if you do, advanced settings are available after you've selected the application pool, either from the Actions category on the right side of Internet Information Services (IIS) Manager or from the context menu.

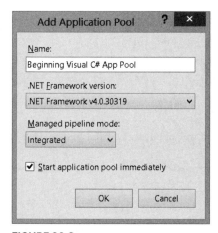

**FIGURE 20-3**

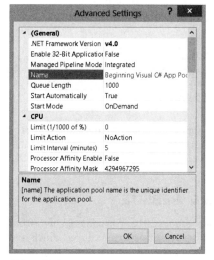

**FIGURE 20-4**

*How It Works*

Application pools make it possible for different websites to run different versions of the ASP.NET runtime, and to have different user accounts and different stability.

After you've configured an application pool, you can create a new web application, as shown in the following Try It Out.

---

**TRY IT OUT** Creating a New Web Application: NewWebSite

**1.** In the IIS Manager, expand the Sites node and select Default Web Site from the tree view.

**2.** Right-click and choose Add Application from the context menu. The Add Application window opens (see Figure 20-5).

**3.** Enter the physical path for the website and the alias name `BeginningVCSharpWebsite`. Select the application pool called Beginning Visual C# App Pool that you just created.

**4.** Click the OK button.

**FIGURE 20-5**

Now the web application is configured, and you can copy or publish web applications from Visual Studio to this website.

---

## COPYING A WEBSITE

With Visual Studio 2012, you can copy files from a source website to a remote website. The source website is the website of your web application, which has been opened with Visual Studio. It is accessed either from the local file system or from IIS, depending on how the web application was created. The remote website to which the files should be copied can be accessed using the file system, the FTP protocol, or FrontPage Server Extensions on IIS.

Copying files can happen in both directions: from the source website to the remote website and vice versa. In the next Try It Out, you use Visual Studio to copy a newly created web application to the website you configured earlier.

> **NOTE** *The Visual Studio menu to copy websites is available only from a website, not from a web project.*

**TRY IT OUT**   Copying a Website: NewWebSite

1. Start Visual Studio 2012 with elevated admin rights by right-clicking on the Start Page and selecting Run as Administrator. Copying a website to the local IIS requires administrator rights.

2. Create a new website with the command File ⇨ New Web Site and select the template ASP.NET Web Forms Site. Select the local file system as the location of this website. This creates a sample site with several pages and styles.

3. Select Website ⇨ Copy Web Site. The window shown in Figure 20-6 appears.

4. Click the Connect button at the top of the window, as shown in Figure 20-6. The Open Web Site window opens.

5. Here you can select files to copy to the local file system, local IIS, FTP sites, and remote sites (those that have FrontPage Server Extensions installed). Select Local IIS, and select the previously created website, `BeginningVCSharpWebsite` (see Figure 20-7). If you're running a Windows Home Edition, you can copy the files only to the local file system because IIS is not available.

6. In the source website list, select the files you want to copy from the source website to the remote website.

7. Click the Copy Selected Files button. This button is located in the middle between the Source view and the Remote view and has an arrow. If you move the mouse over the buttons, a tooltip appears that describes this button. The direction of the arrow shows in which direction the files are copied, from the source to the remote site or vice versa. The button with arrows pointing in both directions verifies which files are newer, and copies the newer files to the other side.

8. Now all the selected files have been copied to the new website. You can open a browser and enter the link `http://localhost/BeginningVCSharpWebsite` to get to the copied website.

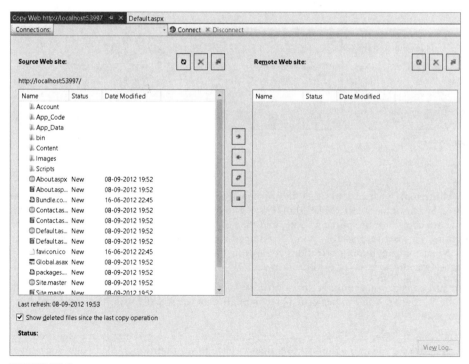

**FIGURE 20-6**

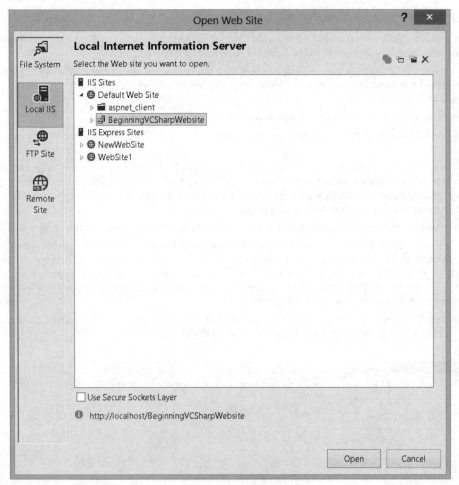

**FIGURE 20-7**

### How It Works

With the Copy Website tool, you can also select files to copy from the remote website to the source website. Selecting the button Synchronize Selected Files shows arrows pointing in both directions; the newer files from the remote website are copied to the source website, and the newer files from the source website are copied to the remote website. This is a very useful option if you have a team web server on which other developers synchronize files. Synchronizing in both directions copies your newer files to the team web server and the files from your colleagues' remote web server to your local site.

When the files are just copied, you cannot be sure if the files can be compiled. Compilation happens when the files are accessed by a browser. You can perform a precompilation of the website using the command-line utility `aspnet_compiler.exe`.

Enter the command `aspnet_compiler -v /BeginningVCSharpWebsite` to precompile the website `BeginningVCSharpWebsite`. This way, the first user doesn't have to wait until the ASPX pages are compiled because they already are.

You can find this utility in the directory of the .NET runtime.

## PUBLISHING A WEB APPLICATION

With a Visual Studio 2012 website, you also have the option to publish the web application. This is the best option if you are not self-hosting IIS and you need to publish the web application to a provider.

Publishing with Visual Studio 2012 gives you several options:

➤ Publish to a file system.

➤ Publish to a server that has the FrontPage Server Extensions installed.

➤ Use FTP.

➤ Use 1-Click publishing, a new feature in Visual Studio 2012. The 1-Click option is available only with hosting partners that support that feature, although the list of such partners is already quite long and can be easily found.

In the next Try It Out, you use the new publish feature of Visual Studio to publish a web application.

> **NOTE** *This example requires the ability to create a SQL Server Database, which is unavailable to the home and express versions of Windows 8 and Visual Studio. If you encountered this problem in Chapter 19, please select the last example from Chapter 19 that you were able to complete and ignore the steps that mention databases.*

**TRY IT OUT** Publishing a Web Application: Chapter19Code\Ex18

1. Open the web project called `EventRegistration` that you created in Chapter 19.

2. Open the Package/Publish web project settings, as shown in Figure 20-8. Check the location where the publish package will be created. Click the link called Open Settings that is next to the Include All Databases Configured in Package/Publish SQL Tab checkbox.

3. The Package/Publish SQL settings are shown (see Figure 20-9). If this is the first time you do this, you might have to click Enable this Page to continue.

4. Click the Import from Web.config button to import the database connection string. The database referenced by the connection string can be deployed as well. Verify the other settings. You can define a connection string to the destination database server where the database data and schema should be written.

5. From the Visual Studio Build menu, choose the Publish Selection menu entry. The Publish Web window shown in Figure 20-10 opens. If the web host you are using supplies a profile you can import, then that is the easiest way to go. Otherwise, you can create a new Profile by selecting New from the dropdown. Do this now and give your profile a name.

6. Next, check the settings of the publish method `Web Deploy`. This is a 1-Click publish option that is available with several hosting providers. At this point you need the information from your hosting provider. Type the service address, site/application name, and destination URLs.

7. Once you have typed the required fields, click Validate Connection. If you can connect, click Next. If not, then you must work with your hosting provider to get access.

8. The Settings page is displayed (see Figure 20-11). Here you can choose the configuration of the web application. Production sites should always use Release configuration, but for testing, Debug is fine as long as you are sure you are not publishing information that a potential hacker could use. Click Next.

9. The final page is the preview page. You can click on the Preview button to see what is going to be published. When you are satisfied you are publishing the correct files, click Publish. Visual Studio now publishes the site to an external vendor, so this can take a while.

10. Check the files that have been published.

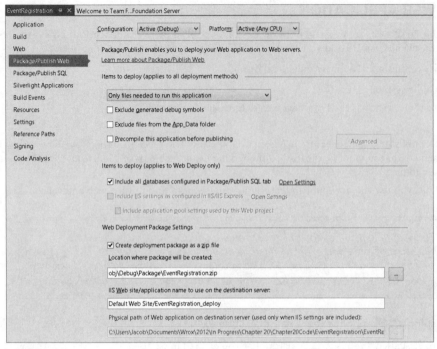

**FIGURE 20-8**

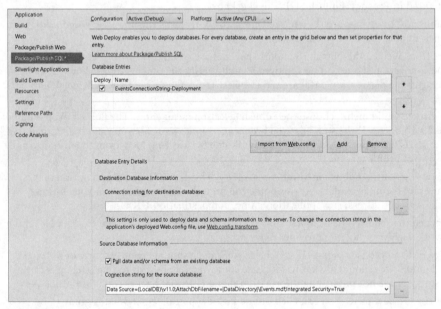

**FIGURE 20-9**

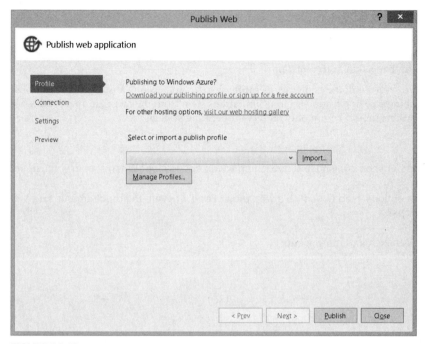

**FIGURE 20-10**

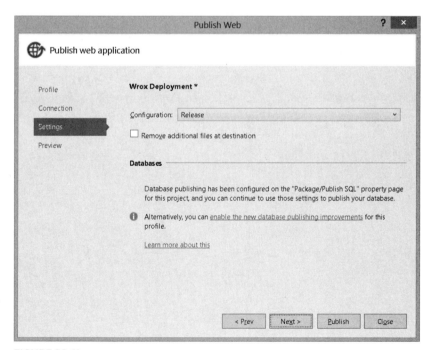

**FIGURE 20-11**

## SUMMARY

This chapter described different options for deploying web applications. The Copy Website tool enables you to copy files to web servers by using file shares, FTP, or FrontPage Server Extensions. You saw that synchronization of files can happen in both directions.

You also saw that there are some limitations on the operating systems and even in Visual Studio editions when dealing with publishing web applications. These limitations stem from the fact that, in a production environment, web applications should be run only on server operating systems.

### EXERCISES

**20.1** What is the difference between copying and publishing a web application? When should you use each?

**20.2** What are the different options used to publish a web project and what are the requirements for these publishing options?

Answers to the exercises can be found in Appendix A.

► **WHAT YOU LEARNED IN THIS CHAPTER**

| TOPIC | KEY CONCEPTS |
|---|---|
| **IIS configuration** | In order to run an ASP.NET web application in IIS, IIS must be configured. The handler mapping defines the classes that are invoked when files with specific file extensions (such as .aspx) are requested. With the application pool configuration, you define the .NET runtime version that is used. |
| **Copying a website** | A simple option to publish a web application is by using a copy. The menu to copy websites is not available with web projects, but only with Visual Studio websites. You can copy files both from the developer machine to the server and vice versa. |
| **Publishing a web application** | If you use a website hoster, a simple option to publish web applications could be a new option with Visual Studio 2012, called 1-Click publishing. Using the publishing menu, you can also publish web applications to FTP servers and to the file system. The database used by the web application can be published as well. |

# PART IV
# Data Access

# 21

# File System Data

## WHAT YOU WILL LEARN IN THIS CHAPTER

➤ What a stream is and how .NET uses stream classes to access files

➤ How to use the `File` object to manipulate the file structure

➤ How to write to and read from a file

➤ How to read and write formatted data from and to files

➤ How to read and write compressed files

➤ How to serialize and deserialize objects

➤ How to monitor files and directories for changes

### WROX.COM CODE DOWNLOADS FOR THIS CHAPTER

You can find the wrox.com code downloads for this chapter at `www.wrox.com/remtitle .cgi?isbn=9781118314418` on the Download Code tab. The code is in the Chapter 21 download and individually named according to the names throughout the chapter.

Reading and writing files are essential aspects of many .NET applications. This chapter shows you how, touching on the major classes used to create, read from, and write to files, and the supporting classes used to manipulate the file system from C# code. Although you won't examine all of the classes in detail, this chapter goes into enough depth to give you a good idea of the concepts and fundamentals.

Files can be a great way to store data between instances of your application, or they can be used to transfer data between applications. User and application configuration settings can be stored to be retrieved the next time your application is run. Delimited text files, such as comma-separated files, are used by many legacy systems, and to interoperate with such systems, you need to know how to work with delimited data. As you will see, the .NET Framework provides you with the necessary tools to use files effectively in your applications.

## STREAMS

All input and output in the .NET Framework involves the use of *streams*. A stream is an abstract representation of a *serial device*. A serial device is something that stores and/or accesses data in a linear manner, that is, one byte at a time, sequentially. This device can be a disk file, a network channel, a memory location, or any other object that supports linear reading, writing, or both. Keeping the device abstract means that the underlying destination/source of the stream can be hidden. This level of abstraction enables code reuse, and enables you to write more generic routines because you don't have to worry about the specifics of how data transfer actually occurs. Therefore, similar code can be transferred and reused when the application is reading from a file input stream, a network input stream, or any other kind of stream. Because you can ignore the physical mechanics of each device, you don't need to worry about, for example, hard disk heads or memory allocation when dealing with a file stream.

There are two types of streams:

➤ **Output**—Output streams are used when data is written to some external destination, which can be a physical disk file, a network location, a printer, or another program. Understanding stream programming opens many advanced possibilities. This chapter focuses on file system data, so you'll only be looking at writing to disk files.

➤ **Input**—Input streams are used to read data into memory or variables that your program can access. The most common form of input stream you have worked with so far is the keyboard. An input stream can come from almost any source, but this chapter focuses on reading disk files. The concepts applied to reading/writing disk files apply to most devices, so you'll gain a basic understanding of streams and learn a proven approach that can be applied to many situations.

## THE CLASSES FOR INPUT AND OUTPUT

The `System.IO` namespace contains almost all of the classes covered in this chapter. `System.IO` contains the classes for reading and writing data to and from files, and you can reference this namespace in your C# application to gain access to these classes without fully qualifying type names. Quite a few classes are contained in `System.IO`, as shown in Figure 21-1, but you will only be working with the primary classes needed for file input and output.

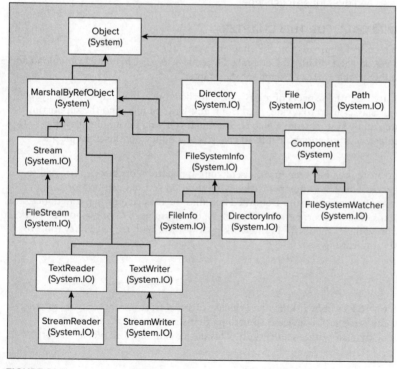

**FIGURE 21-1**

The classes covered in this chapter are described in Table 21-1.

**TABLE 21-1:** File System Access Classes

| CLASS | DESCRIPTION |
| --- | --- |
| File | A static utility class that exposes many static methods for moving, copying, and deleting files. |
| Directory | A static utility class that exposes many static methods for moving, copying, and deleting directories. |
| Path | A utility class used to manipulate path names. |
| FileInfo | Represents a physical file on disk, and has methods to manipulate this file. For any reading from and writing to the file, a Stream object must be created. |
| DirectoryInfo | Represents a physical directory on disk and has methods to manipulate this directory. |
| FileSystemInfo | Serves as the base class for both FileInfo and DirectoryInfo, making it possible to deal with files and directories at the same time using polymorphism. |
| FileStream | Represents a file that can be written to or read from, or both. This file can be written to and read from asynchronously or synchronously. |
| StreamReader | Reads character data from a stream and can be created by using a FileStream as a base. |
| StreamWriter | Writes character data to a stream and can be created by using a FileStream as a base. |
| FileSystemWatcher | The most advanced class you examine in this chapter. It is used to monitor files and directories, and it exposes events that your application can catch when changes occur in these locations. |

You'll also look at the System.IO.Compression namespace, which enables you to read from and write to compressed files. In particular, you will look at the following two stream classes:

➤ DeflateStream—Represents a stream in which data is compressed automatically when writing, or uncompressed automatically when reading. Compression is achieved using the Deflate algorithm.

➤ GZipStream—Represents a stream in which data is compressed automatically when writing, or uncompressed automatically when reading. Compression is achieved using the GZIP algorithm.

Finally, you'll explore object serialization using the System.Runtime.Serialization namespace and its child namespaces. You'll primarily be looking at the BinaryFormatter class in the System.Runtime .Serialization.Formatters.Binary namespace, which enables you to serialize objects to a stream as binary data, and deserialize them again.

## The File and Directory Classes

The File and Directory utility classes expose many static methods for manipulating, surprisingly enough, files and directories. These methods make it possible to move files, query and update attributes, and create FileStream objects. As you learned in Chapter 8, static methods can be called on classes without having to create instances of them.

Some of the most useful static methods of the File class are shown in the Table 21-2.

**TABLE 21-2:** Static Methods of the File Class

| METHOD | DESCRIPTION |
|--------|-------------|
| Copy() | Copies a file from a source location to a target location. |
| Create() | Creates a file in the specified path. |
| Delete() | Deletes a file. |
| Open() | Returns a FileStream object at the specified path. |
| Move() | Moves a specified file to a new location. You can specify a different name for the file in the new location. |

Some useful static methods of the Directory class are shown in Table 21-3.

**TABLE 21-3:** Static Methods of the Directory Class

| METHOD | DESCRIPTION |
|--------|-------------|
| CreateDirectory() | Creates a directory with the specified path. |
| Delete() | Deletes the specified directory and all the files within it. |
| GetDirectories() | Returns an array of string objects that represent the names of the directories below the specified directory. |
| EnumerateDirectories() | Like GetDirectories(), but returns an IEnumerable<string> collection of directory names. |
| GetFiles() | Returns an array of string objects that represent the names of the files in the specified directory. |
| EnumerateFiles() | Like GetFiles(), but returns an IEnumerable<string> collection of filenames. |
| GetFileSystemEntries() | Returns an array of string objects that represent the names of the files and directories in the specified directory. |
| EnumerateFileSystemEntries() | Like GetFileSystemEntries(), but returns an IEnumerable<string> collection of file and directory names. |
| Move() | Moves the specified directory to a new location. You can specify a new name for the folder in the new location. |

The three Enumerate*Xxx*() methods were introduced in .NET 4, and provide better performance than their Get*Xxx*() counterparts when a large amount of files or directories exist.

## The FileInfo Class

Unlike the File class, the FileInfo class is not static and does not have static methods. This class is useful only when instantiated. A FileInfo object represents a file on a disk or a network location, and you can create one by supplying a path to a file:

```
FileInfo aFile = new FileInfo(@"C:\Log.txt");
```

> **NOTE** *You will be working with strings representing the path of a file throughout this chapter, which means a lot of \ characters in your strings. Therefore, you should remember that you can precede a string value with @, which means that the string will be interpreted literally. Thus, \ will be interpreted as \, and not as an escape character. Without the @ prefix, you need to use \\ instead of \ to avoid having this character be interpreted as an escape character. In this chapter you'll stick to the @ prefix for your strings.*

You can also pass the name of a directory to the `FileInfo` constructor, although in practical terms that isn't particularly useful. Doing this causes the base class of `FileInfo`, which is `FileSystemInfo`, to be initialized with all the directory information, but none of the `FileInfo` methods or properties relating specifically to files will work.

Many of the methods exposed by the `FileInfo` class are similar to those of the `File` class, but because `File` is a static class, it requires a string parameter that specifies the file location for every method call. Therefore, the following calls do the same thing:

```
FileInfo aFile = new FileInfo("Data.txt");
if (aFile.Exists)
    Console.WriteLine("File Exists");

if (File.Exists("Data.txt"))
    Console.WriteLine("File Exists");
```

In this code, a check is made to see whether the file `Data.txt` exists. Note that no directory information is specified here, which means that the current *working directory* is the only location examined. This directory is the one containing the application that calls this code. You'll look at this in more detail a little later, in the section "Path Names and Relative Paths."

Most of the `FileInfo` methods mirror the `File` methods in this manner. In most cases it doesn't matter which technique you use, although the following criteria can help you to decide which is more appropriate:

➤  It makes sense to use methods on the static `File` class if you are making only a single method call—the single call will be faster because the .NET Framework won't have to go through the process of instantiating a new object and then calling the method.

➤  If your application is performing several operations on a file, then it makes more sense to instantiate a `FileInfo` object and use its methods—this saves time because the object will already be referencing the correct file on the file system, whereas the static class has to find it every time.

The `FileInfo` class also exposes properties relating to the underlying file, some of which can be manipulated to update the file. Many of these properties are inherited from `FileSystemInfo`, and thus apply to both the `FileInfo` and `DirectoryInfo` classes. The properties of `FileSystemInfo` are shown in Table 21-4.

**TABLE 21-4:** FileSystemInfo Properties

| PROPERTY | DESCRIPTION |
| --- | --- |
| Attributes | Gets or sets the attributes of the current file or directory, using the `FileAttributes` enumeration. |
| CreationTime, CreationTimeUtc | Gets or sets the creation date and time of the current file, available in coordinated universal time (UTC) and non-UTC versions. |
| Extension | Retrieves the extension of the file. This property is read-only. |
| Exists | Determines whether a file exists. This is a read-only abstract property, and is overridden in `FileInfo` and `DirectoryInfo`. |

*continues*

**TABLE 21-4** *(continued)*

| PROPERTY | DESCRIPTION |
|---|---|
| FullName | Retrieves the full path of the file. This property is read-only. |
| LastAccessTime, LastAccessTimeUtc | Gets or sets the date and time that the current file was last accessed, available in UTC and non-UTC versions. |
| LastWriteTime, LastWriteTimeUtc | Gets or sets the date and time that the current file was last written to, available in UTC and non-UTC versions. |
| Name | Retrieves the full path of the file. This is a read-only abstract property, and is overridden in FileInfo and DirectoryInfo. |

The properties specific to FileInfo are shown in Table 21-5.

**TABLE 21-5:** FileInfo Properties

| PROPERTY | DESCRIPTION |
|---|---|
| Directory | Retrieves a DirectoryInfo object representing the directory containing the current file. This property is read-only. |
| DirectoryName | Returns the path to the file's directory. This property is read-only. |
| IsReadOnly | Shortcut to the read-only attribute of the file. This property is also accessible via Attributes. |
| Length | Gets the size of the file in bytes, returned as a long value. This property is read-only. |

A FileInfo object doesn't, in itself, represent a stream. To read or write to a file, you have to create a Stream object. The FileInfo object aids you in doing this by exposing several methods that return instantiated Stream objects.

## The DirectoryInfo Class

The DirectoryInfo class works exactly like the FileInfo class. It is an instantiated object that represents a single directory on a machine. Like the FileInfo class, many of the method calls are duplicated across Directory and DirectoryInfo. The guidelines for choosing whether to use the methods of File or FileInfo also apply to DirectoryInfo methods:

➤ If you are making a single call, use the static Directory class.

➤ If you are making a series of calls, use an instantiated DirectoryInfo object.

The DirectoryInfo class inherits most of its properties from FileSystemInfo, as does FileInfo, although these properties operate on directories instead of files. There are also two DirectoryInfo-specific properties, shown in Table 21-6.

**TABLE 21-6:** Properties Unique to the DirectoryInfo Class

| PROPERTY | DESCRIPTION |
|---|---|
| Parent | Retrieves a DirectoryInfo object representing the directory containing the current directory. This property is read-only. |
| Root | Retrieves a DirectoryInfo object representing the root directory of the current volume—for example, the C:\ directory. This property is read-only. |

## Path Names and Relative Paths

When specifying a path name in .NET code, you can use absolute or relative path names. An *absolute* path name explicitly specifies a file or directory from a known location—such as the `C:` drive. An example of this is `C:\Work\LogFile.txt`—this path defines exactly where the file is, with no ambiguity.

*Relative* path names are relative to a starting location. By using relative path names, no drive or known location needs to be specified. You saw this earlier, where the current working directory was the starting point, which is the default behavior for relative path names. For example, if your application is running in the `C:\Development\FileDemo` directory and uses the relative path `LogFile.txt`, the file references would be `C:\Development\FileDemo\LogFile.txt`. To move "up" a directory, the `..` string is used. Thus, in the same application, the path `..\Log.txt` points to the file `C:\Development\Log.txt`.

As shown earlier, the working directory is initially set to the directory in which your application is running. When you are developing with VS, this means the application is several directories beneath the project folder you created. It is usually located in *ProjectName*`\bin\Debug`. To access a file in the root folder of the project, then, you have to move up *two* directories with `..\..\`. You will see this happen often throughout the chapter.

Should you need to, you can determine the working directory by using `Directory.GetCurrentDirectory()`, or you can set it to a new path by using `Directory.SetCurrentDirectory()`.

## The FileStream Object

The `FileStream` object represents a stream pointing to a file on a disk or a network path. Although the class does expose methods for reading and writing bytes from and to the files, most often you will use a `StreamReader` or `StreamWriter` to perform these functions. That's because the `FileStream` class operates on bytes and byte arrays, whereas the `Stream` classes operate on character data. Character data is easier to work with, but certain operations, such as random file access (access to data at some point in the middle of a file), can be performed only by a `FileStream` object. You'll learn more about this later in the chapter.

There are several ways to create a `FileStream` object. The constructor has many different overloads, but the simplest takes just two arguments: the filename and a `FileMode` enumeration value:

```
FileStream aFile = new FileStream(filename, FileMode.<Member>);
```

The `FileMode` enumeration has several members that specify how the file is opened or created. You'll see the possibilities shortly. Another commonly used constructer is as follows:

```
FileStream aFile = new FileStream(filename, FileMode.<Member>, FileAccess.<Member>);
```

The third parameter is a member of the `FileAccess` enumeration and is a way of specifying the purpose of the stream. The members of the `FileAccess` enumeration are shown in Table 21-7.

**TABLE 21-7:** FileAccess Enumeration Members

| MEMBER | DESCRIPTION |
| --- | --- |
| Read | Opens the file for reading only. |
| Write | Opens the file for writing only. |
| ReadWrite | Opens the file for reading or writing. |

Attempting to perform an action other than that specified by the `FileAccess` enumeration member will result in an exception being thrown. This property is often used as a way to vary user access to the file based on the user's authorization level.

In the version of the `FileStream` constructor that doesn't use a `FileAccess` enumeration parameter, the default value is used, which is `FileAccess.ReadWrite`.

The `FileMode` enumeration members are shown in Table 21-8. What actually happens when each of these values is used depends on whether the filename specified refers to an existing file. Note that the entries in this table refer to the position in the file that the stream points to when it is created, a topic you'll learn more about in the next section. Unless otherwise stated, the stream points to the beginning of a file.

**TABLE 21-8:** FileMode Enumeration Members

| MEMBER | FILE EXISTS BEHAVIOR | NO FILE EXISTS BEHAVIOR |
| --- | --- | --- |
| Append | The file is opened, with the stream positioned at the end of the file. Can be used only in conjunction with `FileAccess.Write`. | A new file is created. Can be used only in conjunction with `FileAccess.Write`. |
| Create | The file is destroyed, and a new file is created in its place. | A new file is created. |
| CreateNew | An exception is thrown. | A new file is created. |
| Open | The file is opened, with the stream positioned at the beginning of the file. | An exception is thrown. |
| OpenOrCreate | The file is opened, with the stream positioned at the beginning of the file. | A new file is created. |
| Truncate | The file is opened and erased. The stream is positioned at the beginning of the file. The original file creation date is retained. | An exception is thrown. |

Both the `File` and `FileInfo` classes expose `OpenRead()` and `OpenWrite()` methods that make it easier to create `FileStream` objects. The first opens the file for read-only access, and the second allows write-only access. These methods provide shortcuts, so you do not have to provide all the information required in the form of parameters to the `FileStream` constructor. For example, the following line of code opens the `Data.txt` file for read-only access:

```
FileStream aFile = File.OpenRead("Data.txt");
```

The following code performs the same function:

```
FileInfo aFileInfo = new FileInfo("Data.txt");
FileStream aFile = aFileInfo.OpenRead();
```

## File Position

The `FileStream` class maintains an internal file pointer that points to the location within the file where the next read or write operation will occur. In most cases, when a file is opened, it points to the beginning of the file, but this pointer can be modified. This enables an application to read or write anywhere within the file, which in turn enables random access to a file and the capability to jump directly to a specific location in the file. This can save a lot of time when dealing with very large files because you can instantly move to the location you want.

The method that implements this functionality is the `Seek()` method, which takes two parameters. The first parameter specifies how far to move the file pointer, in bytes. The second parameter specifies where to start counting from, in the form of a value from the `SeekOrigin` enumeration. The `SeekOrigin` enumeration contains three values: `Begin`, `Current`, and `End`.

For example, the following line would move the file pointer to the eighth byte in the file, starting from the very first byte in the file:

```
aFile.Seek(8, SeekOrigin.Begin);
```

The following line would move the file pointer two bytes forward, starting from the current position. If this were executed directly after the previous line, then the file pointer would now point to the tenth byte in the file:

```
aFile.Seek(2, SeekOrigin.Current);
```

When you read from or write to a file, the file pointer changes as well. After you have read 10 bytes, the file pointer will point to the byte after the tenth byte read.

You can also specify negative seek positions, which could be combined with the SeekOrigin.End enumeration value to seek near the end of the file. The following seeks to the fifth byte from the end of the file:

```
aFile.Seek(-5, SeekOrigin.End);
```

Files accessed in this manner are sometimes referred to as *random access files* because an application can access any position within the file. The StreamReader and StreamWriter classes described later access files sequentially and do not allow you to manipulate the file pointer in this way.

> **NOTE** *.NET 4 introduced a new namespace called* System.IO.MemoryMappedFiles *that includes types (such as* MemoryMappedFile*) that provide an alternative means of random access to extremely large files. This namespace is not covered in this chapter, but it's worth investigating if this is a scenario you are likely to encounter.*

## Reading Data

Reading data using the FileStream class is not as easy as using the StreamReader class, which you will look at later in this chapter. That's because the FileStream class deals exclusively with raw bytes. Working in raw bytes makes the FileStream class useful for any kind of data file, not just text files. By reading byte data, the FileStream object can be used to read files such as images or sound files. The cost of this flexibility is that you cannot use a FileStream to read data directly into a string as you can with the StreamReader class. However, several conversion classes make it fairly easy to convert byte arrays into character arrays, and vice versa.

The FileStream.Read() method is the primary means to access data from a file that a FileStream object points to. This method reads the data from a file and then writes this data into a byte array. There are three parameters, the first being a byte array passed in to accept data from the FileStream object. The second parameter is the position in the byte array to begin writing data to—this is normally zero, to begin writing data from the file at the beginning of the array. The last parameter specifies how many bytes to read from the file.

The following Try It Out demonstrates reading data from a random access file. The file you will read from is actually the class file you create for the example.

**TRY IT OUT** Reading Data from Random Access Files: ReadFile\Program.cs

1. Create a new console application called ReadFile and save it in the directory C:\BegVCSharp\Chapter21.

2. Add the following using directive to the top of the Program.cs file:

```
using System;
using System.Collections.Generic;
using System.Linq;
using System.Text;
using System.Threading.Tasks;
using System.IO;
```

**3.** Add the following code to the `Main()` method:

```
static void Main(string[] args)
{
    byte[] byteData = new byte[200];
    char[] charData = new char[200];

    try
    {
        FileStream aFile = new FileStream("../../Program.cs", FileMode.Open);
        aFile.Seek(144, SeekOrigin.Begin);
        aFile.Read(byteData, 0, 200);
    }
    catch(IOException e)
    {
        Console.WriteLine("An IO exception has been thrown!");
        Console.WriteLine(e.ToString());
        Console.ReadKey();
        return;
    }

    Decoder d = Encoding.UTF8.GetDecoder();
    d.GetChars(byteData, 0, byteData.Length, charData, 0);

    Console.WriteLine(charData);
    Console.ReadKey();
}
```

**4.** Run the application. The result is shown in Figure 21-2.

**FIGURE 21-2**

### How It Works

This application opens its own `.cs` file to read from. It does so by navigating two directories up the file structure with the `..` string in the following line:

```
FileStream aFile = new FileStream("../../Program.cs", FileMode.Open);
```

The two lines that implement the actual seeking and reading from a specific point in the file are as follows:

```
aFile.Seek(144, SeekOrigin.Begin);
aFile.Read(byteData, 0, 200);
```

The first line moves the file pointer to byte number 144 in the file. This is the n of `namespace` in the `Program.cs` file; the 144 characters preceding it are the `using` directives. The second line reads the next 200 bytes into the `byte` array `byteData`.

Note that these two lines were enclosed in `try...catch` blocks to handle any exceptions that are thrown:

```
try
{
    aFile.Seek(113, SeekOrigin.Begin);
    aFile.Read(byteData, 0, 100);
```

```
   }
   catch(IOException e)
   {
      Console.WriteLine("An IO exception has been thrown!");
      Console.WriteLine(e.ToString());
      Console.ReadKey();
      return;
   }
```

Almost all operations involving file I/O can throw an exception of type `IOException`. All production code should contain error handling, especially when dealing with the file system. The examples in this chapter all include a basic form of error handling.

Once you have the `byte` array from the file, you need to convert it into a character array so that you can display it to the console. To do this, use the `Decoder` class from the `System.Text` namespace. This class is designed to convert raw bytes into more useful items, such as characters:

```
Decoder d = Encoding.UTF8.GetDecoder();
d.GetChars(byteData, 0, byteData.Length, charData, 0);
```

These lines create a `Decoder` object based on the UTF-8 encoding schema, which is the Unicode encoding schema. Then the `GetChars()` method is called, which takes an array of bytes and converts it to an array of characters. After that has been done, the character array can be written to the console.

## Writing Data

The process for writing data to a random access file is very similar; a byte array must be created. The easiest way to do this is to first build the character array you want to write to the file. Next, use the `Encoder` object to convert it to a byte array, very much as you used the `Decoder` object. Last, call the `Write()` method to send the array to the file.

Here's a simple example to demonstrate how this is done.

**TRY IT OUT** Writing Data to Random Access Files: WriteFile\Program.cs

**1.** Create a new console application called WriteFile and save it in the directory `C:\BegVCSharp\Chapter21`.

**2.** Add the following `using` directive to the top of the `Program.cs` file:

```
using System;
using System.Collections.Generic;
using System.Linq;
using System.Text;
using System.Threading.Tasks;
using System.IO;
```

**3.** Add the following code to the `Main()` method:

```
static void Main(string[] args)
{
   byte[] byteData;
   char[] charData;

   try
   {
      FileStream aFile = new FileStream("Temp.txt", FileMode.Create);
      charData = "My pink half of the drainpipe.".ToCharArray();
      byteData = new byte[charData.Length];
      Encoder e = Encoding.UTF8.GetEncoder();
      e.GetBytes(charData, 0, charData.Length, byteData, 0, true);

      // Move file pointer to beginning of file.
```

```
                aFile.Seek(0, SeekOrigin.Begin);
                aFile.Write(byteData, 0, byteData.Length);
            }
            catch (IOException ex)
            {
                Console.WriteLine("An IO exception has been thrown!");
                Console.WriteLine(ex.ToString());
                Console.ReadKey();
                return;
            }
        }
```

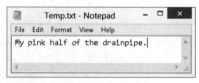

4. Run the application. It should run briefly and then close.

5. Navigate to the application directory—the file will have been saved there because you used a relative path. This is located in the `WriteFile\bin\Debug` folder. Open the `Temp.txt` file. You should see text in the file, as shown in Figure 21-3.

**FIGURE 21-3**

*How It Works*

This application opens a file in its own directory and writes a simple string to it. In structure, this example is very similar to the previous example, except you use `Write()` instead of `Read()`, and `Encoder` instead of `Decoder`.

The following line creates a character array by using the `ToCharArray()` method of the `String` class. Because everything in C# is an object, the text `"My pink half of the drainpipe."` is actually a `string` object (albeit a slightly odd one), so these static methods can be called even on a string of characters:

```
CharData = "My pink half of the drainpipe.".ToCharArray();
```

The following lines show how to convert the character array to the correct byte array needed by the `FileStream` object:

```
Encoder e = Encoding.UTF8.GetEncoder();
e.GetBytes(charData, 0, charData.Length, byteData, 0, true);
```

This time, an `Encoder` object is created based on the UTF-8 encoding. You used Unicode for the decoding as well, and this time you need to encode the character data into the correct byte format before you can write to the stream. The `GetBytes()` method is where the magic happens. It converts the character array to the byte array. It accepts a character array as the first parameter (`charData` in this example), and the index to start in that array as the second parameter (`0` for the start of the array). The third parameter is the number of characters to convert (`charData.Length`—the number of elements in the `charData` array). The fourth parameter is the byte array to place the data into (`byteData`), and the fifth parameter is the index to start writing from in the byte array (`0` for the start of the `byteData` array).

The sixth, and final, parameter determines whether the `Encoder` object should flush its state after completion. This reflects the fact that the `Encoder` object retains an in-memory record of where it was in the byte array. This aids in subsequent calls to the `Encoder` object but is meaningless when only a single call is made. The final call to the `Encoder` must set this parameter to `true` to clear its memory and free the object for garbage collection.

After that, it is a simple matter of writing the byte array to the `FileStream` by using the `Write()` method:

```
aFile.Seek(0, SeekOrigin.Begin);
aFile.Write(byteData, 0, byteData.Length);
```

Like the `Read()` method, the `Write()` method has three parameters: a byte array containing the data to write to the file stream, the index in the array to start writing from, and the number of bytes to write.

## The StreamWriter Object

Working with arrays of bytes is not most people's idea of fun—having worked with the `FileStream` object, you might be wondering whether there is an easier way. Fear not, for once you have a `FileStream` object, you will usually create a `StreamWriter` or `StreamReader` and use its methods to manipulate the file. If you don't need the capability to change the file pointer to any arbitrary position, these classes make working with files much easier.

The `StreamWriter` class enables you to write characters and strings to a file, with the class handling the underlying conversions and writing to the `FileStream` object for you.

There are many ways to create a `StreamWriter` object. If you already have a `FileStream` object, then you can use it to create a `StreamWriter`:

```
FileStream aFile = new FileStream("Log.txt", FileMode.CreateNew);
StreamWriter sw = new StreamWriter(aFile);
```

A `StreamWriter` object can also be created directly from a file:

```
StreamWriter sw = new StreamWriter("Log.txt", true);
```

This constructor takes the filename and a Boolean value that specifies whether to append to the file or create a new one:

➤ If this is set to `false`, then a new file is created or the existing file is truncated and then opened.

➤ If it is set to `true`, then the file is opened and the data is retained. If there is no file, then a new one is created.

Unlike creating a `FileStream` object, creating a `StreamWriter` does not provide you with a similar range of options—other than the Boolean value to append or create a new file, you have no option for specifying the `FileMode` property as you did with the `FileStream` class. Nor do you have an option to set the `FileAccess` property, so you will always have read/write privileges to the file. To use any of the advanced parameters, you must first specify them in the `FileStream` constructor and then create a `StreamWriter` from the `FileStream` object, as you do in the following Try It Out.

**TRY IT OUT**   Writing Data to an Output Stream: StreamWrite\Program.cs

**1.** Create a new console application called StreamWrite and save it in the directory `C:\BegVCSharp\Chapter21`.

**2.** You will be using the `System.IO` namespace again, so add the following `using` directive near the top of the `Program.cs` file:

```
using System;
using System.Collections.Generic;
using System.Linq;
using System.Text;
using System.Threading.Tasks;
using System.IO;
```

**3.** Add the following code to the `Main()` method:

```
static void Main(string[] args)
{
    try
    {
        FileStream aFile = new FileStream("Log.txt", FileMode.OpenOrCreate);
        StreamWriter sw = new StreamWriter(aFile);

        bool truth = true;
        // Write data to file.
        sw.WriteLine("Hello to you.");
        sw.WriteLine("It is now {0} and things are looking good.",
```

```
                     DateTime.Now.ToLongDateString());
          sw.Write("More than that,");
          sw.Write(" it's {0} that C# is fun.", truth);
          sw.Close();
      }
      catch(IOException e)
      {
          Console.WriteLine("An IO exception has been thrown!");
          Console.WriteLine(e.ToString());
          Console.ReadLine();
          return;
      }
  }
```

**4.** Build and run the project. If no errors are found, it should quickly run and close. Because you are not displaying anything on the console, it is not a very exciting program to watch.

**5.** Go to the application directory and find the `Log.txt` file. It is located in the `StreamWrite\bin\Debug` folder because you used a relative path.

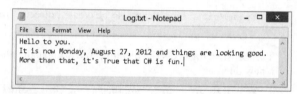

**6.** Open the file. You should see the text shown in Figure 21-4.

### How It Works

**FIGURE 21-4**

This simple application demonstrates the two most important methods of the `StreamWriter` class, `Write()` and `WriteLine()`. Both of them have many overloaded versions for performing more advanced file output, but you used basic string output in this example.

The `WriteLine()` method writes the string passed to it, followed immediately by a newline character. You can see in the example that this causes the next write operation to begin on a new line.

Just as you can write formatted data to the console, you can also write formatted data to files. For example, you can write out the value of variables to the file using standard format parameters:

```
sw.WriteLine("It is now {0} and things are looking good.",
              DateTime.Now.ToLongDateString());
```

`DateTime.Now` holds the current date; the `ToLongDateString()` method is used to convert this date into an easy-to-read form.

The `Write()` method simply writes the string passed to it to the file, without a newline character appended, enabling you to write a complete sentence or paragraph using more than one `Write()` statement:

```
sw.Write("More than that,");
sw.Write(" it's {0} that C# is fun.", truth);
```

Again, you use format parameters, this time with `Write()` to display the Boolean value `truth`—you set this variable to `true` earlier, and its value is automatically converted into the string `"True"` for the formatting.

You can use `Write()` and format parameters to write comma-separated files:

```
[StreamWriter object].Write("{0},{1},{2}", 100, "A nice product", 10.50);
```

In a more sophisticated example, this data could come from a database or other data source.

## The StreamReader Object

Input streams are used to read data from an external source. Often, this will be a file on a disk or network location, but remember that this source could be almost anything that can send data, such as a network application or even the console.

The `StreamReader` class is the one that you will be using to read data from files. Like the `StreamWriter` class, this is a generic class that can be used with any stream. In the next Try It Out, you again construct it around a `FileStream` object so that it points to the correct file.

`StreamReader` objects are created in much the same way as `StreamWriter` objects. The most common way to create one is to use a previously created `FileStream` object:

```
FileStream aFile = new FileStream("Log.txt", FileMode.Open);
StreamReader sr = new StreamReader(aFile);
```

Like `StreamWriter`, the `StreamReader` class can be created directly from a string containing the path to a particular file:

```
StreamReader sr = new StreamReader("Log.txt");
```

---

**TRY IT OUT** Reading Data from an Input Stream: StreamRead\Program.cs

**1.** Create a new console application called StreamRead and save it in the directory `C:\BegVCSharp\Chapter21`.

**2.** Import the `System.IO` namespace by placing the following line of code near the top of `Program.cs`:

```
using System;
using System.Collections.Generic;
using System.Linq;
using System.Text;
using System.Threading.Tasks;
using System.IO;
```

**3.** Add the following code to the `Main()` method:

```
static void Main(string[] args)
{
    string line;

    try
    {
        FileStream aFile = new FileStream("Log.txt", FileMode.Open);
        StreamReader sr = new StreamReader(aFile);
        line = sr.ReadLine();
        // Read data in line by line.
        while(line != null)
        {
            Console.WriteLine(line);
            line = sr.ReadLine();
        }
        sr.Close();
    }
    catch(IOException e)
    {
        Console.WriteLine("An IO exception has been thrown!");
        Console.WriteLine(e.ToString());
        return;
    }
    Console.ReadKey();
}
```

**4.** Copy the `Log.txt` file, created in the previous example, into the `StreamRead\bin\Debug` directory. If you don't have a file named `Log.txt`, the `FileStream` constructor will throw an exception when it doesn't find it.

**5.** Run the application. You should see the text of the file written to the console, as shown in Figure 21-5.

**FIGURE 21-5**

### How It Works

This application is very similar to the previous one, with the obvious difference being that it is reading a file, rather than writing one. As before, you must import the `System.IO` namespace to be able to access the necessary classes.

You use the `ReadLine()` method to read text from the file. This method reads text until a new line is found, and returns the resulting text as a string. The method returns a `null` when the end of the file has been reached, which you use to test for the end of the file. Note that you use a `while` loop, which ensures that the line read isn't null before any code in the body of the loop is executed—that way, only the genuine contents of the file are displayed:

```
line = sr.ReadLine();
while(line != null)
{
    Console.WriteLine(line);
    line = sr.ReadLine();
}
```

## Reading Data

The `ReadLine()` method is not the only way you can access data in a file. The `StreamReader` class has many methods for reading data.

The simplest of the reading methods is `Read()`. It returns the next character from the stream as a positive integer value or a `-1` if it has reached the end. This value can be converted into a character by using the `Convert` utility class. In the preceding example, the main parts of the program could be rewritten as follows:

```
StreamReader sr = new StreamReader(aFile);
int charCode;
charCode = sr.Read();
while(charCode != -1)
{
    Console.Write(Convert.ToChar(charCode));
    charCode = sr.Read();
}
sr.Close();
```

A very convenient method to use with smaller files is the `ReadToEnd()` method. It reads the entire file and returns it as a string. In this case, the earlier application could be simplified to the following:

```
StreamReader sr = new StreamReader(aFile);
line = sr.ReadToEnd();
Console.WriteLine(line);
sr.Close();
```

Although this might seem easy and convenient, be careful. By reading all the data into a string object, you are forcing the data in the file to exist in memory. Depending on the size of the data file, this can be prohibitive. If the data file is extremely large, then it is better to leave the data in the file and access it with the methods of the `StreamReader`.

Another way to deal with large files, which was introduced in .NET 4, is to use the static `File` `.ReadLines()` method. There are, in fact, several static methods of `File` that you can use to simplify reading and writing file data, but this one is particularly interesting in that it returns an `IEnumerable<string>` collection. You can iterate through the strings in this collection to read the file one line at a time. Using this method, you can rewrite the previous example as follows:

```
foreach (string alternativeLine in File.ReadLines("Log.txt"))
   Console.WriteLine(alternativeLine);
```

There are, as you can see, several ways in .NET to achieve the same result—namely, reading data from a file. Choose the technique that suits you best.

## Delimited Files

Delimited files are a common form of data storage and are used by many legacy systems. If your application must interoperate with such a system, you will often encounter the delimited data format. A particularly common form of delimiter is the comma—for example, the data in an Excel spreadsheet, an Access database, or a SQL Server database can be exported as a comma-separated value (CSV) file.

You've seen how to use the `StreamWriter` class to write such files using this approach; it is also easy to read comma-separated files. You might remember from Chapter 5 the `String` class's `Split()` method, which is used to convert a string into an array based on a supplied separator character. If you specify a comma as the separator, it creates a correctly dimensioned string array containing all of the data in the original comma-separated string.

The next Try It Out shows how useful this can be. The example uses comma-separated values, loading them into a `List<Dictionary<string, string>>` object. This example is quite generic, and you might find yourself using the technique in your own applications if you need to work with comma-separated values.

**TRY IT OUT** Working with Comma-Separated Values: CommaValues

**1.** Create a new console application called CommaValues and save it in the directory `C:\BegVCSharp\` `Chapter21`.

**2.** Place the following line of code near the top of `Program.cs`. You need to import the `System.IO` namespace for your file handling:

```
using System;
using System.Collections.Generic;
using System.Linq;
using System.Text;
using System.Threading.Tasks;
using System.IO;
```

**3.** Add the following `GetData()` method into the body of `Program.cs`, before the `Main()` method:

```
private static List<Dictionary<string, string>> GetData(
   out List<string> columns)
{
   string line;
   string[] stringArray;
   char[] charArray = new char[] {','};
   List<Dictionary<string, string>> data =
      new List<Dictionary<string, string>>();
   columns = new List<string>();

   try
   {
      FileStream aFile = new FileStream(@"..\..\SomeData.txt", FileMode.Open);
      StreamReader sr = new StreamReader(aFile);

      // Obtain the columns from the first line.
```

```
            // Split row of data into string array
            line = sr.ReadLine();
            stringArray = line.Split(charArray);

            for (int x = 0; x <= stringArray.GetUpperBound(0); x++)
            {
                columns.Add(stringArray[x]);
            }

            line = sr.ReadLine();
            while (line != null)
            {
                // Split row of data into string array
                stringArray = line.Split(charArray);
                Dictionary<string, string> dataRow = new Dictionary<string, string>();

                for (int x = 0; x <= stringArray.GetUpperBound(0); x++)
                {
                    dataRow.Add(columns[x], stringArray[x]);
                }

                data.Add(dataRow);

                line = sr.ReadLine();
            }

            sr.Close();
            return data;
        }
        catch (IOException ex)
        {
            Console.WriteLine("An IO exception has been thrown!");
            Console.WriteLine(ex.ToString());
            Console.ReadLine();
            return data;
        }
    }
```

4. Add the following code to the Main() method:

```
static void Main(string[] args)
{
    List<string> columns;
    List<Dictionary<string, string>> myData = GetData(out columns);

    foreach (string column in columns)
    {
        Console.Write("{0,-20}", column);
    }
    Console.WriteLine();

    foreach (Dictionary<string, string> row in myData)
    {
        foreach (string column in columns)
        {
            Console.Write("{0,-20}", row[column]);
        }
        Console.WriteLine();
    }
    Console.ReadKey();
}
```

**5.** Add a new text file to the project called SomeData.txt by choosing Text File from the Project ➪ Add New Item window.

**6.** Enter the following text into this new file:

```
ProductID,Name,Price
1,Spiky Pung,1000
2,Gloop Galloop Soup,25
4,Hat Sauce,12
```

**7.** Run the application. You should see the text of the file written to the console, as shown in Figure 21-6.

**FIGURE 21-6**

*How It Works*

Like the previous example, this application reads the file line by line into a string. However, because you know this is a file containing comma-separated text values, you handle it differently. Not only that, you actually store the values you read in a data structure.

First, you need to look at some of the comma-separated data itself:

```
ProductID,Name,Price
1,Spiky Pung,1000
```

The first line holds the names of the columns of data; subsequent lines hold the data. Thus, your procedure is to obtain the column names from the first line of the file and then retrieve the data in the remaining lines.

The GetData() method is declared as static, so you can call this method without creating an instance of your class. This method returns a List<Dictionary<string, string>> object that you create and then populate with data from the comma-separated text file. It also returns a List<string> object containing the header names. The following lines initialize these objects:

```
List<Dictionary<string, string>> data = new List<Dictionary<string, string>>();
columns = new List<string>();
```

columns contains the column names from the first row of the comma-separated text file, and data holds the values on subsequent rows.

You start by creating a FileStream object and then construct a StreamReader around that, as you did in earlier examples. Then you can read the first line of the file and create an array of strings from that one string:

```
line = sr.ReadLine();
stringArray = line.Split(charArray);
```

The Split() method shown in Chapter 5 accepts a character array—in this case, consisting of just "," so that stringArray will hold the array of strings formed from splitting line at each instance of ",". Because you are currently reading from the first line of the file, and this line holds the names of the columns of data, you need to loop through each string in stringArray and add it to columns:

```
for (int x = 0; x <= stringArray.GetUpperBound(0); x++)
{
    columns.Add(stringArray[x]);
}
```

Now that you have the names of the columns for your data, you can read in the data. The code for this is essentially the same as that for the earlier StreamRead example, except for the presence of the code required to add Dictionary<string, string> objects to data:

```
line = sr.ReadLine();
while (line != null)
{
    // Split row of data into string array.
    stringArray = line.Split(charArray);
    Dictionary<string, string> dataRow = new Dictionary<string, string>();

    for (int x = 0; x <= stringArray.GetUpperBound(0); x++)
    {
        dataRow.Add(columns[x], stringArray[x]);
    }

    data.Add(dataRow);

    line = sr.ReadLine();
}
```

For each line in the file, you create a new Dictionary<string, string> object and fill it with a row of data. Each entry in this collection has a key corresponding to a column name, and a value that is the value of the column for that row. The keys are extracted from the columns object you created earlier, and the values come from the string array obtained using Split() for the line of text extracted from the data file.

Once you've read all the data in from the file, you close the StreamReader and return your data. The code in the Main() method obtains the data from the GetData() method in variables called myData and columns, and displays this information to the console. First, the name of each column is displayed:

```
foreach (string column in columns)
{
    Console.Write("{0,-20}", column);
}
Console.WriteLine();
```

The -20 part of the formatting string {0,-20} ensures that the name you display is left-aligned in a column of 20 characters—this helps to format the display.

Finally, you loop through each Dictionary<string, string> object in the myData collection and display the values in that row, once again using the formatting string to format your output:

```
foreach (Dictionary<string, string> row in myData)
{
    foreach (string column in columns)
    {
        Console.Write("{0,-20}", row[column]);
    }
    Console.WriteLine();
}
```

As you can see, it is simple to extract meaningful data from CSV files using the .NET Framework. This technique is also easy to combine with the data access techniques you will learn in later chapters, meaning that data from a CSV file can be manipulated just like any other data source (such as a database). However, no information about the data types of the data is extracted from the CSV file. Currently, you have just been treating all data as strings. For an enterprise-level business application, you need to go the extra step of adding type information to the data you extract. This could come from additional information stored in the CSV file, it could be configured manually, or it could be inferred from the strings in the file, all depending on the specific application.

Even though XML, described in the next chapter, is a superior method of storing and transporting data, CSV files are still quite common and will be for a long time. Delimited files such as comma-separated files also have the advantage of being very terse, and therefore smaller than their XML counterparts.

## Asynchronous File Access

Sometimes—for example, when you are performing a lot of file access operations in one go or are working with very large files—reading and writing file system data can be slow. If this is the case, you might want to perform other operations while you wait. This is especially important with desktop applications, where you want your application to remain responsive to users while you are doing work in the background.

To facilitate this, .NET 4.5 introduces new asynchronous ways to work with streams. This applies to the `FileStream` class, as well as to `StreamReader` and `StreamWriter`. If you have browsed through the definitions of these classes, you might have noticed some methods that end with the suffix `Async`—for example, `StreamReader` has a method called `ReadLineAsync()`, which is an asynchronous version of `ReadLine()`. These methods are designed to be used with the new task-based asynchronous programming model.

Asynchronous programming is an advanced technique that isn't covered in detail in this book. However, if asynchronous file system access is something you are interested in doing then this is the place to start. You might also want to read *Professional C# 2102 and .NET 4.5* by Christian Nagel (Wrox, 2012) for more details.

## Reading and Writing Compressed Files

Often when dealing with files, quite a lot of space is used up on the hard disk. This is particularly true for graphics and sound files. You've probably come across utilities that enable you to compress and decompress files, which are handy when you want to move them around or e-mail them. The `System.IO.Compression` namespace contains classes that enable you to compress files from your code, using either the GZIP or Deflate algorithm—both of which are publicly available and free for anyone to use.

There is a little bit more to compressing files than just compressing them, though. You've probably seen how commercial applications enable multiple files to be placed in a single compressed file, often called an *archive*. There are classes in the `System.IO.Compression` namespace that enable similar functionality. However, to keep things simple for this book you'll just look at one scenario: saving text data to a compressed file. You are unlikely to be able to access this file in an external utility, but the file will be much smaller than its uncompressed equivalent!

The two compression stream classes in the `System.IO.Compression` namespace that you'll look at here, `DeflateStream` and `GZipStream`, work very similarly. In both cases, you initialize them with an existing stream, which, in the case of files, will be a `FileStream` object. After this you can use them with `StreamReader` and `StreamWriter` just like any other stream. All you need to specify in addition to that is whether the stream will be used for compression (saving files) or decompression (loading files) so that the class knows what to do with the data that passes through it. This is best illustrated with the following example.

**TRY IT OUT**　Reading and Writing Compressed Data: Compressor\Program.cs

1. Create a new console application called Compressor and save it in the directory `C:\BegVCSharp\Chapter21`.

2. Place the following lines of code near the top of `Program.cs`. You need to import the `System.IO` namespace for your file handling and `System.IO.Compression` to use the compression classes:

```
using System;
using System.Collections.Generic;
using System.Linq;
using System.Text;
```

```
    using System.Threading.Tasks;
    using System.IO;
    using System.IO.Compression;
```

3. Add the following methods into the body of Program.cs, before the Main() method:

```
static void SaveCompressedFile(string filename, string data)
{
    FileStream fileStream =
        new FileStream(filename, FileMode.Create, FileAccess.Write);
    GZipStream compressionStream =
        new GZipStream(fileStream, CompressionMode.Compress);
    StreamWriter writer = new StreamWriter(compressionStream);
    writer.Write(data);
    writer.Close();
}

static string LoadCompressedFile(string filename)
{
    FileStream fileStream =
        new FileStream(filename, FileMode.Open, FileAccess.Read);
    GZipStream compressionStream =
        new GZipStream(fileStream, CompressionMode.Decompress);
    StreamReader reader = new StreamReader(compressionStream);
    string data = reader.ReadToEnd();
    reader.Close();
    return data;
}
```

4. Add the following code to the Main() method:

```
static void Main(string[] args)
{
    try
    {
        string filename = "compressedFile.txt";

        Console.WriteLine(
            "Enter a string to compress (will be repeated 100 times):");
        string sourceString = Console.ReadLine();
        StringBuilder sourceStringMultiplier =
            new StringBuilder(sourceString.Length * 100);
        for (int i = 0; i < 100; i++)
        {
            sourceStringMultiplier.Append(sourceString);
        }
        sourceString = sourceStringMultiplier.ToString();
        Console.WriteLine("Source data is {0} bytes long.", sourceString.Length);

        SaveCompressedFile(filename, sourceString);
        Console.WriteLine("\nData saved to {0}.", filename);

        FileInfo compressedFileData = new FileInfo(filename);
        Console.WriteLine("Compressed file is {0} bytes long.",
                          compressedFileData.Length);

        string recoveredString = LoadCompressedFile(filename);
        recoveredString = recoveredString.Substring(
            0, recoveredString.Length / 100);
        Console.WriteLine("\nRecovered data: {0}", recoveredString);

        Console.ReadKey();
    }
    catch (IOException ex)
```

```
            {
                Console.WriteLine("An IO exception has been thrown!");
                Console.WriteLine(ex.ToString());
                Console.ReadKey();
            }
        }
```

**5.** Run the application and enter a suitably long string. An example result is shown in Figure 21-7.

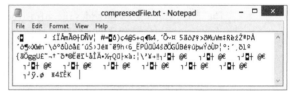

```
file:///C:/BegVCSharp/Chapter21/Compressor/Compressor/bin/Debug/Compres...  -  □  ×
Enter a string to compress (will be repeated 100 times)):
And now as Dawn rose from her couch beside Tithonus, harbinger of light alike to
 mortals and immortals, Jove sent fierce Discord with the ensign of war in her h
ands to the ships of the Achaeans.
Source data is 19400 bytes long.

Data saved to compressedFile.txt.
Compressed file is 255 bytes long.

Recovered data: And now as Dawn rose from her couch beside Tithonus, harbinger o
f light alike to mortals and immortals, Jove sent fierce Discord with the ensign
 of war in her hands to the ships of the Achaeans.
```

**FIGURE 21-7**

**6.** Open compressedFile.txt in Notepad. The text is shown in Figure 21-8.

### How It Works

In this example, you define two methods for saving and loading a compressed text file. The first of these, SaveCompressedFile(), is as follows:

```
compressedFile.txt - Notepad  -  □  ×
File  Edit  Format  View  Help
```

**FIGURE 21-8**

```
static void SaveCompressedFile(string filename, string data)
{
    FileStream fileStream =
        new FileStream(filename, FileMode.Create, FileAccess.Write);
    GZipStream compressionStream =
        new GZipStream(fileStream, CompressionMode.Compress);
    StreamWriter writer = new StreamWriter(compressionStream);
    writer.Write(data);
    writer.Close();
}
```

The code starts by creating a FileStream object, and then uses it to create a GZipStream object. Note that you could replace all occurrences of GZipStream in this code with DeflateStream—the classes work in the same way. You use the CompressionMode.Compress enumeration value to specify that data is to be compressed, and then use a StreamWriter to write data to the file.

LoadCompressedFile() mirrors the SaveCompressedFile() method. Instead of saving to a filename, it loads a compressed file into a string:

```
static string LoadCompressedFile(string filename)
{
    FileStream fileStream =
        new FileStream(filename, FileMode.Open, FileAccess.Read);
    GZipStream compressionStream =
        new GZipStream(fileStream, CompressionMode.Decompress);
    StreamReader reader = new StreamReader(compressionStream);
    string data = reader.ReadToEnd();
    reader.Close();
    return data;
}
```

The differences are as you would expect—different `FileMode`, `FileAccess`, and `CompressionMode` enumeration values to load and uncompress data, and the use of a `StreamReader` to get the uncompressed text out of the file.

The code in `Main()` is a simple test of these methods. It simply asks for a string, duplicates the string 100 times to make things interesting, compresses it to a file, and then retrieves it. In the example, the first sentence of book XI of *The Iliad* repeated 100 times is 19,400 characters long, but when compressed, it takes up only 225 bytes—that's a compression ratio of more than 80:1. Admittedly, this is a bit of a cheat—the GZIP algorithm works particularly well with repetitive data, but it does illustrate compression in action.

You also looked at the text stored in the compressed file. Obviously, it isn't easily readable, which has implications should you want to share data between applications, for example. However, because the file was compressed with a known algorithm, at least you know that it is possible for applications to uncompress it.

## SERIALIZED OBJECTS

Applications, as you have seen, often need to store data on a hard disk. So far in this chapter, you've looked at constructing text and data files piece by piece, but often that isn't the most convenient way of doing things. Sometimes it's better to store data in the form that it is used in—namely, objects.

➤ The .NET Framework provides the infrastructure to serialize objects in the `System.Runtime.Serialization` and `System.Runtime.Serialization.Formatters` namespaces, with specific classes implementing this infrastructure in namespaces below the latter. There is one important implementation available to you in the framework—`System.Runtime.Serialization.Formatters.Binary`. his namespace contains the class `BinaryFormatter`, which is capable of serializing objects into binary data, and vice versa.

> **NOTE** The `IFormatter` interface is also implemented by three other classes in the .NET Framework. The first of these, `ObjectStateFormatter`, is used in ASP.NET for viewstate serialization. The second, `NetDataContractSerializer`, is used for serializing WCF data contracts. The third, `SoapFormatter`, can be used to serialize data to SOAP format XML, but is marked as `Obsolete` in .NET 4.5. Serializing objects to XML is best achieved by means not covered in this chapter.

The `IFormatter` interface provides the methods shown in Table 21-9.

**TABLE 21-9:** IFormatter Methods

| METHOD | DESCRIPTION |
| --- | --- |
| `void Serialize(Stream stream, object source)` | Serializes source into stream |
| `object Deserialize(Stream stream)` | Deserializes the data in stream and returns the resultant object |

Importantly, and conveniently for this chapter, these methods work with streams. That makes it easy to tie these methods into the file access techniques already shown in this chapter—you can use `FileStream` objects.

Serializing using `BinaryFormatter` is as simple as this:

```
IFormatter serializer = new BinaryFormatter();
serializer.Serialize(myStream, myObject);
```

Deserializing is equally easy:

```
IFormatter serializer = new BinaryFormatter();
MyObjectType myNewObject = serializer.Deserialize(myStream) as MyObjectType;
```

Obviously, you need streams and objects to work with, but the preceding holds true for pretty much all circumstances. The following Try It Out shows how this works in practice.

**TRY IT OUT**   Serializing and Deserializing Objects: ObjectStore

**1.**   Create a new console application called ObjectStore and save it in the directory `C:\BegVCSharp\Chapter21`.

**2.**   Add a new class called `Product` to the project, and modify the code as follows:

```
namespace ObjectStore
{
    public class Product
    {
        public long Id;
        public string Name;
        public double Price;

        [NonSerialized]
        string Notes;

        public Product(long id, string name, double price, string notes)
        {
            Id = id;
            Name = name;
            Price = price;
            Notes = notes;
        }

        public override string ToString()
        {
            return string.Format("{0}: {1} (${2:F2}) {3}", Id, Name, Price,
                Notes);
        }
    }
}
```

**3.**   Place the following lines of code near the top of `Program.cs`. You need to import the `System.IO` namespace for your file handling, and the other namespaces for serialization:

```
using System;
using System.Collections.Generic;
using System.Linq;
using System.Text;
using System.Threading.Tasks;
using System.IO;
using System.Runtime.Serialization;
using System.Runtime.Serialization.Formatters.Binary;
```

**4.**   Add the following code to the `Main()` method in `Program.cs`:

```
static void Main(string[] args)
{
    try
    {
        // Create products.
        List<Product> products = new List<Product>();
        products.Add(new Product(1, "Spiky Pung", 1000.0, "Good stuff."));
        products.Add(new Product(2, "Gloop Galloop Soup", 25.0, "Tasty."));
```

```
        products.Add(new Product(4, "Hat Sauce", 12.0, "One for the kids."));

        Console.WriteLine("Products to save:");
        foreach (Product product in products)
        {
            Console.WriteLine(product);
        }
        Console.WriteLine();

        // Get serializer.
        IFormatter serializer = new BinaryFormatter();

        // Serialize products.
        FileStream saveFile =
          new FileStream("Products.bin", FileMode.Create, FileAccess.Write);
        serializer.Serialize(saveFile, products);
        saveFile.Close();

        // Deserialize products.
        FileStream loadFile =
          new FileStream("Products.bin", FileMode.Open, FileAccess.Read);
        List<Product> savedProducts =
            serializer.Deserialize(loadFile) as List<Product>;
        loadFile.Close();

        Console.WriteLine("Products loaded:");
        foreach (Product product in savedProducts)
        {
            Console.WriteLine(product);
        }
    }
    catch (SerializationException e)
    {
        Console.WriteLine("A serialization exception has been thrown!");
        Console.WriteLine(e.Message);
    }
    catch (IOException e)
    {
        Console.WriteLine("An IO exception has been thrown!");
        Console.WriteLine(e.ToString());
    }

    Console.ReadKey();
}
```

**5.** Run the application. The result is shown in Figure 21-9.

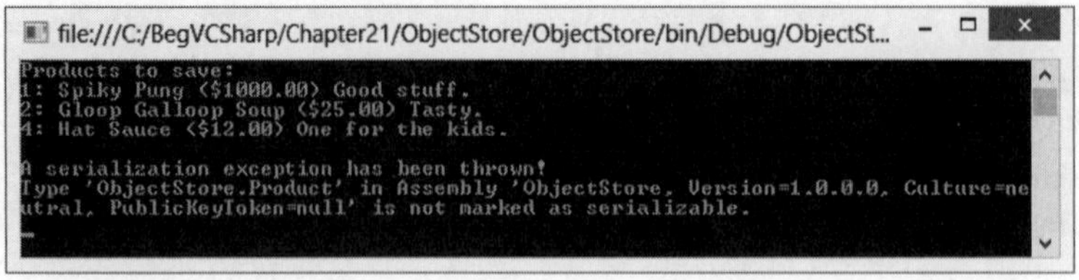

**FIGURE 21-9**

**6.** Modify the code in `Product.cs` as follows:

```
namespace ObjectStore
{
    [Serializable]
```

```
public class Product
{
    ...
}
```

**7.** Run the application again. The result is shown in Figure 21-10.

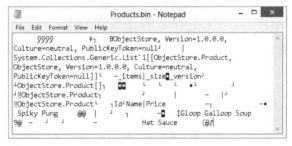

**FIGURE 21-10**

**8.** Open `Products.bin` in Notepad. The text is shown in Figure 21-11.

### How It Works

This example created a collection of `Product` objects, saved the collection to disk, and then reloaded it. The first time you ran the application, though, an exception was thrown because the `Product` object was not marked as *serializable*.

The .NET Framework forces you to mark objects as serializable to enable them to be serialized. There are several reasons for this, including the following:

**FIGURE 21-11**

➤ Some objects don't serialize very well. They might require references to local data that exists only while the objects are in memory, for example.

➤ Some objects might contain sensitive data that you wouldn't want to be saved in an insecure way or transferred to another process.

As shown in the example, marking an object as serializable is straightforward, using the `Serializable` attribute:

```
namespace ObjectStore
{
    [Serializable]
    public class Product
    {
        ...
    }
```

Note that this attribute is not inherited by derived classes. It must be applied to each and every class that you want to be able to serialize. It is also worth noting that the `List<T>` class you used to generate a collection of `Product` objects has this attribute—otherwise, applying it to `Product` wouldn't have helped to make the collection serializable.

When the `products` collection was successfully serialized and deserialized (on the second attempt), another important fact came to light. Only the `Id`, `Name`, and `Price` fields were reconstituted. This is because of another attribute being used, `NonSerialized`:

```
[NonSerialized]
string Notes;
```

Any member can be marked with this attribute and it will not be saved with other members. This can be useful if, for example, just one field or property contains sensitive data.

You also looked at the resultant saved data in the example. Some of the data here is human-readable, which might not be what you desire—or expect. The BinaryFormatter class makes no serious attempt to shield your data from prying eyes. Of course, because you are using streams, it is relatively easy to intercept the data as it is saved to disk or loaded, and apply your own obfuscating or encryption algorithms. The same applies to compression—using the techniques from the last section, you could quite easily compress object data as it is saved to disk.

There is a lot more to the subject of serialization, but you've covered enough information to get the basics. One of the more advanced techniques that you might like to investigate is custom serialization using the ISerializable interface, which enables you to customize exactly what data is serialized. This can be important, for example, when upgrading classes subsequent to release. Changing the members exposed to serialization can cause existing saved data to become unreadable, unless you provide your own logic to save and retrieve data.

## MONITORING THE FILE SYSTEM

Sometimes an application must do more than just read and write files to the file system. For example, it might be important to know when files or directories are being modified. The .NET Framework has made it easy to create custom applications that do just that.

The class that helps you to do this is the FileSystemWatcher class. It exposes several events that your application can catch. This enables your application to respond to file system events.

The basic procedure for using the FileSystemWatcher is simple. First, you must set a handful of properties, which specify where to monitor, what to monitor, and when it should raise the event that your application will handle. Then you give it the addresses of your custom event handlers, so that it can call these when significant events occur. Finally, you turn it on and wait for the events.

The properties that must be set before a FileSystemWatcher object is enabled are shown in Table 21-10.

**TABLE 21-10:** FileSystemWatcher Properties

| PROPERTY | DESCRIPTION |
| --- | --- |
| Path | Must be set to the file location or directory to monitor. |
| NotifyFilter | A combination of NotifyFilters enumeration values that specify what to watch for within the monitored files. These represent properties of the file or folders being monitored. If any of the specified properties change, then an event is raised. The possible enumeration values are Attributes, CreationTime, DirectoryName, FileName, LastAccess, LastWrite, Security, and Size. Note that these can be combined using the binary OR operator. |
| Filter | A filter specifying which files to monitor—for example, *.txt. |

Once these are set, you must write event handlers for four events: Changed, Created, Deleted, and Renamed. As shown in Chapter 13, this is simply a matter of creating your own method and assigning it to the object's event. By assigning your own event handler to these methods, your method will be called when the event is fired. Each event will fire when a file or directory matching the Path, NotifyFilter, and Filter property is modified.

Once you have set the properties and the events, set the EnableRaisingEvents property to true to begin the monitoring. In the following Try It Out, you use FileSystemWatcher in a simple client application to keep tabs on a directory of your choice.

Monitoring the File System: FileWatch

Here's a more sophisticated example using much of what you have learned in this chapter.

**1.** Create a new WPF application called FileWatch and save it in the directory C:\BegVCSharp\Chapter21.

**2.** Modify MainWindow.xaml as follows (the resultant window is shown in Figure 21-12):

```xml
<Window x:Class="FileWatch.MainWindow"
  xmlns="http://schemas.microsoft.com/winfx/2006/xaml/presentation"
  xmlns:x="http://schemas.microsoft.com/winfx/2006/xaml"
  Title="File Monitor" Height="160" Width="300">
  <Grid>
    <Grid.RowDefinitions>
      <RowDefinition Height="Auto" />
      <RowDefinition Height="Auto" />
      <RowDefinition />
    </Grid.RowDefinitions>
    <Grid Margin="4">
      <Grid.ColumnDefinitions>
        <ColumnDefinition />
        <ColumnDefinition Width="Auto" />
      </Grid.ColumnDefinitions>
      <TextBox Name="LocationBox" TextChanged="LocationBox_TextChanged" />
      <Button Name="BrowseButton" Grid.Column="1" Margin="4,0,0,0"
        Content="Browse..." Click="BrowseButton_Click" />
    </Grid>
    <Button Name="WatchButton" Content="Watch!" Margin="4" Grid.Row="1"
      Click="WatchButton_Click" IsEnabled="False" />
    <ListBox Name="WatchOutput" Margin="4" Grid.Row="2" />
  </Grid>
</Window>
```

**3.** Add the following using directives to MainWindow.xaml.cs:

```csharp
using System.IO;
using Microsoft.Win32;
```

**4.** Add a field of type FileSystemWatcher class to the MainWindow class:

```csharp
namespace FileWatch
{
    /// <summary>
    /// Interaction logic for MainWindow.xaml
    /// </summary>
    public partial class MainWindow : Window
    {
        // File System Watcher object.
        private FileSystemWatcher watcher;
```

**FIGURE 21-12**

**5.** Add the following utility method to the class to allow messages to be added to the output from a background thread:

```csharp
private void AddMessage(string formatString,
    params string[] parameters)
{
    Dispatcher.BeginInvoke(new Action(
        () => WatchOutput.Items.Insert(
            0, string.Format(formatString, parameters))));
}
```

6.  Just after the `InitializeComponent()` method call in the window constructor, add the following code. This code is needed to initialize the `FileSystemWatcher` object and associate the events to calls to `AddMessage()`:

```
public MainWindow()
{
    InitializeComponent();

    watcher = new FileSystemWatcher();
    watcher.Deleted += (s, e) =>
        AddMessage("File: {0} Deleted", e.FullPath);
    watcher.Renamed += (s, e) =>
        AddMessage("File renamed from {0} to {1}",
            e.OldName, e.FullPath);
    watcher.Changed += (s, e) =>
        AddMessage("File: {0} {1}", e.FullPath,
            e.ChangeType.ToString());
    watcher.Created += (s, e) =>
        AddMessage("File: {0} Created", e.FullPath);
}
```

7.  Add the `Click` event handler for the `Browse` button. The code in this event handler opens the Open File dialog box, enabling the user to select a file to monitor:

```
private void BrowseButton_Click(object sender, RoutedEventArgs e)
{
    OpenFileDialog dialog = new OpenFileDialog();
    if (dialog.ShowDialog(this) == true)
    {
        LocationBox.Text = dialog.FileName;
    }
}
```

The `ShowDialog()` method returns a `bool?` value reflecting how the user exited the File Open dialog box (the user could have clicked OK or pressed the Cancel button). You need to confirm that the user did not click the Cancel button, so you compare the result from the method call to `true` before saving the user's file selection to the `TextBox`.

8.  Add the `TextChanged` event handler for the `TextBox` to ensure the Watch! button is enabled when the `TextBox` contains text:

```
private void LocationBox_TextChanged(object sender, TextChangedEventArgs e)
{
    WatchButton.IsEnabled = !string.IsNullOrEmpty(LocationBox.Text);
}
```

9.  Add the following code to the `Click` event handler for the Watch! button, which starts the `FileSystemWatcher`:

```
private void WatchButton_Click(object sender, RoutedEventArgs e)
{
    watcher.Path = System.IO.Path.GetDirectoryName(LocationBox.Text);
    watcher.Filter = System.IO.Path.GetFileName(LocationBox.Text);
    watcher.NotifyFilter = NotifyFilters.LastWrite |
        NotifyFilters.FileName | NotifyFilters.Size;
    AddMessage("Watching " + LocationBox.Text);

    // Begin watching.
    watcher.EnableRaisingEvents = true;
}
```

10. Create a directory called `C:\TempWatch` and a file in this directory called `temp.txt`.

11. Run the application. If everything builds successfully, click the Browse button and select `C:\TempWatch\temp.txt`.

**12.** Click the Watch! button to begin monitoring the file. The only change you will see in your application is a message confirming that the file is being watched.

**13.** Using Windows Explorer, navigate to `C:\TempWatch`. Open `temp.txt` in Notepad, add some text to the file, and save it.

**14.** Rename the file.

**15.** You should see a description of the changes to the file you selected to watch, as shown in Figure 21-13.

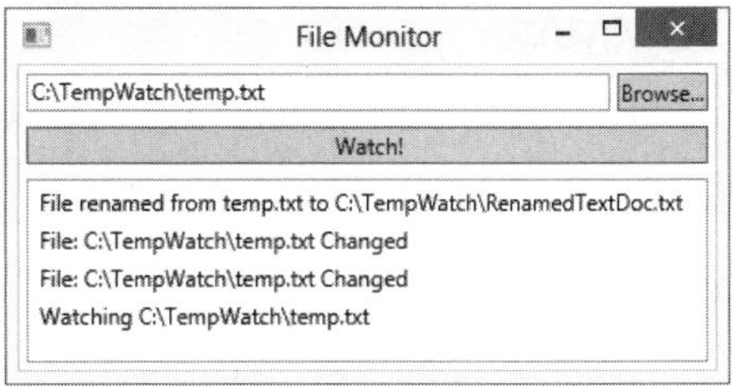

**FIGURE 21-13**

### How It Works

This application is fairly simple, but it demonstrates how the `FileSystemWatcher` works. Try playing with the string you put into the monitor text box. If you specify `*.*` in a directory, it will monitor all changes in the directory.

Most of the code in the application is related to setting up the `FileSystemWatcher` object to watch the correct location:

```
watcher.Path = System.IO.Path.GetDirectoryName(LocationBox.Text);
watcher.Filter = System.IO.Path.GetFileName(LocationBox.Text);
watcher.NotifyFilter = NotifyFilters.LastWrite |
    NotifyFilters.FileName | NotifyFilters.Size;
AddMessage("Watching " + LocationBox.Text);

// Begin watching.
watcher.EnableRaisingEvents = true;
```

The code first sets the path to the directory to monitor. It uses a new object you have not looked at yet: `System.IO.Path`. This is a static class, much like the static `File` object. It exposes many static methods to manipulate and extract information out of file location strings. You first use it to extract the directory name the user typed in the text box, using the `GetDirectoryName()` method.

The next line sets the filter for the object. This can be an actual file, in which case it would only monitor the file, or it could be something like `*.txt`, in which case it would monitor all the `.txt` files in the directory specified. Again, you use the `Path` static object to extract the information from the supplied file location.

The `NotifyFilter` is a combination of `NotifyFilters` enumeration values that specify what constitutes a change. In this example, you have indicated that if the last write time stamp, the filename, or the size of the file changes, your application should be notified of the change. After updating the UI, you set the `EnableRaisingEvents` property to `true` to begin monitoring.

Before that, however, you have to create the object and set the event handlers:

```
watcher = new FileSystemWatcher();
watcher.Deleted += (s, e) =>
    AddMessage("File: {0} Deleted", e.FullPath);
watcher.Renamed += (s, e) =>
    AddMessage("File renamed from {0} to {1}",
        e.OldName, e.FullPath);
watcher.Changed += (s, e) =>
    AddMessage("File: {0} {1}", e.FullPath,
        e.ChangeType.ToString());
watcher.Created += (s, e) =>
    AddMessage("File: {0} Created", e.FullPath);
```

This code uses lambda expressions to create anonymous event handler methods for the events raised by the watcher object when a file is deleted, renamed, changed, or created. These event handlers simply call the `AddMessage()` method with an informative message. Obviously, you could implement a more sophisticated response, depending on your application. When a file is added to a directory, you could move it somewhere else or read the contents and fire off a new process using the information. The possibilities are endless!

## SUMMARY

In this chapter, you learned about streams and why they are used in the .NET Framework to access files and other serial devices. You looked at the basic classes in the System.IO namespace, including the following:

➤ File

➤ FileInfo

➤ FileStream

You saw that the File class exposes many static methods for moving, copying, and deleting files, and FileInfo represents a physical file on disk, and has methods to manipulate this file. A FileStream object represents a file that can be written to, read from, or both. You also explored StreamReader and StreamWriter classes and saw how useful they are for writing to streams, and learned to read and write to random files using the FileStream class. Building on that knowledge, you used classes in the System.IO.Compression namespace to compress streams as you write them to disk, and learned how to serialize objects to files. Finally, you built an entire application to monitor files and directories using the FileSystemWatcher class.

In summary, you learned all of the following in this chapter:

➤ How to open a file, read from a file, and write to a file

➤ The difference between the StreamWriter and StreamReader classes and the FileStream class

➤ How to work with delimited files to populate a data structure

➤ Compressing and decompressing streams

➤ How to serialize and deserialize objects

➤ Monitoring the file system with the FileSystemWatcher class

The remaining chapters in Part 4 of this book look at forms of data that may or may not reside on a file system.

### EXERCISES

**21.1** Which namespace enables an application to work with files?

**21.2** When would you use a FileStream object to write to a file instead of using a StreamWriter object?

**21.3** Which methods of the StreamReader class enable you to read data from files and what does each one do?

**21.4** Which class would you use to compress a stream by using the Deflate algorithm?

**21.5** How would you prevent a class you have created from being serialized?

**21.6** Which events does the FileSystemWatcher class expose and what are they for?

**21.7** Modify the FileWatch application you built in this chapter by adding the capability to turn the file system monitoring on and off without exiting the application.

Answers to the exercises can be found in Appendix A.

## ▶ WHAT YOU HAVE LEARNED IN THIS CHAPTER

| TOPIC | KEY CONCEPTS |
|---|---|
| **Streams** | A stream is an abstract representation of a serial device that you can read from or write to a byte at a time. Files are an example of such a device. There are two types of streams—input and output—for reading from and writing to devices, respectively. |
| **File access classes** | There are numerous classes in the .NET Framework that abstract file system access, including `File` and `Directory` for dealing with files and directories through static methods, and `FileInfo` and `DirectoryInfo`, which can be instantiated to represent specific files and directories. The latter pair of classes is useful when you perform multiple operations on files and directories, as those classes don't require a path for every method call. Typical operations that you can perform on files and directories include interrogating and changing properties, creating, deleting, and copying. |
| **File paths** | File and directory paths can be absolute or relative. An absolute path gives a complete description of a location starting from the root of the drive that contains it; all parent directories are separated from child directories with backslashes. Relative directories are similar, but start from a defined point in the file system, such as the directory where an application is executing (the working directory). To navigate the file system, you often use the `..` parent directory alias. |
| **The `FileStream` object** | The `FileStream` object provides access to the contents of a file, for reading and writing purposes. It accesses file data at the byte level, and so is not always the best choice for accessing file data. A `FileStream` instance maintains a position byte index within a file so that you can navigate through the contents of a file. Accessing a file at any point in this way is known as *random access*. |
| **Reading and writing to streams** | An easier way to read and write file data is to use the `StreamReader` and `StreamWriter` classes in combination with a `FileStream`. These enable you to read and write character and string data rather than working with bytes. These types expose familiar methods for working with strings, including `ReadLine()` and `WriteLine()`. Because they work with string data, these classes make it easy to work with comma-delimited files, which are a common way to represent structured data. |
| **Compressed files** | You can use the `DeflateStream` and `GZipStream` compressed stream classes to read and write compressed data from and to files. These classes work with byte data much like `FileStream`, but as with `FileStream` you can access data through `StreamReader` and `StreamWriter` classes to simplify your code. |
| **Object serialization** | Often, you will want to store and retrieve data that represents the state of an object. Rather than writing your own code to save and load property values, you can instead use serialization techniques to save and load object state automatically. To do this, you must mark the object type as serializable with the `Serializable` attribute. You can also control how members are serialized with other attributes, such as `NonSerialized`, which will prevent a given member from being serialized. |
| **Monitoring the file system** | You can use the `FileSystemWatcher` class to monitor changes to file system data. You can monitor both files and directories, and provide a filter, if required, to modify only those files that have a specific file extension. `FileSystemWatcher` instances notify you of changes by raising events that you can handle in your code. |

# 22

# XML

## WHAT YOU WILL LEARN IN THIS CHAPTER

➤ How to read and write Extensible Markup Language (XML)

➤ The rules that apply to well-formed XML

➤ How to validate your XML documents against two types of schema: XSD and XDR

➤ How to use XML in your applications

➤ How to use .NET to use XML in your programs

➤ How to search through XML documents using XPath queries

## WROX.COM CODE DOWNLOADS FOR THIS CHAPTER

You can find the wrox.com code downloads for this chapter at www.wrox.com/remtitle.cgi?
isbn=9781118314418 on the Download Code tab. The code is in the Chapter 22 download and
individually named according to the names throughout the chapter.

Extensible Markup Language (XML) is a technology that has been receiving great attention for the
past few years. XML is not new, and it was certainly not invented by Microsoft for use in the .NET
environment, but Microsoft recognized the possibilities of XML early in its development. Because of
that you will see it performing a large number of duties in .NET, from describing the configuration of
your applications to transporting information between web services.

XML is a way of storing data in a simple text format, which means that it can be read by nearly any
computer. The versatility of XML has already been demonstrated in this book, where it has been used
to describe user interfaces in WPF and Windows Store applications, as well as to transfer data over
the Internet in web applications. It's even not too difficult for humans to read!

From the first versions of Visual Studio .NET, it has been obvious that Microsoft is putting quite a
lot of effort into developing solutions that use XML. Today most applications in .NET use XML in
some form, from .config files for storing configuration details to XAML files used in Windows Store
applications. Even the document formats introduced with Office 2007 are based on XML, although
the Office applications themselves are not .NET applications.

The ins and outs of XML can be very complicated, so you won't look at every single detail here.
However, the basic format is very simple, and most tasks don't require a detailed knowledge of XML

because Visual Studio typically takes care of most of the work—you will rarely have to write an XML document by hand. Having said that, XML is hugely important in the .NET world because it's used as the default format for transferring data, so it's vital to understand the basics.

During this chapter you will learn how XML documents are structured and how they can be created for use in your own programs. You'll begin by learning how to create XML documents using XML elements and attributes. Next, you will learn how XML documents are structured and how to assign and use namespaces. Before you move on to using XML in your own applications, you will learn about schemas and how to create and use them to ensure validity of documents. Finally, you will see how to use the .NET classes to read and write XML and how to manipulate XML in code.

## XML DOCUMENTS

A complete set of data in XML is known as an *XML document*. An XML document could be a physical file on your computer or just a string in memory. However, it has to be complete in itself, and it must obey certain rules (described shortly). An XML document is made up of a number of different parts. The most important of these are XML elements, which contain the actual data of the document.

## XML Elements

XML elements consist of an opening tag (the name of the element enclosed in angled brackets, such as `<myElement>`), the data within the element, and a closing tag (the same as the opening tag, but with a forward slash after the opening bracket: `</myElement>`).

For example, you might define an element to hold the title of a book like this:

```
<book>Tristram Shandy</book>
```

If you already know some HTML, you might be thinking that this looks very similar—and you'd be right. In fact, HTML and XML share much of the same syntax. The big difference is that XML doesn't have any predefined elements—you choose the names of your own elements, so there's no limit to the number of elements you can have. The most important point to remember is that XML—despite its name—isn't actually a language at all. Rather, it's a standard for defining languages (known as *XML applications*). Each language has its own distinct vocabulary—a specific set of elements that can be used in the document, and the structure these elements are allowed to take. As you'll see shortly, you can explicitly limit the elements allowed in the XML document. Alternatively, you can allow any elements, and have the program using the document determine for itself what the structure is.

Element names are case sensitive, so `<book>` and `<BOOK>` are considered different elements. This means that if you attempt to close a `<book>` element using a closing tag that doesn't have identical case (for example, `</BOOK>`), your XML document won't be legal. Programs that read XML documents and analyze them by examining their individual elements are known as *XML parsers*, and they reject any document that contains illegal XML.

Elements can also contain other elements, so you could modify the `<book>` element to include the author as well as the title by adding two sub-elements:

```
<book>
    <title>Tristram Shandy</title>
    <author>Lawrence Sterne</author>
</book>
```

Overlapping elements aren't allowed, so you must close all sub-elements before the closing tag of the parent element. This means, for example, that you can't do this:

```
<book>
    <title>Tristram Shandy
        <author>Lawrence Sterne
```

```
    </title>
            </author>
    </book>
```

This is illegal because the `<author>` element is opened within the `<title>` element, but the closing `</title>` tag comes before the closing `</author>` tag.

There's one exception to the rule that all elements must have a closing element. It's possible to have "empty" elements, with no nested data or text. In this case, you can simply add the closing tag immediately after the opening element, like this:

```
<book></book>
```

Or you can use a shorthand syntax, adding the slash of the closing element to the end of the opening element:

```
<book />
```

## Attributes

As well as storing data within the body of the element, you can also store data within attributes, which are added within the opening tag of an element. Attributes are in the form

```
name="value"
```

where the value of the attribute *must* be enclosed in either single or double quotes, as in this example:

```
<book title="Tristram Shandy"></book>
```

or

```
<book title='Tristram Shandy'></book>
```

The preceding are both legal, but the following is not:

```
<book title=Tristram Shandy></book>
```

At this point, you may be wondering why you need both ways of storing data in XML. What is the difference between the following?

```
<book>
    <title>Tristram Shandy</title>
</book>
```

and

```
<book title="Tristram Shandy"></book>
```

In fact, there isn't any earth-shattering, fundamental difference between the two. There isn't really any big advantage to using one over the other. Elements are a better choice if there's a possibility that you'll need to add more information about that piece of data later—you can always add a sub-element or an attribute to an element, but you can't do that for attributes. Arguably, elements are more readable and more elegant (but that's really a matter of personal taste). Conversely, attributes consume less bandwidth if the document is sent over a network without compression (with compression there's not much difference), and they are convenient for holding information that isn't essential to every user of the document. Probably the best advice is to use both, selecting whichever you're most comfortable with for storing a particular item of data, but there are no hard-and-fast rules.

## The XML Declaration

In addition to elements and attributes, XML documents can contain a number of constituent parts. These individual parts of an XML document are known as *nodes*. Elements, the text within elements, and attributes are all nodes of the XML document. Many of these are important only if you really want to delve deeply into XML. However, one type of node occurs in almost every XML document: the *XML declaration*. If you include it, it must occur as the first node of the document.

The XML declaration is similar in format to an element but has question marks inside the angled brackets. It always has the name xml, and it always has an attribute named version. Currently there are two possible versions of XML: 1.0 (first edition) and 1.1 (second edition), but perhaps surprisingly Visual Studio does not support the second edition. It should be said that the second edition adds very little to XML that normal use on the Windows platform would demand, and the World Wide Web Consortium (www.w3c.org) encourages you to use the first edition whenever possible. The simplest possible form of the XML declaration is therefore as follows:

```
<?xml version="1.0"?>
```

Optionally, it can also contain the attributes encoding (with a value indicating the character set that should be used to read the document, such as "UTF-16" to indicate that the document uses the 16-bit Unicode character set) and standalone (with the value "yes" or "no" to indicate whether the XML document depends on any other files). However, these attributes are not required.

## The Structure of an XML Document

One of the most important things about XML is that it offers a way of structuring data that is very different from relational databases. Most modern database systems store data in tables that are related to each other through values in individual columns. The tables store data in rows and columns—each row represents a single record, and each column a particular item of data about that record. In contrast, XML data is structured hierarchically, a little like the folders and files in Windows Explorer. Each document must have a single *root element* within which all elements and text data is contained. If there is more than one element at the top level of the document, the document is not legal XML. However, you can include other XML nodes at the top level—notably, the XML declaration. Therefore, this is a legal XML document:

```
<?xml version="1.0"?>
<books>
    <book>Tristram Shandy</book>
    <book>Moby Dick</book>
    <book>Ulysses</book>
</books>
```

The following, however, is not:

```
<?xml version="1.0"?>
<book>Tristram Shandy</book>
<book>Moby Dick</book>
<book>Ulysses</book>
```

Under the root element, you have a great deal of flexibility regarding how you structure the data. Unlike relational data, in which every row has the same number of columns, there's no restriction on the number of sub-elements an element can have. In addition, although XML documents are often structured similarly to relational data, with an element for each record, XML documents don't need any predefined structure at all. This is one of the major differences between traditional relational databases and XML. Whereas relational databases always define the structure of the information before any data can be added, information can be stored in XML without this initial overhead, which makes it a very convenient way to store small blocks of data. As you will see shortly, it is quite possible to provide a structure for your XML, but unlike the relational databases, no one will enforce this structure unless you ask for it explicitly.

## XML Namespaces

As you learned in Chapter 9, anyone can define her own C# classes, and anyone can define her own XML elements, which leads to the obvious problem—how do you know which elements belong to which vocabulary? In a word, *namespaces*. Just as you define namespaces to organize your C# types, you use XML namespaces to define your XML vocabularies. This enables you to include elements from a number of different vocabularies within a single XML document, without the risk of misinterpreting elements because, for example, two different vocabularies define a `<customer>` element. Examples of a languages using XML namespaces in practice are the XAML used in Windows Store applications, WPF, and Silverlight. All of these make extensive use of namespaces to ensure that you can include each part of the framework and even extend it yourself without fear of overwriting any existing parts of the language.

XML namespaces can be quite complex, so this section doesn't go into great detail here, but the basic syntax is simple. Specific elements or attributes are associated with a specific namespace using a prefix, followed by a colon. For example, `<wrox:book>` represents a `<book>` element that resides in the `wrox` namespace. How do you know what namespace `wrox` represents? For this approach to work, you need to be able to guarantee that every namespace is unique. The easiest way to do this is to map the prefixes to something already known to be unique, which is exactly what happens. Somewhere in your XML document you need to associate any namespace prefixes with a *Uniform Resource Identifier (URI)*. URIs come in several flavors, but the most common type is simply a web address, such as www.wrox.com.

To identify a prefix with a specific namespace, use the `xmlns:prefix` attribute within an element, setting its value to the unique URI that identifies that namespace. The prefix can then be used anywhere within that element, including any nested child elements:

```
<?xml version="1.0"?>
<books>
   <book xmlns:wrox="http://www.wrox.com">
      <wrox:title>Beginning C#</wrox:title>
      <wrox:author>Karli Watson</wrox:author>
   </book>
</books>
```

You can use the `wrox:` prefix with the `<title>` and `<author>` elements because they are within the `<book>` element, where the prefix is defined. However, if you tried to add this prefix to the `<books>` element, the XML would be illegal, as the prefix isn't defined for this element.

You can also define a default namespace for an element using the `xmlns` attribute:

```
<?xml version="1.0"?>
<books>
   <book xmlns="http://www.wrox.com">
      <title>Beginning Visual C#</title>
      <author>Karli Watson</author>
      <html:img alt="Cover Image" src="begvcsharp.gif"
               xmlns:html="http://www.w3.org/1999/xhtml" />
   </book>
</books>
```

Here, the default namespace for the `<book>` element is defined as `"http://www.wrox.com"`. Everything within this element will, therefore, belong to this namespace, unless you explicitly specify otherwise by adding a different namespace prefix, as you do for the `<img>` element (when you set it to the namespace used by XML-compatible HTML documents).

## Well-Formed and Valid XML

So far, you've been reading about *legal* XML. In fact, XML distinguishes between two forms of legality: well-formed and valid. Documents that obey all the rules required by the XML standard itself are said to be *well-formed*. If an XML document is not well-formed, parsers will be unable to interpret it correctly, and will reject the document. To be well-formed, a document must conform to the following:

➤   Have one and only one root element

➤   Have closing tags for every element (except for the shorthand syntax mentioned previously)

➤  Not have any overlapping elements—all child elements must be fully nested within the parent

➤  Have all attributes enclosed in quotes

This isn't a complete list, by any means, but it does highlight the most common pitfalls made by programmers who are new to XML. However, XML documents can obey all these rules and still not be valid. Remember that earlier it was mentioned that XML is not itself a language, but a standard for defining XML applications. Well-formed XML documents simply comply with the XML standard; to be valid, they also need to conform to any rules specified for the XML application. Not all parsers check whether documents are valid; those that do are said to be *validating parsers*. To check whether a document adheres to the rules of the application, you first need a way to specify what those rules are.

## Validating XML Documents

XML supports two ways of defining which elements and attributes can be placed in a document and in what order: *Document Type Definitions (DTDs)* and *schemas*. DTDs use a non-XML syntax inherited from the parent of XML and today they are rarely used except when some very specialized functionality is required.

### Schemas

Schemas, unlike DTD, are used frequently—they allow you to specify data types, and they are written in an XML-compatible syntax. Unfortunately, they are very complex and you actually need to be very familiar with XML before you attempt to write a schema, but it is useful to be able to recognize a schema's main elements, so the basic principles are explained here.

To aid in your understanding, you'll look at a sample XSD schema for this simple XML document, which contains basic details about a couple of Wrox's C# books (you can find this XML in `Chapter22Code\XML and Schemas\Books.xml`):

```
<?xml version="1.0"?>
<books>
   <book>
      <title>Beginning Visual C# 2012</title>
      <author>Karli Watson</author>
      <code>7582</code>
   </book>
   <book>
      <title>Professional C# 2012</title>
      <author>Simon Robinson</author>
      <code>7043</code>
   </book>
</books>
```

### XSD Schemas

Elements in XSD schemas must belong to the namespace `http://www.w3.org/2001/XMLSchema`. If this namespace isn't included, the schema elements won't be recognized.

To associate the XML document with an XSD schema in another file, you need to add a `schemalocation` element to the root element:

```
<?xml version="1.0"?>
<books schemalocation=
   "file:// C:\BegVCSharp\Chapter22Code\XML and Schema\C:\BeginVCSharp\Chapter 22\books.xsd">
   .
</books>
```

Take a quick look at an example XSD schema:

```
<schema xmlns="http://www.w3.org/2001/XMLSchema">
    <element name="books">
        <complexType>
            <choice maxOccurs="unbounded">
                <element name="book">
                    <complexType>
                        <sequence>
                            <element name="title" />
                            <element name="author" />
                            <element name="code" />
                        </sequence>
                    </complexType>
                </element>
            </choice>
            <attribute name="schemalocation" />
        </complexType>
    </element>
</schema>
```

The first thing to notice here is that the default namespace is set to the XSD namespace. This tells the parser that all the elements in the document belong to the schema. If you don't specify this namespace, the parser will assume that the elements are just normal XML elements and won't realize that it needs to use them for validation.

The entire schema is contained within an element called <schema> (with a lowercase "s"—remember that case is important!). Each element that can occur within the document must be represented by an <element> tag. This element has a name attribute that indicates the name of the element. If the element is to contain nested child elements, you must include the <element> tags for these within a <complexType> element. Inside this, you specify how the child elements must occur.

For example, you use a <choice> element to specify that any selection of the child elements can occur, or <sequence> to specify that the child elements must appear in the same order as they are listed in the schema. If an element can appear more than once (as the <book> element does), you need to include a maxOccurs attribute within its parent element. Setting this to "unbounded" means that the element can occur unlimited times. Finally, any attributes must be represented by <attribute> elements, including your schemalocation attribute, which tells the parser where to find the schema. Place this after the end of the list of child elements.

Now that you've read the basic theory behind XML, in the following Try It Out you can have a go at creating XML documents. Fortunately, VS does a lot of the hard work for you. It even creates an XSD schema based on your XML document without you having to write a single line of code!

### The XSD dialog box shown in the XmlDocument Class

Usually, the first thing your application will want to do with XML is read it from disk. As described in Table 22-1, this is the domain of the XmlDocument class. You can think of the XmlDocument as an in-memory representation of the file on disk. Once you have used the XmlDocument class to load a file into memory, you can obtain the root node of the document from it and start reading and manipulating the XML:

```
using System.Xml;
.
.
.
XmlDocument document = new XmlDocument();
document.Load(@"C:\BeginVCSharp\Chapter22Code\XML and Schema\books.xml");
```

The two lines of code create a new instance of the XmlDocument class and load the file books.xml into it. Remember that the XmlDocument class is located in the System.Xml namespace, and you should insert a using System.Xml; in the using section at the beginning of the code.

Figure 22-1 includes a long list of schemas recognized by VS, but it will not automatically remember schemas you've used. If you are using a schema repeatedly and don't want to browse for it every time you need it, you can copy it to the following location: C:\Program Files\Microsoft Visual Studio 11.0\ Xml\Schemas. Any schema copied to that location will show up on the Schemas dialog box.

> **TRY IT OUT**     Creating an XML Document in Visual Studio: Chapter22Code\XML and Schema\GhostStories.xml

Follow these steps to create an XML document:

1. Open VS and select File ➪ New ➪ File from the menu. If you don't see this option, create a new project, right-click the project in the Solution Explorer, and choose to add a new item. Then select XML File from the dialog box.

2. In the New File dialog box, select XML File and click Open. VS creates a new XML document for you. As Figure 22-2 shows, VS adds the XML declaration, complete with an encoding attribute (it also colors the attributes and elements, but this won't show up very well in black-and-white print).

3. Save the file by pressing Ctrl+S or by selecting File ➪ Save XMLFile1.xml from the menu. VS asks you where to save the file and what to call the file; save it in the BeginVCSharp\Chapter22 folder as GhostStories.xml.

4. Move the cursor to the line underneath the XML declaration, and type the text **<stories>**. Notice how VS automatically puts the end tag in as soon as you type the greater than sign to close the opening tag.

5. Type this XML file and then click Save:

```
<stories>
    <story>
        <title>A House in Aungier Street</title>
        <author>
            <name>Sheridan Le Fanu</name>
            <nationality>Irish</nationality>
        </author>
        <rating>eerie</rating>
    </story>
    <story>
        <title>The Signalman</title>
        <author>
            <name>Charles Dickens</name>
            <nationality>English</nationality>
        </author>
        <rating>atmospheric</rating>
    </story>
    <story>
        <title>The Turn of the Screw</title>
        <author>
            <name>Henry James</name>
            <nationality>American</nationality>
        </author>
        <rating>a bit dull</rating>
    </story>
</stories>
```

6. It is now possible to let Visual Studio create a schema that fits the XML you have written. Do this by selecting the Create Schema menu option from the XML menu. Save the resulting XSD file by clicking Save as GhostStories.xsd.

**7.** Return to the XML file and type the following XML before the ending `</stories>` tag:

```
<story>
    <title>Number 13</title>
    <author>          <name>M.R. James</name>
        <nationality>English</nationality>
    </author>
    <rating>mysterious</rating>
</story>
```

You are now getting IntelliSense hints when you begin typing the starting tags. That's because Visual Studio knows to connect the newly created XSD schema to the XML file you are typing.

**8.** It is possible to create this link between XML and one or more schemas in Visual Studio. Select XML ➪ Schemas. That brings up the dialog box shown in Figure 22-2. At the top of the long list of schemas that Visual Studio recognizes, you will see `GhostStories.xsd`. To the left of it is a checkmark, which indicates that this schema is being used on the current XML document.

**FIGURE 22-1**

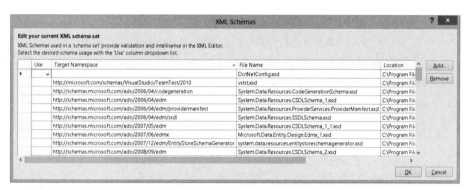

**FIGURE 22-2**

## USING XML IN YOUR APPLICATION

Now that you know how to create XML documents, it is time to put this knowledge to use. The .NET Framework includes a number of namespaces and classes that make it quite simple to read, manipulate, and write XML. The following pages cover a number of these classes and examine how you can use them to create and manipulate XML programmatically.

## XML Document Object Model

The XML Document Object Model (XML DOM) is a set of classes used to access and manipulate XML in a very intuitive way. The DOM is perhaps not the quickest way to read XML data, but as soon as you understand the relationship between the classes and the elements of an XML document, you will find it very easy to use.

The classes that make up the DOM can be found in the namespace `System.Xml`. There are several classes and namespaces in this namespace, but this chapter focuses on only a few of the classes that enable you to easily manipulate XML. These classes are described in Table 22-1.

**TABLE 22-1:** Common DOM Classes

| CLASS | DESCRIPTION |
|---|---|
| XmlNode | Represents a single node in a document tree. It is the base of many of the classes shown in this chapter. If this node represents the root of an XML document, you can navigate to any position in the document from it. |
| XmlDocument | Extends the XmlNode class, but is often the first object you use when using XML. That's because this class is used to load and save data from disk or elsewhere. |
| XmlElement | Represents a single element in the XML document. XmlElement is derived from XmlLinkedNode, which in turn is derived from XmlNode. |
| XmlAttribute | Represents a single attribute. Like the XmlDocument class, it is derived from the XmlNode class. |
| XmlText | Represents the text between a starting tag and a closing tag. |
| XmlComment | Represents a special kind of node that is not regarded as part of the document other than to provide information to the reader about parts of the document. |
| XmlNodeList | Represents a collection of nodes. |

## The XmlDocument Class

Usually, the first thing your application will want to do with XML is read it from disk. As described in Table 22-1, this is the domain of the XmlDocument class. You can think of the XmlDocument as an in-memory representation of the file on disk. Once you have used the XmlDocument class to load a file into memory, you can obtain the root node of the document from it and start reading and manipulating the XML:

```
using System.Xml;
    .
    .
    .
XmlDocument document = new XmlDocument();
document.Load(@"C:\BeginVCSharp\Chapter22Code\XML and Schema\books.xml");
```

The two lines of code create a new instance of the XmlDocument class and load the file books.xml into it. Remember that the XmlDocument class is located in the System.Xml namespace, and you should insert a using System.Xml; in the using section at the beginning of the code.

In addition to loading and saving the XML, the XmlDocument class is also responsible for maintaining the XML structure itself. Therefore, you will find numerous methods on this class that are used to create, alter, and delete nodes in the tree. You will look at some of those methods shortly, but to present the methods properly, you need to know a bit more about another class: XmlElement.

## The XmlElement Class

Now that the document has been loaded into memory, you want to do something with it. The Document Element property of the XmlDocument instance you created in the preceding code returns an instance of an XmlElement that represents the root element of the XmlDocument. This element is important because it gives you access to every bit of information in the document:

```
XmlDocument document = new XmlDocument();
document.Load(@"C:\BeginVCSharp\Chapter22Code\
XML and Schema\books.xml");
XmlElement element = document.DocumentElement;
```

After you have the root element of the document, you are ready to use the information. The XmlElement class contains methods and properties for manipulating the nodes and attributes of the tree. Let's examine the properties for navigating the XML elements first, shown in Table 22-2.

**TABLE 22-2:** XmlElement Properties

| PROPERTY | DESCRIPTION |
|---|---|
| FirstChild | Returns the first child element after this one. If you recall the books.xml file from earlier in the chapter, the root node of the document was called "books" and the next node after that was "book." In that document, then, the first child of the root node "books" is "book."<br><br>      `<books>`      Root node<br>         `<book>`     FirstChild<br><br>FirstChild returns an XmlNode object, and you should test for the type of the returned node because it is unlikely to always be an XmlElement instance. In the books example, the child of the Title element is, in fact, an XmlText node that represents the text Beginning Visual C#. |
| LastChild | Operates exactly like the FirstChild property except that it returns the last child of the current node. In the case of the books example, the last child of the "books" node will still be a "book" node, but it will be the node representing the "Professional C# 2012" book.<br><br>    `<books>` Root node<br>      `<book>` FirstChild<br>        `<title>`Beginning Visual C# 2012`</title>`<br>        `<author>`Karli Watson`</author>`<br>        `<code>`7582`</code>`<br>      `</book>`<br>      `<book>` LastChild<br>        `<title>`Professional C# 2012`</title>`<br>        `<author>`Simon Robinson`</author>`<br>        `<code>`7043`</code>`<br>      `</book>`<br>    `</books>` |
| ParentNode | Returns the parent of the current node. In the books example, the "books" node is the parent of both of the "book" nodes. |
| NextSibling | Where FirstChild and LastChild properties return the leaf node of the current node, the NextSibling node returns the next node that has the same parent node. In the case of the books example, that means getting the NextSibling of the title element will return the author element, and calling NextSibling on that will return the code element. |
| HasChildNodes | Enables you to check whether the current element has child elements without actually getting the value from FirstChild and examining that against null. |

Using the five properties from Table 22-2, it is possible to run through an entire XmlDocument, as shown in the following Try It Out.

**TRY IT OUT**    **Looping through All Nodes in an XML Document: Chapter22Code\LoopThroughXml Document\MainWindows.xaml.cs**

In this example, you are going to create a small WPF application that loops through all the nodes of an XML document and prints out the name of the element or the text contained in the element in the case of an XmlText element. This code uses Books.xml, which you saw in the "Schemas" section earlier; if you didn't create that file as you worked through that section, you can find it in Chapter22Code\XML and Schemas\ in this chapter's downloadable code.

1.  Begin by creating a new WPF project by selecting File ➪ New ➪ Project. In the dialog box that appears, select Windows ➪ WPF Application. Name the project **LoopThroughXmlDocument** and press Enter.

**2.** Design the form as shown in Figure 22-3 by dragging a TextBlock control and a Button control onto the form.

**3.** Name the TextBlock control textBlockResults and name the button buttonLoop. Allow the TextBlock to fill all the space not used by the button.

**4.** Add the event handler for the Click event for the button and enter the code that follows. Don't forget to add using System.Xml; to the using section at the top of the file:

```
private void buttonLoop_Click(object sender, RoutedEventArgs e)
{
    XmlDocument document = new XmlDocument();
    document.LoadbooksFile);
    textBlockResults.Text = FormatText(document.DocumentElement as XmlNode, "", "");
}

private string FormatText(XmlNode node, string text, string indent)
{
    if (node is XmlText)
    {
        text += node.Value;
        return text;
    }

    if (string.IsNullOrEmpty(indent))
        indent = "";
    else
    {
        text += "\r\n" + indent;
    }

    if (node is XmlComment)
    {
        text += node.OuterXml;
        return text;
    }

    text += "<" + node.Name;
    if (node.Attributes.Count > 0)
    {
        AddAttributes(node, ref text);
    }
    if (node.HasChildNodes)
    {
        text += ">";
        foreach (XmlNode child in node.ChildNodes)
        {
            text = FormatText(child, text, indent + "  ");
        }
        if (node.ChildNodes.Count == 1 &&
            (node.FirstChild is XmlText || node.FirstChild is XmlComment))
            text += "</" + node.Name + ">";
        else
            text += "\r\n" + indent + "</" + node.Name + ">";
    }
    else
        text += " />";
    return text;
}

private void AddAttributes(XmlNode node, ref string text)
{
    foreach (XmlAttribute xa in node.Attributes)
```

```
    {
      text += " " + xa.Name + "='" + xa.Value + "'";
    }
  }
```

5. Add the private const that holds the location of the file that is loaded. You can change the location to reflect the location you put the file on your local system:

```
private const string booksFile =
@"C:\BeginVCSharp\Chapter22Code\XML and Schema\Books.xml";
```

6. Run the application and click Loop. You should get a result like the one shown in Figure 22-4.

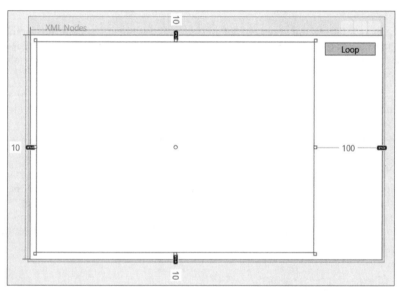

**FIGURE 22-3**

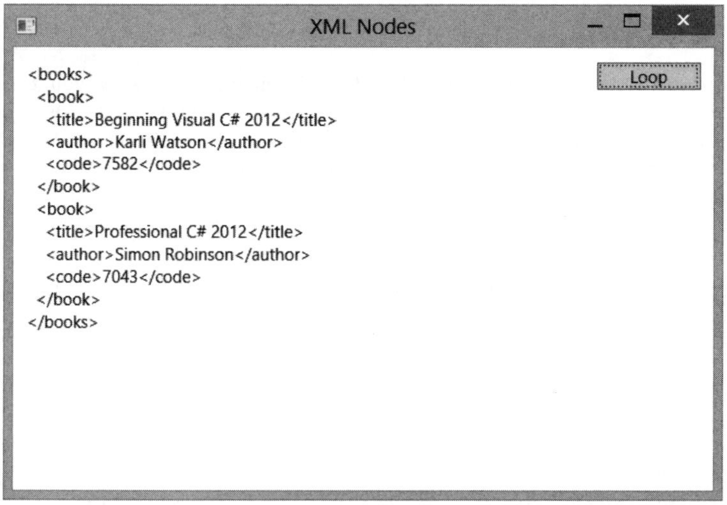

**FIGURE 22-4**

*How It Works*

When you click the button, the XmlDocument method Load is called. This method loads the XML from a file into the XmlDocument instance, which can then be used to access the elements of the XML. Then you call a method that enables you to loop through the XML recursively, passing the root node of the XML document to the method. The root element is obtained with the property DocumentElement of the XmlDocument class. Aside from the check for null on the root parameter that is passed into the FormatText method, the first line to note is the if sentence:

```
if (node is XmlText)
    {
       ...
    }
```

Recall that the is operator enables you to examine the type of an object, and it returns true if the instance is of the specified type. Even though the root node is declared as an XmlNode, that is merely the base type of the objects you are going to work with. By using the is operator to test the type of the objects, you are able to determine the type of the object at runtime and select the action to perform based on that.

Inside the FormatText method you generate the text for the textbox. You have to know the type of the current instance of root because the information you want to display is obtained differently for different elements: You want to display the name of XmlElements and the value of XmlText elements.

## Changing the Values of Nodes

Before you examine how to change the value of a node, it is important to realize that very rarely is the value of a node a simple thing. In fact, you will find that although all of the classes that derive from XmlNode include a property called Value, it very rarely returns anything useful to you. Although this can feel like a bit of a letdown at first, you'll find it is actually quite logical. Examine the books example from earlier:

```
<books>
  <book>
     <title>Beginning Visual C# 2012</title>
     <author>Karli Watson</author>
     <code>7582</code>
  </book>
  <book>
</books>
```

Every single tag pair in the document resolves into a node in the DOM. Remember that when you looped through all the nodes in the document, you encountered a number of XmlElement nodes and three XmlText nodes. The XmlElement nodes in this XML are <books>, <book>, <title>, <author>, and <code>. The XmlText nodes are the text between the starting and closing tags of title, author, and code. Although it could be argued that the value of title, author, and code is the text between the tags, that text is itself a node; and it is that node that actually holds the value. The other tags clearly have no value associated with them other than other nodes.

The following line is in the if block near the top of the code in the earlier FormatText method. It executes when the current node is an XmlText node.

```
text += node.Value;
```

You can see that the Value property of the XmlText node instance is used to get the value of the node.

Nodes of the type XmlElement return null if you use their Value property, but it is possible to get the information between the starting and closing tags of an XmlElement if you use one of two other methods: InnerText and InnerXml. That means you are able to manipulate the value of nodes using two methods and a property, as described in Table 22-3.

**TABLE 22-3:** Three Ways to Get the Value of a Node

| PROPERTY | DESCRIPTION |
|---|---|
| InnerText | Gets the text of all the child nodes of the current node and returns it as a single concatenated string. This means if you get the value of InnerText from the book node in the preceding XML, the string Beginning Visual C# 2012#Karli Watson7582 is returned. If you get the InnerText of the title node, only "Beginning Visual C# 2012" is returned. You can set the text using this method, but be careful if you do so because if you set the text of a wrong node you may overwrite information you did not want to change. |
| InnerXml | Returns the text like InnerText, but it also returns all of the tags. Therefore, if you get the value of InnerXml on the book node, the result is the following string:<br><br>`<title>Beginning Visual C# 2012</title><author>Karli Watson`<br>`</author><code>7582</code>`<br><br>As you can see, this can be quite useful if you have a string containing XML that you want to inject directly into your XML document. However, you are entirely responsible for the string yourself, and if you insert badly formed XML, the application will generate an exception. |
| Value | The "cleanest" way to manipulate information in the document, but as mentioned earlier, only a few of the classes actually return anything useful when you get the value. The classes that will return the desired text are as follows:<br><br>`XmlText`<br>`XmlComment`<br>`XmlAttribute` |

## Inserting New Nodes

Now that you've seen that you can move around in the XML document and even get the values of the elements, let's examine how to change the structure of the document by adding nodes to the books document you've been using until now.

To insert new elements in the list, you need to examine the new methods that are placed on the XmlDocument and XmlNode classes, shown in Table 22-4. The XmlDocument class has methods that enable you to create new XmlNode and XmlElement instances, which is nice because both of these classes have only a protected constructor, which means you cannot create an instance of either directly with new.

**TABLE 22-4:** Methods for Creating Nodes

| METHOD | DESCRIPTION |
|---|---|
| CreateNode | Creates any kind of node. There are three overloads of the method, two of which enable you to create nodes of the type found in the XmlNodeType enumeration and one that enables you to specify the type of node to use as a string. Unless you are quite sure about specifying a node type other than those in the enumeration, use the two overloads that use the enumeration. The method returns an instance of XmlNode that can then be cast to the appropriate type explicitly. |
| CreateElement | A version of CreateNode that creates only nodes of the XmlElement variety. |
| CreateAttribute | A version of CreateNode that creates only nodes of the XmlAttribute variety. |
| CreateTextNode | Creates—yes, you guessed it—nodes of the type XmlTextNode. |
| CreateComment | This method is included here to highlight the diversity of node types that can be created. This method doesn't create a node that is actually part of the data represented by the XML document, but rather is a comment meant for any human eyes that might have to read the data. You can pick up comments when reading the document in your applications as well. |

The methods in Table 22-4 are all used to create the nodes themselves, but after calling any of them you have to do something with them before they become interesting. Immediately after creation, the nodes contain no additional information, and they are not yet inserted into the document. To do either, you should use methods that are found on any class derived from XmlNode (including XmlDocument and XmlElement), described in Table 22-5.

**TABLE 22-5:** Methods for Inserting Nodes

| Method | Description |
|---|---|
| AppendChild | Appends a child node to a node of type XmlNode or a derived type. Remember that the node you append appears at the bottom of the list of children of the node on which the method is called. If you don't care about the order of the children, there's no problem; if you do care, remember to append the nodes in the correct sequence. |
| InsertAfter | Controls exactly where you want to insert the new node. The method takes two parameters—the first is the new node and the second is the node after which the new node should be inserted. |
| InsertBefore | Works exactly like InsertAfter, except that the new node is inserted before the node you supply as a reference. |

In the following Try It Out, you build on the previous example and insert a book node in the books.xml document. There is no code in the example to clean up the document (yet), so if you run it several times you will probably end up with a lot of identical nodes.

**TRY IT OUT**    Creating Nodes: Chapter22Code\LoopThroughXmlDocument\MainWindow.xaml.cs

This example builds on the LoopThroughXmlDocument project you created earlier. Follow these steps to add a node to the books.xml document:

1. Wrap the TextBlock in a ScrollViewer and set its VerticalScrollBarVisibility property to Auto.

2. Add a button beneath the existing button on the form and name it **buttonCreateNode**. Change its Content property to Create.

3. Add the Click event handler to the new button and enter the following code:

```
private void buttonCreateNode_Click(object sender, RoutedEventArgs e)
    {
        // Load the XML document.
        XmlDocument document = new XmlDocument();
        document.Load(booksFile);

        // Get the root element.
        XmlElement root = document.DocumentElement;

        // Create the new nodes.
        XmlElement newBook = document.CreateElement("book");
        XmlElement newTitle = document.CreateElement("title");
        XmlElement newAuthor = document.CreateElement("author");
        XmlElement newCode = document.CreateElement("code");
        XmlText title = document.CreateTextNode("Beginning Visual C# 2010");
        XmlText author = document.CreateTextNode("Karli Watson et al");
        XmlText code = document.CreateTextNode("1234567890");
        XmlComment comment = document.CreateComment("The previous edition");

        // Insert the elements.
        newBook.AppendChild(comment);
        newBook.AppendChild(newTitle);
```

```
                newBook.AppendChild(newAuthor);
                newBook.AppendChild(newCode);
                newTitle.AppendChild(title);
                newAuthor.AppendChild(author);
                newCode.AppendChild(code);
                root.InsertAfter(newBook, root.FirstChild);

                document.Save(booksFile);
            }
```

**4.** Run the application and click Create. Then click Loop, and you should see the dialog box shown in Figure 22-5.

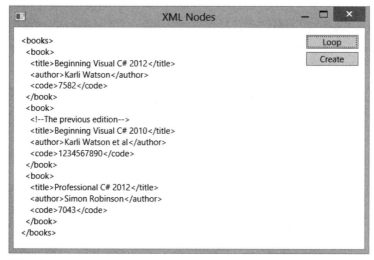

**FIGURE 22-5**

There is one important type of node that you didn't create in the preceding example: the XmlAttribute. That is left as an exercise at the end of the chapter.

### How It Works

The code in the buttonCreateNode_Click method is where all the creation of nodes happens. It creates eight new nodes, four of which are of type XmlElement, three of type XmlText, and one of type XmlComment.

All of the nodes are created with the method of the encapsulating XmlDocument instance. The XmlElement nodes are created with the CreateElement method, the XmlText nodes are created with the CreateTextNode method, and the XmlComment node is created with the CreateComment method.

After the nodes have been created, they still need to be inserted into the XML tree. This is done with the AppendChild method on the element to which the new node should become a child. The only exception to this is the book node, which is the root node of all of the new nodes. This node is inserted into the tree using the InsertAfter method of the root object. Whereas all of the nodes that are inserted using AppendChild always become the last node in the list of child nodes, InsertAfter enables you to position the node where you want it.

### Deleting Nodes

Now that you've seen how to create new nodes, all that is left is to learn how to delete them again. All classes derived from XmlNode include two methods, shown in Table 22-6, that enable you to remove nodes from the document.

**TABLE 22-6:** Methods for Removing Nodes

| Method | Description |
| --- | --- |
| RemoveAll | Removes all child nodes in the node on which it is called. What is slightly less obvious is that it also removes all attributes on the node because they are regarded as child nodes as well. |
| RemoveChild | Removes a single child in the node on which it is called. The method returns the node that has been removed from the document, but you can reinsert it if you change your mind. |

The following short Try It Out extends the application you've been creating over the past two examples to include the capability to delete nodes. For now, it finds only the last instance of the book node and removes it.

**TRY IT OUT** Removing Nodes: Chapter22Code\LoopThroughXmlDocument\MainWindow.xaml.cs

This example builds on the LoopThroughXmlDocument project you created earlier. The following steps enable you to find and remove the final instance of the book node:

1. Add a new button below the two that already exist and name it **buttonDeleteNode.** Set its Content property to Delete.

2. Double-click the new button and enter the following code:

```
private void buttonDeleteNode_Click(object sender, RoutedEventArgs e)
{
    // Load the XML document.
    XmlDocument document = new XmlDocument();
    document.Load(booksFile);

    // Get the root element.
    XmlElement root = document.DocumentElement;

    // Find the node. root is the <books> tag, so its last child
    // which will be the last <book> node.
    if (root.HasChildNodes)
    {
      XmlNode book = root.LastChild;

      // Delete the child.
      root.RemoveChild(book);

      // Save the document back to disk.
      document.Save(booksFile);
    }
}
```

3. Run the application. When you click the Delete Node button and then the Loop button, the last node in the tree will disappear.

### How It Works

After the initial steps to load the XML into the XmlDocument object, you examine the root element to see whether there are any child elements in the XML you loaded. If there are, you use the LastChild property of the XmlElement class to get the last child. After that, removing the element is as simple as calling RemoveChild, which passes in the instance of the element you want to remove—in this case, the last child of the root element.

## Selecting Nodes

You now know how to move back and forth in an XML document, how to manipulate the values of the document, how to create new nodes, and how to delete them again. Only one thing remains in this chapter: how to select nodes without having to traverse the entire tree.

The XmlNode class includes two methods, described in Table 22-7, commonly used to select nodes from the document without running through every node in it: SelectSingleNode and SelectNodes, both of which use a special query language, called XPath, to select the nodes. You learn about that shortly.

**TABLE 22-7:** Methods for Selecting Nodes

| METHOD | DESCRIPTION |
|---|---|
| SelectSingleNode | Selects a single node. If you create a query that fetches more than one node, only the first node will be returned. |
| SelectNodes | Returns a node collection in the form of an XmlNodeList class. |

## XPath

XPath is a query language for XML documents, much as SQL is for relational databases. It is used by the two methods described in Table 22-7 that enable you to avoid the hassle of walking the entire tree of an XML document. It does take a little getting used to, however, because the syntax is nothing like SQL or C#.

> **NOTE** *XPath is quite extensive, and only a small part of it is covered here so you can start selecting nodes. If you are interested in learning more, take a look at* www.w3.org/TR/xpath *and the Visual Studio help pages.*

To properly see XPath in action, you are going to use an XML file called Elements.xml, which contains a partial list of the chemical elements of the periodic table. You will find a subset of that XML listed in the "Selecting Nodes" Try It Out example later in the chapter, and it can be found in the download code for this chapter on this book's website as Elements.xml.

Table 22-8 lists some of the most common operations you can perform with XPath. If nothing else is stated, the XPath query example makes a selection that is relative to the node on which it is performed. Where it is necessary to have a node name, you can assume the current node is the <element> node in the XML document.

**TABLE 22-8:** Common XPath Operations

| PURPOSE | XPATH QUERY EXAMPLE |
|---|---|
| Select the current node. | . |
| Select the parent of the current node. | .. |
| Select all child nodes of the current node. | * |
| Select all child nodes with a specific name—in this case, title. | Title |
| Select an attribute of the current node. | @Type |
| Select all attributes of the current node. | @* |
| Select a child node by index—in this case, the second element node. | element[2] |
| Select all the text nodes of the current node. | text() |
| Select one or more grandchildren of the current node. | element/text() |

*continues*

**TABLE 22-8** *(continued)*

| PURPOSE | XPATH QUERY EXAMPLE |
|---|---|
| Select all nodes in the document with a particular name—in this case, all mass nodes. | `//mass` |
| Select all nodes in the document with a particular name and a particular parent name—in this case, the parent name is element and the node name is name. | `//element/name` |
| Select a node where a value criterion is met—in this case, the element for which the name of the element is Hydrogen. | `//element[name= 'Hydrogen']` |
| Select a node where an attribute value criterion is met—in this case, the Type attribute is Noble Gas. | `//element[@Type='Noble Gas']` |

In the following Try It Out, you'll create a small application that enables you to execute and see the results of a number of predefined queries, as well as enter your own queries.

**TRY IT OUT**    Selecting Nodes: Chapter22Code\XpathQuery\Elements.xml

As previously mentioned, this example uses a new XML file called Elements.xml. You can download the file from the book's website or type part of it in from here:

```
<?xml version="1.0"?>
<elements>
  <!--First Non-Metal-->
  <element Type="Non-Metal">
    <name>Hydrogen</name>
    <symbol>H</symbol>
    <number>1</number>
    <specification>
      <mass>1.007825</mass>
      <density>0.0899 g/cm3</density>
    </specification>
  </element>
  <!--First Noble Gas-->
  <element Type="Noble Gas">
    <name>Helium</name>
    <symbol>He</symbol>
    <number>2</number>
    <specification>
      <mass>4.002602</mass>
      <density>0.1785 g/cm3</density>
    </specification>
  </element>
  <!--First Halogen-->
  <element Type="Halogen">
    <name>Fluorine</name>
    <symbol>F</symbol>
    <number>9</number>
    <specification>
      <mass>18.998404</mass>
      <density>1.696 g/cm3</density>
    </specification>
  </element>
  <element Type="Noble Gas">
    <name>Neon</name>
    <symbol>Ne</symbol>
    <number>10</number>
    <specification>
      <mass>20.1797</mass>
```

```
        <density>0.901 g/cm3</density>
      </specification>
    </element>
  </elements>
```

Save the XML file as `Elements.xml`. Remember to change the path to the file in the code that follows. This example is a small query tool that you can use to test different queries on the XML provided with the code.

Follow these steps to create a WPF application with querying capability:

1. Create a new WPF application and name it **XPath Query**.

2. Create the dialog box shown in Figure 22-6. Name the controls as shown in the figure, except for the button, which should be named **buttonExecute**. Wrap the TextBlock in a ScrollViewer control and set its `VerticalScrollBarVisibility` property to `Auto`.

3. Go to the Code view and include the `using` directive.

4. Add a private field to hold the document, and initialize it in the constructor:

```
private XmlDocument document;


public MainWindow()
{
  InitializeComponent();

  document = new XmlDocument();
  document.Load(@"C:\BeginVCSharp\Chapter22Code\XML and Schema\Elements.xml");
}
```

5. You need a few helper methods to display the result of the queries in the `textBlockResult` TextBlock:

```
private void Update(XmlNodeList nodes)
{
    if (nodes == null || nodes.Count == 0)
    {
      textBlockResult.Text = "The query yielded no results";
      return;
    }
    string text = "";
    foreach (XmlNode node in nodes)
    {
      text = FormatText(node, text, "") + "\r\n";
    }
    textBlockResult.Text = text;
}
```

6. Update the constructor to display the entire contents of the XML file when the application starts:

```
public MainWindow()
    {
      InitializeComponent();
      document = new XmlDocument();
      document.Load(@"C:\BeginVCSharp\Chapter22Code\XML and Schema\Elements.xml");
      Update(document.DocumentElement.SelectNodes("."));
    }
```

7. Copy and paste the two methods `FormatText` and `AddAttributes` from the previous Try It Out sections to the new project.

8. Finally, insert the code that executes whatever the user enters in the text box:

```
private void buttonExecute_Click(object sender, RoutedEventArgs e)
    {
      try
      {
```

```
        XmlNodeList nodes = document.DocumentElement.SelectNodes(textBoxQuery.Text);
        Update(nodes);
    }
    catch (Exception err)
    {
        textBlockResult.Text = err.Message;
    }
}
```

9. Run the application and type the following query into the textBoxQuery textbox to select the element node that contains a node with the text Hydrogen:

```
element[name='Hydrogen']
```

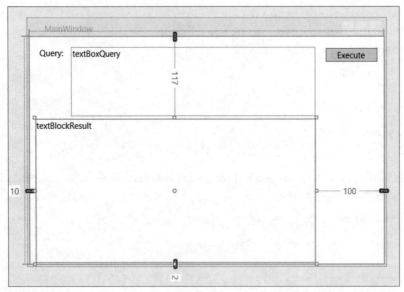

**FIGURE 22-6**

### How It Works

The buttonExecute_Click method performs the queries. Because you can't know in advance if the queries typed into the textBoxQuery are going to yield a single node or multiple nodes, you must use the SelectNodes method. This will either return an XmlNodeList object or throw one of the exceptions regarding XPath if the query used is illegal.

The Update method is responsible for looping through the content of the XmlNodeList selected by SelectNodes. It calls FormatText from the earlier examples with each of the nodes, and FormatText is responsible for recursively traversing the node tree and creating readable text you can use in the textBoxResult control.

In the exercises at the end of the chapter, you will find a number of additional XPath queries to try. Before you enter them into the XPathQuery application to see the result, try to determine for yourself the query's outcome.

## SUMMARY

In this chapter you learned about Extensible Markup Language (XML), a text format for storing and retrieving data. You looked at the rules you need to obey to ensure that XML documents are well-formed, and you learned how to validate them against XSD and XDR schemas.

After learning about the basics of XML, you saw how XML can be utilized through code using C# and Visual Studio. Finally, you learned how to use XPath to make queries in the XML.

In the next chapter, you will learn how to work with a very interesting query language: LINQ. This language can also be used to query XML, but that is beyond the scope of this book. Before you move on, however, try to complete the following exercises.

### EXERCISES

**22.1**  Change the Insert example in the "Creating Nodes" Try It Out section to insert an attribute called `Pages` with the value `1000+` on the book node.

**22.2**  Determine the outcome of the following XPath queries and then verify your results by typing the queries into the XPathQuery application from the "Selecting Nodes" Try It Out. Remember that all of your queries are being executed on the `DocumentElement`, which is the elements node.

```
//elements
element
element[@Type='Noble Gas']
//mass
//mass/..
element/specification[mass='20.1797']
element/name[text()='Neon']
Solution:
```

**22.3**  On many Windows systems the default viewer of XML is a web browser. If you are using Internet Explorer you will see a nicely formatted view of the XML when you load the `Elements.xml` file into it. Why would it not be ideal to display the XML from our queries in a browser control instead of a text box?

Answers to the exercises can be found in Appendix A.

## ▶ WHAT YOU LEARNED IN THIS CHAPTER

| TOPIC | KEY CONCEPTS |
|---|---|
| **XML syntax** | XML documents are created from an XML declaration, XML namespaces, XML elements, and attributes. The XML declaration defines the XML version. XML namespaces are used to define vocabularies and XML elements and attributes are used to define the XML document content. |
| **Well-formed XML** | Well-formed XML adheres to the basic syntax rules of XML. A document is said to be well-formed when there is precisely one root element, and every element has a closing tag, no elements overlap other elements (all child elements must be fully nested within the parent), and all attributes enclosed in quotes. All XML readers can read well-formed XML — but very few if any will allow you to read documents that are not well-formed. Strictly speaking, if a document containing tags isn't well-formed, it is not an XML document. |
| **Valid XML** | Valid XML is well-formed and can be validated by checking that it can be generated from a schema. Ensuring that XML is valid is important because it lets you make assumptions about the content of the XML document, which allows you to work with documents that were generated by others with the knowledge that the structure and names within the document are exactly as expected. |
| **XML schema** | XML schema is used to define the structure of XML documents. Schemas are especially useful when you need to exchange information with third parties. By agreeing on a schema for the data that is exchanged, you and the third party will be able to check that the documents are valid. |
| **XML in your programs** | XML is used extensively throughout the .NET world today, and the .NET Framework provides a host of classes for creating and manipulating XML. You can use XML to store application configuration, persist data to disk, send information across the wire, and so on. |
| **XPath** | XPath is one of the possible ways to query data in XML documents. To use XPath, you must be familiar with the structure of the XML document in order to be able to select individual elements from it. Although XPath can be used on any well-formed XML document, the fact that you must know the structure of the document when you create the query means that ensuring that the document is valid also ensures that the query will work from document to document, as long as the documents are valid against the same schema. |

# 23

# Introduction to LINQ

## WHAT YOU WILL LEARN IN THIS CHAPTER

- ➤ Coding a LINQ query and the parts of a LINQ query statement
- ➤ Using LINQ method syntax versus LINQ query syntax
- ➤ Ordering query results, including ordering on multiple levels
- ➤ When and how to use LINQ aggregate operators
- ➤ Using projection to create new objects in queries
- ➤ Using the `Distinct()`, `Any()`, `All()`, `First()`, `FirstOrDefault()`, `Take()`, and `Skip()` operators
- ➤ Grouping queries
- ➤ Setting operators and joins

## WROX.COM CODE DOWNLOADS FOR THIS CHAPTER

You can find the wrox.com code downloads for this chapter at `www.wrox.com/remtitle .cgi?isbn=9781118314418` on the Download Code tab. The code is in the Chapter 23 download and individually named according to the names throughout the chapter.

This chapter introduces Language Integrated Query (LINQ). LINQ is an extension to the C# language that integrates data query directly into the programming language itself. LINQ solves the problem of dealing with very large collections of data.

In the past, this sort of work required writing a lot of looping code, and additional processing such as sorting or grouping the found objects required even more code, sometimes mixing in a different query language such as SQL (Structured Query Language) typically found in relational databases. LINQ frees you from having to write this extra looping code to filter and sort. It enables you to focus on the objects that matter to your program.

In addition to providing an elegant query language that enables you to specify exactly what objects you are searching for, LINQ offers many extension methods that make it easy to sort, group, and calculate statistics on your query results.

With LINQ, you can query many different data sources in C#, including objects, SQL databases, XML documents, entity data models, and external applications such as web services and corporate directories. The LINQ syntax and methods shown in this chapter are the same for all the different data sources. The LINQ providers for querying different sources are covered in the following chapter, "Applying LINQ."

LINQ is large enough that complete coverage of all its facilities and methods is beyond the scope of a beginning book. However, you will see examples of all of the different types of operators and statements you are likely to need as a user of LINQ, and you will be pointed to resources for more in-depth coverage as appropriate.

# FIRST LINQ QUERY

Let's get started with an example. In the following Try It Out, you use LINQ to create a query to find some data in a simple in-memory array of objects and print it to the console.

**TRY IT OUT** First LINQ Program: 23-1-FirstLINQquery\Program.cs

Follow these steps to create the example in Visual Studio 2012:

1. Create a new console application called 23-1-FirstLINQquery in the directory C:\BegVCSharp\ Chapter23, and then open the main source file Program.cs.

2. Notice that Visual Studio 2012 includes the System.Linq namespace by default in Program.cs:

   ```
   using System;
   using System.Collections.Generic;
   using System.Linq;
   using System.Text;
   using System.Threading.Text;
   ```

3. Add the following code to the Main() method in Program.cs:

   ```
   static void Main(string[] args)
   {
           string[] names = { "Alonso", "Zheng", "Smith", "Jones", "Smythe",
   "Small", "Ruiz", "Hsieh", "Jorgenson", "Ilyich", "Singh", "Samba", "Fatimah" };

           var queryResults =
               from n in names
               where n.StartsWith("S")
               select n;

       Console.WriteLine("Names beginning with S:");

       foreach (var item in queryResults) {
           Console.WriteLine(item);
       }

       Console.Write("Program finished, press Enter/Return to continue:");
       Console.ReadLine();
   }
   ```

4. Compile and execute the program (you can just press F5 for Start Debugging). You will see the names in the list beginning with S in the order they were declared in the array, as shown here:

   ```
   Names beginning with S:
   Smith
   Smythe
   Small
   Singh
   Samba
   Program finished, press Enter/Return to continue:
   ```

Simply press Enter/Return to finish the program and make the console screen disappear. If you used Ctrl+F5 (Start Without Debugging), you may need to press Enter/Return twice. That finishes the program run.

### How It Works

The first step is to reference the `System.Linq` namespace, which is done automatically by Visual Studio 2012 when you create a project:

```
using System.Linq;
```

All the underlying base system support classes for LINQ reside in the `System.Linq` namespace. If you create a C# source file outside of Visual Studio 2012 or edit a project created from a previous version, you may have to add the `using System.Linq` directive manually.

The next step is to create some data, which is done in this example by declaring and initializing the array of names:

```
string[] names = { "Alonso", "Zheng", "Smith", "Jones", "Smythe", "Small",
"Ruiz", "Hsieh", "Jorgenson", "Ilyich", "Singh", "Samba", "Fatimah" };
```

This is a trivial set of data, but it is good to start with an example for which the result of the query is obvious. The actual LINQ query statement is the next part of the program:

```
var queryResults =
            from n in names
            where n.StartsWith("S")
            select n;
```

That is an odd-looking statement, isn't it? It almost looks like something from a language other than C#, and the `from...where...select` syntax is deliberately similar to that of the SQL database query language. However, this statement is not SQL; it is indeed C#, as you saw when you typed in the code in Visual Studio 2012—the `from`, `where`, and `select` were highlighted as keywords, and the odd-looking syntax is perfectly fine to the compiler.

The LINQ query statement in this program uses the LINQ declarative query syntax:

```
var queryResults =
        from n in names
        where n.StartsWith("S")
        select n;
```

The statement has four parts: the result variable declaration beginning with `var`, which is assigned using a *query expression* consisting of the `from` clause; the `where` clause; and the `select` clause. Let's look at each of these parts in turn.

## Declaring a Variable for Results Using the var Keyword

The LINQ query starts by declaring a variable to hold the results of the query, which is usually done by declaring a variable with the `var` keyword:

```
var queryResult =
```

As described in Chapter 14, `var` is a keyword in C# created to declare a general variable type that is ideal for holding the results of LINQ queries. The `var` keyword tells the C# compiler to infer the type of the result based on the query. That way, you don't have to declare ahead of time what type of objects will be returned from the LINQ query—the compiler takes care of it for you. If the query can return multiple items, then it acts like a collection of the objects in the query data source (technically, it is not a collection; it just looks that way).

> **NOTE** *If you want to know the details, the query result will be a type that implements the* IEnumerable<T> *interface. The angle brackets with T(<T>) following* IEnumerable *indicate that it is a generic type. Generics are described in Chapter 12.*
>
> *In this particular case, the compiler creates a special LINQ data type that provides an ordered list of strings (strings because the data source is a collection of strings).*

By the way, the name queryResult is arbitrary—you can name the result anything you want. It could be namesBeginningWithS or anything else that makes sense in your program.

## Specifying the Data Source: from Clause

The next part of the LINQ query is the from clause, which specifies the data you are querying:

```
from n in names
```

Your data source in this case is names, the array of strings declared earlier. The variable n is just a stand-in for an individual element in the data source, similar to the variable name following a foreach statement. By specifying from, you are indicating that you are going to *query* a subset of the collection, rather than iterate through all the elements.

Speaking of iteration, a LINQ data source must be *enumerable*—that is, it must be an array or collection of items from which you can pick one or more elements to iterate through.

> **NOTE** *Enumerable means the data source must support the* IEnumerable<T> *interface, which is supported for any C# array or collection of items.*

The data source cannot be a single value or object, such as a single int variable. You already have such a single item, so there is no point in querying it!

## Specify Condition: where Clause

In the next part of the LINQ query, you specify the condition for your query using the where clause, which looks like this:

```
where n.StartsWith("S")
```

Any Boolean (true or false) expression that can be applied to the items in the data source can be specified in the where clause. Actually, the where clause is optional and can even be omitted, but in almost all cases you will want to specify a where condition to limit the results to only the data you want. The where clause is called a *restriction operator* in LINQ because it restricts the results of the query.

Here, you specify that the name string starts with the letter S, but you could specify anything else about the string instead—for example, a length greater than 10 (where n.Length > 10) or containing a Q (where n.Contains("Q")).

## Selecting Items: select Clause

Finally, the select clause specifies which items appear in the result set. The select clause looks like this:

```
select n
```

The select clause is required because you must specify which items from your query appear in the result set. For this set of data, it is not very interesting because you have only one item, the name, in each element of the result set. You'll look at some examples with more complex objects in the result set where the usefulness of the `select` clause will be more apparent, but first, you need to finish the example.

## Finishing Up: Using the foreach Loop

Now you print out the results of the query. Like the array used as the data source, the results of a LINQ query like this are *enumerable*, meaning you can iterate through the results with a `foreach` statement:

```
Console.WriteLine("Names beginning with S:");

foreach (var item in queryResults) {
        Console.WriteLine(item);
}
```

In this case, you matched five names—Smith, Smythe, Small, Singh, and Samba—so that is what you display in the `foreach` loop.

## Deferred Query Execution

You may be thinking that the `foreach` loop really isn't part of LINQ itself—it's only looping through your results. While it's true that the `foreach` construct is not itself part of LINQ, nevertheless, it is the part of your code that actually executes the LINQ query! The assignment of the query results variable only saves a plan for executing the query; with LINQ, the data itself is not retrieved until the results are accessed. This is called *deferred query execution* or *lazy evaluation* of queries. Execution will be deferred for any query that produces a sequence—that is, a list—of results.

Now, back to the code. You've printed out the results; now it's time to finish the program:

```
Console.Write("Program finished, press Enter/Return to continue:");
Console.ReadLine();
```

These lines just ensure that the results of the console program stay on the screen until you press a key, even if you press F5 instead of Ctrl+F5. You'll use this construct in most of the other LINQ examples as well.

## USING THE LINQ METHOD SYNTAX

There are multiple ways of doing the same thing with LINQ, as is often the case in programming. As noted, the previous example was written using the LINQ *query syntax;* in the next example, you will write the same program using LINQ's *method syntax* (also called *explicit syntax,* but we"ll use the term method syntax is used here).

## LINQ Extension Methods

LINQ is implemented as a series of extension methods to collections, arrays, query results, and any other object that implements the `IEnumerable<T>` interface. You can see these methods with the Visual Studio IntelliSense feature. For example, in Visual Studio 2012, open the `Program.cs` file in the `FirstLINQquery` program you just completed and type in a new reference to the `names` array just below it:

```
string[] names = { "Alonso", "Zheng", "Smith", "Jones", "Smythe", "Small",
"Ruiz", "Hsieh", "Jorgenson", "Ilyich", "Singh", "Samba", "Fatimah" };
```

**names.**

Just as you type the period following `names`, you will see the methods available for `names` listed by the Visual Studio IntelliSense feature.

The `Where<T>` method and most of the other available methods are extension methods (as shown in the documentation appearing to the right of the `Where<T>` method, it begins with `extension`). You can see that they are LINQ extensions by commenting out the using System.Linq directive at the top; you will find that Where<T>, Union<T>, Take<T>, and most of the other methods in the list no longer appear. The from...where...select query expression you used in the previous example is translated by the C# compiler into a series of calls to these methods. When using the LINQ method syntax, you call these methods directly.

## Query Syntax versus Method Syntax

The query syntax is the preferred way of programming queries in LINQ, as it is generally easier to read and is simpler to use for the most common queries. However, it is important to have a basic understanding of the method syntax because some LINQ capabilities either are not available in the query syntax, or are just easier to use in the method syntax.

> **NOTE** *As the Visual Studio 2012 online help recommends, use query syntax whenever possible, and method syntax whenever necessary.*

In this chapter, you will mostly use the query syntax, but the method syntax is pointed out in situations where it is needed, and you'll learn how to use the method syntax to solve the problem.

Most of the LINQ methods that use the method syntax require that you pass a method or function to evaluate the query expression. The method/function parameter is passed in the form of a delegate, which typically references an anonymous method.

Luckily, LINQ makes doing this much easier than it sounds! You create the method/function by using a lambda expression, as described in Chapter 14.

Try this out in an actual program to see this more clearly.

**TRY IT OUT**   Using LINQ Method Syntax: 23-2-LINQMethodSyntax\Program.cs

Follow these steps to create the example in Visual Studio 2012:

1. You can either modify the FirstLINQquery example or create a new console application called 23-2-LINQMethodSyntax in the directory C:\BegVCSharp\Chapter23. Open the main source file Program.cs.

2. Again, Visual Studio 2012 includes the Linq namespace automatically in Program.cs:

   ```
   using System.Linq;
   ```

3. Add the following code to the Main() method in Program.cs:

   ```
   static void Main(string[] args)
   {
           string[] names = { "Alonso", "Zheng", "Smith", "Jones", "Smythe",
   "Small", "Ruiz", "Hsieh", "Jorgenson", "Ilyich", "Singh", "Samba", "Fatimah" };

           var queryResults = names.Where(n => n.StartsWith("S"));

           Console.WriteLine("Names beginning with S:");

           foreach (var item in queryResults) {
               Console.WriteLine(item);
           }

           Console.Write("Program finished, press Enter/Return to continue:");
           Console.ReadLine();
   }
   ```

**4.** Compile and execute the program (you can just press F5). You will see the same output of names in the list beginning with S, in the order they were declared in the array, as shown here:

```
Names beginning with S:
Smith
Smythe
Small
Singh
Samba
Program finished, press Enter/Return to continue:
```

### How It Works

As before, the `System.Linq` namespace is referenced automatically by Visual Studio 2012:

```
using System.Linq;
```

The same source data as before is created again by declaring and initializing the array of names:

```
string[] names = { "Alonso", "Zheng", "Smith", "Jones", "Smythe", "Small", "Ruiz",
    "Hsieh", "Jorgenson", "Ilyich", "Singh", "Samba", "Fatimah" };
```

The part that is different is the LINQ query, which is now a call to the `Where()` method instead of a query expression:

```
var queryResults = names.Where(n => n.StartsWith("S"));
```

The C# compiler compiles the lambda expression `n => n.StartsWith("S")` into an anonymous method that is executed by `Where()` on each item in the names array. If the lambda expression returns `true` for an item, that item is included in the result set returned by `Where()`. The C# compiler infers that the `Where()` method should accept `string` as the input type for each item from the definition of the input source (the `names` array, in this case).

Well, a lot is going on in that one line, isn't it? For the simplest type of query like this, the method syntax is actually shorter than the query syntax because you do not need the `from` or `select` clauses; however, most queries are more complex than this.

The rest of the example is the same as the previous one—you print out the results of the query in a `foreach` loop and pause the output so you can see it before the program finishes execution:

```
foreach (var item in queryResults) {
    Console.WriteLine(item);
}

Console.Write("Program finished, press Enter/Return to continue:");
Console.ReadLine();
```

An explanation of these lines isn't repeated here because that was covered in the "How It Works" section following the first example in the chapter. Let's move on now and explore how to use more of LINQ's capabilities.

## ORDERING QUERY RESULTS

Once you have located some data of interest with a `where` clause (or `Where()` method invocation), LINQ makes it easy to perform further processing—such as reordering the results—on the resulting data. In the following Try It Out, you put the results from your first query in alphabetical order.

---

**TRY IT OUT** Ordering Query Results: 23-3-OrderQueryResults\Program.cs

Follow these steps to create the example in Visual Studio 2012:

1. You can either modify the FirstLINQquery example or create a new console application project called 23-3-OrderQueryResults in the directory C:\BegVCSharp\Chapter23.

2. Open the main source file Program.cs. As before, Visual Studio 2012 includes the using System.Linq; namespace directive automatically in Program.cs.

3. Add the following code to the Main() method in Program.cs:

```
static void Main(string[] args)
{
        string[] names = { "Alonso", "Zheng", "Smith", "Jones", "Smythe",
"Small", "Ruiz", "Hsieh", "Jorgenson", "Ilyich", "Singh", "Samba", "Fatimah" };

            var queryResults =
                from n in names
                where n.StartsWith("S")
                orderby n
                select n;

            Console.WriteLine("Names beginning with S ordered alphabetically:");

            foreach (var item in queryResults) {
                Console.WriteLine(item);
            }

            Console.Write("Program finished, press Enter/Return to continue:");
            Console.ReadLine();
}
```

4. Compile and execute the program. You will see the names in the list beginning with S in alphabetical order, as shown here:

```
Names beginning with S:
Samba
Singh
Small
Smith
Smythe
Program finished, press Enter/Return to continue:
```

### How It Works

This program is nearly identical to the previous example, except for one additional line added to the query statement:

```
var queryResults =
                from n in names
                where n.StartsWith("S")
                orderby n
                select n;
```

---

## UNDERSTANDING THE ORDERBY CLAUSE

The orderby clause looks like this:

```
orderby n
```

Like the where clause, the orderby clause is optional. Just by adding one line, you can order the results of any arbitrary query, which would otherwise require at least several lines of additional code and probably additional methods or collections to store the results of the reordered result, depending on the sorting algorithm you chose to implement. If multiple types needed to be sorted, you would have to implement a set of ordering methods for each one. With LINQ, you don't need to worry about any of that; just add one additional clause in the query statement and you're done.

By default, `orderby` orders in ascending order (A to Z), but you can specify descending order (from Z to A) simply by adding the `descending` keyword:

```
orderby n descending
```

This orders the example results as follows:

```
Smythe
Smith
Small
Singh
Samba
```

Plus, you can order by any arbitrary expression without having to rewrite the query; for example, to order by the last letter in the name instead of normal alphabetical order, you just change the `orderby` clause to the following:

```
orderby n.Substring(n.Length - 1)
```

This results in the following output:

```
Samba
Smythe
Smith
Singh
Small
```

> **NOTE** *The last letters are in alphabetical order* (a, e, h, h, l). *However, you will notice that the execution is implementation-dependent, meaning there's no guarantee of order beyond what is specified in the* orderby *clause. The last letter is the only letter considered, so, in this case, Smith came before Singh.*

## ORDERING USING METHOD SYNTAX

To add capabilities such as ordering to a query using the method syntax, you simply add a method call for each LINQ operation you want to perform on your method-based LINQ query. Again, this is simpler than it sounds, as shown in the following Try It Out.

**TRY IT OUT**    Ordering Using Method Syntax: 23-4-OrderMethodSyntax\Program.cs

Follow these steps to create the example in Visual Studio 2012:

1. You can either modify the 23-2-LINQMethodSyntax example, or create a new console application project called 23-4-OrderMethodSyntax in the directory C:\BegVCSharp\Chapter23.

2. Add the following code to the `Main()` method in `Program.cs`. As in all the examples, Visual Studio 2012 automatically includes the reference to the `System.Linq` namespace.

```
static void Main(string[] args)
{
        string[] names = { "Alonso", "Zheng", "Smith", "Jones", "Smythe",
```

```
            "Small", "Ruiz", "Hsieh", "Jorgenson", "Ilyich", "Singh", "Samba", "Fatimah" };

                var queryResults = names.OrderBy(n => n).Where(n => n.StartsWith("S"));

                Console.WriteLine("Names beginning with S:");

                foreach (var item in queryResults) {
                    Console.WriteLine(item);
                }

                Console.Write("Program finished, press Enter/Return to continue:");
                Console.ReadLine();
        }
```

**3.** Compile and execute the program. You will see the names in the list beginning with S in alphabetical order, as in the output from the previous example.

### How It Works

This example is nearly identical to the previous method syntax example, except for the addition of the call to the LINQ `OrderBy()` method preceding the call to the `Where()` method:

```
            var queryResults = names.OrderBy(n => n).Where(n => n.StartsWith("S"));
```

As you may have seen from the IntelliSense when you typed the code in, the `OrderBy()` method returns an `IOrderedEnumerable<T>`, which is derived from the `IEnumerable<T>` interface, so you can call `Where()` on it just as you can with any other `IEnumerable<T>`.

> **NOTE** The compiler infers that you are working with `string` data, so the data types appear in IntelliSense as `IOrderedEnumerable<string>` and `IEnumerable<string>`.

You need to pass a lambda expression to `OrderBy()` to tell it which function to use for ordering. You pass the simplest possible lambda, `n => n`, because you do not need to order by anything other than the item itself. In the query syntax, you do not need to create this extra lambda expression.

To order the items in reverse order, call the `OrderByDescending()` method:

```
    var queryResults = names.OrderByDescending(n => n).Where(n =>
        n.StartsWith("S"));
```

This produces the same results as the `orderby n descending` clause you used in the query syntax version.

To order by something other than the value of the item itself, you can change the lambda expression passed to `OrderBy()`. For example, to order by the last letter in each name, you would use the lambda `n => n. Substring(n.Length-1)` and pass it to `OrderBy` as shown here:

```
    var queryResults =
        names.OrderBy(n => n.Substring(n.Length-1)).Where(n =>
        n.StartsWith("S"));
```

This produces the same results, ordered by the last letter in each name, as the previous example.

## QUERYING A LARGE DATA SET

All this LINQ syntax is well and good, you may be saying, but what is the point? You can see the expected results clearly just by looking at the source array, so why go to all this trouble to query something that is obvious by just looking? As mentioned earlier, sometimes the results of a query are not so obvious. In the following Try It Out, you create a very large array of numbers and query it using LINQ.

**TRY IT OUT** Querying a Large Data Set: 23-5-LargeNumberQuery\Program.cs

Follow these steps to create the example in Visual Studio 2012:

1. Create a new console application called 23-5-LargeNumberQuery in the directory `C:\BegVCSharp\` `Chapter23`. As before, when you create the project, Visual Studio 2012 already includes the `Linq` namespace method in `Program.cs`:

```
using System;
using System.Collections.Generic;
using System.Linq;
using System.Text;
```

2. Add the following code to the `Main()` method:

```
static void Main(string[] args)
{
        int[] numbers = GenerateLotsOfNumbers(12345678);

        var queryResults =
            from n in numbers
            where n < 1000
            select n
          ;

        Console.WriteLine("Numbers less than 1000:");
         foreach (var item in queryResults)
         {
             Console.WriteLine(item);
         }
         Console.Write("Program finished, press Enter/Return to continue:");
         Console.ReadLine();
}
```

3. Add the following method to generate the list of random numbers:

```
        private static int[] GenerateLotsOfNumbers(int count)
        {
            Random generator = new Random(0);
            int[] result = new int[count];
            for (int i = 0; i < count; i++)
            {
                result[i] = generator.Next();
            }
            return result;
        }
```

4. Compile and execute the program. You will see a list of numbers less than 1000, as shown here:

```
Numbers less than 1000:
714
24
677
350
257
719
584
Program finished, press Enter/Return to continue:
```

### How It Works

As before, the first step is to reference the `System.Linq` namespace, which is done automatically by Visual Studio 2012 when you create the project:

```
using System.Linq;
```

The next step is to create some data, which is done in this example by creating and calling the GenerateLotsOfNumbers() method:

```
int[] numbers = GenerateLotsOfNumbers(12345678);

private static int[] GenerateLotsOfNumbers(int count)
{
    Random generator = new Random(0);
    int[] result = new int[count];
    for (int i = 0; i < count; i++)
    {
        result[i] = generator.Next();
    }
    return result;
}
```

This is not a trivial set of data—there are 12 million numbers in the array! In one of the exercises at the end of the chapter, you will change the `size` parameter passed to the GenerateLotsOfNumbers() method to generate variously sized sets of random numbers and see how this affects the query results. As you will see when doing the exercises, the size shown here of 12,345,678 is just large enough for the program to generate some random numbers less than 1,000, in order to have results to show for this first query.

The values should be randomly distributed over the range of a signed integer (from zero to more than two billion). By creating the random number generator with a seed of 0, you ensure that the same set of random numbers is created each time and is repeatable, so you get the same query results as shown here, but what those query results are is unknown until you try some queries. Luckily, LINQ makes those queries easy!

The query statement itself is similar to what you did with the names before, selecting some numbers that meet a condition (in this case, numbers less than 1,000):

```
var queryResults =
    from n in numbers
    where n < 1000
    select n
```

The `orderby` clause isn't needed here and would add extra processing time (not noticeably for this query, but more so as you vary the conditions in the next example).

You print out the results of the query with a `foreach` statement, just as in the previous example:

```
Console.WriteLine("Numbers less than 1000:");

foreach (var item in queryResults) {
    Console.WriteLine(item);
}
```

Again, output to the console and read a character to pause the output:

```
Console.Write("Program finished, press Enter/Return to continue:");
Console.ReadLine();
```

The pause code appears in all the following examples but isn't shown again because it is the same for each one.

It is very easy with LINQ to change the query conditions to explore different characteristics of the data set. However, depending on how many results the query returns, it may not make sense to print all the results each time. In the next section you'll see how LINQ provides aggregate operators to deal with that issue.

## USING AGGREGATE OPERATORS

Often, a query returns more results than you might expect. For example, if you were to change the condition of the large-number query program you just created to list the numbers greater than 1,000, rather than the numbers less than 1,000, there would be so many query results that the numbers would not stop printing!

Luckily, LINQ provides a set of aggregate operators that enable you to analyze the results of a query without having to loop through them all. Table 23-1 shows the most commonly used aggregate operators for a set of numeric results such as those from the large-number query. These may be familiar to you if you have used a database query language such as SQL.

**TABLE 23-1:** Aggregate Operators for Numeric Results

| OPERATOR | DESCRIPTION |
| --- | --- |
| Count() | Count of results |
| Min() | Minimum value in results |
| Max() | Maximum value in results |
| Average() | Average value of numeric results |
| Sum() | Total of all of numeric results |

There are more aggregate operators, such as `Aggregate()`, for executing arbitrary code in a manner that enables you to code your own aggregate function. However, those are for advanced users and therefore beyond the scope of this book.

> **NOTE** Because the aggregate operators return a simple scalar type instead of a sequence for their results, their use forces immediate execution of query results with no deferred execution.

In the following Try It Out, you modify the large-number query and use aggregate operators to explore the result set from the greater-than version of the large-number query using LINQ.

**TRY IT OUT** Numeric Aggregate Operators: 23-6-NumericAggregates\Program.cs

Follow these steps to create the example in Visual Studio 2012:

1. For this example, you can either modify the LargeNumberQuery example you just made or create a new console project named 23-6-NumericAggregates in the directory `C:\BegVCSharp\Chapter23`.

2. As before, when you create the project, Visual Studio 2012 includes the `Linq` namespace method in `Program.cs`. You just need to modify the `Main()` method as shown in the following code and in the rest of this Try It Out. As with the previous example, the `orderby` clause is not used in this query. However, the condition on the `where` clause is the opposite of the previous example (the numbers are greater than 1,000 (`n > 1000`), instead of less than 1,000):

```
static void Main(string[] args)
{
    int[] numbers = GenerateLotsOfNumbers(12345678);

    Console.WriteLine("Numeric Aggregates");

    var queryResults =
        from n in numbers
        where n > 1000
        select n
        ;

    Console.WriteLine("Count of Numbers > 1000");
    Console.WriteLine(queryResults.Count());

    Console.WriteLine("Max of Numbers > 1000");
```

```
            Console.WriteLine(queryResults.Max());

            Console.WriteLine("Min of Numbers > 1000");
            Console.WriteLine(queryResults.Min());

            Console.WriteLine("Average of Numbers > 1000");
            Console.WriteLine(queryResults.Average());

            Console.WriteLine("Sum of Numbers > 1000");
            Console.WriteLine(queryResults.Sum(n => (long) n));

            Console.Write("Program finished, press Enter/Return to continue:");
            Console.ReadLine();
    }
```

3. If it is not already present, add the same `GenerateLotsOfNumbers()` method used in the previous example:

```
        private static int[] GenerateLotsOfNumbers(int count)
        {
            Random generator = new Random(0);
            int[] result = new int[count];
            for (int i = 0; i < count; i++)
            {
                result[i] = generator.Next();
            }
            return result;
        }
```

4. Compile and execute. You will see the count, minimum, maximum, and average values as shown here:

```
Numeric Aggregates
Count of Numbers > 1000
12345671
Maximum of Numbers > 1000
2147483591
Minimum of Numbers > 1000
1034
Average of Numbers > 1000
1073643807.50298
Sum of Numbers > 1000
13254853218619179
Program finished, press Enter/Return to continue:
```

This query produces many more results than the previous example (more than 12 million). Using `orderby` on this result set would definitely have a noticeable impact on performance! The largest number (maximum) in the result set is over two billion and the smallest (minimum) is just over one thousand, as expected. The average is around one billion, near the middle of the range of possible values. Looks like the `Random()` function generates a good distribution of numbers!

### How It Works

The first part of the program is exactly the same as the previous example, with the reference to the `System.Linq` namespace, and the use of the `GenerateLotsOfNumbers()` method to generate the source data:

```
        int[] numbers = GenerateLotsOfNumbers(12345678);
```

The query is the same as the previous example, except for changing the `where` condition from less than to greater than:

```
        var queryResults =
            from n in numbers
            where n > 1000
            select n;
```

As noted before, this query using the greater-than condition produces many more results than the less-than query (with this particular data set). By using the aggregate operators, you are able to explore the results of the query without having to print out each result or do a comparison in a `foreach` loop. Each one appears as a method that can be called on the result set, similar to methods on a collection type.

Look at the use of each aggregate operator:

➤ `Count()`:

```
Console.WriteLine("Count of Numbers > 1000");
Console.WriteLine(queryResults.Count());
```

`Count()` returns the number of rows in the query results—in this case, 12,345,671 rows.

➤ `Max()`:

```
Console.WriteLine("Max of Numbers > 1000");
Console.WriteLine(queryResults.Max());
```

`Max()` returns the maximum value in the query results—in this case, a number larger than two billion: 2,147,483,591, which is very close to the maximum value of an `int` (`int.MaxValue` or 2,147,483,647).

➤ `Min()`:

```
Console.WriteLine("Min of Numbers > 1000");
Console.WriteLine(queryResults.Min());
```

`min()` returns the minimum value in the query results—in this case, 1,034.

➤ `Average()`:

```
Console.WriteLine("Average of Numbers > 1000");
Console.WriteLine(queryResults.Average());
```

`Average()` returns the average value of the query results, which in this case is 1,073,643,807.50298, a value very close to the middle of the range of possible values from 1,000 to more than two billion. This is rather meaningless with an arbitrary set of large numbers, but it shows the kind of query result analysis that is possible. You'll look at a more practical use of these operators with some business-oriented data in the last part of the chapter.

➤ `Sum()`:

```
Console.WriteLine("Sum of Numbers > 1000");
Console.WriteLine(queryResults.Sum(n => (long) n));
```

You passed the lambda expression `n => (long) n` to the `Sum()` method call to get the sum of all the numbers. Although `Sum()` has a no-parameter overload, like `Count()`, `Min()`, `Max()`, and so on, using that version of the method call would cause an overflow error because there are so many large numbers in the data set that the sum of all of them would be too large to fit into a standard 32-bit `int`, which is what the no-parameter version of `Sum()` returns. The lambda expression enables you to convert the result of `Sum()` to a long 64-bit integer, which is what you need to hold the total of over 13 quadrillion without overflow—13,254,853,218,619,179 lambda expressions enable you to perform this kind of fix-up easily.

> **NOTE** In addition to `Count()`, which returns a 32-bit `int`, LINQ also provides a `LongCount()` method that returns the count of query results in a 64-bit integer. That is a special case, however—all the other operators require a lambda or a call to a conversion method if a 64-bit version of the number is needed.

## QUERYING COMPLEX OBJECTS

The previous examples show how LINQ queries can work with lists of simple types, such as numbers and strings. This section describes how to use LINQ queries with more complex objects. You'll create a simple `Customer` class with just enough information to create some interesting queries.

**TRY IT OUT** Querying Complex Objects: 23-7-QueryComplexObjects\Program.cs

Follow these steps to create the example in Visual Studio 2012:

1. Create a new console application called 23-7-QueryComplexObjects in the directory `C:\BegVCSharp\Chapter23`.

2. Before the start of the `Program` class in `Program.cs`, add the following short class definition for the `Customer` class:

```
class Customer
{
    public string ID { get; set; }
    public string City { get; set; }
    public string Country { get; set; }
    public string Region { get; set; }
    public decimal Sales { get; set; }

    public override string ToString()
    {
        return "ID: " + ID + " City: " + City + " Country: " + Country +
            " Region: " + Region + " Sales: " + Sales;
    }
}
```

3. Add the following code to the `Main()` method of the `Program` class of `Program.cs`:

```
static void Main(string[] args)
{
        List <Customer> customers = new List<Customer> {
            new Customer { ID="A", City="New York", Country="USA",
                                        Region="North America", Sales=9999 },
            new Customer { ID="B", City="Mumbai", Country="India",
                                        Region="Asia", Sales=8888 },
            new Customer { ID="C", City="Karachi", Country="Pakistan",
                                        Region="Asia", Sales=7777 },
            new Customer { ID="D", City="Delhi", Country="India",
                                        Region="Asia", Sales=6666 },
            new Customer { ID="E", City="São Paulo", Country="Brazil",
                                        Region="South America", Sales=5555 },
            new Customer { ID="F", City="Moscow", Country="Russia",
                                        Region="Europe", Sales=4444 },
            new Customer { ID="G", City="Seoul", Country="Korea", Region="Asia",
                                        Sales=3333 },
            new Customer { ID="H", City="Istanbul", Country="Turkey",
                                        Region="Asia", Sales=2222 },
            new Customer { ID="I", City="Shanghai", Country="China", Region="Asia",
                                        Sales=1111 },
            new Customer { ID="J", City="Lagos", Country="Nigeria",
                                        Region="Africa", Sales=1000 },
            new Customer { ID="K", City="Mexico City", Country="Mexico",
                                        Region="North America", Sales=2000 },
            new Customer { ID="L", City="Jakarta", Country="Indonesia",
                                        Region="Asia", Sales=3000 },
            new Customer { ID="M", City="Tokyo", Country="Japan",
                                        Region="Asia", Sales=4000 },
            new Customer { ID="N", City="Los Angeles", Country="USA",
```

```
                                            Region="North America", Sales=5000 },
            new Customer { ID="O", City="Cairo", Country="Egypt",
                                            Region="Africa", Sales=6000 },
            new Customer { ID="P", City="Tehran", Country="Iran",
                                            Region="Asia", Sales=7000 },
            new Customer { ID="Q", City="London", Country="UK",
                                            Region="Europe", Sales=8000 },
            new Customer { ID="R", City="Beijing", Country="China",
                                            Region="Asia", Sales=9000 },
            new Customer { ID="S", City="Bogotá", Country="Colombia",
                                            Region="South America", Sales=1001 },
            new Customer { ID="T", City="Lima", Country="Peru",
                                            Region="South America", Sales=2002 }
        };
        var queryResults =
            from c in customers
            where c.Region == "Asia"
            select c
          ;
        Console.WriteLine("Customers in Asia:");
        foreach (Customer c in queryResults)
        {
            Console.WriteLine(c);
        }
        Console.Write("Program finished, press Enter/Return to continue:");
        Console.ReadLine();
    }
}
```

4.  Compile and execute the program. The result is a list of the customers from Asia:

```
Customers in Asia:
ID: B City: Mumbai Country: India Region: Asia Sales: 8888
ID: C City: Karachi Country: Pakistan Region: Asia Sales: 7777
ID: D City: Delhi Country: India Region: Asia Sales: 6666
ID: G City: Seoul Country: Korea Region: Asia Sales: 3333
ID: H City: Istanbul Country: Turkey Region: Asia Sales: 2222
ID: I City: Shanghai Country: China Region: Asia Sales: 1111
ID: L City: Jakarta Country: Indonesia Region: Asia Sales: 3000
ID: M City: Tokyo Country: Japan Region: Asia Sales: 4000
ID: P City: Tehran Country: Iran Region: Asia Sales: 7000
ID: R City: Beijing Country: China Region: Asia Sales: 9000
Program finished, press Enter/Return to continue:
```

### How It Works

In the Customer class definition, you use the C# automatic properties feature to declare public properties (ID, City, Country, Region, and Sales) for the Customer class without having to explicitly code private instance variables and get/set code for each property:

```
class Customer
{
    public string ID { get; set; }
    public string City { get; set; }
    ...
```

The only extra method you bother to code for the Customer class is an override for the ToString() method to provide a string representation for a Customer instance:

```
public override string ToString()
{
    return "ID: " + ID + " City: " + City + " Country: " + Country +
        " Region: " + Region + " Sales: " + Sales;
}
```

You will use this `ToString()` method to simplify printing out the results of the query.

In the `Main()` method of the `Program` class, you create a strongly typed collection of type `Customer` using collection/object initialization syntax, to avoid having to code a constructor method and call the constructor to make each list member:

```
List <Customer> customers = new List<Customer> {
    new Customer { ID="A", City="New York", Country="USA",
                                Region="North America", Sales=9999 },
    new Customer { ID="B", City="Mumbai", Country="India",
                                Region="Asia", Sales=8888 },
    ...
```

Your customers are located all over the world, with enough geographical information in your data to make interesting selection criteria and groups for queries.

Still in the `Main()` method, you create the query statement—in this case, selecting the customers from Asia:

```
var queryResults =
    from c in customers
    where c.Region == "Asia"
    select c
    ;
```

This query should be very familiar to you by now—it's the same `from...where...select` LINQ query you have used in the other examples, except that each item in the result list is a full-fledged object (a `Customer`), rather than a simple `string` or `int`. Next, you print out the results in a `foreach` loop:

```
Console.WriteLine("Customers in Asia:");
foreach (Customer c in queryResults)
{
    Console.WriteLine(c);
}
```

This `foreach` loop is a little different from the ones in previous examples. Because you know you are querying `Customer` objects, you explicitly declare the iteration variable c as type `Customer`:

```
foreach (Customer c in queryResults)
```

You could have declared c with the variable keyword `var`, and the compiler would have inferred that the iteration variable should be of type `Customer`, but explicitly declaring it makes the code clearer to a human reader.

Within the loop itself, you simply write

```
{
    Console.WriteLine(c);
}
```

instead of explicitly printing out the fields of `Customer` because you added an override to the `Customer` class for the `ToString()` method. If you had not provided a `ToString()` override, then the default `ToString()` method would have simply printed the name of the type, like this:

```
Customers in Asia:
BegVCSharp_23_7_QueryComplexObjects.Customer
BegVCSharp_23_7_QueryComplexObjects.Customer
BegVCSharp_23_7_QueryComplexObjects.Customer
BegVCSharp_23_7_QueryComplexObjects.Customer
BegVCSharp_23_7_QueryComplexObjects.Customer
BegVCSharp_23_7_QueryComplexObjects.Customer
BegVCSharp_23_7_QueryComplexObjects.Customer
BegVCSharp_23_7_QueryComplexObjects.Customer
BegVCSharp_23_7_QueryComplexObjects.Customer
BegVCSharp_23_7_QueryComplexObjects.Customer
Program finished, press Enter/Return to continue:
```

Not what you want at all! Of course, you could always explicitly print the properties of `Customer` that you are interested in:

```
Console.WriteLine("Customer {0}: {1}, {2}", c.ID, c.City, c.Country);
```

However, if you are interested in only a few properties of an object, it is inefficient to pull the entire object into the query. Luckily, LINQ makes it simple to create query results that contain only the items you need—via projection, which you will experiment with in the next section.

## PROJECTION: CREATING NEW OBJECTS IN QUERIES

*Projection* is the technical term for creating a new data type from other data types in a LINQ query. The `select` keyword is the projection operator, which you have used in previous examples. If you are familiar with the SELECT keyword in the SQL data query language, you will be familiar with the operation of selecting a specific field from a data object, as opposed to selecting the entire object itself. In LINQ, you can do this as well—for example, to select only the `City` field from the `Customer` list in the previous example, simply change the `select` clause in the query statement to reference only the `City` property:

```
var queryResults =
        from c in customers
        where c.Region == "Asia"
        select c.City
    ;
```

That produces the following output:

```
Mumbai
Karachi
Delhi
Seoul
Istanbul
Shanghai
Jakarta
Tokyo
Tehran
Beijing
```

You can even transform the data in the query by adding an expression to the `select`, as shown here for a numeric data type:

```
select n + 1
```

Or as shown here for a string data-type query:

```
select s.ToUpper()
```

However, unlike in SQL, LINQ does not allow multiple fields in a `select` clause. That means the line

```
select c.City, c.Country, c.Sales
```

produces a compile error (semicolon expected) because the `select` clause takes only one item in its parameter list.

What you do in LINQ instead is to create a new object on-the-fly in the `select` clause to hold the results you want for your query. You'll do that in the following Try It Out.

**Projection: Creating New Objects in Queries: 23-8-ProjectionCreateNewObjects\Program.cs**

Follow these steps to create the example in Visual Studio 2012:

1. Modify 23-7-QueryComplexObjects, or create a new console application called 23-8-ProjectionCreateNewObjects in the directory `C:\BegVCSharp\Chapter23`.

2. If you chose to create a new project, copy the code to create the `Customer` class and the initialization of the customers list (`List<Customer> customers`) from the 23-7-QueryComplexObjects example; this code is exactly the same as the code previously shown.

3. In the `Main()` method following the initialization of the `customers` list, enter (or modify) the query and results processing loop as shown here:

```
var queryResults =
    from c in customers
    where c.Region == "North America"
    select new { c.City, c.Country, c.Sales }
  ;
foreach (var item in queryResults)
{
    Console.WriteLine(item);
}
```

4. The remaining code in the `Main()` method is the same as the previous examples.

5. Compile and execute the program. You will see the selected fields from the customers in North America listed, like this:

```
{ City = New York, Country = USA, Sales = 9999 }
{ City = Mexico City, Country = Mexico, Sales = 2000 }
{ City = Los Angeles, Country = USA, Sales = 5000 }
Program finished, press Enter/Return to continue:
```

### How It Works

The `Customer` class and `customers` list initialization are the same as in the previous example. In the query, you changed the requested region to North America just to mix things up a bit. The interesting change in terms of projection is the parameter to the `select` clause:

```
select new { c.City, c.Country, c.Sales }
```

You use the C# anonymous-type creation syntax directly in the `select` clause to create a new unnamed object type having the `City`, `Country`, and `Sales` properties. The `select` clause creates the new object. This way, only these three properties are duplicated and carried through the different stages of processing the query.

When you print out the query results, you use the same generic `foreach` loop code that you have used in all the previous examples, except for the `Customers` query:

```
foreach (var item in queryResults)
{
    Console.WriteLine(item);
}
```

This code is entirely generic; the compiler infers the type of the query result and calls the right methods for the anonymous type without you having to code anything explicitly. You did not even have to provide a `ToString()` override, as the compiler provided a default `ToString()` implementation that prints out the property names and values in a manner similar to the object initialization itself.

## PROJECTION: METHOD SYNTAX

The method syntax version of a projection query is accomplished by chaining a call to the LINQ `Select()` method along with the other LINQ methods you are calling. For example, you can get the same query result if you add the `Select()` method call to a `Where()` method call, as shown here:

```
var queryResults = customers.Where(c => c.Region == "North America")
                            .Select(c => new { c.City, c.Country, c.Sales });
```

Although the `select` clause is required in the query syntax, you haven't seen the `Select()` method before because it isn't needed in the LINQ method syntax unless you are actually doing a projection (changing the type in the result set from the original type being queried).

The order of the method calls is not fixed because the return types from the LINQ methods all implement `IEnumerable`—you can call `Select()` on a `Where()` result or vice versa. However, the order may be important depending on the specifics of your query. For example, you could not reverse the order of `Select()` and `Where()` like this:

```
var queryResults = customers.Select(c => new { c.City, c.Country, c.Sales })
                            .Where(c => c.Region == "North America");
```

The `Region` property is not included in the anonymous type `{c.City, c.Country, c.Sales }` created by the `Select()` projection, so your program would get a compile error on the `Where()` method, indicating that the anonymous type does not contain a definition for `Region`.

However, if the `Where()` method were restricting the data based on a field included in the anonymous type, such as `City`, there would be no problem—for example, the following query compiles and executes without a problem:

```
var queryResults = customers.Select(c => new {c.City, c.Country, c.Sales })
                            .Where(c => c.City == "New York");
```

## USING THE SELECT DISTINCT QUERY

Another type of query that those of you familiar with the SQL data query language will recognize is the SELECT DISTINCT query, in which you search for the unique values in your data—that is, values that are not repeated. This is a fairly common need when working with queries.

Suppose you need to find the distinct regions in the customer data used in the previous examples. There is no separate region list in the data you just used, so you need to find the unique, nonrepeating list of regions from the customer list itself. LINQ provides a `Distinct()` method that makes it easy to find this data. You'll use it in the following Try It Out.

---

**TRY IT OUT**    Projection: Select Distinct Query: 23-9-SelectDistinctQuery\Program.cs

Follow these steps to create the example in Visual Studio 2012:

1. Modify the previous example, 23-8-ProjectionCreateNewObjects, or create a new console application called 23-9-SelectDistinctQuery in the directory C:\BegVCSharp\Chapter23.

2. Copy the code to create the `Customer` class and the initialization of the `customers` list (List<Customer> customers) from the 23-7-QueryComplexObjects example; the code is the same.

3. In the `Main()` method, following the initialization of the `customers` list, enter (or modify) the query as shown here:

```
var queryResults = customers.Select(c => c.Region).Distinct();
```

4. The remaining code in the `Main()` method is the same as in the previous example.

5. Compile and execute the program. You will see the unique regions where customers exist:

```
North America
Asia
South America
Europe
Africa
Program finished, press Enter/Return to continue:
```

### How It Works

The `Customer` class and `customers` list initialization are the same as in the previous example. In the query statement, you call the `Select()` method with a simple lambda expression to select the region from the `Customer` objects, and then call `Distinct()` to return only the unique results from `Select()`:

```
var queryResults = customers.Select(c => c.Region).Distinct();
```

Because `Distinct()` is available only in method syntax, you make the call to `Select()` using method syntax. However, you can call `Distinct()` to modify a query made in the query syntax as well:

```
var queryResults = (from c in customers select c.Region).Distinct();
```

Because query syntax is translated by the C# compiler into the same series of LINQ method calls as used in the method syntax, you can mix and match if it makes sense for readability and style.

## USING THE ANY AND ALL METHODS

Another type of query that you often need is for determining whether any of your data satisfies a certain condition, or ensuring that all data satisfies a condition. For example, you may need to know whether a product is out of stock (quantity is zero), or whether a transaction has occurred.

LINQ provides two Boolean methods—`Any()` and `All()`—that can quickly tell you whether a condition is `true` or `false` for your data. That makes it easy to find the data, which you will do in the following Try It Out.

**TRY IT OUT**   Using Any and All: 23-10-AnyAndAll\Program.cs

Follow these steps to create the example in Visual Studio 2012:

1.  Modify the previous example, 23-9-SelectDistinctQuery, or create a new console application called 23-10-AnyAndAll in the directory `C:\BegVCSharp\Chapter23`.

2.  Copy the code to create the `Customer` class and the initialization of the `customers` list (`List<Customer> customers`) from the 23-7-QueryComplexObjects example; this code is the same.

3.  In the `Main()` method, following the initialization of the `customers` list and query declaration, remove the processing loop and enter the code as shown here:

```
bool anyUSA = customers.Any(c => c.Country == "USA");
if (anyUSA)
{
    Console.WriteLine("Some customers are in the USA");
}
else
{
    Console.WriteLine("No customers are in the USA");
}

bool allAsia = customers.All(c => c.Region == "Asia");
if (allAsia)
{
    Console.WriteLine("All customers are in Asia");
}
else
{
    Console.WriteLine("Not all customers are in Asia");
}
```

4.  The remaining code in the `Main()` method is the same as in the previous example.

**5.** Compile and execute the program. You will see the messages indicating that some customers are in the U.S.A., but not all customers are in Asia:

```
Some customers are in the USA
Not all customers are in Asia
Program finished, press Enter/Return to continue:
```

### How It Works

The `Customer` class and `customers` list initialization are the same as in previous examples. In the first query statement, you call the `Any()` method with a simple lambda expression to check whether the Customer Country field has the value `USA`:

```
bool anyUSA = customers.Any(c => c.Country == "USA");
```

The LINQ `Any()` method applies the lambda expression you pass to it—`c => c.Country == "USA"`—against the data in the `customers` list, and returns `true` if the lambda expression is true for any of the customers in the list.

Next, you check the Boolean result variable returned by the `Any()` method and print out a message indicating the result of the query (even though `Any()` is simply returning `true` or `false`, it is performing a query to obtain the `true/false` result):

```
if (anyUSA)
{
    Console.WriteLine("Some customers are in the USA");
}
else
{
    Console.WriteLine("No customers are in the USA");
}
```

Although you could make this message more compact with some clever code, it is more straightforward and readable as shown here. As you would expect, the `anyUSA` variable is set to `true` because there are indeed customers located in the U.S.A. in the data set, so you see the message `"Some customers are in the USA"`.

In the next query statement, you call the `All()` method with another simple lambda expression to determine whether all the customers are located in Asia:

```
bool allAsia = customers.All(c => c.Region == "Asia");
```

The LINQ `All()` method applies the lambda expression against the data set and returns `false`, as you would expect, because some customers are outside of Asia. You then print the appropriate message based on the value of `allAsia`.

## ORDERING BY MULTIPLE LEVELS

Now that you are dealing with objects with multiple properties, you might be able to envision a situation where ordering the query results by a single field is not enough. What if you wanted to query your customers and order the results alphabetically by region, but then order alphabetically by country or city name within a region? LINQ makes this very easy, as you will see in the following Try It Out.

**TRY IT OUT** Ordering By Multiple Levels: 23-11-MultiLevelOrdering\Program.cs

Follow these steps to create the example in Visual Studio 2012:

**1.** Modify the previous example, 23-8-ProjectionCreateNewObjects, or create a new console application called 23-11-MultiLevelOrdering in the directory `C:\BegVCSharp\Chapter23`.

**2.** Create the `Customer` class and the initialization of the `customers` list (`List<Customer> customers`) as shown in the 23-7-QueryComplexObjects example; this code is exactly the same as in previous examples.

**3.** In the `Main()` method, following the initialization of the `customers` list, enter the following query:

```
var queryResults =
    from c in customers
    orderby c.Region, c.Country, c.City
    select new { c.ID, c.Region, c.Country, c.City }
;
```

**4.** The results processing loop and the remaining code in the `Main()` method are the same as in previous examples.

**5.** Compile and execute the program. You will see the selected properties from all customers ordered alphabetically by region first, then by country, and then by city, as shown here:

```
{ ID = O, Region = Africa, Country = Egypt, City = Cairo }
{ ID = J, Region = Africa, Country = Nigeria, City = Lagos }
{ ID = R, Region = Asia, Country = China, City = Beijing }
{ ID = I, Region = Asia, Country = China, City = Shanghai }
{ ID = D, Region = Asia, Country = India, City = Delhi }
{ ID = B, Region = Asia, Country = India, City = Mumbai }
{ ID = L, Region = Asia, Country = Indonesia, City = Jakarta }
{ ID = P, Region = Asia, Country = Iran, City = Tehran }
{ ID = M, Region = Asia, Country = Japan, City = Tokyo }
{ ID = G, Region = Asia, Country = Korea, City = Seoul }
{ ID = C, Region = Asia, Country = Pakistan, City = Karachi }
{ ID = H, Region = Asia, Country = Turkey, City = Istanbul }
{ ID = F, Region = Europe, Country = Russia, City = Moscow }
{ ID = Q, Region = Europe, Country = UK, City = London }
{ ID = K, Region = North America, Country = Mexico, City = Mexico City }
{ ID = N, Region = North America, Country = USA, City = Los Angeles }
{ ID = A, Region = North America, Country = USA, City = New York }
{ ID = E, Region = South America, Country = Brazil, City = São Paulo }
{ ID = S, Region = South America, Country = Colombia, City = Bogotá }
{ ID = T, Region = South America, Country = Peru, City = Lima }
Program finished, press Enter/Return to continue:
```

### How It Works

The `Customer` class and `customers` list initialization are the same as in previous examples. In this query you have no `where` clause because you want to see all the customers, but you simply list the fields you want to sort by in order in a comma-separated list in the `orderby` clause:

```
orderby c.Region, c.Country, c.City
```

Couldn't be easier, could it? It seems a bit counterintuitive that a simple list of fields is allowed in the `orderby` clause but not in the `select` clause, but that is how LINQ works. It makes sense if you realize that the `select` clause is creating a new object but the `orderby` clause, by definition, operates on a field-by-field basis.

You can add the `descending` keyword to any of the fields listed to reverse the sort order for that field. For example, to order this query by ascending region but descending country, simply add `descending` following `Country` in the list, like this:

```
orderby c.Region, c.Country descending, c.City
```

With `descending` added, you see following output:

```
{ ID = J, Region = Africa, Country = Nigeria, City = Lagos }
{ ID = O, Region = Africa, Country = Egypt, City = Cairo }
{ ID = H, Region = Asia, Country = Turkey, City = Istanbul }
{ ID = C, Region = Asia, Country = Pakistan, City = Karachi }
{ ID = G, Region = Asia, Country = Korea, City = Seoul }
```

```
{ ID = M, Region = Asia, Country = Japan, City = Tokyo }
{ ID = P, Region = Asia, Country = Iran, City = Tehran }
{ ID = L, Region = Asia, Country = Indonesia, City = Jakarta }
{ ID = D, Region = Asia, Country = India, City = Delhi }
{ ID = B, Region = Asia, Country = India, City = Mumbai }
{ ID = R, Region = Asia, Country = China, City = Beijing }
{ ID = I, Region = Asia, Country = China, City = Shanghai }
{ ID = Q, Region = Europe, Country = UK, City = London }
{ ID = F, Region = Europe, Country = Russia, City = Moscow }
{ ID = N, Region = North America, Country = USA, City = Los Angeles }
{ ID = A, Region = North America, Country = USA, City = New York }
{ ID = K, Region = North America, Country = Mexico, City = Mexico City }
{ ID = T, Region = South America, Country = Peru, City = Lima }
{ ID = S, Region = South America, Country = Colombia, City = Bogotá }
{ ID = E, Region = South America, Country = Brazil, City = São Paulo }
Program finished, press Enter/Return to continue:
```

Note that the cities in India and China are still in ascending order even though the country ordering has been reversed.

## MULTI-LEVEL ORDERING METHOD SYNTAX: THENBY

Under the covers, things get a bit more complicated when you look at multi-level ordering using the method syntax, which uses the `ThenBy()` method as well as `OrderBy()`. For instance, you get the same query result as the example you just created with the following:

```
var queryResults = customers.OrderBy(c => c.Region)
                    .ThenBy(c => c.Country)
                    .ThenBy(c => c.City)
                    .Select(c => new { c.ID, c.Region, c.Country, c.City });
```

Now it is more apparent why a multi-field list is allowed in the `orderby` clause in the query syntax; you can see it is translated into a series of `ThenBy()` method invocations on a field-by-field basis. The order is important in writing these method calls: You must begin with `OrderBy()` because `ThenBy()` is available only on an `IOrderedEnumerable<T>` interface, which is produced by `OrderBy()`. However, `ThenBy()` can be chained to other `ThenBy()` method calls as many times as necessary. This is a clear case where the query syntax is easier to write than the method syntax.

The descending sort order is specified by calling either `OrderByDescending()` if the first field is to be sorted in descending order, or `ThenByDescending()` if any of the remaining fields are to be sorted in descending order. To sort the country in descending order as in this example, the method syntax query would be as follows:

```
var queryResults = customers.OrderBy(c => c.Region)
                    .ThenByDescending(c => c.Country)
                    .ThenBy(c => c.City)
                    .Select(c => new { c.ID, c.Region, c.Country, c.City });
```

## USING GROUP QUERIES

A group query divides the data into groups and enables you to sort, calculate aggregates, and compare by group. These are often the most interesting queries in a business context (the ones that really drive decision-making). For example, you might want to compare sales by country or by region to decide where to open another store or hire more staff. You'll do that in the next Try It Out.

---

**TRY IT OUT**   **Using a Group Query: 23-12-GroupQuery\Program.cs**

Follow these steps to create the example in Visual Studio 2012:

1. Create a new console application called 23-12-GroupQuery in the directory `C:\BegVCSharp\Chapter23`.

2. Create the `Customer` class and the initialization of the `customers` list (`List<Customer> customers`), as shown in the 23-7-QueryComplexObjects example; this code is exactly the same as previous examples.

3. In the `Main()` method, following the initialization of the `customers` list, enter two queries:

```
var queryResults =
    from c in customers
    group c by c.Region into cg
    select new { TotalSales = cg.Sum(c => c.Sales), Region = cg.Key }
    ;
var orderedResults =
    from cg in queryResults
    orderby cg.TotalSales descending
    select cg
    ;
```

4. Continuing in the `Main()` method, add the following print statement and `foreach` processing loop:

```
Console.WriteLine("Total\t: By\nSales\t: Region\n-----\t ------");
foreach (var item in orderedResults)
{
    Console.WriteLine(item.TotalSales + "\t: " + item.Region);
}
```

5. The results processing loop and the remaining code in the `Main()` method are the same as in previous examples. Compile and execute the program. Here are the group results:

```
Total  : By
Sales  : Region
-----    ------
52997  : Asia
16999  : North America
12444  : Europe
8558   : South America
7000   : Africa
```

### How It Works

The `Customer` class and `customers` list initialization are the same as in previous examples.

The data in a group query is grouped by a key field, the field for which all the members of each group share a value. In this example, the key field is the `Region`:

```
group c by c.Region
```

You want to calculate a total for each group, so you group `into` a new result set named `cg`:

```
group c by c.Region into cg
```

In the `select` clause, you project a new anonymous type whose properties are the total sales (calculated by referencing the `cg` result set) and the key value of the group, which you reference with the special group `Key`:

```
select new { TotalSales = cg.Sum(c => c.Sales), Region = cg.Key }
```

The group result set implements the LINQ `IGrouping` interface, which supports the `Key` property. You almost always want to reference the `Key` property in some way in processing group results, because it represents the criteria by which each group in your data was created.

You want to order the result in descending order by `TotalSales` field so you can see which region has the highest total sales, next highest, and so on. To do that, you create a second query to order the results from the group query:

```
var orderedResults =
    from cg in queryResults
    orderby cg.TotalSales descending
    select cg
;
```

The second query is a standard `select` query with an `orderby` clause, as you have seen in previous examples; it does not make use of any LINQ group capabilities except that the data source comes from the previous group query.

Next, you print out the results, with a little bit of formatting code to display the data with column headers and some separation between the totals and the group names:

```
Console.WriteLine("Total\t: By\nSales\t: Region\n---\t ---");
foreach (var item in orderedResults)
{
    Console.WriteLine(item.TotalSales + "\t: " + item.Region);
};
```

This could be formatted in a more sophisticated way with field widths and by right-justifying the totals, but this is just an example so you don't need to bother—you can see the data clearly enough to understand what the code is doing.

## USING TAKE AND SKIP

Suppose you need to find the top five customers by sales in your data set. You don't know ahead of time what amount of sales qualifies a customer to be in the top five so you can't use a `where` condition to find them.

Some SQL databases, such as Microsoft SQL Server, implement a `TOP` operator, so you can issue a command like `SELECT TOP 5 FROM...` to get the top five customers.

The LINQ equivalent to this operation is the `Take()` method, which takes the first *n* results in the query output. In practical use this needs to be combined with `orderby` to get the top *n* results. However, the `orderby` is not required, as there may be situations for which you know the data is already in the order you want, or, for some reason, you want the first n results without caring about their order.

The inverse of `Take()` is `Skip()`, which skips the first *n* results, returning the remainder. `Take()` and `Skip()` are called *partitioning operators* in LINQ documentation because they partition the result set into the first *n* results (`Take()`) and/or its remainder (`Skip()`).

In the following Try It Out, you use both `Take()` and `Skip()` with the `customers` list data.

**TRY IT OUT**    Working with Take and Skip: 23-13-TakeAndSkip\Program.cs

Follow these steps to create the example in Visual Studio 2012:

1. Create a new console application called 23-13-TakeAndSkip in the directory `C:\BegVCSharp\Chapter23`.

2. Copy the code to create the `Customer` class and the initialization of the `customers` list (`List<Customer> customers`) from the 23-7-QueryComplexObjects example.

3. In the `Main()` method, following the initialization of the `customers` list, enter this query:

```
//query syntax
var queryResults =
    from c in customers
```

```
            orderby c.Sales descending
            select new { c.ID, c.City, c.Country, c.Sales }
        ;
```

**4.** Enter two results processing loops, one using `Take()` and another using `Skip()`:

```
            Console.WriteLine("Top Five Customers by Sales");
            foreach (var item in queryResults.Take(5))
            {
                Console.WriteLine(item);
            }

            Console.WriteLine("Customers Not In Top Five");
            foreach (var item in queryResults.Skip(5))
            {
                Console.WriteLine(item);
            }
```

**5.** Compile and execute the program. You will see the top five customers and the remaining customers listed as shown here:

```
Top Five Customers by Sales
{ ID = A, City = New York, Country = USA, Sales = 9999 }
{ ID = R, City = Beijing, Country = China, Sales = 9000 }
{ ID = B, City = Mumbai, Country = India, Sales = 8888 }
{ ID = Q, City = London, Country = UK, Sales = 8000 }
{ ID = C, City = Karachi, Country = Pakistan, Sales = 7777 }
Customers Not In Top Five
{ ID = P, City = Tehran, Country = Iran, Sales = 7000 }
{ ID = D, City = Delhi, Country = India, Sales = 6666 }
{ ID = O, City = Cairo, Country = Egypt, Sales = 6000 }
{ ID = E, City = São Paulo, Country = Brazil, Sales = 5555 }
{ ID = N, City = Los Angeles, Country = USA, Sales = 5000 }
{ ID = F, City = Moscow, Country = Russia, Sales = 4444 }
{ ID = M, City = Tokyo, Country = Japan, Sales = 4000 }
{ ID = G, City = Seoul, Country = Korea, Sales = 3333 }
{ ID = L, City = Jakarta, Country = Indonesia, Sales = 3000 }
{ ID = H, City = Istanbul, Country = Turkey, Sales = 2222 }
{ ID = T, City = Lima, Country = Peru, Sales = 2002 }
{ ID = K, City = Mexico City, Country = Mexico, Sales = 2000 }
{ ID = I, City = Shanghai, Country = China, Sales = 1111 }
{ ID = S, City = Bogotá, Country = Colombia, Sales = 1001 }
{ ID = J, City = Lagos, Country = Nigeria, Sales = 1000 }
Program finished, press Enter/Return to continue:
```

### How It Works

The `Customer` class and `customers` list initialization are the same as in previous examples.

The main query consists of a `from`...`orderby`...`select` statement in the query syntax, like the ones you have created previously in this chapter, except that there is no `where` clause restriction because you want to get all of the customers (ordered by sales from highest to lowest):

```
var queryResults =
            from c in customers
            orderby c.Sales descending
            select new { c.ID, c.City, c.Country, c.Sales }
```

This example works a bit differently than previous examples in that you do not apply the operator until you actually execute the `foreach` loop on the query results, because you want to reuse the query results. First, you apply `Take(5)` to get the top five customers:

```
        foreach (var item in queryResults.Take(5))
```

Then, you apply `Skip(5)` to skip the first five items (what you already printed) and print the remaining customers from the same original set of query results:

```
foreach (var item in queryResults.Skip(5))
```

The code to print out the results and pause the screen is the same as in previous examples, except for minor changes to the messages, so it isn't repeated here.

## USING FIRST AND FIRSTORDEFAULT

Suppose you need to find an example of a customer from Africa in your data set. You need the actual data itself, not a `true`/`false` value or the result set of all matching values.

LINQ provides this capability via the `First()` method, which returns the first element in a result set that matches the criteria specified. If there isn't a customer from Africa, then LINQ also provides a method to handle that contingency without additional error handling code: `FirstOrDefault()`.

In the following Try It Out, you use both `First()` and `FirstOrDefault()` with the `customers` list data.

**TRY IT OUT**    Using First and FirstOrDefault: 23-14-FirstOrDefault\Program.cs

Follow these steps to create the example in Visual Studio 2012:

1. Create a new console application called 23-14-FirstOrDefault in the directory `C:\BegVCSharp\Chapter23`.

2. Copy the code to create the `Customer` class and the initialization of the `customers` list (`List<Customer> customers`) from the 23-7-QueryComplexObjects example.

3. In the `Main()` method following the initialization of the `customers` list, enter this query:

```
var queryResults = from c in customers
                   select new { c.City, c.Country, c.Region }
                   ;
```

4. Enter the following queries using `First()` and `FirstOrDefault()`:

```
Console.WriteLine("A customer in Africa");
Console.WriteLine(queryResults.First(c => c.Region == "Africa"));

Console.WriteLine("A customer in Antarctica");
Console.WriteLine(queryResults.FirstOrDefault(c => c.Region == "Antarctica"));
```

5. Compile and execute the program. Here's the resulting output:

```
A customer in Africa
{ City = Lagos, Country = Nigeria, Region = Africa }
A customer in Antarctica

Program finished, press Enter/Return to continue:
```

### How It Works

The `Customer` class and `customers` list initialization are the same as in previous examples.

The main query consists of a `from...select` statement in the query syntax, like the ones you have created previously in this chapter, with no `where` or `orderby` clauses. You project the fields of interest with the `select` statement—in this case, the `City`, `Country`, and `Region` properties:

```
var queryResults = from c in customers
                   select new { c.City, c.Country, c.Region }
                   ;
```

Because the `First()` operator returns a single object value, not a result set, you do not need to create a `foreach` loop; instead, you print out the result directly:

```
Console.WriteLine(queryResults.First(c => c.Region == "Africa"));
```

This finds a customer, and the result `City = Lagos, Country = Nigeria, Region = Africa` is printed out. Next, you query for the Antarctica region using `FirstOrDefault()`:

```
Console.WriteLine(queryResults.FirstOrDefault(c => c.Region == "Antarctica"));
```

This does not find any results, so a null (empty result) is returned and the output is blank. What would have happened if you had used the `First()` operator instead of `FirstOrDefault()` for the Antarctica query? You would have received the following exception:

```
System.InvalidOperationException: Sequence contains no matching element
```

Instead of `FirstOrDefault()`, it returns the default element for the list if the search criteria are not met, which is a `null` for this anonymous type. For the Antarctica query, you would have received the exception.

The code to print out the results and pause the screen is the same as in previous examples, except for minor changes to the messages.

## USING THE LINQ SET OPERATORS

LINQ provides standard set operators such as `Union()` and `Intersect()` that operate on query results. You used one of the set operators when you wrote the `Distinct()` query earlier.

In the following Try It Out, you add a simple list of orders that have been submitted by hypothetical customers and use the standard set operators to match the orders with the existing customers.

**TRY IT OUT** Set Operators: 23-15-SetOperators\Program.cs

Follow these steps to create the example in Visual Studio 2012:

1.  Create a new console application called 23-15-SetOperators in the directory `C:\BegVCSharp\Chapter23`.

2.  Copy the code to create the `Customer` class and the initialization of the customers list (`List<Customer>` customers) from the 23-7-QueryComplexObjects example.

3.  Following the `Customer` class, add this `Order` class:

```
class Order
{
    public string ID { get; set; }
    public decimal Amount { get; set; }
}
```

4.  In the `Main()` method, following the initialization of the customers list, create and initialize an orders list with the data shown here:

```
List<Order> orders = new List<Order> {
    new Order { ID="P", Amount=100 },
    new Order { ID="Q", Amount=200 },
    new Order { ID="R", Amount=300 },
    new Order { ID="S", Amount=400 },
    new Order { ID="T", Amount=500 },
    new Order { ID="U", Amount=600 },
    new Order { ID="V", Amount=700 },
    new Order { ID="W", Amount=800 },
    new Order { ID="X", Amount=900 },
    new Order { ID="Y", Amount=1000 },
    new Order { ID="Z", Amount=1100 }
};
```

**5.** Following the initialization of the `orders` list, enter these queries:

```
var customerIDs =
    from c in customers
    select c.ID
    ;
var orderIDs =
    from o in orders
    select o.ID
    ;
```

**6.** Enter the following query using `Intersect()`:

```
var customersWithOrders = customerIDs.Intersect(orderIDs);
Console.WriteLine("Customer IDs with Orders:");
foreach (var item in customersWithOrders)
{
    Console.Write("{0} ", item);
}
Console.WriteLine();
```

**7.** Enter the following query using `Except()`:

```
Console.WriteLine("Order IDs with no customers:");
var ordersNoCustomers = orderIDs.Except(customerIDs);
foreach (var item in ordersNoCustomers)
{
    Console.Write("{0} ", item);
}
Console.WriteLine();
```

**8.** Finally, enter the following query using `Union()`:

```
Console.WriteLine("All Customer and Order IDs:");
var allCustomerOrderIDs = orderIDs.Union(customerIDs);
foreach (var item in allCustomerOrderIDs)
{
    Console.Write("{0} ", item);
}
Console.WriteLine();
```

**9.** Compile and execute the program. Here's the output:

```
Customers IDs with Orders:
P Q R S T
Order IDs with no customers:
U V W X Y Z
All Customer and Order IDs:
P Q R S T U V W X Y Z A B C D E F G H I J K L M N O
Program finished, press Enter/Return to continue:
```

### How It Works

The `Customer` class and `customers` list initialization are the same as previous examples. The new `Order` class is similar to the `Customer` class, using the C# automatic properties feature to declare public properties (`ID`, `Amount`):

```
class Order
{
    public string ID { get; set; }
    public decimal Amount { get; set; }
}
```

Like the `Customer` class, this is a simplified example with just enough data to make the query work.

You use two simple `from...select` queries to get the ID fields from the `Customer` and `Order` classes, respectively:

```
var customerIDs =
    from c in customers
    select c.ID
    ;
var orderIDs =
    from o in orders
    select o.ID
    ;
```

Next, you use the `Intersect()` set operator to find only the customer IDs that also have orders in the `orderIDs` result. Only the IDs that appear in both result sets are included in the intersect set:

```
var customersWithOrders = customerIDs.Intersect(orderIDs);
```

> **NOTE** *The set operators require the set members to have the same type in order to ensure the expected results. Here, you take advantage of the fact that the IDs in both object types are strings and have the same semantics (like foreign keys in a database).*

The printout of the result set takes advantage of the fact that the IDs are only a single character, so you use `Console.Write()` with no `WriteLine()` call until the end of the `foreach` loop to make the output compact and neat:

```
Console.WriteLine("Customer IDs with Orders:");
foreach (var item in customersWithOrders)
{
    Console.Write("{0} ", item);
}
Console.WriteLine();
```

You use this same print logic in the remaining `foreach` loops.

Next, you use the `Except()` operator to find the order IDs that have no matching customer:

```
Console.WriteLine("Order IDs with no customers:");
var ordersNoCustomers = orderIDs.Except(customerIDs);
```

Finally, you use the `Union()` operator to find the union of all the customer ID and order ID fields:

```
Console.WriteLine("All Customer and Order IDs:");
var allCustomerOrderIDs = orderIDs.Union(customerIDs);
```

The IDs are output in the same order in which they appear in the customer and order lists, with duplicates removed.

The code to pause the screen is the same as in previous examples.

---

The set operators are useful, but the practical benefit of using them is limited by the requirement that all the objects being manipulated have the same type. The operators are useful in certain narrow situations where you need to manipulate sets of similarly typed results; but in the more typical case where you need to work with different related object types, you need a more practical mechanism designed to work with different object types, such as the `join` statement.

## USING JOINS

A data set such as the `customers` and `orders` list you just created, with a shared key field (ID), enables a `join` query, whereby you can query related data in both lists with a single query, joining the results together with the key field. This is similar to the `JOIN` operation in the SQL data query language; and as you might expect, LINQ provides a `join` command in the query syntax, which you will use in the following Try It Out.

**TRY IT OUT** Join Query: 23-16-JoinQuery\Program.cs

Follow these steps to create the example in Visual Studio 2012:

1. Create a new console application called 23-16-JoinQuery in the directory `C:\BegVCSharp\Chapter23`.

2. Copy the code to create the `Customer` class, the `Order` class, and the initialization of the `customers` list (`List<Customer> customers`) and orders list (`List<Order> orders`) from the previous example; this code is the same.

3. In the `Main()` method, following the initialization of the `customers` and `orders` list, enter this query:

```
var queryResults =
    from c in customers
    join o in orders on c.ID equals o.ID
    select new { c.ID, c.City, SalesBefore = c.Sales, NewOrder = o.Amount,
                            SalesAfter = c.Sales+o.Amount };
```

4. Finish the program using the standard `foreach` query processing loop you used in earlier examples:

```
foreach (var item in queryResults)
{
    Console.WriteLine(item);
}
```

5. Compile and execute the program. Here's the output:

```
{ ID = P, City = Tehran, SalesBefore = 7000, NewOrder = 100, SalesAfter = 7100 }
{ ID = Q, City = London, SalesBefore = 8000, NewOrder = 200, SalesAfter = 8200 }
{ ID = R, City = Beijing, SalesBefore = 9000, NewOrder = 300, SalesAfter = 9300 }
{ ID = S, City = Bogotá, SalesBefore = 1001, NewOrder = 400, SalesAfter = 1401 }
{ ID = T, City = Lima, SalesBefore = 2002, NewOrder = 500, SalesAfter = 2502 }
Program finished, press Enter/Return to continue:
```

### How It Works

The code declaring and initializing the `Customer` class, the `Order` class, and the `customers` and `orders` lists is the same as in the previous example.

The query uses the `join` keyword to unite the customers with their corresponding orders using the ID fields from the `Customer` and `Order` classes, respectively:

```
var queryResults =
    from c in customers
    join o in orders on c.ID equals o.ID
```

The on keyword is followed by the name of the key field (`ID`), and the `equals` keyword indicates the corresponding field in the other collection. The query result only includes the data for objects that have the same ID field value as the corresponding ID field in the other collection.

The `select` statement projects a new data type with properties named so that you can clearly see the original sales total, the new order, and the resulting new total:

```
select new { c.ID, c.City, SalesBefore = c.Sales, NewOrder = o.Amount,
                        SalesAfter = c.Sales+o.Amount };
```

Although you do not increment the sales total in the `customer` object in this program, you could easily do so in the business logic of your program.

The logic of the `foreach` loop and the display of the values from the query are exactly the same as in previous programs in this chapter.

# SUMMARY

As you have seen, LINQ makes queries written in native C# quite easy and powerful. In the next chapter, you will learn how to apply LINQ to query relational databases and work effectively with large data sets.

There are too many LINQ methods in the method syntax to cover them all in a beginning book. For more details and examples, explore the Microsoft online documentation on LINQ. For short examples of every LINQ method, check out the "101 LINQ Samples" topic in the MSDN help (or online at `http://code .msdn.microsoft.com/101-LINQ-Samples-3fb9811b`).

## EXERCISES

**23.1**   Modify the first example program (23–1-FirstLINQquery) to order the results in descending order.

**23.2**   Modify the number passed to the `GenerateLotsOfNumbers()` method in the large number program example (23–5-LargeNumberQuery) to create result sets of different sizes and see how query results are affected.

**23.3**   Add an `orderby` clause to the query in the large number program example (23–5-LargeNumberQuery) to see how this affects performance.

**23.4**   Modify the query conditions in the large number program example (23–5-LargeNumberQuery) to select larger and smaller subsets of the number list. How does this affect performance?

**23.5**   Modify the method syntax example (23–2-LINQMethodSyntax) to eliminate the `where` clause entirely. How much output does it generate?

**23.6**   Modify the query complex objects program example (23–7-QueryComplexObjects) to select a different subset of the query fields with a condition appropriate to that field.

**23.7**   Add aggregate operators to the first example program (23–1-FirstLINQquery). Which simple aggregate operators are available for this non-numeric result set?

Answers to Exercises can be found in Appendix A.

## ▶ WHAT YOU LEARNED IN THIS CHAPTER

| TOPIC | KEY CONCEPTS |
|---|---|
| **What LINQ is and when to use it** | LINQ is a query language built into C#. Use LINQ to query data from large collections of objects, XML, or databases. |
| **Parts of a LINQ query** | A LINQ query includes the `from`, `where`, `select`, and `orderby` clauses. |
| **How to get the results of a LINQ query** | Use the foreach statement to iterate through the results of a LINQ query. |
| **Deferred execution** | LINQ query execution is deferred until the `foreach` statement is executed. |
| **Method syntax and query syntax** | Use the query syntax for simple LINQ queries, and method queries for more advanced queries. For any given query, the query syntax or the method syntax will give the same result. |
| **Aggregate operators** | Use LINQ aggregate operators to obtain information about a large data set without having to iterate through every result. |
| **Projection** | Use projection to change the data types and create new objects in queries. |
| **Group queries** | Use group queries to divide data into groups, then sort, calculate aggregates, and compare by group. |
| **Ordering** | Use the `orderby` operator to order the results of a query. |
| **Set operators** | Use the `set` operators `Union()`, `Intersect()`, and `Distinct()` to find matching data in multiple result sets. |
| **Joins** | Use the `join` operator to query related data in multiple collections with a single query. |

# 24

# Applying LINQ

## WHAT YOU WILL LEARN IN THIS CHAPTER

- ➤ LINQ varieties
- ➤ How to use LINQ with databases
- ➤ How to navigate database relationships
- ➤ How to use LINQ with XML
- ➤ How to use LINQ to XML constructors
- ➤ How to generate XML from databases
- ➤ How to work with XML fragments

The previous chapter introduced LINQ (Language-Integrated Query) and showed how LINQ works with objects. This chapter teaches you how to apply LINQ to queries and manipulate data from different data sources such as databases and XML (Extensible Markup Language).

## WROX.COM CODE DOWNLOADS FOR THIS CHAPTER

The wrox.com code downloads for this chapter are found at www.wrox.com/remtitle .cgi?isbn=9781118314418 on the Download Code tab. The code is in the Chapter 24 download and individually named according to the names throughout the chapter.

## LINQ VARIETIES

Visual Studio 2012 and the .NET Framework 4.5 come with a number of built-in LINQ capabilities that provide query solutions for different types of data:

- ➤ **LINQ to Objects**—Provides queries on any kind of C# in-memory object, such as arrays, lists, and other collection types. All of the examples in the previous chapter use LINQ to Objects. However, you can use the techniques you learn in this chapter with all of the varieties of LINQ.

- ➤ **LINQ to XML**—Provides creation and manipulation of XML documents using the same syntax and general query mechanism as the other LINQ varieties.

- ➤ **LINQ to ADO.NET**—ADO.NET or Active Data Objects for .NET is an umbrella term that includes all the different classes and libraries in .NET for accessing data in databases, such as Microsoft SQL Server, Oracle, and others. LINQ to ADO.NET includes LINQ to Entities, LINQ to Data Set, and LINQ to SQL.

➤ **LINQ to Entities**—The ADO.NET Entity Framework is the newest set of data interface classes in .NET 4, recommended by Microsoft for new development. In this chapter you will add an ADO.NET Entity Framework data source to your Visual C# project, then query it using LINQ to Entities.

➤ **LINQ to Data Set**—The DataSet object was introduced in the first version of the .NET Framework. This variety of LINQ enables legacy .NET data to be queried easily with LINQ.

➤ **LINQ to SQL**—This is an alternative LINQ interface for .NET 3.5, targeted mainly at Microsoft SQL Server, that has been superseded by LINQ to Entities in .NET 4.0 and 4.5.

➤ **PLINQ**—PLINQ, or Parallel LINQ, extends LINQ to Objects with a parallel programming library that can split up a query to execute simultaneously on a multicore processor.

With so many varieties of LINQ, it is impossible to cover them all in a beginning book, so this chapter shows you how to apply LINQ to the most common data sources of XML and relational database entities. LINQ works very similarly for all data sources, so once you have learned to use two or three LINQ varieties, you will find it easy to apply LINQ to new data sources.

## USING LINQ WITH DATABASES

SQL databases such as Microsoft SQL Server and Oracle are called *relational databases*. Relational databases are built on an *entity-relationship* model, where an *entity* is the abstract concept of a data object such as a customer, which is related to other entities such as orders and products (for example, a customer places an order for products).

Relational databases use the SQL database language (SQL stands for *Structured Query Language*) to query and manipulate their data. Traditionally, working with such a database required knowing at least some SQL, either embedding SQL statements in your programming language or passing strings containing SQL statements to API calls or methods in a SQL-oriented database class library.

Sounds complicated, doesn't it? Well, the good news is that Visual Studio 2012 and the ADO.NET Entity Framework can create C# objects to represent the entities in a database model, then handle all the details of creating and communicating with the SQL database for you! It translates your LINQ queries to SQL statements automatically and enables you and your programs to work simply with C# objects.

Creating the code to make a set of classes and collections that matches the structure of an existing relational table structure is tedious and time-consuming, but with LINQ to Entities object-relational mapping, the classes that match the database table are created automatically from the database itself so you don't have to, and you can start using the classes immediately.

## INSTALLING SQL SERVER AND THE NORTHWIND SAMPLE DATA

To run the examples shown in this chapter, you must install Microsoft SQL Server Express, the lightweight version of Microsoft SQL Server.

> **NOTE** *If you are familiar with SQL Server and have access to an instance of Microsoft SQL Server Standard or Enterprise Edition with the Northwind sample database installed, you can skip this installation, although you will have to change the connection information to match your SQL Server instance and Northwind database. If you have never worked with SQL Server, then go ahead and install SQL Server Express.*

## Installing SQL Server Express

Visual Studio 2012 includes a copy of SQL Server Express LocalDB, the lightweight desktop engine version of Microsoft SQL Server. SQL Server Express LocalDB supports the same SQL syntax as the full Microsoft SQL Server so it is an appropriate version for beginners to learn on.

If you have already installed Visual Studio 2012 but have not installed SQL Server Express Edition, you can download and install it using the following URL: `http://www.microsoft.com/express/sql/default.aspx`.

You will want to download the package titled like this:

```
SQL Server Express with Tools (with
LocalDB, Includes the database engine and
SQL Server Management Studio Express)
```

> **NOTE** *You cannot use Microsoft SQL Server Compact Edition with LINQ to Entities. You must use SQL Server Express LocalDB instead.*

## Installing the Northwind Sample Database

The Northwind sample database for SQL Server is required for the examples in this chapter. A sample database file in SQL Server 2012 LocalDB format is included in the code download for chapter 24. The sample programs assume this file is located at: `C:\BegVCSharp\Chapter24\Database\Northwind.MDF`.

Keep this filename and path handy because you will refer to it later when creating the connection to the database. Now you can have some fun with LINQ to Entities!

## FIRST LINQ TO DATABASE QUERY

In the following Try It Out, you create a simple query to find a subset of customer objects in the Northwind SQL Server sample data using LINQ to SQL, and print it to the console.

**TRY IT OUT** First LINQ to Database Query: BegVCSharp_24_FirstLINQtoDatabaseQuery

Follow these steps to create the example in Visual Studio 2012:

1. Create a new console application project called BegVCSharp_24_1_FirstLINQtoDatabaseQuery in the directory `C:\BegVCSharp\Chapter24`.
2. Press OK to create the project.
3. To add the LINQ to Entities data source for the Northwind database, go to the Solution Explorer pane, click the BegVCSharp_24_1_FirstLINQtoDatabaseQuery C# project, then select Project ➪ Add New Data Source from the menu bar.
4. In the Choose a Data Source Type dialog box, select Database. Click Next.
5. In the Choose a Database Model dialog box, select Entity Data Model. Click Next.
6. In the Choose Model Contents dialog box, select Generate From Database. Click Next.
7. In the Choose Your Data Connection dialog box, select New Connection.
8. In the Choose Data Source dialog box, select Microsoft SQL Server Database File. Click Continue.

9. In the Connection Properties dialog box, click the Browse button next to the Database File Name (this works for a new or existing textbox). Browse to the `C:\BegVCSharp\Chapter24\Database` directory and select `Northwind.MDF` as the database file name. Click OK to close the windows to finish importing the entity model.

10. Click Next. A popup will ask whether you want to copy the database file to your project. Choose No.

11. In the Choose Your Database Objects And Settings dialog box (Entity Data Model Wizard), expand the Tables control, dbo control, and check Customers, Orders, and Order Details. Click Finish and you will now see a diagram of your entity data objects in a window labeled `Model1.edmx`, as shown in Figure 24-1. If VS2012 asks if the location is trusted, answer Yes.

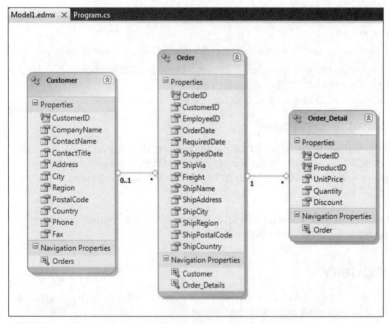

**FIGURE 24-1**

12. Compile the project now so that the `Customer` object will be available when you start entering code in the next step.

    You can see the code for classes generated for your entity model by looking in the `Model1.designer.cs` file, which appears underneath the `Model1.edmx` source file in the Solution Explorer, similar to the way a form's generated code is placed in `<formname>.designer.cs`. However, just as with a form's generated code, you should not modify the designer-generated code, so it best not to open this code in the editor except when you want to verify a class name or check a generated data type.

13. Open the main source file `Program.cs` and add the following code to the `Main()` method:

```
static void Main(string[] args)
{
    NorthwindEntities northWindEntities = new NorthwindEntities();

    var queryResults = from c in northWindEntities.Customers
                       where c.Country == "USA"
                       select new {
                                ID=c.CustomerID,
                                Name=c.CompanyName,
                                City=c.City,
```

```
                             State=c.Region
                  };
        foreach (var item in queryResults) {
            Console.WriteLine(item);
        };

        Console.WriteLine("Press Enter/Return to continue.. ");
        Console.ReadLine();
}
```

**14.** Compile and execute the program (you can just press F5 for Start Debugging). You will see the information for customers in the United States appear as shown here:

```
{ ID = GREAL, Name = Great Lakes Food Market, City = Eugene, State = OR }
{ ID = HUNGC, Name = Hungry Coyote Import Store, City = Elgin, State = OR }
{ ID = LAZYK, Name = Lazy K Kountry Store, City = Walla Walla, State = WA }
{ ID = LETSS, Name = Let's Stop N Shop, City = San Francisco, State = CA }
{ ID = LONEP, Name = Lonesome Pine Restaurant, City = Portland, State = OR }
{ ID = OLDWO, Name = Old World Delicatessen, City = Anchorage, State = AK }
{ ID = RATTC, Name = Rattlesnake Canyon Grocery, City = Albuquerque, State = NM
}
{ ID = SAVEA, Name = Save-a-lot Markets, City = Boise, State = ID }
{ ID = SPLIR, Name = Split Rail Beer & Ale, City = Lander, State = WY }
{ ID = THEBI, Name = The Big Cheese, City = Portland, State = OR }
{ ID = THECR, Name = The Cracker Box, City = Butte, State = MT }
{ ID = TRAIH, Name = Trail's Head Gourmet Provisioners, City = Kirkland,
  State = WA }
{ ID = WHITC, Name = White Clover Markets, City = Seattle, State = WA }
Press Enter/Return to continue…
```

Simply press Enter/Return to finish the program and make the console screen disappear. If you used Ctrl+F5 (Start Without Debugging), you might need to press Enter/Return twice. That finishes the program run. Now let's look at how it works in detail.

### How It Works

The code for this and all other examples in this chapter is similar to the examples described in the introduction to LINQ in Chapter 23. As in that chapter, this code uses extension classes from the System.Linq namespace, which is referenced by a using statement inserted automatically by Visual Studio 2012 when you create the project:

```
using System.Linq;
```

The first step in using the LINQ to Entities classes is to create an instance of the ObjectContext object for the particular database you are accessing, which is the class compiled from the .edmx file created in the data source. This object is the gateway to your database, providing all the methods you need to control it from your program. It also acts as a factory for creating the business objects that correspond to the conceptual entities stored in your database (for example, customers and products).

In your project, the data context class is called NorthwindEntities, compiled from the Model1.edmx file. Your first step in the Main() method is to create an instance of NorthwindEntities as shown here:

```
NorthwindEntities northWindEntities = new NorthwindEntities();
```

When you checked the Customers table into the Choose Your Database Objects pane, a Customer object was added to the LINQ to Entities class in Model1.edmx, and a Customers member was added to the northWindDataEntities object to enable you to query the Customer objects in the Northwind database.

The actual LINQ query statement makes a query using the Customers member of the northWindEntities as the data source:

```
var queryResults = from c in northWindEntities.Customers
                        where c.Country == "USA"
                        select new {
```

```
                                    ID=c.CustomerID,
                                    Name=c.CompanyName,
                                    City=c.City,
                                    State=c.Region
                        };
```

`Customers` is a typed LINQ table (`System.Data.Linq.Table<Customer>`), which is similar to a typed collection of `Customer` objects (like a `List<Table>`), but implemented for LINQ to SQL and filled from the database automatically. It implements the `IEnumerable`/`IQueryable` interfaces so it can be used as a LINQ data source in the `from` clause just like any collection or array.

The `where` clause restricts the results only to customers in the United States. The `select` clause is a projection, similar to the examples you developed in the preceding chapter, that creates a new object having members `ID`, `Name`, `City`, and `State`. Because you know the results are for the United States only, you can rename the `Region` to `State` to more precisely display the results. Finally, you create a standard `foreach` loop like the ones you wrote in Chapter 23:

```
            foreach (var item in queryResults) {
                    Console.WriteLine(item);
            };
```

This code uses the default generated `ToString()` method for each `item` to format the output for the `Console.WriteLine(item)` so you see the values for each projected member instance in curly braces:

```
    { ID=WHITC, Name=White Clover Markets, City=Seattle, State=WA }
```

Finally, the example ends with code to pause the display so you can see the results:

```
            Console.WriteLine("Press Enter/Return to continue.." );
            Console.ReadLine();
    };
```

Now you have created a basic LINQ to SQL query that you can use as a base to build on for more complex queries.

---

## NAVIGATING DATABASE RELATIONSHIPS

One of the most powerful aspects of the ADO.NET Entity Framework is its capability to automatically create LINQ to SQL objects to help you navigate relationships between related tables in the database. In the following Try It Out, you add a related table to the LINQ to Entities class, add code to navigate through the related data objects in the database, and print their values.

**TRY IT OUT** Navigating LINQ to Entities Relationships: BegVCSharp_24_2_NavigatingData

Follow these steps to create the example in Visual Studio 2012:

1. Modify the project from the previous example BegVCSharp_24_1_FirstLINQtoDataQuery in the directory `C:\BegVCSharp\Chapter24`, as shown in the following steps.

2. Open the main source file `Program.cs`. In the `Main()` method, add an `Orders` field to the `select` clause in the LINQ query (don't forget to add a comma following `c.Region` to separate the added field from the rest of the list):

```
    static void Main(string[] args)
    {
        NorthwindDataContext northWindDataContext = new NorthwindDataContext();

        var queryResults = from c in northWindDataContext.Customers
                            where c.Country == "USA"
                            select new {
                                    ID=c.CustomerID,
                                    Name=c.CompanyName,
```

```
                                City=c.City,
                                State=c.Region,
                                Orders=c.Orders
                            };
```

3. Modify the `foreach` clause to print the query results as shown:

```
            foreach (var item in queryResults) {

                Console.WriteLine(
                    "Customer: {0} {1}, {2}\n{3} orders:\tOrder ID\tOrder Date",
                        item.Name, item.City, item.State, item.Orders.Count
                );
                foreach (Orders o in item.Orders) {
                    Console.WriteLine("\t\t{0}\t{1}", o.OrderID, o.OrderDate);
                }

            };

            Console.WriteLine("Press Enter/Return to continue.. ");
            Console.ReadLine();
        }
```

4. Compile and execute the program (you can just press F5 for Start Debugging). You will see the information for customers in the United States and their orders as follows (this is the last part of the output; the first part scrolls off the top of the console window):

```
Customer: Trail's Head Gourmet Provisioners Kirkland, WA
3 orders:        Order ID         Order Date
                 10574    6/19/1997 12:00:00 AM
                 10577    6/23/1997 12:00:00 AM
                 10822    1/8/1998 12:00:00 AM
Customer: White Clover Markets Seattle, WA
14 orders:       Order ID         Order Date
                 10269    7/31/1996 12:00:00 AM
                 10344    11/1/1996 12:00:00 AM
                 10469    3/10/1997 12:00:00 AM
                 10483    3/24/1997 12:00:00 AM
                 10504    4/11/1997 12:00:00 AM
                 10596    7/11/1997 12:00:00 AM
                 10693    10/6/1997 12:00:00 AM
                 10696    10/8/1997 12:00:00 AM
                 10723    10/30/1997 12:00:00 AM
                 10740    11/13/1997 12:00:00 AM
                 10861    1/30/1998 12:00:00 AM
                 10904    2/24/1998 12:00:00 AM
                 11032    4/17/1998 12:00:00 AM
                 11066    5/1/1998 12:00:00 AM
Press Enter/Return to continue…
```

As before, press Enter/Return to finish the program and make the console screen disappear.

### How It Works

You modified your previous program instead of creating a new program from scratch so you did not have to repeat all the steps to create the `Model1.edmx` data source file (note that the sample code has separate projects, each with its own instance of `Model1.edmx`).

By checking the `Orders` table in from the Choose Your Data Objects dialog box, you added the `Order` class to the `Model1.edmx` source file to represent the `Orders` table in your mapping of the Northwind database.

Visual Studio 2012 detected the relationship in the database between `Customers` and `Orders`, adding an `Orders` collection member to the `Customer` class to represent the relationship. All this was done automatically, as when you add new controls to a form.

Next, you added the newly available `Orders` member to the `select` clause of the query:

```
select new {
            ID=c.CustomerID,
            Name=c.CompanyName,
            City=c.City,
            State=c.Region,
            Orders=c.Orders
            };
```

`Orders` is a special typed LINQ set (`System.Data.Linq.EntitySet<Order>`) that represents the relationship between two tables in the relational database. It implements the `IEnumerable/IQueryable` interfaces so it can be used as a LINQ data source itself or iterated with a `foreach` statement just like any collection or array.

Like the `Table` object shown in the previous example, the `EntitySet` is similar to a typed collection of `Order` objects (like a `List<Order>`), but only those orders submitted by a particular customer will appear in the `EntitySet` member for a particular `Customer` instance.

The `Order` objects in the customer's `EntitySet` member correspond to the order rows in the database having the same customer ID as that customer's ID.

Navigating the relationship simply involves building a nested `foreach` statement to iterate through each customer and then each customer's orders:

```
foreach (var item in queryResults) {

        Console.WriteLine(
            "Customer: {0} {1}, {2}\n{3} orders:\tOrder ID\tOrder Date",
                item.Name, item.City, item.State, item.Orders.Count
        );
        foreach (Order o in item.Orders) {
            Console.WriteLine("\t\t{0}\t{1}", o.OrderID, o.OrderDate);
        }
    };
```

Rather than just use the default `ToString()` formatting, you format the output for readability so you can show the hierarchy properly with the list of orders under each customer. The format string `"Customer: {0} {1}, {2}\n{3} orders:\tOrder ID\tOrder Date"` has a placeholder for the name, city, and state of each customer on the first line, and then prints a column header for that customer's orders on the next line. You use the LINQ aggregate `Count()` method to print the count of the number of that customer's orders, and then print out the order ID and order date on each line in the nested `foreach` statement:

```
Customer: White Clover Markets Seattle, WA
14 orders:      Order ID        Order Date
                10269   7/31/1996 12:00:00 AM
                10344   11/1/1996 12:00:00 AM
```

The formatting is still a bit rusty in that you see the time of the order when all that really matters is the date.

Now that you've successfully queried a database, it's time to try a different kind of data source—XML!

## USING LINQ WITH XML

LINQ to XML is not intended to replace the standard XML APIs such as XML DOM (Document Object Model), XPath, XQuery, XSLT, and so on. If you are familiar with these APIs or currently need to use them, you should continue to do so.

LINQ to XML supplements these standard XML classes and makes working with XML easier. LINQ to XML gives you extra options for creating and querying XML data, resulting in simpler code and quicker development for many common situations, especially if you are already using LINQ in your other programs.

## LINQ TO XML FUNCTIONAL CONSTRUCTORS

As shown in previous chapters, one of the themes in C# is easier construction of objects, with features such as object initializers and anonymous types. LINQ to XML continues this theme by introducing a new, easier way to create XML documents called *functional construction* in which the constructor calls can be nested in a way that naturally reflects the structure of the XML document. In the following Try It Out, you use functional constructors to make a simple XML document containing customers and orders.

**TRY IT OUT** LINQ to XML Constructors: BegVCSharp_24_3_LinqtoXmlConstructors

Follow these steps to create the example in Visual Studio 2012:

**1.** Create a new console application called BegVCSharp_24_3_LinqToXmlConstructors in the directory C:\BegVCSharp\Chapter24.

**2.** Open the main source file Program.cs.

**3.** Add a reference to the System.Xml.Linq namespace to the beginning of Program.cs, as shown here:

```
using System;
using System.Collections.Generic;
using System.Linq;
using System.Xml.Linq;
using System.Text;
```

**4.** Add the following code to the Main() method in Program.cs:

```csharp
static void Main(string[] args)
{
        XDocument xdoc = new XDocument(
            new XElement("customers",
                new XElement("customer",
                    new XAttribute("ID", "A"),
                    new XAttribute("City", "New York"),
                    new XAttribute("Region", "North America"),
                    new XElement("order",
                        new XAttribute("Item", "Widget"),
                        new XAttribute("Price", 100)
                    ),
                    new XElement("order",
                        new XAttribute("Item", "Tire"),
                        new XAttribute("Price", 200)
                    )
                ),
                new XElement("customer",
                    new XAttribute("ID", "B"),
                    new XAttribute("City", "Mumbai"),
                    new XAttribute("Region", "Asia"),
                    new XElement("order",
                        new XAttribute("Item", "Oven"),
                        new XAttribute("Price", 501)
                    )
                )
            )
        );
        Console.WriteLine(xdoc);

        Console.Write("Program finished, press Enter/Return to continue:");
        Console.ReadLine();
}
```

**5.** Compile and execute the program (you can just press F5 for Start Debugging). You will see the output shown here:

```
<customers>
  <customer ID="A" City="New York" Region="North America">
    <order Item="Widget" Price="100" />
    <order Item="Tire" Price="200" />
  </customer>
  <customer ID="B" City="Mumbai" Region="Asia">
    <order Item="Oven" Price="501" />
  </customer>
</customers>
Program finished, press Enter/Return to continue:
```

The XML document shown on the output screen contains a very simplified version of the customer/order data you have seen in previous examples. Note that the root element of the XML document is `<customers>`, which contains two nested `<customer>` elements. These in turn contain a number of nested `<order>` elements. The `<customer>` elements have two attributes, `City` and `Region`, and the `<order>` elements have `Item` and `Price` attributes.

Press Enter/Return to exit the program and make the console screen disappear. If you used Ctrl+F5 (Start Without Debugging), you might need to press Enter/Return twice.

### How It Works

The first step is to reference the `System.Xml.Linq` namespace. All of the following examples in this chapter require that you add this line to your program:

```
using System.Xml.Linq;
```

Although the `System.Linq` namespace is included by default when you create a project, the `System.Xml.Linq` namespace is not included; you must add this line explicitly.

Next are the calls to the LINQ to XML constructors `XDocument()`, `XElement()`, and `XAttribute()`, which are nested inside one another as shown here:

```
XDocument xdoc = new XDocument(
    new XElement("customers",
        new XElement("customer",
            new XAttribute("ID", "A"),
            ...
```

Note that the code here looks like the XML itself, where the document contains elements, and each element contains attributes and other elements. Take a look at each of these constructors in turn:

➤ `XDocument()` —The highest-level object in the LINQ to XML constructor hierarchy is `XDocument()`, which represents the complete XML document. It appears in your code here:

```
static void Main(string[] args)
{
    XDocument xdoc = new XDocument(
    ...
    );
```

The parameter list for `XDocument()` is omitted in the previous code fragment so you can see where the `XDocument()` call begins and ends. Like all the LINQ to XML constructors, `XDocument()` takes an array of objects (`object[]`) as one of its parameters so that a number of other objects created by other constructors can be passed to it. All the other constructors you call in this program are parameters in the one call to the `XDocument()` constructor. The first (and only) parameter you pass in this program is the `XElement()` constructor.

➤ XElement() —An XML document must have a root element, so in most cases the parameter list of XDocument() will begin with an XElement object. The XElement() constructor takes the name of the element as a string, followed by a list of the XML objects contained within that element. Here, the root element is "customers", which in turn contains a list of "customer" elements:

```
new XElement("customers",
    new XElement("customer",
...
            ),
...
        )
```

The "customer" element does not contain any other XML elements. Instead, it contains three XML attributes, which are constructed with the XAttribute() constructor.

➤ XAttribute() —Here you add three XML attributes to the "customer" element, named "ID", "City", and "Region":

```
new XAttribute("ID", "A"),
new XAttribute("City", "New York"),
new XAttribute("Region", "North America"),
```

Because an XML attribute is by definition a leaf XML node containing no other XML nodes, the XAttribute() constructor takes only the name of the attribute and its value as parameters. In this case, the three attributes generated are ID="A", City="New York", and Region="North America".

➤ Other LINQ to XML constructors—Although you do not call them in this program, there are other LINQ to XML constructors for all the XML node types, such as XDeclaration() for the XML declaration at the start of an XML document, XComment() for an XML comment, and so on. These other constructors are not used often but are available if you need them for precise control over formatting an XML document.

Finishing up the explanation of the first example, you add two child "order" elements to the "customer" element following the "ID", "City", and "Region" attributes:

```
new XElement("order=",
    new XAttribute("Item", "Widget"),
    new XAttribute("Price", 100)
),
new XElement("order",
    new XAttribute("Item", "Tire"),
    new XAttribute("Price", 200)
)
```

These order elements have "Item" and "Price" attributes but no other children.

Next, you display the contents of the XDocument to the console screen:

```
Console.WriteLine(xdoc);
```

This prints the text of the XML document using the default ToString() method of XDocument().

Finally, you pause the screen so you can see the console output, and then wait until the user presses Enter:

```
Console.Write("Program finished, press Enter/Return to continue:");
Console.ReadLine();
```

After that your program exits the Main() method, which ends the program.

## Constructing XML Element Text with Strings

The example you just performed formatted the XML with no text content in the elements. Often, your XML needs to have text content as well; this is very easy to do with the LINQ to XML `XElement()` constructor. For example, to make the ID the text of the `<customer>` element instead of an attribute, just pass a string in the parameters of the `XElement()` constructor instead of a nested `XAttribute`:

```
XDocument xdoc = new XDocument(
    new XElement("customers",
        new XElement("customer",
        "AAAAAA",
        new XAttribute("City", "New York"),
        new XAttribute("Region", "North America")
    ),
    new XElement("customer",
        "BBBBBB",
        new XAttribute("City", "Mumbai"),
        new XAttribute("Region", "Asia")
    )
  )
);
```

This produces an XML document that looks like this:

```
<customers>
  <customer City="New York" Region="North America">AAAAAA</customer>
  <customer City="Mumbai" Region="Asia">BBBBBB</customer>
</customers>
```

The `XElement()` constructor concatenates all strings in the parameter list into the text section of the element.

## SAVING AND LOADING AN XML DOCUMENT

You might have noticed that when the XML document was displayed to the console screen with `Console.WriteLine()`, it did not display the normal XML declaration that begins with `<?xml version="1.0">`. Although you can create such a declaration explicitly with the `XDeclaration()` constructor, you normally do not need to do so, as it is created automatically when you save an XML document to a file with the LINQ to XML `Save()` method.

In addition, although constructing XML documents in your program is useful for understanding how constructors work, it is not something you will do often. More typically, you load XML documents from an external source such as a file.

You try both of these operations in the following Try It Out.

**TRY IT OUT** Saving and Loading an XML Document: BegVCSharp_24_4_SaveLoadXML

Follow these steps to create the example in Visual Studio 2012:

1. Either modify the previous example or create a new console application called BegVCSharp_24_4_SaveLoadXML in the directory `C:\BegVCSharp\Chapter24`.

2. Open the main source file `Program.cs`.

3. Add a reference to the `System.Xml.Linq` namespace to the beginning of `Program.cs`, as shown here:

```
using System;
using System.Collections.Generic;
using System.Linq;
using System.Xml.Linq;
using System.Text;
```

This will already be present if you are modifying the previous example.

**4.** If not already present, add the XML document constructor and its nested XML element and attribute calls from the preceding example to the `Main()` method in `Program.cs`:

```
static void Main(string[] args)
{
            XDocument xdoc = new XDocument(
                new XElement("customers",
                    new XElement("customer",
                        new XAttribute("ID", "A"),
                        new XAttribute("City", "New York"),
                        new XAttribute("Region", "North America"),
                        new XElement("order",
                            new XAttribute("Item", "Widget"),
                            new XAttribute("Price", 100)
                        ),
                        new XElement("order",
                            new XAttribute("Item", "Tire"),
                            new XAttribute("Price", 200)
                        )
                    ),

                    new XElement("customer",
                        new XAttribute("ID", "B"),
                        new XAttribute("City", "Mumbai"),
                        new XAttribute("Region", "Asia"),
                        new XElement("order",
                            new XAttribute("Item", "Oven"),
                            new XAttribute("Price", 501)
                        )
                    )
                )
            );
```

**5.** After the XML document constructor code is added in the previous step, add the following code to save, load, and display the XML document at the end of the `Main()` method in `Program.cs`:

```
            string xmlFileName = @"c:\BegVCSharp\Chapter24\Xml\example2.xml";

            xdoc.Save(xmlFileName);

            XDocument xdoc2 = XDocument.Load(xmlFileName);


            Console.WriteLine("Contents of xdoc2:");
            Console.WriteLine(xdoc2);

            Console.Write("Program finished, press Enter/Return to continue:");
            Console.ReadLine();
}
```

**6.** Compile and execute the program (you can just press F5 for Start Debugging). You should see the following output in the console window:

```
Contents of xdoc2:
<customers>
  <customer ID="A" City="New York" Region="North America">
    <order Item="Widget" Price="100" />
    <order Item="Tire" Price="200" />
  </customer>
  <customer ID="B" City="Mumbai" Region="Asia">
    <order Item="Oven" Price="501" />
  </customer>
</customers>
Program finished, press Enter/Return to continue:
```

Press Enter/Return to finish the program and make the console screen disappear. If you used Ctrl+F5 (Start Without Debugging), you might need to press Enter/Return twice.

### How It Works

As before, the first step is to reference the `System.Xml.Linq` namespace. Next are the nested calls to the LINQ to XML constructors `XDocument()`, `XElement()`, and `XAttribute()`. See the first example for an explanation of these parts and other code repeated from the first example.

Following the creation of your `XDocument()` object, you specify a filename as a string and save the XML document to a file with this call to the `Save()` method:

```
string xmlFileName = @"c:\BegVCSharp\Chapter24\Xml\example2.xml";

xdoc.Save(xmlFileName);
```

Although in this particular case you save to a specified filename, the `Save()` method also has overloads to save to a `System.IO.TextWriter` or a `System.Xml.XmlWriter`, which might be appropriate if you are writing another program in which you are already using one of those classes to write to a file.

The `Save()` method also has an overload whereby you can specify `SaveOptions` to disable formatting (by default, the XML document is saved with indentation and whitespace to make it look "pretty").

Now that you've saved the document to a file, you load it into a new `XDocument` instance called `xdoc2`:

```
XDocument xdoc2 = XDocument.Load(xmlFileName);
```

The `XDocument.Load()` method is static because it is a factory-type method that creates a new instance of an `XDocument`; you can use this to load a document created by a completely different program.

Next, you display the document just as you did before, only this time using the `xdoc2` instance that you loaded from the file. The rest of the program is the same as the previous example:

```
Console.WriteLine("Contents of xdoc2:");
Console.WriteLine(xdoc2);

Console.Write("Program finished, press Enter/Return to continue:");
Console.ReadLine();
```

## Loading XML from a String

Sometimes instead of loading XML from a file, you receive XML sent from another application as a string, through one or more of your methods. You can create XML documents from strings in LINQ to XML by using the `Parse()` method:

```
XDocument xdoc = XDocument.Parse(@"
    <customers>
        <customer ID=""A"" City=""New York"" Region=""North America"">
            <order Item=""Widget"" Price=""100"" />
            <order Item=""Tire"" Price=""200"" />
        </customer>
        <customer ID=""B"" City=""Mumbai"" Region=""Asia"">
            <order Item=""Oven"" Price=""501"" />
        </customer>
    </customers>
    ");
```

This produces the same result that loading the document from a file does. Just as with `Load()`, `Parse()` is a class-level method that creates a new instance of an `XDocument`; you do not need to construct a new `XDocument` object before calling the `Parse()` method.

> **NOTE** *Although the string literal for the XML in the preceding example has double quotation marks (" "), in the actual contents of the string the quotation marks are not double. The double quotation marks are the convention for including quotation marks in a string literal.*

## Contents of a Saved XML Document

Use Internet Explorer to open the document you just saved with the previous example. Specify the full path name `C:\BegVCSharp\Chapter24\Xml\example2.xml` in the address bar.

Note that the XML document declaration `<?xml version="1.0" encoding="utf-8" ?>` appears at the beginning of the saved document even though it is not displayed when you simply print the `XDocument` object to the screen using `Console.Writeline()`. You needn't worry about the declaration and many other XML details using the defaults supplied by LINQ to XML.

> **NOTE** *The default encoding for XML documents in Windows is UTF-8 (8-bit Unicode Transformation Format). You shouldn't change this except in very unusual situations, such as when creating an ASCII-encoded XML document that would be consumed by a legacy program that doesn't understand UTF-8. In that case, you can add an* `XDeclaration()` *object with the encoding set to ASCII to the beginning of the parameter list for the* `XDocument()` *constructor, or set the* `Declaration` *property of the* `XDocument`:*
>
> ```
> xdoc.Declaration = new XDeclaration("1.0", "us-ascii", "yes");
> ```

## WORKING WITH XML FRAGMENTS

Unlike some XML APIs, LINQ to XML works with XML fragments (partial or incomplete XML documents) in very much the same way as complete XML documents. When working with a fragment, you simply work with `XElement` as the top-level XML object instead of `XDocument`.

> **NOTE** *The only restriction on this is that you cannot add some of the more esoteric XML node types that apply only to XML documents or XML fragments, such as* `XComment` *for XML comments,* `XDeclaration` *for the XML document declaration, and* `XProcessingInstruction` *for XML processing instructions.*

In the following Try It Out, you load, save, and manipulate an XML element and its child nodes, just as you did for an XML document.

**TRY IT OUT**   Working with XML Fragments: BegVCSharp_24_5_XMLFragments

Follow these steps to create the example in Visual Studio 2012:

1. Either modify the previous example or create a new console application called BegVCSharp_24_5_ XMLFragments in the directory `C:\BegVCSharp\Chapter24`.

2. Open the main source file `Program.cs`.

3. Add a reference to the `System.Xml.Linq` namespace to the beginning of `Program.cs`, as shown here:

```
using System;
using System.Collections.Generic;
using System.Xml.Linq;
using System.Text;
```

This will already be present if you are modifying the previous example.

4. Add the XML element without the containing XML document constructor used in the previous examples to the `Main()` method in `Program.cs`:

```
static void Main(string[] args)
{
            XElement xcust =
                new XElement("customers",
                    new XElement("customer",
                        new XAttribute("ID", "A"),
                        new XAttribute("City", "New York"),
                        new XAttribute("Region", "North America"),
                        new XElement("order",
                            new XAttribute("Item", "Widget"),
                            new XAttribute("Price", 100)
                    ),
                    new XElement("order",
                        new XAttribute("Item", "Tire"),
                        new XAttribute("Price", 200)
                    )
                ),
                new XElement("customer",
                    new XAttribute("ID", "B"),
                    new XAttribute("City", "Mumbai"),
                    new XAttribute("Region", "Asia"),
                    new XElement("order",
                        new XAttribute("Item", "Oven"),
                        new XAttribute("Price", 501)
                    )
                )
            )
            ;
```

5. After the XML element constructor code you added in the previous step, add the following code to save, load, and display the XML element:

```
            string xmlFileName = @"c:\BegVCSharp\Chapter24\Xml\example3.xml";
            xcust.Save(xmlFileName);

            XElement xcust2 = XElement.Load(xmlFileName);

            Console.WriteLine("Contents of xcust:");
            Console.WriteLine(xcust);

            Console.Write("Program finished, press Enter/Return to continue:");
            Console.ReadLine();
}
```

6. Compile and execute the program (you can just press F5 for Start Debugging). You should see the following output in the console window:

```
Contents of XElement xcust2:
<customers>
  <customer ID="A" City="New York" Region="North America">
    <order Item="Widget" Price="100" />
    <order Item="Tire" Price="200" />
  </customer>
```

```
    <customer ID="B" City="Mumbai" Region="Asia">
      <order Item="Oven" Price="501" />
    </customer>
  </customers>
  Program finished, press Enter/Return to continue:
```

Press Enter/Return to finish the program and make the console screen disappear. If you used Ctrl+F5 (Start Without Debugging), you might need to press Enter/Return twice.

### How It Works

Both `XElement` and `XDocument` inherit from the LINQ to XML `XContainer` class, which implements an XML node that can contain other XML nodes. Both classes also implement `Load()` and `Save()`, so most operations that can be performed on an `XDocument()` in LINQ to XML can also be performed on an `XElement` instance and its children.

You simply create an `XElement` instance that has the same structure as the `XDocument` used in previous examples but omits the containing `XDocument`. All the operations for this particular program work the same with the `XElement` fragment.

`XElement` also supports the `Load()` and `Parse()` methods for loading XML from files and strings, respectively.

## GENERATING XML FROM DATABASES

XML is often used to communicate data between client and server machines or between "tiers" in a multitier application. It is quite common to query for some data in a database, and then produce an XML document or fragment from that data to pass to another tier. In the following Try It Out, you create a query to find some data in the Northwind sample database, use LINQ to SQL to query the data, and then use LINQ to XML classes to convert the data to XML.

**TRY IT OUT** Generating XML from Databases: BegVCSharp_24_6_XMLfromDatabase

Follow these steps to create the example in Visual Studio 2012:

1. Create a new console application called BegVCSharp_24_6_XMLfromDatabase in the directory `C:\BegVCSharp\Chapter24`.

2. As described in the "First LINQ to Database Query" example at the start of this chapter, add a new data source named `Model1.edmx` to the project, and then add a connection to the Northwind sample database.

3. Compile your program so that the classes and properties defined in `Model1.edmx` will be available via IntelliSense when editing the code in the next steps.

4. Open the main source file `Program.cs`.

5. Add a reference to the `System.Xml.Linq` namespace to the beginning of `Program.cs`, as shown:

```
using System;
using System.Collections.Generic;
using System.Linq;
using System.Xml.Linq;
using System.Text;
```

6. Add the following code to the `Main()` method in `Program.cs`:

```
static void Main(string[] args)
{
            NorthwindEntities northWindEntities = new NorthwindEntities();

            XElement northwindCustomerOrders =
                new XElement("customers",
                  from c in northWindEntities.Customers.AsEnumerable()
```

```
                 select new XElement("customer",
                    new XAttribute("ID", c.CustomerID),
                    new XAttribute("City", c.City),
                    new XAttribute("Company", c.CompanyName),
                      from o in c.Orders
                      select new XElement("order",
                         new XAttribute("orderID", o.OrderID),
                         new XAttribute("orderDay",
                                  o.OrderDate.Value.Day),
                         new XAttribute("orderMonth",
                                  o.OrderDate.Value.Month),
                         new XAttribute("orderYear",
                                  o.OrderDate.Value.Year),
                         new XAttribute("orderTotal",
                             o.Order_Details.Sum(
                                 od => od.Quantity * od.UnitPrice))
                     ) //end order
                  ) // end customer
         ); // end customers

         string xmlFileName =
                   @"C:\BegVCSharp\Chapter24\Xml\NorthwindCustomerOrders.xml";
         northwindCustomerOrders.Save(xmlFileName);

         Console.WriteLine(
             "Successfully saved Northwind customer orders to:");
         Console.WriteLine(xmlFileName);
         Console.Write("Program finished, press Enter/Return to continue:");
         Console.ReadLine();
      }
```

7. Compile and execute the program (you can just press F5 for Start Debugging). You will see the following output:

```
Successfully saved Northwind customer orders to:
C:\BegVCSharp\Chapter24\Xml\NorthwindCustomerOrders.xml
Program finished, press Enter/Return to continue:
```

Simply press Enter/Return to exit the program and make the console screen disappear. If you used Ctrl+F5 (Start Without Debugging), you might need to press Enter/Return twice.

### How It Works

In `Program.cs` you added the reference to the `System.Xml.Linq` namespace in order to call the LINQ to XML constructor classes.

As described in the first part of the chapter, you created a data source for the Northwind sample database and then used Visual Studio 2012 to create a LINQ to Entities object model for the Northwind data. In the main program, you created an instance of the Northwind data context class to use the following mapping:

```
NorthwindEntities northWindEntities = new NorthwindEntities();
```

Your LINQ to Entities query uses the Northwind data context `Customers` member as a data source and drills down through the `Customers`, `Orders`, and `Order Details` tables to produce a list of all customer orders. However, because of deferred execution for LINQ to Entities, you convert the intermediate result to an in-memory LINQ to Objects enumerable type with the `AsEnumerable()` method on the `Customer` object. Finally, the query results are projected in the `select` clause of the query into a nested set of LINQ to XML elements and attributes:

```
         XElement northwindCustomerOrders =
            new XElement("customers",
             from c in northWindDataContext.Customers.AsEnumerable()
             select new XElement("customer",
```

```
                          new XAttribute("ID", c.CustomerID),
                          new XAttribute("City", c.City),
                          new XAttribute("Company", c.CompanyName),
                          from o in c.Orders
                            select new XElement("order",
                                new XAttribute("orderID", o.OrderID),
                                new XAttribute("orderDay",
                                        o.OrderDate.Value.Day),
                                new XAttribute("orderMonth",
                                        o.OrderDate.Value.Month),
                                new XAttribute("orderYear",
                                        o.OrderDate.Value.Year),
                                new XAttribute("orderTotal",
                                    o.Order_Details.Sum(
                                        od => od.Quantity * od.UnitPrice))
                            ) //end order
                        ) // end customer
                );  // end customers
```

To grab all the orders for a customer, you use a second LINQ query (from o in c.Orders...) nested inside the first one (from c in northWindDataContext.Customers...).

You divide the OrderDate field into its month, date, and year components to make the XML easier to query; you will see how this is used in the next example.

Finally, you save the generated XML to file as in the previous example:

```
            string xmlFileName =
                    @"C:\BegVCSharp\Chapter24\Xml\NorthwindCustomerOrders.xml";
            northwindCustomerOrders.Save(xmlFileName);

            Console.WriteLine("Successfully saved Northwind customer orders to:");
            Console.WriteLine(xmlFileName);
```

Now you will write a query against the XML file you just wrote to disk.

## HOW TO QUERY AN XML DOCUMENT

Why would you need to do LINQ queries on an XML document? If your program receives XML generated by another program, you might be looking for specific XML elements or attributes within the received XML to determine how to process it. Your program might be concerned only with a subset of the XML content, or you might need to count elements within the document, or you might need to search for elements or attributes that satisfy a specific condition. LINQ queries provide a powerful solution for situations like these.

To query an XML document, the LINQ to XML classes such as XDocument and XElement provide member properties and methods that return LINQ-queryable collections of the LINQ to XML objects contained within the XML document or fragment represented by that LINQ to XML class.

In the following Try It Out, you use these queryable member methods and properties on the XML document you created in the previous example.

**TRY IT OUT** Querying an XML Document: BegVCSharp_24_7_QueryXML

Follow these steps to create the example in Visual Studio 2012:

**1.** Create a new console application called BegVCSharp_24_7_QueryXML in the directory C:\BegVCSharp\ Chapter24.

**2.** Open the main source file Program.cs.

**3.** Add a reference to the `System.Xml.Linq` namespace to the beginning of `Program.cs`, as shown:

```
using System;
using System.Collections.Generic;
using System.Linq;
using System.Xml.Linq;
using System.Text;
```

**4.** Add the following code to the `Main()` method in `Program.cs`:

```
static void Main(string[] args)
{
    string xmlFileName = @"C:\BegVCSharp\Chapter24\Xml\NorthwindCustomerOrders.xml";
    XDocument customers = XDocument.Load(xmlFileName);

    Console.WriteLine("Elements in loaded document:");
    var queryResult = from c in customers.Elements()
                      select c.Name;
    foreach (var item in queryResult)
    {
        Console.WriteLine(item);
    }
    Console.Write("Press Enter/Return to continue:");
    Console.ReadLine();
}
```

**5.** Compile and execute the program (you can just press F5 for Start Debugging). You will see the following output:

```
Elements in loaded document:
customers
Press Enter/Return to continue:
```

**6.** Press Enter/Return to finish the program and make the console screen disappear. If you used Ctrl+F5 (Start Without Debugging), you might need to press Enter/Return twice.

*How It Works*

As you read through the explanation for each query method, you modify the LINQ to XML query example you just created to use it. Each of these queries returns a collection of LINQ to XML elements or attribute objects having a `Name` property, so your `select` clause simply returns this name to be printed out in the `foreach` loop:

```
var queryResult = from c in customers.Elements()
                  select c.Name;
foreach (var item in queryResult)
{
    Console.WriteLine(item);
}
```

This type of code is what you might first use when developing or debugging a program to see what the queries return. Later, you modify the output to display business results that would be more meaningful to end users.

## USING LINQ TO XML QUERY MEMBERS

This section looks at the LINQ to XML query members that are available to you. Then you can try them out in turn, using the `NorthwindCustomerOrders.xml` file as a data source.

## Elements()

The first LINQ to XML query method you used is the `Elements()` member of the `XDocument` class. This member is also available in the `XElement` class.

Elements() returns the set of all first-level elements in the XML document or fragment. For a valid XML document, such as the NorthwindCustomerOrders.xml file you just created, there is only one first-level element, the root element, which is named customers:

```
<?xml version="1.0" encoding="utf-8" ?>
<customers>
  ...
</customers>
```

All other elements are children of customers, so Elements() returns just one element:

```
Elements in loaded document:
customers
```

An XML fragment can contain multiple first-level elements, but it is usually more useful to query the child elements, which you look at next with the Descendants() member.

## Descendants()

The next LINQ to XML query method is the Descendants() member of the XDocument class. This member is also available in the XElement class.

Descendants() returns a flattened list of all the child elements (at all levels) in the XML document or fragment. Try modifying the BegVCSharp_24_7_QueryXML example as follows:

```
Console.WriteLine("All descendants in document:");
queryResult =
    from c in customers.Descendants()
    select c.Name;
foreach (var item in queryResult)
{
    Console.WriteLine(item);
}
```

Compile and execute. You will see the customer and order element names repeated in the order they appear in the document:

```
All descendants in document:
customer
order
order
...
customer
order
...
customer
order
...
order
order
Press Enter/Return to continue:
```

The output will scroll off the screen, so you might not see the first part of it. This reflects the fact that the NorthwindCustomerOrders.xml file contains only customer and order elements beneath the root customers element:

```
<?xml version="1.0V encoding="utf-8" ?>
<customers>
 <customer ... [{ [SPACE] }] >
  <order ... />
  <order ... />
  ...
 </customer>
```

```
    <customer ... >
    <order ... />
    ...
```

You can make the output more manageable by adding the LINQ `Distinct()` operator to the results processing:

```
        Console.WriteLine("All distinct descendants in document:");
        var queryResult =
            from c in customers.Descendants()
            select c.Name;
        foreach (var item in queryResult.Distinct())
```

This results in a list of only the distinct element names:

```
    All distinct descendants in document:
    customers
    customer
    order
    Press Enter/Return to continue:
```

This is very useful for exploring a document structure the first time you start to work with it, but finding all elements is not a problem you will often need to solve in finished production applications.

A more common scenario involves having to look for descendant elements with a particular name. The `Descendants()` method has an overload that takes the desired element name as a string parameter, as shown here:

```
        Console.WriteLine("Descendants named 'customer':");
        var queryResult =
            from c in customers.Descendants("customer")
            select c.Name;
        foreach (var item in queryResult) // remove Distinct()
        {
            Console.WriteLine(item);
        }
```

This returns just the `customer` elements:

```
    Descendants named 'customer':
    customer
    customer
    customer
    ...
    customer
    customer
    Press Enter/Return to continue:
```

Clearly, this is a more generally useful query. By querying a list of elements of a known type, you can then search for specific attributes, which you will look at next.

> **NOTE** For the sake of completeness, you should know that LINQ to XML also provides an `Ancestors()` method that is the converse of the `Descendants()` method, returning the flattened list of all elements higher than the source element in the tree structure of the XML document. This is not used nearly as often as the `Descendants()` method because developers tend to start processing XML documents at the root, descending from there to the leaf levels of the tree of elements and attributes. The `Parent` property, which points to the single ancestor one level up, is used more often.

## Attributes()

The next LINQ to XML query method to look at is the `Attributes()` member. This returns all the attributes of the currently selected element. To see how this method works, try modifying the BegVCSharp_24_7_QueryXML example as follows:

```
Console.WriteLine("Attributes of descendants named 'customer':");
var queryResult =
    from c in customers.Descendants("customer").Attributes()
    select c.Name;
foreach (var item in queryResult)
{
    Console.WriteLine(item);
}
```

Compile and execute. You should see the names of the attributes of the `customer` elements:

```
Attributes of descendants named 'customer':
ID
City
Company
ID
City
Company
...
ID
City
Company
ID
City
Company
Press Enter/Return to continue:
```

Again the output scrolls off the screen. This query has found the names of the attributes of the `customer` elements:

```
<customer ID= ... City= ... Company= ... >
<customer ID= ... City= ... Company= ... >
<customer ID= ... City= ... Company= ... >
   ...
```

Like the `Descendants()` method, you can pass a specific name to `Attributes()` to search for. In addition, you don't have to restrict the display to the name; you can display the attribute itself. Here is a query that displays the attributes of a customer named `Company`:

```
Console.WriteLine("customer attributes named 'Company':");
var queryResult =
    from c in customers.Descendants("customer").Attributes("Company")
    select c;
foreach (var item in queryResult)
{
    Console.WriteLine(item);
}
```

Compile and execute. You will see the attributes containing the companies for the `customer` elements:

```
...
Company="Toms Spezialitäten"
Company="Tortuga Restaurante"
Company="Tradiçao Hipermercados"
Company="Trail's Head Gourmet Provisioners"
Company="Vaffeljernet"
Company="Victuailles en stock"
Company="Vins et alcools Chevalier"
Company="Die Wandernde Kuh"
Company="Wartian Herkku"
```

```
Company="Wellington Importadora"
Company="White Clover Markets"
Company="Wilman Kala"
Company="Wolski Zajazd"
Press Enter/Return to continue:
```

Here is another example, this time with the `orders` elements and the `orderYear` attribute:

```
Console.WriteLine("order attributes named 'orderYear':");
var queryResult =
    from c in customers.Descendants("order").Attributes("orderYear")
    select c;
foreach (var item in queryResult)
{
    Console.WriteLine(item);
}
```

Compile and execute. Now you see the following:

```
...
orderYear="1998"
orderYear="1998"
orderYear="1998"
orderYear="1996"
orderYear="1997"
orderYear="1997"
orderYear="1998"
orderYear="1998"
orderYear="1998"
orderYear="1998"
Press Enter/Return to continue:
```

You can also get the value of the attribute specifically (here, the year) with the `Value` property:

```
Console.WriteLine("Values of order attributes named 'orderYear':");
var queryResult =
    from c in customers.Descendants("order").Attributes("orderYear")
    select c.Value;
foreach (var item in queryResult)
{
    Console.WriteLine(item);
}
```

Compile and execute. You should see the following:

```
...
1996
1997
1997
1998
1998
1998
1998
Press Enter/Return to continue:
```

Now you can begin to ask specific questions: For example, what was the earliest year in which orders were placed? You can answer that by using the same query but applying the `Min()` aggregate operator on the result instead of the usual `foreach` loop:

```
var queryResult =
    from c in customers.Descendants("order").Attributes("orderYear")
    select c.Value;
Console.WriteLine("Earliest year in which orders were placed: {0}",
                                        queryResult.Min());
```

Compile and execute to see the answer, 1996:

```
Earliest year in which orders were placed: 1996
Press Enter/Return to continue:
```

You can explore more specific questions in the exercises for this chapter.

## SUMMARY

That finishes your exploration of LINQ with databases and XML. As you have seen, LINQ to XML integrates the concepts of LINQ with an easy-to-use alternative XML API that enables quick integration of XML into other programs that use LINQ. This makes queries on XML documents simple and natural for programmers already familiar with LINQ in its other forms.

In this chapter, you learned how to construct XML documents with LINQ to XML functional constructors, and then how to load and save XML documents with LINQ to XML.

You mastered using LINQ to XML to work with incomplete XML documents (fragments), and learned how to easily generate an XML document from a LINQ to SQL or LINQ to Objects query.

Finally, you learned how to query an existing XML document with LINQ to XML, and used advanced LINQ features such as LINQ aggregate operators with LINQ to XML.

### EXERCISES

**24.1**  Create the following XML document using LINQ to XML constructors:

```
<employees>
  <employee ID="1001" FirstName="Fred" LastName="Lancelot">
    <Skills>
      <Language>C#</Language>
      <Math>Calculus</Math>
    </Skills>
  </employee>
  <employee ID="2002" FirstName="Jerry" LastName="Garcia">
    <Skills>
      <Language>French</Language>
      <Math>Business</Math>
    </Skills>
  </employee>
</employees>
```

**24.2**  Write a query against the `NorthwindCustomerOrders.xml` file you created to find the oldest customers (those with orders placed in the first year of Northwind operation, 1996).

**24.3**  Write a query against the `NorthwindCustomerOrders.xml` file to find customers who have placed individual orders over $10,000.

**24.4**  Write a query against the `NorthwindCustomerOrders.xml` file to find the lifetime highest-selling customers—for example, companies with all orders totaling more than $100,000.

**24.5**  Use LINQ to Entities to display detail information from the `Products` and `Employees` tables in the Northwind database.

**24.6**  Create a LINQ to Entities query to show the top-selling products in the Northwind database.

**24.7**  Create a group query to show the top-selling products by country.

Answers to the exercises can be found in Appendix A.

▶ **WHAT YOU LEARNED IN THIS CHAPTER**

| TOPIC | KEY CONCEPTS |
|---|---|
| **The different LINQ varieties** | Each of the different data sources in .NET has a LINQ variety or "flavor" that you can use to query its data. |
| **How to query databases with LINQ** | You can generate a LINQ to Entities class for your database by using the Data Source Configuration Wizard in Visual Studio 2012 (select Data ⇨ Add New Data Source). |
| **How to navigate database relationships with LINQ** | LINQ to Entities classes include navigable instance members for each related data entity (table) that you add to your data source. |
| **How to easily construct XML with LINQ** | LINQ to XML includes very powerful functional constructors to make XML documents from any LINQ query. |
| **How to create XML from databases** | You can construct XML from databases by combining LINQ to Entities, LINQ to Objects, and LINQ to XML in a single query. |
| **How to create XML files and fragments** | LINQ to XML includes methods to load and save XML to files and to manipulate parts of XML documents easily. |

# PART V
# Additional Techniques

# 25

# Windows Communication Foundation

## WHAT YOU WILL LEARN IN THIS CHAPTER

➤ What is WCF?

➤ WCF concepts

➤ WCF programming

## WROX.COM CODE DOWNLOADS FOR THIS CHAPTER

You can find the wrox.com code downloads for this chapter at `www.wrox.com/remtitle` `.cgi?isbn=9781118314418` on the Download Code tab. The code is in the Chapter 25 download and individually named according to the names throughout the chapter.

In recent years, as use of the Internet has become more ubiquitous, there has been a rapid increase in *web services*. A web service is like a website that is used by a computer instead of a person. For example, instead of browsing to a website about your favorite TV program, you might instead use a desktop application that pulled in the same information via a web service. The advantage here is that the same web service might be used by all sorts of applications, and, indeed, by websites. Also, you can write your own application or website that uses third-party web services. Perhaps you might combine information about your favorite TV program with a mapping service to show filming locations.

The .NET Framework has supported web services for some time now. However, in the more recent versions of the framework, web services have been combined with another technology, called *remoting*, to create *Windows Communication Foundation* (WCF), which is a generic infrastructure for communication between applications.

Remoting makes it possible to create instances of objects in one process and use them from another process—even if the object is created on a computer other than the one that is using it. However, remoting on its own is limited, and isn't the easiest thing for a beginner programmer to learn.

WCF takes concepts such as services and platform-independent SOAP messaging from web services, and combines these with concepts such as host server applications and advanced binding capabilities from remoting. The result is a technology you can think of as a superset that includes both web services and remoting, but that is much more powerful than web services and much easier to use than remoting. Using WCF, you can move from simple applications to applications that use a *service-oriented architecture* (SOA). SOA means that you decentralize processing and make use of distributed processing by connecting to services and data as you need them across local networks and the Internet.

This chapter walks you through how to create and consume WCF services from your application code. But just as importantly, it also covers the principles behind WCF, so you understand why things work the way they do.

## WHAT IS WCF?

WCF is a technology that enables you to create services that you can access from other applications across process, machine, and network boundaries. You can use these services to share functionality across multiple applications, to expose data sources, or to abstract complicated processes.

The functionality that WCF services offer is encapsulated as individual methods that are exposed by the service. Each method—or, in WCF terminology, each *operation*—has an endpoint that you exchange data with in order to use it. This data exchange can be defined by one or more protocols, depending on the network that you use to connect to the service and your specific requirements.

In WCF, an endpoint can have multiple *bindings*, each of which specifies a means of communication. Bindings can also specify additional information, such as which security requirements must be met to communicate with the endpoint. A binding might require username and password authentication or a Windows user account token, for example. When you connect to an endpoint, the protocol that the binding uses affects the address that you use, as you will see shortly.

Once you have connected to an endpoint, you can communicate with it by using SOAP messages. The form of the messages that you use depends on the operation you are using and the data structures that are required to send messages to (and receive messages from) that operation. WCF uses *contracts* to specify all of this. You can discover contracts through metadata exchange with a service. One commonly used format for service discovery is the Web Service Description Language (WSDL), which was originally used for web services, although WCF services can also be described in other ways.

When you have identified a service and endpoint that you want to use, and after you know which binding you use and which contracts to adhere to, you can communicate with a WCF service as easily as with an object that you have defined locally. Communications with WCF services can be simple, one-way transactions, request/response messages, or full-duplex communications that can be initiated from either end of the communication channel. You can also use message payload optimization techniques, such as Message Transmission Optimization Mechanism (MTOM), to package data if required.

The WCF service itself might be running in one of a number of different processes on the computer where it is hosted. Unlike web services, which always run in IIS, you can choose a host process that is appropriate to your situation. You can use IIS to host WCF services, but you can also use Windows services or executables. If you are using TCP to communicate with a WCF service over a local network, there is no need even to have IIS installed on the PC that is hosting the service.

The WCF framework has been designed to enable you to customize nearly everything you have read about in this section. However, this is an advanced subject and you will only be using the techniques provided by default in .NET 4.5 in this chapter.

Now that you have covered the basics about WCF services, you will look in more detail at these concepts in the following sections.

## WCF CONCEPTS

This section describes the following aspects of WCF:

➤   WCF communication protocols
➤   Addresses, endpoints, and bindings

➤ Contracts

➤ Message patterns

➤ Behaviors

➤ Hosting

## WCF Communication Protocols

As described earlier, you can communicate with WCF services through a variety of transport protocols. In fact, five are defined in the .NET 4.5 Framework:

➤ **HTTP**—Enables you to communicate with WCF services from anywhere, including across the Internet. You can use HTTP communications to create WCF web services.

➤ **TCP**—Enables you to communicate with WCF services on your local network or across the Internet if you configure your firewall appropriately. TCP is more efficient than HTTP and has more capabilities, but it can be more complicated to configure.

➤ **UDP**—Similar to TCP in that it enables communications via the local network or Internet, but it's implemented in a subtly different way. One of the consequences of this implementation, which you won't look at in detail, is that a service can broadcast messages to multiple clients simultaneously. The UDP protocol is new the .NET 4.5 Framework, although previously third-party implementations were available.

➤ **Named pipe**—Enables you to communicate with WCF services that are on the same machine as the calling code, but reside in a separate process.

➤ **MSMQ**—A queuing technology that enables messages sent by an application to be routed through a queue to arrive at a destination. MSMQ is a reliable messaging technology that ensures that a message sent to a queue will reach that queue. MSMQ is also inherently asynchronous, so a queued message will be processed only when messages ahead of it in the queue have been processed and a processing service is available.

These protocols often enable you to establish secure connections. For example, you can use the HTTPS protocol to establish a secure SSL connection across the Internet. TCP offers extensive possibilities for security in a local network by using the Windows security framework. UDP doesn't support security.

Figure 25-1 illustrates how these transport protocols can connect an application to WCF services in various locations (UDP and TCP connect in a similar way, so only TCP is shown). This chapter describes all of these protocols except for MSMQ, which is a subject requiring a more in-depth discussion.

In order to connect to a WCF service, you must know where it is. In practice, this means knowing the address of an endpoint.

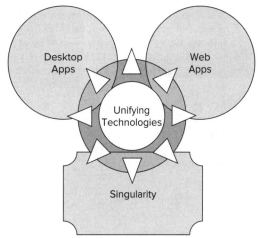

**FIGURE 25-1**

## Addresses, Endpoints, and Bindings

The type of address you use for a service depends on the protocol that you are using. Service addresses are formatted for the three protocols described in this chapter (MSMQ is not covered) as follows:

➤ **HTTP**—Addresses for the HTTP protocol are URLs of the familiar form `http://<server>:<port>/<service>`. For SSL connections, you can also use `https://<server>:<port>/<service>`. If you are hosting a service in IIS, `<service>` will be a file with a .svc extension. IIS addresses will probably include more subdirectories than this example—that is, more sections separated by / characters before the .svc file.

➤  **TCP**—Addresses for TCP are of the form `net.tcp://<server>:<port>/<service>`.

➤  **UDP**—Addresses for UDP are of the form `soap.udp://<server>:<port>/<service>`. Certain `<server>` values are required for multicast communications, but this is beyond the scope of this chapter.

➤  **Named pipe**—Addresses for named pipe connections are similar but have no port number. They are of the form `net.pipe://<server>/<service>`.

The address for a service is a base address that you can use to create addresses for endpoints representing operations. For example, you might have an operation at `net.tcp://<server>:<port>/<service>/operation1`.

For example, imagine you create a WCF service with a single operation that has bindings for all three of the protocols listed here. You might use the following base addresses:

```
http://www.mydomain.com/services/amazingservices/mygreatservice.svc
net.tcp://myhugeserver:8080/mygreatservice
net.pipe://localhost/mygreatservice
```

You could then use the following addresses for operations:

```
http://www.mydomain.com/services/amazingservices/mygreatservice.svc/greatop
net.tcp://myhugeserver:8080/mygreatservice/greatop
net.pipe://localhost/mygreatservice/greatop
```

Since .NET 4, it has been possible to use default endpoints for operations, without having to explicitly configure them. This simplifies configuration, especially in situations where you want to use standard endpoint addresses, as in the preceding examples.

Bindings, as mentioned earlier, specify more than just the transport protocol that will be used by an operation. You can also use them to specify the security requirements for communication over the transport protocol, transactional capabilities of the endpoint, message encoding, and much more.

Because bindings offer such a great degree of flexibility, the .NET Framework provides some predefined bindings that you can use. You can also use these bindings as starting points, tweaking them to obtain exactly the type of binding you want—up to a point. The predefined bindings have certain capabilities to which you must adhere. Each binding type is represented by a class in the `System.ServiceModel` namespace. Table 25-1 lists these bindings along with some basic information about them.

**TABLE 25-1:** Binding Types

| BINDING | DESCRIPTION |
|---|---|
| `BasicHttpBinding` | The simplest HTTP binding, and the default binding used by web services. It has limited security capabilities and no transactional support. |
| `WSHttpBinding` | A more advanced form of HTTP binding that is capable of using all the additional functionality that was introduced in WSE. |
| `WSDualHttpBinding` | Extends `WSHttpBinding` capabilities to include duplex communication capabilities. With duplex communication, the server can initiate communications with the client in addition to ordinary message exchange. |
| `WSFederationHttp Binding` | Extends `WSHttpBinding` capabilities to include federation capabilities. Federation enables third parties to implement single sign-on and other proprietary security measures. This is an advanced topic not covered in this chapter. |
| `NetTcpBinding` | Used for TCP communications, and enables you to configure security, transactions, and so on. |

| | |
|---|---|
| `NetNamedPipeBinding` | Used for named pipe communications, and enables you to configure security, transactions, and so on. |
| `NetPeerTcpBinding` | Enables broadcast communications to multiple clients, and is another advanced class not covered in this chapter. |
| `NetMsmqBinding` and `MsmqIntegrationBinding` | These bindings are used with MSMQ, which is not covered in this chapter. |
| `NetPeerTcpBinding` | Used for peer-to-peer binding, which is not covered in this chapter. |
| `WebHttpBinding` | User for web services that use HTTP requests instead of SOAP messages. |
| `NetTcpContextBinding` | Similar to `NetTcpBinding` but allows context information to be exchanged with SOAP headers. |
| `BasicHttpContext Binding` and `WSHttpContextBinding` | Similar to `BasicHttpBinding` and `WSHttpBinding`, but allows context information to be exchanged with HTTP cookies or SOAP headers, respectively. |
| `NetHttpBinding` and `NetHttpsBinding` | Similar to `BasicHttpBinding` and `WSHttpBinding`, but default to binary message encoding. |
| `UdpBinding` | Allows binding to the UDP protocol. |

Many of the binding classes listed in this table have similar properties that you can use for additional configuration. For example, they have properties that you can use to configure timeout values. You'll learn more about this when you look at code later in this chapter.

Since .NET 4, endpoints have default bindings that vary according to the protocol used. These defaults are shown in Table 25-2.

**TABLE 25-2:** NET Default Bindings

| PROTOCOL | DEFAULT BINDING |
|---|---|
| HTTP | `BasicHttpBinding` |
| TCP | `NetTcpBinding` |
| UDP | `UdpBinding` |
| Named pipe | `NetNamedPipeBinding` |
| MSMQ | `NetMsmqBinding` |

## Contracts

Contracts define how WCF services can be used. Several types of contract can be defined:

➤ **Service contract**—Contains general information about a service and the operations exposed by a service. This includes, for example, the namespace used by service. Services have unique namespaces that are used when defining the schema for SOAP messages in order to avoid possible conflicts with other services.

➤ **Operation contract**—Defines how an operation is used. This includes the parameter and return types for an operation method along with additional information, such as whether a method will return a response message.

➤ **Message contract**—Enables you to customize how information is formatted inside SOAP messages—for example, whether data should be included in the SOAP header or SOAP message body. This can be useful when creating a WCF service that must integrate with legacy systems.

➤ **Fault contract**—Defines faults that an operation can return. When you use .NET clients, faults result in exceptions that you can catch and deal with in the normal way.

➤ **Data contract**—If you use complex types, such as user-defined structs and objects, as parameters or return types for operations, then you must define data contracts for these types. Data contracts define the types in terms of the data that they expose through properties.

You typically add contracts to service classes and methods by using attributes, as you will see later in this chapter.

## Message Patterns

In the previous section, you saw that an operation contract can define whether an operation returns a value. You've also read about duplex communications that are made possible by the `WSDualHttpBinding` binding. These are both forms of message patterns, of which there are three types:

➤ **Request/response messaging**—The "ordinary" way of exchanging messages, whereby every message sent to a service results in a response being sent back to the client. This doesn't necessarily mean that the client waits for a response, as you can call operations asynchronously in the usual way.

➤ **One-way, or simplex, messaging**—Messages are sent from the client to the WCF operation, but no response is sent. This is useful when no response is required. For example, you might create a WCF operation that results in the WCF host server rebooting, in which case you wouldn't really want or need to wait for a response.

➤ **Two-way, or duplex, messaging**—A more advanced scheme whereby the client effectively acts as a server as well as a client, and the server as a client as well as a server. Once set up, duplex messaging enables both the client and the server to send messages to each other, which might not have responses. This is analogous to creating an object and subscribing to events exposed by that object.

You'll see how these message patterns are used in practice later in this chapter.

## Behaviors

Behaviors are a way to apply additional configuration that is not directly exposed to a client to services and operations. By adding a behavior to a service, you can control how it is instantiated and used by its hosting process, how it participates in transactions, how multithreading issues are dealt with in the service, and so on. Operation behaviors can control whether impersonation is used in the operation execution, how the individual operation affects transactions, and more.

Since .NET 4, you can specify default behaviors at various levels, so that you don't have to specify every aspect of every behavior for every service and operation. Instead, you can provide defaults and override settings where necessary, which reduces the amount of configuration required.

Because this chapter is intended to give you a basic understanding of WCF services, you will only see the most basic functionality of behaviors here.

## Hosting

In the introduction to this chapter, you learned that WCF services can be hosted in several different processes. These possibilities are as follows:

➤ **Web server**—IIS-hosted WCF services are the closest thing to web services that WCF offers. However, you can use advanced functionality and security features in WCF services that are much more difficult to implement in web services. You can also integrate with IIS features such as IIS security.

➤ **Executable**—You can host a WCF service in any application type that you can create in .NET, such as console applications, Windows Forms applications, and WPF applications.

➤ **Windows service**—You can host a WCF service in a Windows service, which means that you can use the useful features that Windows services provide. This includes automatic startup and fault recovery.

➤ **Windows Activation Service (WAS)**—Designed specifically to host WCF services, WAS is basically a simple version of IIS that you can use where IIS is not available.

Two of the options in the preceding list—IIS and WAS—provide useful features for WCF services such as activation, process recycling, and object pooling. If you use either of the other two hosting options, the WCF service is said to be *self-hosted*. This isn't necessarily a bad thing, as you might not require the additional functionality that the hosted environments offer. However, self-hosted services do require you to write more code.

## WCF PROGRAMMING

Now that you have covered all the basics, it is time to get started with some code. In this section you'll start by looking as a simple web server–hosted WCF service and a console application client. After looking at the structure of the code created, you'll learn about the basic structure of WCF services and client applications. Then you will look at some key topics in a bit more detail:

➤ Defining WCF service contracts

➤ Self-hosted WCF services

**TRY IT OUT** **A Simple WCF Service and Client: Ch25Ex01Client**

**1.** Create a new WCF Service Application project called Ch25Ex01 in the directory C:\BegVCSharp\ Chapter25.

**2.** Add a console application called Ch25Ex01Client to the solution.

**3.** On the Build menu, click Build Solution.

**4.** Right-click the Ch25Ex01Client project in the Solution Explorer and select Add Service Reference.

**5.** In the Add Service Reference dialog box, click Discover.

**6.** When the development web server has started and information about the WCF service has been loaded, expand the reference to look at its details, as shown in Figure 25-2 (you might have a different port number).

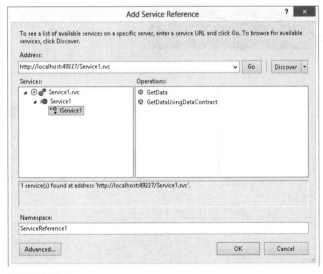

**FIGURE 25-2**

**7.** Click OK to add the service reference.

**8.** Modify the code in `Program.cs` in the Ch25Ex01Client application as follows:

```
using System;
using System.Collections.Generic;
using System.Linq;
using System.Text;
using System.Threading.Tasks;
using Ch25Ex01Client.ServiceReference1;

namespace Ch25Ex01Client
{
    class Program
    {
        static void Main(string[] args)
        {
            string numericInput = null;
            int intParam;
            do
            {
                Console.WriteLine(
                    "Enter an integer and press enter to call the WCF service.");
                numericInput = Console.ReadLine();
            }
            while (!int.TryParse(numericInput, out intParam));
            Service1Client client = new Service1Client();
            Console.WriteLine(client.GetData(intParam));
            Console.WriteLine("Press an key to exit.");
            Console.ReadKey();
        }
    }
}
```

**9.** Right-click the Ch25Ex01Client project in the Solution Explorer and select Set as StartUp Project.

**10.** Run the application. Enter a number in the console application window and press Enter. The result is shown in Figure 25-3.

**FIGURE 25-3**

**11.** Exit the application, right-click the `Service1.svc` file in the Ch25Ex01 project in the Solution Explorer, and click View in Browser.

**12.** Review the information in the window (see Figure 25-4).

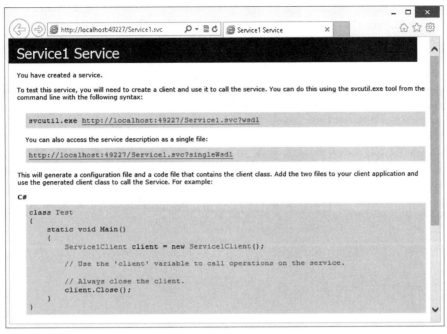

**FIGURE 25-4**

**13.** Click the link at the top of the web page for the service to view the WSDL. Don't panic—you don't need to understand all the stuff in the WSDL file!

*How It Works*

In this example you created a simple web server–hosted WCF service and console application client. You used the default VS template for a WCF service project, which meant that you didn't have to add any code. Instead, you used one of the operations defined in this default template, GetData(). For the purposes of this example, the actual operation used isn't important; here, you are focusing on the structure of the code and the plumbing that makes things work.

First, look at the server project, Ch25Ex01. This consists of the following:

➤ A Service1.svc file that defines the hosting for the service

➤ A class definition, CompositeType, that defines a data contract used by the service (located in the IService1.cs code file)

➤ An interface definition, IService1, that defines the service contract and two operation contracts for the service

➤ A class definition, Service1, that implements IService1 and defines the functionality of the service (located in the Service1.svc.cs code file)

➤ A <system.serviceModel> configuration section (in Web.config) that configures the service

The `Service1.svc` file contains the following line of code (to see this code, right-click the file in the Solution Explorer and select View Markup):

```
<%@ ServiceHost Language="C#" Debug="true" Service="Ch25Ex01.Service1"
   CodeBehind="Service1.svc.cs" %>
```

This is a `ServiceHost` instruction that is used to tell the web server (the development web server in this case, although this also applies to IIS) what service is hosted at this address. The class that defines the service is declared in the `Service` attribute, and the code file that defines this class is declared in the `CodeBehind` attribute. This instruction is necessary in order to obtain the hosting features of the web server as defined in the previous sections.

Obviously, this file is not required for WCF services that aren't hosted in a web server. You'll learn how to self-host WCF services later in this chapter.

Next, the data contract `CompositeType` is defined in the `IService1.cs` file. You can see from the code that the data contract is simply a class definition that includes the `DataContract` attribute on the class definition and `DataMember` attributes on class members:

```
[DataContract]
public class CompositeType
{
    bool boolValue = true;
    string stringValue = "Hello ";

    [DataMember]
    public bool BoolValue
    {
        get { return boolValue; }
        set { boolValue = value; }
    }

    [DataMember]
    public string StringValue
    {
        get { return stringValue; }
        set { stringValue = value; }
    }
}
```

This data contract is exposed to the client application through metadata (if you looked through the WSDL file in the example you might have seen this). This enables client applications to define a type that can be serialized into a form that can be deserialized by the service into a `CompositeType` object. The client doesn't need to know the actual definition of this type; in fact, the class used by the client might have a different implementation. This simple way of defining data contracts is surprisingly powerful, and enables the exchange of complex data structures between the WCF service and its clients.

The `IService1.cs` file also contains the service contract for the service, which is defined as an interface with the `ServiceContract` attribute. Again, this interface is completely described in the metadata for the service, and can be recreated in client applications. The interface members constitute the operations exposed by the service, and each is used to create an operation contract by applying the `OperationContract` attribute. The example code includes two operations, one of which uses the data contract you looked at earlier:

```
[ServiceContract]
public interface IService1
{
    [OperationContract]
    string GetData(int value);

    [OperationContract]
    CompositeType GetDataUsingDataContract(CompositeType composite);
}
```

All four of the contract-defining attributes that you have seen so far can be further configured with attributes, as shown in the next section. The code that implements the service looks much like any other class definition:

```
public class Service1 : IService1
{
    public string GetData(int value)
    {
        return string.Format("You entered: {0}", value);
    }

    public CompositeType GetDataUsingDataContract(CompositeType composite)
    {
        if (composite == null)
        {
            throw new ArgumentNullException("composite");
        }
        if (composite.BoolValue)
        {
            composite.StringValue += "Suffix";
        }
        return composite;
    }
}
```

Note that this class definition doesn't need to inherit from a particular type, and doesn't require any particular attributes. All it needs to do is implement the interface that defines the service contract. In fact, you can add attributes to this class and its members to specify behaviors, but these aren't mandatory.

The separation of the service contract (the interface) from the service implementation (the class) works extremely well. The client doesn't need to know anything about the class, which could include much more functionality than just the service implementation. A single class could even implement more than one service contract.

Finally, you come to the configuration in the `Web.config` file. Configuration of WCF services in config files is a feature that has been taken from .NET remoting, and it works with all types of WCF services (hosted or self-hosted) as well as clients of WCF services (as shown in a moment). The vocabulary of this configuration is such that you can apply pretty much any configuration that you can think of to a service, and you can even extend this syntax.

WCF configuration code is contained in the `<system.serviceModel>` configuration section of `Web.config` or `app.config` files. In this example, there is not a lot of service configuration, as default values are used. In the `Web.config` file, the configuration section consists of a single subsection that supplies overrides to default values for the service behavior `<behaviors>`. The code for the `<system.serviceModel>` configuration section in `Web.config` (with comments removed for clarity) is as follows:

```xml
<system.serviceModel>
  <behaviors>
    <serviceBehaviors>
      <behavior>
        <serviceMetadata httpGetEnabled="true" httpsGetEnabled="true" />
        <serviceDebug includeExceptionDetailInFaults="false" />
      </behavior>
    </serviceBehaviors>
  </behaviors>
</system.serviceModel>
```

This section can define one or more behaviors in `<behavior>` child sections, which can be reused on multiple other elements. A `<behavior>` section can be given a name to facilitate this reuse (so that it can be referenced from elsewhere), or can be used without a name (as in this example) to specify overrides to default behavior settings.

> **NOTE** *If nondefault configuration were being used, you would expect to see a `<services>` section inside `<system.serviceModel>`, containing one or more `<services>` child sections. In turn, the `<service>` sections can contain child `<endpoint>` sections, each of which (you guessed it) defines an endpoint for the service. In fact, the endpoints defined are base endpoints for the service. Endpoints for operations are inferred from these.*

One of the default behavior overrides in `Web.config` is as follows:

```
<serviceDebug includeExceptionDetailInFaults="false"/>
```

This setting can be set to `true` to expose exception details in any faults that are transmitted to the client, which is something you would usually allow only in development.

The other default behavior override in `Web.config` relates to metadata. Metadata is used to enable clients to obtain descriptions of WCF services. The default configuration defines two default endpoints for services. One is the endpoint that clients use to access the service, the other is an endpoint used to obtain metadata from the service. This can be disabled in the `Web.config` file as follows:

```
<serviceMetadata httpGetEnabled="false" httpsGetEnabled="false" />
```

Alternatively, you could remove this line of configuration code entirely, as the default behavior does not enable metadata exchange.

If you try disabling this in the example it won't stop your client from being able to access the service, because it has already obtained the metadata it needed when you added the service reference. However, disabling metadata will prevent other clients from using the Add Service Reference tool for this service. Typically, web services in a production environment will not need to expose metadata, so you should disable this functionality after the development phase is complete.

Without metadata, another common way to access a WCF service is to define its contracts in a separate assembly, which is referenced by both the hosting project and the client project. The client can then generate a proxy by using these contracts directly, rather than through exposed metadata.

Now that you've looked at the WCF service code, it's time to look at the client, and in particular at what using the Add Service Reference tool actually did. You will notice in the Solution Explorer that the client includes a folder called Service References, and if you expand that you will see an item called `ServiceReference1`, which was the name you chose when you added the reference.

The Add Service Reference tool creates all the classes you require to access the service. This includes a proxy class for the service that includes methods for all the operations exposed by the service (`Service1Client`), and a client-side class generated from the data contract (`CompositeType`).

> **NOTE** *You can browse through the code that is generated by the Add Service Reference tool if you want (by displaying all files in the project, including the hidden ones), although at this point it's probably best not to, because it contains quite a lot of confusing code.*

The tool also adds a configuration file to the project, `app.config`. This configuration defines two things:

➤ Binding information for the service endpoint
➤ The address and contract for the endpoint

The binding information is taken from the service description:

```
<configuration>
  <system.serviceModel>
    <bindings>
      <basicHttpBinding>
        <binding name="BasicHttpBinding_IService1" />
      </basicHttpBinding>
    </bindings>
```

This binding is used in the endpoint configuration, along with the base address of the service (which is the address of the .svc file for web server–hosted services) and the client-side version of the contract IService1:

```
    <client>
      <endpoint address="http://localhost:49227/Service1.svc"
        binding="basicHttpBinding"
        bindingConfiguration="BasicHttpBinding_IService1"
        contract="ServiceReference1.IService1"
        name="BasicHttpBinding_IService1" />
    </client>
  </system.serviceModel>
</configuration>
```

Strictly speaking, you could replace this configuration file with the following:

```
<configuration>
  <system.serviceModel>
    <client>
      <endpoint address="http://localhost:51782/Service1.svc"
        binding="basicHttpBinding"
        contract="ServiceReference1.IService1"
        name="BasicHttpBinding_IService1" />
    </client>
  </system.serviceModel>
</configuration>
```

Here, the `<bindings>` section as well as the `bindingConfiguration` attribute of the `<endpoint>` element have been removed, which means that the client will use the default binding configuration.

The `<binding>` element, which has the name `BasicHttpBinding_IService1`, is included so that you can use it to customize the configuration of the binding. There are a number of configuration settings that you might use here, ranging from timeout settings to message size limits and security settings. If these had been specified in the service project to be nondefault values, then you would have seen them in the `app.config` file, since they would have been copied across. In order for the client to communicate with the service, the binding configurations must match. You won't look at WCF service configuration in great depth in this chapter.

This example has covered a lot of ground, and it is worth summarizing what you have learned before moving on:

➤ WCF service definitions:

  ➤ Services are defined by a service contract interface that includes operation contract members.

  ➤ Services are implemented in a class that implements the service contract interface.

  ➤ Data contracts are simply type definitions that use data contract attributes.

➤ WCF service configuration:

  ➤ You can use configuration files (`Web.config` or `app.config`) to configure WCF services.

➤ WCF web server hosting:

  ➤ Web server hosting uses .svc files as service base addresses.

➤ WCF client configuration:

  ➤ You can use configuration files (`Web.config` or `app.config`) to configure WCF service clients.

The following section explores contracts in more detail.

## The WCF Test Client

In the previous Try It Out, you created both a service and a client in order to look at how the basic WCF architecture works and how configuration of WCF services is achieved. In practice, though, the client application you want to use might be complex, and it can be tricky to test services properly.

To ease the development of WCF services, VS provides a test tool you can use to ensure that your WCF operations work correctly. This tool is automatically configured to work with your WCF service projects, so if you run your project the tool will appear. All you need to do is ensure that the service you want to test (that is, the .svc file) is set to be the startup page for the WCF service project. Alternatively, you can run the test client as a standalone application. You can find the test client on 64-bit operating systems at `C:\Program Files (x86)\Microsoft Visual Studio 11.0\Common7\IDE\WcfTestClient.exe`.

If you are using a 32-bit operating system, the path is the same except the root folder is `Program Files`.

The tool enables you to invoke service operations and inspect the service in some other ways. The following Try It Out illustrates this.

**TRY IT OUT**    Using the WCF Test Client: Ch25Ex01\Web.config

1. Open the WCF Service Application project from the previous Try It Out, Ch25Ex01.
2. Right-click the `Service1.svc` service in Solution Explorer and click Set As Start Page.
3. Right-click the Ch25Ex01 project in Solution Explorer and click Set As StartUp Project.
4. In `Web.config`, ensure that metadata is enabled:

   ```
   <serviceMetadata httpGetEnabled="true" httpsGetEnabled="true" />
   ```
5. Run the application. The WCF test client appears, as shown in Figure 25-5 (it takes a moment or two to add the service).

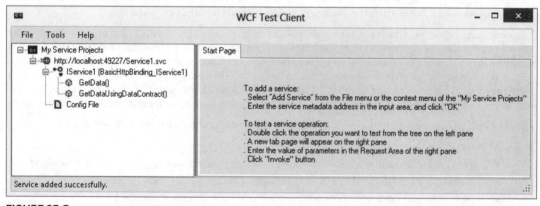

**FIGURE 25-5**

6. In the left pane of the test client, double-click Config File. The config file used to access the service is displayed in the right pane, which is shown in Figure 25-6.

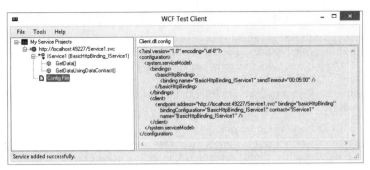

**FIGURE 25-6**

7. In the left pane, double-click the GetDataUsingDataContract() operation.
8. In the pane that appears on the right, change the value of BoolValue to True and StringValue to Test String, and then click Invoke.
9. If a security prompt dialog box appears, click OK to confirm that you are happy to send information to the service.
10. The operation result appears, as shown in Figure 25-7.

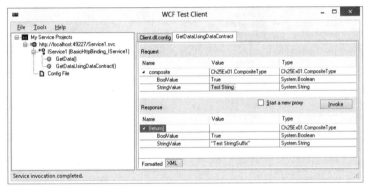

**FIGURE 25-7**

11. Click the XML tab to view the request and response XML, shown in Figure 25-8.

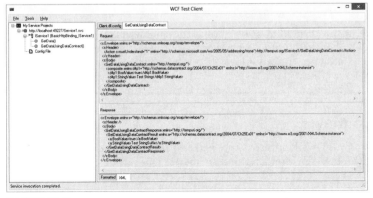

**FIGURE 25-8**

*How It Works*

In this example you used the WCF test client to inspect and invoke an operation on the service you created in the previous Try It Out. The first thing you probably noticed is a slight delay while the service is loaded. This is because the test client has to inspect the service to determine its capabilities. This discovery uses the same metadata as the Add Service Reference tool, which is why you must ensure that metadata is available (it's possible you experimented with disabling it in the previous Try It Out). Once discovery is complete, you can view the service and its operations in the left pane of the tool.

Next, you looked at the configuration used to access the service. As with the client application from the previous Try It Out, this is generated automatically from the service metadata, and contains exactly the same code. You can edit this configuration file through the tool if you need to, by right-clicking on the Config File item and clicking Edit with SvcConfigEditor. An example of this configuration is shown in Figure 25-9, which includes the binding configuration options mentioned earlier in this chapter.

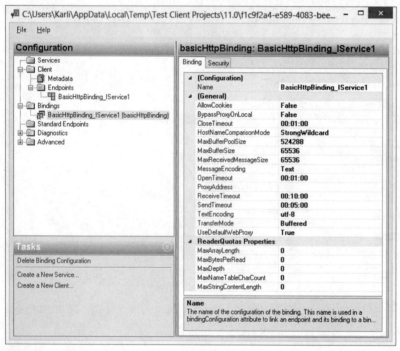

**FIGURE 25-9**

Finally, you invoked an operation. The test client allows you to enter the parameters to use and invoke the method, then displays the result, all without you writing any client code. You also saw how to view the actual XML that is sent and received to obtain the result. This information is quite technical, but it can be absolutely critical when debugging more complex services.

## Defining WCF Service Contracts

The previous examples showed how the WCF infrastructure makes it easy for you to define contracts for WCF services with a combination of classes, interfaces, and attributes. This section takes a deeper look at this technique.

## Data Contracts

To define a data contract for a service, you apply the `DataContractAttribute` attribute to a class definition. This attribute is found in the `System.Runtime.Serialization` namespace. You can configure this attribute with the properties shown in Table 25-3.

**TABLE 25-3:** DataContractAttribute Properties

| PROPERTY | DESCRIPTION |
| --- | --- |
| Name | Names the data contract with a different name than the one you use for the class definition. This name will be used in SOAP messages and client-side data objects that are defined from service metadata. |
| Namespace | Defines the namespace that the data contract uses in SOAP messages. |
| IsReference | Affects the way that objects are serialized. If this is set to `true`, then an object instance is serialized only once even if it is referenced several times, which can be important is some situations. The default is `false`. |

The `Name` and `Namespace` properties are useful when you need interoperability with existing SOAP message formats (as are the similarly named properties for other contracts), but otherwise you will probably not require them.

Each class member that is part of a data contract must use the `DataMemberAttribute` attribute, which is also found in the `System.Runtime.Serialization` namespace. Table 25-4 lists this attribute's properties.

**TABLE 25-4:** DataMemberAttribute Properties

| PROPERTY | DESCRIPTION |
| --- | --- |
| Name | Specifies the name of the data member when serialized (the default is the member name). |
| IsRequired | Specifies whether the member must be present in a SOAP message. |
| Order | An int value specifying the order of serializing or deserializing the member, which might be required if one member must be present before another can be understood. Lower `Order` members are processed first. |
| EmitDefaultValue | Set this to `false` to prevent members from being included in SOAP messages if their value is the default value for the member. |

## Service Contracts

Service contracts are defined by applying the `System.ServiceModel.ServiceContractAttribute` attribute to an interface definition. You can customize the service contract with the properties shown in Table 25-5.

**TABLE 25-5:** ServiceContractAttribute Properties

| PROPERTY | DESCRIPTION |
| --- | --- |
| Name | Specifies the name of the service contract as defined in the `<portType>` element in WSDL. |
| Namespace | Defines the namespace of the service contract used by the `<portType>` element in WSDL. |
| ConfigurationName | The name of the service contract as used in the configuration file. |

*continues*

**TABLE 25-5** *(continued)*

| PROPERTY | DESCRIPTION |
|---|---|
| HasProtectionLevel | Determines whether messages used by the service have explicitly defined protection levels. Protection levels enable you to sign, or sign and encrypt, messages. |
| ProtectionLevel | The protection level to use for message protection. |
| SessionMode | Determines whether sessions are enabled for messages. If you use sessions, then you can ensure that messages sent to different endpoints of a service are correlated—that is, they use the same service instance and so can share state, and so on. |
| CallbackContract | For duplex messaging the client exposes a contract as well as the service. This is because, as discussed earlier, the client in duplex communications also acts as a server. This property enables you to specify which contract the client uses. |

## Operation Contracts

Within interfaces that define service contracts, you define members as operations by applying the `System.ServiceModel.OperationContractAttribute` attribute. This attribute has the properties described in Table 25-6.

**TABLE 25-6:** OperationContractAttribute Properties

| PROPERTY | DESCRIPTION |
|---|---|
| Name | Specifies the name of the service operation. The default is the member name. |
| IsOneWay | Specifies whether the operation returns a response. If you set this to `true`, then clients won't wait for the operation to complete before continuing. |
| AsyncPattern | If set to `true`, the operation is implemented as two methods that you can use to call the operation asynchronously: `Begin<methodName>()` and `End<methodName>()`. |
| HasProtectionLevel | See the previous section. |
| ProtectionLevel | See the previous section. |
| IsInitiating | If sessions are used, then this property determines whether calling this operation can start a new session. |
| IsTerminating | If sessions are used, then this property determines whether calling this operation terminates the current session. |
| Action | If you are using addressing (an advanced capability of WCF services), then an operation has an associated action name, which you can specify with this property. |
| ReplyAction | As with `Action`, but specifies the action name for the operation response. |

> **NOTE** *In the .NET 4.5 Framework, when you add a service reference, VS also generates asynchronous proxy methods to call the service, regardless of whether* `AsyncPattern` *is set to* `true`. *These methods, which have the suffix* `Async`, *use the new asynchronous techniques that are included in .NET 4.5, and are asynchronous only from the point of view of the calling code. Internally, they call the synchronous WCF operations.*

## Message Contracts

The earlier example didn't use message contract specifications. If you use these, then you do so by defining a class that represents the message and applying the `MessageContractAttribute` attribute to the class. You then apply `MessageBodyMemberAttribute`, `MessageHeaderAttribute`, or `MessageHeaderArrayAttribute` attributes to members of this class. All these attributes are in the `System.ServiceModel` namespace. You are unlikely to want to do this unless you need a very high degree of control over the SOAP messages used by WCF services, so details are not provided here.

## Fault Contracts

If you have a particular exception type—for example, a custom exception—that you want to make available to client applications, then you can apply the `System.ServiceModel.FaultContractAttribute` attribute to the operation that might generate this exception. Again, this isn't something you will want to do in ordinary WCF use.

### TRY IT OUT WCF Contracts: Ch25Ex02Contracts

1. Create a new WCF Service Application project called Ch25Ex02 in the directory `C:\BegVCSharp\Chapter25`.

2. Add a class library project called Ch25Ex02Contracts to the solution and remove the `Class1.cs` file.

3. Add references to the `System.Runtime.Serialization.dll` and `System.ServiceModel.dll` assemblies to the Ch25Ex02Contracts project.

4. Add a class called `Person` to the Ch25Ex02Contracts project and modify the code in `Person.cs` as follows:

```
using System;
using System.Collections.Generic;
using System.Linq;
using System.Text;
using System.Threading.Tasks;
using System.Runtime.Serialization;

namespace Ch25Ex02Contracts
{
    [DataContract]
    public class Person
    {
        [DataMember]
        public string Name { get; set; }

        [DataMember]
        public int Mark { get; set; }
    }
}
```

5. Add an interface called `IAwardService` to the Ch25Ex02Contracts project and modify the code in `IAwardService.cs` as follows:

```
using System;
using System.Collections.Generic;
using System.Linq;
using System.Text;
using System.Threading.Tasks;
using System.ServiceModel;

namespace Ch25Ex02Contracts
{
    [ServiceContract(SessionMode=SessionMode.Required)]
    public interface IAwardService
    {
```

```
        [OperationContract(IsOneWay=true,IsInitiating=true)]
        void SetPassMark(int passMark);

        [OperationContract]
        Person[] GetAwardedPeople(Person[] peopleToTest);
    }
}
```

6. In the Ch25Ex02 project, add a reference to the Ch25Ex02Contracts project.

7. Remove `IService1.cs` and `Service1.svc` from the Ch25Ex02 project.

8. Add a new WCF service called `AwardService` to Ch25Ex02.

9. Remove the `IAwardService.cs` file from the Ch25Ex02 project.

10. Modify the code in `AwardService.svc.cs` as follows:

```csharp
using System;
using System.Collections.Generic;
using System.Linq;
using System.Runtime.Serialization;
using System.ServiceModel;
using System.Text;
using Ch25Ex02Contracts;

namespace Ch25Ex02
{
    public class AwardService : IAwardService
    {
        private int passMark;

        public void SetPassMark(int passMark)
        {
            this.passMark = passMark;
        }

        public Person[] GetAwardedPeople(Person[] peopleToTest)
        {
            List<Person> result = new List<Person>();
            foreach (Person person in peopleToTest)
            {
                if (person.Mark > passMark)
                {
                    result.Add(person);
                }
            }
            return result.ToArray();
        }
    }
}
```

11. Modify the service configuration section in `Web.config` as follows:

```xml
<system.serviceModel>
  <protocolMapping>
    <add scheme="http" binding="wsHttpBinding" />
  </protocolMapping>
  ...
</system.serviceModel>
```

12. Open the project properties for Ch25Ex02. In the Web section, make a note of the port used in the hosting settings. If you don't have IIS installed, you can set a specific port for use in the Visual Studio Development Server instead. For example, in Figure 25-10, the port used is 49284.

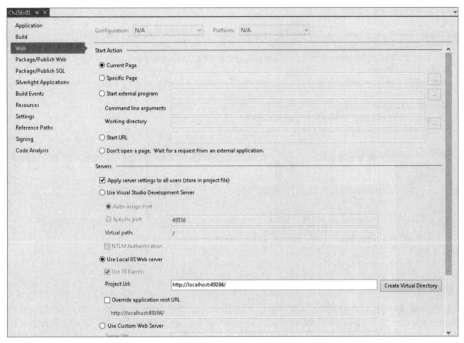

**FIGURE 25-10**

**13.** Add a new console project called Ch25Ex02Client to the solution and set it as the startup project.

**14.** Add references to the System.ServiceModel.dll assembly and the Ch25Ex02Contracts project to the Ch25Ex02Client project.

**15.** Modify the code in Program.cs in Ch25Ex02Client as follows (ensure that you use the port number you obtained earlier in the EndpointAddress constructor, the example code uses port 49284):

```
using System;
using System.Collections.Generic;
using System.Linq;
using System.Text;
using System.Threading.Tasks;
using System.ServiceModel;
using Ch25Ex02Contracts;

namespace Ch25E02Client
{
    class Program
    {
        static void Main(string[] args)
        {
            Person[] people = new Person[]
            {
                new Person { Mark = 46, Name="Jim" },
                new Person { Mark = 73, Name="Mike" },
                new Person { Mark = 92, Name="Stefan" },
                new Person { Mark = 84, Name="George" },
                new Person { Mark = 24, Name="Arthur" },
                new Person { Mark = 58, Name="Nigel" }
            };

            Console.WriteLine("People:");
```

```
            OutputPeople(people);

            IAwardService client = ChannelFactory<IAwardService>.CreateChannel(
                new WSHttpBinding(),
                new EndpointAddress("http://localhost:49284/AwardService.svc"));
            client.SetPassMark(70);
            Person[] awardedPeople = client.GetAwardedPeople(people);

            Console.WriteLine();
            Console.WriteLine("Awarded people:");
            OutputPeople(awardedPeople);

            Console.ReadKey();
        }

        static void OutputPeople(Person[] people)
        {
            foreach (Person person in people)
            {
                Console.WriteLine("{0}, mark: {1}", person.Name, person.Mark);
            }
        }
    }
}
```

**16.** If you are using IIS, simply run the application. If you are using the development server, you must ensure the development server is running for the service, so run the service project first. The result is shown in Figure 25-11.

**FIGURE 25-11**

### How It Works

In this example, you created a set of contracts in a class library project and used that class library in both a WCF service and a client. The service, as in the previous example, is hosted in a web server. The configuration for this service is reduced to the bare minimum.

The main difference in this example is that no metadata is required by the client, as the client has access to the contract assembly. Instead of generating a proxy class from metadata, the client obtains a reference to the service contract interface through an alternative method. Another point to note about this example is the use of a session to maintain state in the service, which requires the WSHttpBinding binding instead of the BasicHttpBinding binding.

The data contract used in this example is for a simple class called Person, which has a string property called Name and an int property called Mark. You used the DataContractAttribute and DataMemberAttribute attributes with no customization, and there is no need to reiterate the code for this contract here.

The service contract is defined by applying the ServiceContractAttribute attribute to the IAwardService interface. The SessionMode property of this attribute is set to SessionMode.Required, as this service requires state:

```
[ServiceContract(SessionMode=SessionMode.Required)]
public interface IAwardService
{
```

The first operation contract, SetPassMark(), is the one that sets state, and therefore has the IsInitiating property of OperationContractAttribute set to true. This operation doesn't return anything, so it is defined as a one-way operation by setting IsOneWay to true:

```
[OperationContract(IsOneWay=true,IsInitiating=true)]
void SetPassMark(int passMark);
```

The other operation contract, GetAwardedPeople(), does not require any customization and uses the data contract defined earlier:

```
[OperationContract]
Person[] GetAwardedPeople(Person[] peopleToTest);
}
```

Remember that these two types, Person and IAwardService, are available to both the service and the client. The service implements the IAwardService contract in a type called AwardService, which doesn't contain any remarkable code. The only difference between this class and the service class you saw earlier is that it is stateful. This is permissible, as a session is defined to correlate messages from a client.

To ensure that the service uses the WSHttpBinding binding, you added the following the Web.config for the service:

```
<protocolMapping>
  <add scheme="http" binding="wsHttpBinding" />
</protocolMapping>
```

This overrides the default mapping for HTTP binding. Alternatively, you could configure the service manually and keep the existing default, but this override is much simpler. However, be aware that this type of override is applied to all services in a project. If you have more than one service in a project, then you would have to ensure that this binding is acceptable to each of them.

The client is more interesting, primarily because of this code:

```
IAwardService client = ChannelFactory<IAwardService>.CreateChannel(
    new WSHttpBinding(),
    new EndpointAddress("http://localhost:49284/AwardService.svc"));
```

The client application has no app.config file to configure communications with the service, and no proxy class defined from metadata to communicate with the service. Instead, a proxy class is created through the ChannelFactory<T>.CreateChannel() method. This method creates a proxy class that implements the IAwardService client, although behind the scenes the generated class communicates with the service just like the metadata-generated proxy shown earlier.

> **NOTE** *If you create a proxy class with* ChannelFactory<T>.CreateChannel(), *the communication channel will, by default, time out after a minute, which can lead to communication errors. There are ways to keep connections alive, but they are beyond the scope of this chapter.*

Creating proxy classes in this way is an extremely useful technique that you can use to quickly generate a client application on-the-fly.

# Self-Hosted WCF Services

So far in this chapter you have seen WCF services that are hosted in web servers. This enables you to communicate across the Internet, but for local network communications it is not the most efficient way of doing things. For one thing, you need a web server on the computer that hosts the service. In addition, the architecture of your applications might be such that having an independent WCF service isn't desirable.

Instead, you might want to use a self-hosted WCF service. A *self-hosted* WCF service exists in a process that you create, rather than in the process of a specially made hosting application such as a web server. This means, for example, that you can use a console application or Windows application to host your service.

To self-host a WCF service, you use the `System.ServiceModel.ServiceHost` class. You instantiate this class with either the type of the service you want to host or an instance of the service class. You can configure a service host through properties or methods, or (and this is the clever part) through a configuration file. In fact, host processes, such as web servers, use a `ServiceHost` instance to do their hosting. The difference when self-hosting is that you interact with this class directly. However, the configuration you place in the `<system.serviceModel>` section of the `app.config` file for your host application uses exactly the same syntax as the configuration sections you've already seen in this chapter.

You can expose a self-hosted service through any protocol that you like, although typically you will use TCP or named pipe binding in this type of application. Services accessed through HTTP are more likely to live inside web server processes, because you get the additional functionality that web servers offer, such as security and other features.

If you want to host a service called `MyService`, you could use code such as the following to create an instance of `ServiceHost`:

```
ServiceHost host = new ServiceHost(typeof(MyService));
```

If you want to host an instance of `MyService` called `myServiceObject`, you could code as follows to create an instance of `ServiceHost`:

```
MyService myServiceObject = new MyService();
ServiceHost host = new ServiceHost(myServiceObject);
```

> **WARNING** Hosting a service instance in a `ServiceHost` works only if you configure the service so that calls are always routed to the same object instance. To do this, you must apply a `ServiceBehaviorAttribute` attribute to the service class and set the `InstanceContextMode` property of this attribute to `InstanceContextMode.Single`.

After creating a `ServiceHost` instance you can configure the service and its endpoints and binding through properties. Alternatively, if you put your configuration in a `.config` file, the `ServiceHost` instance will be configured automatically.

To start hosting a service once you have a configured `ServiceHost` instance, you use the `ServiceHost.Open()` method. Similarly, you stop hosting the service through the `ServiceHost.Close()` method. When you first start hosting a TCP-bound service, you might, if you have it enabled, receive a warning from the Windows Firewall service, as it will block the TCP port by default. You must open the TCP port for the service to begin listening on the port.

In the following Try it Out you use self-hosting techniques to expose some functionality of a WPF application through a WCF service.

Self-Hosted WCF Services: Ch25Ex03

1. Create a new WPF application called Ch25Ex03 in the directory `C:\BegVCSharp\Chapter25`.
2. Add a new WCF service to the project called AppControlService by using the Add New Item Wizard.
3. Modify the code in `MainWindow.xaml` as follows:

```xml
<Window x:Class="Ch25Ex03.MainWindow"
  xmlns="http://schemas.microsoft.com/winfx/2006/xaml/presentation"
  xmlns:x="http://schemas.microsoft.com/winfx/2006/xaml"
  Title="Stellar Evolution" Height="450" Width="430"
  Loaded="Window_Loaded" Closing="Window_Closing">
  <Grid Height="400" Width="400" HorizontalAlignment="Center"
    VerticalAlignment="Center">
    <Rectangle Fill="Black" RadiusX="20" RadiusY="20"
      StrokeThickness="10">
      <Rectangle.Stroke>
        <LinearGradientBrush EndPoint="0.358,0.02"
          StartPoint="0.642,0.98">
          <GradientStop Color="#FF121A5D" Offset="0" />
          <GradientStop Color="#FFB1B9FF" Offset="1" />
        </LinearGradientBrush>
      </Rectangle.Stroke>
    </Rectangle>
    <Ellipse Name="AnimatableEllipse" Stroke="{x:Null}" Height="0"
      Width="0" HorizontalAlignment="Center"
      VerticalAlignment="Center">
      <Ellipse.Fill>
        <RadialGradientBrush>
          <GradientStop Color="#FFFFFFFF" Offset="0" />
          <GradientStop Color="#FFFFFFFF" Offset="1" />
        </RadialGradientBrush>
      </Ellipse.Fill>
      <Ellipse.Effect>
        <DropShadowEffect ShadowDepth="0" Color="#FFFFFFFF"
          BlurRadius="50" />
      </Ellipse.Effect>
    </Ellipse>
  </Grid>
</Window>
```

4. Modify the code in `MainWindow.xaml.cs` as follows:

```csharp
using System.Windows.Shapes;
using System.ServiceModel;
using System.Windows.Media.Animation;

namespace Ch25Ex03
{
    /// <summary>
    /// Interaction logic for MainWindow.xaml
    /// </summary>
    public partial class MainWindow : Window
    {
        private AppControlService service;
        private ServiceHost host;

        public MainWindow()
        {
            InitializeComponent();
        }

        private void Window_Loaded(object sender, RoutedEventArgs e)
```

```
        {
            service = new AppControlService(this);
            host = new ServiceHost(service);
            host.Open();
        }

        private void Window_Closing(object sender,
            System.ComponentModel.CancelEventArgs e)
        {
            host.Close();
        }

        internal void SetRadius(double radius, string foreTo,
            TimeSpan duration)
        {
            if (radius > 200)
            {
                radius = 200;
            }
            Color foreToColor = Colors.Red;
            try
            {
                foreToColor = (Color)ColorConverter.ConvertFromString(foreTo);
            }
            catch
            {
                // Ignore color conversion failure.
            }
            Duration animationLength = new Duration(duration);

            DoubleAnimation radiusAnimation = new DoubleAnimation(
                radius * 2, animationLength);
            ColorAnimation colorAnimation = new ColorAnimation(
                foreToColor, animationLength);
            AnimatableEllipse.BeginAnimation(Ellipse.HeightProperty,
                radiusAnimation);
            AnimatableEllipse.BeginAnimation(Ellipse.WidthProperty,
                radiusAnimation);
            ((RadialGradientBrush)AnimatableEllipse.Fill).GradientStops[1]
                .BeginAnimation(GradientStop.ColorProperty, colorAnimation);
        }
    }
}
```

**5.** Modify the code in `IAppControlService.cs` as follows:

```
[ServiceContract]
public interface IAppControlService
{
    [OperationContract]
    void SetRadius(int radius, string foreTo, int seconds);
}
```

**6.** Modify the code in `AppControlService.cs` as follows:

```
[ServiceBehavior(InstanceContextMode=InstanceContextMode.Single)]
public class AppControlService : IAppControlService
{
    private MainWindow hostApp;

    public AppControlService(MainWindow hostApp)
    {
        this.hostApp = hostApp;
    }
```

```
      public void SetRadius(int radius, string foreTo, int seconds)
      {
         hostApp.SetRadius(radius, foreTo, new TimeSpan(0, 0, seconds));
      }
   }
}
```

7. Modify the code in `app.config` as follows:

```
<configuration>
  <system.serviceModel>
    <services>
      <service name="Ch25Ex03.AppControlService">
        <endpoint address="net.tcp://localhost:8081/AppControlService"
          binding="netTcpBinding"
          contract="Ch25Ex03.IAppControlService" />
      </service>
    </services>
  </system.serviceModel>
</configuration>
```

8. Add a new console application to the project called Ch25Ex03Client.

9. Right-click the solution in the Solution Explorer and click Set StartUp Projects.

10. Configure the solution to have multiple startup projects, with both projects being started simultaneously, as shown in Figure 25-12.

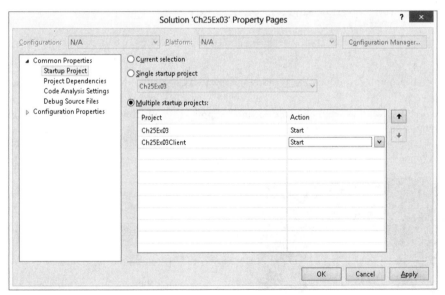

**FIGURE 25-12**

11. Add references to `System.ServiceModel.dll` and Ch25Ex03 to the Ch25Ex03Client project.

12. Modify the code in `Program.cs` as follows:

```
using System;
using System.Collections.Generic;
using System.Linq;
using System.Text;
using System.Threading.Tasks;
using Ch25Ex03;
```

```csharp
using System.ServiceModel;

namespace Ch25Ex03Client
{
    class Program
    {
        static void Main(string[] args)
        {
            Console.WriteLine("Press enter to begin.");
            Console.ReadLine();
            Console.WriteLine("Opening channel.");
            IAppControlService client =
                ChannelFactory<IAppControlService>.CreateChannel(
                    new NetTcpBinding(),
                    new EndpointAddress(
                        "net.tcp://localhost:8081/AppControlService"));
            Console.WriteLine("Creating sun.");
            client.SetRadius(100, "yellow", 3);
            Console.WriteLine("Press enter to continue.");
            Console.ReadLine();
            Console.WriteLine("Growing sun to red giant.");
            client.SetRadius(200, "Red", 5);
            Console.WriteLine("Press enter to continue.");
            Console.ReadLine();
            Console.WriteLine("Collapsing sun to neutron star.");
            client.SetRadius(50, "AliceBlue", 2);
            Console.WriteLine("Finished. Press enter to exit.");
            Console.ReadLine();
        }
    }
}
```

**13.** Run the solution. If prompted, unblock the Windows Firewall TCP port so that the WCF can listen for connections.

**14.** When both the Stellar Evolution window and the console application window are displayed, press Enter in the console window. The result is shown in Figure 25-13.

**FIGURE 25-13**

**15.** Continue pressing Enter in the console window to continue the stellar evolution cycle.

### How It Works

In this example you have added a WCF service to a WPF application and used it to control the animation of an `Ellipse` control. You have created a simple client application to test the service. Don't worry too much about the XAML code in this example if you are not familiar with WPF yet; it's the WCF plumbing that is of interest here.

The WCF service, `AppControlService`, exposes a single operation, `SetRadius()`, which clients call to control the animation. This method communicates with an identically named method defined in the `Window1` class for the WPF application. For this to work, the service needs a reference to the application, so you must host an object instance of the service. As discussed previously, this means that the service must use a behavior attribute:

```
[ServiceBehavior(InstanceContextMode=InstanceContextMode.Single)]
public class AppControlService : IAppControlService
{
   ...
}
```

In `Window1.xaml.cs`, the service instance is created in the `Windows_Loaded()` event handler. This method also begins hosting by creating a `ServiceHost` object for the service and calling its `Open()` method:

```
public partial class Window1 : Window
{
   private AppControlService service;
   private ServiceHost host;

   ...

   private void Window_Loaded(object sender, RoutedEventArgs e)
   {
      service = new AppControlService(this);
      host = new ServiceHost(service);
      host.Open();
   }
}
```

When the application closes, hosting is terminated in the `Window_Closing()` event handler.

The configuration file is again about as simple as it can be. It defines a single endpoint for the WCF service that listens at a `net.tcp` address, on port 8081, and uses the default `NetTcpBinding` binding:

```
<service name="Ch25Ex03.AppControlService">
  <endpoint address="net.tcp://localhost:8081/AppControlService"
    binding="netTcpBinding"
    contract="Ch25Ex03.IAppControlService" />
</service>
```

This matches up with code in the client app:

```
IAppControlService client =
   ChannelFactory<IAppControlService>.CreateChannel(
      new NetTcpBinding(),
      new EndpointAddress(
         "net.tcp://localhost:8081/AppControlService"));
```

When the client has created a client proxy class, it can call the `SetRadius()` method with radius, color, and animation duration parameters, and these are forwarded to the WPF application through the service. Simple code in the WPF application then defines and uses animations to change the size and color of the ellipse.

This code would work across a network if you used a machine name, rather than `localhost`, and if the network permitted traffic on the specified port. Alternatively, you could separate the client and host application further, and connect across the Internet. Either way, WCF services provide an excellent means of communication that doesn't take much effort to set up.

## SUMMARY

In this chapter you looked at the basic techniques for using WCF services to communicate among applications, processes, and computers. You started by learning what a WCF service is and how it differs from a web service or a remoting implementation, and the concepts that you need to know about to use WCF services. You then looked at how to program WCF services, how to consume WCF services in clients, and how to host WCF services in various ways.

What you have learned is the absolute minimum that you need in order to use WCF services in your applications. This chapter barely scratches the surface of what is possible, in particular with .config file configuration and behaviors. The WCF framework enables you to integrate with advanced security infrastructures, and communication can be customized in pretty much any way you can imagine.

If you want to learn more about WCF services, you might like to read *Professional WCF 4* (Wrox, 2010). In the next chapter, you look at the last of the major new technologies introduced with .NET 3.5 (and greatly improved for .NET 4 and .NET 4.5): Workflow Foundation.

### EXERCISES

**25.1** Which of the following applications can host WCF services?

    **a.** Web applications

    **b.** Windows Forms applications

    **c.** Windows services

    **d.** COM+ applications

    **e.** Console applications

**25.2** Which type of contract would you implement if you wanted to exchange parameters of type `MyClass` with a WCF service? Which attributes would you require?

**25.3** If you host a WCF service in a web application, what extension will the base endpoint for the service use?

**25.4** When self-hosting WCF services, you must configure the service by setting properties and calling methods of the `ServiceHost` class. True or false?

**25.5** Provide the code for a service contract, `IMusicPlayer`, with operations defined for `Play()`, `Stop()`, and `GetTrackInformation()`. Use one-way methods where appropriate. What other contracts might you define for this service to work?

Answers to the exercises can be found in Appendix A.

# ▶ WHAT YOU LEARNED IN THIS CHAPTER

| TOPIC | KEY CONCEPTS |
|---|---|
| **WCF fundamentals** | WCF provides a framework for creating and communicating with remote services. It combines elements of the web service and remoting architectures along with new technologies to achieve this. |
| **Communication protocols** | You can communicate with a WCF service by any one of several protocols, including HTTP and TCP. This means that you can use services that are local to your client application, or that are separated by machine or network boundaries. To do this, you access a specific endpoint for the service through a binding corresponding to the protocol and features that you require. You can control these features, such as using session state or exposing metadata, through behaviors. .NET 4.5 includes many default settings to make it very easy to define a simple service. |
| **Communication payload** | Typically, calls to responses from WCF services are encoded as SOAP messages. However, there are alternatives, such as plain HTTP messages, and you can define your own payload types from scratch if you need to. |
| **Hosting** | WCF services might be hosted in IIS or in a Windows service, or they can be self-hosted. Using a host such as IIS enables you to make use of the host's built-in capabilities, including security and application pooling. Self-hosting is more flexible, but it can require more configuration and coding. |
| **Contracts** | You define the interface between a WCF service and client code through contracts. Services themselves, along with any operations they expose, are defined with service and operation contracts. Data types are defined with data contracts. Further customization of communications is achieved with message and fault contracts. |
| **Client applications** | Client applications communicate with WCF services by means of a proxy class. Proxy classes implement the service contract interface for the service, and any calls to operation methods of this interface are redirected to the service. You can generate a proxy by using the Add Service Reference tool, or you can create one programmatically through channel factory methods. In order for communications to succeed, the client must be configured to match the service configuration. |

# 26

# Windows Workflow Foundation

## WHAT YOU WILL LEARN IN THIS CHAPTER

➤  What a workflow is and how to execute one

➤  What an activity is

➤  How to create custom activities

➤  How to send an e-mail from an activity

Windows Workflow Foundation (WF) first appeared with .NET 3.0 and was revised with .NET 3.5 to add some functionality to integrate it with Windows Communication Foundation (WCF) more easily. In .NET 4, Workflow was completely rewritten; while the core concepts are the same as Workflow 3, the implementation is entirely different. This chapter covers Windows Workflow Foundation 4 and 4.5.

A simplified definition of a *workflow* is "a collection of activities," but that's not an entirely satisfying definition. It might be more useful to use an analogy instead.

When you're writing a program, you use statements (such as `if`/`else`) and call functions (`Console .WriteLine`), and you might also execute some code within a loop. You can't expect your end users to understand programming, so they tell you what they want the system to do, and you write the code to achieve those needs.

Now suppose for a moment that you could provide your end users with a vastly simplified programming environment, one in which you pre-build the statements and control flow logic, and all the end users need to do is plug these parts together to get what they want. That's what Workflow can be used for. The statements and control logic are all called *activities*, and these can be plugged together into a workflow.

## HELLO WORLD

Every programming book needs a Hello World example, and this one is no different. However, rather than use a traditional programming language, this example uses Workflow instead. In the following Try It Out, you create a Workflow project, add an activity, and execute the workflow.

**TRY IT OUT** A Simple Workflow Application: 01-HelloWorkflowWorld

1. In Visual Studio 2012, create a new Workflow Console Application project. Ensure that .NET Framework 4.5 is chosen in the drop-down at the top-middle section of the screen, as shown in Figure 26-1.

2. From the Toolbox, drag and drop a `WriteLine` activity onto the main designer area (this activity appears in the Primitives category).

3. Type `"Hello Workflow World"` in the text box (see Figure 26-2), and include the quotes.

4. Run the application to see the output text.

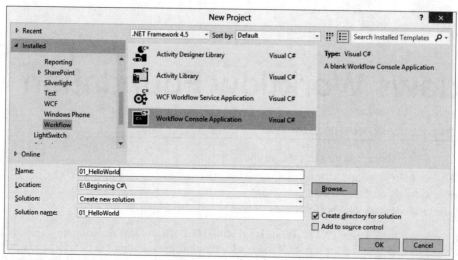

**FIGURE 26-1**

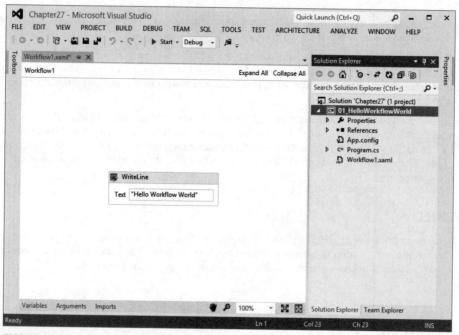

**FIGURE 26-2**

*How It Works*

When the application runs, it executes the activities within the workflow. In this example you have only a single activity that outputs some text; once that activity has completed, the workflow itself completes and therefore the application exits. You will, of course, provide many more activities in a workflow that perform much more useful tasks than writing a message to the console!

## WORKFLOWS AND ACTIVITIES

In the previous section, you saw a trivial example of a workflow that used a simple activity. A workflow is a collection of activities, and the workflow defines the execution order of those activities. The example used a sequential workflow, which is composed of multiple activities executed in sequential order.

An activity is a unit of work, and two types of activity are available. The first is the simple variety you just saw—the WriteLine activity. This activity performs one task only. The other type of activity is a composite activity. There are several examples of these that you might be familiar with, such as the While activity, which effectively contains other child activities.

A workflow, therefore, is similar to a program—it has simple activities that are akin to regular programming language statements, control of flow activities similar to control of flow statements—and is executed much like a program.

If a workflow is similar to a program, then can you create your own functions, like you do in programming? Maybe you need a function that sends an e-mail or one that writes data to an audit trail. This is where custom activities come in—you can write these low-level units of functionality and users can simply plug these into a workflow. Now that's cool!

Windows Workflow Foundation provides many activities, and the following section discusses some of these and shows you how they can be used within a workflow.

## If Activity

This activity works in a similar manner to an if/else statement in C#, and when executed it evaluates a condition and then decides which path the workflow should take based on that condition.

When you use an If activity, it appears within a workflow as shown in Figure 26-3.

The If activity contains a conditional expression that is evaluated at runtime, and placeholders for the Then and Else activities. The Condition property is an expression that evaluates to a Boolean value, so you can include any valid expression here.

**FIGURE 26-3**

> **NOTE** *Workflow 4 included an expression engine that used Visual Basic syntax, however in version 4.5 there is now a C# expression evaluator included. This chapter exclusively uses version 4.5 for the demos, but be warned that if you use version 4.0, the expression engine is different.*

An expression can reference any variables defined in the workflow and access many static classes available in the .NET Framework. So you could, for example, define an expression based on the `Environment .Is64BitOperatingSystem` value, if that were crucial to some part of your workflow. Naturally, you can define arguments that are passed into the workflow and that can then be evaluated by an expression inside an `If` activity. Arguments and variables are covered later in the chapter.

## While Activity

The `While` activity will be familiar to any programmer. It evaluates a condition and while that condition is true, the body of that activity is executed (see Figure 26-4).

`While` supports only one activity within the body, but most programs require more than one statement within any loop, so there must be some way to add more statements, and indeed there is: the `Sequence` activity.

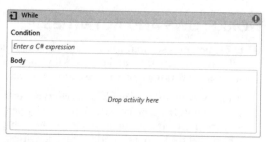

**FIGURE 26-4**

## Sequence Activity

This activity enables you to construct a list of other activities, and when executed it will start with the first child activity and execute each child in turn (see Figure 26-5).

The image in Figure 26-5 shows a `Sequence` activity that contains three child activities—a `WriteLine`, a `While`, and another `WriteLine`. If this workflow were executed, the initial message would be written out to the console. Next, the `While` loop would execute and finally another message would be written to the console. Figure 26-5 also shows another useful feature of the workflow designer, that being the ability to contract (and expand) activities. In this case, the `While` activity has been contracted so you can only see the name—the button on the right side of the activity that shows two chevrons allows you to toggle the visibility of the activity's contents, and the content changes to say "Double-click to View".

This ability to expand and contract an activity is very useful when designing large workflows, as you can contract parts of the workflow you are not actively designing and zoom in on those you are working with.

There are other features of the workflow designer that make it easy to work with. For example, on the bottom right of the designer is the set of controls shown in Figure 26-6.

These controls (from left to right) provide a way to pan around the workflow, zoom to 100%, zoom to a custom level, fit the current workflow to the size of the screen, and show or hide an overview window that displays a thumbnail of the workflow. In addition, you can also double-click on a composite activity such as a `While` or an `If`, which then hides all higher-level activities, leaving only the activity you clicked and its children. A breadcrumb trail at the top left of the screen shows you where you are (see Figure 26-7).

You can click on any item in the breadcrumb, navigating to successively higher levels in the workflow until you reach the top level.

**FIGURE 26-5**

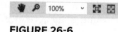

**FIGURE 26-6**

**FIGURE 26-7**

## ARGUMENTS AND VARIABLES

With any normal programming language you can use arguments to pass values into functions (and retrieve responses), and within a function you can define and use variables as temporary storage. Because Workflow is effectively a programming language, the same constructs are available.

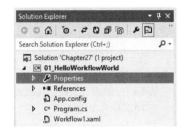

**FIGURE 26-8**

Before examining arguments and variables further, however, consider what a workflow actually consists of. If you display the Solution Explorer in Visual Studio 2012 and look at the solution created in the first part of this chapter, you'll see the file highlighted in Figure 26-8.

Double-clicking `Workflow1.xaml` will display the workflow in the designer. However, this is just a regular XML file, so rather than double-click on it, right-click and choose Open With. From the window that appears, choose XML Editor. This will open the file and show the XML that makes up the workflow:

```xml
<Activity mc:Ignorable="sap sap2010 sads"
  x:Class="_01_HelloWorkflowWorld.Workflow1"
  sap2010:ExpressionActivityEditor.ExpressionActivityEditor="C#"
xmlns="http://schemas.microsoft.com/netfx/2009/xaml/activities"
xmlns:mc="http://schemas.openxmlformats.org/markup-compatibility/2006"
xmlns:sads="http://schemas.microsoft.com/netfx/2010/xaml/activities/debugger"
xmlns:sap="http://schemas.microsoft.com/netfx/2009/xaml/activities/presentation"
xmlns:sap2010=
  "http://schemas.microsoft.com/netfx/2010/xaml/activities/presentation"
xmlns:sco="clr-namespace:System.Collections.ObjectModel;assembly=mscorlib"
xmlns:x="http://schemas.microsoft.com/winfx/2006/xaml">
  <TextExpression.NamespacesForImplementation>
    <sco:Collection x:TypeArguments="x:String">
      <x:String>System</x:String>
      <x:String>System.Collections.Generic</x:String>
      <x:String>System.Data</x:String>
      <x:String>System.Linq</x:String>
      <x:String>System.Text</x:String>
    </sco:Collection>
  </TextExpression.NamespacesForImplementation>
  <TextExpression.ReferencesForImplementation>
    <sco:Collection x:TypeArguments="AssemblyReference">
      <AssemblyReference>Microsoft.CSharp</AssemblyReference>
      <AssemblyReference>System</AssemblyReference>
      <AssemblyReference>System.Activities</AssemblyReference>
      <AssemblyReference>System.Core</AssemblyReference>
      <AssemblyReference>System.Data</AssemblyReference>
      <AssemblyReference>System.Runtime.Serialization</AssemblyReference>
      <AssemblyReference>System.ServiceModel</AssemblyReference>
      <AssemblyReference>System.ServiceModel.Activities</AssemblyReference>
      <AssemblyReference>System.Xaml</AssemblyReference>
      <AssemblyReference>System.Xml</AssemblyReference>
      <AssemblyReference>System.Xml.Linq</AssemblyReference>
      <AssemblyReference>mscorlib</AssemblyReference>
      <AssemblyReference>01-HelloWorkflowWorld</AssemblyReference>
    </sco:Collection>
  </TextExpression.ReferencesForImplementation>
  <WriteLine Text="Hello Workflow World"
    sap2010:WorkflowViewState.IdRef="WriteLine_1" />
  <sap2010:WorkflowViewState.IdRef>_01_HelloWorkflowWorld.Workflow1_1
    </sap2010:WorkflowViewState.IdRef>
  <sap2010:WorkflowViewState.ViewStateManager>
    <sap2010:ViewStateManager>
      <sap2010:ViewStateData Id="WriteLine_1"
```

```
        sap:VirtualizedContainerService.HintSize="211,62" />
      <sap2010:ViewStateData Id="_01_HelloWorkflowWorld.Workflow1_1"
        sap:VirtualizedContainerService.HintSize="251,142" />
    </sap2010:ViewStateManager>
  </sap2010:WorkflowViewState.ViewStateManager>
</Activity>
```

A lot of XML namespaces are referenced in the code, but the main part just shows a `WriteLine` activity with a `Text` property.

To create arguments that are passed into a workflow, you can use the Arguments designer within the Workflow designer. This option appears at the bottom left of the designer surface, as shown in Figure 26-9.

**FIGURE 26-9**

In the following Try It Out section, you create an input argument and a variable and use these in a simple workflow.

**TRY IT OUT**  Using Arguments and Variables: 02-Arguments

1. Create a new Workflow Console Application project in Visual Studio 2012.

2. When the workflow is displayed, click the Arguments button and create a string argument as shown in Figure 26-10. Set the name of the argument to **Name**, the direction to **In**, and its data type to **String**.

3. Add a `Sequence` activity to the workflow, and then add a `WriteLine` activity to the `Sequence` and type **Name** into the expression text box. Note that you shouldn't include quotes, as this is now the name of an argument and not a literal string.

4. Now click the Variables button and define a variable called _uppercaseName of type `String`. You'll use this variable to store the uppercase value of the `Name` argument.

5. Drag an `Assign` activity onto the designer. Set the left text box of the activity to _uppercaseName and set the right side to `Name.ToUpper()`. This activity assigns a value to a variable, and the value in this instance calls a function on the string class that converts it to an uppercase string.

6. Drag a `WriteLine` activity onto the designer and set its text box to _uppercaseName.

7. Now switch to the `MainProgram.cs` file where you will create a value for the `Name` argument and pass this into the workflow. You'll see the following code in that file:

```
class Program
{
    static void Main(string[] args)
    {
        // Create and cache the workflow definition
        Activity workflow1 = new Workflow1();
        WorkflowInvoker.Invoke(workflow1);
    }
}
```

8. The preceding code needs to be modified to pass in a value for the `Name` argument. Change it as follows:

```
class Program
{
    static void Main(string[] args)
    {
        // Create and cache the workflow definition
        Activity workflow1 = new Workflow1();
        Dictionary<string, object> parms = new Dictionary<string, object>();
        parms.Add("Name", "Morgan");
        WorkflowInvoker.Invoke(workflow1, parms);
        Console.ReadLine();
    }
}
```

Substitute your name if you want!

**9.** Build and run the project. You should see two lines, one in uppercase.

**FIGURE 26-10**

### How It Works

When this application executes it passes a string parameter into the workflow. The input parameter is data-bound to the `WriteLine` activity and also the `Assign` activity, where it is altered by an expression into an uppercase version, which is then stored into a local variable. This variable is used by the second `WriteLine` activity.

If you were now to open the `Workflow1.xaml` file from the Try It Out section with the XAML editor, you would see the definition of the argument toward the top of the file:

```
<x:Members>
  <x:Property Name="Name" Type="InArgument(x:String)" />
</x:Members>
```

In addition, you would see the definition of the variable within the sequence:

```
<Sequence.Variables>
  <Variable x:TypeArguments="x:String" Name="_uppercaseName" />
</Sequence.Variables>
```

Just like variables within a regular program, variables in a workflow have a scope that defines when they are available. Once the activity that defines the variable is completed, that variable is destroyed.

In the preceding code example, you created a dictionary of name/value pairs to pass into the workflow and then added a value to the dictionary with the key of Name. The key value you use here must match exactly the argument definition; otherwise, the argument value will not be set correctly and your workflow could execute without the appropriate data.

Another behavior of functions in a normal programming language is that you can return values from them. Similarly, you can pass arguments into a workflow, but also pass arguments out too. In the same way that you created a dictionary to pass values into a workflow, when a workflow completes, any output arguments are returned as a dictionary.

An argument includes the notion of direction, which can be one of the following three values:

➤ **In**—The argument is passed in to the workflow.

➤ **Out**—The argument is returned from the workflow.

➤ **In/Out**—The argument is both passed into the workflow and returned from the workflow when it completes.

Only arguments defined as Out or In/Out will be returned when the workflow completes. In order to read the values returned from the workflow, you can use the following code:

```
IDictionary<string,object> returnValues = WorkflowInvoker.Invoke(new
    Workflow1(), parms);
```

Here, the `returnValues` variable is assigned a dictionary of name/value pairs that will contain all Out and In/Out arguments defined on the workflow.

The following Try It Out shows how you can pass arguments into and out of a workflow.

**TRY IT OUT** Returning Arguments: 03-InOutArgs

**1.** Create a new Workflow Console Application project in Visual Studio 2012.

**2.** Create a string argument on the workflow and define it as an In/Out argument called `Person`.

**3.** Drag a `Sequence` activity onto the workflow.

**4.** Drag a `WriteLine` activity onto the workflow and set its text expression as follows:

```
String.Format ( "Person is called : {0}", Person )
```

> **NOTE** Because this is a C# expression you don't need a semicolon.

**5.** Drag an `Assign` activity onto the workflow. Set the left side to `Person`, and set the right side to be the following expression:

```
String.Format("You entered the name : {0}", Person)
```

You should end up with a workflow that looks like Figure 26-11.

**6.** Alter the main `program.cs` file so that it passes an argument into the workflow and prints out the value of all Out or In/Out arguments, as shown in the following snippet:

```
// Create and cache the workflow definition
Activity workflow1 = new Workflow1();
Dictionary<string, object> parms = new Dictionary<string, object>();
parms.Add("Person", "Morgan");

foreach (KeyValuePair<string, object> kvp in
    WorkflowInvoker.Invoke(workflow1, parms))
{
    Console.WriteLine("{0} = {1}", kvp.Key, kvp.Value);
}
```

When executed, the workflow should output the value of the `Person` argument within the workflow, and then a modified value should be written out from the preceding code. This proves that an argument modified within a workflow will be passed out to the caller once the workflow has completed.

**FIGURE 26-11**

*How It Works*

When this workflow executes it is passed an input argument. This argument is available while the workflow executes, and in this example it's also returned from the workflow when it completes as it was defined as an In/Out argument.

## CUSTOM ACTIVITIES

So far this chapter has used examples only with built-in activities, but Workflow also permits custom activities to be written, which are then used just like the built-in activities.

Earlier in the chapter you learned that there are two broad categories of activity types: singular activities and composite activities. In this section, you create both types.

An activity is scheduled for execution by the workflow (or parent activity) that owns it. What happens next is largely up to the activity writer. In the case of the `WriteLine` activity, you could reasonably expect to find a call to `Console.WriteLine` somewhere within the code for the activity.

When you write an activity you'll typically override the `Execute` method in order to supply your custom code. This method varies according to the base class used for the activity. These base classes and their execute methods are shown in Table 26-1.

**TABLE 26-1:** Activity Execute Methods

| BASE CLASS | EXECUTE METHOD |
|---|---|
| AsyncCodeActivity | IAsyncResult BeginExecute(AsyncCodeActivityContext, AsyncCallback, object) void EndExecute(AsyncCodeActivityContext, IAsyncResult) |
| CodeActivity | void Execute (CodeActivityContext) |
| NativeActivity | void Execute (NativeActivityContext) |
| AsyncCodeActivity<TResult> | IAsyncResult BeginExecute(AsyncCodeActivityContext, AsyncCallback, object)TResult EndExecute(AsyncCodeActivityContext, IAsyncResult) |
| CodeActivity<TResult> | TResult Execute (CodeActivityContext) |
| NativeActivity<TResult> | void Execute (NativeActivityContext) |

The simplest base class to use is `CodeActivity`, and there's also a generic version of `CodeActivity` that accepts a type argument—this is used as the return value from executing that activity. In the same way that a workflow can return arguments, an activity might return a value after it has executed, and this result can be data-bound within the workflow so that the output from one activity can form the input to the next.

Suppose you want to use the current time within a workflow. You could create an activity that would return a `DateTime` value, and when executed it would get this timestamp by calling `DateTime.Now`. Other than writing out a string to the console, this is about as simple as an activity can get! The following Try It Out walks through creating a custom activity.

---

**TRY IT OUT**   Writing a Custom Activity: 04-CustomActivities

1. Create a new Workflow Console Application project in Visual Studio 2012.

2. Add a second project to the solution but use the Activity Library project template for this one. This will create a default activity (`Activity1.xaml`) that you can remove from the project because it will not be used at this point. The example code includes two projects. `04-CustomActivites` contains this code, and `04-WritingCustomActivites` contains the executable that uses the custom activity.

3. Add a new class called `Timestamp` to the class library. The following code is needed:

```
using System;
using System.Activities;
namespace CustomActivities
{
    public class Timestamp : CodeActivity<DateTime>
    {
        protected override DateTime Execute(CodeActivityContext context)
        {
            return DateTime.Now;
        }
    }
}
```

This defines the custom activity and provides an implementation of the appropriate `Execute` method, which returns the current date/time value.

4. Compile the solution and then add a reference from the workflow project to the custom activity project. This enables your custom activity to be used within the workflow project, and adds the custom activity to the Toolbox.

5. Edit the main workflow and drag on a sequence activity. Define a variable of type `DateTime` on the `Sequence` activity. Call this variable `currentDateTime`. You'll need to browse in the variables designer to find the `DateTime` type. You can type part of the type name and all matches will show up.

6. Drag on a `Timestamp` activity and display its properties. You need to alter the `Result` property to `currentDateTime`, which will assign the result value of the activity to this variable. Figure 26-12 shows the property value.

7. Drag on a `WriteLine` activity and set its expression as follows:

```
String.Format ( "The time read from the Timestamp activity is '{0}'",
    currentDateTime)
```

8. Run the workflow. You should see output that describes the current date and time.

### How It Works

When a workflow executes it runs each activity in turn. If the activity is derived from `CodeActivity` then the `Execute` method will be called when the activity is scheduled to run. The activity here has a return value that is set within the `Execute` method to the current date and time. In this Try It Out the value of the `Timestamp` activity is stored in a workflow variable, which is then output to the console using the `WriteLine` activity.

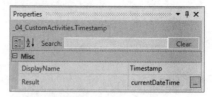

**FIGURE 26-12**

---

The `Timestamp` activity is about as simple as it gets. Typically, you'll create activities that do a bit more work within their `Execute` methods. An activity is generally a self-contained unit, much like a function from a traditional programming language. Functions usually have one or more arguments, and usually these arguments are passed into the function as parameters. Sometimes, however, the function will also receive data via the current application context.

A good example is from ASP.NET. The static property available as `HttpContext.Current` gives you access to various properties such as the current application state, the `HttpRequest`, and the `HttpResponse`. This object is defined by the ASP.NET processing pipeline and is then available to any object called within that pipeline.

A similar facility exists within Workflow using the concept of *extensions*.

# Workflow Extensions

An extension is simply an object that you want to be able to access from an activity within its `Execute` method. Typically, you will define an interface for your extension, and your activity will code against that interface. This enables you to replace the implementation of that extension without needing to recode the entire activity.

As a concrete example, consider an activity that sends an e-mail. You could hard-code the e-mail provider within the activity itself, but then it would work only with that provider. In this instance, it would be beneficial to define an interface that the activity used, and then provide several implementations of that interface—one for sending mail using Outlook, another using Microsoft Exchange, and so on. In short, you could extend the list of e-mail providers without changing the activity.

In order for an e-mail activity to be of any use, you also need to be able to define arguments that are passed into that activity. You certainly wouldn't want to hard-code the e-mail recipient, subject, or body. Just as you did with the `WriteLine` activity, you would like to be able to define properties that can be set on your activity. In order to do that, you need to use classes derived from the `Argument` class, such as `InArgument` and `OutArgument`.

These argument classes are used in place of properties on an activity. The reason why the argument types are used is related to how a workflow stores its state while it is executing, which is covered later in the chapter. For now, go ahead and create your interface and custom activity.

---

**TRY IT OUT**    Defining the ISendEmail Interface and Activity: 05-SharedInterfaces

**1.** Create a new Class Library project with Visual Studio 2012. Call this `SharedInterfaces`. If you wish to look at the example code there is the 05-SharedInterfaces project which contains this code, and the related projects all have the 05-prefix.

**2.** Add an interface to the library called `ISendEmail`, as shown here:

```
/// <summary>
/// Interface used by the SendEmail activity to send an email
/// </summary>
public interface ISendEmail
{
    /// <summary>
    /// Sends an email
    /// </summary>
    /// <param name="sender">The person sending the email</param>
    /// <param name="recipient">The recipient of the email</param>
    /// <param name="subject">The subject</param>
    /// <param name="body">The body</param>
    void SendEmail(string sender, string recipient,
                string subject, string body);
}
```

**3.** Now add a second project to the solution. This time, choose an Activity Library and call it `CustomActivities`. Delete the `Activity1.xaml` file that is automatically created for you.

**4.** Add a new class called `SendEmail` to the project. Define this as shown in the following example. You'll need to reference the `SharedInterfaces` project by the activity library in order to include the definition of the `ISendEmail` interface:

```
public class SendEmail : NativeActivity
{
    public InArgument<string> Sender { get; set; }
    public InArgument<string> Recipient { get; set; }
```

```
public InArgument<string> Subject { get; set; }
public InArgument<string> Body { get; set; }
protected override void Execute(NativeActivityContext context)
{
    context.GetExtension<ISendEmail>().SendEmail
        (Sender.Get(context),Recipient.Get(context),
        Subject.Get(context), Body.Get(context));
}
}
```

The activity defines four input arguments and uses these arguments within the Execute method.

### How It Works

When this activity executes it simply looks up the ISendEmail extension and calls its SendEmail method. There is more functionality needed to get this to send an e-mail, which is the subject of the next two Try It Out sections.

---

When defining the arguments, you should use the generic InArgument<>, OutArgument<>, or InOutArgument<> classes. Within the Execute method, the value of these arguments is retrieved from the current execution context using the somewhat strange syntax Argument.Get(context). This is due to how data is stored within a workflow.

In a traditional class with regular .NET properties, the data for that class is stored within the object instance. This renders that data opaque to an external caller; in cases where this is an activity, it would mean that to store a workflow instance on disk, each activity would need to be serialized in full before the workflow could be stored on disk.

This was how Workflow 3.x worked, and it led to some workflows using a large amount of space on disk. With the new model exposed in Workflow 4, only the data that has changed needs to be persisted, as the context object passed to the activity can keep tabs on the actual values of those arguments. In the SendEmail activity, data is only read from the context using the Get() method, so the state of the workflow is maintained when this activity executes. For example, if you were to call the Set() method, which changes the value of an argument, the workflow execution logic would have a flag set to indicate that something was altered, enabling it to save just those changes to disk. This leads to much better performance in Workflow 4 and potentially a much smaller footprint on disk.

In addition to maintaining the values of all arguments, the context object also includes a collection of extensions. In the preceding code, you can retrieve the ISendEmail interface from the context object by calling the GetExtension<> generic method. Here, you pass in the interface type you're requesting, and the lookup logic within this method will return the extension instance to the code so that you can then call the SendEmail method on that extension.

The next step, as addressed in the following Try It Out, is to add an extension to the workflow. To do this, you can use either the WorkflowInvoker or the WorkflowApplication class.

**TRY IT OUT** Using the WorkflowApplication Class: 05-SendingAnEmail

**1.** Add a third project to the solution. This should be a Workflow Console Application project called SendingAnEmail. Once added, set this as the startup project.

**2.** Add references to the SharedInterfaces and CustomActivities assemblies.

**3.** Add an implementation of the ISendEmail interface as shown here (this won't send an e-mail, but it will at least output the data to the console):

```
public class ConsoleSendEmail : ISendEmail
{
    public void SendEmail(string sender, string recipient, string subject,
    string body)
```

```
        {
            Console.WriteLine("Email to:      {0}", recipient);
            Console.WriteLine("       from:    {0}", sender);
            Console.WriteLine("       subject: {0}", subject);
            Console.WriteLine("       body:    {0}", body);
        }
    }
```

**4.** Add a `SendEmail` activity to the workflow and set all of the properties. The F4 key will display the property grid for the selected activity.

**5.** Modify the `Program.cs` file and use the `WorkflowApplication` class to execute the workflow. This class enables you to add extensions; the `WorkflowInvoker` does not.

```
class Program
{
    static void Main(string[] args)
    {
        WorkflowApplication app = new WorkflowApplication(new Workflow1());
        app.Extensions.Add(new ConsoleSendEmail());
        ManualResetEvent finished = new ManualResetEvent(false);
        app.Completed = (completedArgs) => { finished.Set(); };
        app.Run();
        finished.WaitOne();
        Console.ReadLine();
    }
}
```

Here, you create the `WorkflowApplication` instance and then add the `ConsoleSendEmail` extension to it. Then a `ManualResetEvent` is created and you attach to the `Completed` event that is raised when the workflow completes. The workflow is then executed by calling the `Run` method, and you wait for it to complete by waiting on the event. If you build and run the program, you should see some output on the console matching the value of the properties you set on the `SendEmail` activity.

### How It Works

When a workflow executes, the extensions added to the application are stored in a collection within the `WorkflowApplication` or `WorkflowInvoker` object. The host schedules execution of each activity, and when an activity is executed, a context object is created and passed into the `Execute` method.

The type of context object varies according to which base class you have used for your activity. Because the `SendEmail` activity derives from `NativeActivity`, it is able to call the `GetExtension` method in order to retrieve any extensions added to the workflow application.

If you were to derive from `CodeActivity`, the context object passed into its `Execute` method would not include access to any extensions—indeed, a code activity has very little access to any contextual information, which is by design.

When you call `Run` on a workflow application, a thread pool thread is used to execute the workflow, thereby enabling your code to continue while the workflow executes in the background. The preceding code synchronizes the main application with the completion of the workflow by using the `ManualResetEvent` and setting this within the handler for the `Completed` event.

A `WorkflowApplication` runs asynchronously, whereas the `WorkflowInvoker` runs synchronously. You can use whichever makes sense in your particular scenario.

---

Having tested the preceding, you can confirm that the `SendEmail` activity is working, so now you could create a real implementation of `ISendEmail` using the classes in the `System.Net.Mail` namespace. A great resource for understanding this namespace can be found at `www.systemnetmail.com`.

Another alternative is to use Outlook in order to send an e-mail, which is just what this next example does. At the time of writing, the latest version of Office is 2010; however, this approach may not function correctly on a later version of Word.

**Sending an E-mail Using Outlook: 05-SendingAnEmail**

1. From the Workflow Console Application, add a reference to the Outlook object model. To do so, open the Add Reference window and select the COM tab. Then scroll down until you find the Microsoft Outlook Object Library. The machine used for this example has Microsoft Office 2010 installed, which has a version number of 14.0, so that is what appears in the window shown in Figure 26-13.

2. Create a new class called `OutlookSendEmail` and type in the following code:

```
public class OutlookSendEmail : ISendEmail
{
    public void SendEmail(string sender, string recipient, string subject,
    string body)
    {
        Application app = new Application();
        var mapi = app.GetNamespace("MAPI");
        mapi.Logon(ShowDialog: false, NewSession: false);
        var outbox = mapi.GetDefaultFolder(OlDefaultFolders.olFolderOutbox);

        MailItem email = app.CreateItem(OlItemType.olMailItem);
        email.To = recipient;
        email.Subject = subject;
        email.Body = body;
        email.Send();
    }
}
```

Note that in this instance you don't specify the sender, as the e-mail will be sent using the profile of the currently logged-in user.

3. Alter the `Program.cs` file to use this class as the e-mail extension:

```
app.Extensions.Add(new OutlookSendEmail());
```

You should remove the `ConsoleSendEmail` extension or simply comment it out.

4. Run the program (and ensure that Outlook is running also). If you look into the Sent Items folder, you should see your automatically generated e-mail. If so, congratulations, you've just sent your first automated e-mail message!

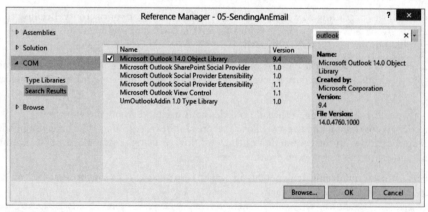

**FIGURE 26-13**

*How It Works*

The `OutlookSendEmail` class uses the Outlook object model to create a new e-mail using the `MailItem` class. In order to send an e-mail with Outlook, you need to construct an instance of the `Application` object and then obtain a reference to the `MAPI` namespace.

If you don't already have Outlook running, then you need to specify your username and password in the call to Login. If it's already running, then you can omit these parameters, and in this case it will use the profile of the currently logged on user.

Once the MailItem has been created you can then specify the recipient by setting the To property. To send to more than one recipient, you can add a semicolon between e-mail addresses. You then need to specify the Body and Subject of the e-mail, and finally call Send(). If you want to send a formatted e-mail, you can alternatively use the HTMLBody property.

---

If you don't see an e-mail in your outbox, or if you received an exception from the code, then you need to be able to track down this exception. In order to do this, you can add some extra code to the Program.cs file, as shown in the next Try It Out.

---

**TRY IT OUT** Processing Workflow Errors: 05-SendingAnEmail

In this example, you see how to trap and process errors in a workflow.

**1.** Using the same project used for the preceding example (example code in 05-SendingAnEmail), alter the Program.cs file so that it looks as follows:

```
static void Main(string[] args)
{
    WorkflowApplication app = new WorkflowApplication(new Workflow1());
    app.OnUnhandledException = (e) =>
        {
            return UnhandledExceptionAction.Abort;
        };
    app.Extensions.Add(new OutlookSendEmail());
    ManualResetEvent finished = new ManualResetEvent(false);
    app.Completed = (completedArgs) => { finished.Set(); };
    app.Aborted = (abortedEventArgs) =>
        {
            Console.WriteLine("Workflow Aborted.\r\n{0}",
                abortedEventArgs.Reason);
            finished.Set();
        };
    app.Run();
    finished.WaitOne();
}
```

The highlighted items have been added.

**2.** Run the application. If an exception occurs, it will be written to the console after a message stating "Workflow Aborted".

*How It Works*

When an unhandled exception occurs in a workflow, the first thing called is the OnUnhandledException delegate. Here, you can choose the action to take: Abort, Cancel, or Terminate. This delegate is passed an instance of the exception so you can decide what action to take based on the type of exception thrown.

If you choose to Abort the workflow, the aborted delegate will subsequently be called. The default is to Terminate the workflow.

---

## Activity Validation

Many activities cannot function without their arguments being defined, and at present you have no way to mark that a given argument is mandatory. You might have noticed an error message showing up within the workflow designer when using some of the standard activities, as these have mandatory arguments.

In order to mark a property as required, you can use the [RequiredArgument] attribute when you define the argument. When you add this to an argument, you'll see an exclamation mark glyph to the right of the activity, as shown in Figure 26-14.

This indicates that one or more properties have errors, and if you hover your cursor over the glyph, a Tooltip will be displayed that describes the error. In the next Try It Out, you'll update the SendMail activity and mark all arguments as mandatory except for Sender.

**FIGURE 26-14**

**TRY IT OUT**   Marking Arguments as Mandatory: 05-CustomActivities

1. Open the SendEmail.cs file and make the following changes:

```
public class SendEmail : NativeActivity
{
    public InArgument<string> Sender { get; set; }
    [RequiredArgument]
    public InArgument<string> Recipient { get; set; }
    [RequiredArgument]
    public InArgument<string> Subject { get; set; }
    [RequiredArgument]
    public InArgument<string> Body { get; set; }
    protected override void Execute(NativeActivityContext context)
    {
        context.GetExtension<ISendEmail>().SendEmail(Sender.Get(context),
            Recipient.

Get(context), Subject.Get(context), Body.Get(context));
    }
}
```

2. Compile the application.

3. Open the Workflow1.xaml file and display the properties of the SendEmail activity. Alter one of the properties that were attributed with [RequiredArgument] and Tab off the text box. You should see the error glyph and be able to hover over it to view the description.

4. Type a value into the required argument and Tab off it again. The error message should be hidden.

*How It Works*

The workflow was designed to inspect activities and look for the RequiredArgument attribute. If any properties are found with this attribute that do not have a value defined, then the designer class will adorn the activity with an error glyph.

You're nearly done with your custom activity. The last task is to create a custom designer that is used to providing a design-time rendering of the activity.

## Activity Designers

When an activity is dragged onto the design surface, the visual representation is provided by a designer. In Workflow 3, this would have been a Windows Forms class. But in Workflow 4 and later, the designer is created using XAML.

XAML is discussed further in Chapter 15 so it isn't all covered again here. Instead, this section concentrates on the important parts as far as custom activities are concerned.

The designer class for an activity is typically created in a separate assembly—it is only needed at design time and not when the activity is executing. Visual Studio 2012 includes an Activity Designer Library project type that provides enough functionality to get you started, and that's what you'll use in the following example.

In addition to providing a visual representation of an activity, the designer can also be used to provide data input fields within itself. Without a designer, all properties of an activity have to be set within the property grid; however, with a custom designer you can opt to include some properties within the design surface itself. This can provide a great design-time experience for the users of your activity.

In the following Try It Out, you update the `SendEmail` activity again to add a custom designer.

**TRY IT OUT**    Adding an Activity Designer: 05-CustomActivities.Design

**1.** Open the earlier solution and then add a new Activity Designer Library project. Call it `CustomActivities.Design`.

**2.** This will create a blank designer for you called `ActivityDesigner1`. You can rename this designer or add a new designer called `SendEmailDesigner`. Either way, you should end up with a designer name similar to that of the activity it is used with.

**3.** The default XAML created provides an empty design surface to which you need to add some text fields and labels. Add the following XAML to the designer XAML file—this defines a set of columns and rows into which you'll place the design elements:

```
<sap:ActivityDesigner x:Class="CustomActivities.Design.SendEmailDesigner"
    xmlns="http://schemas.microsoft.com/winfx/2006/xaml/presentation"
    xmlns:x="http://schemas.microsoft.com/winfx/2006/xaml"
    xmlns:sap="clr-namespace:System.Activities.Presentation;
    assembly=System.Activities.Presentation"
    xmlns:sapv="clr-namespace:System.Activities.Presentation.View;
    assembly=System.Activities.Presentation"
    xmlns:sapc="clr-namespace:System.Activities.Presentation.Converters;
    assembly=System.Activities.Presentation">
    <Grid>
        <Grid.Resources>
            <sapc:ArgumentToExpressionConverter x:Key="argConverter"/>
        </Grid.Resources>
        <Grid.ColumnDefinitions>
            <ColumnDefinition Width="Auto"/>
            <ColumnDefinition Width="*"/>
        </Grid.ColumnDefinitions>
        <Grid.RowDefinitions>
            <RowDefinition Height="Auto"/>
            <RowDefinition Height="Auto"/>
            <RowDefinition Height="Auto"/>
        </Grid.RowDefinitions>
    </Grid>
</sap:ActivityDesigner>
```

Note that the preceding code includes an extra namespace that has also been added to the XAML.

**4.** Add the elements that will be used onscreen to accept user input:

```
        </Grid.RowDefinitions>
        <TextBlock Text="Recipient"/>
        <sapv:ExpressionTextBox Expression="{Binding ModelItem.Recipient,
            Converter={StaticResource argConverter}}"
            OwnerActivity="{Binding ModelItem}" Grid.Column="1"/>
        <TextBlock Text="Subject" Grid.Row="1"/>
        < sapv:ExpressionTextBox Expression="{Binding ModelItem.Subject,
            Converter={StaticResource argConverter}}" Grid.Row="1"
            OwnerActivity="{Binding ModelItem}" Grid.Column="1"/>
        <TextBlock Text="Body" Grid.Row="2"/>
        < sapv:ExpressionTextBox Expression="{Binding ModelItem.Body,
            Converter={StaticResource argConverter}}" Grid.Row="2"
            OwnerActivity="{Binding ModelItem}" Grid.Column="1"/>
    </Grid>
```

These elements define a set of labels and text boxes that are data-bound to the underlying activity — the `ModelItem` prefix is a synonym for the actual activity.

5. You need to associate the designer with the activity. The simplest way is by using the `Designer` attribute. At the top of the `SendEmail` activity, add the following code:

```
using System.ComponentModel;
namespace CustomActivities
{
    [Designer("CustomActivities.Design.SendEmailDesigner,
    CustomActivities.Design")]
    public class SendEmail : NativeActivity
    {
```

The `Designer` attribute is read by Visual Studio and it is used to determine which designer is associated with the activity, and which assembly contains the designer. The string used in the example is the `TypeName` of the designer, and is typically entered as a string so as to avoid having an assembly reference between the design assembly and the activity assembly.

6. Add a reference to the `PresentationCore` assembly from your main workflow assembly, as well as a reference to the `CustomActivities.Design` assembly. If you then compile the solution and open the workflow that contains the `SendEmail` activity, you should see something similar to that in Figure 26-15.

7. This design is functional but not very attractive, and it could benefit from some spacing around the fields. Change the XAML as shown in the following example and you'll get a better design result. You can, of course, add color and graphics to liven up the design experience.

```
<Grid>
    <Grid.Resources>
        <Style TargetType="TextBlock">
            <Setter Property="Margin" Value="0,2,4,2"/>
            <Setter Property="VerticalAlignment" Value="Center"/>
        </Style>
        <Style TargetType="{x:Type sapv:ExpressionTextBox}">
            <Setter Property="Margin" Value="0,2,0,2"/>
        </Style>
    </Grid.Resources>
    <Grid.ColumnDefinitions>
```

These resources define styles that are associated with the text blocks and text boxes. Here, these styles simply apply a uniform margin and alignment so that the activity looks better onscreen.

### How It Works

Visual Studio uses the `Designer` attribute to find a class associated with an activity. If it finds it, then that class is used when showing the activity onscreen.

It is common to use data binding in XAML to link a visual class with a background class — in this instance, the visual class is the designer and the background class is the activity.

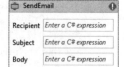

**FIGURE 26-15**

## SUMMARY

In this chapter, you have learned about Windows Workflow Foundation 4. In particular, you learned about the following:

➤ What a workflow is and how to execute one

➤ How to use some of the built-in activities

➤ How to create your own activities

## EXERCISES

**26.1** How can you create a composite activity?

**26.2** Can you expose a workflow over WCF? If so, how?

**26.3** How can you ensure that a workflow can be restarted from where it left off?

Answers to the exercises can be found in Appendix A.

## ▶ WHAT YOU HAVE LEARNED IN THIS CHAPTER

| TOPIC | KEY CONCEPTS |
|---|---|
| **Workflow fundamentals** | Workflows consist of *activities*, and an activity is similar to a statement in a traditional programming language. You can write your own activities and normally a workflow will consist of some built-in activities and some custom activities. |
| **If activity** | This can be used in a workflow to evaluate an expression and choose one of two paths. The expression can be simple or complex, and can reference variables and arguments as necessary. |
| **While activity** | This activity allows you to define a loop inside a workflow. The condition for the loop is an expression, and the activity consists of a single child activity that will typically be a sequence that enables you to add multiple other activities into each iteration of the loop. |
| **Sequence activity** | The Sequence activity allows you to execute a number of child activities in strict top-down order. |
| **Arguments and variables** | You can pass arguments into and out of a workflow, and within a workflow you can define variables that have global or local scope. Arguments are defined by a data type, such as String or Int32 and also a direction. Variables obey the same rules they do in a traditional programming language. |
| **Workflow extensions** | Extensions can be used to change behavior at runtime without having to change the workflow. An extension is typically written as an interface and an implementation of that interface. |
| **Activity validation** | You can define some properties of an activity as mandatory. This allows the end user to see which properties must have values defined. An error glyph is shown on the user interface for any that are not complete. |
| **Activity designers** | A designer can be used to augment the user interface of an activity, to make it easier for the end user to use it. The designer is XAML and you can create any markup you want to show the user interface for a custom activity. |

# Exercise Solutions

There are no exercises in Chapters 1 and 2.

## CHAPTER 3 SOLUTIONS

### Exercise 1

```
super.smashing.great
```

### Exercise 2

b), as it starts with a number, and e), as it contains a full stop.

### Exercise 3

No, there is no theoretical limit to the size of a string that may be contained in a string variable.

### Exercise 4

The * and / operators have the highest precedence here, followed by +, <<, and finally +=. The precedence in the exercise can be illustrated using parentheses as follows:

```
resultVar += (((var1 * var2) + var3) << (var4 / var5));
```

### Exercise 5

```
static void Main(string[] args)
{
    int firstNumber, secondNumber, thirdNumber, fourthNumber;
    Console.WriteLine("Give me a number:");
    firstNumber = Convert.ToInt32(Console.ReadLine());
    Console.WriteLine("Give me another number:");
    secondNumber = Convert.ToInt32(Console.ReadLine());
    Console.WriteLine("Give me another number:");
    thirdNumber = Convert.ToInt32(Console.ReadLine());
    Console.WriteLine("Give me another number:");
```

```
      fourthNumber = Convert.ToInt32(Console.ReadLine());
      Console.WriteLine("The product of {0}, {1}, {2}, and {3} is {4}.",
                  firstNumber, secondNumber, thirdNumber, fourthNumber,
                  firstNumber * secondNumber * thirdNumber * fourthNumber);
   }
```

Note that `Convert.ToInt32()` is used here, which isn't covered in the chapter.

## CHAPTER 4 SOLUTIONS

## Exercise 1

```
(var1 > 10) ^ (var2 > 10)
[AU: wrong sign]
```

## Exercise 2

```
static void Main(string[] args)
{
   bool numbersOK = false;
   double var1, var2;
   var1 = 0;
   var2 = 0;
   while (!numbersOK)
   {
      Console.WriteLine("Give me a number:");
      var1 = Convert.ToDouble(Console.ReadLine());
      Console.WriteLine("Give me another number:");
      var2 = Convert.ToDouble(Console.ReadLine());
      if ((var1 > 10) && (var2 > 10))
      {
         numbersOK = true;
      }
      else
      {
         if ((var1 <= 10) && (var2 <= 10))
         {
            numbersOK = true;
         }
         else
         {
            Console.WriteLine("Only one number may be greater than 10.");
         }
      }
   }
   Console.WriteLine("You entered {0} and {1}.", var1, var2);
}
```

Note that this can be performed better using different logic, for example:

```
static void Main(string[] args)
{
   bool numbersOK = false;
   double var1, var2;
   var1 = 0;
   var2 = 0;
   while (!numbersOK)
   {
      Console.WriteLine("Give me a number:");
      var1 = Convert.ToDouble(Console.ReadLine());
```

```
            Console.WriteLine("Give me another number:");
            var2 = Convert.ToDouble(Console.ReadLine());
            if ((var1 > 10) && (var2 > 10))
            {
                Console.WriteLine("Only one number may be greater than 10.");
            }
            else
            {
                numbersOK = true;
            }
        }
        Console.WriteLine("You entered {0} and {1}.", var1, var2);
    }
```

# Exercise 3

The code should read:

```
int i;
for (i = 1; i <= 10; i++)
{
    if ((i % 2) == 0)
        continue;
    Console.WriteLine(i);
}
```

Using the = assignment operator instead of the Boolean == operator is a very common mistake.

# Exercise 4

```
static void Main(string[] args)
{
    double realCoord, imagCoord;
    double realMax = 1.77;
    double realMin = -0.6;
    double imagMax = -1.2;
    double imagMin = 1.2;
    double realStep;
    double imagStep;
    double realTemp, imagTemp, realTemp2, arg;
    int iterations;
    while (true)
    {
        realStep = (realMax - realMin) / 79;
        imagStep = (imagMax - imagMin) / 48;
        for (imagCoord = imagMin; imagCoord >= imagMax;
            imagCoord += imagStep)
        {
            for (realCoord = realMin; realCoord <= realMax;
                realCoord += realStep)
            {
                iterations = 0;
                realTemp = realCoord;
                imagTemp = imagCoord;
                arg = (realCoord * realCoord) + (imagCoord * imagCoord);
                while ((arg < 4) && (iterations < 40))
                {
                    realTemp2 = (realTemp * realTemp) - (imagTemp * imagTemp)
                        - realCoord;
                    imagTemp = (2 * realTemp * imagTemp) - imagCoord;
                    realTemp = realTemp2;
```

```
                        arg = (realTemp * realTemp) + (imagTemp * imagTemp);
                        iterations += 1;
                    }
                    switch (iterations % 4)
                    {
                        case 0:
                            Console.Write(".");
                            break;
                        case 1:
                            Console.Write("o");
                            break;
                        case 2:
                            Console.Write("O");
                            break;
                        case 3:
                            Console.Write("@");
                            break;
                    }
                }
                Console.Write("\n");
            }
            Console.WriteLine("Current limits:");
            Console.WriteLine("realCoord: from {0} to {1}", realMin, realMax);
            Console.WriteLine("imagCoord: from {0} to {1}", imagMin, imagMax);

            Console.WriteLine("Enter new limits:");
            Console.WriteLine("realCoord: from:");
            realMin = Convert.ToDouble(Console.ReadLine());
            Console.WriteLine("realCoord: to:");
            realMax = Convert.ToDouble(Console.ReadLine());
            Console.WriteLine("imagCoord: from:");
            imagMin = Convert.ToDouble(Console.ReadLine());
            Console.WriteLine("imagCoord: to:");
            imagMax = Convert.ToDouble(Console.ReadLine());
        }
    }
```

## CHAPTER 5 SOLUTIONS

## Exercise 1

Conversions a and c can't be performed implicitly.

## Exercise 2

```
enum color : short
{
    Red, Orange, Yellow, Green, Blue, Indigo, Violet, Black, White
}
```

Yes, as the `byte` type can hold numbers between 0 and 255, so `byte`-based enumerations can hold 256 entries with individual values, or more if duplicate values are used for entries.

## Exercise 3

```
static void Main(string[] args)
{
    imagNum coord, temp;
```

```
        double realTemp2, arg;
        int iterations;
        for (coord.imag = 1.2; coord.imag >= -1.2; coord.imag -= 0.05)
        {
            for (coord.real = -0.6; coord.real <= 1.77; coord.real += 0.03)
            {
                iterations = 0;
                temp.real = coord.real;
                temp.imag = coord.imag;
                arg = (coord.real * coord.real) + (coord.imag * coord.imag);
                while ((arg < 4) && (iterations < 40))
                {
                    realTemp2 = (temp.real * temp.real) - (temp.imag * temp.imag)
                        - coord.real;
                    temp.imag = (2 * temp.real * temp.imag) - coord.imag;
                    temp.real = realTemp2;
                    arg = (temp.real * temp.real) + (temp.imag * temp.imag);
                    iterations += 1;
                }
                switch (iterations % 4)
                {
                    case 0:
                        Console.Write(".");
                        break;
                    case 1:
                        Console.Write("o");
                        break;
                    case 2:
                        Console.Write("O");
                        break;
                    case 3:
                        Console.Write("@");
                        break;
                }
            }
            Console.Write("\n");
        }
    }
```

## Exercise 4

The code will not compile, for the following reasons:

➤ End of statement semicolons are missing.

➤ Second line attempts to access a nonexistent sixth element of `blab`.

➤ Second line attempts to assign a string that isn't enclosed in double quotes.

## Exercise 5

```
static void Main(string[] args)
{
    Console.WriteLine("Enter a string:");
    string myString = Console.ReadLine();
    string reversedString = "";
    for (int index = myString.Length - 1; index >= 0; index--)
    {
        reversedString += myString[index];
    }
    Console.WriteLine("Reversed: {0}", reversedString);
}
```

## Exercise 6

```
static void Main(string[] args)
{
    Console.WriteLine("Enter a string:");
    string myString = Console.ReadLine();
    myString = myString.Replace("no", "yes");
    Console.WriteLine("Replaced \"no\" with \"yes\": {0}", myString);
}
```

## Exercise 7

```
static void Main(string[] args)
{
    Console.WriteLine("Enter a string:");
    string myString = Console.ReadLine();
    myString = "\"" + myString.Replace(" ", "\" \"") + "\"";
    Console.WriteLine("Added double quotes around words: {0}", myString);
}
```

Or using `String.Split()`:

```
static void Main(string[] args)
{
    Console.WriteLine("Enter a string:");
    string myString = Console.ReadLine();
    string[] myWords = myString.Split(' ');
    Console.WriteLine("Adding double quotes around words:");
    foreach (string myWord in myWords)
    {
        Console.Write("\"{0}\" ", myWord);
    }
}
```

## CHAPTER 6 SOLUTIONS

## Exercise 1

The first function has a return type of `bool`, but doesn't return a `bool` value.

The second function has a `params` argument, but this argument isn't at the end of the argument list.

## Exercise 2

```
static void Main(string[] args)
{
    if (args.Length != 2)
    {
        Console.WriteLine("Two arguments required.");
        return;
    }
    string param1 = args[0];
    int param2 = Convert.ToInt32(args[1]);
    Console.WriteLine("String parameter: {0}", param1);
    Console.WriteLine("Integer parameter: {0}", param2);
}
```

Note that this answer contains code that checks that two arguments have been supplied, which wasn't part of the question but seems logical in this situation.

## Exercise 3

```
class Program
{
    delegate string ReadLineDelegate();

    static void Main(string[] args)
    {
        ReadLineDelegate readLine = new ReadLineDelegate(Console.ReadLine);
        Console.WriteLine("Type a string:");
        string userInput = readLine();
        Console.WriteLine("You typed: {0}", userInput);
    }
}
```

## Exercise 4

```
struct order
{
    public string itemName;
    public int    unitCount;
    public double unitCost;

    public double TotalCost()
    {
        return unitCount * unitCost;
    }
}
```

## Exercise 5

```
struct order
{
    public string itemName;
    public int    unitCount;
    public double unitCost;

    public double TotalCost()
    {
        return unitCount * unitCost;
    }

    public string Info()
    {
        return "Order information: " + unitCount.ToString() + " " + itemName +
            " items at $" + unitCost.ToString() + " each, total cost $" +
            TotalCost().ToString();
    }
}
```

# CHAPTER 7 SOLUTIONS

## Exercise 1

This statement is true only for information that you want to make available in all builds. More often, you will want debugging information to be written out only when debug builds are used. In this situation, the Debug.WriteLine() version is preferable.

Using the `Debug.WriteLine()` version also has the advantage that it will not be compiled into release builds, thus reducing the size of the resultant code.

## Exercise 2

```
static void Main(string[] args)
{
    for (int i = 1; i < 10000; i++)
    {
        Console.WriteLine("Loop cycle {0}", i);
        if (i == 5000)
        {
            Console.WriteLine(args[999]);
        }
    }
}
```

In VS, you can place a breakpoint on the following line:

```
Console.WriteLine("Loop cycle {0}", i);
```

The properties of the breakpoint should be modified such that the hit count criterion is "break when hit count is equal to 5000".

## Exercise 3

False. `finally` blocks always execute. This may occur after a `catch` block has been processed.

## Exercise 4

```
static void Main(string[] args)
{
    Orientation myDirection;
    for (byte myByte = 2; myByte < 10; myByte++)
    {
        try
        {
            myDirection = checked((Orientation)myByte);
            if ((myDirection < Orientation.North) ||
                (myDirection > Orientation.West))
            {
                throw new ArgumentOutOfRangeException("myByte", myByte,
                    "Value must be between 1 and 4");
            }
        }
        catch (ArgumentOutOfRangeException e)
        {
            // If this section is reached then myByte < 1 or myByte > 4.
            Console.WriteLine(e.Message);
            Console.WriteLine("Assigning default value, Orientation.North.");
            myDirection = Orientation.North;
        }

        Console.WriteLine("myDirection = {0}", myDirection);
    }
}
```

Note that this is a bit of a trick question. Because the enumeration is based on the `byte` type, any `byte` value may be assigned to it, even if that value isn't assigned a name in the enumeration. In the previous code, you can generate your own exception if necessary.

## CHAPTER 8 SOLUTIONS

### Exercise 1

B, D, and E. Public, private, and protected are all real levels of accessibility.

### Exercise 2

False. You should never call the destructor of an object manually; the .NET runtime environment will do this for you during garbage collection.

### Exercise 3

No, you can call static methods without any class instances.

### Exercise 4

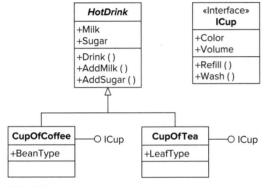

**FIGURE A-1**

### Exercise 5

```
static void ManipulateDrink(HotDrink drink)
{
    drink.AddMilk();
    drink.Drink();
    ICup cupInterface = (ICup)drink;
    cupInterface.Wash();
}
```

Note the explicit cast to ICup. This is necessary as HotDrink doesn't support the ICup interface, but you know that the two cup objects that might be passed to this function do. However, this is dangerous, as other classes deriving from HotDrink are possible, which might not support ICup, but could be passed to this function. To correct this, you should check to see if the interface is supported:

```
static void ManipulateDrink(HotDrink drink)
{
    drink.AddMilk();
    drink.Drink();
    if (drink is ICup)
    {
```

```
            ICup cupInterface = drink as ICup;
            cupInterface.Wash();
        }
    }
```

The is and as operators used here are covered in Chapter 11.

## CHAPTER 9 SOLUTIONS

### Exercise 1

myDerivedClass derives from MyClass, but MyClass is sealed and can't be derived from.

### Exercise 2

You can define a noncreatable class by defining it as a static class or by defining all of its constructors as private.

### Exercise 3

Noncreatable classes can be useful through the static members they possess. In fact, you can even get instances of these classes through these members, as shown here:

```
class CreateMe
{
    private CreateMe()
    {
    }

    static public CreateMe GetCreateMe()
    {
        return new CreateMe();
    }
}
```

Here, the public constructor has access to the private constructor, as it is part of the same class definition.

### Exercise 4

For simplicity, the following class definitions are shown as part of a single code file, rather than listing a separate code file for each:

```
namespace Vehicles
{
    public abstract class Vehicle
    {
    }
    public abstract class Car : Vehicle
    {
    }
    public abstract class Train : Vehicle
    {
    }
    public interface IPassengerCarrier
    {
    }
    public interface IHeavyLoadCarrier
    {
    }
```

```
        public class SUV : Car, IPassengerCarrier
        {
        }
        public class Pickup : Car, IPassengerCarrier, IHeavyLoadCarrier
        {
        }
        public class Compact : Car, IPassengerCarrier
        {
        }
        public class PassengerTrain : Train, IPassengerCarrier
        {
        }
        public class FreightTrain : Train, IHeavyLoadCarrier
        {
        }
        public class T424DoubleBogey : Train, IHeavyLoadCarrier
        {
        }
    }
```

## Exercise 5

```
    using System;
    using Vehicles;

    namespace Traffic
    {
        class Program
        {
            static void Main(string[] args)
            {
                AddPassenger(new Compact());
                AddPassenger(new SUV());
                AddPassenger(new Pickup());
                AddPassenger(new PassengerTrain());
                Console.ReadKey();
            }

            static void AddPassenger(IPassengerCarrier Vehicle)
            {
                Console.WriteLine(Vehicle.ToString());
            }
        }
    }
```

# CHAPTER 10 SOLUTIONS

## Exercise 1

```
    class MyClass
    {
        protected string myString;

        public string ContainedString
        {
            set
            {
                myString = value;
            }
        }
```

```
        public virtual string GetString()
        {
            return myString;
        }
    }
```

## Exercise 2

```
class MyDerivedClass : MyClass
{
    public override string GetString()
    {
        return base.GetString() + " (output from derived class)";
    }
}
```

## Exercise 3

If a method has a return type, then it is possible to use it as part of an expression:

```
    x = Manipulate(y, z);
```

If no implementation is provided for a partial method, then it will be removed by the compiler along with all places where it is used. In the preceding code this would leave the result of x unclear because no replacement for the `Manipulate()` method is available. It might be the case that without this method you would simply want to ignore the entire line of code, but the compiler cannot decide whether this is what you want.

Methods with no return types are not called as part of expressions, so it is safe for the compiler to remove all references to the partial method calls.

Similarly, out parameters are forbidden since variables used as an out parameter must be undefined before the method call and will be defined after the method call. Removing the method call would break this behavior.

## Exercise 4

```
    class MyCopyableClass
    {
        protected int myInt;

        public int ContainedInt
        {
            get
            {
                return myInt;
            }
            set
            {
                myInt = value;
            }
        }

        public MyCopyableClass GetCopy()
        {
            return (MyCopyableClass)MemberwiseClone();
        }
    }
```

The client code:

```
    class Program
    {
        static void Main(string[] args)
```

```
{
    MyCopyableClass obj1 = new MyCopyableClass();
    obj1.ContainedInt = 5;
    MyCopyableClass obj2 = obj1.GetCopy();
    obj1.ContainedInt = 9;
    Console.WriteLine(obj2.ContainedInt);
}
}
```

This code displays 5, showing that the copied object has its own version of the myInt field.

# Exercise 5

```
using System;
using Ch10CardLib;

namespace Exercise_Answers
{
    class Class1
    {
        static void Main(string[] args)
        {
            while(true)
            {
                Deck playDeck = new Deck();
                playDeck.Shuffle();
                bool isFlush = false;
                int flushHandIndex = 0;
                for (int hand = 0; hand < 10; hand++)
                {
                    isFlush = true;
                    Suit flushSuit = playDeck.GetCard(hand * 5).suit;
                    for (int card = 1; card < 5; card++)
                    {
                        if (playDeck.GetCard(hand * 5 + card).suit != flushSuit)
                        {
                            isFlush = false;
                        }
                    }
                    if (isFlush)
                    {
                        flushHandIndex = hand * 5;
                        break;
                    }
                }
                if (isFlush)
                {
                    Console.WriteLine("Flush!");
                    for (int card = 0; card < 5; card++)
                    {
                        Console.WriteLine(playDeck.GetCard(flushHandIndex + card));
                    }
                }
                else
                {
                    Console.WriteLine("No flush.");
                }
                Console.ReadLine();
            }
        }
    }
}
```

This code is looped as flushes are uncommon. You might need to press Return several times before a flush is found in a shuffled deck. To verify that everything is working as it should, try commenting out the line that shuffles the deck.

# CHAPTER 11 SOLUTIONS

## Exercise 1

```
using System;
using System.Collections;

namespace Exercise_Answers
{
    public class People : DictionaryBase
    {
        public void Add(Person newPerson)
        {
            Dictionary.Add(newPerson.Name, newPerson);
        }

        public void Remove(string name)
        {
            Dictionary.Remove(name);
        }

        public Person this[string name]
        {
            get
            {
                return (Person)Dictionary[name];
            }
            set
            {
                Dictionary[name] = value;
            }
        }
    }
}
```

## Exercise 2

```
public class Person
{
    private string name;
    private int age;

    public string Name
    {
        get
        {
            return name;
        }
        set
        {
            name = value;
        }
    }
}
```

```
        public int Age
        {
          get
          {
            return age;
          }
          set
          {
            age = value;
          }
        }

        public static bool operator >(Person p1, Person p2)
        {
          return p1.Age > p2.Age;
        }

        public static bool operator <(Person p1, Person p2)
        {
          return p1.Age < p2.Age;
        }

        public static bool operator >=(Person p1, Person p2)
        {
          return !(p1 < p2);
        }

        public static bool operator <=(Person p1, Person p2)
        {
          return !(p1 > p2);
        }
    }
```

## Exercise 3

```
        public Person[] GetOldest()
        {
          Person oldestPerson = null;
          People oldestPeople = new People();
          Person currentPerson;
          foreach (DictionaryEntry p in Dictionary)
          {
            currentPerson = p.Value as Person;
            if (oldestPerson == null)
            {
              oldestPerson = currentPerson;
              oldestPeople.Add(oldestPerson);
            }
            else
            {
              if (currentPerson > oldestPerson)
              {
                oldestPeople.Clear();
                oldestPeople.Add(currentPerson);
                oldestPerson = currentPerson;
              }
              else
              {
              if (currentPerson >= oldestPerson)
                  {
                    oldestPeople.Add(currentPerson);
```

```
                    }
                }
            }
        }
        Person[] oldestPeopleArray = new Person[oldestPeople.Count];
        int copyIndex = 0;
        foreach (DictionaryEntry p in oldestPeople)
        {
            oldestPeopleArray[copyIndex] = p.Value as Person;
            copyIndex++;
        }
            return oldestPeopleArray;
    }
```

This function is made more complex by the fact that no == operator has been defined for Person, but the logic can still be constructed without this. In addition, returning a People instance would be simpler, as it is easier to manipulate this class during processing. As a compromise, a People instance is used throughout the function, and then converted into an array of Person instances at the end.

## Exercise 4

```
public class People : DictionaryBase, ICloneable
{
    public object Clone()
    {
        People clonedPeople = new People();
        Person currentPerson, newPerson;
        foreach (DictionaryEntry p in Dictionary)
        {
            currentPerson = p.Value as Person;
            newPerson = new Person();
            newPerson.Name = currentPerson.Name;
            newPerson.Age = currentPerson.Age;
            clonedPeople.Add(newPerson);
        }
        return clonedPeople;
    }

    ...
}
```

You could simplify this by implementing ICloneable on the Person class.

## Exercise 5

```
public IEnumerable Ages
{
    get
    {
        foreach (object person in Dictionary.Values)
            yield return (person as Person).Age;
    }
}
```

# CHAPTER 12 SOLUTIONS

## Exercise 1

a, b, and e: Yes

**c and d:** No, although they can use generic type parameters supplied by the class containing them.

**f:** No

## Exercise 2

```
public static double? operator *(Vector op1, Vector op2)
{
    try
    {
        double angleDiff = (double)(op2.ThetaRadians.Value -
            op1.ThetaRadians.Value);
        return op1.R.Value * op2.R.Value * Math.Cos(angleDiff);
    }
    catch
    {
        return null;
    }
}
```

## Exercise 3

You can't instantiate `T` without enforcing the `new()` constraint on it, which ensures that a public default constructor is available:

```
public class Instantiator<T>
    where T : new()
{
    public T instance;

    public Instantiator()
    {
        instance = new T();
    }
}
```

## Exercise 4

The same generic type parameter, `T`, is used on both the generic class and the generic method. You need to rename one or both. For example:

```
public class StringGetter<U>
{
    public string GetString<T>(T item)
    {
        return item.ToString();
    }
}
```

## Exercise 5

One way of doing this is as follows:

```
public class ShortList<T> : IList<T>
{
    protected IList<T> innerCollection;
    protected int maxSize = 10;

    public ShortList()
        : this(10)
    {
```

```
   }

   public ShortList(int size)
   {
      maxSize = size;
      innerCollection = new List<T>();
   }

   public ShortList(IEnumerable<T> list)
      : this(10, list)
   {
   }

   public ShortList(int size, IEnumerable<T> list)
   {
      maxSize = size;
      innerCollection = new List<T>(list);
      if (Count > maxSize)
      {
         ThrowTooManyItemsException();
      }
   }

   protected void ThrowTooManyItemsException()
   {
      throw new IndexOutOfRangeException(
         "Unable to add any more items, maximum size is " + maxSize.ToString()
         + " items.");
   }

   #region IList<T> Members

   public int IndexOf(T item)
   {
      return innerCollection.IndexOf(item);
   }

   public void Insert(int index, T item)
   {
      if (Count < maxSize)
      {
         innerCollection.Insert(index, item);
      }
      else
      {
         ThrowTooManyItemsException();
      }
   }

   public void RemoveAt(int index)
   {
      innerCollection.RemoveAt(index);
   }

   public T this[int index]
   {
      get
      {
         return innerCollection[index];
      }

      set
```

```
      {
         innerCollection[index] = value;
      }
   }

   #endregion

   #region ICollection<T> Members

   public void Add(T item)
   {
      if (Count < maxSize)
      {
         innerCollection.Add(item);
      }
      else
      {
         ThrowTooManyItemsException();
      }
   }

   public void Clear()
   {
      innerCollection.Clear();
   }

   public bool Contains(T item)
   {
      return innerCollection.Contains(item);
   }

   public void CopyTo(T[] array, int arrayIndex)
   {
      innerCollection.CopyTo(array, arrayIndex);
   }

   public int Count
   {
      get
      {
         return innerCollection.Count;
      }
   }

   public bool IsReadOnly
   {
      get
      {
         return innerCollection.IsReadOnly;
      }
   }

   public bool Remove(T item)
   {
      return innerCollection.Remove(item);
   }

   #endregion

   #region IEnumerable<T> Members

   public IEnumerator<T> GetEnumerator()
```

```
    {
        return innerCollection.GetEnumerator();
    }

    #endregion

    #region IEnumerable Members

    IEnumerator IEnumerable.GetEnumerator()
    {
        return GetEnumerator();
    }

    #endregion
}
```

## Exercise 6

No, it won't. The type parameter T is defined as being covariant. However, covariant type parameters can be used only as return values of methods, not as method arguments. If you try this out you will get the following compiler error (assuming you use the namespace VarianceDemo):

```
Invalid variance: The type parameter 'T' must be contravariantly valid on
'VarianceDemo.IMethaneProducer<T>.BelchAt(T)'. 'T' is covariant.
```

## CHAPTER 13 SOLUTIONS

## Exercise 1

```
public void ProcessEvent(object source, EventArgs e)
{
    if (e is MessageArrivedEventArgs)
    {
        Console.WriteLine("Connection.MessageArrived event received.");
        Console.WriteLine("Message: {0}",
                          (e as MessageArrivedEventArgs).Message);
    }
    if (e is ElapsedEventArgs)
    {
        Console.WriteLine("Timer.Elapsed event received.");
        Console.WriteLine("SignalTime: {0}",
                          (e as ElapsedEventArgs ).SignalTime);
    }
}
```

## Exercise 2

Modify Player.cs as follows (one modified method, two new ones—comments in the code explain the changes):

```
public bool HasWon()
{
    // get temporary copy of hand, which may get modified.
    Cards tempHand = (Cards)PlayHand.Clone();

    // find three and four of a kind sets
    bool fourOfAKind = false;
    bool threeOfAKind = false;
    int fourRank = -1;
```

```
int threeRank = -1;

int cardsOfRank;
for (int matchRank = 0; matchRank < 13; matchRank++)
{
    cardsOfRank = 0;
    foreach (Card c in tempHand)
    {
        if (c.rank == (Rank)matchRank)
        {
            cardsOfRank++;
        }
    }
    if (cardsOfRank == 4)
    {
        // mark set of four
        fourRank = matchRank;
        fourOfAKind        if (cardsOfRank == 3)
    {
        // two threes means no win possible
        // (threeOfAKind will be true only if this code
        // has already executed)
        if (threeOfAKind == true)
        {
            return false;
        }
        // mark set of three
        threeRank = matchRank;
        threeOfAKind = true;
    }
}

// check simple win condition
if (threeOfAKind && fourOfAKind)
{
    return true;
}

// simplify hand if three or four of a kind is found,
// by removing used cards
if (fourOfAKind || threeOfAKind)
{
    for (int cardIndex = tempHand.Count - 1; cardIndex >= 0; cardIndex--)
    {
        if ((tempHand[cardIndex].rank == (Rank)fourRank)
            || (tempHand[cardIndex].rank == (Rank)threeRank))
        {
            tempHand.RemoveAt(cardIndex);
        }
    }
}

// at this point the method may have returned, because:
// - a set of four and a set of three has been found, winning.
// - two sets of three have been found, losing.
// if the method hasn't returned then:
// - no sets have been found, and tempHand contains 7 cards.
// - a set of three has been found, and tempHand contains 4 cards.
// - a set of four has been found, and tempHand contains 3 cards.

// find run of four sets, start by looking for cards of same suit
```

```csharp
// in the same way as before
bool fourOfASuit = false;
bool threeOfASuit = false;
int fourSuit = -1;
int threeSuit = -1;

int cardsOfSuit;
for (int matchSuit = 0; matchSuit < 4; matchSuit++)
{
    cardsOfSuit = 0;
    foreach (Card c in tempHand)
    {
        if (c.suit == (Suit)matchSuit)
        {
            cardsOfSuit++;
        }
    }
    if (cardsOfSuit == 7)
    {
        // if all cards are the same suit then two runs
        // are possible, but not definite.
        threeOfASuit = true;
        threeSuit = matchSuit;
        fourOfASuit = true;
        fourSuit = matchSuit;
    }
    if (cardsOfSuit == 4)
    {
        // mark four card suit.
        fourOfASuit = true;
        fourSuit = matchSuit;
    }
    if (cardsOfSuit == 3)
    {
        // mark three card suit.
        threeOfASuit = true;
        threeSuit = matchSuit;
    }
}

if (!(threeOfASuit || fourOfASuit))
{
    // need at least one run possibility to continue.
    return false;
}

if (tempHand.Count == 7)
{
    if (!(threeOfASuit && fourOfASuit))
    {
        // need a three and a four card suit.
        return false;
    }

    // create two temporary sets for checking.
    Cards set1 = new Cards();
    Cards set2 = new Cards();

    // if all 7 cards are the same suit...
    if (threeSuit == fourSuit)
    {
```

```
        // get min and max cards
        int maxVal, minVal;
        GetLimits(tempHand, out maxVal, out minVal);
        for (int cardIndex = tempHand.Count - 1; cardIndex >= 0; cardIndex--)
        {
            if (((int)tempHand[cardIndex].rank < (minVal + 3))
                || ((int)tempHand[cardIndex].rank > (maxVal - 3)))
            {
                // remove all cards in a three card set that
                // starts at minVal or ends at maxVal.
                tempHand.RemoveAt(cardIndex);
            }
        }
        if (tempHand.Count != 1)
        {
            // if more then one card is left then there aren't two runs.
            return false;
        }
        if ((tempHand[0].rank == (Rank)(minVal + 3))
            || (tempHand[0].rank == (Rank)(maxVal - 3)))
        {
            // if spare card can make one of the three card sets into a
            // four card set then there are two sets.
            return true;
        }
        else
        {
            // if spare card doesn't fit then there are two sets of three
            // cards but no set of four cards.
            return false;
        }
    }

    // if three card and four card suits are different...
    foreach (Card card in tempHand)
    {
        // split cards into sets.
        if (card.suit == (Suit)threeSuit)
        {
            set1.Add(card);
        }
        else
        {
            set2.Add(card);
        }
    }

    // check if sets are sequential.
    if (isSequential(set1) && isSequential(set2))
    {
        return true;
    }
    else
    {
        return false;
    }
}

// if four cards remain (three of a kind found)
if (tempHand.Count == 4)
{
```

```
        // if four cards remain then they must be the same suit.
        if (!fourOfASuit)
        {
            return false;
        }
        // won if cards are sequential.
        if (isSequential(tempHand))
        {
            return true;
        }
    }

    // if three cards remain (four of a kind found)
    if (tempHand.Count == 3)
    {
        // if three cards remain then they must be the same suit.
        if (!threeOfASuit)
        {
            return false;
        }
        // won if cards are sequential.
        if (isSequential(tempHand))
        {
            return true;
        }
    }

    // return false if two valid sets don't exist.
    return false;
}

// utility method to get max and min ranks of cards
// (same suit assumed)
private void GetLimits(Cards cards, out int maxVal, out int minVal)
{
    maxVal = 0;
    minVal = 14;
    foreach (Card card in cards)
    {
        if ((int)card.rank > maxVal)
        {
            maxVal = (int)card.rank;
        }
        if ((int)card.rank < minVal)
        {
            minVal = (int)card.rank;
        }
    }
}

// utility method to see if cards are in a run
// (same suit assumed)
private bool isSequential(Cards cards)
{
    int maxVal, minVal;
    GetLimits(cards, out maxVal, out minVal);
    if ((maxVal - minVal) == (cards.Count - 1))
    {
        return true;
```

```
        }
        else
        {
            return false;
        }
    }
```

# CHAPTER 14 SOLUTIONS

## Exercise 1

In order to use an object initializer with a class, you must include a default, parameter-less constructor. You could either add one to this class or remove the nondefault constructor that is there already. Once you have done this, you can use the following code to instantiate and initialize this class in one step:

```
Giraffe myPetGiraffe = new Giraffe
{
    NeckLength = "3.14",
    Name = "Gerald"
};
```

## Exercise 2

False. When you use the `var` keyword to declare a variable, the variable is still strongly typed; the compiler determines the type of the variable.

## Exercise 3

You can use the `Equals()` method that is implemented for you. Note that you cannot use the `==` operator to do this, as this compares variables to determine if they both refer to the same object.

## Exercise 4

The extension method must be static:

```
public static string ToAcronym(this string inputString)
```

## Exercise 5

You must include the extension method in a static class that is accessible from the namespace that contains your client code. You could do this either by including the code in the same namespace or by importing the namespace containing the class.

## Exercise 6

One way to do this is as follows:

```
public static string ToAcronym(this string inputString)
{
    return inputString.Trim().Split(' ')
        .Aggregate<string, string>("",
            (a, b) => a + (b.Length > 0 ?
            b.ToUpper()[0].ToString() : ""));
}
```

Here the tertiary operator prevents multiple spaces from causing errors. Note also that the version of `Aggregate()` with two generic type parameters is required, as a seed value is necessary.

## CHAPTER 15 SOLUTIONS

## Exercise 1

Wrap the TextBlock control in a ScrollViewer panel. Set the VerticalScrollBarVisibility property to Auto to make the scrollbar appear when the text extends beyond the bottom edge of the control.

```
<Window x:Class="Answers.MainWindow"
        xmlns="http://schemas.microsoft.com/winfx/2006/xaml/presentation"
        xmlns:x="http://schemas.microsoft.com/winfx/2006/xaml"
        Title="15.1 Solution" Height="350" Width="525">
  <Grid>
    <Grid.RowDefinitions>
      <RowDefinition Height="75"/>
      <RowDefinition />
    </Grid.RowDefinitions>
    <Label Content="Enter text" HorizontalAlignment="Left" Margin="10,10,0,0"
VerticalAlignment="Top"/>
    <TextBox HorizontalAlignment="Left" Margin="76,12,0,0" TextWrapping="Wrap"
VerticalAlignment="Top" Height="53" Width="423" AcceptsReturn="True"
Name="textTextBox">
    </TextBox>
    <ScrollViewer HorizontalAlignment="Left" Height="217" Margin="10,10,0,0"
Grid.Row="1" VerticalAlignment="Top" Width="489"
VerticalScrollBarVisibility="Auto">
      <TextBlock TextWrapping="Wrap" Text="{Binding ElementName=textTextBox,
Path=Text}"/>
    </ScrollViewer>
  </Grid>
</Window>
```

## Exercise 2

After dragging a Slider and ProgressBar control into the view, set the minimum and maximum values of the slider to 1 and 100 and the Value property to 1. Bind the same values of the ProgressBar to the Slider.

```
<Window x:Class="Answers._15"
        xmlns="http://schemas.microsoft.com/winfx/2006/xaml/presentation"
        xmlns:x="http://schemas.microsoft.com/winfx/2006/xaml"
        Title="15.2 Solution" Height="300" Width="300">
  <Grid>
    <Slider HorizontalAlignment="Left" Margin="10,10,0,0" VerticalAlignment="Top"
Width="264" Minimum="1" Maximum="100" Name="valueSlider"/>
    <ProgressBar HorizontalAlignment="Left" Height="24" Margin="10,77,0,0"
VerticalAlignment="Top" Width="264"
Minimum="{Binding ElementName=valueSlider, Path=Minimum}"
Maximum="{Binding ElementName=valueSlider, Path=Maximum}"
Value="{Binding ElementName=valueSlider, Path=Value}"/>
  </Grid>
</Window>
```

## Exercise 3

You can use a RenderTransform to do this. In Design View, you can position the cursor over the edge of the control and when you see a quarter circle icon for the mouse pointer, click and drag the control to the desired position.

```
<Window x:Class="Answers._15_3"
        xmlns="http://schemas.microsoft.com/winfx/2006/xaml/presentation"
        xmlns:x="http://schemas.microsoft.com/winfx/2006/xaml"
        Title="15.3 Solution" Height="300" Width="300">
```

```xml
    <Grid>
      <Slider HorizontalAlignment="Left" Margin="10,10,0,0" VerticalAlignment="Top"
Width="264" Minimum="1" Maximum="100" Name="valueSlider"/>
      <ProgressBar HorizontalAlignment="Left" Height="24" Margin="-17,125,-10,0"
VerticalAlignment="Top" Width="311"
Minimum="{Binding ElementName=valueSlider, Path=Minimum}" Maximum="{Binding
ElementName=valueSlider, Path=Maximum}"
Value="{Binding ElementName=valueSlider, Path=Value}"
RenderTransformOrigin="0.5,0.5">
        <ProgressBar.RenderTransform>
          <TransformGroup>
            <ScaleTransform/>
            <SkewTransform/>
            <RotateTransform Angle="-36.973"/>
            <TranslateTransform/>
          </TransformGroup>
        </ProgressBar.RenderTransform>
      </ProgressBar>

    </Grid>
  </Window>
```

# Exercise 4

The `PersistentSlider` class must implement the `INotifyPropertyChanged` interface.

Create a field to hold the value of each of the three properties.

In each of the setters of the properties, implement a call to any subscribers of the `PropertyChanged` event. You are advised to create a helper method, called `OnPropertyChanged`, for this purpose.

`PersistentSlider.cs`:

```csharp
using System;
using System.ComponentModel;

namespace Answers
{
  public class PersistentSlider : INotifyPropertyChanged
  {
    private int _minValue;
    private int _maxValue;
    private int _currentValue;

    public int MinValue
    {
      get { return _minValue; }
      set { _minValue = value; OnPropertyChanged("MinValue"); }
    }

    public int MaxValue
    {
      get { return _maxValue; }
      set { _maxValue = value; OnPropertyChanged("MaxValue"); }
    }

    public int CurrentValue
    {
      get { return _currentValue; }
      set { _currentValue = value; OnPropertyChanged("CurrentValue"); }
    }

    public event PropertyChangedEventHandler PropertyChanged;
```

```
      protected void OnPropertyChanged(string propertyName)
      {
        if (PropertyChanged != null)
          PropertyChanged(this, new PropertyChangedEventArgs(propertyName));
      }
    }
  }
```

1.  In the code-behind file, add a field like this:

    ```
        private PersistentSlider _sliderData = new PersistentSlider { MinValue = 1,
    MaxValue = 200, CurrentValue = 100 };
    ```

2.  In the constructor, set the `DataContext` property of the current instance to the field you just created:

    ```
        this.DataContext = _sliderData;

        InitializeComponent();
    ```

3.  In the XAML, change the `Slider` control to use the data context. Only the `Path` needs to be set:

    ```xml
    <Window x:Class="Answers.Window1_15_4"
            xmlns="http://schemas.microsoft.com/winfx/2006/xaml/presentation"
            xmlns:x="http://schemas.microsoft.com/winfx/2006/xaml"
            Title="15.4 Solution" Height="300" Width="300">
      <Grid>
          <Slider HorizontalAlignment="Left" Margin="10,10,0,0" VerticalAlignment="Top"
    Width="264" Minimum="{Binding Path=MinValue}"
    Maximum="{Binding Path=MaxValue}" Value="{Binding Path=CurrentValue}"
    Name="valueSlider"/>
          <ProgressBar HorizontalAlignment="Left" Height="24" Margin="-17,125,-10,0"
    VerticalAlignment="Top" Width="311"
    Minimum="{Binding ElementName=valueSlider, Path=Minimum}"
    Maximum="{Binding ElementName=valueSlider, Path=Maximum}"
    Value="{Binding ElementName=valueSlider, Path=Value}"
    RenderTransformOrigin="0.5,0.5">
            <ProgressBar.RenderTransform>
              <TransformGroup>
                <ScaleTransform/>
                <SkewTransform/>
                <RotateTransform Angle="-36.973"/>
                <TranslateTransform/>
              </TransformGroup>
            </ProgressBar.RenderTransform>
          </ProgressBar>

      </Grid>
    </Window>
    ```

# CHAPTER 16 SOLUTIONS

## Exercise 1

1.  Create a new class with the name `ComputerSkillValueConverter` like this:

    ```csharp
    [ValueConversion(typeof(ComputerSkillLevel), typeof(bool))]
    public class ComputerSkillValueConverter : IValueConverter
    {
        public object Convert(object value, Type targetType, object parameter,
    System.Globalization.CultureInfo culture)
        {
          string helper = parameter as string;
    ```

```
            if (string.IsNullOrWhiteSpace(helper))
              return false;

            ComputerSkillLevel skillLevel = (ComputerSkillLevel)value;
            return (skillLevel.ToString() == helper);
        }

        public object ConvertBack(object value, Type targetType, object parameter,
    System.Globalization.CultureInfo culture)
        {
            string parameterString = parameter as string;
            if (parameterString == null)
              return ComputerSkillLevel.Dumb;

            return Enum.Parse(targetType, parameterString);
        }
    }
```

**2.** Add a static resource declaration to the Options.xaml:

```
<Window.Resources>
  <src:ComputerSkillValueConverter x:Key="skillConverter" />
</Window.Resources>
```

**3.** Change the radio buttons like this:

```
            <RadioButton Content="Dumb" HorizontalAlignment="Left"
Margin="37,41,0,0" VerticalAlignment="Top" Name="dumbAIRadioButton"
IsChecked="{Binding ComputerSkill, Converter={StaticResource skillConverter},
ConverterParameter=Dumb}" />
            <RadioButton Content="Good" HorizontalAlignment="Left"
Margin="37,62,0,0" VerticalAlignment="Top" Name="goodAIRadioButton"
IsChecked="{Binding ComputerSkill, Converter={StaticResource skillConverter},
ConverterParameter=Good}" />
            <RadioButton Content="Cheats" HorizontalAlignment="Left"
Margin="37,83,0,0" VerticalAlignment="Top" Name="cheatingAIRadioButton"
IsChecked="{Binding ComputerSkill,
Converter={StaticResource skillConverter},
ConverterParameter=Cheats}" />
```

**4.** Delete the events from the code-behind file.

## Exercise 2

**1.** Add a new check box to the Options.xaml dialog box:

```
<CheckBox Content="Plays with open cards" HorizontalAlignment="Left"
Margin="10,100, 0,0" VerticalAlignment="Top"
IsChecked="{Binding ComputerPlaysWithOpenHand}" />
```

**2.** Add a new property to the GameOptions.cs class:

```
        private bool _computerPlaysWithOpenHand;
        public bool ComputerPlaysWithOpenHand
        {
          get { return _computerPlaysWithOpenHand; }
          set
          {
            _computerPlaysWithOpenHand = value;
            OnPropertyChanged("PlayWithOpenHand");
          }
        }
```

3. In the `DrawCards` method of the `CardsInHandControl`, change the test for `isFaceUp`:

```
if (Owner is ComputerPlayer)
   isFaceup = (Owner.State == CardLib.PlayerState.Loser ||
Owner.State == CardLib.PlayerState.Winner || ComputerPlaysWithOpenHand);
```

4. Add a new dependency property to the `CardsInHandControl`:

```
public bool ComputerPlaysWithOpenHand
{
  get { return (bool)GetValue(ComputerPlaysWithOpenHandProperty); }
  set { SetValue(ComputerPlaysWithOpenHandProperty, value); }
}

public static readonly DependencyProperty ComputerPlaysWithOpenHandProperty =
    DependencyProperty.Register("ComputerPlaysWithOpenHand", typeof(bool),
typeof(CardsInHandControl), new PropertyMetadata(false));
```

5. Bind the new property to the `CardsInHandControls` on the game client:

```
ComputerPlaysWithOpenHand="{Binding GameOptions.ComputerPlaysWithOpenHand}"
```

# Exercise 3

1. Add a new property to the `GameViewModel` like this:

```
private string _currentStatusText = "Game is not started";
public string CurrentStatusText
{
  get { return _currentStatusText; }
  set
  {
    _currentStatusText = value;
    OnPropertyChanged("CurrentStatusText");
  }
}
```

2. Change the `CurrentPlayer` property like this:

```
public Player CurrentPlayer
{
  get { return _currentPlayer;          {
    _currentPlayer = value;
    OnPropertyChanged("CurrentPlayer");
    if (!Players.Any(x => x.State == PlayerState.Winner))
    {
      Players.ForEach(x => x.State = (x == value ? PlayerState.Active :
PlayerState.Inactive));
      CurrentStatusText = string.Format("Player {0} ready",
CurrentPlayer.PlayerName);
    }
    else
    {
      var winner = Players.Where(x => x.HasWon).FirstOrDefault();
      if (winner != null)
        CurrentStatusText = string.Format("Player {0} has WON!",
winner.PlayerName);
    }
  }
}
```

3. Add this line at the end of the `StartNewGame` method:

```
CurrentStatusText = string.Format("New game stated. Player {0} to start",
CurrentPlayer.PlayerName);
```

**4.** Add a status bar to the game client XAML and set the binding to the new property:

```
<StatusBar Grid.Row="3" HorizontalAlignment="Center" Margin="0,0,0,15"
VerticalAlignment="Center" Background="Green" Foreground="White" FontWeight="Bold">
    <StatusBarItem VerticalAlignment="Center">
      <TextBlock Text="{Binding CurrentStatusText}" />
    </StatusBarItem>
  </StatusBar>
```

# CHAPTER 17 SOLUTIONS

## Exercise 1

**1.** Open the KarliCards game and then open the `MainPage.xaml` file. Insert this XAML code just below the `</Page.Resources>` element:

```
<Page.BottomAppBar>
  <AppBar x:Name="BottomAppBar1" Padding="10,0,10,0" Grid.ColumnSpan="10">
    <Grid>
      <Grid.ColumnDefinitions>
        <ColumnDefinition Width="50*"/>
        <ColumnDefinition Width="50*"/>
      </Grid.ColumnDefinitions>
      <StackPanel x:Name="RightPanel" Orientation="Horizontal"
Grid.Column="1" HorizontalAlignment="Right">
        <Button x:Name="StartGame" Style="{StaticResource
PlayAppBarButtonStyle}" Tag="StartGame" Click="StartGame_Click" />
        <Button x:Name="Settings" Style="{StaticResource
SettingsAppBarButtonStyle}" Tag="Settings" Click="GotoSettings" />
        <Button x:Name="Help" Style="{StaticResource HelpAppBarButtonStyle}"
Tag="Help"/>
      </StackPanel>
    </Grid>
  </AppBar>
</Page.BottomAppBar>
```

**2.** Search for `PlayAppBarButtonStyle` and the other styles in the `StandardStyles.xaml` file and uncomment all you need.

**3.** Add the event handlers on the buttons to the code-behind file. The `StartGame_Click` event handler is already there.

**4.** Open the `GamePage.xaml` page.

**5.** Add this XAML code to the page and add the event handler to the code-behind file:

```
<Page.BottomAppBar>
  <AppBar x:Name="BottomAppBar1" Padding="10,0,10,0" Grid.ColumnSpan="10">
    <Grid>
      <Grid.ColumnDefinitions>
        <ColumnDefinition Width="50*"/>
        <ColumnDefinition Width="50*"/>
      </Grid.ColumnDefinitions>
      <StackPanel x:Name="RightPanel" Orientation="Horizontal"
                  Grid.Column="1" HorizontalAlignment="Right">
        <Button x:Name="Settings" Style="{StaticResource
SettingsAppBarButtonStyle}" Tag="Settings" Click="GotoSettings" />
        <Button x:Name="Help" Style="{StaticResource HelpAppBarButtonStyle}" Tag="Help"/>
      </StackPanel>
    </Grid>
  </AppBar>
</Page.BottomAppBar>
```

## Exercise 2

1. Add a new user control to the project. Name it `SettingsControl.xaml`.

2. Replace the `Grid` control with this:

```xml
<UserControl.Resources>
  <local:SliderComputerSkillToolTipConverter x:Key="intToComputerSkill" />
  <local:ComputerSkillValueConverter x:Key="computerSkillLevel" />
</UserControl.Resources>
<Grid Style="{StaticResource LayoutRootStyle}" Width="346" Margin="0,0,0,0">
  <Grid.ColumnDefinitions>
    <ColumnDefinition Width="73"/>
    <ColumnDefinition Width="3*"/>
    <ColumnDefinition Width="88*"/>
  </Grid.ColumnDefinitions>
  <Grid.RowDefinitions>
    <RowDefinition Height="73"/>
    <RowDefinition Height="32*"/>
    <RowDefinition Height="125*"/>
    <RowDefinition Height="35*"/>
    <RowDefinition Height="118*"/>
    <RowDefinition Height="617*"/>
  </Grid.RowDefinitions>
  <TextBlock Text="Game Options" Style="{StaticResource
PageSubheaderTextStyle}"
Grid.Column="1"  Grid.ColumnSpan="2" Margin="0,0,0,21" Height="30"  />
  <Button x:Name="settingsBackButton" Click="GoBack" IsEnabled="True"
Style="{StaticResource BackButtonStyle}" Grid.Row="0" Grid.Column="0" Margin="14,0,0,10" />
  <TextBlock FontSize="18" Grid.Row="1"
Style="{StaticResource CaptionTextStyle}" Text="Game" FontWeight="Bold"
Padding="10" Grid.RowSpan="5" />
  <StackPanel Grid.Column="2" Grid.Row="2" Grid.RowSpan="4">
    <ToggleSwitch Header="Play Against Computer" HorizontalAlignment="Left"
Margin="0" VerticalAlignment="Top" Height="60" Width="220" OnContent="Yes"
OffContent="No" IsOn="{Binding PlayAgainstComputer, Mode=TwoWay}" />
    <TextBlock Style="{StaticResource ItemTextStyle}"
Text="Number of players"
Padding="0, 4, 0, 0" />
    <ComboBox SelectedValue="{Binding NumberOfPlayers, Mode=TwoWay}"
Margin="0,4,0,0" Width="220" Height="22" HorizontalAlignment="Left"
x:Name="numberOfPlayersCombo" >
        <x:Int32>2</x:Int32>
        <x:Int32>3</x:Int32>
        <x:Int32>4</x:Int32>
    </ComboBox>
  </StackPanel>
  <TextBlock FontSize="18" Grid.Row="3" Style="{StaticResource CaptionTextStyle}"
Text="Computer" FontWeight="Bold" Padding="10" Grid.ColumnSpan="3"
Grid.RowSpan="3"/>
  <StackPanel Grid.Column="2" Grid.Row="4" Grid.RowSpan="2">
    <Grid Height="53"  Width="220" HorizontalAlignment="Left">
      <TextBlock Text="Skill Level" FontSize="12"
HorizontalAlignment="Left" />
      <Slider Minimum="0" Maximum="2" Value="{Binding ComputerSkill,
Mode=TwoWay, Converter={StaticResource computerSkillLevel}}"
ThumbToolTipValueConverter="{StaticResource
ResourceKey=intToComputerSkill}" />
      <TextBlock Text="Dumb" HorizontalAlignment="Left" Margin="0,33,0,0" />
      <TextBlock Text="Good" HorizontalAlignment="Center" Margin="0,33,0,0" />
      <TextBlock Text="Cheats" HorizontalAlignment="Right" Margin="0,33,0,0" />
```

```
        </Grid>
        <ToggleSwitch Header="Computer plays with open cards"
HorizontalAlignment="Left" Margin="0" VerticalAlignment="Top" Height="60"
Width="220" OnContent="Yes" OffContent="No" IsOn="{Binding
ComputerPlaysWithOpenHand, Mode=TwoWay}" />
        </StackPanel>
        <Grid Grid.Row="5" Grid.Column="2" Width="220" HorizontalAlignment="Left">
            <Button Content="Save" HorizontalAlignment="Right"
VerticalAlignment="Top"
Click="Save_Click"/>
        </Grid>
    </Grid>
```

**3.** Add a new class called `SliderComputerSkillToolTipConverter` and add this code:

```
using System;
using Windows.UI.Xaml;
using Windows.UI.Xaml.Data;

namespace KarliCards_Gui
{
  public class SliderComputerSkillToolTipConverter : IValueConverter
  {
    public object Convert(object value, Type targetType, object parameter,
                          string language)
    {
      var currentValue = (double)value;
      if (currentValue == 0)
        return "Dumb";
      if (currentValue == 1)
        return "Good";
      return "Cheats";
    }

    public object ConvertBack(object value, Type targetType, object parameter,
                              string language)
    {
      string currentValue = value as string;
      if (currentValue == null || string.IsNullOrWhiteSpace(currentValue))
        return DependencyProperty.UnsetValue;
      if (currentValue.ToLower() == "dumb")
        return 0D;
      if (currentValue.ToLower() == "good")
        return 1D;
      return 2D;
    }
  }
}
```

**4.** Add a new class called `ComputerSkillValueConverter` and add this code:

```
using System;
using CardLib;
using Windows.UI.Xaml.Data;

namespace KarliCards_Gui
{
  public class ComputerSkillValueConverter : IValueConverter
  {
    public object Convert(object value, Type targetType, object parameter,
                          string language)
    {
      return (double)(int)value;
```

```
  }

  public object ConvertBack(object value, Type targetType, object parameter,
                            string language)
  {
    return (ComputerSkillLevel)System.Convert.ToInt32(value);
  }
  }
}
```

5. Add the event handlers for the `click` event to the `goBack` and `Save` buttons on the `SettingsControl.xaml`.

6. Add this code:

```
private void GoBack(object sender, RoutedEventArgs e)
{
  this.Margin = new Thickness(0, 0, -346, 0);
}

private void Save_Click(object sender, RoutedEventArgs e)
{
  var context = DataContext as GameOptions;
  context.Save();
  this.Margin = new Thickness(0, 0, -346, 0);
}
```

7. Go to the `MainPage.xaml` file and add this to the XAML code above the `VisualStateManager` element:

```
    <local:SettingsControl x:Name="GameSettingsPane"
HorizontalAlignment="Right"
Margin="0, 0, -346, 0" Height="{Binding Height}" Grid.RowSpan="5">
      <local:SettingsControl.Transitions>
        <TransitionCollection>
          <RepositionThemeTransition />
        </TransitionCollection>
      </local:SettingsControl.Transitions>
    </local:SettingsControl>
</local:SettingsControl>
```

8. Go to the `GamePage.xaml` file and then add the same code in the same position as in Step 7.

9. Go to the `MainPage.xaml.cs` code-behind file and add this event handler and method override:

```
    private void MainPage_CommandsRequested(SettingsPane sender,
SettingsPaneCommandsRequestedEventArgs args)
    {
      SettingsCommand cmd = new SettingsCommand("KarliCardsSettings",
"Game Options", (x) =>
      {
        GameSettingsPane.DataContext = new GameOptions();
        GameSettingsPane.Height = Window.Current.Bounds.Height;
        GameSettingsPane.Margin = new Thickness(0, 0, 0, 0);
      });
      args.Request.ApplicationCommands.Add(cmd);
    }

    protected override void OnPointerPressed(PointerRoutedEventArgs e)
    {
      var position = e.GetCurrentPoint(GameSettingsPane).Position.X < 0;
      if (GameSettingsPane.Margin.Right == 0 && position)
      {
        GameSettingsPane.Margin = new Thickness(0, 0, -346, 0);
      }
      base.OnPointerPressed(e);
    }
```

**10.** Change to LoadState, SaveState, and GotoSettings methods like this:

```
protected override void LoadState(Object navigationParameter,
        Dictionary<String, Object> pageState)
{
  SettingsPane.GetForCurrentView().CommandsRequested +=
                MainPage_CommandsRequested;
}
protected override void SaveState(Dictionary<String, Object> pageState)
{
  SettingsPane.GetForCurrentView().CommandsRequested
-= MainPage_CommandsRequested;
}
private void GotoSettings(object sender, RoutedEventArgs e)
{
  Windows.UI.ApplicationSettings.SettingsPane.Show();
}
```

**11.** Go to the GamePage.xaml.cs code-behind file and add this code:

```
protected override void OnPointerPressed(PointerRoutedEventArgs e)
{
  var position = e.GetCurrentPoint(GameSettingsPane).Position.X < 0;
  if (GameSettingsPane.Margin.Right == 0 && position)
  {
    GameSettingsPane.Margin = new Thickness(0, 0, -346, 0);
  }
  base.OnPointerPressed(e);
}

void GamePage_CommandsRequested(SettingsPane sender,
SettingsPaneCommandsRequestedEventArgs args)
{
  SettingsCommand cmd = new SettingsCommand("KarliCardsSettings",
"Game Options", (x) =>
      {
        GameSettingsPane.DataContext = new GameOptions();
        GameSettingsPane.Height = Window.Current.Bounds.Height;
        GameSettingsPane.Margin = new Thickness(0, 0, 0, 0);
      });
  args.Request.ApplicationCommands.Add(cmd);
}
```

**12.** Change the LoadState, SaveState, and GotoSettings methods like this:

```
protected override void LoadState(Object navigationParameter,
Dictionary<String, Object> pageState)
{
  if (pageState != null && pageState["CurrentGame"] != null)
  {
    var context = pageState["CurrentGame"] as GameViewModel;
    if (context != null)
    {
      this.DataContext = context;
      context.ContinueGame();
    }
  }
  else if (navigationParameter != null)
  {
    var players = navigationParameter as string;
    var newGame = new GameViewModel();
    newGame.StartNewGame(PlayerNames.FromString(players));
    DataContext = newGame;
```

```
        }
        SettingsPane.GetForCurrentView().CommandsRequested +=
GamePage_CommandsRequested;
    }
    protected override void SaveState(Dictionary<String, Object> pageState)
    {
        pageState["CurrentGame"] = DataContext as GameViewModel;
        SettingsPane.GetForCurrentView().CommandsRequested -=
GamePage_CommandsRequested;
    }

    private void GotoSettings(object sender, RoutedEventArgs e)
    {
        Windows.UI.ApplicationSettings.SettingsPane.Show();
    }
```

## CHAPTER 18 SOLUTIONS

### Exercise 1

ClickOnce deployment has the advantage that the user installing the application doesn't need administrator privileges. The application can be automatically installed by clicking on a hyperlink. Also, you can configure that new versions of the application to be installed automatically.

### Exercise 2

The application manifest describes the application and required permissions, the deployment manifest describes deployment configuration, such as update policies.

### Exercise 3

If administrator permissions are required by the installation program, the Windows Installer is needed instead of ClickOnce deployment.

## CHAPTER 19 SOLUTIONS

### Exercise 1

Follow these steps to add the username to the master page:

1. Open the previously created web application project named EventRegistration.
2. From Solution Explorer, select the Events.Master page, and display this page in Design View.
3. From the Login GROUP of the Toolbox, drag a LoginName control to the right of the SiteMapPath control, which should already exist on the page. The designer will place this control below the SiteMapDataSource control, which should also already exist.
4. Change the FormatString property of the LoginName control to Hello {0}.
5. Do the same for the LoginView control.
6. From the LoginView Tasks menu that opens when clicking the smart tag of the LoginView control, choose LoggedInTemplate.
7. Start the project. Once logged in, navigate to the Admin/EventManagement.aspx page to view your changes.

## Exercise 2

Follow these steps:

1. Open the previously created web application project named `EventRegistration`.
2. From Solution Explorer, select the `Registration.aspx` page.
3. Before the ending `form` tag, add a `SqlDataSource` control that matches the following.

```
<asp:SqlDataSource ID="SqlDataSource1" runat="server"
    ConnectionString="<%$ ConnectionStrings:EventsConnectionString %>"
    SelectCommand="SELECT [Id], [Title], [Date], [Location] FROM [Events]">
</asp:SqlDataSource>
```

4. Find the events `DropDownList` control on the page, and assign the value of the `SqlDataSource` ID to the `DataSourceID` of the events `DropDownList`.
5. Run the web application and navigate to the Registration page. You will notice the data-bound list of events.

## Exercise 3

Follow these steps:

1. From Visual Studio, create a new project.
2. Choose the `ASP.NET Web Forms Application` project template from the New Project dialog box.
3. Run the new Web Forms application project created from the project template.

# CHAPTER 20 SOLUTIONS

## Exercise 1

Copying the website copies all files required to run the web application. Visual Studio 2012 has a dialog box for a bi-directional copy. Newer files from the target server can be copied locally. If the source code should not be copied to the target web server, publishing allows you to create assemblies. You can then copy just the assemblies to the target web server.

## Exercise 2

The options are to publish to a file system, to publish to a server with FrontPage Server Extensions, to publish via FTP, and to publish with 1-Click publishing. Mainly this depends on the hosting option you are using and what your provider offers. In all cases the virtual directory must have been created on the server. To publish to a file system, you need to have access to the file system. This should be the case if you are running IIS on your own. When you're publishing with FrontPage Server Extensions, the extensions must be installed on the server. To publish via FTP, you must have an FTP server installed on the server. To publish via 1-Click, your provider must support this new publishing option.

# CHAPTER 21 SOLUTIONS

## Exercise 1

`System.IO`

## Exercise 2

You use a `FileStream` object to write to a file when you need random access to files, or when you are not dealing with string data.

## Exercise 3

- ➤ `Peek()`—Gets the value of the next character in the file but does not advance the file position
- ➤ `Read()`—Gets the value of the next character in the file and advances the file position
- ➤ `Read(char[] buffer, int index, int count)`—Reads count characters into `buffer`, starting at `buffer[index]`
- ➤ `ReadLine()`—Gets a line of text
- ➤ `ReadToEnd()`—Gets all text in a file

## Exercise 4

`DeflateStream`

## Exercise 5

Ensure that it doesn't possess the `Serializable` attribute.

## Exercise 6

- ➤ `Changed`—Occurs when a file is modified
- ➤ `Created`—Occurs when a file is created
- ➤ `Deleted`—Occurs when a file is deleted
- ➤ `Renamed`—Occurs when a file is renamed

## Exercise 7

Add a button that toggles the value of the `FileSystemWatcher.EnableRaisingEvents` property.

## CHAPTER 22 SOLUTIONS

### Exercise 1

1. Double-click the Create Node button to go to the event handler doing the work.
2. Below the creation of the `XmlComment`, insert the following three lines:

```
    XmlAttribute newPages = document.CreateAttribute("pages");
    newPages.Value = "1000+";
newBook.Attributes.Append(newPages);
```

### Exercise 2

1. `//elements`—Returns all nodes in the document.
2. `element`—Returns every element node in the document but leaves the element root node out.
3. `element[@Type='Noble Gas']`—Returns every element that includes an attribute with the name `Type`, which has a value of `Noble Gas`.
4. `//mass`—Returns all nodes with the name mass.
5. `//mass/..`—The `..` causes the XPath to move one up from the selected node, which means that this query selects all the nodes that include a mass node.

6. `element/specification[mass='20.1797']`—Selects the specification element that contains a mass node with the value `20.1797`.

7. `element/name[text()='Neon']`—To select the node whose contents you are testing, you can use the `text()` function. This selects the name node with the text `Neon`.

## Exercise 3

Recall that XML can be valid, well formed, or invalid. Whenever you select part of an XML document, you are left with a fragment of the whole. This means that there is a good chance that the XML you've selected is in fact invalid XML on its own. Most XML viewers will refuse to display XML that isn't well-formed, so it is not possible to display the results of many queries directly in a standard XML viewer.

## CHAPTER 23 SOLUTIONS

## Exercise 1

```
static void Main(string[] args)
{
          string[] names = { "Alonso", "Zheng", "Smith", "Jones", "Smythe",
"Small", "Ruiz", "Hsieh", "Jorgenson", "Ilyich", "Singh", "Samba", "Fatimah" };

          var queryResults =
              from n in names
              where n.StartsWith("S")
          orderby n descending
              select n;

          Console.WriteLine("Names beginning with S:");

          foreach (var item in queryResults) {
              Console.WriteLine(item);
          }

          Console.Write("Program finished, press Enter/Return to continue:");
          Console.ReadLine();
}
```

## Exercise 2

Sets smaller than 5,000,000 have no numbers < 1000:

```
static void Main(string[] args)
{
    int[] arraySizes = {    100,    1000,    10000,   100000,
                        1000000, 5000000, 10000000, 50000000 };

    foreach (int i in arraySizes) {
        int[] numbers = GenerateLotsOfNumbers(i);
        var queryResults = from n in numbers
                        where n < 1000
                        select n;
        Console.WriteLine("number array size = {0}: Count(n < 1000) = {1}",
                numbers.Length, queryResults.Count()
        );
    }

    Console.Write("Program finished, press Enter/Return to continue:");
    Console.ReadLine();
}
```

## Exercise 3

Does not affect performance noticeably for n < 1000:

```
static void Main(string[] args)
{

    int[] numbers = GenerateLotsOfNumbers(12345678);

    var queryResults =
        from n in numbers
        where n < 1000
        orderby n
        select n
        ;

    Console.WriteLine("Numbers less than 1000:");
    foreach (var item in queryResults)
    {
        Console.WriteLine(item);
    }

    Console.Write("Program finished, press Enter/Return to continue:");
    Console.ReadLine();
}
```

## Exercise 4

Very large subsets such as n > 1000 instead of n < 1000 are very slow:

```
static void Main(string[] args)
{

    int[] numbers = GenerateLotsOfNumbers(12345678);

    var queryResults =
        from n in numbers
        where n > 1000
        select n
        ;

    Console.WriteLine("Numbers less than 1000:");
    foreach (var item in queryResults)
    {
        Console.WriteLine(item);
    }

    Console.Write("Program finished, press Enter/Return to continue:");
    Console.ReadLine();
}
```

## Exercise 5

All the names are output because there is no query:

```
static void Main(string[] args)
{
        string[] names = { "Alonso", "Zheng", "Smith", "Jones", "Smythe",
"Small", "Ruiz", "Hsieh", "Jorgenson", "Ilyich", "Singh", "Samba", "Fatimah" };

        var queryResults = names;


        foreach (var item in queryResults) {
```

```
                Console.WriteLine(item);
            }

            Console.Write("Program finished, press Enter/Return to continue:");
            Console.ReadLine();
    }
```

# Exercise 6

```
var queryResults =
    from c in customers
    where c.Country == "USA"
    select c
    ;
Console.WriteLine("Customers in USA:");
foreach (Customer c in queryResults)
{
    Console.WriteLine(c);
}
```

# Exercise 7

```
        static void Main(string[] args)
        {
            string[] names = { "Alonso", "Zheng", "Smith", "Jones", "Smythe",
"Small", "Ruiz", "Hsieh", "Jorgenson", "Ilyich", "Singh", "Samba", "Fatimah" };
            // only Min() and Max() are available (if no lambda is used)
            // for a result set like this consisting only of strings
            Console.WriteLine("Min(names) = " + names.Min());
            Console.WriteLine("Max(names) = " + names.Max());
            var queryResults =
                from n in names
                where n.StartsWith("S")
                select n;

        Console.WriteLine("Query result: names starting with S");
         foreach (var item in queryResults)
         {
                Console.WriteLine(item);
         }

        Console.WriteLine("Min(queryResults) = " + queryResults.Min());
        Console.WriteLine("Max(queryResults) = " + queryResults.Max());

         Console.Write("Program finished, press Enter/Return to continue:");
         Console.ReadLine();
        }
```

# CHAPTER 24 SOLUTIONS

# Exercise 1

Use the following code:

```
using System;
using System.Collections.Generic;
using System.Linq;
using System.Xml.Linq;
using System.Text;

namespace BegVCSharp_24_exercise1
```

```
    {
        class Program
        {
            static void Main(string[] args)
            {
                XDocument xdoc = new XDocument(
                    new XElement("employees",
                        new XElement("employee",
                            new XAttribute("ID", "1001"),
                            new XAttribute("FirstName", "Fred"),
                            new XAttribute("LastName", "Lancelot"),
                            new XElement("Skills",
                                new XElement("Language", "C#"),
                                new XElement("Math", "Calculus")
                                )
                            ),
                        new XElement("employee",
                            new XAttribute("ID", "2002"),
                            new XAttribute("FirstName", "Jerry"),
                            new XAttribute("LastName", "Garcia"),
                            new XElement("Skills",
                                new XElement("Language", "French"),
                                new XElement("Math", "Business")
                                )
                            )
                        )
                    );

                Console.WriteLine(xdoc);

                Console.Write(
                  "Program finished, press Enter/Return to continue:");
                Console.ReadLine();

            }
        }
    }
```

## Exercise 2

Use code similar to this:

```
using System;
using System.Collections.Generic;
using System.Linq;
using System.Xml.Linq;
using System.Text;

namespace BegVCSharp_24_exercises
{
    class Program
    {
        static void Main(string[] args)
        {
            string xmlFileName =
                @"C:\BegVCSharp\Chapter24\Xml\NorthwindCustomerOrders.xml";
            XDocument customers = XDocument.Load(xmlFileName);


            Console.WriteLine(
                "Oldest customers: Companies with orders in 1996:");
            var queryResults =
```

```
                from c in customers.Descendants("customer")
                where c.Descendants("order").Attributes("orderYear")
                                     .Any(a => a.Value == "1996")
                select c.Attribute("Company");

            foreach (var item in queryResults)
            {
                Console.WriteLine(item);
            }
            Console.Write("Press Enter/Return to continue:");
            Console.ReadLine();
        }
    }
}
```

# Exercise 3

Here's the code:

```
using System;
using System.Collections.Generic;
using System.Linq;
using System.Xml.Linq;
using System.Text;

namespace BegVCSharp_24_exercises
{
    class Program
    {
        static void Main(string[] args)
        {
            string xmlFileName =
                    @"C:\BegVCSharp\Chapter24\Xml\NorthwindCustomerOrders.xml";
            XDocument customers = XDocument.Load(xmlFileName);

            Console.WriteLine(
                "Companies with individual orders totaling over $10,000");
            var queryResults =
                from c in customers.Descendants("order")
                where Convert.ToDecimal(
                    c.Attribute("orderTotal").Value) > 10000
                select new { OrderID = c.Attribute("orderID"),
                             Company = c.Parent.Attribute("Company") };

            foreach (var item in queryResults)
            {
                Console.WriteLine(item);
            }
            Console.Write("Program finished, press Enter/Return to continue:");
            Console.ReadLine();
        }
    }
}
```

# Exercise 4

Use the following code:

```
using System;
using System.Collections.Generic;
using System.Linq;
using System.Xml.Linq;
```

```
using System.Text;

namespace BegVCSharp_24_exercises
{
    class Program
    {
        static void Main(string[] args)
        {
            string xmlFileName =
                @"C:\BegVCSharp\Chapter24\Xml\NorthwindCustomerOrders.xml";
            XDocument customers = XDocument.Load(xmlFileName);

            Console.WriteLine("Lifetime highest-selling customers:"+
                "Companies with all orders totaling over $100,000");
            var queryResult =
                from c in customers.Descendants("customer")
                where c.Descendants("order").Attributes("orderTotal")
                        .Sum(o => Convert.ToDecimal(o.Value)) > 100000
                select c.Attribute("Company");

            foreach (var item in queryResult)
            {
                Console.WriteLine(item);
            }
            Console.Write("Press Enter/Return to continue:");
            Console.ReadLine();
        }
    }
}
```

## Exercise 5

```
using System;
using System.Collections.Generic;
using System.Linq;
using System.Text;

namespace BegVCSharp_24_exercise1
{
    class Program
    {
        static void Main(string[] args)
        {
            NorthwindEntitiesnorthWindEntities = new NorthwindEntities ();

            Console.WriteLine("Product Details");
            var queryResults = from p in northWindEntities.Products
                        select new
                            {
                                ID = p.ProductID,
                                Name = p.ProductName,
                                Price = p.UnitPrice,
                                Discontinued = p.Discontinued
                            };
            foreach (var item in queryResults)
            {
                Console.WriteLine(item);
            }
            Console.WriteLine("Employee Details");
            var queryResults2 = from e in northWindEntities.Employees
                        select new
                            {
                                ID = e.EmployeeID,
```

```
                                    Name = e.FirstName+" "+e.LastName,
                                    Title = e.Title
                                };
                foreach (var item in queryResults2)
                {
                    Console.WriteLine(item);
                }
                Console.WriteLine("Press Enter/Return to continue…");
                Console.ReadLine();

            }
        }
    }
```

# Exercise 6

Use code similar to this:

```
using System;
using System.Collections.Generic;
using System.Linq;
using System.Text;

namespace BegVCSharp_24_exercise6
{
    class Program
    {
        static void Main(string[] args)
        {
            NorthwindEntitiesnorthWindEntities = new NorthwindEntities ();

            Console.WriteLine("Top-Selling Products (Sales over $50,000) ");
            var queryResults =
             from p in northWindEntities.Products
             where p.Order_Details.Sum(od => od.Quantity * od.UnitPrice) > 50000
             orderby p.Order_Details.Sum(
                     od => od.Quantity * od.UnitPrice) descending
             select new
             {
               ID = p.ProductID,
               Name = p.ProductName,
               TotalSales = p.Order_Details.Sum(
                     od => od.Quantity * od.UnitPrice)
             };
             foreach (var item in queryResults)
             {
               Console.WriteLine(item);
             }

             Console.WriteLine("Press Enter/Return to continue…");
             Console.ReadLine();
        }
    }
}
```

# Exercise 7

```
using System;
using System.Collections.Generic;
using System.Linq;
using System.Text;

namespace BegVCSharp_24_exercise7
```

```
{
    class Program
    {
        static void Main(string[] args)
        {

    NorthwindEntitiesnorthWindEntities = new NorthwindEntities ();

            var totalResults = from od in northWindEntities.Order_Details
                               from c in northWindEntities.Customers
                               where c.CustomerID == od.Order.CustomerID
                               select new
                               {
                                   Product = od.Product.ProductName,
                                   Country = c.Country,
                                   Sales = od.UnitPrice * od.Quantity
                               };

            var groupResults =
                from c in totalResults
                group c by new { Product = c.Product,
                                 Country = c.Country } into cg
                select new {
                    Product = cg.Key.Product,
                    Country = cg.Key.Country,
                    TotalSales = cg.Sum(c => c.Sales)
                }
            ;

            var orderedResults =
                from cg in groupResults
                orderby cg.Country, cg.TotalSales descending
                select cg
             ;

            foreach (var item in orderedResults)
            {
                Console.WriteLine("{0,-12}{1,-20}{2,12}",
                    item.Country, item.Product, item.TotalSales.ToString("C2"));
            }
            Console.WriteLine("Press Enter/Return to continue...");
            Console.ReadLine();

        }
    }
}
```

# CHAPTER 25 SOLUTIONS

## Exercise 1

All of the above.

## Exercise 2

You would implement a data contract, with the DataContractAttribute and DataMemberAttribute attributes.

## Exercise 3

Use the .svc extension.

## Exercise 4

That is one way of doing things, but it is usually easier to put all your WCF configuration in a separate configuration file, either web.config or app.config.

## Exercise 5

```
[ServiceContract]
public interface IMusicPlayer
{
    [OperationContract(IsOneWay=true)]
    void Play();

    [OperationContract(IsOneWay=true)]
    void Stop();

    [OperationContract]
    TrackInformation GetCurrentTrackInformation();
}
```

You would also want a data contract to encapsulate track information; TrackInformation in the preceding code.

# CHAPTER 26 SOLUTIONS

## Exercise 1

A composite activity would typically be created by subclassing the NativeActivity or NativeActivity<TResult>, and then scheduling child activities to run within the Execute() method of the composite activity. The context argument passed to the Execute() method, NativeActivity, is an instance of NativeActivityContext, and it includes methods to schedule child activities to run.

In addition to scheduling execution of child activities, you would also need to tell the workflow engine about these child activities. Typically, you would do so by overriding the CacheMetadata call.

## Exercise 2

Yes, very easily. You'll create a WCF workflow (which has a .xamlx extension). This can be hosted from an ASP.NET site. Alternatively, you can host a workflow yourself using the WorkflowServiceHost class (which is similar to the standard WCF ServiceHost class).

## Exercise 3

You'll need to utilize the persistence capabilities of the framework by adding a persistence provider such as the SqlWorkflowInstanceStore. This provider persists workflows to a SQL Server database.

# INDEX

**E**

## H

## I

## M

properties. *See also specific properties (continued)*
  GameDecks, 462
  implementing, 439–441
  using, 387–388
 described, 159–160
 List<T>, 288
 public, 160, 176, 206, 208, 213
 RadioButton control, 407
 TextBox control, 406
 using fields, methods, properties (Ch10Ex01), 208–210
Properties window, 15, 19, 24
PropertyChangedCallback, 440
propertyChangedCallback, 440
PropertyMetadata, 439
protected, 165, 204
protected internal, 196, 197, 204
proxy classes, 738, 748, 749, 755, 757
public, 160, 162
public abstract access modifier, 180
public access modifier, 180
public fields, 160, 204, 205, 286
public keyword, 90, 178, 180, 202, 204
public methods, 169, 200, 205, 227, 358
public properties, 160, 176, 206, 208, 213
public sealed access modifier, 180
publishing, 1-Click, 597, 601, 815
publishing web application, 597–599, 601
Python, 350

**Q**

qualified name, 43
queries (LINQ queries)
 from clause, 666, 697
 deferred execution, 667, 697
 foreach loops, 667
 group, 687–689, 697
 lazy evaluation, 667
 ordering query results, 669–672
  method syntax, 671–672
  multi-level ordering using method syntax, 687
  by multiple levels, 685–687
 parts, 665–667, 697
 querying complex objects, 678–681
 querying large data set, 672–674
 querying XML documents, 717–718
 result variable declaration, 665–666
 select clause, 666–667, 697
 Select Distinct, 683–684
 where clause, 666, 697
query syntax (LINQ query syntax)
 First LINQ query, 664–665
 method syntax *versus*, 668
 when to use, 697
QuickWatch window, 144

**R**

\r, 35
race car analogy, 158, 159
RadioButton control, 407, 424
RadioButton server control, 545
raised events, 316, 317, 318, 319, 323
random access files, 613–616
Random class, 229, 322
RangeValidator, 554
rank and suit enumerations, 225–226
read(), 613
ReadFile, 613–615
reading and writing compressed data, 625–628
reading data, 620–621
 from input stream, 619–620
 from random access files, 613–615
ReadLine(), 620
ReadLineAsync(), 625
readonly, 204
ReadToEnd(), 620
read/write access, properties, 160
rectangular arrays, 97, 98
ref keyword, 114, 115, 125, 129, 161
refactoring
 class members, 212–213
 defined, 212, 450
 Domain Model, 447–451
reference parameters, 114–115
reference types
 objects, 200
 value types *versus*, 170, 198–200, 257, 281
ReferenceEquals, 183
reflection, 297, 334–335, 338, 350, 354
#region, 28–29
Register(), 439, 440, 460
RegisterAttached(), 439
RegisterUser.aspx, 578–579

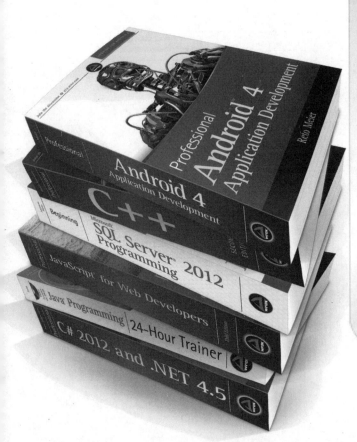